1820 1877

## CULTURAL and TECHNOLOGICAL

1800 Library of Congress established
1807 Robert Fulton launches steamboat *Clermont*
1811 Construction begins on Cumberland Road
1814 Francis Scott Key writes "The Star Spangled Banner"

1821 James Fenimore Cooper, *The Spy*
     Emma Willard founds New York Female Seminary at Troy, New York
1823 James Fenimore Cooper, *The Pioneers*
1824 Hudson River school of landscape painting
1825 Erie Canal completed
1827 *Freedom's Journal* (first Negro newspaper)
     First short-line railroads
1830 First commercial steam locomotive, *Tom Thumb*
1832 Samuel F. B. Morse invents telegraph
1834 Cyrus McCormick patents reaper
1836 Ralph Waldo Emerson, *Nature*
1837 John Deere invents first steel plow
     George Catlin paints *Gallery of Indiana*
1838 Morse code devised
1839 Charles Goodyear produces vulcanized rubber

1844 Morse sends first telegraph message
1846 Elias Howe invents sewing machine
1850 Nathaniel Hawthorne, *The Scarlet Letter*
1851 Melville, *Moby Dick*
     Isaac Singer perfects sewing machine
1852 Harriet Beecher Stowe, *Uncle Tom's Cabin*
     Massachusetts passes first school attendance law
1854 Henry David Thoreau, *Walden*
1855 Walt Whitman, *Leaves of Grass*
1857 Central Park, New York City designed
1861 Mathew Brady begins photographing Civil War
1864 Pullman creates sleeping car

## SOCIAL and ECONOMIC

1801 Gabriel's Rebellion
1803–1806 Louis and Clark expedition
1807 Congress prohibits slave trade
1808–1809 Tecumseh forms confederation
1813 Boston Manufacturing Company formed at Waltham, Massachusetts
1816 Second U.S. Bank
1817 First protective tariff
     American Colonization Society established
1818 First Seminole War
1819–1823 Financial panic and depression

1821 Kentucky abolishes imprisonment for debt
1822 Denmark Vesey's Rebellion
1824 Bureau of Indian Affairs created
1825 Erie Canal opens
1827 Cherokee constitution
     Ten-hour day strike by Boston carpenters
     Mechanics' Union of Trade Association founded in Philadelphia
1828 Tariff of Abominations
1830 Joseph Smith founds Mormon church
1831 Nat Turner's slave rebellion
     William Lloyd Garrison begins publishing *The Liberator*
1832 Jackson vetoes U.S. Bank
1833 American Anti-Slavery Society founded
1834 Lowell mill girls strike
     National Trades Union founded
1836 Specie circular
1837–1844 Panic and Depression
1840 Ten-hour day for federal employees
1841 Frémont expedition to explore route to Oregon
     Great migration over Oregon Trail

1847 Irish potato famine immigration
1848 Women's rights convention, Seneca Falls, New York
1849 California gold rush
1851 Maine prohibition law
1855 First oil business in U.S.
1857 Panic of 1857
1861 First federal income tax
1862 Homestead Act
     Morrill Land-Grant College Act
     Morrill tariff
1865 Freedmen's Bureau established
1865–1866 Black codes
1866 Freedmen's Bureau
1867 Ku Klux Klan formed

## POLITICAL

1798 Undeclared naval war with France
     Alien and Sedition Acts; Naturalization Act
     Virginia and Kentucky resolutions
1800 Thomas Jefferson elected president
1801 John Marshall named Chief Justice
1803 *Marbury v. Madison*
     Louisiana Purchase
1806 Non-Importation Act
1808 James Madison elected president
1809 Non-Intercourse Act
1812 War declared against Britain
1814–1815 Hartford Convention
1814 Treaty of Ghent ends War of 1812
1819 *McCulloch v. Maryland*

1820 Missouri Compromise
1823 Monroe Doctrine
1824 Henry Clay's "American System"
     John Quincy Adams elected president
1825 John Quincy Adams chosen president by House of Representatives
     Texas (Mexican territory) opened to settlement by U.S. citizens
1828 Andrew Jackson elected president
1830 Indian Removal Bill
1832 South Carolina nullification crisis
1833 Force Bill
1834 Whig party formed
1836 Texas declares independence
1838 Cherokee Indian removal
1840 Liberty party formed
1845 United States annexes Texas
1846 Mexican War begins
1848 Wilmot Proviso
     Free-Soil party formed
1850 Treaty of Guadalupe Hidalgo
     Compromise of 1850
1852 Fort Laramie Treaty
1853 Gadsden Purchase
1854 Republican party formed
     Know-Nothing party formed
     Kansas-Nebraska Act

1855–1856 "Bleeding Kansas"
1857 Dred Scott decision
1858 Lincoln-Douglas debates
1859 Raid on Harpers Ferry; John Brown hanged
1860 Abraham Lincoln elected president
1861 Firing on Fort Sumter; Civil War begins
1863 Emancipation Proclamation
1865 Civil War ends
     Lincoln assassinated; Andrew Johnson becomes president
     Thirteenth Amendment abolishes slavery
1867–1877 Congressional Reconstruction
1868 Impeachment attempt against Johnson
     Fourteenth Amendment
1875 Civil Rights Act

1820 1877

# THE
# AMERICAN
# PEOPLE

# THE AMERICAN PEOPLE

## Creating a Nation and a Society

### GENERAL EDITORS

**GARY B. NASH**
*University of California, Los Angeles*

**JULIE ROY JEFFREY**
*Goucher College*

**JOHN R. HOWE**
*University of Minnesota*

**PETER J. FREDERICK**
*Wabash College*

**ALLEN F. DAVIS**
*Temple University*

**ALLAN M. WINKLER**
*University of Oregon*

**Allen Yarnell,** *Administrative Editor*
*University of California, Los Angeles*

**HARPER & ROW, PUBLISHERS, New York**
Cambridge, Philadelphia, San Francisco, Washington
London, Mexico City, São Paulo, Singapore, Sydney,

Sponsoring Editor: Marianne J. Russell
Development Editor: Johnna G. Barto
Project Editor: Jo-Ann Goldfarb
Text and Cover Design: Robert Bull/Design
Text Art: Vantage Art, Inc.
Cartographer: David Lindroth
Photo Research: Elsa Peterson
Production: Willie Lane
Compositor: Black Dot, Inc.
Printer and Binder: Arcata Graphics/Kingsport

Cover Illustration: Thomas P. Otter, *On the Road* (detail), 1860. Nelson-Atkins Museum of Art, Nelson Fund, Kansas City, Mo.

THE AMERICAN PEOPLE: Creating a Nation and a Society

**Library of Congress Cataloging-in-Publication Data**
Main entry under title:

The American people.

    Also issued as two-volume ed.
    Includes bibliographies and index.
    1. United States—History.    I. Nash, Gary B.
II. Jeffrey, Julie Roy.    III.—
E178.1.A49355    1986        973           85-24895
ISBN 0-06-047325-8

87  88  9  8  7  6  5  4  3  2

# CONTENTS IN BRIEF

**PART ONE    A COLONIZING PEOPLE, 1492–1776**

CHAPTER  1   Three Worlds Meet                                            2
CHAPTER  2   Colonizing America                                          30
CHAPTER  3   Mastering the New World                                     62
CHAPTER  4   The Maturing of Colonial Society                            92
CHAPTER  5   Bursting the Colonial Bonds                                130

PORTFOLIO ONE    THE ART OF A COLONIZING PEOPLE    *after page 161*

**PART TWO    A REVOLUTIONARY PEOPLE, 1775–1824**

CHAPTER  6   The American People in Revolution                          162
CHAPTER  7   The Politics of Revolutionary America                      198
CHAPTER  8   Creating a Nation                                          230
CHAPTER  9   The Preindustrial Republic                                 260
CHAPTER 10   Politics and Society in the Early Republic                 296

PORTFOLIO TWO    THE ART OF A REVOLUTIONARY PEOPLE    *after page 333*

**PART THREE    AN EXPANDING PEOPLE, 1820–1877**

CHAPTER 11   Currents of Change in the Northeast and Old Northwest      334
CHAPTER 12   Slavery and the Old South                                  368
CHAPTER 13   Shaping America in the Antebellum Age                      402
CHAPTER 14   Moving West                                                436
CHAPTER 15   The Union in Peril                                         470
CHAPTER 16   Severing the Bonds of Union                                498

PORTFOLIO THREE    THE ART OF AN EXPANDING PEOPLE    *after page 529*

CHAPTER 17   Reconstructing America                                     530

**PART FOUR    AN INDUSTRIALIZING PEOPLE, 1865–1900**

CHAPTER 18   The Farmer's World                                         562
CHAPTER 19   The Rise of Smokestack America                             594
CHAPTER 20   Politics and Protest                                       626
CHAPTER 21   The United States Becomes a World Power                    658

PORTFOLIO FOUR    THE ART OF AN INDUSTRIALIZING PEOPLE    *after page 689*

**PART FIVE    A MODERNIZING PEOPLE, 1900–1945**

CHAPTER 22   The Progressives Confront Industrial America               690
CHAPTER 23   America in the Great War                                   724
CHAPTER 24   Affluence and Anxiety                                      754
CHAPTER 25   The Great Depression and the New Deal                      786
CHAPTER 26   The American People and World War II                       820

PORTFOLIO FIVE    THE ART OF A MODERNIZING PEOPLE    *after page 851*

**PART SIX    AN ENDURING PEOPLE, 1945–1985**

CHAPTER 27   Chills and Fever During the Cold War                       852
CHAPTER 28   The Dreams of Postwar America                              882
CHAPTER 29   From Self-confidence to Self-doubt                         912
CHAPTER 30   Illusion and Disillusionment                               944
CHAPTER 31   Austerity and the American Dream: The United States Since 1976    972

PORTFOLIO SIX    THE ART OF AN ENDURING PEOPLE    *after page 999*

# CONTENTS

Recovering the Past           xviii

Maps           xix

Charts           xxi

Preface           xxv

## PART ONE
## A COLONIZING PEOPLE
## 1492–1776

### CHAPTER 1
### THREE WORLDS MEET
2

The People of America Before Columbus      4

RECOVERING THE PAST / ARCHAEOLOGICAL ARTIFACTS    7a

Africa on the Eve of Contact      9

Europe in the Age of Exploration      11

The Iberian Conquest of America      18

England Goes West      24

Conclusion: Colliding Worlds      28

### CHAPTER 2
### COLONIZING AMERICA
30

The Chesapeake Tobacco Coast      32

The Puritan "City on a Hill"      40

RECOVERING THE PAST / HOUSES    47a

Proprietary New York and Carolina      50

The Quakers' Peaceable Kingdom      54

Conclusion: The Achievement of New Societies      59

## CHAPTER 3
# MASTERING THE NEW WORLD
### 62

Black Bondage 64
Slave Culture 69
The Struggle for Land 74

RECOVERING THE PAST / TOMBSTONES 77a

The Glorious Revolution in America 78
Contending for a Continent 85
Conclusion: Controlling the New Environment 90

## CHAPTER 4
# THE MATURING OF COLONIAL SOCIETY
### 92

America's First Population Explosion 94
A Land of Family Farms 98

RECOVERING THE PAST / TAX RECORDS 99a

The Plantation South 103
The Urban World of Commerce and Ideas 108
The Great Awakening 116
Political Life 122
Conclusion: America in 1750 128

## CHAPTER 5
# BURSTING THE COLONIAL BONDS
### 130

Wars of Empire and Indian Responses 132
The Climactic Seven Years' War 136

RECOVERING THE PAST / HOUSEHOLD INVENTORIES 141a

The Crisis with England 142
The Turmoil of Revolutionary Society 153
Conclusion: Forging a Revolution 159

PORTFOLIO ONE: THE ART OF A COLONIZING PEOPLE, 1492–1776
*after page 161*

# PART TWO
## A REVOLUTIONARY PEOPLE
## 1775–1824

## CHAPTER 6
## THE AMERICAN PEOPLE IN REVOLUTION
### 162

| | |
|---|---|
| The War for American Independence | 164 |
| The Experience of War | 175 |

RECOVERING THE PAST / MILITARY MUSTER ROLLS   *175a*

| | |
|---|---|
| The Revolution and the Economy | 181 |
| Outside the Revolution | 188 |
| Conclusion: The Crucible of Revolution | 196 |

## CHAPTER 7
## THE POLITICS OF REVOLUTIONARY AMERICA
### 198

| | |
|---|---|
| The Ideology of Revolutionary Republicanism | 200 |

RECOVERING THE PAST / POLITICAL DOCUMENTS   *203a*

| | |
|---|---|
| Politicizing the People | 205 |
| Creating Governments in the States | 211 |
| Revolutionary Politics in the States | 216 |
| Toward the Constitutional Convention | 220 |
| Conclusion: The Crosscurrents of Revolution | 228 |

## CHAPTER 8
## CREATING A NATION
### 230

| | |
|---|---|
| The Constitution | 232 |
| Launching the National Republic | 240 |
| The Republic in a Threatening World | 248 |

RECOVERING THE PAST / PATRIOTIC PAINTINGS   *251a*

The Adams Presidency                                      252
Conclusion: Toward the Nineteenth Century                258


CHAPTER 9
# THE PREINDUSTRIAL REPUBLIC
260

The Preindustrial Economy                                262
The Character of Preindustrial Society                   277

RECOVERING THE PAST / CENSUS RETURNS   *277a*

Perfecting Republican Society                            286
Conclusion: Between Two Worlds                           294


CHAPTER 10
# POLITICS AND SOCIETY
# IN THE EARLY REPUBLIC
296

Restoring Republican Liberty                             298
Building an Agrarian Republic                            304
Indian-White Relations in the Early Republic             309

RECOVERING THE PAST / MAPS   *309a*

A Foreign Policy for the Agrarian Republic               318
Culture and Politics in Transition                       326
Conclusion: The Passing of an Era                        331


PORTFOLIO TWO: THE ART OF A REVOLUTIONARY PEOPLE, 1775–1824
*after page 333*

# PART THREE
## AN EXPANDING PEOPLE
## 1820–1877

### CHAPTER 11
## CURRENTS OF CHANGE IN THE NORTHEAST AND OLD NORTHWEST
**334**

| | |
|---|---|
| Economic Growth | 336 |
| The Manufacturing World | 344 |
| The Urban World | 352 |

RECOVERING THE PAST / FAMILY PAINTINGS  *359a*

| | |
|---|---|
| Rural Communities | 362 |
| Conclusion: The Character of Progress | 366 |

### CHAPTER 12
## SLAVERY AND THE OLD SOUTH
**368**

| | |
|---|---|
| Building the Cotton Kingdom | 371 |
| Morning: Master in the Big House | 379 |
| Noon: Slaves in House and Fields | 385 |
| Night: Slaves in Their Quarters | 390 |

RECOVERING THE PAST / FOLKTALES  *393a*

| | |
|---|---|
| Resistance and Freedom | 394 |
| Conclusion: Douglass's Dream of Freedom | 400 |

### CHAPTER 13
## SHAPING AMERICA IN THE ANTEBELLUM AGE
**402**

| | |
|---|---|
| The Political Response to Change | 404 |
| Religious Revival and Reform | 416 |

RECOVERING THE PAST / EUROPEAN TRAVEL JOURNALS  *417a*

| | |
|---|---|
| Utopian Communitarianism | 419 |
| Reforming Society | 423 |

Abolitionism and Women's Rights ................................ 427
Conclusion: Perfecting America .................................. 433

## CHAPTER 14
# MOVING WEST
### 436

Probing the Trans-Mississippi West ............................. 438
Winning the Trans-Mississippi West ............................ 442
Going West ..................................................... 450

RECOVERING THE PAST / PRIVATE SOURCES: DIARIES  *453a*

Living on the Frontier .......................................... 454
The Clash of Cultures .......................................... 463
Conclusion: Fruits of Manifest Destiny ......................... 468

## CHAPTER 15  ✓
# THE UNION IN PERIL
### 470

Slavery in the Territories ....................................... 472

RECOVERING THE PAST / SENATE SPEECHES  *475a*

Political Disintegration ......................................... 477
Kansas and the Two Cultures ................................... 484
Polarization and the Road to War .............................. 488
The Divided House Falls ........................................ 493
Conclusion: The "Irrepressible Conflict" ....................... 496

## CHAPTER 16
# SEVERING THE BONDS OF UNION
### 498

Organizing to Fight the War .................................... 500
Clashing on the Battlefield, 1861–1862 ......................... 505
The Tide Turns, 1863–1865 ..................................... 514
Changes Wrought by War ....................................... 519

RECOVERING THE PAST / PHOTOGRAPHY  *519a*

Conclusion: Union Triumphant .................................. 528

PORTFOLIO THREE: THE ART OF AN EXPANDING PEOPLE, 1820–1877
*after page 529*

## CHAPTER 17
# RECONSTRUCTING AMERICA
### 530

The Bittersweet Aftermath of War                     532
National Reconstruction                              539
Life After Slavery                                   545
Reconstruction in the States                         552

RECOVERING THE PAST / NOVELS   *555a*

Conclusion: The Price of Peace                       559


# PART FOUR
# AN INDUSTRIALIZING PEOPLE
# 1865–1900


## CHAPTER 18
# THE FARMER'S WORLD
### 562

The Modernization of Agriculture                     564
The Second Great Removal                             574

RECOVERING THE PAST / MAGAZINES   *577a*

The New South                                        578
Protesting Farmers                                   586
Conclusion: The Reality of Agricultural America      592


## CHAPTER 19
# THE RISE OF SMOKESTACK AMERICA
### 594

The Character of Industrial Progress                 596
Urban Expansion in the Industrial Age                601

Industrial Work 608
Conflict Between Capital and Labor 614

RECOVERING THE PAST / CONGRESSIONAL HEARINGS 615a

Conclusion: The Complexity of Industrial Capitalism 623


## CHAPTER 20
# POLITICS AND PROTEST
### 626

Politics in the Gilded Age 628
The Life of the Middle Class 639

RECOVERING THE PAST / MATERIAL CULTURE 639a

Middle-Class Reform 647
The Election of 1896 652
Conclusion: Looking Forward 655


## CHAPTER 21
# THE UNITED STATES BECOMES A WORLD POWER
### 658

Steps Toward Empire 659
Expansionist Motives in the 1890s 665
Cuba and the Philippines 670
Roosevelt's Energetic Diplomacy 678

RECOVERING THE PAST / POLITICAL CARTOONS 679a

Conclusion: The Responsibilities of Power 687


PORTFOLIO FOUR: THE ART OF AN INDUSTRIALIZING PEOPLE, 1865–1900
*after page 689*

# PART FIVE
# A MODERNIZING PEOPLE
# 1900–1945

## CHAPTER 22
# THE PROGRESSIVES CONFRONT INDUSTRIAL AMERICA
### 690

The Social Justice Movement                                      692

RECOVERING THE PAST / DOCUMENTARY PHOTOGRAPHS  697a

The Worker in the Progressive Era                               699
Reform in the Cities and States                                 705
Theodore Roosevelt and the Square Deal                          709
Woodrow Wilson and the New Freedom                              718
Conclusion: The Limits of Progressivism                         721

## CHAPTER 23
# AMERICA IN THE GREAT WAR
### 724

The Early Years of the War                                      726
The United States Enters the War                                734
The Military Experience                                         739

RECOVERING THE PAST / FILM AS PROPAGANDA  741a

Domestic Impact of the War                                      744
Planning for Peace                                              749
Conclusion: The Divided Legacy of the Great War                 752

## CHAPTER 24
# AFFLUENCE AND ANXIETY
### 754

Postwar Problems                                                756
The Benefits of Prosperity                                      760
Hopes Raised, Promises Deferred                                 766

RECOVERING THE PAST / ADVERTISING   *767a*

**The Business of Politics**                                              776
**Conclusion: A New Era of Prosperity and Problems**                      784


## CHAPTER 25
# THE GREAT DEPRESSION AND THE NEW DEAL
### 786

**The Great Depression**                                                  788
**Roosevelt and the First New Deal**                                      793
**One Hundred Days**                                                      795
**The Second New Deal**                                                   801
**The End of the New Deal**                                               810
**The Other Side of the Thirties**                                        814

RECOVERING THE PAST / RECREATION: FAIRS   *817a*

**Conclusion: The Ambivalent Character of the Great
Depression**                                                              818


## CHAPTER 26
# THE AMERICAN PEOPLE AND WORLD WAR II
### 820

**The Twisting Road to War**                                              822
**The Home Front During the War**                                         829
**Social Impact of the War**                                              836

RECOVERING THE PAST / ORAL HISTORY   *839a*

**A War of Diplomats and Generals**                                       841
**Conclusion: Peace, Prosperity, and International
Responsibilities**                                                        850


PORTFOLIO FIVE: THE ART OF A MODERNIZING PEOPLE, 1900–1945
*after page 851*

# PART SIX
## AN ENDURING PEOPLE
## 1945–1985

### CHAPTER 27
## CHILLS AND FEVER DURING THE COLD WAR
### 852

| | |
|---|---|
| Origins of the Soviet-American Confrontation | 854 |
| The Beginning of the Cold War | 857 |

RECOVERING THE PAST / PUBLIC OPINION POLLS   *857a*

| | |
|---|---|
| Containing the Soviet Threat | 859 |
| American Policy in Asia, the Middle East, and Latin America | 864 |
| Atomic Weapons and the Cold War | 871 |
| The Cold War at Home | 874 |
| Conclusion: The Cold War in Perspective | 880 |

### CHAPTER 28
## THE DREAMS OF POSTWAR AMERICA
### 882

| | |
|---|---|
| Demobilization and Economic Boom | 885 |
| Consensus and Conformity | 894 |
| Domestic Policy under Truman and Eisenhower | 899 |

RECOVERING THE PAST / POPULAR MUSIC   *899a*

| | |
|---|---|
| The Other America | 903 |
| Conclusion: Qualms amid Affluence | 910 |

### CHAPTER 29
## FROM SELF-CONFIDENCE TO SELF-DOUBT
### 912

| | |
|---|---|
| The Presidency in the Sixties | 914 |
| The New Frontier and Social Reform | 917 |
| The Great Society | 922 |
| The Rising Call for Reform | 929 |
| Intensification of the Cold War | 933 |
| Upheaval at Home | 937 |

RECOVERING THE PAST / TELEVISION   *937a*

| | |
|---|---|
| Conclusion: The Unraveling of the Affluent Society | 942 |

## CHAPTER 30
# ILLUSION AND DISILLUSIONMENT
### 944

| | |
|---|---|
| **Republican Leadership** | 946 |
| **Republican Foreign Policy** | 949 |
| **Searching for Stability** | 953 |

RECOVERING THE PAST / CARTOON HUMOR  *961a*

| | |
|---|---|
| **The Climax of Social Reform** | 963 |
| **Conclusion: The Struggle for Stability** | 970 |

## CHAPTER 31
# AUSTERITY AND THE AMERICAN DREAM: THE UNITED STATES SINCE 1976
### 972

| | |
|---|---|
| **The Disordered Economy** | 974 |
| **The Demographic Transformation** | 979 |

RECOVERING THE PAST / AUTOBIOGRAPHY  *981a*

| | |
|---|---|
| **The Continuing Struggle for Equality** | 983 |
| **The New Reformers** | 988 |
| **The Carter and Reagan Presidencies** | 992 |
| **Conclusion: The Recent Past in Perspective** | 998 |

PORTFOLIO SIX: THE ART OF AN ENDURING PEOPLE, 1945–1985
*after page 999*

# APPENDIX

| | |
|---|---|
| **Declaration of Independence** | A-1 |
| **Constitution of the United States of America** | A-3 |
| **States of the United States** | A-13 |
| **Territorial Expansion of the United States** | A-14 |
| **Presidential Elections** | A-15 |
| **Vice-Presidents, Cabinet Members, and Justices of the Supreme Court** | A-18 |
| **Population of the United States** | A-26 |
| **Demographic Contours of the American People** | A-27 |
| **National Origins of U.S. Immigrants, 1821–1980** | A-28 |
| **Characteristics of the American Work Force** | A-29 |
| **Credits** | C-1 |
| **Index** | I-1 |

# RECOVERING THE PAST

Archaeological Artifacts 7a
Houses 47a
Tombstones 77a
Tax Records 99a
Household Inventories 141a
Military Muster Rolls 175a
Political Documents 203a
Patriotic Paintings 251a
Census Returns 277a
Maps 309a
Family Paintings 359a
Folktales 393a
European Travel Journals 417a
Private Sources: Diaries 453a
Senate Speeches 475a
Photography 519a

Novels 555a
Magazines 577a
Congressional Hearings 615a
Material Culture 639a
Political Cartoons 679a
Documentary Photographs 697a
Film As Propaganda 741a
Advertising 767a
Recreation: Fairs 817a
Oral History 839a
Public Opinion Polls 857a
Popular Music 899a
Television 937a
Cartoon Humor 961a
Autobiography 981a

# MAPS

Migration Routes from Asia to the Americas                                    4
West African Cultures and Slaving Forts                                       9
Oceanic Exploration in the Fifteenth and Sixteenth Centuries                 13
Spanish and Portuguese New World Conquests                                   19
Early Chesapeake Settlement                                                   33
Early New England                                                             44
Early New York, Pennsylvania, and the Carolinas                              51
Origins and Destinations of African Slaves, 1526–1810                        64
France's Inland Empire, 1600–1720                                            87
King William's and Queen Anne's Wars                                         89
Scots-Irish Settlements, 1775                                                95
German Settlements, 1775                                                     95
City Plan of Charleston, 1790                                              109
City Plan of Boston, 1772                                                  113
Seven Years' War                                                           137
Western Land Claims Ceded by the States, 1782–1802                         166
Military Operations in the North, 1776–1780                                169
Military Operations in the South, 1778–1781                                171
Indian Battles, 1775–1783                                                  189
Old Northwest Survey Patterns                                              221
Areas of Settlement and Frontier in 1787                                   222
British and Spanish Claims in Eastern North America, 1783                  224
Federalist and Anti-Federalist Areas, 1787–1790                           239
Presidential Election of 1800                                              257
Growth of Towns in Southeastern Pennsylvania, c. 1800                      266
Rural Industry in the North, c. 1800                                       270
Important Routes Westward                                                  279
Exploring the Trans-Mississippi West, 1804–1807                            307
Indian Land Cessions, 1750–1830                                            310
Tribes of the Old Southeast, c. 1820                                       313
Tribes of the Old Northwest, c. 1809                                       316
The War of 1812                                                            322
Missouri Compromise of 1820                                                329
Growth of the Railroad System, 1840–1870                                   338
Economic Life in the South                                                 372
Southern Cotton Production, 1821–1859                                       373
Concentration of Slavery, 1820–1860                                         375
Religion, Reform, and Utopian Activity, 1830–1850                          421
Expanding Boundaries: The United States in 1853                            439
The Evolution of Texas                                                     443
The Mexican War                                                            446
The Oregon Country                                                         449
Overland Trails, 1840                                                      451

Western Population Advance, 1830–1850 — 452
Western Mining Frontier — 457
Indian Tribes and Culture Areas — 464
The Compromise of 1850 — 475
"Bleeding Kansas" — 486
Secession of the Southern States — 503
Eastern Theater of the Civil War, 1861–1862 — 508
Trans-Mississippi Campaign of the Civil War — 509
The Tide Turns, 1863–1865 — 517
Changes on the Barrow Plantation, 1860–1881 — 548
Sharecropping in the South, 1880 — 549
Return to the Union During Reconstruction — 554
Agriculture in the 1880s — 565
Election of 1896 — 654
United States Territorial Expansion — 662
The Spanish-American War — 673
United States Involvement in Asia, 1898–1909 — 685
Major Parties in the Presidential Election of 1912 — 717
European Alignments in 1914 — 727
United States Involvement in the Caribbean — 733
The Western Front of the Great War in 1918 — 742
The Presidential Election of 1932 — 794
The Tennessee Valley Authority — 799
World War II: Pacific Theater — 843
World War II: European and North African Theaters — 848
Cold War in Europe in 1950 — 863
The Korean War — 866
The Middle East in 1949 — 870
Population Shifts, 1940 to 1950 — 889
The Confusing 1960 Presidential Election — 915
The Vietnam War — 936
Population Shifts, 1970 to 1980 — 980

# CHARTS

Real Wages in England, 1500–1700     **22**
Population of the Chesapeake, 1607–1690     **36**
Population of New England, 1620–1690     **50**
Population of the Restoration Colonies, 1660–1720     **58**
Founding of the British North American Colonies     **60**
Slave Importations, 1451–1810     **65**
Slave Population of British America, 1680–1780     **71**
Rice and Indigo Exports from South Carolina and Georgia, 1698–1775     **106**
Urban Population Growth, 1650–1775     **110**
Wealth Distribution in Colonial America     **114**
Colonial Colleges     **121**
Colonial Foundations of the American Political System     **123**
British Exports to North America, 1756–1775     **148**
Steps on the Road to Revolution     **160**
Diet of Revolutionary War Soldiers     **177**
Exports and Imports, 1768–1783     **181**
Inflation of Wholesale Prices, 1770–1789     **187**
Occupational Composition of Several State Assemblies in the 1780s     **219**
Ratification of the Constitution     **238**
Inflation of Wholesale Prices, 1788–1800     **263**
Agricultural Productivity in 1800 and 1970     **267**
Slave Trade, 1741–1810     **269**
Average Daily Wages in Philadelphia, 1790–1820     **274**
Growth of Trans-Appalachian Population, 1790–1820     **276**
Blacks and Slavery, 1790–1820     **292**
Federal Revenues and Expenditures, 1790–1820     **304**
American Foreign Trade, 1790–1825     **319**
Sources of Population Growth, 1820–1899     **336**
Inland Freight Rates, 1785–1865     **339**
White Secondary School Enrollment, 1840–1860     **341**
Occupational Distribution, 1820–1860     **351**
Ten Largest Cities in the United States, 1810 and 1860     **355**
Wealth Distribution in Three Eastern Cities in the 1840s     **355**
Average Family Size, 1800–1860     **358**
Western Land Sales, 1800–1860     **364**
Diverse Population Patterns in the South: Whites, Slaves, and Free Blacks by State, 1860     **377**
White Class Structure in the South, 1860     **378**
Growth of Black Population: Slave and Free, 1820–1860     **398**
More Americans Vote for President, 1824–1840     **405**
The Second American Party System     **414**

| | |
|---|---|
| Presidential Elections, 1824–1844 | **416** |
| Immigration: Volume and Sources, 1840–1860 | **482** |
| Changing Political Party Systems and Leaders | **483** |
| Presidential Elections, 1848–1860 | **493** |
| Major Causes and Events Leading to the Civil War | **494** |
| Resources: North versus South | **502** |
| Men Present for Duty in the Civil War | **512** |
| War Casualties | **526** |
| Conflicting Goals During Reconstruction | **533** |
| The United States in 1865: Crisis at the End of the Civil War | **535** |
| Reconstruction Amendments | **544** |
| Average Farm Acreage, 1860–1900 | **565** |
| Agricultural Productivity, 1800–1900 | **567** |
| Price of Wheat Flour, 1865–1900 | **568** |
| Percentage of Farms Operated by Tenants, 1880–1900 | **570** |
| Population and Economic Growth, 1855–1919 | **596** |
| Increase in Size of Industries, 1860–1900 | **600** |
| Ten Largest Cities in the United States, 1850 and 1890 | **601** |
| Immigration: Source and Volume, 1870–1900 | **603** |
| Labor Force Distribution, 1870–1900 | **609** |
| Unemployment Rates, 1870–1899 | **611** |
| Status of Young People (12–20) by Ethnicity in Detroit in 1900 | **611** |
| Two Nineteenth-Century Budgets | **622** |
| Presidential Elections, 1872–1892 | **630** |
| Major Legislative Activity of the Gilded Age | **637** |
| Growth of Women in the Labor Force, 1870–1900 | **641** |
| Increase in Higher Education, 1870–1900 | **641** |
| Growth of American Foreign Trade, 1870–1914 | **667** |
| Presidential Elections, 1896–1900 | **677** |
| Union Membership, 1900–1920 | **702** |
| Immigration to the United States, 1900–1920 | **706** |
| Business Mergers, 1895–1905 | **712** |
| Presidential Elections of the Progressive Era | **720** |
| Key Progressive Era Legislation | **721** |
| Motor Vehicle Registration and Sales, 1900–1930 | **762** |
| Ten Largest Cities, 1900–1930 | **764** |
| Telephones in Use, 1900–1930 | **765** |
| Women in the Labor Force, 1900–1930 | **773** |
| Presidential Elections, 1920–1928 | **783** |
| Unemployment Rate, 1929–1940 | **797** |
| Distribution of Income, 1935–1936 | **802** |
| FDR's Successful Presidential Campaigns, 1932–1944 | **810** |
| Key New Deal Legislation | **813** |
| Household Appliance Production, 1929–1939 | **815** |
| Military Expenditures and the National Debt, 1940–1945 | **830** |
| Gross National Product and Unemployment, 1940–1945 | **831** |
| Defense Expenditures, 1945–1960 | **862** |
| Major Events of the Cold War | **879** |
| Weekly Earnings of Manufacturing Workers | **887** |
| Birth and Population Rates, 1900–1960 | **888** |

Growth of Sun Belt Cities, 1920–1980     **889**
Shifts in Population Distribution, 1940–1960     **891**
Occupational Distribution, 1940–1960     **892**
Households Owning Radios and Televisions, 1940–1960     **894**
Presidential Elections, 1948–1956     **902**
The Struggle for Equal Rights     **921**
Federal Aid to Education in the 1960s     **925**
Major Great Society Programs     **926**
Women Working Outside the Home, 1890–1970     **932**
U.S. Troops in Vietnam, 1965–1973     **937**
College Enrollment, 1940–1980     **938**
Rate of Inflation, 1947–1977     **953**
Oil Imports and Gasoline Prices, 1973–1980     **954**
Unemployment Rate, 1940–1982     **954**
Presidential Elections, 1968 and 1972     **961**
Women College Graduates, 1940–1980     **964**
Married Women in the Work Force, 1950–1980     **965**
Share of Total Manufacturing Output of Four Industrial
    Countries, 1950–1977     **975**
Union Membership, 1950–1980     **976**
Farm Indebtedness, 1950–1982     **977**
Immigration: Volume and Sources, 1941–1980     **980**
Changes in Female Employment, 1940–1980     **984**
Black Occupational Progress, 1940–1980     **986**
Federal Budget Surplus or Deficit as Percentage of GNP     **997**
Presidential Elections, 1976–1984     **998**

# PREFACE

The Teton Sioux have a saying that "a people without history is like wind upon the buffalo grass." The Sioux mean by this that the wind will always blow and the grass always grow, but people cannot understand who they are and where they are going without an understanding of the past—where they have been. That is why the Sioux storytellers hand down the history of the tribe from generation to generation.

When we speak of the "people" of American history, we are immediately confronting an extraordinarily complex mixture of human beings. This country's written history began with a convergence of Native Americans, Europeans, and Africans. The United States has always been a nation of immigrants —a magnificent mosaic of cultural backgrounds, religions, and skin shades. This book explores how American society, as it exists today, came to assume its present shape and develop its present forms of government; how as a nation we conduct our foreign affairs and manage our economy; how as a society we live, work, love, marry, raise families, sing, read, study, vote, argue, protest, and struggle—individually and collectively—for fulfillment.

Several special emphases distinguish this book from most textbooks written in the last 20 years. The coverage of presidential elections, diplomatic treaties, and economic legislation is integrated with the human story that underlays these more public aspects of American history. Within a strong chronological framework we have woven together our history as a nation and our history as a people and a society. When a national political event is discussed, for example, we analyze its impact on social and economic life, on life at the state and local level. Wars are described on the battlefield and in the salons of diplomats; but, as history's greatest motors of social change, wars are also discussed on the home front. The interaction of ordinary Americans with extraordinary events runs as a theme throughout the book.

Throughout, we have tried to illuminate the humanness of our history. The authors have often used the words of ordinary Americans and presented their participation in and responses to epic events such as war, industrialization, and reform movements. We have portrayed their material circumstances and woven the experiences of some of them through several chapters. At certain points we have focused on particular communities, describing not only their political, economic, and social contours but also their physical appearances and the rhythm of their everyday life.

## GOALS AND THEMES OF THE BOOK

One of our major goals is to provide students with a rich, balanced, and thought-provoking treatment of the American past. By rich and balanced we mean a history that treats the lives and experiences of Americans of all national origins and cultural backgrounds, at all levels of society, and in all regions of the country. By thought-provoking we mean a history that seeks connections between the multiple factors—political, economic, social, religious, intellectual, and biological—that have operated to mold and remold American society over a period of four centuries. By thought-provoking, we mean also a history that encourages students to consider how we are all legatees of a complicated, achievement-filled, and problem-strewn past. The only history befitting a democratic society and nation is one that inspires students to initiate a frank and searching dialogue with their past. We hope to stimulate such a dialogue here.

We also hope to promote discussion about the major themes we identify running through our history:

* the struggle for national unity and identity amidst cultural diversity and conflict;
* the powerful reform impulse in American society, present from the beginning, that for the last two centuries has worked to fulfill the democratic creed in racial, gender, and social relations;
* the competing claims of liberty and authority—in the family, the school, the workplace, the community, and the nation.

## STRUCTURE OF THE BOOK

**Part Organization**     The chapters of this book are grouped into six parts to reflect major periods in the development of the nation and society. Each part begins with an *introductory essay* that outlines the significant themes and problems explored in the subsequent chapters. Following this introduction is a two-page display of *parallel events* that occurred during that particular period in history. Not only do these chronologies serve as a preview of the section, but they show what was happening simultaneously, in the political, the social and economic, as well as the cultural and technological spheres. They also help give the reader an integrated picture of how these various events converged to make American history.

**Chapter Structure**     Every chapter begins with a *vignette* recalling the experience of an ordinary American. Chapter 1, for example, is introduced with the tragic story of Opechancanough, a Powhatan tribesman whose entire life of nearly 90 years was consumed by a struggle against the land hunger and alien values brought by Spanish and English newcomers. This brief anecdote serves several purposes. First, it introduces the overarching themes and major concepts of the chapter: the clash of three worlds—red, white, and black—in the North American wilderness, each with different cultural values, life styles, and aspirations. Second, the anecdote launches the chapter in a way which facilitates learning—beginning with the student's engagement with a human story. Lastly, the anecdote suggests that history was shaped by and affected ordinary as well as extraordinary Americans. At the end of the vignette, an *overview* relates the particular facts and ideas to the period under review and spells out the major themes of the chapter.

We aim to facilitate the learning process for the students. Every chapter ends with pedagogical features to reinforce and expand the presentation. A *conclusion* briefly summarizes the main concepts of the chapter and serves as a bridge to the following chapter. An annotated list of *recommended readings* provides supplementary sources for further study or research; novels contemporary to the period are often included. A *time line* reviews the major events and developments covered in the chapter.

## SPECIAL FEATURES

A distinctive feature of this book is the two-page *Recovering the Past* presentation in each chapter. These RTPs, as the authors affectionately call them, introduce students to the fascinating variety of evidence—ranging from tax lists, folk tales, and diaries to tombstones, advertising, and house designs—historians have learned to employ in reconstructing the past. Each RTP gives basic information about the source, its use by historians, and then raises questions for students to consider as they study the example reproduced for their inspection.

In addition to the RTPs we have provided other elements that will enable the instructor to use the text as a basis for class discussion or assignments. The program of *color illustrations*—paintings, cartoons, photographs, maps, and charts—amplifies important themes while presenting visual evidence for student reflection and analysis. Each major part of the text includes a *portfolio* on American cultural life. They begin with an essay discussing trends and themes in the art and artifacts of the period and elaborating on the color illustrations displayed.

## SUPPLEMENTAL TEACHING AND LEARNING AIDS

Several companion volumes for both teachers and students have been prepared to enhance this comprehensive presentation of American history.

* Gary B. Nash has selected and edited a two-volume set of readings, entitled **Retracing the Past,** to complement the text. Each reader contains around 25 selections covering political, social, and economic aspects of American history; Volume One focuses on the period until 1877, and Volume Two covers 1865 to the present.

Authors Julie Roy Jeffrey and Peter J. Frederick, both experienced instructional trainers, have written the *Study Guide* and *Instructor's Manual* to accompany the text. Tied closely to the text, both supplements provide a useful basis for reflection and discussion.

* The **Study Guide** (in two volumes) includes chapter outlines, significant themes and highlights, learning goals, list of important dates and names to know, glossary of important terms, learning enrichment ideas, and sample test questions. In addition, the authors provide helpful study hints such as how to underline a chapter.
* For those students who have access to personal computers, the study guide is available on diskettes. **Study-Aid,** a computer program for the Apple II series and the IBM-PC, is keyed directly to the text for learning ease.
* **Teaching the American People** is not merely a file of exam questions for the instructor. It is intended to serve as a resource book for new

teachers *and* for busy and tired veterans as well. This manual contains ideas on ways to use the text to enliven the classroom; suggestions for generating class discussion and involving students in an active learning experience; and a list of resources such as films, slides, and photo collections, records and audiocassettes.

★ A separate **Test Bank** of approximately 1500 items has been prepared by Carol Brown of Houston Community College. Multiple choice, true-false, and essay questions are included to test students' recall and understanding of the text presentation. The *Test Bank* is also available in computerized form *(Microtest)* for both Apple II and IBM-PC.

★ To help you improve your students' geographical and analytical skills, we have also produced a set of color **Transparencies.** For maps showing detailed areas of the country, we have included an inset of the present-day United States with the area under study shaded in. The transparencies also include key charts from the text.

Our aim has been to write a balanced and vivid history of the development of the American nation and its society. We have also tried to provide the support materials to make the teaching and the learning experience enjoyable and rewarding. The reader will be the judge of our success. The authors and Harper & Row welcome your comments.

GBN
JRJ

# ACKNOWLEDGMENTS

During the years that this text was being developed, many of our academic colleagues read and criticized the various drafts of the manuscript. For their thoughtful evaluation and constructive suggestions, the authors wish to extend their gratitude to the following reviewers:

Terry Alford, *Northern Virginia Community College*
Paul Bowers, *Ohio State University*
R. J. Bromert, *Southwestern Oklahoma State University*
Robin Brooks, *San Jose State University*
Carol Brown, *Houston Community College*
Jon Butler, *University of Illinois at Chicago*
Clayborne Carson, *Stanford University*
Lester Cohen, *Purdue University*
Kathleen Neils Conzen, *University of Chicago*
Lewis H. Croce, *Mankato State University*
William Ezzell, *DeKalb Community College*
William Freehling, *Johns Hopkins University*
William Geise, *San Antonio College*
Herbert Gutman, *City University of New York*
Carole Haber, *University of North Carolina at Charlotte*
Mitchell Hall, *University of Kentucky*
Susan Hartmann, *University of Missouri, St. Louis*
Richard J. Hopkins, *Ohio State University*
Richard A. Hunt, *Nassau Community College*
Joseph Illick III, *San Francisco State University*
Frederic Jaher, *University of Illinois, Urbana*
George Juergens, *Indiana University*
Richard Liebermann, *LaGuardia Community College*
Paul R. Lucas, *Indiana University*
Archie P. McDonald, *Stephen F. Austin State University*
Howard Miller, *University of Texas at Austin*
Herbert Parmet, *Queensborough Community College*
Mary Rothschild, *Arizona State University*
Richard T. Ruetten, *San Diego State University*
Ronald E. Shaw, *Miami University*
Richard Sorrell, *Brookdale Community College*
C. James Taylor, *University of South Carolina*
Martin Towey, *St. Louis University*
John Trickel, *Richland College*
Eldon Turner, *University of Florida*
Ronald Walters, *Johns Hopkins University*
Allen Yarnell, *University of California, Los Angeles*
Don Zelman, *Tarleton State University*

# ABOUT THE AUTHORS

GARY B. NASH is a graduate of Princeton University (B.A., 1955; Ph.D., 1964), where he taught for three years. In 1966 he moved to the University of California, Los Angeles, where he teaches colonial and revolutionary American history. Among the books Nash has authored are: *Quakers and Politics: Pennsylvania, 1681–1726* (1968); *Class and Society in Early America* (1970); *Red, White, and Black: The Peoples of Early America* (1974, 1982); *The Urban Crucible: Social Change, Political Consciousness, and the Origins of the American Revolution* (1979); *Race, Class, and Politics: Essays on Colonial and Revolutionary Society* (1985); and *Forging Freedom: The Black Urban Experience in Philadelphia, 1720–1820* (forthcoming). Nash is a recipient of Guggenheim and American Council of Learned Societies fellowships. His scholarship is especially concerned with the role of common people in the making of history. He served as a general editor of this book.

JULIE ROY JEFFREY received her B.A. degree in history and literature from Radcliffe College in 1962 and taught secondary school for several years. She earned her Ph.D. in history from Rice University in 1972, receiving the award for the best American history dissertation. Since 1972 she has taught at Goucher College, offering the American history survey and historic preservation courses. Jeffrey's major publications include: *Education for Children of the Poor: A Study of the Origins and Implementation of the Elementary and Secondary Education Act of 1965* (1978); *Frontier Women: The Trans-Mississippi West, 1840–1880* (1979); and many articles and papers on the lives and perceptions of nineteenth-century women. She is the recipient of fellowships from the NDEA, Rice, Southwest Center for Urban Research, and the Newberry Library. Honored as an outstanding teacher, Jeffrey has been involved in faculty development activities and curriculum evaluation. Her research interest has focused on the relationship of domestic space and family life and the use of buildings as primary sources. She acted as a general editor of this book.

JOHN R. HOWE received his B.A. (1957) from Otterbein College, and his M.A. (1959) and Ph.D. (1962) degrees from Yale University. From 1961 to 1965 he taught at Princeton University; since then he has been on the faculty of the University of Minnesota. His major publications include *The Changing Political Thought of John Adams* (1966), *The Role of Ideology in the American Revolution* (1970), and *From the Revolution Through the Age of Jackson* (1973). Howe has held a Woodrow Wilson fellowship, a faculty research fellowship from the Charles Warren Center at Harvard University, a Guggenheim fellowship, and a Bush Foundation fellowship. His major research currently involves a manuscript entitled "The Transformation of Public Life in Revolutionary America." His special teaching interests include early American politics up to the Civil War, and Indian-white relations in early America.

PETER J. FREDERICK received his B.A. in history from Harvard in 1959, his M.A. in American culture from the University of Michigan in 1960, and his Ph.D. in history from the University of California at Berkeley in 1966. A committed teacher, he began his career as a teaching assistant at Berkeley in 1960; he has taught at San Francisco State and California State College at Hayward, and since 1970 at Wabash College. Frederick's book, *Knights of the Golden Rule: The Intellectual as Christian Social Reformer in the 1890s,* was a runner-up in the Frederick Jackson Turner Award competition in 1974; other writing includes articles on social activism of intellectuals and educational reform. The recipient of several National Endowment for the Humanities fellowships, he held a Fulbright Lectureship in American culture at the University of Vienna in 1982–1983. Frederick has been recognized with several distinguished teaching awards and has conducted teaching workshops around the country. Areas of special research interest include nineteenth-century American social and intellectual history, black history, and biographies. He coordinated and edited all the *Recovering the Past* sections in this book.

ALLEN F. DAVIS is a professor at Temple University where he is the co-director of the Center for Public History and a specialist in American cultural history. He studied at Dartmouth College (A.B., 1953) and the University of Rochester (M.A., 1954) before earning a Ph. D. at the University of Wisconsin (1959). He has also taught at Wayne State University, at the University of Missouri, and as a visiting professor at the University of Texas at Austin. Davis is the author, co-author, or editor of ten books, including *Spearheads for Reform: The Social Settlements and the Progressive Movement; American Heroine: The Life and Legend of Jane Addams; Conflict and Consensus in American History;* and *Generations: Your Family in Modern American History.* Formerly the Executive Director of the American Studies Association, he has lectured widely in the United States and Europe. He has received fellowships from the American Council of Learned Societies, the National Endowment for the Humanities, and the American Philosophical Society. Davis has been honored for his writing by the Friends of Literature, The Society of American Historians, and The Christopher Society. He compiled the six art portfolios and acted as an illustration coordinator for this book.

ALLAN M. WINKLER holds a B.A. degree from Harvard (1966), an M.A. from Columbia (1967), and a Ph.D. from Yale (1974). He was a history faculty member at Yale from 1973 to 1978. He served as Bicentennial Professor of American Studies at Helsinki University before joining the faculty of the University of Oregon in 1979. Winkler was the first recipient of the John Adams Chair in American Civilization at the University of Amsterdam in 1984–1985. He is the author of *The Politics of Propaganda: The Office of War Information, 1942–1945* (1978) and *Modern America: The United States from the Second World War to the Present* (1985). Winkler has received grants from the National Endowment for the Humanities, the Fulbright Commission, the American Council for Learned Societies, and the American Philosophical Society; he has been a Mellon Fellow at the Aspen Institute for Humanistic Studies. Formerly a Peace Corps Volunteer, he is most interested in the connections between public policy and popular mood in the recent past. He is currently studying American atomic energy policy.

# THE
# AMERICAN
# PEOPLE

# PART ONE
# A
# COLONIZING
# PEOPLE

# 1492–1776

America has always been a nation of immigrants, an elaborate cultural mosaic created out of the unending streams of people who for four centuries have flocked to its shores from every corner of the world. It is the colonial roots of this intermingling of people and cultures that provides an organizing framework for the first part of this book. America began with the convergence of people from the three continents of North America, Europe, and Africa. We examine the clash of their values, institutions, and lifeways during the fifteenth and sixteenth centuries in Chapter 1, "Three Worlds Meet." Chapter 2, "Colonizing America," explores four distinct types of settlement in the English colonies. The interplay of religious idealism, economic opportunity, political experimentation, and social adaptation to the new environment are examined on the Chesapeake tobacco coast, in Puritan New England, in proprietary New York and Carolina, and in Quaker Pennsylvania.

The ability to grow from small and struggling settlements in the seventeenth century to thriving, more populous colonies in the early eighteenth century depended above all on exploiting the natural resources of North America. Chapter 3, "Mastering the New World," explores how colonists struggled against Native Americans to expand their land base and turned to slave labor in the southern colonies. While controlling Native Americans and African slaves, the colonists also had to master themselves as social and political tensions grew at the end of the seventeenth century. At the same time, French ambitions in North America challenged the territorial mastery of England's American colonies and involved them in another kind of conflict.

Chapter 4, "The Maturing of Colonial Society," traces the development of the colonies in the first half of the eighteenth century. It stresses the increasingly complex yet unfinished character of colonial society, highlights its regional differences, and shows how economic growth, religious revival, and political maturation brought the colonists by 1750 to a condition of growing preparedness for the epic events that would occur in the next generation. It was this fluidity of colonial society that made the Seven Years' War (1756–1763) and the subsequent coming of the American Revolution such a multifaceted and dynamic period, as Chapter 5, "Bursting the Colonial Bonds," spells out.

# PARALLEL EVENTS

## CULTURAL and TECHNOLOGICAL

- 1450 Printing with movable type perfected
  Missiles propelled by gunpowder begin to transform warfare
- 1477 Marco Polo's *Travels* published in Europe
- 1500 Indian tribes of Southeast attain artistic peak
- 1508 First New World sugar mill established in West Indies
- 1517 Luther launches the Reformation
- 1530s Calvin calls for further religious reforms
- 1539 First printing press in New World established in Mexico City
- 1564 Jacques LeMoyne paints first scenes of Indian life in New World
- 1585 John White, member of Roanoke expedition, paints first scenes of Indian life in area of English settlement
- 1612–1613 John Rolfe's experiments with tobacco develop a hybrid suitable for export
- 1636 Harvard College established
- 1638 First printing press in North America set up in Cambridge
- 1642 Massachusetts passes basic literacy law
- 1643 Roger Williams compiles first American

## SOCIAL and ECONOMIC

- 12,000 B.C. End of Bering Straits migration to New World
- 3000–1000 B.C. Agricultural revolution transforms Native American cultures
- 1420s Portuguese explore west coast of Africa
- 1487 Dias reaches southern tip of Africa
- 1492–1504 Columbus makes four voyages exploring New World
- 1498 Da Gama reaches India by water
- 1515–1565 Spanish explore southern parts of North America
- 1518–1530 European diseases decimate New World native populations in Caribbean and Central America
- 1521–1522 Magellan circumnavigates the world
- 1525–1585 French and English explore northern parts of North America
- 1545–1560 Bonanza silver strikes made in Spanish Mexico and Bolivia
- 1550–1650 Price revolution in western Europe causes widespread distress
- 1616–1621 Decimation of Native Americans in New England by European diseases
- 1617 First Virginia tobacco shipped to England
- 1619 First Africans brought to Virginia
- 1625–1660 Slavery becomes backbone of labor force in English Caribbean
- 1637 Pequot War in New England

## POLITICAL

- 1492 Spain completes expulsion of Moors
- 1493 Pope declares demarcation line in New World
- 1509–1547 Reign of Henry VIII in England
- 1519–1521 Cortés conquers Aztec empire
- 1532–1535 Pizarro conquers Inca empire
- 1558–1603 Reign of Elizabeth I in England
- 1565 Spanish found St. Augustine in Florida
- 1585–1598 England colonizes Ireland
- 1588 Spanish armada attacks England
- 1603–1625 Reign of James I in England
- 1607 Virginia Company of London settles Jamestown
- 1620 Pilgrims establish colony at Plymouth
- 1624 Dutch West India Company settles New Netherland
- 1625–1649 Reign of Charles I in England
- 1630 Puritans migrate to New England under charter to Massachusetts Bay Company
- 1634 Settlement of Maryland begins under charter to Lord Baltimore
- 1636 Settlement of Connecticut and Rhode Island

# 1492–1776

## CULTURAL and TECHNOLOGICAL

1650   Anne Bradstreet publishes first volume of verse written in America

1661   John Eliot's translation of the New Testament into Algonquian becomes first Bible printed in North America

1662   Half-Way Covenant in Massachusetts

1690   First newspaper in colonies published (and quickly suppressed) in Boston

1693   William and Mary College founded

1701   Yale College founded

1721–1722   Inoculation against smallpox creates controversy in colonies

1747   Benjamin Franklin publishes *Poor Richard's Almanack* in Philadelphia

1749   Franklin invents lightning rod

1752   First American hospital established in Philadelphia
   Franklin's *Experiments and Observations in Electricity* published

1754   College of Philadelphia founded

1757   First streetlights in a colonial city installed in Philadelphia

1769   American Philosophical Society founded

1775   Postal system is established by Continental Congress

## SOCIAL and ECONOMIC

1650–1670   Judicial and legislative decisions solidify racial lines in southern colonies

1675–1677   King Philip's War in New England War against Chesapeake tribes associated with Bacon's Rebellion

1690s   South Carolinians begin rice cultivation

1690–1720   Most colonies enact slave codes

1692   Witchcraft hysteria and executions in Salem, Massachusetts

1697–1715   Colonial importations of slaves increase rapidly

1711–1715   Tuscarora and Yamasee wars in the Carolinas

1712   Slave revolt in New York City

1714–1720   Scots-Irish and German immigration begins

1715–1730   Volume of slave trade doubles

1734–1760   Great Awakening in different regions of colonies

1739   Stono Rebellion in South Carolina

1741   Hysteria over suspected slave plot in New York City

1759–1761   Frontier war against Cherokees

1761–1765   Depression hits most colonies

1775   Pennsylvania Abolition Society established

## POLITICAL

1651   First navigation act

1660   Restoration of Stuart monarchy; Charles II installed

1663   Carolina settled under proprietary charter

1664   English conquer New Netherland

1673–1683   French expand into Mississippi valley

1682   Quakers migrate to Pennsylvania under proprietary charter to William Penn

1688–1691   Glorious Revolution in America follows overthrow of James II

1689–1697   King William's War

1702–1703   Queen Anne's War

1732   Georgia founded as colony for English paupers and buffer against Spanish Florida

1744–1748   King George's War

1756–1763   Seven Years' War

1764–1765   Sugar, Stamp, and Currency Acts

1767   Townshend Duties

1773   Tea Act and Boston Tea Party

1774   Coercive Acts and meeting of First Continental Congress

1775   Battles of Lexington and Concord Meeting of Second Continental Congress

1776   Declaration of Independence

# CHAPTER 1
## THREE WORLDS MEET

In the late 1550s, a few years after Catholic King Philip II and Protestant Queen Elizabeth assumed the throne in Spain and England, respectively, Opechancanough was born in Tsenacommacah. In the Algonquian language, the word Tsenacommacah meant "densely inhabited land." Later English colonizers would rename this place Virginia after their monarch, the virgin Queen Elizabeth. Before he died in the 1640s, in the ninth decade of his life, Opechancanough had seen light-skinned, swarthy, and black-skinned newcomers from a half dozen European nations and African kingdoms swarm into his land. Although he could not know it, the Indian leader was witnessing the early moments of European expansion around the globe.

Opechancanough was only an infant when Europeans first reached the Chesapeake Bay region. A small party of Spanish had explored the area in 1561, but they found neither gold, silver, nor anything else of value. Upon departing, they took with them the brother of one of the local chieftains, who was a member of Opechancanough's clan. They left behind something of unparalleled importance in the history of contact between the peoples of Europe and the Americas: a bacterial infection that spread like wildfire through a population that had no immunity against it. Many members of Opechancanough's tribe died, although their casualties were light compared with those of other tribes that caught the deadly European disease.

In 1570, when Opechancanough was young, the Spanish returned and established a Jesuit mission near the York River. Violence occurred, and before the Spanish abandoned the Chesapeake in 1572, they put to death a number of captured Indians, including a chief who was Opechancanough's relative. The Native Americans learned that Europeans, even when they came bearing the crosses of their religion, were a volatile and dangerous people.

Opechancanough was in his forties when three ships of fair-skinned settlers disembarked in 1607 to begin the first permanent English settlement in the New World. For several months, he watched his half brother Powhatan, high chief of several dozen loosely confederated tribes in the region, parry and fence with the newcomers. Then Powhatan sent him to capture the English leader John Smith and escort him to the Indians' main village. Smith was put through a mock execution but then released. He later got the best of Opechancanough, threatening him with a pistol, humiliating him in front of his warriors, and assaulting one of his sons, whom Smith "spurned like a dog."

Opechancanough nursed his wounds for years while Powhatan grew old and the English settlements slowly spread in the Chesapeake region. Then, in 1617, he assumed leadership of the Powhatan Confederacy. Two years later, a Dutch trader sold twenty Africans to the settlers after docking at Jamestown. Three years after that, Opechancanough led a determined assault on the English plantations that lay along the rivers and streams emptying into the bay. The Indians killed nearly one-third of the intruders. But they paid dearly in the retaliatory raids that the colonists mounted in succeeding years.

As he watched the land-hungry settlers swarm in during the next two decades, Opechancanough's patience failed him. Finally, in 1644, now in his eighties, he galvanized a new generation of warriors and led a final desperate assault on the English. It was a suicidal attempt, but the "great general" of the Powhatan Confederacy, faithful to the warrior tradition of his people, counseled death over enslavement and humiliation. Though the warriors inflicted heavy casualties, they could not overwhelm the colonizers, who vastly outnumbered them. For two years, Opechancanough was kept prisoner by the Virginians. Nearly blind and "so decrepit that he was not able to walk alone," he was fatally shot in the back by an English guard in 1646.

3

Over a long lifetime, Opechancanough painfully experienced the meeting of people from three continents. His land was one of many that would be penetrated by Europeans over the next three centuries, as Christian civilization girdled the globe. On the Chesapeake Bay, this clash of cultures formed the opening chapter of what we know as American history. That history, in turn, was one scene in a much broader drama of European colonization and exploitation of many indigenous cultures thousands of miles from the Old World. The nature of this violent intermingling of Europeans, Africans, and Native Americans is an essential part of early American history. But to understand how the destinies of red, white, and black people became intertwined in Opechancanough's land, we must look at the precontact history and cultural foundations of life in the homelands of each of them.

## THE PEOPLE OF AMERICA BEFORE COLUMBUS

Thousands of years before human life existed in the British Isles or in western Europe, the history of humankind in North America began. Nomadic hunting bands from Siberia, pursuing big-game mammals such as bison, caribou, and reindeer, began to migrate across a land bridge connecting northeastern Asia and Alaska. Over many millennia, massive glaciers had covered the northern latitudes, locking up most of the earth's moisture and leaving part of the Bering Sea floor exposed. Geologists believe this land bridge was open for two long periods, from about 32,000 to 36,000 years ago and again from 20,000 to 28,000 years ago. At other times the melting glaciers flooded the land bridge and blocked foot traffic to Alaska. But during these two long intervals, the human history of the Americas began.

### Hunters and Farmers

For thousands of years, these early hunters trekked southward and eastward, following vegetation and game. In time, they reached the tip of South America, 15,000 miles from their Asian homeland, and the eastern edge of North America, 6,000 miles from Siberia. Thus did people from the "Old World" discover the "New World" thousands of generations before Columbus.

Archaeologists have excavated ancient sites of early life in the Americas, unearthing tools, ornaments, and skeletal remains that can be scientifically dated. In this way they have tentatively reconstructed the dispersion of these first Americans over an immense landmass. Although much remains unknown, this archaeological evidence suggests that as centuries

## Migration Routes from Asia to the Americas

Approximate dry land area during ice ages

Glaciers

Modern coastline

4

passed and population increased, the earliest inhabitants evolved into separate cultures, organizing life and adjusting to a variety of environments in distinct ways. Europeans who rediscovered the New World thousands of years later would indiscriminately lump together the myriad societies they found. But by the 1500s, the "Indians" of the Americas were enormously diverse in the size and complexity of their societies, the languages they spoke, and their forms of social organization.

Archaeologists and anthropologists have charted four long phases of "Native American" history. The first, the Beringian epoch, lasted until about 14,000 years ago. Nomadic bands, usually small, pushed farther east and south in the hemisphere, splitting off from one another to form countless new societies.

In the second, Paleo-Indian phase, which lasted until about 8,000 years ago, a technological breakthrough changed the relationship of the migrant bands to their environment. Developing the ability to flake hard stones into spear points, big-game hunters chose "kill sites" where they slew whole herds of Pleistocene mammals. This more reliable food source allowed population growth, and nomadism began to give way to settled habitations or local migration within limited territories.

In a third phase of evolution, the Archaic era, from about 8,000 to 2,500 years ago, great geological changes brought further adaptations to the land. As the massive glaciers of the Ice Age slowly retreated, a warming trend deprived vast areas from Utah to the highlands of Central America of sufficient water and turned them from grasslands into desert. The Pleistocene mammals could not survive the more arid conditions, but human populations ably adapted. They learned to exploit new sources of food, especially plant life. In time this brought about a second technological breakthrough, the "agricultural revolution."

When Native Americans learned to "domesticate" plant life, they began the long process of emancipating themselves from oppression by the physical world. To learn how to harvest, plant, and nurture a seed was to gain partial control over natural forces that before had been ungovernable. Anthropologists believe that this process began independently in widely separated parts of the world—Africa, Asia, Europe, and the Americas—about 7,000 to 9,000 years ago. Though agriculture developed very slowly, everywhere it eventually brought dramatic changes in human societies.

Over the millennia, humans progressed from doorside planting of a few wild seeds to

*Baskets were essential equipment for daily life, as well as an art form, in Native American hunter-gatherer societies.*

systematic clearing and planting of bean and maize fields. As the production of domesticated plant food ended the dependence on gathering wild plants and pursuing game, sedentary village life began to replace nomadic existence. The increase in food supply brought about by agriculture triggered other major changes. As populations grew, large groups split off to form separate societies. Greater social and political complexity developed because not everyone was needed as before to secure the society's food supply. In most areas a sexual division of labor appeared. Men cleared the land and hunted game, while women planted, cultivated, and harvested crops. Many societies empowered religious figures, who organized the common followers, directed their work, and exacted tribute as well as worship from them. In return they were trusted to protect the community from hostile forces.

Everywhere in the Americas, regional trading networks formed. Along trade routes carrying commodities such as salt, obsidian rock for projectile points, and copper for jewelry also traveled technology, religious ideas, and agricul-

*One of the many symbolic mounds built by the Hopewell culture, this one, in the shape of a serpent, is near what is now Cincinnati.*

tural practices. By the end of the Archaic period, about 500 B.C. (to use the Christian European method of dating), hundreds of independent, kin-based groups had learned to exploit the resources of their particular area and to trade with other groups in their region.

## Native Americans in 1600

The last epoch of pre-Columbian development, the post-Archaic phase, occurred during the 2,000 years before contact with Europeans. It involved rapid growth and environmental adaptation among many societies and crisis in some of them. In the American Southwest, for example, the ancestors of the present-day Hopi and Zuni developed carefully planned villages composed of large terraced buildings, each with many rooms. By the time the Spanish arrived in the 1540s, the indigenous Pueblo people were using irrigation canals, check dams, and hillside terracing to bring water to their arid maize fields. In their agricultural techniques, their skill in ceramics, their use of woven textiles for clothing, and their village life, Pueblo society resembled that of peasant communities in most of Europe and Asia.

Far to the east were the mound-building societies of the Mississippi and Ohio valleys. When European settlers first crossed the Appalachian Mountains a century and a half after arriving on the continent, they were astounded to find hundreds of ceremonial mounds, some of them 70 feet high, and gigantic sculptured earthworks in geometric designs or in the shapes of huge humans, birds, or writhing serpents. Believing all "Indians" to be forest primitives, they reasoned that they were gazing at the remains of an ancient civilization that had found its way to North America—perhaps Phoenicians, survivors of the sunken islands of Atlantis, or the Lost Tribes of Israel spoken of in European mythology.

The mound-building "Hopewell" culture of the Ohio valley declined about 1,000 years before Europeans reached the continent, perhaps because of attacks from other tribes or severe climatic changes that undermined agriculture. Several centuries later, another culture, based on intensive cultivation of beans, maize, and squash, began to flourish in the Mississippi valley. Its center, a city of perhaps 20,000, stood near present-day St. Louis. Great ceremonial plazas, flanked by a temple that rose in four terraces to a height of 100 feet, marked this first metropolis in America. This was the urban center of a far-flung "Mississippi" culture that radiated out to encompass thousands of villages from Wisconsin to Louisiana and from Oklahoma to Tennessee.

Several centuries before Europeans arrived in North America, the mound-building cultures of the continental heartlands began to decline. But their influence had already passed eastward to transform the woodlands societies along the Atlantic coastal plain. The numerous small tribes that settled from Nova Scotia to Florida never equaled the larger societies of the mid-continent in earthwork sculpture, architectural design, or development of large-scale agriculture. But they were far from the "savages" that the first European explorers described. They had added limited agriculture to their skill in exploiting natural plants for food, medicine, dyes, and flavoring and had developed food procurement strategies that used all the resources around them—cleared land, forests, streams, shore, and ocean.

Most of the eastern woodlands tribes lived in waterside villages. Locating their fields of maize near fishing grounds, they often migrated seasonally between inland and coastal village sites or situated themselves astride two ecological zones. In the Northeast, their birchbark canoes, light enough to be carried by a single man, gave them a means of trading and communicating over immense territories. In the Southeast, population was denser and social and political organization more elaborate.

As European exploration of the Americas drew near, the continent north of the Rio Grande contained an estimated 5 million people, of whom perhaps 500,000 lived along the eastern coastal plain and in the piedmont region accessible to the early European settlers. Europeans were not coming to a "virgin wilderness," as they often described it, but to a land inhabited for thousands of years by people whose village existence in many ways resembled that of the arriving Europeans.

## Conflicting Values

Colonizing Europeans called themselves "civilized," and they typically described the people they met in the Americas as "savage" or "heathen" or "barbarian." But the gulf that separated people in Europe and North America was not defined so much by how the two cultures extracted a food supply from the land, housed themselves, or organized family life as by how they viewed their relationship to the environment and defined social relations in their communities. In these areas, a wide difference in values existed. This created the potential for a dangerous conflict when the Atlantic Ocean that had separated two ancient civilizations had been transformed from a barrier to a bridge by a technological and scientific leap forward by western Europeans in the fifteenth century.

In the view of Europeans, the natural world was a resource designed for man's use. "Subdue the earth," read the first book of the Old Testament, "and have dominion over every living thing that moves on the earth." God ruled the cosmos, bringing floods, droughts, and earthquakes, but humans could reshape their physical surroundings into a productive and secure world. Man's relationship to the natural environment was a secular matter, even if God, in the sacred sphere, sometimes intervened.

Native Americans, in contrast, were "a people that are contented with Nature as they find her," as one colonist phrased it. In their ethos, every part of the natural environment was sacred. Rocks, trees, and animals all possessed spiritual power, and all were linked to form a sacred whole. To injure the environment, by overfishing or abusing it in any way, was to offend the spiritual power present throughout nature and hence to risk spiritual retaliation. In the villages of Europe, peasant people had similarly believed in spirits residing in trees and rocks, but such "superstition" was fading.

Regarding the soil as a resource to be exploited for man's benefit, Europeans believed that land should be privately possessed. Individual ownership of property became a fundamental concept, and an extensive institutional apparatus grew up to support it. Fences symbolized

# RECOVERING THE PAST

The recovery of the past before there were extensive written records is the domain of archaeology. Virtually our entire knowledge of Indian societies in North America before the arrival of European colonizers is drawn from the work of archaeologists who have excavated the ancient living sites of the first Americans. Many Native Americans today strongly oppose this rummaging in the ancient ancestral places; they particularly oppose the unearthing of burial sites. But the modern search for knowledge about the past goes on.

Historians have relied heavily on archaeological data in attempting to overcome the stereotypic view of Native Americans as a primitive people whose culture was static for thousands of years before Europeans arrived in North America. Such a view allowed historians to argue that the tremendous loss of Native American population and land accompanying the initial settlement and westward migration of white Americans was more or less inevitable. When two cultures, one dynamic and forward-looking and the other static and backward, confronted each other, it was frequently maintained, the more advanced or "civilized" culture usually prevailed.

It will probably never be possible to recapture the elaborate early history of people in the Americas. But many fragments of this long human history are being recovered through archaeological research. Particularly important are studies that reveal how Indian societies were changing during the few centuries immediately preceding the European arrival in the "New World." These studies give us a much better chance to interpret the seventeenth-century interaction of Native Americans and Europeans because they provide an understanding of Indian values, social and political organization, material culture, and religion as they existed when the two cultures first met.

One such investigation has been carried out over the last century near the Mississippi River near modern-day East St. Louis, Illinois. The archaeologists have found the center of a vast "Mississippi" culture that began about A.D. 600, reached its peak about 300 years before Columbus's voyages, and then declined. Cahokia is the name given to the urban center of a civilization that at its height dominated an area as large as New York State. At the center of Cahokia stood one of the largest earth constructions built by ancient man anywhere on the planet. Its base covering 15 acres, this gigantic earthen temple rises in four terraces to a height of 100 feet, as tall as a

Cahokia Mounds Museum Society, Cahokia, Illinois

**Reconstructed view of Cahokia, painting by Valerie Waldorf**

7a

ten-story modern office building. The imaginary drawing shown here indicates some of the dozens of smaller geometric mounds discovered near this major temple. Notice the outlying farms, a sure sign of the settled (as opposed to nomadic) existence of the people who flourished ten centuries ago in this region. How does this depiction of ancient Cahokia change your image of Native American life before the arrival of Europeans?

By recovering artifacts from Cahokia burial mounds, archaeologists have pieced together a picture, still tentative, of a highly elaborate civilization along the Mississippi bottomlands. Cahokian manufacturers mass-produced salt, knives, and stone hoe blades for both local consumption and export. Cahokian artisans made sophisticated pottery, ornamental jewelry, metalwork, and tools. They used copper and furs from the Lake Superior region, black obsidian stone from the Rocky Mountains, and seashells from the Gulf of Mexico, demonstrating that the people at Cahokia were involved in long-distance trade. In fact, Cahokia may have been a crucial crossroads of trade and water travel in the heartland of North America.

The objects shown here, unearthed from graves by archaeologists, are an example of the culture of the Mississippi Mound Builders. The round-faced pottery bottles in the form of heads, each about 6 inches tall and wide, show a sense of humor in early Mississippi culture. Holes in the ears of the bottles and in the armpits and wrists of the woman once held thongs so that the objects could be hung or carried. Other objects, such as a kneeling woman found in Tennessee for example, had holes under the arms for a similar purpose. What other conclusions about Cahokian culture can you draw from figures such as these? Are there archaeological sites in your area that contain evidence of Native American civilization?

The fact that some graves uncovered at Cahokia contain large caches of finely tooled objects while other burial mounds contain many skeletons unaccompanied by any artifacts leads archaeologists to conclude that this was a more stratified society than those the first settlers encountered along the Atlantic seaboard. Anthropologists believe that some of the Mississippi culture spread eastward before Cahokia declined, but much mystery still remains concerning the fate and cultural diffusion of these early Americans.

Museum of the American Indian, Heye Foundation, New York

*Pottery effigy vessels*

private property, inheritance became the mechanism for transmitting these "assets" from one generation to another within the same family, and courts were granted the power to settle property disputes. Property was the basis not only of sustenance but also of independence, material wealth, political status, and personal identity. The social structure directly mirrored patterns of land ownership, with a land-wealthy elite at the apex of the social pyramid and a mass of propertyless individuals forming the broad base.

In the Native American system of values, land invested with sacred qualities could be held only in common. Bands and tribes recognized territorial boundaries, but within these limits, members shared the land. As one German missionary to the Delaware Indians explained their view in the eighteenth century, the Creator "made the Earth and all that it contains for the common good of mankind. Whatever liveth on the land, whatsoever groweth out of the earth, and all that is in the rivers and waters . . . was given jointly to all and everyone is entitled to his share."

Communal ownership sharply limited social stratification in tribal communities. Accustomed to wide disparities of wealth, Europeans often found this remarkable. Observing the Iroquois of the eastern woodlands in 1657, a French Jesuit noted with surprise that they had no almshouses because "their kindness, humanity and courtesy not only makes them liberal with what they have, but causes them to possess hardly anything except in common. A whole village must be without corn, before any individual can be obliged to endure privation." Not all Europeans were acquisitive, competitive individuals. The majority were peasants scratching a subsistence living from the soil, living in kin-centered villages with little contact with the outside world, and exchanging goods and labor through barter. But in Europe's urban centers a wealth-conscious, striving individual who celebrated wider choices and greater opportunities to enhance personal status was coming to the fore. In contrast, Native American traditions stressed the group rather than the individual. Holding land and other resources in common, Indian societies were more egalitarian and their

members more concerned with personal valor than personal wealth.

Exceptions to this cultural system could be found in the highly developed and populous Aztec and Inca empires and, in North America, among a few tribes such as the Natchez. But on the eastern and western coasts of the continent and in the Southwest—the regions of contact in the sixteenth and seventeenth centuries—the European newcomers found a people whose cultural values differed strikingly from theirs.

European colonizers in North America also found disturbing the matrilineal organization of tribal society. Contrary to European practice, family membership among the Iroquois, for example, was determined through the female line. A typical family was composed of an old woman, her daughters with their husbands and children, and her unmarried granddaughters and grandsons. When a son or grandson married, he moved from this female-headed household to one headed by the matriarch of his wife's family. Divorce was also the woman's prerogative. If she desired it, she merely set her husband's possessions outside their dwelling door. Clans were composed of several matrilineal kin groups related by a blood connection on the mother's side. To Europeans this was a peculiar and dangerous reversal of their sexual hierarchy in which men, from time immemorial, had been supreme.

In dividing political power between men and women, Native American societies also differed from those of arriving Europeans. Everywhere in Europe, women were entirely excluded from political affairs. In Native American villages, again to take the Iroquois example, designated men sat in a circle to deliberate and make decisions. But the senior women of the village stood behind the circle of men, lobbying and instructing them. The village chiefs were male, but they were named to their positions by the elder women of their clans. If they moved too far from the will of the women who appointed them, these chiefs were removed—or "dehorned."

The role of women in the tribal economy reinforced the sharing of power between male and female. Men were responsible for hunting, fishing, and clearing land, but women controlled the cultivation, harvest, and distribution of food. When the men were away on hunting expeditions, women directed village life. Europeans, imbued with the idea of male superiority and female subordination, perceived such a degree of sexual equality as another mark of the uncivilized nature of tribal society.

In the religious beliefs of Native Americans, the English saw a final cultural defect. Europeans built their religious life around scriptures, an organized clergy, and churches. Native Americans, lacking this structure and animated by a belief in a spirit power dwelling throughout nature, appeared to Europeans as devil worshipers. European settlers, their fear and hatred of infidels intensified by the Protestant Reformation, saw a holy necessity to convert—or destroy—these enemies of their God.

## AFRICA ON THE EVE OF CONTACT

Half a century before Columbus reached the Americas, a Portuguese sea captain, Antam Gonçalves, made the first European landing on the west coast of sub-Saharan Africa. If he had been able to travel the length and breadth of the immense continent, he would have encountered little to convince him that the rich variety of African peoples suffered a natural inferiority. The notion of their "backwardness" and cultural impoverishment was the myth perpetuated after the slave trade had begun transporting millions of Africans to the New World. But during the period of early contact with Europeans, Africa, like pre-Columbian America, was a diverse continent with a long history of cultural evolution.

### The Kingdoms of Africa

The peoples of Africa, estimated at about 50 million in the fifteenth century when Europeans began making extensive contact with them, lived in vast deserts, grasslands, and tropical forests. As in Europe and the Americas at that time, most people tilled the soil. Part of their skill in farming derived from the development of iron production, which may have begun in West Africa while Europe was still in the Stone Age. More efficient iron implements increased agricultural productivity, which in turn spurred population growth. The pattern was repeated in other parts of the world—the Americas, Europe,

### West African Cultures and Slaving Forts

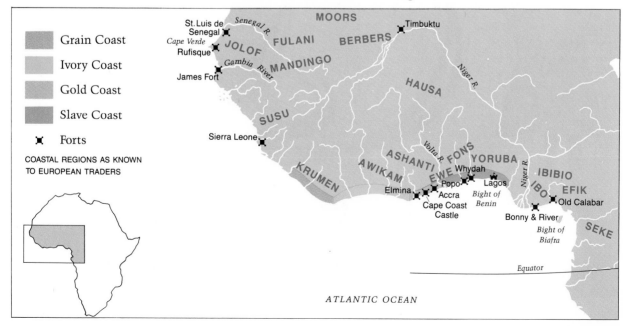

the Far East, and the Middle East—when the agricultural revolution began.

By the time Europeans reached the west coast of Africa, a number of large empires had risen there. The first was the kingdom of Ghana. It embraced an immense territory between the Sahara and the Gulf of Guinea and stretched from the Atlantic Ocean to the Niger River.

The development of large towns, skillfully designed buildings, elaborate sculpture and metalwork depicting humans and animals, long-distance commerce, and a complex political structure came to mark the Ghanaian kingdom from the sixth to eleventh centuries. A thriving caravan trade with Arab peoples across the Sahara to Morocco and Algeria brought extensive Muslim influence by the end of this period. By the eleventh century the king of Ghana boasted an army of 200,000, maintained trading contacts as far east as Cairo and Baghdad, and was furnishing, through Muslim middlemen in North Africa, much of the gold supply for the Christian Mediterranean region.

An invasion of North African Muslim people beginning in the eleventh century intro-

duced a period of religious strife that eventually destroyed the kingdom of Ghana. But in the same region arose the Islamic kingdom of Mali. Prospering through its control of the gold trade, Mali flourished until the fifteenth century. Its city of Timbuktu contained a distinguished faculty of scholars to whom North Africans and even southern Europeans came to study. Traveling there in the 1330s, the Arab geographer ibn-Battutu wrote admiringly of "the discipline of its officials and provincial governors, the excellent condition of public finance, and . . . the respect accorded to the decisions of justice and to the authority of the sovereign."

Lesser kingdoms such as Congo, Songhay, and Benin had also been growing for centuries before Europeans reached Africa by water. In their towns, which rivaled those of Europe in size, lived people who were skilled in metalworking, weaving, ceramics, architecture, and aesthetic expression. Codes of law, regional trade, and effective political organization all developed by the fifteenth century. Finding their way to Africa south of the Sahara, Europeans encountered not a backward area but a densely

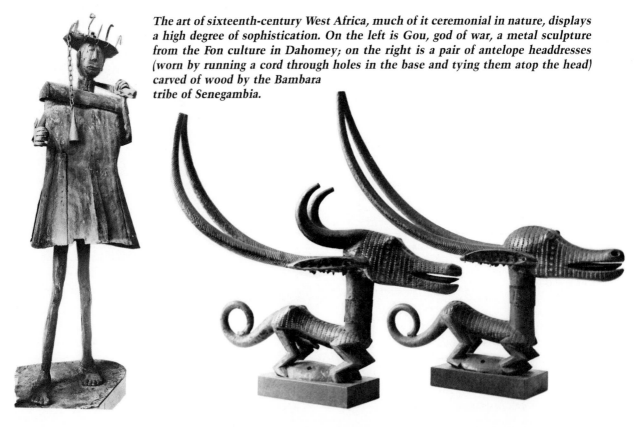

*The art of sixteenth-century West Africa, much of it ceremonial in nature, displays a high degree of sophistication. On the left is Gou, god of war, a metal sculpture from the Fon culture in Dahomey; on the right is a pair of antelope headdresses (worn by running a cord through holes in the base and tying them atop the head) carved of wood by the Bambara tribe of Senegambia.*

settled region with an ancient history of long-distance trade and cultural exchange with other peoples.

Population growth and cultural development in Africa, as elsewhere in the world, proceeded at different rates. Ecological conditions and geography had much to do with this. Where soil was rich, rainfall was adequate, and minerals were abundant, as in western Sudan, population grew and cultures changed rapidly. Where inhospitable desert or impenetrable jungle ruled, societies remained small and changed at a crawl. Isolation from other cultures retarded development, while contact with other regions encouraged change. For example, cultural innovation accelerated in East African, Swahili-speaking societies facing the Indian Ocean after trading contacts began with the Eastern world in the ninth century. At about the same time, trans-Sahara traders from the Arab world began to spread Muslim influence in West Africa.

### The African Ethos

The many peoples of Africa, who were to supply more than half of all the immigrants who crossed the ocean to the Western Hemisphere in the three centuries after Europeans began colonizing there, came from a rich diversity of cultures. But most of them shared certain ways of life that differentiated them from Europeans.

As in Europe, the family was the basic unit of social organization. But in most African societies, as in Native American societies, the family was matrilineal. It traced descent, property rights, and political inheritance through the mother rather than the father. It was not the son of a chief who inherited his father's position but the son of the chief's sister. When a man married, his wife did not leave her family and take his name; the bridegroom left his family to join that of his bride.

West Africans believed in a supreme creator of the cosmos and in an assortment of lesser deities associated with natural forces such as rain, fertility, and animal life. Since these deities could intervene in human affairs, they were elaborately honored. Like most North American Indian societies, the peoples of West Africa held that spirits dwelt in the trees, rocks, and rivers around them, and hence they exercised care in the treatment of these natural objects.

In Africa ancestors were also worshiped, for they mediated between the Creator and the living of the earth. Since the dead played such an important role for the living, relatives held elaborate funeral rites to ensure the proper entrance of a deceased relative into the spiritual world. The more ancient an ancestor, the greater was this person's power to affect the living; thus the "ancient ones" were devoutly worshiped. Deep family loyalty and regard for family lineage flowed naturally from this ancestor worship.

Social organization in much of West Africa by the time Europeans arrived was as elaborate as in fifteenth-century Europe. At the top of society stood the nobility and the priests, usually men of advanced age. Beneath them were the great masses of people. Most of them were farmers, but some worked as craftsmen, traders, teachers, and artists. At the bottom of society resided slaves. As in ancient Greece and Rome, they were "outsiders"—war captives, criminals, or sometimes persons who sold themselves into servitude to satisfy a debt. The rights of slaves were restricted, and their opportunities for advancement were narrow. Nevertheless, as members of the community, they were entitled to protection under the law and allowed the privileges of education, marriage, and parenthood. Their servile condition was not permanent, nor was it automatically fastened onto their children, as would be the fate of Africans enslaved in the Americas.

## EUROPE IN THE AGE OF EXPLORATION

In the ninth century, about the time that the Mound Builders of the Mississippi valley were constructing their urban center at Cahokia and the kingdom of Ghana was rising in West Africa, western Europe was only a dependent frontier of the Muslim world of the Middle East. The great Roman Empire had fallen, and a host of petty principalities with stagnant economies and static populations squabbled among themselves. The center of political power and economic vitality in the "Old World" had shifted eastward to Christian Byzantium, which controlled Asia Minor, the Balkans, and parts of Italy. The other dynamic culture of this age, which was Muslim, had spread through the Middle East, spilled across North Africa, and penetrated Spain and West Africa south of the Sahara.

Over the next six centuries, an epic revitalization of western Europe occurred, creating the conditions that enabled its leading maritime nations vastly to extend their oceanic frontiers. Thence began a 400-year epoch of the militant expansion of European peoples and European culture into other continents. Only in the present century has this process of Europeanization been reversed, as colonized people have regained their autonomy and cultural identity through wars of national liberation.

## The Rise of Europe

The gathering strength of the peoples of western Europe, who began to emerge from the "Dark Ages" in about A.D. 1000, owed much to a revival of long-distance trading from Italian ports on the Mediterranean. The ancient cities of the Roman Empire had stagnated for centuries, but now Venice, Genoa, Pisa, and other Italian ports began to rouse themselves by trading with peoples facing the Adriatic, the Baltic, and the North Sea. These urban commercial centers gradually evolved into merchant-dominated city-states that freed themselves from the rule of feudal lords in control of the surrounding countryside.

While merchants led the emerging city-states, feudal lords in the sparsely populated lands of western Europe were gradually subordinating their individual domains to the centralized authority of a king. For centuries, kings had been weak while the landed aristocracy had been strong. The normal powers of the state, as the modern world knows them—the power to tax, to wage war, and to administer the law—were all exercised locally by private persons who based their claims on extensive property ownership. But as kings asserted themselves in the thirteenth and fourteenth centuries, they began to mend this political fragmentation of feudal Europe. In the fifteenth and sixteenth centuries,

political unification continued, marking the rise of the modern states of England, France, Spain, and Portugal. In these new nation-states, wrote the political theorist Jean Bodin in the late sixteenth century, the sovereign "cannot in any way be subject to the commands of others, for it is he who makes law for the subject, abrogates laws already made, and amends obsolete law."

The emerging monarchies of western Europe were far from stable, however. Peasant revolts erupted throughout western Europe from the thirteenth to the fifteenth centuries as lords increased their demands for labor service from masses of serfs. Wars between the rising monarchies punctuated the era. Widespread drought and crop failure caused famine, and famine was followed by epidemic diseases. From 1346 to 1350, about one of every three people in England and western Europe died miserably of the Black Death. The disease, carried by rats, returned a generation later. Preplague population levels were not reached again in Europe for several hundred years.

## The New Monarchies and the Expansionist Impulse

In the second half of the fifteenth century, ambitious monarchs coming to power in France, England, Aragon, and Castile took steps to bring social order and political stability to their kingdoms. Louis XI in France, Henry VII in England, Isabella of Castile, and Ferdinand of Aragon all created armies and bureaucratic state machinery strong enough to quell internal conflict, such as the English War of the Roses, and to raise taxes sufficient to support their regimes. In all four countries, and in Portugal as well, economic revival and the reversal of more than a century of population decline and civil disorder nourished the impulse to expand into unknown frontiers.

The exploratory urge had two initial objectives: to circumvent Muslim traders by finding an eastward oceanic route to Asia and to tap at its source the African gold trade. Since the tenth century, Muslim middlemen in North Africa had brought the precious metal to Europe from Guinea. Now the possibility arose of bypassing these non-Christian traffickers. Likewise, Christian Europeans dreamed of eliminating Muslim traders from the commerce with Asia. Since 1291, when Marco Polo returned to Venice with tales of Eastern treasures—spices, silks, perfumes, drugs, and jewels—Europeans had bartered with the Orient. But the difficulties of the long eastward overland route through the Muslim world kept alive the hopes of Christian Europeans that an alternative water route could be found. Eventually, Europe's mariners would find they could voyage to Cathay by both eastward and westward water routes, but this took two more centuries to discover.

Portugal seemed the least likely of the rising nation-states to lead the expansion of Europe outside its continental boundaries, yet it forged into the lead at the end of the fifteenth century. A poor and insignificant country of only one million inhabitants, Portugal had gradually overcome Moorish control in the twelfth and thirteenth centuries and, in 1385, had wrenched itself free of domination by neighboring Castile. Led by Prince Henry the Navigator, for whom trade was secondary to the conquest of the Muslim world, Portugal burst through the geo-

graphical unknown. In the 1420s, Henry began dispatching Portuguese mariners, sailing in vessels smaller than today's pleasure yachts, to probe the unknown Atlantic world—the "sea of darkness." His intrepid sailors were aided by important improvements in navigation, mapmaking, and ship design, all promoted by the prince.

Portuguese captains operated at sea on three ancient Ptolemaic principles: that the earth was round, that distances on its surface could be measured by degrees, and that navigators could "fix" their position on a map by measuring the position of the stars. The invention in the 1450s of the quadrant, which allowed a precise measurement of star altitude necessary for determining latitude, represented a great stride forward from the chart-and-compass method of navigation. Equally important was the design of a lateen-rigged caravel, adapted from a Moorish ship design. Its triangular sails permitted ships to sail with a contrary wind, allowing them to beat southward along the African coast—a feat the square-rigged European vessels could never perform.

### Oceanic Exploration in the Fifteenth and Sixteenth Centuries

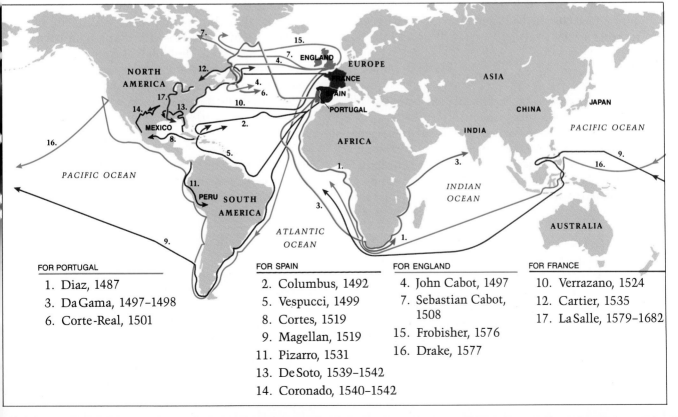

| FOR PORTUGAL | FOR SPAIN | FOR ENGLAND | FOR FRANCE |
|---|---|---|---|
| 1. Diaz, 1487 | 2. Columbus, 1492 | 4. John Cabot, 1497 | 10. Verrazano, 1524 |
| 3. Da Gama, 1497–1498 | 5. Vespucci, 1499 | 7. Sebastian Cabot, 1508 | 12. Cartier, 1535 |
| 6. Corte-Real, 1501 | 8. Cortes, 1519 | 15. Frobisher, 1576 | 17. La Salle, 1579–1682 |
| | 9. Magellan, 1519 | 16. Drake, 1577 | |
| | 11. Pizarro, 1531 | | |
| | 13. De Soto, 1539–1542 | | |
| | 14. Coronado, 1540–1542 | | |

By the 1430s, the ability of Prince Henry's captains to break through the limits of the world known to Europeans had carried them to Madeira, the Canaries, and the Azores, lying off the coasts of Portugal and northwest Africa. These were soon developed as the first European agricultural plantations located on the continent's periphery. From there, the Portuguese sea captains pushed farther south.

By the time of Prince Henry's death in 1460, Portuguese mariners had reached the west coast of Africa, where they began a profitable trade in ivory, slaves, and, especially, gold. By 1500, they had captured control of the African gold trade monopolized for centuries by North African Muslims. The gleaming metal now traveled directly to Lisbon by sea rather than by camel caravan across the Sahara to North African Muslim ports such as Tunis and Algiers.

This enterprise proved so profitable that the Portuguese abandoned attempts to explore any farther south. Not until 1487, when a storm blew Bartolomeu Dias all the way past the tip of Africa, did Prince Henry's original dream of finding a water route to India and the Orient lie within Portuguese grasp. But before Dias's discovery could be exploited, another sailor, who for many years had shipped out of Portugal, announced that he had found the fabled passage to India.

### Reaching the Americas

The marriage of Ferdinand and Isabella in 1469 united the independent states of Aragon and Castile and launched the Spanish nation into its golden age. Leading the way for Spain was an Italian sailor, Christopher Columbus. The son of a poor Genoese weaver, Columbus had married into a prominent family of Lisbon merchants and thus made important contacts at court.

Like many sailors, Columbus had listened to sea tales about lands to the west. He may have encountered Icelandic sagas about the voyages of Leif Ericsson and other Norsemen to an unknown world five centuries before. Others speculated that the Atlantic Ocean terminated in India and eastern Asia. Could one reach the Indies by sailing west rather than by sailing east

around Africa, as the Portuguese were attempting? Columbus hungered to know.

For nearly ten years Columbus failed to secure financial backing and royal sanction in Portugal for exploratory voyages. Many mocked his modest estimates of the distance westward from Europe to Japan. Finally, in 1492, Queen Isabella of Spain commissioned him, and he sailed west with three tiny ships manned by about 90 men.

Strong winds, lasting ten days, blew the ships far into the Atlantic. There they were becalmed. In the fifth week at sea—longer than any European sailors had been out of the sight of land—mutinous rumblings swept through the crews. But Columbus pressed on. On the seventieth day, long after Columbus had calculated he would reach Japan, a lookout sighted land. On October 12, 1492, the sailors clambered ashore on a tiny island in the Bahamas, which Columbus named San Salvador (Holy Savior). Grateful sailors "rendered thanks to Our Lord, kneeling on the ground, embracing it with tears of joy."

Believing he had reached Asia, Columbus explored the island-speckled Caribbean for ten weeks. After landing on heavily populated islands that he named Hispaniola (shared today by Haiti and the Dominican Republic) and Cuba (which he thought was the Asian mainland), he finally set sail for Spain with cinnamon, coconuts, a bit of gold, and several kidnapped natives. While homeward bound, he penned a report of his discoveries. He believed that he had reached Asia and described its hospitable people, fertile soils, magnificent harbors, and gold-filled rivers.

Quickly printed and distributed throughout Europe, Columbus's report brought him financing between 1494 and 1504 for three much larger expeditions to explore the newfound lands. Though at the time his discoveries seemed less significant than the Portuguese exploits in the South Atlantic, he led Spain to the threshold of a mighty empire. He reaped few rewards, however, dying unnoticed and penniless in 1506. To the end he believed that he had found the water route to Asia.

For many generations, other explorers lay in the grasp of this geographical misunderstanding. They could not imagine the Americas blocking the passage to India, nor could they conceive of the great width of the Pacific Ocean lying beyond the American landmass. As late as 1638, the French fur trader Jean Nicolet, reaching Lake Michigan, donned a Chinese robe and prepared to meet the Great Khan of China.

While Spain explored and claimed the overseas lands to the west, Portugal was staking out an empire by sailing east. One year before Columbus's third voyage to the Caribbean in 1498, Vasco da Gama became the first European to sail around the cape of Africa. He landed on the East African coast and there, by a stroke of great luck, encountered the most famous Arab navigator of that generation, Ahmed ibn-Majid. The Muslim mariner expertly guided Da Gama's fleet eastward to India—a fatal stroke for the future of Muslim peoples.

Within a few decades, the Portuguese commanded the Indian Ocean. They defeated the Indian and Egyptian fleet at Diu in 1509, established a trading base at Goa in the next year, and reached the Spice Islands and Guangzhou (Canton) in 1513. They soon controlled the commer-

cial centers of the Muslim-controlled spice trade as far east as Malacca, on the Malay Peninsula. In a single generation, by utilizing their naval superiority, which rested on their development of a heavily gunned merchant ship, they ousted Muslim traders from the lucrative trade that had enlivened the diet of Europeans for generations. Not until the Dutch challenged them in the mid-seventeenth century did the Portuguese fear competition on the rich water routes to the East Indies that brought the pungent nutmeg, cinnamon, ginger, pepper, and cloves to the tables of millions of Europeans.

To Portuguese leaders, the world across the Atlantic being conquered by the Spanish in the early sixteenth century seemed of secondary importance. Trade-conscious Europeans agreed that the Portuguese had gained the greatest prize. By forcing trade concessions in the islands and coastal states of the East Indies, they had unlocked the fabulous Asian treasure houses that since Marco Polo's time had whet the appetites of Europe's seagoing men. The commercial center of Europe had now shifted from the ports of the Mediterranean to the Atlantic ports of Portugal.

### Religious Conflict

While the new worlds being disclosed to the Spanish and Portuguese promised rich frontiers for further stimulating the awakening economies of western Europe, they also beckoned as fields of religious contest. The European discovery of the heavily populated Americas offered an especially rewarding opportunity to convert to Christianity millions of people who might otherwise be seduced by the infidel Muslim world. For many, occupation of the New World signaled a new religious crusade. Conquest of the Americas was carried out in the context of centuries of conflict with the Muslim enemy, especially with the Moors of North Africa. Only in 1492, the year that Columbus reached San Salvador, had Christian Spain finally completed its 800-year struggle to expel the Moors from its southern region.

The Catholic-Protestant division within Christianity complicated Christian dreams of converting a "heathen" continent, however. The

*Theodore De Bry, a Dutch explorer, provided Europeans with some of their first images of the New World. This image of Columbus's third voyage depicts natives with boats filled with pearls on an island that Columbus named Cubagua—island of pearls.*

people of western Europe, at precisely the time they were unlocking the secrets of the new worlds to the east and west in the sixteenth century, were being torn by religious schisms that magnified the era's national rivalries.

### Luther and Calvin

At the heart of Europe's religious strife was a continental movement to cleanse the Christian church of corrupt practices and return it to the purer ways of ancient or "primitive" Christianity. Martin Luther became the first to formulate "Protestant" principles in the early sixteenth century. Within 50 years, he and others had created new systems of Christian doctrine that attracted millions of Europeans and created a violent conflict in the Christian church that today still simmers in some areas such as Ireland.

Luther was preparing for a legal career in 1505 when a bolt of lightning nearly struck him during a violent thunderstorm. Trembling with fear, he vowed to become a monk. But peace of mind eluded him in the mendicant order of Saint Augustine that he joined. Despairing that

*The Reformation, sparked by Martin Luther's protest, brought sweeping change to western Europe in the sixteenth century and eventually led to migrations across the Atlantic. Lucas Cranach the Younger commemorates the movement's leaders in his* Epitaph of the Burgomeisters of Myenburg.

he could earn salvation through any of the age-old rituals of the church—prayer, the Mass, confession, pilgrimages to holy places, even crusades against Muslim infidels—Luther agonized and finally found a new understanding of personal salvation. Discarding the church's teaching that man could earn redemption by these prescribed "works," he reasoned that salvation came through an inward faith, or "grace," that God conferred upon those he chose. Good works, Luther believed, did not earn grace but were only the external evidence of grace won through faith. Luther had taken the revolutionary step of rejecting the church's elaborate hierarchy of officials, who presided over the rituals intended to guide individuals along the path toward salvation.

Luther's doctrine of private "justification by faith" did not immediately threaten the church. But in 1517, he openly attacked the sale of "indulgences" by which the pope raised money for the building of St. Peter's in Rome. By purchasing indulgences, individuals believed they could reduce their time (or that of a deceased relative) in purgatory. Luther drew up 95 arguments against this practice and started publishing tracts in 1520 to gather support. The spread of printing, invented less than 70 years before, allowed for the rapid circulation of his ideas. The printed word—and the ability to read it—were to become revolutionary weapons throughout the world.

Luther's cry for reform soon inspired open revolt among Germans of all classes. He denounced the seven sacraments of the church, calling for a return to baptism and communion, the only sacraments prescribed by the Scriptures. He attacked the clergy for luxurious living and urged celibate prelates to marry. He attacked "the detestable tyranny of the clergy over the laity" and called for a priesthood of all believers. He rejected age-old rituals such as masses and pilgrimages. He urged people to seek faith individually by reading the Bible, which he translated into German and made widely available for the first time in printed form. Most dangerously, he called upon the German princes to assume control over religion in their states. This directly challenged the authority of Rome and further undermined the functions of its clergy.

By the 1530s, Luther's reform movement had gained much ground. Popular resistance to the new religious teachings, however, was widespread. Despite the Lutheran attacks on "pagan" Catholicism, many Germans refused to give up the magical practices and ancient folk rituals that the Catholic church had tolerated.

Lutheranism spawned a variety of sects—Mennonites, Dunkers, Amish, and Schwenkfelders—whose members eventually found their way to the New World. Religious revolt soon brought war to Europe. Individual German states, choosing revolutionary "Protestantism" or remaining loyally "Catholic," fought each other, and other parts of the continent were soon sucked into the conflict.

Building on Luther's redefinition of Christianity, John Calvin, a Frenchman, brought new intensity and meaning to the Protestant Reformation. In 1536, at age 26, he published a ringing appeal to all of Christian Europe. Supporting Luther's reformist work, he called for further change. Calvin believed that the main task of humankind was the glorification of God through earthly works. Since people were deeply depraved and morally helpless, they could never hope to save themselves. Calvin reasoned that God had "elected" some to be saved, though most were not "predestined" for salvation but for damnation. But each person could glorify God in daily conduct, hoping always for the "light of divine providence." Calvin's idea of predestination, which might have led to massive resignation, instead spurred a militant dedication to battle for the Lord because his cause must eventually triumph.

Calvin proposed reformed Christian communities structured around the elect few. To remake the corrupt world and follow God's will, communities of "saints" must control the state, rather than the other way around. Elected bodies of ministers and dedicated laymen, called presbyteries, were to govern the church, directing the affairs of society down to the last detail so that all, whether saved or damned, would work for God's ends.

Calvinism, as a fine-tuned system of self-discipline and social control, was first put into practice in the 1550s in the city-state of Geneva, near the French border of Switzerland. Here the brilliant and austere leader established what he intended to be a model Christian community. A council of 12 elders drove nonbelievers from the city, rigidly disciplined daily life, and stripped the churches of every appeal to the senses—images, music, incense, and colorful clerical costumes. Offenders great and small, from those committing violent acts to those guilty of minor lapses such as frivolous behavior on the Sabbath, were ferreted out and punished. Religious reformers from all over Europe flocked to the new holy community, and Geneva soon became the continental center of the reformist Christian movement. The city, wrote John Knox of Scotland in 1556, "is the most perfect school of Christ that ever was in the earth since the days of the apostles."

From Geneva, Calvinism spread rapidly in the late sixteenth century to eastern Europe, France, England, Scotland, the Lowlands (now Belgium and Holland), and Scandinavia. It made its strongest appeal on the northern and western fringes of Europe, where rulers had not historically benefited from the power and patronage of the Rome-based church, as had the rulers of the Mediterranean societies. Within these areas, it, like Lutheranism, recruited most successfully among the privileged classes of merchants, landowners, lawyers, and the nobility and among the rising middle class of master artisans and shopkeepers.

Although the Protestant revolt against Catholicism initially insisted on freedom of conscience, it soon rejected this founding principle. Burning with the conviction that they had discovered God's plan for the redemption of humankind, Lutherans and Calvinists, as well as Catholics against whom they railed, harshly repressed dissent in the areas they came to dominate. This issue of religious freedom would later be played out in the American colonies.

Catholicism in Spain and Portugal remained almost immune from the Protestant Reformation. So, even while under attack, it swept across the Atlantic almost unchallenged during the century after Columbus's voyages. The massive native population of the Americas, in the eyes of the pope in Rome and the monarchs in Lisbon and Seville, must not only be rescued from heathenism and Islam but also protected from Protestantism.

# THE IBERIAN CONQUEST OF AMERICA

From 1492 to 1518, Spanish and Portuguese explorers opened up vast parts of Asia and the Americas to European knowledge. Yet during this age of exploration, only modest attempts at settlement were made, mostly by the Spanish on the Caribbean islands of Cuba, Puerto Rico, and Hispaniola. The three decades after 1518, however, became an age of conquest. In some of the bloodiest chapters in recorded history, the Spanish nearly exterminated the native peoples of the Caribbean islands, toppled and plundered the great inland empires of the Aztecs and Incas in Mexico and Peru, discovered fabulous silver mines, and built a westward oceanic trade of enormous importance to all of Europe. The consequences of this short era of conquest proved to be immense for the entire world.

Portugal, meanwhile, restricted by one of the most significant lines ever drawn on a map, concentrated mostly on building an eastward oceanic trade to southeastern Asia. In 1493, to settle a dispute, the pope had demarcated Spanish and Portuguese spheres of exploration in the Atlantic. Drawing a north-south line 100 leagues (about 300 miles) west of the Azores, the pope confined Portugal to the European side of the line. One year later, in the Treaty of Tordesillas, Portugal obtained Spanish agreement to move the line 270 leagues farther west. Nobody knew at the time that a large part of South America, as yet undiscovered by Europeans, bulged east of the new demarcation line and therefore fell within the Portuguese sphere. In time, Portugal would develop this region, called Brazil, into one of the most profitable areas of the New World.

## The Spanish Onslaught

Within a single generation of Columbus's death in 1506, Spanish conquistadores explored, claimed, and conquered most of South America (except Brazil), Central America, and the southern parts of North America from Florida to California. Led by audacious explorers and military leaders, they established the authority of Spain and Catholicism over an area that dwarfed

their homeland in size and population. They were motivated by religion, growing pride of nation, and dreams of personal enrichment. "We came here," explained one Spanish footsoldier in Cortés's legion, "to serve God and the king, and also to get rich."

In two bold and bloody strokes, the Spanish overwhelmed the ancient civilizations of the Aztecs and Incas. In 1519, Hernando Cortés set out with 600 soldiers from coastal Veracruz and marched over rugged mountains to attack Tenochtitlan (modern-day Mexico City), the capital of Montezuma's Aztec empire. At its height, centuries before, the ancient city in the Valley of Mexico had contained perhaps 150,000 people. But in 1521, following several years of tense relations between the Spanish and Aztecs, it fell before Cortés's assault. The Spanish use of horses and firearms provided an important advantage, but the alliance of dissident natives oppressed by Montezuma's tyranny was indispensable in overthrowing the Aztec ruler. From the Valley of Mexico, the Spanish extended their dominion over the Mayan people of the Yucatán and Guatemala in the next few decades.

In the second conquest, the intrepid Francisco Pizarro, marching from Panama through the jungles of Ecuador and into the towering mountains of Peru with a mere 168 men, most of them not even soldiers, toppled the Inca empire. Like the Aztecs, the populous Incas lived in a highly organized social system. But also like the Aztecs, they were weakened by violent internal divisions. This ensured Pizarro's success in capturing their capital at Cuzco in 1533. From there, ruthless Spanish soldiers marched farther afield, plundering other gold- and silver-rich Inca cities. Further expeditions into Chile, New Granada (Colombia), Argentina, and Bolivia in the 1530s and 1540s brought under Spanish control an empire larger than any in the Western world since the fall of Rome.

By 1550, Spain had overwhelmed the major centers of native population throughout the Caribbean, Mexico, Central America, and the west coast of South America. A thriving oceanic trade carried gold, silver, dyewoods, and sugar east

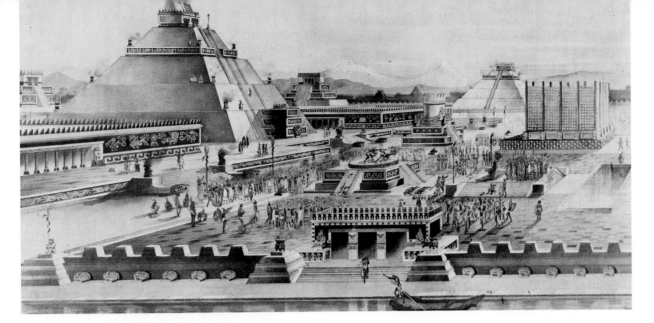

Before the arrival of Cortés in 1519, Tenochtitlán was the capital and showplace of Montezuma's Aztec empire; this modern rendering is based on archaeological evidence.

In this woodcut, published in a German book in 1590, Theodore De Bry depicts Francisco Pizarro's conquest of the Inca capital, Cuzco.

## Spanish and Portuguese New World Conquests

across the Atlantic and transported African slaves, colonizers, and finished goods west. In a brief half century, Spain had exploited the advances in geographical knowledge and marine technology made by their Portuguese rivals and brought into harsh but profitable contact with each other the people of three continents. The triracial character of the Americas had now been established.

For nearly a century after Columbus's voyages, Spain enjoyed almost unchallenged dominion over the fabulous hemisphere newly revealed to Europeans. Greedy buccaneers of various nations snapped at the heels of homeward-bound Spanish treasure fleets with cargoes of silver, but this was little more than a nuisance. France made gestures of contesting Spanish control by planting small settlements in Brazil and on the southern coast of North America in the mid-sixteenth century, but Spanish expeditions quickly wiped them out. England remained island-bound until the 1580s. Until the seventeenth century, only Portugal, which staked out important claims in Brazil in the 1520s, challenged Spanish domination of the New World.

## The Great Dying

Spanish conquest of major areas of the Americas set in motion two of the most far-reaching processes in modern history. One involved microbes, the other precious metal. Spanish contacts with the natives of the Caribbean basin, central Mexico, and Peru in the early sixteenth century triggered perhaps the most dramatic and disastrous population decline ever recorded. The population of the Americas on the eve of European arrival had grown to an estimated 50 million or more. In some areas such as central Mexico, the highlands of Peru, and certain Caribbean islands, population density exceeded that of most of Europe. But though they were less populous than the people of the Americas, the Europeans had one extraordinary biological advantage over them. They were members of a population that for centuries had been exposed to nearly every killer parasite that infects humans on an epidemic scale in the temperate zone. Over the centuries, Europeans had built up immunities to these diseases. Such

*The devastating effects of smallpox on the Native American population were illustrated in this woodcut for a sixteenth-century book about "Nueva España."*

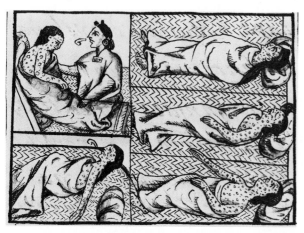

biological defenses did not prevent smallpox, measles, diphtheria, and other afflictions from striking, but they limited their deadly power.

In contrast, the people of the Americas had been geographically sealed off from these diseases. Arriving Europeans therefore unknowingly encountered a huge component of the human race that was utterly defenseless against the "domesticated" microbial infections the explorers, traders, and settlers carried inside their bodies.

The results were catastrophic. On Hispaniola, a population of about one million that had existed when Columbus arrived had only a few thousand survivors by 1530. Of some 25 million inhabitants of the Aztec empire prior to Cortés's arrival, about 90 percent were felled by disease within a half century. Similar demographic disaster struck the equally populous Inca peoples of the Peruvian Andes. The smallpox "spread over the people as great destruction," an old Indian told a Spanish priest in the 1520s. "There was great havoc. Very many died of it. They could not stir; they could not change position, nor lie on one side, nor face down, nor on their backs. And if they stirred, much did they cry out. . . . And very many starved; there was death from hunger, [for] none could take care of [the sick]." Such terrifying sickness led many natives to believe that their gods had failed them and left them ready to acknowledge the greater power of the Christian God that Spanish priests proclaimed.

Wherever Europeans intruded in the hemisphere for the next three centuries, the catastrophe repeated itself. Whether Protestant or Catholic, whether French, English, Spanish, or Dutch, whether male or female, every newcomer from the Old World participated in the germ warfare that typically eliminated, within a few generations, at least two-thirds of the native population. Millions of Native Americans who never saw a European died of their diseases, which swept like wildfire through densely populated regions.

The enslavement and brutal treatment of the native people intensified the lethal effects of European diseases. After their spectacular conquests of the Incas and Aztecs, the Spanish enslaved thousands of native people and fastened upon them work regimens that severely reduced their resistance to disease. Some priests like Bartholme Las Casas waged lifelong campaigns to ameliorate the exploitation of the Indians, but their power to control the actions of their colonizing compatriots was always limited.

## Silver, Sugar, and Their Consequences

The small amount of gold that Columbus brought home from his explorations of the West Indies raised hopes that this metal, which along with silver formed the standard of wealth in Europe, might be found in the transatlantic paradise. Some gold was gleaned from the Caribbean islands and later from Colombia, Brazil, and Peru. But though men pursued it fanatically to the far corners of the hemisphere, more than three centuries would pass before they found gold in windfall quantities on the North American Pacific slope and in the Yukon. It was silver that proved most abundant—so plenteous, in fact that when bonanza strikes were made in Bolivia in 1545, and then in northern Mexico in the next

decade, much of Spain's New World enterprise focused on its extraction. The Spanish empire in America, for most of the sixteenth century, was a vast mining community.

Native people, along with some African slaves, provided the labor supply for the mines. The Spaniards permitted the highly organized Indian societies to maintain control of their own communities but exacted from them huge labor drafts for mining. By imposing themselves at the top of a highly stratified social order that had previously been organized around tributary labor, the Spanish enriched themselves beyond the dreams of even the most visionary explorers. At Potosí, in Bolivia, 58,000 workers labored at elevations of up to 13,000 feet to extract the precious metal from a fabulous sugarloaf "mountain of silver." The town's population reached 120,000 by 1570, making it larger than any in Spain at the time. Thousands of other workers toiled in the mines of Zacatecas, Taxco, and Guanajuato. By 1660, they had scooped up more than 7 million pounds of silver from the Americas, tripling the entire European supply.

The massive flow of bullion from the Americas to Europe triggered profound changes. It financed further conquests and settlement in Spain's American empire, spurred long-distance trading in luxury items such as silks and spices from the Far East, and capitalized agricultural development in the New World of sugar, coffee, cacao, and indigo. The bland diet of Europeans gradually changed as items such as sugar and

*An early eighteenth-century atlas by Hermann Moll included this picture of the Spanish silver mining operation at Potosí, in modern Bolivia.*

spices, previously luxury articles for the wealthy, became accessible to ordinary people.

The enormous increase of silver in circulation in Europe after the mid-sixteenth century also caused a "price revolution." As the supply of silver increased faster than the volume of goods and services that Europeans could produce, the value of the metal declined. Put differently, prices rose. Between 1550 and 1600, they doubled in many parts of Europe and then rose another 50 percent in the next half century. Landowning farmers got more for their produce, and merchants thrived on the increased circulation of goods. But artisans, laborers, and landless agriculture workers (the vast majority of the population) suffered because their wages did not keep pace with rising prices. Skilled artisans, lamented one of the first English immigrants to America, "live in such a low condition as is little better than beggary."

Overall, the "price revolution" brought a major redistribution of wealth and increased the number of people in western Europe living at the margins of society. It thus built up the pressure to emigrate to the Americas, Europe's new frontier. At the same time, rising prices stimulated

commercial development. Expansion overseas fed expansion at home and intensified changes toward capitalist modes of production already under way in the sixteenth century.

While the Spaniards organized their overseas empire around the extraction of silver from the highlands of Mexico and Peru, the Portuguese staked their future on sugar production in the lowlands of Brazil. Spanish colonial agriculture supplied the huge mining centers; but the Portuguese, adapting techniques of cultivation worked out earlier on its Atlantic islands, produced sugar for the export market.

Whereas the Spanish mining operations rested primarily on the backs of the native labor force, the lowland Portuguese sugar planters scattered the indigenous people and replaced them with platoons of African slaves. By 1570, this regimented work force was producing nearly 6 million pounds of sugar annually; by the 1630s, output had risen to 32 million pounds per year. High in calories but low in protein, the sweet "drug food" revolutionized the tastes of millions of Europeans and caused the oceanic transport of millions of African slaves to the coast of Brazil and later to Colombia, Ecuador, and Peru.

From Brazil, sugar production jumped to the island-specked Caribbean. Here, in the early seventeenth century, England, Holland, and France challenged Spain and Portugal for the riches of the New World. Once they secured a foothold in the West Indies, Spain's enemies stood at the gates of the Hispanic New World empire. This ushered in a long period of conflict "beyond the line"—where European treaties had no force. Through contraband trading with Spanish settlements, piratical attacks on Spanish treasure fleets, and outright seizure of Spanish-controlled islands, the Dutch, French, and English in the seventeenth century gradually sapped the strength of the first European empire outside of Europe.

### Spain's Northern Frontier

The crown jewels of Spain's New World empire were silver-rich Mexico and Peru, with the islands and coastal fringes of the Caribbean representing lesser, yet valuable, gemstones. Distinctly third in importance were the north-

### Real Wages in England, 1500–1700

**Sources:** Walton and Shepherd, *The Economic Rise of Early America*, 1979; and Coleman, *The Economy of England: 1450–1750*, 1977.

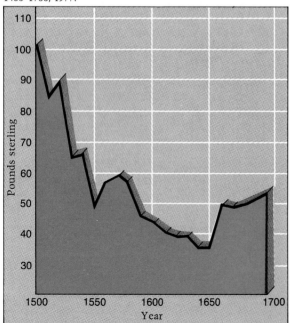

ern borderlands of New Spain—the present-day Sun Belt of the United States. The early Spanish influence in Florida, in the Gulf region, and in Texas, New Mexico, Arizona, and California indelibly marked the history of the United States.

Spanish explorers began charting the southeastern region of North America in the early sixteenth century, beginning with Juan Ponce de León's expeditions to Florida in 1515 and 1521. For the next half century, Spaniards planted small settlements there. They traded some with the natives, but the area was chiefly important to the Franciscan priests who attempted to gather the local tribes into mission villages and convert them to Catholicism.

Several attempts were made to bring the entire Gulf of Mexico region under Spanish control. From 1539 to 1542, Hernando de Soto, a veteran of Pizarro's conquest of the Incas, led an expedition deep into the homelands of the Creeks and explored westward across the Mississippi to Arkansas. In 1559, Spaniards marched northward from Mexico in an attempt to establish their authority in the lower Gulf region. Everywhere they went they enslaved Indians and used them as provision carriers. In 1565, they sought to secure Florida. Feeling threatened by a French settlement planted there, the Spanish built a fort at St. Augustine and evicted their French rivals. The oldest continuously inhabited town in the continental United States, St. Augustine became the center of Spain's southeastern religious frontier. Florida would remain a Spanish possession for more than two centuries.

The Southwest became the second region of Spanish activity in North America. Francisco Vásquez de Coronado explored the region from 1540 to 1542, leading an expedition of several hundred Spanish soldiers and a baggage train of 1,300 friendly Indians, servants, and slaves. Coronado never found the Seven Cities of Cíbola, reported by earlier Spanish explorers to be fabulously decorated in turquoise and gold. But he opened much of Arizona, New Mexico, and Colorado to eventual Spanish control and probed as far north as the Great Plains. His interior explorations, together with the nearly simultaneous expedition of de Soto in the Southeast, established Spanish claims to the southern latitudes of North America and gave them contacts, often bloody, with the populous corn-growing Indian societies of the region.

The Southwest, like Florida, proved empty of the fabled golden cities. Hence, in the seventeenth century the region chiefly interested Jesuit and Franciscan missionaries. The Spanish established presidios, or garrisons, such as those at Santa Fe and Albuquerque, to control these vast regions and serve as trade centers. But the Catholic mission became the primary institution of the Spanish borderlands. In the eighteenth century, the Catholic missions reached northward, bringing most of the Indians of the California coast, from San Diego to the San Francisco Bay, under the control of the Spanish padres.

The Spanish missionary frontier operated differently, depending on the Indian cultures encountered. In Florida and California, where the native people lived in small, often seminomadic tribes, the Spanish used persuasion mixed with force to gather them within the sound of the mission bell. Setting the Indians to agricultural labor, the Spanish attempted slowly to convert them to European ways of life.

In New Mexico, however, missionaries made no attempt to uproot Pueblo people and contain them within the mission walls. The natives they encountered had lived in settled villages and practiced agriculture for centuries, so here the Spanish aimed to graft Catholicism onto Pueblo culture by building churches on the edges of ancient native villages. When they attempted to do more than overlay Indian culture with a veneer of Catholicism, they encountered fierce resistance. Such was the case in 1675, when the Spanish padres tried to root out traditional Pueblo religious practices. In response, a Pueblo leader named Popé led an Indian uprising that destroyed most of the churches in New Mexico and nearly drove the Spanish out of the region.

The Spanish presence in the Southeast and Southwest was numerically insignificant. As late as 1700, no more than about 4,000 Spaniards lived in the northern borderlands of New Spain. But the claims they established in the sixteenth century had repercussions for three centuries, and the cultural influences that stemmed from their long tenure in these regions persist to the present day.

# ENGLAND GOES WEST

By the time England awoke to the promise of the New World, the two Iberian powers were firmly entrenched there. But by the late sixteenth century, the conditions necessary to propel England overseas had ripened. During the seventeenth century, the English, as well as the Dutch and French, began overtaking their southern European rivals. The first challenge came in the Caribbean, where between 1604 and and 1640 the English planted several small colonies producing tobacco and later sugar. Few might have guessed that some secondary and relatively unproductive settlements also being planted on the North American mainland would in time be among England's most prized possessions.

## England Challenges Spain

England was the most backward of the European nations facing the Atlantic in exploring and colonizing the New World. Although far more numerous than the Portuguese, the English in the fifteenth century had little experience with long-distance trade and had made only infrequent contacts with cultures outside their island fastness. Only the voyages of John Cabot (the Genoa-born Giovanni Caboto) gave England any claim to a place in the New World sweepstakes. Even Cabot's voyages to Newfoundland and Nova Scotia a few years after Columbus's first voyage—the first northern crossing of the Atlantic since the Vikings—were never followed up.

At first, England's interest in the far side of the Atlantic centered primarily on fish. This high-protein food supply, which was basic to the European diet, was the gold of the North Atlantic. The early North Atlantic explorers found the waters off Newfoundland and Nova Scotia teeming with fish, not only the ordinary cod but also the delectable salmon. But it was the fishermen of Portugal, Spain, and France, more than those of England, who began making annual spring trips to the offshore fisheries in the 1520s. Not until the end of the century would the French and English drive Spanish and Portuguese fishermen from the Newfoundland Banks.

Exploratory voyages along the eastern coast of North America hardly interested the English. It was for the French that Cartier and Verrazano sailed between 1524 and 1535. Looking for straits westward to India, through the northern landmass, which was still thought to be a large island, they made contact with many Indian tribes and charted the coastline from the St. Lawrence River to the Carolinas. They established the northern latitudes as a suitable place of settlement but found nothing of immediate value to take home. The time had not yet arrived when large numbers of Europeans would leave their homelands to resettle in America rather than go there merely to extract its riches.

Why was England so late to enter the race for New World treasures? Much of the answer resides in the insular history of the English people. Never a seafaring nation, the English had remained relatively isolated from Europe since the end of the Hundred Years' War with France (1337–1453).

Changes occurred in the late sixteenth century, however, that propelled the English overseas. The rising production of woolen cloth, a mainstay of the English economy, had sent merchants scurrying for new markets after 1550. Their success in establishing trading companies in Russia, Scandinavia, the Middle East, and India vastly widened England's commercial orbit and raised hopes that still other spheres could be developed. At the same time, population growth and rising prices depressed the existence of ordinary people and made them look to the transoceanic frontier for new opportunities.

England's challenge to Spain also had a religious dimension. During the sixteenth century, England swayed back and forth between Protestant and Catholic rulers. Henry VIII, who ruled from 1509 to 1547, repudiated the pope's authority in England. But his oldest daughter Mary, who inherited the throne in 1553, was a faithful Catholic. Married to Philip II of Spain, the chief pillar of Catholic power in Europe, Mary tried to wipe out the Protestant heresy. However, upon her death in 1558, Henry VIII's second daughter, Elizabeth, took the throne and restored Protestantism to the realm.

Like her father, Elizabeth was not deeply

*Under the leadership of Elizabeth I, Britain challenged and ultimately overturned Spain's domination of worldwide sea trade.*

religious. She favored Protestantism primarily as a vehicle of national independence. Ambitious and talented, she had to contend with Philip II, king of Spain and her fervently Catholic brother-in-law, whose long reign nearly coincided with hers. Philip regarded Elizabeth as a Protestant heretic and plotted incessantly against her. The pope added to Catholic-Protestant tensions in England by excommunicating Elizabeth in 1571 and absolving her subjects from paying her allegiance. This, in effect, gave them religious license to overthrow her.

The smoldering conflict between Catholic Spain and Protestant England broke into open flames in 1587. Two decades before, Philip II had sent 20,000 Spanish soldiers into his Netherlands provinces to suppress Protestantism. Then, in 1572, he had helped to arrange the massacre of thousands of French Protestants. By the 1580s, Elizabeth was providing covert aid to the Protestant Dutch revolt against Catholic rule. Philip vowed to crush the rebellion and decided as well to launch an attack on England in order to wipe out this growing center of Protestant power.

Elizabeth fed the flames of the international Catholic-Protestant conflict in 1585 by sending 6,000 English troops to aid the Dutch Protestants. Three years later, Philip dispatched a Spanish armada of 130 ships carrying 30,000 men and 2,400 artillery pieces. Sails blazing with crusader's crosses, the fleet set forth to conquer Elizabeth's England. For two weeks in the summer of 1588, a sea battle raged off the English coast. A motley collection of smaller English ships, with the colorful sea dog Francis Drake in the lead, defeated the Armada, sinking many of the lumbering Spanish galleons and then retiring as the legendary "Protestant wind" blew the crippled Armada into the North Sea.

The Spanish defeat prevented a crushing Catholic victory in Europe and brought a temporary stalemate in the religious wars. It also solidified Protestantism in England and brewed a fierce nationalistic spirit there. Shakespeare's love of "this other Eden, this demi-paradise" spread among the people; and with Spanish naval power checked, both the English and the Dutch found the seas more open to their rising maritime and commercial interests.

## The Westward Fever

In the last decades of the sixteenth century, the idea of overseas expansion captured the imagination of important elements of English society. Urging them on were two Richard Hakluyts, uncle and nephew. In the 1580s and 1590s, they devoted themselves to advertising the advantages of colonizing on the far side of the Atlantic. For nobles at court, colonies offered new baronies, fiefdoms, and estates. For merchants, the New World promised exotic produce to sell at home and a new outlet for English cloth and other goods. For the militant Protestant clergy, there awaited a continent filled with heathen people to be saved from both savagery and Catholicism. For the commoner, opportunity beckoned in the form of bounteous land, almost for the taking. In a number of pamphlets the Hakluyts publicized the idea that the time was ripe for England to break the Iberian monopoly on the riches of the New World.

England mounted its first attempts at colonizing, however, in Ireland. In the 1560s and 1570s, the English gradually extended their control over the country through bloody military conquest. Ireland became a turbulent frontier for thousands of career-hungry younger sons of gentry families as well as landless commoners. Many of the leaders first involved in New World colonizing had served in Ireland, and many of their ideas of how to deal with a "savage" and "barbaric" people stemmed from their Irish experience.

The first English attempts at overseas settlement were small, feeble, and ill-fated. Whereas the Spanish encountered unheard-of wealth and scored epic victories over ancient and populous civilizations, the English at first met only with failure in relatively thinly settled lands. Beginning in 1583, they mounted several unsuccessful attempts to settle Newfoundland. Other settlers, organized by Walter Raleigh, planted a settlement from 1585 to 1588 at Roanoke Island, off the North Carolina coast. They apparently perished in attacks by a local tribe whom they had offended. Small groups of men sent out to establish a tiny colony in Guiana, off the South American coast, failed in 1604 and 1609, and another group that set down in Maine in 1607 lasted only a year. Even the colonies founded in Virginia in 1607 and Bermuda in 1612, although they would flourish in time, floundered badly for several decades.

English merchants, sometimes supported by gentry investors, undertook these first tentative efforts. They risked their capital hoping that small-scale ventures in North America might produce the profits of their other overseas commercial ventures. They had little backing from the government, in subsidies, ships, or naval protection, though they had the blessing of their queen. The Spanish and Portuguese colonizing efforts were national enterprises, sanctioned, capitalized, and coordinated by the crown. The English colonies were private ventures, organized and financed by small partnerships of merchants who pooled their slender resources.

Not until these first merchant adventurers solicited the wealth and support of the rising middle class of English society could colonization succeed. This support grew steadily in the first half of the seventeenth century, but even then, investors were drawn far more to the quick profits promised in West Indian tobacco production than to the uncertainties of mixed farming, lumbering, and fishing on the North American mainland. In the 1620s and 1630s, most of the English capital invested overseas went into establishing tobacco colonies in the flyspeck Caribbean islands of St. Christopher (1624), Bar-

bados (1627), Nevis (1628), Montserrat (1632), and Antigua (1632).

Apart from the considerable financing required, the vital element in launching a colony was a suitable body of colonists. About 80,000 streamed out of England between 1600 and 1640, as a combination of economic, political, and religious developments pushed them from their homeland at the same time that dreams of opportunity and adventure pulled them westward. In the next 20 years, another 80,000 departed.

Economic difficulties in England prompted many to try their luck in the New World. More than any other European society, the English had transformed the old feudal system into a new social order, marked by consolidated land ownership and commercial farming. As the size of estates grew after 1550, agricultural productivity increased. But land consolidation also dispossessed many small landowners and thrust off the land swarms of excess laborers, who were free to sell their muscle power if they could find a job or to starve if they could not.

These changes in the agricultural system, when combined with population growth and the unrelenting increase in prices caused by the influx of New World silver, produced a surplus of unskilled labor, squeezed many small producers, and spread poverty and crime. By the late 1500s, the roads, wrote Richard Hakluyt, were swarming with "valiant youths rusting and hurtful for lack of employment," and the prisons were "daily pestered and stuffed full of them." A generation later, beginning in 1618, the renewal of the European religious wars between Protestants and Catholics devastated the continental market for English woolen cloth, bringing widespread unemployment and desperate conditions to the textile regions. Probably half the households in England lived on the edge of poverty, struggling for survival and subject to a punishing economic system in which they had no voice. "This land grows weary of her inhabitants," wrote John Winthop of East Anglia, "so as a man, which is the most precious of all creatures, is near more vile among us than a horse or a sheep."

Religious persecution and political considerations intensified the pressure to emigrate from

England in the early seventeenth century. How this operated in specific situations will be considered in the next chapter. The largest number of emigrants went to the West Indies. The North American mainland colonies attracted perhaps half as many, and the Irish plantations in Ulster and Munster still fewer. For the first time in their history, large numbers of English people were abandoning their island homeland to carry their destinies to new frontiers.

## Anticipating North America

English settlers approaching the North America coast, from the Roanoke settlers in 1585 to the Puritans who flocked to Massachusetts Bay in the 1630s, knew they were entering a New World dominated by Spain. But since they had chosen to settle on the middle part of the Atlantic seaboard, which the Spanish regarded as useless, it was the native occupiers of the land who most concerned the newcomers. What did the English know of these people whom Columbus, thinking he had reached India, mistakenly called Indians? How would they receive the English, and how would the colonizers obtain the possession of the land along the coast?

The early settlers were far from uninformed about the indigenous people of the New World. Beginning with Columbus's first description of the New World, published in several European cities in 1493 and 1494, a mass of reports and promotional accounts had circulated among the participants in early voyages of discovery, trade, and settlement. This literature became the basis for anticipating the world that had been discovered beyond the setting sun.

Most early colonists who read or listened to these accounts probably held a split image of the native people of North America. On the one hand, the Indians were depicted as a gentle people who eagerly received Europeans. Columbus had written of the "great amity towards us" that he encountered in San Salvador in 1492 and had described the Arawaks there as "a loving people" who "were greatly pleased and became so entirely our friends that it was a wonder to see." Verrazano, the first European to touch the eastern edge of North America, wrote with similar optimism about the native people in 1524.

The natives, graceful of limb and tawny-colored, he related, "came toward us joyfully uttering loud cries of wonderment, and showing us the safest place to beach the boat."

This positive image of the Native Americans reflected not only the friendly reception that Europeans often actually received but also the European vision of the New World as an earthly paradise, an exotic place where war-torn, impoverished, or persecuted people could build a new life. The strong desire to trade with the native people also encouraged a favorable view because only a friendly Indian could become a suitable partner in commercial exchange.

A counterimage of the Indian, however, also entered the minds of settlers approaching the coast of North America. It pictured a savage, hostile Indian. Like the positive image, it originated in the early travel literature. As early as 1502, Sebastian Cabot had paraded in England three Eskimos he had kidnapped on an Arctic voyage, and they were described as flesh-eating savages and "brute beasts" who "spake such speech that no man could understand them." Many other accounts portrayed the natives of the New World as crafty, brutal, loathsome halfmen, who lived, as Amerigo Vespucci put it, without benefit of "law, religion, rulers, immortality of the soul, and private property."

Travel tales aside, the English had another reason for believing that all would not be friendship and amiable trading when they came ashore in North America. For years they had read accounts of the Spanish experience in the Caribbean, Mexico, and Peru—and the story was not pretty. A number of books described in gory detail the wholesale violence that occurred when Spaniard met Mayan, Aztec, or Inca. Accounts of Spanish cruelty, even genocide, were useful to Protestant pamphleteers, who labeled the Catholic Spaniards "hell-hounds and wolves." But immigrants embarking for North America might still wonder if the same violent confrontations did not await them.

Another factor nourishing negative images of the Indian stemmed from the Indians' possession of the land necessary for settlement. For Englishmen, rooted in a tradition of the private ownership of property, this presented moral and legal, as well as practical, problems. As early as the 1580s, George Peckham, an early promoter of colonization, had admitted that the English doubted their right to take the land of others. In 1609, the thought was expressed again when an Anglican minister, Robert Gray, asked, "By what right can we enter into the land of these savages, take their rightful inheritance from them, and plant ourselves in their places, being unwronged or unprovoked by them?"

The problem could be partially solved by arguing that English settlers did not intend to take the Indians' land but wanted only to share it with them. In return, they would offer the natives the advantages of a more advanced culture and, most important, the Christian religion. This argument reappeared again and again in the succeeding generations. As the governing council in Virginia put it in 1610, the settlers "by way of merchandizing and trade, do buy of [the Indians] the pearls of earth, and sell to them the pearls of heaven."

A more ominous argument justifying English rights to native soil also arose. By denying the humanity of the Indians, the English, like other Europeans, claimed that the native possessors of the land disqualified themselves from rightful ownership of it. "Although the Lord hath given the earth to children of men," one Englishman reasoned, "the greater part of it [is] possessed and wrongfully usurped by wild beasts and unreasonable creatures, or by brutish savages, which by reason of their godless ignorance and blasphemous idolatry, are worse than those beasts which are of the most wild and savage nature."

Defining the Native Americans as "savage" and "brutish" did not give the English arriving in Opechancanough's land the power to dispossess his people of their soil, but it armed them with a moral justification for doing so when their numbers became sufficient. Few settlers arriving in North America doubted that their technological superiority would be sufficient to establish themselves among the native people. They presumed that if the native people resisted, they could lay waste the country they were entering, as they had done in Ireland.

Two conflicting images of the Indian wrestled for ascendancy in English minds as the first settlers in North America clambered from their boats after long weeks at sea. They viewed the natives as backward but receptive people with whom they could establish friendly and profitable relations. But they also harbored negative images and visions of violence and bloodshed as they arrived in Opechancanough's homeland.

## CONCLUSION: Colliding Worlds

The English migrants who began arriving on the eastern edge of North America in the early seventeenth century came late to a New World that other Europeans had been colonizing for more than a century. The first to come, the immigrants to Virginia, were but a small advance wave of the large, varied, and determined fragment of English society that would flock to England's western Atlantic frontier during the next few generations. Like Spanish, Portuguese, and French colonizers before them, they would establish new societies in the newfound lands in contact with the people of two other cultures—one made up of ancient inhabitants of the lands they were settling and the other composed of those brought against their will across the Atlantic. We turn now to the richly diverse founding experience encountered by English latecomers in the seventeenth century.

## Recommended Reading

The rich pre-Columbian history of the Americas is surveyed in Kenneth Macgowan and Joseph A. Hester, Jr., *Early Man in the New World* (1962) and Jesse Jennings, *The Prehistory of North America* (1968). Another fascinating analysis is Marshall Sahlins, *Stone Age Economics* (1972).

Excellent introductions to early African history include Basil Davidson, *The African Genius* (1969) and J. D. Fage, *A History of West Africa*, 4th ed. (1969).

Europe in the Age of Exploration can be studied in Ralph Davis, *The Rise of the Atlantic Economies* (1973); J. H. Parry, *The Age of Reconnaissance* (1963); Carlo M. Cipolla, *Guns, Sails, and Empire: Technological Innovations and the Early Phases of European Expansion* (1966); and Eric Wolf, *The People Without History* (1983).

A fine corrective to the much romanticized and often distorted story of the Spanish and Portuguese conquest of the Americas is James Lockhart and Stuart B. Schwartz, *Early Latin America* (1983). Also valuable are J. H. Elliott, *Imperial Spain, 1469–1716* (1963); J. H. Parry, *The Spanish Seaborne Empire* (1966); Charles Gibson, *Spain in America* (1966); and C. R. Boxer, *The Portuguese Seaborne Empire, 1415–1825* (1972).

The shape of English society and England's belated intervention in the Americas is detailed in C. R. Elton, *England Under the Tudors* (1955); A. G. Dickens, *The English Reformation* (1964); Peter Clark and Paul Slack, eds., *Crisis and Order in English Towns, 1500–1700* (1972); A. L. Rowse, *The Expansion of Elizabethan England* (1955); Nicholas P. Canny, *The Elizabethan Conquest of Ireland* (1976); and David B. Quinn, *England and the Discovery of America, 1481–1620* (1974).

## TIME LINE

| | |
|---|---|
| Pre-Columbian epochs | |
| 12,000 B.C. | Beringian epoch ends |
| 6,000 B.C. | Paleo-Indian phase ends |
| 500 B.C. | Archaic era ends |
| 500 B.C.–A.D.1500 | Post-Archaic era in North America<br>Kingdoms of Ghana, Mali, Songhay in Africa |
| 1420s | Portuguese sailors explore west coast of Africa |
| 1492 | Christopher Columbus lands on Caribbean islands<br>Spanish expel Moors (Muslims) |
| 1494 | Treaty of Tordesillas |
| 1497–1585 | French and British explore northern part of the Americas |
| 1498 | Vasco da Gama reaches India after sailing around Africa |
| 1513 | Portuguese explorers reach China |
| 1515–1565 | Spanish explore Florida and southern part of North America |
| 1520s | Luther's attacks on Catholicism |
| 1521 | Cortés captures Mexico City, conquering the Aztecs |
| 1530s | Calvin's calls for religious reform |
| 1533 | Pizarro captures Cuzco, conquering the Incas |
| 1558 | Elizabeth I crowned queen of England |
| 1585 | Roanoke Island settlement |
| 1588 | Spanish armada defeated by English |
| 1603 | James I succeeds Elizabeth I |
| 1607 | English begin settlement at Jamestown, Virginia |

# CHAPTER 2
## COLONIZING AMERICA

PENNS TREATY with the INDIANS, made 1681 with out an Oath, and never broken. The foundation of Religious and Civil LIBERTY, in the U.S. of AMERICA.

By 1637, after five years in New England, John Mason knew both the prospects and perils of England's new overseas frontier. In his early thirties, Mason had emigrated from southeastern England. He was part of the flock of John Warham, a Puritan minister from the village of Dorchester. In Massachusetts, the group commemorated their origins by giving the name Dorchester to the area assigned to them. Here, 6 miles south of Boston, they built a crude church, assigned town lots and outlying farms, and began the work of serving their God in the wilderness of North America.

Like many Puritans, Mason had thrilled at the sight of southern New England's game-filled forests and fish-filled streams, the fields cleared and tilled by Algonquian agriculturalists, the lush meadows available for grazing stock. Though the winters were inhospitable, it seemed this might be the Promised Land where Puritan refugees could plant their New World Zion. But Mason also recognized that these lands were not vacant. From the earliest days of the Pilgrim settlers at Plymouth in 1620, it was evident that the native occupiers of the region, whose claim went back a hundred generations, stood in the way of the Puritan "errand into the wilderness."

It was this tension between English colonizers and Native Americans defending their homelands that brought John Mason to the Mystic River in Connecticut in May 1637. The previous fall, he had followed many of his Dorchester friends out of Massachusetts. In search of better land and restless with the political squabbling in the Massachusetts Bay Colony, the Dorchester settlers set out for the Connecticut River, 100 miles to the west. For 14 days, stung by the frost of late autumn, they trekked wearily along Indian paths, carrying their meager possessions. At their journey's end they founded the town of Windsor, on the west bank of the Connecticut.

Six months later, when his new village was no more than a collection of crude lean-tos, John Mason marched south against the Pequots. He owed his militia captaincy to military experience in the Netherlands, where thousands of English soldiers had gone in the 1620s to help the Protestant Dutch break the yoke of Catholic Spain in the Lowlands. Now he commanded several hundred men whom the fledgling Connecticut River towns had dispatched to drive the Pequots from the area. In the years before the English arrival, the powerful Pequots had formed a network of tributary tribes. Finding it impossible to placate the English as they swarmed into the Connecticut River valley, the Pequots chose resistance.

At dawn on May 26, 1637, Captain Mason and his troops approached a Pequot village on the Mystic River. Supported by Narragansett allies, the English slipped into the town. After a few scuffles in the half-light, Mason cried out, "We must burn them," and his men began torching the Pequot wigwams. Then they rushed from the fortified village. As flames engulfed the huts, the Pequots fled the inferno, only to be cut down with musket and sword by the English soldiers who had ringed the community. Most of the terrified victims were noncombatants—old men, women, and children—for the Pequot warriors were preparing for war at another village about 5 miles away.

Before the sun rose, a major portion of the Pequot tribe had been exterminated. The resistance of the others crumbled when they learned the fate of their families. "It was a fearful sight to see them thus frying in the fire," wrote one Puritan, "and horrible was the stink and scent thereof; but the victory seemed a sweet sacrifice, and they gave the praise thereof to God, who had wrought so wonderfully for them." Mason himself wrote that God had "laughed at his enemies and the enemies of his people, . . . making them as a fiery oven."

Captain John Mason was a God-fearing Puritan and a man highly esteemed by his fellow colonists. His actions at the Mystic River, just seven years after the great Puritan migration to New England began in 1630, testify that the European colonization of America involved a violent confrontation of two cultures. We often speak of the "discovery" and "settlement" of North America by English and other European colonists. But the penetration of the eastern edge of what today is the United States might more accurately be called "the invasion of America."

Yet mixed with violence was utopian idealism. In the New World, Puritans—and countless waves of immigrants who followed them—sought both spiritual and economic renewal. Settlement in America represented a chance to escape European war, despotism, material want, and religious corruption. The New World was a place to rescue humankind from the ruins of the Old World. This chapter reconstructs the manner of settlement and the character of immigrant life in four areas of early colonization: the Chesapeake Bay, southern New England, New York and the Carolinas, and Pennsylvania. A comparison of these various colonies will show how the colonizers' backgrounds, ideologies, goals, and modes of settlement produced distinctly different societies along the Atlantic seaboard in the seventeenth century.

## THE CHESAPEAKE TOBACCO COAST

In 1584, England gained a first foothold in a hemisphere dominated by Spanish and Portuguese colonizers. A reconnaissance expedition organized by Walter Raleigh, one of Queen Elizabeth's favorite courtiers, scouted the Carolina coast, surveyed Roanoke Island in Albemarle Sound, and then hastened homeward carrying two natives and a string of tales about rich soil, friendly Indians, and mineral wealth. A second voyage in 1585 and a third in 1587, composed of 91 men, 17 women, and 9 children, planted a small colony on Roanoke Island. But the enterprise failed. The voyages to Roanoke were too small and poorly financed to plant successful settlements. They served only as tokens of England's rising challenge to Spain in North America and as a source of valuable information for colonists later settling the area.

The Roanoke colony also failed resoundingly as the first sustained contact between English and Native American peoples. Although one member of the first expedition reported that "we

*As seen in this sixteenth-century watercolor by John White, the first Englishmen in the Roanoke region found the natives peaceful, friendly, and orderly.*

found the people most gentle, loving, and faithful, void of all guile and treason," relations with the local tribes quickly soured and then turned violent. Charges flew back and forth; the English believing that the local Indians had stolen a silver cup and the Indians angered by English raids on their winter supply of corn. Aware of their numerical disadvantage and afraid of a coordinated attack against them, the English employed their muskets to intimidate the natives with their superior technology. In 1591, when a relief expedition reached Roanoke, none of the settlers could be found. It is likely that in spite of their Iron Age weaponry, these "lost colonists" of Roanoke succumbed to Indian attacks. It was an ominous beginning for England's overseas ambitions.

### Jamestown

In 1607, a generation after the first Roanoke expedition, a group of merchants established the first permanent colony in North America at Jamestown, Virginia. Under a charter from James I, they operated as a joint-stock company, an early form of the modern corporation that allowed them to sell shares of stock in their company and use the pooled investment capital to outfit and supply overseas expeditions. Although the king's charter to the Virginia Company of London began with a concern for bringing Christian religion to native people who "as yet live in darkness and miserable ignorance of the true knowledge of God," most of the settlers probably agreed with Captain John Smith, who emerged as their strongest leader. "We did admire," he wrote, "how it was possible such wise men could so torment themselves with such absurdities, making religion their colour, when all their aim was profit."

Profits in the early years proved elusive, however. Hoping to find gold and other minerals, anticipating a rewarding trade with Indians for beaver and deer skins, and, best of all, hoping to discover the fabled passage through the North American continent to China, the original investors and settlers received a rude shock. Rather than duplicating the remarkable success of the Spanish and Portuguese in Mexico, Peru, and Brazil, the early Virginia colonists died miserably of dysentery, malaria, and malnutrition. More than 900 settlers, mostly men, arrived in the colony between 1607 and 1609; only 60 survived.

Seeking occupational diversity, the Virginia Company sent French silk artisans, Italian glassmakers, and Polish potash burners to Jamestown. But one-third of the first three groups of immigrants were gold-seeking adventurers with unroughened hands, a proportion of gentlemen six times as great as in the English population. Many others were unskilled servants, some with criminal backgrounds, who "never did knowe what a days work was," observed John Smith. Both types adapted poorly to wilderness conditions, leaving Smith begging for "but thirty carpenters, husbandmen, gardeners, fishermen, and blacksmiths" rather than "a thousand such gallants as were sent to me, that would do nothing but complain, curse and despair, when they saw . . . all things contary to the report in England."

The Jamestown colony, in addition to its unproductive mix of settlers, was hampered by the common assumption that Englishmen could exploit the Indians of the region. Cortés

### Early Chesapeake Settlement

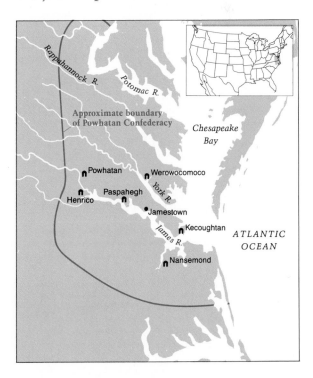

### NOVA BRITANNIA.

# OFFERING MOST

Excellent fruites by Planting in
VIRGINIA.

Exciting all such as be well affected
to further the same.

LONDON
Printed for SAMVEL MACHAM, and are to be sold at
his Shop in Pauls Church-yard, at the
Signe of the Bul-head.
1 6 0 9.

To the worthy Gentlemen, Adventurers and Planters in *VIRGINIA*.

My loving Friends:

 Thought it convenient heere briefly to minde
you of those Necessaries, that if wanted there,
would greatly prove your prejudice, and render you obnoxious to many evils, which are
these.

*Necessaries for Planters.*

For Aparell: Provide each man 1. Monmouth Cap, 1. Wast-
coat, 1. Suit of Canvase, Bands, Shirts, Shooes, Stockings, Canvase to make sheets, with Bed and Bolster to fill in Virginia,
1. Rugge, and Blankets.
For Armes: Provide 1. Suit of compleat light Armour, and
each man 1. Sword, 1. Musket or Fowling Peece, with Powder
and Shot convenient.
For Houshold stuffe: Provide one great Iron Pot, large and
small Kettles, Skellets, Frying pannes, Gridiron, Spit, Platters,
Dishes, Spoons, Knives, Sugar, Spice, Fruit, and Strong water at Sea for sicke men.
For Tools: Provide Howes broad and narrow, Axes broad
and narrow, Handsawes, two-hand-sawes, whipsaws, Hammers,
Shovels, Spades, Augors, Piercers, Gimblets, Hatchets, Handbills, Frowes to cleave pale, Pickaxes, Nayls of all sorts, 1. Grind-
stone, Nets, Hooks, Lines, Plowes: All which accommodation
wherewith each to be well furnished, together with his Transportation,

*The title page of a 1609 book on the New World could easily serve as an advertisement to recruit settlers (top left); by 1650, the hardships endured by many had given another author reason to include a list of necessary equipment in his book, Virginia (bottom left).*

and Pizarro had conquered the mighty Aztec and Inca empires with a few hundred soldiers and then turned the labor of thousands of natives to Spanish advantage. Why, the early settlers mused, should it not be so in Virginia?

But in the Chesapeake the English found that the indigenous peoples were not densely settled and could not easily be subjugated. Contrary to expectations, no wealthy Indian empire lay waiting to be conquered. Nor could some 20,000 Powhatan Indians of the region be molded into a labor force to serve the Virginians because the English, unlike the Spanish, brought neither an army of conquistadores nor an army of priests to subdue the natives.

Instead, relations with some 40 small tribes, grouped into a confederacy led by the able Powhatan, turned bitter almost from the beginning. Powhatan brought supplies of corn to the sick and starving Jamestown colony during the first autumn. However, John Smith, whose military experience in eastern Europe schooled him in dealing with people he regarded as "barbarians,"

*No one knows exactly what the Jamestown colony looked like in its early years; this twentieth-century mural by Sidney King is a conjectural rendering based on archaeological evidence.*

raided Indian corn supplies and tried to cow the local tribes by shows of force. Powhatan responded by withdrawing from trade with the English and by sniping at their flanks. Many settlers died in "the starving times" of the first years.

Despite these early failures, merchants of the Virginia Company of London poured more money and settlers into the venture. Understanding the need for ordinary farmers who could raise the food necessary to sustain the colony, they reorganized the company in 1609. By promising free land at the end of seven years' labor for the company, they enticed many new settlers. In 1618, they sweetened the terms by offering 50 acres of land outright to anyone journeying to Virginia. To thousands of people on the margins of English society, such an offer seemed irresistible. More than 9,000 crossed the Atlantic between 1610 and 1622 to begin life anew in Virgina. Yet only 2,000 were still alive at the end of that period. "Instead of a plantation," wrote one English critic, "Virginia will shortly get the name of a slaughter house."

## Sot Weed and Indentured Servants

The promise of free land in Virginia lured a steady stream of settlers to Virginia, even

*More a curiosity than a cash crop, "Tabaco, or Henbane of Peru" was included in a 1633 history of plants. A second variety, "Trinidada," soon became famous as the finest for smoking.*

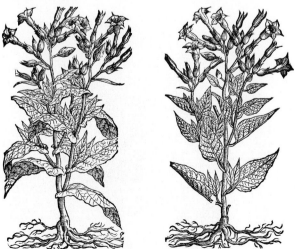

though the colony proved a burial ground for most immigrants within a few years of arrival. Also crucial to the continued migration was the discovery that tobacco grew splendidly in Chesapeake soil. Tobacco had been first brought to Portugal from Florida in the 1560s. But it was Francis Drake's boatload of the "jovial weed," so named for its intoxicating effect, procured in the West Indies in 1586, that popularized it among the upper class and launched it on its long history as a European social addiction.

Even James I's denunciation of smoking as "loathsome to the eye, hateful to the nose, harmful to the brain, and dangerous to the lungs" failed to halt the smoking craze. It proved to be Virginia's salvation. The first crop was shipped in 1617, and thereafter the cultivation of tobacco spread rapidly. Commanding the handsome price of 3 shillings per pound in England, tobacco allowed a profit sufficient for settlers to plant it even in the streets and marketplace of Jamestown. By 1624, Virginia was exporting 200,000 pounds of the "stinking weed"; by 1638, though the price had plummeted, the crop exceeded 3 million pounds. Tobacco became to Virginia in the 1620s what sugar was to the West Indies and silver to Mexico and Peru. In London, men gibed that Virginia was built on smoke.

While launching Virginia on an era of sustained growth, the cultivation of tobacco also obliged Virginia's planters to find a reliable supply of cheap labor. The "sot weed" required intensive care through the various stages of planting, weeding, thinning, suckering, worming, cutting, curing, and packing. To fill their need, planters recruited immigrants in England and Ireland and a scattering from Sweden, Portugal, Spain, Germany, and even Turkey and Poland. Such people, called indentured servants, willingly sold a portion of their working lives in exchange for free passage across the Atlantic. About four of every five seventeenth-century immigrants to Virginia—and later Maryland—came in this status. Nearly three-quarters of them were male, and most of them were between 15 and 24 years old.

Many of the indentured servants came from the armies of the unemployed. Others were orphans, political prisoners, or common criminals swept out of the jails and given a choice of transportation or the gallows. Some were of the "middling sort," younger sons unlikely to inherit a father's farm or shop, or young men eager to leave behind an unfortunate marriage. Others were drawn simply by the prospect of adventure in a "strange new land." But overwhelmingly, indentured servants had occupied the lower rungs of the social ladder in their place of origin.

Life for indentured servants often turned into a nightmare. Only a handful, perhaps one in 20, realized the dream of achieving freedom and acquiring land. If malarial fevers or dysentery did not quickly kill them, servants often succumbed to the brutal work routine imposed by harsh masters. Even by the middle of the seventeenth century, when the "starving times" were only a memory, about half died during the first few years of "seasoning." Masters bought and sold their servants as pieces of property, gambled for them at cards, and worked them to death since there was little motive for keeping them alive beyond their term of labor. "My Master Adkins," wrote one servant in 1623,

"hath sold me for £150 like a damned slave." When servants neared the end of their contract, masters found ways to add time and were backed by courts controlled by the planter class.

Contrary to English custom, masters often put women servants to work at the hoe. Sexual abuse by masters was common. Servant women paid dearly for illegitimate pregnancies. The courts fined them heavily and ordered them to serve an extra year or two to repay the time lost during pregnancy and childbirth. Mothers were often deprived of their illegitimate children by the courts, which indentured them out at an early age. For many servant women, marriage was the best release from this hard life. Many willingly accepted the purchase of their indenture by any man who suggested marriage.

### Expansion and Indian War

As Virginia's population increased, spurred by the growth of tobacco production, violence mounted between white colonizers and the Pow-

## Population of the Chesapeake, 1607–1690
**Source:** U.S. Bureau of the Census.

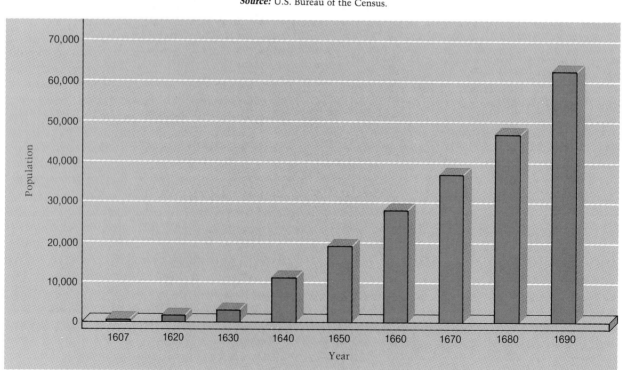

hatan tribes. In 1614, the sporadic hostility that had marred relations in the early years ended temporarily with the arranged marriage of Powhatan's daughter, the fabled Pocahontas, to planter John Rolfe. However, the profitable cultivation of tobacco created an intense demand for land. As more and more settlers pushed up the rivers that flowed into Chesapeake Bay, the local tribes worried that the previous abrasive and sometimes bloody contact might become a disastrous one.

In 1617, when Powhatan retired, the leadership of the Chesapeake tribes fell to Opechancanough. This proud and talented leader began building military strength for an all-out attack on his English enemies. The English murder of Nemattanew, a Powhatan war captain and religious prophet, triggered a fierce Indian assault on Good Friday in 1622 that dealt Virginia a staggering blow. More than one-quarter of the white population fell before the marauding tribesmen; the casualties in cattle, crops, and buildings were equally severe.

The devastating attack led to the bankruptcy of the Virginia Company. Two years later, the king annulled its charter and established a royal government, which allowed the elected legislative body established in 1619 to continue to function as a House of Burgesses that made laws in concert with the royal governor and his council.

The Indian assault of 1622 fortified the determination of the surviving planters to pursue a ruthless new Indian policy. John Smith, writing from England two years later, noted the grim satisfaction that had followed the Indian attack. Many, he reported, believed that it "will be good for the plantation, because now we have just cause to destroy them by all means possible." Bolstered by instructions from London to "root out [the Indians] from being any longer a people," the Virginians adopted a policy of annual military expeditions against the native villages west and north of the settled areas. The "flood of blood," as the English poet John Donne called it, in 1622 cost the colony dearly and doomed the Virginia Company of London. Yet it justified a policy of "perpetual enmity," even though several leaders admitted that the Indians had at-tacked in 1622 because of "our own perfidious dealing with them."

Population growth after 1630 and the recurrent need for fresh land by settlers who planted soil-exhausting tobacco intensified the pressure on Indian land. With their land running out, the tough, ambitious planters encroached on Indian territories, provoking war in 1644 and again in 1675. In each of these conflicts, the colonizers proved superior. Greatly outnumbering their opponents, they reduced the native population of Virginia to less than 1,000 by 1680. The Chesapeake tribes, Virginians came to believe, had little to contribute to the goals of English colonization; they were merely obstacles to be removed from the path of English settlement.

## Proprietary Maryland

By the time Virginia had achieved commercial success in the 1630s, another colony on the Chesapeake took root. Rather than hoping for profit, the founder sought to establish a religious refuge for Catholics and a New World version of the English manorial countryside.

George Calvert, an English nobleman, was the designer and promoter of Virginia's Chesapeake neighbor. Closely connected to the royal family, he had received a huge grant of land in Newfoundland in 1628, just three years after James I had elevated him to the peerage as Lord Baltimore. In 1632, Charles I, James's son, prepared to grant him a more hospitable domain of 10 million acres. He named it Terra Maria after the king's Catholic wife, Queen Maria. In English it became Maryland.

Catholics were an oppressed minority in England, and Lord Baltimore planned his colony as a place where they could start anew without fear of harassment. But knowing that he needed more than a small band of Catholic settlers, the proprietor planned to invite others as well. Catholics would never form a majority in his colony. They were quickly overwhelmed by Protestants who jumped at the offer of free land with only a modest yearly fee to the proprietary family (a "quitrent") of 2 shillings per 100 acres.

George Calvert died while the charter for his colony was being drawn up in 1632, leaving his

26-year-old son, Cecilius Calvert, to carry out his plans. The charter guaranteed the proprietor control over all branches of government, but Calvert learned that his colonists could not be satisfied with fewer political liberties than they enjoyed at home or could find in other colonies. Hence the Lords Baltimore were obliged to give up their charter-given right to initiate all colonial laws, subject only to the advice and consent of the people.

In land policy, Calvert's heirs found it impossible to carry out his plan for establishing feudalism in the woodlands of eastern North America. His design of 6,000-acre manors for his relatives and 3,000-acre manors for lesser aristocrats, each to be ruled by provincial nobles and worked by flocks of serflike tenants, was blithely ignored by the immigrants, who began arriving in 1634. They took up their free land, imported as many indentured servants as they could afford, maintained generally peaceful relations with local Indian tribes, began to grow tobacco on scattered riverfront plantations like their Virginia neighbors, and governed themselves locally as much as possible. In time, they created their own social hierarchy, not with assigned social roles but with status determined by the ability of some to rise above others in the competitive tobacco economy. Although Maryland grew slowly at first—in 1650 it had a population of only 600—it developed rapidly in the second half of the seventeenth century. By 1700, its population of 33,000 was half that of Virginia's.

## Daily Life on the Chesapeake

Though immigrants to the Chesapeake Bay region dreamed of bettering the life they had known in England, existence for most of them was dismally difficult. Males who reached their twenty-second birthday were middle-aged because life expectancy was about 43 years. Only a small minority of them could expect to take a wife and sire a family because marriage had to be deferred until after the indenture was completed, and there were only enough women for about one-third of the men. Once made, marriages were fragile. Either husband or wife was likely to

succumb to disease within about seven years. The vulnerability of pregnant women to malaria frequently terminated marriages in the first few years, and death claimed half the children born before they reached adulthood. Few children could expect to have both parents alive while growing up, and grandparents were almost unknown.

In a society with such a preponderance of men, widowed women were prized and remarried quickly. Such conditions produced complex families, full of step children and step parents, half sisters and half brothers. In the common case of marriage between a widow and widower, each with children from an early marriage, the web of family life became particularly complex, and the tensions attending child rearing unusually thick.

The tangled family relationships in this death-filled society is illustrated by the household of Robert Beverley of Middlesex County. When Beverley married Mary Keeble in 1666, she was a 29-year-old widow who had borne seven children during her first marriage. At least four of them were still alive to join the household of their mother's new husband. They gained five half brothers and half sisters during their mother's 12-year marriage to Beverley. When Mary Keeble Beverley died at age 41, her husband quickly remarried a recent widow, Katherine Hone. Beverley's second wife brought her son into the household and in the next nine years produced four more children with Beverley before his death in 1687. Thus between 1666 and 1687, Beverley had married two widows who bore him nine children and had been stepfather to the eight children his two wives had produced with previous husbands. Not one of these 17 children, from an interlocking set of four marriages, reached adulthood with both a living mother and father.

Plagued by such mortality, the Chesapeake remained, for most of the seventeenth century, a land of immigrants rather than a land of old settled families. Social institutions such as churches and schools took root very slowly amid such fluidity. The instability of community life was further increased by the large number of indentured servants. Strangers in a household, they served their time and moved on. Other strangers, purchased as they clambered off boats fresh from England, replaced them.

The fragility of life in the tobacco-growing Chesapeake world showed clearly in the region's architecture. As in nearly every New World colony, the settlers at first erected only primitive huts and shanties, hardly more than windbreaks. After establishing crops, most planters improved their habitats but still built no more than ramshackle, one-room dwellings. "Their houses," it was observed in 1623, "stand scattered one from another, and are only made of wood . . . so as a firebrand is sufficient to consume them all." Even as Virginia and Maryland matured, cheaply built and cramped houses remained the norm. Life was too uncertain, the tobacco economy too volatile, and the desire to invest every available shilling in field labor too great for men to build more than small, rough-hewn wooden structures, usually no larger than 16 by 24 feet. In England, solidly framed buildings erected on stone foundations had become the rule several centuries before. But throughout

*This clapboard church is typical of the rudimentary buildings erected by early colonists in the Chesapeake region.*

the Chesapeake, "earthfast" flimsy cabins and houses were built directly on the ground or on posts.

Even by the early eighteenth century, most Chesapeake families were "pigg'd lovingly together," as one planter said, in a crude house with no interior partitions. Eating, dressing, working, and loving all took place with hardly a semblance of privacy. For nearly two centuries, most ordinary Virginians and Marylanders lived in such crowded, unfinished quarters. "Like a flock of sheep in a fold," an eighteenth-century traveler described the family he bedded down with, 16 to a room, on the Virginia frontier. Even prosperous planters did not begin constructing fully framed, substantial homesteads until a century after the colony was founded.

The crudity of life also showed in the household possessions of the Chesapeake colonists. The houses of struggling farmers and tenants were likely to contain only a straw mattress, a crude storage chest, and the tools necessary for food preparation and eating—a mortar and pestle to grind corn, knives for butchering, a pot or two for cooking stews and porridges, wooden trenchers and spoons for eating. Most ordinary settlers owned no chairs, no dressers, no plates or silverware. Among middling planters the standard of living was raised only by possession of a flock mattress, coarse earthenware for milk and butter, a few pewter plates and porringers, a frying pan or two, and a few rough tables and chairs.

Even one of Virginia's wealthiest planters, the prominent Robert Beverley, had "nothing in and about his house but what was necessary . . . good beds . . . but no curtains, and instead of cane chairs, he hath stools made of wood." To be near the top of Chesapeake society meant to enlarge one's living space to three or four rooms, to sleep more comfortably, to sit on chairs rather than squat on the floor, and to acquire such ordinary decencies as chamber pots, candlesticks, bed linen, a chest of drawers, and a desk. But only the affluent few could boast luxury items such as clocks, window curtains, punch bowls, wine glasses, and imported furniture. Four generations elapsed in the Chesapeake settlements before the frontier quality of life slowly gave way to more refined living.

# THE PURITAN "CITY ON A HILL"

While some English settlers in the reign of James I (1603–1625) scrambled for wealth on the Chesapeake, others in England were seized by the spirit of religion. They looked to the wilds of North America as a place to build a tabernacle to God. The society they fashioned aimed at unity of purpose and utter dedication to reforming the corrupt world. American Puritanism would powerfully affect the nation's history, especially in planting the seeds of a belief in America's special mission in the world. Yet "the New England way" only partially prefigured the pathways of American development because Puritanism represented a visionary attempt to banish diversity on a continent where the arrival of streams of immigrants from around the globe was destined to become a primary phenomenon.

## Puritanism in England

England had been officially Protestant since the reign of Henry VIII. Many English in the late sixteenth century, however, thought the Church of England was still ridden with Catholic elements. Detesting such remnants of Catholicism as vestments and rituals that lingered on in the reign of Elizabeth (1558–1603), some voices demanded the end of every taint of "the Bishop of Rome and all his detestable enormities." Because they wished to purify the Church of England, they were dubbed Puritans.

The people attracted to the Puritan movement were not only religious reformers but also men and women who hoped to find in religion an antidote to the changes sweeping over English society. Many feared for the future as they witnessed the growth of turbulent cities, the increase of wandering poor, rising prices, and the accelerating pace of commercial activity. In general, they disapproved of the growing freedom from the restraints of gentry-dominated medieval institutions such as the church, guilds, and local government.

The concept of the individual operating as freely as possible, maximizing both opportunities and personal potential, is at the core of our modern system of beliefs and behavior. But many in England cringed at the crumbling of traditional restraints on individual action. They worried that individualistic behavior would undermine the notion of community—the belief that people were bound together by reciprocal rights, obligations, and responsibilities. Especially they decried the "degeneracy of the times," which they saw in the defiling of the Sabbath by maypole dancing, card playing, fiddling, bowling, and all the rest of the roistering and erotic behavior captured in Shakespeare's dramatic portrayals of Merrie England. Puritans vowed to reverse the march of disorder, wickedness, and disregard for community by imposing a new discipline. They intended not only to purify the Church of England but to reform society at large as well.

One part of their plan was a social ethic stressing work as a primary way of serving God. Derived from the Calvinist concept of "calling," this emphasis on work made the religious quest of every member of society equally worthy. The labor of a mason was just as valuable in God's sight as that of a merchant, and so was his soul. The "work ethic" would banish idleness and impart discipline and purpose throughout the community. Second, Puritans organized themselves into religious congregations in which each member hoped for personal salvation but also supported all others in their quest. Third, Puritans assumed responsibility for all the "unconverted" people around them. They were convinced that others who could not find Christian truth in their hearts might have to be coerced and controlled, as in Calvin's Geneva. Religious reform and social vision were in this way interlocked.

When King James VI of Scotland succeeded the childless Elizabeth as James I of England in 1603, he spoke stridently for the divine right of the monarch. Claiming responsibility only to God, James collided with the rising power of the Puritans. They had occupied the pulpits in hundreds of churches, gained control of several colleges at Oxford and Cambridge, and recruited large numbers to their cause. Translating their religious appeal into political power, the Puritans obtained many seats in Parliament and aggressively challenged the king's power. James responded by harassing them, removing dozens of Puritan ministers from their pulpits, and threatening many others. "I will harry them out of the land," he vowed, "or else do worse."

When Charles I succeeded to the throne in 1625, the situation worsened for Puritans. Determined to strengthen the monarchy and stifle dissent, the king summoned a new Parliament in 1628 and one year later adjourned this venerable body (which was the Puritans' main instrument of reform) when it would not accede to royal demands. The king then appointed William Laud, the bishop of London, to high office and turned him loose on the Puritans, whom Laud called "wasps" and "the most dangerous enemies of the state."

By 1629, when the king began ruling without Parliament, some Puritans were turning their eyes to the New World. They were convinced that God intended them to carry their religious and social reforms beyond the reach of persecuting authorities. The state of the economy added to their discouragement about their homeland, for England was suffering a depression in the cloth trades, most severely in Puritan

strongholds. To some distant shore, many Puritans decided, they would transport a fragment of English society and carry out the completion of the Protestant Reformation. As they understood history, God had assigned them a special task in his plan for the redemption of humankind.

## Puritan Predecessors in New England

Puritans were not the first Europeans to reach the shores of New England. Fishermen of various Eurropean nations had been working the fishing banks off Newfoundland and drying the cod they caught on the coast of Cape Cod and Maine since the early 1500s. On many occasions they had made contact with the Algonquian-speaking tribes of the area. A short-lived attempt at settlement on the coast of Maine had also been made in 1607. Seven years later, the aging Chesapeake war dog, John Smith, hired to hunt whales off the North American coast, coined the term "New England" after visiting the area. In his *Description of New England*, published in 1616, he excited considerable interest in "the Paradise of these parts."

No permanent settlement took root, however, until the Pilgrims arrived in Plymouth in

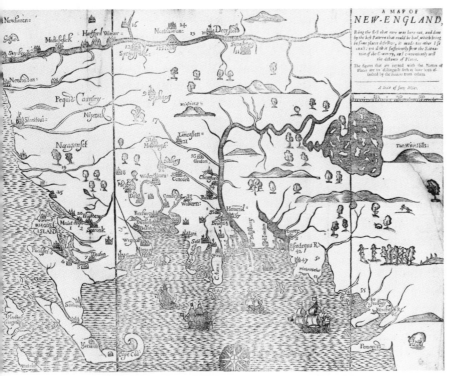

*John Foster, a schoolmaster, engraved this first published map of New England in 1677; it appeared in a contemporary history of King Philip's War.*

1620. Unlike the Puritans who would follow, these humble Protestant farmers did not expect to convert a sinful world. Rather, they wanted to be left alone to realize their radical vision of a pure and primitive life. Rather than reform the Church of England, they left it and hence were called Separatists. They had first fled from England to Amsterdam in 1608, then to Leyden when they found the commercial capital of Holland too corrupt, and finally, in 1620, to North America.

When they arrived at the northern tip of Cape Cod in November of that year, the Pilgrims were weakened from the stormy nine-week voyage and ill-prepared for the harsh winter ahead. Misled by John Smith's glowing report of a fertile country at the same latitude as southern France, they discovered instead a severe climate and a rockbound coast. By the following spring, half of the *Mayflower* passengers were dead, including 13 of the 18 married women.

The survivors, led by the redoubtable William Bradford, settled at Plymouth. Squabbles soon erupted wih local Indians, whom Bradford considered "savage and brutish men, which range up and down, little otherwise than the wild beasts." In 1622 they found themselves nearly overwhelmed by the arrival of 60 non-Pilgrims, sent out by the London Company, which had helped the Pilgrims finance their colony. For two generations the Pilgrims tilled the soil and fished while trying to keep intact their religious vision. But with the much larger Puritan migration that began in 1630, the Pilgrim villages nestled on the shores of Cape Cod Bay became a backwater of the thriving, populous Massachusetts Bay Colony that absorbed them in 1691.

### Errand into the Wilderness

In 11 ships, 1,000 Puritans set out from England in 1630 for the Promised Land. They were the vanguard of a movement that by 1642 had brought about 18,000 colonizers to New England's shores. Led by John Winthrop, a talented Cambridge-educated member of the English gentry, they operated under a charter from the king to the Puritan-controlled Massachusetts Bay Company. The Puritans set about building their utopia with a fervor possible only

to those who regarded themselves as providentially blessed and charged with divine tasks.

Their intention was to establish communities of pure Christians who collectively swore a covenant with God to work for his ends. To accomplish this, the Puritan fathers agreed to employ severe means. Their historic mission was too important, they believed, to allow the luxury of diversity of opinion in religious matters. Likewise, participation in government must be limited to those admitted to their churches. Civil and religious transgressors must be rooted out and severely punished. Their emphasis was on homogeneous communities where the good of the group outweighed individual interests. "We must delight in each other, make others' conditions our own, rejoice together, mourn together, labor and suffer together," counseled Winthrop.

To realize their utopian goals, the Puritans willingly gave up freedoms that their compatriots sought. An ideology of rebellion in England,

*Always searching himself as well as others for signs of weakness, John Winthrop was named governor of the Massachusetts Bay Colony.*

Puritanism in America became an ideology of control. Much was at stake, for as Winthrop reminded the first settlers, "we shall be as a city upon a hill [and] the eyes of all people are upon us." That visionary sense of mission would help to shape a distinctive American self-image in future generations.

As in Plymouth and Virginia, the first winter tested the strongest souls. More than 200 of the first 700 arrivers perished, and 100 others, disillusioned and sickened by the forbidding climate, returned to England the next spring. But Puritans kept coming. They "hived out" along the Back Bay of Boston, the port capital of the colony, along the rivers that emptied into the bay, south into what became Connecticut and Rhode Island a few years later, and north along the rocky Massachusetts coast.

Energized by their militant work ethic and sense of mission, led by men experienced in local government, law, and the uses of exhortation, the Puritans thrived almost from the beginning. The early leaders of Virginia were soldiers of fortune or roughneck adventurers with predatory instincts, men who had no families or had left them at home. The ordinary Chesapeake settlers were mostly young men with little stake in English society who sold their labor to cross the Atlantic. In Massachusetts, the early leaders were university-trained ministers, experienced members of the lesser gentry, and men with a compulsion to fulfill what they knew was God's prophecy for New England. The ordinary settlers came as families, men and women in nearly equal numbers, and almost all of them free. Trained artisans and farmers from the middling rank of English society, they established tight-knit communities in which, from the outset, the brutal exploitation of labor rampant in the Chesapeake had no place.

### The Elusive Utopia

The Massachusetts Bay Colony flourished at first. The Puritans built a sound economy based on agriculture, fishing, timbering, and trading for beaver furs with local Indians. Even before leaving England, the directors of the Massachusetts Bay Company transformed their commercial charter into a rudimentary government and transferred the charter to New England. Once

there, the elements of self-government were constructed. Free male church members annually elected a governor and deputies from each town who formed one house of a colonial legislature. The other house was composed of the governor's assistants, later to be called councillors. Consent of both houses was required to pass laws.

The Puritans also established the first printing press in North America and even planted the seed of a university, Harvard College, which opened its doors in 1636 for the training of prospective clergymen. The Puritan leaders also launched a brave attempt in 1642 to create a tax-supported school system so that all children might gain "the ability to read and understand the principles of religion and the capital laws of this country." In 1647, the government ordered every town with 50 families to establish an elementary school and every town with 100 families a secondary school as well, open to all who wished to take advantage of this education.

In spite of these accomplishments, the Puritan colony suffered many of the tensions peculiar to those bent on perfecting the human condition. Also, its inhabitants proved no better than their less religious countrymen on the Chesapeake in reaching an accommodation with the Native Americans. Surrounded by what seemed boundless land, Puritan leaders found it difficult to stifle acquisitive instincts and to keep families closely confined in compact communities. Restless souls looked to more distant valleys. "An over-eager desire after the world," wrote an early leader, "has so seized on the spirits of many as if the Lord had no farther work for his people to do, but every bird to feather his own nest." Others, remaining at the nerve center in Boston, agitated for broader political rights and even briefly ousted Winthrop as governor in 1635, when the colony's clergy backed the stiff-necked Thomas Dudley. After a few years in Zion, Governor Winthrop wondered if the Puritans had not gone "from the snare to the pit."

Winthrop's troubles multiplied in 1633 when Salem's Puritan minister, Roger Williams, began to voice disturbing opinions on church and government policies. Now the colony's leaders faced a contentious and visionary young man who argued that the Massachusetts Puritans were not truly pure because they would not completely separate themselves from the polluted Church of England (which most Puritans still hoped to reform). Williams also denounced mandatory worship, which he said "stinks in God's nostrils," and argued that government officials should not interfere with religious matters but confine themselves to civil affairs. Later to be celebrated as the earliest spokesman for the separation of church and state, Williams seemed in 1633 to strike at the heart of the Bible commonwealth, whose leaders regarded the interpenetration of civil and religious affairs as essential. Williams also charged the Puritans with illegally intruding on Indian land.

Winthrop and others spent two years plying Williams with both sweet reason and threats, but they could not quiet the determined young man. Convinced that he would split the colony into competing religious groups and undermine authority, the magistrates vowed to deport him to England. Warned by Winthrop, Williams fled southward through winter snow with a small band of followers to found Providence, a settlement on Narragansett Bay in what would become Rhode Island.

Even as they were driving Williams out, the Puritan authorities confronted another threat. This time it was a woman of extraordinary talent and intellect. Anne Hutchinson was as devoted a Puritan as any who came to the colony. Arriving in 1634 with her husband and seven children, she gained great respect among Boston's women as a practiced midwife, healer, and spiritual counselor. She soon began to discuss religion, suggesting that the "holy spirit" was absent in the preaching of some ministers.

**Early New England**

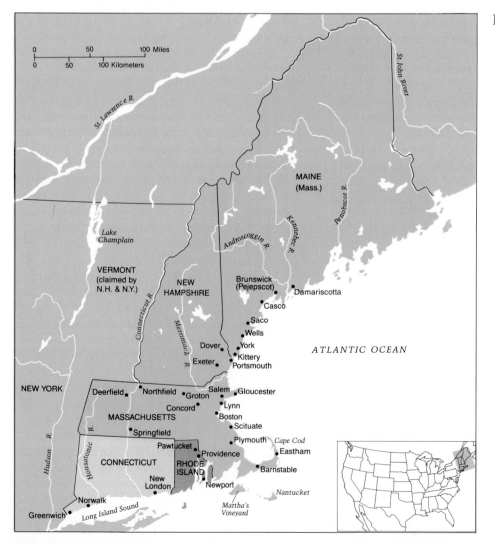

Before long Hutchinson was leading a movement labeled antinomianism, an interpretation of Puritan doctrine that had a powerful emotional appeal in stressing the mystical nature of God's free gift of grace while discounting the efforts the individual could make to gain salvation.

By 1636, Boston was dividing into two camps, those who followed the male clergy and those who cleaved to the theological views of a gifted though untrained woman with no official standing. Her followers included most of the community's malcontents—merchants who chafed under the price controls imposed in 1635 by the magistrates, young people resisting the rigid rule of their elders, women disgruntled by male authority, and artisans who resented wage controls designed to arrest growing inflation. Hutchinson doubly offended the male leaders of the colony because she boldly stepped outside the subordinate position expected of women. "The weaker sex" set her up as "a priest" and "thronged" after her, wrote one male leader. Another described a "clamour" in Boston that "New England men [should] usurp over their wives and keep them in servile subjection."

Determined to remove this nettle from their sides, the clergy and magistrates put Hutchinson on trial in 1637. After two long interrogations, she was convicted of sedition and contempt in a civil trial and banished from the colony "as a woman not fit for our society." Six months later, the Boston church excommunicated her for preaching 82 erroneous theological opinions. She had "highly transgressed and offended and troubled the church," intoned the presiding clergyman, and "therefore in the name of our Lord Jesus Christ, I do cast you out and deliver you up to Satan and account you from this time forth to be a heathen and a leper." In the last month of her eighth pregnancy, Hutchinson, with a band of supporters, followed the route of Roger Williams to Rhode Island, the catch basin for Massachusetts Bay's dissidents.

But ideas proved harder to banish than people. The magistrates could never enforce uniformity of belief. Neither could they curb the appetite for land. Growth, geographic expansion, and commerce with the outside world all eroded the ideal of integrated, self-contained communities permeated with religious piety and dedicated to holding spiritual values above material gain. Leaders never wearied of reminding Puritan settlers that "the care of the public must oversway all private respects." But they faced the difficult, almost impossible, task of containing land-hungry immigrants in an expansive region. By 1636, groups of Puritans had swarmed not only to Rhode Island but to Hartford and New Haven, where Thomas Hooker and John Davenport led new Puritan settlements.

### Puritans and Indians

The charter of the Massachusetts Bay Company proclaimed that the "principal end of this plantation" was "to win and incite the natives to the knowledge and obedience of the only true God and Saviour of mankind and the Christian faith." But the instructions that Governor John

*By the late seventeenth century, "troubles with the Indians" were a major factor in discussions of New England, as indicated by the descriptive title of William Hubbard's book, published in Boston and London in 1677.*

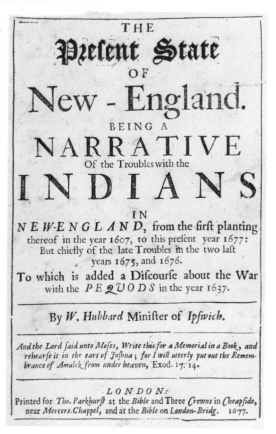

THE

**Present State**

OF

New - England.

BEING A

NARRATIVE

Of the Troubles with the

INDIANS

IN

NEW-ENGLAND, from the first planting thereof in the year 1607, to this present year 1677:
But chiefly of the late Troubles in the two last years 1675, and 1676.

To which is added a Discourse about the War with the PEQUODS in the year 1637.

By *W. Hubbard* Minister of *Ipswich*.

*And the Lord said unto Moses, Write this for a Memorial in a Book, and rehearse it in the ears of Joshua; for I will utterly put out the Remembrance of Amalek from under heaven,* Exod. 17. 14.

LONDON:
Printed for *Tho. Parkhurst* at the *Bible* and *Three Crowns* in *Cheapside*, near *Mercers-Chappel*, and at the *Bible* on *London-Bridge*. 1677.

Winthrop carried from England reveal other Puritan thoughts about the native inhabitants. According to Winthrop's orders, all men were to receive training in the use of firearms, which was a reversal of the sixteenth-century English policy of disarming the citizenry in order to quell public disorders. In addition, Indians were to be prohibited from entering Puritan towns, and any colonist selling arms to an Indian or instructing one in their use was to be deported immediately.

Only sporadic conflict with local tribes occurred at first because disease had catastrophically struck the Native American population of southern New England, which may have numbered as many as 125,000 in 1600, and left much of their land vacant. English fishermen, stopping along the coast in 1616, triggered an outbreak of respiratory viruses or smallpox among a population with no immunity against European microbes. From Massachusetts Bay to Plymouth, entire towns of Indians died in an epidemic carnage that wiped out about half the population. Five years later, an Englishman exploring the area wrote that the Indians "died on heapes, as they lay in their houses" and described walking through a forest where human skeletons covered the ground.

When smallpox returned in 1633, killing thousands more natives, it again relieved pressure for land. The Puritans saw the disease as proof that God had intervened on their side, just when a flood of new settlers was causing trouble over rights to land. "Without this remarkable and terrible stroke of God upon the natives," reported the Charlestown settlers, "[we] would with much more difficulty have found room, and at far greater charge have obtained and purchased land." Many surviving Indians welcomed the Puritans because they now had surplus land and through trade hoped to gain English protection against tribal enemies to the north.

The immigrant pressure for new land, however, soon reached into areas not touched by disease. When land hunger mingled with the Puritan sense of mission, it proved an explosive mix. To a people charged with messianic zeal, the heathen Indians represented a mocking challenge to attempts to build a religious common-

wealth that would "shine as a beacon" back to decadent England. How could order and discipline be brought to their New Jerusalem unless its original inhabitants were tamed and "civilized"? If the natives could not be converted to civility and Christianity, the Puritans would have demonstrated their failure to control the land to which God had directed them. God, they knew, would answer such a failure with his wrath.

Making the "savages" of New England strictly accountable to the ordinances that governed white behavior was part of this quest for fulfilling their mission. In this the Puritans succeeded with the smaller, disease-ravaged tribes of eastern Massachusetts. But their attempts to control the stronger Pequots led to the bloody war in 1637 in which John Mason was a leader. The Puritan victory in that war assured English sovereignty over all the tribes of southern New England except the powerful Wampanoags and Narragansetts of Rhode Island and removed the last obstacle to expansion into the Connecticut River valley. Missionary work, led by John Eliot, began among the remnant tribes in the 1640s. After a decade of effort, about 1,000 Indians had been settled in four "praying villages," learning to live according to the white man's ways.

### The Web of Village Life

The village was the vital center of Puritan life. Unlike the Chesapeake tobacco planters, who dispersed along the streams and rivers of their area, the Puritans planted small, tightly settled villages. Most pursued "open field" agriculture, trudging out from the village each morning to farm narrow strips of land that radiated out from the town. They grazed their cattle on common meadow and cut firewood on common woodland. Such a system re-created agricultural life in many parts of England.

In other towns Puritans employed the "closed field" system of self-contained farms that they had known at home. But in either system, families lived close together in compact towns built around a common, where the meetinghouse and tavern were located. These small, communal villages kept families in close touch so that each could be alert not only to its own transgressions but also to those of its neighbors. "In a multitude of counsellors is safety," Puritan ministers were fond of advising, and the little villages of 50 to 100 families perfectly served the need for moral surveillance, or "holy watching."

Determined to achieve godliness and communal unity, Puritans also prohibited single men and women from living by themselves, for this would put individuals beyond patriarchal authority and group observation. Only such self-imposed togetherness would maintain uniformity of thought and godly behavior. Left to themselves, men and women would stray from the path, for, as Thomas Hooker put it, "every natural man and woman is born full of sin, as full as a toad of poison." In Virginia, the leading planters counted the absence of restraint as a blessing. In New England, it was feared as the Devil.

At the center of every Puritan village stood the meetinghouse. These plain wooden structures, sometimes called "Lord's barns," gathered within them every soul in the village, not just once but twice on the Lord's day and during midweek as well. No man stood higher in the community than the minister. He was the spiritual leader in these small, family-based, community-oriented settlements that viewed life as a Christian pilgrimage.

The unique Puritan mixture of strict authority and incipient democracy, of hierarchy and equality, can be seen in the way the Massachusetts town distributed land and devised local government. Each town was founded by a grant of the colony's General Court, sitting in Boston. These settlement grants were made only to groups of Puritans who had signed a compact signifying their unity of purpose. "We shall by all means," read the town of Dedham's covenant, "labor to keep off from us such as are contrary minded, and receive only such unto us as may be probably of one heart with us."

After receiving a grant, townsmen met to parcel out land. They awarded individual grants according to the size of a man's household, his

*The similarity in settlement patterns between England and New England is seen in a modern rendering of early seventeenth-century Rowley, Massachusetts (left) and a 1591 plan of Chelmsford, Essex (right).*

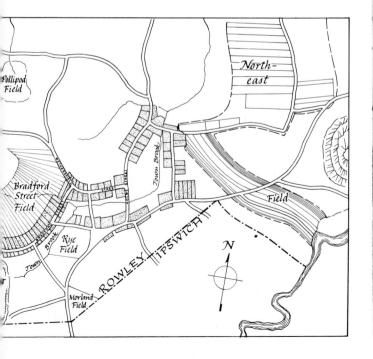

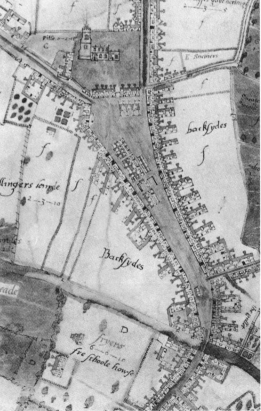

# RECOVERING THE PAST

Homesteading is central to our national experience. For 300 years after the founding of the first colonies, most Americans were involved in taming and settling the land. On every frontier, families faced the tasks of clearing the fields, beginning farming operations, and building shelter for themselves and their livestock. What kind of structures they built depended on available materials, their resources and aspirations, and their notions of a "fair" dwelling. The plan of a house and the materials used in its construction reveal much about the needs, resources, priorities, and values of the people who built it.

By examining archaeological remains of early ordinary structures and by studying houses that are still standing, historians are reaching new understandings of the social characteristics of pioneering societies. During the past 20 years, archaeologists and architectural historians have been studying seventeenth-century housing in the Chesapeake Bay and New England regions. They have discovered a familiar sequence of house types—from temporary shanties and lean-tos to rough cabins and simple frame houses to larger and more substantial dwellings of brick and finished timber. This hovel-to-house-to-

home pattern existed on every frontier, as sodbusters, gold miners, planters, and cattle raisers secured their hold on the land and then struggled to move from subsistence to success.

What is unusual in the findings of the Chesapeake researchers is the discovery that the second phase in the sequence—the use of temporary, rough-built structures—lasted for more than a century. While many New Englanders had rebuilt and extended their temporary clapboard houses into timber-framed, substantial dwellings by the 1680s, Chesapeake settlers continued to construct small, rickety buildings that had to be repaired continually or abandoned altogether every 10 to 15 years.

The William Boardman house, built around 1687, is an example of the "orderly, fair, and well-built" houses of late seventeenth-century Massachusetts. Its plan shows a typical arrangement of space: the hall, used for cooking, eating, working, and socializing; the parlor; a sleeping room for the parents; and a lean-to for kitchen chores and activities such as dairying. The great central chimney warmed the main downstairs room. Upstairs were two rooms used for both storage and sleeping. As you examine the exterior of the

Society for the Preservation of New England Antiquities, Boston; photo by Marcus Whiffen

**William Boardman house, Saugus, Massachusetts, c. 1687**

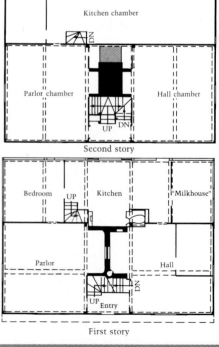

Plan from HABS, Library of Congress

**William Boardman house, floor plan**

47a

building, note the materials that have been used and the arrangement and treatment of windows, doors, and chimney. What impression of the Boardman family might visitors have as they approached the house? What kind of privacy and comfort did the house provide for family members?

The second house is a typical reconstructed tobacco planter's house. It has some of the same features as the Boardman house, for both are products of an English building tradition. But there are some major differences between the two. In the Chesapeake house, the chimney is not built of brick but of mud and wood; there is no window glass, only small shutters. The exterior is rough, unfinished planking. The placement of doors and windows and the overall dimensions indicate that this house has only one room downstairs and a loft above. The builders of this house clearly enjoyed less privacy and comfort than the Boardmans.

Historians have puzzled over this contrast between the architecture of the two regions. Part of the explanation may lie in the different climatic conditions and different emigration patterns of New England and the Chesapeake. In the southern region, disease carried off thousands of settlers. The imbalance of men and women produced a stunted and unstable family life, hardly conducive to an emphasis on constructing fine homes. In New England, good health prevailed almost from the beginning, and the family was at the heart of society. It made more sense, in this environment, to make a substantial invest-ment in larger and more permanent houses. Some historians, moreover, argue that the Puritan work ethic impelled New Englanders to build solid homes as contrasted with the culturally backward, "lazy" South.

Archaeological evidence combined with data recovered from land, tax, and court records, however, suggests another reason for the impermanence of housing in the Chesapeake region. Living in a labor-intensive tobacco world, it is argued, planters large and small economized on everything possible in order to buy as many indentured servants and slaves as they could. Better to live in a shanty and have ten slaves than to have a handsome dwelling and nobody to cultivate the fields. As late as 1775, the author of *American Husbandry* calculated that in setting up a tobacco plantation, five times as much ought to be spent on purchasing 20 black fieldhands as on the "house, offices, and tobacco-house."

When the Chesapeake region emerged from its prolonged era of mortality and sexual imbalance, and when a mixed economy of tobacco, grain, and cattle replaced the tobacco monoculture, the rebuilding of the region belatedly began. This occurred in the period after 1720, as excavated house sites reveal. The rhythms of home building and the social and economic history of a society, as new research is revealing, were closely interwoven. What do houses today reveal about the resources, economic livelihood, priorities, and values of contemporary Americans? Do class and regional differences in house design continue?

Photo by Julie Roy Jeffrey

*Reconstructed Chesapeake planter's house*

47b

wealth, and his usefulness to the church and town. Such a system perpetuated existing differences in wealth and status. Yet some towns wrote language into their covenants that to the moden ear has an almost socialistic ring. "From each according to his ability to each as need shall require," read one. It was not socialism that the Puritans had in mind. Rather, they believed that the community's welfare transcended individual ambitions or accomplishments and that unity demanded limits on the accumulation of wealth. Every family should have enough land to sustain it, and prospering men were expected to use their wealth for the community's benefit, not for conspicuous consumption. Repairing the meetinghouse, building a school, aiding a widowed neighbor—such were the proper uses of wealth.

Having felt the sting of centralized power in church and state, Puritans emphasized local exercise of authority. Until 1684, only male church members could vote; this excluded at least half the adult men. These voters elected selectmen, who allocated land, passed local taxes, and settled disputes. Once a year, all townsmen gathered for the town meeting, called later by Thomas Jefferson "the wisest invention ever devised by the wit of man for the perfect exercise of self-government." At the town meeting, the citizens selected town officers for the next year and decided matters large and small: Should the playing of football in the streets be prohibited? Might Widow Thomas be allowed £10 for a kidney stone operation for her son? What salary should the schoolteacher be paid?

Participation in local government was also strengthened by the appointment of many citizens to minor offices—surveyors of hemp, informers about deer, purchasers of grain, town criers, measurers of salt, fence viewers, and many others. Complaints about officialdom rarely grew into political bitterness in such a system. All officeholders were annually subject to electoral approval, and about one out of every ten adult males in many towns was selected each year for some office, large or small. In New England, nobody could acquire a reputation for sobriety and industry without finding himself elected to a local post.

The cohesion of Puritan village life was

## Population of New England, 1620–1690

*Source:* U.S. Bureau of the Census.

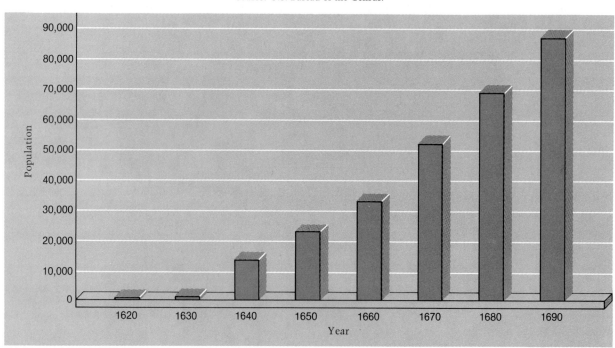

fostered not only by unswerving commitment to social order but also by the demographic characteristics of society. Whereas the Chesapeake was populated mostly by one fragment of English society—young, mobile, lower-class males—Massachusetts from the beginning was composed of families. Settlers kept kinship networks and even old neighborhood associations intact as they moved from Hingham in Norfolk County, England, to Hingham, Massachusetts, or from Sudbury in Suffolk County, England, to their new home in Sudbury, Massachusetts.

Strengthening this family orientation was the remarkably healthy environment of the Puritans' American Israel. While the germs carried by English colonizers devastated neighboring Indian societies, the effect on the newcomers of entering a new environment was the opposite. The low density of settlement prevented infectious diseases from spreading, while the isolation of the New England villages from the avenues of Atlantic commerce, along which diseases as well as cargo flowed, minimized biological hazards in the seventeenth century.

The result was a spectacular natural increase in the population and a longevity unknown in Europe. At a time when the population of western Europe was barely growing—deaths almost equaled births—the population of New England, discounting new immigrants, doubled every 27 years. The difference was not a higher birthrate. New England women typically bore about seven children during the course of a marriage, but this barely exceeded the European norm. The crucial factor was that chances for survival after birth were far greater than in England. In most of Europe, only half the babies born lived long enough to produce children themselves. Life expectancy for the population at large was less than 40 years. In New England, nearly 90 percent of the infants born in the seventeenth century survived to marriageable age, and life expectancy was above 60 years—longer than for the American population as a whole at any time until the early twentieth century. About 25,000 people immigrated to New England in the seventeenth century, but by 1700 they had produced a population of 100,000. By contrast, some 75,000 immigrants to the Chesapeake colonies had yielded a population of about 70,000 by the end of the century.

Women played a vital role in this family-centered society. In the household economies of the Puritan villages, the woman was not only wife, mother, and housekeeper but also custodian of the vegetable garden, processor of salted and smoked meats, dairy products, and preserved vegetables, and spinner, weaver, and clothesmaker.

The presence of women and a stable family life strongly affected New England's regional architecture. As communities formed, the Puritans converted early economic gains into more substantial housing rather than investing in bound labor as in the Chesapeake colonies, where family formation was retarded and the economy unstable. Well-constructed one-room houses with sleeping lofts quickly replaced the early "wigwams, huts, and hovels." Families then added parlors and lean-to kitchens as soon as they could. Within a half century, New En-

*Primers such as this served to instill religious values as well as literacy in the Puritan colonies.*

*Noah* did view
The old World & new

Young *Obadias,*
*David, Jcfias,*
All were pious.

*Peter* deny'd
His Lord, and cry'd.

Queen *Efther* fues,
And faves the *Jews.*

Young pious *Ruth,*
Left all for Truth.

Young *Samuel* dear
The Lord did fear.

gland immigrants accomplished a general rebuilding of their living structures, while the Chesapeake lagged far behind.

A final binding element in Puritan communities was the uncommon stress on literacy and education, eventually to become a hallmark of American society. Placing religion at the center of their lives, Puritans emphasized the ability to read catechisms, psalmbooks, and especially the Bible. Literacy could instill the basic precepts of life in all. "Thy life to mend, this book attend" went one verse in a children's schoolbook. In literacy and books Puritans saw guarantees that they would not succumb to the savagery they saw all around them in the new land. They also trusted that through education they could preserve the central values of their struggle to redeem humankind in the North American wilderness.

The Puritan migration to New England halted abruptly after civil war broke out in England in 1642 between parliamentary and royal forces. By that time about 20,000 English immigrants had settled from Maine to Long Island. Governor Winthrop of Massachusetts lamented the dispersion, and Roger Williams condemned the "depraved appetite" for new and better land. Yet, in a terrain so rock-strewn that its pastures were said to produce Yankee sheep with sharpened noses, it was natural that men should seek better plow land.

To combat dispersion, Puritan leaders established a broad intercolony political structure in 1643 called the Confederation of New England. Designed to coordinate government among the various Puritan settlements and especially to provide greater defense against the French, the Dutch, and the Indians, the pact bound together Massachusetts, Plymouth, the small colony of New Haven, and the river towns of Connecticut.

This first American attempt at federalism functioned fitfully for a generation, though Massachusetts, the strongest and largest member, often refused to abide by group decisions when they ran counter to its objectives.

Although the Puritans fashioned stable communities, developed the economy, and constructed effective government, their leaders, as early as the 1640s, complained that the founding vision of Massachusetts Bay was faltering. Material concerns seemed to transcend religious commitment; the individual prevailed over the commonweal. In 1638, the General Court declared a day of humiliation and prayer to atone for the colony's "excess idleness and contempt of authority." A generation later, the synod of 1679—a convention of Puritan churches—cried out that "the church, the commonwealth and the family are being destroyed by self-assertion." By this time the work of salvaging western Protestantism by example was rarely mentioned. Instead, Puritan leaders concentrated on keeping their children on the straight and narrow road.

Frequent complaints about moral laxness notwithstanding, New England had achieved economic success and political stability by the end of the seventeenth century. Towns functioned efficiently, poverty was uncommon, public education had been mandated, and family life was stable. If social diversity increased and the religious zeal of the founding generation waned, that was only to be expected. One second-generation Bay colonist put the matter bluntly. His minister had noticed his absence in church and found him late that day at the docks, unloading a boatload of cod. "Why were you not in church this morning?" asked the clergyman. Back came the reply: "My father came here for religion, but I came for fish."

## PROPRIETARY NEW YORK AND CAROLINA

By the mid-seventeenth century, the Chesapeake and New England regions each contained about 50,000 settlers. Between them lay the mid-Atlantic area controlled by the Dutch, who had planted a small colony named New Netherland at the mouth of the Hudson River in 1624 and in the next four decades had extended their control to the Connecticut and Delaware river valleys. To the south of the Chesapeake lay a vast territory where only the Spanish, on their mission frontier in Florida, challenged the power of Native American tribes.

These two areas, north and south of the Chesapeake, became strategic zones of English colonizing activity after the end of England's civil war in 1660 brought the reinstallation of the English monarchy that had been eclipsed in 1649 by the execution of Charles I. Commercial rivals with the Dutch and religious and economic enemies of the Spanish, England moved to cement its claims on the North American coast.

## England Challenges the Mighty Dutch

Although for generations they had been the Protestant bulwarks in a mostly Catholic Europe, England and Holland became bitter commercial rivals in the mid-seventeenth century. By the time the Puritans arrived in New England, the Dutch had become the mightiest carriers of seaborne commerce in western Europe. By one contemporary estimate, Holland owned 16,000 of Europe's 20,000 merchant ships. They had also muscled in on Spanish and Portuguese transatlantic commerce, trading illegally with Iberian colonists who gladly violated their government's commercial policies in order to obtain cloth and slaves more cheaply.

By 1650, the Dutch had overwhelmed the Portuguese in Brazil, and soon their vast trading empire reached the East Indies, Ceylon, India, and Formosa. The best shipbuilders, mariners, and businessmen in western Europe, they had put into practice the dictum of Sir Walter Raleigh that "whosoever commands the sea commands the trade; whosoever commands the trade of the world commands the riches of the world, and consequently the world itself."

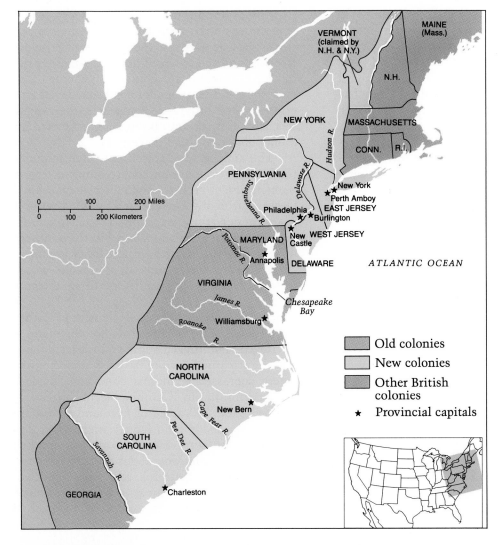

**Early New York, Pennsylvania, and the Carolinas**

In North America, the Dutch West India Company's colony at New Netherland was small but profitable. Agents fanned out from Fort Orange and New Amsterdam, later to become Albany and New York City, into the river valleys of the Hudson, Connecticut, and Delaware. There they established a lucrative fur trade with local tribes. While the Dutch never settled more than 10,000 people in their mid-Atlantic colonies, their commercial and naval power was impressive. The Virginians learned as much in 1667 when brazen Dutch raiders captured 20 tobacco ships on the James River and confiscated virtually the entire tobacco crop for that year.

By 1650, England was ready to challenge Dutch maritime supremacy. Three times between 1652 and 1675, war broke out between the two Protestant competitors for control of the emerging worldwide capitalist economy. In the second and third wars, the Dutch colony on the Hudson River became an easy target for the English. They captured it in 1664 and then, after it fell to the Dutch in 1673, recaptured it almost immediately. By 1675, the Dutch had been permanently dislodged from the North American mainland. But they remained mighty commercial competitors of the English in Europe, Africa, the Far East, and the Caribbean.

New Netherland, where from the beginning Dutch, French Huguenots, Walloons from present-day Belgium, Swedes, Portuguese, Finns, English, refugee Portuguese Jews from Brazil, and Africans had commingled in a babel of languages and religions, now became New York. It was so named because the king made a proprietary grant of the territory, along with the former Dutch colonies on the Delaware River, to James, duke of York, the king's brother and heir to the English throne.

Under English rule, the former Dutch colonists retained much of their ethnic identity for several generations. They spoke their native language, worshiped in their Dutch Reformed Calvinist churches, perpetuated Dutch architecture, and made their peace with their new rulers. In time, the Dutch would be overwhelmed by English immigrants, and gradual intermarriage between the Dutch, the French Huguenots, and the English, the three main groups, would dilute the ethnic loyalty of New Yorkers. But the polyglot, religiously tolerant character of New York would remain, and New Yorkers would never allow religious concerns or utopian plans to interfere with the pragmatic conduct of business.

## A Restoration Reward

In 1663, three years after he was restored to the throne taken from his father, Charles II granted a vast territory named Carolina to a group of men who had supported him when he was in exile. Its boundaries extended from ocean to ocean and from Virginia to central Florida. Within this miniature empire, eight proprietors, including several involved in Barbados sugar plantations, gained large powers of government and semifeudal rights to the land. For settling their royal reward, they constructed a system of government with both feudal and modern features. To lure settlers, they promised religious freedom and offered land not at a bargain price but for nothing at all. Onto this generous land offer they grafted plans for a semimedieval government that provided themselves, their deputies, and a small number of noblemen with a monopoly of political power.

The architects of Carolina, which included the brilliant young John Locke, were reacting to a generation of violence and radical social experiments during the English civil war (1642–1649). They intended their design for Carolina to guarantee social and political stability in the southern wilds of North America. A hereditary aristocracy of wealthy manor lords, they thought, would check the boisterous multitude of small landholders.

However, the reality of settlement in Carolina bore faint resemblance to what the planters envisaged. The rugged sugar and tobacco planters who streamed in from Barbados and Virginia, where depressed economic conditions made a new beginning in Carolina seem attractive, claimed their 150 acres of free land (and additional acreage for each family member or servant they brought). But they blithely ignored proprietary regulations about settling in compact rectangular patterns and reserving two-fifths of every county for an appointed nobility.

In government they also did as they pleased. When they met in assembly for the first time in 1670, they refused to accept the proprietors' Fundamental Constitutions of 1667 and ignored the orders of the governor appointed in London. In shaping local government, the planters were guided mostly by their experience in the slave society of Barbados, whence most of them had come.

## The Indian Debacle

Carolina was the most elaborately planned colony in English history but the least successful in achieving amicable relations with Native Americans. The proprietors in London intended otherwise. Mindful of the violent encounters that had plagued other English settlements, they projected a well-regulated Indian trade limited to their appointed agents. But the aggressive settlers streaming in from the West Indies and the Chesapeake openly flouted proprietary policy. Those from Barbados, accustomed to exploiting African slave labor, saw that if the major tribes of the Southeast—the Cherokees, Creeks, and Choctaws—could be drawn into trade, the planters might reap vast wealth. The Spanish in Florida had done little to tap this potential gold mine; their main goal had been protecting their territorial claim by establishing missions that gathered local Indians into a sedentary, agricultural life.

It was not the beaver that beckoned in the Indian trade, as in the North, but the deerskin, much desired in Europe for making warm and durable clothing. "There is such infinite herds [of deer]," wrote one early leader in 1682, "that the whole country seems but one continued [deer] park." What began as a trade for the skins of deer, however, soon became a trade for the skins of Indians. Much to the consternation of the London proprietors, capturing Indians for sale in New England and the West Indies became the cornerstone of commerce in Carolina in the early years.

The Indian slave trade plunged Carolina into a series of wars. Local planters and merchants selected a tribe, armed it, and rewarded it handsomely for bringing in captives from another. Even the stronger tribes that allied for trade with the Carolinians found that after they had used English guns to enslave their weaker neighbors, they themselves were sometimes scheduled for elimination. The colonists justified the policy by claiming that "thinning the barbarous Indian natives" was necessary to make room for white settlement. The "thinning" was so thorough that by the early eighteenth century, the two main tribes of the coastal plain, the Westos and the Savannahs, were nearly extinct.

## Early Carolina Society

Carolina's fertile land and warm climate convinced many that it was "a Country so delicious, pleasant, and fruitful that were it cultivated doubtless it would prove a second Paradize." Into the country came Barbadians, Swiss, Scots, Irish, French Huguenots, English, and even migrants from New England, New York, and New Jersey. But far from creating paradise, this ethnically and religiously diverse people rubbed abrasively against each other in an atmosphere of fierce competition, brutal race relations, and stunted social institutions.

For the land-hungry white cattle raisers and rice growers of coastal South Carolina, the Indian slave trade had no direct benefits, since the profits flowed entirely to the merchants of Charleston, the main port and seat of government. They reaped important secondary advantages, however. As the Indian population of the coastal region fell sharply, expansion from the initial settlements around Charleston became easier. Along the twisting rivers that flowed to the coast, planters staked out claims and experimented with a variety of exotic crops, including sugar, indigo, tropical fruits, tobacco, and rice. It was this last that, after much experimentation, proved to be the staple crop upon which a flourishing economy could be built.

The cultivation of rice required much backbreaking labor to drain the swampy lowlands, build dams and levees, and hoe, weed, cut, thresh, and husk the crop. Since many of the early settlers had experience with African slaves in Barbados, their early reliance on slave labor came naturally to them. On widely dispersed plantations, black labor came to predominate. In 1680, four-fifths of South Carolina's population was white. But by 1720, when the colony had grown to 18,000, black slaves outnumberd whites two to one.

As in Virginia and Maryland, the low-lying areas of coastal Carolina were so disease-ridden that population grew only slowly in the early years. "In the spring a paradise, in the summer a hell, and in the autumn a hospital," remarked one traveler. Malaria and yellow fever, especially dangerous to pregnant women, were the twin killers that retarded population growth, while the scarcity of women further limited natural increase. Like the West Indies, the rice-growing region of Carolina was at first more a place to accumulate a fortune than to raise a family.

In the northern part of Carolina, mostly pine barrens along a sandy coast, a different kind of society emerged. Populated largely by small tobacco farmers from Virginia seeking free land,

the Albemarle region developed a mixed economy of livestock grazing, tobacco and foodstuffs production, and the mining of the pine forests for naval stores—turpentine, resin, pitch, tar, and lumber. In 1701, North and South Carolina became separate colonies; but before that their distinctiveness had emerged. Slavery took root only slowly in North Carolina, which was still 85 percent white in 1720. A land of struggling white settlers (called "Lubberland" by one prosperous Virginia planter), its healthier climate and settlement by families rather than by single men with servants and slaves gave it a greater potential for sustained growth. But in both North and South Carolina, several factors inhibited the growth of a strong corporate identity: the pattern of settlement, the ethnic and religious diversity, and the lack of shared assumptions about social and religious goals.

## THE QUAKERS' PEACEABLE KINGDOM

Of all the utopian dreams imposed on the North American landscape in the seventeenth century, the most remarkable was that of the Quakers. During the English civil war, the Society of Friends, as the Quakers called themselves, had sprung forth as one of the many radical sects searching for a more just society and a purer religion. Their visionary ideas and their defiance of civil authority cost them dearly in fines, brutal punishment, and imprisonment. After Charles II and Parliament began stifling radical dissent in the 1660s, they too sent many converts across the Atlantic. In America they swam against the tide of their times, attempting to perfect social relations among religiously and ethnically diverse people. The reformist imprint they placed on the larger society is still vibrant today in spite of their small number. Moreover, the society they founded in Pennsylvania foreshadowed more than any other colony the future religious and ethnic pluralism of the United States.

### The Early Friends

Like their Puritan cousins, the Quakers regarded the English Protestant church (called the

Church of England) as corrurpt and renounced its formalities and rituals, which smacked of Catholicism. But they carried the Puritan revolt against the Church of England to the extreme. They foreswore all church officials and institutions standing between the lone individual and God. The Quakers were persuaded that every believer could find grace through the "inward light," a spark of redemption that resided in every man and woman, unaided by priests, ministers, liturgy, or other human devices. By discarding the ideas of original sin and eternal predestination, they offered a radically liberating alternative to the reigning Calvinist doctrine.

Quakers were persecuted in England after their movement, led by George Fox and Margaret Fell, gathered momentum in the 1650s. Other Protestants looked upon them as dangerous fanatics, for the Quakers' egalitarian doctrine of the light within elevated all lay persons to the position of the clergy and denied the primary place accorded the Scriptures. They seemed to threaten the stability of the organized church.

Equally threatening was the Quakers' social radicalism. They refused to observe the customary marks of deference, such as doffing one's hat to a superior, for they believed that in God's sight no social distinctions existed. They used the familiar *thee* and *thou* instead of the formal and deferential *you*, they resisted taxes supporting the Church of England, and they refused to sign witnesses' oaths on the Bible, regarding this as profane. They also shocked a world conditioned to violence by renouncing the use of force in human affairs. Their pacifism carried them into a refusal to perform militia service. Garbing themselves in plain black cloth and practicing civil disobedience, the Quakers presented a threat to social hierarchy and order in every community they entered.

By conferring on women a more equal place than anywhere in the English-speaking world, the Quakers also affronted traditional views. They insisted on the spiritual equality of the sexes and the right of women to participate in church matters on an equal, if usually separate, footing with men. The Puritans had granted spiritual equality to women but excluded them from preaching, electing ministers, admitting others to membership, and other churchly functions. They had excommunicated Anne Hutchinson, who had defied these rules in Massachusetts, with the words, "You have stepped out of your place, you have rather been a husband than a wife, and a preacher than a hearer."

The Quaker leader George Fox renounced such discrimination. "Now Moses and Aaron and the 70 elders did not say to those assemblies of women: 'we can do our work ourselves and you are more fit to be at home to wash the dishes,' but they did encourage them in the work and service of God." Quaker leaders urged women to preach and help govern within meetings. Among Quakers who fanned out from England to preach the doctrine of the "inward light," 26 of the first 59 to cross the Atlantic were women. All but four of them were unmarried or without their husbands and therefore living, traveling, and ministering outside the bounds of male authority.

Intensely committed to converting the rest of the world to their beliefs, the Quakers ranged westward to North America and the Caribbean in the 1650s and 1660s. Nearly everywhere they were reviled, mutilated, imprisoned, and deported. Puritan Massachusetts warned them that their liberty in that colony consisted of "free

liberty to keep away from us and such as will come to be gone as fast as they can, the sooner the better." Hungering to serve in what they called "the Lamb's War," the Quakers vowed to test the Puritans' resolve and kept coming.

The Bay Colony magistrates were desperate to rid themselves of such a dangerous threat to religious conformity and civil authority. Finally, in 1659, they hanged two Quaker men on the Boston Common and went through the motions of hanging Mary Dyer, an old woman who had followed Anne Hutchinson a quarter century before. Escorted from the colony, Mary Dyer returned the next year to defy the Massachusetts ban. Undaunted, she met her death at the end of a rope.

### Early Quaker Designs

By the 1670s, the English Quakers were looking for a place in the New World to carry out their millennial dreams. In England, fears of a Catholic conspiracy centered in the royal family led to severe religious repression of all dissenting groups in the late 1670s. Thousands of Quakers were jailed and fined heavily for practicing their faith.

Emerging as their leader in this dark period was William Penn, whose background made him an unlikely Quaker. Penn was the son of Admiral Sir William Penn, who by capturing Jamaica from the Spanish in 1654 had placed in English hands one of the most productive sugar-growing sites in the world. Young William had been groomed for life in the English aristocracy. But when sent to Oxford, he found it a "hellish darkness and a debauchery." He rebelled against his parents' designs for him in one of the professions; then, at age 23, he was converted by a spellbinding speech about the power of the Quaker inward light.

After joining the Society of Friends in 1666, Penn devoted himself to their cause. He defended Quakers arrested for religious nonconformity and trekked through England, Ireland, Holland, and Germany spreading the Quaker faith. In 1674, Penn joined other Friends in establishing their own colony, between the Hudson and Delaware rivers.

The area south of New York had originally been part of the Dutch New Netherland colony, but it was only sparsely settled. Following the English capture of New Netherland in 1664, Charles II granted the area, divided into two large tracts called West and East Jersey, as a royal gift to Lord John Berkeley and Sir George Carteret. Little interested in managing his half of the 4,600-square-mile territory, Berkeley sold his rights to West Jersey to a group of Quakers in 1674. William Penn was among them.

One of England's most active pamphleteers on the side of religious toleration and parliamentary rights in the 1670s, Penn now helped fashion an extraordinarily liberal constitution for the budding Quaker colony. Legislative power and the authority to constitute courts were vested in an assembly chosen annually by virtually all free males in the colony. Election of justices of the peace and local officeholders was also mandated. Settlers were guaranteed freedom of religion and trial by jury. As Penn and the other trustees of the colony explained, "We lay a foundation for after ages to understand their liberty as men and Christians, that they may not be brought in bondage, but by their own consent; for we put the power in the people."

The last phrase, summing up the document, would have shocked anyone of property and power in England or America at the time. Most regarded "the people" as ignorant, dangerous, and certain to bring society to a state of anarchy if entrusted with the right to rule themselves. Nowhere in the English world had ordinary citizens, including even those who owned no land, enjoyed such extensive privileges. Nowhere had a popularly elected legislature received such broad authority.

Despite these idealistic plans, West Jersey sputtered at first. Only 1,500 immigrants arrived in the first five years, and the colony for several decades was caught up in legal complications caused by the tangled claims to the land and government. The focus of Quaker hopes lay across the Delaware River where in 1681 Charles II granted William Penn a vast territory, almost as large as England itself. The grant extinguished a large royal debt to Penn's father, but the crown may also have seen it as a way of getting the pesky Quakers out of England. To the Quakers' great fortune, the territory granted to Penn, the last unassigned segment of the eastern coasts of North America, was also one of the most fertile.

### Pacifism in a Militant World: Quakers and Indians

On the day Penn received his royal charter for Pennsylvania, he wrote a friend, "My God that has given it to me will, I believe, bless and make it the seed of a nation." The nation that Penn envisioned was unique among colonizing schemes. Penn intended to make his colony an asylum for the persecuted, a refuge from arbitrary state power. Puritans strove to nurture social homogeneity and religious uniformity, excluding all not of like mind. In the Chesapeake and Carolina colonies, aggressive, unidealistic men sought to enrich themselves by exploiting the region's resources. But Penn dreamed of inviting to his sylvan woods people of all religions and national backgrounds and blending them together in peaceful coexistence. His state would claim no authority over the consciences of its citizens nor demand military service of them.

The Quakers who began streaming into

*Although most immigrants to Pennsylvania preferred to settle on isolated farmsteads, the city of Philadelphia was one of the largest in the colonies by 1720.*

Pennsylvania in 1682 quickly absorbed earlier Dutch, Finnish, and Swedish settlers. Primarily farmers, they fanned out from the capital city of Philadelphia. They participated in the government by electing representatives, who initiated laws (which also required the approval of the proprietary governor, Penn's appointee, and his council). Like colonists elsewhere, they avidly acquired land, purchasing it from Penn at reasonable rates. But unlike other colonizers, the Quakers practiced pacifism, holding the ethic of love and nonresistance embodied in the Sermon on the Mount as literally binding on them.

Even before arriving, Penn laid the foundation for peaceful relations with the Delaware tribe inhabiting his colony. He wrote to the Delaware chiefs: "The king of the Country where I live, hath given me a great Province; but I desire to enjoy it with your Love and Consent, that we may always live together as Neighbors and friends." In this single statement Penn dissociated himself from the entire history of European colonization in the New World and from the negative view of Native Americans so common whenever the two cultures met. Recognizing the Indians as the rightful owners of the land inluded in his grant, Penn pledged not to sell one acre until he had first purchased it from local chiefs. He also promised strict regulation of the Indian trade and a ban on the sale of alcohol. Voltaire was later moved to write, although not with strict accuracy, that this was "the only league between those [Indian] nations and the Christians that was never sworn to, and never broken."

The Quaker accomplishment is sometimes belittled with the claim that there was little competition for land in eastern Pennsylvania between the natives and the newcomers. However, a comparison between Pennsylvania and South Carolina, both Restoration colonies, shows that religious belief had the power to dictate outcome. A quarter century after initial settlement, Pennsylvania had a population of about 20,000 whites. Penn's Indian policy had so impressed Native American tribes that Indian refugees began migrating into Pennsylvania from all sides. During the same quarter century, South Carolina had grown to only about 4,000 whites, but the area had become a cauldron of violence. Carolinians spread arms through the region to facilitate slave dealing, shipped some 10,000 members of local tribes off to New England and the West Indies as slaves, and laid waste to the Spanish mission frontier in Florida.

As long as the Quaker philosophy of pacifism and friendly relations with the Delawares and Susquehannocks held sway, interracial relations in the Delaware River valley contrasted sharply with those in other parts of North America. Long after Penn left his colony in 1701, the native people cherished in tradition his fair treatment and genuine regard for them. Ironically, the Quaker policy of toleration, liberal government, and exemption from military service attracted to the colony, especially in the eighteenth century, thousands of immigrants whose land hunger and disdain for Indians undermined Quaker trust and friendship. Germans and Scots-Irish flooded in, swelling the population to 20,000 by 1708. Neither of these groups shared Quaker idealism about racial harmony. Driven from their homelands by hunger and war, they cared only about tilling the soil in Pennsylvania. Pressing inland, they encroached on the lands of the local tribes, sometimes encouraged by the land agents of Penn's heirs. This created conflict with the natives who had sought sanctuary in Pennsylvania. By the mid-eighteenth century, a confrontation of displaced persons, some red and some white, was occurring in Pennsylvania.

### Building the Peaceable Kingdom

Although Pennsylvania came closer to matching its founder's goals than any other European colony, Penn's dream of a society that banished violence, religious intolerance, and arbitary authority never completely materialized. Nor was he able to convince people to settle in compact villages, which he believed necesary for his "holy experiment." The plain Quaker farmers scattered across the countryside and built simple farmsteads on their land. Instead of agricultural villages with meetinghouses at their centers, as in New England, they created open country networks without any particular centers or boundaries. Yet a sense of common endeavor persisted.

While Penn's official settlement policies carried "no more weight than the East Wind," Quaker farmers prized family life and emigrated almost entirely in kinship groups. At first, people from the same region clustered together—the Welsh in "the Welsh tract," the Rhinelanders in Germantown, the Cheshire immigrants in Chester County. In time, intermarriage and sale of land to newcomers created a patchwork of national and religious groups across Pennsylvania's countryside. The Quakers maintained their distinctive identity, however, allowing marriage only within their society, carefully providing land for their offspring, and guarding against too great a population increase (which would cause too rapid a division of farms) by limiting the size of their families.

Settled by religiously dedicated farming families and favored by rich grainlands, Pennsylvania's countryside blossomed. The colony avoided the "starving period" known in other areas and achieved economic success from the beginning. The colony's port capital of Philadelphia also grew rapidly. By 1700, it had overtaken New York City in population, and a half century later it was the largest city in the colonies, bustling with a wide range of artisans, merchants, and professionals.

## The Limits of Perfectionism

In spite of commercial success and peace with Native Americans, not all was harmonious in early Pennsylvania. Promotional literature described a "precious harmony" in meetings of the legislature and a "heavenly authority" that bound settlers in common purpose. But in reality, political affairs were often turbulent.

In part, dissension arose because of Pennsylvania's weak leadership. Penn was a much-loved proprietor, but he did not tarry long in his colony to guide its course. He returned to England in 1684, visited his colony briefly in 1700, and then left forever. The leadership vacuum he left was never filled.

A more important cause of disunity resided in the Quaker attitude toward authority. In England, balking at authority was almost a daily part of Quaker life. To be a Quaker was to refuse to bear arms, to disobey the law prohibiting nonconformists to hold religious services, to deny the Bible as revealed truth, to reject the traditional role assigned women, and to violate social custom obliging inferiors to defer to their superiors. The Quaker was the supremely "inner-directed" person, fired by an apocalyptic

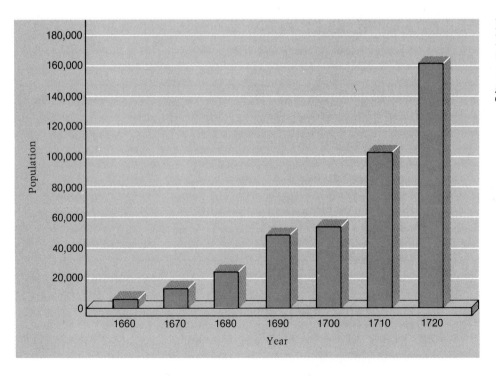

**Population of the Restoration Colonies, 1660–1720**

**Source:** U.S. Bureau of the Census.

view of the world and bound to other Quakers by decades of persecution.

In Pennsylvania, the absence of persecution eliminated a crucial binding element. In their own colony, Quakers had no need to cling together in mutual defense. The factionalism that developed among them demonstrated that people never unify so well as when under attack. Rather than looking inward and banding together, they looked outward to an environment filled with opportunity. Their squabbling filled Penn with dismay. Why, he asked, were his settlers so "governmentish, so brutish, so susceptible to scurvy quarrels that break out to the disgrace of the Province?"

Pennsylvania proved to be different from other colonies in several but not all respects. The Quaker New World immigrant was just as eager to acquire land and build an estate as his Puritan counterpart. In fact, Quaker industriousness and frugality led to such material success that after a generation, their social radicalism and religious evangelicalism began to fade. As in other colonies, settlers discovered the door to prosperity wide open and surged across the threshold.

Where Pennsylvania differed from New England and the South was in its relations with Native Americans, at least for the first few generations. It also departed from the Puritan colonies in its immigration policy. Pennsylvania, it is said, was the first community since the Roman Empire to allow people of different national origins and religious persuasions to live together under the same government on terms of near equality. English, Highland Scots, French, Germans, Irish, Welsh, Swedes, Finns, and Swiss all settled in Pennsylvania. This ethnic mosaic was further complicated by a religious division that included Mennonites, Lutherans, Dutch Reformed, Quakers, Baptists, Anglicans, Presbyterians, Catholics, Jews, and a sprinkling of mystics and hermits. If their relations were not always friendly, at least few attempts were made to drive dissenting groups out or to discriminate against them. Pennsylvanians never sought religious or ethnic uniformity and never cast out malcontents and dissenters. Consequently, they laid the foundations for the pluralism that was to become the hallmark of American society.

## CONCLUSION: The Achievement of New Societies

Nearly 200,000 immigrants who had left their European homelands reached the coast of North America in the seventeenth century. Coming from a variety of social backgrounds and spurred by different motivations, they represented the rootstock of distinctive societies that would mature in England's colonies. For three generations, North America served as a social laboratory for religious and social visionaries, political theorists, fortune seekers, social outcasts, and, most of all, ordinary men and women seeking a better life than they had known in their European homelands.

Nearly three-quarters of them came to the Chesapeake and Carolina colonies. Most of them found this region a burial ground rather than an arena of opportunity. Disease, stunted family life, and the harsh work regimen imposed by the planters who commanded the labor of the vast majority ended the dreams of most who came. Yet population inched upward, and the bone and sinew of a workable economy formed. In the northern colonies, to which the fewest immigrants came, life was more secure. Organized around family and community, favored by a healthier climate, and motivated by religion and social vision, the Puritan and Quaker societies thrived. Utopian expectations were never completely fulfilled. But nowhere else in the Western world at that time could they even have been attempted. What did succeed was the rooting of agricultural life based on family farms and the establishment of locally oriented political institutions marked by widespread participation. Thus, as the seventeenth century progressed, the scattered settlements along the North American coast, largely isolated from one another, pursued their separate paths of development.

## Founding of the British North American Colonies

| COLONY | CAPITAL | CHARTER DATE | TYPE |
|---|---|---|---|
| Virginia | Williamsburg | 1607 | Self-governing 1607–1624; royal 1624–1776 |
| Massachusetts | Boston | 1629 | Self-governing 1629–1691; royal 1691–1776 |
| New Hampshire | Portsmouth | 1622 | Proprietary 1622–1641; annexed by Massachusetts 1641–1680; royal 1680–1776 |
| New York | New York City | 1624 | Dutch 1624–1664; proprietary 1664–1685; royal 1685–1776 |
| Delaware | New Castle | 1631 | Dutch 1631–1682; annexed by Pennsylvania 1682–1703; self-governing 1703–1776 |
| Maryland | Annapolis | 1634 | Proprietary 1634–1691; royal 1691–1715; proprietary 1715–1776 |
| Rhode Island | Newport | 1636 | Self-governing 1636–1663; royal 1663–1776 |
| Connecticut | Hartford; New Haven | 1636 | Self-governing 1636–1776 |
| New Jersey | Perth Amboy; Burlington | 1676 | Proprietary 1676–1702; royal 1702–1776 |
| North Carolina | New Bern | 1663 | Proprietary 1663–1729; royal 1729–1776 |
| South Carolina | Charleston | 1669 | Proprietary 1669–1729; royal 1719–1776 |
| Pennsylvania | Philadelphia | 1681 | Proprietary 1681–1776 |
| Georgia | Savannah | 1732 | Proprietary 1732–1754; royal 1754–1776 |

## Recommended Reading

The early settlement of the Chesapeake is the subject of much exciting new research. Among the older treatments, the soundest is Wesley F. Craven, *The Southern Colonies in the Seventeenth Century* (1949). New works include Edmund S. Morgan, *American Slavery, American Freedom: The Ordeal of Colonial Virginia* (1975); Thad W. Tate and David L. Ammerman, eds., *The Chesapeake in the Seventeenth Century* (1979); David B. Quinn, ed., *Early Maryland in a Wider World* (1982); Gloria L. Main, *Tobacco Colony: Life in Early Maryland* (1982); and Darrett B. Rutman and Anita H. Rutman, *A Place in Time: Middlesex County, Virginia, 1650–1750* (1984).

A good introduction to English Puritanism is Christoper Hill, *Society and Puritanism in Pre-Revolutionary England*, 2d ed. (1967). For information on the Puritans in their early New England communities, consult John Demos, *A Little Commonwealth* (1970); Kenneth Lockridge, *A New England Town* (1970); Philip Greven, Jr., *Four Generations* (1970); Stephen Innes, *Labor in a New Land* (1983); and Darrett B. Rutman, *Winthrop's Boston* (1965). Illuminating biographies of early Puritan leaders are Edmund S. Morgan, *The Puritan Dilemma: The Story of John Winthrop* (1958); Richard S. Dunn, *Puritans and Yankees* (1962); and Robert Middlekauff, *The Mathers* (1971). For rich analyses of Puritan-Indian relations, see Neal Salisbury, *Manitou and Providence* (1982) and William Cronon, *Changes in the Land: Indians, Colonists, and the Ecology of New England* (1983). Another fascinating study is John Demos, *Entertaining Satan: Witchcraft and the Culture of Early New England* (1982).

Proprietary New York and Carolina are treated in Robert C. Ritchie; *The Duke's Province* (1977); Allen W. Trelease, *Indian Affairs in Colonial New York* (1960); M. Eugene Sirmans, *Colonial South Carolina* (1966); and Verner Crane, *The Southern Frontier, 1670–1732* (1929).

Quaker Pennsylvania is the subject of Frederick B. Tolles, *Meeting House and Counting House: The Quaker Merchants of Colonial Philadelphia* (1948) and Gary B. Nash, *Quakers and Politics* (1968).

## TIME LINE

|  |  |
|---|---|
| 1590 | Roanoke Island colony fails |
| 1607 | Jamestown settled |
| 1616–1621 | Native American population in New England decimated by European diseases |
| 1617 | First tobacco crop shipped from Virginia |
| 1619 | First blacks arrive in Jamestown |
| 1620 | Pilgrims land in Massachusetts |
| 1622 | Powhatan tribes attack Virginia settlements |
| 1624 | Dutch colonize mouth of Hudson River |
| 1630 | Puritan migration to Massachusetts Bay |
| 1632 | Maryland grant to Lord Baltimore (George Calvert) |
| 1633–1634 | Native Americans in New England again struck by European diseases |
| 1635 | Roger Williams banished to Rhode Island |
| 1636 | Anne Hutchinson exiled to Rhode Island |
| 1637 | New England wages war against the Pequot tribe |
| 1640 | English Civil War ends great migration to New England |
| 1643 | Confederation of New England |
| 1659 | Two Quaker men hanged on Boston Common |
| 1660 | Restoration of King Charles II in England |
| 1663 | Carolina charter granted to eight proprietors |
| 1664 | English capture New Netherland and rename it New York<br>Royal grant of the Jersey lands to proprietors |
| 1681 | William Penn receives Pennsylvania grant |

# CHAPTER 3
## MASTERING THE NEW WORLD

Anthony Johnson, an African, arrived in Virginia in 1621 with only the name "Antonio." Caught as a young man in the Portuguese slave-trading net, he had passed from one trader to another in the New World until he reached Virginia. There he was purchased by Richard Bennett and sent to work at Warrasquoke, Bennett's tobacco plantation situated on the south side of the James River.

In the next year, Antonio was brought face to face with the world of triracial contact and conflict that would shape the remainder of his life. On March 22, 1622, the Powhatan tribes of tidewater Virginia fell upon the white colonizers in a determined attempt to drive them from the land. Of the 57 persons on the Bennett plantation, only black Antonio and four others survived.

Antonio—anglicized to Anthony—labored on the Bennett plantation for some 20 years, slave in fact if not in law, for legally defined bondage was still in the formative stage. During this time he married Mary, another African trapped in the labyrinth of servitude, and fathered four children. In the 1640s, Anthony and Mary Johnson gained their freedom after half a lifetime of servitude. Probably at this point they chose the surname Johnson to signify their new status. Already past middle age by seventeenth-century standards, the Johnsons began carving out a niche for themselves on Virginia's eastern shore. By 1650, they owned 250 acres, a small herd of cattle, and two black servants. In a world in which racial boundaries were not yet firmly marked, the Johnsons had entered the scramble of small planters for economic security.

By schooling themselves in the workings of the English legal process, by carefully cultivating white patronage, and by working industriously on the land, the Johnsons gained their freedom, acquired property, established families, warded off contentious neighbors, and hammered out a decent existence. But by the late 1650s, as the lines of racial slavery tightened, the customs of the country began closing in on Virginia's free blacks.

In 1664, convinced that ill winds were blowing away the chances for their children and grandchildren on Virginia's eastern shore, the Johnsons began selling their land to white neighbors. The following spring, most of the clan moved northward to Maryland, where they rented land and again took up farming and cattle raising. Five years later, Anthony Johnson died, leaving four children and his wife, who lived another ten years. The growing racial prejudice of Virginia followed Johnson beyond the grave. A jury of white men in Virginia declared that because Johnson "was a Negroe and by consequence an alien," the 50 acres he had deeded to his son Richard before moving to Maryland should be taken from his family and awarded to a local white planter.

Johnson's children and grandchildren, born in America, could not duplicate the modest success of the African-born patriarch. By the late seventeenth century, people of color faced much greater difficulties in extricating themselves from slavery. When they did, they found themselves forced to the margins of society. Anthony's sons never rose higher than tenant farmer or small freeholder. John Johnson moved farther north into Delaware in the 1680s, following a period of great conflict with Native Americans in the Chesapeake region. Members of his family married local Indians and became part of a triracial community that has survived to the present day. Richard Johnson stayed behind in Virginia. When he died in 1689, just after a series of colonial insurrections connected with the overthrow of James II in England, he had little to leave his four sons. They became tenant farmers and hired servants, laboring on plantations owned by whites. By now, in the early eighteenth century, slave ships were pouring Africans into Virginia and Maryland to replace white indentured servants, the backbone of the labor force for four generations. To be black had at first been a handicap. Now it became a fatal disability, a practically inescapable mark of degradation and bondage.

Mastering the New World environment involved two main processes that would echo down the corridors of American history: the defeat of Native American tribes who contested white expansion and the molding of an African labor force. Both developments occurred in the lifetimes of Anthony and Mary Johnson and their children. Both involved a level of violence that made this frontier of European expansion not a zone of pioneer equality and freedom but one of growing inequality and servitude.

This chapter surveys the fluid, conflict-filled era from 1675 to 1715. It was a time when European colonizers struggled to dominate land and labor and when Native Americans and Africans struggled to cope with a radically transformed triracial world. For the European settlers, who had established their racial mastery by the early eighteenth century, the era brought unprecedented disruptions. Learning to exploit black labor, reared amid Indian wars and internal upheavals, they developed a race-conscious mentality and a robust aversion to distant authority that indelibly marked their future.

## BLACK BONDAGE

For almost four centuries after Columbus's voyages to the New World, European colonizers forcibly transported Africans out of their homelands, using their labor to produce wealth in their colonies. Estimates vary widely, but the number of Africans who immigrated involuntarily to the New World was probably not less than 12 million. Millions more lost their lives while being marched from the African interior to coastal trading forts or during the "middle passage" across the Atlantic. Of all the immigrants who peopled the New World between the fifteenth and eighteenth centuries, the Africans were by far the most numerous, probably outnumbering Europeans two to one.

European slave traders carried a large majority of the slaves to the West Indies, Brazil, and Spanish America. Not more than one out of

### Origins and Destinations of African Slaves, 1526–1810

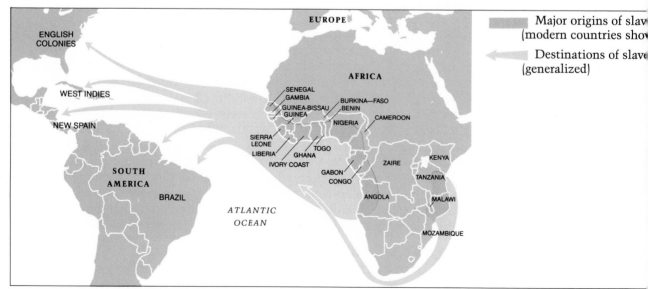

every 12 reached North America, which remained a fringe area for slave traders until the eighteenth century. Yet those who came to the American colonies, about 10,000 in the seventeenth century and 350,000 in the eighteenth, profoundly affected the destiny of American society. In a prolonged period of labor scarcity, their labor and skills were indispensable to colonial economic development. Their African culture mixed continuously with that of their European masters. And the race relations that grew out of slavery so deeply marked society that the problem of race has continued ever since to be "the American dilemma."

## The Slave Trade

The African slave trade did not begin as a part of the colonization of the Americas but rather as an attempt to fill a labor shortage in the Mediterranean world. As early as the eighth century, Arab and Moorish traders had driven slaves across Saharan caravan trails for delivery to Mediterranean ports. Seven centuries later, Portuguese merchants became the first Europeans involved in the slave trade. Reaching the west coast of Africa by water, they began buying slaves captured by other Africans and transporting them home by ship. These slaves were mostly criminals consigned to bondage in their own society or unfortunate individuals captured in tribal wars. This early trade in black Africans satisfied the modest labor needs of the Portuguese, just as their slave trade in whites of the

Black Sea area had done earlier in the fifteenth century.

More than anything else, sugar transformed the African slave trade. For centuries, sugarcane had been grown in the Mediterranean countries to sweeten the diet of the wealthy. As its popularity grew, the center of production shifted to Portuguese Madeira, an island off the coast of Africa. Here in the sixteenth century, a European nation for the first time established an overseas colony organized around slave labor. From Madeira the cultivation of sugar spread to Portuguese Brazil and Spanish Santo Domingo. By the seventeenth century, with Europeans developing a taste for sugar almost as insatiable as their craving for tobacco, they vied fiercely for possession of the tiny islands dotting the Caribbean and for control of the trading forts on the West African coast. African kingdoms, eager for European trade goods, warred against each other in order to supply the "black gold" demanded by white ship captains.

Europeans of many nations competed for trading rights on the West African coast. In the seventeenth century, when about one million Africans were brought to the New World, the Dutch replaced the Portuguese as the major supplier. The English, meanwhile, hardly counted in the slave trade. Not until the 1690s did the English challenge the Dutch as they pursued their centurylong rise to maritime greatness. By the 1790s, the English were the foremost slave-trading nation in Europe. In the eighteenth century, European traders carried at least 6 million

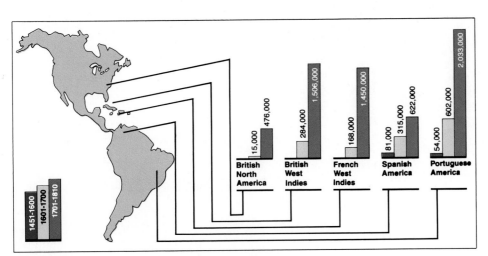

**Slave Importations, 1451–1810**

*Source:* Curtin, *The Atlantic Slave Trade: A Census,* 1969.

Africans to the Americas, probably the greatest forced migration in history. By this time African slave labor figured so importantly in the colonial world that one Englishman called slavery "the strength and the sinews of this western world."

No accounts of the slave trade, no matter how vivid, can convey the pain and demoralization that must have accompanied the initial capture and subsequent march to slave-trading forts on the West African coast or the dreaded middle passage across the Atlantic. Olaudah Equiano, an eighteenth-century Ibo from what is now Nigeria, described how he was kidnapped with his younger sister when only 11 years old by raiders from another tribe. He passed from one trader to another while being marched to the coast. Many slaves attempted suicide or died from exhaustion or hunger on these forced marches from the interior. But Equiano survived. Reaching the coast, he encountered the next humiliation, confinement in barracoons, fortified enclosures on the beach where a surgeon from an English slave ship inspected him. Equiano was terrified by the light skins, language, and long hair of the English and was convinced that he "had got into a world of bad spirits and that they were going to kill me."

More cruelties followed. After purchase by European traders, African slaves were often branded with a hot iron to indicate which company had procured them. The next trauma came with the ferrying of slaves in large canoes to the ships anchored in the harbor. An English captain recounted the desperation of Africans who were about to lose touch with their ancestral homeland and embark upon a vast ocean that many had never seen. "The Negroes are so loath to leave their own country, that they have often leaped out of the canoes, boat and ship, into the sea, and kept under the water till they were drowned."

Conditions aboard the slave ships were miserable, even though the traders' goal was to deliver alive as many slaves as possible to the other side of the Atlantic. Equiano recounted the scene below decks, where manacled slaves crowded together like corpses in coffins. "With the loathsomeness of the stench, and crying together, I became so sick and low that I was not able to eat, nor had I the least desire to taste anything." The refusal to take food was so common that ship captains devised special techniques to cope with slaves who were determined to starve themselves to death rather than reach the New World in chains. Slavers flogged their captives brutally and applied hot coals to their

*One of the most dehumanizing aspects of slavery was the auctioning of newly arrived Africans at dockside.*

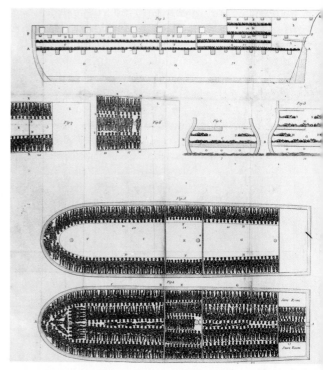

*Diagrams such as this, useful to captains wishing to take advantage of "tight packing," were printed as late as the nineteenth century.*

lips. If this did not suffice, they employed a specially devised mouth wrench to pry apart the jaws of resistant Africans for forced feeding.

The Atlantic passage usually took four to six weeks. It was so physically depleting and psychologically wrenching that one of every seven captives died en route. Many others arrived in the Americas deranged or near death. In all, the relocation of any African may have averaged about six months from the time of capture to the time of arrival at the plantation of a colonial buyer. During this protracted personal crisis, the slave was completely cut off from the moorings of a previous life—language, family and friends, tribal religion, familiar geography, and status in a local community. Still facing these victims of the European demand for cheap labor was adaptation to a new physical environment, a new language, a new work routine, and a life in which bondage for themselves and their children was unending.

## The Southern Transition to Black Labor

Even though they were familiar with Spanish, Dutch, Portuguese, and French use of black slaves, English colonists on the mainland of North America turned only slowly to Africa to solve their labor problem. Like other Europeans, they first regarded Native Americans as the obvious source of labor. But European diseases ravaged native societies, and the American Indian, far more at home in the environment than the white colonizer, proved difficult to subjugate. Indentured white labor provided the best way to meet the demand for labor during most of the seventeenth century. Beginning in 1619, a small number of Africans entered Virginia and Maryland to labor in the tobacco fields alongside white servants. But as late as 1671, when some 30,000 slaves toiled in English Barbados, fewer than 3,000 served in Virginia. They were still outnumbered there three to one by white indentured servants.

The transformation of the southern labor force, from one in which many whites and a few black servants labored side by side to one in which black slaves performed most of the field labor, began only in the last quarter of the seventeenth century. Three reasons explain this shift, which figured momentously in the history of the United States. First, the rising commercial power of England, at the expense of the Spanish and Dutch, greatly increased English participation in the African slave trade. Beginning in the 1680s, southern planters could purchase slaves more readily and cheaply than before. Second, the supply of white servants from England began drying up. Those who did arrive fanned out among a growing number of colonies. Finally, white servant unrest and a growing population of ex-servants who were landless, discontented, and potential challengers to established white planters led the southern elite to welcome a more pliable labor force. Consequently, by the 1730s, the number of white indentured servants had dwindled to insignificance. Black hands, not white, tilled and harvested Chesapeake tobacco and Carolina rice. Nothing had greater priority in starting a plantation than procuring slave labor. "If any one designs to make a plantation in this province," wrote Thomas Nairne from South Carolina in 1710, "the first thing to be done is, after having cut down a few trees, to split palisades or clapboards and therewith make small houses or huts to shelter the slaves."

In enslaving Africans, English colonists merely copied their European rivals in the New World. Making it all the more natural for American planters to adopt this labor system was the precedent their countrymen had set in the English West Indies. From the 1630s onward, the English imported Africans in huge numbers in Barbados, Jamaica, and the Leeward Islands. Through brutal repression, they molded them into a sugar-producing slave labor force. Human bondage would later become the subject of intense moral debate. But in the seventeenth century, all but a few whites readily accepted it.

## Slavery in the Northern Colonies

Slavery never became the foundation of the northern colonial work force, for labor-intensive crops could not survive in colder climates. On the smaller family farms, household labor and occasional hired hands sufficed. Only in the cities, where slaves worked as artisans and domestic servants, and in a few scattered rural areas did slavery take substantial root.

Although the northern colonists did not employ slaves to any significant extent, their economies were becoming enmeshed in the larger commercial network of the Atlantic basin that depended on slavery and the slave trade. New England's merchants eagerly pursued profits in the slave trade as early as the 1640s, when their ships began supplying Barbados with Africans. By 1676, New England slavers were packing their holds with slaves from Madagascar, off the coast of East Africa, and transporting their human cargoes 6,000 miles to the western side of the Atlantic. Rhode Island became so involved in the dirty business that by 1750 half the merchant fleet of Newport reaped profits from carrying human cargo. In New York and Philadelphia, the building and outfitting of slave vessels was vital to the waterfront economy.

New England's involvement in the international slave trade deepened with the growth of its seaports as centers for the distilling of rum—the "hot, hellish and terrible liquor." Made from West Indian sugar, rum became one of the principal commodities traded for slaves on the African coast. As the number of slaves to be fed in the Caribbean multiplied—from about 50,000 in 1650 to 500,000 in 1750—the West Indies became a favorite market for the codfish hauled in by New England's extensive fishing fleet. Wheat from the middle colonies and barrel staves and hoops from North Carolina also fed into the slave-based West Indies economy. Hence, as the plantation South became most directly involved in an international system of racial exploitation, every other North American colony also participated in it.

## The System of Bondage

The first Africans brought to the American colonies came as bound servants. They served for a number of years; then, like Anthony and Mary Johnson, many of them eventually gained their freedom. Once released, they could own land, hire out their labor, and move as they pleased. Their children, like those of white indentured servants, were born free. Gradually during the seventeenth century, Chesapeake planters began to draw tighter lines around the activities of black servants. By the 1640s, Virginia forbade blacks, free or bound, to carry firearms. In the 1660s, marriages between white women and black servants were called "shameful matches" and "the disgrace of our Nation." Bit by bit, the association between black skin and slave status grew in the white colonists' minds. This mental connection between color and degraded status arose in part because European colonists were culturally conditioned to see evil and ugliness in blackness, whereas white stood for purity, beauty, and virtue.

By the middle of the seventeenth century, perpetual bondage was becoming firmly embedded in the minds of the colonizers as the appropriate status for black servants. By the end of the century, when incoming Africans increased from a trickle to a torrent, even the small number of free blacks found themselves pushed to the margins of society. Slavery, which had existed for centuries in many societies as the lowest social status, was becoming in the Americas a racial caste reserved for those with black skin. Step by step, the black servant was transformed, in the eyes of society and the law, from a human being to a piece of chattel property.

In this dehumanization of Africans, which the English copied largely from their colonial rivals, the key step was instituting hereditary lifetime service. Once servitude became perpetual, relieved only by death, the elimination of all other privileges followed quickly. When the slave condition of the mother legally fell upon the black infant, slavery became self-perpetuating, passing automatically from one generation to the next.

Slavery existed not only as a system of forced labor but also as a pattern of human relationships eventually legitimated by law. By the early eighteenth century, most provincial legislatures were enacting laws for controlling black rights and activities. Borrowed largely from the statute books of England's Caribbean colonies, these "black codes" forced Africans into a more and more limited world. Slaves were forbidden to testify in court, engage in commercial activity, hold property, participate in the political process, congregate in public, travel without permission, or engage in legal marriage or parenthood. Nearly stripped of human status, they became defined as a form of property.

Restraints upon the master's freedom to deal with his slave property in any way he saw fit gradually disappeared.

Annulling all slave rights had both pragmatic and psychological dimensions. Every black man and woman in chains was a potential rebel. So the rapid increase in the slave population brought anxious demands to bring slaves under strict control. The desire to stifle black rebelliousness mingled with a need to justify brutal behavior toward slaves by defining them as less than human. "The planters," wrote one Englishman in Jamaica, "do not want to be told that their Negroes are human creatures. If they believe them to be of human kind, they cannot regard them as no better than dogs or horses."

This tendency to define slaves in nonhuman terms contained one of the great paradoxes of modern history. Many Old World immigrants imagined the Americas as a liberating and regenerating arena. Yet the opportunity to exploit its resources led to a historic world process by which a mass of people were wrenched from their homelands and forced into a system of slavery that could be maintained only by the systematic use of intimidation and brutality.

## SLAVE CULTURE

For Africans toiling on plantations 5,000 miles from their homes, the basic struggle was to create strategies for living as satisfactorily as possible despite harsh regimens. The master hoped to convert the slave into a mindless drudge who obeyed every command and worked efficiently for his profit. But the attempt to cow slaves rarely succeeded completely. Masters could set the external boundaries of existence for their slaves, controlling physical location, work roles, diet, and shelter. But the authority of the master class impinged far less on how slaves established friendships, fell in love, formed kin groups, raised children, worshiped their gods, buried their dead, and organized their leisure time.

In these aspects of daily life, slaves in America drew upon their African heritage to shape their existence to some degree. In doing so, they laid the foundations for an Afro-American culture. At first this culture was very diverse because slaves came from many cultural areas in Africa and lived under different conditions in the colonies. But common elements emerged, led by developments in the South, where about 90 percent of American slaves labored in the colonial period.

### The Growth of Slavery

In contrast to other areas of the New World, in North America Africans reached a relatively healthy environment. The West Indies became a graveyard for both whites and blacks. In South America, tropical diseases swept away slaves like leaves in a windstorm. In the southern American colonies, where the ghastly mortality of the early decades had subsided by the time Africans were arriving in large numbers, their chances for survival were much better. A simple comparison makes the point. Colonizers in Virginia and Jamaica each owned about 200,000 slaves in 1775. But to attain that number, more than three times as many Africans had been imported into the West Indies as into the Chesapeake colony during the eighteenth century. This environmental advantage, combined with a more even sex ratio, led to a natural increase in the American slave population that was unparalleled elsewhere.

In 1675, about 4,000 slaves were scattered across Virginia and Maryland. Most were men. They toiled with their masters and a larger number of white indentured servants, clearing the land, planting, hoeing, and harvesting tobacco. A half century later, with the decline of white servitude, 45,000 slaves were laboring on Chesapeake plantations. By 1760, when their number exceeded 185,000, the Chesapeake plantations relied almost entirely on black labor.

Although the passing of slave codes severely restricted the lives of slaves, the possibility for family life increased as the southern colonies matured. Larger plantations employed dozens and even hundreds of slaves, and the growth of roads and market towns permitted them greater opportunities to forge relationships beyond their own plantation. By the 1740s, a growing proportion of Chesapeake slaves were American-born, had established a family, and were living in plantation outbuildings where from sundown to sunup they could fashion a personal life of their own.

In South Carolina, African slaves drew upon agricultural skills they had practiced on the other side of the Atlantic and made rice the keystone of the coastal economy by the early eighteenth century. Their numbers increased rapidly, from about 4,000 in 1708 to 90,000 on the eve of the American Revolution. Working mostly on large plantations in swampy lowlands, they endured the most life-sapping conditions on the continent. But in the coastal low country they outnumbered whites three to one by 1760 and hence were able to maintain more of their African culture than did slaves in the Chesapeake. South Carolina, one European observed in 1737, "looks more like a negro country than like a country settled by white people."

Many slaves spoke Gullah, a "pidgin" or mixture of several African languages. They often gave African names to their children, names like Cudjoe, Cuffe, Quashey, and Phibbi. And they kept alive their African religious customs.

In the northern colonies, where no labor shortage existed and the climate did not allow the cultivation of staple crops, slaves made up less than 10 percent of the population. They typically worked as artisans, farmhands, or personal servants. Mingled among them were occasional Indian slaves. Whereas about two-thirds of all southern slaves worked on plantations with at least ten of their fellows by the 1720s, in the North the typical slave labored alone or with only a few others. Living in the same house as the master, slaves adapted to European ways much faster than in the South, where the slave quarters were places for perpetuating African folkways. Slavery was also less repressive in the North than in the South. Slaves were more widely dispersed among the white population, and black-white contact was so extensive that African culture faded more quickly.

*The physical appearance of blacks captured the imaginations of many European and American artists. John Singleton Copley (American),* Head of a Negro *(left); John Greenwood (American),* Jersey Nanny *(center); Théodore Géricault (French),* Portrait of a Negro *(right).*

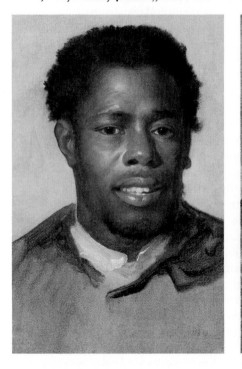  

Slavery spread more extensively in the northern port cities than across the countryside. Artisans found it profitable to invest in slaves whom they could work on a year-round basis. Ship captains purchased them for maritime labor. And an emerging urban elite of merchants, lawyers, and landlords displayed their wealth and status by employing slaves as liveried coachmen and house servants. By the beginning of the eighteenth century, more than 40 percent of New York City's households owned slaves. Boston's slave population rose from 350 in 1710 to 1,374 in 1742. Even in Quaker Philadelphia, slaveholding increased sharply in the eighteenth century. Struggling white artisans resented slave workers for undercutting their wages, and the white citizenry felt threatened by potential black arsonists and rebels. Yet where labor demand was high, the desire for lifelong servants, who could be purchased for a mere two years of a free white laborer's wages, outweighed these reservations.

### Slave Population of British America, 1680–1780

*Source:* U.S. Bureau of the Census.

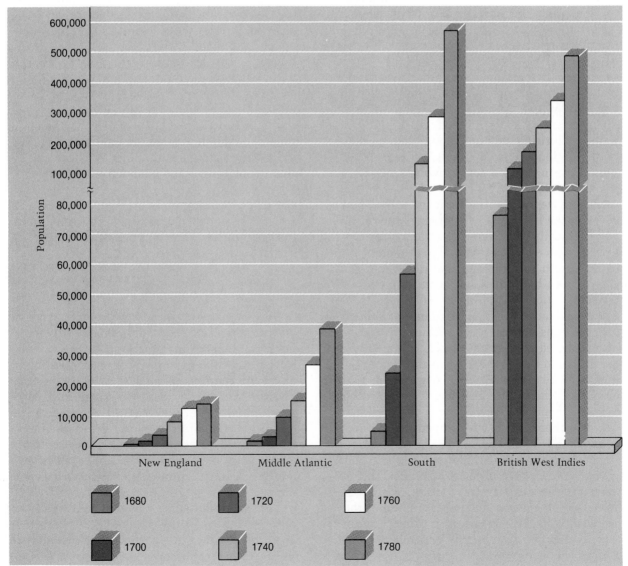

## Resistance and Rebellion

While struggling to adapt to bondage in various regions of British America, African-born and Creole slaves also resisted and rebelled in ways that constantly reminded their masters that slavery's price was eternal vigilance. Slave owners preferred to interpret rebelliousness as evidence of the "barbarous, wild savage natures" of Africans, as a South Carolina law of 1712 phrased it. Some planters, like Virginia's Landon Carter, believed that "slaves are devils and to make them free is to set devils free." But from the African point of view, the struggle against enslavement was essential to maintaining meaning and dignity in a life of degrading toil.

"Saltwater" Africans fresh from their homelands often resisted slavery fiercely. "You would really be surprised at their perseverance," wrote one observer. "They often die before they can be conquered." Commonly this initial resistance took the form of escaping to the frontier to begin renegade Maroon colonies, to Indian tribes in the interior that sometimes offered refuge, or to Spanish Florida. Open rebellions, such as those at Stono, South Carolina, in 1739 and in New York City in 1712, mostly involved newly arrived slaves.

There was no North American parallel, however, for the massive slave uprisings that erupted periodically in the West Indies and Brazil. Nor was there an American parallel to the semistates in the South Atlantic sugar world, where runaway slaves built their own communities and resisted periodic assaults by colonial troops. Slaves had far better chances to mount successful rebellions in these areas because they vastly outnumbered their masters and, in the case of Brazil, could flee to the rugged interior to join unconquered Indian tribes. "The greater number of blacks which a frontier has," remarked one colonist, "and the greater the disproportion is between them and her white people, the more danger she is liable to."

In North America, slaves rarely outnumbered whites except in South Carolina, and the master class carefully cultivated tension between local Indians and slaves so that they would be "a check upon each other," as one worried planter explained. When rebellion did occur, white colonizers used every available means to quell it. They tried to intimidate all slaves by torturing, hanging, dismembering, and even burning captured rebels at the stake. After a rumored uprising was disclosed near Charleston, South Carolina, in 1740, for example, 50 blacks were tortured and hanged. Their decapitated heads, impaled on posts, gave warning to other potential insurrectionists.

Open rebelliousness often gave way to more subtle forms of resistance as slaves acquired English, adjusted to the routines of shop, farm, and plantation, and began forming families. Dragging out the job, shamming illness, pretending ignorance, and breaking tools were strategies for avoiding physical exhaustion and also indirect forms of opposing slavery itself.

Slaves resisted more directly through truancy, arson directed against the master's barns and houses, crop destruction, pilfering to supplement their food supply, and direct assaults on the lives of masters, overseers, and drivers. Slave masters extracted labor and obedience from their slaves in an overall sense. If they had not, the slave system would have collapsed. But they did so only with great difficulty. Masters learned that to push slaves too hard could be costly. One South Carolina planter drove his slaves late into the night cleaning and barreling a rice crop in 1732. When he awoke in the morning, he found his barn, with the entire harvest in it, reduced to ashes.

## Black Religion and Family

Resistance and rebellion represented attacks on the institution of slavery. But the balance of power was always massively stacked against the slaves. Only the most desperate were willing to challenge the system directly. Much more importantly historically was the struggle of Afro-Americans to find meaning and worth in their existence, no matter how brutal and discouraging the slave system that manacled them. In this quest, religion and family played a central role—one destined to continue far into the postslavery period.

Africans brought a complex religious heritage to the New World. No amount of desolation or physical abuse could wipe out these deeply rooted beliefs. People enduring the daily travail that accompanied the master-slave relationship typically turned to their deepest emotional sources for relief. Coming from cultures where the division between sacred and secular activities was less clear than in Europe, slaves made religion central to their existence. The black Christianity that emerged in the eighteenth century blended African religious practices and the religion of the master class. It laid the foundations for the black church that in later generations became the central institution in Afro-American life.

Slave masters were not eager to see their slaves exposed to Christianity because of its potentially dangerous notions of brotherhood and its prohibition against enslaving other Christians. On the other hand, Christianity's emphasis on meekness and obedience might restrain black rebelliousness. Gradually in the eighteenth century, slaves gained exposure to Christianity. They used it both to light the spark of resistance and to find comfort from oppression.

The religious revival that began in the 1720s in the northern colonies and spread southward thereafter made important contributions to Afro-American religion. Evangelicalism stressed personal rebirth, used music and body motion, and caught individuals up in an intense emotional experience. The dancing, shouting, rhythmic clapping, and singing that came to characterize slaves' religious expression represented a creative mingling of Christianity and West African religion.

Besides religion, the slaves' greatest refuge from their dreadful fate lay in their families. In West Africa, all social relations were centered in kinship lines, which stretched backward to include dead ancestors. Torn from their native societies, slaves therefore placed great importance on rebuilding extended kin groups.

Most English colonies prohibited slave marriages. But in practice, domestic life was an area in which slaves and masters struck a bargain. Masters found that slaves would work harder if they were allowed to form families. Moreover, family ties stood in the way of escape or rebellion, for few slaves wanted to leave loved ones at the mercy of an angry master. For their part,

slaves valued family life so highly that they were willing to risk almost everything to secure the right to marry and parent children.

But slaves did not find it easy to fashion a family life. The general practice of importing three male slaves for every two females stunted family formation. Female slaves, much in demand, married in their late teens, but males usually had to wait until their mid- to late twenties. As natural increase swelled the slave population in the eighteenth century, however, the sex ratio became more even.

The sale of either husband or wife could abruptly sever their fragile union. Broken marriages were frequent, especially when a deceased planter's estate was divided among his heirs or his slaves were sold to his creditors to satisfy debts. Young children usually stayed with their mothers, but at about age 8 they were frequently torn from their families through sale, often to small planters needing only a hand or two. Few were the slaves who did not suffer separation from family members at some time during their lives.

White male exploitation of black women presented another barrier to satisfactory family life. How many black women were assaulted or lured with favors into sexual relations with white masters and overseers cannot be known. But the sizable mulatto population at the end of the eighteenth century indicates that the number was large. Interracial liaisons, frequently coerced, were widespread, especially in the Lower South. In 1732, the South Carolina *Gazette* called racial mixing an "epidemical disease." It was a malady that had traumatic effects on slave attempts to build stable relationships because the male head of the black family was usually powerless to defend those closest to him.

Not all interracial relationships were cruel. In some cases black women sought the liaison, hoping to gain advantages for themselves or their children. These unions nonetheless threatened both the slave community and the white plantation ideal. They bridged the supposedly unbridgeable gap between the slave and free parts of society and produced children who lived in a racial twilight zone, even though they were legally slaves.

Despite such obstacles, slaves fashioned intimate ties as husband and wife, parent and child. If monogamous relationships did not last as long as in white society, much of the explanation lies in matters beyond the control of those caught in slavery's net: the shorter life span of Afro-Americans, the shattering of marriage through sale of one or both partners, and the call of freedom that impelled some slaves to run away.

While slave men struggled to preserve their family role, black women assumed a position in the family and in the black community that differed strikingly from that of white women. Many plantations' mistresses worked hard in helping to manage estates, but nonetheless the ideal grew that they should remain in the house to guard white virtue and set the standards for white culture. In contrast, the black woman remained indispensable to both the work of the plantation and the stability of the slave community. She toiled in the fields and worked in the slave cabins. Paradoxically, black women's roles, which required constant labor, made them more equal to men than was the case of women in white society.

The family history of Daphne, a slave in Virginia, illustrates the kinship networks that formed in Afro-American society. Born about 1736 on the plantation of the wealthy Robert Tyler, Daphne was the youngest of five children living with her mother Nan. When their master died in 1738, the family was split up. Three children went to the nearby farm of Tyler's granddaughter. Daphne and her mother remained on the estate of Tyler's widow. There Daphne lived for the next 51 years, though the plantation passed from one member of the Tyler family to another.

After marrying in about 1753, Daphne bore ten children. Before the end of the American Revolution, some of her daughters bore children, who lived on the same plantation with their maternal grandmother. But in 1779, when Robert Tyler III, the grandson of Daphne's first master, died, he bequeathed her children and grandchildren to his son and daughter. Daphne's oldest four children, aged from 20 to 25, remained on the plantation with their mother and families. Her youngest six children, aged 7 to 19, were sent to the plantation of the daughter of Robert Tyler III, several miles away. Thus, Daphne had grown children and grandchildren living on her plantation; she had sisters, brothers, nieces, and nephews nearby; and she had children and grandchildren on another plantation in the area. Absent from the surviving records are any traces of her husband's fate and that of other family members who were sold or bequeathed from the original Tyler estate.

Above all, slavery was a set of power relationships designed to extract the maximum labor from its victims. Hence it regularly involved cruelties that filled family life with tribulation. But slaves in America were unusually successful in establishing families because they lived in a healthier environment, toiled in less physically exhausting circumstances than slaves on sugar and coffee plantations, and were better clothed, fed, and treated than Africans in the West Indies, Brazil, and other parts of the hemisphere. In these more tropical areas, plantation owners found it profitable to import large numbers of male slaves, literally work them to death, and then purchase replacements from Africa. Family life in the American colonies brimmed over with uncertainty and sorrow, but slaves nonetheless made it the greatest monument to their will to endure captivity and eventually gain their freedom.

## THE STRUGGLE FOR LAND

In the same period that slavery gained a permanent foothold in North America, both New England and Virginia fought major wars against Native Americans. The desire for land, a cause of both wars, produced a similar conflict somewhat later in South Carolina. The conflicts brought widespread destruction to the towns of both colonizers and Indians, inflicted heavy human casualties, and left a legacy of bitterness on both sides. For the coastal tribes, it was a disastrous time of defeat and decline. For the colonists, the wars contributed to the turbulence of the late seventeenth and early eighteenth centuries, but they also established in the colonial mind the superiority of white military force.

### King Philip's War in New England

Following the Pequot War of 1637 in New England, the Wampanoags and Narragansetts, whose fertile land lay within the boundaries of Plymouth and Rhode Island, attempted to maintain their distance from the New England colonists. But the New Englanders coveted Indian territories. As they quarreled among themselves over provincial boundaries, they gradually reduced the Indians' land base.

By the 1670s, when New England's population had grown to about 50,000, younger Indians began brooding over their situation. Their lead-er, Metacomet (named King Philip by the English), was the son of Massasoit, the Wampanoag who had allied himself with the first Plymouth settlers in 1620. Metacomet had watched his older brother preside over the deteriorating position of his people after their father's death in 1661. A year later, Metacomet's brother died mysteriously while Plymouth officials questioned him about a rumored Indian conspiracy. As the Wampanoag leader, Metacomet faced one humiliating challenge after another.

In 1671, Plymouth forced Metacomet to surrender a large stock of guns and accept a treaty of submission acknowledging Wampanoag subjection to English law. Convinced that more setbacks would follow and humiliated by the discriminatory treatment of Indians brought before English courts, Metacomet began recruiting for a resistance movement.

The triggering incident of King Philip's War was the trial of three Wampanoags who were

*The Wampanoags led New England tribes in a tenacious campaign of resistance against the white settlers. Metacomet (left), called King Phil-*

*ip by the English, was leader of the Wampanoags; Ninigret (right), chief of the Nipmucks, fought with the Wampanoags.*

dragged before a Puritan court for an act of tribal revenge against John Sassamon, a Christianized Indian educated at Harvard. Sassamon was a man caught between two cultures. Though he had fled white society after his college experience, he warned the Plymouth government in 1675 that the Wampanoags were preparing a general attack on the English settlements. When Sassamon was found murdered shortly afterward, Plymouth officials produced an Indian who claimed he had witnessed the murder and could identify the felons. As a result, three Wampanoags swung at the end of English ropes in June 1675.

The execution of the three tribesmen was the catalyst, but the root cause of the war that erupted was the rising anger of the young Wampanoag males. As would happen repeatedly in the next two centuries as Americans pushed westward, these younger Native Americans refused to imitate their fathers, who had watched the colonizers erode their land base and compromise their sovereignty. Rather than put themselves under white authority, they attempted a pan-Indian offensive against an intruder with far greater numbers and a much larger arsenal of weapons. For the young tribesmen, revitalization of their ancient culture through war became as important a goal as defeating the enemy.

Early in the war, the Wampanoags unleashed daring hit-and-run attacks on villages in the Plymouth colony. By autumn of 1675, many of the small New England tribes, as well as the powerful Narragansetts, had joined King Philip's warriors. Towns all along the frontier reeled under Indian attacks. "We were too ready to think that we could easily suppress that flea," confessed John Eliot, who had worked to convert the Indians to Christianity, "but now we find that all the craft is in catching them, and that in the meantime they give us many a sore nip." By the time the first snow fell in November, mobile Indian warriors had laid waste to the entire upper Connecticut River Valley.

By March 1676, King Philip's forces were attacking less than 20 miles from Boston and Providence. Assumptions about English military superiority faded as one Indian success followed another. Desperate to reverse the course of the war, New England officials passed America's first draft laws. Evasion was widespread, however, with eligible men—all those between 16 and 60—"skulking from one town to another." Political friction among the New England colonies also hampered a united counteroffensive.

King Philip's offensive faltered in the spring of 1676. Food shortages and disease, as well as intertribal divisions, sapped Indian strength. By summer, groups of Indians were surrendering, while some moved westward seeking shelter among other tribes. King Philip fell in a battle near the Wampanoag village in Rhode Island where the war began. The head of this "hellhound, fiend, serpent, caitiff and dog," as one colonial leader branded him, was carried triumphantly back to Plymouth, where it remained on display for 25 years.

At the end of the war, several thousand colonists and perhaps twice that many Indians lay dead. Of some 90 Puritan towns, 52 had been attacked and 13 completely destroyed by the "tawny serpents." Some 1,200 homes lay in ruins, and 8,000 cattle were destroyed. The estimated cost of the war exceeded the value of all personal property in New England. Not for 40 years would the frontier advance beyond the line it had reached in 1675. Indian society was devastated even more completely. Nearly an entire generation of young men had been annihilated. Many of the survivors, including Metacomet's wife and son, were sold into slavery in the West Indies.

### Bacon's Rebellion Engulfs Virginia

While New Englanders fought local tribes in 1675 and 1676, the Chesapeake colonies became locked in a struggle involving both a war between the red and white populations and civil war within the colonizers' society. Before it ended, hundreds of whites and Indians lay dead in Virginia and Maryland, Virginia's capital of Jamestown lay smoldering, and English troops were crossing the Atlantic to suppress what the king labeled an outright rejection of his authority. This deeply tangled conflict was called Bacon's Rebellion after the fiery Cambridge-educated planter Nathaniel Bacon, who arrived in Virginia at age 28.

Bacon and many other ambitious young planters detested the Indian policy of Virginia's royal governor, Sir William Berkeley. In 1646, at the end of the second Indian uprising against the Virginians, the Powhatan tribes had accepted a treaty granting them exclusive rights to territory north of the York River, beyond the limits of white settlement. Stable Indian relations suited the established planters but became obnoxious to new settlers arriving in the 1650s and 1660s. Nor did it please the white indentured servants who had served their time and were hoping to find cheap frontier land.

Land hunger and dissatisfaction with declining tobacco prices, rising taxes, and lack of opportunity erupted into violence in the summer of 1675. A group of frontiersmen used an incident with a local tribe as an excuse to launch an attack on the Susquehannocks, whose rich land they coveted. Governor Berkeley denounced the attack, but few supported his position. He faced, he said, "a people where six parts of seven at least are poor, indebted, discontented, and armed."

Despite overwhelming odds against them, the Susquehannocks prepared for war. Virginians girded themselves for the southern version of what they heard was occurring in New England. Rumors swept the colony that the Susquehannocks were offering large sums to western Indian nations to join in attacking the colonists. Some even said that King Philip had formed a confederacy with the Chesapeake tribes.

Thirsting for revenge, the Susquehannocks attacked during the winter of 1675–1676 and killed 36 Virginians. That spring, the hot-blooded Nathaniel Bacon became the frontiersmen's leader. Joined by hundreds of runaway servants and some slaves, he launched a campaign of indiscriminate warfare on friendly and hostile Indians alike. When Governor Berkeley refused to sanction these attacks, the fiery Bacon ignored his authority. The governor then declared Bacon a rebel and sent out 300 militiamen to drag him to Jamestown for trial. Bacon headed into the wilderness for "a more agreeable destiny" and recruited more followers, including many substantial planters. Frontier skirmishes with Indians had turned into civil war.

During the summer of 1676, Bacon's and Berkeley's troops maneuvered around each other, while Bacon's men continued their forays against local Indian tribes. In one bold move, Bacon and his followers captured the capital at Jamestown. They razed the statehouse, church, and other buildings and put Governor Berkeley to flight across the Chesapeake Bay.

Time was on the governor's side, however. Once they had crushed the Indians, Bacon's followers began drifting home to tend their crops. Meanwhile, Berkeley's reports of the rebellion brought the dispatch of 1,100 royal troops from England. By the time they arrived, in January 1677, Nathaniel Bacon lay dead of swamp fever and most of his followers had melted back into the frontier. Berkeley had time after Bacon's death in October 1676 to round up 23 rebel leaders and hang them without benefit of civil trial.

Many Virginians, established planters as well as "the scum of the country," as a supporter of Berkeley called the Baconians, had chafed under the governor's rule. High taxes, an increase in the governor's powers at the expense of local officials, and his monopoly of the Indian trade were especially unpopular. This opposition surfaced in the summer of 1676 as Berkeley's and Bacon's troops pursued each other through the wilderness. Berkeley tried to rally public support by holding new assembly elections and extending the vote to all freemen, whether they owned property or not. The new assembly promptly turned on the governor, passing a set of reform laws intended to make government more responsive to the common people and to end rapacious officeholding.

Reflecting the widespread hatred of Indians, the assembly also made legal the enslavement of Native Americans. Nonetheless, it was primarily the governor's conciliatory Indian policy before the first bloodshed and his unaggressive course of action thereafter that fueled the insurrection. Spurred on by their numerical superiority, frontiersmen demanded a war of extermination.

Royal investigators who arrived in 1677 remarked on this genocidal mentality. They denounced the "inconsiderate sort of men who so rashly and causelessly cry up a war and seem

Historians have used funeral orations, gravestone designs and inscriptions, and handbooks on how to die to gain insight into early American culture. Tombstone markings—"graven images," they have been called—provide a particularly fascinating body of evidence. At first, Puritans in New England marked their graves only with wooden rails and posts. But in the 1670s, carved headstones filled with symbolic images began to appear, and they became a regular feature of New England graveyards after that. Hardly any Puritan family thereafter, one historian noted, was "ready to commit its loved ones to the cold earth without an appropriate cluster of symbols hovering protectively over the grave." How the symbols carved on them changed tells much about how people's attitudes and values shifted. "There is no better place in all New England to stand face to face with the past," it has been said, "than in the old burying grounds."

The tombstone shown here shows vividly the intensity with which Puritans faced death. To die was to be called to final account by a just and merciful God, and the way one died gave evidence of one's self-discipline and faith. The scrolled pediment on this gravestone signifies the doorway between earthly life and spiritual rebirth through which Joseph Tapping's relatives hoped he passed. The grim winged skull represents the soul of the dying man in transition. This death's-head motif was widely used on seventeenth-century gravestones. It conveys much of the Puritans' intense concern that life is transitory (note the hourglass) and that salvation is not automatically granted to those who believe in Christ. This emphasis on life as a preparation for afterlife is reinforced by the Latin mottoes on the right side of the stone: *Vive memor loethi* ("Live mindful of death") and *Fugit hora* ("The hour flies"). At bottom center of the stone is an image of Time fending off Death as Death tries to snuff out the candle of Life. Note Father Time's symbols—the hourglass and scythe—in the background.

The Puritans' fixation on death has also been noted in the elaborate and expensive funerals they often conducted and in the content of funeral sermons and handbooks on how to die well. In a popular book on advice for the young, *Token for Children*, published first in England in 1671 and in an American edition in 1700, James Janeway described the "Joy and holy Triumph" of a 12-year-old girl's death. As a model of faith in God's mercy, without yielding to pride or certainty of salvation in her last hours, this young girl

> spake with a holy Confidence in the Lord's Love to her Soul, and was not in the least daunted

Photo by Daniel Farbe

***Joseph Tapping headstone, Boston, 1678***

when she spake of her Death; but seemed greatly delighted in the Apprehension of her nearness to her Father's House: And it was not long before she was fill'd with Joy unspeakable in believing.

Still obsessed with death, but with a less joyful view, was Michael Wigglesworth's *Day of Doom* (1662), an account of the Judgment Day in verse intended to reinvigorate Puritan spirituality. *Day of Doom* was New England's first best-seller. The verses reprinted here may suggest why.

By the second quarter of the eighteenth century, attitudes toward death were changing, as the gravestone iconography after about 1730 testifies. The epitaphs stressing mortality appeared much less frequently, and the ever-present foreboding death's-head, shovels, and hourglass symbols of the seventeenth century began to be replaced by smiling cherubs, angels, natural objects, and sentimentalized willow and urn motifs.

Note the details shown here from an eighteenth-century gravestone compared to those on the Tapping

## DAY OF DOOM

MICHAEL WIGGLESWORTH (1662)

### 56

Now it comes in, and every sin
  unto men's charge doth lay;
It judgeth them and doth condemn,
  though all the world say nay.
It so stingeth and tortureth,
  it worketh such distress,
That each man's self against himself
  is forcèd to confess.

### 57

It's vain moreover for men to cover
  the least iniquity;
The Judge hath seen, and privy been
  to all their villainy.
He unto light and open sight
  the work of darkness brings;
He doth unfold both new and old,
  both known and hidden things.

### 58

All filthy facts and secret acts,
  however closely done
And long concealed, are there revealed
  before the mid-day sun.
Deeds of the night, shunning the light,
  which darkest corners sought,
To fearful blame and endless shame
  are there most justly brought.

### 59

And as all facts and grosser acts,
  so every word and thought,
Erroneous notions and lustful motion,
  are unto judgment brought,
No sin so small and trivial
  but hither it must come,
Nor so long past, but now at last
  it must receive a doom. . . .

### 188

The Judge is strong; doers of wrong
  cannot his power withstand.
None can by flight run out of sight
  nor 'scape out of his hand.
Sad is their state, for advocate
  to plead their cause there's none—
None to prevent their punishment,
  or misery bemoan.

### 189

O dismal day! wither shall they
  for help and succor flee?
To God above, with hopes to move
  their greatest enemy?
His wrath is great, whose burning heat
  no floods of tears can slake:
His word stands fast, that they be cast
  into the burning lake.

stone. A winged image of Mrs. Betsy Shaw (Plymouth, Massachusetts, 1795) optimistically represents the flight of her soul heavenward. This romantic design tells us much about the secularization of New England society and the passing of the early Puritans' intense seriousness about their godly mission in America to redeem humankind. As the funerary handiwork of stonecarvers tells us, the Puritans' early providential self-image had been transformed. Less piety and morbid introspection, more worldliness and individual hopefulness had spread through the Puritan Holy Commonwealth. Can you point out how these changes are reflected on the Shaw and Tapping gravestones? What do the markings, inscriptions, and design of tombstones in cemeteries near you reveal about the changing experience and values of later Americans?

Photo by Daniel Farber

***Betsy Shaw headstone, Plymouth, 1795***

to wish and aim at an utter extirpation of the Indians." Even a royal governor could not restrain such men, bent on pursuing their hopes of land ownership and independence. To them, Indians were only "wolves, tigers, and bears," as Bacon charged, "which daily destroyed our harmless and innocent lambs."

The blind hatred of Indians bred into white society during the war became a permanent feature of Virginia life. A generation later, in 1711, the legislature spurned the governor's plea for quieting the Indian frontier with a program of educational missions and regulated trade. Instead, the legislators voted military appropriations of £20,000 "for extirpating all Indians without distinction of Friends or Enemys." The Indians learned that even when white society was divided, the tribes could be outmatched. The remnants of the once populous Powhatan Confederacy lost their last struggle for the world they had known. Now they moved farther west or submitted to a life on the margins of white society as tenant farmers, day laborers, or domestic servants.

In the aftermath of Bacon's Rebellion, most of the reform laws of 1676 were annulled and government by an emerging planter aristocracy regained its former place. But the war relieved much of the social tension among white Virginians. Newly available Indian land created fresh opportunities for small planters and former servants. Equally important, Virginians with capital to invest were turning from the impoverished rural villages of England and Ireland to the villages of West Africa to supply their labor needs. This halted the influx of poor white servants who, once free, formed a discontented mass at the bottom of Chesapeake society. A racial consensus, uniting whites of different ranks in the common pursuit of a prosperous, slave-based economy, began to take shape.

North and south of Virginia, Bacon's Rebellion caused insurrectionary rumblings. Many of Bacon's compatriots took refuge after his death in North Carolina's Albemarle County, the "backside of Virginia." There they joined dissident tobacco farmers, who were distressed by recent Indian uprisings, export duties on tobacco, and quitrents controlled by a mercenary elite. Led by George Durant and John Culpeper, they drove the governor from office and briefly seized the reins of power.

In Maryland, Protestant settlers chafed under high taxes, quitrents, and officeholders regarded as venal, Catholic, or both. Declining tobacco prices and a fear of Indian attacks increased their touchiness. This volatile mix soon produced sparks. One month after Bacon razed Jamestown, insurgent small planters tried to seize the Maryland government. Two of their leaders were hanged for the attempt. In 1681, Josias Fendall and John Coode, "two rank Baconists" according to Lord Baltimore, led another abortive uprising. After their attempt to kidnap the Catholic proprietor failed, Fendall was executed and Coode banished from the colony.

In all three southern colonies, the volatility of late seventeenth-century life owed much to the region's peculiar social development. Where family formation was retarded by imbalanced sex ratios and fearsome mortality, and where geographic mobility was high, little social cohesion or attachment to community could grow. Missing in the southern colonies were the stabilizing power of mature local institutions, a vision of a larger purpose, and the presence of experienced and responsive political leaders.

## THE GLORIOUS REVOLUTION IN AMERICA

A dozen years after the major Indian wars in New England and Virginia, a series of small insurrections and a major witchcraft incident rumbled through colonial society. These outbursts reflected the social strains besetting society in the expanding seaboard colonies and their uneasy adjustment to attempts in England to create a more disciplined colonial empire. The rebellions were all triggered by the Revolution of 1688, known in England thereafter as the Glorious Revolution because it ended forever the notion that kings ruled by a God-given "divine right" and marked the last serious Catholic challenge to Protestant supremacy.

## Organizing the Empire

From the earliest attempts at colonization, the English assumed that overseas settlements would not only benefit the emigrants but also promote the national interest at home. Colonies served as outlets for English manufactured goods, provided foodstuffs and raw materials, stimulated trade (and hence promoted a larger merchant navy), and contributed to the royal coffers by paying duties on exported commodities such as sugar and tobacco.

England proceeded slowly in the seventeenth century to regulate its colonies and mold them into a unified empire. A first small step was taken in 1621, when the king's council forbade tobacco growers to export their crop to anywhere but England. Three years later, when the Virginia Company of London plunged into bankruptcy, the crown made Virginia a royal colony, the first of many to come. However, not until 1651, when the colonists traded freely with the commercially aggressive Dutch, did Parliament take the first step toward regulating colonial affairs. It passed a navigation act requiring that English or colonial ships, manned by English or colonial sailors, carry all goods entering England, Ireland, and the colonies, no matter where those goods originated. These were the first steps toward a regulated empire and the first steps to place the states' power behind national economic development.

In 1660, after the monarchy was restored, Parliament passed a more comprehensive navigation act that listed colonial products (tobacco, sugar, indigo, dyewoods, cotton) that could be shipped only to England or to other English colonies. Like its predecessor, the act took dead aim at Holland's domination of Atlantic commerce while increasing England's revenues by imposing duties on the enumerated articles. In the following decades, other navigation acts closed loopholes in the 1660 law and added other enumerated articles. It was a form of regulation that bore lightly on the colonists because the laws lacked enforcement mechanisms.

After 1675, international competition and war, rather than a desire to regulate the internal affairs of overseas colonies, led England to impose greater imperial control. That year marked the establishment of the Lords of Trade, a committee of the king's privy council vested with power to make and enforce decisions regarding the management of the colonies. Chief among their goals was the creation of more uniform governments in North America and the West Indies that would answer to the crown's will. Although this movement toward the central administration of empire often sputtered, the trend was unmistakable, especially to colonists who felt the sting of royal customs agents sent to enforce the navigation acts. England was becoming the shipper of the world, and its state-regulated policy of economic nationalism, duplicating that of the Dutch, was essential to this rise to commercial greatness.

## Uprising in New England

When Charles II died in 1685, his brother, the duke of York, assumed the throne as James II. This set in motion a train of events that nearly led to civil war. Like his brother, James II professed the Catholic faith. But unlike Charles II, who had disclosed this only on his deathbed, the new king announced his faith immediately

*The center of government and official news in colonial New England was Boston's town house, built in 1657.*

upon assuming the throne. Consternation ensued. Protestant England recoiled even more when James issued the Declaration of Indulgence, which granted liberty of worship to all. Although religious toleration is cherished today, it was unacceptable to most English Protestants 300 years ago. Belief that the declaration was primarily a concession to Catholics hardened when the king began creating Catholic peerages to fill the House of Lords, appointed Catholics to high government posts, including command of the English navy, and demanded that Oxford and Cambridge open their doors to Catholic students. In 1687, the king dismissed a resistant Parliament. When his wife, believed to be too old for further childbearing, gave birth to a son in 1688, a Catholic succession loomed.

Appalled by James's policies, and sniffing a Catholic conspiracy, a group of Protestant leaders secretly plotted his downfall. In 1688, led by the earl of Shaftesbury, they invited William of Orange, king of the Netherlands, to invade England and take the throne with his wife Mary, James's Protestant daughter. James abdicated rather than fight. It was a bloodless victory for Protestantism, for parliamentary power and the limitation of kingly prerogatives, and for the propertied merchants and gentry of England who stood behind the revolt.

The response of New Englanders to these events stemmed from their previous experience with royal authority and their fear of "papists." New England became a prime target for reform when the administrative reorganization of the empire began in 1675, for an independent spirit

and widespread evasion of commercial regulations had prevailed there for two generations. In 1684, Charles II had annulled the Massachusetts charter. Two years later, James II appointed Sir Edmund Andros, a crusty professional soldier and former governor of New York, to rule over the newly created Dominion of New England that soon gathered under one government the colonies of New Hampshire, Massachusetts, Connecticut, Plymouth, Rhode Island, New York, New Jersey, and part of Maine. Puritans were now forced to swallow the bitter fact that they were subjects of London bureaucrats who cared more about shaping a disciplined empire than they did about the special religious vision of one group of overseas subjects.

At first Andros was peacefully accepted, if not welcomed. But he soon earned the New Englanders' hatred by stepping heavily on freedoms they had come to cherish. He imposed taxes without legislative consent, ended trial by jury, abolished the General Court of Massachusetts (which had met annually since 1630), muzzled Boston's town meeting, and challenged the validity of all land titles. He mocked the Puritans by converting a Boston Puritan church into an Anglican chapel and holding services there on Christmas Day. In Puritan nostrils, this gesture stank of popery. Adding to Puritan outrage, Andros rejected their practice of suppressing religious dissent.

When news reached Boston in April 1689 that William of Orange had landed in England, ending James II's hated Catholic regime, Bostonians streamed into the streets to the beat of

*The ousting of the Dutch government at New Amsterdam in 1664 was an early incident in England's struggle for dominance in North America, furthered in King William's and Queen Anne's wars.*

drums. They imprisoned Andros, a suspected papist, and forced the surrender of the fort in Boston harbor, which held most of the governor's small contingent of red-coated royal troops. Andros escaped but was quickly recaptured, disguised in women's clothing. Boston's ministers, along with merchants and former magistrates, led the rebellion, but city folk of the lower orders supplied the footsoldiers. For three years Massachusetts would be ruled by an interim government while awaiting a new royal charter and a royal governor.

Although Bostonians had dramatically rejected royal authority, which to them represented the "bloody Devotees of Rome" as well as arbitrary power, no real internal revolution occurred. However, growing social stratification and the emergence of a political elite led to some disturbing effects. Some citizens challenged the traditional view that those at the top of society were the true guardians of the public interest. They argued that men of modest means but common sense might better be trusted with power. *Anarchy* was the word chosen by Samuel Willard, minister of Boston's Third Church, to tar the popular spirit he saw unloosed in Boston in the aftermath of Andros's ouster. But such egalitarian rumblings came to little.

## Leisler's Rebellion in New York

In New York, the Glorious Revolution was similarly bloodless at first but far more disruptive. It was not necessary to overthrow royal government when news arrived of James II's abdication. It simply melted away. When a local militia captain, the German-born Jacob Leisler, appeared at Fort James at the lower tip of Manhattan, Governor Francis Nicholson made only a token show of resistance before quietly stepping down. Displacing the governor's "popishly affected dogs and rogues," Leisler established an interim government and ruled with an elected Committee of Safety for 13 months until a governor appointed by King William arrived.

Leisler's government enjoyed popularity among small landowners and urban laboring people. Most of the upper echelon, however, regarded him with distaste. They remembered that he had come to New Amsterdam in 1660 as a common footsoldier of the Dutch West India Company and three years later had leapfrogged into the merchant class by marrying a wealthy widow. After the English took over the Dutch colony in 1664, he was often at odds with New Yorkers of the upper rank, who regarded him as a boor. "Up jump into the saddle hott brain'd Capt. Leisler," sneered one aristocrat after Leisler's takeover. Thereafter the Leislerians were often labeled as people of "mean birth, and sordid education and desperate fortunes."

Much of this antipathy originated in the smoldering resentment lower- and middle-class Dutch inhabitants felt toward the town's English elite. Many Dutch merchants had readily adjusted to the English conquest of New Netherland in 1664, and many incoming English merchants had married into Dutch families. But beneath the upper class, where economic success softened ethnic friction, incidents of Anglo-

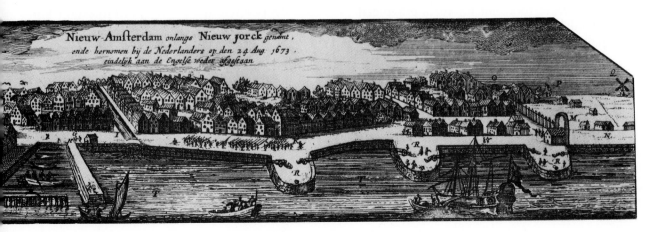

Dutch hostility were common. The feeling rose in the 1670s and 1680s among ordinary Dutch families that the English were crowding them out of the society they had built.

The Glorious Revolution provided a spark to ignite this smoldering social conflict. Leisler shared Dutch hostility toward New York's English elite, and his sympathy for the common people, mostly Dutch, earned him the hatred of the city's oligarchy. Leisler freed imprisoned debtors, planned a town-meeting system of government for New York City, and replaced merchants with artisans in important official posts. By the autumn of 1689, Leislerian mobs were attacking the property of some of New York's wealthiest merchants. Two merchants, refusing to recognize Leisler's authority, were jailed.

Leisler's opponents, accustomed to controlling government, were horrified at the power of what one called the "rabble" and another the "tumultuous multitude." They believed that ordinary people had the right neither to rebel against authority nor to exercise political power. When a new English governor arrived in 1691 to take charge, the anti-Leislerians embraced him and charged Leisler and seven of his assistants with treason for assuming the government without royal instructions.

In the ensuing trial, Leisler and Jacob Milbourne, his son-in-law and chief lieutenant, were convicted of treason and hanged. Leisler's popularity among the artisans of the city was evident when his wealthy opponents, having sentenced him to death, could find no carpenter in the city who would furnish a ladder to use at the scaffold. After his execution, peace gradually returned to New York, but for years provincial and city politics reflected the deep rift between Leislerians and anti-Leislerians.

### Southern Rumblings

The Glorious Revolution also gave dissatisfactions a focus in several southern colonies. Since Maryland was ruled by a Catholic proprietary family, the Protestant majority predictably seized upon word of the Glorious Revolution and used it for their own purposes. Lord Baltimore had returned to England in 1684. In 1688, when his instructions to his colony to honor

William and Mary were delayed, leading officials and planters formed a Protestant Association. Seizing control of the government in July 1689, they vowed to cleanse Maryland of its popish hue and also to reform a corrupt customs service, cut taxes and fees, and extend the rights of the representative assembly. John Coode, formerly a fiery Anglican minister who had already been involved in a brief rebellion in 1681, assumed the reins of government and held them until the arrival of Maryland's first royal governor in 1692.

In neighboring Virginia, the wounds of Bacon's Rebellion were still healing when word of the Glorious Revolution arrived. The fact that Virginia lived under the governorship of the Catholic Lord Howard of Effingham, who had installed a number of Catholic officials, made it easy for rumors to spread that a Catholic conspiracy was hatching. News of the revolution in England led a group of planters, who had suffered a prolonged drop in tobacco prices, to attempt an overthrow of the governor. The uprising quickly faded when the governor's council asserted itself and took its own measures to remove Catholics from positions of authority.

The Glorious Revolution brought political changes to several colonies. The Dominion of New England was shattered, and each of its parts hereafter would be supervised by a royal governor appointed in England. In Massachusetts, a new royal charter in 1691 eliminated church membership as a voting requirement. The Maryland proprietorship was abolished (to be restored in 1715 when the Baltimore family became Protestant), and Catholics were barred from office. Everywhere the liberties of Protestant Englishmen were celebrated.

### The Social Meaning of the Glorious Revolution

Although the colonial insurrections associated with the Glorious Revolution sought primarily to overthrow arbitrary royal governors and foil papist plots (most of them imaginary), they revealed social and political tensions that accompanied the transplanting of English society to the North American wilderness. Still hardly beyond the frontier stage, the immature societies along the coast were highly fluid and competitive. They lacked the stable political systems and acknowledged leadership class thought necessary for maintaining social order.

The colonial elite tried, of course, to foster social and political stability. The best insurance of this, they believed, was the maintenance of a stratified society where children were subordinate to parents, women to men, servants to masters, and the poor to the rich. Only well-knit societies had coherence and balance, the upper echelon believed. Amid the barbarizing conditions of the New World, where anarchy lurked just beyond every threshold, it was especially vital to reproduce the social arrangements of the Old World.

Hence, in every settlement leaders tried to maintain a system of social gradations and subordination. Puritans did not file into church on Sundays and occupy the pews in random fashion. Rather, the seats were "doomed," or assigned according to customary yardsticks of respectability—age, parentage, social position, wealth, and occupation. Even in fluid Virginia, lower-class persons were haled before courts for horse racing because this was a sport by law reserved for men of social distinction.

This social ideal proved difficult to transplant to North American soil, however. Regardless of previous rank, settlers rubbed elbows so frequently and faced such raw conditions together that those without pedigrees often saw little reason to defer to men of superior rank. "In Virginia," explained John Smith, "a plain soldier that can use a pickaxe and spade is better than five knights." Colonists everywhere learned that basic lesson. They gave respect not to those who claimed it by birth but to those who earned it by deed.

Adding to the difficulty of reproducing a traditional social order in the colonies was the obvious social fluidity in frontier society. A native aristocracy gradually formed, but it had no basis, as in Europe, in legally defined and hereditary social rank. Planters and merchants, gradually accumulating large estates, aped the English gentry by cultivating the arts, building fine houses, and acquiring symbols of respectability such as libraries, coaches, and racehorses. Yet their place was rarely secure. In the race to drag wealth from the resource-rich environment, new competitors nipped constantly at their heels.

Amid such social flux, the elite could never command general allegiance to the ideal of a fixed social structure. Ambitious men on the rise such as Nathaniel Bacon and Jacob Leisler, and thwarted men below them who followed their lead, rose up against the constituted authorities, though they almost certainly would not have dared to do so in their homelands. When they gained power during the Glorious Revolution, in every case only briefly, the leaders of these uprisings linked themselves with a tradition of English struggle against tyranny and oligarchical power. They vowed to make government more responsive to the ordinary people, who composed most of their societies.

In both North and South this earned parvenu leaders the epithet "Masaniello" after the peasant fish seller of Naples who in 1647 had mobilized ordinary people against exploitation by the rich. Masaniello briefly controlled the city, momentarily stood the political order on its head, and became an Italian Robin Hood. In America, Bacon's Rebellion was likened to Masaniello's revolt by the royal governor. In New York, Leisler was labeled a local Masaniello by his wealthy enemies. In Maryland, John Coode proudly called himself a Chesapeake Masaniello. The comparisons were far from exact, but references to the Italian folk hero indicate that colonists from all ranks recognized that social relations in their competitive and open society were subject to violent alterations that violated the ideal of a fixed and orderly social system.

### Witchcraft in Salem

The greatest internal conflict of the late seventeenth century came not as a part of the Glorious Revolution in America but was indirectly nourished by the governmental instability associated with it. In Massachusetts, the deposing of Andros left the colony in political limbo for three years, and this allowed what might have been a brief outbreak of witchcraft in the little community of Salem to escalate into a bitter and bloody battle that the provincial government, caught in transition, reacted to only belatedly.

On a winter's day in 1692, 9-year-old Betty Parris and her 11-year-old cousin Abigail Williams began to play at magic in the kitchen of a small house in Salem, Massachusetts. They enlisted the aid of Tituba, the slave of Betty's father, Samuel Parris, the minister of the small community. Tituba told voodoo tales handed down from her African past and baked "witch cakes." The girls soon became seized with fits and began making wild gestures and speeches. Before long, other young girls in the village were behaving strangely. Village elders forced from them confessions that they were being tormented by Tituba and two other women, one a decrepit pauper and the other a disagreeable old woman.

What began as the innocent play of young girls attempting to foresee their futures turned into a ghastly rending of a farm community capped by the execution of 20 villagers accused of witchcraft. The incident displayed, in exaggerated form, the tensions that beset the lives of obscure, ordinary individuals in England's late seventeenth-century colonies.

Belief in the supernatural, and in witchcraft, was ancient. For centuries throughout western Europe, people had believed that witches followed Satan's bidding and could spread his evil to anyone he designated. Communities had accused and sentenced women more often than men to death for witchcraft. In the seventeenth century, people still took literally the biblical injunction "Thou shalt not suffer a witch to live." In Massachusetts more than 100 people, mostly older, shrewish women, had been accused of witchcraft before 1692, and more than a dozen had been hanged.

In Salem, the initial accusations against three older women quickly multiplied. Within a matter of weeks, as fear gripped the town, dozens had been charged with witchcraft, including several prominent members of the community. But formal prosecution of the accused witches could not proceed because neither the new royal charter of 1691 nor the royal governor to rule the colony had yet arrived. For three months, while charges spread, local authorities could only send the accused to jail without trial. When Governor William Phips arrived from England in May 1692, he ordered a special court to try the accused, but by now events had careened out of control. All through the summer the court listened to testimony. By September it had condemned about two dozen villagers. Nineteen of

*Witch hangings were commonplace in Europe as well as the colonies; this woodcut appeared in a book on injustices in England's coal industry, published in 1655.*

them were hanged on barren "Witches Hill" outside the town, and 80-year-old Giles Corey was crushed to death under heavy stones. The trials rolled on into 1693, but by then colonial leaders, including many of the clergy, recognized that a feverish fear of one's neighbors, rather than witchcraft itself, had possessed the little village of Salem.

Many factors contributed to the hysteria. Among them were generational strife, old family animosities, tensions between agricultural Salem Village and the nearby commercial center called Salem Town, and even an outbreak of food poisoning that may have caused hallucinogenic behavior. Probably nobody will ever fully understand the underlying causes, but the fact that the accusations of witchcraft kept spreading suggests the anxiety of this tumultuous era, marked by war, economic disruption, the political takeover of the colony by Andros and then his overthrow, and the erosion of the early generation's utopian vision.

The family history of Thomas Putnam, Jr., shows how these forces became entangled in the lives of a single family and led to the hangman's noose. Putnam was the grandson of an early settler in Salem Village. His grandfather had left 800 acres of farmland to his three sons when he died in 1662, and these three heirs produced 11 sons. No amount of hard work on the marginal family lands could glean a living for that many farmers and their families.

Thomas Putnam, Jr., and his brother were two of those 11 grandsons. Their father was a substantial member of the village and frequently held local offices. When his wife died in 1666, he married the widow of a prosperous ship captain from nearby Salem Town. To them was born a son, Joseph, three years later. Whether his step brothers resented Joseph as a young boy is not known. But when their father died in 1686,

Thomas Putnam, Jr., and his brother were shocked to find that he had willed most of his estate to their step mother and young Joseph. Their fortunes already eroded by the generational effects of too many sons dividing too few acres, they now saw their inheritance fall mostly into the hands of a teenage step brother.

Thomas and his brother tried unsuccessfully to break their father's will. Their pique only grew a few years later when their step brother Joseph, now 21, married the daughter of one of the most prominent families in Salem Town. By 1692, young Joseph had been chosen for the town committee, an office that the elder Putnam brothers were accustomed to holding. It was at this time that witchcraft accusations were first raised in the village.

The wife, daughter, and servant girl of Thomas Putnam, Jr., were among the first to allege that they had been bewitched. His daughter Ann was perhaps the most afflicted person in the town. She testified against 21 persons whom she believed had tried to kidnap her soul. Her father testified against 12 and signed complaints against another dozen. Thomas Putnam's brother Edward participated in 13 cases that went before the special court. One of young Ann's cousins, who lived in Putnam's house, named 16 persons who had demonically assaulted her in 1692.

No direct link can be made between the declining fortunes and status of the Putnam family and their belief that they had been besieged by witches. But their family history, which was one small example of some larger trends in the agricultural villages of late seventeenth-century New England, provides insights into how personal disappointment and bitterness could be displaced onto others in the community when a crisis occurred.

## CONTENDING FOR A CONTINENT

At the end of the seventeenth century, following an era of Indian wars and internal upheaval, the colonists for the first time confronted an extended period of international war. North America

was less an arena of armed rivalry among the European powers than were the sugar-rich islands of the Caribbean. Nonetheless, the global struggle for control of land and sea that erupted late in the seventeenth century—the beginning of a century of conflict—reached to the doorsteps of those who thought that in immigrating to North America they had left dynastic wars behind.

### Anglo-French Rivalry

The French were a force in the New World long before the English. Their early overseas activities revolved around fishing and trading settlements. Winning handsome profits for the mother country rather than establishing populous agricultural communities was the guiding principle. After the Portuguese and Spanish had wiped out their small settlements at the mouth of the Rio de Janeiro and in Florida in the 1560s, France concentrated its overseas effort in the northern latitudes of North America. In the waters of the northwestern Atlantic and in the vast region watered by the St. Lawrence River, France launched a commercial empire based on fish and furs.

The farming of offshore waters for fish, of growing importance as a protein source for legions of slaves in the West Indies, proved a valuable enterprise. But the fur trade became even more profitable. It was not necessary to conquer eastern Canada and Nova Scotia or even to plant large settlements. An extensive fur trade could be coordinated from small trading posts where Indian trappers would come from vast distances to exchange the pelts of the beaver for manufactured iron and woolen goods.

By the early seventeenth century, however, the French realized that without a more substantial population base their trading posts would fall to Dutch and English rivals. Thus they began planting permanent settlements in North America. The small colonies established at Port Royal, Nova Scotia, in 1604 and at Quebec in 1608 were designed to solidify French claims to the northern part of the continent. Their mere presence incited the English on the Chesapeake in 1613 to mount a campaign of extermination against such pretensions of Catholic France. But the colony survived, and during the next half century the French slowly nurtured their tiny settlements. As late as 1643, however, not more than 400 Frenchmen inhabited "Nova Gallia," or New France. Most of them were Indian traders or Jesuit priests. As one royal governor of New France remarked, only two kinds of business existed there: the conversion of beaver and the conversion of souls.

In 1661 Louis XIV ushered in a new era for New France. Determined to make his country the most powerful in Europe, the king regarded

*A seventeenth-century French engraving depicts a frontier settlement in what is now Texas.*

North America and the Caribbean with renewed interest. New France's timber resources would build the royal navy; its fish would feed the growing mass of slaves in the French West Indies; and its fur trade, if greatly expanded, would fill the royal coffers.

Under the leadership of able governors such as Count Frontenac, New France grew in population, economic strength, and ambition in the late seventeenth century. In the 1670s, Louis Jolliet and Father Jacques Marquette, a Jesuit priest, explored an immense territory watered by the Mississippi and Missouri rivers, previously unknown to Europeans. A decade later, military engineers and priests began building forts and missions, one complementing the other, throughout the Great Lakes region and the Mississippi valley.

Visions of an extraordinary inland empire grew in the 1680s when René Robert de La Salle canoed down the Mississippi all the way to the Gulf of Mexico and planted a settlement in Texas at Matagorda Bay. The dream of connecting Canada and Louisiana by a chain of forts and trading posts would not be realized for another half century. But it was the French, with a colonial population of only 12,000, rather than the English, with colonies inhabited by 200,000, who controlled the interior of North America in 1690.

The growth of French strength and ambitions brought New England and New France

### France's Inland Empire, 1600–1720

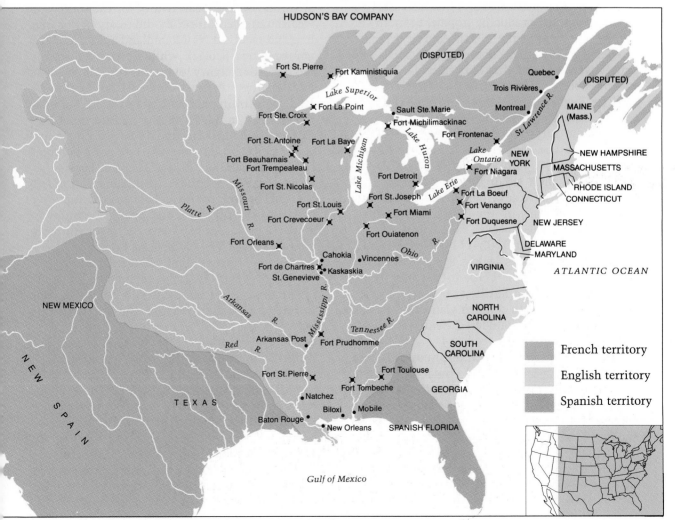

into deadly conflict for a generation beginning in the late seventeenth century. Religious hostility overlaid commercial rivalry. Protestant New Englanders regarded popish New France as a satanic challenge to the historic mission God had assigned them. When the European wars of Louis XIV began in 1689, armed conflict between England and France quickly extended into every overseas theater where the two powers had colonies. In North America the battle zone was New York, New England, and eastern Canada.

In two wars, from 1689 to 1697 and 1702 to 1713, the English and French sought to oust each other from the New World. The zone of greatest importance was the Caribbean. Both home governments understood that the importance of the North American colonies lay chiefly in supplying the timber and fish necessary to sustain the sugar-producing tropical economy of the West Indies. In the North American zone, problems of weather, disease, transport, and supply were so great that only irregular warfare was possible.

The English struck three times at the centers of French power—Port Royal, which commanded the access to the St. Lawrence River, and Quebec, the administrative center of New France. In 1690, during King William's War (1689–1697), their small flotilla captured Port Royal, the hub of Acadia (which was returned to France at the end of the war). The English assault on Quebec, however, failed disastrously. In Queen Anne's War (1702–1713), New England launched three attacks against Port Royal before finally capturing it in 1710. In the next year, when England sent a flotilla of 60 ships and an army of 5,000 men to conquer Canada, the land and sea operations foundered before reaching their destinations.

With European-style warfare miserably unsuccessful, both England and France attempted to subcontract military tasks to their Indian allies. Here was a new aspect of the meeting of cultures—the use of Native Americans as mercenaries in an international conflict. This policy occasionally succeeded, especially with the French, who gladly sent their own troops into the fray alongside Indian partners. The French and Indians wiped out the frontier outpost of

Schenectady, New York, in 1690; razed Wells, Maine, and Deerfield, Massachusetts, in 1703; and battered other towns along the New England frontier throughout both wars. In retaliation, the Iroquois, supplied by the English, stung several French settlements and left New France "bewildered and benumbed" after a massacre near Montreal in 1689. The Iroquois sat out the second war in the early eighteenth century, however, convinced that neutrality better served their purposes than acting as mercenaries for the English.

## The Costs of War

The Peace of Utrecht in 1713, which brought international hostilities to a close, signaled the centurylong rise of England and the decline of Spain in the European rivalry for the sources of wealth outside Europe. By the treaty provisions, England received Newfoundland and Acadia (renamed Nova Scotia), while France recognized English sovereignty over the fur-rich Hudson Bay territory. France retained Cape Breton Island, controlling the entrance to the St. Lawrence River. In the Caribbean, France yielded St. Kitts and Nevis to England. In Europe, Spain lost its provinces in Italy and the last of its holdings in the Netherlands to the Austrian Hapsburgs. Spain also surrendered Gibraltar and Minorca to the English and awarded England the lucrative privilege of supplying the Spanish empire in America with African slaves, a favor formerly enjoyed by the French Senegal Company.

Though England rebuffed France after a generation of war, New England suffered grievously. In time Nova Scotia would provide a new frontier for Puritan farmers. But the two wars between 1689 and 1713 struck hard at New England's economy. Massachusetts bore the brunt of the burden. Probably one-fifth of all able-bodied males in the colony participated in the Canadian campaigns, and of these about one-quarter never lived to tell the terrors of New England's first major experience with international warfare. At the end of the first war in 1697, one leader bemoaned that Massachusetts was left "quite exhausted and ready to sink under the calamities and fatigue of a tedious consuming war." The war debt was £50,000 sterling in Massachusetts alone, a greater per capita burden than the national debt today.

At the end of the second conflict in 1713, war widows were so numerous that the Bay Colony faced its first serious poverty problem. In addition, taxes to pay for the military campaigns had "much impoverished and enfeebled" the people, and price inflation had eaten deeply into the pocketbooks of most working families. Pamphleteers in New England's principal port wrote of "the present melancholy circumstances" and "the distressed state of the Town of Boston."

The colonies south of New England remained on the sidelines during most of the war. But war at sea between European rivals affected even those who sat out the land war. In Queen Anne's War, New York lost one of its best grain markets when Spain, allied with France, outlawed American foodstuffs in its West Indian

colonies. The French navy plucked off nearly 30 New York merchant vessels, about one-quarter of the port's fleet, and disrupted the vital sea lanes between the mainland and the Caribbean, to the detriment of Philadelphia's grain merchants as well.

One lesson of war, to be repeated many times in succeeding generations, was that the burdens and rewards fell unevenly upon the participants. Some lowborn men could rise spectacularly. William Phips, the twenty-sixth child in his family, had been a poor sheep farmer and ship's carpenter in Maine who seemed destined to go nowhere. Then he won a fortune by recovering a sunken Spanish treasure ship in the West Indies in 1687. For that feat he was given command of the expedition against Port Royal in 1690. Victory there catapulted him to the governorship of Massachusetts in 1691, and thereafter his status was secure.

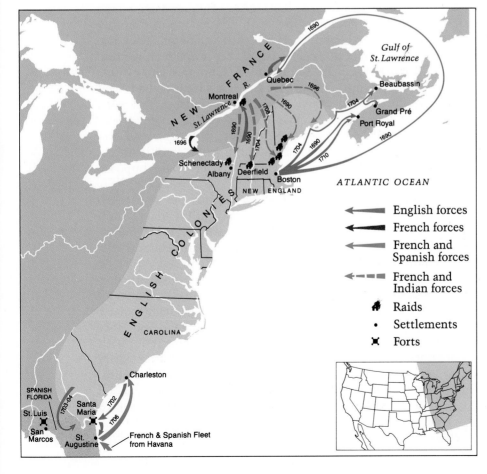

**King William's and Queen Anne's Wars**

English forces
French forces
French and Spanish forces
French and Indian forces
Raids
Settlements
Forts

Other men, already rich, multiplied their wealth. Andrew Belcher of Boston, who had grown wealthy on provisioning contracts during King Philip's War in 1675 and 1676, combined patriotism with profit in King William's and Queen Anne's wars by supplying warships and outfitting the New England expeditions to Canada. As one of the favored recipients of the fruits of war, Belcher became a local titan, riding through Boston's crooked streets in London-built coaches, erecting a handsome mansion on State Street, and purchasing slaves to symbolize his rise to the pinnacle of New England society.

Most men, especially those who did the fighting, gained little, however, and many lost all. It was from the ranks of the least securely placed New Englanders—indentured servants, apprentices, recently arrived immigrants, unskilled laborers, fishermen, and ordinary farmers —that most troops were recruited or pressed involuntarily into service. Once in the army or navy, they died in proportions that seem staggering today. Fervent antipopery, dreams of glory, and promises of plunder from the commercial centers of French Canada lured most of them into uniform. Having achieved no place on the paths leading upward, they grasped at straws. A hefty percentage of those who sailed in the naval expeditions against Port Royal or plodded overland to attack Montreal and Quebec never lived even to collect their meager wages. None found the advertised booty, which turned out to be only a sugarplum dangled by military recruiters.

## CONCLUSION: Controlling the New Environment

By the second decade of the eighteenth century, the 12 English colonies on the eastern edge of North America had secured footholds in the hemisphere and erected the basic scaffolding of colonial life. With the aid of the mother country, they had ousted the Dutch from their mid-Atlantic perch. They had fought the French to a draw. The coastal Indian tribes were reeling from disease and a series of wars that secured the colonists' land base along 1,000 miles of coastal plain. The powerful Indian tribes of the interior had been brought within a profitable trading orbit. The scarcity of labor had been overcome by copying the rest of the European colonists in the hemisphere, who had linked the west coast of Africa to the New World through the ghastly trade in human flesh. Finally, the colonists had engaged in a rash of insurrections against what they regarded as arbitrary and tainted governments imposed by England.

The embryo of America that the colonists carried into the eighteenth century contained peculiarly mixed features. Still physically isolated from Europe, the colonists developed by necessity a large measure of self-reliance. Slowly, they began to identify themselves as the permanent inhabitants of a new land rather than transplanted English, Dutch, or Scots-Irish. Viewing land and labor as the indispensable elements of a fruitful economy, they learned to exploit without apologies the land of one dark-skinned people and the labor of another. Yet even as they attained a precarious mastery in a triracial society, they were being culturally affected by the very people whose land and labor they had laid claim to. Although utopian visions of life in America still reverberated in the heads of some, most colonists had awakened to the reality that life in the New World was a puzzling mixture of unpredictable opportunity and sudden turbulence, unprecedented freedom and debilitating wars, racial intermingling and racial separation. It was a New World in much more than a geographic sense, for the people of three cultures who now inhabited it had remade it; and, while doing so, they were remaking themselves.

## Recommended Reading

The Atlantic slave trade, which spanned four centuries, is explored in Philip Curtin, *The Atlantic Slave Trade* (1969); Martin Kilson and Robert I. Rotberg, eds., *The African Diaspora* (1976); and Basil Davidson, *The African Slave Trade* (1961).

The origins and early history of slavery in the Americas, long-controversial topics, are studied in Frank Tannenbaum, *Slave and Citizen* (1956); Carl N. Degler, *Neither Black nor White: Slavery and Race Relations in Brazil and the United States* (1971); H. Hoetink, *Slavery and Race Relations in the Americas* (1973); David B. Davis, *The Problem of Slavery in Western Culture* (1966); and Richard S. Dunn, *Sugar and Slaves* (1972).

For slavery in the American colonies, a fine introduction is Ira Berlin, "Time, Space, and the Evolution of Afro-American Society in British Mainland America," *American Historical Review*, 85 (1980). Other valuable studies include Peter H. Wood, *Black Majority* (1974); Gerald Mullins, *Flight and Rebellion* (1972): and Winthrop D. Jordan, *White over Black* (1968).

Relations between colonizers and Native Americans after the founding period are examined in James Axtell, *The European and the Indian* (1981); Wilcomb Washburn, *The Governor and the Rebel* (a history of Bacon's Rebellion), (1957); Douglas Leach, *Flintlock and Tomahawk: New England in King Philip's War* (1958); Francis Jennings, *The Invasion of America* (1975): and Gary B. Nash, *Red, White, and Black* (1974, 1982).

For the Glorious Revolution in America and the era of instability at the end of the seventeenth century, consult David Lovejoy, *The Glorious Revolution in America* (1972); Jerome Reich, *Leisler's Rebellion* (1953); and Paul Boyer and Steven Nissenbaum, *Salem Possessed: The Social Origins of Witchcraft* (1974).

## TIME LINE

| | |
|---|---|
| 1600–1700 | Dutch monopolize slave trade |
| 1619 | First Africans imported to Virginia |
| 1637 | Pequot War in New England |
| 1640s | New England merchants enter slave trade <br> Virginia forbids blacks to carry firearms |
| 1650–1670 | Judicial and legislative decisions in Chesapeake solidify racial lines |
| 1660 | Parliament passes first Navigation Act |
| 1664 | English conquer New Netherland |
| 1673–1685 | French expand into Mississippi valley |
| 1675–1677 | King Philip's War |
| 1676 | Bacon's Rebellion in Virginia |
| 1684 | Massachusetts charter recalled |
| 1686 | Dominion of New England |
| 1688 | Glorious Revolution in England, followed by accession of William and Mary |
| 1689 | Overthrow of Governor Andros in New England <br> Leisler's Rebellion in New York |
| 1689–1697 | King William's War |
| 1692 | Witchcraft crisis in Salem |
| 1702–1713 | Queen Anne's War |
| 1713 | Peace of Utrecht |

# CHAPTER 4
## THE MATURING
## OF COLONIAL SOCIETY

As a youth, Devereaux Jarratt knew only the isolated life of the small southern planter. Born in 1733 on the Virginia frontier, he was the third son of an immigrant yeoman farmer. In New Kent County, where Jarratt grew up, class status showed in a man's dress, his leisure habits, his house, even in his religion. A farmer's "whole dress and apparel," Jarratt recalled later, "consisted in a pair of coarse breeches, one or two shirts, a pair of shoes and stockings, an old felt hat, and a bear skin coat." In a maturing colonial society that was six generations old by the mid-eighteenth century, such simple folk stepped aside and tipped their hat when prosperous neighbors went by. "A periwig, in those days," recollected Jarratt, "was a distinguishing badge of gentle folk—and when I saw a man riding the road, near our house, with a wig on, it would so alarm my fears . . . that, I dare say, I would run off, as for my life."

As the colonies grew rapidly after 1700, economic development brought handsome gains for some, opened modest opportunities for many, but produced disappointment and privation for others. Jarratt remembered that his parents "neither sought nor expected any title, honors, or great things, either for themselves or their children. They wished us all brought up in some honest calling that we might earn our bread, by the sweat of our brow, as they did." But Jarratt was among those who advanced. His huge appetite for learning was apparent to his parents when as a small child he proved able to repeat entire chapters of the Bible before he had learned to read. That earned him some schooling. But at age 8, when his parents died, he had to take his place behind the plow alongside his brothers. Then, at 19, Jarratt was "called from the ax to the quill" by a neighboring planter's timely offer of a tutoring position.

Tutoring put Jarratt in touch with the world of wealth and status. Gradually he advanced to positions in the households of wealthy Virginia planters. His modest success also introduced him to the world of evangelical religion. In the eighteenth century, an explosion of religious fervor dramatically reversed the growing secularism of the settlers. Jarratt first encountered evangelicalism in the published sermons of George Whitefield, an English clergyman. But it was later, at the plantation of John Cannon, "a man of great possessions in lands and slaves," that he personally experienced conversion under the influence of Cannon's wife. Jarratt later became a clergyman in the Anglican church, which was dominated in the South by wealthy and dignified planters. But he never lost his religious zeal and desire to carry religion to the common people. In this commitment to spiritual renewal, he participated in the first mass religious movement to occur in colonial society.

Colonial America in the first half of the eighteenth century was a thriving, changing set of regional societies that had developed from turbulent seventeenth-century beginnings. New England, the mid-Atlantic colonies, and the Upper and Lower South were all distinct regions. Even within regions, diversity increased in the eighteenth century as incoming streams of immigrants, mostly from Africa, Germany, and Ireland, added new pieces to the emerging American mosaic. In nobody's mind did the concept of a distinctly American society yet exist.

Despite their bewildering diversity and lack of cohesion, the colonies along the Atlantic seaboard were similarly affected by population growth and economic development. Everywhere except on the frontier, class differences grew. A commercial orientation spread from north to south, especially in the towns, as local economies matured and forged links with the network of trade in the Atlantic basin. The exercise of political power of elected legislative assemblies and local bodies produced seasoned leaders, a tradition of local autonomy, and a widespread belief in a political ideology stressing the liberties that freeborn Englishmen should enjoy. And all regions experienced a deep-running religious awakening that was itself connected to the secular changes occurring and had important political implications. All of these themes will be explored as we follow the way that scattered frontier settlements developed into mature provincial societies.

## AMERICA'S FIRST POPULATION EXPLOSION

In 1680, 150,000 colonizers clung to the eastern edge of North America. By 1750, they had swelled sevenfold to 1 million. This growth rate, never experienced in Europe, staggered English policymakers. Perceptive observers understood that the gap between the population of England and its American colonies was closing rapidly. Benjamin Franklin's prediction in 1751—that before his grandchildren died, the colonies would outstrip the mother country in population—proved correct.

The population boom was fed from both internal and external sources. Among the white colonial population, a high marriage rate, large families, and lower mortality than in Europe prevailed by the 1720s. Natural increase accounted for much of the population boom in all the colonies and nearly all of it in New England, where immigrants arrived only in a trickle in the eighteenth century. The black population also began to increase naturally by the 1720s. American-born slaves, forming families and producing as many children as white families, soon began to outnumber slaves born in Africa.

### The New Immigrants

While expanding through natural increase, the colonial population also received waves of new immigrants. They were not English, however. The last sizable group of settlers from England had arrived at the end of the seventeenth century. The eighteenth-century newcomers, who far outnumbered those emigrating before 1700, came overwhelmingly from Germany, Switzerland, Ireland, and Africa, and they were mostly indentured servants and slaves. Africans, who numbered about 15,000 in 1690, grew to 80,000 in 1730 and 325,000 in 1760. By the last date, when they composed one-fifth of the colonial population, their numbers were growing far more from natural increase than from importation. Of all the groups arriving in the eighteenth century, the Africans were the largest.

German-speaking settlers, about 90,000 strong, flocked to the colonies in the eighteenth century. Most were Protestant farmers of Swiss and French extraction, fleeing "God's three arrows"—famine, war, and pestilence. Drifting down the Rhine to Rotterdam, they crowded onto ships and began the long voyage to America. Once in the colonies, they hurried to areas where promoters promised them cheap and fertile land, low taxes, and freedom from military duty. Most settled between New York and South Carolina, with Pennsylvania claiming the largest number of them. Coming mostly in families, they turned much of the mid-Atlantic hinterland into a German-speaking region. Place names still mark their zone of settlement: Mannheim, New Berlin, and Herkimer, New York; Bethlehem, Ephrata, Nazareth, and Hanover, Pennsylvania; Hagerstown and Frederick, Maryland; Mecklenberg and New Hanover, North Carolina.

Outnumbering the Germans were the Protestant Scots-Irish. Several thousand from Northern Ireland arrived each year after the Peace of Utrecht in 1713 reopened the Atlantic sea lanes. Mostly poor farmers, they streamed into the same backcountry areas where Germans were settling, though more of them followed the mountain valleys south into the Carolinas and Georgia. Occasionally mingling with the Germans, these Ulster families washed over the ridges of Appalachia until their appetite for land brought them face to face with the ancient occupiers of the land. No major Indian wars occurred between 1715 and 1754, but the frontier bristled with tension as the new settlers pushed westward.

In the enormous buildup of population that occurred after 1715, the region southward from Pennsylvania witnessed the most spectacular growth. New England nearly tripled in population, but the middle and southern colonies quadrupled, though in the South the fast-growing slave population accounted for much more of the growth than in the mid-Atlantic. Pennsylvania, with its fertile lands and open door policy, grew fastest of all. Between 1720 and 1760,

## Scots-Irish Settlements, 1775

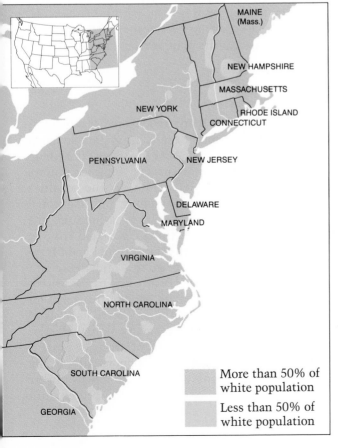

## German Settlements, 1775

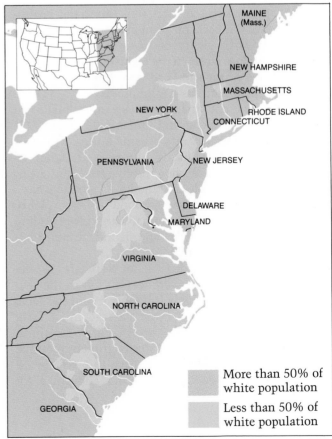

its population mushroomed from 30,000 to 180,000. Virginia, with a population of nearly half a million by 1760, remained by far the largest colony.

## New Classes of Newcomers

The social background of these new European immigrants differed substantially from their seventeenth-century predecessors. In the first century of colonization, a number of men from the upper levels of the English social pyramid came to America: university-trained Puritan ministers, sons of wealthy gentry, and merchants. In the eighteenth century, few such men arrived.

The seventeenth-century immigrants had also included many from the middle rungs of the English social ladder—yeomen farmers, skilled craftsmen, and shopkeepers. In America, they formed the backbone of the provincial churches and participated actively in community politics. Through "shipboard mobility" they moved up a notch or two on the western side of the Atlantic. Many lived to see their sons enter the professions or embark on a mercantile career in a society with plenty of room at the top. Such people came rarely in the eighteenth century, for religious persecution had waned in England, and material conditions had improved.

Slaves and indentured servants made up most of the incoming human tide after 1713. The traffic in servants became a regular part of the commerce linking Europe and America. Shipowners made their profits fetching sugar, fish, furs, rice, tobacco, and forest products eastward. Then, on the westbound voyages, plenty of room remained for human cargo after loading the less bulky textiles and manufactured products colonists desired.

Shipboard conditions for servants in the eighteenth century were worse than in the seventeenth and hardly better than aboard the slave ships. How wretched the passage must have been can be judged by the attempt at reform in the 1720s when the British government required an increase in horizontal space to 6 feet by 18 inches per passenger, with no allowance for children.

Such limited attempts to reduce "tight packing" did little to improve shipboard life. Crammed between decks in stifling air, servants suffered from smallpox and fevers, rotten food, impure water, cold, and lice. "Children between the ages of one and seven seldom survive the sea voyage," bemoaned one German immigrant, "and parents must often watch their offspring suffer miserably, die, and be thrown into the ocean." One expedition of 3,000 Palatinate immigrants in 1717 lost 470 en route, and another 250 succumbed shortly after reaching American soil. The misery would be repeated hundreds of times in the next two centuries. The average shipboard mortality rate of about 15 percent in the colonial era meant that this was the most unhealthy of all times to seek American shores.

Like indentured servants in the seventeenth century, the servant immigrants who poured ashore after 1715 came mostly from the lower ranks of society. As earlier, some were petty criminals, political prisoners, and the castoffs of the cities. Yet they were bold and ambitious souls. "Men who emigrate," an Englishman commented, "are from the nature of their circumstances, the most active, hardy, daring, bold and resolute spirits, and probably the most mischievous also."

## A Land of Opportunity?

Once ashore, many indentured servants, especially males, found the labor system so harsh that they ran away. Advertisements for them filled the colonial newspapers alongside notices for escaped slaves. Servants knew the penalties if they were caught: whipping and additional service, usually reckoned at twice the time lost to the master but sometimes calculated at a 5 to 1 or 10 to 1 ratio, as in Pennsylvania and Maryland. When war came in the mid-eighteenth century, hundreds of servants fled to the British army, not known for its kindly treatment of soldiers but preferable in many servants' eyes to four or five years under a harsh colonial master.

The goal of every servant was to secure a foothold on the ladder of opportunity. "The hope of buying land in America," a New Yorker noted, "is what chiefly induces people into

America." However, many servants died before serving out their time. Others won freedom only to toil for years as poor day laborers and tenant farmers. Only a small proportion achieved the dream of becoming independent landholders. The indentured servants in the seventeenth-century Chesapeake world suffered fearful mortality rates, but those who survived often rose in society. Among the eighteenth-century servants, ironically, the chances of living long enough to complete the labor contract were much better, but the opportunity to climb into the propertied ranks was less favorable. The chief beneficiaries of the system of bound white labor were not the laborers but their masters.

### Africans in Chains

Among the thousands of ships crossing the Atlantic in the eighteenth century, those that were fitted out as seagoing dungeons for slaves were the most numerous. The slave trade to the southern colonies after the Peace of Utrecht expanded so sharply that within two generations what had been a society with many slaves became a society built on slavery. From 1690 to 1715, annual importations rarely exceeded 1,000, but in the next 15 years the number probably doubled. The generation after 1730 witnessed the largest influx of African slaves in the colonial period, averaging about 5,000 a year. For the entire period from 1700 to 1775 more than 250,000 African slaves entered the American colonies.

Most of these miserable captives were auctioned off to southern planters. Some, however, landed in the northern cities, especially New York and Philadelphia. Merchants sold them there to artisans, farmers, and upper-class householders seeking domestic servants.

Even as the traffic in slaves peaked, a religious and humanitarian opposition to slavery emerged. A few individuals, mostly Quaker, had objected to slavery on moral grounds since the late seventeenth century. But the idea grew in the 1750s that slavery contradicted the Christian concept of brotherhood and the Enlightenment notion of the natural equality of all humans. Abolitionist sentiment was also fed by the growing belief that the master's authority

*New-Providence Township, Philadelphia County, December 19th, 1772.*

RUN AWAY from the subscriber, living in the aforesaid township, on Monday the fourteenth instant, an indented Irish servant man named BARNABAS KELLY, about five feet three inches high, and twenty one years of age, his left eye blind and is near-sighted with the other, has long black hair which he wears tied behind: Had on an old great coat, and a blue cut velvet jacket without buttons, a red outside jacket, and a white linen one without sleeves, an old pair of leather breeches, black stockings, and a pair of new shoes with strings. He took with him about Four or Five Pounds in money, and his own and his master's part of his indentures; also a grey HORSE, which trots mostly and paces a little. Whoever will take up the said servant, and secure him in any gaol, so that I may get him again, shall have FORTY SHILLINGS, and FORTY SHILLINGS more for the horse, and reasonable charges, paid by
EDWARD ROBERTS.

*Like slaves, indentured servants often found it difficult to tolerate the conditions of their employment. Advertisements for the recovery of runaway servants (left) were plentiful in colonial newspapers. No explanation is given for the sale of this servant's time (right). Was her performance unsatisfactory? Did her master unexpectedly need cash?*

TO BE SOLD,
The TIME of an IRISH
SERVANT GIRL,
WHO has about three years to serve. Enquire of the Printers.

"depraved the mind," as the Quaker John Woolman argued. An introspective tailor from New Jersey, Woolman gave his life over in the 1750s to a crusade against slavery. He traveled thousands of miles on foot through the colonies, determined to convince personally every Quaker slaveholder of his or her wrongdoing. Only a few hundred masters freed their slaves in the mid-eighteenth century, but men such as Woolman had nevertheless planted the seeds of abolitionism.

## A LAND OF FAMILY FARMS

Population growth and economic development gradually transformed the landscape of eighteenth-century America. Three variations of colonial society emerged: the farming society of the North, the plantation society of the South, and the urban society of the seaboard commercial towns. Although they shared some important characteristics, each was distinct.

### Northern Agricultural Society

In the northern colonies, especially New England, tightknit farming families, organized in communities of several thousand people, dotted the landscape by the mid-eighteenth century. New Englanders staked their future on a mixed economy. They cleared forests for timber used in barrels, ships, houses, and barns. They plumbed the offshore waters for fish that fed both local populations and the ballooning slave population of the West Indies. And they cultivated and grazed as much of the thin-soiled, rocky hills and bottomlands as they could recover from the forest.

The farmers of the middle colonies—Pennsylvania, Delaware, New Jersey, and New York—set their wooden plows to much richer soils than did New Englanders. They enjoyed the additional advantage of settling an area cleared by Native Americans who had relied more on agriculture than New England tribes. Thus favored, mid-Atlantic farm families produced modest surpluses of corn, wheat, beef, and pork. By the mid-eighteenth century, New York and Philadelphia ships were carrying these foodstuffs not only to the West Indies, always a primary market, but also to areas that could no longer feed themselves—England, Spain, Portugal, and even New England.

In the North, the widespread ownership of land distinguished farming society from every other agricultural region of the Western world. Although differences in circumstances and ability led gradually toward greater social stratification, in most communities the truly rich and abjectly poor were few and the gap between them small compared to European society. Most men other than indentured servants lived to purchase or inherit a farm of at least 50 acres. With their family's labor they could earn a decent existence and provide a small inheritance for each of their children. Settlers valued land highly, for freehold tenure ordinarily guaranteed both economic independence and political rights.

In spite of widespread property ownership, a rising population pressed against a limited land supply by the eighteenth century, especially in New England. Family farms could not be divided and subdivided indefinitely, for it took at least 50 acres (of which only a quarter could be cropped on most farms) to support a single family. In Concord, Massachusetts, for example, the founders had worked farms averaging about 250 acres. A century later, in the 1730s, the average farm had shrunk by two-thirds, as Concordians struggled to provide an inheritance for the three or four sons that the average marriage produced.

The decreasing fertility of the soil compounded the problem of dwindling farm size. When land had been plentiful, farmers planted crops in the same field for three years and then let it lie fallow in pasturage seven years or more until it regained its fertility. But on the smaller farms of the eighteenth century, the land could be rested less often, and farmers had reduced fallow time to only a year or two. Inevitably, such intense use of the soil reduced crop yields, thus forcing farmers to plow marginal land or shift to livestock production. Such was the process that led Jaret Eliot, New England's first agricultural essayist, to refer to "our old land which we have worn out."

The diminishing size and productivity of New England family farms forced many men to move to the frontier or out of the area altogether in the eighteenth century. "Many of our old towns are too full of inhabitants for husbandry, many of them living on small shares of land," bemoaned one resident of eastern Massachusetts. In Concord, one of every four adult males migrated from town every decade from the 1740s on, and in many towns out-migration was even greater. Some drifted south to New York and Pennsylvania. Others sought opportunities as artisans in the coastal towns or took to the sea. More headed for the colony's western frontier or for the northern frontier of New Hampshire and the eastern frontier of Maine. Several thousand New England families migrated even farther north, to the Annapolis valley of Nova Scotia. Throughout New England after the early eighteenth century, most farmers' sons learned to expect that future prospects lay in moving away from their place of birth.

Wherever they took up farming, northern cultivators engaged in agricultural work routines that were far less intense than in the South. The growing season was much shorter, and the cultivation of cereal crops required incessant labor only during spring planting and autumn harvesting. This less burdensome work rhythm led many northern cultivators to fill out their calendars with intermittent work as clockmakers, shoemakers, carpenters, and weavers.

## Changing Values

Boston's weather on April 29, 1695, began warm and sunny, noted the devout merchant Samuel Sewall in his diary. But by afternoon thunder, lightning, and hailstones "as big as pistol and musket bullets" pummeled the town. Sewall dined that evening with Cotton Mather, New England's most prominent Puritan clergyman. Mather wondered why "more ministers houses than others proportionately had been smitten with lightning." The words were hardly out of his mouth before hailstones began to shatter the windows of Sewall's house, "flying to the middle of the room or farther." Sewall and Mather fell to their knees and broke into prayer together "after this awful Providence."

These two third-generation Massachusetts Puritans understood that God was angry with New England—and angry with them as leaders of a people whose piety and moral rectitude were being overtaken by worldliness. Even if farms were getting smaller and open land scarcer, growth and success had undermined early utopian dreams and made Massachusetts "sermon-proof," as one dejected minister put it.

In other parts of the North, the expansive environment and the Protestant emphasis on self-discipline and hard work were also breeding qualities that would become hallmarks of American culture: an ambitious outlook, individualistic behavior, and a love of material things. In Europe, most tillers of the soil expected little from life. With no frontier lands ripe for exploitation, impoverished peasant farmers viewed life not as a quest for achievement but as a deadly struggle against famine and disease. In America, starvation was almost unknown, and few obstacles held people back from uncharted expanses of land once they had overwhelmed the Native Americans. "Every man," one colonist remarked, "expects one day or another to be upon a footing with his wealthiest neighbor."

Religion and commitment to family and community did not disappear in the eighteenth century. Intimate ties of family, church, and locality bound the lives of most. But fewer men and women saw daily existence as a preparation for afterlife. They began to regard land not simply as a source of livelihood but as a commodity to be bought and sold for profit. "Every man is for himself," sighed a Philadelphia leader only a generation after Penn had planted his "holy experiment." A few decades later, a New Yorker wrote that "the only principle of life propagated among the young people is to get money, and men are only esteemed according to what they are worth, that is, the money they are possessed of."

A slender almanac, written by the twelfth child of a poor Boston candlemaker, captured the

In recent years, historians have borrowed methods of analysis from economics and sociology to study social and economic patterns, divisions of wealth within society, the degree of mobility between social ranks, and the pattern of recruitment of elite groups. Understanding how to use quantitative indicators is important because social changes, working silently beneath the surface of public events and involving masses of people, often bring about political tensions that culminate in protest, reform, and sometimes revolution.

In colonial America, contemporary opinion varied widely on how much equality and opportunity existed. Writing from Philadelphia in 1756, a recent German immigrant, Gottlieb Mittelberger, exclaimed, "Even in the humblest or poorest houses, no meals are served without a meat course." Yet the Quaker John Smith noted in his diary, "It is remarkable what an increase of the number of beggars there is about this town this winter." Thomas Hutchinson, one of Boston's wealthiest merchants, believed in 1768 that "in some towns you see scarce a man destitute;" yet in that very year, hundreds of indigent Massachusetts people were wandering into Boston in search of work, and magistrates were dispensing poor relief to approximately one out of every ten adults in the town.

To go beyond such contradictory literary sources, historians have turned to previously unexamined sources such as tax lists and probate records to gain a more precise and verifiable picture of how the structure of wealth and opportunity was changing in eighteenth-century America. These sources are often incomplete and difficult to interpret. But when used cautiously and subjected to modern techniques of statistical analysis, they can provide insights into how the lives of colonial Americans were changing before the Revolution.

Tax records are among the most accessible and useful sources for studying the social structure. A tax assessor's list gives a snapshot of a community's social profile by indicating how much taxable wealth each inhabitant possessed. The list usually included land, houses and barns, rental property, horses and cattle, and servants and slaves. By comparing a series of lists for a single community, historians have been able to measure the degree and pace of change for a number of important social indicators: the proportion of residents owning no land, the changing size of farms and urban properties, the concentration of wealth, and the ownership of indentured servants and slaves.

Two tax-list fragments are reproduced here. One is for a street in Upper Delaware Ward in Philadelphia. It was drawn up to determine the taxes residents owed

## TAX LIST, UPPER DELAWARE WARD, 1767

| | |
|---|---:|
| Leonard Hammond | |
| 1 Negro | £8 |
| William Hodge, merchant | |
| 6 Negroes, 1 horse | 24-13 |
| £18 of Edward Gallean—Southwark | 10-16 |
| £18 of Robt Willson—Southwark | 10-16 |
| £18 of William Gordon—Southwark | 10-16 |
| £18 of Patrick McGavock—Southwark | 10-16 |
| 3 acres of meadow—Moyamensin | 2-5 |
| half a house—Frankford Road | 8 |
| | 78-2 |
| | |
| Arthur Barnes        mariner | 5 |
| William Coon        cordwainer | 3 |
| Joseph Norris        ship carpenter | 4 |
| John Clinton | 3 |
| Thomas Vaughan | 3 |
| Tobias Barthson for George Vanlears Estate | |
| £20 of Tobias Barthson in No. Lib. | 12 |
| £5-10 of Elizabeth Arins in No. Lib. | 3-6 |
| | 15-6 |
| | |
| Thomas Brice        mariner | 5 |
| Edward Beach        cooper | |
| 2 Negroes, 1 horse | 8-13 |
| 2 Servants | 3 |
| Thomas Thompson | 4 |
| Robert Waln        merchant | |
| Dwelling—£80 | 48 |
| 3 Negroes, 1 horse | 12-13 |
| £30 of Isaac Cathrell | 19 |
| £30 of Zachariah Martin | 19 |
| £15 of | 9 |
| £40 of Catherine Hesbruck | 24 |
| £12 of Philip Leary | 7 |
| . . . | |
| | 255 |
| | |
| Isaac Catherall        cooper | 5 |
| Mary McCulloch | 3 |
| William Pollard        merchant | 10 |
| Martha Green | 15 |
| John Pearson        cordwainer | 2 |
| | |
| Stephen Hutchins | 3 |
| Benjamin Worthington | 10 |
| A small shop        £15-9 | |
| William Howard | 2 |

the colonial government to enable it to meet expenses of the Seven Years' War. The assessment was, of course, expressed in pounds and shillings. As you look through the list, you can see that some residents, like William Hodge, had several tenants. Edward Gallean, who rented one of Hodge's houses, paid him £18 for property in Southwark. If you rank the residents in order of their wealth, you can determine how large the gap is between the richest and poorest taxpayers and can see how many people fall into various wealth categories. The list also gives occupations for some of the taxpayers, thus allowing you to make some inferences about the connection between occupation and wealth. It also shows who owns slaves and the number of women who lived on their own.

The second fragment is from rural Chester County, a few miles outside Philadelphia. Even though the categories (land, servants, Negroes, cattle, horses, sheep, mills, etc.) are different, by comparing this information with that for Upper Delaware Ward, you can draw some conclusions about the composition of a rural community and the ways its social structure differed from that of the city. Is wealth more concentrated in the city or the country? Are the gaps between rich and poor similar in both places? Where did slavery appear more common? What generalizations can be made about economic equality and opportunity for eighteenth-century Americans?

## ASSESSOR'S RETURN, CHESTER COUNTY, PENNSYLVANIA, 1759

| | Land | Sow'd | Servants | Negroes | Ages | Cattle | Horses | Sheep | Mills | £ | S | D |
|---|---|---|---|---|---|---|---|---|---|---|---|---|
| Burnett James | 200 | 12 | — | — | — | 7 | 4 | 8 | — | 1 | 17 | 9 |
| Barnard Isaac | 160 | 5 | — | 1 | 16 | 5 | 2 | 6 | — | 1 | 8 | — |
| Connaly Edward | 7 | — | — | — | — | 2 | 2 | — | — | — | 5 | — |
| Carter Jacob Stiller | 66 | 6 | — | — | — | 3 | 2 | 4 | — | — | 10 | — |
| Carter Joseph | 66 | — | — | — | — | 2 | 4 | — | 1 | — | 13 | — |
| Crage James | 50 | 6 | — | — | — | 3 | 2 | 9 | — | — | 12 | — |
| Carter Joseph Smith | 150 | 10 | — | — | — | 4 | 3 | — | — | 1 | 7 | — |
| Cambel John | 50 | 6 | — | — | — | 2 | 2 | 6 | — | — | 11 | — |
| Chamberlin Joseph | 200 | — | — | — | — | — | — | — | — | 1 | 7 | — |
| Chamberlin Isaac | 141 | 16 | — | — | — | 2 | 2 | 6 | — | 1 | 5 | — |
| Carter Samuel | 90 | 8 | — | — | — | 2 | 3 | — | — | — | 15 | — |
| Caldwell Margrat | 100 | — | — | — | — | 1 | — | — | — | — | 12 | 6 |
| Dinge Christopher | 120 | 15 | — | — | — | 4 | 3 | 7 | — | 1 | 4 | — |
| Dutton Joseph Mill Wright | 68 | 4 | — | — | — | 1 | 1 | 4 | — | — | 9 | 9 |
| Darragh John | 100 | 10 | — | — | — | 2 | 1 | 4 | — | — | 18 | — |
| Dutton Kingsman | 6 | 5 | — | — | — | 1 | 1 | — | — | — | 3 | 6 |
| Dutton Richard | 200 | 12 | 1 | — | — | 5 | 3 | 8 | — | 1 | 19 | — |
| Eleson Jared | 100 | 6 | — | — | — | 1 | 1 | — | — | — | 14 | 9 |
| Farra Oliver | — | — | — | — | — | 2 | 1 | — | — | — | 2 | 6 |
| Gillieson John | 50 | — | — | — | — | 4 | 2 | — | — | — | 1 | Free Man |
| Griffith William | 150 | 10 | — | — | — | 3 | 2 | 6 | — | 1 | 2 | — |
| Harclay Thomas | 100 | 11 | — | — | — | — | — | — | — | — | 14 | — |
| Johnson James | — | — | — | — | — | 1 | 1 | — | — | — | 5 | — |
| Linn Hugh | 100 | 7 | — | — | — | 4 | 2 | 6 | — | — | 17 | 6 |
| Lindsay James | 150 | 10 | — | — | — | 6 | 3 | 12 | — | 1 | 9 | — |
| Martin Abraham | 200 | 12 | 1 | — | — | 5 | 3 | 8 | — | 1 | 19 | — |
| Myer Hanry | 100 | 9 | — | — | — | 3 | 3 | — | — | — | 18 | 3 |
| McCloskey Joseph | 130 | 10 | — | — | — | 2 | 2 | 2 | — | 1 | 1 | |
| McMinn John | 50 | 8 | — | — | 51 | — | — | — | — | — | 12 | — |
| Noblet William | 100 | — | — | — | 47 | 4 | 2 | — | — | — | 11 | 9 |
| Peters William | 300 | 20 | 1 | 4 | 36 | 9 | 4 | 14 | 2 | 3 | 13 | 9 |
| Pike Abraham | 29 | 10 | — | — | 12 | 2 | 2 | 2 | — | — | 7 | 6 |
| Perkins John a house and Garden | — | — | — | — | — | — | — | — | — | — | 3 | 9 |
| Richards Edward | — | — | — | 1 | 30 | 2 | — | 6 | — | — | 7 | 6 |
| Reed John | — | 9 | — | — | — | 2 | 1 | — | — | — | 2 | — |
| Richards Jacob | 170 | 13 | — | — | — | 6 | 4 | 7 | — | 1 | 12 | 9 |
| Richards John | 80 | — | — | — | — | — | — | — | — | 1 | Free Man | |
| Richards Jonathan | 130 | 8 | — | — | — | 5 | 1 | 4 | — | 1 | 1 | — |
| Ratten John | 100 | 8 | — | — | — | 3 | 2 | 5 | — | — | 16 | — |
| Shelley Nathan | — | — | — | — | — | 1 | — | — | — | | Poor | |
| Smith Richard | 100 | 3 | — | — | — | 2 | 1 | 2 | — | — | 12 | — |
| Thomson William | 100 | 8 | — | — | — | 2 | 2 | 2 | — | — | 18 | — |
| Tayler Elizabeth | 125 | — | — | — | — | — | — | 1 | — | — | 15 | — |
| Withrow Alexander | — | — | — | — | — | 2 | 1 | — | — | — | 5 | — |
| Withrow William | — | — | — | — | — | 2 | 1 | — | — | — | 5 | — |
| Phillip Taylers Children | 180 | — | — | — | — | — | — | — | — | 1 | 3 | — |

| | Land | Cattle | Horses | £ | S | D |
|---|---|---|---|---|---|---|
| **INMATES** | | | | | | |
| John Bean | — | — | — | — | 3 | 6 |
| Samuel Farra | — | 1 | 1 | — | 5 | — |
| John Farra | — | 2 | — | — | 4 | — |
| Jacob Pike | — | 1 | 1 | — | 5 | — |
| **FREEMEN** | | | | | | |
| Thomas Johnson | | | | 1 | — | — |
| Andrew McMin | | | | 1 | — | — |
| Hugh Redden | | | | 1 | — | — |
| Thomas Marshall | | | | 1 | — | — |
| Rees Peter | | | | 1 | — | — |
| John Lindsey | | | | 1 | — | — |

new outlook with wit and charm. Born in 1706, Benjamin Franklin had climbed the ladder of success spectacularly. Running away from a harsh apprenticeship to an older brother when he was 16, he abandoned a declining Boston for a rising Philadelphia. By 23, he had learned the printer's trade and was publishing the *Pennsylvania Gazette.* Three years later, he began *Poor Richard's Almanack,* next to the Bible the most widely read book in the colonies.

Franklin spiced his annual almanac—the ordinary person's guide to weather and useful information—with quips, adages, and homespun philosophy. Eventually this homely material added up to a primer for success published in 1747 as *The Way to Wealth.* "The sleeping fox gathers no poultry" and "Lost time is never found again," advised Poor Richard, emphasizing that time is money. "It costs more to maintain one vice than to raise two children," he counseled, advocating not morality but practicality. "Sloth makes all things difficult but industry all easy," he assured his readers, while gibing that "God heals, and the doctor takes the fees."

Ever cocky, the individualistic Franklin caught the spirit of the rising secularism of the eighteenth century. He embodied the growing utilitarian doctrine that the good is whatever is useful and the notion that the community is best served through efforts at individual self-improvement and accomplishment.

*Boston-born Benjamin Franklin's wit and pragmatic wisdom made his* **Almanack** *the most widely read book in the colonies after the Bible.*

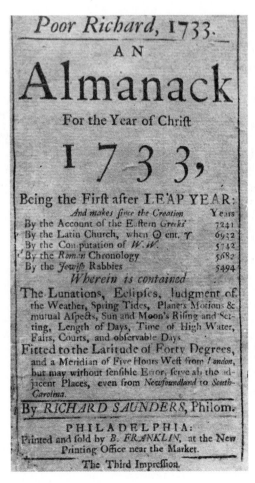

## Woman's Place

In 1662, Elnathan Chauncy, a Massachusetts schoolboy, copied into his writing book that "the soul consists of two portions, inferior and superior; the superior is masculine and eternal; the feminine inferior and mortal." This lesson had been taught for generations on both sides of the Atlantic. It was part of a larger conception of a world, of God's design, that assigned degrees of status and stations in life to all persons. In such a world, the place of women was, by definition, subordinate to that of men. From infancy, women were taught to be modest, patient, compliant. Regarded by men as weak of mind and large of heart, they existed for and through men. As daughters they were subject to their fathers, as wives to their husbands. John Winthrop reflected the common view that such submission was natural and hence "a true wife accounts her subjection her honor."

European women usually accepted these narrowly circumscribed roles. Few complained that their work was generally limited to housewifery and midwifery. Few objected to exclusion from the early public schools or to laws that transferred to their husbands any property or income they brought into marriage. Fewer still objected that women could not speak in church or participate in governing it and had no legal voice in political affairs. Nor did most women expect to choose a husband for love, for parental guidance prevailed in a society in which producing legal heirs was the means of transmitting property. Once wed, women expected to remain so until death, for they could rarely obtain a divorce.

On the colonial frontier, women's lives changed in modest ways. In Europe, about one woman in every ten did not marry. But in the colonies, where men outnumbered women for the first century, a spinster was almost unheard of, and widows remarried with astounding speed. "A young widow with 4 or 5 children, who among the middling or inferior ranks of people in Europe would have little chance for a second husband," observed one Englishman, "is in America frequently courted as a sort of fortune." *Wife* and *woman* thus became nearly synonymous.

*Childbirth was an oft-repeated event in the lives of most colonial wives; note the consistency in age difference among the nine Cheney children.*

A second difference concerned property rights. Single women and widows in the colonies, as in England, could make contracts, convey property, represent themselves in court, and conduct business. Under English law, a woman forfeited these property rights when she married. In the colonies, however, legislatures and courts gave wives more control over property brought into marriage or left at their husbands' death. They also enjoyed broader rights to act for and with their husbands in business transactions. In addition, young colonial women slowly gained the right of consenting to a marriage partner—a right that came by default to the thousands of female indentured servants who completed their labor contracts and had no parents within 3,000 miles to dictate to them.

While colonial society did not encourage or reward female individuality and self-reliance, women acted in competent and complementary ways. Women had limited career choices and rights but broad responsibilities. Moreover, the work spaces and daily routines of husband and wife overlapped and intersected far more than they do today. A farm wife helped with planting and harvesting, milked cows, made butter and cheese, smoked meat, made cloth, and sometimes marketed farm products. The merchant wife kept shop, handled accounts when her husband voyaged abroad, and helped supervise the servants and apprentices. "Deputy husbands" and "yoke mates" were revealing terms used by New Englanders to describe eighteenth-century wives.

In neighborhood life, women also played a central role. Within female networks, dictated by custom rather than by law, older women shaped the behavior of young women, aided the needy, and subtly affected menfolk, who held the formal reins of authority. In church life, where they outnumbered men, women worked privately in their families to promote religion in outlying areas, to seat and unseat ministers, and to influence the community's moral life. Periodically they appeared as visionaries and mystics. Schooled to believe they were inferior and subordinate, women nonetheless operated within their families and localities to shape the world around them.

As midwives, women played one of their most important roles. Until the late eighteenth century, the "obstetrick art" was almost entirely in women's hands. Midwives such as Anne Hutchinson counseled pregnant women, delivered babies, supervised postpartum recovery, and participated in ceremonies of infant baptism and burial. Mrs. Phillips, an immigrant to Boston in 1719 who delivered more than 3,000 infants in her 42-year career, was a familiar figure in town as she hurried through the streets to attend the lying-in of about 70 women each year. Since colonial women were pregnant or nursing infants for about half of the years between 20 and 40 and because childbirth was a recurring and dangerous crisis, the circle of female friends and relatives who attended childbirth created strong networks of mutual assistance.

In her role as wife and mother, the eighteenth-century northern woman differed somewhat from her English counterpart. Whereas English women married in their mid-twenties, American women typically took husbands a few years earlier. This head start increased their childbearing years. Hence the average colonial family included five children (two more typically died in infancy), whereas the English family contained fewer than three. Gradually, as the coastal plain filled up in the eighteenth century and older family farms were divided and subdivided among descendants of the early settlers, marriage age crept up and the number of children per family inched down.

Northern child-bearing patterns differed considerably. In the seventeenth century, stern fathers dominated Puritan family life, and few were reluctant to punish unruly children. "Better whip'd than damn'd," advised Cotton Mather, the minister who served as the Puritan conscience of New England. Many parents believed that breaking the young child's will created a pious and submissive personality. In Quaker families, however, mothers played a more active role in child rearing. More permissive, they relied on tenderness and love rather than guilt to mold their children. Attitudes toward choosing a marriage partner also separated early Puritan and Quaker approaches to family life. Puritan parents usually arranged their children's marriages but allowed them the right to veto. Young Quaker men and women made their own matches, subject to parental veto.

Despite this initial diversity in child rearing, the father-dominated family of New England gradually declined in the eighteenth century. In its place rose the mother-centered family, in which affectionate parents encouraged self-expression and independence in their children. This "modern" approach, which was on the rise in Europe as well, brought the colonists closer to the parenting methods of the coastal Native Americans, who initially had been widely disparaged for their lax methods of rearing their young.

## THE PLANTATION SOUTH

Between 1680 and 1750, the white tidewater settlements of the southern colonies made the transition from a frontier society marked by a high immigration rate, a surplus of males, and an unstable social organization to a settled society composed mostly of native-born families. Scots-Irish and German immigrants flooded into the backcountry of Virginia and the Carolinas after 1715, creating a new southern frontier. But between the piedmont region and the ocean, a mature southern culture took form.

### The Tobacco Coast

Tobacco production in Virginia and Maryland expanded rapidly in the seventeenth century, with exports reaching 25 million pounds annually during the 1680s. But war in Europe and the Americas for the two decades bridging the turn of the century drove up transportation costs and dampened the demand for tobacco. Stagnation in the tobacco market lasted from the mid-1680s until about 1715.

Yet it was precisely in this period that the colonies of the Upper South underwent a profound social transformation. First, slaves replaced indentured servants so rapidly that by 1730 the unfree labor force was almost entirely black. Second, the planters responded to the dull tobacco market by diversifying their crops. They shifted some of their tobacco fields to grain, hemp, and flax; increased their herds of cattle and swine; and became more self-sufficient by developing local industries to produce iron, leather, and textiles. By the 1720s, when a profitable tobacco trade with France created a new period of prosperity, their economy was much more diverse and resilient than in the seventeenth century.

Third, the structure of the population changed rapidly. Black slaves grew from about 7 to 35 percent of the region's population between 1690 and 1750, and the drastic imbalance between white men and women disappeared. Families rather than single men now dominated the Chesapeake landscape. The earlier frontier society of white immigrants who mostly lived short and unrewarding lives as indentured servants grew into an eighteenth-century plantation society of native-born freeholder families.

Notwithstanding the rapid influx of Africans, slave-owning was far from universal. As late as 1750, a majority of families owned no slaves at all. Among slave owners, not more than one-tenth operated plantations with more than 20 slaves. Nonetheless, the common goal was the large plantation where black slaves made the earth yield up profits to support an aristocratic existence for their masters. One Virginia minister observed that "the custom of the country is such that without slaves a man's children stand but a poor chance to marry in reputation."

The Chesapeake planters who acquired the best land and accumulated enough capital to invest heavily in slaves created a gentry life style, setting them apart from ordinary farmers such as Devereaux Jarratt's father. By the eighteenth century, the economic development of the northern colonies had produced prosperous farmers worth several thousand pounds. But such wealth paled by comparison with the estates of men such as Charles Carroll of Maryland or Robert "King" Carter and William Byrd of Virginia. These Chesapeake planters counted their slaves by the hundreds, their acres by the thousands, and their fortunes by the tens of thousands of pounds.

Ritual display of wealth marked southern gentry life. Racing thoroughbred quarter horses and gambling on them recklessly, sometimes for purses of £100 (at a time when a laboring man earned £40 per year) became common sport for young gentlemen, who had often been educated in England. Planters began to construct stately brick Georgian mansions, some designed by imported English architects. These "great houses," similar in style to the houses of English gentry, were filled with imported furniture, attended by liveried black slaves, and graced by formal gardens and orchards.

Hospitality became a hallmark of the genteel southern life style. Philip Fithian, the tutor for a wealthy Virginia planter's children, described the cultivation of this quality. "Whenever any person or family move into a house, or repair [remodel] a house they have been living in before, they make a ball & give a supper . . . in compliance with custom, to invite . . . neighbours and dance and be merry." Even poor planters, "who have but one bed," wrote the colony's first historian, "will sit up . . . all night to make room for a weary traveller."

Some observers saw the cultivated aristocratic life style as a veneer. "If a [man] has Money, Negroes, and Land enough," scoffed a Scottish newcomer, "he is a complete Gentleman. These hide all his defects, usher him into the best of company, and draw upon him the smiles of the fair Sex." Affected or not, the emerging Chesapeake planter elite controlled the county courts, officered the local militia, ruled the parish vestries of the Anglican church, and made law in their legislative assemblies. To their sons they passed the mantle of political and social leadership.

For all their social display, southern planter squires were essentially agrarian businessmen. They spent their days obtaining credit, dealing in land and slaves, scheduling planting and harvesting routines, conferring with overseers, disciplining slaves, and arranging leases with tenants. Cultivating tobacco was a particularly demanding enterprise and a highly personal one. Whereas other staple crops such as wheat and corn required intensive labor only during the planting and harvesting seasons, tobacco demanded the planter's attention throughout the year as the crop moved through the many stages of planting, transplanting, topping, cutting, curing, and packing. A planter's reputation was tied up with the quality of his crop, and so personalized was the culture of tobacco that planters stamped their hogsheads of leaf with their initials or emblem. "Question a planter on the subject," explained one observer, "and he will

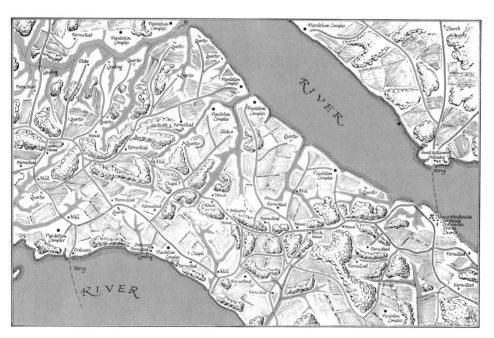

*The distribution of cultivated fields, dwellings, and commercial buildings in the tidewater landscape created "communities" without towns (rendered from historical and archaeological evidence).*

*Westover, the home of William Byrd II, is typical of a later colonial plantation manor.*

tell you that he cultivates such or such a kind [of tobacco], as for example, 'Colonel Carter's sort, John Cole's sort' or [that of] some other leading crop master.''

Planters' wives also shouldered many responsibilities. They superintended cloth production and the processing and preparation of food while ruling over households crowded with children, slaves, and visitors. An aristocratic veneer gave the luster of gentility to plantations from Maryland to North Carolina, but it could not disguise the fact that these were large working farms, often so isolated from each other that the planter and his wife lived a "solitary and unsociable existence," as one phrased it. With only infrequent contact with the outside world, they learned to be independent as they managed their own little communities of servants, slaves, and family members. Patriarchs on their estates, southern planters were "haughty and jealous of

*An idyllic depiction of a backcountry plantation shows the function of the river for transportation, commerce, and communication; power for the mill wheel; and source of fresh fish to help feed the household.*

their liberties, impatient of restraint, and can scarcely bear the thought of being controlled by any superior power," noted Andrew Burnaby, a mid-eighteenth-century visitor.

### The Rice Coast

The plantation economy of the Lower South in the eighteenth century rested on the production of rice and indigo. Rice exports surpassed 1.5 million pounds per year by 1710 and reached 80 million pounds by the eve of the Revolution. Indigo, a blue dye obtained from plants for use in textiles, became a staple crop in the 1740s after Eliza Lucas Pinckney, a wealthy South Carolina planter's wife, experimented successfully with its cultivation. Within a generation, indigo production had spread into Georgia. It soon ranked among the leading colonial exports.

The expansion of rice production transformed the swampy coastal lowlands. In the rice-producing region radiating out from Charleston, planters imported huge numbers of African slaves after 1720; by 1740, they composed nearly 90 percent of the region's inhabitants. White population declined as wealthy planters left their estates in the hands of resident overseers. They wintered in cosmopolitan Charleston and summered in Newport, Rhode Island, their refuge from seasonal malaria along the rice coast. Rice converted the eighteenth-century Carolina coast into a tropical plantation regime similar to that of the sugar-producing West Indies. At mid-century, a shocked New England visitor described it as a society "divided into opulent and lordly planters, poor and spiritless peasants, and vile slaves."

Throughout the plantation South, the courthouse became a central gathering place. Court day brought together people of all classes. They came to settle debts, dispute land boundaries, sue and be sued. When court was over, a multitude lingered on, drinking, gossiping, and staging horse races, cockfights, wrestling matches, footraces, and fiddling contests. Competition

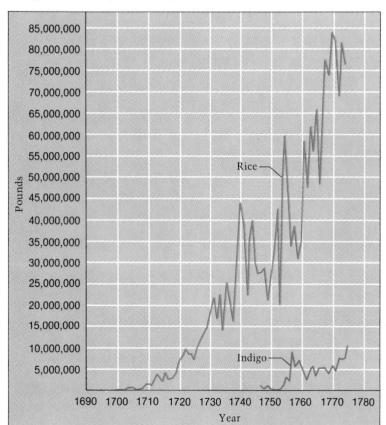

### Rice and Indigo Exports from South Carolina and Georgia, 1698–1775

*Source:* U.S. Bureau of the Census.

*The Carolina lowlands became a vital source of indigo dye for British textile mills in the eighteenth century.*

and assertiveness lay at the heart of all these demonstrations of male personal prowess.

The church, almost always Anglican in the South before 1750, also became a center of community gathering. Philip Fithian described the animated socializing before worship, men "giving and receiving letters of business, reading advertisements, consulting about the price of tobacco and grain, and settling either the lineage, age, or qualities of favourite horses." Then, as the hour of service approached, people filed into church. Reaffirming the social gradation of their rank-conscious society, the lower and middling planters entered first. They stood attentively until the wealthy gentry, striding in together "in a body," took their pews at the front. After church, socializing continued, with young people strolling together and older ones extending invitations to Sunday dinner. The pious Sabbath atmosphere perpetuated in New England was little in evidence.

## The Backcountry

While a stable southern gentry matured along the tobacco and rice coasts, settlers poured into the upland region known as the backcountry. As late as 1730, only hunters and Indian fur traders had known this vast expanse of hilly red clay and fertile limestone soils, stretching from Pennsylvania to Georgia. Over the next four decades it attracted some 250,000 inhabitants, including nearly half the southern white population.

Thousands of land-hungry German and Scots-Irish settlers spilled into the interior valleys running along the eastern side of the Appalachians. They squatted on land wherever they could, lived tensely with neighboring Indians in a region where boundaries were shadowy, and created a subsistence society of small farms. Gradually acquiring slaves, this "mixed medley from all countries and the off scouring of America," as one colonist reported, pursued mixed farming and cattle raising. Their enclaves remained isolated from the coastal region for several generations; and these pioneers clung fiercely to the folkways they had known on the other side of the Atlantic.

The crudity of backcountry life appalled many visitors from the more refined seaboard. In 1733 William Byrd described a large Virginia frontier plantation as "a poor, dirty hovel, with hardly anything in it but children that wallowed about like so many pigs." He sneered at the disorder. "Both cattle and hogs ramble in the neighboring marshes and swamps, where they maintain themselves the whole winter long and are not fetched home til spring." Charles Woodmanson, a stiff-necked Anglican minister who spent three years tramping between settlements in the Carolina upcountry, could hardly find words to express his shock. "Through the licentiousness of the people," he wrote, "many hundreds live in concubinage—swopping their wives as cattle and living in a state of nature more irregularly and unchastely than the Indians."

What Byrd and Woodmason were really observing was the poverty of frontier life and the lack of schools, churches, and towns. Most families plunged into the backcountry with only a few crude household possessions and farm tools, perhaps a pair of oxen, a few chickens and swine, and the clothes on their backs. They lived in rough-hewn log cabins—"cold cabins, unfloored and almost open to the sky," Woodmason observed—and planted their corn, beans, and wheat between the stumps of trees they had felled. Women toiled alongside men, in the fields, forest, and homestead. For a generation, these settlers endured a poor diet, endless work, and meager rewards.

As the Revolution approached, the southern backcountry began to emerge from the frontier stage. Small marketing towns such as Camden, South Carolina; Salisbury, North Carolina; Winchester, Virginia; and Fredericktown, Maryland, became centers of craft activity, church life, and local government. Farms began producing surpluses for shipment east. Density of settlement increased, creating a social life known for harvest festivals, logrolling contests, horse races, wedding celebrations, dances, and prodigious drinking bouts during which hard cider, whiskey, and apple and peach brandy flowed freely. Class distinctions remained narrow compared with the older seaboard settlements, but many backcountry settlements acquired the look of permanence.

## Family Life in the South

As the South emerged from the early era of withering mortality and stunted families, male and female roles gradually became more physically and functionally separated. In most areas, the white sex ratio reached parity by the 1720s. Women lost the leverage in the marriage market that scarcity had provided earlier. With the growth of slavery the work role of white women also changed. The wealthy planter's wife became the domestic manager in "the great house." In a description of his daughters' daily routine, William Byrd II pointed to the emerging female identity: "They are every day up to their elbows in housewifery, which will qualify them effectually for useful wives and if they live long enough for notable women."

The balanced sex ratio and the growth of slavery also brought changes for southern males. The planter's son had always been trained to operate in the world beyond the plantation-house doors. Learning horsemanship, the use of a gun, and the rhythms of agricultural life was as important a part of a young man's education as lessons with tutors such as Jarrett and Fithian. Ordering and disciplining slaves also became a part of the southern youth's education. Many had slaves of their own before reaching adulthood. Some planters worried that this would lead, as Thomas Jefferson would later write, to "odious peculiarities" in the character of southern men since slavery involved "a perpetual exercise of the most boisterous passions" by white masters "nursed, educated, and daily exercised in tyranny." But bred to command, southern planters' sons also developed a self-confidence and authority that would propel many of them into leadership roles during the American Revolution.

On the small farms of the tidewater region and throughout the back settlements, women's roles closely resembled those of northern women. Work assignments were rarely segregated by sex, for women's labor in the fields alongside their menfolk was indispensable. "She is a very civil woman," noted an observer of a southern frontierswoman, "and shows nothing of ruggedness or immodesty in her carriage; yet she will carry a gun in the woods and kill deer and turkeys, shoot down wild cattle, catch and tie hogs, knock down beeves with an ax, and perform the most manful exercises as well as most men in those parts."

Marriage and family life were also more informal in the backcountry. With vast areas unattended by ministers of any religion and courthouses out of reach, most couples married or "took up" with each other in matches unsanctioned by state or church. The arrival of an itinerant clergyman on horseback typically brought forth dozens of couples living in common-law marriage who asked to have vows performed and their children legitimized by baptism. Respectable clergymen saw the frontier settlers living in lascivious abandon. But the poor upcountry hunters and farmers were really only the first of many generations of pioneers who made do as best they could on the forest's edge, where the institutions of settled society had not yet arrived.

## THE URBAN WORLD OF COMMERCE AND IDEAS

Only about 5 percent of the eighteenth-century colonists lived in towns as large as 2,500, and none of the commercial centers boasted a population greater than 16,000 in 1750 or 30,000 in 1775. Yet the urban societies were the cutting edge of social change. Almost all the alterations associated with the advent of "modern" life occurred first in the seaport towns and then radiated outward to the villages, farms, and plantations of the hinterland. In the seaboard centers, the transition first occurred from a barter to a commercial economy, from a social order based on assigned status to one based on achievement, from a rank-ordered and deferential politics to a participatory and contentious politics, and from small-scale craftsmanship to factory production. In addition, the cities were the centers of intellectual life and the conduits through which European ideas flowed into the colonies.

## Sinews of Trade

In the half century after 1690, Boston, New York, and Philadelphia blossomed from urban villages into thriving commercial centers. This urban growth accompanied the development of

## City Plan of Charleston, 1790

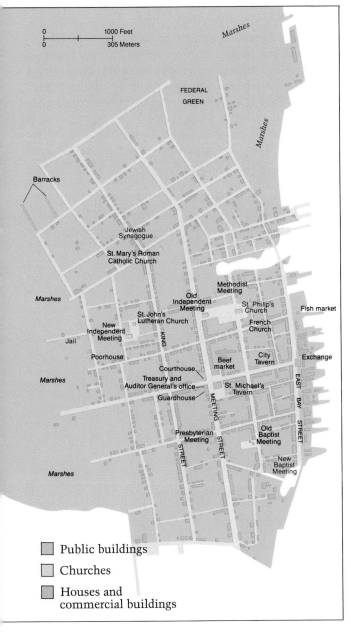

Public buildings

Churches

Houses and commercial buildings

the agricultural interior, to which the seaports were closely linked. As the colonial population rose and spread geographically, minor seaports such as Newport, Providence, Baltimore, Annapolis, Norfolk, and Charleston gathered 10,000 or more inhabitants.

Trade was indispensable to colonial economic life, and cities were trade centers. Through them flowed colonial export staples such as tobacco, rice, wheat, timber products, and fish as well as the imported goods that colonists needed. The imports included manufactured and luxury goods from England such as glass, paper, iron implements, and cloth; wine, spices, coffee, tea, and sugar from other parts of the world; and the human cargo so widely desired to fill the labor gap.

By the eighteenth century, the American economy was integrated into the Atlantic basin trading system that connected Great Britain, western Europe, Africa, the West Indies, and Newfoundland. In the seaboard commercial centers, the pivotal figure was the merchant. He provided the bridge between producers and consumers, coordinating a commercial network that reached from the coastal city to the interior villages, plantations, and frontier trading posts and stretched outward across the Atlantic. Often engaged in both retail and wholesale trade, the merchant was also moneylender (for no banks yet existed), shipbuilder, insurance agent, and often coordinator of artisan production.

The colonists could never produce enough exportable raw materials to pay for the imported goods they craved, so they had to earn credits in England by supplying the West Indies and other areas with foodstuffs and timber products. They also accumulated credit by providing shipping and distributional services. New Englanders became the most ambitious participants in the carrying trade. Sailing from Boston, Salem, Newbury, Marblehead, Newport, and Providence, Yankee merchant seamen, manning Yankee-built ships, dominated the traffic along the Atlantic seaboard, the Caribbean trade, and the transatlantic commerce. A much higher proportion of New England's population made their living in maritime enterprise than in any other colonial region.

## The Artisan's World

Though merchants stood first in wealth and prestige in the colonial towns, artisans were far more numerous. About two-thirds of urban adult males, slaves excluded, labored at handicrafts. By the mid-eighteenth century, the colonial cities contained scores of specialized "leather apron men," not only the proverbial butcher, baker, and candlestick maker but also carpenters and coopers (who made barrels); shoemakers and tailors; silver-, gold-, pewter-, and blacksmiths; mast and sail makers; masons, plasterers, weavers, potters; and many more. Handicraft specialization increased as the cities matured, but every artisan worked with hand tools, usually in small shops, as had generations of craftsmen before him.

Work patterns for artisans were irregular, dictated by weather, hours of daylight, erratic delivery of raw materials, and shifting consumer demand. When the cost of fuel for artificial light exceeded the extra income that he could earn from laboring before dawn or after dusk, what artisan would not shorten his day during winter? When ice blocked northern harbors, mariners and dockworkers endured slack time. If prolonged rain delayed the slaughter of cows in the country or made impassable the rutted roads into the city, the tanner laid his tools aside for lack of hides, and the shoemaker was also idle. The hatter depended upon the supply of beaver skins, which could stop abruptly if disease struck an Indian tribe or war disrupted the fur trade. Every urban artisan knew "broken days," slack spells, and dull seasons. Ordinary laborers dreaded winter, for it was a season when cities had "little occasion for the labor of the poor," and firewood to heat a small house could cost several months' wages.

Urban artisans took fierce pride in their crafts. They saw themselves as the backbone of

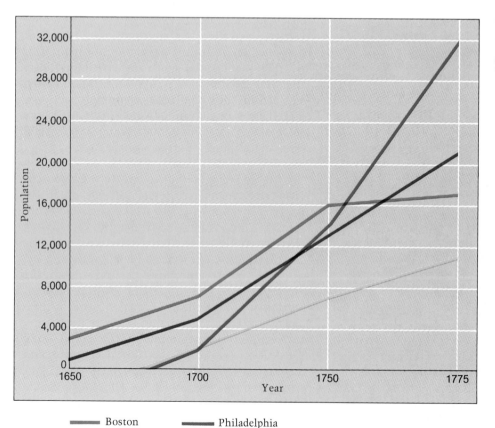

**Urban Population Growth, 1650–1775**

**Source:** Nash, *The Urban Crucible*, 1979.

Boston    Philadelphia

New York    Charleston

the community, contributing essential products and services. "Our professions rendered us useful and necessary members of our community," the Philadelphia shoemakers asserted; "proud of that rank, we aspired to no higher." This artisan self-esteem and desire for community recognition sometimes jostled with the upper-class view of artisans as mere mechanics, part of the "vulgar herd."

In striving for respectability, artisans placed a premium on achieving economic independence. Every craftsman began as an apprentice, spending five or more teenage years learning the "mysteries of the craft" in the shop of a master "mechanick." After fulfilling his contract, the young artisan became a "journeyman." He sold his labor to a master craftsman, often lived in his house, ate at his table, and sometimes mar-

*Working under supervision was thought of as a temporary status by most artisans, who aspired to self-employment. In a high-capital industry such as shipbuilding, only a few attained this goal.*

ried his daughter. The journeyman hoped to complete within a few years the three-step climb from servitude to self-employment. After setting up his own shop, he could control his work hours and acquire the respect that came from economic independence. In trades requiring greater organization and capital, such as distilling and shipbuilding, the rise from journeyman to master proved impossible for many artisans. Nonetheless, the ideal of the independent craftsman prevailed.

In good times, ubran artisans fared well. They expected to earn "a decent competency" and eventually to purchase a small house. In Philadelphia, about half the artisans living in the first half of the eighteenth century left personal property worth between £50 and £200 sterling, an amount signifying a comfortable standard of living. Another quarter left in excess of £200, often including slaves and indentured servants. New England's artisans did not fare so well, for their economy was weaker in the eighteenth century. But in all cities, artisans took pride in their life of productive labor. "The meanest [of them] thinks he has a right of civility from the greatest" person in the city, wrote one city dweller.

The careers of two immigrant families in Philadelphia demonstrate how differently urban artisans fared. Francis Richardson, a Quaker mariner from England, emigrated in the 1680s. He acquired land in Penn's colony, bought several slaves, and at his death in 1688 left his wife and young son in comfortable circumstances. Richardson's widow married a Quaker merchant, and when her son, Francis, Jr., grew of age, he learned the silversmith's trade. Francis, Jr., married Elizabeth Growdon, the daughter of a wealthy Bucks County landowner and passed on to his sons, Francis and Joseph, a place among the Philadelphia Quaker elite when he died in 1729. Francis III practiced silversmithing like his father, but his assets allowed him to engage in mercantile and real estate ventures that made him wealthy enough to retire to a country estate at age 54 and spend the remainder of his life in philanthropic and civic affairs. The Richardsons had risen from mariner to country gentleman, from subsistence to affluence, in three generations.

César Ghiselin, a French Huguenot, also came to America in the 1680s. Establishing himself in Philadelphia as a silversmith, he prospered modestly, ranking just below Francis Richardson, Jr., on the city tax list in 1709. Nine years later he moved to Maryland, but he returned to the Quaker city in 1728 after his wife's death. When he died in 1733, he left a considerable estate. But then the family fortunes collapsed. César's sons, Nicholas and William, made inconspicuous marriages, and though one of them carried on his father's silversmithing trade, they could not consolidate or extend their father's material gains. William's son, named César after his grandfather, became a barber in Philadelphia. By the bitter winter of 1761, his family was receiving aid from the Committee to Alleviate the Miseries of the Poor. The grandson of the first Francis Richardson was on the committee that distributed blankets and firewood to the grandson of the first César Ghiselin. The Ghiselins had declined from silversmith to barber and from middle class to near poverty in three generations.

These two vignettes remind us that in colonial cities, success was far from automatic, even for those following all of Poor Richard's advice about hard work and frugal living. Nor did urban growth and economic expansion guarantee success. An advantageous marriage, luck in avoiding illness, and the size of an inheritance were often the critical factors in whether an artisan moved up or down the ladder of success.

## Urban Social Structure

Population growth, economic development, and a series of wars that punctuated the period from 1690 to 1765 altered the urban social structure. Stately townhouses rose as testimony to the fortunes acquired in trade, shipbuilding, war contracting, and urban land development. This last may have been the most profitable of all. "It is almost a proverb," a Philadelphian observed in the 1760s, "that every great fortune made here within these 50 years has been by land." Some merchants amassed fortunes. A merchant's estate of £2,000 sterling was counted impressive in the early eighteenth century. Two generations later, some commercial titans had become America's first millionaires by accumulating estates of £10,000 to £20,000 sterling.

The rise of Thomas Hancock, upon whose fortune his less commercially astute nephew, John Hancock, would later construct a shining political career, provides a glimpse of how war could catapult the enterprising trader to great wealth. Hancock, a minister's son, became a bookseller in Boston. An opportune marriage to the daughter of a prosperous merchant provided a toehold in commerce and enough capital to invest in shares in several vessels. By 1735, Hancock had made enough money, much of it from smuggling tea, to build a large house on Beacon Hill.

When war broke out with Spain in 1739, Hancock seized new opportunities. Through his connections with the governor, he obtained lucrative supply contracts for military expeditions to the Caribbean and Nova Scotia. He also invested heavily in privateers, who engaged in private warfare against enemy shipping and sold at auction the enemy vessels they overpowered. When peace returned in 1748, all Boston witnessed what war had done for a well-connected merchant. The man who had sold books from a tiny shop on Drawbridge Street 15 years before now imported a four-horse chariot from London with the interior lined in scarlet and the doors emblazoned with a heraldic shield. Hancock also imported a proper English coachman; a man of his affluence could no longer make do with a body servant recruited from the lower class of Boston.

Alongside urban wealth grew urban poverty. From the beginning, every city had its disabled, orphaned, and widowed who required aid. But after 1720, poverty marred the lives of many more city dwellers. Many were war widows with numerous children and no means of support. Others were rural migrants seeking opportunities in the city. Some were recent immigrants, who found fewer chances for employment than earlier. Boston was hit especially hard. Its economy stagnated in the 1740s, and the taxpayers strained under the burden of paying for heavy war expenditures. The overseers of the poor groaned that their relief expenditures were double the outlays of any town of equal size "upon the face of the whole earth."

Burdened with mounting poor taxes, cities devised new ways of helping the poor. Rather than support the impoverished in their homes with "outrelief" payments, officials built large almshouses where the poor could be housed and fed more economically. Many of the indigent preferred "to starve in their homes" rather than leave their neighborhoods to suffer the discipline and indignities of the poorhouse. Boston's poor women also resisted laboring in the linen

**City Plan of Boston, 1772**

Charlestown

Charles River

North Writing School

Christ Church

NORTH BATTERY

North Grammar School

New North Meeting

Second Baptist Meeting

Bennet Street Meeting (Mather's Church)

Mill Pond

First Baptist Meeting

Old North Meeting

New Brick Meeting

West Church

OLD WHARF

Manifesto Church

Powder House

Beacon Hill

Writing School

Faneuil Hall

The Harbor

QUEEN STREET

LONG        WHARF

Prison and courthouse

KING STREET

Almshouse

King's Chapel

First Church

Town House

Bridewell

Friends Meeting

STREET

Workhouse

South Grammar

School Street Meeting

OLD WHARF

Town Granary

Province House

Old South Meeting

Common

South Writing School

MARLBOROUGH

SOUTH BATTERY

THE MALL

Trinity Church

Irish Meeting

Fort Hill

NEWBURY STREET

New Baptist Meeting

Hollis Street Meeting

Boston Neck

Public buildings

Churches

Houses and commercial buildings

factory that was built in 1750 to enable them to contribute to their own support through spinning and weaving. Despite the warnings of Boston's ministers that "if any would not work, neither should they eat," they refused to leave their children at home to labor in America's first textile factory.

The increasing gap between the wealthy and the poor in the colonial cities was recorded in the eighteenth-century tax lists. The urban elite —the top 5 percent of taxpayers—increased their share of the cities' taxable assets from about 30 percent to 50 percent between 1690 and 1770. The bottom half of the taxable inhabitants saw their share of the wealth shrink from about 10 percent to 4 percent. The urban middle classes,

### Wealth Distribution in Colonial America

*Percentage of wealth held by the richest 10% and the poorest 30% of the population in two cities and one rural area*

| YEAR | RICHEST 10% | POOREST 30% |
| --- | --- | --- |
| *Boston* | | |
| 1684–1699 | 41.2 | 3.3 |
| 1700–1715 | 54.5 | 2.8 |
| 1716–1725 | 61.7 | 2.0 |
| 1726–1735 | 65.6 | 1.9 |
| 1736–1745 | 58.6 | 1.8 |
| 1746–1755 | 55.2 | 1.8 |
| 1756–1765 | 67.5 | 1.4 |
| 1766–1775 | 61.1 | 2.0 |
| *Philadelphia* | | |
| 1684–1699 | 36.4 | 4.5 |
| 1700–1715 | 41.3 | 4.9 |
| 1716–1725 | 46.8 | 3.9 |
| 1726–1735 | 53.6 | 3.7 |
| 1736–1745 | 51.3 | 2.6 |
| 1746–1755 | 70.1 | 1.5 |
| 1756–1765 | 60.3 | 1.1 |
| 1766–1775 | 69.9 | 1.0 |
| *Chester County, Pennsylvania* | | |
| 1693 | 23.8 | 17.4 |
| 1715 | 25.9 | 13.1 |
| 1730 | 28.6 | 9.8 |
| 1748 | 28.7 | 13.1 |
| 1760 | 29.9 | 6.3 |
| 1782 | 33.6 | 4.7 |

*Source:* Nash, *the Urban Crucible*, 1979.

except in Boston, continued to make gains. But the growth of princely fortunes amid growing poverty made some urban dwellers reflect on how the conditions of the Old World seemed to be reappearing in the New.

### The Entrepreneurial Ethos

As the colonial cities grew, new values took hold. In the older "corporate" view of society, medieval in origin, economic life ideally operated according to what was equitable, not what was profitable. Citizens usually agreed that government should provide for the general welfare by regulating prices and wages, setting quality controls, licensing providers of service such as tavernkeepers and ferrymen, and supervising public markets where all food was sold. Such regulation seemed natural because a community was defined not as a collection of individuals, each entitled to pursue separate interests, but as a single body of interrelated parts where individual rights and responsibilities formed a seamless web.

In America, as in Europe, new ideas about economic life were gathering support. The subordination of private interests to the commonweal became viewed as a lofty but unrealistic ideal. Prosperity required the encouragement of acquisitive appetites rather than self-denial, for ambition would spur economic activity as more people sought more goods. According to the new view, if people were allowed to pursue their own material desires in open competition, they would collectively form a natural market of producers and consumers. Though impersonal, this market would operate to everyone's advantage.

As the colonial port towns took their places in the Atlantic world of commerce, merchants became accustomed to making decisions according to the emerging commercial ethic that rejected traditional restraints on entrepreneurial activity. If wheat fetched 8 shillings a bushel in the West Indies but only 5 in Boston, a grain merchant felt justified in sending all he could purchase from local farmers to the more distant buyer. The new transatlantic marketplace was indifferent to individuals and local communities. It responded only to the invisible laws of supply and demand.

The underlying tension between the new economic freedom and the older concern for the public good erupted only with food shortages or galloping inflation. Since the American colonies experienced none of the punishing famines that plagued Europe in this period, such crises occurred rarely, usually during war, when demand for provisions rose sharply.

Such a moment struck in Boston during Queen Anne's War. Merchant Andrew Belcher contracted to ship large quantities of wheat to the Caribbean, where higher prices guaranteed him greater profit than he could obtain in Boston. Ordinary neighbors, threatened with a bread shortage and angered that a leading townsman would put profit ahead of community needs, attacked one of Belcher's grain-laden ships in 1710. They sawed through the rudder and tried to run it aground in order to seize the grain. Invoking the older ethic that the public welfare outweighed private interests, they took the law into their own hands. Even the grand jury, composed of substantial members of the community, hinted its approval of the violent action against Belcher by refusing to indict the rioters.

The two conceptions of community and economic life rubbed against each other for many decades. Urban merchants, shopkeepers, land speculators, and ambitious artisans—participants in England's rising commercial empire—cleaved more and more to the new economic formulas, although they continued to voice respect for the old precepts of the corporate community. The clergy continued to preach the traditional message: "Let no man seek his own, but every man another's wealth." But by the mid-eighteenth century, the pursuit of a profitable livelihood, not the social compact of the community, animated most city dwellers.

## The American Enlightenment

Not only ideas about economic life but also about the nature of the universe and improving the human condition reached across the Atlantic to the colonies. In the eighteenth century, an American version of the European intellectual movement called the Enlightenment occurred, and the cities became centers for disseminating these new ideas.

European thinkers, in what is called the Age of Reason, rejected the pessimistic Calvinist concept of innate depravity, replacing it with the optimistic notion that a benevolent God had blessed man with the supreme gift of reason. Thinkers like John Locke, in his influential *Essay on Human Understanding,* argued that God had not predetermined the contents of the human mind but furnished it with the capacity to acquire knowledge. All Enlightenment thinkers prized this acquisition of knowledge, for with its application to human affairs humankind could improve its condition. Through systematic investigation, the secrets of the physical universe might be unlocked, as mathematicians and astronomers such as René Descartes (1596–1650) and Isaac Newton (1642–1727) were showing. Beyond this, scientific knowledge could be applied to human institutions in order to improve society.

The number of educated colonists who read the books of the Enlightenment thinkers was small, but in the eighteenth century they began to make significant contributions to the advancement of science. Naturalists such as John Bartram of Philadelphia ranged the eastern part of the continent gathering and describing American plants as part of the transatlantic attempt to classify all plant life into one universal system of classification. Professor John Winthrop III of Harvard made an unusually accurate measurement of the earth's distance from the sun. Standing above them all was Benjamin Franklin, whose spectacular (and highly dangerous) experiments with electricity, whose properties were just becoming known, gave him an international reputation.

Franklin's true genius as a figure of the Enlightenment came, however, in his practical application of scientific knowledge in the service of an improved life. Among his inventions were the lightning rod, which nearly ended the age-old danger of fires when lightning struck wooden buildings; bifocal spectacles; and an iron stove that heated rooms—in an age when firewood was a major item in the household budget—far more efficiently than the open fireplace commonly used. Franklin also made his adopted home of Philadelphia a center of the American Enlightenment. He played a leading role in founding America's first circulating library in 1731, an artisans' debating club for "mutual improvement" through discussion of the latest ideas from Europe, and an intercolonial scientific society that would emerge in 1769 as the American Philosophical Society. Though most colonists were not educated enough to participate actively in the American Enlighten-

ment, the efforts of men such as Franklin exposed thousands, especially in the cities, to new currents of thought. This led to the growing sense that the colonists, blessed by their abundant environment, might truly inhabit the part of the world where the Enlightenment ideal of achieving a perfect society might be fulfilled.

## THE GREAT AWAKENING

Many of the social, economic, and political changes occurring in the eighteenth-century colonies converged in the Great Awakening, the first of many religious revivals that would sweep American society during the next two centuries. The timing, as well as the religious and social character of the Awakening, varied from region to region. But North and South, from seaboard to frontier, this quest for spiritual renewal challenged old sources of authority and produced patterns of thought and behavior that helped fuel a revolutionary movement in the next generation.

### Fading Faith

Colonial America in the early eighteenth century remained an overwhelmingly Protestant culture. The Puritan, or Congregational, church dominated all of New England except Rhode Island. Anglicanism held sway in much of New York and throughout the South except the backcountry. In the mid-Atlantic and in the back settlements commingled a polyglot of German Mennonites, Dunkers, Moravians, and Lutherans; Scots-Irish Presbyterians; and English Baptists and Quakers.

Yet these diverse groups commanded the allegiance of only about one-third of the colonists. Those who did not belong or went to no church at all remained the majority. In many areas, ministers and churches were simply unavailable. In Virginia, the most populous colony, only 60 clergymen in 1761 served a population of 350,000—one parson for every 5,800 people.

By the eighteenth century, most colonial churches had become voluntary or gathered ("congregated") groups. Congregations formed

for reasons of conscience, not because of government compulsion. Catholics, Jews, and nonbelievers could not vote or hold office. But the persecution of Quakers and Catholics had largely passed, and some dissenting groups by 1720 had gained the right to use long-obligatory church taxes to support their own congregations.

The clergy often found administering their congregations difficult. Anglicans and several German sects maintained close ties to mother churches across the Atlantic, while other denominations made attempts to centralize authority. However, efforts to tighten organization and discipline proved mostly ineffective. For example, Anglican ministers had to be ordained in England and make regular reports to the bishop of London. But once installed in a parish, an Anglican priest found he was hardly in command. In Virginia, to take one case, wealthy planters controlled the vestry (the local church's governing body), and the vestry set the minister's salary and made a habit of driving out ministers who challenged them too forcefully. In Connecticut, the Saybrook Platform of 1708 created a network, or "consociation," of Congregational churches, but individual churches still preserved much of their autonomy.

Though governing their churches frustrated many clergymen, religious apathy was a far more pressing problem in the early eighteenth century. As early as the 1660s, the Congregational clergy of New England had attempted to return wandering sheep to the fold by adopting the Half-Way Covenant. It specified that children of church members, if they adhered to the "forms of godliness," might join the church even if they could not demonstrate that they had undergone a conversion experience. They could not, however, vote in church affairs or take communion.

Adopted in 1662, this compromise kept in the church many children of the founders, and they in turn could pass church membership on to their children. Some ministers took other measures to increase their flocks. Solomon Stoddard, for 60 years patriarch of the Congregational church in Northampton, Massachusetts, gave communion to every professing Christian and used an emotional style of preaching to reap annual "harvests" of souls.

Despite compromises and innovations, most church leaders saw creeping religious apathy when they surveyed their towns. An educated clergy, its energies often drained by doctrinal disputes within denominations, appealed too much to the mind and not enough to the heart. In such a state, as one Connecticut leader remembered it, "the spirit of God appeared to be awfully withdrawn."

## The Awakeners' Message

The Great Awakening was not a homogeneous movement but rather a series of revivals that swept different regions between 1720 and 1760 with varying degrees of intensity. The first stirrings came in the 1720s in New Jersey and Pennsylvania. Theodore Frelinghuysen, a Dutch Reformed minister newly arrived from Holland, fired his congregation through emotional preaching. Avoiding theological abstractions, he concentrated on arousing a need to be "saved" among his parishioners. A neighboring Presbyterian, Gilbert Tennent, soon took up the Dutchman's techniques and enjoyed similar success.

From New Jersey the Awakening spread to Pennsylvania in the 1730s, especially among Presbyterians, and then broke out in the Connecticut River valley. There it was led by Jonathan Edwards, who had succeeded his grandfather, Solomon Stoddard, in Northampton's church. Edwards later became a philosophical giant in the colonies. But as a young man, he gained renown by lambasting his parishioners and promising them that hell awaited unrepentant sinners. "How manifold have been the abominations of your life!" Edwards declared from the pulpit. "Are there not some here that have debased themselves below the dignity of human nature, by wallowing in sensual filthiness, as swine in the mire . . . ? How much of your precious time have you spent away at the tavern, and in drinking companies, when you ought to have been at home seeking God and your salvation!" Edwards paraded one sin after another before his trembling congregants: "God and your own consciences know what abominable lasciviousness you have practised in things not fit to be named, when you have been alone; when you ought to have been reading, or meditating, or on your knees before God in secret prayer."

After cataloging his parishioners' wicked thoughts and deeds, Edwards drew such graphic pictures of the hell awaiting the unrepentant that his Northampton neighbors were soon throwing themselves into preparing for the conversion experience by which they would be "born again." Edwards's *Faithful Narrative of the Surprizing Work of God* (1736), which described his town's awakening, was the first published revival narrative. This literary form would be used many times in the future to fan the flames of evangelical religion.

In 1739, these regional brushfires of evangelicalism began to spread. Instrumental in drawing together the separate local revivals and in inspiring a more scorching religious enthusiasm was a 24-year-old Anglican priest from England named George Whitefield. Inspired by John Wesley, the founder of English Methodism, Whitefield became a master of emotional open-air preaching.

Whitefield made the first of seven barnstorming tours along the American seaboard in 1739 and 1740. Thousands turned out to see him, and with each success his fame and influence grew. Especially in the cities, his effect was extraordinary. People fought for places in the churches when he spoke and gathered by the tens of thousands in open fields to hear his message. Even in sedate Philadelphia, he turned skeptics into true believers, "so that one could not walk thro' town, in an evening," claimed the unreligious Benjamin Franklin, "without hearing psalms sung in different families of every street." In Boston, Whitefield preached to 19,000 in three days. Then, at a farewell sermon, he left 25,000 writhing in fear of damnation. In his wake came American preachers, mostly young men like Devereaux Jarrett, whom he had inspired.

Some of Whitefield's appeal lay in his genius for dramatic performance, some in his tactic of advanced publicity, and some in his ability to simplify theological doctrine and focus people's attention on one facet of religious life, the conversion experience. In electrifying performances, he cast away the conventional written sermon in favor of spontaneous preaching. Using wild body movements and his magnificent voice, he filled thousands with the desire to "fly to Christ."

The appeal of the Awakeners lay not only in the medium but also in the message. They preached that the established, college-trained

*George Whitefield, who first toured the American colonies in 1739 and 1740, inflamed thousands with his emotional sermons.*

clergy was too intellectual and tradition-bound to bring faith and piety to a new generation. Congregations were dead, Whitefield declared, "because dead men preach to them." "The sapless discourses of such dead drones," cried another Awakener, were worthless. The fires of Protestant belief could be reignited only if people individually assumed greater responsiblity for their own conversion.

One of the main forms of individual participation was "lay exhorting." In this personal religious testimony, any person—young or old, female or male, black or white—might rise spontaneously to recount his or her conversion experience and preach "the Lord's truth." This horrified most established clergymen. They allowed no place within the church for lay persons to compete with the educated ministry in preaching the word of God. Lay exhorting shattered the monopoly of the trained clergy on religious discourse and put all people on the same plane. It gave new importance to the oral culture of common people, whose spontaneous outpourings contrasted sharply with the controlled literary culture of the gentry. Through lay exhorting, ordinary men and women, and even children, servants, and slaves, crossed class lines and defied assigned roles.

How religion, social change, and politics became interwoven in the Great Awakening can be seen by examining two regions swept by revivalism. Both Boston, the heartland of Puritanism, and interior Virginia, a land of struggling small planters and slave-rich aristocrats, experienced the Great Awakening, but in different ways and at different times.

### The Urban North

In Boston, revivalism ignited in the midst of political controversy. Since 1739, the citizens had argued strenuously about remedies for the severe depreciation of the province's paper currency, which had been issued for years to finance military expeditions against French Canada. The English government insisted that Massachusetts retire all paper money by 1741. Searching for a substitute circulating medium, one group proposed a land bank to issue private bills of credit backed by land. Another group proposed a silver bank to distribute bills of credit backed by silver. Controversy over the land and silver banks swept politics in 1740 and 1741, pitting large merchants, who preferred the fiscally conservative silver bank, against local traders, artisans, and the laboring poor, who preferred the land bank.

Whitefield's arrival in Boston coincided with the currency furor. He first preached shortly after leading merchants announced they would not accept land bank bills for payment. His stay in Boston overlapped with attacks on these merchants as "gripping and merciless usurers" who "heaped up vast estates" at the expense of the common people. At first Boston's elite applauded Whitefield's ability to call the masses to worship. The master evangelist, it seemed, might restore social harmony by redirecting people from earthly matters such as the currency dispute to concerns of the soul.

When Whitefield left Boston in 1740, he was succeeded by Gilbert Tennent, whom he had instructed "to blow up the divine fire lately kindled there." Tennent deeply offended the town's upper class and the clergy. During an unusually harsh winter, thousands of Bostonians stood in deep snow to hear his attacks on the "unconverted" clergy, on aristocratic fashion, and on the self-indulgent accumulation of wealth.

James Davenport, who arrived in 1742, pushed such denunciations farther. His great-grandfather had been a founder of New Haven, and his father was a respected Congregational minister in Stamford, Connecticut. But the 25-year-old Davenport, who had been inspired by Whitefield, appeared anything but respectable to the elite. He arrived with a reputation for barnstorming performances that turned into street singing, all-night revival meetings, and emotional outpourings that went far beyond religion.

In Boston, Davenport found every church closed to him, even those whose clergy had embraced the Awakening. This mattered little to the young spellbinder, for his natural amphitheater was the street or field. Moreover, the condemnation from the top of society was a recommendation to the bottom, where deference was crumbling among "God's people," as the radical revivalists called the poor. Davenport's daily appearances on Boston Common aroused religious ecstasy among thousands and

stirred up feeling against Boston's leading figures. Respectable people grew convinced that revivalism had gotten out of hand, for by this time ordinary people were verbally attacking opponents of the land bank in the streets as "carnal wretches, hypocrites, fighters against God, children of the devil, cursed Pharisees." A revival that had begun as a return to religion among backsliding Christians had overlapped with political affairs. Hence it threatened polite culture, which stressed order and discipline from ordinary people.

### The Rural South

The Great Awakening was subsiding in New England and the middle colonies by 1744, although aftershocks continued for another generation. But in Virginia, where the initial religious earthquake was barely felt, tremors of enthusiasm rippled through society from the mid-1740s onward. As in Boston, the Awakeners challenged and disturbed the gentry-led social order.

Whitefield stirred some religious fervor during his early trips through Virginia. But the first large outburst came in 1742, when William Robinson began preaching in frontier settlements. Traveling "New Light" preachers, led by the brilliant orator Samuel Davies, were soon gathering large crowds both in the backcountry and in the traditionally Anglican parishes of the older settled areas.

By 1747, worried Anglican clergyman convinced the governor to issue a proclamation restraining strolling preachers. As in other colonies, officers of Virginia's government despised traveling evangelists, for like lay exhorters, these roving Awakeners conjured up a world without properly constituted authority. As one critic in Virginia put it in 1745, the wandering preachers were "those who have turned the world upside down." When the Hanover County court gave the fiery James Davenport a license to preach in 1750, the governor ordered the suppression of all circuit riders.

New Light Presbyterianism, which challenged the religious monopoly of the gentry-dominated Anglican church, continued to spread in the 1750s. The evangelical cause advanced further with the rise of the Baptists in the 1760s. Renouncing finery, attacking ostentatious display, addressing each other as "brother" and "sister," and committing themselves to a new spirit of community, the Baptists reached out to thousands of unchurched people. As among earlier northern revivalists, they focused on the conversion experience. Many of their preachers were uneducated ordinary farmers and artisans who called themselves "Christ's poor." They stressed a general equality in human affairs and insisted that heaven was always more populated by the humble poor than by the purse-proud rich. Among the poorest of all, Virginia's 140,000 slaves in 1760, the evangelical message penetrated deeply.

The insurgent Baptist movement in rural Virginia was both a quest for a personal, emotionally satisfying religion among ordinary folk and a rejection of the gentry's social values. It brought from the pulpits of the established clergy the same denunciations that had been voiced earlier in urban New England. In both regions, social changes had weakened the cultural authority of the upper class and, in the context of religious revival, produced a vision of a society drawn along different, more equal lines.

### The Awakening's Legacy

By the time George Whitefield returned to America for his third tour in 1745, the revival had burned out in the North. Its effects, however, were long-lasting. The Awakening promoted religious pluralism and nourished the idea that all denominations were equally legitimate; none had a monopoly on the truth. Whitefield had anticipated this tendency when he called out during a sermon: "Father Abraham, whom have you in heaven? Any Episcopalians? And the answer came back, No! Any Presbyterians? No! Any Independents or Methodists? No, no, no! Whom have you there? And the final answer came down from heaven, We don't know the names here. All who are here are Christians."

By legitimizing the dissenting Protestant groups that had sprung up in seventeenth-century England, the Great Awakening gave competing Protestant churches, which had rubbed abrasively for generations, a theory for living together in relative harmony. From this framework of denominationalism came a second change—the separation of church and state. Once a variety of churches gained legitimacy, it was hardly possible for any one church to claim special privileges. In the seventeenth century, Roger Williams had tried to sever church and state because he believed that ties with civil bodies would corrupt the church. But during the Awakening, groups such as the Baptists and Presbyterians in Virginia constituted their own religious bodies and broke the Anglican monopoly as *the* church in the colony. This undermining of the church-state tie would be completed during the Revolutionary era.

A third effect of the revival was to bolster the view that diversity within communities, for better or worse, could not be prevented. Almost from the beginning, Rhode Island, the Carolinas, and the middle colonies had recognized this. But homogeneity had been prized elsewhere, especially in Massachusetts and Connecticut. In these colonies, the Awakening split even Congregational churches into New Lights and Old Lights. Mid-Atlantic Presbyterian churches were similarly beset by schisms. And everywhere the Baptists, once a small persecuted sect, made spectacular gains. In hundreds of rural communities by the 1750s, two or three churches existed where only one had stood before. People learned that the fabric of community could be woven from threads of more than one hue.

New eighteenth-century colonial colleges reflected the religious pluralism symbolized by the Great Awakening. Before 1740 there existed only three. Harvard and Yale had been founded in 1636 and 1701, respectively, to provide New England with educated ministers, and William and Mary had been chartered in 1696 as an Anglican institution. To these small seats of higher education were added six new colleges between 1746 and 1769.

In spite of ties to particular denominations, none of the new colleges was controlled by an established church, all had governing bodies composed of men of different faiths, and all admitted students regardless of religion. Eager for students and funds, they made nonsectarian appeals and constructed classical curricula mixed with natural sciences and natural philosophy.

Yale College, founded in 1701, was one of only three institutions of higher learning in the colonies before the Great Awakening.

## Colonial Colleges

| NAME | COLONY | FOUNDING DATE | DENOMINATIONAL AFFILIATION |
|---|---|---|---|
| Harvard College | Massachusetts | 1636 | Congregational |
| College of William and Mary | Virginia | 1693 | Anglican |
| Yale College | Connecticut | 1701 | Congregational |
| College of New Jersey (Princeton) | New Jersey | 1746 | Presbyterian |
| College of Philadelphia (University of Pennsylvania) | Pennsylvania | 1754 | Secular |
| King's College (Columbia) | New York | 1754 | Anglican |
| College of Rhode Island (Brown) | Rhode Island | 1764 | Baptist |
| Queen's College (Rutgers) | New Jersey | 1766 | Dutch Reformed |
| Dartmouth College | New Hampshire | 1769 | Congregational |

Last, the Awakening nurtured a subtle change in values that crossed over into politics and daily life. Especially for ordinary people, the revival experience created a new feeling of self-worth. People flocked to spontaneous meetings, assumed new responsibilities in religious affairs, and became skeptical of dogma and authority. The multitudes moved by the Awakeners learned to take some matters into their own hands. Many of them, most notably among the fast-growing Baptists, decried the growing materialism and deplored the new acceptance of self-interested behavior. He who was "governed by regard to his own private interest," Gilbert Tennent preached, was "an enemy to the public," for in true Christian communities "mutual love is the band and cement." By learning to oppose authority and to take part in the creation of new churches, thousands of colonists unknowingly rehearsed for revolution.

## POLITICAL LIFE

"Were it not for government, the world would soon run into all manner of disorders and confusions," wrote a Massachusetts clergyman early in the eighteenth century. "Men's lives and estates and liberties would soon be prey to the covetous and the cruel," and every man would be "as a wolf" to his neighbors. Few colonists, wherever they lived, would have disagreed. On both sides of the Atlantic, it was widely believed that government must be erected to protect life, liberty, and property.

How to guarantee these protections was a thorny question, however, for history recorded many forms of government. American colonists naturally drew heavily upon inherited political ideas and institutions. These were almost entirely English in origin because English charters sanctioned settlement, English governors ruled the colonies, and English common law governed the courts. But in a new environment, where they met unexpected circumstances, the colonists modified familiar political forms to suit their needs.

### Structuring Colonial Governments

As in all societies, determining the source of political authority was fundamental. In England, the notion of the God-given supreme authority of the monarch had disintegrated long before the planting of the colonies. In its place stood the belief that stable and enlightened government depended on balancing the interests of monarchy, aristocracy, and democracy. Each of these pure forms of government would degenerate into oppression if unleavened by the other two. Monarchy, the rule of one, would become despotism. Aristocracy, the rule of the few, would turn into corrupt oligarchy. Democracy, the rule of the many, would descend into anarchy or mob rule. The Revolution of 1688 in England, by thwarting the king's pretensions to greater power, seemed to most colonists a vindication and strengthening of a carefully balanced political system.

In colonial governments, political balance was contrived somewhat differently. The governor was the king's agent or, in proprietary colonies, the agent of the king's delegated authority. The council, composed of wealthy appointees of the governor in most colonies, was a pale equivalent of the English House of Lords. The assembly, elected by the white male freeholders, functioned as a replica of the House of Commons. "The concurrence of these three forms of government," wrote a Bostonian in 1749, "seems to be the highest perfection that human civil government can attain to."

Bicameral legislatures developed in most of the colonies in the seventeenth century. The lower houses, or assemblies, represented the local interests of the people at large. The upper houses, or councils (which also sat as the highest courts), represented the nascent aristocracy. Except in Rhode Island and Connecticut, every statute required the governor's assent and all colonial laws required final approval from the king's privy council. This royal check on colonial lawmaking operated imperfectly, however. It took many months to send laws to England, to consider them there, and to return word concerning final approval or rejection. In the meantime, the laws set down in the colonies took force.

Behind the formal structure of politics stood the rules governing who could participate in the political process. In England since the fifteenth century, the ownership of land had largely defined electoral participation (women and non-Christians were uniformly excluded). Only those with property sufficient to produce an annual rental income of 40 shillings could vote or hold office. The colonists closely followed this principle, except in Massachusetts, where it took until 1691 to break the requirement of church membership for suffrage. As in England, the poor and propertyless were excluded, for they lacked the "stake in society" that supposedly transformed unpredictable, ignorant creatures into thoughtful and responsible voters.

Whereas in England the 40-shilling freehold requirement was intended to restrict the size of the electorate, in the colonies, because of the cheapness of land, it conferred the vote on a large proportion of adult males. Between 50 and 75 percent of the adult free males could vote in most colonies. As the proportion of landless colonists increased in the eighteenth century, however, the franchise slowly became more limited.

## Colonial Foundations of the American Political System

| | |
|---|---|
| 1606 | Virginia companies of London and Plymouth granted patents to settle lands in North America. |
| 1619 | First elected colonial legislature meets in Virginia. |
| 1634 | Under a charter granted in 1632, Maryland's proprietor is given all the authority "as any bishop of Durham" ever held–more than the king possessed in England. |
| 1635 | The council in Virginia deports Governor John Harvey for exceeding his power, thus asserting the rights of local magistrates to contest authority of royally appointed governors. |
| 1643 | The colonies of Massachusetts, Plymouth, Connecticut, and New Haven draw up articles of confederation and form the first intercolonial union, the United Colonies of New England. |
| 1647 | Under a charter granted in 1644, elected freemen from the Providence Plantations draft a constitution establishing freedom of conscience, separating church and state, and authorizing referenda by the towns on laws passed by the assembly. |
| 1677 | The Laws, Concessions and Agreements for West New Jersey provide for a legislature elected annually by virtually all free males, secret voting, liberty of conscience, election of justices of the peace and local officeholders, and trial by jury in public so that "justice may not be done in a corner." |
| 1689 | James II deposed in England in the Glorious Revolution, and royal governors, accused of abusing their authority, ousted in Massachusetts, New York, and Maryland. |
| 1701 | First colonial unicameral legislature meets in Pennsylvania under the Frame of Government of 1701. |
| 1735 | John Peter Zenger, a New York printer, acquitted of seditious libel for printing attacks on the royal governor and his faction, thus widening the freedom of the press. |
| 1754 | First congress of all the colonies meets at Albany (with seven colonies sending delegates) and agrees on a Plan of Union (which is rejected by the colonies and the English government). |
| 1765 | The Stamp Act Congress, the first intercolonial convention called outside England's authority, meets in New York. |

Though voting rights were broadly based, most men assumed that only those of substantial wealth and social status were entitled to hold positions of political power. Lesser men, it was held, ought to defer to their betters. Balancing this elitist conception of politics, however, was the notion that the entire electorate should periodically judge the performance of those they entrusted with political power and reject those who represented them inadequately. Unlike the members of the English House of Commons, who by the seventeenth century thought of themselves as representing the entire nation, the colonial representatives were expected to reflect the views of those who elected them locally. Believing this, their constituents judged them accordingly.

When were citizens entitled to defy those who ruled them? The answer to this vexing question followed English precedent: the people were justified in badgering their leaders, protesting openly, and, in extreme cases of abuse of power, assuming control in order to rectify the situation. The uprisings in the colonies associated with England's Glorious Revolution represented such moments when the deferential mass transformed itself into a purposeful crowd in order to overthrow those who trampled on their traditional English liberties.

## The Crowd in Action

What gave special power to the common people when they assembled to protest oppressive authority was the general absence of effective police power. In the countryside, where most colonists lived, only the county sheriff, with an occasional deputy, insulated civil leaders from angry farmers. In the towns, police forces were still unknown. Only the sheriff, backed up by the night watch, safeguarded public order. As late as 1757, the night watch of New York was described as a "parcell of idle, drinking vigilant snorers, who never quelled any

*The Philadelphia Paxton incident, in which townspeople "did decline / For to Go to the Barracks their duty to Do/over some Indians, who never were true," exemplifies the conflicts that arose within settler society as the colonies matured.*

nocturnal tumult in their lives." In theory the militia stood ready to suppress public disturbances, but both urban and rural crowds usually included many of the very people who composed the militia.

Since agencies of law enforcement were weak, the potential for political action outside formal legislative channels was never so great as in the colonial period. Crowd action, frequently effective, gradually achieved a kind of legitimacy. The assembled people became perceived as the watchdog of government, ready to chastise or drive from office those who violated the collective sense of what was right and proper.

Boston's impressment riot of 1747 vividly illustrates the people's readiness to resist incursions on their inherited privileges and the weakness of law enforcement. It began when Commodore Charles Knowles, commander of the British Royal Navy in North American waters, brought his fleet to Boston for reprovisioning—and to replenish the ranks of mariners thinned by desertion. England was at war with France, and the fleet was being readied for engagements against the enemy. Hence, Knowles sent press gangs out on a chill November evening with orders to fill the crew vacancies from Boston's waterfront population. They operated under a hated English law authorizing ship captains to press into service as many colonial subjects as they required. The British dragnet scooped up artisans, laborers, servants, and slaves, as well as merchant seamen from ships riding at anchor in the harbor.

But before the press gangs could hustle their victims back to the British men-of-war, a crowd of angry Bostonians seized several British officers; surrounded the governor's house, where other naval officers had taken refuge; and demanded the release of their townsmen. When the sheriff and his deputies attempted to intervene, the mob mauled them. The militia, called to arms by the governor to "suppress the mob by force, and if need be to fire upon 'em with ball," refused to respond. By dusk a crowd of several thousand, defying the governor's orders to disperse, had stoned the windows of the governor's house and dragged a royal barge from one of the British ships into the courtyard of his house. There they burned it amid cheers.

Enraged by the defiant Bostonians, Commodore Knowles threatened to bombard the town. Only determined negotiations, conducted during several days of further tumult, averted a showdown. Finally, Knowles released the impressed Bostonians. In the aftermath of the riot, a young politician named Samuel Adams defended Boston's defiance of royal authority. The people, he argued, had "a natural right" to band together against press gangs that deprived them of their liberty. Local magnates who supported the governor in this incident were labeled "tools to arbitrary power."

## The Growing Power of the Assemblies

Incidents such as the Boston impressment riot of 1747 dramatically demonstrated the touchiness of England's colonial subjects. But a more gradual and restrained change—the growing ambition and power of the legislative assemblies—was far more important. For most of the seventeenth century, royal and proprietary governors had exercised greater power in relation to the elected legislatures than did the king in relation to Parliament. The governors could dissolve the lower houses and delay their sitting, control the election of their speakers, and in most colonies initiate legislation with their appointed councils. Colonial governors also had authority to appoint and dismiss judges at all levels of the judiciary and to create chancery courts, which sat without juries. Governors also controlled the expenditure of public monies and had authority to grand land to individuals and groups, which they sometimes used to confer vast estates upon their favorites.

By the 1730s, many of the proprietary governments had been replaced by royal governments. In the seventeenth century, Virginia, Massachusetts, and New York had become royal colonies, with governors appointed by the crown. In the eighteenth century, royal government came to New Jersey (1702), South Carolina (1719), and North Carolina (1729).

Many of the royal governors were competent military officers or bureaucrats, but often they were simply recipients of patronage posts. They were rewarded for who they knew, not what they had done or might accomplish. A few were psychologically damaged, like Sir Danvers Osborn, who committed suicide a week after arriving in New York in 1753. Many were corrupt, such as Pennsylvania's William Denny, who tried to build a fortune in the 1750s by selling flags of truce to merchants, which enabled them to ship goods to the enemy under the pretext of engaging their vessels in prisoner exchanges. Some governors never took up their posts at all, preferring, like the earl of Orkney, Virginia's royal governor from 1705 to 1737, to pocket the salary and pay a part of it to other men who went to the colony as lieutenant governor. But most governors were neither crazy, corrupt, nor absent; they were merely mediocre.

In the eighteenth century, elected colonial legislatures challenged the swollen executive powers of these colonial governors. The governors lacked the extensive patronage power that in England enabled ministers of government to manipulate elections and buy off opposition groups. They could therefore contest but not prevent encroachments on their power. Bit by bit, the representative assemblies won new rights—to initiate legislation, to elect their own speakers, to settle contested elections, to discipline their membership, and to nominate provincial treasurers who controlled the disbursement of public funds. The most important gain of all was acquiring the "power of the purse"—the authority to initiate money bills, which specified how much money should be raised by taxes and how it should be spent.

Originally thought of as advisory bodies, the elected assemblies gradually transformed themselves into governing bodies reflecting the interests of the electorate. The Glorious Revolution had eroded royal power in England in the late seventeenth century. Thereafter, colonial executive power, an extension of royal power in the colonies, also gave ground to the ambitious legislative assemblies. Governors complained bitterly about the "levelling spirit" and "mutinous and disorderly behavior" of the assemblies, but they could not stop their rise.

## Local Politics

Binding elected officeholders to their constituents became an important feature of the colonial political system. In England, the House of Commons was filled with representatives from "rotten boroughs," ancient places left virtually uninhabited by population shifts, and with men whose vote was in the pocket of the ministry because they had accepted crown appointments, contracts, or gifts. The American assemblies, by contrast, contained mostly representatives sent by voters who instructed them on particular issues and held them accountable for serving local interests.

Royal governors and colonial grandees who sat as councillors often deplored this localist, popular orientation of the people's representatives. The assemblies, sniffed one aristocratic New Yorker, were crowded with "plain, illiterate husbandmen [small farmers], whose views seldom extended farther than the regulation of highways, the destruction of wolves, wildcats, and foxes, and the advancement of the other little interests of the particular counties which they were chosen to represent." In actuality, the voters mostly sent merchants, lawyers, and substantial planters and farmers to represent them in the lower houses, and by the mid-eighteenth century in most colonies these men had formed political elites. But it was true that they represented the local interests of their constituents. They prided themselves on doing so, for they saw themselves as bulwarks against oppression and arbitrary rule, which history taught them were most frequently imposed by monarchs and their appointed agents.

Local government was usually more important to the colonists than provincial government. In the North, local political authority generally rested in the towns. The New England town meeting decided a wide range of matters. In making decisions, the meeting strived for consensus, searching and arguing until it could express itself as a single unit. "By general agreement" and "by the free and united consent of the whole" were phrases denoting a decision-making process that sought participatory assent rather than a democratic competition among differing interests and points of view.

In the South, the county constituted the primary unit of government. No equivalent of the town meeting existed for placing local decisions before the populace. The planter gentry ruled the county courts, as they did the legislature, while substantial farmers served in minor offices such as road surveyor and deputy sheriff. At court sessions, usually convened four times a year, deeds were read aloud and then recorded, juries impaneled and justice dispensed, elections held, licenses issued, and proclamations read aloud. On election days, gentlemen treated their neighbors (upon whom they depended for votes) to "bumbo," "kill devil," and other forms of alcoholic treats. By the mid-eighteenth century, a landed squirearchy of third- and fourth-generation families had achieved political dominance.

## The Spread of Whig Ideology

Whether in local or provincial affairs, a political ideology called Whig or "republican" had become embedded in the minds of most people as the colonies reached the middle of the eighteenth century. The canons of this body of thought, inherited from England, flowed from the belief that concentrated power was historically the enemy of liberty and that too much power lodged in any person or group inevitably brought corruption and tyranny. The best defenses against concentrated power were balanced government, elected legislatures adept at checking executive authority, prohibition of standing armies (almost always controlled by tyrannical monarchs to oppress the people), and eternal vigilance by the people in watching their leaders for telltale signs of corruption.

Much of this Whig ideology reached the people through the newspapers that began appearing in the seaboard towns in the early eighteenth century. The first was the *Boston News-Letter*, founded in 1704. By 1763, 23 papers circulated in the colonies. Though limited to a few pages and published only once or twice a week, the papers passed from hand to hand and were read aloud in taverns and coffeehouses. In this way their contents probably reached most households in the towns and a substantial minority of farmsteads in the countryside.

By the 1730s, newspapers had become an important conduit of Whig ideology. Many of them reprinted material from English Whig writers who railed against corruption and creeping despotism in the reign of George II (1727–1760). Particularly popular were the essays of John Trenchard and Thomas Gordon, whose *Cato's Letters* and *Independent Whig* found their way into the private libraries of many colonists and were widely reprinted in the newspapers.

The new power of the press and its importance in guarding the people's liberties against would-be tyrants, such as abrasive royal governors, was vividly illustrated in the Zenger case in New York. Young John Peter Zenger, a printer's apprentice, had been hired in 1733 by the antigovernment faction of Lewis Morris to start a newspaper that would publicize the tyrannical actions of Governor William Cosby. In Zenger's *New-York Weekly Journal*, salvos were rapidly fired at Cosby's interference with the courts and his alleged corruption in giving important offices to his henchmen. New Yorkers believed, said one essay published by Zenger, "that their LIBERTIES and PROPERTIES are precarious, and that SLAVERY is like to be tailed on them and their posterity if some things past are not amended."

This and other bruising indictments of the governor led to Zenger's arrest for seditious libel. He was rescued from an early end to his career by the brilliant defense of Andrew Hamilton, a Philadelphia lawyer hired by the Morris faction to convince the jury that Zenger was innocent of everything but trying to inform the people of attacks on their liberties. Although Zenger was acquitted, the libel laws remained very restrictive. But the acquittal did reinforce the notion that the government was the people's servant, and it brought home the point that public criticism was an effective tool in keeping people with political authority responsible to the people they ruled.

## CONCLUSION: America in 1750

The American colonies, robust and expanding, matured rapidly in the first half of the eighteenth century. Transatlantic commerce linked them closely to Europe, Africa, and other parts of the New World. Churches, schools, and towns—the visible marks of the receding frontier—appeared everywhere. A balanced sex ratio and stable family life had been achieved throughout the colonies. Seasoned political leaders and familiar political institutions functioned from Maine to Georgia.

Yet the sinew, bone, and muscle of American society had not yet fully knit together. The polyglot population, one-fifth of it bound in chattel slavery and its Native American component still unassimilated and uneasily situated on the frontier, was a kaleidoscopic mixture of ethnic and religious groups. Its economy, while developing rapidly, showed weaknesses, particularly in New England, where land resources had been strained. The social structure reflected the colonizers' emergence from a frontier stage, but the consolidation of wealth by a landed and mercantile elite was matched by pockets of poverty appearing in the cities and some rural areas. Full of strength yet marked by awkward incongruities, colonial Americans in 1750 approached an era of strife and momentous decisions.

## Recommended Reading

James A. Henretta provides a good introduction to the growth and development of eighteenth-century colonial society in *The Evolution of American Society* (1973). On immigration and immigrant groups, see Stephanie G. Wolf, *Urban Village: Population, Community, and Family Structure in Germantown, Pennsylvania* (1977); Jon Butler, *The Huguenots in Colonial America* (1983); and Ned Landsman, *Scotland and Its First American Colony* (1985).

On the development of the northern colonies, rich material can be found in Richard Bushman, *From Puritan to Yankee* (1967); Christopher M. Jedrey, *The World of John Cleaveland* (1979); Laurel T. Ulrich, *Good Wives* (1982); Sung Bok Kim, *Landlord and Tenant in the Colony of New York* (1976); and James Lemon, *The Best Poor Man's Country* (1972).

The transformation of eighteenth-century southern society is the subject of Paul Clemens, *The Atlantic Economy and Colonial Maryland's Eastern Shore* (1980); Carville Earle, *The Evolution of a Tidewater Settlement System* (1975); and Rhys Isaac, *The Transformation of Virginia* (1982).

For commercial and intellectual life in the cities, much can be learned from Bernard Bailyn, *The New England Merchants in the Seventeenth Century* (1955); Gary M. Walton and James F. Shepherd, *The Economic Rise of Early America* (1979); J. E. Crowley, *This Sheba Self: The Conceptualization of Economic Life in Eighteenth-Century America* (1974); and Gary B. Nash, *The Urban Crucible* (1979). Henry May addresses the American Enlightenment in *The American Enlightenment* (1976).

Excellent treatments of religious life and the Great Awakening include Perry Miller, *From Colony to Province* (1953); Alan Heimert, *Religion and the American Mind* (1966); Edwin Gaustad, *The Great Awakening in New England* (1957); J. M. Bumsted and John Van de Wetering, *What Must I Do to Be Saved?* (1976); and Patricia Tracy, *Jonathan Edwards, Pastor* (1979).

The maturing colonial political systems involved many variations, which can be followed in Bernard Bailyn, *The Origins of American Politics* (1968); Charles Sydnor, *American Revolutionaries in the Making* (1965); Jack P. Greene, *The Quest for Power* (1963); Edward M. Cook, Jr., *The Fathers of the Towns* (1976); and Patricia Bonomi, *A Factious People: Politics and Society in Colonial New York* (1977).

## TIME LINE

| | |
|---|---|
| 1662 | Half-Way Covenant in New England |
| 1685–1715 | Stagnation in tobacco market |
| 1704 | *Boston News-Letter*, first colonial newspaper, published |
| 1713 | Beginning of Scots-Irish and German immigration |
| 1715–1730 | Volume of slave trade doubles |
| 1720s | Black population begins to increase naturally |
| 1734–1736 | Great Awakening begins in Northampton, Massachusetts |
| 1735 | Zenger acquitted of seditious libel in New York |
| 1739–1740 | Whitefield's first American tour spreads Great Awakening |
| | Slaves compose 90 percent of population on Carolina rice coast |
| 1740s | Indigo becomes staple crop in Lower South |
| 1747 | Benjamin Franklin publishes first *Poor Richard's Almanack* |
| | Impressment riot in Boston |
| 1760 | Africans compose 20 percent of American population |

# CHAPTER 5
## BURSTING THE COLONIAL BONDS

The BLOODY MASSACRE perpetrated in King—ſ—Street BOSTON on March 5th 1770 by a party of the 29th REGt.

BUTCHER'S HALL

Engrav'd Printed & Sold by PAUL REVERE BOSTON

Unhappy BOSTON! ſee thy Sons deplore,
Thy hallow'd Walks beſmear'd with guiltleſs Gore,
While faithleſs P—n and his ſavage Bands,
With murd'rous Rancour ſtretch their bloody Hands;
Like fierce Barbarians grinning o'er their Prey,
Approve the Carnage and enjoy the Day.

If ſcalding drops from Rage from Anguiſh Wrung,
If ſpeechleſs Sorrows lab'ring for a Tongue,
Or if a weeping World can ought appeaſe
The plaintive Ghoſts of Victims ſuch as theſe:
The Patriot's copious Tears for each are ſhed,
A glorious Tribute which embalms the Dead.

But know FATE ſummons to that awful Goal,
Where JUSTICE ſtrips the Murd'rer of his Soul:
Should venal C—ts the ſcandal of the Land,
Snatch the relentleſs Villain from her Hand,
Keen Execrations on this Plate inſcrib'd,
Shall reach a JUDGE who never can be brib'd.

The unhappy Sufferers were Meſſrs. SAML. GRAY, SAML. MAVERICK, JAMS. CALDWELL, CRISPUS ATTUCKS & PATK. CARR
Killed. Six wounded; two of them (CHRIST'R. MONK & JOHN CLARK) Mortally

In 1758, when he was 21 years old, Ebenezer MacIntosh of Boston laid down his shoemaker's awl and enlisted in the Massachusetts expedition against the French on Lake Champlain. The son of a poor Boston shoemaker who had fought against the French in a previous war, MacIntosh had known poverty all his life. Service against the French offered the hope of plunder or at least an enlistment bounty worth half a year's wages. One among thousands of colonists who fought against "the Gallic menace" from 1755 to 1763 in the French and Indian War, MacIntosh contributed his mite to the climactic Anglo-American struggle that drove the French from eastern North America.

But a greater role lay ahead for the poor Boston shoemaker. Two years after the Peace of Paris in 1763, England imposed a stamp tax on the American colonists. In the massive protests that followed, MacIntosh emerged as the street leader of the Boston crowd. In two nights of the most violent attacks on private property ever witnessed in America, a Boston crowd nearly destroyed the houses of two of the colony's most important officials. On August 14, they tore through the house of Andrew Oliver, a wealthy merchant and the appointed distributor of stamps for Massachusetts. Twelve days later, MacIntosh led the crowd in attacking the home of Thomas Hutchinson, a wealthy merchant who served as lieutenant governor and chief justice of Massachusetts. "The mob was so general," wrote the governor, "and so supported that all civil power ceased in an instant."

For the next several months, the power of the poor Boston shoemaker grew. Called "General" MacIntosh and "Captain-General of the Liberty Tree" by his townspeople, he soon sported a militia uniform of gold and blue and a hat laced with gold. Two thousand townsmen followed his commands on November 5, when they marched in orderly ranks through the crooked streets of Boston to demonstrate their solidarity in resisting the hated stamps.

Five weeks later, a crowd publicly humiliated stamp distributor Oliver. Calling on him to announce his resignation before the assembled citizenry, they marched him across town in a driving December rain. With MacIntosh at his elbow, he finally reached the "Liberty Tree," which had become a symbol of resistance to England's new colonial policies. There on the home ground of the radical working people, the aristocratic Oliver ate humble pie. He concluded his resignation remarks with bitter words, hissing sardonically that he would "always think myself very happy when it shall be in my power to serve the people."

"To serve the people" was an ancient idea embedded in English political culture, but it assumed new meaning in the American colonies during the epic third quarter of the eighteenth century. Few colonists in 1750 held even a faint desire to break the connection with England, and fewer still might have predicted the form of government that 13 independent states and an independent nation might fashion. Yet in a whirlwind of events, 2 million colonists moved haltingly toward a showdown with mighty England. Little known men like Ebenezer MacIntosh struggled individually and in groups. Collectively, their personal dramas influenced—and sometimes even dictated—the revolutionary movement in the colonies. Though we read and speak mostly of a small group of "founding fathers," the wellsprings of the American Revolution can be fully discovered only among a variety of people from different social groups, occupations, regions, and religions.

This chapter addresses the tensions in late colonial society, the imperial crisis that followed the Seven Years' War (in the colonies often called the French and Indian War), and the tumultuous decade that led to "the shots heard round the world" fired at Concord Bridge in April 1775. It portrays the origins of a dual American Revolution. Ebenezer MacIntosh, in leading the Boston mob against crown officers and colonial collaborators who tried to implement a new colonial policy after 1763, helped set in motion a revolutionary movement to restore ancient liberties thought by the Americans to be under deliberate attack in England. This movement eventually escalated into the War of American Independence.

But MacIntosh's Boston followers were also venting years of resentment at the accumulation of wealth and power by Boston's aristocratic elite. Behind every swing of the ax, every shattered crystal goblet and splintered mahogany chair, lay the fury of a Bostonian who had seen the city's conservative elite try to dismantle the town meeting, had suffered economic hardship, and had lost faith that opportunity and equitable relations still prevailed in his town. This sentiment, which called for the regeneration of a colonial society that had become corrupt, self-indulgent, and elite-dominated, fed an idealistic commitment to reform American society even while severing the colonial bond. As distinguished from the War for Independence this was the American Revolution.

## WARS OF EMPIRE AND INDIAN RESPONSES

After the Glorious Revolution of 1688, England began constructing a more coherent imperial administration. Major new instruments for governing the colonies were introduced. In 1696, a professional Board of Trade replaced the old Lords of Trades; the Treasury strengthened the customs service; and Parliament created overseas vice-admiralty courts, which functioned without juries to prosecute smugglers who evaded the trade regulations set forth in the Navigation Acts. Royal governors received greater powers and more detailed instructions and came under more insistent demands from the Board of Trade to enforce policies set in London. The machinery of imperial management and a corps of colonial civil servants were quietly being put into place.

### War and the Management of Empire

The best test of an effectively organized state was its ability to wage war. Four times between 1689 and 1763, England matched its strength against France, its archrival in North America and the Caribbean. These wars of empire had tremendous consequences for all involved—the home governments, their colonial subjects, and the Indian tribes that were drawn into the bloody conflicts.

We have already seen (in Chapter 3) how the growing resources and markets vital to the strength of home governments twice brought England's and France's North American colonies into conflict between 1689 and 1713. The Peace of Utrecht that ended Queen Anne's War (1702–1713) brought victor's spoils of great importance to England. From France, the English acquired Hudson's Bay, rich in furs; Newfoundland, rich in fish; and Nova Scotia, a new frontier for New England's growing population. From Spain, England received Gibraltar, which commanded the entrance to the Mediterranean; several Caribbean islands; and a monopoly on supplying Spain's colonies with African slaves.

The generation of peace that followed the signing in Utrecht in 1713 was really only a time-out between wars. Both England and France used the years until 1739 to strengthen their war-making capacity, to which productive and efficiently governed New World colonies made important contributions. The decades after 1713, though known as a period of "salutary neglect," were not really years when the crown and Parliament ignored the colonies. In fact, this was an era when king and Parliament competed for power in managing colonial affairs.

Parliament had already begun playing a more active role after the reign of Queen Anne (1702–1714) and continued to do so when weak, German-speaking King George I came to the throne. Its main concern was economic regulation. New articles such as furs, copper, hemp, tar, and turpentine were added to the list of enumerated items produced in America that had to be shipped to England before being exported to another country. Acts were passed to curtail colonial production of articles important to England's economy: woolen cloth in 1699, beaver hats in 1732, and finished iron products in 1750. Most important, Parliament passed the Molasses Act in 1733. Attempting to stop the trade between New England and the French West Indies, where Yankee traders exchanged fish, beef, and pork for molasses to convert into rum, Parliament imposed a prohibitive duty of 6 pence per gallon on molasses imported from the French islands. The main result was to turn many of New England's largest merchants and distillers into smugglers and to school them for a generation, along with their ship captains, crews, and allied waterfront artisans, in defying royal authority.

The generation of peace ended abruptly in 1739 when England declared war on Spain. The immediate cause of hostilities was the ear of an English sea captain, Robert Jenkins. He had been deprived of that appendage eight years before by Spanish authorities, who charged him with smuggling in the Spanish colonies. With encouragement from his government, Jenkins brought his severed ear before the public in 1738 as a way of whipping up war fever against Spain, whom English policymakers decided must be chastened for transferring certain commercial privileges from England to France.

The real cause of the war, however, was England's determination to continue its drive toward commercial domination of the Atlantic basin. Five years after the war with Spain began in 1739, it merged into a much larger conflict between England and France that lasted until 1748. Then, after a brief period of peace, France and England fought around the globe in the Seven Years' War.

The scale of King George's War (1744–1748) and the Seven Years' War (1756–1763) that followed it far exceeded the conflicts of the preceding generations. As military priorities became paramount, the need increased for discipline and cooperation within the empire. In addition, unprecedented military expenditures brought pressure to enlarge colonial revenues. England's West Indian and American colonies were asked to share in the costs of defending—and extending—the empire and to tailor their behavior to the needs of the home country.

### Iroquois and Creek Diplomacy

The struggle for ascendancy in trade and territory in the Caribbean and North America brought the contending European powers—England, France, and Spain—into close contact with the powerful Indian tribes of interior North America. These tribes—principally the Iroquois, Cherokee, Creek, and Choctaw—were far stronger than the smaller coastal tribes that had succumbed to the colonizers in the previous century. They were therefore better able to defend their territory and political sovereignty while interacting with Europeans as military allies, trading partners, and diplomats. The interior tribes would eventually suffer from involvement in the European wars. But at the time, the tribes derived many advantages from allying with one European nation or another.

During the late seventeenth century, European policymakers and their colonial bureaucrats moved armies and navies across the Atlantic, engaged thousands of people in the manufacture and transport of Indian trade goods, and struggled against each other for control of North America. Meanwhile, the preliterate woodlands Iroquois, never numbering more than 12,000 people, played a crucial role in shaping the history of French Canada and the northern English colonies.

In the two wars between 1689 and 1713, the

English and French discovered that staggering problems of weather, disease, transport, and supply made European-style warfare impossible in the North American wilderness. They therefore sought to subcontract military tasks to Indian allies. The Iroquois, calculating their own interests, sometimes agreed to play the role of English mercenaries for handsome rewards. But early in the eighteenth century, they decided to pursue a policy of neutrality. Iroquois strength could better be preserved by promising not to fight for the French than by going to war for a price in trade goods.

Both the English and French maneuvered to keep the Iroquois from joining the other side. The Iroquois, noted the governor of Quebec in 1711, were "more to be feared than the English colonies." A decade later, a New Englander wrote that visiting Iroquois chiefs in Boston were "courted and caressed like the potentates of the earth." Controlling the trade routes to the north and west of the French and English fur posts, the Iroquois skillfully played the French and English off against each other, maintaining their territory and political independence until the outbreak of the American Revolution.

Like the Iroquois, the Creek Confederacy of the Southeast mastered the principles of *Realpolitik* in the eighteenth century. Capitalizing on contacts with the Spanish, French, and English settlers on their borders, the Creek deftly extended and withdrew promises of trade and military assistance while maintaining a balance of power in their region. The Creek chief Brims was so skillful a diplomat that one Englishman called him "as great a politician as any governor in America." His emissaries ranged thousands of miles to parley with the Spanish in St. Augustine, Veracruz, and Mexico City; with the French at their fort on the Alabama River; and with the English in Charleston and even in London.

*The Creek nation practiced a highly successful diplomacy with European colonists for generations. Tomochichi and his nephew (left) sat for this portrait in 1734. Joseph Brant was a Mohawk who fought against the colonists in the American Revolution. His grandfather (right) was a chief who traveled to England in 1710 to treat with the English government.*

After Brims's death in the early 1730s, the Creek continued their policy of neutrality. In 1739, when England declared war on Spain, the South Carolina government pressured the Creek to join General James Oglethorpe, founder of the colony of Georgia, in an assault on Spanish St. Augustine. A scattering of Creek joined Oglethorpe in the disastrous expedition, but most remained out of the fray. They followed the policy of trading with all European powers but allying militarily with none. In the 1740s, the Creek again resisted English entreaties to join an attack against the French at Fort Toulouse. They told the English bluntly that they were welcome to trade in Creek country but could not build forts nor expect Creek support for military expeditions against the Spanish or the French.

## Cultural Changes
## Among Interior Tribes

During the first half of the eighteenth century, the inland tribes proved their capacity to adapt to the contending European colonizers in their region while maintaining their independence. Yet extensive contact with the French, Spanish, and English slowly transformed Indian ways of life in a manner that boded ill for the future.

The introduction of European trade goods, especially iron implements, textiles, firearms and ammunition, and alcohol, inescapably changed Indian lifeways. Subsistence hunting, limited to satisfying the food requirements of a tribe, turned into commercial hunting, restricted only by the quantity of trade goods desired. Indian males spent far more time away from the villages trapping and hunting, and the increased importance of this activity to tribal life undermined the former matrilineal basis of society. Women were also drawn into the new economic activities. Once killed, the beaver, marten, and fox had to be skinned and the pelts then scraped, dressed, trimmed, and sewed into robes. Among some tribes, the trapping, preparation, and transporting of skins became so time-consuming that they had to procure food resources from other tribes.

Involvement in the fur trade also altered the spiritual ethos that had long governed hunting.

Native Americans had traditionally believed that the destinies of humans and animals were closely linked, for both inhabited a spiritual world governed by a Great Creator. This imposed obligations on both hunters and animals. The hunter knew that he must never kill more animals than he needed and must treat their bodies with respect. The animals in return must not resist capture. When trappers and hunters declared all-out war on the beaver and other fur-bearing animals to provide pelts for the European traders who offered attractive trade goods, they began to ignore the age-old custom of merging sympathetically with the environment.

The fur trade also heightened intertribal tensions, often to the point of war. Conflict between tribes long preceded the arrival of Europeans, but trade frequently flowed between cooperating tribes. As settlers of different nationalities competed for client tribes in the fur trade, however, the tribes were sucked into their patron's rivalry. Also, tribes became accustomed to certain trade articles. When furs became depleted in their hunting grounds, they could maintain their trade only by conquering more remote tribes with fertile hunting grounds or by forcibly intercepting the furs of other tribes as they were carried to European trading posts. The introduction of European weaponry, which Indians quickly mastered, further intensified intertribal conflict.

Tribal political organization among the interior tribes also changed in the eighteenth century. Most tribes had earlier been loose confederations of villages and clans, each exercising considerable local autonomy. The Creek, Cherokee, and Iroquois gave their primary loyalty to the village, not to the tribe or confederacy. But trade, diplomatic contact, and war with Europeans required more coordinated policies. To deal effectively with traders and officials, the villages gradually adjusted to more centralized leadership.

Cherokee political organization in the eighteenth century illustrates the changes overcoming tribal societies. Early in the century, the nearly autonomous village formed the basic unit of political authority. But tension with Creek neighbors and intermittent hostilities with English traders and settlers pressed home the need for coordinated decision making. By 1750, the Cherokee had formed an umbrella political organization that under the leadership of Chief Old Hop gathered together the fragmented authority of the villages and formed a more centralized tribal "priest state." When even this proved inadequate, warriors began to assume the dominant role in tribal councils, replacing the civil chiefs. By this process the Cherokee reorganized their political structure so that dozens of scattered villages could amalgamate their strength.

While incorporating trade goods into their material culture and adapting their economies and political structures to new situations, the interior tribes held fast to tradition in many ways. Unimpressed with most settler practices, they saw little reason to replace what they valued in their own culture. When they observed the colonists' systems of law and justice, religion, education, family organization, and child rearing, Native Americans often concluded that their own ways were superior.

English missionaries, eager to win Native Americans from "savage" ways, were frustrated by the Indians' refusal to accept the superiority of white culture. Some colonists understood that the white behavior observed by natives cast doubts on the notion that Indians were of an inferior race. A Carolinian admitted that "they are really better to us than we are to them. We look upon them with scorn and disdain, and think them little better than beasts in human shape, though if well examined, we shall find that, for all our religion and education, we possess more moral deformities and evils than these savages do."

Despite maintaining many cultural practices, the interior Indian tribes suffered from the commercial, diplomatic, and military contact with the colonizers. Decade by decade, the fur trade spread epidemic diseases, raised the level of warfare, depleted their lands of game animals, and drew the Native Americans into a market economy where their trading partners gradually became trading masters.

## THE CLIMACTIC SEVEN YEARS' WAR

During the first half of the eighteenth century, the powerful Indian tribes of the interior maintained equilibrium with colonizing Europeans by artfully playing off one settler society against another. "To preserve the balance between us and the French," wrote New York's white Indian secretary, "is the great ruling principle of modern Indian politics." But after 1750, a European showdown for control of eastern North America, accompanied by the rapid increase of the colonial population, undermined this balance of power.

### Outbreak of Hostilities

The spectacular growth of the English colonies transformed a society of a quarter million in 1700 to one of 1.25 million in 1750 and then added another half million in the next decade. Three-quarters of the increase came in the colonies south of New York. Such growth propelled thousands of land-hungry settlers toward the mountain gaps in the Appalachians in search of farmland.

Promoting this westward rush were eastern merchants and speculators. Fur traders in their employ penetrated a French-controlled region, where they made trading agreements by offering better prices and higher-quality goods than the French provided. In the 1740s and 1750s, speculators formed land companies to capitalize on the population explosion. Many of the future leaders of the Revolution were heavily involved in establishing companies that raced to establish claims to millions of acres of western land. The farther west the settlement line moved, the closer it came to the western trading empire of the French and their Indian allies.

Colonial penetration of the Ohio valley in the 1740s established the first English outposts in the continental heartland. This challenged the French where their interest was vital. While the English controlled most of the eastern coastal plain of North America, the French had nearly encircled them to the west by building a chain of trading posts and forts along the St. Lawrence River, through the Great Lakes, and southward into the Ohio and Mississippi valleys.

Challenged by the English, the French chose resistance. They attempted to block further English expansion by constructing new forts in the Ohio valley and by prying some tribes loose from their new English connections. The English, a French emissary warned a western tribe in the 1750s, "are much less anxious to take away your peltries than to become masters of your lands, and your blindness is so great that you do not perceive that the very hand that caresses you will scourge you like negroes and slaves, so soon as it will have got possession of your lands."

By 1755, the French had driven the English traders out of the Ohio valley and established forts as far east as the forks of the Ohio River, near present-day Pittsburgh. It was there, at Fort Duquesne, that the French smartly rebuffed an ambitious young Virginia militia colonel named George Washington, dispatched by his colony's government to expel them from the region.

The decision to force a showdown in the interior of North America was made in the capitals of Europe, not in the colonies. England's powerful merchants, supported by American clients, had been emboldened by English success in the previous war against the French. Now they argued that the time was ripe for the further destruction of French overseas trade. Convinced, the English ministry ordered several thousand troops to America in 1754; in France, 3,000 regulars embarked to meet the English challenge.

With war looming, the colonial governments attempted to coordinate their efforts. Representatives of seven colonies met with 150 Iroquois chiefs at Albany, New York, in June 1754. The twin goals were to woo the powerful Iroquois out of their neutrality and to perfect a plan of colonial union. Both failed. The Iroquois left the conference with 30 wagonloads of gifts but made no firm commitment to fight against the French. Benjamin Franklin designed a plan for an intercolonial government that would manage Indian affairs and defense and have the power to pass laws and levy taxes. But even the clever woodcut displayed in the *Pennsylvania Gazette* that pictured a chopped-up snake with the insignia "Join or Die" failed to overcome the longstanding jealousies that had thwarted previ-

## Seven Years' War

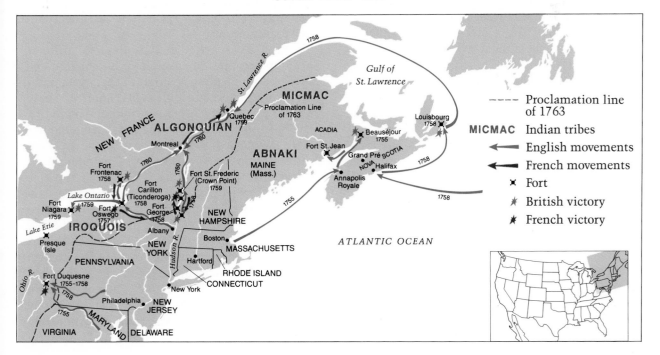

ous attempts at intercolony cooperation. "Everyone cries a union is necessary," sighed Franklin, "but when they come to the manner and form of the union, their weak noodles are perfectly distracted."

With his British army and hundreds of American recruits, General James Braddock slogged his way across Virginia in the summer of 1755, cutting a road through forests and across mountains at a few miles a day. A headstrong professional soldier who regarded his European battlefield experience as sufficient for war in the American wilderness, Braddock had contempt for the woods-wise French regiments and their stealthy Indian allies.

Only 10 miles from his objective of Fort Duquesne, defended by only 100 French regulars and 150 Canadian militiamen, the French and their Indian allies ambushed Braddock's reputedly invincible army. Two-thirds of the English were killed or wounded. Braddock fell mortally wounded, and Washington, his uniform pierced by four bullets, had two horses shot from beneath him.

Throughout the summer, French-supplied Indian raiders put the torch to the Virginia and Pennsylvania backcountry. Frontier settlers fled their farms to the extent that "the roads are full of starved, naked, indigent multitudes." One French triumph followed another during the next two years. The victory over Braddock's army had brought almost every tribe north of the Ohio River to the French side. Never was disunity within the English colonies so painfully evident. With its Indian allies, French Canada, only 70,000 inhabitants strong, had badly battered a million and a half colonists supported by the British army.

The turning point in the war came after the energetic William Pitt became England's prime minister in 1757. Proclaiming "I believe that I can save this nation and that no one else can," he abandoned Europe as the main theater of action against the French and threw his nation's military might into the American campaign.

The forces dispatched by Pitt to America dwarfed all preceding commitments. About 23,000 British troops landed in America in 1757 and 1758, and the huge naval fleet that arrived in the latter year included 14,000 mariners. Even

forces of this magnitude, when asked to engage the enemy in the forests of North America, were not necessarily sufficient to the task without Indian support, or at least neutrality. "A doubt remains not," proclaimed one English official in the colonies, "that the prosperity of our colonies on the continent will stand or fall with our interest and favour among them."

## Tribal Strategies

Anglo-American leaders knew that in a war fought mainly in the northern colonies, the support of the Iroquois Confederacy and their tributary tribes was crucial. Iroquois allegiance could be secured in only two ways, through purchase or by a demonstration of power that would convince the tribes that the English would prevail with or without their assistance. The first stratagem failed in 1754 when colonial negotiators heaped gifts on the Iroquois chiefs at the Albany Congress but received in return only tantalizing half promises of support against the French. The second alternative proved impossible because the English proved militarily inferior to the French in the first three years of the war. Hence, the westernmost of the Iroquois Six Nations, the Seneca, fought with the French in the campaigns of 1757 and 1758, while the Delaware, a tributary tribe, harassed the Pennsylvania frontier.

In 1758, when the huge English military buildup began to produce victories, the Iroquois finally shifted their position. The largest military force ever assembled in America, some 15,000 British and American soldiers, including the Bostonian Ebenezer MacIntosh, suffered terrible casualties and withdrew from the field after attempting to storm Fort Ticonderoga on Lake Champlain in June 1758. Then the tide turned. Troops commanded by Sir Jeffrey Amherst captured Louisbourg, on Cape Breton Island, and Fort Duquesne fell to an army of 6,000 led by General John Forbes. The resolute Pitt had mobilized the fighting power of the English nation and put more men in the field than existed in all of New France. The colonists, in turn, had put aside intramural squabbling long enough to overwhelm the badly outnumbered French.

The victories of 1758 finally moved the Iroquois away from neutrality. Incentive to join the English was increased by the royal navy's control of the St. Lawrence River. By late 1758, the English had bottled up French shipping, cutting the Iroquois off from French trade goods. By the next spring, understanding that the French were going down to defeat in North America, the Iroquois pledged 800 warriors for an attack on Fort Niagara, the strategic French trading depot on Lake Ontario. As always, their policy had been to assess the shifting military balance between rival European powers and to formulate their strategy accordingly.

Even dramatic Anglo-American victories did not always guarantee Indian support. In the South, backcountry skirmishes with the Cherokee from Virginia to South Carolina turned into a costly war from 1759 to 1761. In 1760, the Cherokee mauled a British army of 1,300 under Amherst. The following summer, a much larger Anglo-American force invaded Cherokee country, burning towns and food supplies. By this time, English control of the sea had interrupted the Indians' supply of French arms. Struggling against food shortages, lack of ammunition, and a smallpox epidemic, the Cherokee finally sued

*The taking of Quebec in 1759 was the decisive blow in England's campaign to end French domination of Canada, the Caribbean, and lands west of the Appalachians.*

for peace.

Other Anglo-American victories in 1759, "the year of miracles," decided the outcome of the bloodiest war yet known in the New World. The capture of Fort Niagara, the critical link in the system of forts that joined the French inland empire with the Atlantic, was followed by the conquest of sugar-rich Martinique in the West Indies. The culminating stroke came with a dramatic victory at Quebec. Led by 32-year-old General James Wolfe, 5,000 troops scaled a rocky cliff and overcame the French on the Plains of Abraham. When Montreal fell, late in 1760, French power was shattered in North America. The theater of operations shifted to the Caribbean, where fighting continued, as in Europe, for three years longer. But in the American colonies, the ancient dream of ridding the continent of "the Gallic menace" had finally come true.

## Consequences of War

For the interior Indian tribes, the Treaty of Paris ending the Seven Years' War in 1763 dealt a harsh blow. Unlike the coastal Native Americans, whose population and independence had ebbed rapidly through contact with the colonizers, the inland tribes had maintained their strength and sometimes even grown more unified through relations with settlers. Although they came to depend on European trade goods, Native Americans had turned this commercial connection to their advantage so long as more than one source of trade goods existed.

The Indian play-off system ended with the French defeat. By the terms of the Treaty of Paris, France ceded Canada and all territory east of the Mississippi, except for New Orleans, to England. To Spain went New Orleans and France's trans-Mississippi empire. Spain yielded Florida to England. For the interior tribes, only one source of trade goods remained. Two centuries of European rivalry for control of eastern North America ended abruptly. Iroquois, Cherokee, Creek, and other interior peoples were now forced to adjust to this reality.

After concluding peace with the French, the English government launched a new policy in North America designed to separate Native Americans and colonizers by creating a racial

*Under the leadership of Ottawa Chief Pontiac, the tribes of the Great Lakes region formed a unified front of resistance against English encroachment into their lands.*

boundary roughly following the crestline of the Appalachian Mountains from Maine to Georgia. The Proclamation of 1763 ordered the colonial governors to reserve all land west of the line for Indian nations. White settlers already living beyond the Appalachians were charged to withdraw to the east.

Though well intended, this attempt to legislate interracial accord failed completely. Even before the proclamation was issued, the Ottawa Chief Pontiac had gathered together many of the northern tribes that had aided the French assaults on the English forts from the Great Lakes as far south as Pittsburgh. Although Pontiac's pan-Indian movement to drive the British out of the Ohio valley collapsed in 1764, it served notice that the interior tribes would not passively watch the invasion of their lands after the French withdrawal from North America.

The English government could issue stern commands to colonial governors to observe the Proclamation of 1763, but it could not enforce its policy. Staggering under an immense wartime debt, England decided to maintain only small army garrisons in America to regulate the interior. Nor could royal governors stop land speculators and settlers from privately purchasing land from trans-Appalachian tribes or from simply encroaching on their land. Under such circumstances, the western frontier seethed with tension after 1763.

While the Seven Years' War marked an epic victory of Anglo-American arms over the French and redrew the map of North America, it also had important social and economic effects on colonial society. The war convinced the colonists of their growing strength, yet left them debt-ridden and weakened in manpower. The wartime economy spurred economic development and poured British capital into the colonies, yet rendered them more vulnerable to cyclic fluctuations in the British economy.

Military contracts, for example, brought prosperity to most colonies during the war years. Huge orders for ships, arms, uniforms, and provisions enriched many northern merchants and provided good prices for farmers as well. Urban artisans enjoyed full employment and high wages, as tailors' needles flashed to meet clothing contracts, shoemakers stitched for an unprecedented demand for shoes, and bakers found armies clamoring for bread. Privateers—privately outfitted ships licensed by colonial governments to attack enemy shipping—enriched the fortunate few. On a single voyage in 1758, John MacPherson snared 18 French ships. The prize money was lavish enough to allow this son of a Scottish immigrant to pour £14,000 into creating a country estate outside Philadelphia, to which he retired in splendor.

The war, however, required heavy taxes and took a huge human toll. Privateering carried many fortune seekers to a watery grave, and the wilderness campaigns from 1755 to 1760 claimed the lives of thousands. Garrison life was wracked with killing fevers (which claimed more victims than enemy weapons), and battlefield medical treatment was too primitive to save many of the wounded. Boston's Thomas Hancock accurately predicted at the beginning of the war that "this province is spirited to [send] every third man to do the work of the Lord." But the Lord's work was expensive. Thomas Pownall, assuming the governorship of Massachusetts in August 1757, found not the "rich, flourishing, powerful, enterprizing" colony he expected but a province "ruined and undone."

The magnitude of the human losses in Boston indicates the war's impact. The census takers in 1764 found equal numbers of males and females under 16 years of age, but adult females outnumbered adult males 3,612 to 2,941. The wartime muster lists show that nearly every working-class Bostonian tasted military service at some point during the long war. When peace came, Boston had a deficit of almost 700 men in a town of about 2,000 families. The high rate of war widowhood produced a feminization of poverty and required expanded poor relief for the maintenance of husbandless women and fatherless children.

Peace ended the casualties but also brought depression. The British forces in the American theater numbered about 40,000 at the conclusion of the North American campaigns; with their departure for the Caribbean in 1760, the economy slumped badly, especially in the coastal towns. "The tippling soldiery that used to help us out at a dead lift," mused a New York merchant, "are gone to drink it [rum] in a warmer region, the place of its production."

The greatest hardships after 1760 fell upon the laboring classes, although even some wealthy merchants went bankrupt. Those with the smallest wages had the thinnest savings to cushion them against hard times. How quickly their security could evaporate showed in Philadelphia, where early in the contractionary cycle "many very poor people," unable to pay their property taxes, were "disposing of their huts and lots to others more wealthy than themselves." The economic security of the middle sector of society also slipped, as established craftsmen and shopkeepers found themselves caught between rising prices and reduced demand for their goods and services. A New York artisan expressed a common lament in 1762. Thankfully, he still had employment, he wrote in a letter to the *New-York Gazette.* But despite every effort at unceasing labor and frugal living, he had fallen into poverty and found it "beyond my ability to support my family . . . [which] can scarcely appear with decency or have necessaries to subsist." His situation, he added, "is really the case with many of the inhabitants of this city."

In spite of its heavy casualties and economic repercussions, the Seven Years' War paved the way, though not foreseen at the time, for a far larger conflict in the next generation. The legislative assemblies, for example, which had been flexing their muscles at the expense of the governors in earlier decades, accelerated their bid for political power. During wartime, knowing that their governors must obtain military appropriations, they extracted concessions as the price for raising revenues. The war also trained a new group of military and political leaders. In carrying out military operations on a scale unknown in the colonies and in shouldering heavier political responsibilities, men such as George Washington, Samuel Adams, Benjamin Franklin, Patrick Henry, and Christopher Gadsden acquired the experience that would serve them well in the future.

The Seven Years' War, in spite of the severe costs, left many of the colonists with a sense of buoyancy. New Englanders rejoiced at the final victory over the "Papist enemy of the North." Frontiersmen, fur traders, and land speculators also celebrated the French withdrawal, for the West now appeared open for exploitation. This "Garden of the World," trumpeted a Boston almanac publisher, was larger than France, Germany, and Poland combined "and all well provided with rivers, a very fine wholesome air, a rich soil, . . . and all things necessary for the conveniency and delight of life." A new frontier now seemed to await those whom opportunity had passed by on the crowded seaboard.

The colonists also felt a new sense of their identity after the war. Surveying a world free of French and Spanish threats, they could not help but reassess the advantages and disadvantages of subordination to England. The colonists would soon discover, a French diplomat predicted at the war's end, "that they stand no longer in need of your protection. You will call on them to contribute towards supporting the burden which they have helped to bring on you; they will answer you by shaking off all dependence."

Probate records of deceased property holders are an important source used by historians to examine the social changes occurring in American society. They include wills, the legal disposition of estates, and household inventories taken by court-appointed appraisers that detail the personal possessions left at death. Inventories have been especially valuable in tracing many aspects of the transformation of colonial communities as they evolved from tiny frontier settlements to established eighteenth-century communities.

Like tax lists, inventories can be used to show changes in a community's distribution of wealth. But they are far more detailed than tax lists, providing a kind of snapshot of how people lived at the end of their life. Inventories list and value almost everything a person owned—household possessions, equipment, books, clothes and jewelry, cash on hand, livestock and horses, crops and stored provisions, and other items. Hence through inventories we can measure the quality and style of life at different levels of society in various regions. We can also witness how people made choices about how to invest their savings—in capital goods of their trade such as land, ships, and equipment; in personal goods such as household furnishings and luxurty items; or in real property such as land and houses.

Studied systematically (and corrected for biases, which infect this source as well as others), inventories show that by the early eighteenth century, ordinary householders were improving their standard of living. Finished furniture such as cupboards, beds, tables, and chairs turn up in inventories with increasing frequency. Pewter dinnerware replaces wooden bowls and spoons, bed linen makes an appearance, and occasionally books and pictures are found.

Among an emerging elite before the Revolution, much more fashionable articles of consumption appear. The partial inventory of Robert Oliver, a wealthy merchant and officeholder living in a Boston suburb, is reproduced here. You can get some idea of the dignified impression Oliver wished to make by looking at his furniture and dishes and by noticing that he owned a mahogany tea table, damask linen, and a bed with curtains. The inventory further suggests the spaciousness of Oliver's house and shows how he furnished each room.

It is helpful when studying inventories to categorize the goods in the following way: those that are needed to survive (basic cooking utensils, for example); those that make life easier or more comfortable (enough plates and beds for each member of the family, for example); and those that make life luxurious (slaves, silver plates, paintings, mahogany furniture, damask curtains, spices, wine, and so forth). Oliver had many luxury goods as well as items that contributed to his use of leisure time and his personal enjoyment. Which items in his inventory do you think were needed only to survive comfortably? Which were luxuries? What other conclusions can you draw about the life style of rich colonial merchants like Oliver?

Beyond revealing the growing social differentiation in colonial society, the inventories help the historian understand the reaction during the Great Awakening to what appeared to many ordinary colonists as sinful pride and arrogance displayed by the elite. By the 1760s, this distrust of affluence among simple folk had in some areas led to outright hostility toward men who surrounded themselves with the trappings of aristocratic life while their poorer neighbors suffered. Even the ambitious young John Adams, a striving lawyer, was shocked at what he saw at the house of a wealthy merchant in Boston. "Went over the House to view the Furniture, which alone cost a thousand Pound sterling," he exclaimed. "A seat it is for a noble Man, a Prince. The Turkey Carpets, the painted Hangings, the Marble Tables, the rich Beds with crimson Damask Curtains . . . are the most magnificent of any Thing I have ever seen."

Such a description takes on its fullest meaning only when contrasted with what inventories tell us about life at the bottom of society. The hundreds of inventories for Bostonians dying in the decade before the American Revolution show that fully half of the people died with less than £40 personal wealth and one-quarter with £20 or less. The inventories and wills of Jonathan and Daniel Chandler of Andover, Massachusetts, show the material circumstances of less favored Americans. The Chandler brothers' inventories show the material circumstances of those who suffered from the economic distress afflicting New England since the 1730's. Note that Daniel Chandler, like Ebenezer MacIntosh, was a shoemaker. How do the possessions of these brothers compare with Oliver's partial inventory? An examination of these contrasting inventories helps explain the class tension that figured in the Revolutionary experience.

## HOUSEHOLD INVENTORY OF ROBERT OLIVER, WEALTHY MERCHANT

Dorchester Jan^ry 11^th 1763.

Inventory of what Estates Real & Personall, belonging to Coll^o Robert Oliver [Esquire] late of Dorchester Deceased, that has been Exhibited to us the Subscribers, for Apprizement. Viz^t

**In the Setting Parlour Viz^tt**

| | | |
|---|---|---|
| a looking Glass | £ | 4. —. — |
| a Small Ditto | | 0. 6. 0 |
| 12 Metzitens pictures Glaz'd· | @ 6/ | 3. 12. — |
| 8 Cartoons D^o Ditto | | 4. —. — |
| 11 small Pictures | | —. 4. — |
| 4 Maps | | —. 10. — |
| 1 Prospect Glass | | —. 10. — |
| 2 Escutchons Glaz'd | | —. 4. — |
| 1 pair small hand Irons | | —. 6. — |
| 1 Shovel & Tongs | | —. 8. — |
| 1 Tobacco Tongs | | —. 1. — |
| 1 pair Bellowes | | —. 2. — |
| 1 Tea Chest | | —. 2. — |
| 2 Small Waters [waiters?] | | —. 1. — |
| 1 Mehogony Tea Table | | 1. —. — |
| 8 China Cups & Saucers | | —. 2. — |
| 1 Earthen Cream Pott | | —. —. 1 |
| 1 Ditto. Sugar Dish | | —. —. 4 |
| 1 Black Walnut Table | | 1. —. — |
| 1 Black Ditto Smaller | | 0. 6. — |
| 1 Round painted Table | | 0. 1. — |
| 7 Leather Bottom Chairs | @ 6/ | 2. 2. — |
| 1 Arm^d Chair Common | | 1. 3. — |
| 1 Black Walnut Desk | | 1. 12. — |
| 1 pair Candlesticks snuffers & Stand Base Mettle | | —. 4. — |
| 6 Wine Glasses 1 Water Glass | | —. 1. — |
| à parcell of Books | | 1. —. — |
| a Case with Small Bottles | | 0. 4. — |
| | | 22. 1. 5 |

**In the Marble Chamber Viz^t** £

| | | |
|---|---|---|
| 1 Bedstead & Curtains Compleat | £ | 8. —. — |
| 1 feather bed, Bolster & 2 pillows | | 8. —. — |
| 1 Chest of Drawers | | 2. 8. — |
| 1 Buroe Table | | 1. —. — |
| 6 Chairs Leather'd Bottoms | @ 6/ | 1. 16. — |
| 1 Small dressing Glass | | —. 6. — |
| 1 Small Carpett | | 1. —. — |

| | | |
|---|---|---|
| 1 White Cotton Counterpin | | —. 18. — |
| 1 pair Blanketts | | 1. 12. — |
| 1 pair holland Sheets | | 1. 4. — |
| 3 pair Dowlases D^o New | 12^s/p^r | 1. 16. — |
| 3 pair & 1 Ditto Coarser | 4/ | 0. 14. — |
| 3 pair Cotton & Linnen D^o | 3/ | 0. 9. — |
| 4 pair Servants Ditto | 2/ | 0. 8. — |
| 4 Coarse Table Cloths | 1/ | 0. 4. — |
| 10 Ditto Kitchen Towels | 1 | 0. 1. — |
| 5 Diaper Table Cloths | 12/ | 3. —. — |
| 6 Damask Table Cloths | @ 18/ | 5. 8. — |
| 4 N: England Diaper D^o | 3/ | 0. 12. — |
| 4 pair Linnen pillow Cases | 2/ | 0. 8. — |
| 5 Coarser Ditto | 1/ | 0. 5. — |
| 6 Diaper Towels | 6^d | 0. 3. — |
| 7 Damask Ditto | 2/ | 0. 14. — |
| 2 doz^n & 9 Damask Napkins | @ 24 ℔ loz^n | 3. 6. — |
| 1 Gauze Tea Table Cover | | 0. 1. — |
| | | 43. 13. 0 |

£

**In the Entry & Stair Case Viz^t**

| | |
|---|---|
| 17 Pictures | £ 0.10.— |
| | 0.10.0 |

**In the Kitchen Chamber Viz^t**

| | |
|---|---|
| a Bedstead & Curtains Compleat | £ 4. —. — |
| a Bed Bolster & 2 pillows | 5. —. — |
| a Under Bed & 1 Chair | 0. 1. — |
| 2 Rugs & 1 Blankett @ 6/ | 0. 18. — |
| | 09. 19. 0 |

**In the Dining Room Viz^t**

| | |
|---|---|
| 1 pair an Irons | £ 0. 3. — |
| 7 Bass Bottoms Chairs 1/ | 0. 7. — |
| 1 Large Wooden Table | 0. 3. — |
| 1 Small Ditto Oak | 0. 1. — |
| 1 Small looking Glass | 0. 6. — |
| 1 Old Desk | 0. 6. — |
| 1 Case with 2 Bottles | 0. 2. — |
| 1 Warming pan | 0. 12. — |
| | 2. 0. 0 |

## HOUSEHOLD INVENTORY OF JONATHAN CHANDLER (d1745)

| | |
|---|---|
| Cash | £ 18 |
| Gun | 1 |
| Psalmbook | 8 p |
| | £ 19 |
| Debts | £ 5 |
| Total | £ 14 |

## HOUSEHOLD INVENTORY OF DANIEL CHANDLER (d 1752) SHOEMAKER

| | |
|---|---|
| Bible | |
| Shoe knife | |
| Hammer | Total £ 12 |
| Last (shoe shaper) | |
| Various notes | |

## THE CRISIS WITH ENGLAND

George Grenville became England's prime minister at the end of the Seven Years' War. He inherited a national debt that had billowed from £75 million to £145 million during the war and a nation of wearied taxpayers. To reduce the debt, Grenville proposed new taxes in England and others in America, where the colonists were asked to bear their share of running the empire. Grenville's particular concern was financing the 10,000 British regulars left in North America after 1763 to police French-speaking Canada and the frontier and to remind the unruly American subjects that they were still beholden to the crown. It was Grenville's revenue program that initiated a rift between England and its colonies that a dozen years later would culminate in revolution.

### Sugar, Currency, and Stamps

In 1764, Grenville pushed through Parliament several bills that in combination pressed hard against the economic system of the colonies. First came the Revenue Act (or Sugar Act) of 1764. While reducing the tax on imported French molasses from 6 to 3 pence per gallon, it added a number of colonial products to the list of enumerated commodities that could be sent only to England. It also required American shippers to post bonds guaranteeing observance of the trade regulations before loading their cargoes. Finally, it strengthened the vice-admiralty courts, where violators of the trade acts were prosecuted.

Many of the colonial legislatures grumbled about the Sugar Act because a strictly enforced duty of 3 pence per gallon on molasses pinched more than the loosely enforced 6-pence duty. But only New York objected that *any* tax by Parliament to raise revenue (rather than to control trade) violated the rights of overseas English subjects who sent no representatives to Parliament.

On the heels of the Sugar Act came the Currency Act. In 1751, the New England colonies had been forbidden to issue paper money as legal tender, and now Parliament extended that

prohibition to all the colonies. In a colonial economy chronically short of hard cash, this was a trade-constricting measure.

The move to tighten up the machinery of empire confused the colonists because many of the new regulations came from Parliament, which usually had been content to allow the king, his ministers, and the Board of Trade to run overseas affairs. In a world where history taught that power and liberty were perpetually at war, generations of colonists had viewed Parliament as a bastion of English liberty, the bulwark against despotic political rule. The Parliament upon which colonial legislatures had modeled themselves in the past now began to seem like an oppressive violator of colonial rights.

In protesting new parliamentary regulations, colonial leaders were hobbled by uncertainty concerning where Parliament's authority began and ended in administering the colonies. The colonists had always implicitly accepted parliamentary power overseas because it was easier to evade distasteful trade regulations than to contest this power. But the exact limits of that authority were vague.

After Parliament passed the Sugar Act in 1764, Grenville announced his intention to extend to America the stamp duties that had already been imposed in England. However, he gave the colonies a year to suggest alternative ways of raising revenue. The colonies spent the time objecting strenuously to the proposed stamp tax, but none provided another plan. Knowing that colonial property taxes were slight compared to those in England, Grenville dismissed the petitions that poured in from the colonies and drove the bill through Parliament. The Stamp Act, to go into effect in November 1765, required revenue stamps on every newspaper, pamphlet, almanac, legal document, liquor license, college diploma, pack of playing cards, and pair of dice.

Colonial reaction to the Stamp Act ranged from disgruntled submission to mass defiance. The breadth of the reaction shocked the British government—and many Americans as well.

Lieutenant Governor Hutchinson of Massachusetts believed that "there is not a family between Canada and Pensacola that has not heard the name of the Stamp Act and but very few . . . but what have some formidable apprehensions of it." In many cases, resistance involved not only discontent over England's tightening of the screws on the American colonies but internal resentments born out of the play of local events. Especially in the cities, the defiance of authority and destruction of property by people from the middle and lower ranks redefined the dynamics of politics, setting the stage for a ten-year internal struggle for control among the various social elements alarmed by the new English policies.

### Stamp Act Riots

The Virginia House of Burgesses was the first legislature to react to the news of the Stamp Act, which arrived in April 1765. Virginia was already on edge because a severe decline in tobacco prices and heavy war-related taxes had mired most planters in debt. In late 1764, the burgesses had strenuously objected to the proposed stamp tax, citing the economic hardship it would cause and arguing that it was their "inherent" right to be taxed only by their own consent.

The Stamp Act enraged a group of Virginia's young burgesses. In May 1765, led by 29-year-old Patrick Henry, a fiery lawyer newly elected from a frontier county, the House of Burgesses debated seven strongly worded resolutions. Old-guard burgesses regarded some of them as treasonable. The legislature finally adopted the four more moderate resolves, including one proclaiming Virginia's right to impose taxes. But they rejected the other resolves, which declared it "illegal, unconstitutional, and unjust" for anybody outside Virginia to lay taxes; asserted that Virginians did not have to obey any externally imposed tax law; and labeled as "an enemy to this, his Majesty's colony" anyone denying Virginia's exclusive right to tax its inhabitants.

Since many burgesses had left for home before Henry introduced his resolutions, less

*From the time of his election to the Virginia House of Burgesses at the age of 29, Patrick Henry was an outspoken proponent of American autonomy.*

than a quarter of Virginia's legislators voted for the four moderate resolves. But within a month, all seven resolutions were broadcast in the newspapers of other colonies. Henry and the aggressive young burgesses had hurled words of defiance at Parliament for other colonies to reflect on and match.

Governor Francis Bernard of Massachusetts called the Virginia resolves "an alarm bell for the disaffected." The events in Boston in August 1765 amply confirmed his view. On August 14, Bostonians awoke to find an effigy of stamp distributor Andrew Oliver, dressed in rags, hanging from a huge elm tree in the south end of town. When the sheriff tried to remove it at the order of Chief Justice and Lieutenant Governor Thomas Hutchinson, Oliver's brother-in-law, a hostile crowd intervened. In the evening, working men began gathering for a mock funeral. Led by Ebenezer MacIntosh, they cut down Oliver's effigy and boisterously carried it through the streets. Then they leveled Oliver's new brick office on the wharves, rumored to be the distribution point for the hated stamps.

When night fell, the crowd reduced Oliver's luxurious mansion to a shambles. The stamp distributor promptly asked to be relieved of his commission. Twelve days later, MacIntosh led the crowd again in an all-night bout of destruction of the handsomely appointed homes of two British officials and Chief Justice Hutchinson, a haughty man who was as unpopular with the common people as his great-great-grandmother, Anne Hutchinson, had been popular. Military men "who have seen towns sacked by the enemy," one observer reported, "declare they never before saw an instance of such fury."

In attacking the property of men associated with the stamp tax, the Boston crowd under MacIntosh demonstrated its opposition to parliamentary policy. But the crowd was also expressing hostility toward a British-aligned local elite that for years had disdained lower-class political participation and had publicly denounced the working poor for their supposed lack of industry and frugality. For decades, ordinary Bostonians had aligned politically with the Boston "caucus," which led the colony's "popular party" against conservative aristocrats such as Hutchinson and Oliver. They had also read in the *Boston Gazette* that the new parliamentary legislation had been proposed by "mean mercenary hirelings among yourselves, who for a little filthy lucre would at any time betray every right, liberty, and privilege of their fellow subjects."

But "the rage-intoxicated rabble" had suddenly broken away from the leaders of the popular party and gone farther than they had intended. Thomas Hutchinson was one of their main targets. Characterized in the diary of a young lawyer named John Adams as "very ambitious and avaricious," Hutchinson was chief among the "mean mercenary hirelings" in the popular view. In the aftermath of the destruction of his house—what Governor Bernard called "a war of plunder, of taking away the distinction between rich and poor"—the more cautious political leaders knew they would have to struggle to regain control of the protest movement.

Violent protest against the Stamp Act also wracked New York and Newport, Rhode Island. Leading the resistance were groups calling themselves the Sons of Liberty, composed mostly of artisans, shopkeepers, and ordinary citizens. Protest took a more dignified form at the Stamp Act Congress, called by Massachusetts and attended by representatives of nine colonies who met in New York in October 1765. English authorities regarded this first self-initiated intercolonial convention as a "dangerous tendency." The delegates formulated 12 restrained resolutions that accepted Parliament's right to legislate for the colonies but denied its right to tax them directly.

All over America by late 1765, effigy-burning crowds had convinced stamp distributors to resign their commissions. The colonists defied English authority even more directly by forcing most customs officers and court officials to open the ports and courts for business after November 1 without using the hated stamps required after that date. It often took months of pressure, sometimes accompanied by mob action, to convince justices to open their courts. But the Sons of Liberty, often led by new faces in local politics, ultimately got their way by going outside the law.

In March 1766, Parliament debated the surprising American reaction to the Stamp Act and voted to repeal it. Some members warned that to retreat before colonial defiance of the law would ultimately be fatal. But the legislators bowed to expediency. They satisfied themselves with passing the Declaratory Act, which asserted Parliament's power to enact laws for the colonies in "all cases whatsoever." The crisis had passed. Yet nothing was really solved. In America, an image had appeared of a grasping government trampling its subjects' rights. The Stamp Act, one New England clergyman foresaw, "diffused a disgust through the colonies and laid the basis of an alienation which will never be healed."

In the course of challenging parliamentary authority, the Stamp Act resisters politicized their communities as never before. The established leaders, generally cautious in their protests, were often displaced by those beneath them on the social ladder. Men such as New York ship captains Alexander McDougall and Isaac Sears mobilized common citizens and raised political consciousness, employing mass demonstrations and street violence to humble stamp distributors and force open the courts and seaports. Scribbled John Adams in his diary: "The people have become more attentive to their liberties, . . . and more determined to defend them. . . . Our presses have groaned, our pulpits have thundered, our legislatures have resolved, our towns have voted; the crown officers have everywhere trembled, and all their little tools and creatures been afraid to speak and ashamed to be seen."

## An Uncertain Interlude

Ministerial instability in England hampered the quest for a coherent, workable American policy. To manage the colonies more effectively, the Pitt-Grafton ministry that the king had appointed in 1767 obtained new laws to reorganize the customs service, establish a secretary of state for American affairs, and install three new vice-admiralty courts in the port cities. Still hard pressed for revenue—for at home the government faced severe unemployment, tax protests, and riots over the high price of corn—the ministry also pushed through Parliament the Townshend duties on paper, lead, painters' colors, and tea. A final law suspended New York's assembly until that body ceased its noncompliance with the Quartering Act of 1765, which required public funds for support of British troops garrisoned in the colony since the end of the Seven Years' War.

Colonial reaction to the Townshend Acts, centered in Massachusetts, was more restrained than in 1765. New York buckled under to the Quartering Act rather than see its assembly suspended. But the Massachusetts House of Representatives sent a circular letter to each colony objecting to the new Townshend duties,

*This wood engraving, published in an 1829 history of the United States, recalls a New Hampshire riot in which a stamp master was lynched and stoned in effigy.*

small though they were. Written by Samuel Adams, the letter attacked as unconstitutional the plan to underwrite salaries for royal officials in America from customs duties. Under instructions from England, Governor Bernard dissolved the legislature after it refused to rescind the circular letter. "The Americans have made a discovery," declared Edmund Burke before Parliament, "that we mean to oppress them; we have made a discovery that they intend to raise a rebellion. We do not know how to advance; they do not know how to retreat."

While most of the colonists only grumbled and petitioned, Bostonians protested stridently. In the summer of 1768, after customs officials seized a sloop owned by John Hancock for a violation of the trade regulations, an angry crowd mobbed them. They were forced to flee to a British warship in Boston harbor and remain there for months. The newspapers hounded overeager revenue officers who extracted money for the maintenance of "swarms of officers and pensioners, and an enormous train of underlings and dependents"; it also warned of new measures designed "to suck the life blood" from the people and predicted that troops would be sent "to dragoon us into passive obedience." In the minds of many colonists, the belief grew that the English were plotting "designs for destroying our constitutional liberties."

Troops indeed came. The attack on the customs officials brought a resolute response from England, where the Bostonians' action was regarded as insubordinate and selfish. The ministry dispatched two regiments from England and two more from Nova Scotia. The intention was to bring the Bostonians to a proper state of subordination and make them an example to the rest of the colonies. Now cries went up against maintaining standing armies in peacetime, but radical Bostonians who proposed force to prevent the troops from landing got little support from delegates called to a special provincial convention. On October 1, 1768, red-coated troops marched into the town without resistance.

After the troops occupied Boston, the colonists' main tactic of protest against the Townshend Acts became economic boycott. First in Boston and then in New York and Philadelphia, merchants and consumers adopted nonimportation and nonconsumption agreements. They pledged neither to import nor to use British articles. These measures promised to bring the politically influential English merchants to their aid, for half of British shipping was engaged in commerce with the colonies, and one-quarter of all English exports were consumed there.

Many colonial merchants, however, especially those tied to the government's interest,

*The occupation of Boston by British troops in 1768 never quelled disorder as King George III had hoped.*

had no intention of being bound by a community compact that had no force in law. They had to be persuaded otherwise by street brigades, usually composed of artisans who warmly supported nonimportation as a boon to home manufacturing. Crowd action welled up again in the seaports, as determined patriot bands attacked the homes and warehouses of offending merchants and "rescued" incoming contraband goods seized by zealous customs officials. When the southern colonies also adopted nonimportation agreements in 1768, a new step toward intercolonial union had been taken.

England's attempts to discipline its American colonies and oblige them to share the costs of governing an empire that brought advantages as well as obligations lay in shambles by the end of the 1760s. The employment of troops to restore order undermined the respect for the mother country on which colonial acceptance of its authority ultimately depended. American newspapers denounced new extensions of British authority. Colonial governors quarreled with their legislatures. Customs officials met with determined opposition and were widely accused of arbitrary actions and excessive zeal in enforcing the Navigation Acts. The Townshend duties had failed miserably, yielding less than £21,000 by 1770 while costing British business £700,000 through the colonial nonimportation movement.

In London, on March 5, 1770, Parliament repealed all the Townshend duties except the one on tea (which the new minister of state, Lord North, explained was retained "as a mark of the supremacy of Parliament and an efficient declaration of their right to govern the colonies."). On that same evening in Boston, British troops fired on an unruly crowd of heckling citizens. For months, Bostonians had been baiting the "lobsterbacks," as they dubbed the redcoated British soldiers. They hated them for competing with townspeople for menial jobs when off duty, as well as for their military presence. On this evening, a taunting crowd had first hurled insults and snowballs and then surged toward a sentry. After a squad of redcoats joined the sentry, someone cried, "Fire!" When the smoke cleared, five bloody bodies, including that of Ebenezer MacIntosh's brother-in-law,

stained the snow-covered street. Bowing to furious popular reaction, Thomas Hutchinson, recently appointed governor, ordered the British troops out of town and arrested the commanding officer and the soldiers involved. They were later acquitted, two young patriot lawyers, John Adams and Josiah Quincy, Jr., having provided a brilliant defense.

In spite of the potential of the "Boston massacre" for galvanizing the colonies into further resistance, opposition to English policies, including economic boycotts, subsided in 1770. Popular leaders such as Samuel Adams in Boston and Alexander McDougall in New York, who had made names for themselves as the standard-bearers of American liberty, had few issues left to exploit. They were further handicapped by the end of the depression that had previously helped sow discontent. Yet the fires of revolution had been not extinguished but merely dampened.

### The Growing Rift

From 1770 to 1772, relative quiet descended over the colonies. Not until June 1772 did England provide another inflammatory issue. Then, by announcing that it would pay the salaries of the royal governor and superior court judges in Massachusetts rather than allow the provincial legislature to continue supporting these positions, the crown created a new furor. Even though the measure saved the colony considerable money, it was seen as a "dangerous innovation" because it undermined a right set forth in the colony's charter and hence was interpreted as a design to impose a despotic government on the colony. Judges paid from London, it was assumed, would respond to London.

Boston's town meeting protested loudly and created a committee of correspondence "to state the rights of the colonists . . . and to communicate and publish the same to the several towns and to the world." Crown supporters called the committee "the foulest, subtlest, and most venomous serpent ever issued from the egg of sedition." By the end of 1772, 80 other towns in Massachusetts had created committees. In the next year, all but three colonies established committees of correspondence within their legislatures.

Samuel Adams was by now the leader of the Boston radicals, for the influence of men like Ebenezer MacIntosh had been quietly neutralized. Adams was experienced in caucus politicking, a skilled political journalist, and a man with deep roots among the laboring people despite his Harvard degree. He organized the working ranks through the taverns, clubs, and volunteer fire companies and also secured the support of wealthy merchants such as John Hancock, whose ample purse financed patriotic celebrations and feasts that kept politics on everyone's mind and helped to build interclass bridges. In England, Adams was known as one of the most dangerous firebrands in America.

In 1772, a band of Rhode Island colonists gave Adams new material to work with when they attacked a royal warship. The British commander of the *Gaspee* was roundly hated for hounding the fishermen and small traders of Narragansett Bay. When his ship ran aground while pursuing a suspected smuggler, Rhode Islanders took their revenge. Clambering aboard the stranded vessel, they burned it to the water's edge. Adding insult to injury, a Rhode Island

court convicted the *Gaspee's* captain of illegally seizing what he was convinced was smuggled sugar and rum. The government in London reacted with cries of high treason. Finding the lips of Rhode Islanders sealed regarding the identity of the arsonists, an investigating committee could do little. The event was tailor-made for Samuel Adams, who used it to "awaken the American colonies, which have been too long dozing upon the brink of ruin."

In early 1773, Parliament's passage of the Tea Act precipitated the final plunge into revolution. The act allowed the East India Company, which was on the verge of bankruptcy, to ship its tea directly to America. By eliminating English middlemen and English import taxes, this provided Americans with the opportunity to buy their tea cheaply from the company's agents in the colonies. Even with the small tax to be paid in the colonies, Indian tea would now undersell smuggled Dutch tea. The Americans would get inexpensive tea, the crown would derive a modest revenue, and the East India Company would obtain a new lease on life. The company soon had 600,000 pounds of tea in 2,000 chests ready for shipment to America.

Parliament monumentally miscalculated

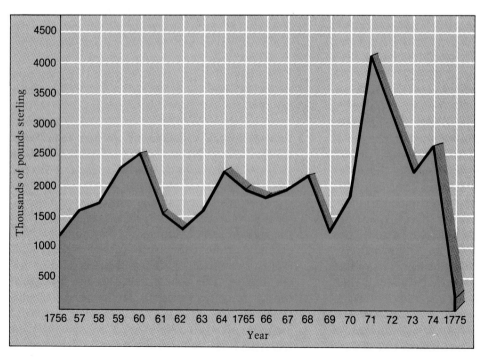

**British Exports to North America, 1756–1775**

*Source:* U.S. Bureau of the Census.

the American response. For several years, merchants in Philadelphia and New York had been flagrantly smuggling Dutch tea. As a consequence, imports of English tea in the two seaports plummeted from 500,000 pounds in 1768 to a mere 650 pounds in 1772. The merchants bitterly denounced the new act for giving the East India Company a monopoly on the American tea market. Other monopolies would follow, they predicted, and middlemen of all kinds would be eliminated. Objections were also raised that the government was shrewdly trying to gain implicit acceptance of Parliament's taxing power by offering tea at a new reduced rate. When Americans drank the taxed tea, they would also be swallowing the English right to impose taxes.

The colonists quickly demonstrated that their principles were not entirely in their pocketbooks. Mass meetings in the port towns soon forced the resignation of the East India Company's agents, and vows rang forth that the obnoxious tea making its way across the Atlantic would be stopped at the water's edge.

Governor Hutchinson of Massachusetts brought the tea crisis to a climax. He decided that to yield once more to popular pressure would be the final blow to English sovereignty in America. The popular party led by Samuel Adams had been urging the citizenry to demonstrate that they were not yet prepared for the "yoke of slavery" by sending the tea back to England. Hutchinson's refusal to grant the tea ships clearance papers to return to England with their cargoes finally led to dramatic action. Buoyed by resolutions from surrounding towns, 5,000 Bostonians packed Old South Church on December 16, 1773. The meeting passed resolutions urging the governor to clear the ships. But Hutchinson could not be swayed by the town's determination to resist what they regarded as another affront to their liberties. "This meeting," despaired Samuel Adams, "can do no more to save the country."

At nightfall, a band of Bostonians, dressed as Indians, boarded the tea ships, broke open the chests of tea, and flung £10,000 worth of the East India Company's property into Boston harbor. George Hewes, a 31-year-old shoemaker, recalled how he had garbed himself as a Mo-

hawk, blackened his "face and hands with coal dust in the shop of a blacksmith," and joined men of all ranks in marching stealthily to the wharves to do their work.

Now the die was cast. Lord North, the king's chief minister, called the Bostonians "fanatics" and argued that the dispute was no longer about taxes but about whether England had any authority at all over the colonies. George III put it succinctly: "We must master them or totally leave them to themselves and treat them as aliens."

Thoroughly aroused, Parliament passed a set of stern laws, which Bostonians promptly labeled the "Intolerable Acts." The port of Boston was ordered closed to all shipping until the colony paid for the destroyed tea. British soldiers and officials were declared immune from local court trials for acts committed while suppressing civil disturbances. To hamstring the colony's truculent political assemblies, the act amended the Massachusetts charter to transform the council from an upper legislative chamber, elected by the lower house, to a body appointed by the governor. This stripped the council of its veto power over the governor's decisions.

The act also struck at local government by authorizing the governor to prohibit all town meetings except for one annual meeting in each town to elect local officers of government. Finally, General Thomas Gage, commander in chief of British forces in America, replaced Thomas Hutchinson as governor. "This is the day, then," declared Edmund Burke in the House of Commons, "that you wish to go to war with all America, in order to conciliate that country to this."

The English plan to strangle Massachusetts into submission and hope for acquiescence elsewhere in the colonies proved popular in England. Earlier, the colonies had gained supporters in Parliament for their resistance to what many regarded as attacks on their fundamental privileges. Now this support evaporated. After a decade of debating constitutional rights and mobilizing sentiment against what many believed was a systematic plot to enslave freeborn citizens, the Americans found their maneuvering room severely narrowed.

When the Intolerable Acts arrived in May 1774 aboard the *Harmony*, Boston's town meeting reacted belligerently. A circular letter was dispatched to all the colonies urging an end to trade with England. This met with faint support; but a second call, for a meeting in Philadelphia of delegates from all colonies, received a better response. The Continental Congress, as it was called, now began to transform a ten-year debate conducted by separate colonies into a unified American cause.

Fifty-five delegates from all the colonies except Georgia converged on Carpenter's Hall in Philadelphia in September 1774. The discussions centered not on how to prepare for a war, which many sensed was inevitable, but on how to resolve differences that most delegates feared were irreconcilable. As important as the formal debates was overcoming sectional hostilities and prejudices. New Englanders were especially eyed with suspicion for their reputed intolerance and self-interest. "We have numberless prejudices to remove here," wrote John Adams from Philadelphia. "We have been obliged to keep ourselves out of sight, and to feel pulses, and to sound the depths; to insinuate our sentiments, designs, and desires by means of other persons, sometimes of one province, and sometimes of another."

The Continental Congress was by no means a unified body. Some delegates, led by cousins Samuel and John Adams from Massachusetts and Richard Henry Lee and Patrick Henry of Virginia, argued for outright resistance to Parliament's Coercive Acts. Moderate delegates from the middle colonies, led by Joseph Galloway of Pennsylvania and James Duane of New York, urged restraint and further attempts at reconciliation. After weeks of debate, the delegates did agree to issue a restrained Declaration of Rights and Resolves. It attempted to define American grievances and to justify the colonists' defiance of English policies and laws by appealing to the "immutable laws of nature, the principles of the English constitution, and the several [colonial] charters and compacts" under which they lived. More concrete was Congress's agreement on a plan of resistance. If England did not rescind the Intolerable Acts by December 1, 1774, a ban on all imports and exports between the colonies and Great Britain, Ireland, and the British West Indies would take effect. Some exceptions were made for the export of southern staple commodities in order to keep reluctant southern colonies in the fold.

By the time the Congress adjourned in late October, leaders from different colonies had learned of one another's conditions, measured one another's rhetoric and temperament, and transformed what had been primarily Boston's cause into a national movement. "Government is dissolved [and] we are in a state of nature," argued the fiery Patrick Henry. "The distinctions between Virginians, Pennsylvanians, New Yorkers, and New Englanders, are no more. I am not a Virginian, but an American." Many of Henry's fellow delegates were a long way from converting their provincial identities to a national one, but in adjourning, Congress agreed to reconvene in May 1775.

Even before the Second Continental Congress met, the fabric of government had been badly torn in most colonies. Revolutionary committees, conventions, and congresses, entirely unauthorized by law, were replacing legal governing bodies. Assuming authority in defiance of royal governors, who suspended truculent legislatures in many colonies, they often operated on instructions from mass meetings where the legal franchise was ignored. These extralegal bodies created and armed militia units, bullied merchants and shopkeepers refusing to conform to popularly authorized boycotts, levied taxes, operated the courts, and obstructed the work of English customs officials. By the end of 1774, all but three colonies defied their own charters by appointing provincial assemblies without royal authority. In the next year, this independently created power became evident in the nearly complete cessation of trade with England.

### The Final Rupture

The culminating spark to the revolutionary powder keg was struck in the spring of 1775. General Gage had assumed the governorship of Massachusetts 11 months earlier and occupied Boston with 4,000 troops—one for every adult male in the town. In April 1775, Gage was ordered by the government in London to arrest "the principal actors and abettors" of insurrection in Massachusetts. As a first step, he sent 700 redcoats out of Boston under cover of night to seize colonial arms and ammunition in nearby Concord. But Americans learned of the plan. When the troops reached Lexington at dawn, 70 "Minutemen"—townsmen available on a minute's notice—occupied the village green. In the skirmish that ensued, 18 Massachusetts farmers fell, 8 of them mortally wounded.

Marching 6 miles west, the British entered Concord, where another firefight broke out. Withdrawing, the redcoats made their way back to Boston, harassed by militiamen firing from farmhouses and barns and from behind stone walls. Before the bloody day ended, 273 British and 95 American casualties were recorded. News of the bloodshed swept through the colonies. Within weeks, one colonist reported that wherever one traveled "you see the inhabitants training, making firelocks, casting mortars, shells, and shot."

The outbreak of fighting vastly altered the debates of the Second Continental Congress that assembled in Philadelphia in May 1775. The Congress had the same slim powers as its predecessor, but it had awesome new responsibilities. Many delegates knew one another from the earlier Congress. But fresh faces appeared, including Boston's wealthy merchant, John Hancock; a tall, young planter-lawyer from Virginia, Thomas Jefferson; and the much-applauded Benjamin Franklin, who had arrived from London only four days before Congress convened.

The Congress had no power to legislate or command; it could only request and recommend. Delegate John Adams worried that such a body could form a constitution "for a great empire," while "at the same time they have a country of 1,500 miles to fortify, millions to arm and train, a naval power to begin, an extensive commerce to regulate, numerous tribes of Indians to negotiate with, a standing army of 27,000 men to raise pay, victual, and officer."

Another 14 months elapsed before Congress issued a formal declaration of independence, but the war with England—and a civil war in America—had already begun. Meeting in the statehouse in Philadelphia, where the king's arms hung over the entrance and the inscription

on the tower bell read "Proclaim liberty throughout the land unto all the inhabitants thereof," the Second Congress set to work. It authorized a continental army of 20,000, chose George Washington as commander in chief, issued a "Declaration of Causes of Taking-up Arms," sent the king an "Olive Branch Petition" humbly begging him to remove the obstacles to reconciliation, made moves to secure the neutrality of the interior Indian tribes, issued paper money, erected a postal system, and approved plans for a military hospital.

While debate continued over whether the colonies ought to declare themselves independent, military action grew hotter. The fiery Ethan Allen and his Green Mountain boys from eastern New York captured Fort Ticonderoga, controlling the Champlain valley, in May 1775. On New Year's Day in 1776, the British shelled Norfolk, Virginia. Yet many members of the Congress dreaded a final rupture and still hoped for reconciliation with England. Such hopes crumbled at the end of 1775 when news arrived that the king, rejecting the Olive Branch Petition, had dispatched 20,000 additional British troops to quell the American insurrection and had proclaimed the colonies in "open and avowed rebellion." Those fatal words made all of Congress's actions treasonable and turned all who obeyed them into traitors.

By the time Thomas Paine's fiery pamphlet *Common Sense* appeared in Philadelphia on January 9, 1776, members of Congress were talking less gingerly about independence. Paine's blunt words and compelling rhetoric smashed through the remaining reserve. "O ye that love mankind! Ye that dare oppose not only the tyranny, but also the tyrant, stand forth!" wrote Paine. Within weeks the pamphlet was in bookstalls all over the colonies. "The public sentiment which a few weeks before had shuddered at the tremendous obstacles, with which independence was envisioned," declared Edmund Randolph of Virginia, now "overleaped every barrier."

Congress continued to debate independence during the spring of 1776, even as the war became bloodier. While the delegates talked, men under arms acted. The army that Washington had gathered in Massachusetts forced the

British to evacuate Boston in March. Several months later, an American assault on Quebec failed. England embargoed all trade to the colonies and ordered the seizure of American ships. That convinced Congress to declare its ports open to all countries. "Nothing is left now," Joseph Hewes of North Carolina admitted before Congress, "but to fight it out." It was almost anticlimactic when Richard Henry Lee introduced his resolution in Congress on June 7 calling for a declaration of independence. After two days of debate, Congress ordered a committee chaired by Jefferson to begin drafting the document.

Though it would become revered as the new nation's birth certificate, the declaration was not a highly original statement. It drew heavily upon the addresses that Congress had been issuing to justify American resistance, and it presented a theory of government that was em-bedded in the scores of pamphlets that had issued from the colonial presses over the previous decade. The ringing phrases that "all men are created equal, that they are endowed by their Creator with certain unalienable Rights, that among these are Life, Liberty and the pursuit of Happiness" were familiar in the writing of many pamphleteers, including John Adams, Thomas Paine, and James Wilson.

Jefferson's committee brought its handiwork before the Congress on June 28. The proposals were read and ordered "to lie on the table" until the following Monday, July 1. "This morning is assigned for the greatest debate of all," noted John Adams, when the Congress reconvened. "May Heaven prosper the new-born republic, and make it more glorious than any former republics have been." At the end of the day, nine colonies voted to adopt the declaration, two voted against, one delegation split, and one abstained.

*In Common Sense, **Thomas Paine dared to articulate, in muscular language, the thoughts of rebellion and independence that others had alluded to.***

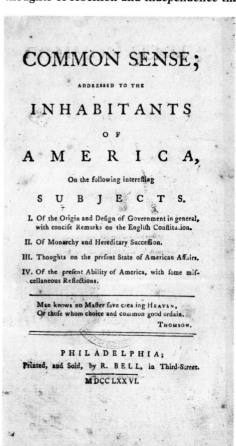

The next day, July 2, 12 delegations voted yes, with New York's abstaining, thus allowing the Congress to say that the vote for independence was unanimous. Two days more were spent cutting and polishing the document. The major change was the elimination of a long argument blaming the king for slavery in America.

On July 4, the Declaration of Independence was sent to the printer. Four days later, Philadelphians thronged to the statehouse to hear it read aloud. They huzzahed the reading, tore the king's arms from above the statehouse door, and later that night, amid cheers, toasts, and clanging church bells, tossed this symbol of more than a century and a half of colonial dependency to England into a roaring bonfire.

## THE TURMOIL OF REVOLUTIONARY SOCIETY

The long struggle with England over colonial rights between 1764 and 1776 did not occur within a unified colonial society. Social and economic change, which accelerated in the late colonial period, brought deep unrest and calls for reform from many quarters. By the end of the Seven Years' War, faith in the internal social systems of the colonies had waned among many colonists, just as allegiance to the mother country and to the British mercantile system had worn thin.

Among colonists who struggled for security in the aftermath of the Seven Years' War, many hoped that migration to frontier land would improve their fortunes. The flood of new immigrants from Ireland and Germany after the Treaty of Paris in 1763 added to the pressure to reach the trans-Appalachian river valleys. However, the western option involved much violence with Indian tribes unreceptive to the encroaching settlers. So most colonists chose to work out their destinies within their own communities or in other eastern communities to which they migrated in search of opportunity.

As agitation against English policy became more intense and the rhetoric of protest more inflated, previously acquiescent people took an active interest in politics. In such a charged atmosphere, the constitutional struggle with England spread quickly over its original boundaries into uncharted territory. Groups emerged —slaves, urban laboring people, backcountry farmers, evangelicals, women—who enunciated goals of their own that were sometimes only loosely connected to the struggle with England. The stridency and potential power of these groups raised for many upper-class leaders the frightening specter of a radically changed society. Losing control of the protests they had initially led, many of them would abandon the resistance movement against England.

### Republicanism and Revolutionary Ideology

In the years after 1763, the colonists responded to a variety of ideas that gave meaning to the events and conditions they were experiencing. Most of these ideas were formally expressed, in hundreds of newspaper articles and pamphlets, by educated lawyers, clergymen, and planters. These Americans had learned much earlier from English Whig writers that corrupt and power-hungry men were slowly extinguishing the lamp of liberty in England. The so-called "country" party represented by these Whig pamphleteers proclaimed itself the guardian of the true principles of the English constitution and opposed the "court" party representing the king and his appointees.

When the king's ministers began a new program for disciplining the empire after 1763, American Whig writers were intellectually prepared to view the new laws and policies as attacks on such traditional English liberties as balanced government, representative rights, and disestablishment of standing armies in peacetime. Even Parliament, traditionally the preserver of the rights of the people against tyrannical executive power, seemed to threaten a despotism of its own in its alliance with the monarchy. Every ministerial policy and parliamentary act in the decade after the Stamp Act appeared as a subversion of English liberties. Resistance to such blows against liberty seemed wholly justified to most Americans.

The belief that England was carrying out "a deep-laid and desperate plan of imperial despotism . . . for the extinction of all civil liberty," as the Boston town meeting expressed it in 1770, spread rapidly in the next few years. By 1774, John Adams was writing of "the conspiracy against the public liberty [that] was first regularly formed and begun to be executed in 1763 and 1764." From London, America's favorite writer, Benjamin Franklin, described the "extreme corruption prevalent among all orders of men in this old rotten state." Another pamphleteer reached the conclusion that England was no longer "in a condition at present to suckle us, being pregnant with vermin that corrupt her milk and convert her blood and juices into poison."

Among many Americans, especially merchants and others, the attack on constitutional rights blended closely with the encroachments on their economic interests that the tough new trade policies represented. Merchants saw a coordinated attack on their "lives, liberties, and property," as they frequently phrased it. If a man was not secure in his property, he was not secure in his political citizenship, for it was property that allowed a man the independence to shape his identity rather than be controlled by external forces.

The continuing crises over the imperial relationship inspired many colonists to resist impending tyranny—and nothing more. But the revolutionary mentality of others was also nourished by a belief that an opportunity was at hand to revitalize American society. They believed that the colonies had been undergoing a silent transformation in the previous generations and that the growing commercial connection with the decadent and corrupt mother country had injected deadly fluids into the American bloodstream. They anguished over the luxury and vice they saw around them and came to believe that resistance to England would return American society to a state of civic virtue, spartan living, and godly purpose.

The fervent support of the patriot movement by much of the colonial clergy, especially in New England, and the clergy's importance as writers of protest pamphlets helped to give a high-toned moral character to colonial protest. As in most revolutionary movements, the notion of moral regeneration, of a societywide rebirth through battle against a corrupt enemy, ennobled the cause. Such appeals resonated most strongly in New England, where even so secular a man as John Adams groaned at the "universal spirit of debauchery, dissipation, luxury, effeminacy and gaming." But they also inspired people in areas that had been affected a generation before by the Great Awakening.

The growth of a revolutionary spirit among common people also owed much to the rhetoric and plain style of polemic writers such as Thomas Paine and Patrick Henry. Paine's *Common Sense* transformed the terms of the imperial argument by attacking monarchy itself. But its astounding popularity—it went through 25 editions in 1776 and sold more copies than any printed piece in colonial history—stemmed not only from its argument but also from its style. Paine wrote for the common people, assuming their knowledge of nothing more than the Bible. Using biblical imagery and plain language, he appealed to their Calvinist heritage and their belief in their providential destiny. After savagely attacking the king, whom he called "a royal brute," Paine appealed to millennial yearnings: "We have it in our power to begin the world over again. The birthday of a new world is at hand," if only the Americans would stand up for liberty, the goddess whom "Europe regards . . . like a stranger, and England hath given . . . warning to depart."

Paine avoided the legalistic, logical style of most of the pamphlets written in the previous decade by lawyers and clergymen. His language could be understood on the docks, in the taverns, on the streets, and in the farmyards. Many Whig leaders found his pungent language and egalitarian call for ending hereditary privilege and concentrated power too strong. They denounced the disheveled immigrant with "genius in his eyes" as "a crack-brained zealot for democracy" and a dangerous man who appealed to "every silly clown and illiterate mechanic." But thousands read or listened to *Common Sense* and were radicalized by it. Gradually the colonists were piecing together a political ideology of their own, borrowed partly from English political thought, partly from the theories of the Enlightenment, and partly from their own experience. (A full discussion of this appears in Chapter 7.)

## Urban People

Although the cities contained only about 5 percent of the colonial population, they formed the vital cores of revolutionary agitation. As centers of communications, government, and commerce, they led the way in protesting English policy, and they soon contained the most politicized citizens in America. Local politics could be rapidly transformed as the struggle against England became interconnected with calls for internal reform.

In Philadelphia, for example, craftsmen had usually acquiesced in politics to the merchant and lawyer politicos before the Seven Years' War. But economic difficulties in the 1760s and 1770s convinced them to concert themselves within both their craft and their community. Artisans played a central role in forging a nonimportation agreement in 1768, calling public meetings, pub-

lishing newspaper appeals, organizing secondary boycotts against foot-dragging merchants, and ferreting out and tarring and feathering opponents to their policies. Cautious merchants complained that mere artisans had "no right to give their sentiments respecting an importation" and called the craftsmen "a rabble." But artisans, casting off their customary deference, forged ahead.

By 1772, artisans were filling elected municipal positions and insisting on their right to participate equally with their social superiors in nominating assemblymen and other important officeholders. Inspired by electing their own kind to important offices, they began lobbying for reform laws. The craftsmen called for elected representatives to be more accountable to their constituents, for publication of assembly debates and roll calls on important issues, and for construction of public galleries in the legislative chamber. Genteel Philadelphians muttered that "it is time the tradesmen were checked—they ought not to intermeddle in state affairs—they will become too powerful."

By 1774, working-class intermeddling in state affairs had taken a bold new step—the de

*Public sentiment against the importation of tea and other British goods often found expression in a coat of tar and feathers applied to the bare skin of the offending importer. A broadside from the "Committee for Tarring & Feathering" (left) exhorts pilots on the Delaware to watch for an arriving tea ship. Note the symbols in the painting (right)* The Bostonian's Paying the Excise-Man: *dumping tea into the harbor, the Liberty Tree with hangman's noose and overturned copy of the Stamp Act.*

## TO THE
# Delaware Pilots.

WE took the Pleasure, some Days since, of kindly admonishing you *to do your Duty*; if perchance you should meet with the *(Tea,)* SHIP POLLY, CAPTAIN AYRES; a THREE DECKER which is hourly expected.

We have now to add, that Matters ripen fast here; and that *much is expected from those Lads who meet with* a Ship.----There is some Talk of A HANDSOME REWARD FOR THE PILOT WHO GIVES THE FIRST GOOD UNS OF HER.----How that may be, we cannot *for certain* determine: But ALL agree, that TAR and HERS will be his Portion, who pilots her into this Harbour. And we will answer for ourselves, that ver is committed to us, as an Offender against the Rights of *America*, will experience the utmost Ex-of our Abilities; as

THE COMMITTEE FOR TARRING AND FEATHERING.

facto assumption of governmental powers by committees called into being by the people at large. Craftsmen had first clothed themselves in such extralegal authority in policing the nonimportation agreement in 1769. Five years later, in response to the Intolerable Acts, they put forward a radical slate of candidates for a committee to enforce a new economic boycott. Their ticket drubbed one nominated by the city's conservative merchants.

The political mobilization and heightened consciousness of laboring Philadelphians continued as the impasse with England reached a climax in 1775. Many pacifist Quaker leaders of the city had abandoned politics by this time, and other conservative merchants had also concluded that mob rule had triumphed. Into the leadership vacuum stepped a group of radical men of middle ranks: the fiery Scots-Irish doctor, Thomas Young, who had agitated in Boston and Albany before migrating to Philadelphia; Timothy Matlack, a hardware retailer who was popular with the lower classes for matching his prize bantam cocks against those of New York's aristocratic James Delancy; James Cannon, a young schoolteacher; Benjamin Rush, whose new medical practice took him into the garrets and cramped rooms of the city's poor; and Thomas Paine, a recent immigrant seeking something better in America than he had found as an ill-paid excise officer in England.

The political support of the new radical leaders was centered in the 31 companies of the Philadelphia militia, composed mostly of laboring men, and in the extralegal committees now controlling the city's economic life. Their leadership helped to overcome the conservatism of the regularly elected Pennsylvania legislature, which was restraining the movement of the Continental Congress toward independence. In addition, the new radical leaders demanded internal reforms: opening up opportunity; curbing the accumulation of vast wealth by "our great merchants" who were "making immense fortunes at the expense of the people"; abolishing the property requirement for voting; allowing militiamen to elect all their officers; and imposing stiff fines, to be used for the support of the families of poor militiamen, on all men who refused militia service.

Philadelphia's radicals at no time controlled the city. They always jostled for position with prosperous artisans and shopkeepers of more moderate views and with cautious lawyers and merchants. But mobilization among artisans, laborers, and mariners, in other cities as well as Philadelphia, was indispensable to the flow of events that led toward independence. Whereas most of the patriot elite fought only for redress of grievances with regard to English colonial policy, the populace of the cities also struggled for internal reforms and raised notions of how an independent American society might be reorganized.

Women also played a vital role in the urban crucible of revolutionary activity. They signed nonimportation agreements, harassed noncomplying merchants, and helped organize "fast days" when communities prayed for deliverance from English oppression. But the women's most important role was in facilitating the economic boycott of English goods. The success of the nonconsumption pacts depended on substituting homespun cloth for English textiles on which colonists of all classes had always relied. From Georgia to Maine, women and children

*This British cartoon, showing a group of North Carolina ladies signing an antitea agreement, takes a derisive view of political activities in the colonies.*

began spinning yarn and weaving cloth. "Was not every fireside, indeed a theatre of politics?" John Adams remembered after the war. Towns often vied patriotically with each other in the manufacture of cotton, linen, and woolen cloth, the women staging open-air spinning contests to publicize their commitment. In 1769, the women of tiny Middletown, Massachusetts, set the standard by weaving 20,522 yards of cloth, about 160 yards each.

After the Tea Act in 1773, the interjection of politics into the household economy increased as patriotic women boycotted their favorite drink. Newspapers carried recipes for tea substitutes and recommendations for herbal teas. In Wilmington, North Carolina, women paraded solemnly through the town and then made a ritual display of their patriotism by burning their imported tea. Many women could agree with one Rachel Wells: "I have done as much to carry on the war as many that set now at the helm of government."

## Protesting Farmers

In most of the agricultural areas of the colonies, where the majority of settlers made their livelihoods, passions concerning English policies were aroused only slowly. After about 1740, farmers had benefited from a sharp rise in the demand for foodstuffs in England, southern Europe, and the West Indies. Rising prices and brisk markets brought a higher standard of living to thousands of rural colonists, especially south of New England. Living far from harping English customs officers, impressment gangs, and occupying armies, the colonists of the interior had to be drawn gradually into the resistance movement by their urban cousins. Even in Concord, Massachusetts, only a dozen miles from the center of colonial agitation, townspeople found little to protest in English policies until England closed the port of Boston in 1774. They concerned themselves with local issues—roads, schools, the location of churches—but rarely with the frightful offenses to American liberty that Bostonians perceived.

Yet some parts of rural America seethed with social tension in the prewar era. The dynamics of conflict, shaped by the social development of particular regions, eventually became part of the momentum for revolution. In three western counties of North Carolina and in the Hudson River valley of New York, for example, widespread civil disorder marked the pre-Revolutionary decades. The militant rhetoric and tactics used by small farmers in combating exploitation formed rivulets that fed the main stream of revolutionary consciousness.

For years, the small farmers of western North Carolina had suffered exploitation by corrupt county court officials appointed by the governor and a legislature dominated by eastern planter interests. Sheriffs and justices, allied with land speculators and lawyers, seized property when farmers could not pay their taxes and sold it, often at a fraction of its worth, to their cronies. The legislature turned a deaf ear to western petitions for lower taxes, paper currency, and lower court fees. In the mid-1760s, frustrated at getting no satisfaction from legal forms of protest, the farmers organized associations of so-called Regulators that forcibly closed the courts, attacked the property of their enemies, and whipped and publicly humiliated judges and lawyers. When their leaders were arrested, the Regulators stormed the jails and released them.

In 1768 and again in 1771, Governor William Tryon led troops against the Regulators. Bloodshed was averted on the first occasion, but on the second, at the Battle of Almance, two armies of more than 1,000 opened fire on each other. Nine men died on each side before the Regulators fled the field. Seven leaders were executed in the trials that followed. Though the Regulators lost on the field of battle, their protests became part of the larger revolutionary struggle. They railed against the self-interested behavior of a wealthy elite and asserted the necessity for people of humble rank to throw off deference and assume political responsibilities.

Rural insurgency in New York flared up in the 1750s, subsided, and then erupted again in 1766. The conditions under which land was held precipitated the violence. The Hudson River valley had long been controlled by a few wealthy families with enormous landholdings, which they leased to small tenant farmers. The Van Rensselaer manor totaled a million acres, the

Phillipses' manor nearly half as much. Hundreds of tenants with their families paid substantial annual rents for the right to farm on these lands, which had been acquired as virtually free gifts from royal governors. When tenants resisted rent increases or purchased land from Indians who swore that manor lords had extended the boundaries of their manors by fraud, the landlords began evicting their leaseholders.

As the wealthiest men of the region, the landlords had the power of government, including control of the courts, on their side. Organizing themselves and going outside the law became the tenants' main strategy, as with the Carolina Regulators. By 1766, while New York City was absorbed in the Stamp Act furor, tenants led by William Prendergast began resisting sheriffs who tried to evict tenants from lands they claimed. The militant tenants threatened landlords with death and broke open jails to rescue their friends. British troops from New York were employed to break the tenant rebellion. Prendergast, brought to trial, was sentenced to be hanged, beheaded, and quartered. Although he was pardoned, the bitterness of the Hudson River tenants endured through the Revolution when most of them, unlike the Carolina Regulators, fought with the British because their landlords had joined the patriot cause.

### The First Abolitionists

In developing a rationale for resisting English policies after 1763, colonial leaders adopted a vocabulary and phraseology that emphasized natural rights, the consent of the governed, the naturalness of equality, and the need to resist corrupt and despotic power. The stirring phrases that flowed from the press led to a consideration of slavery. Catchwords such as *slavery* and *tyranny*, employed to describe the effects of British policies, readily brought to mind that chattel slavery held one-fifth of America's population in chains. Seeing themselves as the protectors of liberty in the 1770s, the Americans were forced to look at an ugly contradiction between their rhetoric and the plain facts of their labor system.

By midcentury in the northern colonies, Quakers and a few others made the morality of

slavery a public issue for the first time since Africans had been brought to Jamestown in 1619. After 1765, a score of New England ministers, black spokesmen, and some revolutionary radicals joined these early abolitionists. All of them argued that slavery was immoral, destructive of virtue in slaveholders, and irreconcilable with the principles of liberty that Americans heralded in their society.

Writers on both sides of the Atlantic and on both sides of the imperial argument pointed to the contradiction of the colonists' building a society on slave labor while they argued about British violations of inalienable rights. How could Americans treat Negroes "as a better kind

*The New England slave John Jack, who eventually bought his own freedom, died in 1773 and was buried with an abolitionist epitaph that concludes, "He practised these virtues / without which kings are but slaves."*

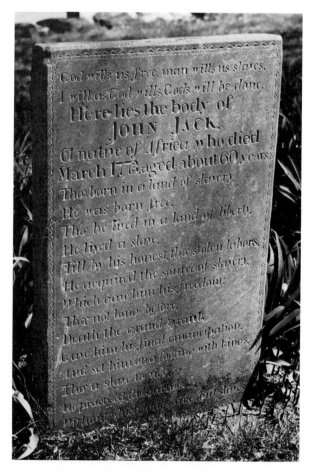

of cattle, while they are bawling about the rights of human nature?" queried an English official. Samuel Hopkins, a New England clergyman, chided his compatriots for "making a vain parade of being advocates for the liberties of mankind, while . . . you at the same time are continuing this lawless, cruel, inhuman, and abominable practice of enslaving your fellow creatures."

Brought face to face with white racial prejudice and the insult that slavery represented to the principles Americans proclaimed in resisting English policies, many northern colonies abolished the slave trade or taxed it out of existence before the Declaration of Independence was signed. Slavery itself, however, was not eliminated. In the South, the abolitionists had little impact. The 1760s witnessed the largest importations of slaves in colonial history. By the eve of the Revolution, 200,000 slaves toiled in Virginia, more than in any of England's 22 Western Hemisphere colonies.

## CONCLUSION: Forging a Revolution

The colonial Americans who lived in the third quarter of the eighteenth century participated in an era of political tension and conflict that changed the lives of nearly all of them. The Seven Years' War removed French and Spanish challengers and nurtured the colonists' sense of separate identity. Yet it left them with difficult economic adjustments, heavy debts, and growing social divisions. The Treaty of Paris in 1763 was heralded as the dawning of a new era; but it led to a reorganization of England's triumphant, yet debt-torn empire that had profound repercussions in America.

In the pre-Revolutionary decade, as England and the colonies moved from crisis to crisis, a dual disillusionment with the mother country penetrated ever deeper into the colonial consciousness. Pervasive doubt arose concerning both the colonies' role, as assigned by England, in the economic life of the empire and the sensitivity of the government in London to the colonists' needs. At the same time, the colonists began to perceive British policies—instituted by Parliament, the king, and his advisers—as a systematic attack on the fundamental liberties and natural rights of British subjects in America.

The fluidity and diversity of colonial society and the differing experiences of Americans during and after the Seven Years' War evoked varying responses to the disruption that accompanied the English reorganization of the empire. In the course of resisting English policy, many previously inactive groups entered public life to challenge gentry control of political affairs. Often occupying the most radical ground in the opposition to England, they simultaneously challenged the concentration of economic and political power in their own communities.

When Congress turned the 15-month undeclared war into a formally declared struggle for national liberation in July 1776, they steered their compatriots onto turbulent and unknown seas. Writing to his wife Abigail from his Philadelphia boardinghouse, the secularized Puritan John Adams caught some of the peculiar blend of excitement and dread that thousands shared. "You will think me transported with enthusiasm but I am not. I am well aware of the toil and blood and treasure that it will cost us to maintain this Declaration, and support and defend these States. Yet through all the gloom I can see the rays of ravishing light and glory. I can see that the end is more than worth all the means. And that posterity will triumph in that day's transactions, even although we should rue it, which I trust in God we shall not."

### Steps on the Road to Revolution

| | |
|---|---|
| 1763 | Treaty of Paris ends Seven Years' War between England and France; France cedes Canada to England. |
| | Proclamation of 1763 forbids white settlement west of Appalachian Mountains. |
| 1764 | Sugar Act sets higher duties on imported sugar and lower duties on molasses and enlarges the power of vice-admiralty courts. |
| | Currency Act prohibits issuance of paper money by colonies. |
| 1765 | Stamp Act requires printed documents to affix revenue-raising stamps purchased from British-appointed stamp distributors. |
| | Stamp Act Congress meets in New York. |
| | Quarterly Act requires colonies to furnish British troops with housing and certain provisions. |
| | Sons of Liberty formed in New York City and thereafter in many towns. |
| 1766 | Declaratory Act asserts Parliament's sovereignty over the colonies after repealing Stamp Act. |
| | Rent riots by New York tenant farmers. |
| 1767 | Townshend Revenue Acts impose duties on tea, glass, paper, paints, and other items. |
| | South Carolina Regulators organize in backcountry. |
| 1768 | British troops sent to Boston. |
| 1770 | British troops kill four and wound eight American civilians in Boston Massacre. |
| 1771 | Battle of Alamance pits frontier North Carolina Regulators against eastern militia led by royal governor. |
| 1772 | British schooner *Gaspee* burned in Rhode Island. |
| | Committee of correspondence formed in Boston and thereafter in other cities. |
| 1773 | Tea Act reduces duty on tea but gives East India Company right to sell directly to Americans. |
| | Boston Tea Party dumps £10,000 of East India Company tea into Boston harbor. |
| 1774 | Coercive Acts close port of Boston, restrict provincial and town governments in Massachusetts, and send additional troops to Boston. |
| | Quebec Act attaches trans-Appalachian interior north of Ohio River to government of Quebec. |
| | First Continental Congress meets and forms Continental Association to boycott British imports. |
| 1775 | Battles of Lexington and Concord cause 93 American and 272 British casualties; Fort Ticonderoga taken by Americans. |
| | Second Continental Congress meets and assumes many powers of an independent government. |
| | Dunmore's Proclamation in Virginia promises freedom to slaves and indentured servants fleeing to British ranks. |
| | Prohibitory Act embargoes American goods. |
| | George III proclaims Americans in open rebellion. |
| 1776 | Thomas Paine publishes *Common Sense*. |
| | British troops evacuate Boston. |

## Recommended Reading

Further knowledge of the long, exhausting wars of empire that embroiled the colonies for four generations before 1763 can be derived from Douglas E. Leach, *Arms for Empire* (1973); Francis Jennings, *The Ambiguous Iroquois Empire* (1984); William Eccles, *The Canadian Frontier*, rev. ed. (1983); David H. Corkran, *The Cherokee Frontier* (1962); and Lawrence H. Gipson's exhaustive *The British Empire Before the American Revolution*, 15 vols. (1936–70).

The administration of the British Empire and the difficulties surrounding the Seven Years' War are addressed in Michael Kammen, *Empire and Interest* (1970); Ian R. Christie, *Crisis of Empire* (1966); Jack M. Sosin, *Whitehall and the Wilderness* (1961); Howard Peckham, *Pontiac and the Indian Uprising* (1947); and John R. Alden, *John Stuart and the Southern Colonial Frontier* (1944).

For different points of view on the origins of the American Revolution, see John Brewer, *Party Ideology and Popular Politics at the Accession of George III* (1976); Bernard Bailyn, *The Ideological Origins of the American Revolution* (1967); Gary B. Nash, *The Urban Crucible* (1979); Edmund S. Morgan and Helen M. Morgan, *The Stamp Act Crisis* (1953); Joseph A. Ernst, *Money and Politics in America, 1755–1775* (1973); David Ammerman, *In the Common Cause* (1974); and Pauline Maier, *From Resistance to Rebellion* (1972). Merrill Jensen gives a comprehensive view in *The Founding of a Nation* (1968).

Rich local studies of the revolutionary crisis include Robert Gross, *The Minutemen and Their World* (1976); Dirk Hoerder, *Crowd Action in Revolutionary Massachusetts* (1977); Eric Foner, *Tom Paine and Revolutionary America* (1976); and Edward Countryman, *A People in Revolution* (1981). Excellent essays on various aspects of the coming of the Revolution can be found in Stephen G. Kurtz and James H. Hutson, eds., *Essays on the American Revolution* (1973) and Alfred F. Young, ed., *The American Revolution* (1976).

## TIME LINE

| | |
|---|---|
| 1696 | Parliament establishes Board of Trade |
| 1701 | Iroquois set policy of neutrality |
| 1702–1713 | Queen Anne's War |
| 1713 | Peace of Utrecht |
| 1733 | Molasses Act |
| 1739–1740 | Creeks maneuver to maintain neutrality |
| 1744–1748 | King George's War |
| 1754 | Albany conference |
| 1755 | Braddock defeated by French and Indian allies |
| 1756–1763 | Seven Years' War |
| 1759 | Wolfe defeats the French at Quebec |
| 1759–1761 | Cherokee War against the English |
| 1760s | Economic slump |
| 1763 | Treaty of Paris ends Seven Years' War  Proclamation line limits westward expansion |
| 1764 | Sugar and Currency Acts  Pontiac's Rebellion in Ohio valley |
| 1765 | Stamp Act resisted by colonists  Virginia House of Burgesses issues Stamp Act resolutions |
| 1766 | Declaratory Act  Tenant rent war in New York  Slave insurrections in South Carolina |
| 1767 | Townshend duties imposed |
| 1768 | British troops occupy Boston |
| 1770 | "Boston massacre"  Townshend duties repealed (except on tea) |
| 1771 | Carolina Regulators defeated |
| 1772 | *Gaspee* incident in Rhode Island |
| 1773 | Tea Act provokes Boston Tea Party |
| 1774 | "Intolerable Acts"  First Continental Congress meets |
| 1775 | Second Continental Congress meets  Battles of Lexington and Concord  Fear of slave revolts spreads |
| 1776 | Tom Paine publishes *Common Sense*  Declaration of Independence |

# PORTFOLIO ONE

## THE ART OF
## A COLONIZING PEOPLE

### 1 4 9 2 – 1 7 7 6

The early settlers of Massachusetts and Virginia were not interested in fine art; their main concern was survival. But when they erected houses, barns, and public buildings, even when they fashioned simple household utensils, they adopted the forms familiar to them from their experience in Europe. In the beginning, most of the forms were medieval in origin.

As other people came to the American colonies, they brought their own concept of design with them. The Germans, settling mostly in Pennsylvania, built houses and barns quite different from those in New England, and their elaborately decorated chests stood in marked contrast to the more simple New England versions. Most settlers brought a few prized or practical objects with them—a chest, a few tools, some cooking utensils. Among the early settlers, only the black Africans were deprived of the chance to bring familiar objects to America. But the slaves brought mental images of how things should look and feel, and they translated these conceptions into ceramic pots, grave markers, and other objects in the New World. The European settlers had little appreciation for American Indian culture, already established in North America, but the various Native American tribes that spanned the continent had well-developed concepts of design, expressed most frequently in blankets, baskets, belts, clothes, pipes, and pots made by women.

Each group of settlers brought its own perception of art and design, but gradually an American style developed. Regional and ethnic distinctions remained, however, and styles mixed. Even Indian basketry and blankets were influenced by European culture. There was never quite a melting pot of art, any more than there was a melting pot of ethnic groups in America. But imperceptibly, almost unconsciously, an American style of building and painting emerged, still influenced by Europe but owing much to the American environment.

Although American society remained more fluid and democratic than that in Europe, class differences developed in the American colonies and were often expressed in art and furniture. For the wealthy throughout the colonial period, art remained something that was imported from Europe. Prominent American families had their portraits painted in England, used imported china and silverware, and sat in elegant English chairs. Yet by the eve of the Revolution, especially in the major port cities, skilled American craftsmen were producing furniture and silver of exquisite and expensive design, still patterned after European models but with differences. Even more distinctive in some ways were the simple objects and primitive paintings turned out by artisans and ordinary citizens. The quilt or coverlet, the gravestone, the pottery bowl, even the plain chairs and tables found in all parts of the American colonies had developed an American form, even before most colonists thought of themselves as distinctly American.

Anonymous, *Mrs. Elizabeth Freake and Baby Mary*, c. 1674.
Worcester Art Museum, Worcester, Massachusetts.

Anonymous, *Magdalena Douw (Gansevoort)*, c. 1740.
Henry Francis du Pont Winterthur Museum, Winterthur, Delaware.

Although colonial America produced a few artists who achieved world fame, most
notably John Singleton Copley and Benjamin West, the colonies also supported
hundreds of lesser artists, many of them unidentified, who did portraits of individuals
and family groups. Many of these primitive paintings have a charm and freshness that is
appealing, but they also give us insight into a world quite different from our own.
Studying the portrait of a mother and child done in Boston about 1674, it is difficult to
believe that the unknown artist believed in infant depravity. The portrait of a young
girl, painted by a Dutch colonist in the Hudson River region, shows the colonial love of
color and decoration and contrasts with the somber image we often have of the early
New England settlers.

Anonymous, *The Old Plantation*, n.d.
Abby Aldrich Rockefeller Center for American Folk Art, Williamsburg, Virginia.

For years most scholars assumed that the African slaves brought little cultural heritage with them to the New World and that what few African ways they remembered were entirely lost after a generation or two. Recently, however, a number of authorities have begun to trace the African influence on music, religion, house and boat design, and a number of artifacts including ceramic jugs and quilts. The African memory mixed with the American influence to form a unique Afro-American culture.

The eighteenth-century watercolor by an anonymous artist records a group of slaves on a South Carolina plantation singing and dancing. One of the musicians is playing a banjolike instrument with a gourd body. Some experts think the design of the American banjo originated in Africa and was brought to this continent by slaves. In fact, until the middle of the nineteenth century, the banjo seems to have been played almost exclusively by blacks. The drumsticks in the picture appear to be made of twisted leather, just as African drumsticks are often made.

Many black women were expert weavers before they were taken out of Africa, and their knowledge and artistry were put to use by slave owners. The two examples of slave-made fabrics display sophistication of technique and, notably in the gold-and-black coverlet, an aesthetic sense that owes little to European models.

Reverse-weave bedspread, made near Macon, Georgia.
Old Slave Mart Museum, Charleston, South Carolina.
Photo Mrs. Judith W. Chase.

Woven coverlet, made near La Grange, Georgia.
Old Slave Mart Museum, Charleston, South Carolina.
Photo Mrs. Judith W. Chase.

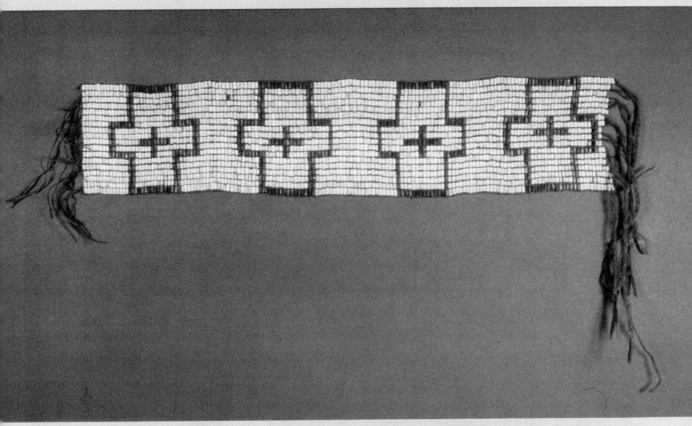

Lenape wampum belt believed to have been given to William Penn at the signing of the Treaty of Shakamaxon, 1683.
Museum of the American Indian, Heye Foundation, New York.

American Indian artifacts, now in great demand by collectors and recognized for their skill and design, were ignored for years by Americans and Europeans alike. All the Indian nations—the Iroquois and Algonquian of the Northeast as well as the more advanced groups of the Southwest—produced beautiful artwork that began to attract recognition only in the late nineteenth century, often by artists fascinated by the abstract designs. The fabrics, baskets, and beaded articles were made predominantly by women.

Lenape quilled deerskin bag.
Museum of the American Indian,
Heye Foundation, New York.

Brewster chair, Massachusetts, c. 1650.
Metropolitan Museum of Art, New York.
Gift of Mrs. J. Insley Blair.

The early settlers in the colonies often copied English medieval furniture such as the solid and elaborate Brewster chair from Massachusetts. But much more common were simple benches and stools. By the middle of the eighteenth century, however, skilled colonial craftsmen were creating their own versions of European styles for wealthy American families. Within the colonies, regional variations existed. At the left is a rather stiff Chippendale chair from New Hampshire, in the center a more ornate Philadelphia version, and at the right a gracefully curved Queen Anne chair from New York.

The chest was one of the most common pieces of furniture in colonial America. In the days before closets and elaborate bureaus, the chest was an all-purpose storage place for clothes, linens, and valuables. It could also be used as a table, and some versions served as seats as well. The first example, from seventeenth-century New Hampshire, shows a style of construction and decoration often seen in the New England colonies. The second, more elaborate and colorful example shows the German influence in Pennsylvania.

Chippendale side chair,
New Hampshire, c. 1775.
Metropolitan Museum of Art, New York.
Gift of Mrs. J. Insley Blair.

Chippendale side chair, attributed to
Thomas Fisher, Philadelphia, 1772.
Metropolitan Museum of Art, New York.
Anonymous gift in memory of Elizabeth Snow Bryce.

Queen Anne side chair, made for the
Apthorp family, New York, 1750–1770.
Metropolitan Museum of Art, New York.
Gift of Mr. and Mrs. Benjamin Ginsburg.

Joined chest, Portsmouth, New Hampshire, 1687.
Museum of Fine Arts, Boston.

Chest with drawers, Pennsylvania, 1780–1790.
Philadelphia Museum of Art. Gift of Mrs. J. Stogdell Stokes.

# PART TWO
# A REVOLUTIONARY PEOPLE

# 1775–1824

The American Revolution not only represented an epic military victory over the powerful mother country but also set the course of national development in ways that still affect American society. The Revolutionary generation was inspired by the idea that once they were free from England, they would build a model society based on principles of freedom and equality. Even as the battle for independence raged, they were embarked on the task of building new forms of government and forging new social, religious, and economic institutions. This attempt to construct a *novus ordo seclorum*, a new secular order, continued beyond the Revolutionary era and continues yet today.

Chapter 6, "The American People in Revolution," traces the impact of the Revolutionary call to arms on the various groups that made up American society and shows the paradoxical result of the Revolution for blacks and Native Americans. Chapter 7, "The Politics of Revolutionary America," delves into the exhilarating yet divisive work of constructing state and national governments, an exercise in nation building that brought into contention the diverse views of different social groups concerning how power should be shared and governmental decisions made. This search for a national identity and a shared understanding about what government ought to be and do continued in the years after the Treaty of Paris ended the war with England in 1783. This is the focus of Chapter 8, "Creating a Nation," which discusses the "Great Debate" that emerged over replacing the Articles of Confederation with a new constitution and a stronger national government. Out of this momentous decision came the development of a two-party system, created in an atmosphere charged with reverberations from the French Revolution and fierce disagreements about the government's role in economic affairs of the nation.

Chapters 9 and 10, overlapping in time, should be considered as a pair. Chapter 9, "The Preindustrial Republic," evaluates the underlying social and economic changes that were occurring in the early decades of the republic. It examines regional patterns of life and the experience of different social groups in an era poised between a preindustrial economy and the industrializing world of the nineteenth century. It also investigates how the American people began to think of perfecting their republican society to rid it of some of the contradictions it posed to the lofty Revolutionary principles that they espoused. Chapter 10, "Politics and Society in the Early Republic," delves into the political and diplomatic developments of the first three decades of the nineteenth century when the young nation expanded rapidly beyond the Appalachians, acquired vast new territories, fought a series of wars with Indian tribes and a second war against England, and moved toward a new party system under the presidencies of three Virginia Democratic-Republicans—Jefferson, Madison, and Monroe—and one New Englander, John Quincy Adams.

## CULTURAL and TECHNOLOGICAL

1775 Mercy Warren, *The Group*

1780 American Academy of Arts and Sciences
1781 Massachusetts Medical Society
New Jersey Society for Promoting Agriculture
1782 Crevecoeur, *Letters from an American Farmer*
John Trumbull, *M'Fingal*
First Catholic parochial school established in Philadelphia
1783 Noah Webster's *American Spelling Book*
1784 Jefferson's *Notes on Virginia*

1787 John Fitch launches first American steamboat
Royal Tyler, *The Contrast*
Joel Barlow, *Vision of Columbus*
1789 State University of North Carolina begins instruction
Thanksgiving first celebrated as national holiday
Protestant Episcopal Church established

1790 Roman Catholic episcopate created
Federal Copyright Act
First federal patent issued
1791 Susannah Rowson, *Charlotte Temple*
William Bartram, *Travels*
Anthracite coal discovered in Pennsylvania
First macadam road opens in Pennsylvania
Franklin's *Autobiography* published in France
1792 Robert Thomas founds *The Farmer's Almanac*
Joel Barlow, *Advice to the Privileged Orders*
1793 Eli Whitney perfects cotton gin
1794 Charles Willson Peale establishes Philadelphia Museum
William Billings composes *The Continental Harmony*

## SOCIAL and ECONOMIC

1775 Lord Dunmore's proclamation
Philadelphians organize first antislavery society

1780 Pennsylvania begins gradual abolition of slavery
1781 Bank of North America

1784 *Empress of China* sails to Canton
Treaty of Fort Stanwix
1785 Treaty of Hopewell
1786 Virginia Statute of Religious Freedom
1787 Free African School established in New York City

1789 Gustavus Vasa's *Narrative*
Fort Harmar Treaty

1790 Non-Intercourse Act regulates treaty making by states
Samuel Slater's cotton mill
1791 Haitian rebellion begins
Benjamin Banneker publishes first almanac

1792 New York Stock Exchange established

1793 Yellow fever epidemic hits Philadelphia
Battle of Fallen Timbers
1794 Richard Allen establishes Bethel African Methodist Episcopal Church
Federated Society of Journeyman Cordwainers established in Philadelphia

## POLITICAL

1776 Cherokee War
Declaration of Independence
British evacuate Boston and occupy New York
Thomas Paine publishes *Common Sense*
Adam Smith publishes *Wealth of Nations*
1777 Burgoyne defeated at Saratoga
Washington's army encamps at Valley Forge
1778 Treaty of alliance with France
British peace commission fails
1779 Sullivan's expedition against the Iroquois

1780 British capture Charleston
1781 Cornwallis surrenders at Yorktown
Articles of Confederation ratified
Robert Morris named superintendent of finance
1782 British evacuate Savannah and Charleston
Great Seal of the United States adopted
1783 Treaty of Paris with Great Britain ends Revolutionary War
Continental army disbands; Washington resigns

1785 Congress adopts Land Ordinance
Jay-Gardoqui negotiations
1786 Annapolis Convention
1786–1787 Shays's Rebellion
1787 Northwest Ordinance
Constitutional Convention in Philadelphia
1788 *The Federalist* published by Hamilton, Jay, and Madison
Constitution ratified
1789 George Washington inaugurated; national government organizes in New York
French Revolution begins

1790 Congress adopts Hamilton's funding and assumption program

1791 Bill of Rights becomes part of Constitution
First U.S. Bank established

1792 Washington reelected

1793 Democratic-Republican societies founded
Washington issues Neutrality Proclamation
First Fugitive Slave Act
Citizen Genêt affair
Wars of French Revolution begin
1794 Whiskey Rebellion

# 1775–1824

## CULTURAL and TECHNOLOGICAL

- 1797 Great Revivals begin on western frontier
- 1799 Nathaniel Bowditch, *Practical Navigator*
- 1800 Library of Congress established
- 1807 Robert Fulton launches steamboat *Clermont*
- 1811 Construction begins on Cumberland Road
- 1812 Benjamin Rush, *Diseases of the Mind*
- 1814 Francis Scott Key writes "The Star Spangled Banner"
- 1821 James Fenimore Cooper, *The Spy*; Emma Willard founds New York Female Seminary at Troy, New York

## SOCIAL and ECONOMIC

- 1795 Treaty of Greenville
- 1796 Congress establishes Indian factory system
- 1801 Gabriel's Rebellion
- 1801–1803 Handsome Lake's Gospels
- 1807 Congress prohibits slave trade
- 1808 John Jacob Astor founds American Fur Company
- 1808–1809 Tecumseh forms confederation
- 1811 Battle of Kithtippecanoe
- 1813 Boston Manufacturing Company formed at Waltham, Massachusetts; Battle of the Thames
- 1814 Jackson defeats Creek Indians at Horseshoe Bend
- 1817 American Colonization Society established
- 1818 First Seminole War
- 1821 Kentucky abolishes imprisonment for debt; Colonized American blacks settle at Monrovia, Liberia; Benjamin Lundy begins publication of *The Genius of Universal Emancipation*
- 1822 Denmark Vesey's Rebellion
- 1824 Bureau of Indian Affairs created; Female weavers strike at Pawtucket, Rhode Island; Auburn Penitentiary built
- 1825 Erie Canal opens
- 1826 Robert Owen begins New Harmony
- 1827 Sequoyah devises Cherokee alphabet; Cherokee constitution

## POLITICAL

- 1795 Jay's treaty with Great Britain
- 1796 Washington's Farewell Address
- 1797 John Adams elected president; XYZ affair
- 1798 Undeclared naval war with France; Alien and Sedition Acts; Naturalization Act; Virginia and Kentucky resolutions
- 1800 Thomas Jefferson elected president
- 1801 John Marshall named Chief Justice
- 1803 *Marbury v. Madison*; Louisiana Purchase
- 1803–1806 Louis and Clark expedition
- 1804 Jefferson reelected
- 1806 Non-Importation Act
- 1807 Embargo Act; *Chesapeake-Leopard Affair*
- 1808 James Madison elected president
- 1809 Non-Intercourse Act
- 1810 Macon's Bill No. 2; West Florida annexed
- 1812 Madison reelected; War declared against Britain
- 1814 Treaty of Ghent ends War of 1812
- 1814–1815 Hartford Convention
- 1816 Second U.S. Bank; First protective tariff; James Monroe elected president
- 1819 *McCulloch v. Maryland*; Adams-Onis Treaty with Spain
- 1819–1823 Financial panic and depression
- 1820 Missouri Compromise; Monroe reelected
- 1822 Recognition of Latin American republics
- 1823 Monroe Doctrine
- 1824 Henry Clay's "American System"; John Quincy Adams elected president; *Gibbons v. Ogden*

# CHAPTER 6
## THE AMERICAN PEOPLE
## IN REVOLUTION

Among the Americans wounded and captured at the Battle of Bunker Hill in the spring of 1775 was Lieutenant William Scott of Peterborough, New Hampshire. Asked by his captors how he had come to be a rebel, "Long Bill" Scott replied:

> The case was this Sir! I lived in a Country Town; I was a Shoemaker, & got [my] living by my labor. When this rebellion came on, I saw some of my neighbors get into commission, who were no better than myself. . . . I was asked to enlist, as a private soldier. My ambition was too great for so low a rank. I offered to enlist upon having a lieutenant's commission, which was granted. I imagined myself now in a way of promotion. If I was killed in battle, there would be an end of me, but if my Captain was killed, I should rise in rank, & should still have a chance to rise higher. These Sir! were the only motives of my entering into the service. For as to the dispute between Great Britain & the colonies, I know nothing of it; neither am I capable of judging whether it is right or wrong.

People fought in America's Revolutionary War for many reasons: fear, ambition, principle. We have no way of knowing whether Long Bill Scott's motives were typical. Certainly many Americans knew more than he about the colonies' struggle with England. But many did not.

In the spring of 1775, the Revolutionary War had just begun. So, as it turned out, had Long Bill's adventures. When the British evacuated Boston a year later, Scott was taken prisoner and transported to Halifax, Nova Scotia. After more than a year's captivity, he managed to escape, secure passage on a ship, and make his way home to fight once more. He was recaptured in November 1776 near New York City, when its garrison fell to a surprise British assault. Again Scott escaped, this time by swimming the Hudson River at night with his sword tied around his neck and his watch pinned to his hat.

During the winter of 1777, he returned to New Hampshire to recruit his own militia company. It included two of his eldest sons. In the fall he joined in the defeat of Burgoyne's army near Saratoga, New York, and later took part in the fighting around Newport, Rhode Island. When his light infantry company was ordered to Virginia in early 1778, Scott's health broke, and he was permitted to resign from the army. After only a few months of recuperation, however, he was at it again. During the last year of the war, he served as a volunteer on a navy frigate.

For seven years the war held Scott in its harsh grasp. Scott's oldest son died of camp fever after six years of service. In 1777, Long Bill sold his New Hampshire farm, to meet family expenses. The note he took in exchange turned into a scrap of paper when the dollar of 1777 became worth less than 2 cents by 1780. He lost a second farm in Massachusetts, when his military pay depreciated similarly. After his wife died, he helplessly turned their younger children over to his oldest son and set off to beg a pension or job from the government. When his son, whose corn crop was killed by a late frost, begged Scott for help, he could only advise handing the children over to the town of Peterborough.

Long Bill's saga was still not complete. In 1792, he gained notoriety by rescuing eight people from drowning when their boat capsized in New York harbor. Two years later, he landed a job as deputy storekeeper for the military garrison at West Point. In 1795, General Benjamin Lincoln took Scott with him to the Ohio country, where they negotiated with the Indians and surveyed land that was opening for white settlement. At last he had a respectable job and even a small government pension for his nine wounds. But trouble would still not let him go. While surveying on the Black River near Sandusky, Scott and his colleagues contracted "lake fever." Though ill, he guided part of the group back to Fort Stanwix in New York, then returned for the others. It was his last heroic act. A few days after his second trip, on September 16, 1796, he died.

The Revolutionary War was not as hard on everyone as it was on Long Bill Scott. Yet it transformed the lives of all Americans. It lasted for seven years, longer than any other of America's wars until Vietnam nearly 200 years later. And unlike the nation's twentieth-century contests, it was fought on American soil, among American people. It called men by the thousands from shops and fields, disrupted families, killed many civilians, spread disease, and made a shambles of the economy. The war dominated the lives of Americans who lived through it. But it had different consequences for men than for women, for black slaves than for their white masters, for Native Americans than for frontier settlers, for overseas merchants than for urban workers. Our understanding of the Revolution must begin with the war, what it was like, and what it did to the American people, for liberty came at a high cost.

## THE WAR FOR AMERICAN INDEPENDENCE

On the afternoon of October 19, 1781, near the Virginia hamlet of Yorktown, Lord Charles Cornwallis, commander of His Majesty's army in the southern states, surrendered. His decision followed nearly three weeks of close, bitter fighting. While a military band played "The World Turned Upside Down" and hundreds of civilians looked on, British troops, nearly 7,000 in number, marched out to lay down their arms.

Learning the news of Yorktown a month later, Lord North, the king's chief minister, exclaimed, "Oh, God! It is all over." On February 27, 1782, the House of Commons voted against further support of the war, and the next month, Lord North resigned. In Philadelphia, citizens poured into the streets to celebrate while Congress assembled for a solemn ceremony of thanksgiving. Sporadic fighting continued for another year; not until November 1782 were the preliminary articles of peace signed. But everyone knew after Yorktown that the war was over. Americans had won their independence.

### Creating an Independent Government

America's military victory over mighty England was all the more remarkable given the weak and uncompleted national government that directed the war effort. For six years, the American cause depended on the inadequately empowered and uncertain Continental Congress. It operated under a document called the Articles of Confederation that was not even ratified until seven months before Yorktown.

Prior to independence, the colonies had typically gone their own ways. Most often, in fact, they had competed with one another for territory, new settlers, control of the fur trade, and commercial advantage within the British Empire. The crisis with England, however, forced them together, first to protest England's efforts at imperial reform and then to carry on the war. The Continental Congress was the first embodiment of that union. The First Continental Congress met for only seven weeks and limited itself to sending resolutions of protest to England and calling on the people to support the Continental Association. It functioned, in short, as a temporary assembly.

The Second Continental Congress, however, behaved quite differently. It convened, in May 1775, in the midst of a war crisis that required it to exercise some of the most basic responsibilities of a sovereign government: defense and the conduct of diplomatic relations. The Second Congress, however, had no more legal standing than its predecessor. Its powers were unclear, its legitimacy uncertain. While hopes of reconciliation with England remained, these limitations were acceptable, for they seemed temporary. But as independence loomed and prospects of an extended war increased, the need to establish the Congress on a sounder footing became urgent. On June 20, 1776, shortly before independence was declared, Congress appointed a committee, chaired by John Dickinson of Pennsylvania, to draw up a plan of perpetual union. So urgent was the crisis that the committee responded in exactly a month's time, and debate on its proposed Articles of Confederation quickly began.

While the war erupted around them, the delegates struggled with the new and difficult problem of creating a permanent government. The debate quickly revealed that the delegates disagreed whether there should be a strong, consolidated regime or a loosely joined confederation of sovereign states. Those differences sharpened as the discussion continued.

The Dickinson draft outlined a government of considerable power. Each state was to retain "the sole and exclusive regulation and government of its internal police," but only in "matters that shall not interfere with the Articles of Confederation." The only unqualified restriction on Congress was that it might never impose taxes or duties except in managing the post office. Dickinson's proposals, however, met determined opposition. North Carolina's Thomas Burke, fearful of the centralizing tendencies of the war, insisted that the Congress be subordinate to the states.

As finally approved, the Articles fell between Dickinson's and Burke's positions. Article 9 gave Congress sole authority to regulate foreign affairs, declare war, mediate boundary disputes between the states, manage the post office, and administer relations with Indians living outside state boundaries. The Articles also stipulated that the citizens of each state were to enjoy "the privileges and immunities" of the citizens of every other state. Embedded in that clause was the basis for national, as distinguished from state, citizenship. Given the experience out of which it came, the Articles were surprisingly strong. Their strength evidenced the desperate crisis the American people faced.

Events, however, quickly proved that the Articles were flawed. Most important, Congress could raise neither troops nor revenue on its own. It could not tax or lay tariffs on imported goods, except with the unanimous agreement of the states. To run the war, Congress could only lay assessments on the states, hoping they would comply.

Article 2 spelled out the intended balance between state and national government. Each of the states was to "retain its sovereignty, freedom and independence, and every power, jurisdiction, and right which is not by this confederation expressly delegated to the United States in Congress assembled." Nor could these puny powers be easily enlarged, since the Articles could be amended only by the unanimous agreement of the 13 states.

Though the Articles were sent to the states for approval in November 1777, they did not gain ratification until March 1781. Several reasons explain the delay. They required the unanimous approval of the 13 states, and that was hard to obtain. In addition, state leaders were reluctant to ratify the new government until satisfied that their state's interests were sufficiently protected. New York, for example, sought assurances that Congress would not support Vermont's attempt to break away and form a separate state, while Pennsylvania asked for guarantees concerning its longstanding boundary disputes with Connecticut and Maryland.

Ratification bogged down most deeply, however, in the dispute over state versus federal ownership of western lands. The controversy pitted states such as Virginia, South Carolina, and New York, which had vast western claims tracing back to their colonial charters, against states such as Maryland and New Jersey, which had none. Representatives of the six "landless" states argued that the trans-Appalachian region should be common property because it was being "wrested from the common enemy by the blood and treasure of the thirteen states." In December 1778, the Maryland assembly announced that it would not ratify the Articles until all the western lands had been ceded to the Congress. It was the most powerful trump card that landless Maryland could play.

Land speculators, such as the Indiana and Illinois-Wabash companies, also worked actively for state cession, hoping that Congress would honor the land purchases they had already made from interior tribes such as the Shawnee and Miami.

For several years, ratification hung in the balance while politicians and speculators jockeyed for advantage. A breakthrough finally came in February 1780, when New York offered to transfer its western claims to Congress. Virginia, however, held out, and its lands were so vast that no solution was possible unless they were ceded as well. In September, the Virginia assembly agreed to turn over its western claims, but only on condition that Congress not recognize any of the Indian purchases that the land compa-

nies had made. The speculators were furious. They signed petitions, circulated pamphlets, and distributed company stock among influential congressmen in a vain effort to prevent acceptance of Virginia's restrictions.

In early 1781, the Maryland assembly accepted Virginia's conditions and approved the Articles, though the vote was close because a number of assemblymen had investments in the companies. Ratification was now assured. In September 1783, Congress finally agreed to Virginia's condition, and in 1784 the actual transfer of land occurred.

Congress, of course, could not sit idly by during the struggle over ratification, for the war would not wait. It did the best it could, using the unratified Articles as a guide. Events quickly

### Western Land Claims Ceded by the States, 1782–1802

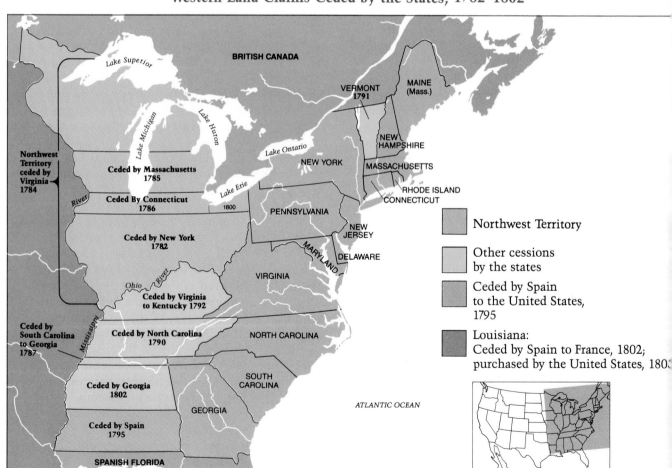

proved the inadequacy of the powers allowed the Congress. It could not legislate; it could only pass resolutions and ask the states for support. If they refused, as they frequently did, the Congress could only protest and urge cooperation. Its ability to function was further limited by the requirement that each state's delegation could cast but one vote. On a number of occasions, disagreements within state delegations prevented them from voting at all. That could paralyze the Congress, since most important decisions required a nine-state majority.

During the war, Washington repeatedly criticized the Congress for its failure to support the army adequately. In 1778, acknowledging its own ineffectiveness, the body temporarily granted Washington extraordinary powers and asked him to manage the war on his own. Congress did, of course, survive because the states realized that disaster would follow its collapse and because enough of its members were determined to see things through.

*Europeans watched in fascination as news of the colonies' rebellion against England reached them. Here, a French and a German artist portray the American forces confronting British troops at Lexington in April 1775.*

## The War in the North

Under such an imperfectly formed government, the war proceeded. Few Americans escaped the war's effects altogether, though some felt it more powerfully than others, either because of who they were or where they lived. It began, as we know, in Massachusetts in 1775. Within a year, the center of fighting shifted to the middle states. After 1779, the South was the primary theater. Why did this geographic pattern develop, what was its significance, and why did the war end in American victory?

For a brief time following Lexington and Concord, British officials thought of launching forays out from Boston into the surrounding countryside. General Gage was eager to gain revenge for the embarrassment the Minutemen had caused him, and it was important to reestablish British control beyond that one beseiged city. They soon reconsidered, however, for the growing size of the continental army and the absence of significant Loyalist strength in the New England region suggested caution. Even more important, the Americans' successful emplacement of artillery on the strategic

Dorchester Heights overlooking the city made its continued occupation untenable. So on March 7, 1776, the new British commander, General William Howe, decided to evacuate. Perhaps 1,000 New England Loyalists accompanied him, the first of a continuing tide of emigrants.

People worried that Howe would set fire to the city as he departed. The city, however, was not burned, nor were civilians transported against their will. Howe feared retaliation against Loyalist property and wished not to destroy any lingering hopes of reconciliation. But the town had been treated badly enough. British officers had taken over the homes of John Hancock, James Bowdoin, and 100 others. Dragoons had used the Old South Meeting House as a riding school, after tearing out the pews. The West Street and Hollis Street churches had served as barracks; the Old North Church had been demolished for firewood. All around lay trampled gardens, uprooted trees, and filth. The city, one resident lamented, was not "that agreeable place it once was. Almost everything here, appears Gloomy and Melancholy."

For a half dozen years after Boston's evacuation, British ships prowled the New England coast from Maine to Connecticut attacking American commerce, confiscating supplies, and destroying towns. Yet away from the coast there was little fighting at all. New Englanders had reason to be thankful for their good fortune.

When they evacuated Boston, British officials established their military headquarters in New York City. Their decision was strategically sound. New York was more centrally located and had earlier served as headquarters for British forces during the Seven Years' War. Moreover, its harbor was more spacious than Boston's and overlooked the mouth of the Hudson River, the major transportation route northward into the interior. Control of New York would, in addition, ensure access to the grain and livestock of the Middle Atlantic states. Finally, Loyalist sentiment ran wide and deep among the inhabitants of the city and its environs. Both politically and militarily, New York offered advantages that Boston did not.

In the summer of 1776, Washington moved his troops south from Boston and positioned them on Manhattan and Long Island. Encouraged by the outcome in Massachusetts, he decided to challenge the British for control of the city. It proved a terrible mistake. Outmaneuvered and badly outnumbered, he suffered defeat, first at the Battle of Long Island and then in Manhattan itself. By late October, the city was firmly in British hands and would remain so until the war's end.

In the fall of 1776, George III instructed two of his commanders in North America, the brothers General William and Admiral Richard Howe, to make a final effort at reconciliation with the colonists. They carried authority to pardon all Americans who acknowledged allegiance to the king and to negotiate with any colony that dissolved its revolutionary committees. In early September, the Howes met on Staten Island, in New York harbor, with three delegates from the Congress. The outcome was not long in doubt, for when the Howes demanded revocation of the Declaration of Independence before negotiations could continue, the Americans walked out. It was clear from that point on that the war would be long and difficult.

For the next two years, the war swept back and forth across New Jersey and Pennsylvania. Reinforced by German mercenaries hired in Europe, the British moved virtually at will. Neither the state militias nor the continental army, now weakened by losses, low morale, and inadequate supplies, could offer serious opposition. At Trenton in December 1776 and again at Princeton in the following month, Washington surprised the British and scored important victories; they probably prevented the Americans' collapse. But for the rebels, survival remained the primary goal.

American efforts during the first year of the war to invade Canada and bring that British colony into the rebellion also fared badly. In November 1775, American forces under General Richard Montgomery had taken Montreal. But the subsequent assault against Quebec ended in disaster, with almost 100 Americans killed or wounded and more than 300 taken prisoner. The American cause, Washington realized, could not survive many such losses.

At New York, Washington had learned the painful lesson that his troops were no match for the British in frontal combat. If the continental army was defeated and scattered, a prospect that these early defeats made real, American independence would almost certainly be lost. Above all, the army must be preserved. Thus Washington adopted a strategy of caution and delay. He would harass the British, make the war as costly for them as possible, and protect the civilian population as best he could. But above all, he would avoid major battles. For the remainder of the war, Washington's posture was primarily defensive and reactive.

As a consequence, the war's middle years turned into a deadly game of chase, one that neither side proved able to win. In September 1777, the British took Philadelphia, sending the Congress fleeing into the countryside, but then proved unable to press their advantage. British

## Military Operations in the North, 1776–1780

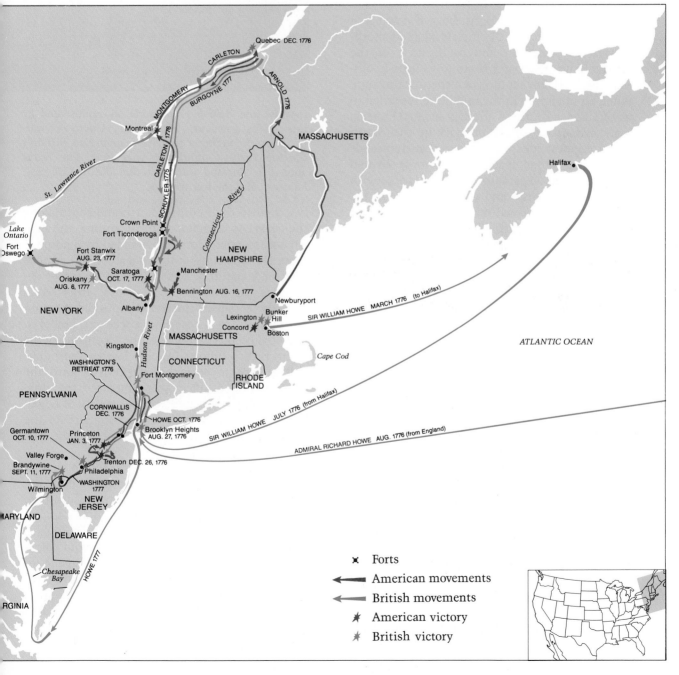

| | |
|---|---|
| ✗ | Forts |
| ⬅ | American movements |
| ⬅ | British movements |
| ✸ | American victory |
| ✸ | British victory |

commanders repeatedly hesitated to act, either reluctant to move through the hostile countryside or uncertain of their instructions. Countering the British domination of the Middle Atlantic region was the American victory at Saratoga, New York, where 5,700 British soldiers under General Burgoyne surrendered in October 1777.

## The War Moves South

As the war in the North bogged down in a costly stalemate, British officials adopted another strategy: invasion and pacification of the South. From the war's beginning, British officials had talked about a southern campaign. When rapid victory in the middle states failed to materialize, a southern strategy seemed increasingly attractive. Royal officials in the South encouraged the idea with reports that thousands of Loyalists stood ready to fight once British authority was reestablished. Moreover, with their long coastline and numerous rivers, the southern states offered maximum advantage to British naval strength. Then there were the slaves, that vast but imponderable force in southern society. If they could be lured to the British side, the balance might tip in Britain's favor. In any case, the threat of slave rebellions would weaken the ability of white southerners to resist. Persuaded by these arguments, British policymakers decided first to reestablish royal authority in Georgia and the Carolinas, then gradually extend British control northward. During the final years of the war, the southern states became the primary theater of military operations.

Georgia—small, isolated, and largely defenseless—was the initial target. In December 1778, Savannah, the state's major port town, fell before a seaborne attack of 3,500 men. For nearly two years, the Revolution in the state virtually ceased. Encouraged by their success, the British turned to the Carolinas. British achievements there were also impressive. On May 12, 1780, Charleston surrendered after a month's siege. At a cost of only 225 casualties, the British captured the entire 5,400-man American garrison. It was the costliest American defeat of the war.

After securing Charleston, the British quick-

*Loyalist and British propaganda, as represented by this 1778 woodcut, played on American war-weariness in urging a positive response to Britain's Carlisle Peace Commission that year. The terms offered by England were unacceptable to Congress, however, and the war went on.*

ly extended their control north and south along the coast. At Camden, South Carolina, the British commander, Cornwallis, aided by a corps of mounted dragoons, killed nearly 1,000 Americans and captured 1,000 more, effectively destroying the southern continental army. With scarcely a pause, the British pushed on into North Carolina. These early successes, however, proved deceptive. Though they controlled the coast, British officers quickly learned how difficult it was to extend their control into the interior. The distances were too large, the problems of supply too great, the reliability of Loyalist troops too problematic, and support for the Revolutionary cause among the people too strong.

In October 1780, Washington sent Nathanael Greene south to replace Horatio Gates at the head of the continental forces. It was a fortunate choice, for Greene knew the region and understood the kind of war that had to be fought. Determined, like Washington, to avoid large-scale encounters whenever possible, Greene divided his army into small, highly mobile bands. Employing what today would be called guerrilla tactics, he harassed the British and their Loyalist allies at every opportunity, striking by surprise and then disappearing into the interior. No-where was the war more fiercely fought than through the Georgia and Carolina countryside. Neither British nor American authorities could restrain the violence. Bands of private marauders, who roved the land seizing whatever advantage they could from the war's confusion, compounded the chaos.

In time, the tide began to turn. At Cowpens, South Carolina, in early 1781, American general Daniel Morgan won a decisive victory, suffering fewer than 75 casualties to 329 British deaths

and taking 600 men prisoner. In May, at Guilford Court House in North Carolina, Cornwallis won the day, but at a cost that forced his retreat to safety at Wilmington, near the sea. By the fall of 1781, the British held only Charleston and its immediate vicinity.

In April 1781, convinced that British authority could not be restored in the Carolinas while Virginia remained a supply and staging area for the Americans, Cornwallis moved north out of the Carolinas. With a force of 7,500, he raided deep into Virginia. In June, his forces sent Gov-

## Military Operations in the South, 1778–1781

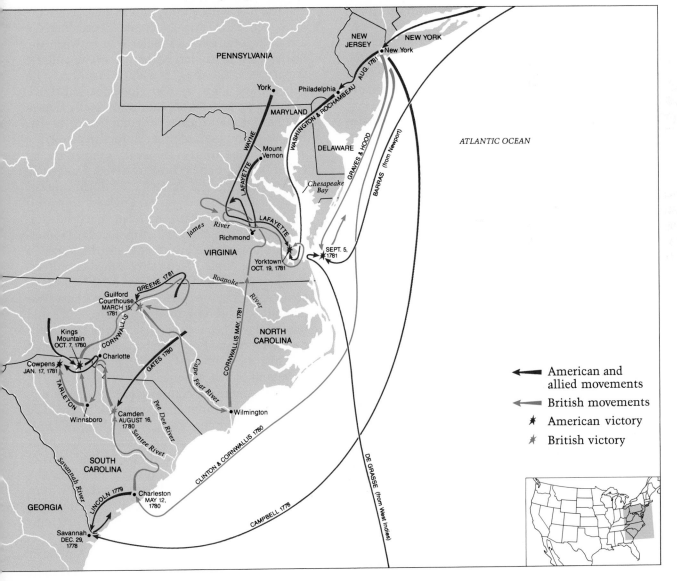

ernor Jefferson and the Virginia legislature fleeing from Charlottesville into the mountains. But again Cornwallis found the costs of victory high, and again he turned toward the coast for protection and resupply. This time his goal was Yorktown, where he arrived on August 1.

As long as the British fleet controlled the waters of Chesapeake Bay, his position was secure. That advantage, however, did not last long. In 1778, the French government, still smarting from its defeat by England in the Seven Years' War and persuaded by the American victory at Saratoga in 1777 that the rebellion against Great Britain might succeed, had signed a treaty of alliance with the American Congress, promising to send its naval forces into the war. Initially, the French concentrated their fleet in the West Indies, where they hoped to seize some of the rich British sugar islands. After repeated American urging, however, the French finally

*This close-up rendering of Lord Cornwallis surrendering his sword to General Washington and Count de Rochambeau at Yorktown in 1781 was engraved for Edward Barnard's* History of England *(1783).*

sailed north, and on August 30 Comte de Grasse arrived off Yorktown. Reinforced by a second French squadron from the North, De Grasse established clear naval superiority in the region.

As Washington had foreseen, French entry into the war turned the tide decisively in the Americans' favor. Cut off from the sea and caught on a peninsula between the York and James rivers by 17,000 French and American troops, Cornwallis's fate was sealed. On October 17, 1781, he opened negotiations for surrender.

## Negotiating Peace

The following spring, informal peace discussions began in Paris. Not until September did actual negotiations get under way between the British commissioner, Richard Oswald, and the American emissaries, Benjamin Franklin, John Adams, and John Jay. On November 30, 1782, preliminary articles of peace were finally signed.

The negotiations were complicated by the fact that a number of other European countries, seeking opportunity to weaken and contain Great Britain, had become involved. France had entered the war in February 1778. Eight months later, Spain declared war on England, though it declined to recognize American independence. Between 1780 and 1782, Russia, the Netherlands, and six other European countries joined in a League of Armed Neutrality aimed at protecting their maritime trade against British efforts to control it. Thus America's Revolutionary War had quickly become internationalized. It could hardly have been otherwise, given England's centrality to the European balance of power and the historical interest of the major European powers in North America.

The American commissioners quickly discovered how complicated peacemaking could be under such circumstances. Franklin, Adams, and Jay carried instructions from the Congress obligating them to follow the advice and counsel of Vergennes, the French foreign minister. The Congress had agreed to this under pressure from its French ally. It could hardly have refused, given American dependence on French economic, military, and diplomatic support.

As the treaty talks began, the American commissioners learned to their distress that

Vergennes was in no hurry to negotiate. He was quite prepared to let the exhausting war continue a while longer in order to weaken England further and tighten America's dependence on France. Even more alarming, while Vergennes reassured his allies of his commitment to American independence, he suggested that the new nation's western boundary ought to be set no farther inland than the crest of the Appalachian Mountains. In addition, he hinted that the British should retain the territories they controlled at the war's end. That would have left New York City and other coastal enclaves in British hands. As Franklin and his colleagues realized, the French alliance brought dangers as well as advantages.

In the end, the American commissioners ignored their instructions and, without a word to Vergennes, arranged a provisional peace agreement with the British emissaries. Fortunate it was that they did so, for the British were prepared to be generous. England agreed, fully and without qualification, to recognize American independence and set the western boundary of the United States at the Mississippi River. Moreover, Britain promised that U.S. fishermen would have the "right" to fish the waters off Newfoundland and that its own land and sea forces would evacuate American territory "with all convenient speed" once hostilities had ceased. In return, Congress agreed to recommend that the states restore the rights and property of the Loyalists. Both sides agreed that all prewar debts owed the citizens of one country by the citizens of the other would remain valid. Each of these issues would trouble Anglo-American relations in the decades ahead, but for the moment it seemed a splendid outcome to a long and difficult struggle.

### The Ingredients of Victory

How were the weak and disunited American states able to defeat Great Britain, the most powerful nation in the Atlantic world? Certainly the Dutch and French loans, war supplies, and military forces were crucially important. More decisive, though, was the American people's determination not to submit. Often the Americans were disorganized and uncooperative. Repeatedly, it seemed that the war effort was about to collapse as continental troops drifted away, state militias refused to march, and military supplies failed to materialize. Neither Congress nor the states, which often squabbled with each other, provided consistent direction to the strug-

*John Jay, John Adams, and Benjamin Franklin (the three figures on the left) meet with their British counterparts to negotiate preliminary conditions of peace in this unfinished painting by Benjamin West.*

gle. Yet as the war progressed, the people's estrangement from England and their commitment to the "glorious cause" increased. To subdue the colonies, England would have had to occupy the entire eastern third of the continent, and that it could not do.

State militias frequently refused to go beyond their own state borders, and after the first months of the war, they engaged in relatively few battles. Yet the militia provided a vast reservoir of manpower available to control the countryside, intimidate Loyalists and deprive the British of their support, and harass British forces. All of this occupied British troops that would otherwise have been free to engage the continental army.

The American victory owed much to the extraordinary administrative and organizational talents of Washington. Against massive odds, he held the continental army together, often, it seemed, only by the force of his will. In the face of inadequate supplies, low pay, high rates of turnover among the troops, ineffective support from Congress, and lack of cooperation from the states, he successfully fashioned a military force capable of winning selected encounters and, more important, of surviving over time. Had he failed, the Americans could not possibly have defeated the British.

In the end, however, it is as accurate to say that Britain lost the war as that the United States won it. In 1776, with its vast economic and military resources, Britain enjoyed clear military superiority over the American states. Its troops, including the German auxiliaries hired in Europe, were more numerous, better armed and supplied, and more professionally trained. Until the closing months of the contest, Britain enjoyed naval superiority as well. As a consequence, its forces could move up and down the coast virtually at will.

England, however, could not capitalize sufficiently on its advantages. It proved too difficult to extend command structures and supply routes across several thousand miles of ocean. Information flowed erratically back and forth across the water. As a result, strategic decisions made in London were often based on faulty or outdated intelligence. Given the difficulties of supply over such distances, British troops often

had to live off the land. This reduced their mobility and increased the antagonism of the people whose crops and animals they commandeered.

In addition, British leaders were frequently inept or overly cautious. Burgoyne's attempt in 1777 to isolate New England by invading from Canada failed because Sir William Howe decided to attack Philadelphia rather than move northward up the Hudson River to join him. Thus ended England's hope of dividing the new nation in two and forcing an early surrender. Similarly, neither Howe nor Cornwallis pressed his advantages in the central states during the middle years of the war, when more aggressive action might have defeated and scattered the continental force.

British commanders also generally failed to adapt their battlefield tactics to the realities of the American war. This was perhaps their greatest shortcoming. They continued to fight in the European style, away from civilian populations, during specified times of the year, and using set formations of troops deployed in formal battlefield maneuvers. The war of American independence required different tactics. Much of the terrain was rough and wooded and thus better suited to the use of smaller units and irregular troops. More important, Washington and Greene pursued a patient strategy of raiding, harassment, and strategic retreat. Behind it lay a willingness, grounded in necessity, to allow England control of considerable territory, especially along the coast. But it was based as well on the conviction that popular support for the Revolutionary cause would persist and that over time the costs of subduing the colonial rebellion would be greater than the British government could bear. As a much later American war in Vietnam would also reveal, a guerrilla force can win if it does not lose; a regular army loses if it does not consistently win.

The American strategy proved sound. As the war dragged on and its costs escalated, Britain's will to continue wavered. After France and Spain entered the conflict, Britain's problems increased, for its government then had to worry about Europe, the Caribbean, and even the Mediterranean as well as North America. Given all these commitments, the drain on the nation's resources was immense. As the costs in money and lives rose and the prospects of victory waned, political support for the war gradually eroded. With the defeat at Yorktown, it collapsed. Britain's effort to retain its 13 North American colonies had failed.

## THE EXPERIENCE OF WAR

The Revolutionary War often seems strange and far away. Compared to modern weapons of mass destruction, its muskets and cannon appear puny, even amusing. How seriously can one take a war in which Benjamin Franklin urged the widespread use of bows and arrows? "Nothing terrifies enemies more," he explained, "than the deadly silent flight of a volley of arrows." In terms of the loss of life or destruction of property, the Revolutionary War hardly compares with America's wars of more recent vintage. Yet such comparisons are misleading, for the War of American Independence was terrifying and destructive to the people caught up in it.

### Recruiting an Army

No one, of course, was affected more directly by the war than the combatants. Estimates vary, but on the American side as many as 250,000 men may at one time or another have borne arms. That would amount to about one out of every four or five adult males. Before the war's end, Concord, Massachusetts, had provided 875 soldiers, more than 2½ times its eligible male population on the eve of the war. Concord's experience was not unique.

Tens of thousands served in the state militias. Each of the colonies had required adult males between the ages of 15 and 60 to enroll in their local militia company, provide themselves with a weapon, attend the monthly drill, and turn out when called upon. At the time of independence, however, the militia in most of the states was not a very effective fighting force. This was especially true in the South where Nathanael Greene complained that the men came "from home with all the tender feelings of domestic life." They were not by experience or training "sufficiently fortified . . . to stand the shocking scenes of war, to march over dead men, to hear without concern the groans of the wounded. Few men can stand such scenes unless steeled by habit or fortified by military pride." Fighting, as Greene knew, was neither a pleasant nor a heroic business.

The militia did serve effectively as a ready-made recruitment system. Men were already enrolled, companies were organized, and arrangements were in place for calling them into the field on short notice. This was of special importance during the early months of the war, before the continental army took shape. Given its grounding in local community life, the mili-

*The "American Rifle Man," even when idealized in an engraving, lacked the pomp and formality—and often the discipline—of the British soldier.*

*A Real American Rifle Man*

In almost all of America's wars, patriotism has run high, and bombastic rhetoric has inspired citizens to arms. The American Revolutionary War was no exception. But people fought for other than patriotic reasons, as the account of "Long Bill" Scott makes clear. It is always difficult to assess human motivations. Nor do we know just how many Americans bore arms during the struggle for independence, but it was probably between 20 and 25 percent of adult males. Who were these people? An answer to that question will help us understand why people fought and perhaps even what the war meant to them.

As we see in this chapter, the social composition of the Revolutionary army changed markedly as the war went along. At the beginning, men from all walks of life and every class fought in defense of American liberty. Within a short time, however, that began to change. As the war lengthened and its costs increased, men who could afford to do so hired substitutes or arranged to go home, while men of less wealth and influence increasingly carried the burden of fighting. Many of them did so out of choice, for the army promised adventure, an escape from the tedium of daily life, a way to make a living, and even, as for "Long Bill" Scott, the chance to rise in the world. And so thousands of poorer men hired out to defend American liberty. Such a decision, of course, was more attractive to them because other opportunities were limited.

One source for studying the social history of the Revolutionary War is the muster rolls and enlistment lists of the continental army and the state militias. Although eighteenth-century records are imperfect by modern standards, recruiting officers did keep track of the men they signed up so that bounties and wages could be paid accurately. Customarily, these lists show the recruit's name, age, occupation, place of birth, place of residence, and length of service, including time of desertion if that occurred (as it frequently did).

Such lists exist for many of America's early wars, from the seventeenth century into the nineteenth. The muster rolls for New York City and Philadelphia during the Seven Years' War, for example, show that these two cities contributed no more than 300 and 180 men per year, respectively, to the war effort. Most of the enlistees were immigrants—about 90 percent of New York's recruits and about 75 percent of Philadelphia's. Their occupations—mariner, laborer, shoemaker, weaver, tailor—indicate that they came primarily from the lowest ranks of the working class. Many were former indentured servants, and many others were servants running away from their masters to answer the recruiting sergeant's drum. In these

## NEW YORK LINE—1ST REGIMENT
### CAPTAIN JOHN H. WENDELL'S COMPANY, 1776–1777

| MEN'S NAMES | AGE | OCCUPATION | PLACE OF BIRTH | PLACE OF ABODE |
|---|---|---|---|---|
| Abraham Defreest | 22 | Yeoman | N. York | Claverack |
| Benjamin Goodales | 20 | do [ditto] | Nobletown | do |
| Hendrick Carman | 24 | do | Rynbeck | East Camp |
| Nathaniel Reed | 32 | Carpenter | Norwalk | Westchester |
| Jacob Crolrin | 29 | do | Germany | Bever Dam |
| James White | 25 | Weaver | Ireland | Rynbeck |
| Joseph Battina | 39 | Coppersmith | Ireland | Florida |
| John Wyatt | 38 | Carpenter | Maryland | Alb^y |
| Jacob Reyning | 25 | Yeoman | Amsterdam | Albany |
| Patrick Kannely | 36 | Barber | Ireland | N. York |
| John Russell | 29 | Penman | Ireland | N. York |
| Patrick McCue | 19 | Tanner | Ireland | Schohary |
| James J. Atkson | 21 | Weaver | do | Stillwater |
| William Burke | 23 | Chandler | Ireland | N. York |
| W^m Miller | 42 | Yeoman | Scotland | Claverack |
| Ephraim H. Blancherd | 18 | Yeoman | Ireland | White Creek |
| Francis Acklin | 40 | Cordwainer | Ireland | Claverack |
| William Orr | 29 | Cordwainer | Ireland | Albany |
| Thomas Welch | 31 | Labourer | N. York | Norman's Kill |
| Peter Gasper | 24 | Labourer | N. Jersey | Greenbush |
| Martinis Rees | 19 | Labourer | Fishkill | Flatts |
| Henck Able | 24 | do | Albany | Flatts |
| Daniel Spinnie | 21 | do | Portsmouth | |
| Patrick Kelly | 23 | Labourer | Ireland | Claverack |
| Rich^d James Barker | 12 | do | America | Rynbeck |
| John Patrick Cronkhite | 11 | | | Claverack |
| William Dougherty | 17 | | Donyal, Ireland | Sch^ty |

Middle Atlantic port towns, successful, American-born artisans left the bloody work of bearing arms against the French to those beneath them on the social ladder. Enlistment lists for Boston, however, reveal that soldiers in the 1750s came from higher social classes.

Similarly, a comparison of the Revolutionary War muster rolls from different towns and regions provides a penetrating view of the social composition of the Revolutionary army and how that changed over time. It also offers clues to social conditions in different regions during the war and how that might have affected military recruitment.

The lists shown here of Captain Wendell's and Captain White's companies from New York and Virginia give "social facts" on 81 men. What kind of group portrait of these units can you draw from the data? Some occupations, such as tanner, cordwainer, and chandler, may be unfamiliar, but they are defined in standard dictionaries. How many of the recruits come from middling occupations (bookkeeper, tobacconist, shopkeeper, and the like)? How many are skilled artisans? How many are unskilled laborers? What proportions are foreign and native-born? Analyze the ages of the recruits; what does that tell you about the kind of fighting force that was assembled? How do the New York and Virginia companies differ

## VIRGINIA LINE—6TH REGIMENT
### CAPTAIN TARPLEY WHITE'S COMPANY, DECEMBER 13TH 1780

| | | | WHERE BORN | | PLACE OF RESIDENCE | |
| NAMES | AGE | TRADE | STATE OR COUNTRY | TOWN OR COUNTY | STATE OR COUNTRY | TOWN OR COUNTY |
| --- | --- | --- | --- | --- | --- | --- |
| Wm Balis.    Serjt | 25 | Baker | England | Burningham | Virg. | Leesburg |
| Arthur Harrup. " | 24 | Carpenter | Virg. | Southampton | " | Brunswick |
| Charles Caffatey " | 19 | Planter | " | Caroline | " | Caroline |
| Elisha Osborn " | 24 | Planter | New Jersey | Trenton | " | Loudon |
| Benj Allday | 19 | " | Virg. | Henrico | " | Powhatan |
| Wm Edwards Senr | 25 | " | " | Northamberland | " | Northumberland |
| James Hutcherson | 17 | Hatter | Jersey | Middlesex | " | P. Williams |
| Robert Low | 31 | Planter | " | Powhatan | " | Powhatan |
| Cannon Row | 18 | Planter | Virg. | Hanover | Virg. | Louisa |
| Wardon Pulley | 18 | " | " | Southampton | " | Hallifax |
| Rich'd Bond | 29 | Stone Mason | England | Cornwell | " | Orange |
| Tho' Homont | 17 | Planter | Virg. | Loudon | " | Loudon |
| Tho' Pope | 19 | Planter | " | Southampton | " | Southampton |
| Tho' Morris | 22 | Planter | " | Orange | " | Orange |
| Littlebury Overby | 24 | Hatter | " | Dinwiddie | " | Brunwick |
| James [Pierce] | 27 | Planter | " | Nansemond | " | Nansemond |
| Joel Counsil | 19 | Planter | " | Southamton | " | Southamton |
| Elisha Walden | 18 | Planter | " | P. William | " | P. William |
| Wm Bush | 19 | S Carpenter | " | Gloucester | " | Gloucester |
| Daniel Horton | 22 | Carpenter | " | Nansemond | " | Nansemond |
| John Soons | 25 | Weaver | England | Norfolk | " | Loudon |
| Mora Lumkin | 18 | Planter | Virg. | Amelia | " | Amelia |
| Wm Wetherford | 27 | Planter | " | Goochland | " | Lunenburg |
| John Bird | 16 | Planter | " | Southamton | " | Southamton |
| Tho' Parsmore | 22 | Planter | England | London | " | Fairfax |
| Josiah Banks | 27 | Planter | Virg. | Gloucester | " | Gloucester |
| Rich'd Roach | 28 | Planter | England | London | " | Culpeper |
| Joseph Holburt | 33 | Tailor | " | Middlesex | " | Fredericksb'g |
| Henry Willowby | 19 | Planter | Virg. | Spotsylvania | " | Spotsylvania |
| Thos Pearson | 22 | Planter | | Pennsylvany | " | Loudon |
| Jno Scarborough | 19 | Planter | Virg. | Brunswick | " | Brunswick |
| Chas Thacker | 21 | Planter | " | " | " | " |
| Nehemiah Grining | 20 | Planter | Virg. | Albemarle | Virg. | Albemarle |
| Ewing David | 19 | Planter | " | King Wm | " | Brunswick |
| Isaiah Ballance | 17 | Shoemaker | " | Norfolk | " | Norfolk |
| Wm Alexander | 20 | Planter | Virg. | Northumbl'd | Virg'a | Nothumb'd |
| Wm Harden | 26 | Planter | " | Albemarle | " | Albemarle |
| John Ward | 20 | Sailor | England | Bristol | " | Nothumbl'd |
| Daniel Cox | 19 | Planter | Virg. | Sussex | " | Sussex |
| George Kirk | 21 | Planter | " | Brunswick | " | Brunswick |
| John Nash | 19 | Planter | " | Nothuml'd | " | Northumbl'd |
| Wm Edwards. Jr | 19 | Planter | " | Northuml'd | " | Northumbl'd |
| John Fry | 20 | Turner | " | Albemarle | " | Albemarle |
| Jno Grining | 25 | Hatter | " | " | " | " |
| Daniel Howell | 30 | Planter | " | Loudon | " | Loudon |
| Milden Green | 25 | Planter | " | Sussex | " | Sussex |
| Matthias Cane | 32 | Planter | " | Norfolk | " | Norfolk |
| Wm Mayo | 21 | Joiner | " | Dinwiddie | " | Dinwiddie |
| Jas Morgan | 25 | Shoemaker | England | Shropshire | " | Stafford |
| Mathew Carsan | 19 | Planter | Pennsylvania | York | " | Berkly |
| Wm B[rown] | 22 | Planter | | | " | |
| Rich'd Loyd | 42 | Planter | Virg. | Surry | " | Surry |
| Abram Foress | 33 | Planter | " | Gloster | " | Gloster |
| Wm White | 19 | Planter | | | " | |

in terms of these social categories and occupations? How would you explain these differences?

To extract the full meaning of the soldiers' profile, you would have to learn more about the economic and social conditions prevailing in the communities from which these men were drawn. But already you have glimpsed how social historians are trying to go beyond the history of military strategy, tactics, and battles to understand the "internal" social history of the Revolutionary War.

How would social historians describe and analyze a more recent American war? What would a social profile of soldiers who fought in Vietnam, including their age, region, race, class, extent of education, and other differences, suggest to a social historian of this recent war?

tia served to legitimize the war among the people and secure their commitment to the Revolutionary cause. What better way, as well, to separate Patriots (those who supported the cause of independence) from Tories (those who did not support the cause) than by mustering the local company and seeing who turned out?

During the first year of the war, enthusiasm ran high, and quotas were quickly filled. Men of all ranks—rich and middle-class as well as poor —volunteered to fight the British. Even under conscription, which soon became necessary, the militia was at first broadly representative of American society. But as the war proceeded, as its personal costs increased and community quotas grew, its social character changed. Initially fought by volunteers, the war soon became a battle by conscripts. Eventually it was transformed, as wars so often are, into a poor man's fight. Middle- and upper-class men increasingly hired substitutes to replace them, and communities such as Concord filled their quotas with strangers lured by the promise of enlistment bonuses. The "three-year men" who enlisted in 1777 were generally poor, but they were at least from the town. Three years later, however, only 8 of the 16 men who signed up had any local connection. For Concord, as for countless communities across the states, the Revolution was becoming a war by proxy.

This social transformation was even more dramatically true of the continental army. Congress had no power to conscript men; it could only assign states a proportion of the troops requested by Washington and hope they would respond. They generally did so as best they could, but they constantly sought lower quotas because they were easier to fill. The continental army's longer terms, stiffer discipline, and often distant battlefields discouraged the enlistment of men who could avoid it.

For the poor and the jobless, whose ranks the war rapidly expanded, bonus payments and the promise of army board and keep proved attractive. But often the bonuses failed to materialize, and pay was long overdue. Moreover, life in the camps was harsh, while soldiers frequently heard from their wives about the distress suffered by their families at home. Faced with such trials, soldiers often became disgruntled and

insubordinate. As the war progressed, Washington imposed harsher discipline on the continental troops in an effort to hold them in line.

Occasionally frustration and despair spilled over into open revolt. Sergeant Samuel Glover of the North Carolina line learned in 1779 what the costs of such behavior were. He was executed for leading a group of soldiers, unpaid for 15 months, that, in Glover's words, "demanded their pay, and refused to obey the commands of their superior officer, and would not march until they had justice done them." His widow later apologized to the North Carolina assembly for her husband's conduct but begged leave to ask "what must the feeling of the man be who fought at Brandywine, at Germantown, and at Stony Point and did his duty, and when on another march in defense of his country, with poverty staring him full in the face, he was denied his pay?" Poor soldiers, she explained to the assembly, were "possessed of the same attachment and affection for their families as those in command."

Throughout the war, soldiers suffered from severe and continuing shortages of supplies. At Valley Forge during the terrible winter of 1777– 1778, men hobbled about without shoes or coats. From the midst of that winter's gloom, Washington wrote, "There are now in this army 4000 men wanting blankets, near 2000 of which have never had one, altho' some of them have been 12 months in service." "The army," despaired another soul, "grow sickly from the continual fatigues they have suffered in the Campaign. I am sick, discontented, and out of humour. Poor food, hard lodging, cold weather, fatigue, nasty cloathes, nasty cookery, vomit half my time, smoaked out of my senses. The Devil's in't, I can't Endure it. Why are we sent here to starve and freeze?"

The states possessed food and clothing enough. But they were often reluctant to strip their own people of wagons and livestock, blankets and shoes for use elsewhere. Moreover, state jealousies, mismanagement, and difficulties in transportation stood in the way. Neither the state governments nor Congress had the ability to administer a war effort of such magnitude. Throughout the war, Congress experimented with a variety of quartermaster and commissary arrangements, but none proved adequate. Most American supplies, moreover, were produced in homes or small shops and could not easily be increased in quantity. Wagon transport was slow and costly, while the presence of the British fleet made water transportation along the coast perilous. Though many individuals served honorably as supply officers, others took personal advantage of the army's distress. Washington commented bitterly on the "speculators, various tribes of money makers, and stock-jobbers of all denominations" whose "avarice and thirst for gain" threatened the country's ruin.

## The Casualties of Conflict

Even though the weaponry of the eighteenth century was limited in range and firepower, it killed and maimed when it hit. Medical treatment, whether for wounds or diseases (such as smallpox, dysentery, and typhus) that raged continuously through the camps, did little to help. Casualties poured into hospitals, overcrowding them beyond capacity. Dr. James Tilton, the prescribing physician at Princeton, commented after the battles of Brandywine and Red Bank that with the "sick & wounded, flowing promiscuously without restraint into the hospital, it soon became infectious and was attended with great mortality." Dr. Jonathan Potts, the attending physician at Fort George in New York, reported that "we have at present upwards of one thousand sick crowded into sheds & labouring under the various and cruel disorders of dysentaries, bilious putrid fevers and the effects of a confluent smallpox; to attend to this large number we have four seniors and four mates, exclusive of myself, and our little [apothecary] shop does not afford a grain of jalap, ipecac, bark, salt, opium and sundry other capital articles and nothing of the kind [is] to be had in this quarter."

Surgeons, operating without anesthetics and with the crudest of instruments, as readily threatened life as preserved it. Few understood the causes and treatment of infection. Doctoring consisted mostly of bleeding, blistering, vomiting (which was "deemed of excellent use, by opening and squeezing all the glands of the body,

### Diet of Revolutionary War Soldiers

—————— *French and English repatriates, 1780* ——————

3,100 calories per day
7 pounds of bread weekly
7 pounds of beef weekly
3½ gallons of beer weekly

—————— *Continental army rations, 1780* ——————

2,600–4,000 calories per day
7 pounds of bread or flour weekly
1¾ pounds of cornmeal weekly
7 pounds of beef or 6⅛ pounds of pork weekly

—————— *Tory prisoners in Maryland, 1776* ——————

3,600–4,200 calories per day
7 pounds of bread or flour weekly
3 pints of peas weekly
1 quart of cornmeal weekly
7 pounds of beef or 5¼ pounds of pork weekly
7 gills of molasses weekly
7 gills of vinegar weekly

—————— *Continental army rations, 1775* ——————

3,000–5,400 calories per day
7 pound of bread or flour weekly
3 pints of peas or beans weekly
1 pint of cornmeal or ½ pint of rice weekly
7 pounds of beef or 5¼ pounds of pork weekly
1¾ gallons of beer or ⅝ gallon of molasses weekly
⅞ gallon of milk weekly

*Source:* U.S. Bureau of the Census.

*The Revolutionary War surgeon, with his chest of unsterilized knives, saws, and lancets, often did as much to threaten soldiers' lives as to save them.*

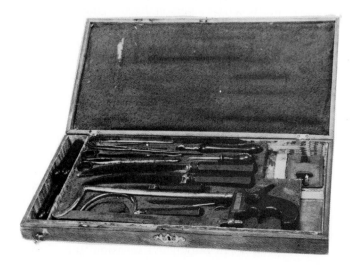

& then shaking from the nervous system, the contaminating poison"), and diarrhetics. Mercury was a commonly administered drug. One doctor had "no hesitation in declaring . . . that we lost no less than from 10 to 20 of camp diseases, for one by weapons of the enemy."

How many soldiers actually died we do not know, for no one kept accurate records. But the most conservative estimate runs over 25,000. That amounts to a higher percentage of the total population than for any other American conflict except the Civil War. About 12 percent of American soldiers died of wounds or disease, a rate virtually the equivalent of the Civil War and higher than any of America's other conflicts. For the Revolutionary War soldier, death was real and imminent.

The death that soldiers dispensed to each other on the battlefield was intensely personal. Because of the small scale of most battles and limits of the weaponry—the effective range of muskets was little more than 100 yards—combat was typically at close quarters. That meant that soldiers came virtually face to face with the men they killed. According to eighteenth-century military conventions, armies formed on the battlefield in ranks and fired in unison. After massed volleys, the lines often closed for hand-to-hand combat with knives and bayonets. Such encounters were powerfully etched in the memory of individuals who survived them. The partisan warfare in the South, with its emphasis on ambush and small group actions and its cyclic patterns of revenge and counterrevenge, personalized combat even more. British officers, used to more distanced and dispassionate styles of warfare, were shocked at the ferocity with which Americans often fought. One attributed to the American troops "a sort of implacable ardor and revenge, which happily are a good deal unknown in the prosecution of war in general."

The American fervor in battle is also largely explained by the fact that this was in part a civil war. Not only did Englishmen fight Americans, but American Loyalists and Patriots fought each other as well. As many as 50,000 colonists fought for the king and were engaged in some of the war's most bitter encounters. They figured importantly in Burgoyne's invasion from Cana-

da and in the attacks on Savannah and Charleston. Benedict Arnold led a force of Loyalists on raids through the Connecticut and James river valleys, while Loyalist militia joined Indian allies in destructive sweeps through central New York and Pennsylvania and the backcountry of the Carolinas and Kentucky. Throughout America, communities and even families divided against each other. The war's violent temper reflected this civil conflict.

Moreover, the war was fought in the midst of American society. It destroyed towns and property and killed civilians. When war came to a locality, soldiers found themselves fighting for their own and their families' survival. Finally, Americans believed intensely in the importance of their Revolutionary cause. The struggle, as they understood it, was between irreconcilable principles—their own liberty and the tyranny that Britain threatened. In such a crusade, against such a foe, nothing was to be spared that might bring victory.

## Civilians and the War

Though the soldiers found themselves most tightly in the war's grip, noncombatants also experienced the reality of war. Unlike America's twentieth-century conflicts, the Revolution was fought at home. The American people quickly learned what the consequences of that would be.

Though the war's impact varied from place to place, it struck hardest in the most densely settled areas along the coast. England focused its military efforts there because the coastal communities were the political, economic, and cultural centers of American life. Moreover, along the coast, England could bring its naval power directly to bear. At one time or another, British troops occupied every major port city—Boston for a year at the war's start, New York from 1777 to 1783, Philadelphia over the winter and spring of 1777–1778, Charleston in 1780–1781, and Savannah two years before. The resulting disruptions of urban life were profound. Overseas commerce, the economic lifeblood of these centers, was interrupted, and churches, schools, and other social institutions were disturbed.

The chaos in New York was typical. In September 1776, a fire consumed 500 houses, nearly a quarter of the city's dwellings. Most were not rebuilt until the war was over. About half the town's inhabitants fled when the British occupation began and were replaced by an almost equal number of Loyalists who streamed in from the surrounding countryside. Ten thousand British and German troops added to the crowding. The growing numbers of poor erected makeshift shelters of sailcloth and timbers. "Canvass Town" was the name people gave to the region stretching along Broadway. At the war's end, an American officer somberly reported what he found as his troops entered the city: "Close on the eve of an approaching winter, with an heterogeneous set of inhabitants, composed of almost ruined exiles, disbanded soldiery, mixed foreigners, disaffected Tories, and the refuse of the British army, we took possession of a ruined city."

In Philadelphia, the occupation was shorter and the disruptions were less severe, but still the shock of invasion was real. Elizabeth Drinker, living alone after local Patriots had exiled her Quaker husband, found herself the unwilling landlady of a British officer, Major Crammond, and his friends. The major's presence may have protected her from the more severe plundering that went on all around. She was, however, constantly anxious, confiding to her journal that

"I often feel afraid to go to Bed." During the occupation, British soldiers frequently took what they wanted, tore down fences for their campfires, and confiscated food to supplement their own tedious fare. Even the Loyalists commented on the "dreadful consequences" of occupation.

More than the port cities was at risk, however, for the entire coastal plain lay open to British attack. Landing parties descended without warning to capture supplies or terrorize the inhabitants. Charlestown, Massachusetts, was almost entirely consumed by shelling and fire during the Battle of Bunker Hill. In 1780 and 1781, the British mounted a sustained, punitive attack along the Connecticut coast in an effort to divert American troops from the defense of Virginia. Over 200 buildings in Fairfield were burned, and much of nearby Norwalk was destroyed three days later.

To the south, the Americans were even more vulnerable to attack. From 1779 to 1781, the Virginia tidewater region lay open to the British. In December 1780, Arnold ravaged the James River valley, uprooting tobacco, confiscating slaves, and creating panic among the white population. Similar devastation befell the coasts of Georgia and the Carolinas.

The relentlessness of these British attacks

*In September 1776, as American troops fought unsuccessfully for control of New York, nearly a quarter of the city was destroyed by fire. Not until the war ended did reconstruction and cleanup of the ruins begin.*

sent civilians fleeing into the interior for safety. During the first years of the war, the port cities lost nearly half their population. Inland communities strained to cope with the thousands of migrants who streamed into them. Concord eventually supported 82 poverty-stricken Bostonians. So many refugees had crowded in by July 1775 that they decided to hold a Boston town meeting there! By March 1776, Concord's population had grown by 25 percent, creating major problems of housing, social order, and public health. Communities to the north of New York City absorbed even larger numbers of refugees from the British-occupied city and its surrounding counties.

Not all the traffic was inland, away from the coast. To the west, in New York, Pennsylvania, Virginia, and the Carolinas, numerous frontier settlements collapsed in the face of British and Indian attack. West along the Mohawk River from Albany, New York, vicious fighting devastated the countryside. By 1783, the white population in the region had declined from 10,000 to scarcely a third as many. According to one observer, after nearly five years of warfare in Tryon County, 12,000 farms had been abandoned, 700 buildings burned, hundreds of thousands of bushels of grain destroyed, nearly 400 women widowed, and perhaps 2,000 children orphaned. Some of the war's most brutal atrocities occurred in the Wyoming valley of northeastern Pennsylvania. On July 3, 1778, Sir John Butler led Loyalists and Indians in a sweep through the region, while at Cherry Valley, New York, 40 survivors of a Loyalist and Indian attack were massacred after they had surrendered.

Within the Revolutionary state governments, representatives from the interior protested bitterly the lack of protection afforded their regions, while easterners replied that they were doing what they could and had to guard first of all against British threats along the coast. That controversy between coastal region and the interior would echo through state politics for years to come.

Wherever the armies went, they generated a swirl of refugees, who spread vivid tales of the war. This refugee traffic, added to the constant movement of soldiers back and forth between army and civilian life, brought the war home even to people who did not experience it at first hand.

Disease followed the armies like an avenging angel, ravaging civilians and soldiers alike. And wherever they went, the armies lived off the land, commandeering the supplies they needed. During the desperate winter of 1778–1779, in an effort to protect the surrounding population, Washington issued an order prohibiting his troops from roaming more than a half mile from camp. State militias were even less disciplined than the continentals, especially when away from their own localities.

In New Jersey, Britain's German mercenaries generated special fears among the citizenry. The Patriot press was filled with lurid stories of attacks on American civilians, especially women. Lord Rawdon, a British commander stationed nearby on Staten Island, wrote with arrogant amusement to a relative in London, "A girl cannot step into the bushes to pluck a rose without running the most immanent risk of being ravished, and they are so little accustomed to these vigorous methods that they don't bear with them with the proper resignation, and of consequence we have most entertaining courts martial every day."

In April 1777, a committee of the Congress, appointed to inquire into the conduct of British troops, took affidavits from women who had suffered rape. The committee reported that it had "authentic information of many instances of the most indecent treatment, and actual ravishment of married and single women; but, such is the nature of that most irreparable injury that the persons suffering it, though perfectly innocent, look upon it as a kind of reproach to have the facts related and their names known." Whether the report had any effect is unknown. American troops were not without guilt, but their behavior was less often publicized.

## THE REVOLUTION AND THE ECONOMY

The Revolutionary War altered people's lives in ways that reached beyond the sounds and sights of battle. Before the war was over, major sectors of the American economy lay in shambles. Recovery would come, and, in time, America's economy would enter a new and more dramatic phase of development. That future, however, was not evident amid the confusion of the war years.

Even had England allowed the colonies to depart the empire in peace, the consequences of independence for the American economy would have been severe. The American colonies had developed within the context of England's imperial system. Its laws and regulations had shaped American economic life. Independence broke those ties of dependence and subordina-

tion and thus fundamentally altered the context of American economic activity. The consequences were immediate and far-reaching. Independence brought the American people important gains in economic freedom, but, as they quickly discovered, breaking with England had severe costs as well. Americans, moreover, faced the new problem of surviving in an Atlantic world divided into exclusive, competing, and often warring empires.

England, of course, did not let the colonies go without a fight. And so the American people experienced the economic shocks of warfare as well—the destruction of property, loss of human life, diversion of productive labor into the army, rampant inflation, and collapse of the monetary system. Together, independence and war worked

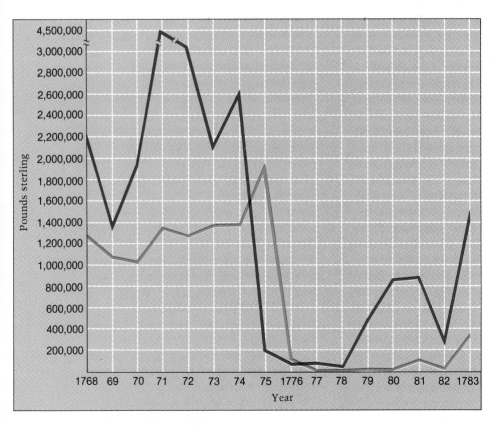

**Exports and Imports, 1768–1783**

*Source:* U.S. Bureau of the Census.

Exports     Imports

profound changes on the economic affairs of the American people. No other American war has been more universally disruptive.

### Interruption of Trade

Waterborne commerce—across the ocean to England and Europe, along the North American coast, and down to the West Indies—had been the lifeblood of the colonial economy. It carried away America's agricultural exports and brought back manufactured goods. It provided jobs for sailors and ship captains, carpenters and sailmakers, lumbermen and provisioners. During the imperial crisis, nonimportation had temporarily interrupted this trade. Independence and the war brought it virtually to a halt.

Gone after 1776 were the familiar overseas markets in England and the British West Indies for such staple exports as New England fish, Pennsylvania wheat, and Chesapeake tobacco. Gone were most of the English manufactured goods that had dominated American imports. Gone were the business connections with English bankers, wholesalers, and insurance brokers who had supported American commerce. Gone as well was the protection of the British fleet, for it was now the enemy, blockading the coast, attacking coastal towns, and sweeping American merchantmen from the sea.

To be sure, the end of British mercantile restrictions opened new trade possibilities. American merchants could now deal directly with Europe, Africa, and Asia, as well as the French and Dutch West Indies. France and the Netherlands were especially eager to buy American raw materials and sell their own manufactured goods. And though England's naval blockade was effective, it was not complete. The Atlantic was too vast to police, even by England's fleet.

A certain amount of trade continued with England during the war, because American buyers could always be found for English goods. In 1782, Jonathan Amory, a Boston merchant, advised his brother, who had remained in London as agent for the family business, that "English goods . . . are prohibited by Congress; yet I think they might be so managed that by Invoice and mixed with Holland goods, there would be but little difficulty, and English goods sell best." For some merchants, this illicit trade proved highly profitable. "The prospect of peace," declared one New York merchant, "has given more general discontent than anything that has happened in a long time; particularly among the mercantile part of the community."

In addition, some merchants and ship captains found profit in privateering, the chartering of private vessels by state or Congress to prey on English merchantmen. Some privateering ventures were extraordinarily successful. Elias Derby of Salem, Massachusetts, became one of New England's richest merchants in this way. The risks, however, were high, and the majority of ventures did not return a profit. In the end, the gain from privateering made up only a fraction of the nation's commercial losses. On balance, American overseas commerce declined dramatically during the war, while the height-

*Merchants who continued to stock English goods during the war faced boycotts, social ostracism, and sometimes tarring and feathering.*

*WILLIAM JACKSON,*

an *IMPORTER*; at the

*BRAZEN HEAD,*

*North Side of the* TOWN-HOUSE,

and *Oppofite the Town-Pump, in*

*Corn-hill,* BOSTON.

It is defired that the SONS and DAUGHTERS of *LIBERTY,* would not buy any one thing of him, for in fo doing they will bring Difgrace upon *themfelves,* and their *Pofterity,* for *ever* and *ever,* AMEN.

ened costs of insurance and shipping reduced profits on the trade that did get through.

Up and down the coast, communities whose livelihoods depended on the sea felt the war's impact. New England's fishing industry, once a central part of that region's economy, was decimated. Countless small but once thriving fishing centers, such as Wellfleet on Cape Cod, never recovered. Commercial communities, such as Newburyport, Massachusetts, just up the coast from Boston, struggled to survive. When economic recovery eventually came to Newburyport during the 1790s, it would be fashioned by an entirely new group of merchants. In the interval, countless laborers and artisans, sailors and dockworkers were cut adrift, their always tenuous livelihoods taken away. Many moved into Boston and New York seeking work or inland seeking land. Others stayed where they were, struggling to survive.

*Private vessels known as privateers, chartered by Congress and the new state governments, engaged in piratelike attacks against British merchantmen, confiscating goods and occasionally turning handsome profits for their owners.*

Once the war was over, American traders sought to rebuild their overseas trade, though with difficulty. Familiar English goods flooded American markets; few American goods, however, flowed the other way. John Adams learned why. In 1785, he arrived in London as the first American minister to England. Congress had assigned him the task of negotiating a commercial treaty, but he soon discovered the unlikelihood of accomplishing that. After endless rebuffs and delays, he wrote home in frustration that England had no intention of opening the empire's ports to American shipping. English officials reminded him that Americans had desired independence and must now live with its consequences. They pointed out, moreover, that British goods could command the American market without England's needing to grant any concessions in return.

During the mid-1780s, Americans had some success in their search for new commercial arrangements; progress, however, was slow. After independence had been won, France and Spain gradually withdrew the special trading privileges they had extended during the war and returned to their policy of mercantile restrictions. The New York merchant ship *Empress of China* made the first American voyage to China in 1784, and others soon followed. The successful development of that trade, however, would not come until the nineteenth century.

By the mid-1790s American commerce had regained its prewar level, but the American population had also increased substantially, and on a per capita basis American commerce continued to languish. Between 1770 and 1790, the per capita value of American exports fell by a startling 30 percent. Nearly a decade after the fighting had stopped, the country's commercial recovery was still incomplete.

### Boom and Depression in Agriculture

Agriculture was second only to commerce in its importance to the American economy, and it suffered the effects of independence and war as well. On the eve of independence, northern agriculture was prosperous. New England farmers exported livestock, salted meat, and other foodstuffs to the southern colonies and the West

Indies. Pennsylvania wheat and corn found expanding and highly profitable markets in Europe, in part because of a series of bad harvests there. From Maryland southward, a system of plantation agriculture dominated the economy. Black slaves, rather than free labor, supported the production and export of staple commodities —tobacco and wheat in Maryland and Virginia, rice and indigo in South Carolina and Georgia. South Carolina's exports found a ready market in Europe. In the Chesapeake region, even though the price of tobacco had softened on the world market, exports remained high, and English credit continued to support crop expansion.

Independence threw American agriculture into disarray. No area was hit harder than the Chesapeake. With the loss of English markets, tobacco production dropped precipitously, and a deep depression settled across the region. Not until 1790 did tobacco exports regain their pre-war level. South Carolina's rice continued to command a good price in Europe when it could be slipped through the British blockade. It remained an important export until cotton supplanted it early in the nineteenth century. But once British markets and financial incentives were removed, the production of indigo, the state's second most valuable export commodity, virtually ceased. To the north, Pennsylvania's overseas trade to Europe in wheat and corn declined, while New England farmers staggered under the loss of their lucrative West Indies provisioning trade.

Armies and navies, of course, have to eat. The large number of men in the field and at sea—British, German, and French as well as American—sharply increased the demand for agricultural produce. As a consequence, agricultural prices rose and farmers often prospered when the armies were nearby. Such was the case in New England during the first years of the war. At one point Congress called upon New England farmers to provide 1,000 head of cattle weekly for the army's use. When the fighting shifted to the South, however, New England agriculture slipped into a depression from which it did not recover for more than a decade.

Farmers often received fair compensation for their commodities. French and British purchasing agents were regarded as especially good customers, because they frequently paid in gold and silver coin, something American commissaries often could not do. But as the war went on, farmers increasingly received payment in continental dollars that depreciated in value before they could be spent, or in various kinds of governmental IOUs that carried only the most distant prospect of redemption. When things got difficult, as they so often did, military commanders simply seized what they needed—corn, hay, livestock, wagons—and went on their way.

Agricultural productivity almost certainly declined during the war. The supply of agricultural labor decreased, and its cost rose as men were called into the army and as large numbers of southern slaves slipped behind British lines or ran away. Farm property was confiscated and destroyed, and few persons had money to pay for its replacement. Throughout the colonial period, American farmers had increased production by bringing new acreage under cultivation, as land long cultivated declined in productivity. During the war, however, crop acreage actually decreased, and virtually no new lands came under the plow.

Farmers found ways to compensate for the losses they suffered. For example, they withheld their produce from local markets until prices rose, thus angering nearby urban dwellers. Or they shifted from crops to the more lucrative production of livestock, or supplemented their incomes by smithing or cabinetmaking. During the war, the labor of farm women increased substantially in value, for shirts, blankets, and other objects of domestic manufacture were much in demand.

Most farmers and planters, however, did not prosper. The average real worth per farm, as measured by the combined value of farm implements, livestock, and crops, declined. When the war ended, farmers and planters almost unanimously lamented their heavy personal debts and the uncertainty of their future. In 1785, an English traveler visited a Rhode Island farm, where he found 11 people struggling for a living on 76 acres of land. The farmers here, he wrote, "are miserably poor and in debt." For agriculturalists everywhere, independence and the war took a heavy toll. As we shall see in Chapter 7, the hard times that accompanied the agricultural depression inflamed state politics throughout the Revolution.

## Manufacturing and Wartime Profits

Breaking with the empire caused little hardship for most American manufacturers. They had often ignored English regulations and had generally sold their goods in local, colonial markets. Several industries, however, were hard hit, shipbuilding most dramatically. On the eve of independence, New England constructed about 50 percent of the merchant tonnage carrying cargo within England's Atlantic empire. During the war, shipbuilding virtually ceased. For towns such as Boston and Newburyport, the results were disastrous. Hundreds of people—ship captains, ropemakers, blacksmiths, sailmakers, shipwrights, and sailors—lost their livelihoods. Many drifted away into the army, but others stayed where they were, frustrated and restless, wondering what benefits independence held for them. The construction of a few naval vessels under contract from the Congress or state governments offered some relief, but they were few in number, and their completion was often delayed because of insufficient funds.

Overall, however, the war stimulated American manufacturers. With British goods excluded, American producers moved to take up the slack. Patriotism as well as necessity argued for the use of domestic goods. (The familiar slogan "Buy American!" has a long tradition.) As during the years of protest before independence, wearing homespun signified one's commitment to the Revolutionary cause. Women continued to spin more thread, weave more cloth, and fashion it into clothes appropriate for republican citizens to wear.

It was hard to increase production rapidly, however, for artisans and craftsmen, working at home or in small shops, fashioned virtually everything by hand, using traditional tools. In Pennsylvania, the most skilled gunsmiths could produce no more than 50 muskets a year, for each part had to be made and fitted individually. Moreover, with so many men in the army, the cost of labor increased, a problem intensified by the wartime cutoff of immigration. Finally, though the country's shops and mills were widely scattered across the land, they were most numerous in the coastal areas, where the war's destruction was heaviest.

Still, there were profits to be made, especially by opportunistic merchants with the right political connections. The largest returns came from government contracting. Too often the search for profits shaded over into outright profiteering. An "insatiable thirst for riches," lamented George Washington in 1779, "seems to have got the better of every other consideration and almost of every order of men." Merchants with valuable wares did not always make nice distinctions among their customers, trading as freely with the English army as with the Patriots. Members of the military were not immune from the temptation. General Henry Knox, commander of the continental artillery, observed to a friend that he was "exceedingly anxious to effect something in these fluctuating times, which may make . . . [me] lazy for life."

Then as now, the boundaries between individuals' private interests and their public responsibilities were often difficult to discern. Silas Deane capitalized on his position as congressional purchasing agent in France by using public money to arrange lucrative trading ventures of his own. The Congress finally called the unscrupulous Deane home to explain, but many others acted much the same while charting their course more carefully than he.

Robert Morris, an eminent Philadelphia merchant, insisted on his right to continue his private ventures after he became treasurer of the Congress, and the Congress agreed. Several of Morris's chief business partners were themselves members of that body. Morris explained to one of them, "You may depend that the pursuit of . . . [our] plan deserves your utmost exertion & attention so far as your mind is engaged in making money, for there never has been so fair an oppert'y of making a large fortune since I have been conversant in the world." At the same time, the public benefited immeasurably from Morris's services, for he worked mightily to stabilize congressional finances and at several critical moments committed his own sizable fortune to support the tottering credit of the Congress.

When peace returned, America's manufacturing boom collapsed. As French and English soldiers withdrew and American troops returned home, the demand for war materiel dropped. At the same time, long-excluded English goods came flooding into the American market, driving the cruder American goods from the stores. American merchants welcomed that renewal of English trade. But artisans, who found their livelihoods endangered by English competition, were alarmed.

## Financial Chaos

The war left America's financial arrangements in a state of chaos that would take more than a decade to repair. Historically, the American people had conducted their economic affairs via a confusing array of their own currencies and coin, as well as English, Spanish, Dutch, and French emissions. When public expenditures increased, as for example during the Seven Years' War, colonial governments had printed paper money, used it to pay soldiers or purchase supplies, and then tried to withdraw it quickly from circulation through taxation before people lost confidence in its value.

The Revolutionary War required unprecedented governmental expenditures. Faced with the rapid and seemingly uncontrollable escala-

*Lacking sufficient gold and silver to cover the costs of war, Congress printed massive amounts of paper money, which rapidly depreciated in value.*

tion of costs, Congress and the states acted as American governments have done ever since: they printed money. Within the first year of the war, Congress and the states together issued more than $400 million in various kinds of paper, and that was only the beginning. By the end of the war, they had pumped countless additional millions in state and continental issues into the economy in payment for military supplies and salaries. Nothing supported its value but the citizens' willingness to accept it in their dealings with the government and each other.

That willingness rapidly disappeared as the flood of paper expanded and efforts to retrieve it through taxation lagged. The result was a headlong collapse of the currency's value and an equally precipitous upward spiral of inflation. Congressional bills of credit that in 1776 were pegged against gold at the ratio of 1.5 to 1 had slipped five years later to 147 to 1. State currencies depreciated even more alarmingly. In 1780, most states called in their old depreciated money and issued new currency, hoping that this would bring stability. New York pegged the exchange rate at 128 to 1, North Carolina at 800 to 1, and Virginia at 1,000 to 1.

The situation offered wonderful opportunities for the unscrupulous. In May 1781, the exchange rate in Boston between continental bills of credit and gold was 75 to 1; in Philadelphia it was three times that rate. The road between the two cities, observed one bemused Bostonian, was crowded with "numbers of men, loaded with the old currency; among the rest a Mr. Tim Palmer who has made three tours to Philadelphia."

For most Americans, however, this flood of depreciated paper had anything but beneficial consequences. What was one to do when goods, services, and wages had no consistent value, when the idea of saving made no sense, when even the incentive to work disappeared? James Lovell observed uneasily that "sailors with clubs parade the streets" of Boston "instead of working for paper." How could individuals make plans or conduct economic transactions under such conditions? Often they could not.

The price inflation accompanying the currency collapse was staggering. In Massachusetts, a bushel of corn that sold for less than a dollar in 1777 went for nearly $80 two years later, while in Maryland, the price in paper money of a bushel of wheat increased by several thousand times. In Boston, a crowd of women, angered by the escalating costs of food and other necessities, tossed a merchant suspected of monopolizing commodities into a cart and dragged him through the city's streets while "a large concourse of men stood amazed."

Runaway inflation transformed relationships between creditors and debtors. More than once, people observed the curious sight of debtors relentlessly pursuing their creditors, seeking to pay off their obligations in money worth but a fraction of its former value. Depreciating currency could change an individual's circumstances quickly and dramatically. John Witherspoon remarked to a friend that his son-in-law had sold all his furniture before leaving Virginia to come to Philadelphia. The several thousand pounds' worth of continental bills of credit that he received for it soon depreciated to nothing. His loss was virtually complete. With property values in disarray, people's social positions, then as now largely defined by property, were uncertain as well. At times it seemed as if the very foundations of society were becoming unhinged.

Thomas Paine described the situation in 1777 to his friend Elbridge Gerry. "The war," he wrote, "has thrown property into channels where before it never was. . . . Moneys in large sums . . . enables . . . [profiteers] to roll the snow ball of monopoly and forestalling; and . . . while these people are heaping up wealth . . . the remaining part are jogging on in their old way, with few or no advantages."

Though many people were hurt, the poor suffered most. During the best of times they lived at the margins of subsistence. More than others, they were vulnerable to losses in the purchasing power of their wages or military pay. The poor, however, were not alone. Farmers and merchants, planters and artisans faced increas-

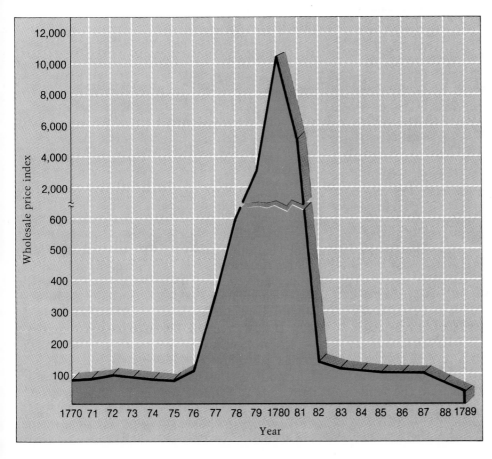

**Inflation of Wholesale Prices, 1770–1789**

*Note:* 1850–1859 = 100
*Source:* U.S. Bureau of the Census.

ing debt and uncertainty. Rarely has the American economy been in such disarray as it was at the nation's founding. Independence and the war virtually halted the economic expansion of the previous half century. By the 1790s, that expansion would be under way once again, but until then America's economic affairs remained deeply troubled.

## OUTSIDE THE REVOLUTION

Many people in America—black slaves, Native Americans, white Loyalists—found themselves outsiders during the Revolution. They suffered its effects but reaped few of its rewards. Each group experienced the Revolution differently, and each played a role in its outcome, but each found itself the victim of events it could not control.

### Native Americans and the Revolution

The American Revolution had powerful consequences for Native Americans. It could hardly have been otherwise, for the lives of Indians and colonists had been intimately connected since the first white settlements more than a century and a half before.

By the middle of the eighteenth century, the coastal tribes were mostly gone, victims of white settlement and the ravages of European disease. In the interior region stretching from the Appalachian Mountains west to the Mississippi River, however, powerful tribes remained. In the Northeast, the Iroquois Six Nations occupied the area from Albany, New York, to the Ohio country. Formed into an imposing confederation, they numbered perhaps 15,000 people. Their size, location, and fighting ability enabled them to dominate the entire northeastern region, while years before they had established control over the "western" tribes of the Ohio valley—the Shawnee and the Delaware, the Wyandotte and the Miami. From their strategic geographic position, they had regulated the flow of furs from the interior tribes to the colonists along the coast.

In the Southeast, five tribes dominated the interior, the Choctaw and Chickasaw, the Seminole, the Creek, and the Cherokee. They totaled perhaps 60,000 people and together occupied a vast region between the western Carolinas and the Mississippi, the Ohio River and the Gulf of Mexico.

When the Revolutionary War began, both British and American officials urged the Indians to remain neutral. The British, expecting the conflict to be short, wished to disrupt the interior as little as possible. The Americans urged neutrality because they feared Indian attacks from the west while they faced the British threat along the coast. In July 1775, Congress passed a resolution stating that "securing and preserving the friendship of Indian nations, appears to be a subject of the utmost moment to these colonies."

Up and down the interior, Native Americans debated their situation. All recognized they had a considerable stake in the conflict. At a council in Albany, New York, in August 1775, representatives of the Six Nations listened while American commissioners urged them to remain at home and keep the hatchet buried deep. The tribes' answer was returned by Little Abraham, a Mohawk leader. "The determination of the Six Nations," he declared, "[is] not to take any part; but as it is a family affair, to sit still and see you fight it out." The Iroquois would remain neutral as long as neither side sent troops across their land. Neutrality, however, did not last long. The Native Americans were too important militarily to be ignored, and both the British and the Americans feared that the other would be first to recruit them. By the spring of 1776, both sides were actively seeking Indian alliances.

In the Southeast, the tribes moved quickly to take advantage of the situation. Increasingly alarmed by the westward advance of white settlement from Virginia and the Carolinas, a band of Cherokee, led by the warrior Dragging Canoe, launched a series of raids in July 1776 against white settlements in what is today eastern Tennessee. The American response was quick and devastating. Fearing a general uprising of the Cherokee while they were preoccupied with Britain along the coast, the Virginia and Carolina governments sent militia to lay waste a group of Cherokee towns. Thomas Jefferson expressed satisfaction at the outcome. "I hope that the Cherokees will now be driven beyond the Mississippi," he wrote, "and that this in the future will be declared to the Indians the invariable consequence of their beginning a war. Our contest with Britain is too serious, and too great to permit any possibility of [danger] . . . from the Indians. This then is the reason for driving them off."

During the winter of 1780–1781, American militia once more ravaged Cherokee towns. Though sporadic raiding continued throughout the war, the Cherokee never again mounted a sustained military effort against the Patriots. Seeing what had become of their neighbors, the Creek stayed aloof. Their time for resistance would come several decades later, in the early

nineteenth century, when white settlers began to push aggressively into their lands. In November 1785, the Treaty of Hopewell formally ended the conflict between the Cherokee and the new American nation. In the decade that followed, they ceded away much of their land through treaty agreements, while white settlements crowded around them. By the turn of the century, war and disease had reduced their population by nearly half.

### The Devastation of the Iroquois

As the war spread throughout the Northeast, Iroquois neutrality also fell by the wayside. American troops raided deep into Mohawk territory west of Albany in 1776. The British, newly alarmed, argued with words, rum, and trade goods for Iroquois involvement against the rebels. At the Oswego Council in the summer of 1777, most of the Iroquois abandoned neutrality and joined the struggle against the Americans. They did so at the urging of Joseph Brant, a Mohawk warrior who had several years before

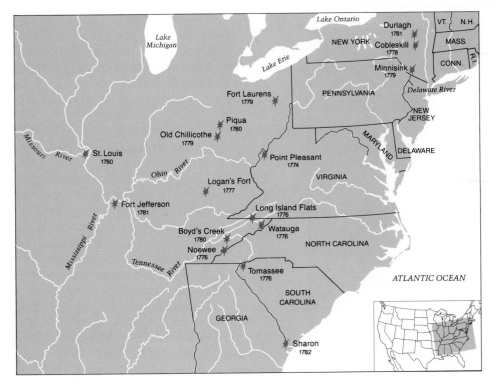

**Indian Battles, 1775–1783**

visited England and who argued England's importance as an ally against American expansion.

It was a fateful decision for Indians and whites alike. Over the next several years, the Iroquois and their English and Tory allies devastated large areas in central New York and Pennsylvania, destroying property, terrorizing the inhabitants, and disrupting the entire region. An officer of the Pennsylvania militia reported somberly, "Our country is on the eve of breaking up. There is nothing to be seen but disolation, fire & smoak. As the inhabitants is collected at particular places [for safety], the enemy burns all their houses that they have evacuated."

The Americans' revenge came swiftly. During the summer of 1779, General John Sullivan led a series of punishing raids into Iroquois country, burning the Iroquois villages, killing men, women, and children, destroying fields of corn, and cutting down orchards. His motto for

*Mohawk chief Joseph Brant (Tayadaneega) was of prime influence in the Iroquois' decision to enter the war on the side of Britain. Brant's ties with England went back to the days of his grandfather (see Chapter 5, p. 134).*

the campaign was blunt: "Civilization or death to all American savages." Two of the Iroquois nations, the Oneida and the Tuscarora, had allied with the Americans, and their villages were spared. The British and other Iroquois tribes, however, destroyed them in turn. The Iroquois recovered sufficiently to conduct punishing counterraids during the final years of the war, but their losses in human lives and property were great.

When peace came, the Indians' interests were totally ignored. No mention of them was made at Paris by their British allies. No compensation for their losses was provided, nor any guarantees of their land, for the boundary of the United States was set far to the west, at the Mississippi. Most of the Indians had had good reason for choosing England as their ally, for England had provided them with trade goods, gifts, and arms. England, moreover, had offered them protection against the expansionist Americans, as the Proclamation Line of 1763 had demonstrated. England, however, lost the war and so, as a consequence, did their Indian allies.

Defeat cost the Iroquois dearly. Their confederation, divided and defeated, lay in ruins. Unable any longer to protect their client tribes in the Ohio valley from white advances, their western influence was broken. Some Iroquois fled into Canada, but others stayed on. Pressed by Congress and the New York government, they rapidly deeded away most of their land. At the Treaty of Fort Stanwix in 1784, the first American treaty with an Indian tribe, the American commissioners refused to recognize the Iroquois Confederacy, demanding instead to negotiate separately with each tribe. Under the threat of continued war, the Six Nations made peace, yielded their western lands to the United States, and took up residence on small reservations. Though the Iroquois would later renounce the Treaty of Fort Stanwix because it was made under duress, the damage had been done. By the mid-1790s, little remained of the once extensive Iroquois domain but a few islands in a spreading sea of white settlement. On those islands—"slums in the wilderness," they have been called—the Iroquois struggled for survival against disease and poverty, their traditional lifeways gone, their self-confidence broken.

The Revolution left behind a legacy of bitterness for both Indians and whites: for Indians because they had suffered both betrayal and defeat, for white Americans because the Indians had sided with England and had threatened the success of the Revolutionary cause. This bitterness would deeply affect Indian-white relations during the years ahead.

## Blacks and the Revolution

The Revolution was accompanied by the largest slave rebellion in American history prior to the Civil War. Once independence had been declared and the war was under way, blacks found a variety of ways to turn the Revolution to their own advantage. For some, this meant applying Revolutionary principles to their own lives and calling for their freedom from the Patriots. For others, it meant an opportunity for seeking liberty behind English lines or in the continent's interior. Not all American blacks found their lives changed, but thousands did in important and lasting ways.

Blacks had no voice in the decision for independence. Most were slaves and lacked political standing. Their presence, however, affected the decisions of both sides throughout the war, especially in the southern states, where most blacks lived. Southern Patriots worried that their slaves would take advantage of a war with England and rise against them. They had reason to be alarmed, for wherever the British army went, slaves fled their masters to take advantage of British offers of freedom.

During the pre-Revolutionary decade, as their white masters talked excitedly about liberty, the dignity of mankind, and the nobility of opposing despotism, increasing numbers of black Americans questioned their own oppression. Some slaves petitioned legislatures in the North to set them free. In the South, pockets of insurrection appeared. In 1765, more than 100 South Carolina slaves fled to the interior, where they tried to establish a Maroon colony. The next year, slaves paraded through the streets of Charleston, chanting, "Liberty, liberty!"

In November 1775, Lord Dunmore issued a proclamation offering freedom to all of Virginia's slaves and servants, "able and willing to bear arms," who left their masters and joined the British forces in Norfolk. Within weeks, 500 to 600 slaves had responded. Among those who demonstrated their commitment to freedom by traveling through the hostile, Patriot-controlled countryside was Thomas Peters, a slave from Wilmington, North Carolina.

Brought to America by a French slave trader, Peters was sold in Louisiana about 1760. Kidnapped from the Yoruba tribe in what is now Nigeria, he resisted enslavement so fiercely in Louisiana that his master sold him into the English colonies. By 1770, Peters belonged to William Campbell, an immigrant Scots planter on North Carolina's Cape Fear River. Here Peters toiled while the storm brewed between England and the colonies.

Peters's plans for his own declaration of independence may have ripened as a result of the rhetoric of liberty he heard around his master's house. William Campbell had become a leading member of Wilmington's Sons of Liberty by 1770 and talked much about inalienable rights. By mid-1775, the Cape Fear region, like

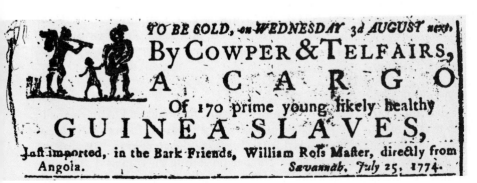

TO BE SOLD, on WEDNESDAY 3d AUGUST next. By COWPER & TELFAIRS, A CARGO Of 170 prime young likely healthy GUINEA SLAVES, Just imported, in the Bark Friends, William Ross Master, directly from Angola.     Savannah, July 25, 1774.

*The ideals and rhetoric of liberty did not escape the notice of slaves in the years before the Revolution, though few slave owners gave serious thought to extending these principles to include blacks.*

most areas from Maryland to Georgia, was filled with rumors of slave uprisings. Importations of new slaves were banned, and patrols were dispatched to disarm all blacks in the area. In July, the state's Revolutionary government imposed martial law when the British commander of Fort Johnston at the mouth of the Cape Fear River near Wilmington gave "encouragement to Negroes to elope from their masters." Four months later, Dunmore issued his dramatic proclamation.

Thomas Peters struck his blow for freedom in March 1776, when 20 British ships entered the Cape Fear River and disembarked royal troops, who quickly established control over the surrounding countryside. Peters seized the moment to redefine himself as a man instead of William Campbell's property and made good his escape. During the war, he fought with the British-officered Black Pioneers.

How many American blacks such as Peters sought liberty behind British lines is unknown, but as many as 20 percent may have done so. In dramatic contrast to their white masters, blacks saw in England the promise of freedom, not tyranny. As the war dragged on, English commanders pressed blacks into service, usually in support roles but also as combatants. From the first group of Virginia slaves who fled in 1775 after Dunmore's proclamation, a regiment of black soldiers was formed and marched into battle, their chests covered with sashes on which were emblazoned "Liberty to Slaves." Some of the blacks who joined England and fought for their freedom achieved it. At the war's end, several thousand evacuated with the British to Nova Scotia, where they established their own settlements. Their reception by the white inhabitants there, however, was generally hostile. By the end of the century, most had left Canada, this time to become founders of the free black colony of Sierra Leones on the west coast of Africa. Thomas Peters was a leader among them.

Many of the slaves who fled behind English lines, however, never won their freedom. At the end of the war, as the British prepared to evacuate the port cities, blacks from the surrounding countryside crowded in, begging to be taken away. Against their appeals for liberty, British commanders had to balance the terms of the peace treaty, which stipulated that the British were to evacuate "with all convenient Speed and without causing any destruction or carrying away any Negroes or other Property of the American Inhabitants." In the end, hundreds of slaves were returned to their American owners. Several thousand others, their value as fieldhands too great to be ignored, were transported to the West Indies and the harsher slavery of the sugar plantations there. For many, it was evident that England had not entered the war to abolish slavery.

Other blacks chose not to flee to the British but took advantage of the war's confusion to drift away into the towns or the countryside, seeking the opportunity to establish a new life. Some sought refuge among the Indians, though not always with success. The Seminoles of Georgia and Florida generally welcomed black runaways and through intermarriage absorbed them into tribal society. The blacks' reception by the Cherokees and Creeks, however, was more uncertain. Some were taken in, but others were returned to their white owners in return for bounties, while still others were held in slave-like conditions by new Indian masters. Numerous other blacks made their way north, following rumors that slavery had been abolished there. Whatever their destination, thousands of American blacks acted to throw off the bonds of slavery.

Many fewer blacks fought on the American side than on England's. In part this was because neither Congress nor the states were eager to see blacks armed. Faced with the increasing need for troops, however, Congress and each of the states except Georgia and South Carolina relented and pressed blacks into service. Of the blacks who served the Patriot cause, many received the freedom they were promised. The patriotism of countless others, however, went unrewarded.

## Slavery Under Attack

The Revolution affected black Americans in two other ways as well. First, it sharply reduced and ultimately ended the slave trade. During the several decades preceding the imperial crisis, the trade in human chattels had thrived. The war halted that trade almost completely. Once the war was over, southern planters sought to replace the slaves they had lost, and for several years the trade revived. Everywhere but in South Carolina, however, the revival was of short duration. Revolutionary principles, the reduced need for fieldhands in the depressed tobacco economy, a continuing increase in the slave population through natural reproduction, and post-Revolutionary anxiety over black rebelliousness argued for its extinction. By 1790, each of the states, with the notable exceptions of South Carolina and Georgia, had outlawed slave importations. Though some merchants up and down the coast continued the nefarious practice, the transatlantic traffic in humans was nearly over.

The consequences were profound. The renewed demand for field labor generated by the expansion of cotton production during the first half of the nineteenth century would have to be met domestically. This would give rise to the internal slave trade between the Chesapeake, with its excess of slaves, and the developing regions of Mississippi and Alabama, where the demand was high and cotton planters were willing to pay a top price. That internal, forced migration would affect the lives of countless black Americans and exacerbate the sectional crisis between North and South.

Just as important, termination of the slave trade reduced the infusion of new Africans into the black population. This meant that over time, an even higher proportion of blacks were American-born and had no personal recollections of their African homeland, thus speeding the process of cultural transformation by which Africans became Afro-Americans.

Finally, the institution of slavery itself came under attack during the Revolutionary era. The consequences, both for black Americans and for the nation's future, were immense. In South Carolina and Georgia, the Revolution brought no change at all. In those states, blacks outnumbered whites more than two to one. Believing strongly in their racial superiority and fearing the black majority, whites shuddered at the prospect of black freedom. Moreover, slave labor remained essential to their rice economy. In response to the dangers generated by the war, whites tightened the local slave codes even more.

In Virginia and Maryland, change did occur, as some leaders argued that slavery and republican liberty were incompatible. During the 1780s, both state legislatures openly debated the question of the abolition of slavery. The depression in the tobacco economy and the accompanying decline in demand for slave labor made that debate easier. Neither state came close to universal abolition. Both did, however, pass laws making it easier for individual slave owners to free their slaves, and during the last two decades of the century, many owners did so. Moreover, increasing numbers of blacks took advantage of the more flexible public mood to petition for their own freedom or to purchase it from their masters. The result was a rapid increase in the free black population throughout the Chesapeake region. By 1800, more than one of every ten blacks was free, a dramatic increase over 30 years before. The majority lived and worked in Baltimore, Richmond, and other towns scattered throughout the area. There they formed communities that became centers of an expanding Afro-American social and cultural life and havens for runaway slaves from the countryside. For countless blacks in the Chesapeake region, the conditions of life slowly changed for the better.

The most dramatic breakthroughs, however, occurred in the North. There slavery was either abolished or put on the road to extinction. Abolition was easier in the North because there were fewer blacks. Except for a few cities and rural areas in Rhode Island and along the Hudson River in New York, blacks constituted no more than 4 percent of the northern population. As a consequence, slavery did not have the economic or social importance that it did in the South. Awareness that slavery was incompatible with the principles of the Revolution, however, had important consequences as well.

Northern blacks joined in the attack on slavery. Following independence, they frequently petitioned the state assemblies for their freedom. "Every Principle from which America has acted in the course of their unhappy difficulties with Great Britain," declared one group of Philadelphia blacks, "pleads stronger than a thousand arguments in favor of our petition."

Pennsylvania acted first, in response to both black initiatives and the promptings of radical leaders in the state government. Though the Quakers had by now lost political power, they also continued to oppose slavery. In 1780, the Pennsylvania assembly passed a law stipulating that all newborn blacks were to be free when they reached age 28. It was a cautious but decisive step. Other northern states in the decades ahead adopted similar policies of gradual emancipation, although it took another half century for the complete extinction of slavery.

Though opposition to slavery among northern whites was real, commitment to racial equality was much less evident. Even as freemen, blacks continued to encounter pervasive discrimination. Still, remarkable progress had occurred. Prior to the Revolution, slavery had been an accepted fact of northern life; after the Revolution, it no longer was. The change made a vast difference in the circumstances of black life and in the ways in which blacks and whites interacted.

The abolition of slavery in the North also increased the sectional divergence between North and South. The consequences of that would become more apparent in the nineteenth century. In addition, there now existed a coherent and publicly proclaimed antislavery argument, one closely linked in Americans' minds with the nation's founding. The first antislavery organizations had been created as well. Although another half century would transpire before antislavery became a force in national political life, the groundwork for slavery's final abolition had been laid.

## The Loyalists

On September 8, 1783, Thomas Danforth, formerly a lawyer from Cambridge, Massachusetts, appeared in London before the King's Commission of Enquiry into the Losses and Services of the American Loyalists. Danforth was there to seek compensation for the losses he had suffered at the hands of the American revolutionaries because of his loyalism. As with other Loyalists who appealed to the commission, Danforth began by explaining his position in colonial Massachusetts and the consequences of his loyalty to the crown. "Having devoted his whole life . . . in preparing himself for future usefulness," he began,

> . . . now he finds himself near his fortieth year, banished under pain of death, to a distant country, where he has not the most remote family connection . . . cut off from his profession—from every hope of importance in life, and in a great degree from social enjoyments. And where . . . he shall be unable . . . to procure common comforts and conveniences, in a station much inferior to that of a menial servant, without the assistance of government.

Danforth then proceeded to detail his losses. The commission's response is unknown, but if it treated him as it did many of the several thousand Loyalists who appeared before it, it reimbursed him for about one-third of his actual losses. At least it was something, and more in fact than most Loyalist refugees could expect, for relatively few ever appeared before the commission. It hardly compensated him adequately, however, for what he had endured—the confiscation and sale of his house and property, expulsion from his native land, ostracism and attack by his former neighbors, and the trauma of relocation in a distant and unfamiliar land.

How many white American men and women remained loyal to England can only be estimated because, again, complete records were not kept. We do know that tens of thousands left with the British troops from ports such as New York, Charleston, and Savannah at the end of the war. At least as many slipped away to England, Canada, or the West Indies while the fighting was still under way. Thousands of others never left, but stayed on in the new nation and struggled to rebuild their lives. There were many more who wished in their hearts that independence had never come but who, out of prudence or fear, kept their views to themselves and tried to stay out of trouble.

The problem of numbers is further complicated by the fact that individuals might be accused of loyalism simply because they seemed insufficiently ardent in support of the Revolution or because some personal antagonist sought revenge on them. No count, then, can be exact. As many as 80,000 men, women, and children, however, may have departed the new nation, while several hundred thousand more remained in the United States. These are substantial figures when set against the total American population, black and white, of about 2.5 million souls. The incidence of loyalism differed dramatically from region to region. There were fewest Loyalists in New England and most in and around New York City. Not surprisingly, they tended to congregate near the British army and where British authority was most stable.

Why did so many Americans remain loyal, often at the cost of considerable personal danger and loss? Some, appointed to office in the king's name, had a special incentive to loyalism. Customs officers, members of the governors' councils, and Anglican clergymen most often remained with the crown. Loyalism was common as well among groups who depended on British authority to protect their interests within American society—for example, settlers on the Carolina frontier who believed themselves mistreated by the politically dominant planter elite along the coast and who looked to the royal governor for help; or ethnic minorities, such as the Germans in the middle states, who feared domination by the Anglo-American majority; or tenants on some of the large estates along the Hudson River, who had struggled for years with their landlords over the terms of their leaseholds and who regarded English officials as potential allies.

For many other colonists, the prospect of confronting English military power, however correct they believed the American position to be, was sufficiently daunting. Others doubted the ability of a new, weak nation to survive in an Atlantic world dominated by competing empires, even if independence could be won.

The Loyalist position was often principled as well. Samuel Seabury emphasized the duty of obedience to English law. "Every person," he wrote in 1775, "owes obedience to the laws of the government . . . and is obliged in honour and duty to support them. Because if *one* has a right to disregard the laws of the society to which he belongs, *all* have the *same* right; and then government is at an end. . . . And you are

so far from being bound in honour to obey *any* determinations of the Congress, which interfere with the laws of the government, that you are really bound in honour to *oppose* them."

William Eddis wondered what kind of society independence would bring when Revolutionary crowds showed no respect for the rights of Loyalist dissenters such as he. "If I differ in opinion from the multitude," he asked, "must I therefore be deprived of my character, and the confidence of my fellow-citizens; when in every station of life I discharge my duty with fidelity and honour?" Whatever their motives, the Loy-

*Loyalists, or Tories, found that the Patriots' interpretation of liberty did not include the freedom to honor the British crown. Harassment drove many to resettle in Canada, England, or other parts of the British Empire.*

alists believed themselves advocates of reason and moderation and the rule of law in the midst of revolutionary confusion. Tens of thousands of Americans believed strongly enough in their position to sacrifice home, community, and personal safety on its behalf.

Many who faced exile successfully established new lives in other parts of the empire. The majority settled in the Maritime Provinces of Canada. But even under the best of circumstances, forced resettlement was traumatic. Most of the several thousand or so who made it all the way to England met something other than the warm and grateful reception they had hoped for. Try as they might to be English, they quickly discovered that they were not; and so, along with Thomas Danforth, they remained on the fringes of English society, their financial affairs troubled, their futures uncertain.

How many Loyalists returned after the war was over is not known. Clearly, some did. During the late 1780s, the Connecticut assembly specifically invited certain individuals to come back, apparently hoping that their skills and experience would help in the task of economic recovery. But there is no evidence that the number returning was large.

Loyalists came from all social classes, but they were most numerous among the upper and middle ranks of society, where individuals were most likely to have direct political and social connections with English officials. In localities where they were numerous, their departure opened positions of social and political leadership and increased the tempo of social change. More generally, given their adherence to monarchical government and its values of hierarchy and subordination, their loss weakened the forces of social conservatism in America and facilitated the progress of revolutionary reform.

## CONCLUSION: The Crucible of Revolution

The Revolutionary War, though it ended in victory, disrupted countless American lives. No region escaped its ravages entirely. Tens of thousands of men answered the call to arms and helped bring a nation into existence. On the home front, many experienced hardship and impoverishment, while some made fortunes. By all, the war would be indelibly remembered.

The war changed the relationship between Native Americans and the former colonists. It opened the floodgates of western expansion, previously held back by British policy, and removed a powerful overseas government that had at least partially recognized the natives' territorial claims. For black Americans, the Revolution had paradoxical results. It produced an ideology that decried slavery of all sorts and marked the first general debate over abolishing the oppressive institution. Yet the Revolutionary generation took steps to eradicate slavery only where it was least important, in the North, while guaranteeing its future in the region where it was most important, the South.

Military victory assured independence for an American nation. But the American people had to solve a host of problems in the midst of the war. No longer governed by England, they had to decide how to govern themselves. No longer a colonial society, they had to define what kind of society they wanted to be. Tom Paine put the matter simply: "The answer to the question, can America be happy under a government of her own, is short and simple—as happy as she pleases; she hath a blank sheet to write upon." How Americans labored to decide what to write upon that blank sheet is the subject of the next chapter.

## Recommended Reading

Standard accounts of the Revolutionary War can be found in Don Higginbotham, *The War of American Independence* (1971) and Robert Middlekauff, *The Glorious Cause* (1982). In *A People Numerous and Armed* (1976), John Shy deals with the social dimensions of military conflict, while Charles Royster's *A Revolutionary People at War* (1979) explains how the continental army embodied the Revolution's social and ideological goals. Richard Van Alstyne, *Empire and Independence: The International History of the American Revolution* (1965) and Richard Morris, *The Peacemakers: The Great Powers and American Independence* (1965) offer skillful discussions of Revolutionary War diplomacy.

The most vivid description of Native American involvement in the Revolution can be found in Anthony Wallace, *The Death and Rebirth of the Seneca* (1969). James O'Donnell discusses the situation in the Southeast in *Southern Indians in the American Revolution* (1973). Several books offer starting points for further examination of the tangled history of slavery, race, and the Revolution: Winthrop Jordan, *White over Black: American Attitudes Toward the Negro, 1550–1812* (1968); Duncan MacLeod, *Slavery, Race, and the American Revolution* (1974); Ira Berlin and Ronald Hoffman, eds., *Slavery and Freedom in the Age of the American Revolution* (1983); and Jeffrey Crow, *The Black Experience in Revolutionary North Carolina* (1977).

Two excellent recent books examine the Revolutionary experience of women: Linda Kerber, *Women of the Republic* (1980) and Mary Beth Norton, *Liberty's Daughters* (1980). Robert Calhoon, *The Loyalists in Revolutionary America, 1760–1781* (1973) and Mary Beth Norton, *The British-Americans: The Loyalist Exiles in England, 1774–1789* (1972) deal with the experiences of Loyalist Americans. Robert Gross, *The Minutemen and Their World* (1976) offers a vivid portrayal of the Revolution's impact on the daily lives of ordinary people in Concord, Massachusetts. The essays in Jeffrey Crow and Larry Tise, eds., *The Southern Experience in the American Revolution* (1978) offer similar insights for the South.

For a deeper understanding of the Continental Congress and the Articles of Confederation, see Merrill Jensen, *The Articles of Confederation* (1940) and Jack Rakove, *The Beginnings of National Politics: An Interpretive History of the Continental Congress* (1979).

## TIME LINE

| | |
|---|---|
| 1775 | Lord Dunmore's proclamation to slaves and servants in Virginia<br>Congress resolves on Indian friendship<br>Iroquois Six Nations pledge neutrality |
| 1776 | British evacuate Boston<br>Declaration of Independence<br>Cherokee raids and American retaliations |
| 1777 | British occupy Philadelphia<br>Iroquois (except Tuscarora and Oneida) join the British<br>British surrender at Saratoga<br>Washington's army winters at Valley Forge |
| 1778 | War shifts to the South<br>Savannah falls to the British<br>French Treaty of Alliance and Commerce |
| 1778–1779 | Massacres of civilians by Loyalists and Indians<br>German mercenaries spread fear in New Jersey |
| 1779 | Sullivan destroys Iroquois villages in New York |
| 1780 | Charleston surrenders to the British<br>Nathanael Greene begins partisan warfare in the South<br>Pennsylvania begins gradual abolition of slavery |
| 1780s | Virginia and Maryland debate abolition of slavery<br>Destruction of Iroquois Confederacy |
| 1781 | Cornwallis surrenders at Yorktown |
| 1783 | Treaty of Paris<br>Massachusetts judiciary abolishes slavery<br>King's Commission on American Loyalists begins work |
| 1784 | Treaty of Fort Stanwix with Iroquois |
| 1785 | Treaty of Hopewell with Cherokee |
| 1790 | Slave trade outlawed in all states but Georgia and South Carolina |

# CHAPTER 7
## THE POLITICS
## OF REVOLUTIONARY AMERICA

Dirck Brinckerhoff of Dutchess County, New York, was a Dutchman and a farmer. His ancestors had come from Holland to New Netherland in the seventeenth century, before the English took over the colony and called it New York. Unlike some of their more clannish compatriots, the Brinckerhoffs accommodated to English rule, learned the language, and secured their place on the land.

Dutchess County, which stretched along the east bank of the Hudson River for 50 miles between Albany and New York City, was Brinckerhoff's home. In the 1760s, tenants, leasing small plots of land from wealthy families such as the Beekmans and the Philipses, farmed much of the county. Brinckerhoff was more fortunate, for, he owned his land outright and was reasonably prosperous. In 1768, he paid as much provincial tax as anyone in the river town of Poughkeepsie where he lived and had money left over to put out in mortgages.

Like most of his middle-class neighbors, Brinckerhoff was uneasy when several thousand tenants on the Philips patent rioted in 1766 over the "largeness of rents and shortness of leases" that bedeviled them. He was even more alarmed by the mobs that restored dispossessed tenants to their lands and then marched to the outskirts of New York City, seeking support from the Sons of Liberty there.

Yet Brinckerhoff understood the tenants' plight for he shared their resentment at the arrogance of the great landed families and their tight control over county affairs. So he allied himself with the tenants. With their support, he defeated the wealthy Robert Livingston for election to one of Dutchess County's two seats in the assembly, though, as Brinckerhoff observed, Livingston "had everything in his favor which power could give him." For two decades, Dirck represented ordinary constituents, first in the contest with Great Britain, then in the subsequent struggle for control of the Revolution within Dutchess County itself.

During the Revolutionary War, as British forces threatened to overrun the state, Brinckerhoff and other popular leaders worked closely with the county's wealthy Patriots. But in 1779, the Revolutionary movement in Dutchess County divided over a number of explosive issues: fair pay for the militia, control of skyrocketing prices, and the confiscation of Loyalist property. On each issue, Brinckerhoff spoke up for the common people. He opposed efforts by worried conservatives, such as James Duane, to replace the county's popularly elected militia officers with leaders appointed from above. "Licentiousness," wrote Duane, "can only be guarded against by placing the command of the troops in the hands of men of property and rank." Where Duane saw licentiousness and disloyalty, Brinckerhoff found ordinary men, faithful to the Revolution, calling for adequate pay and fair treatment.

In 1779, Brinckerhoff supported the creation of a county committee to limit the profits of merchants and shopkeepers accused of profiteering. In the state assembly, he worked tirelessly for passage of a law to regulate prices. Most important, he supported a bill to confiscate the estates of Dutchess County Loyalists and sell them to former tenants and farmers. No issue aroused greater alarm among the more conservative supporters of American independence, not only because confiscation threatened to redistribute property but because it would bring a broader sharing of political power as well.

With the help of Brinckerhoff and other popular leaders, an act providing for the confiscation and sale of Loyalist property passed the state assembly in 1780. As a result, almost half the tenants in southern Dutchess County gained ownership of their farms. Because they now owned property, these new landholders could also vote. Four hundred voters were added during the 1780s to the 1,800 who voted in Dutchess County before the Revolution.

Within several decades' time, three remarkable changes transformed the political world of Dirck Brinckerhoff and his fellow Americans. Political beliefs, systems of government, and ways of conducting elections—all were permanently altered. Independence forced the American people to explain their rebellion and define the principles on which their new nation was to be founded. They did that in the powerful and distinctive language of Revolutionary republicanism. All Americans could agree on many elements of the republican ideology. But there were many points of conflict as well, especially such explosive notions as political equality and the relationship between liberty and power. Continuing debate over the meaning of republicanism lay at the center of the Revolutionary experience.

The Revolution also changed political behavior. Large numbers of people—women, blacks, Native Americans—continued to be excluded from office-holding and voting, for republican reform did not carry that far. Among white males, however, political participation increased dramatically as farmers, artisans, and shopkeepers gained a degree of political power they had never enjoyed. Under the pressure of revolutionary events, people turned increasingly to politics to solve their problems and achieve their goals. As they did, they found themselves clashing over the most basic issues of public policy.

Finally, independence required the creation of new governments. In the states, the old colonial regimes were replaced by new ones based explicitly on republican principles. The Revolutionary generation also set about the more difficult task of fashioning a national government. Both efforts generated controversy, for in creating new governments the American people had to decide how power would be shared and governmental decisions made. The difficulties were compounded by the fact that the extraordinary demands of the war transformed the place of government in American society and changed people's notions of what government should be and do. By 1786, American politics and government were far more open and responsive—in a word, more democratic—than before.

## THE IDEOLOGY OF REVOLUTIONARY REPUBLICANISM

In times of danger and uncertainty, people often seek security and understanding in the realm of ideas. So it was in the world of Revolutionary America. We learned in Chapter 5 that on the eve of independence, Americans expressed their ideas about politics and society in the language of the English "country" tradition. In the crucible of Revolution, those ideas fused into the powerful and transforming ideology of Revolutionary republicanism. Much of that ideology was broadly shared among the American people. At the same time, people quickly disagreed once they started debating republican principles and trying to put them into effect.

### Creating a New Identity

The decision for independence was the central, defining experience in the lives of the Revolutionary generation. It set them apart, in their own minds and in the annals of history, from those who had come before and those who would follow. John Adams, writing to his wife Abigail, described his feelings as Congress debated independence. "Yesterday," he exulted, "the greatest question was decided which ever was debated in America, and a greater, perhaps, never was nor will be decided among men. The second day of July, 1776," he continued, will be the most memorable epocha in the history of America. . . . It ought to be commemorated as the day of deliverance, by solemn acts of devotion to God Almighty. It ought to be solemnized with pomp and parade, with shows, games, sports, guns, bells, bonfires, and illuminations, from one end of this continent to the other, from this time forward for evermore.

Adams was wrong about the day that Americans would recognize as the nation's anniversary, but his hope that they would celebrate what the Congress had done was fulfilled. Towns and hamlets throughout the states celebrated the event with bells and gun salutes, bonfires and parades. Ministers uttered solemn prayers that "He who putteth down potentates and setteth up States may guard and protect the United States of America." Everywhere people raised toasts to the great event: "Liberty to those who have the spirit to preserve it." "May the Crowns

*The first published announcement of the decision to declare independence appeared in Philadelphia's German-language newspaper, the* Pennsylvanischer Staatsbote. *Dated July 5, it translates: "Yesterday the Honorable Congress of this Continent declared the united colonies free and independent states." The paper goes on to promise that the entire declaration will appear in print "today or tomorrow."*

ral-Adjudant) und Capitain Burr, welche zu Quebec zu gefangenen gemacht wurden als der würdigste General Montgomery daselbst ein opfer der Ministerialischen rache wurde, jetzt an bord der Ministerialischen flotte zu Sandy-Hook sind.

Die rede gehet durchgängig, daß unsere kreuzfahrer 30 transportschiffe gegen Osten zu genommen haben.

Philadelphia, den 5 July.

Gestern hat der Achtbare Congreß dieses Vesten Landes die Vereinigten Colonien Freye und Unabhängige Staaten erkläret.

Die Declaration in Englisch ist jetzt in der Presse; sie ist datirt, den 4ten July, 1776, und wird heut oder morgen im druck erscheinen.

of Tyrants be crowns of thorns." And "May Liberty expand sacred wings, and, in glorious effort, diffuse her influence o'er and o'er the globe."

The Patriots of '76, they called themselves. One had to have shared the thrill of independence to be among their number. Their sense of uniqueness is understandable, for they were creating a new nation and entering a dangerous and uncertain world. Life for them would never again be the same.

As daunting as independence seemed, its declaration also brought a sense of relief. For several years, the American people had lived partly within the empire and partly without. While professing to accept English authority, they had increasingly opposed it. While hoping for reconciliation, they had become more and more skeptical that accommodation was possible. While seeking relief through traditional channels of petition and remonstrance, they had resorted to illegal forms of protest. Independence cut through those uncertainties in a stroke. Taking their fate decisively in their own hands, they declared, publicly and unequivocally, that America and England were separate. No longer English, they were now Americans; but what exactly did that mean? While creating a new nation, they would have to fashion a new identity as well.

Throughout history, as people have moved from colonialism to independence, they have had to create new identities. Where differences of race or culture have distinguished colonizers from colonized, as in Asia and Africa, racial and cultural uniqueness have dominated such efforts at self-definition. The American colonists, however, did not differ dramatically either in race or culture from their English masters. Slaves excluded, most were of British descent. Their culture consisted of variations on English themes. Most spoke English as their native language and looked to England for literary and artistic standards. Their laws and religion resembled England's, and their leaders affected English dress and mimicked English ways.

When the Revolutionary generation talked about American uniqueness, when they described their revolution and who they now were, they used the language of politics. "Our style and manner of thinking," observed Thomas Paine in amazement, "have undergone a revolution. . . . We see with other eyes, we hear with other ears, and think with other thoughts, than those we formerly used." Revolutionary republicanism constituted that revolution in thought.

Their republican ideology is not easy to understand. Its vocabulary is often unfamiliar, its meanings grounded in a historical experience different from our own. Yet it provides a key to what the Revolution was about. Moreover, republican ideology would reappear and be redefined throughout the nineteenth century as Americans struggled to deal with vast economic and social changes. (See Chapters 11, 15, and 18.)

### Rejecting Monarchy

The rejection of monarchy was one basic component of America's republican faith. "The word *republic*," explained Thomas Paine, "means the public good of the whole, in contradistinction to the despotic form which makes the good of the sovereign, or of one man, the only object of government." The American people did not easily turn away from the English monarchy. Up to the moment of independence,

they had celebrated England's "mixed and balanced" government with its combination of king, Lords, and Commons. They had thought England's limited monarchy, when properly administered, the safest and most stable form of government ever devised. America's problems with England had arisen not because of the monarchy but because the king and Parliament, corrupted by their own power, had turned their backs on the English constitution and attacked the liberties it was intended to protect.

Only at the very end of the imperial crisis, after they had already repudiated Parliamentary authority, did the colonists attack the king. It was Paine's unsparing rejection of monarchy, his denial that it was in any way compatible with liberty, that made his pamphlet *Common Sense* so radical. "Of more worth is one honest man to society, and in the sight of God," he scoffed, "than all the crowned ruffians that ever lived." Americans were not accustomed to using such language in reference to the king.

In rejecting monarchy, the American people also rejected the system of hierarchical authority on which the monarchy was based. They set aside the belief that political authority grew out of governmental power and the doctrine that in return for the king's protection the people owed him loyalty and obedience. Therein lay much of the true radicalism of their republican faith.

*In celebration of American independence, patriots and their slaves in New York City toppled the statue of King George III that stood at Bowling Green.*

## Balancing Liberty and Power

Revolutionary republicanism emphasized not the benefits of governmental power but its dangers. Political power—the ability to influence and control others—was understood to entice people and ultimately to corrupt them. Those possessing power inevitably used it for their own advantage rather than for the general good. Given human nature, this was unavoidable, for power charmed even the best-intentioned.

In the republican world view, liberty was seen as the opposite of power: freedom from the controlling influence of others and the ability to govern one's own life. Republicanism assumed that liberty and power were in perpetual conflict in human affairs, because power was expansive and always threatening to grow at liberty's expense. The Revolutionary generation believed that this tension between power and liberty was the central theme of human history. Their recent experience with England burned the lesson indelibly into their minds. Thus their overriding concern in thinking about politics and government was to find ways of controlling power and maximizing liberty.

The Revolutionary generation acknowledged that excessive liberty could degenerate into political chaos. History and their own experience, however, told them that trouble arose most often not from excessive liberty but from too much governmental power. "It is much easier to restrain the people from running into licentiousness," went the common refrain, "than power from swelling into tyranny and oppression."

Given the dangers of governmental power and the need to limit it, how could political order be maintained? The Revolutionary generation offered an extraordinary answer to that question. Order was not to be imposed from above through such traditional agencies of control as monarchies, centralized governments, or standing armies. In republican systems, political order flowed upward from the responsible, self-regulated behavior of the people, especially from their willingness to put the public good before their own private interests. In a republic, explained one pamphleteer, "each individual gives up all private interest that is not consistent with the general good." The term for this extraordinary self-denial was "public virtue." It formed the core of the Revolution's republican faith.

In placing responsibility for political order with the people and counting on them to act for the good of the whole, Americans made a revolutionary change in the location of authority. Some seventeenth-century visionaries had talked of placing "the power in the people"; but now a nation was being founded on such a principle. The dangers in redefining so radically the location of authority were obvious. If the people proved unworthy, as some believed they would, chaos would ensue. If the attempt was made, warned one alarmed soul, "the bands of society would be dissolved, the harmony of the world confused, and the order of nature subverted." A strong incentive toward Loyalism lurked in such concerns.

Few Patriots were so naive as to believe that the American people were uncompromisingly virtuous. Wartime profiteering, political squabbling, and the occasional reluctance of state militias to fight beyond their own borders rid people of that notion. But during the first years of independence, when Revolutionary enthusiasm ran high, most Americans believed that "public virtue" was sufficiently widespread to support republican government. Religion and education could instruct citizens in virtuous behavior. More than that, the American people would learn virtue by its practice. The Revolutionary struggle would serve as a "furnace of affliction," refining the American character as it tested and strengthened people's capacity for virtuous behavior. It was an extraordinarily hopeful but risk-filled undertaking.

Republicanism posed another problem for the Revolutionary generation. Republics, given their lack of strong, central government, were understood to be vulnerable to internal decay and external attack. The concern over internal decay centered on the problem of "faction," or organized political interests. History taught that internal divisions had destroyed every republic in the past. Faction was the "mortal disease under which popular governments have everywhere perished." In a monarchy, the crown, the army, or the church might control factional

In their effort to recover the story of the American Revolution, historians turn not only to muster rolls and battle strategies but also to such well-known political documents as the Declaration of Independence. As we see in this chapter, republican ideology provided the basic language that members of the Revolutionary generation used in explaining their decision for independence and their thoughts about political principles to guide the new nation's future. No single document has had as much influence on the political rhetoric and ideals of American history as the Declaration of Independence. In the past 200 years, its impact has spread around the world as well, calling other peoples to the ideals of political autonomy, the right of revolution, and the self-evident rights of life, liberty, and the pursuit of happiness. Such a document is worth studying and knowing well.

The declaration's author, Thomas Jefferson, was no ordinary American, nor was the document intended for ordinary purposes. He was a Virginian of considerable wealth and education at a time when most of his countrymen were poor and uneducated. Even though Jefferson was not one of the common people, he was in touch with the aspirations of ordinary Americans. He believed firmly in popular government and had a unique ability to express in a few succinct phrases both broadly shared lofty ideals and the "common sense" of an issue. This helps to explain why the declaration was widely read and quickly became the essential statement of American revolutionary principles. In many ways a masterful piece of propaganda, the declaration was intended to be read in the capitals of Europe as well as in the towns and hamlets of America. In an effort to secure support, the document sought to explain why the American people had taken the unprecedented and dangerous step of separating from England.

The full text of the Declaration of Independence, an amazingly compact and carefully crafted piece of literature, is found in the appendix of this book. You should read and study it in its entirety, asking yourself how it reflects the historical context in which it was written and noting the nature of the language and arguments. How would you describe it? What do you think is the major purpose of the declaration? Who is the primary intended audience? What kinds of arguments—even particular phrases and sentences—indicate that Jefferson had in mind a wide audience and lofty purposes? Who would have been impressed by which arguments and appeals?

The rhetorical structure of the Declaration of Independence is very clear and contributes to the overall impact. After a brief preamble stating the intentions of the document and the source of the ideological principles embodied in it, the declaration has three major sections. In the first, Jefferson states the "self-evident" truths and the political philosophy of revolutionary republicanism that led the American people to "dissolve the political bonds" between them and England. Then he launches into a lengthy recital of the "repeated injuries and usurpations," or "Facts," by which King George III threatened to impose "an absolute Tyranny" over the American colonies. The document concludes with the actual declaration of independence, dissolving the "political connection" with Great Britain and setting up "Free and Independent States." Weaving these three parts together are two transition sections that describe how long-suffering the American people had been and why rebellion was the only just alternative to slavery. Can you detect these different parts?

Now look at some particularly important sections of the declaration, beginning with the political philosophy in the second paragraph. What do you think Jefferson meant by the phrase "all men are created equal"? What did he not mean? In an earlier draft, Jefferson listed "life, liberty, and property" as the three "unalienable rights" of men. Why do you suppose he replaced "property" with "pursuit of happiness" in the final version? What did this phrase mean to him and his contemporaries? What do you think about his argument justifying "the Right of the People to alter or to abolish" their form of government? How do you think Englishmen responded to it? How would our own government respond to that justification now? Who else has used similar arguments in recent years?

Independence National Historical Park Collection, Philadelph

**Edward Savage, Congress Voting Independence, 1785**

# POLITICAL DOCUMENTS

Shifting to the middle section of the declaration, why does Jefferson emphasize the crimes of George III and ignore Parliament? By the summer of 1776, were the colonists' grievances against the king or Parliament? As you read the list of charges against George III, ask yourself what specific instances in the crisis with England Jefferson had in mind and what positive political principle each of the charges represents. How valid do you think the charges were, especially the last three—those about "transporting large Armies

... to compleat the works of death, desolation and tyranny" and about exciting "domestic insurrections" and the attacks of "merciless Indian Savages"? How do you think colonial Americans might have responded to Jefferson's language in those items?

Finally, ask yourself if you would have signed the Declaration of Independence. Why or why not? Would you sign it today? A few years ago, a reporter in Miami approached 50 people and invited them to sign a typed copy of the declaration, and only one person did so.

Independence National Historical Park Collection, Philadelphia

**Facsimile of the Declaration of Independence**

203b

disputes and maintain order. In a republic, however, no such agencies of control existed, and factional conflict, once begun, could easily spin out of control.

The only way to master the demon was to avoid its causes, and that was possible only where societies were small and homogeneous, free of serious economic, social, or religious conflicts. It was impossible to measure exactly how much internal division a republic could tolerate. Some people worried that the larger states, such as New York and Pennsylvania, were already too diverse, but most assumed that the familiar colonial boundaries could safely be used to separate one republican state from another. Few Americans during the early years of independence believed that a single, unified continental republic was possible. The nation would have to be organized differently, as a confederation of individual republican states. The problem of faction and its control would trouble American politics throughout the years of the nation's founding.

Republics were understood to be vulnerable to enemies on the outside as well. Lacking strong central authority, republics throughout history had succumbed to domination by stronger neighbors. The Revolutionary generation was painfully aware of the dangers confronting their republics in the threatening world of the late eighteenth century.

### Debate over Political Equality

Political equality was the other great principle at the heart of the nation's republican faith. No doctrine was more fundamental—or, as things soon proved, more controversial. Republicanism's rejection of monarchy and its emphasis on individual liberty were accompanied by the belief that republican citizens must watch over their governments in order to protect their own rights. That meant that every citizen must have a political voice. Virtually everyone agreed that republican governments had to be grounded in popular consent, that frequent elections were needed, and that public officials should be accountable to the people.

The doctrine of political equality, however, generated sharp debate. Some Americans took

the principle literally, arguing that no one should have more political power than anyone else. This position found its greatest support among groups that prior to the Revolution had been largely outside the political process—farmers and tenants in the interior, workers and artisans in the coastal towns and cities.

Republican equality, however, meant something quite different to other revolutionaries. More cautious Patriots talked about order as well as liberty, arguing that each was essential to the other and that both depended on the leadership of persons wise in the ways of politics and experienced in government. While rejecting European-like aristocracies and their legally es-

*John Trumbull's engraving of a New England town meeting captures the mood of dissension that often prevailed as citizens, unaccustomed to political participation, expressed their individual views on how the new nation should be governed.*

tablished privileges and political power, conservative republicans emphasized the importance of what they called an "aristocracy of talent"—that is, of ability, wisdom, and public virtue. That argument was voiced most frequently by individuals and groups who already enjoyed political power—merchants, planters, larger commercial farmers. They saw no need to alter radically the existing political system.

When confronted by the harsh realities of war, America's initial Revolutionary idealism would wane. During the first years of independence, however, the new republican faith glowed with an almost utopian fervor. "How few of the human race," marveled one Patriot, "have enjoyed an opportunity of making an election of government . . . for themselves or their children." It was an awesome and exhilarating responsibility, for the Revolutionary generation firmly believed that on their shoulders rested the future of human liberty. And so they set about the task of creating what they called their "republican experiments." Only the test of experience would finally determine whether they could succeed where all other republics had failed.

## POLITICIZING THE PEOPLE

The Revolution transformed patterns of political behavior as well as the content of political thought. Under the pressure of Revolutionary events, politics came to absorb people's energies and attention as never before. Elbowing their way into a political system in which they had never been centrally involved, ordinary people shaped the Revolutionary process in vital ways.

### The Politics of Press and Pulpit

The flood of printed material inundating the states stimulated the Revolutionary generation's political consciousness. There were only 37 newspapers, most of them weeklies, at the time of Lexington and Concord. During the war, nearly 70 papers appeared at one time or another. Circulating more widely among the people, they contained news and opinions of the Revolution rather than reports from European capitals, as the pre-Revolutionary papers often had.

Even more pervasive were the swarms of political pamphlets and broadsides issuing from American presses. More than 1,500 of them, dealing with the imperial crisis alone, appeared between 1750 and 1783. Countless others focused on the domestic concerns of state and nation. It was, declared one contemporary in amazement,

> a spectacle . . . without a parallel on earth. . . . Even a large portion of that class of the community which is destined to daily labor have free and constant access to public prints, receive regular information of every occurrence, [and] attend to the course of political affairs. Never . . . were [political pamphlets] . . . so cheap, so universally diffused, so easy of access.

During the Revolutionary era, religion and politics were intimately joined. They had never been sharply separated during the colonial period, but the Revolution intensified their connection. The Great Awakening had strengthened Americans' belief that Christ would soon return to establish his kingdom on earth. America's separation from a corrupt England fanned these millennialist beliefs and seemed further evidence that God intended America as the place of Christ's Second Coming. Even Americans whose religion was less apocalyptic thought of America as a New Israel, a covenanted people specially chosen by God to preserve liberty in a dark and threatening world.

Throughout the war, ministers of every denomination emphasized the religious dimensions of political belief. Loyalist Anglican clergy, such as the Reverend Jonathan Boucher of Maryland, warned parishioners of their divine obligation to support the king as head of the church. During the months preceding independence, as the local committee of safety interrupted worship to harass him, Boucher carried a loaded pistol into the pulpit while he preached obedience and submission to royal authority.

Congregational, Presbyterian, and Baptist clergy, on the other hand, preached just as ardently that God required his people to oppose royal tyranny. In countless recruiting, election, and "fast day" sermons, they called the American people to repentance for the sins that had caused God to visit English tyranny upon them and to rededicate themselves to God's law by fighting for American freedom. It was language that everyone nurtured in Puritan piety and the Great Awakening instinctively understood.

The belief that God sanctioned their revolution strengthened American resolve in the face of English might. It also posed dangers, however, for it encouraged them to equate their national interest with divine intent, and thus provided justification for whatever they believed necessary to do. It was not the last time such confusion would lead Americans to make historic decisions.

### The People Mobilized

The politicization of the American people was most evident in new patterns of political behavior. Except when the war interrupted the political process, as it frequently did during the late 1770s, elections attracted much larger turnouts than before. The situation varied from state to state, but by the 1780s, more than twice as many voters were casting ballots than a decade

earlier. In addition, elections were now more frequently contested and more often turned on issues of Revolutionary policy than on candidates' names or social standing. Archibald Stuart of Virginia observed in 1785 that "competition for seats in the House runs higher than ever it did under the old government." American politics would never be the same.

Even more dramatic evidence of America's expanding Revolutionary politics appears in the array of extralegal committees, conventions, and spontaneous gatherings that erupted continuously across the states during the 1770s and 1780s. Electoral politics simply could not contain the political energies and conflicts generated by the Revolution, and so people devised more direct forms of political action.

Earlier in the imperial crisis, people had frequently gathered "out of doors," that is, outside the regular processes of politics and government, to organize protests against measures like the Stamp Act (see Chapter 5). That practice accelerated as the war continued. People formed committees and held meetings, sometimes with the approval of state authorities and sometimes without, to enforce nonimportation, regulate prices and wages, intimidate Loyalists, levy taxes, administer justice, and, as one individual protested, even to direct "what we shall eat, drink, wear, speak, and think"—all on behalf of the Revolution.

*Ordinary men and women participated in public gatherings, such as this Philadelphia parade of 1780 in which Benedict Arnold, an American general who deserted to the British, was burned in effigy.*

Among the more radical republicans, such activity appeared to be the most direct and purest expression of the popular will. More conservative republicans, however, believed such behavior threatened the very stability of the new republics. Direct action by the people had been necessary in the struggle against England. But why such restlessness now when the threat of tyranny had disappeared and republican governments were in place? Even Thomas Paine was concerned. "It is time to have done with tarring and feathering," he wrote in 1777. "I never did and never would encourage what may properly be called a mob, when any legal mode of redress can be had."

This sudden and dramatic expansion of popular politics resulted naturally from the momentous process of rebellion and war. People took seriously all the talk about liberty, natural rights, and government by consent and applied those principles to their own circumstances. The outcome was a growing demand for access to the political process. In addition, Patriot leaders, recognizing that a successful struggle for independence required broad support among the people, had worked hard to organize committees of safety and correspondence as ways of stimulating popular participation.

The expanded activities of state governments also encouraged political participation. Independence freed those governments from the restraints of English law and administrative control. Not only did they now have responsibility for the full range of governmental duties, but the war also vastly expanded their activities. As the fighting continued, the states had to tax and spend on an unprecedented scale, raise troops by the thousands for the militia and the continental army, control the Tories, regulate prices and wages, establish a stable money supply, and deal with the powerful issues of slavery and the relationship between church and state. It was a large and explosive agenda.

As the tempo and scope of governmental activity increased, so too did the people's determination to have a voice in what government did. Groups of all sorts—farmers, working people, women—many of them formerly on the periphery of political life, pushed their way into the political arena, asserted their right as republican citizens to a voice in public affairs and demanded consideration of their special needs.

*The role of government, and the level of individual citizens' participation in it, changed profoundly and permanently during the Revolution. State capitols, such as Pennsylvania's State House (later called Independence Hall), became centers of intense political activity.*

Never had the reach of governmental action been so wide. Never again would it be so narrow as it had been before.

## The Limits of Citizenship

Revolutionary politics, however, was not open to everyone, for lawmakers imposed limits on who could claim the rights of republican citizenship and thus participate in politics. Those limits almost entirely excluded blacks and Native Americans.

Most Native Americans lived outside the boundaries of white society and politics. That was by their own and white Americans' choice. The Revolution did nothing to change that. By the standards of white society, Native Americans continued to be regarded as "uncivilized" and "savage." Most white observers considered their systems of politics and government primitive and anarchic. After all, they had no written codes of law or legislative assemblies as "civilized" people did. Moreover, Native Americans had almost unanimously chosen to support England in the great struggle (see Chapters 5 and 6).

The Revolutionary generation did retain a certain fascination with Native Americans. Their reputation for bravery and their image as simple, uncorrupted "children of nature" appealed to white Americans' sense of their own innocence and virtue. The Indian woman became the earliest model for Columbia, the figure devised to represent the new united republic. Few people, however, gave serious thought to including Native Americans in political life. The differences of culture and behavior were too great. Moreover, the tribes occupied the interior lands, lying between the Appalachians and the Mississippi, that the American people coveted. Obtaining that land would be easier if they remained outside politics, where they could be dealt with as separate nations.

Even the most sympathetic whites believed that before Native Americans could join white society they would have to undergo a long process of cultural transformation. They would have to become "civilized" and "Christianized" —which is to say that they would have to cease being Indian. Actually, most whites gave little thought to incorporating Native Americans into their own society, even in the distant future.

George Washington bluntly expressed the dominant view. "The gradual extension of our settlements," he explained, "will as certainly cause the savage as the wolf to retire; both being beasts of prey though they differ in shape." Faced with such attitudes, the tribes had ample reason for remaining apart.

Nor did the Revolutionary generation seriously consider incorporating blacks into the political community. Certainly not black slaves, for they lacked the most essential attributes of republican citizenship—personal autonomy and political independence. The colonists had struggled to free themselves from the "slavery" threatened by England. Freedom and liberty, the watchwords of republicanism, had no relevance for people who were physically and legally enslaved.

But what of the growing number of free blacks in the northern states and the Chesapeake area? Unlike most Native Americans, blacks lived within the boundaries of white society and were subject to the actions of state governments. Free black citizenship was an issue of considerable difficulty and importance.

In some states, such as Pennsylvania, New York, and North Carolina, blacks did occasionally vote. This was usually the result, however, of inadvertence and haste in constitution writing rather than conscious intent. The first draft of the Massachusetts constitution excluded blacks and mulattoes as well as Indians from the vote. When it was made public, Reverend William Gordon voiced his protest. "Would it not be ridiculous, inconsistent and unjust to exclude freemen from voting . . . though otherwise qualified, because their skins are black, tawny or reddish? Why not [be] disqualified for being long-nosed, short-faced, or higher or lower than five feet nine? A black, tawny or reddish skin is not so unfavorable a hue to the genuine son of liberty as a tory complexion." In the end, Massachusetts's constitution made no mention of race, and during the 1780s a few blacks did cast votes.

But black participation in the North was scattered and temporary. In the South, it was altogether missing. Nor could blacks count on such basic rights of citizenship as protection of their persons and property before the law. No matter that the bills of rights appended to most state constitutions specified such rights. In spite of the gains that had been made against slavery, blacks remained almost entirely without political voice, except in the petitions against slavery and mistreatment that they frequently pressed upon the state regimes.

## Republican Women

The boundaries of republican politics were not even broad enough to include all white Americans. Only persons with property could vote, because people continued to believe that at least some property was necessary to ensure a person's commitment to the local community and to support the independence of judgment that republican citizenship required. Most states reduced property requirements for the franchise and often did not enforce them consistently. But nowhere were they abolished altogether. Even in Pennsylvania and Vermont, where political reform carried furthest, servants, dependent sons, and persons too poor to pay taxes could not vote.

*Abigail Adams, like many women of the Revolutionary generation, saw the contradiction in men's subordination of women while they extolled the principles of liberty and equality.*

Even more significant, republican citizenship was denied to women. Except on scattered occasions, women had neither voted nor held public office during the colonial period. Nor did they in Revolutionary America, except in New Jersey. The New Jersey constitution of 1776 declared that "all free inhabitants" meeting the property and residency requirements should be allowed to vote. During the 1780s, a number of property-owning women took advantage of the loophole to participate in local elections. In 1790, the New Jersey assembly adopted an election law that explicitly referred to voters as "he or she," thus legitimating what had become common practice.

The experiment, however, did not last long. One political leader thought it a "mockery," even "perfectly disgusting" to watch female voters cast their ballots. "It is evident," he asserted, "that women, generally, are neither by nature, nor habit, nor education . . . fitted to perform this duty with credit to themselves, or advantage to the public." In 1807, the New Jersey assembly concurred, passing a bill specifically disenfranchising women. Its author, John Condict, had several years earlier narrowly escaped defeat when a number of women voted for his opponent. In no other state did women even temporarily secure the vote.

Most women did not press for political equality, for the idea flew in the face of long-standing social convention, and its advocacy exposed a person to public ridicule. But some women did make the case, most often with each other or their husbands. "I cannot say, that I think you are very generous to the ladies," Abigail Adams chided her husband John. "For whilst you are proclaiming peace and good will to men, emancipating all nations, you insist upon retaining an absolute power over all wives." John consulted Abigail on many things but turned this admonition quickly aside. Not until the twentieth century would the female half of the American people secure that most basic attribute of republican citizenship, the vote.

Even though denied a formal political voice, women developed a new relationship to the public realm during the Revolution. Prior to independence, both women and men had accepted the principle that political discussion as well as participation fell outside the feminine sphere. Women, however, felt the urgency of the Revolutionary crisis just as much as men. "How shall I impose a silence upon myself," wondered Anne Emlen in 1777, "when the subject is so very interesting, so much engrossing conversation—& what every member of the community is more or less concerned in?"

Not all women asked, as did she, for "divine prudence, which may prove a stay to my mind & a bridle to my tongue." With increasing frequency, women wrote and spoke to each other about public events, especially as they affected their own lives. Declared Eliza Wilkerson of South Carolina during the British invasion of 1780, "None were greater politicians than the several knots of ladies, who met together. All trifling discourses of fashions, and such low chat was thrown by, and we commenced perfect statesmen."

As the war progressed, increasing numbers of women ventured their opinions publicly. Though risks were involved, some attended public meetings. A few, such as Esther DeBerdt Reed of Philadelphia, published essays explaining women's urgent need to contribute to the Patriot cause. In her 1780 broadside "The Sentiments of an American Woman," she declared that women were determined to do more than offer "barren wishes" for the Revolution's success. Instead, they wanted to be "useful," like "those heroines of antiquity, who have rendered their sex illustrious." Anyone denying women that opportunity, she insisted, was not "a good citizen."

Reed called upon women to renounce "vain ornament" as they had earlier renounced tea and English finery. The money no longer spent on clothing and hair styles would be "the offering of the Ladies" to Washington's army. Within two weeks, a group of middle- and upper-class Philadelphia women outlined an organization whose purpose was nothing less than the mobilization of the nation's entire female population. The project never fully materialized, but in several places women, traveling in pairs, canvassed neighborhoods, requesting offerings from "each woman and girl without any distinction." In Philadelphia, they collected $300,000 in continental currency from over 1,600 individuals. Moreover, they refused Washington's proposal that the money be mixed with general funds in the national treasury, insisting instead on using it themselves to purchase materials for shirts so that each soldier might know he had received a contribution specifically from the women.

Women's activities took on political dimension in other ways as well. Within the context of the Revolution, traditional female roles took on new political meanings. With English imports cut off and the army badly in need of clothing, spinning and weaving assumed increased importance. Often coming together under the banner Daughters of Liberty, women made shirts, stockings, and other items of clothing. Charity

*The outpouring of politically oriented broadsides from American presses between 1750 and 1783 signified a concern with government that had never before existed for the average citizen. This notice, dated 1770, calls for the "tea-drinking ladies of New-York" to cool their demand for the imported brew.*

New-York May 10th 1770.

**The FEMALE PATRIOT, No. I.**

ADDRESSED TO THE

TEA-DRINKING LADIES of NEW-YORK.

WHEN Adam first fell into Satan's Snare,
    And forfeited his Bliss to please the Fair;
God from his Garden drove the sinful Man,
And thus the Source of human Woes began.
'I was weak in Adam, for to please his Wife,
To lose his access to the Tree of Life:
His dear bought Knowledge all his Sons deplore,
Death their Inheritance, and Sin their Store.
But why blame Adam, since his Brainless Race
Will lose their All to obtain a beautious Face;
And will their Honour, Pride, and Wealth lay down,
Rather than see a lovely Woman frown.
The Ladies are not quite so compliant,
If they want Tea, they'll storm and rave and rant,
And call their Lordly Husbands Ass and Clown,
The jest of Fools and Sport of all the Town.
A pleasant Story lately I heard told
Of Mad'am Hornbloom, a noted Scold,
Last Day her Husband said, " My dearest Life,
My Kind, my Fair, my Angel of a Wife;
Just now, from London, there's a Ship come in
Brings noble News will raise us Merchants Fame,
The Fruits of our non-importation Scheme.
The Parliament, dear Saint, may they be blest
Have great part of our Grievances redrest:"
" Have they indeed," replies the frowning Dame,
" Say, is there not some Tea and China come."
" Why, no! We can't import that Indian Weed;
That Duty's still a Rod above our Head."
"Curse on your Heads, you nasty fumbling Crew,
Then round his Shoulders the hard Broom-Stick flew,
Go, dirty Clod-pole! get me some Shufhong,
This Evening I've invited Madam Strong.
— Silence — you Blockhead — hear, the Lady
    knocks!
Get to your Cock-Loft or expect some Strokes."
— " Your Servant Madam, Tea is on the Board
really who't you once had broke your Word."
" I ask your Pardon, dear Miss Hornbloom,
My sprightly Brats kept me so long at Home;
My stupid Husband too has gone astray
To wait upon the Sons of Liberty."

*The symbolic figure of Columbia, typically in the form of an Indian maiden embodying the innocence and freedom of the new republic, was popularized from the time of the Revolution. This French engraving dates from the decade after 1810.*

Clarke, a New York teenager who knitted "stockens" for the soldiers, acknowledged that she "felt Nationaly." Though "heroines may not distinguish themselves at the head of an army," she informed an English cousin, women could still contribute to America's defense. A "fighting army of amazons . . . armed with spinning wheels" would emerge in America. "Though this body is not clad with silken garments," she concluded, "these limbs are armed with strength, the soul is fortified by virtue, and the love of liberty is cherished within this bosom."

Finally, that most traditional of female roles, the care and nurture of children, also took on political overtones during the Revolutionary era. How could the republic be sustained once independence had been won? Only by a rising generation of republican citizens schooled in the principles of public virtue and ready to assume the task. How would they be prepared? During their earliest years by their republican mothers, the women of the Revolution.

In a variety of ways, women developed new connections with the public realm during the Revolutionary years. Those connections remained limited, for the assumption that politics and government belonged to men, not women, did not die easily. But challenges to that assumption would come, and when they did, women found guidance in the principles that the women of the Revolution had helped to define.

## CREATING GOVERNMENTS IN THE STATES

On the night of June 8, 1775, Lord Dunmore, Virginia's royal governor, fled the capital at Williamsburg and took refuge on a British man-of-war anchored in the James River near Norfolk. His departure signaled the final collapse of British authority in that colony. During the months leading up to independence, similar scenes occurred up and down the coast as royal authority dissolved in each colony. As the colonial assemblies had become bolder in their challenges to English authority, the governors had sent their members home and refused to reconvene them. Well before independence, the regular processes of government had come to a halt.

The assemblymen, however, not content to disband, had continued to meet extralegally, as provincial congresses, to deal with the deepening imperial crisis. They made no claim to governmental status but regarded themselves as temporary bodies whose activities would end once England repealed the hated legislation and things returned to normal.

The outbreak of war in April 1775 dramatically changed their situation. Now the provincial congresses had to mobilize the militia, gather money and supplies, and look after the public safety. Thus, they began to act not as temporary bodies but as sovereign governments.

As independence loomed, the American people had to begin thinking about replacing these congresses with more permanent governments. They knew it would be a perilous task. One person thought it the "most difficult and dangerous business" they had to do, because it would require redefining the rights and duties of citizens, the powers of government, and the balance between individual liberty and public order. Nothing in the entire Revolutionary agenda was more important or more controversial than creating new republican governments in the states.

## Writing Constitutions

In November 1775, the Continental Congress had urged the states to establish new governments "such . . . as in their judgment will best produce the happiness of the people, and most effectually secure peace and good order." When independence finally came, they set about the business of government making in earnest. Connecticut and Rhode Island continued under their colonial charters, simply deleting all references to the British crown. The other 11 states, however, set their charters aside and started anew. Within two years, all but Massachusetts had completed the task. By 1780, it had done so as well.

The work was not easy, for the American people had no experience with government making on such a scale. Each colony had existed under a charter granted many years before. Not only were Americans inexperienced, but they had to rebuild their governments while embroiled in war. Moreover, they were sharply divided over the kind of government they wished to create. In the debates over the new state constitutions, the political divisions that had been simmering during the prewar decades burst through the surface of political life.

Given the promptings of republican theory and their own recent experience with England, the Revolutionary generation began with two overriding concerns: to limit the powers of government and to hold governmental officials accountable. The only certain way of accomplishing these goals was by creating a fundamental law, in the form of a written constitution, that could serve as a standard for regulating governmental behavior.

Americans were familiar with the idea of a constitution. They had based much of their defense against the king and Parliament on their rights under English constitutional law. England's constitution, however, had provided inadequate protection for their liberties. It was vague and inexact, consisting of common law, judicial rulings, Parliamentary statutes, and historical documents such as the Magna Charta and the Revolutionary Settlement of 1688. American constitutions would be much clearer and more specific and would be written down for everyone to understand.

In most states, the provincial congresses wrote the first constitutions, along with everything else they had to do. This seemed easiest, for the congresses were in place, had been elected by the people, and were regarded as representing the popular will. As the process went along, however, people became increasingly uneasy. Constitutions were intended to define and control government, but if government-like bodies wrote the documents, they could change them as well. If they could do that, what guarantee would the constitutions be against the abuse of governmental power? Some way had to be found of grounding them directly in the people's sovereign will.

Massachusetts was the first state to perfect the new procedures. In 1778, its citizens rejected a proposed constitution, in part because the provincial congress had drawn it up. A year later the congress asked the voters to elect a special constitutional convention for the sole purpose of preparing a new and more satisfactory document. Elections were held, the convention did its work, and the resulting constitution was returned to the people for ratification, this time successfully.

Through trial and argumentation, the Revolutionary generation worked out a practical understanding of what a constitution was and how it should be developed. In the process it established some of the most basic doctrines of American constitutionalism: that sovereignty resides in the people; that written constitutions, produced by specially elected conventions and then ratified by the people, embody their sovereign will; and that government comes into being only after a constitution has been created and functions strictly according to its terms. No doctrines have been more important to the preservation of American liberty.

## Redistributing Power

The new state constitutions redefined American government in fundamental and lasting ways. For one thing, the new governments were considerably more democratic than the colonial regimes had been. Gone were the crown's appointed officials: governors, councillors, and customs officers. Most officials were now elected, many of them annually rather than every two or three years as before.

Just as important, most of the new constitutions sharply reduced the governors' powers and increased the powers of the assemblies. "The executive power," warned one commentator, "is ever restless, ambitious, and grasping at increases." He had in mind both the king and the royally appointed colonial governors. Most of the states did not strip the new governors entirely of their authority, but all except Massachusetts restricted such traditional executive powers as setting the time and meeting place of the assemblies, declaring war, coining money, creating courts, and pardoning crimes. Above all, the documents sharply reduced the governors' powers of appointment. "He who has the giving of . . . places in the government," went the common refrain, "will always be master."

The assemblies absorbed most of the powers stripped from the governors. Not only were the assemblies more powerful, they were larger and more representative as well. Reflecting the spirit of republican reform, the assemblies grew in size by half or more. Their growth resulted as well from the demands of groups such as farmers and artisans for a voice in public affairs.

Changes in attitudes toward representation further reduced the distance between government and citizens. Prior to the Revolution, most voters believed that assemblymen, once elected, should have considerable independence in carrying out their duties. This reflected the prevailing notion that public office was primarily the domain of the "better sort"—persons of wealth and experience who knew best what to do.

The Revolution, however, transformed the relationship between rulers and ruled. Inspired by republican beliefs and concerned increasingly about governmental power, people adopted a more watchful stance toward their representatives. Increasingly, people came to view their representatives not as independent agents acting on their behalf but as direct extensions of the people's will. Vigilance, even outright suspicion of officials' behavior, became the hallmark of the true republican.

## Different Paths to the Republican Goal

The reform of state government, however, did not come easily or without controversy, for people vigorously disagreed about how democratic the new governments should be. Republican theory gave only the most general guidance. "What is called a republic," explained one individual, "is not any particular form of government."

Conservatives such as James Duane of New York, who had opposed England primarily because its actions threatened their control of local affairs, urged that the new governments resemble the colonial regimes as much as possible, allowing only for the most necessary republican changes. More radical republicans, how-

## Occupational Composition of Several State Assemblies in the 1780s (percentage)

|  | MASS. | N.Y. | PA. | S.C. | VA. |
|---|---|---|---|---|---|
| Farmer | 47.0 | 37.1 | 36.7 | 13.8 | 19.9 |
| Planter or large landowner | 1.0 | 8.2 | 2.3 | 32.4 | 36.3 |
| Artisan, manufacturer, miscellaneous nonfarmer | 12.0 | 9.9 | 21.7 | 3.2 | 3.0 |
| Doctor, laywer, other professional | 13.0 | 18.1 | 15.0 | 14.9 | 21.4 |
| Entrepreneur, innkeeper, shopkeeper | — | — | 13.5 | 1.6 | 3.0 |
| Merchant or trader | 20.0 | 19.4 | 6.6 | 11.7 | 6.5 |
| Unknown | 7.0 | 7.3 | 4.2 | 22.3 | 10.0 |

*Source:* Main, *Political Parties Before the Constitution*, 1973.

ever, sought to redistribute political power and build the principle of political equality into the very structure of the new regimes.

The outcomes differed from state to state, depending on the local balance of political power and the extent of the war's disruption. Two examples, Pennsylvania and Massachusetts, illustrate how different those outcomes could be.

In Pennsylvania, a coalition of western farmers and Philadelphia artisans and shopkeepers, allied with a group of radical leaders such as Thomas Paine, Timothy Matlack, and Thomas Young, pushed through the most democratic state constitution of all. Drafted less than three months after independence, during the most intense period of republican reform, it rejected the familiar English model of a mixed and balanced government of two legislative houses and an independent executive. Such complexity, radicals argued, had always protected the power of monarchs and aristocrats and robbed the people of their liberties. Republican governments, by contrast, should be simple, easily understood, and directly responsive to the people.

The architects of Pennsylvania's constitution provided for a single, all-powerful legislative house, its members elected annually, its debates open to the public. There was to be no governor and thus no executive veto of legislation. Legislative committees would assume executive duties. A truly radical assumption underlay this design: that only the "common interest of society" and not "separate and jarring private interests" should be represented in public affairs. There was thus no need for a separate governor or upper legislative house to represent different interests or balance against the popular will.

Property-holding requirements for public office were abolished, and the franchise was opened to every white male over 21 who paid taxes. In addition, citizens were to elect a council of censors to review the government's performance every seven years and determine if it had violated the constitution. The bill of rights introducing the document guaranteed every citizen religious freedom, trial by jury, and freedom of speech.

The most radical proposal of all called for the redistribution of property within the state.

Even the most conservative republicans agreed that republican liberty depended on the widespread ownership of land. But the radicals were calling for the actual redistribution of property. "An enormous proportion of property vested in a few individuals," declared the proposed constitution, "is dangerous to the rights, and destructive of the common happiness of mankind; and therefore every free state hath a right by its laws to discourage the possession of such property." No clause created more alarm. By marshaling all their strength, Pennsylvania's conservatives just managed to defeat it.

Debate over the constitution divided the state deeply. Opponents, led by men of wealth, condemned the document's supporters as "coffee-house demagogues" and "political upstarts," accusing them of wanting a "tyranny of the people." The constitution's proponents—tradesmen, farmers, and other small producers—shot back that their critics were "the rich and great men and the wise men, the lawyers and doctors," who thought they had no "common interest with the body of the people."

In 1776, the radicals had their way, for the Pennsylvania constitution—together with its counterparts in Vermont and Georgia—represented the most radical thrust of Revolutionary republicanism. Its guiding principle, declared Thomas Young, one of the constitution's most ardent supporters, was that "the people at large [are] the true proprietors of governmental power." The struggle for control of the Revolution in Pennsylvania was not over, for in 1790 a considerably more moderate document would replace this one. For the moment, however, the lines of political authority had been decisively redrawn in Pennsylvania.

In Massachusetts, constitution making followed a different path. There the disruptions of the war were less severe and the continuity of political leadership and control much greater. Though the Revolution brought western farmers and Boston artisans into state politics, it did not dramatically alter the balance of political power. As a consequence, the new Massachusetts constitution embodied a much more cautious vision of what republican government should be.

No one had a more important role in shaping that constitution than John Adams. He readily admitted that the new government must be firmly grounded in the people. "All power," he wrote, "residing originally in the people and being derived from them, the several magistrates and officers of government . . . are their subordinates and agents, and are at all times accountable to them." Yet Adams urged moderation in forming the new government. There was danger, he believed, in reckless experimentation. A balance between two legislative houses and an independent executive was essential to preserve liberty, for "power must be opposed to power, force to force . . . interest to interest . . . and passion to passion."

Adams had something else in mind in arguing for a balanced government. Society, he believed, was inescapably divided between "democratic" and "aristocratic" forces. Believing that each was dangerous if it became dominant, Adams sought to isolate them in separate legislative houses where they could watch and balance each other. The assembly, he explained, should be "an exact portrait, in miniature" of the people; it should "think, feel, act, and reason" like them. The senate, on the other hand, should constitute a "natural aristocracy" of

*Massachusetts was the first state to elect a special convention to draw up a new constitution. That convention met in the State House in Boston in 1779 and 1780.*

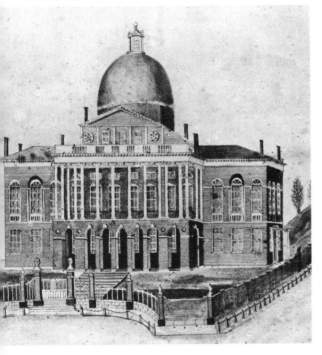

wealth, talent, and good sense. Following Adams's advice, the Massachusetts convention provided for a popular, annually elected assembly and a senate based on wealth, its members apportioned according to the amount of taxes paid in special senatorial districts. Since the senators' function was to balance the popular excesses of the assembly and look after the interests of property and social position, they were required to own three times as much property as assemblymen were.

The Massachusetts constitution also provided for a powerful, independent governor. The chief executive could veto legislation, make appointments, serve as commander in chief of the militia, and oversee state expenditures. "The dignity of the Commonwealth," Adams noted, was embodied in the character of its chief magistrate. The requirement that gubernatorial candidates be worth at least £1,000 ($100,000 in today's money) indicated how dignified the governor was to be.

On March 2, 1779, the convention sent the document to the town meetings for approval, and for the next three months the citizenry debated it vigorously. Many among the farmers of the interior and the artisans and working people of Boston thought the document too "aristocratic," too much like the old colonial regime. The citizens of Richmond criticized the property requirement for the franchise because it would "exclude many good members of society." Only "misbehavior" or "vicious conduct," they thought, should deprive a person of the "free liberty to vote." Given the impact of the war on ordinary people's lives and the increasing number of the poor, warned the citizens of Dorchester, disfranchisement under the proposed constitution "may increase in such proportion, that one half the people of this commonwealth will have no choice in any branch of the general court."

The inhabitants of Petersham feared that with a strong governor the people would be "droved into parties by the influence of the rich and powerful men who will act in competition with each other and spread the corruption that naturally flows from bribery and undue influence." A "republican monarch," they protested, should have no place in the new system. Controversy erupted as well over the senate's special character as the defender of property and social standing.

No complete tally of the towns' responses was ever taken. But when the convention reconvened in July 1779, it declared the constitution approved. In spite of the many objections, it was enough for the moment simply to have a new, republican government in place.

## REVOLUTIONARY POLITICS IN THE STATES

During the Revolutionary era, the assemblies—expanded in power, increased in size, and more responsive to the people's will—became potent and controversial instruments of popular government. How potent and how controversial become apparent as we examine the politics that swirled around them.

Revolutionary politics seemed chaotic to those caught up in it. Partly that was because so many more people and conflicting interests were now involved. Partly it was because the expanded assemblies were filled with new and inexperienced legislators. It was due as well to the fact that the old assembly leadership in many states disappeared as eager and committed new leaders thrust aside Loyalists and more cautious Patriots. No wonder political alignments were unclear and the sources of political control uncertain.

The confusion was compounded because political parties capable of organizing and disciplining the political process did not exist. Nor were they considered desirable. The concept of "party" was equated in people's minds with "faction," that perpetual enemy of republican virtue. Benjamin Franklin warned in 1779 against "the infinite mutual abuse of parties, tearing to pieces the best of characters." Not until the early nineteenth century would political parties as we know them achieve either ideological legitimacy or organizational form.

Political alignments varied from state to state, depending on local circumstances. But beneath the apparent confusion were two recurring patterns, both reflecting fundamental divisions within Revolutionary society. Neither was new to American politics, but the experience of revolution clarified and intensified them both.

The first pattern set persons of wealth and influence against those with little or none. The second was regional in character, arraying people living in commercially oriented communities along the coast against people in the more isolated, noncommercial communities of the interior. These two alignments often pulled in conflicting directions. But they had a common element, for they both pitted groups formerly excluded from the political process but now demanding access to it—small farmers and tenants, urban artisans and laborers, religious and ethnic minorities—against groups, such as merchants and planters and large commercial farmers, who had traditionally controlled political life. In practical terms, the struggle was over political power and the protection of specific interests. In terms of principle, it was over the meaning of political equality.

Time and again these divisions broke through the surface of Revolutionary politics as people struggled to cope with the consequences of independence and war. Nothing revealed them more clearly than the issues of Loyalism, the separation of church and state, and management of the wartime economy.

### Loyalists and the Public Safety

Emotions ran high between Patriots and Loyalists in Revolutionary America. "The rage of civil discord," lamented one individual, "hath advanced among us with an astonishing rapidity. The son is armed against the father, the brother against the brother, family against family." The security, perhaps the very survival of the republic required stern measures against the counterrevolutionaries in the Revolution's midst. Security, however, was not the only motive at work, for the Patriots were also determined to exact revenge on those whose "disloyalty" threatened the Revolutionary cause.

During the war, each of the states passed a series of laws to control the Loyalist menace. In 1778, the Georgia assembly declared 117 persons guilty of treason, banished them from the state upon pain of death, and declared their possessions subject to seizure and sale. Four years later, the assembly extended the act to anyone "deemed responsible" for committing "murder, rapine, and devastation" during the recent British occupation.

In 1776, the Connecticut assembly passed a remarkably punitive law threatening anyone who criticized either the assembly or the Continental Congress with immediate fine and imprisonment. In every state, individuals whose Revolutionary fervor was suspect were publicly forced to forswear loyalty to the crown and pledge allegiance to the new regime. Those who refused lost the vote, the opportunity to hold office, and the protection of the law. Probably not more than a few dozen Tories died at the hands of the Revolutionary regimes, but hundreds found their livelihoods destroyed, their families ostracized, and themselves subject to physical attack.

Punishing Loyalists—or persons accused of loyalism—was a popular activity, especially since Loyalists were most numerous among the upper classes. Yet for many of the more conservative Patriots, troublesome questions surfaced. How safe would anyone's property be if some

*This nineteenth-century print gives "A Correct View of the Old Methodist Church in John Street, New York. The first erected in America. Founded A.D. 1768." Methodists and Baptists were among the "dissenting" religious groups tolerated, though not encouraged, in the eighteenth century.*

people's property was confiscated and sold? Did not American liberty rest on the principle that property rights were fundamental to all others? And were not everyone's rights threatened when the rights of some were disregarded, especially when it was often difficult to tell who actually was a Loyalist and who was not?

The continuing eruption of mob activity was equally disturbing. Some Patriots tried to distinguish between "public mobs," which punished enemies of the people, and "private mobs," which took advantage of the Revolutionary crisis to settle personal scores. The distinction, however, was not easily sustained. Caught up in the Revolution's turmoil, many argued that the Loyalists had put themselves outside the protection of American law and thus deserved whatever treatment they got. But others worried about the implications of setting aside the protections of the law, even for Loyalists. Republics, after all, were supposed to be "governments of law, and not of men." Once that distinction disappeared, no one would be safe.

After the war ended and passions cooled, most states repealed their anti-Tory legislation. In the midst of the Revolution, however, no issue raised more troublesome questions or more clearly divided the Patriots from each other.

## Church and State

The relationship between church and state generated controversy as well, for it touched on the sensitive issue of religious freedom. In most of the colonies prior to the Revolution, one religious group had enjoyed the special benefits of endorsement by the government and public tax support for its clergy. At the time of independence, these religious establishments were no longer as restrictive as they once had been. The upheavals of the Great Awakening had divided the churches and undermined notions of religious uniformity (see Chapter 4). In each of the colonies, moreover, "dissenting" groups such as the Methodists and the Baptists were increasing in number, especially among the lower classes of city and countryside. While authorities did not encourage them, they did allow them to function. Toleration, however, as the dissenters pointed out, was not religious freedom, for that required the complete separation of church and state and the guarantee that conscience, not compulsion, would govern religious life.

With independence, pressure built for severing church and state completely. Republican theory warned that such alliances had been instruments of oppression throughout history and argued that voluntary choice was the only safe basis for religious association. Even before independence, Rhode Island, New Jersey, Pennsylvania, and Delaware had established full religious liberty. In five additional states, the Anglican church collapsed when English support was withdrawn. In the other four, however, dissenters clashed with the defenders of religious privilege.

In Massachusetts, Connecticut, and New Hampshire, the Congregationalists fought to retain their special privileges. Most major political leaders were Congregationalists who ardently supported the church. To separate church and state, they argued, was to invite infidelity and disorder. Isaac Backus, the most outspoken of New England Baptists, disagreed. He and his supporters unrelentingly criticized the Congregational order. "Many, who are filling the nation with the cry of *liberty* and against oppressors," he cried, "are at the same time themselves violating that dearest of all rights, *liberty of conscience.*"

Massachusetts's new constitution guaranteed everyone the right to worship God "in the manner and season most agreeable to the dictates of his own conscience." But as Backus pointed out, it also empowered the legislature to require the towns to lay taxes for "the public worship of *God*, and for the support and maintenance of public protestant teachers of piety, religion, and morality. . . ." The legislature, moreover, was authorized to compel church attendance.

The dangers in these arrangements were readily apparent. The town meeting of Middleborough worried that individuals would be pressured to violate their consciences, while the citizens of Granville denied that the people "have a right to invest their legislature with a power to interfere in matters that properly belong to the Christian Church." During the decades following independence, New England's

Congregational establishment continued to weaken. But not until the early nineteenth century—in Massachusetts not until 1833—were the laws linking church and state finally repealed.

In Virginia, the Baptists pressed their cause against the Protestant Episcopal church, successor to the Church of England. The Episcopalians, fighting to retain their special privileges, proposed in 1784 a "general tax assessment" to be distributed among all Christian churches. Even that cautious proposal failed. In 1786, the adoption of Thomas Jefferson's Bill for Establishing Religious Freedom, which rejected all connections between church and state and removed all religious tests for public office, finally settled the issue. Three years later, that statute served as a model for the First Amendment to the new federal Constitution.

Even most supporters of religious freedom, however, were not prepared to extend it universally. It was typically limited to "Christians" or "Protestants" or, in one case, even to "trinitarians." The people of Northbridge, Massachusetts, while opposing the Congregational establishment, wanted to prevent "Roman Catholics pagons or Mahomitents from having any seat in government, from which the People of God have so much suffred in past ages." Legal disestablishment did not end religious discrimination. But it did implant the principle of religious liberty firmly in American constitutional law.

## The Politics of Economic Policy

Revolutionary politics also had to deal with the economic disruptions of independence and war. Price and wage inflation, collapse of the currency, skyrocketing taxation, mushrooming private and public debt—all touched many lives and demanded attention. Americans discovered that these issues offered no easy solutions, for their complexity often defied understanding, lay beyond the reach of state action, or exceeded the capacity of politics for compromise and solution. Thus they continued on the public agenda through the 1770s and 1780s, heightening class and regional tensions.

As the war progressed, state governments increased their spending dramatically. They covered much of the cost by printing paper money and issuing massive amounts of public securities. As a result, public debt soared. Managing this debt during the war and struggling to reduce it afterward became the central dilemma of Revolutionary politics.

Some argued that the public debt should be honored at only a fraction of its face value because of inflation and because speculators had purchased large amounts of public securities at a discount from their original owners, hoping to redeem them at full value. Partial redemption seemed only fair to state militiamen and continental soldiers, urban workers and rural farmers who had often had to sell their securities at pennies on the dollar simply to support their families. Full repayment would only raise their taxes.

Most of the arguments for honoring the full public debt came from the states' major creditors, merchants and other persons of wealth who had loaned money to the states and had bought up large amounts of securities at deep discounts. These people spoke earnestly of upholding the public honor and giving fair return to those who had committed their own resources at critical moments to the Revolutionary cause.

The issue of taxation generated even hotter debate. The conflict with England had been triggered by opposition to taxes. No governmental power more alarmed the Revolutionary generation, for none offered greater opportunity for abuse. As the costs of the war mounted, so did the tax burden. From 1774 to 1778, Massachusetts officials levied a total of £408,976 in taxes, a dramatic increase over colonial days. Between 1783 and 1786, as the state struggled to reduce its accumulated debt, assessments jumped again, to £662,476. Taxes, complained one anguished soul, now equaled nearly one-third of the inhabitants' incomes. Massachusetts was not unique.

As taxes rose, so did clashes over tax policy. Farmers, artisans, and other people of modest means argued that taxes should be payable in depreciated paper money or government securities rather than only in specie, as some state laws required. Most of them had no gold or silver coin and thus faced the prospect of having their property foreclosed when they could not meet their tax obligations. Government officials, on

the other hand, protested that to allow payment in depreciated paper was to deprive the governments of badly needed revenue.

People also argued over how the staggering tax burden should be apportioned. In the New York assembly, men of property urged continuing dependence on the poll tax, a uniform assessment levied on all males 16 years of age and older. Working people, however, protested the inequity of a tax that fell on everyone equally. They argued that taxes should bear some relationship to people's ability to pay and thus should be based on differences in property. As the demand for public revenue increased, pressure for taxing property rather than people grew. The change, however, was bitterly contested.

Merchants and shopkeepers argued that agricultural property—land, crops, livestock—should bear the primary burden of taxation. Farmers replied that commercial goods such as ships, store inventories, and money on loan should carry the load. The disagreements did not stop there. Large landowners insisted that agricultural land be assessed at a uniform rate, regardless of location, value, or productivity, and that unimproved land, which they held as an investment, should not be taxed at all. Smaller farmers, on the other hand, whose lands were often of poorer quality and who had to cultivate most of them in order to make ends meet, protested the inequities of such a policy. With taxes reaching ever more deeply into people's pockets, the stakes were obviously high for everyone.

Controversy swirled around the states' efforts to control soaring prices as well. Each of the states experimented with price controls at one time or another. Seldom were such efforts effective; always they generated political storms.

In general, the poor and those not yet integrated into the market economy supported price controls. Faced with escalating prices, they had difficulty simply making ends meet. Such people, moreover, continued to believe that buying and selling had moral and social dimensions, for they involved intensely personal, face-to-face agreements among neighbors. These notions of a "moral economy" were guided by the doctrine of a "just price," a price not determined by the goal of maximizing profit but one deemed fair to buyer and seller alike. Government had a responsibility to regulate prices in this way for the public good. In keeping with these principles, a crowd in New Windsor, New York, in 1777 seized a shipment of tea bound for Albany and sold it for what they deemed a fair offering.

Merchants, shopkeepers, and others caught up in the commercial economy, however, looked at things differently. For them, the exchange of goods and services was primarily an economic transaction and should be controlled only by the laws of supply and demand. "It is contrary to the nature of commerce," declared Benjamin Franklin, "for government to interfere in the prices of commodities." Attempts to regulate prices only created a disincentive to labor, which was "the principal part of the wealth of every country."

The argument over price controls revealed not just the competing interests of buyers and sellers but fundamentally different understandings of how economic relations should be conducted. That argument would continue to echo through American politics during the years ahead.

## TOWARD THE CONSTITUTIONAL CONVENTION

As long as the war lasted, the pressures of popular politics continued, and the state governments remained broadly responsive to the people's needs. With victory over England secured, however, the tide of popular politics began to wane as people turned their attention toward ordering their own disrupted lives. At the same time, Congress's ability to manage the nation's affairs, always shaky at best, eroded further. A series of difficult problems that beset the weak national government in the mid-1780s strengthened the hands of more conservative leaders who were calling for an end to republican experimentation and replacement of the Articles of Confederation by a stronger central government.

### Demobilizing the Army

Demobilization of the army presented the Confederation government with some of its most difficult moments. When the fighting stopped, many of the troops refused to disband and go home until Congress redressed their grievances. Trouble first arose in early 1783 among the officers at the continental army camp in Newburgh, New York. In January, they sent a delegation to Congress to complain about arrears in pay, unsettled food and clothing allowances, and failure to make provision for the lifetime pensions that Congress had promised them during the dark days of 1780. Congress responded by calling for the army to be decommissioned. Almost immediately, an anonymous address circulated among the officers, attacking the "coldness and severity" of the Congress, calling on the officers to assemble and draw up a "last remonstrance," and hinting darkly at more direct action if their grievances were not met.

Several members of the Congress encouraged the officers' mutterings, hoping the crisis would add urgency to their own calls for a strengthened central government. Most, however, were alarmed by this challenge to the Congress's authority. Washington was disturbed as well, and he moved quickly to calm the situation. Promising that Congress would treat the officers justly, he counseled patience and urged his comrades not to tarnish the victory they had so recently won. His efforts succeeded, for the officers soon reaffirmed their confidence in the Congress and agreed to disband.

The officers were not the only ones to take action. In June, several hundred disgruntled continental soldiers and Pennsylvania militiamen demonstrated in front of Independence Hall, where both Congress and Pennsylvania's executive council were meeting. When the state authorities would not guarantee the Congress's safety, it fled in confusion to Princeton, New Jersey. Once there, it eased the tension by issuing the soldiers three months' pay and furloughing them until they could be fully discharged. By early November, the crisis was over.

During the mid-1780s, the Congress shuffled between Princeton and Annapolis, Trenton and New York, its transiency visible evidence of its steadily eroding authority. A hot-air balloon, scoffed the *Boston Evening Herald*, would "exactly accommodate the itinerant genius of Congress," since it could then "float along from one end of the continent to the other . . . and when occasion requires . . . suddenly pop down into any of the states they please." Congress had been criticized before, but never so mockingly.

## Opening the West

Congress was not without important accomplishments during the 1780s, however. Most notable were the two great land ordinances of 1785 and 1787. The first provided for the systematic survey and sale of the region west of New York and Pennsylvania and north of the Ohio River. The area was to be laid out in townships 6 miles square, which were in turn to be subdivided into lots of 640 acres each. Thus began the rectangular grid pattern of land survey and settlement that to this day characterizes the nation's Midwest and distinguishes it so markedly from the irregular settlement patterns of the older colonial areas along the coast.

Two years later, Congress passed the Northwest Ordinance. It provided for the political organization of the same interior region, first as territories with elected assemblies and congressionally appointed governors and ultimately as new states to be incorporated into the Union "on an equal footing with the original states in all respects whatsoever." Together these two pieces of legislation provided the legal mechanism for the nation's dramatic territorial expansion during the nineteenth century.

Congress was able to pass these bills because they served so many people's interests. They opened land to settlers and profits to speculators, while the income from land sales promised to help reduce the national debt. The Northwest Ordinance, moreover, while permitting slave owners already living north of the Ohio River to retain their slaves, prohibited the importation of new slaves into the region. This made the area much more attractive to white farmers from the Northeast who worried about their ability to compete with slave labor and were disinclined to live among blacks. Southern delegates in the Congress accepted the restriction because their constituents could look forward to slavery's expansion south of the Ohio. During the 1780s, the country's interior seemed sufficiently large for everyone's needs.

## Old Northwest Survey Patterns

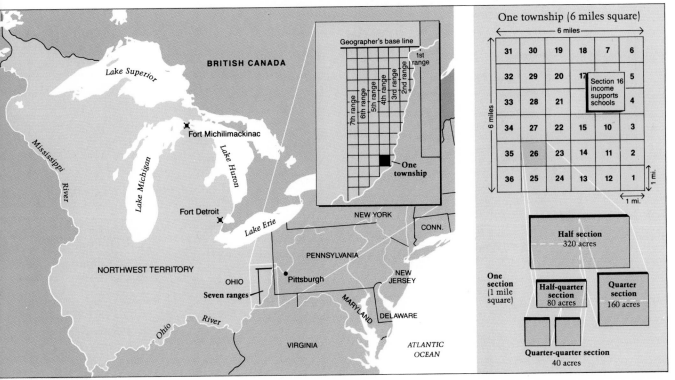

Despite Congress's success in providing for the settlement of the trans-Appalachian frontier, however, many Americans doubted that it could successfully promote the nation's territorial growth. It had neither secured removal of the British troops from the western posts after 1783 nor guaranteed free navigation of the Mississippi. Nor could it clear the tribes of the Ohio region out of the white settlers' way.

During the immediate postwar years, Congress operated as if the Native Americans of the interior were "conquered" peoples. As allies of England, they had lost the war and thus came under the American government's control. The Treaty of Paris, American officials insisted, gave the United States political sovereignty over the tribal territory south of the Great Lakes and east of the Mississippi, as well as actual ownership of the land.

For a few years, that strategy seemed to work. During the mid-1780s, Congress negotiated several important land treaties with the interior tribes. At Fort Stanwix, in October 1784, the Iroquois Nation ceded to the United States all its lands west of the Niagara River. In January 1785, representatives of the Wyandotte, Chippewa, Delaware, and Ottawa tribes relinquished claim to most of present-day Ohio.

## Areas of Settlement and Frontier in 1787

But the treaties did not hold, for they were exacted under the threat of force and accepted by only a few tribal leaders. At Fort Stanwix, negotiations were held at gunpoint, and hostages were taken in order to coerce the delegates. Native Americans regarded the attitude of the Congress's commissioners as insulting and arbitrary. Some of the disgusted delegates, including the Mohawk chief Joseph Brant, left before the agreement was signed. As Brant remarked before his departure, "We are sent in order to make peace and . . . are not authorized to stipulate any particular cession of land." Two years later, the Iroquois openly repudiated the treaty, asserting that they were still sovereigns of their own soil and "equally free as . . . any nation under the sun."

By the mid-1780s, most tribal groups both above and below the Ohio River were resisting white expansion onto their land. In the summer of 1786, the Creek resumed hostilities in the backcountry of Georgia, while north of the Ohio, the Shawnee, Delaware, Wyandotte, and Miami moved to strengthen their Western Confederacy and prepare for the defense of their common homeland. That fall, the confederacy rejected the whites' conquest theory, declared the Treaty of Fort Stanwix invalid, asserted that the Ohio River was the proper boundary between them and the United States, and insisted on a new treaty between the combined tribes of the confederacy and the United States. When white settlers continued to press into the region, Native Americans launched a series of devastating raids, virtually halting white settlement. By

1786, the entire region from the Great Lakes to the Gulf of Mexico was embroiled in warfare. With the continental army disbanded and the nation in no position to raise a new one, Congress could do little about it.

Congress's inability to open up the interior alarmed many Americans—speculators threatened with the loss of their investments, farmers wanting to leave the crowded lands of the east, Revolutionary soldiers eager to start afresh on the rich soil of Kentucky and Ohio, and leaders such as Thomas Jefferson who believed that republican liberty depended on an expanding nation of yeoman farmers. With the Confederation Congress unable to act effectively, each of these groups found value in proposals for a stronger national government.

Settling the interior, the indispensable land reserve for the fast-growing nation, also involved relations with other nations. Here, too, Congress proved weak and ineffective.

In June 1784, Spain—still in possession of Florida, the Gulf Coast, and the trans-Mississippi West—closed the outlet of the Mississippi River at New Orleans to American shipping. Spain's action raised a storm of protest, especially among settlers in the West who counted on the interior river system to float their produce to outside markets. Land speculators from Virginia to South Carolina were aroused as well, for closure of the Mississippi would discourage development of the southern backcountry. Rumors spread that Spanish agents were urging backcountry American settlers to seek affiliation with Spain. Washington commented uneasily that the settlers there were "on a pivot. The touch of a feather," he feared, "would turn them away."

For more than a year, Foreign Secretary John Jay negotiated with the Spanish ambassador to the United States, Don Diego de Gardoqui, in an effort to reopen that vital commercial outlet. When Gardoqui held firm, Jay switched tactics and offered to relinquish American claims to free transit of the Mississippi in return for a new commercial treaty opening Spanish ports to American shipping. The northern states, excited at the prospect of Spanish trade, supported the bargain, but the southern states, angry at Jay's betrayal of their interests, refused. Thus stalemated, Congress could take no action at all.

## "Utmost Good Faith" Clause from the Northwest Ordinance

The following articles shall be considered as articles of compact between the original States and the people and States in the said territory and forever remain unalterable, unless by common consent, to wit:

> The utmost good faith shall always be observed towards the Indians; their land and property shall never be taken from them without their consent; and, in their property, rights, and liberty, they shall never be invaded or disturbed, unless in just and lawful wars authorized by Congress; but laws founded in justice and humanity, shall from time to time be made for preventing wrongs being done to them, and for preserving peace and friendship with them.

## Postwar Commercial and Financial Problems

Congress also proved less and less able to lead the economic recovery that all Americans expected after the war. That was in large part because of its weak diplomatic position. Independence dramatically transformed America's relationships with the outside world. It shattered longstanding American assumptions about friends and enemies, allies and antagonists. England, once the nurturing mother country, had become a tyrannical parent bent on enslaving its own children. Just as bewildering, France, the traditional enemy, was now the ally. Yet France was at best a strange and uncomfortable friend. With an empire of its own, France was no more sympathetic to colonial rebellions than England. Moreover, the French king and aristocracy regarded republicanism as subversive. French aid had been essential to achieving American independence, but France's efforts to manipulate the peace process for its own interests had provided a hard lesson in the realities of power diplomacy.

Independence, moreover, did not change European imperial ambitions in North America. France had lost its North American possessions following the Seven Years' War, but before the century was over, it would gain title to most of the continent beyond the Mississippi River. England's Union Jack continued to fly over eastern Canada just north of the American border. English troops, moreover, retained possession of a number of strategic outposts on American soil—at Detroit, Michilimackinac, and Niagara. Spain was no longer as powerful as before but, as the Jay-Gardoqui affair made evident, still conjured up memories of New World conquests.

The reason for America's diplomatic troubles was clear: The country was new, weak, and republican in a world dominated by strong monarchic governments. Although formally independent, the United States remained under the diplomatic and economic domination of Europe.

While struggling with this diplomatic weakness, Congress was also attempting to obtain the states' cooperation in a program of national economic recovery. In 1784, it failed in a renewed attempt to obtain authorization from the states to regulate foreign commerce; each state wanted to channel its own trade for its own advantage. As a result, Congress could not negotiate satisfactory commercial agreements abroad. Overseas trade continued to languish, bringing economic hardship, especially to coastal communities. In Philadelphia, only 13 ships were built in 1786, compared to three times as many just two years before. Merchants and artisans, carpenters and storekeepers, sailors and dockworkers—all dependent on shipbuilding and overseas commerce—suffered.

In an Atlantic world divided into exclusive imperial trading spheres, the United States stood alone, lacking both the political unity and the economic power to protect its interests. That made many Americans yearn for a stronger national government.

The new nation's commercial development was hobbled as well by Congress's inability to deal with the massive war debt, an issue that preoccupied Congress and demonstrated its weakness during the postwar years. No one knew how large the public debt actually was at

### British and Spanish Claims in Eastern North America, 1783

the war's end, but it probably stood at about $35 million. Much of it was held abroad by French and Dutch bankers. Not only was Congress unable to make regular payment against the loan's principal, but it had to borrow additional money abroad simply to pay the accumulating interest. At home, things were no better. In response to the incessant demands of its creditors, the government could only delay and try to borrow more.

In 1781, Congress had appointed Robert Morris, a wealthy and influential Philadelphia merchant, as superintendant of finance and had given him broad authority to deal with the nation's troubled affairs. Morris persuaded the states to stop issuing paper money and obtained a demand from Congress that they pay their requisitions in specie. In addition, he arranged for Congress to charter the Bank of North America and take steps to make federal bonds more attractive to investors.

Morris made considerable progress, but the government's finances remained shaky. In February 1781, New Jersey flatly refused to make payment on a new congressional requisition. In October, desperate for resources, Congress requested an additional $8 million from the states.

*Congress's futile efforts to secure revenue by printing paper money and apportioning taxes to the states generated anger and derision.*

Philadelphia, Sept. 22, 1779.

TAXATION ROYAL TYRANNY,
the errors of the American Congreſs demonſtrated by a geometrical axiom.

ƲPPOSE the congreſs emitted two years ago thirteen millions, but now the emiſſions amount to one hundred and eighty millions of greſs paper dollars.

t two years ago one million was worth twenty millions of this day's greſs paper dollars; then it geometrically follows, that the ſaid one dred and eighty millions is worth no more than nine millions was years ago, and by ſuch depreciation the congreſſal government never get in debt; conſequently there is no need of a tax; for one dred and eighty millions divided by twenty quotes nine millions ; *ergo* ſaid congreſſal government have gained by ſaid depreciation millions of congreſſal paper dollars. If the beſt man in congreſs any ſtronger demonſtration for tax, I hope he will produce them; if as not I make no doubt, but he will defend theſe as ſufficient proofs is congreſſal errors, or honeſtly give up the argument of taxation. This point being eſtabliſhed, the next queſtion is whether the ral wealth, value and reſource of the" profits of the confiſcated vn land and king's quit rents will be equal to the debt. To this greſs ſay nothing.    VOX POPULI.

Two and a half years later, less than $1.5 million of it had come in. Late in 1783, Morris overdrew his personal account in Europe in an effort to find money for the army's demobilization. In January 1784, he resigned, partly in despair over the government's continuing financial situation and partly to recoup his personal fortunes.

By 1786, total federal revenue amounted to no more than $370,000 a year, not a sufficient amount, as one official lamented, to provide for "the bare maintenance of the federal government on the most economical establishment, and in a time of profound peace." "The crisis has arrived," declared a congressional committee in February 1786, when Americans

> must decide whether they will support their rank as a nation, by maintaining the public faith at home and abroad; or whether, for want of . . . a general revenue . . . they will hazard not only the existence of the Union, but of the great and invaluable privileges for which they have so arduously and so honorably contended.

Not all Americans were so alarmed. Many people, including some state leaders and most small farmers of the interior, continued to believe that the Articles, though needing revision, were fundamentally sound. In their minds, the states remained the key to republican self-government. Congress seemed to them far away and largely irrelevant to their daily lives. Growing numbers, however, believed that the Confederation was on the verge of collapse and that its replacement by a new kind of central government was essential.

### Shays's Rebellion

Servicing an immense war debt had weighty implications at the state and local levels as well. The war vastly expanded the burden of private debt throughout American society. Increasing numbers of people found that they had to borrow just to pay their taxes or support their families. Others borrowed to speculate in western land or government securities or to finance the sale of goods to the army.

Since there were no commercial banks, people borrowed from each other in a complicated pyramid of private credit. At the top of the pyramid were the wealthiest merchants, who both borrowed and loaned the largest amounts. Below them stretched descending layers of borrowers and lenders. In each of the states, the top of the credit pyramid was located in the commercial regions along the coast. Its base lay in the less commercialized regions of the interior.

The system was not only complicated but also inherently unstable. If small debtors fell on hard times and could not pay their accounts, creditors above them were quickly affected and had trouble meeting their own obligations, sending trouble echoing upward toward the top. If major creditors, such as the wealthiest merchants in the port cities, ran into difficulty and began calling in their loans, a crisis could spread in the opposite direction.

Such a crisis occurred shortly after the war's end. As peace returned, English goods once again flooded the American market. Strong demand encouraged American importers to borrow heavily in England and expand their purchases, which they sold to retailers at a handsome profit. Some of those profits they loaned to the retailers so they could sell even more goods. The retailers in turn extended credit to their customers.

The system held together reasonably well for several years, but the flood of English goods eventually glutted the American market and forced prices down. By 1785, a number of English banking houses, heavily overcommitted in America, were in trouble. In an effort to survive, they called in their American loans. American merchants in turn tried to collect the debts due them, thus setting off a spiraling crisis of credit throughout the economy.

The crisis was most acute at the bottom of the pyramid, among the small farmers and laboring people of country and town. Caught in a tightening bind, they did what people had become accustomed to doing: they turned to their state governments for relief, asking for "stay laws" suspending the collection of private debts. If not granted relief, they faced the certain foreclosure and loss of their shops and farms. They also pressed for new issues of paper money so that they would have something with which to pay both private debts and public taxes.

Creditors, however, most of whom lived in the commercial areas to the east, fought these relief proposals. They opposed stay laws because

they had loaned out large sums of money and wanted to be able to call them in. They argued vigorously against new paper money because they feared it would once again depreciate and further confound economic affairs. Sound commerce, they argued, demanded a stable, specie-based money supply.

The situation was most explosive in Massachusetts. By 1786, heavy private debt and a lingering agricultural depression had made many farmers desperate. In words that echoed the colonial protests of the 1760s, they petitioned their government for relief. Their appeals, however, fell on deaf ears, for commercial and creditor interests now controlled the state regime. The farmers' call for new paper money was quickly rejected. To their appeal for tax relief, the government responded by passing a law setting the state debt at full face value, calling for its rapid repayment, and levying a heavy new round of taxes. No matter that the citizens of interior towns such as Conway complained bitterly of "the great difficulty we labor under in regard to paying our taxes" or that Peter Wood, tax collector for the town of Marlborough, reported that "there was not . . . the money in possession or at command among the people . . . to discharge taxes" or that between 1784 and 1786, some 29 towns declared their inability to meet their obligations.

As frustrated citizens had done before and would do again when the law proved unresponsive to their needs, Massachusetts farmers stepped outside the law and took matters into their own hands. A Hampshire County convention of 50 towns condemned the state senate, lawyers, court fees, and the tax system. It advised against violence, but mobs soon began to form.

The county courts drew much of the farmers' wrath because they issued the writs of foreclosure that both the state and private creditors so relentlessly demanded. On August 31, 1786, armed men prevented the county court from sitting at Northampton, and on September 5, angry citizens closed down the court at Worcester. When farmers threatened similar actions elsewhere, an alarmed Governor James Bowdoin dispatched 600 militiamen to protect the Supreme Court, then on circuit at Springfield.

About 500 insurgents had gathered near there under the leadership of Daniel Shays, a popular Revolutionary War captain recently fallen on hard times. A "brave and good soldier," Shays had mustered out of the army in 1780 and returned home, like thousands of other tired and frustrated soldiers, to await payment for his military service. Like the others, he had a long wait. In the meantime, his farming went badly, his debts accumulated, and, as he later recalled, "the spector of debtor's jail always hovered close by." Most of the men who gathered around Shays were debtors and veterans also.

Worried about a possible raid on the federal arsenal at Springfield and encouraged by the Massachusetts delegates to take the affair seriously, the Continental Congress authorized 1,300 troops, ostensibly for service against the Indians but actually to be ready for use against Shays and his rebels. For a few weeks, Massachusetts seemed poised on the brink of civil war.

In late November, the insurrection collapsed in eastern Massachusetts, but things were far from over in the west. When several insurgent groups refused to disband at the governor's command, Bowdoin called out a force of 4,400 men, financed and led by worried eastern merchants. On January 26, 1787, Shays led 1,200 men toward the federal arsenal. Frightened by the siege,

*The Massachusetts farmers' rebellion against foreclosures and taxes, led by Daniel Shays, generated considerable alarm throughout the state. Grateful citizens of Springfield commissioned Paul Revere to make this silver punch bowl for General William Shepard, who was credited with defeating the insurgents.*

its defenders opened fire, killing four of the attackers and sending the Shaysites into retreat.

Over the next several weeks, the militia chased the remnants of Shays's followers across the state and sent Shays himself fleeing into Vermont for safety. By the end of February, the rebellion was over. In March, the legislature pardoned all but Shays and three other leaders; in another year, they too had been forgiven.

Massachusetts experienced the most dramatic instance of agrarian protest. But similar challenges to public authority erupted in at least half the states. In Maryland in June 1786, a "tumultuary assemblage of the people" rushed into the Charles County courthouse and closed it down. Like the Massachusetts rebels, they demanded the suspension of debt proceedings and new paper money. In Cecil County, farmers circulated unsigned handbills threatening state officers if they seized people's property for unpaid taxes. The governor condemned the "riotous and tumultuous" proceedings and warned against further "violence and outrages." In South Carolina in May 1785, sheriffs were "threatened in the execution of their duty" as they attempted to foreclose several properties. In one incident, Colonel Hezekiah Mayham, "being served by the sheriff with a writ obliged him to eat it on the spot." Warned Judge Aedanus Burke, not even "5,000 troops, the best in America or Europe, could enforce obedience" to the court. Across the nation, state politics was in turmoil.

## The Federalists and the Internal Crisis

By the late 1780s, supporters of a stronger national government were calling themselves Federalists (leading their opponents to adopt the name Anti-Federalists). Led by Washington, Hamilton, Madison, and Jay, they believed that the nation was in the midst of a social and political crisis that threatened its very survival. "Our affairs seem to lead to some crisis, some revolution," wrote Jay. Such men had never been comfortable with the more radical aspects of the Revolution. While supporting the principles of moderate republicanism, they continued to believe in an aristocracy of talent and to place high value on social order and the rights of property.

They were now persuaded that social and political change had been carried too far, "natural" distinctions among the people were being ignored, and the bases of social and political stability were in danger of collapse. The Revolution, Jay lamented, "laid open a wide field for the operation of ambition," especially for "men raised from low degrees to high stations and rendered giddy by elevation." It was time, he insisted, to find better ways of protecting "the worthy against the licentious."

The Federalist leaders feared for their own social and political security. But they were concerned more generally about the collapse of the orderly world they believed essential to the preservation of republican liberty. There should be clear limits, they thought, to notions of political equality. Even more limited should be talk of erasing social distinctions. In 1776, American liberty had needed protection from English power. Danger now, however, came from too much liberty threatening to degenerate into license. "We have probably had too good an opinion of human nature in forming our Consti-tution," wrote Washington. "Experience has taught us, that men will not adopt and carry into execution measures the best calculated for their own good, without the intervention of a coercive power." In the Federalists' minds, power no longer stood as liberty's antagonist but as its guarantor. What America needed was "a strong government, ably administered."

Much of the Federalists' determination to strengthen the central government stemmed from apparent disorder in the states, especially the renewed pressure for debt relief and paper money so evident in Shays's Rebellion. These seemed to threaten the security of property on which the Federalists believed liberty depended. The Federalists did not see Shays's uprising in Massachusetts and similar outbursts elsewhere as evidence of genuine distress but as threats to social order. While they were reassured by the speed with which the Shaysites were dispatched, that episode persuaded them of the need for a stronger national government managed by the "better sort."

## CONCLUSION: The Crosscurrents of Revolution

The Revolution changed many aspects of American life, but none more profoundly than politics. Faced with the need to define a new national identity, the Revolutionary generation fashioned a distinctive republican ideology. Republican principles formed the basis for new state regimes, which were directly responsive to the citizenry and much more active in people's lives than the colonial governments had ever been. In the process of creating a new political system, Americans clarified many of the basic constitutional principles that have protected our liberties ever since. Through it all, politics came to play a more central role in American life than ever before.

As with so much else during these Revolutionary years, the changes did not come easily. Americans argued over what republican liberty meant and how much political democracy there should be. As the state governments reached ever more deeply into people's lives, the people struggled with each other for political power and the ability to influence what government did. Rich and poor, powerful and weak, male and female, black and white, merchant and farmer, dissenter and defender of religious privilege—all sought a voice in deciding what these Revolutionary republics should be.

By the late 1780s, many of the original decisions seemed to be unraveling. Protests such as Shays's Rebellion in Massachusetts expressed the frustration many Americans, especially farmers of the interior, felt at the state governments' increasing insensitivity to their needs. At the same time, the Articles of Confederation seemed on the verge of collapse, and increasing numbers of people in the more commercial areas along the coast were calling for its reform. As 1786 began, all of these anxieties converged in a momentous debate over the national government. In the next chapter, we examine that debate and its consequences for the future course of America's republican experiment.

## Recommended Reading

For further information about the ideology of Revolutionary republicanism, see Bernard Bailyn, *The Ideological Origins of the American Revolution* (1967); Gordon Wood, *The Creation of the American Republic, 1776–1787* (1969); and Morton White, *The Philosophy of the American Revolution* (1978).

State constitution making is discussed in many of the books listed, but see especially Gordon Wood, *The Creation of the American Republic, 1776–1787* (1969) and Willi Paul Adams, *The First American Constitutions* (1980). The writing on Revolutionary state politics is rich and exciting. Among the most important books are Ronald Hoffman, *A Spirit of Dissension: Economics, Politics and the Revolution in Maryland* (1973); David Szatmary, *Shays' Rebellion: The Making of an Agrarian Insurrection* (1980); Edward Countryman, *A People in Revolution: The American Revolution and Political Society in New York, 1760–1790* (1981); Eric Foner, *Tom Paine and Revolutionary America* (1976); Stephen Patterson, *Political Parties in Revolutionary Massachusetts* (1973); and Jackson T. Main, *Political Parties Before the Constitution* (1973). See also the essays in Ronald Hoffman and Peter Albert, eds., *Sovereign States in an Age of Uncertainty* (1981).

Among the major works dealing with the Articles of Confederation and the movement toward a stronger national government are Gordon Wood, *The Creation of the American Republic, 1776–1787* (1969); Merrill Jensen, *The New Nation: A History of the United States During the Confederation, 1781–1789* (1950); H. James Henderson, *Party Politics in the Continental Congress* (1974); and Jack Rakove, *The Beginnings of National Politics: An Interpretive History of the Continental Congress* (1979).

Among many readable and informative biographical accounts are Pauline Maier, *The Old Revolutionaries: Political Lives in the Age of Samuel Adams* (1980); Norman Risjord, *Representative Americans: The Revolutionary Generation* (1980); Fawn Brodie, *Thomas Jefferson: An Intimate History* (1974); Gerald Stourzh, *Alexander Hamilton and the Idea of Republican Government* (1970); Claude Lopez and Eugenia Herbert, *The Private Franklin: The Man and His Family* (1975); Peter Shaw, *The Character of John Adams* (1976); and Marcus Cunliffe, *George Washington: Man and Monument* (1958).

## TIME LINE

| | |
|---|---|
| 1775 | Continental Congress urges "states" to establish new governments |
| 1776 | Declaration of Independence<br>States pass laws against Loyalists<br>Eight states draft constitutions |
| 1778 | People of Massachusetts reject proposed constitution |
| 1779 | Massachusetts state constitutional convention |
| 1780 | Massachusetts constitution ratified |
| 1781 | Articles of Confederation ratified by states<br>Western lands ceded by states to Congress |
| 1784 | Treaty of Fort Stanwix with Iroquois<br>Spain closes Mississippi River to American navigation |
| 1784–1786 | Agrarian protest in several states |
| 1785 | Land Ordinance for Northwest Territory |
| 1786 | Virginia adopts "Bill for Establishing Religious Freedom"<br>Annapolis Convention calls for revision of Articles of Confederation |
| 1786–1787 | Shays's Rebellion |
| 1787 | Northwest Ordinance |

# CHAPTER 8
## CREATING A NATION

In October 1789, David Brown arrived in Dedham, Massachusetts. Born about 50 years before in Bethlehem, Connecticut, Brown had served in the Revolutionary army and after the war had shipped out on an American merchantman to see the world. His travels, as he later reported, took him to "nineteen different . . . Kingdoms in Europe, and nearly all the United States." For two years before settling in Dedham, he visited scores of Massachusetts towns, supporting himself as a day laborer while discussing the troubled state of public affairs with local townspeople.

Initially the people of Dedham took little notice of Brown, but he soon made his presence felt. Though he had little formal schooling, he was a man with powerful opinions and considerable natural ability. His reading and personal experience had persuaded him that government was a conspiracy of the rich to exploit farmers, artisans, and other common folk, and he was quick to make his opinions known.

"The occupation of government," Brown declared bluntly in one of his numerous pamphlets, "is to plunder and steal." The object of his wrath was the central government recently established under the new national constitution. The leaders of government, he charged, were engrossing the nation's western lands for themselves. "Five hundred [people] out of the union of five millions receive all the benefit of public property and live upon the ruins of the rest of the community." Brown warned that such policies would not last long, because no government could survive "after the confidence of the people was lost, for the people are the government."

In the highly charged political climate of the 1790s, Brown's radical language and exaggerated attacks on the new government's leaders brought a sharp response. In 1798, John Davis, the federal district attorney in Boston, issued a warrant for Brown's arrest on charges of sedition, while government-supported newspapers attacked him as a "rallying point of insurrection and disorder." Fearing arrest, Brown fled to Salem, but there he was caught and charged with intent to defame the government and aid the country's enemies. For want of $400 bail, he was clapped in prison.

In June 1799, Brown came before the U.S. Circuit Court, Justice Samuel Chase presiding. Chase was anything but judicial. Persuaded that critics of the administration were also enemies of the republic, Chase was determined to make Brown an example of what the government's opponents could expect. Confused and hoping for leniency, Brown pleaded guilty; for Chase, however, that made no difference. Ignoring Brown's plea, he directed the federal prosecutor to "examine the witness . . . that the degree of his guilt might be duly ascertained." Before sentencing him, Chase demanded that Brown provide the names of his accomplices and a list of subscribers to his writings. When Brown refused, protesting that he would "lose all my friends," Chase sentenced him to a fine of $480 and 18 months in jail. No matter that Brown could not pay the fine and faced the prospect of indefinite imprisonment.

In rendering judgment, Chase castigated Brown for the "vicious industry" with which he had circulated his "disorganizing doctrines and . . . falsehoods, and the very alarming and dangerous excesses to which he attempted to incite the uninformed part of the community." Not all citizens, Chase thought, should be allowed to comment on public affairs. For nearly two years, Brown languished in prison. Not until the Federalist party was defeated in the election of 1800 and the Jeffersonian Republicans had taken office was he freed.

D avid Brown discovered how easy it was for critics of the government to get into trouble during the 1790s, a decade of extraordinary political controversy. Even though the Revolutionary War was long past, the debate over Revolutionary principles continued. That debate now came to focus on the national government. In May 1787, as the crisis surrounding the Articles of Confederation deepened, a special convention gathered in Philadelphia to consider proposals for the Articles' revision. After weeks of heated argument, the Convention produced a constitution laying out an entirely new and far stronger national government. When sent to the states for ratification, it generated fierce debate among the people, for it raised again the familiar concerns about power, political equality, and the proper role of central government in a republican society.

As the new government got under way during the 1790s, that debate intensified, catching up countless people like David Brown in its toils. Issues of domestic and foreign policy fueled the controversy, but at its center lay disagreements over economic interests and the nature of the new republic's government. Benjamin Rush, Philadelphia physician and Revolutionary Patriot, explained the situation. "The American War is over," he wrote, "but this is far from being the case with the American revolution. On the contrary, nothing but the first act of the great drama is closed. It remains . . . to establish and perfect our new forms of government."

As the decade proceeded and the political debate escalated, Americans divided into two opposing political camps—the Federalists, supporters of the presidential administrations of George Washington and John Adams, and the Jeffersonian Republicans, the Federalists' increasingly vocal critics. Seldom has American political discourse been so virulent; rarely has the very survival of the republic seemed to hang more clearly in the balance.

In this chapter, we examine the movement toward a stronger national government, the Philadelphia Convention and the constitution that it produced, the debate over ratification, the swirl of political controversy that surrounded the new government's first decade of operation, and the election of 1800, which brought the Federalists' defeat and Thomas Jefferson's election to the presidency.

## THE CONSTITUTION

The first step toward governmental reform came in September 1786, when delegates gathered in Annapolis, Maryland, to discuss ways of promoting interstate commerce. Nine states had agreed to attend, but only four were actually represented. Persuaded that it was useless to continue with so few in attendance, the 12 delegates prepared an address to the states. Written by the ardent nationalist Alexander Hamilton, it called for a new convention to gather in Philadelphia in May 1787 to discuss all matters necessary "to render the constitution of the

federal government adequate to the exigencies of the Union." In February 1787, the Confederation Congress cautiously endorsed the idea of a convention to revise the Articles of Confederation. Before long, however, it became clear that more than revision was under way.

### The Grand Convention

At the end of May, the 55 delegates, representing every state except Rhode Island, began assembling in Philadelphia. The city bustled with excitement as they gathered. The convention's roster read like an honor role of the Revolution. Certainly it was a more impressive gathering than the old Congress, still sitting 100 miles away in New York City. From Virginia came Washington, Madison, and George Mason. Jefferson would certainly have been there had he not been abroad as minister to France. Patrick Henry had declined election, fearing what the convention was likely to do and wanting no part of it.

From Pennsylvania came the venerable Franklin, too old any longer to contribute to the debates but able still to lend his presence to the occasion. His colleagues from Pennsylvania included the lawyer James Wilson and the merchant Robert Morris. The New York assembly sent a powerful, though deeply divided delegation. There was no more committed advocate of stronger national government (Federalist) at Philadelphia than Hamilton, nor any more vocal opponents of broad governmental reform (Anti-Federalists) than Robert Yates and John Lansing. Massachusetts was ably represented by Elbridge Gerry and Rufus King. South Carolina sent John Rutledge and Charles Pinckney.

The convention elected Washington as its presiding officer, adopted rules of procedure, and, after spirited debate, voted to close the doors and do the convention's business in secret. For nearly four months, the delegates debated the nation's future while the public waited and wondered what was happening.

Debate focused first on the so-called Virginia Plan, introduced by Edmund Randolph on May 29. It outlined a new and truly national government. According to its provisions, there would be a bicameral congress, with the lower house elected by the people and the upper house, or senate, elected by the lower house from nominees proposed by the state legislatures. The plan also proposed a president chosen by the congress; a national judiciary; and a council of revision, consisting of the executive and several members of the judiciary, whose task was to review the constitutionality of legislation.

Opposition to the Virginia Plan came chiefly from the smaller states and centered on the provision for proportional rather than equal congressional representation for the states. On June 15, William Paterson introduced a counterproposal, the New Jersey Plan. It urged retention of the Articles as the basic structure of government but conferred on the congress the long-sought powers to tax and regulate foreign and interstate commerce, as well as authority to appoint a veto-less executive and a supreme court. After three days of heated debate, by a vote of seven states to three, the delegates adopted the Virginia Plan as the basis for further discussions. It was now clear that the convention would recommend replacing the Articles of Confederation with a much stronger national government. For the next four months, the convention struggled to give that new government shape and definition.

*An unknown artist depicted the Constitutional Convention of 1787 as an august assembly, with George Washington occupying the place of honor. The proceedings actually went on behind closed doors.*

On July 12, as part of what has become known as the Great Compromise, the delegates settled one major point of controversy by agreeing that representation in the lower house should be based on the total of each state's white population and three-fifths of its black population. Though blacks were not accorded citizenship and could not vote, the southern delegates argued that they should be fully counted for this purpose. Delegates from the northern states, where relatively few blacks lived, did not want them counted at all, but the bargain was struck. As part of this compromise, the convention agreed that direct taxes would also be apportioned on the basis of population and that blacks would be counted similarly in that calculation as well. On July 16, the convention accepted the principle that each state should have only one vote in the senate. Thus the interests of both large and small states were effectively accommodated.

The convention then submitted its work to a committee of detail for drafting in proper constitutional form. That group reported on August 6, and for the next month the delegates hammered out the document's seven articles. On several occasions, differences seemed so great that it was uncertain whether the convention could proceed. In each instance, however, agreement was reached, and the discussion continued.

The Federalists were determined to separate the new government from the people to ensure the stability the state governments lacked. They thus created an electoral process designed to bring only persons of standing and experience into national office. They described it as a "filtration of talent." An electoral college of wise and experienced leaders would choose the president. They were to meet without instructions and select the president on their own. The process functioned exactly that way during the first several presidential elections.

Selection of the new Senate was to be similarly indirect, for its members were to be named by the state legislatures. Not until 1913, when the Seventeenth Amendment to the Constitution was ratified, would the people elect their senators. Even the House of Representatives, the only popularly elected branch of the new government, was to be filled with persons of standing and wealth, for the Federalists were confident that only familiar and experienced leaders could attract the necessary votes.

The delegates' final set of compromises touched the fate of black Americans. At the urging of southerners, the convention agreed that the slave trade could not formally end for another 20 years. The delegates never used the words *slavery* or *slave trade* at all but spoke more vaguely about not prohibiting, prior to 1808, "the migration or importation of such persons as any of the states now existing shall think proper to admit." Their meaning, however, was entirely clear.

Similarly, the convention quickly and firmly set aside a proposal to abolish slavery altogether. In so doing, the delegates tacitly acknowledged slavery's legitimacy. More than that, they provided for slavery's protection, for Section 2 of Article 4 of the Constitution stated: "No person held to service or labour in one state, . . . [and] escaping into another, shall, in consequence of any law . . . therein, be discharged from such service, but shall be delivered up on claim of the party to whom such service or labour may be due." The delegates thus provided federal sanction for the capture and return of runaway slaves. This fugitive slave clause would return to haunt northern consciences in the years ahead, but at the moment it seemed a small price to pay for sectional harmony and a new government. Northern accommodation to the demands of the southern delegates was eased, moreover, by knowledge that southerners in the Confederation Congress had just agreed to prohibit slaves from entering the Northwest Territory.

The document that emerged from the Philadelphia Convention, then, represented compromises between large states and small, as well as between North and South. Some of those compromises came at the expense of black Americans, who had no voice either in the Constitution's drafting or its approval.

Although the Constitution called for shared responsibilities between the central government and the states, it clearly shifted the balance in the national government's favor. Congress would now have authority to levy and collect taxes, regulate commerce with foreign nations and between states, devise uniform rules for naturalization, administer national patents and copyrights, and control the special federal district in which it would eventually be located. Restrictions on the government's authority were limited and specific. Conspicuously missing was any statement reserving to the states all powers not explicitly conferred on the central government, which had been a crippling limitation of the Articles. On the contrary, the Constitution contained a number of clauses bestowing general grants of power on the new government. Section 8 of Article 1, for example, contained phrases granting Congress authority to "provide for the . . . general welfare of the United States" as well as "to make all laws . . . necessary and proper for carrying into execution . . . all . . . powers vested by this Constitution in the government of the United States." Later generations would call these phrases "elastic clauses" and would use them to expand the government's activities. The Federalists anticipated the need for such expansion. A final measure of the Federalists' determination to make the new government supreme over the states was the assertion in Article 6 that the Constitution and all

*Symbolism was important in the new republic. Congress adopted the Great Seal in 1782, a half decade before the Philadelphia Convention.*

laws passed under it were to be regarded as "the supreme Law of the Land."

When the convention had finished its business, 3 of the 42 remaining delegates refused to sign the document. The other 39, however, affixed their names and forwarded it to the Congress along with their request that it be sent on to the states for approval. On September 17, the Grand Convention adjourned.

## Debate over the Constitution

Ratification presented the Federalists with more difficult problems than they had faced at Philadelphia. Now the debate moved into the open and shifted to the states, where sentiment was sharply divided and the situation more difficult to control. The Federalists, though, had thought carefully about securing ratification. Recognizing the unlikelihood of gaining quick agreement from all 13 states, they provided that the Constitution should go into effect when any nine agreed to it. Other states could then enter the Union as they were ready. They also arranged for ratification by specially elected conventions rather than the state assemblies, since under the Constitution the assemblies would lose substantial amounts of power. Ratification by convention was also more constitutionally sound, since it would give the new government its own grounding in the people and free it from dependence on the states.

When the convention reported its work to the Confederation Congress, opponents attempted to censure it for exceeding its authority. But after a few days' debate, Congress dutifully forwarded the document to the states for consideration. Word of the dramatic changes being proposed spread rapidly. In each state, Federalists and Anti-Federalists, the latter now actively opposing the Constitution, prepared to debate the new articles of government.

Federalist and Anti-Federalist strength differed from place to place, but in most of the states, opposition to the Constitution was widespread and vocal. Some criticized it out of fear that a stronger central government would threaten state interests or their own political power. Others charged the Federalists with betraying the essentials of Revolutionary republicanism. Like all "vigorous" and "energetic" governments, they warned, the new one would be corrupted by its own power. Far from the watchful eyes of the citizenry, its officials would behave as power wielders always had. American liberty, so recently preserved at such a high cost, would once again come under attack.

The Anti-Federalists were aghast at the Federalists' vision of an expanding "republican empire." "The idea of . . . [a] republic, on an average of 1000 miles in length, and 800 in breadth, and containing 6 millions of white inhabitants all reduced to the same standards of morals . . . habits . . . [and] laws," exclaimed one critic incredulously, "is itself an absurdity, and contrary to the whole experience of mankind." Such an attempt would guarantee factional conflict and disorder. The Anti-Federalists continued to believe that republican liberty could be preserved only in simple, homogeneous societies, where faction was absent and public virtue guided people's behavior.

Nor did the Anti-Federalists believe arguments that the separation of executive, legislative, and judicial powers and the balancing of state and national governments would prevent power's abuse. Government, they insisted, must be kept simple, for complexity only confused the people and provided opportunity for the free play of selfish ambition. No system of checks and balances, however ingeniously contrived, could long preserve liberty.

Federalist spokesmen moved quickly to counter the Antis' criticism. The Federalists' most important effort was a series of essays penned by James Madison, Alexander Hamilton, and John Jay and published in New York under the pseudonym Publius. The *Federalist Papers*, as they were called, were written to promote ratification in New York but were quickly reprinted by Federalists elsewhere.

Madison, Hamilton, and Jay moved systematically through the proposed Constitution, explaining its virtues and responding to the Anti-Federalists' attacks. In the process, they described a political vision fundamentally different from that of their Anti-Federalist opponents.

No difference was more dramatic than the Federalists' discussion of governmental power. Power, the Federalists now argued, was not the enemy of liberty but its guarantor. Nothing was more dangerous than the "mischievous effects of unstable government." Where government was not "energetic" and "efficient" (these were favorite Federalist words), demagogues and disorganizers did their work. It is far better, Hamilton wrote in *Federalist* No. 26, "to hazard the abuse of . . . confidence than to embarrass the government and endanger the public safety by impolitic restrictions of . . . authority".

Federalists found it difficult to counter the Anti-Federalists' warning that no republic could safely incorporate the country's economic and social diversity, for the accusation was grounded in both republican theory and Americans' traditional localism. The authors of the *Federalist Papers* did so, however, by turning the classic republican argument on its head. Factional divisions, they explained, could never be avoided, even in the smallest societies, because they were the inevitable by-products of economic and social development. Faction, moreover, was the necessary accompaniment of human liberty. Wrote Madison in *Federalist* No. 10: "Liberty is to faction what air is to fire, an aliment without which it instantly expires." To suppress faction was to destroy liberty itself.

Earlier emphasis on public virtue, the Federalists explained, had been naive, for most people did not place the public good ahead of their own interests. Politics had to heed this harsh fact and provide for peaceful compromise among conflicting interests. That could best be accomplished, they insisted, by expanding the nation so that it included innumerable factional interests. Out of the clash and accommodation of social and economic interests, then, would emerge public order and the best available approximation of the public good.

The Federalists' argument established the basic rationale for modern democratic politics, but it left the Antis sputtering in frustration. Where in the Federalists' scheme was that familiar abstraction, the public good? Who would look after it? What place was there for public virtue in a system built on the notion of competing private interests? In such a free market of competition, the Anti-Federalists warned, only the wealthy and powerful would benefit, while ordinary folk would suffer.

The Anti-Federalists accused their opponents as well of elitism, of wishing to join the government to wealth and privilege. Not all the Antis were democrats. Many of their leaders held slaves, and their appeals to local authority did not always mean support for social and political equality. Yet given their warnings against wealth and power and their distrust of centralization, the Anti-Federalists were consistently more sympathetic to democratic principles than were their Federalist opponents. Certainly they believed more firmly that for government to be safe, it must be tied intimately to the people.

As the ratification debate revealed, the Federalists and Anti-Federalists held distinctly different visions of the new republic. The Antis remained much closer to the original republicanism of 1776, with its suspicion of power and wealth, its emphasis on the primacy of local government, and its fears of national development. They envisioned a decentralized republic filled with self-reliant citizens whose ambitions were limited, whose activities were guided by public virtue, and whose destiny was determined by what happened in the states rather than the nation. Anxious about what the future might bring, they wanted to keep their world much as it had been.

The Federalists, on the other hand, arguing that America's situation had changed dramatically since 1776, embraced the idea of nationhood and looked forward with anticipation to the development of a rising "republican empire" based on commercial development and led by men of wealth and talent. Both Federalists and Anti-Federalists claimed to be heirs of the Revolution, yet they differed on what the Revolution had meant.

## The Struggle for Ratification

It is impossible to know with certainty what most Americans thought of the proposed Constitution. Probably no more than several hundred thousand participated in the elections for the state ratifying conventions, and many of the delegates carried no binding instructions from their constituents on how they should vote. No national plebiscite on the Constitution was ever taken. Had one been, a majority of the people would probably have opposed the document, out of either indifference or alarm. Fortunately for the Federalists, they did not have to persuade most Americans; they needed only secure majorities in nine of the state ratifying conventions, a much less formidable task.

They set about it with determination. As soon as the Philadelphia convention adjourned, its members hurried home to organize the ratification movement in their states. In Delaware and Georgia, New Jersey and Connecticut, where the Federalists were confident of their strength, they pressed quickly for ratification. Where the outcome was uncertain, as in New York and Virginia, they delayed, hoping that word of ratification elsewhere would work to their benefit.

It took less than a year from the time the document left Congress to secure approval of the necessary nine states. Delaware, Pennsylvania, and New Jersey ratified first, in December 1787. Approval came a month later in Georgia and Connecticut. Massachusetts was next to ratify, but only after considerable political maneuvering. When the Massachusetts convention gathered in Boston on January 9, the Anti-Federalists enjoyed a solid majority. In an effort to woo Anti-Federalist delegates and persuade the uncommitted, Federalist leaders agreed to forward a set of amendments describing a federal "bill of rights" along with notice of ratification. The strategy worked, for it brought Samuel Adams and John Hancock into line, and with them the crucial convention votes that they controlled.

Maryland and South Carolina were the seventh and eighth states to approve. That left New Hampshire and Virginia as the most likely candidates for the honor of being ninth and putting the Constitution over the top. In both states, however, there was determined opposition. The New Hampshire convention met on February 13. Sensing that they lacked the necessary votes, the Federalists arranged for an adjournment until mid-June and began working feverishly to build support. When the convention reconvened, it took but three days to secure a Federalist majority. New Hampshire ratified on June 21.

Two massive gaps in the new union

remained—Virginia and New York. Clearly, the government could not endure without them. In Virginia, Madison nailed down Jefferson's support by promising that the new Congress would immediately consider a federal bill of rights. Other Federalists tried to weaken the opposition by spreading the rumor that Patrick Henry, most influential of the Anti-Federalist leaders, had changed sides. Henry loudly denied the charge, but his eloquence proved no match for the careful politicking of Madison and the others. On June 25, the Virginia convention voted to ratify by the narrow margin of ten votes.

The New York convention met on June 17 at Poughkeepsie, with the Anti-Federalist followers of Governor George Clinton firmly in command. Hamilton worked for delay, hoping that news of the results in New Hampshire and Virginia would turn the tide. For several weeks, approval hung in the balance while the two sides argued and maneuvered for support. On July 27, approval squeaked through, 30 to 27. That left two states still uncommitted. North Carolina finally ratified in November 1789; Rhode Island did not enter the Union until May 1790, more than a year after the new government had gotten under way.

### The Social Geography of Ratification

A glance at the geographic pattern of Federalist and Anti-Federalist strength in the states indicates how different were the sources of their political support. Federalist strength was concentrated in areas along the coast and navigable rivers and was strongest of all in cities and towns. The centers of Anti-Federalist support, on the other hand, lay away from the coast, in the interior of New England, upstate New York, the Virginia piedmont and south, and the western regions of the Carolinas. Georgia was the most notable exception to this otherwise general pattern. Unable alone to subdue the Creek Indians on their frontier and hoping desperately for help from a strengthened central government, Georgians gave almost uniform support to the Constitution.

Merchants and businessmen supported the Constitution most ardently. Enthusiasm also ran high among urban laborers, artisans, and shopkeepers, however, which was rather surprising given the Anti-Federalists' criticism of wealth and power and their emphasis on political equality. City artisans and workers, after all, had been in the vanguard of political reform during the Revolution. But in the troubled circumstances of the late 1780s, they worried about their livelihoods and believed that a stronger government could better promote overseas trade and protect American artisans from foreign competition.

On July 4, 1788, a grand procession celebrating the Constitution's ratification wound through the streets of Philadelphia. Seventeen thousand strong, it graphically demonstrated working-class support for the Constitution. At

### Ratification of the Constitution

| STATE | DATE | VOTE | |
|---|---|---|---|
| | | FOR | AGAINST |
| Delaware | December 1787 | 30 | 0 |
| Pennsylvania | December 1787 | 46 | 23 |
| New Jersey | December 1787 | 38 | 0 |
| Georgia | January 1788 | 26 | 0 |
| Connecticut | January 1788 | 128 | 40 |
| Massachusetts | February 1788 | 187 | 168 |
| Maryland | April 1788 | 63 | 11 |
| South Carolina | May 1788 | 149 | 73 |
| New Hampshire | June 1788 | 57 | 47 |
| Virginia | June 1788 | 89 | 79 |
| New York | July 1788 | 30 | 27 |
| North Carolina | November 1789 | 194 | 77 |
| Rhode Island | May 1790 | 34 | 32 |

the head of the line marched lawyers, merchants, and others of the city's elite, but close behind came representatives of virtually every trade in the city, from ship's carpenters to shoemakers, each with floats, flags, and mottoed banners. "May commerce flourish and industry be rewarded," declared the mariners and shipbuilders. "May the federal government revive our trade," exclaimed the bakers. "May industry ever be encouraged," urged the porters. "Home-brewed is best," insisted the maltsters.

For one day, declared Benjamin Rush in amazement, "rank . . . forgot all its claims. Hand in hand marched merchants and seamen, shopkeepers and artisans." Within a few years, political disputes would again divide them. For the moment, however, people of all ranks joined in celebrating the new Constitution.

The Constitution found support as well in the countryside, especially close to the coast among commercial farmers and southern planters eager for profit and anxious about overseas

## Federalist and Anti-Federalist Areas, 1787–1790

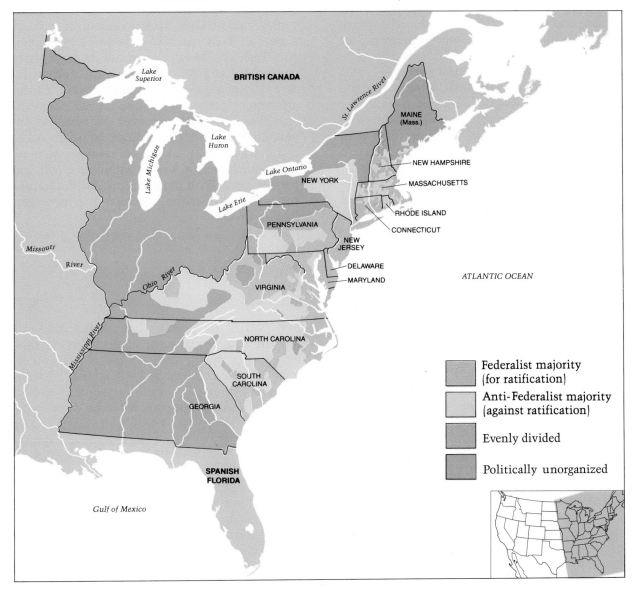

Federalist majority (for ratification)

Anti-Federalist majority (against ratification)

Evenly divided

Politically unorganized

markets. But Federalist enthusiasm waned and Anti-Federalist sentiment increased in the interior. Among most ordinary farmers living outside the market economy and immersed in their own localities, the republicanism of 1776 outweighed their interest in national affairs. They found the Federalist vision of an "American empire" both strange and alarming.

Why were the Federalists finally successful? The political cards certainly seemed to be stacked against them. The Anti-Federalists had only to defend the status quo, arouse people's deep-seated fears of central government, and play upon their local loyalties. The Federalists, on the other hand, had to explain how republicanism had suddenly become compatible with national power and expansion. Moreover, they faced the complicated political task of coordinating ratification in the various states.

The Federalists' task was simplified by the fact that many Americans agreed that the Articles needed strengthening. Given the troubles of the Confederation, the Federalists were able to argue that the Revolution was doomed to failure unless something dramatic was done.

Most of all, however, the Federalists succeeded because of their determination and political skill. They included most of the Revolution's major leaders, men such as Washing-ton, Adams, Franklin, and Jay. Time and again these heroes spoke out for the Constitution in the state ratifying debates, and time and again their support proved decisive. Their experience as army officers and as members of the Continental and Confederation Congresses caused these men to identify with the nation and what it might become. They brought their vision to the ratification process and asked others to share it with them.

Nor were they above tough political maneuvering. In New York, the Federalists warned darkly that if opposition persisted, they would carry the city and its surrounding counties out of the state and ratify on their own. In Pennsylvania, Federalist leaders in the assembly sent out a gang of their supporters to round up several Anti-Federalist legislators who were desperately trying to leave town in order to deprive the assembly of a quorum and thus prevent it from arranging elections for a state ratifying convention. The Federalists retrieved their hapless opponents, plunked them down in their seats, counted a quorum, and moved ratification on its way. Altogether, it was an impressive political performance. With their success, the Federalists turned the American republic in a new and fateful direction.

## LAUNCHING THE NATIONAL REPUBLIC

Once ratification was achieved, opposition to the Constitution weakened, and many of the Anti-Federalists seemed ready to give the new experiment a chance. They were determined, however, to watch it closely and raise the alarm at the first sign of danger. It was not many months before those alarms began to be heard.

### Getting the Government Under Way

On April 16, 1789, George Washington started north from Virginia toward New York City to be inaugurated as the first president of the United States. The first electoral college convened under the Constitution had unanimously elected him to the nation's highest of-fice. Nearly six years earlier, Washington had left the continental army camp believing that his years of public service were over. His feelings now were mixed as he set forth. "I bade adieu to Mount Vernon, to private life, and to domestic felicity," he confided to his diary, "and with a mind oppressed with more anxious and painful sensations than I have words to express, set out for New York . . . with the best disposition to render service to my country in obedience to its call, but with less hope of answering its expectations." Events would soon show that he had good reason for such forebodings.

Washington's journey through the countryside resembled a royal procession, for he was the object of constant adulation along the way.

Local militias turned out to escort him. In villages and towns, guns boomed their salutes, children danced in the streets, church bells pealed, and dignitaries toasted his arrival. On April 23, the president-elect and his entourage reached the northern New Jersey shore, where awaited an elegant barge, festooned with flowers and attended by 11 ship's captains. People crowded the shore as Washington climbed aboard and, accompanied by a flotilla of boats, was rowed across the harbor to New York City. There, throngs of citizens and newly elected members of Congress greeted the weary traveler. Over the streets of the city stretched gaily decorated arches. During the parade uptown to the governor's mansion, young women in white flowing robes preceded him, strewing flowers in his path. That night, bonfires illuminated the city.

Already the transition from the old Confederation Congress to the new government was under way. Back on October 2, the Congress had moved from its home in New York's City Hall so it could be redecorated and prepared for the new government's beginning. On October 10, the old Congress transacted its last official busi-

*This imaginative scene of President-elect Washington's trip from Virginia to New York City for his inauguration reveals much about the popular adulation he encountered as well as the different political roles of men and women.*

ness and adjourned *sine die.* Before doing so, it set March 4, 1789, as the day for the new Congress to assemble.

Inaugural day was April 30. Shortly after noon, on a small balcony overlooking a Wall Street thronged with people, Washington took the oath of office. "It is done," exulted New York's chancellor, Robert Livingston. "Long live George Washington, President of the United States!" With the crowd roaring approval and 13 guns booming in the harbor, the president bowed his way off the balcony and into Federal Hall. The rest of the day and late into the night, celebrations filled the air.

Great hopefulness and excitement surrounded the new government's beginning. But its first weeks were not easy, for so much had to be done and so many decisions had to be made. It seemed especially important that the government start on a proper, republican footing. "Many things which appear of little importance in themselves and at the beginning," the president warned, "may have great and durable consequences from their having been established at the commencement of a new general government."

When Washington decided to address the Congress, republican purists complained that it smacked too much of the English monarch's speech from the throne at the opening of Parliament. His appearance, moreover, confronted Congress with the question of how it should address the president in its reply and thus opened the sensitive issue of using titles in a republican government. Some congressmen pointed out that state governors and foreign ambassadors carried the title of "Excellency" and argued that the American president deserved a more exalted title than that. Vice-president Adams proposed "His Most Benign Highness." Others offered the even gaudier suggestion: "His Highness, the President of the United States, and Protector of the Rights of the Same." Both generated howls of outrage from those who thought titles had no place in a republic.

In the end, republican principles prevailed, and Congress settled on the simple and now familiar "Mr. President." But not before the House and Senate had spent days debating the matter. During these early years, every decision, no matter how trivial, seemed filled with significance, for people believed they were setting the direction and character of the new government for years to come. That belief gave special intensity to the politics of the time.

### The Bill of Rights

Among the new government's first items of business were the amendments that several states had made conditions of their ratification. The government's supporters were eager to keep their promise that this would be done, because it would reassure the fearful, weaken calls for a second constitutional convention, and build support for the new regime. After considerable debate, Congress reached agreement on 12 amendments and sent them on to the states, which ratified ten of them. These ten became the Bill of Rights. Among other things, they guaranteed freedom of speech, press, and religion; pledged the right of trial by jury, the right to bear arms, and the right to due process of law; and forbade both "unreasonable searches and seizures" and compulsion to testify against oneself in criminal cases. These constitutional amendments have protected individuals' basic rights throughout the nation's history.

During its first months in office, Washington's administration enjoyed almost universal support, both in the Congress and among the people. The honeymoon, however, did not last long. Within a year, as the administration's policies took shape, differences sprang up as people moved into opposition on a variety of issues and for a variety of reasons. By the middle of the decade, opposition groups came together in a political coalition known as the Jeffersonian Republicans. As they did, the administration's remaining supporters rallied under the name of Federalists. By 1800, the Federalists were so reduced in number and so badly divided that their Jeffersonian opponents gained control of the government. The political conflict of this first decade revealed the fragility but also the resilience of this new government.

### The People Divide

Disagreement began in June 1790, when Secretary of the Treasury Alexander Hamilton submitted the first of several major reports, the "Report on the Public Credit," to the Congress. Seldom in the nation's history has a single official so dominated public affairs as did Hamilton during these first years. He was a man of extraordinary intelligence and ambition who preferred not to seek elective office but to act behind the scenes, where he could shape events beyond the public eye. His instincts for locating and seizing the levers of political power were unerring.

Hamilton was a nationalist and a proponent of America's economic development. Perhaps more clearly than anyone else among the nation's founders, he foresaw the country's future strength and was determined to promote its growth. The United States, he was fond of saying, was "a Hercules in the cradle." Domestic manufacturing and overseas commerce, he believed, were the ways to promote America's economic development and build national wealth. Competitive self-interest he thought the

*Alexander Hamilton used both the office of secretary of the treasury and his personal relationship with President Washington to shape national policy during the 1790s.*

surest guide to behavior, whether of nations or individuals.

The proper role of the new government, he argued, was to promote economic enterprise. The people he most admired were men of wealth, ambitious entrepreneurs eager to tie their own fortunes to America's rising empire. Hamilton regarded a close alliance between these people and government officials as essential to achieving American greatness.

If Hamilton's economic policies were liberal in looking forward to enhanced economic opportunity, his politics were profoundly conservative. He had supported the colonies' break with England and had served meritoriously in the Revolutionary War. But he continued to be deeply impressed with England's political system, especially the stability of the monarchy and the confident governing style of the upper class. At bottom, Hamilton distrusted the people. He doubted their wisdom and feared their purposes. "The people," he asserted, "are turbulent and changing; they seldom judge or determine right." That stark belief guided much of what he did.

In the Philadelphia convention, Hamilton had urged that power be concentrated in the hands of the "rich and well-born" so that they could "check the unsteadiness" of the people. When the convention rejected his proposal for a Senate and president elected for life, Hamilton withdrew, persuaded that the convention would fail. The Constitution that emerged he thought not "high-toned" enough to meet the crisis in the nation's affairs. But he believed it was a considerable improvement over the Confederation and worked hard for its ratification. With that accomplished, he set about to find ways of giving it proper direction. His opportunity came when Washington named him secretary of the treasury. Recognizing the potential importance of his office, he determined to use it to build the kind of nation he thought America should be.

Hamilton's objectives were five: to stabilize the government's finances and establish its credit; to demonstrate its power; to tie the interests of the rich and wellborn to the national government; to promote the country's commercial expansion overseas and its economic development at home; and to anchor the nation's foreign relations in a commercial and diplomatic

alliance with England. All were essential to the nation's survival; each, in his own mind, was closely tied to the others.

In his first "Report on the Public Credit," submitted to Congress in January 1790, Hamilton recommended funding the remaining Revolutionary War debt by enabling the government's creditors to exchange their badly depreciated securities at full face value for new interest-bearing government bonds. The foreign debt, held chiefly in France and the Netherlands, Hamilton set at $11.7 million. The domestic debt, including back interest, he fixed at $40.4 million. Second, he proposed that the federal government assume responsibility for the $21.5 million in remaining state war debts. In all of this, he hoped to revive confidence in the government at home and abroad and tie business and commercial interests, which held most of the outstanding securities, firmly to the new government.

The proposal to fund the foreign debt aroused little controversy, but Hamilton's plans for handling the government's domestic obligations generated immediate opposition. In the House, James Madison protested the unfairness of funding depreciated securities at their face value, especially since speculators, anticipating Hamilton's proposals, had bought most of them up at a fraction of their initial worth. In addition, Madison and many of his southern colleagues knew that northern businessmen held most of the securities and that funding would bring little benefit to the South.

Hamilton was not impressed. The speculators, he observed, "paid what the commodity was worth in the market, and took the risks." They should therefore "reap the benefit." If his plan served the interests of the wealthy, that bothered him little; indeed, it was exactly as he intended, for it would further strengthen the tie between wealth and national power. After a bit of grumbling, Congress firmly endorsed the funding plan.

Federal assumption of the remaining state debts, another important part of Hamilton's program, aroused even greater criticism. States with the largest remaining unpaid obligations, such as Massachusetts, thought assumption a splendid idea. But others, such as Virginia and Pennsylvania, which had already retired much of their debt, were not eager to help cover others' indebtedness as the assumption scheme demanded. Critics also pointed out that assumption would strengthen the central government at the expense of the states, for wealthy individuals would now look to it rather than the states for a return on their investments. Moreover, the federal government, with its increased need for revenue, would now have reason to exercise its newly acquired power of taxation. That was exactly what Hamilton intended.

Once again, Congress supported Hamilton's bill. Both Madison and Jefferson approved it as part of an agreement to move the seat of government from New York, first to Philadelphia and then, after 1800, to a special federal district on the Potomac River. Southerners, disturbed by the early growth of federal power, hoped that locating the government away from northern commercial centers would enable them to control its development and keep it more closely aligned with southern, agrarian interests.

Despite this congressional agreement, opposition to the funding and assumption scheme did not die, especially in the southern states. In December 1790, the Virginia assembly passed a series of resolutions, framed by that old republican Patrick Henry, warning that a monied aristocracy was taking control of the government, that agriculture was being subordinated to commerce, and that the government's powers were expanding dangerously. Nothing in the Constitution, the assembly protested, authorized Congress to assume the states' debts. Hamilton wrote privately to a friend upon hearing of the Virginia resolutions: "This is the first symptom of a spirit which must either be killed, or will kill the Constitution." The contest for control of the new government was now clearly joined.

In December 1790, Hamilton introduced the second phase of his financial program when he proposed a national bank capable of handling the government's financial affairs and pooling private investment capital for economic development. Though he was careful not to mention it publicly, he had the example of the Bank of England and its ties with the royal government clearly in mind.

Congressional opposition to the bank was largely sectional. Only one vote was cast against it by a northern delegate; all the others came from the South. It seemed obvious that the bank would serve far better the needs of northern merchants and manufacturers than of southern agrarians. In February 1791, Congress approved the bank bill.

Before signing it, Washington asked his cabinet for their advice. Following the constitutional doctrine of "implied powers"—the principle that the government possessed the authority to make any laws "necessary and proper" for exercising the tasks granted to it—Hamilton argued that Congress could charter such a bank under its power to collect taxes and regulate trade. Secretary of State Jefferson, however, disagreed and urged the president to veto the bill. He saw in Hamilton's argument a blueprint for the indefinite expansion of federal authority and argued instead that the Constitution should be narrowly construed and the government allowed only those powers specifically granted to it. Since the Constitution said nothing at all about chartering banks, the bill was unconstitutional and should be rejected.

*Overcoming opposition led by Secretary of State Jefferson, Hamilton secured congressional approval of a national bank in 1791. The first bank building was erected in Philadelphia four years later.*

Jefferson also opposed the bank because he feared the rapid development of commerce and domestic manufacturing that the bank was intended to promote. He opposed Hamilton's goal of a commercial republic filled with merchants and a dependent laboring class and sought instead an agrarian republic populated by yeoman farmers committed to economic and political equality. Only among agrarians, "the chosen people of God," could republican liberty be sustained. To Jefferson's distress, Washington followed Hamilton's advice and signed the bank bill into law.

In December 1790, in his second "Report on the Public Credit," Hamilton broached the issue of federal taxation. He proposed a series of excise taxes, including one on the manufacture of distilled liquor. By this so-called Whiskey Tax he

*The revolutionary generation found inspiration in the republican eras of ancient Greece and Rome. This bust of Thomas Jefferson was completed in 1789 by the French sculptor Jean-Antoine Houdon.*

intended both to signal the government's intention to use its new taxing authority and to increase federal revenue. The power to tax and spend, Hamilton knew, was the power to govern. The Whiskey Tax became law in March 1791.

Finally, in his "Report on Manufactures," issued in December 1791, Hamilton called for a system of protective tariffs for American industry, bounties to encourage the expansion of commercial agriculture, and a network of federally sponsored internal improvements such as roadways and lighthouses. These were intended to stimulate commerce and bind the nation more tightly together. Hamilton's economic program had now been fully presented.

All the while, criticism of it continued to grow. In October 1791, opposition leaders in Congress established a newspaper, the *National Gazette*, and mounted increasingly vigorous attacks on the administration's program. Hamilton responded with a series of anonymous articles in the administration's paper, *The Gazette of the United States*, in which he directly attacked his cabinet colleague, Jefferson, accused him (inaccurately) of having opposed the Constitution, and charged him (also inaccurately) of fomenting opposition to the government. Alarmed at the division within his administration, Washington pleaded unsuccessfully for restraint.

Congressional criticism of Hamilton's policies reached a climax in January 1793 when Representative William Branch Giles of Virginia introduced a series of resolutions calling for an inquiry into the condition of the Treasury, accusing Hamilton of using the office for his own benefit, and urging censure of the secretary's conduct. Hamilton vigorously defended both his policies and his personal conduct, and none of Giles's accusations passed the House. The monthlong debate, however, showed just how embittered political discourse at the seat of government had already become.

The debate was now spreading beyond the circle of governing officials in Philadelphia. Among ordinary Americans, Hamilton's financial program drew a mixed response. In northern towns and cities, artisans and other working people generally approved. Tied closely to the expansion of commerce and manufacturing, they supported efforts to improve credit and stimulate economic development. With their own economic circumstances improving, they seemed undisturbed by the special benefits that funding, assumption, and the bank brought to a few. Within several years, many of them would move into political opposition, but for the moment their support of the government was secure.

### The Whiskey Rebellion

The farmers of western Pennsylvania provided the most dramatic expression of popular discontent with government policies. Its focus was the Whiskey Tax. Ever since the trouble with England 30 years before, Americans had been sensitive to the issue of taxation and suspicious of its connections with governmental power. The farmers of western Pennsylvania had special reason to dislike this particular tax. Their livelihood depended on their ability to transport surplus grain eastward across the mountains to market. To ship it in bulk was prohibitively expensive, so they distilled the grain and moved it in the more cost-efficient form of whiskey.

Hamilton's tax threatened to make this practice unprofitable. He knew that but cared little what the farmers thought; the government needed revenue, and the farmers would have to bear the cost. George Clymer, federal supervisor of revenue for Pennsylvania, was equally unsympathetic to the farmers and their situation. Referring to the "moral and personal weakness" of the "lesser folk," Clymer publicly castigated the "sordid shopkeepers" who retailed Pennsylvania whiskey and the "greatly depraved" farmers who produced it. The farmers resented the Federalists' arrogance as much as the tax and quickly made their resentment known.

Trouble was brewing by the summer of 1792 as angry farmers and their supporters gathered in mass meetings across western Pennsylvania. In August, a convention at Pittsburgh drew up a series of resolutions denouncing the tax and declaring that the people would prevent its collection. The convention's pronouncements echoed the Anti-Federalists' arguments against the Constitution. They had warned that once the central government secured the power to tax, a swarm of excise officers would descend like locusts on the people, consuming their property and offering nothing in return. If given the chance, one Anti-Federalist had warned, the central government would "monopolize every source of revenue [and] . . . demolish the state governments." To Pennsylvania's farmers, those predictions rang true. Like opponents of the Stamp Act in 1765, they decided that repression would follow if resistance did not soon begin.

Alarmed by the convention's resolutions, Washington quickly issued a proclamation warning against such "unlawful" gatherings and insisting on the enforcement of the excise. As tax collections began, the farmers took more direct action. They complained not only about the excise but also about the requirement that persons charged with evading the tax must stand trial in federal court. This seemed further evidence of the government's efforts to intimidate its critics. Moreover, the nearest federal court was hundreds of miles away, over the mountains, in Philadelphia.

In July 1794, federal marshal David Lennox, in company with John Neville, a local excise inspector, attempted to serve papers on several western farmers commanding their appearance in court at Philadelphia. An angry crowd gathered and stood in the way. Soon 500 armed men surrounded Neville's home just outside Pittsburgh and, in a scene that echoed the Stamp Act riots of 1765, demanded that he resign his commission. Learning that Neville had left, they ordered the dozen soldiers trapped in the house to lay down their arms and come out. Fearing for their safety, the soldiers refused, and for several hours the two sides exchanged rifle fire. After several men had been wounded, the soldiers finally surrendered, whereupon Neville's house was put to the torch. Similar episodes involving angry crowds, liberty poles, and placards carrying such slogans as "Liberty and No Excise. O Whiskey!" erupted across the state.

Alarmed that the protests might spread through the entire whiskey-producing backcountry stretching from New York to Georgia,

Washington issued another stern proclamation ordering the insurgents home and calling out troops from Pennsylvania and the surrounding states to restore order. For more than a year, Hamilton had been urging the use of force against the protestors. He viewed the insurrection not as evidence of an unjust policy needing change but as a test of the administration's ability to govern. Firmly suppressing the rebellion, Hamilton explained, "will do us a great deal of good and add to the solidity of everything in this country." He eagerly volunteered to accompany a federal army west.

In late August, a force of nearly 13,000 men, larger than the average strength of the continental army during the Revolutionary War, moved toward western Pennsylvania. At its center was Colonel William McPherson's "Pennsylvania Blues," an upper-class and strongly Federalist cavalry regiment. At its head rode the president of the United States and the secretary of the treasury. Washington soon returned to Philadelphia, persuaded by his aides of the danger to his safety, but Hamilton pressed ahead. When later criticized for accompanying the army to Pittsburgh, he replied that he had "long since . . . learned to hold public opinion of no value." The battle that Hamilton had anticipated, however,

never materialized, for as the federal army approached, the "Whiskey Rebels" dispersed, their two chief leaders, David Bradford and James Marshall, fleeing for safety across the Ohio River. The federal army managed to take 20 prisoners. Two were convicted of high treason and sentenced to death. Later, in a calmer mood, Washington pardoned them both.

As people quickly realized, the "Whiskey Rebellion" had never threatened the government's safety. "An insurrection was announced and proclaimed and armed against," Jefferson scoffed, "but could never be found." Hamilton, he charged, was merely pursuing his "favorite purpose of strengthening government" under "the sanction of a name [Washington's] which has done too much good not to be sufficient to cover harm also." Even as ardent a Federalist as Fisher Ames was uneasy at the sight of federal troops marching against American citizens. Though a government "by overcoming an unsuccessful insurrection becomes stronger," he noted, "elective rulers can scarcely ever employ the physical force of a democracy without turning the moral force, or the power of public opinion, against the government." Americans would soon have additional reason to ponder Ames's warning.

*President Washington and Secretary of the Treasury Hamilton led a federal army of nearly 13,000 into the whiskey-producing region of western Pennsylvania in 1794. Rebelling farmers, protesting the government's excise tax on whiskey, dispersed as the army approached.*

# THE REPUBLIC IN A THREATENING WORLD

During the 1790s, because the nation was so new and the outside world so threatening, issues of foreign policy generated extraordinary excitement. This was especially so after the tumultuous events of the French Revolution and the accompanying European war burst upon the international scene. In the arguments over the revolution in France and its implications for the new American republic, the American people revealed once again how sharply they differed in values and beliefs.

## The Promise and Peril of the French Revolution

France's revolution began in 1789 as an effort to reform an arbitrary monarchy weakened by debt and administrative decay. Pent-up demands for social justice, however, quickly outran the initial attempts at moderate, constitutional reform. By the early 1790s, France was embroiled in a genuinely radical social revolution. In January 1793, the monarch, Louis XVI, was beheaded. While the rest of Europe watched in horror and fascination, the forces of revolution and reaction struggled in bloody encounter for the nation's soul.

As the revolution grew and extended its attack upon the aristocracy, the monarchy, and the Catholic church, the forces of conservatism across the continent gathered in opposition, their fears fueled by the appeals of French aristocrats who had fled their homeland for safety. Finding itself surrounded and facing assault by Austria and Prussia, France's revolutionary government launched a series of military thrusts into Belgium and Prussia. The result was a general declaration of war. By the end of 1793, Europe was locked in a deadly struggle between revolutionary France and a counterrevolutionary coalition led by Prussia and Great Britain.

For more than a decade, the French Revolution dominated European affairs. Before it was finished, it would transform the entire course of European history. The revolution cut like a ploughshare through the surface of American politics as well, dividing Americans more deeply

against each other. Not only did it raise immediate threats to the nation's security, but it also captured people's imaginations and polarized the debate over what the American republic should be.

The outbreak of European war posed a number of thorny problems for Washington's administration. Both England and France wanted access to America's raw materials and were determined to prevent them from reaching the other. American merchants, on the other hand, were eager to profit from trade with both sides. According to international law, neutral nations in time of war could continue to trade with belligerent powers, as long as it did not involve goods directly related to the war effort. Neither France nor England, however, was willing to tie itself down with legal formalities when locked in deadly combat. So both nations attempted to control American trade for their own advantage by stopping American ships headed for the other's ports and confiscating American cargoes.

America's relations with England were further complicated by its practice of impressing American sailors into service aboard ships of the Royal Navy to meet its growing demand for seamen. Washington faced the problem of upholding the country's neutral rights and protecting its citizens without getting drawn into the European war.

The government's dilemma was compounded by the old French alliance of 1778. If still in effect, it seemed to require the United States to aid France, much as France had assisted the American states a decade and a half before. Persons sympathetic to the French cause argued that America's commitment still existed. Others, however, fearing the consequences of American involvement and the political infection that closer ties with revolutionary France might bring, insisted that the old treaty had been dissolved when the French monarchy had been overthrown.

The American people's intense reaction to the European drama further complicated the situation. Though they were an ocean away, Americans followed France's revolution with fascination, for they believed they had an important stake in its outcome. At first, virtually everyone enthusiastically supported the revolution because it seemed an extension of their own struggle for liberty. Even the swing toward social revolution did not immediately dampen American enthusiasm.

By the mid-1790s, however, especially after France's revolutionary regime launched its attacks on organized Christianity, many Americans began to pull back in alarm. This certainly did not resemble their own revolution. What connection could there possibly be between the principles of 1776 and the chaos of revolutionary France? "There is a difference between the French and the American Revolution," insisted *The Gazette of the United States*. "In America no barbarities were perpetrated—no men's heads were stuck upon poles—no mangled ladies' bodies were carried thro' the streets in triumph. . . . Whatever blood was shed, flowed gallantly in the field." The writer ignored the harsh violence meted out by the supporters of monarchy in France and betrayed a selective memory of the character of America's revolution. But the differences were indeed profound.

For the Federalists, revolutionary France now symbolized social anarchy and threatened the collapse of the European order on which they believed America's commercial and diplomatic well-being depended. With increasing vigor, they castigated the revolution, championed England as the defender of European civilization, and sought ways of linking England and the United States more closely.

Many Americans, however, continued to support France. While decrying the revolution's excesses, they noted how deeply entrenched the forces of reaction had been and how difficult it was to root them out. Moreover, they retained the belief that republican liberty would ultimately emerge from the turmoil. Jefferson wrote that while he regretted the shedding of innocent blood, he believed it necessary if true liberty was to be achieved. John Bradford, editor of the *Kentucky Gazette*, declared, "Instead of reviling the French republicans as monsters, the friends of royalty in this country should rather admire their patience in so long deferring the fate of their perjured monarch, whose blood is . . .

considered . . . atonement for the safety of many guilty thousands that are still suffered to remain in the bosom of France." In Bradford's judgment, England was not a bastion of order but the defender of arbitrary privilege and despotic government.

## Citizen Genêt and the Democratic-Republican Societies

Popular associations known as the Democratic-Republican societies offered most vocal support for revolutionary France. As early as 1792, ordinary citizens had begun to establish "constitutional societies" for the purpose of "watching over the rights of the people, and giving an early alarm in case of governmental encroachments." During the government's first years, several dozen such societies formed to oppose Hamilton's financial program. Modeling themselves on the Sons of Liberty (see Chapter 5), they kept their membership secret, appealed to the people for support, and established networks of correspondence.

It was the French Revolution, however, that kindled democratic enthusiasm and stimulated the societies' growth. The arrival in April 1793 of Citizen Edmund Genêt, minister from the French republic to the United States, provided the spark. Genêt landed first at Charleston, South Carolina, to a tumultuous reception. His instructions were to woo public support and negotiate a commercial treaty with Washington's administration. It quickly became evident, however, that he had other plans as well. Immediately after his arrival in Charleston, he began commissioning American privateers to prey on British shipping in the Caribbean and enlisting American seamen for expeditions against Spanish Florida, a clear violation of American neutrality.

As he traveled northward toward Philadelphia, Genêt met enthusiastic receptions all along the way. His popularity, though, soon led him beyond the bounds of diplomatic propriety. When, at Washington's insistence, Secretary of State Jefferson warned Genêt that granting military commissions infringed American sovereignty and must stop, he threatened to appeal over the president's head to the people. In open defiance of diplomatic protocol, he urged Congress to reject Washington's recently issued neutrality proclamation and side with revolutionary France. That was the final straw. On August 2, the president demanded Genêt's recall, charging that his conduct threatened "war abroad and anarchy at home."

If Genêt had little success as a diplomat, he did fan popular enthusiasm for revolutionary France. In June 1793, with his open encouragement, the largest and most influential of the new societies, the Democratic Society of Pennsylvania, was founded in Philadelphia. It called immediately for the formation of similar societies elsewhere to join in supporting France and promoting "the spirit of freedom and equality" at home. People across the land, it declared, should join in the effort everywhere to "erect the temple of *liberty* on the ruins of palaces and thrones." Washington and his colleagues might wonder if that challenge was also aimed at them.

Although a full network of popular societies never developed, about 40 organizations scattered from Maine to Georgia sprang up during the next several years. Federalist critics derided their members as "the lowest orders of mechanics, laborers and draymen . . . butchers, tinkers, broken hucksters, and trans-Atlantic traitors." Working people—mechanics, artisans and laborers in the cities, small farmers and tenants in the countryside—did provide the bulk of membership. The leaders, however, were individuals of acknowledged "respectability," such as doctors, lawyers, tradesmen, and landowners. They were united by a common dedication to what they called the "principles of '76" and a determination to preserve those principles against the "royalizing" tendencies of Washington's administration.

Lamenting the decline of republicanism, the societies worked actively for its reinvigoration. They organized public celebrations of the nation's birth, printed circulars, issued addresses to the people, and framed petitions to the president and Congress, almost all sharply critical of administration policies. They labeled Washington's Neutrality Proclamation a "pusillanimous truckling to Britain, despotically conceived and unconstitutionally promulgated." Neutrality toward England and revolutionary France, they

insisted, was impossible, for if Britain should succeed in Europe, America would again feel its wrath. Declared the New York society: "We firmly believe that he who is an enemy to the French revolution cannot be a firm republican; and therefore . . . ought not to be entrusted with the guidance of any part of the machine of government." Several of the societies openly urged the United States to enter the war on France's behalf.

The local societies took up other issues as well. In western areas they agitated against the continuing British occupation of the frontier posts and berated Spain for closing the Mississippi. In the East they castigated England for its "piracy" against American shipping. In the Carolinas they demanded fuller representation for the growing backcountry in the state's assembly. And almost to a person they protested the

*Heralded as the first president and worshiped by later generations, George Washington left office in 1796 amid vicious criticism.*

Excise Tax, opposed the administration's overtures to England, and demanded that public officials, state and federal alike, attend to the people's wishes.

Finally, they campaigned for a press free from the political control of Federalist "aristocrats." "The greater part of the American newspapers," they protested, "seem to be lock, stock, and barrel in the hands of the anti-democrats." Declared William Manning, a Massachusetts farmer who had marched to the "Concord fight" in 1775 and continued to praise the principles for which he had then fought: "A labouring man may as well hunt for pins in a haymow as to try to collect the knowledge necessary for him to have from such promiscuous piles of contradictions" as appeared in the Federalist press.

President Washington and his supporters reacted with alarm to such attacks. They were incensed by the societies' unwavering support of Genêt and their criticism of the government's domestic program. The "real design" of the societies, thundered the staunch Federalist Fisher Ames, was "to involve the country in war, to assume the reins of government and tyrannize over the people." As "nurseries of sedition," they were bent on revolutionizing America as the Jacobins had revolutionized France. Writing in the *Virginia Chronicle* of January 17, 1794, "Xantippe" berated Kentucky's Democratic Society as "that horrible sink of treason, that hateful synagogue of anarchy, that odious conclave of tumult, that frightful cathedral of discord, that poisonous garden of conspiracy, that hellish school of rebellion and opposition to all regular and well-balanced authority!" Such polemics illustrated how inflamed public discourse had become.

To Washington's supporters, the critics seemed dangerous radicals intent on importing social revolution and spreading it across the land. In turn, those critics, now beginning to coalesce under the name of Jeffersonian Republicans, attacked the Federalists as defenders of special privilege, as antirepublicans eager to return the United States to monarchy and subject it once again to British control. The language of political attack on both sides was wildly exaggerated, but in the volatile political climate of the 1790s, when the nation was new and its very survival seemed on the line, it was easy to believe the worst of one's opponents.

### Jay's Controversial Treaty

Controversy over Jay's treaty with England further heightened tensions at mid-decade. Alarmed by the worsening relations with England, Washington sent John Jay to London in the spring of 1794 with instructions to negotiate on a wide range of troublesome issues. Ever since the American Revolution, tension had been building over continued British occupation of the western posts and the failure of England to honor other clauses in the peace treaty of 1783. British interference with American neutral shipping and impressment of American seamen added to the rising tide of anti-English sentiment.

Early in 1795, Jay returned home with a treaty that resolved almost none of America's grievances. England finally agreed to vacate the western posts, but not for another year and then only if it had uninterrupted access to the fur trade. Jay also failed to secure compensation for American slaves carried off by the British at the end of the Revolution. Nor would the British foreign minister offer guarantees against the future impressment of American seamen. England refused as well to compromise on the issue of neutral rights, in effect declaring that it would decide what America's rights would be. Finally, England declined to open the West Indies to American shipping.

When the terms of the treaty were made public, they triggered an explosion of protest. The administration's pleas that the agreement headed off an open breach with England and was the best that could be obtained failed to pacify the critics. In New York City, Hamilton was stoned when he defended the treaty at a noonday mass meeting. The "rabble," sniffed a Federalist newspaper, attempted "to knock out Hamilton's brains to reduce him to an equality with themselves." Southern planters were angry because the agreement brought no compensation for their slaves. Westerners complained that the British were not evacuating the posts, while merchants and sailors railed against Jay's capitulation on the West Indies trade and impress-

# RECOVERING THE PAST

The questions that historians ask are limited only by their imagination and the historical evidence left behind for them to study. We have seen how historians use different kinds of written evidence—household inventories and political documents—as well as material artifacts such as tombstones and house designs. They also use artistic visual evidence like paintings and sculptures, for these too can provide insights into the life and culture of the past. With the proper mixture of care and ingenuity, historians can often tease surprising amounts of information out of materials that at first glance seem silent and unrewarding.

Paintings, for example, offer unique insights into the past. They can tell us most obviously about the history of art itself, the development over time of artistic styles and techniques. Paintings also offer a window into the past for cultural and social historians. They reveal how people lived and looked, what the landscape was like, and what the dominant values and attitudes of the time were.

The paintings of the Revolutionary era, for example, celebrated patriotic values of the war for independence and the heroic wisdom of the founding fathers. John Trumbull, Gilbert Stuart, and Charles Willson Peale all sought to reflect and inspire patriotism and national pride in their paintings of the great moments and great men of the Revolutionary generation. In 1776, Congress commissioned Peale to do a portrait of George Washington. As a member of the Pennsylvania militia, Peale carried paintbrushes and canvases along with his musket as he followed Washington throughout the war. Before it was over, he had done five paintings of the general. We see here a portrait done in 1776 at a point when the war was not going particularly well for the Patriot cause. How would you describe the Washington in this painting—is he conquered or confident, pursued or proud, hassled or heroic?

The art of the early national era was no less celebratory and patriotic. The second piece displayed here is an engraving by Enoch G. Gridley. Its title, *Mourning Piece for George Washington*, and its in-

*Charles Willson Peale*, George Washington, *1776*

251a

scription, "Sacred to the Memory of the truly Illustrious," tell us much about it. Although Washington left office in 1797 in a storm of controversy, when he died in 1799 the entire nation mourned his passing. During the first year after his death, countless sermons and eulogies praised his accomplishments and celebrated him as "the Father of his Country," a man "first in war, first in peace, and first in the hearts of his countrymen." Everywhere people organized memorial processions and decked themselves out in black crepe, gold mourning rings, and funeral medals. In New York, an enterprising bookseller named Mason Weems had a popular biography ready at the great hero's death, and this became an instant best-seller. Complete with invented accounts of the cherry tree episode and the story of Washington throwing a silver dollar across the Delaware River, by 1824 Weems's book had gone through 40 editions, with 40 more to follow.

Gridley's engraving was part of the mythologiz-

ing of Washington that occurred immediately after his death. Why do you think such exaggerated veneration of Washington took place? The artist has constructed his painting very carefully. Examine each element in the scene, and think about why it is there and what it is meant to show. What impression is the overall arrangement intended to convey? Do you think Washington is represented primarily as an American patriot, a Roman hero, or a medieval religious saint?

Examine further the classical and religious images in the painting. How many specifically religious symbols can you discover? How many classical ones? Notice the arch at the top: What do you think it represents? To what extent is Washington celebrated here as a military rather than a presidential figure? Notice the two grieving figures at the bottom of the painting: What do you think they represent and why were they chosen? What does the painting suggest about American attitudes toward women in 1810?

*Enoch G. Gridley,* **Mourning Piece for George Washington,** *1810*

251b

ment. After a long and acrimonious debate, the Senate finally ratified the treaty, but only by the narrowest of margins.

By mid-decade, political harmony had entirely disappeared, and the American people stood sharply divided on almost every significant issue of foreign and domestic policy. Frustrated by the president's increasing dependence on Hamilton and increasingly estranged from administration policy, Jefferson resigned as secretary of state in July 1793. He soon joined politicians such as Madison and Albert Gallatin of Pennsylvania in open opposition to the Federalist administration. By 1796, the cabinet contained only the most ardent Federalists.

The presidential election that year reflected the political storms buffeting the nation. In 1792, Washington and Adams had been reelected without significant opposition; four years later, however, the situation had changed. In September, in what came to be called his Farewell Address, Washington announced that he would not accept a third term. He had long been contemplating retirement, for he was now 64 and was exhausted by the political controversy swirling about him. Even the Great Patriot was no longer immune to attack. The nadir of abuse came in July 1796 in an open letter published by that old revolutionary Thomas Paine in the Philadelphia *Aurora*. "As to you, sir," Paine fumed, "treacherous in private friendship . . . and a hypocrite in public life, the world will be puzzled to decide, whether you are an apostate or an imposter; whether you have abandoned good principles, or whether you ever had any." Seldom has an American president been subjected to such public abuse as was Washington during his final year in office.

## THE ADAMS PRESIDENCY

With Washington removed from the scene, the contest quickly narrowed to Vice-President Adams and Jefferson. Though Jefferson did not publicly oppose Adams, his followers campaigned on his behalf. Adams and Jefferson had once been comrades in the struggle for American independence; the election's outcome bound them together once again, but this time in a strained alliance. Adams received 71 electoral votes and was declared president. Jefferson came in second with 68 and, according to the practice then specified by the Constitution, became vice-president. The narrowness of Adams's majority—his enemies constantly reminded him that he was only "a President of three votes"—was a measure of the Federalists' weakness and the growing strength of the Jeffersonians. Adams later recalled his inaugural day. "A solemn scene it was indeed, and it was made more affecting by the presence of the General, whose countenance was as serene and unclouded as the day. He seemed to enjoy a triumph over me. Methought I heard him say, 'Ay! I am fairly out and you fairly in! See which of us will be the happiest.'" The answer to that was not long in coming.

*Washington's vice president, John Adams, was narrowly elected to the presidency in 1796. His administration was plagued by political turmoil.*

## War Crisis with France

Adams had no sooner taken office than he confronted a deepening crisis with France. Hoping to ease diplomatic relations between the two countries, Adams sent off a three-person commission to try to negotiate an accord.

When the commissioners arrived in Paris, three agents of the French foreign minister, Talleyrand, visited them and made it clear that the success of the negotiations depended on a prior loan to the French government and a $240,000 gratuity for them. The two staunchly Federalist commissioners, John Marshall and Charles Pinckney, indignantly rejected the demands and sailed home. The third commissioner, Elbridge Gerry, stayed behind, still hoping for an accommodation and alarmed by Talleyrand's intimation that if all the Americans left, France would declare war.

When Adams submitted a report to Congress on this so-called XYZ affair, Americans were outraged. The episode served the Federalists' purposes wonderfully well, and they made the most of it. Secretary of State Pickering urged an immediate declaration of war, while Federalist congressmen thundered against the insult to American honor and demanded action. "Millions for defense, but not one cent for tribute" became their rallying cry. Adams now found himself an unexpected hero. When he attended the theater in Philadelphia, audiences cheered themselves hoarse with cries of "Adams and Liberty!" Deeply caught up in the anti-French furor, the president lashed out at "enemies" both at home and abroad. In response to the countless petitions of support that flooded in, he warned that the country had never been in greater danger. "In the last extremity," he declared ominously, "we shall find traitors who will unite with the invading enemy and fly within their lines."

For the moment, the Republicans were in disarray. Publicly they deplored the French government's behavior and joined in pledges to uphold the nation's honor; they could do nothing else. But among themselves they talked with alarm about the Federalists' intentions. They had good reason for concern, because the Federalists quickly mounted a crash program to repel foreign invaders and roust out traitors in the country's midst.

## Alien and Sedition Acts

In May 1798, Congress created a Navy Department and called for the rapid development of a naval force to defend the American coast against French attack. In July, Congress unilaterally repealed the treaty of 1778, thus moving France and the United States closer to an open breach, and then approved a 10,000 man army.

*This Federalist cartoon from the late 1790s depicts Thomas Jefferson and Citizen Genèt trying to prevent the provisional army, led by Washington, from stopping the imagined invading French.*

(The Federalists' initial goal had been 50,000 men.) The army's mission was to defend the country against an expected French invasion. The Jeffersonians, however, feared otherwise. Given France's desperate struggle in Europe, its diversion of troops to North America seemed inconceivable. Moreover, memories of the speed with which the Federalists had used force against the Whiskey Rebels made the Jeffersonians wonder about the army's intended use now.

As criticism of the army bill mounted, Adams had second thoughts. He was still enough of an old revolutionary to worry about the domestic dangers of standing armies. The navy, he believed, should be America's first line of defense, and he ardently supported that part of the program. But the army alarmed him. "This damned army," he burst out, "will be the ruin of the country." Much to the dismay of the Federalists, he delayed its organization by issuing only a few of the officers' commissions that Congress had authorized. Without officers, the troops could not be mobilized.

Fearful of foreign subversion and aware that French immigrants were active in the Jeffersonian opposition, the Federalist-dominated Congress moved in the summer of 1798 to curb the flow of aliens into the country. The Naturalization Act extended from 5 to 14 years the residence requirement for citizenship, while the Alien Act authorized the president to expel "all such aliens as he shall judge dangerous to the peace and safety of the United States." Imprisonment and permanent exclusion from citizenship awaited individuals who were warned to leave but refused to go. Another bill, the Alien Enemies Act, empowered the president in time of war to arrest, imprison, or banish the subjects of any hostile nation without specifying charges against them or providing opportunity for appeal. The Federalist congressman Harrison Gray Otis explained that there was no need "to invite hordes of Wild Irishmen, nor the turbulent and disorderly of all parts of the world, to come here with a view to distract our tranquility. . . ."

The implications of these acts for basic political liberties were ominous, but the Federalists had not yet finished. In July 1798, Congress passed the Sedition Act, aimed directly at the Jeffersonian opposition. The bill made it a high misdemeanor, punishable by fine and imprisonment, for anyone, citizen or alien, to conspire in opposition to "any measure or measures of the government" or to aid "any insurrection, riot, unlawful assembly, or combination." Fines and imprisonment were provided as well for persons who "write, print, utter, or publish . . . any false, scandalous and malicious writing" having the effect of bringing the government, Congress, or president into disrepute.

The boldness of the Federalist moves stunned the Jeffersonians, for they threatened to smother political opposition. The Federalists left no room for doubts on the matter. With an open declaration of war, predicted Congressman James Lloyd of Delaware, "traitors and sedition mongers who are now protected and tolerated, would . . . be easily restrained or punished." The Federalists now equated preservation of their own political power with the nation's survival.

Under the terms of the Alien Act, Secretary of State Pickering began an elaborate system of investigations designed to force the registration of all foreigners. The act's chilling effects were widespread. In July, Pickering noted approvingly that large numbers of aliens, especially persons of French ancestry, were leaving the country. Several prosecutions were started, but the individuals involved went into hiding before they could be caught. Prosecutions under the Sedition Act were more numerous. Twenty-five individuals, including David Brown of Dedham, were arrested and charged with violating the act. Fifteen were indicted and ten were ultimately convicted, the majority of them Jeffersonian printers and editors.

### Local Reverberations

Luther Baldwin discovered how little it took even for ordinary people to get into trouble with the Federalist authorities. On July 27, 1798, President and Mrs. Adams passed through Newark, New Jersey, on their way from Philadelphia to their home in Quincy, Massachusetts. As the chief magistrate entered Broad Street around 11 o'clock that morning, he was greeted by the firing of cannon, the ringing of church bells, and the cheers of the citizenry. The president's entourage did not stop but continued through town, the cannon booming a final 16-gun salute as he left.

Not all Newark's residents shared in the moment's enthusiasm. Luther Baldwin happened to be coming toward John Burnett's dram shop when one of the tavern's customers, noting that the cannon continued to fire after the president had passed by, observed, "There goes the President and they are firing at his a——." According to the Newark *Centinel of Freedom*, Baldwin, being "a little merry" with drink, replied that "he did not care if they fired thro' his a——." At that point, the Federalist tavernkeeper cried out that Baldwin had spoken sedition, whereupon "a considerable collection gathered—and the . . . Federalists, being much disappointed that the president had not stopped that they might have had the honor of kissing his hand, bent their malice on poor Luther and the cry was, that he must be punished."

Within two months, the local grand jury indicted Baldwin on charges of sedition. The following year, he was hailed before the federal Circuit Court. After changing his plea from not guilty to guilty, Baldwin was convicted of speaking "seditious words tending to defame the President and Government of the United States," fined, assessed court costs, and committed to jail until both fine and fees were paid.

Baldwin's trial gave the local Jeffersonians a field day. The New York *Argus* confessed "astonishment . . . on hearing the peculiarity of the expressions for which so formal a trial was instituted. . . . Can the most enthusiastic Federalists and Tories suppose that those who are opposed to them would feel any justification in firing at such a disgusting target as the a—— of J. A.?" But the Jeffersonians saw danger as well in the Federalists' use of informers and their zealous overreaction. "When cognizance is taken of such a ridiculous expression," the *Argus* concluded, every Republican could see "the extraordinary malignancy of the federal faction."

Passage of the Alien and Sedition Acts generated a firestorm of protest. The Virginia and Kentucky assemblies challenged the Federalist laws most directly. The Kentucky Resolutions, drafted by Jefferson and passed on November 16, 1798, declared that the national government had violated the Bill of Rights. Faced with the arbitrary exercise of federal power, the resolutions continued, each state "has an equal right to judge by itself . . . infractions . . . [and] the mode and measure of redress." Nullification was the "rightful remedy" for unconstitutional laws. The Virginia Resolutions, authored by Madison and passed the following month, asserted that when the central government threatened the people's liberties, the states "have the right and are in duty bound to interpose for arresting the progress of the evil." It would not be the last time that state leaders would claim authority to set aside a federal law.

The Kentucky and Virginia resolutions received little support elsewhere. Neither state, moreover, attempted to obstruct enforcement of the acts. Still, the resolutions indicated the depth of popular opposition to the Federalists' program. As the Federalists pressed ahead, some Jeffersonians prepared for open conflict. The Virginia assembly called for the formation of a state arsenal at Harpers Ferry, reorganization of the militia, and a special tax to pay for these preparations. In Philadelphia, armed Federalist patrols walked the streets to protect government officials against angry crowds. The turmoil prompted President Adams to smuggle arms into his residence as a precaution. As 1799 began, the country seemed poised on the brink of upheaval.

Within a year, the cycle turned again, this time decisively against the Federalists. The break came with Adams's dramatic decision to send a new emissary to France. Adams's son, John Quincy Adams, was in Europe and sent his father assurances that Talleyrand, wishing to avoid war, was ready to negotiate an honorable accord. Adams seized the opening eagerly. He was alarmed at the political furor consuming the nation and feared that war with France "would convulse the attachments of the country." Opposition to the war program was spreading rapidly, even among some of the administration's supporters. "The end of war is peace," Adams explained, "and peace was offered me." Moreover, he had concluded that his only chance of reelection lay in fashioning a peace coalition out of both parties.

Adams's cabinet knew nothing of his inten-

*French foreign minister Talleyrand's willingness to negotiate with the United States enabled Adams to avert war in 1800, a decision that enraged extremists within Adams's own Federalist party.*

tions until he told them of the new mission. When they learned of it, they were enraged, for the entire war program depended on the credibility of the French crisis. When Secretary of State Pickering repeatedly ignored the president's orders to send the new commissioners on their way, Adams dismissed him and personally ordered the commissioners to depart. By year's end, they had secured an agreement releasing the United States from the 1778 alliance and providing for the restoration of peaceful relations between the two nations.

### The "Revolution of 1800"

As the election of 1800 approached, the Federalists were in political disarray. They had squandered the political advantage handed them by France in 1798 and now, with peace a reality, stood before the nation charged with the unconstitutional exercise of federal power, the suppression of political dissent, and the intention of using the federal army against American citizens. The Federalists never recovered.

The party, moreover, was bitterly divided. The Hamiltonians were furious at Adams's "betrayal" and demanded that he not seek reelection in 1800. The only chance for the Federalists' survival was for Adams to decline the presidency after his term ended. When Adams did not withdraw, the Hamiltonians plotted his defeat.

Emotions continued to run high as the election approached. Fisher Ames berated the Federalists' opponents as "fire-eating salamanders, poison-sucking toads," while the Jeffersonians returned the abuse in kind. Both sides fully believed that the republic's survival hung in the balance. The election, Jefferson declared, would "fix our national character" and "determine whether republicanism or aristocracy" would prevail. The Federalists saw the choice as between republicanism and "anarchy." In Virginia, rumors of a slave insurrection briefly interrupted the feuding. Only something that ominous could calm the political waters. But the scare passed quickly, and the Federalists and Jeffersonians were soon at each others' throats again.

Election day was tense throughout the nation but passed without serious interruption. As the results were tallied, it became clear that the Jeffersonians had handed the Federalists a decisive defeat. The presidential outcome was surprisingly close. When the electoral votes were counted, the two Republican candidates, Jefferson and the New Yorker Aaron Burr, each had 73, so tightly disciplined had the Jeffersonians become. Adams followed with 65. His peace initiative had been effective but was too late to overcome the excesses of the Federalists' war program.

Because of the tie vote, the election was thrown into the existing House of Representatives, where a deadlock quickly developed. In spite of considerable pressure from Jefferson's supporters, Burr refused to give way. The Federalist caucus decided to back Burr, believing him less of a Francophile than Jefferson and more sympathetic to Federalist principles. Hamilton, however, distrusted Burr intensely. Though he believed Jefferson dangerous, he was even more fearful of Burr's ambition. In part through Hamilton's bàckstairs maneuvering, the House finally elected Jefferson, ten states to four, on the thirty-sixth ballot. The magnitude of the Federalists' defeat was more evident in the congressional elections, where they lost their majorities in both House and Senate.

The election's outcome revealed the strong sectional divisions now evident in the country's politics. The Federalists remained dominant in New England because of regional loyalty to Adams, the importance of the area's commercial ties with England, and fears, fed by ministers and politicians alike, that the Jeffersonians intended to import social revolution. From Maryland south, Jeffersonian control was almost as complete. South Carolina was the exception. There, the white society's fears of the surrounding black majority smothered every tendency toward political division, and the Federalists remained solidly in control. But elsewhere, loyalty to Jefferson, strong anti-British and pro-

French sentiment, and suspicion of the commercially oriented Federalists kept power in the hands of the Jeffersonians.

In the middle states, Federalists and Jeffersonians were more evenly balanced, because economic and social differences in the mid-Atlantic region were greater and the issues of foreign and domestic policy cut across society in more complicated ways. As a result, political activity in these states was most intense, and the election most fiercely fought. This sectional pattern would remain permanently embedded in American politics.

The distinctions between Federalists and Jeffersonians, however, were grounded in social divisions as well. The Federalists were strongest among merchants, manufacturers, and commercial farmers located within easy reach of the coast—groups that had supported the Constitution in 1787 and 1788. "Here [in Connecticut] as everywhere," claimed one Federalist leader, "the men of talents, information, and property . . . are found among the Federalists." The Jeffersonians concurred with such claims. In his state, one Pennsylvanian conceded, the Federalists commanded the support of "everything that consid-

*Remembered later as the man who shot Alexander Hamilton in a duel in 1804, Aaron Burr came within a few votes of defeating Thomas Jefferson for the presidency in 1800.*

## Presidential Election of 1800

Electoral Votes for:

Jefferson (Republican)

Adams (Federalist)

Vote divided

ers itself a part of the natural aristocracy," including "nearly all the lawyers, nearly all the merchants, most of the patrons, [and] many of the physicians." In both New York City and Philadelphia, the Federalists were strongest in the wards where assessments were highest, houses largest, and addresses most fashionable.

The Jeffersonians drew their strength from different segments of the population. They counted most of the old Anti-Federalists among their numbers and found their major support among agriculturalists in both North and South. But they had significant support in urban areas as well. Their opposition to Federalist elitism, support for revolutionary France, and defense of republican liberty attracted countless urban workers and artisans, many of whom had once been staunch Federalists. They attracted as well individuals who felt threatened by the Federalists' domestic programs, people such as Irish and French immigrants and religious minorities—Baptists, Jews, and Catholics—restive under the lingering religious establishments.

The political alignment of 1800 resembled, but was not identical to, the Federalist–Anti-Federalist division from 1786 to 1789. The Jeffersonian coalition was much broader than the Anti-Federalists, had been, for it included countless individuals, from urban workers to leaders such as Madison and Jefferson, who had supported the Constitution and helped set the new government on its feet. Unlike the Anti-Federalists, the Jeffersonians were ardent supporters of the Constitution. They had no desire to return to the Articles; they sought instead the proper management of the new government, consistent with principles of liberty, political equality, and a strong dependence on state authority. Within the nation as a whole, the Jeffersonians now enjoyed a clear political majority. Their coalition would dominate American politics well into the nineteenth century.

## CONCLUSION: Toward the Nineteenth Century

The election of 1800 was a remarkable outcome to more than a decade of continuous political crisis. The series of events had begun in the late 1780s with the intensifying debate over the Articles of Confederation and the movement toward a stronger central government. Then had come the heated contest over ratification of the new Constitution. Scarcely had the new government gotten under way than divisions began to form, first within Congress, then, increasingly, among the people. Hamilton's domestic policies first generated opposition, but it was foreign affairs—the French Revolution, the European war, Jay's Treaty, and the prospect of a war with France—that galvanized political energies and set the Federalists and Jeffersonians adamantly against each other.

In 1800, control of the federal government passed for the first time from one political party to another, not easily but peacefully and in legal fashion. "The Revolution of 1800," the Jeffersonians called it—"as real a revolution in the principles of our government as that of 1776 was in its form." Only the future would show whether the Jeffersonians were correct. But for the moment the crisis had passed, the Federalists had been defeated, and the government was in new hands.

## Recommended Reading

The Philadelphia convention and new national constitution are examined in Gordon Wood, *The Creation of the American Republic, 1776–1787* (1969); Jackson T. Main, *The Anti-Federalists: Critics of the Constitution, 1781–1788* (1961); and Clinton Rossiter, *1787: The Grand Convention* (1961).

Important discussions of politics in the states during the heated decade of the 1790s include Alfred Young, *The Democratic Republicans of New York: The Origins, 1763–1797* (1967); Richard Beeman, *The Old Dominion and the New Nation, 1788–1801* (1972); Norman Risjord, *Chesapeake Politics, 1781–1800* (1978); and Paul Goodman, *The Democratic Republicans of Massachusetts* (1964).

For cogent discussions of the ideological debates between Federalists and Jeffersonians, see Joyce Appleby, *Capitalism and a New Social Order: The Republican Vision of the 1790s* (1984); Lance Banning, *The Jeffersonian Persuasion: The Evolution of a Party Ideology* (1978); and John Zvesper, *Political Philosophy and Rhetoric: A Study of the Origins of American Party Politics* (1977).

Party development during the 1790s can be followed in Noble Cunningham, *The Jeffersonian-Republicans: The Formation of Party Organization, 1789–1801* (1957); Richard Hofstadter, *The Idea of a Party System* (1970); William Nisbet Chambers, *Political Parties in a New Nation: The American Experience, 1776–1809* (1963); Joseph Charles, *The Origins of the American Party System* (1956); and Merrill Peterson, *Thomas Jefferson and the New Nation* (1970).

The Bill of Rights and the problem of civil liberties are treated by Bernard Schwartz, *The Great Rights of Mankind* (1977); James M. Smith, *Freedom's Fetters: The Alien and Sedition Laws and American Civil Liberties* (1956); and Leonard Levy, *Legacy of Suppression: Freedom of Speech and Press in Early American History* (1960).

For a fuller understanding of foreign policy issues, turn to Harry Ammon, *The Genêt Mission* (1973); Jerald Combs, *The Jay Treaty* (1970); Alexander DeConde, *Entangling Alliance: Politics and Diplomacy Under George Washington* (1958) and *The Quasi-War: The Politics and Diplomacy of the Undeclared War with France, 1797–1801* (1966); Felix Gilbert, *To the Farewell Address: Ideas of Early American Foreign Policy* (1961); and Bradford Perkins, *The First Rapprochement: England and the United States, 1795–1805* (1955).

## TIME LINE

|  |  |
|------|-------|
| 1786 | Annapolis Convention |
| 1787 | Constitutional Convention<br>*Federalist Papers* published by Hamilton, Jay, and Madison |
| 1788 | Constitution ratified |
| 1789 | George Washington inaugurated as first president<br>Outbreak of French Revolution |
| 1790 | Hamilton's "Reports on the Public Credit" |
| 1791 | Bill of Rights ratified<br>Whiskey Tax and national bank established |
| 1792 | Washington reelected |
| 1793 | Outbreak of war in Europe |
| 1794 | Whiskey Rebellion in Pennsylvania<br>Controversy over Citizen Genêt's visit |
| 1795 | Jay's treaty with England divides nation |
| 1796 | Washington's Farewell Address<br>John Adams elected president |
| 1797 | XYZ affair in France |
| 1798 | Naturalization Act; Alien and Sedition Acts<br>Virginia and Kentucky resolutions |
| 1799 | Trials of David Brown and Luther Baldwin |
| 1800 | Adams achieves "peace" with France<br>Jefferson elected president by House of Representatives |

# CHAPTER 9
## THE PREINDUSTRIAL REPUBLIC

In April 1795, Ben Thompson started north from Queen Anne's County, Maryland, for New York City. Since Ben knew little about making a living beyond farming, he first supported himself by common labor on the city's docks. Ben, however, was ambitious and resourceful. He listened carefully to the ships' captains who talked enthusiastically about life at sea while they recruited men for their crews. Ben was lucky, for he arrived in New York just as American overseas commerce, stimulated by renewed war in Europe, was entering a decade of unprecedented prosperity. Sailors were in demand, pay was good, and few questions were asked.

For five years, Ben sailed the seas. Several times his ship narrowly escaped capture by British and French men-of-war. Having enough of travel, he returned to New York, gathered his meager savings together, and hired out as an apprentice to a ship's carpenter.

About the same time, Phyllis Sherman left her home in Norwalk, Connecticut. She also headed for New York, where she took a job as a maid in the household of one of the city's wealthy merchants. As fate would have it, Phyllis and Ben met, fell in love, and, in the spring of 1802, were married.

There is little of note in all this, except that Ben and Phyllis were former slaves and were married in the new African Methodist Episcopal Zion Church. Ben had set aside his slave name, Cato, as a sign of his liberation, while Phyllis kept the name her master had given her. Ben was doubly fortunate, for his master had allowed him to buy his freedom and move north just as cotton production was beginning to spread through the Chesapeake region. In another few years, he would have faced greater trouble securing his freedom. Phyllis had been freed as a child when slavery ended in Connecticut. As she grew up, she tired of living as a servant with her former owner's family and longed for the companionship of other black people. She had heard that there were people of color in New York City, and she was correct. In 1800, it contained 6,300 blacks, more than half of them free.

Though life in New York was better than either Ben or Phyllis had known before, it was hardly easy. Along with most blacks, and many white families as well, they shared only marginally in the commercial prosperity and struggled just to get along. In 1804, they watched helplessly as yellow fever carried off their daughter and many of their friends. And while they found support in the expanding black community and solace in their church, they constantly encountered the disdain of the city's white majority. They had to be on guard, moreover, because slave ships still moved in and out of the port, and runaways from the South were pursued in the city's streets. New York still contained 2,800 slaves, a fact that constantly reminded them of their tenuous freedom.

Still, they persevered. All about them they heard white Americans talking about social equality and economic opportunity, and like other Americans, white as well as black, they struggled to understand what those words meant for them. Like others, Ben and Phyllis also tried to deal with the economic and social forces that were beginning to change their community. Though they scarcely understood it, they were living in a time of transition between two contrasting ways of life—the rural, preindustrial world of the eighteenth century and the increasingly urban, industrial world of nineteenth-century America.

During the nineteenth century, industrialization, urbanization, large-scale immigration, and westward expansion would revolutionize American economic and social life. These transformations and their consequences make up the essential story of nineteenth-century America. By 1820, the effects of economic and social change were already becoming evident, though they had not yet carried far enough to displace earlier ways of life. In economic and social affairs, as in government and politics, the years of the early republic were years of beginnings, of transitions between old ways of life and new. If we are to understand this nineteenth-century transformation, we must first understand the world that was transformed.

In this chapter, we first examine the underlying changes that between 1790 and 1820 began to remake American life. We turn next to a discussion of preindustrial society and how people lived within its distinctive regions and local communities. Finally, we examine the new ways in which the American people were beginning to think about their republican society and their first efforts at republican social reform.

## THE PREINDUSTRIAL ECONOMY

In early nineteenth-century America, most people went about their economic affairs much as their parents had done before them. The economy still depended on overseas trade, while agriculture, which occupied nearly 90 percent of the people, differed little from decades earlier. Change, however, was afoot: in commerce, where merchants began operating on a larger scale; in agriculture, where cotton became the South's new staple crop; and especially in manufacturing, where merchant capitalists began to reorganize industries and redefine the nature of work.

### The Return of Commercial Prosperity

On August 14, 1801, the merchant ship *Arabella*, captain Charles Adams in command, left New York bound for Liverpool, England. The hold of the *Arabella* was filled with a cargo of flour from Pennsylvania, tobacco from the Chesapeake, and sugar from the West Indies. Adams and his crew were uneasy as the coast dropped out of sight because the North Atlantic was a dangerous as well as profitable place for American merchantmen.

Both danger and profit arose from the same circumstance—European war. That had often been the case during the colonial period, given

Europe's insistent demand for America's staple commodities and the colonies' role as pawns in the European game of power politics. It was little different now that independence had been achieved.

We saw in Chapter 8 how powerfully the outbreak of European war in 1793 had affected American politics. It had equally important consequences for the economy. In 1790, the nation's merchants were still struggling to rebuild overseas trade to its pre-Revolution levels. By the end of the decade, however, American commerce was booming, and the country was in the midst of prosperity undreamed of but a few years before.

In part, the newfound prosperity stemmed from actions of the national government taken under the direction of Secretary of the Treasury Hamilton. He had quickly implemented his policies of funding and assumption to establish American credit and restore the confidence of investors, both foreign and domestic. The Federalists, moreover, worked hard to rebuild commercial ties with England, America's traditional trading partner.

Decisions made in the capitals of Europe, rather than in America, however, lay behind the country's surging commercial expansion. England and France, locked in deadly struggle, sought North America's raw materials, especially its foodstuffs and naval stores. Each was anxious to keep American goods out of the hands of the other. As Europe's war-induced demand for American commodities grew, the price of those goods increased. As prices rose, so did profits and so, in turn, did the willingness of American merchants to risk capture on the high seas.

According to established practice, neutral nations in time of war could trade with the belligerents as long as two conditions were met. First, the goods that were exchanged could not include arms or other war matériel; second, the trade connections must predate the outbreak of hostilities. American commerce met both those conditions. Both England and France, however, were determined to control America's trade for their own advantage. To back up that determination, each sent armed cruisers to prowl the Atlantic and intercept American merchant ships believed headed for the other's ports.

For nearly two decades following 1793, England and France continued their desperate struggle. The losses in American ships and cargoes during these years were alarmingly high and included the *Arabella*, which ran afoul of a British cruiser off southern France and was lost to its owners. The costs of doing business in the North Atlantic were further increased by escalating insurance rates and the high wages needed to lure American sailors into the risky trade.

The profits waiting for cargoes that got through, however, more than compensated for the risks. And so American exports surged upward, more than tripling in value between 1793 and 1807. These swollen trade earnings financed the importation of an increasing volume of European manufactured goods. Stimulated by this direct trade and the replacement of European ships by neutral American vessels throughout the Atlantic, American tonnage increased dramatically. By 1800, American bottoms were carrying 92 percent of all commerce between America and Europe. Between 1790 and 1808, ships sailing under American registry rose from 355,000 tons to over a million tons. The freight earnings from this expanded fleet added further to the country's newfound prosperity.

The main beneficiaries were the merchants who built the ships, gathered the cargoes, and

## Inflation of Wholesale Prices, 1788–1800

*Note:* 1821–1825 = 100
**Source:** U.S. Bureau of the Census.

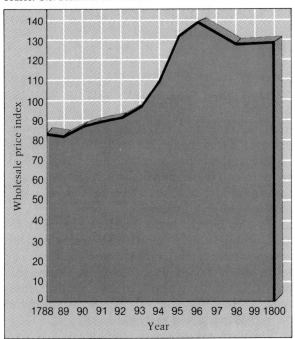

*Merchant ships, such as the one depicted in this 1800 scene of a bustling Philadelphia wharf, brought renewed prosperity during the 1790s.*

dispatched them to the waiting markets in Europe. As the nineteenth century began, men such as E. H. Derby of Salem, John Jacob Astor of New York, and Stephen Girard of Philadelphia were amassing impressive fortunes. But America's booming commerce benefited others as well, especially in the port cities, where nearly everyone was affected by overseas trade. The expansion of commerce stimulated insurance and banking activities, for ships had to be protected and financed. By 1800, some 33 insurance companies were in operation. State chartered banks proliferated even more rapidly.

The dramatic increase in commerce also brought the shipbuilding industry out of its long doldrums. Employment for rope and sail makers, ship carpenters, and metalsmiths boomed. Even sailors found advantage, for work was steady and wages high. As merchants' profits and the wages of artisans and other workers increased, so did their spendable income, and so, as a result, did the fortunes of tavernkeepers, grocers, and landlords.

Though America's surging prosperity was most evident in the port cities, its effects radiated into the countryside, where the cargoes of agricultural and forest goods and the provisions required by the ships' crews were produced. Not everyone benefited equally; some Americans—blacks, unskilled laborers, and others living at the bottom of society—did not benefit at all. But the nation as a whole was thriving. Not within living memory had times been so good.

In spite of the prosperity, however, escape from England's empire had not fundamentally changed the realities of American economic life. Its export trade continued to depend on European demand for America's raw materials. American consumers, moreover, still preferred English and European manufactured goods to cruder American products. As yet, the United States had insufficient population, investment capital, manufacturing capability, transportation systems, and levels of labor productivity to support its own internally generated economic development. Not until the second quarter of the nineteenth century would it finally escape this colonial-like dependence on Europe and develop the capacity for self-sustained economic growth.

While commerce continued in its traditional channels, a few merchants experimented with new forms of business organization, notably the use of incorporation. It had two chief advantages. First, a charter of incorporation from a state government often brought certain privileges with it, such as the exclusive right to carry on certain activities for a number of years or special tax incentives. Second, corporations could sell stock and thus accumulate capital for investment. Between 1776 and 1800, the states chartered some 300 commercial, banking, and manufacturing enterprises. That was a striking change from the eighteenth-century practice of reserving charters almost exclusively for towns, colleges, and philanthropic organizations.

Most merchants, however, still operated their business individually or in simple partnerships. Even the largest mercantile houses employed no more than a half dozen clerks. Moreover, they usually marketed their goods in familiar, informal ways. In New York, the merchant community developed a more centralized auction system for selling cargoes, but merchants elsewhere continued to depend on their own personal ties with wholesalers and shopkeepers.

As we shall see, many of the profits generated by the new prosperity would soon be used in new and innovative ways. The commercial activity that produced them, however, remained firmly rooted in the past.

## Agriculture in the North

During the early years of the republic, the vast majority of Americans drew their living from the land. In 1800, fully 83 percent of the labor force was engaged in agriculture; as late as 1820, that figure had hardly changed. For American farmers, the dimensions of economic life—planting and harvesting, buying and selling—remained largely unaltered.

In the North, many farmers produced an agricultural surplus, which they exchanged in nearby markets for commodities such as tea, sugar, window glass, or special tools. During the early nineteenth century, more agriculturalists came within the market's reach. In southern New England, along the Hudson River in New York, and in southeastern Pennsylvania, access to urban and even European markets stimulated production for commercial sale. In New England, where the soil was poor, farmers turned fields into pasture and switched to more profitable dairying and livestock raising. New York and Pennsylvania farmers cultivated the land more intensively, virtually ending the earlier practice of allowing worn-out fields a fallow period to recover their fertility. During the eighteenth century, the rural landscape had looked cluttered and unkempt, with areas still covered by timber and fallow lands lapsing back into brush. Now, however, the countryside was clean and orderly, with most of the fields under regular cultivation and their boundaries marked by permanent hedges or stone walls.

The wills and estate inventories of farmers around the turn of the century indicate that many of them enjoyed new comforts. After 1800, farm families were much more likely to possess table linens and china bowls, store-bought furniture and fancier clothes than 50 years before. But this prosperity was modest because agricultural opportunities remained limited. As the term *surplus* indicates, most farmers still took to market only what was left over after they had first met their family's needs. As late as 1820, no more than 25 percent of agricultural output was available for export. The rest was consumed on the country's farms or used in local exchange.

Custom dictated that farm families strive for self-reliance. "The great effort," reported a European traveler, "was for every farmer to produce anything he required within his own family; and he was esteemed the best farmer, to use a phrase of the day, 'who did everything within himself.'" Self-improvement meant primarily the acquisition of land rather than money or consumer goods. The goal of most farmers was to achieve a "pleasing competence" and transmit family farms intact to their children.

Across much of the country, cash still played only a small part in economic exchanges. "Instead of money going incessantly backwards and forwards into the same hands," declared an observant Frenchman in 1790, people "supply their needs in the countryside by direct reciprocal exchanges. The tailor and the bootmaker go and do the work of their calling at the home of the farmer . . . who most frequently provides the raw material for it and pays for the work in goods . . . They write down what they give and receive on both sides, and at the end of the year they settle a large variety of exchanges with a very small quantity of coin."

*An illustration from P. Campbell's* Travels in North America *(1793)* shows a newly cleared farm in the wilderness, complete with birchbark canoes carrying Indians and a white passenger to and fro on the adjoining river.

Most farms were not large. By 1800, the average size in the longer-settled areas of New England and the Middle Atlantic states was no more than 100 to 150 acres, down substantially from 50 years before. Even the cargoes of wheat exported from Philadelphia and Baltimore came from the surpluses of small producers, not from large-scale farmers.

Northern farms were not only small but limited in productivity as well, even in southeastern Pennsylvania, probably the richest and most productive area in the North. Unlike New England, where settlement had concentrated in town centers and farmers worked in the surrounding fields, the people of southeastern Pennsylvania lived on isolated farmsteads. A combination of circumstances contributed to their prosperity: the people's industriousness, fertile and well-watered lands, a lengthy growing season, and a growing demand for wheat in Philadelphia and abroad. In spite of the slowness and high costs of wagon transport, grain from as far inland as 100 miles found its way profitably to market. There were few persons of real wealth in the region, but most lived in reasonable comfort. During the eighteenth century, people

had called it "the best poor man's country" in America.

As the nineteenth century began, however, economic opportunity was declining in southeastern Pennsylvania. The average farm was no larger than 125 acres, barely above the margin of profitability. This was due to two reasons: the growing population and the continuing division of farm property from fathers to sons. By 1800, nearly 20 percent of the taxpayers were single freemen, clear evidence that young men were finding it harder to establish themselves on the land before taking a wife. Moreover, in certain areas of the region as many as 30 percent of the married taxpayers were landless. Some worked in the region's towns, but more were tenants and rural laborers. Declining productivity plagued inhabitants as well. Long and continuous cropping had robbed the soil of its fertility, and as population increased, farmers were forced to bring marginal land under cultivation.

Although some of the region's farmers showed interest in new, "scientific" theories of fertilization, crop rotation, and selective animal breeding, most farmers changed their ways only slowly. One disillusioned soul spoke bitterly of

## Growth of Towns in Southeastern Pennsylvania, c. 1800

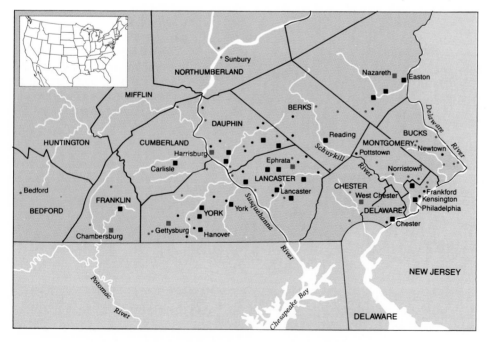

those "who turn a deaf or incredulous ear to all instructions; who condemn new things because they are new . . . who keep themselves aloof and warn others of the specious and dangerous novelty." Among farmers of that time, tradition died hard.

In an effort to compensate for declining yields, most followed the self-defeating strategy of keeping their fields under constant cultivation. They continued to sow their grain broadcast and plant their corn in widely separated hills, one worker hoeing open a hole and another following behind to drop in the kernels and close the soil with his heel. Farmers knew that fertilizing with manure increased crop yields, but few had enough animals to produce a sufficient supply.

Nor had agricultural technology changed significantly from a century before. Farmers still worked the land with crude, wooden plows that required several yoke of oxen and two or three men to use and frequently broke when run against the rocks and tree stumps that dotted the fields. In 1807, Charles Newbold of Burlington, New Jersey, patented a cast-iron plow, but it was expensive and dulled easily. Not until the 1830s did efficient metal plows come into general use.

The costs of agricultural labor limited output as well. As landlessness increased, more people offered to work for wages, and farmers depended increasingly on hired help. But only the more prosperous could afford it. At planting and harvest time, moreover, when extra labor was most needed, the cost increased. On most farms, the acreage under cultivation was limited by the family's ability to plant and harvest the crop.

One mark of increasing commercialization was greater dependence on livestock and dairying. Most farmers, however, owned only a few animals—perhaps several horses, four or five cattle, some pigs, and a flock of chickens. Few farmers knew much about scientific breeding; even fewer practiced it. Animals typically grazed together in common fields or were allowed to forage for themselves in the countryside. Even in winter, many farmers neither sheltered their animals nor provided them with fodder. An animal's hardiness was valued as highly as its weight or productivity. One observer remarked that "it is a very pitiable sight to go about our country and see the condition of multitudes of cattle and sheep which fill almost every farmer's yard in the spring of the year. The severity of our winters, with bad management are . . . the cause of so much poverty among our cattle."

By 1820, Pennsylvania's farmers were producing considerably more than 50 years before, but that was because there were more of them cultivating more land, not because there had been significant changes in the agricultural economy. It would be another several decades before the North's agricultural revolution got solidly under way.

## The South Embraces Cotton

As the eighteenth century ended, southern agriculture was still in disarray. Falling prices, worn-out lands, and the destruction wrought during the Revolutionary War had left the Chesapeake's tobacco economy in a shambles. The extensive loss of slaves added to the region's woes.

## Agricultural Productivity in 1800 and 1970

| | WHEAT | | COTTON | |
|---|---|---|---|---|
| | WORKER-HOURS PER ACRE | YIELD PER ACRE | WORKER-HOURS PER ACRE | YIELD PER ACRE |
| 1800 | 56 | 15 bushels | 185 | 147 pounds |
| 1970 | 3 | 31 bushels | 24 | 438 pounds |

*Source:* U.S. Bureau of the Census.

Even before the Revolution, Virginia and Maryland planters had begun to diversify their crops in an effort to escape dependence on tobacco and bolster their sagging fortunes. Those efforts continued during the 1780s and 1790s. As agriculture became diversified, so did the rest of the region's economy, for grain required milling, packaging, and transporting before it could be exported. At the same time, grain absorbed fewer man-days of labor than tobacco, thus freeing slaves for other employment.

As the new century began, southern planters turned back to single-crop agriculture, only this time the crop was cotton, not tobacco. Planters in both the Chesapeake and South Carolina had experimented with cotton before the Revolution, but their efforts increased after the war. They were most successful in cultivating the long-staple variety. Its long, silky fibers were highly valued and could easily be separated from the cotton's seeds. The delicate long-staple plant, however, grew only where soil and climate were exactly right—on the sea islands off the coast of Georgia and South Carolina.

There was an alternative—the hardier short-

*Although the cotton gin, invented in 1793, simplified one step of cotton processing, much of the work on a plantation continued to be done with rudimentary tools by slave labor. Here Benjamin Latrobe sketches "An Overseer Doing His Duty."*

staple variety, which could be successfully cultivated across large areas of the South. Its fibers, however, clung tenaciously to the plant's sticky, green seeds and could be separated from them only with great difficulty. A slave could clean only a pound of short-staple cotton a day.

Demand for cotton of all sorts was growing, especially in England, where new textile factories, with their weaving and spinning machines, created an insatiable appetite for the crop. Demand and supply began to come together in 1793 when Eli Whitney, a Yankee schoolteacher seeking employment in the South, set his mind to the problem of short-staple cotton and its seeds. Within a few days, he had designed a functioning model of what he called a "cotton gin." In conception it was disarmingly simple, nothing more than a box containing a roller, equipped with wire teeth, designed to pull the fibers through a comblike barrier, thus stripping them from the seeds. A hand crank activated the mechanism. The implications of Whitney's invention were immediately apparent, for with this crude device a slave could clean up to 50 pounds of short-staple cotton per day.

During the next several decades, southern cotton production soared. In 1790, the South produced only 3,135 bales. By 1800, output had grown to 73,145 bales, and by 1820 it had mushroomed to 334,378. In 1805, cotton already accounted for 30 percent of all agricultural exports; by 1820, it exceeded half. Across both the old, coastal South and the newly developing interior states of Tennessee, Alabama, and Mississippi, cotton was becoming king. The growing demand of England's textile mills provided the stimulus, but a fortuitous combination of factors made possible the South's dramatic response: wonderfully productive virgin soil; a long and steamy growing season; the availability of ample, well-trained slave labor; and the long experience of southern planters with the production and marketing of staple crops.

As we shall see in later chapters, the swing to cotton marked a momentous turning point for both the South and the nation. Perhaps most important, it breathed new life into the institution of slavery, for as cotton production increased, so did the value of prime fieldhands. Some of the escalating demand for slave labor was met from overseas. In 1803 alone, Georgia and South Carolina imported 20,000 new slaves as southern planters and northern merchant-suppliers rushed to fill the need before the slave trade finally ended in 1807. Much of the labor demand, however, would be met by domestic reproduction and the internal slave trade that moved blacks from the worn-out lands of the Chesapeake to the booming "black belt" of the deep South.

## Preindustrial Manufacturing and Merchant Capitalism

The pace of economic change was more rapid in the manufacturing sector during the early nineteenth century. The majority of American goods continued to be produced at home or in small shops by artisans and their journeyman apprentices. Merchant capitalists, however, seeking investment opportunities for their commercial profits, began to buy into and consolidate various industries, among them textiles and shoes. Development of the factory system that would revolutionize manufacturing still lay in the future, but the early nineteenth century brought the first steps toward industrialization.

How much of the American work force was involved in manufacturing is difficult to determine, since most people did a variety of jobs. In the rural North, for example, farmers augmented their income by running grist mills, fashioning cabinets, or repairing wagons. Their wives contributed as well by making clothes for sale or exchange with neighbors. "Almost all the farmers of the United States," declared one

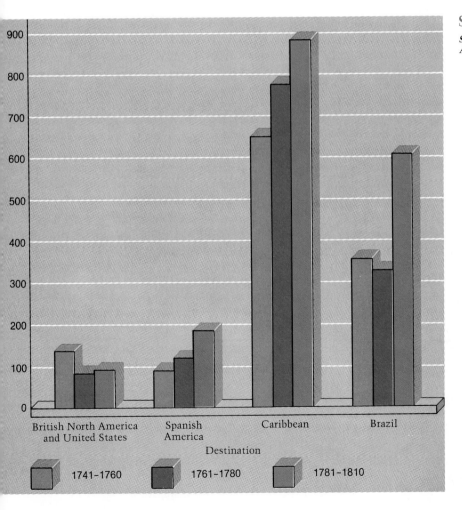

### Slave Trade, 1741–1810

**Source:** Curtin, *The Atlantic Slave Trade: A Census,* 1969.

European visitor, "combine some trade with agriculture." In older regions, where the land was worn and farms were small, such work was essential for survival. Elijah Norton of Westhampton, Massachusetts, observed that he could "carry on his farm" only by making shoes for his neighbors in return for their labor.

Unlike later years, when industry was larger and became concentrated in the cities, manufacturing in preindustrial America was small in scale and highly decentralized. The rural landscape was dotted with small enterprises of one kind or another—stores and shops, grain mills

*In the economy of the early republic, women continued to produce clothing and other household goods in traditional ways.*

### Rural Industry in the North, c. 1800

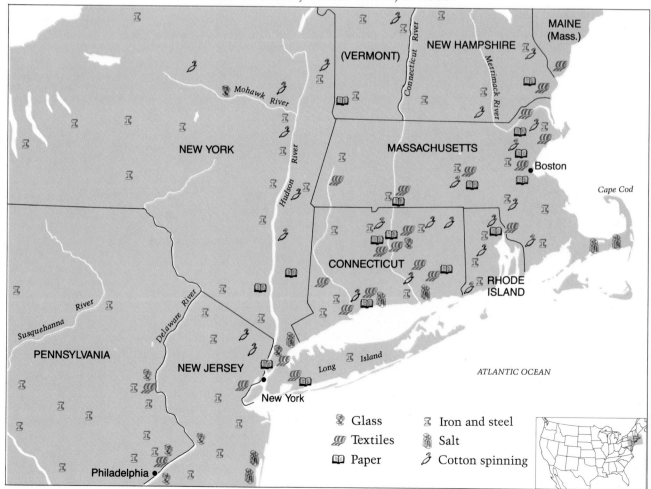

Glass
Textiles
Paper
Iron and steel
Salt
Cotton spinning

and sawmills, potash works and iron forges—that employed three or four workers and served people in the immediate vicinity. In the South, planters trained some of their slaves as artisans and set them to work producing commodities needed on the plantation.

In the shops of both North and South, artisans made goods much as they had for decades—slowly, by hand, and with the simplest of tools. Where more than human power was required, as in milling grain or sawing wood, waterwheels provided it. Not only was manufacturing small in scale, it was intensely personal as well. Since artisans fashioned products for sale to their neighbors, they took pride in the quality of their work. To offer shoddy goods was to risk losing the community's confidence and with it the chance to make a reasonable living.

In the small shops of preindustrial America, labor and management were closely aligned. Artisans occupied both roles, working side by side with their journeymen helpers but also managing the enterprise. They owned their shops, which were often directly attached to their houses; they hired their help; and they made their living from profits rather than wages.

Though artisans worked hard, they could control their work schedule and tempo; indeed, they frequently adjusted both to suit their needs.

During the first several decades of the nineteenth century, this decentralized, artisan-based manufacturing system slowly began to change. By the 1820s, industrialization was sufficiently advanced to indicate the more rapid and dramatic transformation that lay ahead. The explanation for these changes is to be found, once again, in America's continuing involvement with Europe.

In an attempt to prevent the United States from becoming more deeply embroiled in the ongoing European war, President Jefferson in 1807 declared an embargo, cutting off American trade across the Atlantic. The effect was immediate and far-reaching. In one year, the value of American exports declined nearly 80 percent.

When the embargo was lifted in 1809, American trade gradually recovered. In 1812, however, Britain and the United States once again went to war. During the next three years, while Britain blockaded the coast and captured nearly 1,400 American merchantmen, overseas trade sank to its lowest level in recorded history. Even

*In the early nineteenth century, older cities like Philadelphia continued to grow but were as yet little changed by the forces of industrialization.*

after the war's end in 1815, American commerce languished, largely because England's new Corn Laws prohibited the importation of American grain.

The consequences of these trade disruptions for American manufacturing were immense. With prospects for profits from overseas trade drastically reduced, merchants sought other investment opportunities. Domestic manufacturing was attractive, especially since the embargo had also prevented the importation of British manufactured goods. As the domestic demand for American goods increased and prices rose, the shift in investment from commerce to manufacturing grew apace.

Merchants brought organizational skills as well as ambition and surplus capital to American manufacturing. They used all three to consolidate America's decentralized, inefficient industries. The merchant capitalists' strategy was to gain control of both the raw materials from which goods were fashioned—leather in the case of shoes; cotton, flax, and wool for textiles—and the arrangements for marketing the finished products. Some steps in the manufacturing process they farmed out to workers in shops and homes, paying them on a piecework basis. Other steps they consolidated in their own central shops. Their wealth, connections, and organizational skills allowed them to absorb smaller producers and increase their control over different industries. Textiles and shoes attracted the greatest attention from the merchant capitalists because they had the largest potential market and offered the best prospects for consolidation.

### Shoes and Textiles

The development of the early shoe industry in Lynn, Massachusetts, illustrates the merchant capitalists' techniques. During the eighteenth century, Lynn's farmers learned to augment their income by making shoes. By 1800, Lynn had become a center of shoe production, the town's many small shops turning out one pair of shoes for every five people in the country.

At first, individual shopkeepers commissioned shoemakers to fill specific orders, which the shopkeepers then sold. But seeing the vast potential in shoe manufacturing, merchant capitalists soon began to take control of the industry. In the years following 1805, they developed central shops where the leather was cut into pieces and then "put out" to hundreds of workers, many of them women laboring in their homes, who sewed the pieces together. The completed "uppers" were then returned to the central shops, checked, and sent out again, this time to male workers who attached the soles. The finished shoes were then gathered, given a final inspection, and packed for shipment all over the country.

The process was efficient and turned a handsome profit for the merchant capitalists who managed it. It had serious implications, however, for the master craftsmen who had formerly dominated the trade. With manufacturing increasingly under the control of the merchants and focused around the central shops, the masters lost both their own independence and their influence over their journeyman apprentices.

A few, such as Chris Robinson, prospered under the new system. In 1818, he made shoes in a 10-foot-long shop attached to the back of his home. Within four years he was able to build a new shop measuring 16 by 28 feet. A decade later, now with a partner, Robinson erected a wooden factory on one side of the town common. Among artisans, however, Robinson was the exception. Most shoemakers either entered the central shops or continued to work at home, no longer as independent producers but as dependent wage earners. Less and less often did they make important production decisions; those were reserved for the "bosses" who ran the enterprise. Moreover, the workers could be "turned away" for bringing in unsatisfactory work and thus deprived of their livelihood. By the 1820s, shoemaking in Lynn was no longer controlled by individual artisans.

Industrial consolidation went even further in textiles, where the various steps in the manufacturing process were first gathered into one unified operation. Historically, spinning and weaving had been done in the home, mostly by women who fashioned cloth and made articles for family use and local sale. In the late eighteenth century, however, a number of entrepreneurs began to experiment with new wooden "spinning jennies" like those being developed in England. Often they sought the help of British emigrants who had the practical experience and technical know-how no American possessed. In 1789, William Ashley and Moses Brown, two Rhode Island merchants, hired 21-year-old Samuel Slater, a former apprentice with an English cotton textile firm, to devise a water-powered yarn-spinning machine. Slater did that, but he also developed a machine capable of carding, or straightening the cotton fibers. Within a year, Ashley and Brown's spinning mill had begun operations in Pawtucket, Rhode Island. Its initial work force consisted of nine children, ranging in age from 7 to 12. Ten years later, their number had grown to over 100.

Textile mills soon sprang up all across the New England and the Middle Atlantic states, for they contained swift-flowing streams to power the mills, children and women to tend the machines, capitalists eager to finance the ventures, and numerous cities and towns with ready markets for cheap textiles. The early mills were small affairs, containing only the machines for carding and spinning. The thread was then put out to home workers to be woven into cloth. The early mechanization of cloth production did not replace home manufacture but supplemented it.

Already under way, however, were experiments that would further transform the industry. Closeted in the attic of a Boston house in 1813, Francis Cabot Lowell, a merchant, and Paul Moody, a mechanic, worked to devise a power loom capable of weaving cloth. Lowell's study of mechanical looms during his earlier tour of English and Scottish cotton factories guided their work. Eventually they succeeded, and the loom they devised was soon installed in a mill at Waltham, Massachusetts, capitalized at $300,000 by Lowell and his Boston Associates.

The most important innovation of the Waltham operation was Lowell's decision to bring all the steps of cotton production together under one roof. The Waltham mill thus differed from those in Rhode Island and Great Britain, where spinning and weaving were separate operations. With the entire manufacturing process and work force centralized in one place, factory production of cheap cloth designed for the mass market could now be efficiently and profitably organized. In 1823, the Boston Associates moved their operations to East Chelmsford on the Merrimack River, a town they renamed Lowell.

*Samuel Slater was said to have "smuggled a textile mill out of England in his head." The Pawtucket mill, established in 1789, was the first of hundreds to mechanize the tedious operation of spinning cotton into thread.*

## The Panic of 1819

In spite of the success of the Lynn and Lowell operations, Americans continued to produce most of their goods by hand, in households and artisans' shops. The industrialization of the economy had scarcely begun. Following 1815, even consolidation under the limited system of merchant capitalism had slowed, for following the end of America's second war with England, British goods again flooded American markets and the manufacturing boom collapsed.

In 1815, the value of imported goods had zoomed upward to $113 million, and the following year rose to over $30 million more. Because England's industrial revolution was further along and its factories were more efficient, its products sold competitively in the United States, even with the added costs of transportation across the Atlantic. The shoe industry and the textile mills at Lynn and Pawtucket survived, but hundreds of other infant industries did not.

In 1819, the economy suffered a severe financial panic. Only a few commercial banks had existed anywhere in the country in 1790. By 1818, stimulated by commercial prosperity and the growth of manufacturing, the number had risen to 392. Many, however, were insufficiently capitalized and irresponsibly managed. Caught up in the commercial and manufacturing booms, their directors extended credit and printed money without retaining sufficient specie in their vaults to cover their obligations. It was a financial system waiting to collapse, and in 1819 it did when the Bank of the United States, which had been rechartered by Congress in 1816, forced the state banks to redeem their note issues in specie. Many could not meet the demands, thus triggering a sequence of bank failures and the collapse of credit.

The panic and the depression that followed left in their wake an unprecedented stream of bankruptcies and shattered fortunes. Across New England and the Middle Atlantic states, businesses failed and unemployment soared. In Massachusetts, wages plummeted in less than a year from $1.50 per day to 53 cents, while in upstate New York the daily pay of unskilled turnpike workers dropped from 75 cents to 12 cents. Philadelphia businesses that at the end of the war had employed 9,700 workers hired only

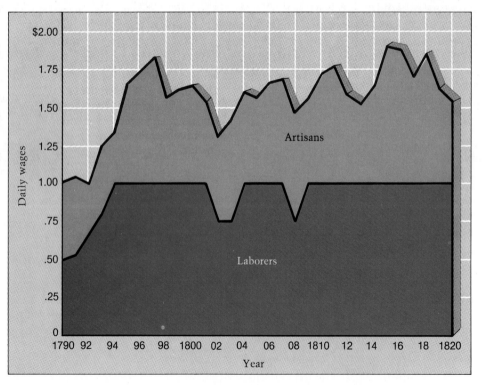

**Average Daily Wages in Philadelphia, 1790–1820**
*Source:* U.S. Bureau of the Census.

2,100 in 1819. In the trans-Appalachian West, land sales plummeted from $13.6 million in 1818 to $1.7 million the following year. William Greene, secretary to the governor of Ohio, reported in 1820 that "the greater part of our mercantile citizens are in a state of bankruptcy," while "the citizens of every class are uniformly delinquent in discharging even the most trifling of debts." In the South, farms and plantations stood abandoned as cotton and tobacco exports fell.

By the early 1820s, recovery was under way, and the stage had been set for the second and more dramatic phase of America's epic industrial revolution. The panic, however, demonstrated how unstabilizing that transformation could be and how powerfully its effects would be felt in the lives of individual Americans.

## An Ideology of Expectant Capitalism

The American people had long embraced the basic principles of capitalism: commitment to private property, individual enterprise, and the accumulation of wealth. During the colonial period, however, the circumstances of economic life had dampened the capitalist spirit. English mercantilism had stressed the subordination of colonial to British enterprise and the supremacy of the community's good over individual economic interests. More important, the eighteenth century had offered most Americans living outside the urban centers limited opportunities and thus curbed economic incentives. While many colonists, especially southern tobacco and rice planters and northern merchants, accumulated significant wealth, most ordinary Americans did not; nor did they expect to. Given the realities of daily life, farmers, artisans, and other workers hoped only for what was sometimes called a "pleasing mediocrity."

Attitudes began to change, however, late in the eighteenth century. Among artisans and commercial farmers as well as merchants and planters, earlier preoccupation with the limits of economic opportunity gave way to a newly expansive economic spirit. Several developments accounted for the change. The break with England enhanced Americans' sense of economic freedom and autonomy. Beyond that, they shared the attitudes toward economic affairs

that Adam Smith elevated to an ideology in his *Wealth of Nations*, published in England in 1776. Smith launched a frontal assault on the restrictive, controlling assumptions of mercantilism. He argued first of all that economic behavior was governed by consistent and knowable laws, just as was physical nature. He asserted that individual self-interest was the only reliable guide to human behavior and that the public good was best served by the free and unregulated play of individual ambition within the marketplace. Government, Smith explained, should not control economic affairs but act only to guarantee the free working of supply and demand. Smith's doctrines suited the circumstances of the new republic wonderfully, for they emphasized the importance of international free trade, provided a rationale for the rapid exploitation of the continent, and explained, in terms congenial with republican principles, that government's task was to nurture individual opportunity.

The booming prosperity at the turn of the century also fanned American imaginations and persuaded people that economic opportunity was real. Not all Americans shared in this newly expansive spirit. Black slaves had little reason for enthusiasm, and many American farmers continued to labor in an agricultural world of constraints. Most women, moreover, continued to be closely dependent on the men around them. Still, countless Americans found their circumstances improved and believed that economic opportunities were expanding.

The new spirit was fed, finally, by the accelerating pace of westward settlement. In 1790, only 100,000 white settlers lived in the nation's interior beyond the Appalachian Mountains. By 1800, their numbers had swollen to nearly a million; and by 1820, to over 2 million.

They came by wagon along Zane's Trace and other tortuous routes into Kentucky and Tennessee and clambered aboard flatboats at Pittsburgh to float down the Ohio river to destinations at Wheeling, Marietta, Louisville, and Cincinnati. The human tide seemed to grow with each passing year. "Genesee fever" brought thousands of settlers surging onto the rich lands of western New York. A traveler in 1797 counted 500 wagons a day on the road west from Albany. "The woods are full of new settlers," wrote an observer near Batavia, New York, in 1805. "Axes are resounding, and the trees literally falling about us as we passed." By 1812, some 200,000 souls lived in the western part of the state, where scarcely 30,000 had lived 20 years before.

Every spring, when the water was high and settlers were anxious to get west and plant their new land, the Ohio was crowded with flatboats carrying people, animals, and a few valued family possessions downriver. "America is breaking up and going west!" declared the British traveler Morris Birkbeck. To many people at the time, it certainly seemed so.

Settlers were drawn by the promotions of countless speculators seeking fortunes in the sale of western land. Between 1790 and 1820, land companies boomed vast areas of New York and Ohio, Kentucky and Alabama to prospective settlers back east. The Holland Land Company, financed by a consortium of Dutch bankers, bought 2.5 million acres of prime land in western New York and another 1.5 million in Pennsylvania. Many of the most extravagant ventures failed, their plans too ambitious even for the surging tide of settlement. But many succeeded,

returning handsome profits to their investors. Individual settlers shared in the speculative fever, going into debt to buy extra land so that they might sell it at a profit when population increased and land prices rose. For years, land had offered the promise of economic security. In the expanding republic, it stimulated economic ambitions as well.

Even the panic and depression of 1819 failed to dampen for long the exuberance of America's expansionary capitalist faith. Out of the depression came not despair and greater caution but renewed and even more reckless ambition. Indicative of this was the move in many states to ease bankruptcy laws so that entrepreneurs come upon hard times were not put in jail but were left free to try their fortunes again. Before long, bankruptcy would lose most of its earlier stigma.

In 1820, the American economy stood poised at a historic divide. Behind it lay the traditional world of preindustrial America; ahead loomed the emerging industrial world of the future. The details of that new order were not yet clear, but its outlines were coming into view.

### Growth of Trans-Appalachian Population, 1790–1820

| | 1790 | 1800 | 1810 | 1820 |
|---|---|---|---|---|
| *Old Northwest* | | | | |
| Ohio | — | 45,365 | 230,760 | 581,434 |
| Indiana | — | 5,641 | 24,520 | 147,178 |
| Illinois | — | — | 12,282 | 55,211 |
| Michigan | — | — | 4,762 | 8,896 |
| Total | — | 51,006 | 272,324 | 792,719 |
| *Old Southwest* | | | | |
| Kentucky | 73,677 | 220,955 | 406,511 | 564,317 |
| Tennessee | 35,691 | 105,602 | 261,727 | 422,823 |
| Alabama | — | 1,250 | 9,046 | 127,901 |
| Mississippi | — | 7,600 | 31,306 | 75,448 |
| Total | 109,368 | 335,407 | 708,590 | 1,190,489 |
| *Trans-Mississippi West* | | | | |
| Louisiana | — | — | 76,556 | 153,407 |
| Arkansas | — | — | 1,062 | 14,273 |
| Missouri | — | — | 19,783 | 66,586 |
| Total | — | — | 97,401 | 234,266 |

*Source:* U.S. Bureau of the Census.

# THE CHARACTER OF PREINDUSTRIAL SOCIETY

Just as America's preindustrial economy differed from the later industrial order, so did the preindustrial society of the early republic. During the nineteenth century, the combined forces of industrialization, urban growth, large-scale immigration, and westward expansion would transform American social life. By 1820, enough had changed to make clear that a new social order was in the making. At the same time, the traditional social relationships defined by family, community, class, gender, and race were slow to alter, considerably slower than ways of producing and marketing goods. If the future was increasingly on people's minds, the past was still evident in their daily lives.

It requires considerable imagination on our part to understand that preindustrial society, so different was it from our own. We must do so, however, if we are to grasp the revolutionary changes that the nineteenth century would bring.

## A Nation of Regions

Were we to be transported back to that preindustrial world, much about it would seem strange and unfamiliar. Probably nothing would impress us more than the smallness of American communities and the isolation of people from each other. In the early nineteenth century, community and region were much more real to most Americans than was the sense of nationhood.

The country was divided first by distinct and separate regions. The regional differences between North and South that began during the colonial period persisted and even increased during the early nineteenth century. The northern states continued down the path of economic diversification, with their mixed farming, commerce, fishing, and manufacturing. The North's denser population and relatively broad distribution of wealth generated a growing demand for consumer goods. Moreover, the kinds of commodities produced in the North—grain, dried fish, forest and manufactured goods—generated jobs and stimulated numerous support indus-

tries. The production of dried fish, for example, required boats and nets, salt and barrels, sails and docks. Finally, the region's topography, combining agricultural lands, rapidly flowing rivers, and easy access to the sea, promoted economic diversification.

The South, by contrast, focused increasingly on the cultivation and export of cotton. Unlike many of the commodities produced in the North, cotton generated few economic "linkages," for it required little processing and stimulated few local industries. The South's relative advantage lay in expanding its staple-crop agriculture rather than in economic diversification.

As the two regions' economies diverged, so did their societies. In the North, wealth was far from equally distributed, but the free-labor system did reward most people for their work. In the South, on the other hand, the slave-labor system produced a dramatically uneven distribution of wealth, for the masters reaped most of the profit from the slaves' labor. Even within white society, class differences were expanding. As cotton took hold, people without slaves or with access only to marginal lands fell rapidly behind.

America's regional diversity now included the vast area of trans-Appalachia as well. During the first years of settlement on that rapidly moving frontier, life was hard as settlers struggled to clear the land and get their first crops in the ground. Their task was made more difficult because they initially shied away from the "oak openings" and prairie lands, believing that heavily forested areas were most fertile.

As population increased, however, and the rich virgin soil began to bloom, trans-Appalachia began to grow. North of the Ohio River, settlement followed the grid pattern prescribed in the Northwest Ordinance of 1787, while south of the Ohio people distributed themselves more randomly across the land, much as their ancestors had done back east. Above the Ohio, mixed, free-labor agriculture quickly appeared as farmers worked to reproduce the life they had known in Pennsylvania or New England. In short order, towns such as Columbus and Cin-

From the seventeenth century to the twentieth, the American population has changed dramatically, not only in size and location but also in demographic characteristics such as birth and death rates, marriage age, and family size. In the early nineteenth century, for example, the average life expectancy of white Americans was about 45 years, and men tended to outlive women. In our own time, the average life expectancy has reached 74, and women on the average now live longer than men. Population characteristics have differed as well in different regions, within urban and rural settings, and among racial, ethnic, and class groups.

Changes in demographic traits often have an immense impact on the character and quality of social life. Demographic information can tell us a great deal about the life experiences of ordinary Americans, for example, the effects of the baby boom generation and its children on today's youth. Indeed, demographic data is often the major source of historical information about otherwise anonymous individuals. In recent years, historians have paid increasing attention to the analysis of populations, their characteristics during given periods, and their patterns of change over time.

Two kinds of demographic data have proved most important. One consists of birth, death, and marriage records, often contained in church and government registers. These record the basic events in people's lives. If they are complete and continuous enough, they allow historians to follow the life course of individuals and to reconstruct patterns of family and community life.

Here we offer an example of the second kind of demographic data, a census. The material is from the federal census of 1820. Article 1, Section 2 of the Constitution called for an enumeration (or counting) of the nation's population within three years after the first meeting of Congress, and then every ten years "in such manner as they shall by law direct." The first decennial census was taken in 1790. The information was necessary to determine the periodic reapportionment of the House of Representatives and the allocation of direct taxes to the states.

Compared to modern census inquiries, the first federal censuses were very simple and collected a limited amount of information. The 1790 census, for example, gathered data under the following headings only: "Name of Head of Family," "Free White Males, 16 Years and Upward," "Free White Males, Under 16," "Free White Females," "All Other Free Persons," and "Slaves." As the nation grew, however, the demands for information increased. In 1820, Congress for the first time called for the collection of various kinds of economic data, and in the decades that followed the categories of economic data were expanded.

Here we see aggregate data for two Ohio counties and the city of Cincinnati from the 1820 federal census. Ashtabula County, settled mostly by migrants from New England, is in the northeastern part of Ohio, along Lake Erie. Hamilton County is in the southwestern part of the state, near Cincinnati, across the Ohio River from Kentucky.

The actual census schedules broke free white males and females, male and female slaves, and male and female free colored persons into several age categories. We have combined those age categories. Why do you suppose the headings were defined as they were? How did the three local populations compare in terms of race, gender, and immigration? How can you explain the differences? Why are there no slaves? What can you conclude about the ways people earned their livings in the three localities? How would the 1980 census returns for your own town or county compare with these data from 1820?

# CENSUS RETURNS

### Ashtabula County

| | | |
|---|---|---|
| 1. | Free white males | 3,878 |
| 2. | Free white females | 3,493 |
| 3. | Foreigners not naturalized | 16 |
| 4. | Numbers of persons engaged in agriculture | 1,499 |
| 5. | Number of persons engaged in commerce | 19 |
| 6. | Number of persons engaged in manufacturing | 271 |
| 7. | Male slaves | 0 |
| 8. | Female slaves | 0 |
| 9. | Free male colored persons | 3 |
| 10. | Free female colored persons | 1 |
| 11. | All other persons except Indians not taxed | 7 |
| | Total* | 7,382 |

### Hamilton County

| | | |
|---|---|---|
| 1. | Free white males | 16,262 |
| 2. | Free white females | 14,869 |
| 3. | Foreigners not naturalized | 303 |
| 4. | Numbers of persons engaged in agriculture | 4,127 |
| 5. | Number of persons engaged in commerce | 389 |
| 6. | Number of persons engaged in manufacturing | 1,548 |
| 7. | Male slaves | 0 |
| 8. | Female slaves | 0 |
| 9. | Free male colored persons | 328 |
| 10. | Free female colored persons | 305 |
| 11. | All other persons except Indians not taxed | 0 |
| | Total* | 31,764 |

### City of Cincinnati

| | | |
|---|---|---|
| 1. | Free white males | 4,919 |
| 2. | Free white females | 4,290 |
| 3. | Foreigners not naturalized | 241 |
| 4. | Numbers of persons engaged in agriculture | 99 |
| 5. | Number of persons engaged in commerce | 313 |
| 6. | Number of persons engaged in manufacturing | 753 |
| 7. | Male slaves | 0 |
| 8. | Female slaves | 0 |
| 9. | Free male colored persons | 219 |
| 10. | Free female colored persons | 214 |
| 11. | All other persons except Indians not taxed | 0 |
| | Total* | 9,642 |

*The totals exclude categories 3 through 6, since the people listed in them are also included in the other categories.

cinnati emerged to provide services and cultural amenities for the surrounding population. In Kentucky and Tennessee, mixed agriculture also took hold, but it was soon challenged by the spread of slave-based cotton.

As people continued to spill into the region, they established churches and courts, schools and even colleges (Transylvania University, founded in Lexington, Kentucky, in 1780, was the first college west of the Appalachians). Even so, trans-Appalachia retained a reputation for its rough and colorful quality of life. Life could be depressingly lonesome for families lost in the hollows of the Cumberland mountains of eastern Tennessee. In the river towns along the Ohio River, on the other hand, boatmen and gamblers, con men and speculators gave civic life a raucous quality; and everywhere the transiency, youthfulness, and predominant maleness of the population kept society unsettled.

The constant drama of migration and the grandeur of the natural surroundings fed people's imaginations. No characters were more famous in popular folklore than westerners like Daniel Boone, who fought the Indians, explored the country, and founded frontier settlements. None were more colorful than the mythical riverman, Mike Fink, who boasted that he was "half man, half alligator" and could "whip his weight in grizzly bears." And nothing revealed more graphically the West's rawness than the slashing, eye-gouging, ear-biting, no-holds-barred "rough and tumble" brawls that erupted regularly.

## A Nation of Communities

If regional identity was important in Americans' lives, social existence centered even more tightly on their local communities, for most people spent their years—growing up and marrying, raising families and dying—within the physical and social boundaries of their localities. In the early republic, the social world of most Americans was intimate and self-contained.

The point is best made by noting what we would find missing were we to visit the nation's villages and farms around 1800. We would note first the absence of communication systems such as today join the American people closely together. The written word was the only way people could communicate across space.

Newspapers and the mail provided the major information links between communities. From 1790 to 1820, both systems expanded greatly. Ninety-two newspapers circulated, mostly in towns along the coastal plain, as the new government got under way. By 1820, the number had risen to 512, and they were now widely scattered through the interior. The number of post offices and the flow of mail increased even more dramatically. When Washington was inaugurated, only 75 post offices existed in the entire nation; 30 years later there were nearly 8,500. Over those same three decades, the number of letters sent through the postal system increased ninefold.

Improvements in communication, however, were not as dramatic as these figures at first

*By 1800, Cincinnati had already become an important port on the Ohio River between Pittsburgh and Louisville and was providing services for surrounding farms.*

*The turnpike system, begun in the 1790s, reduced travel time through the countryside. Tree stumps were cut low enough to clear under a wagon's axles, and log bridges were kept in passable repair. Here an express coach makes its way through the forest.*

suggest. Though newspapers were more numerous, they still had limited distribution, primarily because of the high costs of production. As late as 1820, the average circulation was only 800. Most papers, moreover, appeared only once or twice a week; not until midcentury would new, high-speed presses reduce printing costs sufficiently to make possible the production of daily mass-circulation papers.

Though the flow of mail grew significantly, expanded business activity rather than personal correspondence accounted for most of the increase. The average cost of mailing a single-page letter declined by one-third during the first quarter of the nineteenth century. Even so, it still cost 25 cents to send a letter 30 miles or more. At a time when the daily wage averaged about a dollar, that was prohibitively expensive for many people.

Overland travel also improved during these years. In 1800, it took two days to go by horseback or coach from New York to Philadelphia, four days to Boston, and more than a week to Pittsburgh in western Pennsylvania. By 1820, those travel times had been halved, especially north of Virginia and east of the Appalachians,

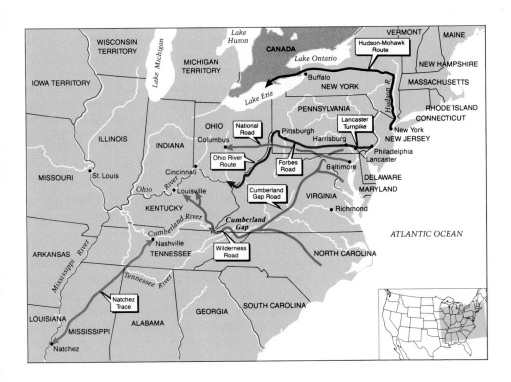

**Important Routes Westward**

where the roads were better. Beginning in the 1790s, a flurry of "turnpike" construction began in the Northeast. The first one of any length opened between Philadelphia and Lancaster, Pennsylvania, in 1794. It immediately proved profitable, and soon dozens of similar projects were under way. By 1811, New York had chartered 137 turnpike companies, and the New England states 200 more. In 1806, Congress authorized construction of the National Road westward from Cumberland, Maryland. By 1818, it had penetrated as far as Wheeling on the Ohio River and had reduced travel time along its length from eight days to three.

Even the turnpikes, though, would seem crude to the modern traveler, for constructing most of them involved little more than smoothing the dirt roadway, trimming back the bushes along its sides, and cutting off the tree stumps at 16 inches, just low enough for most wagon axles to clear. Turnpikes, moreover, were few; most often people had to make their way along crude pathways or wagon trails that wound across the countryside, skirting lakes and hills, following the path of least topographic resistance. In the summer, travel along these byways raised clouds of choking dust; in the spring, they dissolved into mud. People often preferred to travel in the winter if the weather was mild, for sleds and sleighs moved more easily than wagons. In the mountainous areas of western Pennsylvania, whole hillsides were denuded of trees cut by anxious travelers to drag behind their wagons as makeshift brakes on the jolting ride downhill. The usual pace of travel, whether on foot or horseback, was no more than 3 or 4 miles an hour. At that rate, a trip of 25 miles filled a day, and even that was impossible if there were mountains to cross or rivers to ford.

The contrast with modern times is staggering. It has been estimated that within half an hour of President Kennedy's assassination in 1963, 68 percent of the American people had learned about it. When George Washington died in December 1799 in Alexandria, Virginia, it took five days for the news to reach Philadelphia, 11 days to get as far as Boston, and over three weeks to penetrate west to Lexington, Kentucky.

By 1810, steamboats were beginning to appear along the Atlantic coast and on the Ohio and Mississippi rivers. In 1807, Robert Fulton had launched his 160-ton sidewheeler *Clermont* on the Hudson River and demonstrated the feasibility of steam travel. Four years later, the *New Orleans*, a crude sternwheeler built at Pittsburgh, made the first successful run over the falls of the Ohio River at Cincinnati and down the Mississippi to New Orleans. Following the War of 1812, new shallow-draft hulls and more powerful engines brought a surge of steamboat construction in fast-growing river towns such as Pittsburgh, Louisville, and Cincinnati. Within a few decades, steamboats would revolutionize transportation on the nation's vast, interior river system. For the moment, however, most westerners still depended on flatboats to carry them downstream and keelboats for the laborious task of poling upriver.

Missing as well from America's preindustrial communities were regional and national organizations such as today knit localities together. Churches, schools, fire companies, laboring men's associations, militia companies—all were tightly bounded by the local community and had but tenuous connections with similar groups elsewhere. During the second quarter of the nineteenth century, political parties, religious denominations, reform societies, and countless other associational groups would begin to bring American communities into closer contact. That process of organization building was a fundamental part of America's national development. But in the early years of the republic, the organizational as well as informational boundaries of community life were tightly drawn.

## Lives of Intimacy and Quietness

Life within these preindustrial communities was intimate and highly personal. The vast majority of America's 5.2 million people in 1800 lived on farms and plantations or in villages of no more than a few hundred souls. Only ten places in the entire country held as many as 5,000 people. The two largest, New York and Philadelphia, at about 60,000, were the size of present-day Brownsville, Texas. All the towns of 2,500 or more taken together accounted for only 7 percent of the population.

In these rural and small-town settings, people encountered each other frequently. They went to church together, shared the joys of birth and the sorrows of death, exchanged goods, and gossiped at village stores. The continuity of local populations also contributed to this dense and intensely personal network of social relations. As the nineteenth century proceeded, the geographic mobility of the American people increased. The accelerating migration westward was one major cause, but the movement of people from countryside to town also contributed to it. This intraregional traffic was especially heavy in New England, where young men and women, finding it increasingly difficult to get a start on the crowded and rock-strewn soil, sought opportunity in Boston and emerging mill towns such as Waltham, Lowell, and Pawtucket. But it was evident in the Middle Atlantic states as well. Between 1790 and 1820, the nation's cities grew at a rate nearly twice that of the population as a whole, something entirely new in the American experience. Part of the increase came from immigration, now beginning again after a quarter century's interruption. Much of it, however, resulted from movement from the surrounding countryside.

Most people, however, did not move far or often during their lifetimes. Prior to 1820, persistence rates—people's tendency to stay in the same community over a decade's time—changed little from the eighteenth century. As a result, generational continuity, family stability, and extended kin networks continued to characterize community life. In the intimate communities of preindustrial America, people encountered faces, voices, and patterns of behavior that were reassuringly familiar.

Life within the communities of preindustrial America was remarkably quiet as well. We who live in an environment filled with the relentless noise of engines and machinery, portable tape decks and piped-in Muzak, would be amazed, perhaps even unnerved, by the quietness of that bygone day. In the world of preindustrial America, silence, not sound, was the regular accompaniment of daily life.

When the enveloping silence was interrupted, it was by the pealing of church bells or the clopping of horses' hoofs or the unmagnified sounds of human voices conversing. People labored to the accompaniment of a waterwheel's creaking or the pang of a blacksmith's hammer or the clacking of a hand loom—nothing more. Out in the endless countryside where most Americans lived, the sounds were nature's own—the wind blowing in the trees, a summer thunderstorm, the lowing of a cow, the call of a catbird seeking its mate.

The slowness and unscheduled character of

*The pace of life on a farm in 1800, though far from leisurely, was largely determined by the rhythms of nature.*

life's pace would impress a modern visitor as well. Difficulties of transportation were in part responsible, for every trip required effort and was subject to interruption by a winter's storm, a lame horse, or a dying wind. It was common experience for storekeepers not to know when their new goods would arrive, for families to be uncertain whether relatives were coming for a visit, for merchants to wonder if their cargoes had reached their destination. In the face of such realities, it made little sense for people to try to schedule their lives too closely.

Work patterns were similarly deliberate and informal. Since most Americans gained their living from the land, they were bound by the unhurried cycle of the seasons. Planting, cultivating, and harvesting followed regularly, one upon the other, but they could not be speeded by human effort. At harvest time, the tempo of farm life picked up, for wheat and other grains could spoil if left too long in the field. Corn, however, could wait, and root crops could even survive a frost.

Farm families certainly worked hard. When not tending their crops, men found more than enough to do repairing the barn, shoeing a horse, or rooting out tree stumps from a field. Farm women also worked long and difficult hours cultivating the garden, raising children, preserving food, and making clothes. Though the hours were long and arduous, the pace was slow, and schedules were almost nonexistent.

Nonagricultural work patterns, at least outside the few machine-based textile and shoe factories, would also seem to us slow and inefficient. Working by hand with the simplest tools and for limited markets, artisans gave little thought to maximizing output. Instead, they worked when there were orders to fill and closed their shops when there were none. Seldom did either craftsmen or merchants keep regularly scheduled hours, nor did their customers expect it of them.

Nothing illustrates life's unscheduled pace more vividly than the ways people reckoned time. For most Americans, life went on in the absence of clocks and timepieces. Not until the 1830s did they become cheap enough for most families to own. Nor did most communities have public clocks, either on church towers or

public buildings, to show and chime the hours. There was no use for them, for in the early nineteenth century, standard time did not exist. Even in the same community, clocks often told widely different times, and no one seemed to mind. Most people were content to estimate the time of day by the position of the sun. At night, they simply waited for the dawn. The tolling of a bell might indicate when church was to begin or a town meeting to convene, but estimates were generally sufficient for organizing life. Days, months, and seasons of the year were meaningful measures of human activity; hours and minutes often were not.

## Lives of Difficulty and Trial

As modern visitors to the communities of preindustrial America, we would be impressed as well by the rigors of daily life. Though most Americans were better off than their colonial ancestors, their lives were hardly comfortable. They lacked virtually all the conveniences of housing and diet that we take for granted today, and disease and death were their constant companions.

Most people's housing offered limited space and few amenities. Its quality varied enormously from place to place and class to class. The wealthy lived comfortably enough, for they could afford fine townhouses or elegant plantation mansions. Most Americans, however, could not. For southern slaves, frontier settlers, and the urban poor, housing meant cramped and filthy spaces; dirt floors; small window openings, often lacking glass; and only the roughest and most rudimentary furniture. For the urban poor, even firewood was often too expensive to buy, forcing them to scavenge their neighborhoods for waste materials to burn.

Even the wealthy depended on fireplaces or stoves for heat and had no indoor plumbing. After dark, people used candles and firelight for illumination. During the winter months, when the sun set early and the nights were cold, evening activities were curtailed and people sought warmth in bed.

People's diet was limited as well. Farm and small-town families enjoyed regular access to fresh fruits and vegetables, dairy products, domestic animals, and wild game. In the cities, many families still maintained small garden plots, a few chickens, perhaps even a cow. But as the cities grew and land values increased, that became increasingly difficult. Ice for refrigeration was often scarce; as a consequence, every city dweller knew the familiar taste of sour milk and the smell of rancid butter. Each city had its vegetable stands to which farmers brought their produce and markets where the meat of animals driven in from the countryside was sold. But prices were high and supplies often uncertain. Fresh meats and vegetables, to say nothing of milk and butter, were but occasional parts of most urban dwellers' diets. Far more common were bread, potatoes, onions, and salt pork.

Even in the countryside, fresh fruits and vegetables disappeared during the winter months, and people turned to the dried fruits and root vegetables they had stored away. Coffee, sugar, and spices were expensive enough that most people could enjoy them only occasionally.

Alcohol was a central part of the diet. During the early nineteenth century, the consumption of alcohol, especially in the form of distilled spirits, skyrocketed. In 1790, the annual per capita consumption of spirits stood at about 2.6 gallons. By 1830, Americans were consuming 5.2 gallons of hard liquor for every man, woman, and child in the nation, nearly triple today's rate. Whiskey was the most popular drink, with hard cider close behind. In 1820, there were over 1,000 licensed distilleries in New York alone. Not until midcentury, after large numbers of Germans had entered the country and distilling techniques had changed, did the consumption of beer begin to grow.

Then, as now, drinking patterns differed across social boundaries. Among whites, the heaviest drinking was done by young, lower-class males. Drinking rates were high as well among the foreign-born and people living in the West. The consumption of alcohol was lowest, on the other hand, among middle-aged, native-born New England farmers.

Women drank less extravagantly than men but still consumed from an eighth to a quarter of the nation's liquor. Ideals of femininity discouraged public tippling; women were supposed to show restraint, consistent with their higher virtue and delicacy. Still, many women found solace in the private consumption of alcohol-based medicines ostensibly taken for their health. On some occasions women imbibed publicly. Eastern upper-class women frequently drank in mixed company at dinner parties, while at frontier dances the whiskey bottle was "passed pretty briskly from mouth to mouth, exempting neither age nor sex." Even infants were often taught to imbibe. "I have frequently seen fathers," wrote one traveler, "wake their child of a year from a sound sleep to make it drink rum or brandy."

Improvements in distilling contributed to the increase in liquor consumption. From 1802 to 1815, the federal government issued more than 100 patents for distilling devices. The rapid opening of the West, where farmers grew corn and turned it into whiskey before sending it east to market, was a factor as well. As output increased, prices dropped, further promoting consumption. In the early 1820s, whiskey sold at retail for as little as 25 to 50 cents per gallon.

As the consumption of alcohol grew, so did public concern. Washington thought that distilled spirits were "the ruin of half the workmen in this country," while Jefferson feared that raw whiskey was "spreading through the mass of our citizens." Anne Royall, who spent much of her life crisscrossing the country in stage coaches, observed, "When I was in Virginia, it was too much whiskey—in Ohio, too much whiskey—in Tennessee, it is too, too much whiskey!" By the 1830s, concern would change to alarm. As we shall see in Chapter 13, nothing aroused more zeal among reformers during the second quarter of the nineteenth century than demon rum.

## Birth, Death, and Disease

The quality of life in early nineteenth-century America was also affected by the constant presence of disease and death. The rigors of daily life and limitations of diet and medical care meant dramatically shorter life spans than we enjoy today. At the turn of the century, only half the people could expect to live to age 45. Unlike today, women on the average died sooner than men, their bodies weakened by the rigors of frequent childbirth. Though birthrates were declining, white women could expect to give birth to four to eight children, and immigrant and black women averaged even more. Male physicians, such as Dr. William Shippen of Philadelphia, were increasingly overseeing the birth process. Whether that made childbirth less risky is uncertain. It did, however, reduce the role of female midwives and increasingly remove birthing from the realm of shared female experiences.

Disease constantly threatened human life. Medical knowledge and care had improved little over a century's time. Germ theories of infection were still unknown, and hospitals and trained physicians were few. Most Americans, especially among the lower and middle classes, had little access to doctors, depending instead on self-medication, home remedies, and prayer. That probably was not all bad at a time when the standard treatment for most diseases still included bleeding, purging, and blistering.

Diseases such as diphtheria and tuberculosis took a steady toll of human life, and epidemics of smallpox and yellow fever periodically raced through the population with devastating results. Today, through programs of inoculation and public health, we have largely eliminated disease epidemics. In the early nineteenth century, however, they visited men, women, and children with terrifying regularity.

During the 1790s, yellow fever struck the coastal cities repeatedly. The most devastating attack hit Philadelphia in 1793. Within months, nearly 10 percent of the city's population died. Those who could afford to fled the city, seeking refuge in the surrounding countryside. Those who could not stayed in their homes, venturing out only as necessary to secure food and water. No one was immune, though the poor and the elderly fared worst because they could not as readily escape and were physically more vulnerable. Blacks also died in large numbers when the Free African Society, responding to appeals from the mayor, supplied nurses and men for burial duty. The common belief that blacks were naturally immune to the fever's ravages turned out to be tragically false.

The authorities made efforts to deal with the devastation by setting up hospitals to hold the sick and establishing quarantines to restrict movement in and out of the cities. After the crisis passed, city officials took steps to improve sanitation by cleaning the streets of their usual filth. Such efforts, however, were inadequate, for garbage continued to litter the streets, animals

*In a world where neither medicine nor hygiene could be depended on to save lives, the commonly held view of earthly existence was as an inexorable journey toward the grave.*

still roamed freely through the cities, the collection of human excrement remained sporadic, and the wells from which people drank were often polluted. Yellow fever returned to Philadelphia in 1796 and 1797 and hit hard at other seaboard cities as well.

Disease and death, then, were regular visitors to community and family life. Scarcely anyone could expect more than a few years to pass without suffering the loss of a family member or close friend.

## Patterns of Wealth and Poverty

One of the defining features of any society is its pattern of social class—that is, the way in which wealth, and thus power and status, is distributed among its people. During the nineteenth century, class distinctions increased as industrialization redrew the contours of economic and social life.

As the century began, property was already unequally distributed across gender and racial lines. Women continued to hold far less property than men. The large majority of blacks, moreover, were slaves; for them, ownership of anything more than the smallest items of personal property was beyond reach. Though the condition of free blacks was better, they too held little of the country's wealth.

Among white males, property was most equally shared in rural areas of the North, where free-labor and family-farm agriculture predominated, and least equally in the South, where control of slave labor and the best land gave tobacco, rice, and cotton planters opportunity to monopolize the region's wealth.

The class structure was also sharply drawn in the port cities. There, merchant capitalists controlled the sources of commercial and manufacturing wealth, while small artisans, sailors, and unskilled workers lived at the margins of the economy, their lives taken up almost entirely by a struggle for survival. Perhaps the most even distribution of property existed on the edges of settlement in the trans-Appalachian frontier, but that was an equality of want. As that region developed, differences in wealth appeared there as well.

Taking the country as a whole, the pattern of wealth distribution had not changed much from pre-Revolutionary times. In 1800, the top 10 percent of property holders controlled about 42 percent of the nation's wealth, very close to what it had been 50 years before. By 1850, that figure would reach 70 percent as industrialization reshaped economic life and separated capital from labor.

When the century opened, not many Americans were truly rich. Even the wealthiest, such as the Boston merchant Francis Lowell and the South Carolina planter Charles Manigault, could not match the grandeur of English landed aristocrats or the great London merchants. Nor did their wealth begin to approach the fortunes accumulated by America's captains of industry during the last half of the nineteenth century. Neither did America contain a large, destitute underclass such as could be found in the cities and countryside of Europe. By comparison with England and France, property in the United States was broadly shared.

Poverty, however, existed and was increasing. In the South, it was most evident among slaves and poor whites living on the sandy pine barrens of the backcountry. In the North, the port cities housed growing numbers of the poor. The commercial prosperity of the 1790s was widely shared, but it did not benefit everyone. In Boston, for example, artisans and shopkeepers, who together had owned 20 percent of the city's wealth in 1700, held scarcely half that much as the nineteenth century began.

In the centers of commercial bustle, substantial numbers of people struggled to survive, their task actually made more difficult by the inflation of rent and food prices that prosperity brought. The commercial recession following Jefferson's embargo in 1807 hit the urban poor with particular force, for they felt the effects of unemployment most directly. Winter seasons regularly brought hard times for many as shipping slowed and jobs disappeared. During the winter months of 1805, New York's mayor, De Witt Clinton, worried publicly about the fate of 10,000 impoverished New Yorkers and asked the state legislature for help. During the winter of 1814–1815, relief agencies assisted nearly one-fifth of the city's population.

Even in rural New England and southeastern

Pennsylvania, a lower class of transient and propertyless people was growing. The "strolling poor," they were called—men, and sometimes women as well, unable to secure land of their own and thus forced to roam the countryside searching for work.

Three other groups were conspicuous among the nation's poor. One consisted of old Revolutionary War veterans, men like Long Bill Scott, who had found poverty as well as adventure in the war. Just how many there were is not known, but state and federal governments were peppered with petitions from grizzled veterans describing their misery and asking for relief. Women and children also suffered from poverty. Annual censuses of almshouse residents in New York City from 1816 to 1821 consistently listed more women and children than men.

Nothing more clearly illustrated poverty's grip or the vulnerability of many Americans to economic hard times than the depression following the Panic of 1819. Hardest hit were the West and South, where land speculation had been rampant and wildcat banking the most uncontrolled. When the financial bubble burst and depression settled in, a tide of foreclosures swept across the West, destroying the livelihoods of farmers and speculators alike. Residents of the port cities felt the harsh grip of depression as well, as commerce slowed, banks collapsed, and businesses shut down, leaving thousands without employment.

Poverty was a continuing reality in the early nineteenth century. And for every American who actually suffered its effects, there were several others living just beyond its reach, their margin of safety alarmingly thin.

## PERFECTING REPUBLICAN SOCIETY

During the Revolutionary era, politics and government had preoccupied the American people. There was concern as well, however, about the proper functioning of republican society. Between 1790 and 1820, some Americans turned their thoughts to issues of social change and reform, for if their experiment was to succeed, society would have to be republicanized as well. Behind their reformist efforts lay a cluster of beliefs regarding the unique character of the newly emerged American people.

### The Youthfulness of America

The reformist impulse that emerged in the 1790s had roots deep in the colonial past. From the first days of colonial settlement, European immigrants had thought of America as a place free of Old World social rigidities and open to new ways of life. We have seen, however, that by the middle of the eighteenth century, many colonists feared that American society was becoming more like Europe's and that social opportunities were disappearing. That perception fed their worry over the corrupting effects of

their ties with England and helped inspire the movement toward independence.

Separation from England persuaded Americans that they were casting off the burden of their European past and launching a new and glorious future. They called their new society *novus ordo seclorum*, a new secular order. That motto expressed their sense of new beginnings and their belief that reason rather than habit or tradition would now guide America's social development.

These attitudes appeared in the growing emphasis on youthfulness that characterized American attitudes during these years. America, people repeatedly insisted, was a "young" and "rising" republic, a "new nation" taking its place among the "old" and "decadent" empires of Europe.

The emphasis on youthfulness reflected the widely shared belief that nations followed a cyclic course of birth, growth, maturity, decline, dissolution, and death—much like human beings. This cyclic understanding of history helped explain America's birth as a new nation. England, aged and corrupted by its own power, had begun its decline, while the United States, youthful and vigorous, had entered its upward cycle of social development.

## The Meaning of Social Equality

Equality was the second element of America's new social faith. By social equality, most people did not mean an actual equality of social condition. They meant two other things instead.

The first was equality of opportunity. We have seen in Chapter 8 how reluctant the Federalists were to give up their familiar notions of social privilege. But we have also seen that it became increasingly difficult for them to support such doctrines openly. In a republican society, social differences were not to be based on privilege or inherited position but on ability. For that to be true, society had to provide people with the opportunity to rise as far as their abilities and ambition allowed. The emphasis on equality of opportunity was attractive to social democrats, for it spoke of setting privilege aside and giving everyone an equal chance. Social conservatives, however, could embrace it as well, for it could be used to explain continuing social inequalities, implying that people who fell behind did not have the ability to succeed.

The doctrine of equal opportunity had little relevance for the actual life circumstances of many Americans. Slaves, women, and working-class men understood all too well the limits of opportunity in preindustrial America. But the principle was bold and inspiring for countless others.

Social equality had a powerful moral dimension as well, for it implied an equality of social worth among individuals, no matter what their wealth or social standing might be. Though ordinary Americans generally accepted inequalities of wealth and social position, they were much less willing to tolerate social pretension or the arrogant assumption that differences in social standing signified differences in people's value.

That attitude showed up repeatedly in daily encounters, but nowhere more vividly than in an episode that took place in New York City in 1795. Thomas Burke and Timothy Crady, two recent Irish immigrants, ran a ferry across the East River between lower Manhattan and Brooklyn. One day in early November, Gabriel Furman, a merchant and Federalist alderman, arrived on the Brooklyn shore a bit before the scheduled departure time. Impatient to get across, Furman instructed the ferrymen to leave early. When they refused, he upbraided the "rascals" for their disrespect and threatened to have them arrested. Crady was especially angered by the alderman's arrogance. He and Burke, Crady exploded, "were as good as any buggers," and he threatened to use his boathook on anyone who tried to arrest him. When the ferry landed on the Manhattan shore, Furman called the constable and had the two arrested, brandishing his cane at them as they were led off to jail, where they were charged with vagrancy. Their employer offered bail, but Furman refused to allow it, and so they remained 12 days in Bridewell prison awaiting trial.

Both Crady and Burke were eventually hauled before Mayor Varick and three other Federalist aldermen, sitting as the Court of General Sessions. There was no jury. The judges quickly decided to make examples of the two insolent Irishmen. "You rascals, we'll trim you," Varick allegedly said; "we'll learn you to insult men in office." The two ferrymen were not allowed to speak in their own behalf, nor were friendly witnesses permitted to testify. The magistrates quickly found the two guilty on charges of insulting an alderman and threatening the constable, sentenced them to two months at hard labor, and ordered 25 lashes for Crady as well.

Within a month, the two ferrymen had bolted from jail and disappeared into Pennsylvania, never to be heard from again. The episode, however, was not yet over, for a young Jeffersonian lawyer named William Keteltas took up the case and in time carried it all the way to the New York assembly. In a two-column newspaper account signed "One of the People," he castigated "the tyranny and partiality of the court" and concluded that Burke and Crady had been punished to "gratify the pride, the ambition and insolence of men in office." That, he argued, was intolerable in a republican society. The assembly, he charged, was protecting the mayor to save his reputation. But what of the ruined reputations of the ferrymen? Were they not just as important?

Before it was over, the incident generated wide public anger, and Keteltas earned a jail sentence for lambasting the legislature's failure to address the case. Over 2,000 citizens crowded the assembly chamber when Keteltas was sentenced and then carried him in a chair through the streets chanting "The Spirit of '76." Once released, he was paraded through the streets by a throng carrying American and French flags and a banner inscribed "What you rascal, insult your superiors?" In the early republic, notions of equal social worth spread rapidly.

## The Doctrine of Individualism

The doctrine of individualism was the third element in America's new social faith. It asserted that society's basic purpose was to promote the interests of its individual members. That idea had been voiced during the colonial years, but then it had been carefully balanced by the opposing view that individuals existed only as parts of a larger social order and must subordinate themselves to the good of society.

Revolutionary republicanism, with its emphasis on public virtue, initially reinforced the doctrine that the public good outweighed the interests of individuals. The Revolutionary experience, however, moved the balance in the other direction, in favor of an emphasis on the primacy of the free and unfettered individual. The stress on natural rights had that effect, as did the widespread questioning of authority that occurred.

Equality of opportunity and moral worth, individualism, and a belief that society could be shaped in ways to increase human liberty all combined to create a dramatically new social vision that Americans carried with them into the nineteenth century.

## Alleviating Poverty and Distress

It was a heady brew, this new combination of social beliefs, and it underlay early nineteenth-century efforts at social reform. Most of these reforms also drew nourishment from the perfectionist emphasis of the Second Great Awakening (see Chapter 10). By the 1830s, American reform would be in full swing. During the early years of the century, the goals and accomplishments of reform were more modest, but a clear start was made toward perfecting republican society.

The alleviation of poverty was one goal of these early social reformers. A few individuals, such as Benjamin Rush of Philadelphia, believed that poverty could be permanently reduced, and he proposed programs of education for the poor designed to achieve that end. Many Americans, however, took a more limited view, continuing to believe that poverty was inevitable, that its primary causes were hard drink and moral indolence, and that the most that could be done was to offer selective relief to deserving individuals. In New York City during the early decades of the century, private and public authorities established more than 100 charitable and relief agencies to aid orphans and widows, aged females and young prostitutes, immigrants and imprisoned debtors, juvenile delinquents and poverty-stricken seamen.

Most of these ventures distinguished between the "worthy poor," respectable folk who were victims of circumstance and merited assistance, and the "idle" or "vicious poor," who lacked character and thus deserved their fate. Many Americans thought such distinctions were real and discoverable. No matter that a New York commission in 1823 found only 43 able-bodied adults (37 women and 9 men) among the 851 inmates of the city's almshouses; or that a census of homes for the indigent in 1813 listed people such as Susanne Wilson, a blind pauper, aged 76, who first entered the almshouse in 1761; or that another listing included a variety of disabled Revolutionary War veterans, abandoned infants, illegitimate children, and indigent immigrants recently arrived from Europe. New Yorkers had not yet connected pauperism with the changing conditions of urban, commercial life.

Poverty was not the only object of public and private reform. Municipal and state authorities as well as private charities established orphanages for children, asylums for the insane, and hospitals for the sick. Most of these institutions were small and short-lived, but they provided a beginning for the more ambitious reform efforts that were to come.

### Educating the Republic's Children

A virtuous republic required above all the education of its citizens so that they would be honest, hard-working, and civic-minded. Educating the "rising generation" of young Americans involved not just the three R's but, as Noah Webster explained, "an acquaintance with ethics and . . . the general principles of law, commerce, money and government"—in other words, the basic doctrines of republican society.

Except in New England, which had a long tradition of public schooling, education in the colonial era had been largely left to individual families. Typically that meant that only the children of the well-to-do, who could pay the costs of tutors or academies, received even the most rudimentary education.

Following the Revolution, however, state legislatures, led by Massachusetts in 1789, began for the first time to appropriate tax revenues for the support of free public education. In 1795, Governor George Clinton of New York complained that education was "confined to the children of the opulent" and urged state aid to common schools. Over the next five years, the legislature appropriated $50,000 a year to be divided among local common school committees. Tax-shy legislatures and deep-seated devo-

tion to local control often frustrated the efforts of educational reformers, but the new principle that the state had an obligation to educate its citizens had been declared. In the meantime, free charity schools, financed by churches and private philanthropists and organized to train the children of the poor in responsible republican citizenship, took up some of the slack.

Colleges were also affected by the new attention to education. When the Revolution began, only nine colleges existed in the colonies. By 1800, that number had increased to 25—including the first state universities in North Carolina (1789), Georgia (1801), and Virginia (1819)—and by 1820 to more than twice that many. In most of them, traditional education, based on classical languages and theology and designed primarily for the training of clergymen, was broadened to include geography, natural sciences, and European languages, subjects deemed more useful for republican leaders.

Zest for the diffusion of knowledge was also revealed in the founding of scientific organizations, natural history museums, and medical and philosophical societies. Drawing on the optimism of the Enlightenment, the new republic's intellectual leaders saw these organizations as instruments for improving American life. Boston's Academy of Arts and Sciences (1780), the New Jersey Society for the Promotion of Agriculture, Commerce, and Art (1781), and the Philadelphia Natural History Museum (founded in 1794 by Charles Willson Peale, one of the nation's most accomplished artists) were only a few of the many organizations that sprang up between 1780 and 1820.

### Women in Republican Society

Reform in the early republic also focused on women. Though women's lives did not change dramatically during these early years, changes that helped set the stage for later, more dramatic breakthroughs did occur.

Divorce was one area where women achieved somewhat more equal treatment. When a neighbor asked John Backus, a silversmith in Great Barrington, Massachusetts, why he kicked and struck his wife, John replied that it was partly owing to his education, for his

*Ludwig (Lewis) Miller, who painted many watercolors of his life in York County, Pennsylvania, here shows himself giving a music lesson to the students in the coeducational Lutheran school in 1805.*

father often treated his mother in the same manner. We don't know whether John's mother tolerated such abuse, but his wife did not. She complained of cruelty, desertion, and adultery, and obtained a divorce. Her reaction was not unique, for during the late eighteenth and early nineteenth centuries, increasing numbers of women followed her example.

Many demonstrated their unwillingness to stay with a bad marriage by walking out. We know this from the increasing number of newspaper notices taken out by deserted husbands announcing that their wives had left bed and board. Some women filed directly for divorce. The process was not easy, for most states allowed divorce only on the single ground of adultery, and South Carolina did not permit it at all. Moreover, women typically had to present detailed evidence of their husbands' infidelities and face the discomfort of an all-male court, while a wife's transgressions could be more easily established and might include disobedience as well as more serious offenses such as adultery. Amos Bliss believed he had a valid complaint against his wife, Phebe, because, as his divorce petition stated, she "behaved herself unfriendly and unsubjectedly toward him," had "linked herself in friendship with her father's family against him," and was "wasteful and careless of his provisions and goods." Marriage may have been a contract, but it remained a contract of unequals.

Still, divorce was somewhat more available to women. In Massachusetts during the decade after independence, 50 percent more women than men filed for divorce, with almost exactly the same rate of success. Part of the explanation no doubt lies in the war's disruptions, which led larger numbers of men to desert their wives and thus larger numbers of women to take action. It is just as likely that women shared the new notions of individualism and social equality and from them developed rising expectations of marriage. Finally, the increasingly sympathetic treatment of women's divorce petitions, at least in Massachusetts, suggests that their complaints were being taken more seriously and that their status within the family had risen.

Changes also occurred in women's education. This was part of the general enthusiasm for educational reform, but it reflected a special concern for women's place in the new republic. Given women's role as keepers of public morality and nurturers of future citizens, their education was a subject of general concern. If the republic was to fulfill its destiny, young women would have to prepare for the responsibilities that motherhood would bring. During the 1790s, Judith Sargeant Murray published a series of essays, gathered under the title *The Gleaner*, in which she decried the antiegalitarian habit of assuming that a genteel education in music and needlework was superior to a practical one. She was also critical of parents who "pointed their daughters" toward marriage and dependence. "I would give my daughters every accomplishment which I thought proper," Murray wrote. "They should be enabled to procure for themselves the necessaries of life; independence should be placed within their grasp. A woman," she concluded, "should reverence herself."

Between 1790 and 1820, a number of female academies were established. Most, such as Susanna Rowson's Young Ladies Academy of Philadelphia, were located in northeastern cities. Timothy Dwight, the future president of Yale, opened his academy at Greenfield Hill in Connecticut to girls and taught them the same subjects he taught boys, at the same time and in the same room; but he was the exception. Most proposals for female education assumed that the curriculum should be different and less demanding than that provided boys.

Benjamin Rush, in his essay "Thoughts upon Female Education" (1787), prescribed bookkeeping, reading, grammar, penmanship, geography, natural philosophy, vocal music ("because it soothes cares and is good for the lungs"), and history. But he argued that female education should be condensed so that young women could marry in a timely way. Traditionalists such as Boston minister Rev. John Gardiner were decidedly less sympathetic. "Women of masculine minds," he warned, "have generally masculine manners, and a robustness of person ill calculated to inspire the tender passions." Even the *Lady's Magazine* counseled that while learning was the road to preferment for men, "consequences very opposite were the result of the same quality in women."

The prediction that intellect would unsex women was accompanied by the warning that educated women would abandon their proper sphere as mothers and wives. In the face of that threatening charge, even the most ardent supporters of female learning insisted that they sought education so that they might function more effectively within their traditional sphere. As Judith Sargeant Murray explained, the happiness of the nation depended on the happiness of families, and that is based in turn on women who are "properly methodical, and economical in their . . . expenditures of time." As "daughters of Columbia," educated women would "fill with honor the parts allotted them." It was a lofty but limited vision of what women's place in the republic should be. Even that vision,

*Thomas and Sarah Mifflin, a well-to-do Quaker couple, sat for this portrait by John Singleton Copley. Note that Mrs. Mifflin's hands are busy weaving thread into a strip of fringe, while her husband marks his place in the book he is reading. Literacy for women was not considered a necessity until well into the nineteenth century.*

however, was restricted mostly to white, urban, middle- and upper-class young ladies.

## The Limits of Reform: Race and Slavery

Early nineteenth-century reform made only limited progress in ameliorating the twin evils of slavery and racism. Slavery's inconsistency with republican principles continued to be pointed out after 1790, but with much less urgency than before, while the prospects of further abolition became increasingly faint. In spite of Ben Thompson's experience, manumission of individual slaves by private owners slowed as well.

The reasons were several. The gradual abolition of slavery in the North soothed many consciences, while in the South, the spread of cotton increased the value of slave labor. Equally important in shaping white attitudes, however, were two slave rebellions, one bloody and successful on the Caribbean island of Hispaniola (which later became Haiti and the Dominican Republic) in 1791, the other, smaller and unsuccessful but still bloody enough, near Richmond, Virginia, nearly a decade later.

Panic-stricken whites fleeing Hispaniola for their lives carried word to the North American mainland of the black Haitians' successful rebellion against a French colonial army of 25,000. The news spread terror, especially through Georgia and the Carolinas, where rumors abounded that Haitian incendiaries would soon be landing. Immediately, southern whites tightened their black codes, cut the importation of new slaves from the Caribbean, and quizzed their slaves in an effort to root out malcontents and suspected Haitian revolutionaries. The bloody rebellion and the prospect of a nearby island nation governed by blacks frightened northern whites as well. Colonial rebellions were noble, but not when they set blacks against white authority.

A second shock followed in the summer of 1800, when another rebellion, this time just outside Richmond, was nipped in the bud. Gabriel Prosser, a 24-year-old free black, had fashioned a plan to arm 1,000 slaves for an assault on Richmond. Prosser and his immediate accomplices were all native-born Americans who spoke English, worked at skilled jobs that gave them considerable personal freedom (and thus opportunity to lay their plans), and knew enough about American independence to speak confidently of freedom and equality. A drenching downpour delayed the attack, giving time for several loyal, black house servants to sound the alarm before the conspirators could act. No white lives were lost, but blacks paid a heavy cost, for alarmed white Virginians exacted their revenge. Scores of slaves and free blacks were arrested, and 25 suspects, including Gabriel Prosser, were hanged at the personal order of Governor James Monroe.

The carnage saddened Thomas Jefferson. "There is strong sentiment that there has been hanging enough," he wrote to his young friend Monroe. "The other states and the world at large will forever condemn us if we indulge in a principle of revenge, or go one step beyond absolute necessity." In the midst of panic, however, necessity was hard to define, and the fateful steps had already been taken.

In the early nineteenth century, antislavery appeals all but disappeared from the South, while proslavery arguments increased. "A large majority of the people of the southern states," declared Congressman Peter Early of Georgia in 1806, "do not consider slavery as a crime. They do not consider it immoral to hold human flesh in bondage. Many deprecate slavery as an evil, as a political evil," he continued, "but not as a crime." White southerners at the time of the Civil War would be saying much the same thing.

In the North, antislavery attitudes were increasingly conciliatory toward slave owners and unsympathetic toward blacks. Most of slavery's critics assumed that private manumission was the only safe approach, that it should be gradual so as to avoid social turmoil, and that it should be accompanied by the colonization of freed blacks in Africa. The American Colonization Society, founded in 1816, typified these attitudes. Many of its supporters genuinely hated slavery but believed the two races could never coexist without it. Others were slaveholders who saw in colonization a convenient way of

## Blacks and Slavery, 1790–1820

*Source:* U.S. Bureau of the Census.

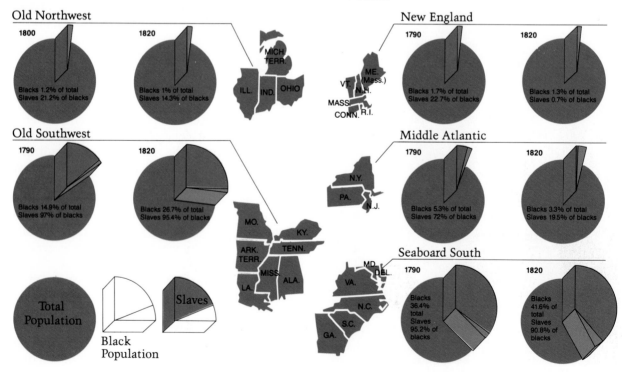

reducing the free black population and eliminating troublesome bondsmen. The Colonization Society never sent many blacks abroad, but it did help allay white anxieties.

Nor did free blacks, living in the North, find their lives much improved by the first stirrings of republican reform. During the half century following independence, strong and growing black communities appeared in the northern port cities. Emancipation in the North and the Upper South enabled increasing numbers of blacks to leave their masters' homes and establish their own households. The majority did so in the major port cities of Boston, New York, Philadelphia, and Baltimore.

Fed by people like Phyllis Sherman coming in from the northern countryside and Ben Thompson making his way up from the South, black communities began to grow. On the eve of independence, 4,000 slaves and a few hundred free blacks had called the four port cities home; 50 years later, more than 30,000 free blacks did so.

The men who came sought employment as laborers or sailors, the women as domestics. They sought as well the companionship of other people of color. There were hundreds like Alexander Giles, a free black Philadelphia seaman

who had been born in 1777 in nearby Kent County, Delaware, and Randall Shepherd, who had made his way north from Nansemond County, Virginia, in 1798.

The development of black neighborhoods was a result both of white discrimination and the black desire for community. In rural areas, free blacks lived in relative isolation and were largely defenseless against white hostility. In the cities, however, numbers provided some protection and greatly improved the chances of finding a marriage partner, establishing a family, and participating in the activities of black organizations. Family formation was eased by the fact that many of the migrants were women, thus correcting a longstanding urban imbalance.

Even so, the process of forming families often took years. After extricating themselves from their masters, former slaves typically established extended households that included relatives, friends, and boarders. As circumstances allowed, single family units were formed. In the northern cities by 1820, most blacks belonged to autonomous households.

As their numbers increased, blacks fashioned community institutions. In 1794, Richard Allen and Absalom Jones founded the first two black churches in Philadelphia. By 1813, the two

*In this watercolor of a black Methodist church meeting, Paul Svinin, a traveler from Russia, reveals his amazement at the physical emotion displayed by the worshipers. "African" churches, schools, and other organizations were rare before 1800 but grew steadily in the ensuing decades.*

congregations contained over 1,800 people. "African" schools, mutual-aid societies, and fraternal associations followed, first in Philadelphia and Boston, more slowly in New York and Baltimore, where slavery lingered longer.

By 1820, a rich institutional and cultural life had taken root in the black neighborhoods of the port cities. White hostility, however, remained. Slavery's abolition actually increased rather than diminished white enmity in the North, in part because it pitted free blacks more directly against white laborers for employment, especially during the hard times following the embargo and the War of 1812. Working-class whites were unnerved as well by the growing black competition for cheap housing. Open expressions of violence against free blacks were infrequent during the early decades of the century, but even so, blacks found themselves increasingly segregated in residence, employment, and social life. Race, as well as gender and class, continued to separate Americans from each other and reveal the limits of America's new social faith.

## CONCLUSION: Between Two Worlds

The years between 1790 and 1820 were years of transition between preindustrial America and the industrializing world of the nineteenth century.

America's renewed commercial prosperity was grounded in traditional dependence on Europe, yet its profits financed the beginnings of industrialization. Northern agriculture remained largely unchanged, but the continuing spread of commercial agriculture would soon launch a revolution in agricultural productivity. Staple agriculture still dominated the South, but cotton would transform the region and powerfully affect the entire nation. Perhaps most important, the separation from England, the surge of commercial prosperity, and the accelerating pace of westward expansion created a new and exuberant spirit of economic opportunity that would dominate the years ahead.

Region and locality still shaped people's lives, while differences of race, class, and gender remained largely unchanged. And yet even here, old ways of life were giving way, and new ones were forming. Social ideals and expectations were changing most rapidly of all, as an emphasis on youthfulness and change, social equality and individualism shaped Americans' attitudes toward their society and its possibilities.

Life in the early republic still echoed the past but pointed unmistakably toward the future. In Chapter 10 we shall examine how religious and political life, relations with Europe and the rest of the Americas, and the interaction between whites and Native Americans changed during these years of transition.

### Recommended Reading

Valuable information on America's preindustrial economy can be found in Stuart Bruchey, *The Roots of American Economic Growth, 1607–1861* (1965); Curtis Nettels, *The Emergence of a National Economy 1775–1815* (1962); and Louis Hartz, *Economic Policy and Democratic Thought: Pennsylvania, 1776–1860* (1948).

For illuminating discussions of merchant capitalism and early industrialization, see Jonathan Prude, *The Coming of Industrial Order: Town and Factory Life in Rural Massachusetts, 1810–1860* (1983); Susan Hirsch, *Roots of the American Working Class: The Industrialization of Crafts in Newark, 1800–1860* (1978); Howard Rock, *Artisans of the New Republic:*

The Tradesmen of New York City in the Age of Jefferson (1979); and Bruce Laurie, Working People of Philadelphia, 1800–1850 (1980). Early nineteenth-century agriculture is examined in Percy Bidwell and John Falconer, History of Agriculture in the Northern United States, 1620–1860 (1925) and James Lemon, The Best Poor Man's Country: A Geographical Study of Early Southeastern Pennsylvania (1972).

Important information on the trans-Appalachian West can be found in Malcolm Rohrbough, The Trans-Appalachian Frontier: People, Societies, and Institutions, 1775–1850 (1978); Richard Wade, The Urban Frontier: The Rise of Western Cities, 1790–1830 (1959); and Ray Billington, Westward Expansion, 4th ed. (1974). Changes in transportation and communication are traced in Alan Pred, Urban Growth and the Circulation of Information: The United States System of Cities, 1790–1840 (1973) and Ronald Shaw, Erie Water West: A History of The Erie Canal, 1792–1854 (1966).

Themes of class and wealth are dealt with in Sean Wilentz, Chants Democratic: New York City and the Rise of the American Working Class, 1788–1850 (1984); Robert Doherty, Society and Power: Five New England Towns, 1800–1860 (1977); and Raymond Mohl, Poverty in New York, 1783–1825 (1971).

Among important works on women are Nancy Cott, The Bonds of Womanhood: "Woman's Sphere" in New England, 1780–1835 (1977); and Carl Degler, At Odds: Women and the Family in America from the Revolution to the Present (1980). On race and slavery, see Gerald Mullin, Flight and Rebellion (1972); Robert McColley, Slavery and Jeffersonian Virginia (1964); and Leon Litwack, North of Slavery: The Negro in the Free States, 1790–1860 (1961).

Recent books on early education include Carl Kaestle, Pillars of the Republic: Common Schools and American Society, 1780–1860 (1983); Lawrence Cremin, American Education: The National Experience, 1783–1876 (1980); Howard Miller, The Revolutionary College: American Presbyterian Higher Education, 1707–1837 (1976); and Stephen Novak, The Rights of Youth: American Colleges and Student Revolt, 1798–1815 (1977).

## TIME LINE

| | |
|---|---|
| 1776 | Adam Smith publishes Wealth of Nations |
| 1790 | First textile mill established in Pawtucket, Rhode Island |
| 1790s | Turnpike construction in Northeast<br>Yellow fever epidemics in cities<br>Female academies founded<br>Cotton production booms in the South |
| 1791 | Black rebellion begins in Haiti |
| 1793 | Eli Whitney invents the cotton gin<br>Europe embroiled in war |
| 1794 | First Afro-American churches founded |
| 1800 | Gabriel's rebellion in Virginia |
| 1807 | Robert Fulton launches first steamboat<br>Cast-iron plow patented<br>Jefferson declares trade embargo<br>U.S. slave trade ends |
| 1809 | Embargo lifted |
| 1811 | Successful trip of steamboat from Ohio River to New Orleans |
| 1812–1814 | War with Great Britain |
| 1815 | Waltham textile mills established |
| 1816 | American Colonization Society formed |
| 1819 | Panic of 1819 |

# CHAPTER 10
## POLITICS AND SOCIETY
## IN THE EARLY REPUBLIC

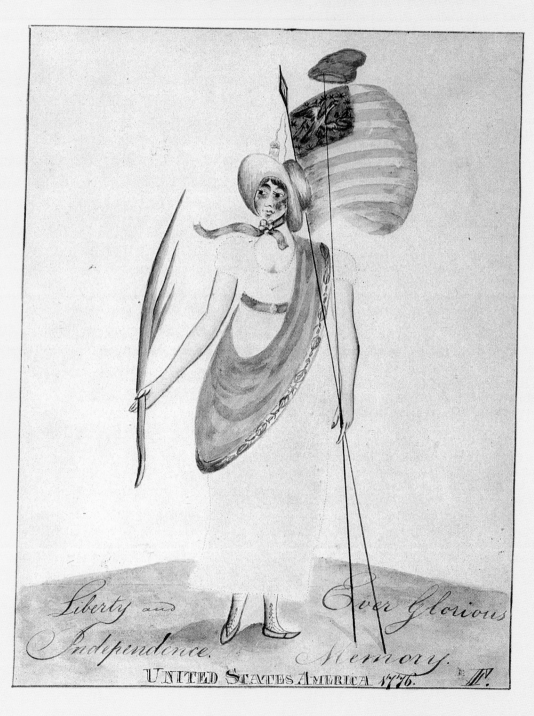

Liberty and Independence. Ever Glorious Memory.
UNITED STATES AMERICA 1776.

In June 1799, a middle-aged Seneca named Handsome Lake, living on a tiny reservation in western New York, began to preach a message of hope and redemption to his people. Like so many of his tribe, Handsome Lake had been beaten down by the experiences of the preceding 30 years. As a young warrior in 1776, he had joined England in the fight against American independence. Wounded on several occasions, his spirit broken by the American victory, he had watched helplessly as the Senecas' land was taken and his people were confined on reservations. Handsome Lake's own life had crumbled as well. On several occasions, alcohol and depression brought him close to death.

As he lay on his bunk, scarcely breathing, Handsome Lake experienced a vision. Out of that vision and others like it, he fashioned a message of renewal for the Seneca people. The Great Spirit, he explained, had given him two "gospels" to share with them. The first was a religious or apocalyptic gospel. In it Handsome Lake preached the imminence of the world's destruction; the dangers of spiritual sins such as witchcraft, abortion, and drunkenness; and the promise of salvation through the rituals of *Gaiwiio*, a new form of worship combining Christian elements with the great ceremonies of the Seneca's traditional religious calendar.

Handsome Lake also preached a "social gospel," offering guidance for the reconstruction of Seneca life. Here again he called for a mingling of old ways and new. Drawing ideas from the federal officials who encouraged his revival movement and the example of nearby Quaker missionaries, Handsome Lake emphasized the importance of temperance, peace, land retention, acculturation, and domestic morality.

Though in time his dictatorial manner alienated many supporters, his message inspired a dramatic revitalization of the Seneca nation. In 1800, the Seneca people were hungering for leadership. The traumatic changes of the late eighteenth century had run their course, their lives had stabilized, and they could once more imagine a better future. Handsome Lake offered them hope and renewed pride. His gospels, moreover, originated in a vision transmitted by the Great Spirit. In Seneca culture, no source of truth was more powerful or certain. He also commanded the attention of his people because he had shared with them the humiliation of defeat and the poverty of reservation life. Finally, his gospels had effect because they were supported by other tribal leaders, especially his half sister Gayantgogwus, who spoke for the tribal women before the Great Council, and Cornplanter, political leader of the community and Handsome Lake's half brother.

Revitalization was one strategy of survival followed by Native Americans during the early nineteenth century. There were others, including armed resistance. Most Native Americans lived at the margins of white society, near the frontier of settlement, which pushed steadily westward. Their relations with white settlers and with state and national governments reveal much about the nation's early history—its dynamic expansion, commercial and agrarian values, and definitions of republican liberty. We shall examine what those relations were like.

There were other changes as well that continued to transform American life between 1800 and 1824. After their victory over the Federalists in 1800, the Jeffersonian Republicans reshaped the national government and implemented their vision of an expanding, agrarian republic. The Jeffersonians also transformed America's diplomatic relations with Europe and the rest of the Western Hemisphere. As Americans struggled to make the nation secure, they also worked to create a new cultural identity consistent with their republican values.

Finally, American politics continued to evolve during the years of Jeffersonian ascendency. At the local level this meant the increasing democratization of political life. Nationally these years brought the collapse of the Federalist-Jeffersonian party system of the 1790s, and set the stage for the dramatically new political era that Andrew Jackson's election to the presidency in 1828 would usher in.

## RESTORING REPUBLICAN LIBERTY

The Jeffersonians entered office in March 1801 with several clear objectives in mind: calming the political storms that had threatened to rend the country, consolidating their recent victory, purging the government of Federalist impurities, and setting it on a proper republican course. They set about these tasks with eager determination.

### The Jeffersonian Republicans Take Control

The government had moved from Philadelphia to the new capital in the District of Columbia in November 1800, while John Adams was still president. When the politicians arrived in Washington, they were stunned by its primitiveness and isolation. In New York and Philadelphia, where the national government had met since 1789, politicians could find comfortable (though expensive) accommodations, enjoy the companionship of merchants and others of note, and keep abreast of news brought into those

busy ports by ships from around the Atlantic world. The new capital, however, was little more than a swampy clearing on the banks of the Potomac River, lost among the woods of Maryland and northern Virginia.

Congress, boasting that the new governmental community would become "the Rome of the New World," had commissioned the Frenchman Pierre L'Enfant to develop a plan for the capital. L'Enfant produced a magnificent design, replete with central plazas and broad boulevards radiating outward from a government center anchored by the capitol building and the presidential mansion. At the time Adams moved there, however, little of the grand design had materialized. The Capitol wing containing the House chamber was finished, but the Senate chamber was still under construction. The president's mansion also remained unfinished.

Congress had expected that income from the sale of residential and commercial plots would pay for the government's resettlement. After an initial flurry of interest, however, sales sagged

*Pierre L'Enfant's grand design for the new capital city was published in the* Columbian Magazine *of March 1792. Ten years later, however, little of the plan had been completed.*

*Although hardly a wilderness outpost, Washington boasted few of the comforts to be found in more established cities. This* View of the Suburbs, *c. 1800, gives a vivid impression of the capital's newness.*

and people stopped coming. As late as 1820, Washington remained a sleepy town of only 10,000 people. Congressmen complained constantly about the heat, poor accommodations, and isolation from family and home community. They did more than complain; they fled the capital at every opportunity to tend to their personal and financial affairs and refused, with disturbing regularity, to stand for reelection.

In keeping with his desire to rid the government of Federalist embellishments, Jefferson planned a simple inauguration. What might have been an awkward encounter was eased when an embittered President Adams slipped out of Washington early on the morning of inauguration day. Shortly before noon on March 4, the president-elect walked to the Capitol from his temporary lodgings at a nearby boardinghouse. "His dress," noted one observer, "was, as usual, that of a plain citizen, without any distinctive badge of office." Jefferson read his short inaugural address in a voice so low that some in attendance had difficulty hearing. When he had finished, Chief Justice John Marshall, a Virginian but a staunch Federalist as well, administered the oath of office, a company of militia fired a 16-gun salute, and the ceremony ended.

Though simple, the inauguration was filled with significance. The last years of Adams's presidency had been tempestuous, and people were uncertain what the new administration would bring. This was the first time in the nation's brief history that control of the government had shifted from one political party to another. Some wondered if the change could be accomplished peacefully. Mrs. Samuel Harrison Smith, wife of the editor of the Washington *National Intelligencer*, described the occasion's drama: "I have this morning witnessed one of the most interesting scenes a free people can ever witness," she wrote a friend. "The changes of administration, which in every . . . age have most generally been epochs of confusion, villainy, and bloodshed, in this our happy country take place without any species of distraction or disorder." Many Americans shared her sense of relief and pride.

In his inaugural speech, Jefferson enumerated "the essential principles of republican government" that would guide his administration:

"equal and exact justice to all"; support of the states as "the surest bulwarks against antirepublican tendencies"; "absolute acquiescence" in the decisions of the majority; supremacy of civil over military authority; reduction of government spending; "honest payment" of the public debts; freedom of the press; and "freedom of the person under the protection of the *habeas corpus*." Though Jefferson never mentioned the Federalists by name, his litany of principles echoed with the dark experience of the 1790s. His followers could rest assured that the government was finally in safe, republican hands.

The president spoke also of political reconciliation. Everyone, Federalists and Jeffersonians alike, he declared, must "unite in common efforts for the common good." "Every difference of opinion," he explained "is not a difference of principle. We have called by different names brethren of the same principles. We are all republicans—we are all federalists."

Not all his followers welcomed that final flourish, for many were eager to root the Federalists out and scatter them to the political winds. Memories of the 1790s were still too fresh, the stakes too high, and differences of principle too great to talk about reconciliation. Jefferson, however, was not naive. His goal was to absorb the moderate Federalists, isolate the extremists, and destroy the Federalist party as a political force. That was essential, he believed, to the continuing supremacy of his own party and the safety of the republic. His strategy worked, for never again did the Federalists regain control of the national government.

## Cleansing the Government

Having swept both houses of Congress as well as the presidency in 1800, the Jeffersonians claimed a mandate to cleanse the government of Federalist corruptions. How could they make the necessary changes, though, if Federalist officeholders remained in place? The Jeffersonians were especially outraged by a flurry of last-minute appointments President Adams had pushed through the lame-duck Federalist Congress during the closing days of his administration in an effort to reward party loyalists and deny the Jeffersonians full control of the government.

Jefferson decided to withhold the commissions not yet delivered; but what about the Federalists already in place? In Connecticut, where the Jeffersonian party was still struggling to take hold, his supporters demanded control of local federal offices such as that of the collector of customs and the inspectors of the port of New Haven. A letter signed by the state's Jeffersonian leaders bluntly told the president, "Even if it should be judged good policy in all other States, to retain the Federalists . . . yet in this State . . . such a policy [would bring] only the certain ruin of republicanism." Jefferson reluctantly agreed that "a general sweep" of Federalist officeholders was necessary. By July 1803, only a third of appointive federal officials were Federalists; by 1808, virtually all government personnel were solid Republicans.

## The Judiciary and the Principle of Judicial Review

Having lost Congress and the presidency, the Federalists turned to the judiciary for protection against the expected Jeffersonian onslaught. Late in Adams's administration, the Federalists had introduced a new Judiciary Act calling for the expansion of the number of circuit courts and judges, each court with its array of federal marshals, attorneys, and clerks. Congress passed the bill in February 1801, just before adjourning. This blatant effort to pack the judiciary aroused the Jeffersonians' wrath. "The Federalists," observed Jefferson bitterly, "defeated at the polls, have retired into the Judiciary, and from that barricade . . . hope to batter down all the bulwarks of Republicanism."

A Federalist judiciary was especially obnoxious because during the 1790s, Federalist judges had expanded their jurisdiction by invoking principles of the English common law, which they held to be still in force in areas where Congress had not legislated. England's common law, protested the Jeffersonians, was a product of monarchic government and was incompatible with republican liberty. "The revolution [of 1800]," declared Representative William Branch Giles, "is incomplete so long as that strong

fortress [the judiciary] is in possession of the enemy." Something had to be done.

In January 1802, Senator John Breckenridge of Kentucky introduced a bill calling for repeal of the Judiciary Act of 1801. A staunch opponent of common law, he was also angry because in the land controversies wracking his state, federal district courts had consistently ruled against Kentucky settlers and in favor of absentee Virginia landlords holding patents granted years earlier when Kentucky was still part of Virginia. The law of 1801, moreover, was a "wanton waste of the public treasure. . . . The time will never arrive," Breckenridge asserted, "when America will stand in need of 38 federal judges."

In reply, the Federalists insisted that the real issues were the judiciary's security from political attack and its ability to oppose democratic excesses. Gouverneur Morris, Federalist senator from New York, declared that an independent judiciary was necessary "to save the people from their most dangerous enemy, themselves." The Constitution, he explained, had provided for a judicial branch to "stop you short" if you "trench upon the rights of your fellow citizens, by passing an unconstitutional law."

The Jeffersonians responded by asking who would "check the courts when they violate the Constitution?" Granting the courts sole power to nullify legislation would give them "the absolute direction of the Government." Each branch of the government—executive and legislative as well as judicial—must have the right to decide on the validity of an act. Some among the Jeffersonians also argued that judges should be elected by the people rather than appointed, so that they could be held more closely accountable.

Congressional debate over repeal of the Judiciary Act generated wide public attention, for it offered a vivid contrast between Federalist and Jeffersonian notions of republican government. The House was deluged with petitions supporting and opposing repeal. Opposition came from 225 Philadelphia merchants and "sundry counsellers at law" in New Jersey, while support was voiced at public meetings in Baltimore and elsewhere.

In February 1802, by a strict party vote, Congress repealed the Judiciary Act. "Should

Mr. Breckenridge now bring forward a resolution to repeal . . . the Supreme Court of the United States," declared the editor of the *Washington Federalist*, "we should only consider it a part of the system to be pursued. . . . We sincerely expect it will be done next session. . . . Such is democracy." Jeffersonians, on the other hand, declared jubilantly that democracy had been saved.

The Jeffersonians also sought to purge several highly partisan Federalist judges from the bench. In March 1803, the House of Representatives voted to impeach federal District Judge John Pickering of New Hampshire. The grounds were not "high crimes and misdemeanors" as the Constitution required but erratic judicial behavior, especially the Federalist diatribes with which Pickering regularly assaulted defendants and juries. In their rush to remove Pickering, the Jeffersonians asserted that impeachment was not a criminal process and thus did not require evidence of a crime. Declared Representative William Branch Giles of Virginia, it is "nothing more than a declaration by Congress" that an individual holds "dangerous opinions" that, if allowed to go into effect, "will work the destruction of the Union." Although these phrases echoed the language of repression used by Federalists a half decade before, the Senate convicted Pickering, again by a strict party vote.

Spurred on by success, the Jeffersonians brought impeachment charges against Supreme Court Justice Samuel Chase, one of the most notorious Republican baiters. The indictment charged Chase with "intemperate and inflammatory political harangues," delivered "with intent to excite the fears and resentment of the . . . people . . . against the Government of the United States." The trial, however, revealed that Chase had committed no impeachable offense. He was acquitted on every count and returned triumphantly to the federal bench.

Chase was a sorry hero, but constitutional principles are often established in the defense of other than heroic people. Had Chase's impeachment succeeded, Chief Justice Marshall would almost certainly have been next, and that would have created a political and constitutional crisis. Sensing the danger, the Jeffersonians pulled back, content to allow time and the regular turnover of personnel to cleanse the bench of Federalist control.

Repeal of the Judiciary Act did not settle the issue of judicial review. That came in several important Supreme Court decisions. In *Marbury v. Madison* (1803), Chief Justice Marshall laid down in unmistakable terms the principle of exclusive judicial review. "It is emphatically the province and duty of the judicial department," he declared, "to say what the law is." In another landmark decision, *McCulloch v. Maryland* (1819), the court struck down as unconstitutional a Maryland law taxing the Baltimore branch

*John Marshall, appointed by President Adams in 1801, served as chief justice of the Supreme Court for 34 years. During that time, his decisions established some of the most basic principles of American constitutional law.*

of the Second Bank of the United States. No state, explained Chief Justice Marshall, possessed the right to tax a nationally chartered bank, for "the power to tax involves the power to destroy." In the *McCulloch* decision, Marshall also affirmed the constitutionality of the bank's congressional charter and laid down the constitutional argument for broad congressional authority. Let congressional intent "be within the scope of the Constitution," he wrote, "and all means which are appropriate . . . which are not prohibited, but consist with the letter and spirit of the Constitution, are constitutional." These two decisions established some of the most fundamental principles of American constitutional law.

## Dismantling the Federalist War Program

The Jeffersonians had regarded the Federalists' war program as a threat to republican liberty, so they moved quickly to dismantle it. Rather than wait for repeal of the hated Sedition Act, Jefferson simply stopped prosecutions under it and freed its victims. In 1802, the Sedition Act silently lapsed. The Jeffersonians, however, were not thoroughgoing civil libertarians. More than a few Federalist newspaper editors felt the government's displeasure during the early nineteenth century. But Jefferson never duplicated the Federalists' campaign to stifle dissent.

Jefferson handled the Alien Acts similarly, not bothering to seek their repeal but dismantling the Federalists' inspection system and allowing enforcement to lapse. In 1802, Congress passed a new and more liberal naturalization law, requiring only 5 rather than 14 years of residence for citizenship. The Federalists' provisional army also fell before the Jeffersonians' attack. By 1802, land forces numbered only 3,400, most of them assigned to "Indian duty" in the West. No longer would federal troops intimidate American citizens. The excise tax came under fire as well. Jefferson wanted to end it immediately, but Secretary of the Treasury Albert Gallatin argued that its revenues could help reduce the national debt. Jefferson agreed to leave it in place until it expired in 1802.

Finally, the Jeffersonians sought ways to reduce the size of the federal government. An active, expanding government they thought dangerous because it required revenue, generated taxes, added to the number of officeholders, and increased governmental power. The central government, Jefferson declared in his first message to Congress in 1801, was "charged with the external and mutual relations only of these states. The principal care of our persons, our property, and our reputation, constituting the great field of human concerns," should be left to the states because they were more closely attuned to the people's needs and could be held more closely accountable.

In actuality, the government inherited by the Jeffersonians was already small by modern standards. In 1802, the fourteenth year of its existence, it had fewer than 3,000 civilian employees from the lowest clerk to the president. That amounted to one federal public official for every 1,914 citizens, compared with one for every 62 citizens today. There were only 300 officials in Washington, half of them congressmen. Even so, Jefferson wrote his son-in-law that after carefully surveying government personnel, his administration was "hunting out and abolishing multitudes of useless offices, striking off jobs, etc., etc." As late as 1816, the government employed only 5,000 civilians, more than two-thirds of them in the post office.

In terms of domestic policy, the federal government did little more than deliver the mail, deal with Native Americans, and administer the public lands. Congress ordinarily sat only during the winter months, nor were the president or his cabinet around for much of the summer. "This government, if put to the test," declared one congressman, "is by no means calculated to endure . . . [because] it is a government not having a common feeling and a common interest with the governed." He may have overstated, but not by much.

Not everything the Jeffersonians did was consistent with strict notions of limited government. As the nation grew, so did pressures for a federal program of internal improvements. That reflected in part the growing political influence of the West, for the new states forming beyond the Appalachians were strongly nationalist in

### Federal Revenues and Expenditures, 1790–1820
### (in thousands of dollars)

| YEAR | REVENUES | | EXPENDITURES | |
|---|---|---|---|---|
| 1790 | Customs | 4,399 | Military | 634 |
| | Other | 19 | Interest on | |
| | | 4,418 |   public debt | 2,349 |
| | | | Other | 1,426 |
| | | | | 4,409 |
| 1800 | Customs | 9,081 | Military | 6,010 |
| | Internal revenue | 809 | Interest on | |
| | Other | 793 |   public debt | 3,375 |
| | | 10,848 | Other | 1,466 |
| | | | | 10,851 |
| 1810 | Customs | 8,583 | Military | 3,948 |
| | Internal revenue | 7 | Interest on | |
| | Sale of public lands | 697 |   public debt | 2,845 |
| | Other | 793 | Other | 1,447 |
| | | 10,080 | | 8,240 |
| 1820 | Customs | 15,006 | Military | 7,018 |
| | Internal revenue | 106 | Interest on | |
| | Sale of public lands | 1,636 |   public debt | 5,126 |
| | Other | 2,769 | Other | 9,324 |
| | | 19,517 | | 21,468 |

*Source:* U.S. bureau of the Census.

sentiment and sought closer ties of trade and communication with the East. The government responded by launching construction of several western routes, including the National Road (in 1811) connecting Cumberland, Maryland, with Wheeling, on the Ohio River. The states, however, carried the major responsibility for internal improvements.

The Jeffersonians were successful as well in reducing the national debt. In spite of the extraordinary costs of the Louisiana Purchase (1803), the debt dropped from $83 million in 1801 to $57 million a decade later. Renewed prosperity following the Panic of 1819 brought what one Senate committee described as "the serious inconvenience of an overflowing Treasury." Though the Jeffersonians may not have "revolutionized" the government as they claimed, they clearly changed its character and direction.

## BUILDING AN AGRARIAN REPUBLIC

The Jeffersonians did far more than reverse Federalist initiatives, for they worked vigorously to implement their own distinctive vision of an expanding, agrarian nation uniquely suited to the preservation of republican liberty. That vision guided Jeffersonian policies for over two decades, through the presidential administrations of Jefferson (1800–1808), James Madison (1808–1816), and James Monroe (1816–1824).

### The Jeffersonian Vision

Political liberty, the Jeffersonians believed, could survive only under conditions of broad economic and social equality. When wealth and social power became consolidated in the hands of a few, so did political power, and when power increased, liberty was threatened. The central task of Jeffersonian statecraft was thus to maintain on open and roughly equal society. The task was believed difficult because as societies grew in wealth and power, equality eroded and liberty was snuffed out. England offered ample evidence of that. Even in France, where the Jeffersonians had expected the cycle of oppression to be broken, the story was much the same. By 1799, the French Revolution had ended in Napoleon's dictatorship, and the dream of republican liberty lay shattered.

The Jeffersonians, however, continued to believe that America, if properly guided, could escape Europe's fate. The Federalists had sought to build the American nation through commerce, manufacturing, and a strong central government, and had regarded the resulting economic and social inequalities as both inevitable and good. The Jeffersonians' strategy for securing America's future was fundamentally different. They suspected commercial wealth, feared concentrated power, and distrusted social inequality. The central actor in the Jeffersonians' social and political drama was neither merchant nor banker but the independent yeoman farmer —self-reliant, secure in person and possessions, enterprising and yet filled with concern for the public good. Such people exemplified the qualities essential to republican citizenship.

The Jeffersonian vision threatened to become clouded, however, because industriousness generated wealth, and wealth bred inequality. In short, economic and social development threatened to destroy the social bases of republicanism. Human nature could not be changed, but the economic and social environment might be arranged to minimize concentrations of wealth, dampen personal ambitions, and thus preserve republican liberty.

The solution to the problem of economic and social development, the Jeffersonians believed, lay in rapid territorial expansion. Land, constantly expanding and readily available to the nation's yeoman citizens, would offer opportunity to a restless people, draw them out of the cities and off the crowded lands of the East, and

preserve the social equality that republican liberty required. While promoting habits of thrift and industry, the agrarian life would neither stimulate personal ambitions nor encourage the competition that in more crowded, commercial regions inflamed passions and set people against one another. Instead, exposure to the ordered regularity of nature would cleanse and calm the human spirit. Thus the republic's growth across the North American continent would prevent, or at least indefinitely delay, the cyclic process of growth, maturity, and decay through which all past societies had traveled.

Expanding America's land base was given added urgency by the arguments of an English clergyman and political economist named Thomas Malthus. In 1798, Malthus published an essay that jolted Europeans and Americans alike. Observing the growing population and increasingly crowded condition of his native England, Malthus offered ominous predictions about the future of English society and, by implication, of other societies as well.

Given the remarkable fecundity of human beings, Malthus argued, population increased more rapidly than agricultural production. "The power of population," he wrote in characteristically stark prose, "is definitely greater than the power in the earth to produce subsistence for man." Optimistic Enlightenment notions of the steadily improving quality of human life, he warned, were a delusion, for the future would be filled with increasing misery and exploitation as population outran food. The future was most clear in Europe, where land was limited and poverty widespread, but the same fate awaited America. Talk of its "perpetual youth" was nonsense.

Jefferson took Malthus's warnings seriously but refused to believe that the Englishman correctly understood America, whose vast reservoir of land would enable its people to escape Europe's fate. "The differences of circumstance between this and the old countries of Europe," Jefferson explained, "will . . . produce . . . a difference of result. There . . . the quantity of food is fixed . . . [while] supernumerary births add only to mortality. Here the immense extent of uncultivated and fertile lands enables every one who will labor, to marry young, and to raise a family of any size. Our food, then, may increase geometrically with our laborers, and our births, however multiplied, become effective."

Rapid and continuing national expansion was thus indispensable to the Jeffersonian vision of the agrarian republic. Occupation of the West was also essential to secure America's borders against continuing threats from England, France, and Spain. The rapid sale of new public lands would in addition provide revenue for reducing the national debt. Finally, the Jeffersonians calculated that westward expansion would strengthen their political control of the nation and assure the Federalists' demise.

## The Windfall Louisiana Purchase

Securing the agrarian republic by rapid territorial expansion was the Jeffersonians' fundamental goal. It explains Jefferson's most dramatic accomplishment, his purchase of the vast Louisiana Territory in 1803.

In 1800, at the urging of Napoleon, who was eager to rebuild France's New World empire, Spain ceded the vast trans-Mississippi region known as Louisiana to France. When Jefferson learned of the secret agreement in 1801, he was profoundly disturbed. His fears were well grounded, for in October 1802 the Spanish commander at New Orleans, which Spain had retained, closed the Mississippi River to American commerce, thus depriving westerners of the major outlet for their agricultural produce. Spain's action caused consternation both in Washington and in the West. Especially upsetting were rumors that Spain would soon transfer New Orleans to France. "The day that France takes New Orleans," Jefferson wrote, "we must marry ourselves to the British fleet and nation."

In January 1803, the president sent his young associate James Monroe to Paris with instructions to purchase New Orleans and West Florida, which contained Mobile, the only good harbor on the Gulf Coast, and the mouths of several rivers that drained the southern interior. Congress appropriated $2 million for the purchases, but Jefferson authorized Monroe to go as high as $10 million if necessary.

When Monroe arrived, he found the French Foreign Minister Talleyrand ready to sell all of Louisiana. The recent failure to oust Toussaint L'Ouverture, leader of the black rebellion against the French in Haiti, had deprived Napoleon of the military base necessary to mount an effective occupation of Louisiana; nor did he any longer need those lands to provide food for

*The American eagle extends its wings over New Orleans following the Louisiana Purchase in this 1803 panorama by Boqueto de Woiserie.*

Haitian slaves. Expecting a renewed war with England at any moment, moreover, Napoleon was eager to concentrate French troops in Europe. In addition, he feared American designs on Louisiana and knew he would not be able to keep American settlers away. In an effort to cut his losses, Napoleon decided to get what he could from the eager Americans and vacate North America.

In April, the deal was struck. For $15 million, the United States obtained all of Louisiana, nearly 830,000 square miles, in one stroke doubling the nation's size. It was a magnificent acquisition that would profoundly shape the nation's future. So important was Louisiana to Jefferson that he brushed aside complaints that the Constitution did not give the president authority to purchase additional territory. He urged Congress to ignore "metaphysical subtleties" and "throw themselves on their country for doing for them, unauthorized, what we know they would have done for themselves had they been in a situation to do it." Some within Jefferson's party questioned the legality of Jefferson's act, but the public's response was overwhelmingly favorable, and Congress readily approved the purchase.

The Federalists, however, reacted with alarm to the acquisition. They feared that the new states ultimately to be carved from Louisiana would be staunchly Jeffersonian and that rapid expansion of the frontier would "decivilize" the nation. In New England, Federalist extremists talked of forming a northern confederacy and seceding from the Union. Their conspiracy included plans to enlist the support of

### Exploring the Trans-Mississippi West, 1804–1807

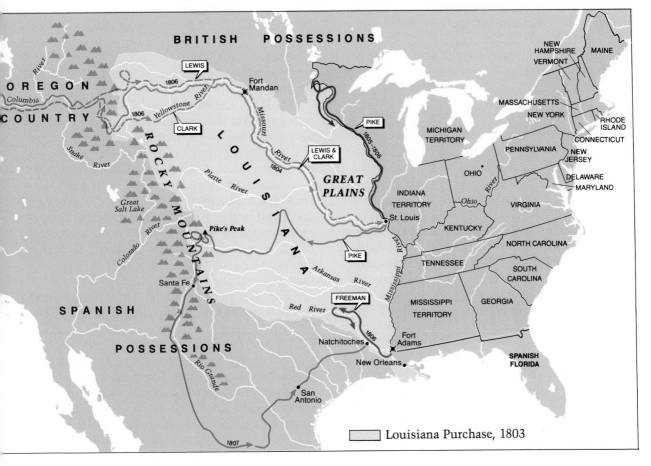

Vice-President Aaron Burr, now in open conflict with Jefferson because of his refusal to step aside in Jefferson's favor in the election of 1800. The secessionist scheme failed because it lacked public support and because key Federalist leaders, including Alexander Hamilton, refused to endorse it. Within another decade, however, New England would again echo with threats of disunion.

The nation's expansion did not stop with Louisiana. In 1810, American adventurers fomented a revolt in Spanish West Florida, captured the fort at Baton Rouge, proclaimed an independent republic, and sought annexation by the United States. In May 1812, over vigorous Spanish objections, Congress formally annexed West Florida. In 1819, pressured by southern expansionists and facing a rising tide of rebellion throughout its Latin American colonies, Spain ceded East Florida as well. As part of that agreement, the United States also extended its territorial claims beyond the original western boundary of Louisiana to include the Pacific Northwest. It was an impressive accomplishment that set the stage for the final surge of continental expansion during the 1840s.

## Exploring and Opening the New West

If America's vast new domain was to serve the needs of the agrarian republic, it would have to be explored and made ready for settlement. In the spring of 1804, Jefferson dispatched an expedition led by his personal secretary, Meriwether Lewis, and William Clark, a young army officer, to explore the Far Northwest, make contact with the Native Americans there, and bring back scientific information about the area. For nearly 2½ years the intrepid band of explorers, assisted by the Shoshoni woman Sacajawea, made its way across thousands of miles of unmapped and hostile terrain—up the Missouri River, through the Rockies via the Bitterroot Valley and Lolo Pass, down the Columbia to the Pacific coast, and back again—finally reemerging at St. Louis in September 1806. Lewis and Clark's reports of their journey fanned American interest in the trans-Mississippi West, established an American presence in the region, and demonstrated for the first time the feasibility of an overland route to the Pacific.

In 1805 and 1806, Lieutenant Zebulon Pike explored the sources of the Mississippi as far as Leech Lake in northern Minnesota. He followed that trek with an equally bold venture into New Mexico and Colorado, where he explored and named Pike's Peak. Although interest in western exploration waned after 1807 while the government was preoccupied with foreign affairs and the War of 1812, it revived in 1815. Over the next decade, the government established a string of military posts from Fort Snelling, at the confluence of the Minnesota and Mississippi rivers, to Fort Atkinson on the Missouri and Fort Smith on the Arkansas. They were intended to secure the American frontier, promote the fur trade, and support white settlement.

The Jeffersonians' agrarian vision also guided federal land policy. In the Land Act of 1796, the Federalists had set the minimum per-acre price for federal land at $2 and the standard purchase at 640 acres. Their primary objective had been to produce government revenue. The Jeffersonians desired revenue to reduce the national debt, but they were even more interested in settling people on the land. High prices and large purchase requirements hindered that objective.

In 1801, the Republican Congress passed a new Land Act that reduced the minimum allowable purchase to 320 acres, established a four-year credit system, and provided 8 percent discounts for cash sales. In addition, Congress established new land offices at Chillicothe, Marietta, and Steubenville, Ohio. Over the next year and a half, settlers, speculators, and land companies purchased nearly 400,000 acres of federal land, more than four times as much as during the entire 1790s. The amounts increased geometrically in the following decade.

The transfer of federal land into private hands was not tidy. Ownership was often confused in a tangle of conflicting titles, and the liberal credit system established in 1801 encouraged widespread speculation. In 1819, Secretary of the Treasury William Crawford reported that the government had disposed of $44 million worth of land since 1789 but had actually taken in only half that amount. In an effort to rectify that problem, the Land Act of 1820 abolished the credit system but further reduced the purchase price to $1.25 and the minimum purchase area to 80 acres. During the 1820s, several additional principles were added to federal land policy: preemption, which for the first time enabled squatters to secure title to land, and gradation in pricing, whereby lands that did not readily sell were offered at less than the established price or even given away. All were efforts to speed the transfer of public land into private hands.

Once again, northeastern Federalists, anxious about the West's growing political power and concerned that eastern labor costs would rise as workers sought new opportunities beyond the mountains, opposed these policies. Senator Samuel Foot of Connecticut even proposed a moratorium on the sale of public lands, an idea that Congress quickly rejected.

In the early nineteenth century, few activities of the federal government were as important to the American people as the expansion, exploration, and sale of the public domain. Though it frequently proved wasteful and inefficient, fostered widespread speculation, and contributed to the Panic of 1819, federal land policy ably served the Jeffersonians' goal of expanding the agrarian republic.

## INDIAN-WHITE RELATIONS IN THE EARLY REPUBLIC

As white settlers surged across the interior, they found not empty space but a land already occupied by Native American peoples. By 1800, white settlement, disease, and warfare had decimated Native Americans along the Atlantic coast, leaving only a few tribal remnants scattered from Maine to Georgia. Powerful tribes, however, still controlled much of the trans-Appalachian interior. North of the Ohio River, the Shawnee, Delaware, Miami, and Pottawatomie were allied in a Western confederacy capable of mustering several thousand warriors. South of the Ohio lived five major tribal groups, the Cherokee, Creek, Choctaw, Chickasaw, and Seminole. Together these southern tribes totaled nearly 60,000 people.

The years from 1790 to the 1820s brought a decisive shift in Indian-white relations throughout the trans-Appalachian interior. In 1790, the region was aflame with raids and warfare. As the pressures of white expansion increased, tribal groups devised various strategies of resistance and survival. Handsome Lake led the Seneca toward cultural revitalization. The Cherokee, followed a different path of peaceful accommodation. Others, like the Shawnee and Creek, rose in armed resistance. None of the strategies was altogether successful, for by the 1820s the balance of power had shifted, and the Indians faced a bleak future of continued acculturation, military defeat, or forced migration to new lands west of the Mississippi.

### Land and Trade

Between 1790 and 1820, the government established a set of policies that would guide Indian-white relations for the rest of the century. Federal policymakers tried to balance a number of conflicting goals. They attempted to protect Native Americans from exploitation by unscrupulous traders and aggressive settlers, and to Christianize and civilize them in preparation for their ultimate admission into white society. Yet the overriding goal of territorial expansion and officials' sensitivity to the demands of western settlers for Indian land created irresistible pressure to move the Indians out of the white settlers' way.

The acquisition of Native American land was the dominant objective of federal Indian policy. By 1790, the government had given up its earlier "conquest" theory, recognized Indian rights to the soil, and declared that land transfers would henceforth be accomplished through treaty agreements. Those new principles had been made explicit in the Treaty of Fort Harmar, concluded with the Iroquois and Northwestern Confederacy in 1789. In the Intercourse Act of 1790, the government also stipulated that land treaties made between states and Indian tribes had to be approved by Congress—a requirement that few states would bother to observe.

Responsibility for the management of Indian affairs rested with the War Department. Henry

# RECOVERING THE PAST

As we have seen, President Jefferson and other government officials eagerly sent exploring expeditions into the trans-Mississippi West. The Lewis and Clark expedition (1803–1806) was the most important of these ventures. It proved the feasibility of an overland route to the Pacific; produced scientific information on the topography, flora, and fauna of the region; established official government contact with the Native Americans of the area; and helped stimulate westward expansion. Many of the place names that the explorers gave to rivers and other features are still used.

During their travels, Meriwether Lewis, William Clark, and others in their party kept extensive journals in which they recorded their experiences and observations. These journals, first published during the nineteenth century and now available in a variety of printed forms, provide a remarkably full account of the expedition, including information on the landscape through which Lewis and Clark passed and the Native Americans they encountered. The journals also reveal a great deal about the explorers themselves, their interests, values, and attitudes.

The accompanying brief selection from one of these journals not only shows the diverse topography and beauty of the American West, as described by Lewis at two locations in what is now Montana, but also reveals the value of journals to historians. Even from this short excerpt, what do you learn about Lewis's attitudes toward the land and its people?

As suggested by Lewis's concern to acquire the data necessary to fix his latitude and longitude, the expedition produced many maps. These cartographic records also tell us a great deal about the experiences, perceptions, and values of the explorers, as well as about the regions through which they passed.

Examine the two maps shown here. The first is an example of the sketch maps that William Clark drew as the expedition made its way across the country. The second is a composite map put together by Clark after the journey was over, copied by another mapmaker in more finished form, and finally published in a popular history of the expedition in 1814. Because these maps were quite large, we have shown here only the eastern third of the composite map. It includes the area covered by the smaller sketch map. Mapmaking has changed dramatically since Clark's early efforts. Over the years, changes have occurred in cartographic theory, mapmaking techniques, our knowledge of the earth's surface, and the ways in which people view the landscape.

To imagine Clark's mapmaking difficulties, as

## MERIWETHER LEWIS'S JOURNAL

July 27th 1805.—
We arrived at 9. A.M. at the junction of the S.E. fork of the Missouri and the country opens suddonly to extensive and bea[u]tifull plains and meadows which appear to be surrounded in every direction with distant and lofty mountains; supposing this to be the three forks of the Missouri I halted the party on the Lard shore for breakfast. and walked up the S.E. fork about ½ a mile and ascended the point of a high limestone clift from whence I commanded a most perfect view of the neighbouring country. . . . believing this to be an essential point in geography of this western part of the Continent I determined to remain at all events untill I obtained the necessary data for fixing it's latitude Longitude &c.

well as to appreciate his accomplishment, try this experiment: Without consulting anything but your own memory and past experience, try to draw a map of the region you passed through on your way to college. Include the major topographical or other interesting features on the route, and also indicate the groups of people you met or passed near. As an alternative, draw a map of the area around your hometown, again including the major features, inhabitants, and travel routes. Make your scale as good as possible to aid others who will depend on the accuracy of your map for their own travels. With an appreciation for Clark's momentous task and achievement, we can now examine his maps.

First, consider how these maps were created, especially how the data they contain were gathered and the conditions in which representations were put on paper. How accurate do you suppose they are? How accurate would they have had to be in order to be useful to people in the early nineteenth century? Second, look at the content of the maps. What information do they contain? What are their dominant features? Why are some features so conspicuously displayed? What is missing that you might have expected to find on such a map? How would a modern map of the same region be different? What would it include that Clark's maps do not? How different would the scale be?

Finally, consider the impact and significance of these maps and journals. What was the effect of the Lewis and Clark expedition on the course of American history in succeeding years? How did it change the "map" of the United States?

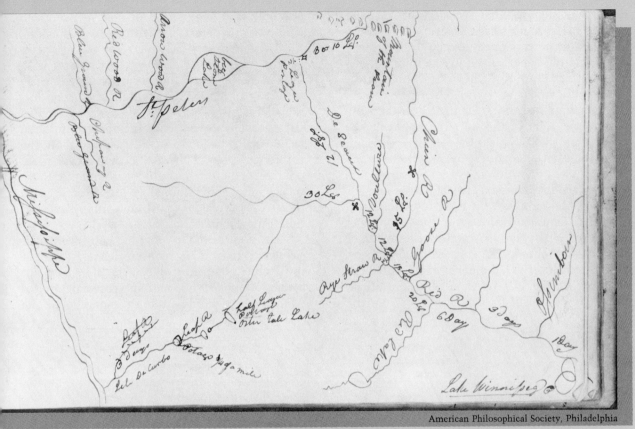

**William Clark, sketch map of Red and St. Peter's Rivers**

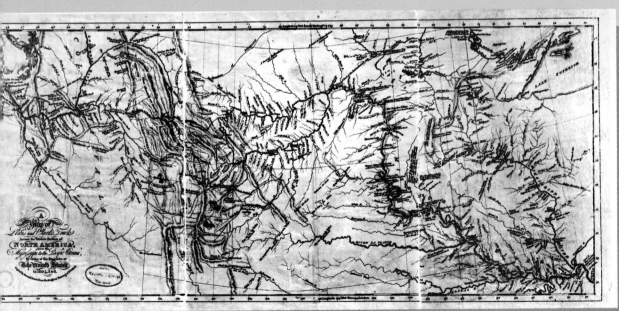

**Composite map of Lewis and Clark's track**

*309b*

Knox, Washington's first secretary of war, laid out the government's basic positions in 1789. A just nation, he explained, should "reject every proposition to benefit itself by the injury of any neighboring community, however contemptible and weak it might be." The Indians, he continued, "being the prior occupants of the soil, possess the right of the soil." It should not be taken from them "unless by their free consent, or by the right of conquest in case of just war." To dispossess them for any other reason would violate "the fundamental laws of nature and . . . justice." Maintaining "the right of conquest in case of just war" provided a gigantic loophole in the protection of Native American rights during the century ahead. Few of the land treaties negotiated after 1789, moreover, represented the "free consent" of Native American people. Still, Knox had established a new and more humane

principle, the acquisition of Native American land by formal treaty agreement.

The new treaty-based strategy was effective. Native American leaders were frequently willing to cede land in return for trade goods, yearly annuity payments, and assurances that no further demands would be made on them. When tribal leaders proved reluctant, they could often be persuaded to cooperate by warnings about the inevitable spread of white settlement, or more tractable chieftains could be found. In these ways, state and national governments gained title to vast areas of tribal land throughout the trans-Appalachian interior.

The continuing loss of land had severe consequences for the Native Americans. It brought the decline of hunting, one of the Indians' major means of subsistence and an essential way for young boys to demonstrate their manhood. The

Indian Land Cessions, 1750–1830

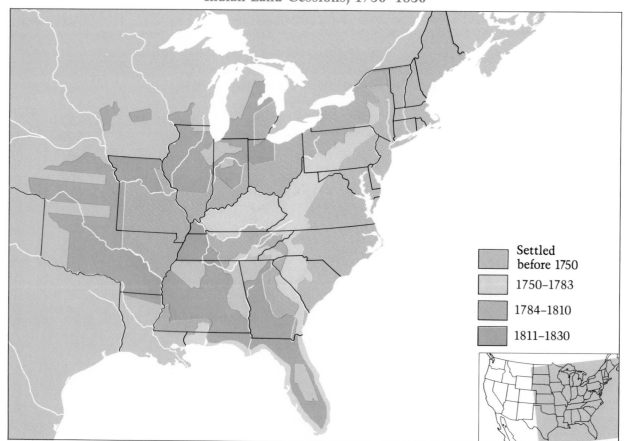

Settled before 1750

1750–1783

1784–1810

1811–1830

*Treaty between the United States and the Cherokees.*

*Nb.* 2. A treaty of peace and friendship, made and concluded between the president of the United States of America, on the part and behalf of the said states, and the undersigned chiefs and warriors of thef Cherokee nation of Indians, on the part and behalf of the said nation. . . .

*Perpetual peace and friendship.*

ART. 1. There shall be perpetual peace and friendship between all the citizens of the United States of America, and all the individuals composing the whole Cherokee nation of Indians.

*Cherokees under the protection of the United States; and not to treat with other powers, etc.*

ART. 2. The undersigned chiefs and warriors, for themselves and all parts of the Cherokee nation, do acknowledge themselves and the said Cherokee nation, to be under the protection of the United States of America. . . .

*Boundary between the United States and the Cherokee nation.*

ART. 4. The boundary between the citizens of the United States and the Cherokee nation, is and shall be as follows: [detailed description] . . .

*Extinguishment of Cherokee claims. The United States to deliver goods, and pay $1,000 annually to the Cherokees. Cherokee cession of land.*

And in order to extinguish forever all claims of the Cherokee nation . . . to any of the land lying to the right of the line above described, . . . it is hereby agreed, that . . . the United States will cause certain valuable goods to be immediately delivered to the undersigned chiefs and warriors, for the use of their nation; and the said United States will also cause the sum of one thousand dollars to be paid annually to the said Cherokee nation. And the undersigned chiefs and warriors do hereby, for themselves and the whole Cherokee nation, their heirs and descendants, for the considerations abovementioned, release, quit claim, relinquish, and cede, all the land to the right of the line described, and beginning as aforesaid. . . .

*Guarantee of Cherokee lands.*

ART. 7. The United States solemnly guaranty to the Cherokee nation, all their lands not hereby ceded.

*Citizens settling on Cherokee lands, outlawed.*

ART. 8. If any citizen of the United States, or other person, not being an Indian, shall settle on any of the Cherokees' lands, such person shall forfeit the protection of the United States, and the Cherokees may punish him or not, as they please.

*No citizen to hunt on Cherokee land. Passports to go into the Cherokee country.*

ART. 9. No citizen or inhabitant of the United States, shall attempt to hunt or destroy the game on the lands of the Cherokees; nor shall any citizen or inhabitant go into the Cherokee country, without a passport first obtained from the governor of some one of the United States, or territorial districts, or such other person as the president of the United States may, from time to time, authorize to grant the same. . . .

In witness of all and every thing herein determined between the United States of America and the whole Cherokee nation, the parties have hereunto set their hands and seals, . . . this second day of July, in the year of our Lord one thousand seven hundred and ninety-one.

loss of land also altered the balance of power among tribal groups. As tribes were forced to migrate farther west, moreover, they frequently intruded on the lands of other Native Americans, thus generating conflict.

Regulating the fur trade was also of concern to the national government. By 1790, most of the trans-Appalachian tribes served as middlemen for hunters farther to the west. Handsome profits from the trade encouraged private companies such as John Jacob Astor's American Fur Company (1808) to expand their operations into the interior. Access to the western trade was also a continuing point of contention between England and the United States in the Great Lakes region. Both Native Americans and whites entered willingly into the trade. In return for furs, which they had in abundance, the Indians secured highly valued goods such as blankets, guns, rum, and ironware. White traders, on the other hand, acquired valuable furs in exchange for the relatively inexpensive items of trade. Both sides, moreover, used the trade to cement diplomatic relations with each other.

The trade served white society very well. It had severe costs, however, for Native Americans. Trade goods frequently transmitted diseases such as smallpox and measles that decimated tribal populations. The trade generated patterns of dependence as well, for it offered the only certain supplies of rum, firearms, and other goods increasingly important to Indian life. As the demand for furs and pelts increased, moreover, Native Americans repeatedly overtrapped their hunting grounds, forcing them to reach farther west for fresh sources of supply. That process disturbed longstanding patterns of trade and diplomatic relations among tribes.

In 1790, in an effort to increase profits, prevent fraud and misdealing, and cement peaceful relations with tribal groups, Congress required the licensing of all private traders. The law, however, proved ineffective, for enforcement was difficult, and the profits to be realized from unscrupulous behavior were more tempting than many traders could resist. In 1796, Congress created a system of government trading posts, or "factories," where Indians could come for fair treatment. The system lasted until 1822 but never supplanted private traders as Congress had expected.

## Civilizing a "Savage" People

Another major objective of federal Indian policy was to civilize and Christianize the Native Americans and ultimately to assimilate them into white society. In the trans-Appalachian West, where whites and Native Americans struggled openly for survival, most people believed that the Indians would always remain "savage" and thus unsuited for republican citizenship. They regarded Indians as impediments to be moved out of white settlement's way. Different attitudes, however, were evident in the East, where the Indian "problem" seemed more distant. There, clergymen and government officials, newspaper editors and ordinary citizens displayed greater sympathy for the Native Americans' well-being.

Policymakers and church officials often distinguished between the capacities of blacks and Native Americans for republican citizenship. Perhaps because the bias against blackness was so deeply rooted in American culture and slavery was so much a part of American life, blacks were almost uniformly regarded as destined to perpetual subordination. The color of Native Americans, on the other hand, was not so dark, or so filled with cultural significance. Indians, moreover, were the country's original inhabitants and had lived free if "uncivilized" lives. While fearing the Indians' "savagery," white Americans admired their "bravery" and "independence," their stoicism in the face of pain, and their "simplicity" of life—qualities deemed important among republican citizens.

Even the most enthusiastic advocates of Indian assimilation believed the process would take generations to accomplish. Language, religion, dress, family arrangements, social customs —all the Indians' "savage" ways would have to be replaced by white modes of living. Given time and the right circumstances, however, Native Americans might eventually share the blessings of republican liberty, American civilization, and Christianity.

A policy of assimilation seemed to offer hope for the Indians' survival in the face of continuing warfare, disease, and white expansion. Although the assimilationists cared deeply about the physical and spiritual fate of Native American people, they had little sympathy for

Indian society or culture, for they demanded that Native Americans cease being Indian and adopt the ways of white society instead. Assimilation or continuing destruction were the alternatives posed by even the most benevolent whites.

Education and Christianization were the major instruments of assimilationist policy. After the Revolution, mission activity increased dramatically as Moravians, Quakers, Baptists, Congregationalists, and Dutch Reformed church members launched mission efforts of their own or joined together in bodies such as the Society for Propagating the Gospel Among Indians (1787). Together they sent scores of missionaries to live among the Indians, preach the gospel, and teach the benefits of white civilization. Among them was the Baptist missionary Isaac McCoy. Born in Pennsylvania and entirely self-educated, McCoy moved to Indiana, where from 1817 to 1829 he ministered to the Shawnee tribe. John Stewart, a freeborn mulatto who was himself part Indian, was another. From 1815 to his death in 1821, he preached to the Wyandotte near Sandusky, Ohio. Among the most selfless were the Quaker missionaries who labored with the Iroquois in New York, attempting by hard work and Christian humility to inspire conversion and improve the conditions of Iroquois life.

*Few government officials or other white Americans saw any reason to gain an understanding of Native American customs, such as the Choctaw ceremonial dances shown in this painting by George Catlin.*

The missionaries' greatest success occurred where Indians had succumbed to white control or when missionaries blended Indian beliefs with the basic tenets of Christianity. Even so, most Native Americans remained aloof, for the chasm between Christianity and their own religions was wide (see Chapter 1), and the missionaries' denigration of Indian culture was evident.

Education was the other weapon of the assimilationists. In 1793, Congress appropriated $20,000 for the promotion of literacy, agriculture, and vocational instruction. Church groups established schools as well, believing that literacy would enhance Native Americans' ability to read the Scriptures and increase the likelihood of their conversion. In 1819, the government handed over to the churches full responsibility for Indian education. Because federal officials thought that Christianity and civilization went hand in hand, they encouraged missionaries to teach their Indian students religious doctrine as well as reading, writing, and vocational skills.

## Strategies of Survival: The Cherokee

Faced with the steady loss of land and autonomy, Native Americans devised various strategies of resistance and survival. The Cherokee followed the path of accommodation. Their goal was not assimilation into white society and disappearance as a distinct people but the redefinition of Cherokee life through a combination of white and Native American ways.

## Tribes of the Old Southeast, c. 1820

As the nineteenth century began, the Cherokee still controlled millions of acres in Tennessee, Georgia, and the western Carolinas. Their land base, however, was shrinking. By 1800, more than 40 Cherokee towns had disappeared, and over two-thirds of all Cherokee families had been forced to move into the increasingly crowded settlements that remained.

Southern state governments, responding to the demands of their white constituents for Indian lands, put increasing pressure on tribal autonomy. In 1801, the Tennessee legislature unilaterally expanded the boundaries of several counties to include Cherokee land and then claimed that the Indians fell under the authority of state law. As violence escalated along the borders between white and Indian settlements, state authorities demanded that Native Americans accused of horse stealing and other crimes be handed over for trial in state courts. The Cherokee, declaring that they had their own system of justice and distrusting the state courts with their all-white juries and exclusion of Indian testimony, rejected the whites' demands.

Within Cherokee councils, a group of full-blood leaders argued for armed resistance. Better to stand and fight, they insisted, than follow the false path of accommodation. Others, however, including mixed-bloods such as John Ross, pointed out the futility of fighting and argued that accommodation offered the only hope for survival. The son of a mixed-blood mother and a Scots father who had lived for years as a trader among the Cherokee, Ross had been educated at a mission academy and moved easily between white and Native American societies. In the early 1800s, after a bitter struggle for tribal control, the accommodationists won out.

Their first goal was to bring the tribe's scattered villages under a common government so that they might better defend their freedom and prevent the further loss of land. In 1808, the Cherokee National Council adopted a written legal code combining elements of white and Indian law, and in July 1827, they devised a written constitution patterned after those of nearby states, complete with executive, legislative, and judicial branches of government. They accompanied it with a bold declaration of their standing as an independent nation holding full sovereignty over their lands in Tennessee, North Carolina, Alabama, and Georgia.

Their action alarmed southern whites, for it posed a direct challenge to state authority. White concerns proved well founded. In 1829, the Cherokee government formalized the "blood law," making it an offense punishable by death for any tribe member to transfer land to white ownership without the consent of tribal authorities.

Meanwhile, the process of social and cultural accommodation, encouraged by Cherokee leaders such as Ross and promoted by white missionaries and government agents, went forward. Missionaries opened a school for Cherokee youth on the Hiwanee River in 1804 and established a boarding school near present-day Chattanooga 12 years later. They stepped up their religious activities as well, baptizing countless Cherokee into the Christian faith.

As the Cherokee changed from a mixed hunting, gathering, and farming economy to one based predominantly on settled agriculture, many of them moved out from the traditional

*Sequoyah, famed for devising the Cherokee alphabet, sat for this portrait in 1838.*

town settlements onto individual farmsteads. Others established sawmills and gristmills, country stores and blacksmiths' shops. In contrast to traditional Cherokee practices of sharing and the communal ownership of property, notions of private property took hold.

The majority of Cherokee people continued to inhabit crude log cabins no more than 15 by 25 feet and live a harsh, hand-to-mouth existence. Some however, prospered, especially mixed-bloods who spoke English and understood how to deal with white society. A few of the most successful lived as well as upper-class whites. Joseph Vann, known as "Rich Joe," accumulated hundreds of acres of fertile land, scores of black slaves, and an assortment of mills, stores, and river ferries. While most Cherokee continued to wear hip-length buckskin shirts and moccasins, the families of people such as Vann and John Ross dressed in cloth trousers, leather shoes, long dresses, and fancy hats.

Changes in the Cherokee economy altered their relations with blacks as well. Since the mid-eighteenth century, the Cherokee had held a few blacks in slavelike conditions. During the early nineteenth century, however, Cherokee slavery expanded and became more harsh. By 1820, there were nearly 1,300 black slaves leading increasingly restricted lives in the Cherokee nation. A Cherokee law of 1824 forbade intermarriage and prohibited blacks from owning livestock. Three years later, a tribal court declared that "negroes and descendants of white or Indian men by negro women who may have been set free" could not vote in tribal elections or "hold any office of profit, honor or trust under this government."

Such changes came about primarily because the spread of cotton cultivation increased the demand for slave labor among Cherokee as well as whites. As accommodation to white society increased, moreover, the ownership of slaves became a mark of social standing, and Cherokee assertions of black inferiority were a way of making common cause with whites.

By 1820, the strategy of peaceful accommodation had brought obvious rewards. Tribal government was stronger, the standard of living higher, and the sense of Cherokee identity reasonably secure. In the end, however, the Cherokee's success proved their undoing, for as their self-confidence grew, so did the hostility of southern whites, who were increasingly impatient to get them out of the way. That hostility would soon erupt in a final campaign to remove the Cherokee from their land forever (see Chapter 14).

## Patterns of Armed Resistance: The Shawnee and the Creek

Not all tribes of the interior proved so accommodating to the pressures of white expansion. Faced with growing threats to their political and cultural survival, the Shawnee and Creek nations rose in armed resistance. Conflict was smoldering as the nineteenth century began; it burst into open flame during the War of 1812.

In the late 1780s, the tribes of the Old Northwest, led by chieftains such as Joseph Brant of the Mohawk, Little Turtle of the Miami, and Blue Jacket of the Shawnee, had launched a series of devastating raids across Indiana, Ohio, and western Pennsylvania, creating panic among white settlers and openly challenging the federal government's control of the region. In September 1790, a force of 1,500, dispatched by President Washington to quell the uprising, fell into an ambush in northwestern Ohio, losing nearly 200 men. The following year, another army of 6,000 troops, led by Ohio's territorial governor, Arthur St. Clair, met a similar fate. Buoyed by their victories, the Shawnee and their allies followed up with a furious assault, virtually clearing northern and central Ohio of white settlement.

Faced with two humiliating defeats, Washington determined to smash the Indians' resistance once and for all. In the autumn of 1793, General Anthony Wayne led a third army of conquest into the Ohio wilderness. The following year, Wayne's army clashed with over 2,000 Indian warriors in the decisive Battle of Fallen Timbers. This time the Americans won a complete victory. After the smoke of battle had cleared, Wayne wrung from the assembled chiefs an agreement ceding the entire southern two-thirds of Ohio. In return, he offered $20,000 in trade goods and a $10,000 annual annuity. It was the largest single transfer of Indian land yet, and it opened the heart of the Old Northwest to white control.

In subsequent years, additional treaties further reduced the Indians' land base, driving the Shawnee and Delaware, the Miami and Wyandotte more tightly in upon each other. A turning point came with the Treaty of Fort Wayne in 1809, which opened to white settlement 3 million additional acres of Delaware and Pottawatomie land in Indiana. Shortly afterward, two Shawnee leaders, the brothers Tecumseh and Elskwatawa, the latter known to whites as "the Prophet," began to travel among the region's tribes warning of their common dangers and forging an alliance against the invading whites. In 1809, they established headquarters at an ancient Indian town named Kithtippecanoe in northern Indiana. Soon it became a gathering point for Native Americans from across the entire region as they responded to the messages of cultural pride, land retention, and pan-Indian resistance presented by the Shawnee brothers.

Between 1809 and 1811, Tecumseh carried his message of Indian nationalism and military resistance south to the Creek and the Cherokee. His speeches rang with bitter denunciations of white Americans. "The white race is a wicked race," he told his listeners.

> Since the days when the white race first came in contact with the red men, there has been a continual series of aggressions. The hunting grounds are fast disappearing, and they are driving the red men farther and farther to the west. The mere presence of the white men is a source of evil. . . . His whiskey destroys the bravery of our warriors, and his lust corrupts the virtue of our women. The only hope . . . is a war of extermination against the paleface.

The southern tribes refused to join, but by 1811, over 1,000 fighting men had gathered at Kithtippecanoe.

Alarmed by the Indians' growing militance, the governor of the Indiana Territory, William Henry Harrison, decided to act. Mustering a force of 1,000 soldiers, Harrison surrounded the Indian stronghold at Kithtippecanoe. He carried with him full authority from Secretary of War William Eustis to do whatever was necessary to secure the frontier. At dawn on November 7, 1811, some 400 Indian warriors assaulted Harrison's lines. For hours the battle raged, and by day's end Harrison counted over 150 warriors dead and countless others wounded. Before retiring to the territorial capital at Vincennes, he burned Kithtippecanoe to the ground.

Over the next several months, Tecumseh's followers, aided by British troops from Canada, carried out devastating raids across Indiana and southern Michigan. Together they crushed American armies at Detroit and Fort Nelson and followed up with forays against Fort Wayne. At the Battle of the Thames near Detroit, the tide finally turned, for there Harrison inflicted a grievous defeat on a combined British and Indian force. Among those slain was Tecumseh.

The American victory at the Thames signaled the collapse of Tecumseh's confederacy and an end to Indian resistance in the Old Northwest. Beginning in 1815, American settlers surged once more across Ohio and Indiana, only now they pressed on unimpeded into Illinois and Michigan. The balance of power had permanently shifted.

## Tribes of the Old Northwest, c. 1809

To the south, the Creek challenged white intruders for control of their homeland as well. As the nineteenth century began, white settlers were pushing onto Creek lands in northwestern Georgia and central Alabama. While some Creek leaders urged accommodation, others, called Red Sticks, prepared to fight. The embers of this smoldering conflict were fanned into flame by an aggressive Tennessee militia commander named Andrew Jackson. Citing Creek atrocities "which bring fresh to our recollection the influence . . . that raised the scalping knife and tomahawk against our defenseless women and children," Jackson in 1808 urged President Jefferson to endorse a campaign against the Creek. The Tennessee militia, Jackson reported, "pant for the orders of our government to punish a ruthless foe."

Bristling at their treatment by Georgia and Alabama, the Red Sticks carried out a series of violent frontier raids in the spring and summer of 1813, killing and scalping two white families and taking one of the women captive. They capped their campaign with an assault on Fort Mims on the Alabama River, where they killed as many as 500 people, women and children among them. News of that tragedy raised bitter cries for revenge. The Tennessee legislature denounced the "horrid and inhuman murders" and called for proper "atonement," while frontier editors warned that "when the tomahawk and the scalping knife are drawn in the cabins of our peaceful and unsuspecting citizens, it is time, high time to prepare . . . for defense."

At the head of 5,000 Tennessee and Kentucky militia, augmented by Cherokee, Choctaw, and Chickasaw warriors eager to punish their traditional Creek enemies, Jackson launched his long-awaited attack. As he moved south, the ferocity of the fighting grew. David Crockett, one of Jackson's soldiers, later reported that the militia volunteers shot down the Red Sticks "like dogs." The Indians gave like measure in return.

The climactic battle of the Creek War came in March 1814 at Horseshoe Bend, on the Tallapoosa River in central Alabama. There, in the fortified town of Tohopeka, 1,000 Creek warriors made their stand against 1,400 state troops and 600 Indian allies. While American cannonfire raked the Creek defenses, the allied Indians crossed the river to cut off retreat. In the battle that followed, over 800 Native Americans died, more than in any other single battle in the history of Indian-white warfare. Jackson followed up his victory with a scorched-earth sweep through the remaining Red Stick towns. With no hope left, Red Eagle, one of the few remaining Red Stick leaders, walked alone into Jackson's camp and addressed the American commander:

> General Jackson, I am not afraid of you. I fear no man, for I am a Creek warrior. I have nothing to request in behalf of myself; you can kill me if you desire. But I come to beg you to send for the women and children of the war party, who are now starving in the woods . . . without an ear of corn. I am now done fighting. The Red Sticks are nearly all killed. If I could fight you any longer I would most heartily do so. Send for the women and children. They never did you any harm. But kill me, if the white people want it done.

The war against the Creek was finished, and Jackson allowed Red Eagle to return home.

The general, however, was not quite done. He had fulfilled his vow to march to the Hickory Ground, the most sacred spot of the Creek nation. There he constructed Fort Jackson, where, in August 1814, he exacted his final revenge. Making clear that he held the entire Creek nation responsible for the Red Sticks' insurgency, he seized 22 million acres of their land, nearly two-thirds of their domain. Before his Indian-fighting days were over, Jackson would acquire through treaty and military conquest nearly three-fourths of Alabama and Florida, a third of Tennessee, and a fifth of both Georgia and Mississippi.

Just as Tecumseh's death had signaled the end of Indian resistance in the North, so the Creek's defeat at Horseshoe Bend broke the back of Indian defenses in the South. With all possibility of armed resistance gone, the Native Americans of the Old Southwest gave way before the swelling tide of white settlement.

# A FOREIGN POLICY FOR THE AGRARIAN REPUBLIC

During the early decades of the nineteenth century, the Jeffersonians struggled to fashion a new foreign policy appropriate for the expanding agrarian republic. They had several major goals: protecting American interests on the high seas during a period of continuing European war, clearing America's western territories of foreign troops and influence, and breaking free from the country's historic dependence on Europe. Those goals were not easily accomplished, yet by the 1820s, aided by changes taking place in Europe, the Jeffersonians had fashioned a new set of relationships with Europe. In the Monroe Doctrine of 1823, they projected as well a momentous new role for the United States within the Americas.

## Jeffersonian Principles

Jeffersonian foreign policy was based on the doctrine of "no entangling alliances" with Europe that Washington had articulated in his Farewell Address of 1796. In the Jeffersonians' minds, England was still the prime enemy, but France was now suspect as well. By the time the Jeffersonians took office, the French Revolution had run its course and ended in the consulate of Napoleon. While some Jeffersonians still harbored hopes for French liberty, most were sobered by Napoleon's dictatorial rule. They no longer needed Federalist warnings to believe that France should be held at arm's length.

Second, the Jeffersonians emphasized the importance of overseas commerce to the security and prosperity of the agrarian republic. The prosperity of the 1790s had demonstrated the importance of overseas trade. The needs of the expanding agrarian republic argued the point as well, for the slave populations of the West Indies and the crowded cities of Europe offered crucial markets for American agricultural exports. Without those markets, what incentive would there be for American farmers to occupy the West and make it bloom?

Overseas commerce was almost as important for what it brought in return. The American ships that carried away agricultural commodities fetched back European manufactured goods. The Federalists had nurtured domestic manufacturing by offering tariff protection against European competition. The Jeffersonians, however, hoped to keep large-scale manufacturing in Europe, since they feared the concentrations of wealth and the dependent working classes that domestic manufacturing would bring.

Maintaining peace was a third major goal of Jeffersonian foreign policy. The Jeffersonians were not pacifists, but they pursued peace with special urgency because they feared war's effects on republican liberty. War not only killed people and destroyed property, it also inflamed politics, stifled freedom of speech, disrupted the economy, increased the public debt, and expanded governmental power. The Jeffersonians understood the dangers lurking throughout the Atlantic world, and knew that protecting the nation's interests might require the use of force. Between 1801 and 1805, Jefferson dispatched naval vessels to the Mediterranean to defend American commerce against the Barbary States (Algiers, Morocco, Tripoli, and Tunis). War, however, was to be a policy of last resort. The Jeffersonians' handling of the crisis leading into the War of 1812 against Great Britain illustrates how eagerly, and in this case how futilely, they sought to avoid conflict.

## Struggling for Neutral Rights

After a brief interlude of peace, European war resumed in 1803. Once again England and France seized American shipping, and England's overwhelming naval superiority made its attacks especially serious. British impressment of American seamen and continued occupation of the Great Lakes posts also increased tension between the two nations.

In the *Essex* decision of 1805, a British court, resurrecting the so-called Rule of 1756, declared that European powers could not open their colonies to trade with neutral nations during war if such trade was prohibited during times of peace. The clear intention was to close down the American practice of carrying cargoes from the French and Spanish West Indies to American ports, reloading them, and then shipping them to Europe as American neutral goods. Following the *Essex* decision, British seizures of American shipping increased dramatically. As they did, American anger grew as well.

When England disregarded American protests over such "unprovoked aggression," the Jeffersonians decided on a strategy of economic coercion. In April 1806, Congress passed the Non-Importation Act prohibiting the importation of English goods that could be produced domestically or acquired elsewhere. On May 16, in one of several orders in council, Britain replied by declaring a full blockade of the European coast. Threatened by Britain's action, Napoleon answered with the Berlin Decree, forbidding all commerce and communication with the British Isles. Americans were further angered by Britain's refusal to deal in good faith on issues of impressment and the reopening of the West Indian trade.

During 1807, the pressure on American shipping increased as Britain and France escalated their economic warfare against each other. Tension between England and the United States reached the breaking point in June, when the British warship *Leopard* stopped the American frigate *Chesapeake* off the Virginia coast. The British captain claimed that four *Chesapeake* crew members were British deserters and demanded their surrender. When the American commander refused, the *Leopard* opened fire, killing 3 men and wounding 18, and removed the alleged deserters. After the *Chesapeake* limped back into port with the story, cries of outrage rang across the land.

Fearing the approach of war and recognizing that the United States was not prepared to confront England, Jefferson decided to withdraw

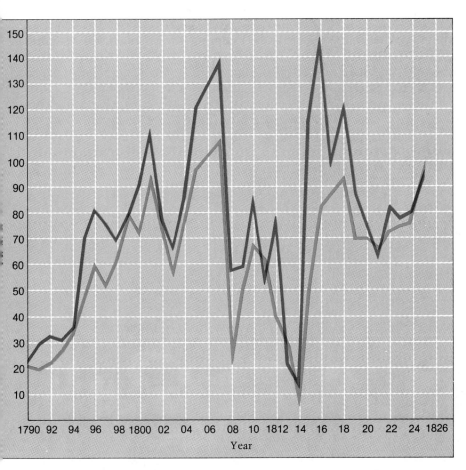

**American Foreign Trade, 1790–1825**

*Source:* U.S. Bureau of the Census.

Exports    Imports

American ships from the Atlantic. In December 1807, Congress passed the Embargo Act, forbidding all American vessels from sailing for foreign ports. It was one of the most ill-fated decisions Jefferson ever made.

The embargo had relatively little effect on England. British shipping actually profited from the withdrawal of American competition, and British importers supplied their agricultural needs from Latin America. Moreover, as word of the impending embargo spread, American merchantmen left port in order to escape confinement, while ships bound for the United States changed course and docked in Canada or the West Indies so that they could continue to sail.

The embargo's domestic impact, however, was immediate and far-reaching. American exports fell 80 percent in a year, while imports dropped by more than half. New England was hardest hit. In ports such as Salem, Boston, and Providence, depression settled in as ships rocked idly at the wharves and thousands went unemployed.

Up and down the coast, communities dependent on overseas commerce for their livelihood openly challenged the embargo and opposed efforts to enforce it. Federalists, eager to embar-

rass the administration, were behind much of the opposition, but resistance came from Republicans as well. The government's efforts to police the embargo proved futile, for it could not effectively patrol either the Atlantic coast or the long Canadian border, across which large quantities of American goods were smuggled.

In an effort to uphold federal authority, the government acted with an increasingly heavy hand. At Plattsburgh, New York, on Lake Champlain, federal officials declared martial law and sent in federal troops in an effort to stop the smuggling into Canada. The result was guerrilla skirmishing as local citizens fired on U.S. revenue boats, recaptured confiscated goods, and ignored curfews. Equally ominous was the government's use of federal marshals to seize private goods on the suspicion that they might be smuggled abroad.

Throughout the Northeast, bitterness threatened to escalate into open rebellion. Town meetings attacked the embargo; state legislatures questioned its constitutionality. Governor Jonathan Trumbull of Connecticut, in words reminiscent of the Virginia and Kentucky resolutions, warned that whenever Congress exceeded its authority, the states were duty-bound "to interpose their protecting shield between the rights and liberties of the people and the assumed power of the general government." Timothy Pickering, a leading Federalist of Mas-

*The tranquility of Crowninshield Wharf in Salem, Massachusetts, is deceptive: this engraving shows the ships idled and docks emptied by Jefferson's embargo.*

sachusetts, openly proposed a New England nullifying convention.

In the election of 1808, the Federalists rebounded after nearly a decade's decline. James Madison handily succeeded Jefferson in the presidency, but the Federalist candidates, C. C. Pinckney and Rufus King, garnered 47 electoral votes, and their party also made gains in Congress and recaptured several state legislatures.

Faced with the embargo's ineffectiveness abroad and its disastrous consequences at home, Congress repealed the measure in 1809, replacing it with the Non-Intercourse Act, which reopened trade with everyone except England and France and authorized the president to resume commerce with either of them that ceased its hostile behavior. It proved equally futile and was also soon repealed.

In 1810, Congress tried another tactic. In Macon's Bill No. 2, it authorized the president to reopen trade with France and Great Britain, then reinstitute an embargo against either of them that continued to attack American shipping. It was an ingenious attempt to shape French and English behavior, but it proved too clever by half. Napoleon, sensing an opportunity to drive a further wedge between England and the United States, informed the American government—falsely, as eventually became clear—that he had repealed France's trade restrictions. Madison rose to the bait, reopened trade with France, and set a date for halting all commerce with England unless it rescinded its restrictions as well. England, however, angry at France's duplicity and stung by Madison's threat, stepped up its campaign of impressment and confiscation while American war fever continued to grow.

## The War of 1812

The most vocal calls for war came from the West and the South. The election of 1810 had brought to Congress a new group of western and southern leaders, firmly Republican in their party loyalty but impatient with the administration's bumbling policy and convinced of the need for tougher measures. The War Hawks, they were called, and an impressive group they proved to be: Henry Clay and Richard Johnson of Kentucky, John Calhoun and Langdon Cheves from South Carolina, Felix Grundy of Tennessee, and Peter Porter from western New York.

For too long, the War Hawks cried, the United States had tolerated Britain's presence on American soil, encouragement of Tecumseh's confederation, and attacks on American commerce. Their language echoed as well with talk of territorial expansion, north into Canada and south into Florida.

Most of all, these young, highly nationalistic War Hawks resented English arrogance and America's continuing humiliation. No government, they warned, could long survive unless it protected the interests of its people and upheld the nation's honor. Among the first of a post-Revolutionary generation of political leaders to achieve national office, they took upon themselves responsibility for facing down England and completing the struggle for American independence. Their overriding goals were to secure the republic and demonstrate the Republican party's ability to govern.

Responding to the growing pressure, Madison finally asked Congress for a declaration of war on June 1, 1812. Opposition came entirely from the New England and Middle Atlantic states—ironically, the regions most adversely affected by British policies—while the South and West voted solidly for war. Seldom had the sectional alignment of congressional politics been clearer.

Seldom also had American foreign policy proved more ineffective. Madison decided to set economic coercion aside just as it seemed about to succeed, for the revival of the American trade embargo under Macon's bill, together with the increasing effectiveness of Napoleon's continental blockade, was creating havoc in the English economy. By the spring of 1812, the British government was under increasing pressure to seek accommodation. In an effort to make England's position clear, Foreign Secretary Castlereagh suspended the orders in council. His move was too late, for three days later, unaware of Castlereagh's action, the United States declared war.

The war itself was a curious affair, for its causes were uncertain and its goals unclear. England successfully fended off several American forays into Canada. In spite of American braggadocio, Canada proved quite secure. As the war progressed, England launched a series of attacks south from Canada, along the Gulf Coast, and inland from the Atlantic. The British navy once again blockaded American coastal waters, while British landing parties launched punishing attacks up and down the east coast. On August 14, a British force occupied Washington, torched the Capitol and president's house

## The War of 1812

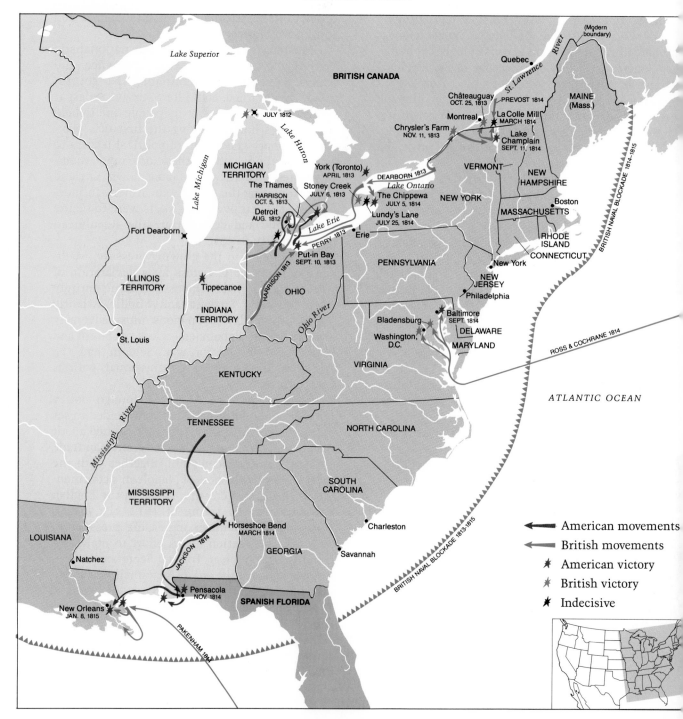

Legend:

← American movements
← British movements
✳ American victory
✳ British victory
✳ Indecisive

(it became known as the White House after being repaired and painted white), and sent the president, Congress, and a panic-stricken American army fleeing into Virginia. England, however, did not press its advantage, for it was preoccupied with Napoleon's armies in Europe and wanted to end the American quarrel. Throughout the contest, the American government struggled to coordinate the war effort, but with limited success, for it was too weak, the country too large, and communication too slow.

Emotions ran high among both the war's Federalist critics and Republican supporters. In Baltimore, on the night of June 22, 1812, a Republican crowd demolished the printing office of the *Federal-Republican*, a local Federalist newspaper. The attack reflected not only partisan politics but also Republican working-class animosity toward Federalist "aristocrats" and the eagerness of working people for war-related jobs.

In late July, after copies of the *Federal-Republican* again appeared on Baltimore's streets, a mob of 1,000 men and women once more surrounded the paper's office. This time 50 armed Federalists were there to defend it. When the Federalist defenders opened fire, the crowd rolled up a cannon and fired a round of grapeshot into the building. Several people lay dead on

*A British cartoon shows James Madison spilling official papers as he flees the burning President's Mansion, while citizens react with sarcastic comments during the British attack on Washington in 1814.*

both sides before the militia finally arrived to cart the Federalists off to the safety of jail.

The bloody encounter was not over yet, however, for on the following night a crowd reassembled in front of the city jail, brushed aside the mayor's pleas to disperse, and seized ten of the prisoners, including former congressman Richard Bland Lee and James Lingan, an old Revolutionary War general. Lee escaped, but Lingan and several others were beaten to death by the enraged mob. It left their bodies, stripped of their fine clothing, sprawling in the street.

Though the Baltimore riots were not duplicated elsewhere, emotions ran high throughout the country. In Federalist-dominated New England, organized opposition to the war veered toward outright disloyalty. The governors of Massachusetts and Connecticut refused to furnish the government with troops or supplies, while New England merchants continued a brisk, illegal trade with Canada.

In December 1814, delegates from the five New England states met at Hartford, Connecticut, to debate proposals for secession. Cooler heads prevailed, but before adjourning, the convention asserted the right of a state "to interpose its authority" against "unconstitutional" acts of the government. Now it was New England's turn to play with the nullification fire. The Federalist gathering also prepared a list of constitutional amendments designed to reshape the union to New England's liking. As the war dragged on, Federalist fortunes soared in the Northeast, while elsewhere bitterness grew over New England's disloyalty.

Before the war ended, American forces won several impressive victories, among them Commander Oliver Hazard Perry's defeat of the British fleet on Lake Erie in 1813. The most dramatic American triumph was Andrew Jackson's smashing victory in 1815 over an attacking British force at New Orleans. It had nothing to do with the war's outcome, however, for it occurred after preliminary terms of peace had already been signed.

Tiring of the contest and increasingly concerned about affairs in Europe, Lord Castlereagh offered to negotiate peace. Madison accepted eagerly, and on Christmas Eve in 1814, at Ghent, Belgium, the two sides reached agree-

**The Battle of Lake Erie, in which the American fleet under Commodore Matthew C. Perry defeated the British, was one of several spectacular victories in the War of 1812.**

ment. The treaty resolved almost nothing, for it ignored impressment, blockades, neutral rights, and American access to Canadian fisheries. Nor did it address England's concern about military control of the Great Lakes or its proposal for a neutral Indian buffer state around them. England did finally agree to evacuate the western posts, but other than that the treaty simply ended the conflict, provided for an exchange of prisoners and the restoration of conquered territory, and called for the creation of several joint commissions to deal with the remaining disputes.

The war did leave its mark on the American nation. It made Andrew Jackson a military hero and established him as a national political leader of great promise. The American people, moreover, regarded the contest as a "Second War of American Independence." Jackson's resounding victory at New Orleans enabled them to believe that they had whipped the British once again. Moreover, the republic now seemed finally secure. No longer would Americans have to worry about the vulnerability of their republican "experiment" to outside attack.

The years following 1815, moreover, brought an end to America's colonial-like dependence on Europe. In part that was because the United States was now economically stronger and more self-reliant and was focusing its energies increasingly on the tasks of internal

## The Hartford Convention

*Resolved*, That the following amendments of the constitution of the United States be recommended to the states. . . .

*First.* Representatives and direct taxes shall be apportioned among the several states . . . according to their respective numbers of free persons . . . excluding Indians not taxed, and all other persons.

*Second.* No new state shall be admitted into the Union by Congress . . . without the concurrence of two thirds of both houses.

*Third.* Congress shall not have power to lay any embargo on the ships or vessles of the citizens of the United States, in the ports or harbours thereof, for more than sixty days. . . .

*Fifth.* Congress shall not make or declare war, or authorize acts of hostility against any foreign nation, wihtout the concurrence of two thirds of both houses, except such acts of hostility be in defence of the territories of the United States when actually invaded.

*Sixth.* No person who shall hereafter be naturalized, shall be eligible as a member of the senate or house of representatives of the United States, no capable of holding any civil office under the authority of the United States.

*Seventh.* The same person shall not elected president of the United States a second time; nor shall the president be elected from the same state two terms in succession.

development—occupying the continent, industrializing the economy, and reforming American society.

America's diplomatic reorientation was also speeded by changes taking place in Europe, where problems of industrialization, social change, and national unification absorbed governmental energies. Following the end of the Napoleonic wars in 1815, moreover, Europe entered nearly a century free from general war. In the past, European wars had involved the American people; in the twentieth century, they would do so again. For the remainder of the nineteenth century, however, that fateful link was missing. Finally, the focus of European colonialism was shifting away from the Americas to Africa and Asia. From the 1820s on, Europe left the Americas relatively alone. All these circumstances combined to end the United States' historic dependence on Europe and free it for the task of developing its own continental empire.

## The United States and the Americas

While disengaging from Europe, the Jeffersonians fashioned new policies for Latin America that would guide the United States' hemispheric relations for years to come. Prior to 1800, the American people gave little thought to Europe's Latin American colonies. The Caribbean islands were of concern because of their trade, but Central and South America were not.

When those colonies began their struggles for independence from Spain and Portugal in 1808, however, Americans voiced their enthusiastic support. It was flattering to have leaders such as Simon Bolivar hold the United States up as a model for Latin American liberation, and North Americans were happy to see European colonialism weakened. Latin American independence, moreover, carried with it the prospect of increased trade.

In 1818, Henry Clay proposed that the United States recognize the newly independent governments of Colombia, Mexico, Chile, and Argentina. Initially, President Monroe was slow to act, primarily for fear of disrupting the ongoing efforts to secure Florida from Spain. In March 1822, he finally sent Congress a message proposing formal recognition of the new Latin American republics. Congress quickly agreed, and over the next several years, the United States established diplomatic relations with seven Latin American nations.

Though Latin American independence seemed to offer the United States many advantages, it raised one troublesome question. What would the United States do if Spain or Portugal attempted to reestablish colonial control? It was more than a hypothetical question, for in November 1822, the Holy Alliance (France, Austria, Russia, and Prussia) talked of a plan to help Spain regain its American colonies. Prospects of a resurgent Spanish empire alarmed Great Britain as well. In August 1823, the British foreign secretary, George Canning, broached the idea of a common Anglo-American policy.

Secretary of State John Quincy Adams opposed the idea. Son of the former Federalist president, Adams had joined the Jeffersonian camp some years before as part of the continuing

*John Quincy Adams, son of John and Abigail Adams and secretary of state under James Monroe, developed the basic principles of the famous Monroe Doctrine.*

exodus from the Federalist party. Adams inherited from his father a deep suspicion of Europe and its purposes in the New World. He also shared the new spirit of nationalism so evident following the War of 1812. The United States, Adams declared, should not "come in as a cockboat in the wake of the British man-of-war." He urged independent action based on two principles: a sharp separation between the Old World and the New, and the United States' dominance in the Western Hemisphere.

Monroe soon agreed that the United States should issue a policy statement of its own. In his annual message of December 1823, he outlined a new Latin American policy. Though that policy is known as the Monroe Doctrine, its content was of Adams's devising.

Monroe asserted four basic principles: (1) the American continents were now closed to European colonization; (2) the political systems of the Americas were separate from those of Europe; (3) the United States would consider as dangerous to its peace and safety any attempts to extend Europe's political influence into the Western Hemisphere; and (4) the United States would neither interfere with existing colonies in the New World nor meddle in the internal affairs of Europe.

When Monroe issued his doctrine, it amounted to little more than a statement of principles. Europeans ignored it, and the United States had neither the economic nor military power to enforce it. By the end of the nineteenth century, however, when the country's economic and military power had increased, it would become clear what a fateful turning point in the history of the Americas Monroe's declaration had been.

## CULTURE AND POLITICS IN TRANSITION

Americans' determination to break their historic pattern of subordination to Europe and complete their struggle for independence was evident as well in their efforts to fashion a distinctive republican cultural identity. The task was not easy, for people disagreed over the extent to which Anglo-European standards of art and literature should prevail and whether American culture should be grounded in the experience of ordinary people or an elite. Jeffersonians and Federalists differed almost as sharply over definitions of republican culture as they did over republican politics. During the early nineteenth century, American politics continued to evolve as well. By the mid-1820s, the Federalist-Jeffersonian party system was in disarray, a new party alignment was beginning to form, and the very character of political life was changing.

*Industry was valued over art in the first half century of independence; nevertheless, artists like Charles Willson Peale achieved a measure of success.* Self portrait of the Artist in His Museum *shows Peale unveiling a corridor of his Natural History Museum, which featured the bones of a woolly mammoth.*

## The Tensions of Republican Culture

Many among the Revolutionary generation believed that once independence was achieved, there would be an outpouring of republican cultural creativity. The expected cultural flowering, however, did not occur, in part because America's commercial spirit and growing preoccupation with the practical tasks of national development drained energy away from literature and the arts. In the expanding world of early nineteenth-century America, commerce and technology counted for more than literature or painting. Novelists such as Charles Brockden Brown and Susanna Haswell Rowson found limited audiences for their works, while painters such as Gilbert Stuart and Thomas Sully turned to portraiture in order to make a living. The painter and naturalist Charles Willson Peale found success with his immensely successful natural history museum in Philadelphia, complete with the bones of an ancient mammoth, "the LARGEST of terrestrial beings," the "ninth wonder of the world!!!"

In their effort to forge an American cultural identity, artists and writers frequently turned to American themes in their work. Jonathan Trum-

*The popular revivalism of the Second Great Awakening, beginning in the 1790s, set aside theological subtleties and emphasized the believers' immediate, emotional communion with God. This Anabaptist ceremony of baptism by immersion was painted by the Russian traveler Paul Svinin.*

bull recorded the great events of the nation's founding on a series of massive canvases depicting the Battle of Bunker Hill, Cornwallis's surrender, and the Declaration of Independence. The poet Joel Barlow fashioned a sprawling epic poem, *The Vision of Columbus* (1787), in which he traced the flight of liberty to America's shores and enthused over the nation's boundless future, while Noah Webster sought in his *Spelling Book* (1783) and *American Dictionary of the English Language* (1828) to standardize American styles of spelling and pronunciation and rid them of English affectations. By midcentury, schoolchildren and adults had purchased nearly 15 million copies of Webster's *Speller.*

Sharp disagreement arose over the continuing suitability of English cultural standards for republican America, as well as over the connections between culture and social class. The conservative Connecticut Wits—a group of Federalist poets and essayists including Timothy Dwight, David Humphries, and Lemuel Hopkins—consciously employed English Augustan literary styles in their satires on public education, popular religion, and what they called Jeffersonian mob rule. Many Americans, however, rejected English cultural standards just as they had rejected English politics and spurned the arts as artifacts of wealth, social privilege, and moral decadence. That belief was deeply rooted in republican values and in the historic sponsorship of high culture by monarchs and aristocrats in Europe. Viewed in this way, painting, sculpture, and imaginative literature seemed incompatible with republican simplicity, social equality, and moral virtue.

Tensions between what might be called high and popular culture were evident as well in American religious life. Beginning in the 1790s, a swelling tide of popular revivalism known as the Second Great Awakening swept across the nation, catching people by the thousands in its grasp. The Awakening's theology, articulated most powerfully by itinerant Methodist and Baptist preachers who moved tirelessly across the land, was simple and direct. In contrast with the intricate theological arguments of the Great Awakening a half century before, it emphasized the immediacy of every believer's encounter with God, rejected predestination in favor of universal salvation, and proclaimed the responsibility of each individual for his or her own soul. Such beliefs were fully consistent with popular republicanism.

The Awakening took hold first among ordinary people in the farms and villages of the West. One of the most spectacular outpourings of religious enthusiasm occurred in 1801 at Cane Ridge, Kentucky, where for six frenetic days 10,000 people gathered to exalt God and wrestle with the Devil. With hundreds shouting at once, the uproar could be heard for miles around. "The noise," declared James Finley, an observer and participant, "was like the roar of Niagara." He counted as many as seven ministers preaching at once, while some of the people sang, others prayed, and still others cried out for mercy "in the most pitiable accents." "My heart beat tumultuously," recalled Finley, "my knees trembled, my lips quivered, and I felt as though I must fall to the ground." Stepping onto a log for a better view, he saw "at least five hundred swept down in a moment, as if a battery of a thousand guns had been opened upon them, and then immediately followed shrieks . . . that rent the very heavens." Finding it too much to endure, Finley fled to the surrounding woods, wishing he had stayed at home.

In time the revivals would penetrate eastern and urban churches as well. When they did, many clergymen from long-established Presbyterian, Congregational, and Episcopalian churches were aghast at the doctrinal and social disorder the revivals seemed to represent. Where would America end, they wondered, if this was what republican religion was to become?

### Politics in Transition

By the 1820s, the Federalist-Jeffersonian party system was in disarray, setting the stage for a new era of politics. The Federalist party, its reputation damaged by charges of disloyalty during the War of 1812 and its continuing anti-democratic image, lay shattered as a national political force. Even in New England, long the bastion of Federalist strength, the party was in retreat.

The Jeffersonian Republicans, on the other hand, stood triumphant, their ranks swollen by fresh recruits, including ex-Federalists, in the East and the admission of new states in the West. The Jeffersonians' success, however, proved their undoing, for no single party could contain the nation's growing diversity of economic and social interests, sectional differences, and individual ambitions. Increasingly divided among themselves, the Jeffersonians found it ever more difficult to chart a consistent course or govern effectively.

Following the War of 1812, largely in response to growing pressures from the West and the Northeast, the government launched a program of national economic development. Wartime disorganization of the currency had demonstrated the need for a new national bank to replace the First Bank of the United States, whose charter had expired in 1811. In March 1816, President Madison signed a bill creating a second bank, intended to stimulate economic expansion and regulate the loose currency-issuing practices of the country's countless state-chartered banks. In his final message to Congress in December 1816, Madison called for a tariff to protect the country's infant industries from European competition. Congress responded with the first truly protective tariff in American history, a set of duties on imported woolen and cotton goods, iron, leather, hats, paper, and sugar.

The administration's program of national economic development drew sharp criticism from so-called Old Republicans, who regarded themselves as keepers of the Jeffersonian conscience. Speaking in opposition to the bank bill in 1816, Congressman John Randolph of Virginia warned that "the question is whether . . . we are willing to become one great consolidated nation . . . whether the state governments are to be swept away; or whether we . . . still . . . regard their integrity and preservation as part of our policy." Thirty-three Old Republicans voted against the bank bill, a significant showing, but not enough to prevent passage. Over the next decade, their strength dwindled, even as their cries of alarm became increasingly shrill.

Madison also recommended construction of

a federally subsidized network of roads and canals to speed economic development and enhance national security but warned that a constitutional amendment authorizing such action would first be necessary. Unwilling to delay, Representatives John Calhoun and Henry Clay pushed an internal-improvements bill through Congress. In the end, Madison vetoed the bill on constitutional grounds, but proposals for federal programs of national development would not die. By the early 1820s, Henry Clay and others, taking up the name National Republicans, were proposing an ambitious "American system" of tariffs and internal improvements.

## The Specter of Sectionalism

Sectional tensions added to the growing disorganization of American politics around 1820.

Congressional debates over the tariff, internal improvements, and the national bank echoed with the clash of sectional interests, while New England's opposition to the War of 1812 continued to fester. It was the Missouri crisis of 1819–1820, however, that revealed how deep-seated sectional tensions had become.

Ever since 1789, politicians had labored to keep the explosive issue of slavery beneath the surface of political life, for they recognized how quickly it could jeopardize national unity. Their fears were borne out in 1819 when Missouri applied for admission to the Union and raised anew the question of slavery's expansion. In the Northwest Ordinance of 1787, Congress had limited slavery north of the Ohio River while allowing its expansion to the south. But what about the vast new territory west of the Mississippi?

### Missouri Compromise of 1820

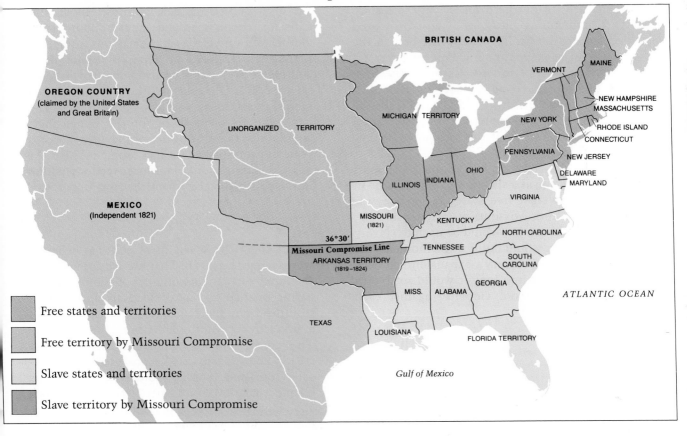

Seizing the opportunity to deal with that question, Senator Rufus King of New York demanded that Missouri prohibit slavery before entering the Union. His proposal triggered a fierce debate over the merits of slavery and Congress's authority to prevent its spread. Southerners were adamant that Congress could not close the trans-Mississippi West to their slave property and were determined to maintain a balance between slave and free states in the Senate. Already by 1819, the North's more rapidly growing population had given it a 105 to 81 advantage in the House of Representatives. Equality in the Senate offered the only sure protection of southern interests against an increasingly active central government. Northerners, on the other hand, were determined to keep the trans-Mississippi West open to free labor. That meant closing it to slavery.

For nearly three months, Congress angrily debated the issue. During much of the time, the House gallery was filled with free blacks listening intently to northern antislavery speeches. "This momentous question," worried the aged Jefferson at Monticello, "like a fire-bell in the night, [has] awakened and filled me with terror." Northerners were similarly alarmed. The Missouri question, declared the editor of the New York *Daily Advertiser,* "involves not only the future character of our nation, but the future weight and influence of the free states. If now lost—it is lost forever."

In the end, compromise prevailed. Missouri gained admission as a slave state, Maine came in as a counterweight free state, and a line was drawn west from Missouri at latitude 36° 30', dividing the lands that would be open to slavery from those that would not. For the moment, the explosive issue of slavery's expansion had been put to rest, but before long it would set North and South even more violently against each other.

### Collapse of the Federalist-Jeffersonian Party System

The final collapse of the Federalist-Jeffersonian party system came with the presidential election of John Quincy Adams in 1824.

In that year, contenders representing every wing of the Jeffersonian party competed for the presidential office. Of the five candidates, Adams of Massachusetts and Henry Clay of Kentucky advocated strong federal programs of economic development. William Crawford of Georgia and Andrew Jackson of Tennessee clung to traditional Jeffersonian principles of limited government, agrarianism, and states' rights. Somewhere in between stood John Calhoun of South Carolina, just beginning his fateful passage from nationalism to southern nullification.

When none of the candidates secured a majority of electoral votes, the election moved, as in 1800, into the House of Representatives. There an alliance of Adams and Clay supporters gave the New Englander the election, even though he had trailed Jackson in electoral votes, 84 to 99. The Jacksonians' charges of a "corrupt bargain" were given credence by Adams's appointment of Clay as secretary of state.

Adams's ill-fated administration revealed the disarray in American politics. His stirring calls for federal road and canal building, standardization of weights and measures, establishment of a national university, promotion of commerce and manufacturing, and governmental support for science and the arts quickly fell victim to sectional conflicts, political factionalism, and his open scorn for the increasingly popular democratic politics of the day. Within a year, his administration had foundered. For the rest of his term, politicians jockeyed for position in the political realignment that was under way.

### A New Style of Politics

By the 1820s, patterns of political behavior were changing as well. That was most evident in the rapidly expanding number of people participating in state and local elections. In part that resulted from the removal of property-holding and taxpaying requirements from the franchise. The constitutions of Indiana (1816), Illinois (1818), and Alabama (1819) provided for universal white male suffrage; older states such as Connecticut, Massachusetts, and New York abolished property requirements as well. Women, blacks, and Native Americans continued to be excluded from voting, but men flocked to the polls in unprecedented numbers.

At least as important in stimulating voter participation in the states were the growing strength of democratic beliefs; the active role of state governments in building roads and canals, selling public land, chartering corporations, and dealing with Native Americans; and the competition between Federalists and Jeffersonians for voter support. As popular politics grew and traditional distrust of "party faction" and open campaigning faded, a new generation of state political leaders—men such as Martin Van Buren of New York, Levi Woodbury of New Hampshire, and Lewis Cass of Ohio—perfected their skills in the techniques of mass politics, including voter registration drives, party conventions, and popular campaigning. Even some of the younger Federalists, learning from their defeats at the hands of the Jeffersonians, followed along. By the 1820s, politicians of every persuasion vied with each other for voters' support. The result was an extraordinary outpouring of interest in state elections. Participation frequently climbed well above 50 percent of eligible voters; in the New Hampshire gubernatorial election of 1814, it soared as high as 81 percent, and on one occasion in Alabama to over 90 percent.

During the first quarter of the nineteenth century, the politics of mass participation developed in the states and localities where government affected people's lives directly and the new techniques of political organization could be perfected. In the decades immediately ahead, leaders would fashion a new, national system of democratic politics and forever change the course of American political life.

## CONCLUSION: The Passing of an Era

During the first quarter of the nineteenth century, Americans reshaped the geographical and political dimensions of their republic. The nation's territory more than doubled in size, reaching for the first time to the Pacific shore. Safely in control of the federal government, the Jeffersonians labored to set it on a proper republican course. In the process, they fashioned domestic policies designed to promote agrarian expansion and foreign policies that transformed the country's relations with Europe and the Americas. They also sought, much less successfully, to reconcile Native American rights with national expansion and to fashion a distinctive cultural identity.

The 1820s brought the United States to another turning point in its development, for the decade marked an end to the era of founding. That was dramatized on July 4, 1826, the fiftieth anniversary of American independence, when two of the remaining Revolutionary patriarchs, John Adams and Thomas Jefferson, died within a few hours of each other. "The sterling virtues of the Revolution are silently passing away," wrote George McDuffie of South Carolina, "and the period is not distant when there will be no living monument to remind us of those glorious days of trial." A new era was at hand.

## Recommended Reading

Drew McCoy, *The Elusive Republic* (1980) describes the importance of agrarian expansion for the Jeffersonians. For Jeffersonian politics and government, see also Noble Cunningham, *The Jeffersonians in Power* (1963) and *The Process of Government Under Jefferson* (1978); James Young, *The Washington Community, 1800–1828* (1966); Richard Buel, *Securing the Revolution* (1972); and Daniel Jordan, *Political Leadership in Jefferson's Virginia* (1983). Discussions of the Federalists can be found in James Banner, *To the Hartford Convention* (1969); Linda Kerber, *Federalists in Dissent* (1970); and David H. Fischer, *The Revolution of American Conservatism: The Federalist Party in the Era of Jeffersonian Democracy* (1965).

Bernard Sheehan, *Seeds of Extinction: Jeffersonian Philanthropy and the American Indian* (1973) describes the intellectual bases of early Indian policy. Robert Berkhofer discusses white attitudes toward Native Americans in *The White Man's Indian* (1978). See also Reginald Horsman, *Expansion and American Indian Policy, 1783–1812* (1967) and William McLoughlin, *Cherokees and Missionaries, 1789–1839* (1984).

Foreign policy issues and the politics surrounding them are portrayed by Bradford Perkins, *Prologue to War: England and the United States, 1805–1812* (1961); Reginald Horsman, *The War of 1812* (1969); Roger Brown, *The Republic in Peril: 1812* (1964); and Ernest May, *The Making of the Monroe Doctrine* (1975).

On politics and the Supreme Court, see Charles Haines, *The Role of the Supreme Court in American Government and Politics, 1789–1835* (1944); R. Kent Newmyer, *The Supreme Court Under Marshall and Taney* (1968); and Richard Ellis, *The Jeffersonian Crisis: Courts and Politics in the Young Republic* (1971).

Donald Jackson, *Thomas Jefferson and the Stony Mountains: Exploring the West from Monticello* (1981) discusses Jefferson's fascination with the West. On the Great Awakening, see John Bole, *The Great Revival, 1787–1805* (1972) and Donald Mathews, *Religion in the Old South* (1977). For problems of cultural nationalism, see Neil Harris, *The Artist in American Society: The Formative Years, 1790–1860* (1966); Joseph Ellis, *After the Revolution: Profiles of Early American Culture* (1979); and Russell Nye, *The Cultural Life of the New Nation, 1776–1830* (1960).

The following books provide perspective on the 1820s: George Dangerfield, *The Era of Good Feelings* (1949); S. F. Bemis, *John Quincy Adams* (1951); and Glover Moore, *The Missouri Controversy* (1953).

## TIME LINE

| | |
|---|---|
| 1789 | Treaty of Fort Harmar<br>Knox's reports on Indian Affairs |
| 1790s | Second Great Awakening begins |
| 1794 | Battle of Fallen Timbers |
| 1795 | Treaty of Greenville |
| 1800 | Capital moves to Washington<br>Thomas Jefferson elected president |
| 1801 | Judiciary Act<br>New Land Act |
| 1802 | Judiciary Act repealed |
| 1803 | *Marbury* v. *Madison*<br>Louisiana Purchase |
| 1803–1806 | Lewis and Clark expedition |
| 1803–1812 | Napoleonic Wars resume<br>British impress American sailors |
| 1804 | Jefferson reelected |
| 1805–1806 | Pike's explorations in the West |
| 1806 | Non-Importation Act |
| 1807 | Embargo Act |
| 1808 | James Madison elected<br>Cherokee legal code established |
| 1809 | Tecumseh's confederacy formed<br>Non-Intercourse Act |
| 1810 | Macon's Bill No. 2 |
| 1811 | Battle of Kithtippecanoe |
| 1812 | Madison reelected<br>West Florida annexed<br>War declared against Great Britain |
| 1813 | Battle of the Thames |
| 1813–1814 | Creek War |
| 1814 | Treaty of Ghent |
| 1814–1815 | Hartford Convention |
| 1815 | Battle of New Orleans<br>U.S. establishes military posts in<br>trans-Mississippi West |
| 1816 | James Monroe elected |
| 1819 | Transcontinental Treaty with Spain<br>Spain cedes East Florida to U.S.<br>*McCulloch* v. *Maryland* |
| 1820 | Land Act<br>Missouri Compromise |
| 1823 | Monroe Doctrine proclaimed |
| 1824 | John Quincy Adams elected |
| 1827 | Cherokee adopt written constitution |
| 1829 | Cherokee "blood law" |

# PORTFOLIO TWO

# THE ART OF
# A REVOLUTIONARY
# PEOPLE

## 1 7 7 5 – 1 8 2 4

The American Revolution was one of those profound events that had an impact on all aspects of American life, even on art and design. By announcing their independence from Great Britain, Americans declared cultural independence as well, and they tried to paint American pictures, build American houses, and design American furniture. This did not mean that they were untouched by European movements; in fact, for some, like Benjamin West and John Singleton Copley, England seemed a much more congenial place to practice their art. And for some prominent American families who could afford to buy the best, the only furniture and art that mattered was that produced in Europe.

Yet the American Revolution caused many artists to rethink what it meant to be an American. European artists and writers had been fascinated with the New World almost from the moment of discovery, and they had used a variety of symbols, including the Indian, to represent the terror and opportunity in the wilderness. The new country, searching for other symbols to represent its national spirit, chose a new flag in 1777 and selected the eagle, the personification of Zeus, as the national bird. The eagle quickly appeared on the official coins. It also became a popular patriotic decoration for furniture and architecture, and women across the nation frequently worked it into the design of the quilts and coverlets they made.

The eagle was not the only symbol for the new nation. Gradually the figure of a young white woman representing liberty, but also freedom and wisdom, began to be used in a variety of illustrations. But every country needs a hero as well as a heroine, and the United States found that hero in George Washington. Even before his death, some Americans looked upon Washington as almost godlike; after he died in 1799, his image came to represent all the republican virtues. Washington's likeness appeared in paintings and lithographs. Horatio Greenough carried the Washington cult to a climax in 1840 by creating a heroic sculpture of the first president bare from the waist up and dressed in a Roman toga.

It was no accident that Greenough made Washington into a Roman. The art of ancient Greece and Rome was frequently used as models for the new nation. The ancient world seemed to represent tradition, rationality, freedom, and grandeur. The new country without a past found legitimacy by comparing itself to the glory that was Greece and the grandeur that was Rome. Thomas Jefferson, the leading architect of his day as well as the third president of the United States, borrowed from Roman architecture in designing his home at Monticello and the campus of the University of Virginia. But it was to the Greek temples that most architects turned as they tried to create an American architecture. Classical revival styles influenced the simple farmhouses of New England and the Midwest, the plantation houses in the South, and banks, schools, and churches throughout the nation. The classical style also provided the unifying theme for the new capital of the United States. Classical motifs also influenced interior design and the furniture of Duncan Phyfe and other furniture manufacturers.

John Singleton Copley, *Paul Revere*, 1768–1770.
Museum of Fine Arts, Boston.
Gift of Joseph W., William B., and Edward H. R. Revere.

John Singleton Copley (1738–1815), one of colonial America's outstanding artists, painted this portrait of Paul Revere in 1770. Revere was well known in Boston as a silversmith long before he made his famous midnight ride, and the painting shows the kind of simple, elegant silver for which he was famous. Copley left Boston in 1774, on the eve of the Revolution, to live permanently in London. Charles Willson Peale (1741–1827) studied in London with Benjamin West, another expatriate American, but settled in Philadelphia, where he founded an academy and several museums and helped Philadelphia to replace Boston as the cultural capital of the nation in the period from 1790 to 1820. This painting shows Peale's fresh, informal style. He could also paint in the more formal "European" style, as may be seen in his portraits of prominent families from South Carolina to New York. Peale's influence extended beyond his death, for he established a dynasty of "painting Peales." His sons Raphaelle and Rembrandt became outstanding artists. Several of his daughters were also accomplished painters, and his niece, Sara Miriam Peale (1800–1885), became the leading portrait painter in Baltimore and St. Louis.

Charles Willson Peale, *Staircase Group*, 1795.
Philadelphia Museum of Art, The George W. Elkins Collection.

Samuel Jennings,
*Liberty Displaying the Arts
and Sciences*, 1792.
Library Company of Philadelphia.

Quilt, initials C.A.C., 1853.
National Gallery of Art, Washington. Index of American Design.

**Patriotic symbols—the eagle, the flag, the young woman representing Liberty—were enthusiastically adopted by the new nation. A Philadelphian who was studying art in London presented this highly allegorical tableau to the Library Company of Philadelphia in 1792. As evidenced in the other two examples, symbolism also found its way into the decoration of everyday objects, helping to stir the pride and create the unity that fostered nationalism for generations after the American Revolution.**

Chest, possibly made in Ohio, c. 1860.
From the Collections of Henry Ford Museum and Greenfield Village,
Dearborn, Michigan.

Mary Wiggin, sampler, 1797.
Philadelphia Museum of Art.
Whitman Sampler Collection,
given by Pet Inc.

Young American girls often spent the winter months embroidering samplers and memorial pictures. The samplers, thousands of which have survived, range from the simple to the ornate and constitute a fascinating form of folk art. Mourning pictures served as an emotional outlet, like the one painted by 15-year-old Harriett Moore of Massachusetts to express her grief over the death of two friends. The classic urns evidence the early nineteenth-century fascination with Greek and Roman forms.

Harriett Moore,
*Richardson Memorial*, c. 1817.
New York State Historical Association,
Cooperstown.

SACRED
to the Memory of
WASHINGTON
OB 14 Dec D 1799
Æ 68

One spring day in 1839, Persis Edwards, a New Hampshire mill girl, started a letter to her cousin, Sabrina Bennett. Persis described her job in the Nashua textile mills and admitted that she liked it "very well—enjoy myself much better than I expected." But the work had disadvantages, for Persis found herself "very much confined, could wish to have my liberty a bit more." Yet, on the whole, she decided, "I can put up with that as I am favored with other privileges." As Persis was finishing her letter, Malenda Edwards, her 29-year-old aunt, added a postscript. Malenda was also a mill girl, and she shared Persis's mixed feelings about the work. "I have wished you were here too," she told Sabrina, "but I suppose your mother would think it far beneath your dignity to be a factory girl. There are very many young ladies at work in the factories that have given up millinery, dress-making and school keeping for to work in the mill but I should not advise anyone to do it for I was so sick of it at first. I wished a factory had never been thought of but the longer I stay the better I like [it]."

Although neither Malenda nor Persis worked at the mills for more than a few years, their letter hints at some of the adjustments that were necessary during an era when vast changes were taking place in American life. Industrialization and new job opportunities that lured the two young women to the mills were just two of the components contributing to the transformation of the United States during the first half of the nineteenth century. In these decades, but particularly after 1839, the country experienced rapid economic growth and a steady rise in the standard of living. Population patterns changed as the Old Northwest was settled and as more Americans moved to cities. The makeup of the American people was altered by European immigrants who poured into the country in the 1840s and 1850s. By the 1860s, foreigners comprised 10 percent of the American population and 20 percent of the population in the Northeast. Even the rhythms of country life were modified as many more farmers began to produce for the market and to participate in a national economy.

This chapter focuses on the economic and social transformations in the Northeast and Old Northwest between 1820 and 1860. The chapter explores antebellum economic growth, investigates the new industrial world, and then considers urban and rural life. The chapter highlights the impact of economic growth on different groups of Americans, in different settings, and examines their responses to change.

## ECONOMIC GROWTH

Between 1820 and 1860, the American economy lurched from boom to bust. Years of rapid growth, from 1820 to 1834 and from the mid-1840s to the late 1850s, saw expanding agricultural and industrial production, high prices, ready money, and lively land speculation. Then overproduction and overspeculation caused contraction, bank failures, depression, and deflation. Widespread unemployment accompanied

these downward lurches, with at times as much as a third of the working class unemployed. Despite this cyclic pattern, however, the overall growth rate was impressive: real per capita output grew an average of 2 percent annually between 1820 and 1840 and slightly less between 1840 and 1860. These rates meant the doubling of per capita real income over the 40-year period.

### Sources of Population Growth, 1820–1899
***Source:*** U.S. Bureau of the Census.

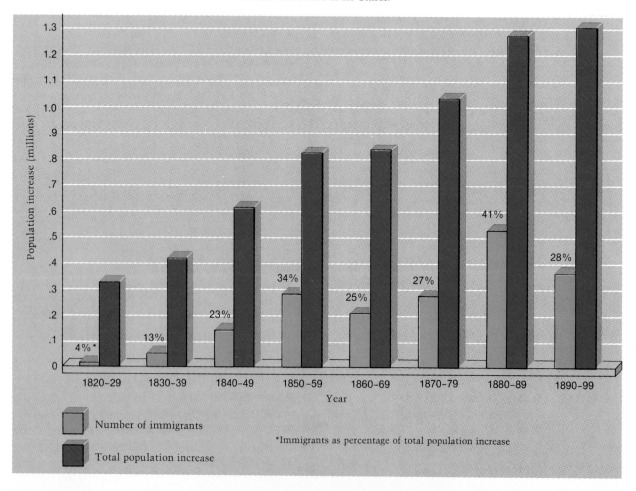

Year

Number of immigrants

Total population increase

*Immigrants as percentage of total population increase

## Natural Resources and Population

What accounted for this extraordinary increase in productivity and national wealth? The United States, of course, had abundant natural resources: vast stands of timber for buildings and machines, valuable minerals, rich soils for crops, rushing rivers for power. The Louisiana Purchase in 1803 had enormously increased these resources by adding 828,000 square miles to the public domain.

As the country's base of natural resources expanded, its population soared, from 9 million in 1820 to over 30 million in 1860. The accompanying chart illustrates that until the 1840s, most of the growth came from natural increase. But as the size of American families gradually shrank (in 1800, the average white woman bore seven children; by 1860, the number had declined to five), foreign immigrants, mostly young men from Ireland and Germany, took up the slack. During the 1850s, they accounted for almost a quarter of the total increase in population. These swelling numbers contributed to economic growth by providing workers, consumers, and new households to produce and purchase the new goods of the age.

*The Erie Canal, most famous of the many canals built between 1820 and 1840, boosted the growth of production and commerce across New York State.*

## Transportation: The Critical Factor

Improved transportation was the most important factor behind economic and geographic expansion. Early in the century, it cost more for two yoke of oxen to haul a ton of iron 10 miles than to ship it across the Atlantic. These high freight rates discouraged production for distant domestic markets, and primitive transportation hindered western settlement. In 1820, only one American in five lived west of the Appalachians. During the 1820s and 1830s, however, canal-building projects changed this situation dramatically.

The completion in 1825 of the Erie Canal, connecting New York City to the Great Lakes and the Old Northwest by water, helped set off the canal boom. Stretching 363 miles between Albany and Buffalo, the canal carried travelers along at the pace of 4 miles an hour for only 4 cents a mile. Transportation rates, which had discouraged farmers in western New York from shipping agricultural products to Manhattan, tumbled by 90 percent. The volume of trade and production increased accordingly. By 1837, the canal was carrying over 665,000 tons annually; by midcentury, it carried about 2 million tons a year.

The Erie Canal and hundreds of others, often built with the help of state subsidies, bound the country together in a new way. Canals provided farmers, merchants, and manufacturers with cheap and reliable access to distant markets and goods. They encouraged Americans to settle the frontier and bring new lands into cultivation. By 1860, almost half of the American people lived west of the Appalachians.

Even at the height of the canal boom, some Americans were urging the construction of railroads. In 1835, Jesse Williams, chief engineer of Indiana, described the spirited lobbying in his state capital. "It would awake you to be here, and witness the extravagant ideas and plans entertained in regard to Internal Improvement," he remarked. "The members [of the legislature] came here this winter full of the spirit of internal improvement, and a great many of them, full of the belief that rail roads were far superior to anything else."

Despite the avid interest in improving trans-

# Growth of the Railroad System, 1840–1870

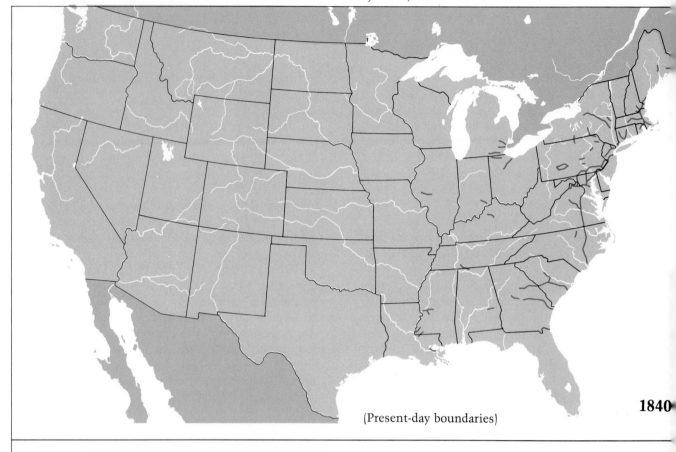

(Present-day boundaries)

**1840**

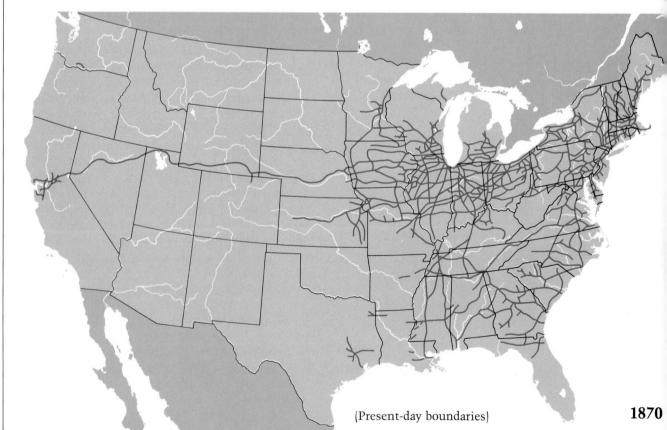

(Present-day boundaries)

**1870**

portation, railroad construction at first lagged far behind that of canals. Between 1828 and 1830, only 73 miles of tracks were laid. Early trains did not prove successful; they jumped their tracks and spewed sparks that set nearby fields ablaze. Technical difficulties were soon resolved, however. By 1840, there were 3,000 miles of track, most in the Northeast. Another 5,000 miles were laid during the 1840s, and by the end of the 1850s, total mileage soared to

*Like canals, railroads provided fast, economical transportation to and from areas lacking navigable natural waterways.*

30,000. Much of the new track was in the Old Northwest and linked that area firmly with the East.

As the railroads followed—or led—settlers westward, they exerted an enormous influence. The route a railway chose to follow could determine whether a city, town, or even homestead would survive. The railroad transformed Chicago from an insignificant settlement into a tremendous commercial and transportation center. In 1850, the city contained not one mile of track, but within five years, 2,200 miles of track serving 150,000 square miles terminated in Chicago.

The dramatic rise in railroad construction in the two decades before the Civil War probably accounts for faster economic growth after 1839. Goods, people, commercial information, and mail flowed ever more predictably and rapidly. In 1790, it had taken two weeks to send an order from Boston to Philadelphia; in 1836, it took only 36 hours. Ultimately, goods also moved relatively cheaply by railroad.

Improved transportation stimulated both agricultural expansion and regional specialization. Farmers began to plant larger crops for the market, concentrating on those for which their soil and climate were best suited. By the late 1830s, the Old Northwest had become the country's granary, while New England farmers abandoned cereal crops for dairy or produce farming. Some

### Inland Freight Rates, 1785–1865

**Source:** North, *Growth and Welfare in the American Past*, 1974.

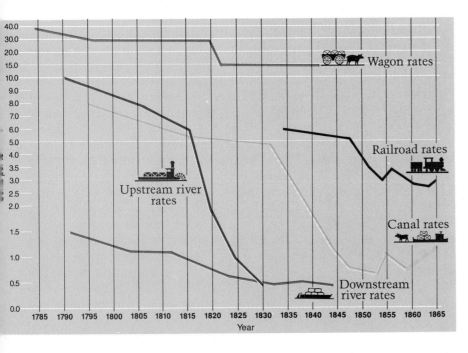

gave up their farms altogether and moved to the cities or to the frontier. By 1860, American farmers were producing four to five times as much wheat, corn, cattle, and hogs as they had in 1810. Their achievements meant abundant, cheap food for American workers and more income for farmers to spend on the new goods of the age.

## Capital Investment

Internal improvements, the exploitation of natural resources, and the cultivation of new lands all depended on capital. Much of it came from European investors. Between 1790 and 1861, over $500 million flowed into the United States from Europe. Foreign investors financed as much as a third of the cost of canal construction and bought about a quarter of all railroad bonds.

American mercantile capital fueled growth as well. As pointed out in Chapter 9, the merchant class prospered in the half century after the Revolution. Now merchants invested in schemes ranging from canals to textile factories. Many ventured into the production of goods and became manufacturers themselves.

Americans of means eagerly sought opportunities to make their capital work for them. Two New Yorkers, Arthur Bronson and his partner Charles Butler, exemplify the speculative outlook that nurtured economic development. Intrigued by the Northwest's investment possibilies, Bronson and Butler toured the region in 1833 to assess its future. Conditions were often primitive. "We have become accustomed & familiarized to scenes, & things which we never dreamed of before leaving home, & which then should have revolted at," wrote Butler. But despite discomfort, both men saw wonderful opportunities. Detroit, Butler concluded, "is destined to be a very great city," while Chicago "presents one of the finest fields in America for industry & enterprise." Each channeled funds into numerous western projects. Bronson's investments ranged from Ohio banks to farmland in Wisconsin Territory, Illinois, Michigan, Ohio, and Indiana to real estate in Chicago and Detroit, all in addition to his holdings in New York ironworks and banks.

Bronson's investment in banks derived from his appreciation of their role in stimulating economic growth. He also actively promoted the creation of life insurance companies, which, unlike commercial banks, lent money on a long-term basis. These kinds of financial institutions, Bronson realized, served as intermediaries, funneling into economic enterprises the capital of people with neither the time nor the expertise to invest their money themselves.

## The Role of Government

Local, state, and federal governments played an important part in fostering economic development. States often passed laws of incorporation that helped new ventures raise capital and gave special privileges to entrepreneurs. They also underwrote bonds for improvement projects, which increased their investment appeal and provided loans for internal improvements. New York, Pennsylvania, Ohio, Indiana, Illinois, and Virginia publicly financed almost 75 percent of the canal systems in their states between 1815 and 1860.

The national government also supported economic expansion. Its tariff policy shielded American products, and the second U.S. Bank provided financial stability so crucial to investors. Even as late as 1837, the Treasury distributed its surplus to several states for internal improvements. So widespread was the consensus that growth was desirable that the line separating the public sector from the private often became unclear.

Law as well as public policy played a part in promoting economic growth. Judicial decisions created a new and dynamic understanding of property rights. The case of *Palmer* v. *Mulligan*, decided by the New York State Supreme Court in 1805, laid down the principle that property ownership included the right to develop property for business purposes. Land was increasingly defined as a productive asset to be exploited, not merely to be enjoyed, as earlier judicial rulings had suggested. Legal decisions thus supported an aggressive attitude toward property.

Investors and businessmen alike wanted to increase predictability in the conduct of business. Contracts lay at the heart of business and commercial relationships. At the beginning of the nineteenth century, however, contract law hardly existed. It soon began to develop rapidly. In a series of important decisions between 1819 and 1824, Chief Justice John Marshall and the Supreme Court established the basic principle that contracts were binding. In *Dartmouth College* v. *Woodward*, the Court held that a charter granted by a state could not be modified without the agreement of both parties, while the Court declared in *Sturges* v. *Crowninshield* that a New York law allowing debtors to repudiate their debts was unconstitutional.

## The Innovative Mentality

As the discussion of the relationship between law and economic growth suggests, increasing productivity depends on intangible factors as well as the more obvious ones such as improved transportation. The entrepreneurial mentality that encouraged investment, new business ventures, and land speculation was just such an intangible component of antebellum economic development.

Europeans often noted another intangible factor when they described Americans as energetic and oriented toward change. As one Frenchman explained in 1834, "All here is circulation, motion, and boiling agitation. Experiment follows experiment; enterprise succeeds to enterprise." Former United States Bank head Nicholas Biddle agreed. "Every man seems born with some steam engine within him, driving him into an incessant and restless activity of body and mind . . . every head and every hand busy, with a thousand projects, and only one holiday—the 4th of July—working from morning till night with the most intense industry."

Others pointed to an American mechanical "genius." The American was "a mechanic by nature," one Frenchman insisted. "In Massachusetts and Connecticut, there is not a labourer who had not invented a machine or tool." Although this observer no doubt exaggerated, every new invention brought imitators and heated patent fights. In 1854, the government patent office issued 56 patents for harvesting implements and 39 for seed planters; a year later, 40 patents were issued for sewing machines.

Mechanical Americans turned their attention to developing more efficient and productive tools and machines. The McCormick harvester, the Colt revolver, Goodyear vulcanized rubber products, and the sewing machine were developed, refined, and developed further. Such improvements cut labor costs and increased efficiency. By 1840, for example, the average American cotton textile mill was about 10 percent more efficient and 3 percent more profitable than its British counterpart.

Although little in the way of formal technical training existed, adult lectures and lyceums fed the American taste for practical information. A series of pragmatic lectures at Boston's Lowell Institute, for example, drew thousands of people eager to hear about scientific subjects. As one of the institute's benefactors had requested, the lectures stressed "applications" and presented information of "particular utility to men."

The shortage of labor in the United States stimulated technological innovation by encouraging experiments to replace humans with machines. But the rapid spread of education after 1800 also promoted innovation and increased productivity. Clearly, the nineteenth-century American population was remarkably well educated. By 1840, more than 90 percent of northern whites and more than 80 percent of southern whites were literate.

The proliferation of public schools, which nationwide educated 37 percent of white children between the ages of 5 and 19 in 1840 (but under 20 percent in the South), suggests a relationship between education and economic

### White Secondary School Enrollment, 1840–1860

*Percent of white population between 5 and 19 years of age*

|                | 1840  | 1850  | 1860  |
|----------------|-------|-------|-------|
| New England    | 81.4% | 76.1% | 73.8% |
| Middle Atlantic| 54.7  | 61.9  | 61.3  |
| North Central  | 29.1  | 52.4  | 69.4  |
| South Atlantic | 16.2  | 29.7  | 31.4  |
| South Central  | 13.4  | 31.0  | 38.6  |
| Total          | 38.4  | 50.4  | 57.0  |

*Source:* Niemi, *U.S. Economic History,* 1975.

growth. The growth of the Massachusetts common school system illustrates that school reformers thought there was a connection.

Although several states had decided to use tax monies for education by 1800, Massachusetts moved first toward mass education by mandating in 1827 that public schools be entirely paid for by taxes. Several years later, the state set up a permanent elementary education fund and in 1836 forbade factory managers to hire children who had not spent 3 of the previous 12 months in school. Despite the legislation, the Massachusetts school system did not function well. School buildings were often run-down and even unheated. Because school curricula were virtually nonexistent, students often lounged idly at their desks.

With the formation of the first state board of education, with Horace Mann as its secretary, in 1837, the reform of state education for white children got under way. Mann and others sought to strengthen public education by introducing graded schools, uniform curricula, and teacher training; by reducing the power of local districts over their schools; and by luring more students into the schools. His campaigns helped to make the Massachusetts system a model for reformers everywhere. For the first time in American history, primary education became the rule for the majority of children between 5 and 19 in most parts of the country outside of the South, and a whole new career, mostly for women, was created.

Mann thought education promoted inventiveness and economic growth. "Education," he said, "had a market value." Businessmen often agreed. A questionnaire given to prominent industrialists in the 1840s revealed that factory owners believed literate workers could handle complex machinery without undue supervision and were superior employees—reliable, punctual, industrious, and sober. Manufacturers valued education not merely because of its intellectual content but because it encouraged habits essential to a disciplined and productive work force.

## Ambivalence Toward Change

Many nineteenth-century Americans supported education as a means to economic growth. They also firmly believed in its social value. Public schools could mold student character and promote a "just disposition, virtuous habits, and rational self-governing" behavior. Many school activities were designed to teach good habits. Students learned facts by rote because memory work and recitation taught them discipline and concentration. Nineteenth-century schoolbooks reinforced the classroom message. "It is a great sin to be idle," children read in one 1830 text, while another encouragingly pointed out, "He who rises early and is industrious and temperate will acquire health and riches." A third warned flatly, "Poverty is the fruit of idleness." "Light" reading contained similar messages and painted dreadful pictures of the consequences of ignoring them.

The concern with education and character indicate that much as Americans welcomed economic progress, they also feared its results. The much-heralded improvements in transportation that facilitated trade and settlement

*The common-school movement brought free primary education to both young men and young women, but private schools such as the Emerson School for "young ladies" in Boston existed as well.*

caused some to wonder whether civilization might disintegrate as people moved far from their place of birth and from familiar institutions. Others worried that the American family was collapsing under the impact of rapid change and feared that children would turn into barbarians. Schools, which taught students to be deferential, obedient, and punctual, could counter the worst by-products of change. Schools were as much a defence against change as they were its agents. Fear and confidence were two sides of the coin of economic transformation.

There were other signs of cultural uneasiness. In the eighteenth century, Benjamin Franklin popularized the importance of hard work in his celebrated *Poor Richard's Almanack*. In the 1830s, a group of popularizers restated Franklin's message. As the publishing revolution speeded the production of printed material and lowered costs, these authors poured out tracts, stories, and manuals on how to get ahead. They claimed that hard work and good character were the keys to success and lavished praise on the virtues of diligence, persistence, punctuality, temperance, and thrift. These habits probably did assist economic growth. Slothful workers are seldom very productive. Industry and perseverance often pay off. But the success of economic ventures in the early nineteenth century frequently depended on the ability to take risks, to think daringly. The emphasis given to the safe but stolid virtues suggests the fear of social disintegration that ran through antebellum society. New notions about women's duties and responsibilities, discussed later in this chapter, show a similar concern. By insisting on the necessity of responsible behavior, publicists hoped to counter unsettling effects of change and ensure the dominance of middle-class values.

## The Advance of Industrialization

One of the significant sources of the country's economic growth between 1820 and 1860 came through the reorganization of production. As we saw in Chapter 9, before industrialization, individual artisans fashioned their goods with hand tools. Many American families also manufactured necessary articles; as late as 1820, Americans made two-thirds of all their clothes at home.

Factory production reorganized work by breaking down the manufacture of an article into discrete steps. At first, manufacturers often relied on the putting-out system. Eventually they centralized all the steps of production under one roof, where hand labor gradually gave way to power-driven machinery. As the factory worker replaced the artisan and the home manufacturer, the volume of goods rose and prices dropped dramatically. The price of a yard of cotton cloth fell from 18 cents to 2 cents over the 45 years preceding the Civil War.

The transportation improvements that were so fundamental to economic development helped to foster industrialization. Although factories appeared as early as the 1790s, the opportunity to reach large markets after 1820 encouraged the reorganization of the production process and the use of machinery. The simple tastes and rural character of the American people suggested the wisdom of manufacturing inexpensive, everyday goods like cloth and shoes rather than luxuries for the rich.

Between 1820 and 1860, textile manufacturing became the country's leading industry. Mills rose along dozens of rivers in New England and the Middle Atlantic states. Most New England mills produced cheap cloth, following the system used at Lowell, where all the steps in manufacturing cloth had been brought together in one factory. In the Middle Atlantic states, the textile industry was more varied. Philadelphia was a center for fine textiles like gingham and carpets, while Rhode Island factories produced less expensive materials. Maryland manufacturers, like those in Philadelphia, focused on quality goods. The cumulative impact of the rise of the textile industry was to supplant the home production of cloth, even though some women would continue to weave for their families for some years to come, and hand-loom weavers would survive for another generation. In the process, Americans were transformed from a people clad in earth-colored homespun into a nation decked out in gayer, more colorful, and newer clothing.

Textile mills helped to account for the increasingly industrial character of the Northeast, although other manufacturing concerns, such as shoemaking, also contributed to the region's economy. By 1860, 71 percent of all manufacturing workers were located in the Northeast.

Other important manufacturing operations reached west and south from New England. The processing of wheat, timber, and hides using power-driven machinery was common in most communities of 200 families or more. Although a third of them were clustered in Philadelphia, paper mills were widespread. The iron and metalworking industry stretched from Albany, New York, south to Maryland and west to Cincinnati. The manufacturing of shoes centered in New England.

## THE MANUFACTURING WORLD

Because industrialization created a more efficient means of production, more goods could be produced at much lower cost than had been possible in the homes and small shops of an earlier day. Philadelphian Samuel Breck's diary gives some idea of the profusion and range of goods that industrialization made available. "Went to town principally to see the Exhibition of American Manufactures at the Masonic Hall," he noted in 1833. "More than 700 articles have been sent. Among this great variety, I distinguished the Philadelphia porcelains, beautiful Canton cotton, made at York in this state, soft and capacious blankets, silver plate, cabinet ware, marble mantels, splendid pianos and centre tables, chymical drugs, hardware, saddlery, and the most beautiful black broadcloth I ever saw."

### The Impact of Industrialization

Two examples illustrate how industrialization transformed American life. Before the nineteenth century, local printing shops produced books, newspapers, and journals through processes that substantially depended on manual labor. The cost of reading material was high enough to make a library a sign of wealth. Many literate families of moderate means had little in their homes to read other than a family Bible and an almanac.

Between 1830 and 1850, however, the print-

*Printed cloth, called calico, was a new and popular consumer item. In 1854, this calico factory employed about 2,000 workers, 1,250 of them female.*

ing and publishing industries were revolutionized as Americans adopted and improved on British inventions, as they had already done in the textile industry. Like other changes in production, the transformation of publishing was not only technological. It involved managerial, marketing, and business changes as well. From a $2.5 million market in 1830, the book business soared to become a $12.5 million enterprise by 1850.

As books and magazines dropped in cost and grew in number, far more people could afford them. No longer dependent solely on the words of the "better sort" for information, people could now begin to form their views on the basis of what they read. Books and magazines spread norms, values, and ideas to households all over the country. Even on the frontier, pioneer women could study inexpensive ladies' magazines and books of domestic advice while their husbands kept up with the latest political news or theories about scientific farming and their children learned their letters from McGuffey readers. The proliferation of printed matter had an enormous impact on people's values, their stock of information, their tastes, and their use of leisure time. It also contributed to the rising literacy rate among white Americans.

The revolution in printing had other important cultural consequences. With the expansion of the reading public, American literature flowered. Most of the literature was romantic in spirit, emphasizing emotion over reason, nature over civilization. American writers had much in common with their European counterparts, but they often chose American themes for their novels. As Ralph Waldo Emerson, thinker and writer, explained, "We shall yet have an American genius."

James Fenimore Cooper was among the first to develop American themes. In a period when familiar ways of life were in the midst of change, Cooper explored societies in transition. His Leatherstocking novels, *The Pioneers* (1823), *The Last of the Mohicans* (1826), *The Prairie* (1827), *The Pathfinder* (1840), and *The Deerslayer* (1841), portrayed the meeting of Indian and white culture and the passage from barbarism to civilization. Cooper's appreciation of the natural world and of the "noble savages" meant that he

could not accept their destruction as an unmitigated good. Like other thoughtful Americans, he was sensitive to and fearful about some of the costs of "progress."

Nathaniel Hawthorne also found his subject in the American past. He had little interest in "minute fidelity," for he wished to convey "a severer truth . . . the truth of the human heart." In *The Scarlet Letter* (1850) he sympathetically told the story of a Puritan woman's adultery, while in *The House of the Seven Gables* (1851) he depicted the decline of an old Salem, Massachussetts, family unable to escape the heavy hand of history. Grim though these novels were, they attracted a large audience of readers.

Herman Melville dedicated *Moby Dick* (1851) to Hawthorne but told him, "Dollars damn me. What I feel most moved to write, that is banned,—it will not pay." This novel of hunting the great white whale, Moby Dick, was a study of good and evil, of bravery and weakness, as well as a rousing story of whaling on the high seas. The novel's denseness, however, discouraged readers. The promise of a mass audience was not always fulfilled; although today we consider *Moby Dick* one of the masterpieces of nineteenth-century literature, Melville fell out of popularity and died almost unknown.

Just as printed materials wrought great changes in American life, the making of inexpensive timepieces affected its pace and rhythms. Before the 1830s, when few Americans could afford a clock, it was difficult to make exact plans, even if only to organize work at home more efficiently or to arrive promptly at an event like a church or town meeting. But the production of timepieces soared in the 1830s, and by midcentury, inexpensive, mass-produced ones could be found everywhere. As one observer of frontier life pointed out, "In Kentucky, in Indiana, in Illinois, in Missouri, and here in every dell in Arkansas, and in cabins where there was not a chair to sit on, there was sure to be a Connecticut clock." Free of nature's irregular divisions of the day, Americans could plan exactly how to use their time and coordinate their activities. Clocks encouraged people to think about and use time in a more disciplined way. They also undergirded some of the economic changes taking place. Timepieces, for

*Acclaimed as a model of industrialism, Lowell, Massachusetts, was planned and built in the 1820s expressly as a site for textile mills.*

example, were essential for the successful operation of railroads, which ran on schedules.

Clocks also imposed a new rhythm in many workplaces. For some Americans the clock represented a form of oppression rather than liberation. An early mill song put it directly: "The factory bell begins to ring / And we must all obey, / And to our old employment go / Or else be turned away."

## A New England Textile Town

To understand the process of industrialization and its impact on work and the work force, let us examine Lowell, the "model" Massachusetts textile town, and Cincinnati, a bustling midwestern industrial center. Though there were some similarities between the process of industrialization in these two communities, there were also significant differences. The example of Cincinnati shows that industrialization was often an uneven and complex process, while Lowell points out the importance of women like Persis Edwards in the early manufacturing work force.

Lowell was a new town, planned and built expressly for industrial purposes in the 1820s. Planners gave most attention to the shops, mills, and workers' housing, but the bustling town had a charm that prompted visitors to see it as a model factory community. In 1836, Lowell, with 17,000 inhabitants, aspired to become the "Manchester of America." It was the country's most important textile center.

By 1830, nearly 70 percent of the Lowell textile work force was women, with men and children filling the remaining positions. The women who came to Lowell for jobs were the first women to labor outside their homes in large numbers. They were also among the first Americans to experience the full impact of the factory system.

Because water was the least expensive source of energy, early manufacturers built their factories along rushing rivers and then had to attract workers to them. Lowell's planners realized the difficulty of persuading men to leave farming for mill work but saw that they might recruit unmarried women relatively cheaply for a stint of mill work. Unlike mill owners farther south, they decided not to depend on child labor. By hiring women who would work only until marriage, they hoped to avoid the kind of permanently depressed work force so evident in Great Britain. Early conversations among the planners focused on the depraved character of European industrialism. New England factory communities, they hoped, because of their special arrangements, would become models for the world.

## Working and Living in a Mill Town

Persis Edwards was typical of the young women drawn to work in Lowell and other New England textile towns. Most of the women, as the planners had anticipated, were unmarried and young. In 1830, more than 63 percent of Lowell's population was female. Most were between the ages of 15 and 29.

These women, from New England's middling rural families, came to the mills for a variety of reasons, but desperate poverty was not among them. The decline of home manufacture did mean that many women, especially daughters, in farming families had lost their traditional productive role. Mill work offered them the possibility of economic independence. As Sally Rice from Vermont explained, "I am almost nineteen years old. I must of course have something of my own before many more years have passed over my head. And where is that something coming from if I go home and earn nothing." Mill work paid women relatively well in the 1820s and 1830s. Domestic servants' weekly wages hovered around 75 cents and seamstresses' 90 cents, while in the mid-1830s women could make between $2.40 and $3.20 a week in the mill. The lure of the "privileges" of the new environment also drew young women to Lowell. As Sally Rice informed her parents, "You may think me unkind but how can you

blame me for wanting to stay here. I have but one life to live and I want to enjoy myself as well as I can."

Few considered their decision to come to Lowell as a permanent commitment. Most young women came to work for a few years, felt free to go home or to school for a few months, and then to return to mill work again. Once married—and the majority of women did so—they left the mill work force forever. In 1847, Sally Rice, presumably with a good dowry saved up, accepted the marriage proposal of a brother of one of her co-workers and moved away from Lowell.

Persis Edwards mentioned the mill's lack of "liberty," while Malenda Edwards had confessed she initially "wished a factory had never been thought of." Such responses were understandable, for new manufacturing work was regimented and exhausting. The day began at dawn or even earlier and ended about seven in the evening. Twelve hours a day, six days a week, with only a half hour for breakfast and lunch, were standard. The clock tower atop the attractive four- to six-story brick mills symbolized the new control of work.

Within the factory, space was organized to facilitate production. In the basement was the waterwheel, the source of power. Above, successive floors were completely open, each containing the machines necessary for the different steps of cloth making: carding, spinning, weaving, and dressing. Elevators moved materials from one floor to another. On a typical floor, rows of similar machines stretched the length of the low room, tended by operatives who might watch over several machines at the same time. At the end of the room, the overseer's elevated desk provided him with a view of the work space. The male supervisor and two or three children roamed the aisles to survey the work and to help out. The rooms were noisy, poorly lit, and badly ventilated. Overseers, believing that humidity would prevent threads from breaking, often nailed the windows shut.

Although machines, not operatives, did the basic work of production, workers had to ensure that their machines worked properly. The lowest-paid women workers who watched over the spinning frames and drawing frames were

*The factory bell set the daily schedule for hundreds of workers. Morning starting times varied with the seasons: in midwinter one had until 7 A.M. to be at work, whereas in summer the day began at 5.*

## TIME TABLE OF THE LOWELL MILLS,

To take effect on and after Oct. 21st, 1851.

The Standard time being that of the meridian of Lowell, as shown by the regulator clock of JOSEPH RAYNES, 43 Central Street

| | From 1st to 10th inclusive. | | | From 11th to 20th inclusive. | | | From 21st to last day of month. | | |
|---|---|---|---|---|---|---|---|---|---|---|
| | 1st Bell | 2d Bell | 3d Bell | Eve.Bell | 1st Bell | 2d Bell | 3d Bell | Eve.Bell | 1st Bell | 2d Bell | 3d Bell | Eve.Bell |
| January, | 5.00 | 6.00 | 6.50 | *7.30 | 5.00 | 6.00 | 6.50 | *7.30 | 5.00 | 6.00 | 6.50 | *7.30 |
| February, | 4.30 | 5.30 | 6.40 | *7.30 | 4.30 | 5.30 | 6.25 | *7.30 | 4.30 | 5.30 | 6.15 | *7.30 |
| March, | 5.40 | 6.00 | | *7.30 | 5.20 | 5.40 | | *7.30 | 5.05 | 5.25 | | 6.35 |
| April, | 4.45 | 5.05 | | 6.45 | 4.30 | 4.50 | | 6.55 | 4.30 | 4.50 | | 7.00 |
| May, | 4.30 | 4.50 | | 7.00 | 4.30 | 4.50 | | 7.00 | 4.30 | 4.50 | | 7.00 |
| June, | " | " | | " | " | " | | " | " | " | | " |
| July, | " | " | | " | " | " | | " | " | " | | " |
| August, | " | " | | " | " | " | | " | " | " | | " |
| September, | 4.40 | 5.00 | | 6.45 | 4.50 | 5.10 | | 6.30 | 5.00 | 5.20 | | *7.30 |
| October, | 5.10 | 5.30 | | 6.30 | 5.20 | 5.40 | | *7.30 | 5.35 | 5.55 | | *7.30 |
| November, | 4.30 | 5.30 | 6.10 | *7.30 | 4.30 | 5.30 | 6.20 | *7.30 | 5.00 | 6.00 | 6.35 | *7.30 |
| December, | 5.00 | 6.00 | 6.45 | *7.30 | 5.00 | 6.00 | 6.50 | *7.30 | 5.00 | 6.00 | 6.50 | *7.30 |

* Excepting on Saturdays from Sept. 21st to March 20th inclusive, when it is rung at 20 minutes after sunset.

### YARD GATES,

Will be opened at ringing of last morning bell, of meal bells, and of evening bells; and kept open Ten minutes.

### MILL GATES.

Commence hoisting Mill Gates, Two minutes before commencing work.

### WORK COMMENCES,

At Ten minutes after last morning bell, and at Ten minutes after bell which "rings in" from Meals.

### BREAKFAST BELLS.

During March "Ring out".........at....7.30 a. m..........."Ring in" at 8.05 a. m.
April 1st to Sept. 20th inclusive.....at....7.00 " " ........ " " at 7.35 " "
Sept. 21st to Oct. 31st inclusive.....at....7.30 " " ........ " " at 8.05 " "
Remainder of year work commences after Breakfast.

### DINNER BELLS.

" Ring out"...... ............. ........12.30 p. m........."Ring in".... 1.05 p. m.

In all cases, the *first* stroke of the bell is considered as marking the time.

responsible for piecing together broken yarn once the machines had automatically halted. The better-paid weavers made skillful interventions in the production process, repairing warp yarns and rapidly replacing shuttle bobbins when they ran out of yarn so that production would slow down only momentarily. "I can see myself now," recalled Harriet Robbins, "racing down the alley, between the spinning frames, carrying in front of me a bobbin-box bigger than I was. These mites had to be very swift . . . so as not to keep the spinning-frames stopped long."

Involving an adaptation to a completely new work situation, mill work also entailed an entirely new living situation for women operatives. The companies provided substantial quarters for their overseers and housing for male workers and their families. Hoping to attract a respectable female work force, the Lowell mill

*The promise of a personal nest egg and a degree of autonomy convinced many young women to endure long hours of regimented work in the mills. Labor-saving machinery resulted in much of the work being tedious and repetitive.*

owners also constructed company boarding-houses for their women workers. Women employees had to live in them unless they resided with their own families. Headed by female housekeepers, the boardinghouse maintained strict rules, including a ten o'clock curfew. Owners wanted a respectable and well-rested work force. Little personal privacy was possible in the crowded 2- to 3½- story buildings. Normally, four or six girls shared a small room, which contained little more than the double beds in which they slept together.

Amid such intimate working and living conditions, young women formed close ties with one another and developed a strong sense of community. Some of this sense of collectivity was apparent in strong group norms dictating acceptable behavior, clothing, and speech and in shared leisure activities at lectures, night classes, sewing and literary circles, and church. It also shaped conduct at work. Experienced operatives initiated newcomers into the mysteries of tending machines, which involved working together for weeks or months. Women stood in for each other and shared work assignments.

### Female Responses to Work

Although mill work offered better wages than other occupations open to women, all female workers shared limited job mobility. The small number staying in the mills for more than a few years did receive increases in pay and promotions to more responsible positions. A top female wage earner took home 40 percent more than a newcomer. But she never could earn as much as the male employees, who at the top of the job ladder earned 200 percent more than men at the bottom. Because only men could hold supervisory positions, economic and job discrimination was built into the American industrial system from its early days.

Job discrimination generally went unquestioned, for most female operatives accepted sexual differences as part of life. But the sense of sisterhood so much a part of the Lowell work experience supported open protest, most of it focused against a system that workers feared was turning them into a class of dependent wage earners. Lowell women's critique of the new industrial order drew on the sense of female community as well as the Revolutionary tradition.

Trouble broke out when hard times hit Lowell in February 1834. Falling prices, poor sales, and rising inventories prompted managers to announce a 15 percent wage cut. This was their way of protecting profits—at the expense of their employees. The mill workers sprang into action. Petitions circulated threatening a strike. Meetings followed. At one lunchtime gathering, the company agent, hoping to end the protests, fired an apparent ringleader. But, as the agent reported, "she declared that every girl in the room should leave with her," then "made a signal, and . . . they all marched out & few returned the ensuing morning." The strikers roamed the streets appealing to other workers and visited other mills. In all, about a sixth of the town's work force turned out.

Though this work stoppage was brief and failed to prevent the wage reduction, it demonstrated women workers' concern about the impact of industrialization on the labor force. Strikers, taunted as unfeminine for their "amazonian display," refused to agree that workers were inferior to bosses. As one of the protest songs proclaimed, "The overseers they need not think, / Because they higher stand; / That they are better than the girls / That work at their command."

Pointing out that they were daughters of free men, strikers sought to link their protest to Revolutionary ideology:

Let oppression shrug her shoulders,
And a haughty tyrant frown,
And little upstart Ignorance,
In mockery look down.
Yet I value not the feeble threats
Of Tories in disguise,
While the flag of Independence
O'er our noble nation flies.

The women viewed threatened wage reductions as an unjust attack on their economic independence and also on their claim to equal status with their employers. Revolutionary rhetoric took on new economic overtones as Lowell women confronted industrial work.

During the 1830s, wage cuts, long hours, increased work loads, and production speed-ups, mandated by owners' desires to protect profits, constantly reminded Lowell women and other textile workers of the possibility of "wage slavery." In Dover, New Hampshire, 800 women turned out and formed a union in 1834 to protest wage cuts. In the 1840s, women in several New England states agitated for the ten-hour day, while petitions from Lowell prompted the Massachusetts legislature to hold the first government hearing on industrial working conditions.

## The Changing Character of the Work Force

Most protest efforts met with limited success. The short tenure of most women mill workers prevented permanent labor organizations. Protests mounted in hard times often failed because mill owners could easily replace striking workers. Increasingly, owners found that they could do without the Yankee women altogether. The waves of immigration that deposited so many penniless foreigners in northeastern cities in the 1840s and 1850s created a new pool of labor. The newcomers were desperate for jobs and would accept lower wages than New England farm girls. Gradually, the Irish began to replace Yankee women in the mills. Representing only 8 percent of the Lowell work force in 1845, the Irish composed nearly half the workers by 1860.

As the ethnic makeup of the work force changed, so did its gender composition. More men came to work in the mills. By 1860, 30 percent of the Lowell workers were male. All these changes made the women expendable and the costs of going "against the mill" high.

It was easy for New England women to blame the Irish for declining pay and worsening conditions. Gender no longer unified women workers, not only because there were more men in the mills but also because Irish women and New England women had little in common. The Irish mill girl who started working as early as age 13 to earn money for her family's survival had a different perspective on work than the older Yankee women who were earning money

*This 1848 view of Cincinnati shows a commercial city barely recognizable from the frontier town pictured in Chapter 9, p. 278.*

for themselves. Segregated living conditions further divided the work force and undermined the likelihood of united worker actions in the 1850s.

Lowell itself changed as the Irish crowded into the city, and New England women gradually left the mills. With owners no longer feeling the need to continue paternalistic practices, boardinghouses disappeared. A permanent work force, once a nightmare to owners, had become a reality by 1860, and Lowell's reputation as a model factory town faded away.

### Factories on the Frontier

Cincinnati, a small riverfront settlement of 2,540 in 1810, grew to be the country's third largest industrial center by 1840. With a population of 40,382, it contained a variety of industries at different stages of development. Cincinnati manufacturers who turned out machines, machine parts, hardware, and furniture were quick to reorganize and introduce machinery for increased volume and profits. Other trades like carriage making and tobacco moved far more slowly toward mechanization before 1860. Alongside these concerns, artisans like coopers, blacksmiths, and riverboat builders still labored in small shops using traditional hand tools. The new and the old ways coexisted in Cincinnati, as they did in most manufacturing communities.

There was no uniform work experience in

Cincinnati as there was in Lowell. The size of the shop, the nature of work, the skills required, and the rewards all varied widely. In 1850, most Cincinnati workers worked in small or medium-size shops, but almost 20 percent labored in factories with over 100 employees. Some craftsmen continued to use a wide array of skills as they produced goods in the time-honored ways. Others used their skills in new factories, but they tended to focus on more specialized and limited tasks. In furniture factories, for example, machines did the rough work of cutting, boring, and planing while some artisans worked exclusively as varnishers, others as carpenters, and still others as finishers. No single worker made a chair from start to finish. But they still used some of their skills and earned steady wages. Though in the long run machines threatened to replace them, these skilled factory workers often had reason in the short run to praise the factory's opportunities.

Less fortunate was the new class of unskilled factory laborers who performed limited operations at their jobs either with or without the assistance of machinery. In the meatpacking industry, for example, workers sat at long tables. Some cleaned the ears of the hogs, others scraped the bristles, others had the unenviable task of gutting the dead animals. The meatpacking industry as a whole profited from efficient new operations. But its workers received low wages and had little job security. Since they had no skills to sell, they were easily replaced and casually dismissed during business slow-downs.

Still other Cincinnati residents were "out-workers" who labored at home or in small shops. Cincinnati's growing ready-to-wear clothing industry depended on outworkers. Manufacturers purchased cloth and had it cut into basic patterns. Contractors then took the material and subcontracted the work to tailors and women to finish. Paid by the piece, these outworkers, mostly female, were among the most exploited of all Cincinnati's workers. Their marginality suggested what was typical for women working for wages: not the Lowell experience, but low pay, poverty, and limited options.

The invention of the sewing machine in the mid-1840s worsened the situation of outworkers. The pool of potential workers increased now that the sewing machine made stitching easier. The volume of work expected by bosses grew. Tasks were even further subdivided, making work more monotonous. As one Cincinnati citizen explained, "as many as 17 hands" were "employed upon a single pair of pants."

Because outwork allowed women to labor at home, it was a common form of employment for women in Cincinnati as in other cities. In 1840, only about 10 percent of all women, most unmarried, labored in the official work force, usually as servants. Domestic ideology prescribed home, not paid employment, for wives. When they had to supplement their family income, however, married women took work into their homes and thereby honored social norms.

Cincinnati employers were quick to claim that the new industrial order offered great opportunities to most of the city's male citizens. They insisted that manufacturing work encouraged the "manly virtues" so necessary to the "republican citizen." Not all Cincinnati workers agreed. Like workers in Lowell and other manufacturing communities, Cincinnati's laborers rose up against their bosses in the three decades before the Civil War.

The analysis of the workingman's plight that Cincinnati labor leaders developed had much in common with the analyses of labor activists elsewhere. Even though a manufacturing job provided a decent livelihood for some, the new industrial order seemed to be changing the nature of the laboring class itself. A new kind of worker had emerged. Rather than selling the products of his skills, he had only his raw labor to sell. His "wage slavery," or dependence on wages, promised to be lifelong. The reorganization of work signaled the end of the progression from apprentice to journeyman to master and undermined traditional skills. Few could expect to rise to the position of independent craftsman. Most would only labor for others. Nor would wages bring to most that other form of independence, home ownership. The slogan "wage slavery" contained a deep truth about the changed conditions of many American working-men.

Workers also resented the ways masters tried to control their lives. In the new factories, owners insisted on a steady pace of work and uninterrupted production. Artisans who were used to working in spurts, stopping for a few moments of conversation or a drink, disliked the new routines. Those who took a dram or two at work found themselves discharged. Even outside the workplace, manufacturers attacked Cincinnati working-class culture. Crusades to abolish volunteer fire companies and to close down saloons, both attacked as nonproductive activities, suggested how little "equality" the Cincinnati worker enjoyed in an industrializing society.

The fact that workers' wages in Cincinnati, as in other cities, rose more slowly than food and housing costs compounded discontent over changing working conditions. The working class sensed it was losing ground at the very time the city's rich were visibly growing richer. In 1817,

## Occupational Distribution, 1820–1860

|              | 1820   | 1840   | 1860   |
|--------------|--------|--------|--------|
| Agriculture  | 78.8%  | 63.1%  | 52.9%  |
| Mining       | 0.4    | 0.6    | 1.6    |
| Construction | —      | 5.1    | 4.7    |
| Manufacturing| 2.7    | 8.8    | 13.8   |
| Trade        | —      | 6.2    | 8.0    |
| Transport    | 1.6    | 1.8    | 2.0    |
| Service      | 4.1    | 5.0    | 6.4    |
| Other        | 12.4   | 9.4    | 10.6   |

*Source:* U.S. Bureau of the Census.

the top tenth of the city's taxpayers owned over half of the wealth, while the bottom half possessed only 10 percent. In 1860, the share of the top tenth had increased to two-thirds, while the bottom share had shrunk to 2.4 percent. Cincinnati workers may not have known these exact percentages, but they could see growing social and economic inequality in the luxurious mansions the city's rich were building and in the spreading blight of slums.

In the decades before the Civil War, Cincinnati workers formed unions, turned out for fair wages, and rallied in favor of the ten-hour day. Like the Lowell mill girls, they cloaked their protest with the mantle of the Revolution. Striking workers staged parades with fifes and drums and appropriated patriotic symbols to bolster their demands for justice and independence. Although they did not see their bosses as a separate or hostile class, labor activists insisted that masters were denying workers a fair share of profits. This unjust distribution held them in economic dependency. Since the republic depended on a free and independent citizenry, the male workers warned that their bosses' policies threatened to undermine the republic itself.

Only in the early 1850s did Cincinnati workers begin to suspect that their employers formed a distinct class of parasitic "nonproducers." Although most strikes still revolved around familiar issues of better hours and wages, signs appeared of the more hostile labor relations that would emerge after the Civil War.

As elsewhere, skilled workers were in the forefront of Cincinnati's labor protest and union activities. But their victories proved temporary. Depression and bad times always harmed labor organizations and destroyed concessions made by employers. Furthermore, Cincinnati workers did not readily unite to protest new conditions. The uneven pace of industrialization meant that Cincinnati workers, unlike the Lowell mill girls, did not have a common working experience. Moreover, differences in the workplace were compounded by growing cultural and ethnic diversity within the work force. By 1850, almost half the people in the city were foreign-born, whereas only 22 percent had been in 1825.

As the heterogeneity of the American people increased, ethnic and religious tensions simmered. Immigrants, near the bottom of the occupational ladder, had limited job choices and often experienced hostility from American workers, who were suspicious of immigrants' faith, habits, and culture. Protestant workers frequently felt that they had more in common with their Protestant bosses than with Irish or German fellow workers. These tensions boiled over in Cincinnati in the spring of 1855. Americans attacked barricades erected in German neighborhoods with the cry "Kill the Dutch!" Their wrath visited the Irish as well. Although immigration contributed to economic growth, it also introduced a new and divisive element into American life.

## THE URBAN WORLD

It was in the cities that Americans experienced the impact of economic growth most dramatically. In the four decades before the Civil War, the rate of urbanization in the United States was faster than ever before or since. In 1820, about 9 percent of the American people lived in cities (defined as areas containing a population of 2,500 or more). Forty years later, almost 20 percent of them did. Older cities like Philadelphia and New York mushroomed in size, while new cities like Cincinnati, Columbus, and Chicago sprang up "as if by enchantment." Al-

though urban growth was not confined to the East, it was most dramatic there. By 1860, more than a third of the people living in the Northeast were urban residents, while only 14 percent of westerners and 7 percent of southerners were.

### The Process of Urbanization

Better transportation stimulated urban growth at the same time that urbanization fostered transportation improvements. Cities vying for commercial supremacy made substantial investments in transportation to secure trade. Baltimore merchants, for example, began construction of the Baltimore and Ohio Railroad in the 1820s to counter the advantage its rival, New York City, gained from the Erie Canal. As better transportation encouraged the easy flow of people and goods, cities capitalized on new commercial and industrial opportunities and markets. Outfitting and providing service for pioneers provided a basis for prosperity and expansion in cities like Pittsburgh, which first imported eastern goods but then turned to manufacturing. New Orleans and Mobile, Alabama, profited from their cotton trade, while Rochester, New York, took advantage of the new accessibility of rural hinterlands and began processing and marketing agricultural products.

Although industrialization contributed to the expansion of cities like Cincinnati, it was less important to growth than these new commercial opportunities. Most factories relied on water power and located along rushing streams and rivers rather than in crowded cities. Only when steam power became economically viable would industries routinely select urban locations.

Urbanization also helped to generate economic growth. City dwellers, who rarely had gardens or animals, had to purchase their food. Their needs encouraged farmers to turn to commercial farming. Cities also provided a growing market for other products like shoes, clothing, furniture, and carriages. The iron industry sold more than a half million cast-iron stoves yearly, mainly to city dwellers, while city governments purchased cast-iron pipes for sewers and the water supply, and city merchants erected cast-iron buildings.

Until 1840, the people eagerly crowding into cities came mostly from the American countryside. Then ships began to spill their human cargoes into seaboard cities, and a growing number of immigrants began their lives anew in the United States. Those who could afford to leave the crowded port cities for the interior did so. Germans and Scandinavians often headed for farms and towns in the West. But those who arrived almost penniless had little choice but to remain in eastern cities, search for work there, and begin forming ethnic neighborhoods. By 1860, fully 20 percent of the people living in the Northeast were immigrants; in some of the largest cities, they and their children comprised more than half the population. The Irish, fleeing famine and poverty at home, were the largest foreign group in the Northeast.

A look at Philadelphia helps to show the character, rhythms, rewards, and tensions of urban life during the antebellum period. The city was one of the giants of the age. An inland port, a bustling mercantile city, a center of shops producing textiles, metals, and a host of other products, Philadelphia stood second only to New York. As Philadelphia grew, the city steadily pushed its boundaries outward. Though William Penn's town had been admired for its attractive appearance and orderly planning, the nineteenth-century city merited little praise. Speculators interested only in profit relied on the grid pattern as the cheapest and most efficient way to divide land for development. Monotonous miles of new streets, new houses, new alleys, with "not a single acre left for public use, either for pleasure or health," as merchant Samuel Breck observed, were built.

Not all citizens enjoyed the benefits of urban life. Overwhelmed by rapid growth, city governments provided few of the services we consider essential today. What services they did offer usually went only to those who paid for them. Water is a case in point. By 1801, Philadelphia had constructed a system of waterworks that drew water from the Schuylkill River, then pumped it through wooden pipes to street hy-

### Ten Largest Cities in the United States, 1810 and 1860

| 1810 | 1860 |
| --- | --- |
| 1. New York | 1. New York |
| 2. Philadelphia | 2. Philadelphia |
| 3. Baltimore | 3. Baltimore |
| 4. Boston | 4. Boston |
| 5. Charleston | 5. New Orleans |
| 6. New Orleans | 6. Cincinnati |
| 7. Salem | 7. St. Louis |
| 8. Providence | 8. Chicago |
| 9. Richmond | 9. Buffalo |
| 10. Albany | 10. Newark |

*Source:* U.S. Bureau of the Census.

drants. Only by paying a special fee could Philadelphians have water brought into their homes, so most of the city's residents went without. In the 1820s, the city expanded the water system by constructing the Fairmount waterworks, but the more abundant supply of water again benefited those who could afford to have it piped into their homes.

In 1849, Isaac Parrish's report on the sanitary conditions in Philadelphia lamented some of the consequences. "There is . . . a general absence of bathing apparatus, and even of hydrants," he wrote, "in the houses of the poorer classes, and especially in confined courts and alleys of the populous districts of the city." An earlier inspection, carried out by Mathew Carey in 1837, had pointed to an even more basic problem: 253 persons crowded into 30 tenements without even one privy. Not just comfort but health itself was closely related to the urban dweller's ability to pay for services.

### Class Structure in the Cities

The drastic differences in the quality of urban life reflected the growing economic inequality that characterized Philadelphia and other American cities. In sharp contrast to the colonial period, the first half of the nineteenth century witnessed a dramatic rise in the concentration of wealth in the United States. The pattern was most extreme in cities.

Because Americans believed that profits belonged to the people who worked for them and because affluent Americans possessed so many advantages in the rush for riches, the well-to-do profited handsomely from this period of growth, while workers comparatively lost ground. The merchants, brokers, lawyers, bankers, and manufacturers composing Philadelphia's upper class gained control of more and more of the city's wealth. By the late 1840s, the wealthiest 4 percent of the population held about two-thirds of the wealth. The economic pattern was similar in other American cities, as the accompanying chart suggests.

This widening social gap between the upper class and the working class did not translate into mass suffering because more wealth was being generated. But the growing inequality hardened class lines, nourished social tensions, and contributed to the labor protests of the antebellum period.

Between 1820 and 1860, Philadelphia's

*Philadelphia's grid pattern, a source of order in Penn's original design, was expanded and exploited by developers with little thought to attractiveness or availability of services.*

working class, like Cincinnati's, was transformed. As preindustrial ways of producing goods yielded to factory production, some former artisans and skilled workers climbed into the middle class, becoming businessmen, factory owners, mill supervisors, and shopkeepers. Urban growth provided many opportunities. Perhaps 10 to 15 percent of Philadelphians in each decade before the Civil War improved their occupations and places of residence. But downward occupational mobility increased over the period. Fed by waves of immigrants, the lower class was growing at a faster and faster rate. Moreover, within the working class itself, the percentage of unskilled wage earners who lived in poverty or on its brink increased from 17 percent to 24 percent between 1820 and 1860. At the same time, the proportion of craftsmen, once the heart of the laboring class, shrank from 56 percent to 47 percent.

## Homes in the City

As with so much else in urban life, housing reflected these social and economic divisions. The poorest had the least desirable housing, renting quarters in crowded, flimsily constructed shacks, shanties, and two-room houses. Because much of the worst housing was in back alleys or even in backyards, it was concealed by the more substantial houses fronting the main streets. Many visitors did not even realize there were slums behind the rows of brick housing, nor did they suspect the uncollected garbage, privy runoffs, and fetid decay in the dark, unpaved alleys. In his diary, Philadelphia shopkeeper Joseph Sill left a description of living conditions at the bottom. "In the afternoon," he wrote, "Mrs. S & I went to the lowest part of the City to see some poor persons who had call'd upon us for Charity. We found one woman, with two children, & expecting soon to be confined, living in a cellar, part of which was unfloored, & exhibited much wretchedness; but it was tolerably clean. Her husband is a Weaver, & had his loom in the Cellar, but has only occasional work."

A member of the comfortable middle class like Joseph Sill lived in a pleasantly furnished brick house. Rooms devoted to particular activities like cooking or eating were usual. Middle-class families enjoyed more space, more privacy, and more comfort than the less affluent. Franklin stoves gave warmth in winter, and iron

### Wealth Distribution in Three Eastern Cities in the 1840s

| LEVEL OF WEALTH | PERCENTAGE OF POPULATION | APPROXIMATE NONCORPORATE WEALTH OWNED | PERCENTAGE NONCORPORATE WEALTH |
|---|---|---|---|
| *Brooklyn in 1841* | | | |
| $50,000 or more | 1% | $10,087,000 | 42% |
| $15,000 to $50,000 | 2 | 4,000,000 | 17 |
| $ 4,500 to $15,000 | 9 | 5,730,000 | 24 |
| $ 1,000 to $ 4,500 | 15 | 2,804,000 | 12 |
| $ 100 to $ 1,000 | 7 | 1,000,000 | 4 |
| Under $100 | 66 | — | — |
| *New York City in 1845* | | | |
| $55,000 or more | 1 | 85,804,000 | 40 |
| $20,000 to $55,000 | 3 | 55,000,000 | 26 |
| *Boston in 1848* | | | |
| $90,000 or more | 1 | 47,778,500 | 37 |
| $35,000 to $90,000 | 3 | 34,781,800 | 27 |
| $ 4,000 to $35,000 | 15 | 40,636,400 | 32 |
| Under $4,000 | 81 | 6,000,000 | 4 |

*Source:* Pessen, *Wealth, Class, and Power Before the Civil War,* 1973.

cookstoves made cooking easier. Conveniences like Astral lamps made it possible to read after dark. Bathing stands and bowls ensured higher standards of cleanliness. Rugs muffled sounds and kept in the heat.

The houses of the city's elite were spacious and filled with new conveniences. Samuel Breck's detailed description of the house he purchased in 1839 gives a picture of elegance and luxury:

> It is a first rate house, of the first class in size etc., being nearly 25 feet front, 4 stories high, covered with zinc, fine kitchen (dining room etc. in back buildings), splendid white Italian carved mantel pieces in other parlours. Parlours 14 feet high, a marble Portico to this and the adjoining house that cost upwards of three thousand dollars, exceeding fine cellars, with cistern and furnaces, water closet and shower and common bath up stairs, marble mantels and fireplaces in dressing rooms, as well as in the rooms to which they are an appendage, and finally the gas at the door, which has been introduced into the next house, and can be (as I intend) introduced into mine, and has been done. This splendid house cost upwards of $25,000. I bought it for $22,500.

Three weeks later, he purchased the adjoining lot for a garden, paying another $8,000 for it.

For the urban middle and upper class, residential comfort, choice, and stability were the rewards of economic success. But working-class renters moved often, from one cramped lodging to another. This common pattern of repeated mobility made it difficult to create close-knit neighborhoods in urban settings.

## The Ideals of Middle-Class Life

Although growth provided more goods for more Americans, the dramatic increase in the concentration of wealth favored the middle and upper classes in antebellum America. Theirs were the houses with new conveniences like stoves and ice chests in the 1830s and bathrooms, gas lighting, and matching sets of furniture in the 1840s.

As the gap between classes widened, new middle-class norms emerged. They seemed best suited to the rhythms of middle-class urban life,

but they also had an impact on working people and rural Americans.

New expectations about middle-class family life were an outgrowth of the period's changing economy. In the seventeenth and eighteenth centuries, many American families operated as an economic unit. Even though men and women, adults and children were hardly equal, they all performed complementary tasks in the family's struggle to get ahead. Better transportation, new products, and the rise of factory production and large businesses changed the family economy. Falling prices for manufactured goods like soap, candles, clothing, and even bread made it unnecessary for women, except on the frontier, to continue making these goods at home. As men became increasingly enmeshed in a money economy, whether through trade and commerce or through market farming, women's and children's contributions to the family economy became relatively less significant. Although middle-class women and children still worked in their homes as their husbands left to "bring home the bacon," they often neither produced vital goods nor earned money. Even the rhythm of their lives, oriented to housework rather than the demands of the clock, separated them from the bustling commercial world where their husbands now labored. By 1820, the notion emerged that the sexes occupied separate spheres.

If men were in the public world, pursuing the dream of success, what was woman's sphere and what were her responsibilities? Sarah Hale, editor of the popular magazine *Godey's Lady's Book*, and Catherine Beecher, well-known lecturer and writer, argued that woman's sphere was at home. There she would work not as producer but as housekeeper, creating a clean, wholesome, and private setting for family life.

But women were more than housekeepers; they were also their families' moral and cultural guardians. Arguing that women had different characters than men, that they were innately pious, virtuous, unselfish, and modest, publicists extended the argument developed during the Revolutionary era. By training future citizens and workers to be obedient, moral, patriotic, and hardworking, mothers would ensure the welfare of the republic. Just as important, they would be preserving important values in a time of rapid change. It was each wife's responsibility, for example, to help her husband cope with the temptations and tensions of the new, fast-paced economic order. As one preacher explained, a wife was the guardian angel who "watches over" her husband's interests, "warns him against dangers, comforts him under trial; and by . . . pious, assiduous, and attractive deportment, constantly endeavors to render him more virtuous, more useful, more honourable, and more happy."

This view, which characterized women as morally superior to and different from men, had important consequences for women's lives. The separation of the male and female worlds and the shift in women's status often meant that women had more in common with one another than with men. Similar social experiences and perspectives made female friendships central for many women. With men away from home for most of the day, women naturally turned to each other. Much evidence suggests that women found comfort, security, and happiness in their relations with other women rather than with their husbands.

They also experienced pleasure and frustration in their role as housekeepers. Publicists proclaimed the importance of housekeeping, but the new standards of cleanliness and order were often impossible to achieve. Moreover, efforts to create a perfect home often worked against attempts to nourish a harmonious family life.

Although the concept of domesticity seemed to confine women to the domestic sphere and to emphasize the private nature of family life, it actually prompted women to take on activities in the outside world. If women were the guardians of morality, why should they not carry out their tasks in the public sphere? This reasoning lay behind the tremendous growth of voluntary female associations in the early decades of the century. Initially most were religious and charitable in nature. They supported orphanages, paid for and distributed religious tracts and Bibles, established Sunday schools, and ministered to the poor. The associations provided women with congenial companions and suitable tasks for their "moral character." Sometimes the women recognized special interests that men did not share. In the 1830s, as we shall see in Chapter 13, women added specific moral concerns like the abolition of slavery to their missionary and benevolent efforts. As these women took on more active and controversial tasks, they often clashed with men and with social conventions about "woman's place."

Domesticity described norms, not the actual conduct of middle-class women. Obviously not all women were pious, disinterested, selfless, virtuous, cheerful, and loving. But these ideas influenced how women thought of themselves and promoted "female" behavior by encouraging particular choices. Domestic ideals helped many women make psychological sense of their lives.

The new norms, so effectively spread by the publishing industry, also influenced rural women and urban working women. The insistence on marriage and service to family discouraged married women from entering the work force. Those who had to work often bore a burden of guilt. Many took in poorly paid piecework so that they could remain at home.

*Erastus Salisbury Field (1805-1900), an accomplished folk artist, painted this middle-class family in Ware, Massachusetts, in 1839. The family portrait is stylized, but it represents some of the expectations of roles for husband, wife, and children.*

Though the new feminine ideal may have seemed noble to middle-class women in cities and towns, it created difficult tensions in the lives of working-class women.

As family roles were reformulated, a new view of childhood emerged. Since middle-class children were no longer expected to contribute economically to their families, childhood now appeared as a special stage of life, a period of preparation for adulthood. In the child's earliest years, mothers were to impart important values, including the necessity of behaving in accordance with gender prescriptions. Harsh punishments lost favor because they suited neither a mother's character nor the delicate task at hand. As Catherine Beecher explained, "Affection can govern the human with a sway more powerful than the authority of reason or [even] the voices of conscience." Schooling also contributed to preparing a child for the future, and urban middle-class parents supported the public school movement.

Children's fiction, which poured off the printing presses, also helped socialize children. Stories pictured modest youngsters who happily made the correct choices of playmates and activities, obeyed their parents, and were dutiful, religious, loving, and industrious. Occasionally, as in The Child at Home (1833), the reader could discover the horrible consequences of wrongdoing. The young girl who refused to bring her sick mother a glass of water saw her parent promptly die. Heavy-handed moralizing made sure that children got the proper message.

The growing publishing industry played an important part in spreading new ideas about family roles and appropriate family behavior. Novels, magazines, etiquette and child-rearing manuals, and schoolbooks all carried the message from northern and midwestern centers of publishing to the South, to the West, and to the frontier. Probably few Americans lived up to the new standards established for the model parent or child, but they were increasingly influenced by them.

New notions of family life supported the widespread use of contraception for the first time in American history. Since children required so much loving attention and needed to be prepared so carefully for adulthood, many parents desired smaller families. The declining birthrate was evident first in the Northeast,

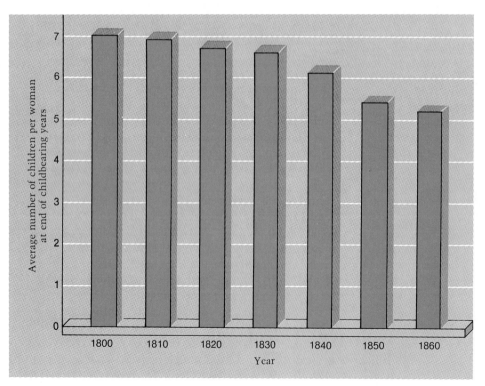

**Average Family Size, 1800–1860**
*Source:* U.S. Bureau of the Census.

particularly in cities and among the middle class. Contraceptive methods included abortion, which was legal in many states until 1860. Perhaps as many as a third of all pregnancies were terminated by this medical procedure. Other birth control methods included coitus interruptus and abstinence. The success of these methods for family limitation suggests that many women had adopted the new definitions of their sex as naturally affectionate but passionless and sexually restrained.

## Mounting Urban Tensions

The social and economic changes transforming American cities in the half century before the Civil War produced recurrent urban violence on a scale never before witnessed in America, not even during the Revolution. Festering ethnic and racial tensions often triggered mob actions. Cities, which were lightly governed in this period, lacked police forces able to quell urban riots or protect citizens' property. Although a modern uniformed police force had been established in London in 1829, American cities only slowly followed the English example. Most still had the traditional constable-and-watch system. The night watch lit city streetlights and patrolled the streets to preserve order and arrest suspicious persons. During the day, constables were charged with eliminating health hazards, carrying out court orders, and apprehending criminals once a complaint had been lodged. Neither group tried to prevent crimes or discover offenses. Neither wore uniforms. Certainly neither was able to "prevent a tumult." Each chaotic event, however, made the London model more attractive.

With a large black community, Philadelphia's disorders were partly due to racial tensions. A brief analysis of that city's unsavory riot in August 1834, however, reveals other important sources of social antagonism as well as the inability of its police force to control disorder.

One hot August evening, several hundred Philadelphians wrecked a building on South Street that contained the "Flying Horses," a merry-go-round patronized by blacks and whites. A general melee followed. As the *Phila-*

*delphia Gazette* reported, "At one time it is supposed that four or five hundred persons were engaged in the conflict, with clubs, brickbats, paving stones, and the materials of the shed in which the flying horses were kept." Spurred by the taste of blood, the mob moved into the center of the crowded and decaying racially mixed neighborhood, where they continued their orgy of destruction, looting, and intimidation. Similar mayhem followed on the next two nights. Intermittent rioting broke out the succeeding night as well, but the presence of 300 special constables, a troop of mounted militia, and a company of infantry prevented the violence from reaching the pitch of the previous nights.

The destructive force of the mob was substantial. An investigation following the riots revealed that at least $4,000 of damage had occurred. Two black churches and more than 36 private homes had been harmed or destroyed. At least one black had been killed, and numerous others had been injured. As one shocked eyewitness reported, "The mob exhibited more than fiendish brutality, beating and mutilating some of the old, confiding and unoffending blacks with a savageness surpassing anything we could have believed men capable of."

Many rioters bragged that they were "hunting the nigs." Riots, however, are complicated events, and this racial explanation does not reveal the range of causes underlying the rampage of violence and destruction. As the papers of the time noted and as recent historical study has substantiated, the rioters were young and generally of low social standing. Many were Irish. Some had criminal records. A number of those arrested, however, were from "a class of mechanics of whom better things are expected": weavers, house painters, a cabinetmaker, a carpenter, a blacksmith, and a plasterer. No professional people or businessmen seem to have been involved. Accompanying the rioters, however, were onlookers who egged the mob on. As one paper reported, these onlookers "countenanced" the operations of the mob "and in one or two instances coincided with their conduct by clapping." The rioters revealed that in the event of "an attack by the city police, they confidently counted" on the assistance of these bystanders.

# RECOVERING THE PAST

Although paintings are often admired and studied for artistic reasons alone, their value as historical sources should not be overlooked. In an age before the camera, paintings, sketches, and even pictures done in needlework captured Americans at different moments of life and memorialized their significant rituals. Paintings of American families in their homes, for example, reveal both an idealized conception of family life and the details of its reality. In addition, the paintings provide us with a sense of what the houses of the middle and upper class (who could afford to commission art) were like.

Although artists trained in the European tradition of realism painted family scenes and portraits, many painters of family life lacked formal academic training and have thus been called "primitive" artists. Their art was "unreal" or abstract in the sense that artists tended to emphasize what they knew or felt rather than what they actually saw.

Some of these primitive artists were women who had received some drawing instruction at school. They often worked primarily for their own pleasure. Other artists, however, were craftsmen, perhaps house or sign painters, who painted pictures in their leisure time. Some traveling house decorators made a living by doing paintings and wall decorations. Many primitive paintings are unsigned, and even when we know the painter's identity, we often know little more than a name and perhaps a date. After flourishing in the first three-quarters of the nineteenth century, primitive artists eventually lost the market for their paintings with the appearance of the camera and inexpensive prints.

We see here a painting of the Sargent family done by an unknown artist around 1800. Although it is not an exact representation of reality, it does convey what the artist and the buyer considered important. Like any piece of historical evidence, this painting must be approached critically and carefully. The following questions focus on four areas: (1) the individual family members and their treatment, (2) the objects associated with each, (3) the implied or apparent re-

**Anonymous, The Sargent Family, 1800**

359a

# FAMILY PAINTINGS

lation ship between family members, and (4) the domestic environment. The painting gives us an idealized version of what both the painter and the subjects felt ought to be as well as what actually was.

First, study the family itself. Describe what you see. How many family members are there, and what is each one doing? What seems to be the relationship between husband and wife? Why do you think Mr. Sargent is painted with his hat on? Who seems to dominate the painting, and how is this dominance conveyed (positioning, attitude or facial expression, eye contact, clothing)? What can you conclude about different "spheres" and roles for men and women?

Why do you think the artist painted two empty chairs and included a ball and a dog in this scene of family life? What do these choices suggest about attitudes toward children and their upbringing? What seems to be the role of the children in the family? What does the painting suggest about how this family wished to be viewed? How do your conclusions relate to information discussed in this chapter?

Take a look at the room in which the Sargents are gathered. Make an inventory of the objects and furnishings in it. The room seems quite barren in comparison to present-day interiors. Why? Why do you think the chairs are placed near the window and door? What kind of scene does the window frame?

*The Family at Home*, painted by H. Knight in 1836, is a more detailed painting showing a larger family gathering almost 40 years later. Similar questions can be asked about this painting, particularly in relationship to the different treatment of boys and girls and the positioning and objects associated with each sex. There are many clues about the different socialization of male and female children. The family's living room can be contrasted to the Sargent family's room to reveal some of the changes in the home brought about by industrialization.

Finally, how do these nineteenth-century homes and sex roles differ from those in colonial New England and the Chesapeake?

Photograph Hirschl & Adler Galleries, Inc., New York

*H. Knight,* **The Family at Home,** *1836*

359b

The mob's composition hints at some of the reasons for participation. Many of the rioters were at the bottom of the occupational and economic ladder and were in competition with blacks for jobs. This was particularly true of the newly arrived Irish immigrants, who were attempting to replace blacks in low-status jobs. That economic rivalry was an important component of the riot was borne out by violence against blacks soon afterward. "Colored persons, when engaged in their usual vocations," the *Niles Register* observed, "were repeatedly assailed and maltreated. . . . Parties of white men have insisted that no blacks shall be employed in certain departments of labor."

If blacks threatened the dream of advancement of some whites, this was not quite the complaint of the skilled workers. These men were more likely to have been experiencing the negative impact of a changing economic system that was undermining the small-scale mode of production. The dream of a better life seemed increasingly illusory as their declining wages drew them closer to unskilled workers than to the middle class. Like other rioters, they were living in one of the poorest and most crowded parts of the city. Their immediate scapegoats were blacks, but for them the real but intangible villain was the economic system itself. Trade union organizing and a general strike a year later would highlight the grievances of this group.

Urban expansion also figured as a factor in the racial violence. Most of the rioters lived either in the riot area or nearby. All had experienced the overcrowded and inadequate living conditions caused by the city's rapid growth and indifference to planning. The racial tensions generated by squalid surroundings and social proximity go far to explain the outbreak of violence. The same area would become the scene of race riots and election trouble later and became infamous for harboring criminals and juvenile gangs. The absence of middle- or upper-class participants did not mean that these groups were untroubled during times of growth and change. But their material circumstances cushioned them from some of the more unsettling forces.

The city's police force proved unable to control the mob, thus prolonging the violence.

Philadelphia, like other eastern cities, was in the midst of creating its police force, but change was very slow. In 1833, a small, police force had been added to the constable-and-watch system. The new force was moving toward a preventive role, for these policemen were supposed to deter crime by walking the city streets. But their small size rendered them powerless in the face of the angry mob. The next year, the city government reduced their numbers, complaining of the excessive expense of the day force. Only continued rowdiness, violence, and riots would convince residents and city officials in Philadelphia (and in other large cities) to support an expanded, quasi-military, preventive police force in uniforms. By 1855, most sizable eastern cities had established such a force.

Finally, the character of the free black community itself was a factor in producing those gruesome August events. Not only was the community large and visible, but it also had created its own institutions and its own elite. Much of the mob's rage was vented against affluent blacks or their property. Many of the houses destroyed on the second night of rioting were solid brick houses, and middle-class blacks were robbed of silver and watches. Black wealth threatened the notion of the proper social order held by many Philadelphians and seemed unspeakable when whites could not afford life's basic necessities or lacked jobs. As one white noted critically, "In the older times, dressy blacks and dandy coloured beaux and belles, as we see them issuing from their proper churches, were quite unknown."

## The Black Underclass

Events in Philadelphia showed how hazardous life for free blacks could be. Few enjoyed the rewards of economic expansion and industrial progress. Northern whites, like southerners, believed in black inferiority and depravity and at the same time feared black competition for jobs and resources. Although northern states had passed gradual abolition acts in the 1780s and the national government had banned slaves from entering new states to be formed out of the Northwest Territory, nowhere did any government extend equal rights and citizenship or economic opportunities to the free blacks in their midst.

For a time in the early nineteenth century, some blacks living in the North were permitted to vote, but they soon lost that right. Beginning in the 1830s, in part because of the influx of fugitive slaves and manumitted blacks without property or jobs, Pennsylvania, Connecticut, and New Jersey disenfranchised blacks. New York allowed only those with three years' residence and property valued at $250 or more to vote. Only the New England states (with the exception of Connecticut), which had tiny black populations, preserved the right to vote regardless of color. By 1840, 93 percent of the northern free black population lived in states where law or custom prevented them from voting.

Black civil rights were also restricted. In five northern states, blacks could not testify against whites or serve on juries. In most states, the two races were thoroughly segregated. Blacks had to endure separate and inferior facilities in railway cars, steamboats, hospitals, prisons, and other asylums. In some states they could enter public buildings only as personal servants of white men. They sat in "Negro pews" in churches and were permitted to take communion only after whites had left the church. Although most Protestant religious denominations in the antebellum period split into northern and southern branches over the issue of slavery, most northern churches were not disposed to welcome blacks as full members.

As the Philadelphia riot revealed, whites were driving blacks from their jobs. In 1839, *The Colored American* blamed the Irish. "These impoverished and destitute beings . . . are crowding themselves into every place of business . . . and driving the poor colored American citizen out." The paper's accusation reflected reality. Increasingly after 1837, these "white niggers" became coachmen, stevedores, barbers, cooks, house servants—all occupations once held by blacks.

Educational opportunities for blacks were also severely limited. Only a few school systems admitted blacks, and they provided separate facilities. The case of Prudence Crandall illustrates the lengths to which northern whites would go to maintain racial segregation. In 1833, Crandall, a Quaker schoolmistress in Canterbury, Connecticut, announced that she would admit "young colored ladies and Misses" to her school. The outraged townspeople, fearful that New England would become the "Liberia of America," tried everything from persuasion to intimidation to induce Crandall to abandon her project.

Nonetheless, Crandall opened the school. Hostile citizens harassed and insulted students and teachers, refused to sell them provisions, and denied them medical care and admission to churches. Ministers degraded Crandall's efforts in their sermons, and local residents poured manure in the school's well, set the school on fire, and knocked in walls with a battering ram. Crandall was arrested, and after two trials—in which free blacks were declared to have no citizenship rights—she finally gave up and moved to Illinois.

Crandall would not have found the Old Northwest much more hospitable. The fast-growing western states were intensely committed to white supremacy and black exclusion. In Ohio, the response to talk of freeing the slaves was to pass "black laws" excluding them from the state. Said one Ohioan, "The banks of the Ohio would be lined with men with muskets to keep off the emancipated slaves." In 1829 in Cincinnati, where evidence of freedom papers

*Life was often hazardous for urban blacks. This 1827 broadside mockingly describes a Boston riot in which "a great number de white Trucker-man got angry wid count I spose many bad girl who lib here" in the black section of town.*

**Dreadful Riot on Negro Hill!**

Read wid detention de Melancholly Tale and he send you yelling to your bed!

and $500 bond was demanded of blacks who wished to live in the city, white rioters ran nearly 2,000 blacks out of town.

As an Indiana newspaper editor observed in 1854, informal customs made life dangerous for blacks. They were "constantly subject to insults and annoyance in traveling and the daily avocations of life; are practically excluded from all social privileges, and even from the Christian communion." An Indiana senator said in 1850 that a black could "never live together equally" with whites because "the same power that has given him a black skin, with less weight or volume of brain, has given us a white skin with greater volume of brain and intellect." A neighboring politician, Abraham Lincoln of Illinois, would not have disagreed with this assessment.

# RURAL COMMUNITIES

Although the percentage of families involved in farming fell from 72 percent to 60 percent between 1820 and 1860, Americans remained a rural people. Agriculture persisted as the country's most significant economic activity, and farm products still made up most of the United States' exports. The small family farm still characterized eastern and western agriculture.

Even though farming persisted as the dominant way of life, agriculture changed in the antebellum period. Railroads, canals, and better roads pulled rural Americans into the orbit of the wider world. Some crops were shipped to regional markets; others, like grain, hides, and pork, stimulated industrial processing. Manufactured goods flowed in return to farm families. Like city dwellers, farmers and their families read books, magazines, and papers that exposed them to new ideas. Commercial farming encouraged different ways of thinking and acting and lessened the isolation so typical before 1820.

## Farming in the East

During the antebellum period, economic changes created new rural patterns in the Northeast. Marginal lands in New England, New York, and Pennsylvania, cultivated as more fertile lands ran out, yielded discouraging returns. Gradually after 1830, farmers abandoned these farms, and the New England hill country began a slow decline. By 1860, almost 40 percent of people who had been born in Vermont had left their native state; elsewhere in New England, the out-migration hovered around 30 percent. A popular song of the 1840s caught the pattern of flight. "Come, all ye Yankee farmers who wish to change your lot, / Who've spunk enough to travel beyond your native spot. / And leave behind the village where Pa and Ma do stay, / Come follow me, and settle in Michigan, yea, yea."

Northern farming was in the midst of a transformation. By the 1830s, eastern farmers were realizing that they could not compete with western grain. Therefore, they sought new agricultural opportunities created by better transportation and growing urban markets.

One of the demands was for fresh milk. By the 1830s, some eastern cities had grown so large that milk was turning sour before it could be delivered to central marketplaces. To meet the desire for milk, several cities, including New York City, started urban dairies. Barns were erected for cows who fed on garbage and slop from distilleries and breweries. As railroad lines extended into rural areas, farmers living as far away as Vermont and upper New York State realized that they could ship cooled milk to urban centers and have it arrive fresh. In 1842 and 1843, the Erie Railroad carried 750,000 gallons of milk to New York City. As they turned to dairy farming, these farmers eventually drove the city dairies out of business. City residents had fresher and cheaper milk and drank more of it as a result.

Urban appetites encouraged other farmers to cultivate fruit and vegetables. Every city was surrounded by farmers raising produce for urban consumption. Railroads also prompted farmers miles away to turn to specialized farming. Upper New York State farmers began to raise and ship quantities of apples, while New Jersey and Delaware farmers became famous for their peaches. Thus, in July 1837, a Boston housewife could buy at the central market a wide variety of fresh vegetables and fruits, ranging from peas, summer squash, and cauliflower to grapes, cherries, and raspberries.

As northern farmers adopted new crops, they began to use their land more intensively. Increasingly they became interested in scientific farming as a means of making their land more productive. After 1800, northern farmers began to use manure as fertilizer rather than disposing of it as a smelly nuisance. By the 1820s, some farmers were rotating their crops and planting new grasses and clover to restore fertility to the soil. Worn-out wheat and tobacco lands in Maryland and Delaware were recovered for livestock farming in this way. Calculation began to replace "habit and prejudice . . . the powerful opponents of improvement."

Farmers in the Delaware River valley were leaders in adopting new methods, but interest in scientific farming was widespread. By 1860, American farmers had developed thousands of varieties of plants especially suited for local conditions. Many improvements resulted from experimentation, but farmers also enjoyed more and better information. New journals like the

*Improved transportation to urban markets made it profitable for eastern farmers to produce perishables such as eggs, milk, vegetables, and fruit. Note the live chickens, which are also packed in a crate for the trip to market.*

*New England Farmer,* the *Farmers' Register,* and the *Cultivator* informed readers of modern farming practices, fertilizers, scientific breeding, and methods for treating fruits and vegetables. Following New York's lead in 1819, many states established agricultural agencies to propagate new ideas. Although wasteful farming practices did not disappear, they became less characteristic of the Northeast. Improved farming methods contributed to increased agricultural output and helped to reverse a 200-year decline in farm productivity in some of the oldest areas of settlement. A "scientific" farmer in 1850 could probably produce two to four times as much as a farmer had been able to produce in 1820.

Farmers in the fertile area around Northampton, Massachusetts, illustrate the American farmer's adjustment to new economic conditions. As early as 1800, farming families there began to overcome rural isolation as roads were improved, a turnpike was built, and stage routes were introduced. Canal improvements and then railroads strengthened new contacts. With markets ever more accessible, farmers began to change their patterns of agriculture. Rather than raising crops and animals for home use or for local barter, farmers began to cultivate crops "scientifically" in order to increase profits. Farming was becoming a business. At home, women found themselves freed from many of their traditional tasks. Peddlers brought goods to the door. The onerous duty of making cloth and clothing disappeared with the coming of inexpensive ready-made cloth and even ready-made clothes in the 1820s. Daughters liberated from the chores of home manufacturing went off to the mills or earned money by taking in piecework from local merchants.

As the rhythms of rural life in the Connecticut River valley quickened, attitudes also changed. Cash transactions replaced the exchange of goods. Country stores became more reluctant to accept wood, rye, corn, oats, and butter as payment for goods instead of cash. Among some of the farmers, the ethic of getting ahead became evident, even if the motive was not entrepreneurial but rather a desire to provide for family material comfort.

Traditional attitudes did not wither completely, however. Some farmers continued to be content with making a living rather than chasing a profit. "Reason's whole pleasure, all the joys of sense / Lie in three words, health, peace and competence" was still the motto for some of the valley's farmers.

One of these old-fashioned farmers, Moses Goodell, was described by his son as "always . . . too honest to get along in the world and get very rich. . . . He managed somehow to just about hold his own, but I suppose it has been tight work for the past few years." Some farmers prospered as they became involved in the market economy; others, like Goodell, just got along. Wealth inequality increased near Northampton, as it did elsewhere in the rural Northeast.

## Frontier Families

Some of the people who left the North during these years intended to farm on the expanding frontier. After the War of 1812, Americans moved into the Old Northwest. Early communities dotted the Ohio River, the link to the South. Concentrating on corn and pork, settlers sent their products down the Ohio and Mississippi rivers to southern buyers. By 1820, less than one-fifth of the American population lived west of the Appalachians; in 1860, almost half would.

By 1830, the southern parts of Ohio, Indiana, and Illinois were heavily settled, but Michigan, northern Illinois, Wisconsin, and parts of Iowa and Missouri were still frontier. Chicago was only a town of 250. Conditions were often primitive, as Charles Butler and Arthur Bronson discovered during their 1833 trip. Their hotel in Michigan City, Indiana, was "a small log house, a single room, which answered the purpose of drawing room, sitting room, eating room & sleeping room; in this room some eleven or twelve persons lodged in beds & on the floor."

During the 1830s, the Old Northwest experienced a boom in land sales and settlement. Changes in federal land policy, which reduced both prices and the minimum acreage a settler had to buy, were partly responsible for the rapid movement west. The accompanying chart shows the rise in land sales as government policy changed. Eastern capital contributed to the boom with loans, mortgages, and speculative buying. Speculators frequently bought up large tracts of land from the government, then subdivided them and sold parcels off to settlers.

Internal improvement schemes after 1830 also contributed to new settlement patterns and tied the Old Northwest firmly to the East. Erasmus Gest, who as a 17-year-old had worked on canal projects in Indiana, recalled the settlers' enthusiasm for improvements: "We Engi-

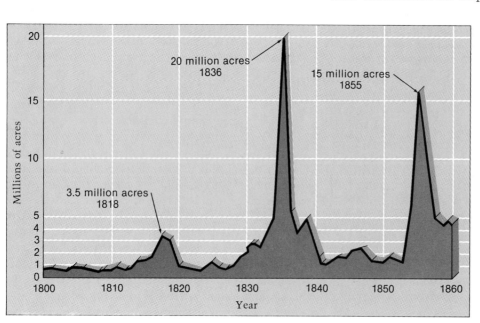

### Western Land Sales, 1800–1860

**Source:** Riegel and Athern, *America Moves West,* 1971.

neers were favorites with the People wherever we went."

Wheat for the eastern market rather than corn and hogs for the southern market became increasingly important with the transportation links eastward. Between 1840 and 1860, Illinois, southern Wisconsin, and eastern Iowa turned into the country's most rapidly growing grain regions. In the 1850s, these three states accounted for 70 percent of the increase in national wheat production.

Although the Old Northwest passed rapidly through the frontier stage between 1830 and 1860, its farming families faced severe challenges. Catharine Skinner, who moved from New York to Indiana with her husband when she was 24, described her rigorous existence. "We are poor and live in the woods where deers roam plentifully and the wolf is occasionally heard," she wrote to her sister in 1849. "We are employed in honest business and trying to do the best we can; we have got 80 acres of land in the woods of Indiana, a very level country; we have got two acres cleared and fenced and four more pirty well under way; we have got about five acres of wheat in the ground; we raised corn enough for our use and to fat our pork . . . we have a cow so that we have milk and butter and plenty of corn bread but wheat is hard to be got in account of our not having money."

The Skinners were typical. Western farms were small, for there were clear limits to what a family with hand tools could manage. A family with two healthy men could care for about 50 acres. In wooded areas, it took several years to get even that much land under cultivation, for only a few acres could be cleared during the year. The Skinners' target was to clear 10 acres during the first 12 months, if, as Catharine said, "health permit." At this rate, it could take ten years for settlers in forested areas to get a farm in full operation. On the prairies, the typical settler would need only half that time.

Catharine Skinner mentioned the shortage of money and described her family as "poor." Although money was in short supply in the Northwest, she probably overstated her family's poverty. It took capital to begin farming—a minimum initial investment of perhaps $100 for 80 acres of government land, $300 for basic farming equipment, and another $100 or $150 for livestock. To buy an already "improved" farm cost more, and free bidding at government auctions could drive the price of unimproved federal land far above the minimum price. Once farmers moved onto the prairies of Indiana and Illinois, they needed an initial investment of about $1,000 since they had to buy materials for fencing, housing, and, expensive steel plows.

## Opportunities in the Old Northwest

It was possible to begin farming with less, however. Some farmers borrowed from relatives, banks, or insurance companies like the Ohio Life Insurance and Trust Company. Others rented land from farmers who had bought more acres than they could manage. Tenants who furnished their own seeds and animals could expect to keep about a third of the yield. Within a few years, some saved enough to buy their own farms. Even those without any capital could work as hired hands. Since labor was scarce, they earned good wages. In Indiana, German settler Jacob Schramm hired men "to help with heavy labors of lumbering and field work, ditch-digging, and so on." Five to ten years of frugal living and steady work for men like Schramm would bring the sum needed to get started.

Probably about a quarter of the western farm population consisted of young men laboring as tenants or hired hands. Although they stood on the bottom rung of the agricultural ladder, their chances of moving up and joining the rural middle class were excellent. Western rural communities were characterized by widespread ownership of land, and they knew no growing class of propertyless wage earners as existed in the cities.

But inequalities existed in the Old Northwest, just as they did in eastern cities and agricultural areas. In Butler Country, Ohio, for example, 16 percent of people leaving wills in the 1830s held half of the wealth. By 1860, the wealthiest 8 percent held half the wealth. In a Wisconsin frontier county in 1860, the richest tenth owned 40 percent of all property. While wealth was not as concentrated in rural areas as in the cities, a few were benefiting far more from rapid economic development than others.

Nevertheless, the Northwest offered many American families the chance to become independent producers and to enjoy "a pleasing competence." The rigors of frontier life faded with time. As Catharine Skinner wrote to her sister from her new Illinois home in 1850, "We here have meetings instead of hearing the hunters gun and the woo[d]man's ax on the sabbath."

Commercial farming brought money to spend on new goods. As early as 1836, the *Dubuque Visitor* was advertising the availability of ready-made clothing and "Calicoes, Ginghams, Muslins, Cambricks, Laces and Ribbands." The next year the *Iowa News* told of the arrival of "Ready Made Clothing from New York."

## CONCLUSION: The Character of Progress

Between 1820 and 1860, the United States experienced tremendous growth and economic development. Transportation improvements facilitated the movement of people, goods, and ideas. Larger markets stimulated both agricultural and industrial production. There were more goods and ample food for the American people. Cities and towns were established and throve. Visitors constantly remarked on the amazing bustle and rapid pace of American life. The United States was, in the words of one Frenchman, "one gigantic workshop, over the entrance of which there is the blazing inscription 'NO ADMISSION HERE, EXCEPT ON BUSINESS.'"

Although the wonders of American development dazzled foreigners and Americans alike, economic growth had its costs. Expansion was cyclic, and financial panics and depression punctuated the period. Industrial profits were partly based on low wages to workers. Time-honored routes to economic independence disappeared, and a large class of unskilled, impoverished workers appeared in American cities. Growing inequality characterized urban and rural life, prompting some labor activists to criticize new economic and social arrangements. But workers, largely still unorganized, did not speak with one voice. Ethnic and religious diversity divided Americans in new and troubling ways.

Yet a basic optimism and sense of pride also characterized the age. To observers, however, it frequently seemed as if the East and the Old Northwest were responsible for the country's achievements. During these decades, many noted that the paths between the East, Northwest, and South seemed to diverge. The rise of King Cotton in the South, where slave rather than free labor formed the foundation of the economy, created a new kind of tension in American life, as the next chapter will show.

## Recommended Reading

Two useful introductions to economic change during this period are Stuart Bruchey, *The Roots of American Economic Growth, 1607–1861* (1965) and Albert W. Niemi, *U.S. Economic History: A Survey of the Major Issues* (1975).

The significance of changes in transportation forms the basis for George R. Taylor's *The Transportation Revolution, 1815–1860* (1951). Thomas C. Cochran provides an overview of industrial development in *Frontiers of Change: Early Industrialism in America* (1981), while technological innovation is the subject of Nathan Rosenberg, *Technology and American Economic Growth* (1972) and David J. Jeremy, *Transatlantic Industrial Revolution: The Diffusion of Textile Technology Between Britain and America, 1790–1830* (1981).

A number of useful studies focus on economic change in individual communities. Thomas Dublin gives a picture of life and work in Lowell in *Women at Work: The Transformation of Work and Community in Lowell, Massachusetts, 1826–1860* (1979). He has also edited primary sources in *Farm to Factory: Women's Letters, 1830–1860* (1981). Alan Dawley portrays the reorganization of work in the shoe industry in *Class and Community: The Industrial Revolution in Lynn* (1976). Essays on Philadelphia can be found in Allen F. Davis and Mark H. Haller, eds., *The Peoples of Philadelphia: A History of Ethnic Groups and Lower-Class Life, 1790–1940* (1973). Steven J. Ross deals with a midwestern city in *Workers on the Edge: Work, Leisure, and Politics in Industrializing Cincinnati, 1788–1890* (1985).

Alexis de Tocqueville analyzes American society in the 1830s in *Democracy in America* (1957 ed.). Edward Pessen shows the growth of inequality in four cities in *Riches, Class, and Power Before the Civil War* (1973). Changes in middle-class housing are described in Russell Lynes, *The Domesticated Americans* (1957). Mary P. Ryan focuses on the middle-class family in *Cradle of the Middle Class: The Family in Oneida County, New York, 1790–1865* (1981). For a more complete understanding of family life, see Tamara K. Hareven, ed., *Family and Kin in Urban Communities, 1700–1930* (1977) and Robert V. Wells, *Revolutions in Americans' Lives: A Demographic Perspective of the History of Americans, Their Families, and Their Society* (1982). For a view of immigrant life, see Stephan Thernstrom, ed., *Harvard Encyclopedia of American Ethnic Groups* (1980).

For an understanding of the midwestern frontier, two useful overviews are Paul W. Gates, *The Farmer's Age: Agriculture, 1815–1860* (1960) and Clarence Danhof, *Changes in Agriculture: The Northern United States, 1820–1870* (1969). Don H. Doyle provides an excellent community study in *The Social Order of a Frontier Community: Jacksonville, Illinois, 1825–1870* (1978).

## TIME LINE

| | |
|---|---|
| 1805 | *Palmer* v. *Mulligan* |
| 1819 | *Dartmouth College* v. *Woodward* |
| 1820 | Lowell founded by Boston Associates<br>Land Act of 1820<br>The expression "woman's sphere" becomes current |
| 1824–1850 | Construction of canals in the Northeast |
| 1825–1856 | Construction of canals linking the Ohio, the Mississippi, and the Great Lakes |
| 1828 | Baltimore and Ohio Railroad begins operation |
| 1830 | Preemption Act |
| 1830s | Boom in the Old Northwest<br>Increasing discrimination against free blacks<br>Public education movement spreads |
| 1833 | Philadelphia establishes small police force |
| 1834 | Philadelphia race riots<br>Lowell work stoppage |
| 1837 | Thomas Mann becomes secretary of Massachusetts Board of Education |
| 1837–1844 | Financial panic and depression |
| 1840 | Agitation for ten-hour day |
| 1840s–1850s | Rising tide of immigration |
| 1841 | Distributive-Preemption Act |

# CHAPTER 12
## SLAVERY AND THE OLD SOUTH

As a young slave boy, Frederick Douglass was sent by his master to live in Baltimore. When he first met his mistress, Sophia Auld, she appeared to be "a woman of the kindest heart and finest feelings." He was "astonished at her goodness" as she began to teach him to read. Her husband, however, ordered her to stop because Maryland law forbade teaching slaves to read. A literate slave was "unmanageable," utterly "unfit . . . to be a slave." From this episode Douglass learned to set inverse goals from Master Auld's wishes. "What he most dreaded, that I most desired . . . and the argument which he so warmly urged, against my learning to read, only served to inspire me with a desire and determination to learn."

In the seven years he lived with the Aulds, young Frederick used "various strategems" to teach himself to read and write. In the narrative of his early life, written after his dramatic escape to the North, Douglass acknowledged that his master's "bitter opposition" had been as beneficial to him as Mrs. Auld's "kindly aid" in achieving his eventual freedom.

Most slaves did not, like Douglass, escape to freedom. But all were as inextricably tied to their masters as Douglass was to the Aulds. Nor could whites in antebellum America escape the pervasive influence of slavery. Otherwise decent people were often compelled by the "peculiar institution" to act inhumanely. After her husband's interference, Sophia Auld, Douglass observed, was transformed from an angel into a demon by the "fatal poison of irresponsible power." Her formerly tender heart turned to "stone" as she ceased teaching him. "Slavery proved as injurious to her," Douglass wrote, "as it did to me."

Such was also the case in Douglass's relationship with Mr. Covey, a slavebreaker to whom he was sent in 1833 to have his will broken. Covey succeeded for a time, Douglass reported, in breaking his "body, soul, and spirit" by brutal hard work and discipline. But one hot August day in 1833, the two men fought a long, grueling battle, which Douglass won. His victory, he said, "rekindled the few expiring embers of freedom, and revived within me a sense of my own manhood." Although it would be four more years before his escape to the North, the young man never again felt like a slave. The key to Douglass's successful resistance to Covey's power was not just his strong will, nor even a magical root he carried in his pocket, but rather his knowledge of how to jeopardize Covey's reputation and livelihood as a slavebreaker. The oppressed survive by knowing their oppressors.

Similarly, in slave folktales, where the clever Brer Rabbit usually outwits the more powerful animals, masters and slaves were so intimately bound together that roles were also often reversed. After quarreling with a house servant, one plantation mistress complained that she "exercises dominion over me—or tries to do it—one would have thought . . . that I was the Servant, she the mistress." Many whites lived in constant fear of a slave revolt, sleeping behind barricaded doors with pistols under their pillows or hiding out in caves or temporary forts during Christmas week when the slaves were drinking and relaxing. A Louisiana planter recalled that he had "known times here when there was not a single planter who had a calm night's rest; they then never lay down to sleep without a brace of loaded pistols at their sides."

As Mrs. Auld and Covey also discovered, as long as some people were not free, no one was free. Douglass observed that "you cannot outlaw one part of the people without endangering the rights and liberties of all people. You cannot put a chain on the ankle of the bondsman without finding the other end of it about your own necks." Slavery was an intricate series of human relationships as well as a labor system. After showing the economic growth and devlopment of the Old South, in which slavery and cotton played a vital role, this chapter will emphasize the daily lives and relationships of those masters and slaves who, like Douglass and the Aulds, lived, loved, learned, worked, struggled, and sometimes fought with one another for two generations before the Civil War.

*Frederick Douglass, photographed here in about 1855, spent his life working for freedom and improved opportunities for blacks after his own escape to freedom as a young man in 1838.*

Perhaps no issue in American history has generated quite as many interpretations or as much emotional controversy as slavery. As American attitudes toward that institution have changed over the years, three interpretive schools have developed, each adding to our knowledge of the "peculiar institution." The first saw slavery as a relatively humane and reasonable institution in which plantation owners took care of helpless and childlike slaves. The second depicted slavery as a harsh and cruel system of oppressive exploitation. The third, and most recent, interpretation described the slavery experience from the perspective of the slaves, who did indeed suffer brutal treatment in slavery but who also survived with individual self-esteem and a sense of community and culture.

The first and second interpretive schools emphasized workaday interactions among masters and slaves, while the third focused on life in the slave quarters from sundown to sunup. This chapter follows these masters and slaves through their day, from morning in the Big House through hot afternoon in the fields to the slave cabins at night. But although slavery was the most unique and central institution in defining the Old South, many other social groups and patterns contributed to the tremendous economic growth of the South from 1820 to 1860. We will look first at these diverse aspects of antebellum southern life.

## BUILDING THE COTTON KINGDOM

The vast region of the antebellum South was not a monolithic society filled only with large cotton plantations worked by hundreds of slaves. The realities of the South and slavery were much more complex. Large-plantation agriculture was a dominant force in the antebellum South, but most southern whites were not even slaveholders, much less large planters. Most southern farmers lived not in mansions but in dark, cramped, two-room cabins. Cotton was a crucial cash crop in the South, but it was not the only crop grown there. Some masters were kindly, but many were not; some slaves were contented, but most were not.

There were many Souths, encompassing several geographic regions, each with different economic bases and social structures and each reflecting its own cultural and political values. The older Upper South of Virginia, Maryland, North Carolina, and Kentucky grew different staple crops from those grown in the newer, Lower or "Black Belt" South that stretched from South Carolina to eastern Texas. Within each state, moreover, the economies differed between flat, coastal areas and inland, upcountry forests and pine barrens. A still further diversity existed between these areas and the Appalachian highlands of northern Alabama and Georgia, eastern Tennessee and Kentucky, and western Virginia and North Carolina. Finally, the cultural and economic life of New Orleans, Savannah, and Richmond differed dramatically from rural or frontier areas of the South.

Although the South was diverse, agriculture dominated industry and commerce. In 1859, a Virginia planter complained about a neighbor who was considering abandoning his farm to become a merchant. "To me it seems to be a wild idea," the planter wrote in his diary, hoping that his friend would "give it up and be satisfied to farm." As Jeffersonians, southerners placed a high value on agricultural labor, as evidenced by their use of over 75 percent of their slaves in farming. Slavery was, therefore, primarily a way of organizing agricultural workers to produce wealth for those who owned the land and the labor. Although slavery in older areas had become paternalistic, with masters and slaves owing mutual obligations to each other, increasingly it became a capitalistic enterprise intended to maximize productivity and profits.

## Economic Expansion

In the 20 years preceding the Civil War, the South's economy grew slightly faster than the North's. Personal income in 1860 was 15 percent higher in the South than in the prosperous states of the Old Northwest. If the South had become an independent nation in 1860, it would have ranked as one of the wealthiest countries in the world in per capita income. One dramatic technological breakthrough, the cotton gin, was fundamental to this economic growth. The cotton gin had two momentous effects: first, it tied the southern economy to cotton production for the next century; second, it allowed the expansion of slavery into vast new territories.

As we learned in Chapter 9, most cotton farmers planted "long staple" cotton prior to the invention of Eli Whitney's cotton gin in 1793. After the cotton gin, the "short staple" variety, which could grow anywhere in the South, predominated. But only large plantation owners could afford to buy gins and purchase the fertile bottomlands of the Gulf states. Thus the plantation system spread with the rise of cotton.

Since cotton could be grown all over the South after the perfection of the cotton gin, men rushed westward to fresh, fertile lands. Large-scale farming increased and demanded more and more slave labor. As a valuable capital resource, slaves received a degree of care and protection. But despite the abolition of slavery in the North and occasional talk of emancipation in the South, slavery became more deeply entrenched, seemingly a permanent part of southern life. Any doubts whispered about ending it could be dispelled by one word: "cotton."

Although corn was a larger crop than cotton in total acreage, cotton was the largest cash crop and for that reason was called "king." In 1820, the South became the world's largest producer of cotton, and from 1815 to 1860 cotton represented more than half of all American exports. The economic growth spurred on by cotton helped not only the South but also the North and the Midwest. Northern merchants gained by shipping, insuring, and marketing southern cotton. Western farmers found a major market for their foodstuffs. Cotton was the mainstay of the southern economy, but it was also a crucial link in the national economy.

The supply of cotton from the South grew at an astonishing rate. Cotton production soared from 461,000 bales in 1817 to 1.35 million bales

## Economic Life in the South

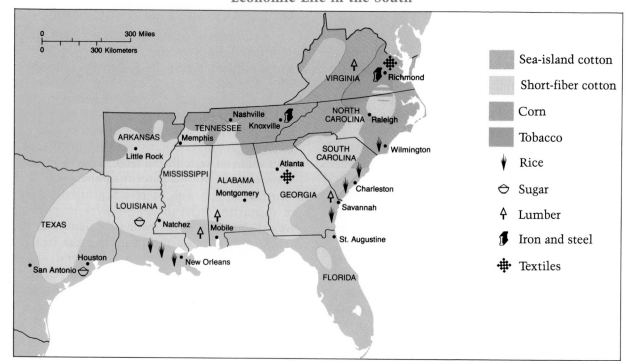

in 1840. A cotton "boom" started in 1849 when output reached 2.85 million bales and continued until 1860, when production peaked at 4.8 million bales. In the period from 1817 to 1860, cotton production jumped over tenfold. This rapid growth was stimulated by world demand, especially from English textile mills. The availability of new lands, a self-reproducing supply of cheap slave labor, and low-cost steamboat trans-

portation down the Mississippi River to New Orleans helped to keep cotton king.

## White and Black Migrations

Southerners migrated southwestward in huge numbers between 1830 and 1860 to grow more and more cotton. Seeking profits from the worldwide demand for cotton, they pushed the

**Southern Cotton
Production, 1821–1859**

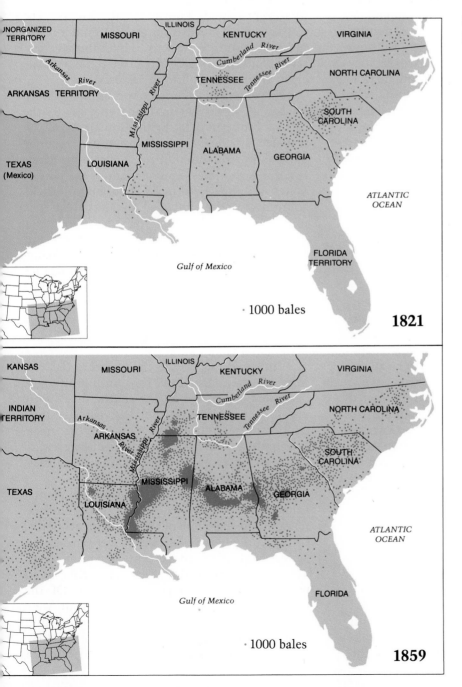

southeastern Indians and the Mexicans in Texas out of the way and were still moving into Texas as the Civil War began. The migration process made many planters rich.

Southern cotton growers, like northern grain farmers, followed parallel migration paths westward. While New Englanders moved into the Midwest, southerners migrated from the coastal states westward into the Lower South. By the 1830s, the center of cotton production had shifted from South Carolina and Georgia to Alabama and Mississippi. This process continued in the 1850s as southerners forged into Arkansas, Louisiana, and eastern Texas. As they moved, they carried their values and institutions, including slavery, with them. Usually, a father and his sons would go west first, find land and clear it, plant some corn, and begin to raise a cabin. Leaving the sons to finish, the father would return east, where his wife and daughters had been managing the farm, pack up the household, and bring it to the new home. Thus in November 1835, one extended family of nearly 50 persons left South Carolina for Alabama. "We bade adieu to friends," a daughter wrote, "and left the old homestead never to look upon it again."

These migrating southern families were not only attracted by the pull of fresh land and cheap labor but were also pushed westward by worsening economic conditions and other pressures in the older Atlantic states. Beginning in the 1820s, the states of the Upper South underwent a long depression affecting tobacco and cotton prices. Moreover, years of constant use had exhausted their lands. With land scarce, families living in a democratized society that valued land ownership had several choices. One was to move west. Another was to stay and diversify. Therefore, the older states of the Upper South continued to shift to grains, mainly corn and wheat. Because these crops required less labor than tobacco, slave owners began to sell excess slaves to the growing Black Belt area of the Lower South.

The internal slave trade from Virginia "down the river" to the Old Southwest thus became a multimillion-dollar "industry" in the 1830s. Between 1830 and 1860, an estimated 300,000 Virginia slaves were transported south for sale. One of the busiest routes was from Alexandria, Virginia, almost within view of the nation's capital, to a huge depot near Natchez, Mississippi. Although most southern states attempted from time to time to outlaw or control the traffic in slaves, these efforts were poorly enforced and usually short-lived. Besides, the reason for outlawing the slave trade was generally not humanitarian but rather originated in a fear of a rapid increase in the slave population, especially of "wicked" slaves sent south because they were considered unmanageable. Alabama, Mississippi, and Louisiana all banned the importation of slaves after the Nat Turner revolt in Virginia in 1831 (described later in this chapter). But all three states permitted the slave trade again during the profitable 1850s.

The external slave trade was formally ended by act of Congress on January 1, 1808, the earliest time permitted by the Constitution. The British Navy, however, was primarily responsible for stopping this traffic in slaves from Africa and the West Indies. Enforcement by the United States was weak, and many thousands of blacks continued to be smuggled to North America until the end of the Civil War. The tremendous increase in the slave population was the result not of this illegal trade but of natural reproduction, often encouraged by slave owners eager for more laborers and internally salable human property.

## The Dependence on Slavery

The rapid increase in the number of slaves, from 1.5 million in 1820 to 4 million in 1860, paralleled the growth of the southern economy and its dependence on the slave labor system, mainly in agriculture but also in other areas. Economic growth and migration southwestward changed the geographic distribution of slaves, thus hindering the cause of abolition.

Although most slaves worked on plantations and medium-size farms, they could be found in all segments of the southern economy. In 1850, 75 percent of all slaves were engaged in agricultural labor, 55 percent in cotton alone. Ten percent produced tobacco, while another 10 percent grew rice, sugar, and hemp. Of the remaining one-fourth, about 15 percent were domestic servants, and the remainder were in mining, lumbering, construction, and industry.

The 300,000 slaves in 1850 who were not

# Concentration of Slavery, 1820–1860

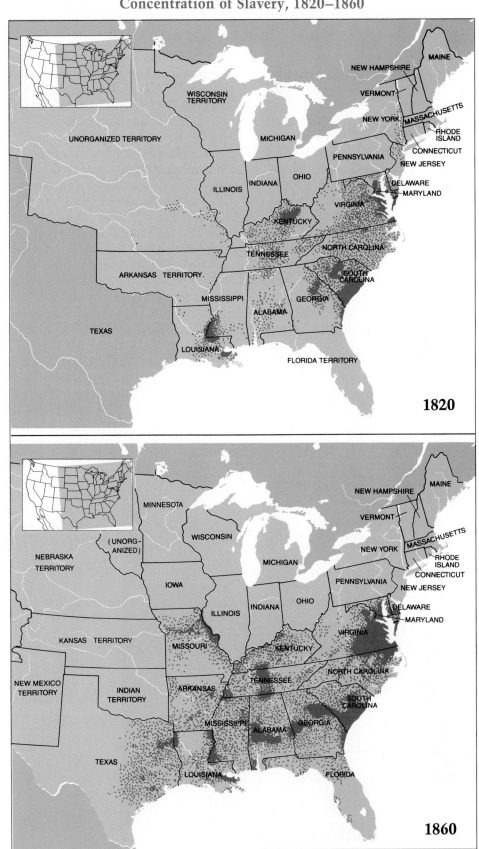

domestics or agricultural laborers worked as lumberjacks and turpentine producers in Carolina and Georgia forests; gold, coal, and salt miners in Virginia and Kentucky; boiler stokers and deckhands on Mississippi River steamships; toilers on road and railroad construction gangs in Georgia and Louisiana; textile laborers in Alabama cotton mills; dockworkers in Savannah and Charleston; and tobacco and iron workers in Richmond factories. A visitor to Natchez in 1835 observed slaves working as "mechanics, draymen, hostelers, labourers, hucksters, and washwomen, and the heterogeneous multitude of every other occupation, who fill the streets of a busy city—for slaves are trained to every kind of manual labour."

Slaves were also used in the industrial sector. The Tredegar Iron Company of Richmond decided in 1847 to shift from white labor "almost exclusively" to slave labor. In this way the company hoped to destroy the potential power of organized workers, avert strikes, and "compete with other manufacturers." Tredegar's decision, though localized, had enor-

mous implications for the future relationship of black and white workers. White perceptions of threats to their job security by black workers, slave or free, continue to this day.

Whether in iron factories, coal mines, or cotton fields, slavery was profitable as a source of labor and as a capital investment. In 1859, the average plantation slave produced $78 in cotton earnings for his master annually while costing only about $32 to be fed, clothed, and housed. Despite maintenance costs, debts from the purchase of land and more slaves, and the declining price of cotton, the "crop value per slave" increased from about $15 in 1800 to $125 in 1860. Slaves were also a good investment. In 1844, a "prime field hand" sold for $600. A cotton boom beginning in 1849 raised this price by 1860 to $1,800. A slave owner could prosper by buying slaves, working them for several years, then selling them for a profit. The rising price of slaves reflected the optimism the planter class had in the future of the system. By the same token, any threat to slavery would be viewed by the planters as threatening their investment.

*Slaves were found in nearly every kind of labor in the South. These Virginia dockworkers were photographed about 1860 in Alexandria, Virginia, by Mathew Brady.*

The economic growth of the slaveholding South was impressive, but it was limited because of the dependence on slavery. Generally, agricultural growth leads to the rise of cities and industry, facilitating sustained economic growth. In the planter-dominated antebellum South, however, agricultural improvements did not lead to industrialization and urbanization. In 1860, the South had 35 percent of the country's population and only 15 percent of its manufacuring establishments. On the eve of the Civil War, one southerner in 14 was a city dweller, compared to one of every three people in the North. The South would be economically backward as long as the whites with capital insisted on putting all their business energies toward cotton production.

Some southerners were aware of the dangers of following a single path to wealth. J. D. B. DeBow created a journal in 1846 dedicated to trade, commerce, and manufacturing. *DeBow's Review* called for greater economic independence in the South through the diversification of agriculture, the development of industry, and an improved transportation system. A believer in slavery, DeBow thought that slave labor could fuel the industrial revolution in the South. But the planter class had little enthusiasm for such plans. As long as money could be made through an agricultural slave system, plantation owners saw no reason to venture capital in new areas. One effect of this attitude was to block the economic opportunity of other white southerners.

## Class Levels in the South

Slavery was more than an economic institution, for it also served a social purpose. Although three-fourths of all southern families owned no

## Diverse Population Patterns in the South: Whites, Slaves, and Free Blacks by State, 1860

*Source:* U.S. Bureau of the Census.

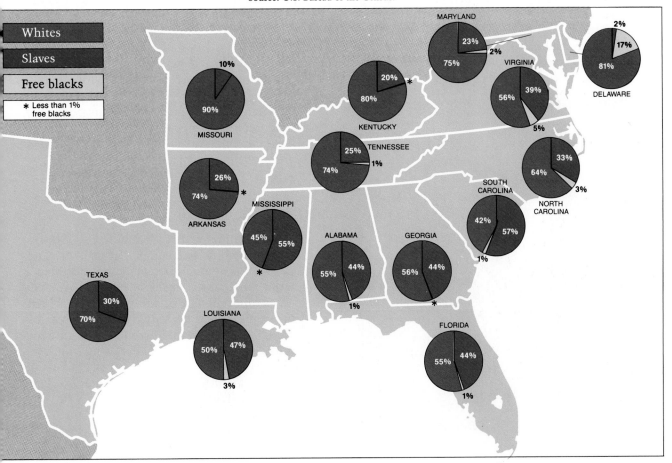

slaves, the idea of slave ownership determined the hierarchical character of the southern social structure. At the top stood the planter aristocracy, much of it new wealth, elbowing its way among the old established families like the Byrds and Carters of Virginia. Some 10,000 rich families owned 50 or more slaves in 1860; about 3,000 of these owned over 100. Below them was a slightly larger group of small planters who held from 10 to 50 slaves. But the largest group, 70 percent of all slaveholders in 1860, comprised 270,000 middle-level farm families who owned fewer than ten slaves. The typical slaveholder worked a small family farm of about 100 acres with eight or nine slaves, perhaps members of the same family. The typical slave, however, was more likely to be in a group of 20 or more other slaves on a large farm or small plantation.

In 1841, a young, white North Carolinian, John Flintoff, went to Mississippi to fulfill his dream of wealth and prestige. Beginning as an overseer managing an uncle's farm, he bought "a negro boy 7 years old" even before he owned any land. After several years of unrewarding struggle, Flintoff married and returned to North Carolina. There he finally bought 124 acres and a few more cheap, young blacks, and by 1860 he had a

## White Class Structure in the South, 1860

**Source:** U.S. Bureau of the Census.

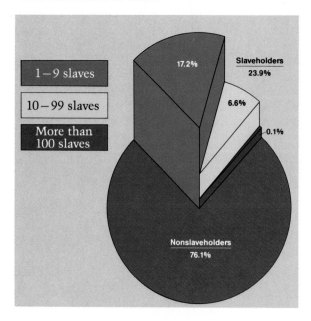

modest farm with several slaves growing corn, wheat, and tobacco. Although he never became as prosperous as he had dreamed, his son went to college, and his wife, he reported proudly, "has lived a *Lady*."

For the middle-level farmer like John Flintoff, who had only a few slaves, as well as for those who owned none, slavery was a powerful force in their lives. Upward economic mobility, social prestige, and political influence were determined by ownership of slaves. Many whites like John Flintoff hoped to purchase one slave, perhaps a female who would bear children, and then begin to climb the economic and social ladder of southern society. White southerners, therefore, supported slavery whether or not they owned slaves.

They also defended the institution because it gave them a sense of superiority over at least one group and a sense of kinship, if not quite equality, with other whites. Although there was always a small element of southern society that believed in emancipation, most southerners did not. A small Alabama farmer told a northern visitor in the 1850s that if the slaves were given their freedom, "they'd all think themselves just as good as we. . . . How would you like to hev a nigger feelin' just as good as a white man." Another said that he wished "there warn't no niggers here." But he did not know anybody who favored freeing them, because if someone was to "make 'em free and leave 'em here . . . they'd steal everything we made. Nobody couldn't live here then."

### The Other White South

Below Flintoff and other middle-class whites lived most white southerners, who owned no slaves but were equally, or even more, antiblack. Newton Knight, for example, worked a harsh piece of land cut out of the pines of southern Mississippi. He and his wife lived in a crude log cabin, scratching out their livelihood by growing corn and sweet potatoes and raising chickens and hogs. A staunch Baptist given to fits of violence, Knight had once killed a black.

The 75 percent of southern whites who, like Newton Knight and his family, owned no slaves were scattered throughout the South. Most lived in the foothills of the mountains and worked generally poorer land than the large planters. They did not need to be near commercial centers because they were largely self-sufficient. Working together as a family, they raised mostly corn and wheat, hogs, enough cotton for their own clothes and a little cash, and subsistence vegetable crops. These yeoman farmers maintained a household economy, making soap, shoes, candles, whiskey, coarse textiles, and ax handles, and trading hogs, eggs, small game, or homemade items for cash and other goods. They lived in two-room log houses separated by a "dog run." Cooperation with neighbors brightened the yeoman farmer's drab and isolated life. Families gathered at corn huskings or quilting parties, logrolling and wrestling matches, and political stump and revivalist camp meetings.

In many ways the yeoman farmers were the solid backbone of the South. In 1860 in North Carolina, 70 percent of the farmers held less than 100 acres, while in Mississippi and Louisiana, reputedly large plantation states, over 60 percent of the farms were under 100 acres. Fiercely proud of their independence, the yeoman farmers had a share of political power, voting overwhelmingly for Andrew Jackson. Al-

*Southern yeoman farm families lived self-sufficient lives of relative isolation. Gatherings such as this quilting party provided welcome social contact as well as the means to accomplish a large task in a short time.*

though some resented the tradition of political deference to "betters," these farmers were not yet ready to challenge planters for political power. Yeoman farmers fought with the Confederacy during the Civil War; but some, like Newton Knight, refused to fight against the Union and ended up organizing a guerrilla band of Unionists in southern Mississippi.

Another little-known group of southern whites were the herdsmen who raised hogs and other livestock. Living among the plantations and small farms, they supplied bacon and pork to local slaveholders (who often thought hog growing was beneath their dignity) and drove herds of hogs to stockyards in Nashville, Louisville, and Savannah. The South raised two-thirds of the nation's hogs. In 1860, the value of southern livestock was $500 million, twice that of cotton. Although much of the corn crop fed the hogs, many herdsmen preferred to let their stock roam loose in the woods. As one South Carolinian explained, "We raise our hogs by allowing them to range in our woods, where they get fat . . . on acorns," which he and others considered a better diet for bacon and pork than corn. However valuable the total size of the hog business, individual hog herdsmen did not stand very high on the southern social ladder.

Below them were the poor whites of the South, about 10 percent of the population. Often sneeringly called "hillbillies," "dirt eaters," "crackers," or "poor white trash," they were victims of their environment. Living in isolated, inhospitable areas of the South, they eked out a living from the poor soil of pine barrens, sand hills, and marshes. Although they grew a little corn and vegetables, their livelihood came mostly from fishing, hunting small game, and raising a few pigs. Some made corn whiskey, and many hired themselves out as farmhands for an average wage, with board, of about $14 per month. Because of poor diet and bad living conditions, these poor whites often suffered from diseases such as hookworm and malaria. This, plus the natural debilitation of heat and poverty, led to their reputation as lazy, shiftless, and illiterate. An English visitor, Fanny Kemble, described them as "the most degraded race of human beings claiming an Anglo-Saxon origin that can be found on the face of the earth."

The poor whites were kept poor in part because the slave system allowed the planter class to accumulate a disproportionate amount of land and political power. High slave prices made entry into the planter class increasingly diffficult, thus increasing class tensions within the South. Because the larger planters dominated southern life and owned the most slaves, an understanding of the character of slavery and the relationships between masters and slaves is best accomplished by looking at plantation life during a typical day from morning to night.

## MORNING: MASTER IN THE BIG HOUSE

It is early morning on the southern plantation. Imagine four scenes. In the first, William Waller of Virginia and a neighbor are preparing to leave with 20 choice slaves on a long trip to the slave market in Natchez, Mississippi. Waller is making this "intolerable" journey, as he calls it, to sell some of his slaves in order to ease his heavy debts. Although he "loaths the vocation of slave trading," he must recover some money out of a "sense of duty" to see his family "freed from my bondage" of indebtedness. To ease his conscience, he intends to supervise the sale personally, thus securing the best possible deal not only for himself but also for his departing slaves.

On another plantation, owned by James Hammond of South Carolina, the horn blows an hour before daylight to awaken the slaves for work in the fields. Hammond rises soon after, ever aware that "to continue" as a wealthy master, he must "draw the reign tighter and tighter" to hold his slaves "in complete check." He is as good as his word, recommending that "in general 15 to 20 lashes will be sufficient flogging" for most offenses, but that "in extreme cases" the punishment "must not exceed 100 lashes in one day." On a Mississippi plantation, the slaves are awakened by a bell, and a visitor hears "the tramp of the laborers passing" on their way to the fields. He does not hear singing.

On an Alabama plantation, Hugh Lawson is up early, writing a sorrowful letter to Susanna Clay, telling her of the death of a "devotedly attached and faithful" slave, Jim. "I feel desolate," Hugh writes, "my most devoted friend is gone and *his place* can never be supplied by another." As Lawson pens his letter, another slave has already awakened and "walked across a frosty field in the early morning and gone to the big house to build a fire" for her mistress. As the mistress wakes up to a warming house, she says to the slave, "Well, how's my little nigger today?"

In a fourth household, this one a medium-size farm in upcountry Georgia, not far from Hammond's huge plantation, Charles Brock wakes up at dawn and joins his two sons and four slaves to work his modest acreage of grains and sweet potatoes, while Brock's wife and a female slave tend the cows that provide milk and butter. On small and medium-size family farms, with five or fewer slaves, blacks and whites commonly worked together, as one observer noted, with "the axe of master and man [slave] falling with alternate strokes . . . [and] ploughing side by side."

As these scenes suggest, slavery thoroughly permeated the lives of southern whites. For the slaves, morning was a time for getting up and going to work. But for southern whites, morning involved contact with slaves in many ways: as burdens of figuring profit and loss, as objects to be kept obedient and orderly, as intimates and fellow workers, and as ever-present reminders of fear, hate, and uncertainty.

### The Burdens of Slaveholding

Robert Francis Withers Allston (1801–1864) was a major rice planter in the Georgetown district of South Carolina, a low, swampy, mosquito-infested tidal area where four rivers empty into Winyah Bay. It was a perfect spot for growing rice, but so unhealthy that few whites wanted to live there. In 1840, a total of 18,274 slaves toiled in the Georgetown district, but only 2,193 whites. By 1860, in part because of the appalling death rate among the slaves, the ratio of blacks to whites fell to 6 to 1. Robert was the fifth generation of Allstons to live in this inhospitable land. By 1860, he owned seven plantations along the Peedee River, totaling some 4,000 acres, in addition to another 9,500 acres of pasture and timber lands. He held nearly 600 slaves, 236 of whom worked at the home plantation, Chicora Wood. The total value of his land and slaves in the 1850s was approximately $300,000. Rich in land and labor, he nevertheless had large mortgages and outstanding debts.

Allston was an enlightened, talented, public-spirited man. Educated at West Point but also trained in the law, he did far more than practice agriculture. He served in the South Carolina state senate for 24 years and as governor from 1856 to 1858. His political creed, he wrote in 1838, was one of "virtue and purity" based on "the principles of Thomas Jefferson." The core of his conviction was "a plain, honest, common-sense reading of the Constitution," which for Allston clearly meant the constitutionality of slavery and nullification and the illegitimacy of abolitionism and the United States Bank.

Allston also reflected Jefferson's humane side. He was an ardent reformer, advocating liberalization of South Carolina's poor laws; an improved system of public education open to rich and poor alike; humanitarian care of the deaf, blind, insane, and other disabled persons; and the improvement of conditions on the reservations of the Catawba Indians. He was active in the Episcopal church and gave money generously to support ministerial students.

In 1832, Allston married Adele Petigru, an equally enlightened and hardworking person. She participated fully in the management of the plantation and ran it while Robert was away on politics. In a letter to her husband, written in 1850, Adele demonstrated her diverse interests by reporting on family affairs and the children's learning, sickness among the slaves, the status of spring plowing, the building of a canal and causeway, her supervision of the bottling of some wine, and her thoughts on "Mr. Clay's compromise" (the Great Compromise of 1850). After Robert's death during the Civil War, she assumed control of the Allston plantations, which had been abandoned when Union troops moved through the area. The difficulties of Reconstruction, however, led her to sell most of the estate at auction, holding on only to Chicora Wood, which she managed with her daughter, Elizabeth, until her death in 1896.

State politics lured Robert from his land for part of each year, but he was by no means an absentee owner. Except when living away in order to escape the worst periods of mosquitoes and heat, the Allstons were fully engaged in the operation of their plantations. Managing thousands of acres was a major undertaking, and

*Robert F. W. Allston married Adele Petigru in 1832. They shared the work of managing the rice plantation; after Robert's death in the Civil War, his widow continued the work for nearly 30 years.*

owning slaves a serious burden and duty. Although the size of Robert Allston's acreage and slave population were larger than those of most big planters, and he grew rice rather than cotton, his concerns were typical.

Allston's letters frequently expressed problems of owning slaves. Although he was careful to distribute enough cloth, blankets, and shoes to his slaves and to give them sufficient rest, the sickness and death of slaves, especially young fieldworkers, headed his list of concerns. "I lost in one year 28 negroes," Allston complained, "22 of whom were task hands." He tried to keep slave families together but sold slaves when necessary. For several months, he faced a suit over his sale of a young girl medically determined to be "thoroughly unsound" and unfit for work. In a letter to his son Benjamin, he expressed concern over the bad example set by a slave driver who was "abandon'd by his hands" because he had not worked with them the previous Sunday. In the same letter Allston urged Benjamin to keep up the "patrol duty," less to guard against runaway slaves, he said, than to restrain the excesses of "vagabond whites." Thus the planter class felt a duty to control lower-class whites as well as black slaves.

Other planters shared Allston's concerns, seeing slavery as both a duty and a burden. A Louisiana planter, in financial difficulty, wrote how much he dreaded "the miserable occupation of seeing to negroes, and attending to their wants and sickness and to making them do their duty—and after all have no prospect of being paid for my trouble." Many planters insisted that they worked harder than their slaves to feed and clothe them and to make their lives "as comfortable as possible." Some accepted this as part of their responsibility, while others complained loudly. R. L. Dabney of Virginia exclaimed that "there could be no greater curse inflicted on us than to be compelled to manage a parcel of Negroes." Curse or not, Dabney and other planters profited from their burdens, a point they seldom admitted.

Their wives experienced other kinds of burdens. "The mistress of a plantation," wrote Susan Dabney Smedes, "was the most complete slave on it." Southern women were expected to adhere to the cult of domesticity both by im-

proving their husbands' morals, which often meant restraining them from excessive cruelty toward slaves, and by beautifying their parlors. Moreover, plantation mistresses suffered under a double standard of sexuality. They were expected to act always as chaste ladies, while their husbands, whether they acted on it or not (and they often did), had virtually unrestrained sexual access to slave women. "God forgive us, but ours is a monstrous system," Mary Boykin Chesnut wrote in her diary. "Like the patriarchs of old, our men live all in one house with their wives and their concubines; and the mulattoes one sees in every family partly resemble the white children. Any lady is ready to tell you who is the father of all the mulatto children in everybody's household but her own. Those, she seems to think, drop from the clouds."

Chesnut called the sexual dynamics of slavery "the sorest spot." There were others. Unlike northern women, plantation mistresses had to tend to the food, clothing, health, and welfare of not just their husbands and children but of the plantation slave population as well. Adele Allston, we saw, added plantation management to these duties. The son of a Tennessee slaveholder remembered his mother and grandmother as "the busiest women I ever saw." One woman, who spent the night sitting up to attend a slave birth, complained to a northern visitor: "It is the slaves who own me. Morning, noon, and night, I'm obliged to look after them, to doctor them, and attend to them in every way." The plantation mistress, then, served many roles: as a humanizing influence on men; as a tough, resourceful, responsible manager of numerous plantation affairs; and as a victim herself.

## Justifying Slavery

The cruel behavior of Douglass's mistress, Sophia Auld, suggests another way in which slavery victimized southern women. Whether they acted humanely or not, slavery burdened slaveholders. Increasingly attacked as immoral, they felt compelled to justify their institution. Until the 1830s, this defense was put primarily in terms of slavery as a "necessary evil." After the abolitionists stepped up their attack in that decade, however, the justification shifted to a

## Agreement to Purchase Slaves, January 25, 1859

Agreed to purchase from Dr. Forster Forty one Negroes of Mrs. Withers of the "remainder" from the Estate of the late Francis Withers, to be deliver'd in all this week at $500. Titles to Ben Allston his Bond and mine payable in 8, 10, 12 yrs. secured by mortgage of the property, viz

| $1000[1] | 1 | Andrew | 38 | yrs. | | had | Blanket | in | 1858 | |
|---|---|---|---|---|---|---|---|---|---|---|
| 800 | 2 | Serena | 36 | " | " | " | " | | 56 | |
| 400 | 3 | Jos. | 10 | " | " | " | " | | 57 | |
| 300 | 4 | Judy | 8 | " | " | " | " | | 57 | |
| 200 | 5 | Henry | 5 | " | " | " | " | | 54 | |
| 1000 | 6 | Jack[2] | 30 | " | " | " | " | | 1858 | |
| 800 | 7 | Patience | 27 | " | " | " | " | | 56 | pregnant |
| 400 | 8 | Daniel | 11 | " | " | " | " | | 49 | |
| 300 | 9 | Prince | 9 | " | " | " | " | | 1850 | |
| 250 | 10 | Phyllis | 5 | " | " | " | " | | 54 | |
| 200 | 11 | Bess | 3½ | " | " | " | " | | 55 | |
| 800 | 12 | James* | 28 | " | " | " | " | | 56 | carpenter, Drinks, delicate |
| 800 | 13 | Hagar | 24 | " | " | " | " | | 56 | pregnant, near time of delivery |
| 1200 | 14 | Joe | 39 | " | " | " | " | | 56 | carpenter and cooper |
| 800 | 15 | Levi | 50 | " | " | " | " | | 1858 | |
| 500 | 16 | Betsey† | 40 | " | " | " | " | | 57 | delicate |
| 400 | 17 | Murria‡ | 18 | " | " | " | " | | 58 | |
| 400 | 18 | Toby | 14 | " | " | " | " | | 57 | |

\*Has Epileptic attacks produced by drink, would be valuable if kept from drink.
†With this family there is the incumbrance of an old man of 80 years, father of Betsey.
‡Murria is half witted.

| 1000 | 19 | Paris | 35 | " | " | " | " | 58 | |
|---|---|---|---|---|---|---|---|---|---|
| 800 | 20 | Hannah | 33 | " | " | " | " | 56 | |
| 800 | 21 | Frank | 16½ | " | " | " | " | 58 | |
| 500 | 22 | William | 14 | " | " | " | " | 56 | |
| 350 | 23 | Caty | 9 | " | " | " | " | 50 | |
| 300 | 24 | Michael | 6 | " | " | " | " | 53 | |
| 150 | 25 | Eleanor | 3½ | " | " | " | " | 55 | |
| 50 | 26 | Dandy | 1 | " | " | " | " | 57 | |

[1]The prices have been taken from a second list, also some of the remarks concerning individuals.
[2]The heavy lines probably indicate family groups.

| 800 | 27 | Strophon | 50 | yrs. | had | Blanket | in | 56 | |
|---|---|---|---|---|---|---|---|---|---|
| 700 | 28 | Lucy | 18 | " | " | " | " | 56 | |
| 500 | 29 | Judy | 14 | " | " | " | " | 57 | |
| 1000 | 30 | Toney | 38 | " | " | " | " | 56 | an indifferent carpenter |
| 800 | 31 | Betty | 35 | " | " | " | " | 58 | |
| 800 | 32 | Daniel | 16½ | " | " | " | " | 56 | 3 years with Bricklayers to mix mortar |
| 200 | 33 | Francis | 4½ | " | " | " | " | 52 | |
| 100 | 34 | Caesar | 1½ | " | " | " | " | 56 | |
| 500 | 35 | O Sary | 50 | " | " | " | " | 56 | cook and washer |
| 1000 | 36 | Israel | 31 | " | " | " | " | 57 | |
| 800 | 37 | Esther | 28 | " | " | " | " | 57 | |
| 100 | 38 | William | 1½ | " | " | " | " | 57 | |
| 800 | 39 | Dinah | 18½ | " | " | " | " | 58 | |
| 500 | 40 | Quash | 14½ | " | " | " | " | 56 | |
| 300 | 41 | William | 9" | " | " | " | " | 56 | |

defense of slavery, in John C. Calhoun's words, as "a positive good." Various arguments were used: biblical, historical, constitutional, scientific, and sociological.

The biblical justification was based in part on the curse of Canaan, the son of Ham, who was condemned to eternal servitude because his father had looked on Noah's nakedness. Furthermore, in various places both the Old and New Testaments admonished servants to obey their masters and accept their earthly lot. When Hagar, the maidservant of Abraham's wife Sarah, ran away, an angel of the Lord came and told her to "return to thy mistress, and submit thyself under her hands." It did not matter whether or not this biblical interpretation was religiously "correct" but that southern slaveholders believed it was.

Southern apologists also cited historical arguments. Slavery had existed throughout history. In fact, the greatest civilizations—Egypt, Greece, and Rome—had all built their strength and grandeur in part on slave labor, thus relieving the educated elite of manual labor and freeing them for art, law, and military glory. No less a figure than Aristotle taught that in society men of superior talents would become masters over those who were inferior.

A third argument justified slavery on legal grounds. Southerners pointed out that the United States Constitution did not forbid slavery. In fact, although slavery was not mentioned by name, three passages in the original document clearly implied its constitutionality. First, slaves, called "all other Persons," were counted as three-fifths of a person for purposes of representation. Second, the overseas slave trade was protected for 20 years from congressional abolition. Third, the Constitution mandated the return of runaway slaves from one state to another.

A fourth justification was scientific. Until the 1830s, most white southerners believed that blacks were a degraded race as a result not of nature but environment. The retarded mental and moral development of Africans, the argument went, derived from the special conditions and circumstances of African climate and American slavery. But with the "positive good" defense in the 1830s, southern ethnologists

increasingly argued that blacks had been created separately (a theory called "polygenesis") and were an inherently inferior race. Through a study of cranial shapes and sizes, called "niggerology" by one doctor, southern scientists maintained that in the black "the animal parts of the brain preponderate over the moral and intellectual, which explains why he is deficient in reason, judgement and forecast." Therefore, the destiny of the inferior Africans was to serve the superior Caucasians (the "Adamic race") in work and then become extinct. At best, the patriarchal slave system would domesticate uncivilized blacks. As Allston put it, "The educated master is the negro's best friend upon earth."

Allston's point suggested a paternalistic sociological defense of slavery. George Fitzhugh, a leading advocate of this view, argued that "the Negro is but a grown child and must be governed as a child." Therefore, he needed the paternal guidance, restraint, and protection of his white masters. What would happen, apologists asked, if the slaves were freed? Many southerners believed that chaos would ensue. Allston wrote that emancipation "cannot be contemplated," for it would lead to "giving up our beautiful country to the ravages of the black race and amalgamation with savages." Fitzhugh was a little less direct. He compared the treatment of southern slaves favorably to that of free blacks and of free laborers working in northern factories. These "wage slaves," he argued, worked as hard as slaves, yet with their paltry wages they had to feed, clothe, and shelter themselves. Southern masters took care of all these necessities. Emancipation, therefore, would be heartless and unthinkable, a burden to both blacks and whites.

Southern apologists for slavery faced the difficult intellectual task of justifying a system that ran counter to the main ideological directions of nineteenth-century American society: the expansion of individual liberty, mobility, economic opportunity, and democratic political participation. Moreover, the southern defense of slavery had to take into account the 75 percent of white families who owned no slaves and who were envious of those who did. Because of the potential for class antagonisms among whites, wealthy planters developed a justification of slavery that deflected class differences by maintaining that all whites were superior to all blacks but equal to one another. The theory of democratic equality among whites, therefore, was made consistent with racism and the holding of slaves.

However couched in the language of science, law, history, or religion, the underlying motive of these various justifications, though rarely admitted, was that slavery was profitable. As the southern defense of slavery intensified in the 1840s and 1850s, it aroused greater opposition

from northerners and from slaves themselves. Although slavery was cruel in many ways, perhaps its worst feature was not physical but psychological: to be enslaved at all and barred from economic advancement in a nation that put a high value on freedom and equality of opportunity. "One of the grossest frauds committed upon the down-trodden slave," Douglass wrote, was to encourage such drunken dissipation during holidays that slaves would be disgusted "with freedom" and would look forward to marching back "to the field."

## NOON: SLAVES IN HOUSE AND FIELDS

It is two o'clock on a hot July afternoon on the plantation. The midday lunch break is over, and the slaves are returning to their work in the fields. Lunch was the usual fare of cornmeal and pork. The slaves return to work slowly and listlessly, not because of innate laziness but because of a lack of stamina resulting from deficient diet and the suffocating heat and humidity in the fields. Douglass remembered that "we worked all weathers. . . . It was never too hot, or too cold" for toiling in the fields. Mary Reynolds of Louisiana recalled that she "hated most" having to pick cotton "when the frost was on the bolls," which made her hands "git sore and crack open and bleed."

### Daily Toil

The daily work schedule for most slaves, whether in the fields or the Big House, was long and demanding. Aroused by a bell or horn before daybreak, they worked on an average day 14 hours in the summer and 10 hours in the winter. During harvest time it was not uncommon to work for 18 hours. Depending on the size of the work force and the crop, the slaves were organized either in gangs or according to tasks. The gangs, usually of 20 to 25, worked their way along the cotton rows under the watchful eye and quick whip of a driver. Ben Simpson, a Georgia slave, remembered vividly how his master would use a "great, long whip platted out of

rawhide" to hit a slave in the gang who would "fall behind or give out."

Under the task system, each slave had a specific task to complete daily. This system gave slaves the incentive to work hard enough to finish early, but it meant that they were constantly checked on the quality of their work. An overseer's weekly report to Robert Allston in 1860 noted that he had "flogged for hoeing corn bad Fanny 12 lashes, Sylvia 12, Monday 12, Phoebee 12, Susanna 12, Salina 12, Celia 12, Iris 12." The black slave driver, George Skipwith, was no less rigorous in his expectations of work from fellow slaves. In 1847, he reported to his master that several slaves working under him "at a reasonable days work" should have plowed 7 acres apiece but had only done 1 1/2. Therefore, George proudly reported, "I gave them ten licks a peace upon their skins [and] I gave Julyann eight or ten licks for misplacing her hoe."

An average slave was expected to pick 130 to 150 pounds of cotton per day. The work on sugar and rice plantations was even harder. Sugar demanded constant cultivation and the digging of drainage ditches in snake-infested fields. At harvest time, cutting, stripping, and carrying the cane to the sugar house for boiling was extremely strenuous work. In addition, huge quantities of firewood had to be cut and carried. Working in the low-country rice fields was worse. So much water was needed for rice growing that the slaves spent long hours standing in water up to their knees.

House slaves had relatively easier assignments than the field slaves, even though they were usually called on to help with the harvest. Their usual work was in or near the Big House as housemaids, cooks, seamstresses, laundresses, coachmen, drivers, gardeners, and mammies. Most of the artisanal work on the plantation was also done by slaves, many of whom became skilled carpenters, blacksmiths, stonemasons, weavers, mechanics, and millers. More intimacy between whites and blacks occurred near the house. House slaves ate and dressed better than their fellow slaves in the fields.

But there were also disadvantages. House slaves were more closely watched, were on call at all hours of the day and night, and were more often involved in personality conflicts in the white household and with one another. As one house servant put it, "We were constantly exposed to the whims and passions of every member of the family." This meant everything from assignment to petty jobs to insults, spontaneous angry whippings, and sexual assault. The most feared punishment for a house slave, however, other than sale to the Deep South, was to be sent to the fields.

### Slave Health

Although it was in the self-interest of slave owners to keep their slaves healthy by providing adequate care, and many masters did, in general slaves led sickly lives. Home was a crude, one-room log cabin with a dirt floor; some such houses were well made, but most were full of cracks and holes. Pesky mosquitoes came in at night, making sleep difficult in the summer months. Most cabins had a fireplace for heat and cooking. Typical furnishings included a table, some stools or boxes to sit on, an iron pot and wooden dishes, and perhaps a bed. Some slaves slept on the ground on mattresses of corn shucks, using burlap bags for blankets. The cabins were crowded, with usually more than one family living in each. Slave clothing was shabby and uncomfortable. Each man usually was issued two cotton shirts and two pairs of cotton or woolen pants each fall and spring and a pair of stout shoes once a year. Women were given cotton and woolen cloth twice a year with which to make their own and their children's clothes.

Studies on the adequacy of slave diet disagree, some showing that the food most slaves ate was deficient in calories and vitamins, others claiming that the energy value of the slave diet exceeded that of free whites in the general population. Compared to Latin American slavery, where the ratio of male slaves to white residents was much higher than in the United States, American slaves were well fed. Once a week, each slave was issued an average ration: a peck of cornmeal, 3 to 4 pounds of salt pork or bacon, some molasses, and perhaps some sweet potatoes. The main regimen, however, was "corn, at every meal, from day to day, and week to week."

*The slave family, though disrupted by separations and the sexual domination of slave owners, still provided a source of love and support for slaves.*

This bland fare was supplemented for some slaves, with the master's permission, by vegetables grown in a small garden and by fishing or hunting small game.

Most slaves, however, rarely enjoyed fresh meat, dairy products, fruits, or vegetables. To make up for these deficiencies, they sometimes stole from the master's kitchen, gardens, and barnyard. Such offenses were frequent, and just as frequently punished. A Louisiana planter told a neighbor, "I beg to regrets that two of my men have been found guilty of killing one of your calves," and another complained of many acts of theft committed by "famished negroes." Inadequate diet, moreover, led some slaves to become dirt eaters, which gave them worms and "swollen shiny skin, puffy eyelids, pale palms and soles." Others suffered regularly from skin disorders, cracked lips, and sore eyes. Many slaves, like poor whites, came down with diet-deficient diseases such as rickets, pellagra, beriberi, scurvy, and even mental illness.

Women slaves especially suffered from the weaknesses caused by diet insufficiency, hard work, and disease. They were expected to do the same tasks in the fields as the men, as well as cooking, sewing, child care, and traditional female jobs in the quarters when the fieldwork was finished. "Pregnant women," the usual rule stated, "should not plough or lift but must be kept at moderate work until the last hour" and were given a three-week recovery period after giving birth. But these guidelines were more often violated than honored. Infant mortality of slave children under 5 years of age was twice as high as for white children.

Life expectancy for American slaves was longer than for those in Latin America and the Caribbean, but not very high for either blacks or whites in the antebellum South (21.4 for blacks and 25.5 for whites in 1850). In part because of poor diet and climate, slaves were highly susceptible to epidemic diseases. Despite some resistance as a result of the sickle-cell gene, many slaves still contracted and died from malaria, yellow fever, cholera, and other diseases caused by mosquitoes or bad water, especially in the dangerous low-lying rice fields of the Georgia coast and the sugar fields of Louisiana. Slaves everywhere suffered and died from intestinal ailments in the summer and respiratory diseases in the winter. An average of 20 percent (and sometimes 50 to 60 percent) of the slaves on a given plantation would be sick at one time, and

### An Overseer's Report
*W. Sweet to Adele Petigru Allston*

N[ightin]gale hall, 14th September, 1864.

DEAR MADAM I comence my harvest on last saterday on Boath Plantations the weather is very fin for harvest so far I will Bring some Rice in to the Barn yard at N[ightin]gale hall to Day and at ganderloss to morrow. I think that I will make about 2 Barrels of Syrrup on Each Place I finish grinding at ganderloss to Day I will not finish at Nightingale hall until the last of next weeak. litle Dianah was confind with a boy child on the 9 I am very sorry to say to you that one of Prisilia children a boy name July Dide on 12th with fits a[nd] fever I have had a grea[t] deal of fever among the children But not much among the grone negroes. old Rose is Stil quite sick mr Belflowers sent toney to mee on friday last I have concluded to let toney wife stay whare she is for a while as I understand that she is Pregnant and will not Be much survice in the harvest if I am Rong for soe Doing Pleas let mee know. the negroes all sends thare love to you an family my self and family is very un well.

N[ightin]gale hall

| 8th September | all hands hoing Bancks and grinding shugar cain no sick |
| 9th September | all hands hoing Bancks grind shugar cain no sick |
| 10th September | all hands cu[tt]ing Rice grinding shugar cain no sick |
| 12th September | all hands harvesting grinding shugar cain 3 women with sick children |
| 13th September | all hands harvesting grinding shugar cain 3 women with sick children |
| 14th September | all hands harvesting grinding shugar cain 1 woman with sick child |

no overseer's report was complete without an account of sickness and the number of days of lost labor.

The relatively frequent incidence of whippings and other physical punishments added to the poor physical condition of the slaves. Many slaveholders offered rewards—a garden plot, an extra holiday, hiring oneself out, or passes—as inducements for faithful labor. For punishments they would withhold these privileges rather than resort to the lash. But southern court records, newspapers, plantation diaries, and slave memoirs reveal that sadistic slave punishments were frequent and harsh.

The slave William Wells Brown reported that on his plantation the whip was used "very frequently and freely" for inadequate or uncompleted work, stealing, running away, and even insolence and lying. Whippings ranged from 10 to 100 strokes of the lash, occasionally even more. Former slaves described a good owner as one who did not "whip too much" and a bad owner as one who "whipped till he'd bloodied you and blistered you." Slaveholders had many theories on the appropriate kind of lash to inflict sufficient pain and punishment without damaging a valuable laborer. Other forms of punishment included isolation and confinement in stocks and jails during leisure hours, chains, muzzling, salting lash wounds, branding, burning, and castration.

Nothing testifies better to the physical brutality of slavery than the advertisements for runaways that slaveholders printed in antebellum newspapers. In searching for the best way to describe the physical characteristics of a missing slave, slave owners unwittingly condemned their own behavior. One Mississippi slave had "large raised scars . . . in the small of his back and on his abdomen nearly as large as a person's finger." Another, a Georgia female, was "considerably marked by the whip." Still another, who according to his North Carolina master had a "remarkably bad temper," was described by the "marks of the lash upon his back." Slaves who were branded were even easier to identify in these advertisements. One fugitive, Betty, was described as recently "burnt . . . with a hot iron on the left side of her face." "I tried to make the letter M" her master admitted in his diary.

## Slave Law and the Family

One can almost imagine Betty's master agonizingly applying his brand. Complicating master-slave relationships was the status of slaves as both persons and property, a legal and psychological ambiguity the South never resolved. On the one hand, the slaves had names, personalities, families, and wills of their own. This required dealing with them as fellow humans. But on the other hand, they were items of property, purchased and maintained to perform specific profit-making tasks. As a Kentucky court put the problem in 1836, "Although the law of this state considers slaves as property, . . . it recognizes their personal existence, and, to a qualified extent, their natural right."

This ambiguity led to confusion in the laws governing treatment of slaves. Until the early 1830s, some southern abolitionist activity persisted, primarily in the Upper South. Slaves had slight expectations that they might be freed, if not by state action then by individual manumission. But along with this ray of hope, they suffered careless and often brutal treatment in matters of food, housing, work load, and punishments. This confusion changed with the threatening convergence in 1831 of Nat Turner's revolt and William Lloyd Garrison's publication of the abolitionist *Liberator*. After 1831, the South tightened up the slave system. Laws prohibiting manumission were passed, and the slaves' expectation of freedom other than by revolt or escape vanished. At the same time, laws protecting them from overly severe treatment were strengthened, and material conditions generally improved.

But whatever the law said, the practice was always more telling. Treatment varied with individual slaveholders and depended on their mood and other circumstances. This was especially true with regard to the slave family. Most planters, like Robert Allston, generally encouraged their slaves to marry and did all they could to keep families intact. They believed that families made black males more docile and less inclined to revolt or run away. But some masters failed to respect slave marriages or broke them up because of financial problems. This tendency was supported by southern courts and legislatures, which did not legally recognize slave marriages or the right to family unity. As a North Carolina supreme court justice said in 1853, "Our law required no solemnity or form in regard to the marriage of slaves."

Adding to the pain of forced breakup of the slave family was the sexual abuse of black women. Although the frequency of such abuse is unknown, the presence of thousands of mulattoes in the antebellum era is testimony to this practice. White men in the South abused black slave women in several ways: by offering gifts for sexual "favors," by threatening those who refused with physical punishment or the sale of a child or loved one, by purchasing concubines, or by rape. As Frederick Douglass put it, the "slave woman is at the mercy of the fathers, sons or brothers of her master."

Because of the need to obtain cheap additional slaves for the work force, slaveholders encouraged slave women to bear children, whether married or not. The slaves' choice of a mate was sometimes influenced by their masters, who often insisted on permitting marriages only among their own slaves as a means of maintaining better control over them. Some-

*The breakup of families and friendships was an ever-present fear for slaves, who might be sold for purely economic reasons as well as in retribution for uncooperative behavior.*

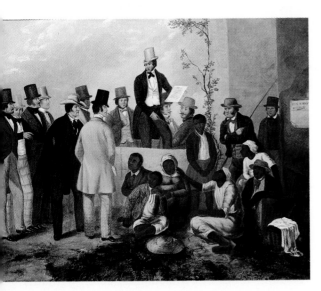

times, masters chose mates and foisted them upon slave women. Massa Hawkins, for example, selected Rufus to live with 16-year-old Rose Williams, as she recalled many years later. She resisted the attempted liaison with unmistakable clarity: "I puts de feet 'gainst him and give him a shove and out he go on de floor 'fore he knew what I's doin'." When Rufus persisted, Rose took a poker and "lets him have it over de head." Hawkins then threatened Rose with a "whippin' at de stake" or with sale away "from my folks." This was too much for her. "What am I's to do? So I 'cides to do as de massa wish and so I yields."

Unlike the case of Rose and Rufus, however, slaves usually chose their own mates based on mutual attraction. As among poor whites, premarital intercourse was frequent, but promiscuous behavior was rare. Most couples maintained affectionate, lasting relationships. This too led to numerous sorrows in slavery. Members of slave families had to witness the flogging or physical abuse of a loved one and were powerless to interfere. William Wells Brown remembered that "cold chills ran over me and I wept aloud" when he saw his mother whipped for being late into the fields for work. For this reason, some slaves preferred to marry a spouse from a different plantation than their own.

Parenting challenged the resourcefulness of slaves. Their children were often denied proper physical care and emotional support by the absence of their parents during most of the working day. Diet suffered, along with proper supervision. But the slaves adapted. The husband might work extra time so that his wife could be with the children. Or young teenagers might be put in charge. New mothers often had to choose between taking their babies into the hot fields to be fed or to leave them with others. Some masters would provide time off for nursing mothers, but the more common practice was for them to work in the fields with their newborn infants lying nearby, wrapped in cloth to protect them from the sun.

The most traumatic problem for slaves was the separation of families through the internal slave trade. This haunting fear was rarely absent from slave consciousness. Although many slaveholders began with both moral and economic reasons to maintain families, inevitably they found themselves destroying them. One study, compiling 30 years of data from three Deep South states, shows that masters dissolved one-third of all slave marriages. Even then, the slaves tried to maintain contact. In 1858, Abream Scriven informed his wife Dinah of his sale to a trader in New Orleans. He had no idea where he would be sold but promised to "write and let you know where I am. My Dear I want to Send you Some things . . . I will try to get them to you and my children. Give my love to my father & mother and tell them good Bye for me. . . . My Dear Wife for you and my Children my pen cannot Express the griffe I feel to be parted from you all."

There was much basis in fact for the aboli-tionists' contention that slavery was a harsh, brutal system. However, two points need to be emphasized. First, although slavery was a barba-rous institution that led otherwise decent human beings to commit inhumane acts, many slaveholders throughout the South were neither sadistic nor cruel but did what they could to provide decent care and humane treatment for their slave laborers. Second, despite the travail of slavery, whether under relatively kind or cruel masters, the slaves endured with dignity, communal sensitivity, and even some joy. If daytime in the fields serves to describe a view of slavery at its worst, nighttime in the quarters, as examined from the black perspective, reveals the slaves' survival powers and their capacity to mold an Afro-American culture under slavery.

## NIGHT: SLAVES IN THEIR QUARTERS

It is near sundown, and the workday is almost over. Some of the slaves begin singing the gentle spiritual "Steal Away to Jesus," and others join in. Or perhaps they sing, "dere's a meeting here tonight." To the unwary overseer or master, the humming, soothing sound of the song suggests happy slaves, content with their earthly lot and looking forward to deliverance in heaven, "in the sweet bosom of Jesus." To the slaves, howev-er, the songs are a signal that, as an ex-slave, Wash Wilson, put it, they are to "steal away to Jesus" because "dere gwine be a 'ligious meetin' dat night." When evening arrived on the planta-tion, after a hard day of work in the hot sun or in the Big House, the slaves returned to their own quarters. There, as Wilson said, "sometimes us sing and pray all night."

In the slave quarters, away from white mas-ters, overseers, and the burdens of daily work, existed an elaborate black community that helped the slaves make sense out of their lives. In family life, religion, song, dance, the playing of musical instruments, and the telling of stor-ies, the slaves both described their experiences and sought release from hardship and suffering. However burdensome their lives were from sunup to sundown, after work the slaves were able to experience enjoyment and a sense of self-worth, hope, and group identity in their quarters.

### Black Christianity

As in Africa, religion was an indispensable part of antebellum life for both free and enslaved blacks. Slaves brought many forms of religious expression to America and blended them with Christianity. Thus West African practices such as ancestor worship, extended funerals, folk be-liefs like voodoo, magical charms and herbs, the ecstatic behavior of spirit possession, and the significance of dance, drumming, and shouting during worship all survived and were adapted to fit Christianity and the slave experience. The practice of voodoo, for example, evolved into the magical root work of the plantation conjurer, who healed wounds and warded off harm.

Black religious institutions in North Ameri-ca were both visible and invisible. From the 1790s, the widespread increase in evangelical-ism led to the founding of several independent black churches. These visible churches, most of them Baptist and African Methodist Episcopal (AME), nourished an influential group of black preachers and leaders like Richard Allen and Absalom Jones of Philadelphia, Peter Williams of New York, and Andrew Marshall of Savannah. Serving both slaves and free blacks, these separate churches had to steer a careful path to maintain their freedom and avoid white civic and ecclesiastical interference. Free blacks, however, were a small minority in the South, and most blacks attended the churches of their masters.

Robert Allston built a prayer house for his slaves, reporting with pride that they were "attentive to religious instruction, and greatly improved in intelligence and morals." For the slaveholders, religion often represented a form of social control. Despite the presence of illiterate but eloquent slave preachers on the plantation, who frequently played a prominent role in administering baptisms, weddings, and funerals, white masters sought to direct the purposes of religion to their own ends. Black religious gatherings were usually forbidden except when white observers were present or, preferably, when white preachers led them. Whether in slave or white churches (where blacks sat in the back), preachers often delivered sermons from the text "Servants, obey your masters." These sermons emphasized the importance of work, obedience, honesty, and respect for the master's property. One former slave complained that "all that preacher talked about was for us slaves to obey our masters and not to lie and steal."

As the comment suggests, there were limits to the effectiveness of paternal control. Although some slaves accommodated themselves to the master's brand of Christianity and patiently waited for heavenly deliverance, others rebelled and sought earthly liberty. Not far from Allston's plantation, several slaves were discovered (and imprisoned) for singing "We'll soon be free / We'll fight for liberty / When de Lord will call us home." Douglass had an illegal Sabbath school on one plantation, where he and others risked being whipped while learning about Christianity and how to read. "The work of instructing my dear fellow-slaves," he wrote, "was the sweetest engagement with which I was ever blessed."

In religious schools and meetings like these, the slaves created an "invisible" church. On Sunday morning they sat dutifully through the master's service and waited for the "real meetin' " and "real preachin' " later that night. Sarah Fitzpatrick, an Alabama slave, recalled that the slaves wanted so much to "go to church by de'selves" that they were willing to sit through the "white fo'ks' . . . service in de mornin.' " But when evening came, "a'ter dey clean up, wash de dishes, an' look a'ter ever'thing," the slaves would "steal away" to the nearby woods for their own service.

Long into the night they would sing, dance, shout, and pray. "Ya' see," Sarah explained, "niggers lack ta shout a whole lot an' wid de white fo'ks al'round 'em, dey couldn't shout jes' lack dey want to." But at night they could,

*Religious meetings provided an outlet for emotions hidden all day from the overseer. At the Christmas holidays, music and dancing continued day and night.*

taking care to deafen the sound to keep the whites away. One method was to hang a curtain from the trees. Another, an African custom, was to turn over a pot to "catch the sound." Another African form, the frenetic dancing of the ring shout, survived in adapted form. Dance, forbidden by Methodists, was transformed into the "ecstatic shout," praising the Lord. The religious ceremony itself, with its camp meeting features, relieved the day's burdens and expressed communal religious values. "At night," another ex-slave recalled with pride, "was when the darkies really did have they freedom of spirit."

Although many of the expressive forms were African, the message reiterated over and over in the invisible slave church was the Christian theme of suffering and deliverance from bondage. Slaves identified with the children of Israel and with the Exodus story, as well as with the suffering Jesus and the inner turmoil of an unconverted "trebbled spirit." "We prayed a lot to be free," Anderson Edwards recalled, but the freedom the slaves sought was a complex blend of a peaceful soul and escape from slavery. Nothing illustrated both the communal religious experience and these mixed Christian themes of suffering and redemption better than slave spritituals.

### The Power of Song

A group of slaves gathers in the dark of night in the woods behind their quarters to sing and shout together:

> O brothers, don't get weary
> O brothers, don't get weary
> O brothers, don't get weary
> We're waiting for the Lord.
> We'll land on Canaan's shore
> We'll land on Canaan's shore
> When we land on Canaan's shore
> We'll meet forever more.

Then, after moaning of being stolen from Africa and sold in Georgia, with families "sold apart," they sing:

> There's a better day a-coming,
> Will you go along with me?
> There's a better day a-coming,
> Go sound the jubilee!

Music was a crucial form of expression in the slave quarters on both secular and religious occasions. The slaves were adept at creating a song, as one slave woman recalled, "on de spurn of de moment." Jeanette Robinson Murphy described a process of spontaneous creation that, whether in rural church music or urban jazz, describes black music to this day. "We'd all be at the 'prayer house' de Lord's day," she said, when all of a sudden, perhaps even in the midst of a white preacher's sermon, "de Lord would come a-shinin' thoo dem pages and revive dis ole nigger's heart, and I'd jump up dar and den and holler and shout and sing and pat, and dey would all cotch de words and I'd sing it to some ole shout song I'd heard 'em sing from Africa, and dey'd all take it up and keep at it, and keep a-addin' to it, and den it would be a spiritual."

Although the spirituals were composed for many purposes, they returned again and again to one basic Christian theme: a chosen people, the children of God, were held captive in bondage but would be delivered. The titles and lyrics reveal the message: "We Are de People of de Lord," "To the Promised Land I'm Bound to Go," "Go Down, Moses, " "Who Will Deliver Po' Me?" What they meant by "deliverance" was not always clear and often had a double meaning: freedom in heaven and freedom in the North. Where, exactly, was the desired destination of "Oh Canaan, sweet Canaan / I am bound for the land of Canaan"? Was it heaven, where one would meet lost relatives again? A vague symbol for freedom "anyplace else but here"? A literal reference to the end of the underground railroad? For different slaves, and at different times for the same person, it meant all of these.

"The songs of the slave," Douglass wrote, "represent the sorrows of his heart." Indeed, they often expressed the sadness of broken families and the burdens of work. The songs were filled with images of trouble, toil, and homelessness. But they also expressed joy, triumph, and deliverance. Each expression of sorrow usually ended in an outburst of eventual affirmation and justice. "O nobody knows a who I am" resolved itself on "judgment morning" when one heard the "bells a-ringing in my soul." The sadness of "Nobody knows the trouble I've seen" was lightened by happening upon some juicy berries hanging down "just as sweet as de honey in de comb." And the deep sorrow of "Sometimes I feel like a motherless chile," as terrible a situation as any person could endure, was transformed later in the song into "Sometimes I feel like / A eagle in de air. . . . / Gonna spread my wings an' / Fly, fly, fly."

Slave songs were not always filled with so many hidden meanings. Sometimes slaves gathered simply for music, to play fiddles, drums, and other instruments fashioned by local artists in imitation of West African models. Some musicians were so talented that whites invited them to perform at ceremonies and parties. But most played for the slave community. Sacred and secular events such as weddings, funerals, holiday celebrations, family reunions, and the completion of the harvest were all occasions for a communal gathering, usually with music. So also was news of external events that affected their lives—a crisis in the master's situation, a change in the slave code, the outcome of a battle during the Civil War, or emancipation itself.

### The Enduring Family

The role of music in births, weddings, funerals, and other milestones of family life suggests that the family was central to life in the slave quarters. Although the pain of sexual abuse and family separation was present in the experience of all slaves, as a threat if not in actuality, so also was the hope for some continuity in slave families. The study of naming practices, for example, shows that children were connected to large extended families. In the records of one plantation for the century from 1760 to the eve of the Civil War, some 175 men, women, and children were found to be linked together by blood and marital ties, respecting taboos against marrying first cousins.

The benefits of family cohesion were like those in any society: love, protection, education, moral guidance, the transmission of culture, and the provision of status, role models, and basic support. All of these existed in the slave quarters. As the slaves gathered together at the end of the working day, parents passed on to their children the family story, language patterns and words, recipes, folktales, religious and musical traditions, and strong impressions of strength and beauty. In this way they preserved cultural tradition, which enhanced the identity and self-esteem of parents and children alike. Parents taught their children how to survive in the world and how to cope with life under slavery. As the young ones neared the age when they would work full time in the fields, their parents instructed them in the best ways to pick cotton or corn, how to avoid the overseer's whip, whom to trust and learn from, and ways of fooling the master.

Opportunities existed on many plantations for fathers, and mothers as well, to improve the welfare of the family by working extra to earn money to buy scarce items like sugar or

*This 1862 photograph shows five generations of a slave family, all born on the plantation of J. J. Smith of Beaufort, South Carolina.*

A frequent activity of family life in the slave quarters was telling stories. The folktale was an especially useful and indirect way in which older slaves could express hostility toward their masters, impart wisdom to the young, teach them how to survive, portray and mock their own weaknesses, and entertain themselves. Folktales served the slaves as schooling, recreation, group therapy, and how-to-survive manual. Thus they reveal to historians a great deal about the slaves' view of their experience.

Although the tales took many forms, perhaps the best known were the "Brer Rabbit" animal stories. The trickster rabbit, who existed originally in African folklore, was weak, careless, and looked down on by the other animals. Like the slaves, he was a victim. But he was also clever, boastful, and full of mischief and knew how to use his cunning to outwit stronger foes, usually by knowing them better than they knew him, a psychological necessity for all who are oppressed.

In one story, the powerful Brer Tiger took all the water and food for himself during a time of terrible famine, leaving the weaker animals miserable. Brer Rabbit, however, turned things around. He played on Brer Tiger's fears that he would be blown away by a "big wind," secretly manufactured by the rabbit. The tiger was so afraid of the wind (perhaps the winds of revolt?) that he begged Brer Rabbit to tie him "tightly" to a tree to keep from being blown away. Brer Rabbit was happy to oblige, after which all the creatures of the forest were able to share the cool water and juicy pears.

In another folktale, Brer Rabbit fell in a well but then got out by tricking Brer Wolf into thinking it was more desirable to be in the cool bottom of the well than outside where it was hot. As the wolf lowered himself down in one bucket, Brer Rabbit rose up in the other, laughingly saying as he passed Brer Wolf, "Dis am life; some go up and some go down." In these stories, the slaves vicariously outwitted their more powerful masters and even reversed roles. The tiger was bound to the tree while Brer Rabbit and the other

## TAR BABY

Brer Wolf studied and studied to find a way to catch Brer Rabbit. He scratched his head, and he pulled his chin whiskers until by and by he said, "I know what I'll do. I'll make me a tar baby, and I'll catch that good-for-nothing rabbit."*

And so Brer Wolf worked and worked until he had made a pretty little girl out of tar. He dressed the tar baby in a calico apron and carried her up to the well, where he stood her up and fastened her to a post in the ground so that nobody could move her. Then Brer Wolf hid in the bushes and waited for Brer Rabbit to come for some water. But three days passed before Brer Rabbit visited the well again. On the fourth day, he came with a bucket in his hand.

When he saw the little girl, he stopped and looked at her. Then he said, "Hello. What's your name? What are you doing here, little girl?"

The little girl said nothing.

This made Brer Rabbit angry, and he shouted at her, "You no-mannered little snip, you! How come you don't speak to your elders?"

The little girl still said nothing.

"I know what to do with little children like you. I'll slap your face and teach you some manners if you don't speak to me," said Brer Rabbit.

Still the little girl said nothing.

And then Brer Rabbit lost his head and said, "Speak to me, I say. I'm going to slap you." With that, Brer Rabbit slapped the tar baby in the face, bam, and his right hand stuck.

"A-ha, you hold my hand, do you? Turn me loose, I say. Turn me loose. If you don't, I'm going to slap you with my left hand. And if I hit you with my left hand, I'll knock the daylights out of you."

But the little girl said nothing. So Brer Rabbit drew back his left hand and slapped the little girl in her face, bim, and his left hand stuck.

"Oh, I see. You're going to hold both my hands, are you? You better turn me loose. If you don't, I'm going to kick you. And if I kick you, it's going to be like thunder and lightning!" With that, Brer Rabbit drew back his right foot and kicked the little girl in the shins with all his might, blap! Then his right foot stuck.

"Well, sir, isn't this something? You better turn my foot loose. If you don't, I've got another foot left, and I'm going to kick you with it, and you'll think a cyclone hit you." Then Brer Rabbit gave that little girl a powerful kick in the shins with his left foot, blip! With that, his left foot stuck, and there he hung off the ground, between the heavens and the earth. He was in an awful fix. But he still thought he could get loose.

*Tar was often spread on fences by masters to catch slaves who, out of hunger or mischief, would sneak into fields and orchards to steal food. Tar stuck on the hands would betray the "guilty" slave.

William J. Faulkner, *The Days When the Animals Talked.* Copyright © 1977 by William J. Faulkner. Used by permission of Modern Curriculum Press, Inc.

creatures were free, not to take revenge but simply to survive. In telling these stories, the slaves revealed much about their experience under slavery and their aspirations for freedom.

The accompanying excerpt is from perhaps the most famous animal tale, "The Tar Baby Tricks Brer Rabbit." This version is by William J. Faulkner, who after he retired as minister and dean of men at Fisk University, gathered and recorded the folktales he had heard in his youth in South Carolina as told by an ex-slave, Simon Brown. Rev. Faulkner opposed telling the stories in dialect because he believed readers formed stereotyped judgments from the dialect and missed the significance of the tale itself.

As you read the folktale, ask yourself what the message of the story is, how it reveals what slavery was like, and how it might have provided a sense of identity and self-worth for the slaves who heard it. We enter the story as an angry Brer Wolf has decided on a plan to catch the lazy Brer Rabbit, who refused to help the wolf build a well and has been fooling him by drinking from the well while Brer Wolf was asleep.

When you have finished reading the story, consider the following questions: What did you learn about slavery from this story? Did violence work for Brer Rabbit, or did it only make things worse? Notice the resourcefulness and survival instincts of the rabbit. He was in a terrible fix, but he got out. What finally worked? How do you interpret the ending? Brer Rabbit is returned to the briar patch, "the place where I was born." But is the briar patch, with all its thorns, scratches, and roots, Africa or slavery? Or what?

Finally, reflect on the stories *you* heard as a child or now find yourself telling others. What are they? How do they express the realities, flaws, values, and dreams of the American people? The basic question to ask of the folktales and stories that we tell is a question we could ask as well of the songs we sing, the art we make, the rhythms we move to, and the jokes we tell: What do they tell us about ourselves and our values? In answering these questions, we deepen the knowledge of our own history.

---

So he said to the little girl, "You've got my feet and my hands all stuck up, but I've got one more weapon, and that's my head. If you don't turn me loose, I'm going to butt you! And if I butt you, I'll knock your brains out." Finally then, Brer Rabbit struck the little girl a powerful knock on the forehead with his head, and it stuck, and there he hung. Smart old Brer Rabbit, he couldn't move. He was held fast by the little tar baby.

Now, Brer Wolf was hiding under the bushes, watching all that was going on. And as soon as he was certain that Brer Rabbit was caught good by his little tar baby, he walked over to Brer Rabbit and said, "A-ha, you're the one who wouldn't dig a well. And you're the one who's going to catch his drinking water from the dew off the grass. A-ha, I caught the fellow who's been stealing my water. And he isn't anybody but you, Brer Rabbit. I'm going to fix you good."

"No, sir, Brer Wolf, I haven't been bothering your water. I was just going over to Brer Bear's house, and I stopped by here long enough to speak to this little no-manners girl," said Brer Rabbit.

"Yes, you're the one," said Brer Wolf. "You're the very one who's been stealing my drinking water all this time. And I'm going to kill you."

"Please, sir, Brer Wolf, don't kill me," begged Brer Rabbit. "I haven't done anything wrong."

"Yes, I'm going to kill you, but I don't know how I'm going to do it yet," growled Brer Wolf. "Oh, I know what I'll do. I'll throw you in the fire and burn you up."

"All right, Brer Wolf," said Brer Rabbit. "Throw me in the fire. That's a good way to die. That's the way my grandmother died, and she said it's a quick way to go. You can do anything with me, anything you want, but please, sir, don't throw me in the briar patch."

"No, I'm not going to throw you in the fire, and I'm not going to throw you in the briar patch. I'm going to throw you down the well and drown you," said Brer Wolf.

"All right, Brer Wolf, throw me down the well," said Brer Rabbit. "That's an easy way to die, but I'm surely going to smell up your drinking water, sir."

"No, I'm not going to drown you," said Brer Wolf. "Drowning is too good for you." Then Brer Wolf thought and thought and scratched his head and pulled his chin whiskers. Finally he said, "I know what I'm going to do with you. I'll throw you in the briar patch."

"Oh, no, Brer Wolf," cried Brer Rabbit. "Please, sir, don't throw me in the briar patch. Those briars will tear up my hide, pull out my hair, and scratch out my eyes. That'll be an awful way to die, Brer Wolf. Please, sir, don't do that to me."

"That's exactly what I'll do with you," said Brer Wolf all happy-like. Then he caught Brer Rabbit by his hind legs, whirled him around and around over his head, and threw him way over into the middle of the briar patch.

After a minute or two, Brer Rabbit stood up on his hind legs and laughed at Brer Wolf and said to him, "Thank you, Brer Wolf, thank you. This is the place where I was born. My grandmother and grandfather and all my family were born right here in the briar patch."

And that's the end of the story.

clothing, by hunting and fishing to add protein to the diet, or by working a small garden to grow vegetables. J. W. C. Pennington proudly recalled helping his "father at night in making straw hats and willow-baskets, by which means we supplied our family with little articles of food, clothing and luxury."

Slaves were not always totally at the mercy of abusive masters and overseers. Occasionally, one family member could intervene to prevent the abuse of another. When emotional appeals for mercy did not work, or when the subtle magical effects of the conjurer's bag of herbs hung around the neck did not suffice, some slaves resorted to physical force. In 1800, a slave called Ben shot and killed a white man for living with his wife, but not without first tragically poisoning his wife by mistake in an earlier murder attempt. Another slave killed his overseer in 1859 for raping his wife, but the court ruled that his action was unjustified. The love and affection that slaves had for each other was sometimes a liability. Many slaves were reluctant to run away because they did not want to leave their families. Those who fled were easily caught because, as an overseer near Natchez, Mississippi, told a northern visitor, they "almost always kept in the neighborhood, because they did not like to go where they could not sometimes get back and see their families."

As these episodes suggest, the stability of slave families was constantly threatened by violence, sexual abuse, and separation. But despite these serious restraints, slave parents were able to serve as protectors, providers, comforters, transmitters of culture, and role models for their children. The slave family, though constantly endangered, played a crucial role in helping blacks adapt to slavery and achieve a sense of self-esteem.

## RESISTANCE AND FREEDOM

Songs, folktales, and other forms of cultural expression enabled slaves to articulate their resistance to slavery. For example, Old Jim was going on a "journey" to the "kingdom" and, as he invited others to "go 'long" with him, he taunted his owner: "O blow, blow, Ole Massa, blow de cotton horn / Ole Jim'll neber wuck no mo' in de cotton an' de corn." From refusal to work it was a short step to outright revolt. In another song, "Samson," the slaves clearly stated their determination to abolish the house of bondage: "An' if I had-'n my way / I'd tear the buildin' down! / . . . And now I got my way / And I'll tear this buildin' down." Every hostile song, story, or event, like Douglass's victory over Covey, was an act of resistance by which the slaves asserted their dignity and gained a measure of freedom. Some escaped slavery altogether to achieve such autonomy as was possible for free blacks in the antebellum South.

### Forms of Black Protest

One way slaves protested the burdensome demands of continuous forced labor was in various "day to day" acts of resistance. These ranged from breaking tools to burning crops, barns, and houses, from stealing or destroying animals and food to defending fellow slaves from punishment, from self-mutilation to deliberate work slowdowns. Two favorite techniques were to pretend sickness during periods when the overseers were driving the hardest and to misplace tools or deliberately leave them in the fields so that they would have to be "hunted all over the place when wanted."

Overseers also suffered from these little acts of disobedience, for their job depended on productivity, which in turn depended on the goodwill of the slave workers. No one knew this better than the slaves themselves, who adeptly played on the frequent struggle between overseer and master. Often the conflicts ended with the firing of a bad overseer and the hiring of a more suitable replacement. Many slaveholders eventually resorted to the use of black drivers rather than overseers, but this created other problems.

The slave drivers were "men between," charged with the tricky job of getting the master's work done without alienating fellow slaves or compromising their own values. Although some drivers were as brutal as white overseers, many became leaders and role models for other slaves. A common practice of the drivers was to appear to punish without really doing so. Solomon Northrup reported that he "learned to handle the whip with marvellous dexterity and precision, throwing the lash within a hair's breadth of the back, the ear, the nose, without, however, touching either of them." As he did this, the "punished" slave would howl in pretended pain and complain loudly to his master about his harsh treatment.

Another form of resistance was to run away. So many blacks ran off that a southern doctor coined a new word, *drapetomania*, which meant "the disease causing negroes to run away." The typical runaway was a young male, who ran off alone and hid out in a nearby wood or swamp. He left to avoid a whipping or because he had just been whipped, to protest excessive work demands, or, as one master put it, for "no cause" at all. But there was a cause—the need to experience a period of freedom away from the restraints and discipline of the plantation. Many runaways would sneak back to the quarters at night for food, and after a few days, if not tracked down by hounds, they would return, perhaps to be whipped but also perhaps with some concessions for better treatment in the future.

Some slaves ran away again and again. Remus and his wife Patty ran away from their master, James Battle, in Alabama. They were caught and jailed three times, but each time they escaped again. Battle urged the next jailer to "secure Remus well." Some runaways, called "Maroons," hid out for months and years at a time in communities of runaway slaves. Several Maroon colonies were located in the swamps and mountains of the South, especially in Florida, where Seminole and other tribes befriended them. In these areas, blacks and Indians sharing a common hostility to local whites, frequently intermarried.

The means of escape were manifold: forging passes, posing as master and servant, disguising one's sex, sneaking aboard ships, and pretending loyalty until taken by the master on a trip to the North. One slave even hid in a large box and had himself mailed to the North. The underground railroad, organized by abolitionists, was a series of safe houses and stations where runaway slaves could rest, eat, and spend the night before continuing. Harriet Tubman, who led some 300

*Working with tools and machinery enabled slaves to engage in silent protests by misplacing or sabotaging a piece of equipment. Work could not continue in its monotonous way until the tool was found or the broken machine repaired.*

slaves out of the South on 19 separate trips, was the railroad's most famous "conductor." It is difficult to know exactly how many slaves actually escaped to the North and Canada, but the numbers were not large. One estimate suggests that in 1850 about 1,000 slaves (out of over 3 million) attempted to run away, and most of them were returned.

Other ways in which slaves sought their freedom included petitioning Congress and state legislatures, bringing suit against their masters that they were being held in bondage illegally, persuading masters to provide for emancipation in their wills, and purchasing their own freedom by hiring out to do extra work at night and on holidays.

### Slave Revolts

The ultimate act of resistance, of course, was rebellion. Countless slaves committed individual acts of revolt. In addition, there were hundreds of conspiracies to revolt, whereby a group of slaves met and planned a group escape and often the massacre of whites. Most of these conspiracies, however, never took place, either because circumstances changed or the slaves lost the will to follow through, or, more often, because some fellow slave—perhaps planted by the master—betrayed the plot to white officials ahead of time. In this way the elaborate conspiracies of Gabriel Prosser (Richmond, Virginia, 1800) and Denmark Vesey (Charleston, South Carolina, 1822) were thwarted. Both resulted in severe reprisals by whites, including mass executions of leaders and the random killing of countless innocent blacks. The severity and intensity of the white response indicated the enormous fear southern whites had of a slave revolt.

Only a few organized revolts, in which slaves threatened white lives and property, ever actually took place. Latin American slaves challenged their masters more often than their North American counterparts. Weaker military control, easier escape to rugged interior areas, the greater imbalance of blacks to whites, and the continued dependence of Latin American slaveholders on the African slave trade for their supply of mostly male workers helped to explain this pattern. Nearly 80 percent of the Africans imported into Brazil in the 1830s and 1840s were male, and as late as 1875, only one in six Brazilian slaves was recorded as married. The imbalance of males to females (156 to 100 in Cuba in 1860, for example, compared to a near one to one ratio in the United States) weakened family restraints on violent revolts.

Although Vesey's South Carolina conspiracy in 1822 was more extensively planned, the most famous slave revolt in North America, led by Nat Turner, occurred in Southampton County, Virginia, in 1831. Turner was an intelligent, skilled, unmarried, religious slave who had experienced many visions of "white spirits and black spirits engaged in battle." He believed that he was "ordained for some great purpose in the hands of the Almighty."

On a hot August night, Turner and a small band of fellow slaves launched their revolt. They intended, as Turner said, "to carry terror and devastation" throughout the county. They crept into the home of Turner's master, Joseph Travis, who Nat said was "a kind master" with "the greatest confidence in me," and killed the entire family. Before the revolt was finally put down, 55 white men, women, and children had been murdered and as many blacks killed in the aftermath. Turner hid in a hole in the woods for two weeks before he was apprehended and executed, but not before dictating a chilling confession to a white lawyer. The Nat Turner revolt was a crucial moment for southern whites. A Virginia legislator said that he suspected there was "a Nat Turner . . . in every family." Rarely thereafter would slaveholders go to sleep without the Southampton revolt in mind.

The fact that Turner was an intelligent and trusted slave, with "no cause to complain" of his master's treatment, and yet led such a terrible revolt suggests again how difficult it is to generalize about slavery and slave behavior. Slaves, like masters, showed diverse personalities and moods, changing from one day to the next, depending on relationships with others, the weather, the amount of work to be done, and personal inner compulsions. Their behavior could not be easily predicted. Sometimes humble and deferential, at other times obstinate and rebellious, the slaves made the best of a bad situation and did what they needed to do to survive and achieve a measure of self-worth.

## Free Blacks: Becoming One's Own Master

No matter how well they coped with their bondage, the slaves obviously preferred freedom. As Frederick Douglass said of the slave, "Give him a *bad* master, and he aspires to a *good* master; give him a good master, and he wishes to become his *own* master." When Douglass himself had successfully forged a free black's papers as a seaman and sailed from Baltimore to become his own master in the North, he found "great insecurity and loneliness." Apart from the immediate difficulties of finding food, shelter, and work, he realized that he was a fugitive in a land "whose inhabitants are legalized kid-nappers" who could at any moment seize and return him to the South. Apart from this fear, which haunted blacks in the North, what was life like for the just over 11 percent of the total black population who in 1860 were not slaves?

Between 1820 and 1860, the number of free blacks in the United States doubled, from 233,500 to 488,000. This increase was the result of natural increase, successful escapes, "passing" as whites, purchasing one's freedom, and a continuation of some manumissions despite legal restriction in most states after the 1830s. Despite the increase, the proportion of free blacks in the total black population decreased from 13.2 percent in 1820 to a little more than 11 percent in 1860. Thus the number of blacks who were slaves grew faster than those who were free. More than half the free blacks were in the South, and most of these (85 percent in 1860) lived in the Upper South. (The life of free blacks in the North is described in the next chapter.)

*Nat Turner's Revolt in 1831, the most famous American slave uprising, left 55 whites dead as Turner's band carried "terror and devastation" throughout Southampton County, Virginia.*

Since free blacks represented a constant reminder of freedom to slaves and feared reenslavement themselves, they were found least frequently in the Black Belt of the Lower South. They lived, rather, away from the dense plantation centers, scattered on impoverished rural farmlands and in small towns and cities. One-third of the southern free blacks lived in cities such as Baltimore, Richmond, Charleston, and New Orleans. In part because it took a long time to buy one's freedom, they tended to be older, more literate, and more skilled than other blacks. They were more often women and light-skinned, reflecting the favored privileges, including manumission, these blacks received from slaveholders. In 1860, over 40 percent of the free blacks were mulattoes (compared to 10 percent of the slaves).

Most southern free blacks were poor, laboring as farmhands, day laborers, or woodcutters. In the cities, they lived in appalling poverty and

## Growth of Black Population: Slave and Free, 1820–1860

*Source:* U.S. Bureau of the Census.

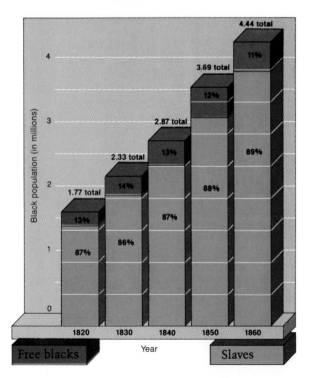

worked in factories. A few skilled jobs, such as barbering, shoemaking, and plastering, were reserved for black men; they were barred from more than 50 other trades. Women worked as cooks, laundresses, and domestics. The 15 percent of free blacks who lived in the Lower South were divided into two distinct castes. Most were poor. But in New Orleans a small, mixed-blood class of free blacks emerged as an elite group, closely connected to white society and removed from the mass of poor blacks. A handful even owned land and slaves. One white observed that these blacks were "respectable" and enjoyed "their rights."

Most free blacks, however, had no such privileges. "We reside among you . . . surrounded by the freest people and most republican institutions in the world," a Baltimore black paper said in 1826, pointing out that free blacks were not yet citizens and enjoyed "none of the immunities of freedom. . . . Though we are not slaves, we are not free." Southern state laws seriously limited the mobility, rights, and opportunities of free blacks. In most states they could not vote, bear arms, buy liquor, assemble, speak in public, form societies, or testify against whites in court.

One reason for these restrictions was that urban white southerners feared the influence of free blacks, who mixed with whites in working-class grogshops, gambling halls, and brothels. Richmond police closed one house of ill fame where "men and women of diverse colors . . . congregate for most unhallowed purposes." Efforts were made to confine the free blacks to certain sections of the city or, increasingly by the 1850s, to compel them to leave the city, county, or state altogether. Those who stayed had trouble finding work, were required to carry licenses and freedom papers to be surrendered on demand, and often needed a white guardian to approve their actions.

However threatening free blacks were to southern standards of separatism and white supremacy, whites were even more afraid of contact between free blacks and slaves. Black ghettos were created by a combination of black needs to be together and white aversion to racial intermingling. As in the slave quarters of the plantation, blacks in cities developed a strong sense of identity and community life. Freemen and bondsmen often worked together in factories and fields, attended the same churches and places of entertainment, and sometimes even married.

The center of urban black community was the church. Martin Delaney wrote to Douglass in 1849 that "among our people . . . the Church is the Alpha and Omega of all things." The church not only performed the usual religious ritual functions and guarded moral discipline and community values but also provided and promoted education, social insurance, fraternal associations, and picnics, concerts, and other forms of recreation. Besides the church, black community identity and pride revolved around the African schools and various burial and benevolent societies for self-help and protection against poverty, illness, and other disasters. Like their counterparts among whites, these societies grew and took on a new and significant social importance in the two decades before the Civil War. African Methodist Episcopal bishop Henry

M. Turner proudly claimed in the 1850s that "we, as a race, have a chance to be Somebody, and if we are ever going to be a people, now is the time."

In part because free blacks were becoming more of "a people," they faced a crisis of extinction in the 1850s. Growing prosperity and the worsening conflict between North and South over slavery in the territories caused many white southerners to be even more concerned than usual with the presence of free blacks in their midst. North Carolina whites complained in 1852 that free blacks were "a perfect nuisance" because they attempted "in divers ways to equalize themselves with [the] white population." Pressures increased in the late 1850s either to deport the free blacks or to enslave them. In the wake of increasing threats to their already precarious free status, some black leaders not surprisingly began to look more favorably on migration to Africa. That quest was interrupted, however, by the outbreak of the Civil War, rekindling again in Douglass and others the "expiring embers of freedom."

*Churches for free blacks, rare before 1800, increased and became a major source of social as well as religious activity by the 1840s.*

## CONCLUSION: Douglass's Dream of Freedom

Frederick Douglass eventually won his freedom by forging a free black sailor's pass and escaping through Chesapeake Bay to New York. In a real sense, he wrote himself into freedom. *Narrative of the Life of Frederick Douglass,* "written by himself" in 1845, was a way of both exposing the many evils of slavery and of creating his own identity, even to the point of choosing his own name. Ironically, Douglass had learned to value reading and writing, we recall, from his Baltimore masters, the Aulds. This reminds us again of the intricate and subtle ways in which the lives of slaves and masters were tied together in the antebellum South. Our understanding of the complexities of this relationship is enhanced as we consider the variations of life in the Big House in the morning, in the fields during the afternoons, in the slave quarters at night, and in the degrees of freedom blacks achieved through resistance, revolt, and free status.

In a poignant moment in his *Narrative,* Douglass described his dreams of freedom as he looked out at the boats on the waters of Chesapeake Bay as a boy. Contrasting his own enslavement with the boats he saw as "freedom's swift-winged angels," Douglass vowed to escape: "This very bay shall yet bear me into freedom. . . . There is a better day coming." As we will see later, southern white planters also bemoaned their lack of freedom relative to the North and made their own plans to achieve an independent status through secession. Meanwhile, as that struggle brewed beneath the surface of antebellum life, many other Americans were dismayed by various evil aspects in their society, slavery among them, and sought ways of shaping a better America. We turn to these other dreams in the next chapter.

## Recommended Reading

Gavin Wright provides a difficult but thorough analysis of the economic development of the Old South in *The Political Economy of the Cotton South: Households, Markets, and Wealth in the Nineteenth Century* (1978). For a spirited argument of the economics of slavery, read the controversial *Time on the Cross: The Economics of American Negro Slavery* (1974), by Robert Fogel and Stanley Engerman, and two highly critical rejoinders, Herbert Gutman and Richard Sutch, *Slavery and the Numbers Game* (1975) and Paul David et al., *Reckoning with Slavery: A Critical Study of the Quantitative History of American Negro Slavery* (1976). Nonagricultural slaves are dealt with in Robert Starobin, *Industrial Slavery in the Old South* (1970) and Richard Wade, *Slavery in the Cities* (1964). The most readable story of the lives of nonslaveholding whites in the South is an old one, Frank Owsley, *Plain Folk in the Old South* (1949).

The standard picture of slavery from the point of view of its defenders is in two works by Ulrich B. Phillips, *American Negro Slavery* (1919) and *Life and Labor in the Old South* (1929). A brilliant study of racism in America, including excellent chapters on the southern justification of slavery, is George Fredrickson, *The Black Image in the White Mind: The Debate on Afro-American Character and Destiny, 1817–1914* (1971). A fascinating insight into the life of southern white women is Catharine Clinton, *Plantation Mistress* (1983).

Of the many collections of primary source documents about slavery, the best is Willie Lee Rose, *A Documentary History of Slavery in North America* (1976). The three most accurate and sensitive surveys of slavery are Kenneth Stampp, *The Peculiar Institution* (1956); Eugene Genovese, *Roll, Jordan, Roll: The World the Slaves Made* (1974); and John Blassingame, *The Slave Community,* rev. ed. (1979). Various as-

By the 1840s, the frontier was retreating across the Mississippi. As Americans contemplated the lands west of the great river, they debated the question of expansion. Some, like Michigan's senator Lewis Cass, saw the Pacific Ocean as the only limit to territorial expansion. Cass believed that the West represented not only economic opportunity for Americans but political stability for the nation as well. People crowded into cities and confined to limited territories endangered the republic, he told fellow senators. But if they headed west to convert "the woods and forests into towns and villages and cultivated fields" and to extend "the dominion of civilization and improvement over the domain of nature," they would find rewarding personal opportunities that would ensure political and social harmony.

Cass's arguments supporting the righteousness and necessity of westward expansion were echoed again and again in the 1840s. Yet even supporters of expansion admitted some disadvantages. In a letter written to his wife Mary less than a month after Cass's speech, Thomas Gibson, a captain of Indiana volunteers fighting in the Mexican War, described some of the costs of territorial acquisition. The battlefield, he wrote, was "still covered with . . . [Mexican] dead and the stench is most horrible." Friends had been killed; Gibson himself had narrowly escaped. "The ball struck me a glancing blow on the head and knocked me down but it did not hurt me." The weather was foul, and so too was the food, "hard biscuit full of black bitter bugs." Still, Gibson did not challenge the war and even bragged that "our little army could go out tomorrow in a fair field of battle and whip fifty thousand of the best Mexican troops that ever were on a field of battle. One thing is certain, we would be willing to try it."

For Mary Gibson, waiting anxiously for news in Charlestown, Indiana, the main question was simply whether her husband was dead or alive. "May God bless you and send you home," she wrote. Yet, with all her worries and prayers for a rapid end to the war, she offered support for the Mexican adventure. She had heard that Indiana soldiers "shode themselves great cowards by retreating during battle" and disapproved. "We all would rather you had stood like good soldiers since you have gone there," she told Tommy.

Lewis Cass, Thomas and Mary Gibson, and thousands of others all played a part in the nation's expansion into the trans-Mississippi West. The differences and similarities in their perspectives and in their responses to territorial growth unveil the complex nature of the western experience. Lewis Cass's speech illustrates the hold the West had on people's imagination and how some Americans linked expansion to individual opportunity and national progress. His reference to its riches reminds us of the gigantic contribution western resources made to national development and wealth. Yet his assumption that the West was vacant points to the costs of white expansion for Hispanic-Americans and Native Americans. The Gibsons's letters show similar preconceptions and racial prejudices. They also portray the winning of the West on a human level: the anxieties, worries, enthusiasm, and optimism felt by those who fought for and settled in the West.

This chapter concerns the movement into the trans-Mississippi West between 1830 and 1865. First, we will consider how and when Americans moved west, by what means the United States acquired the vast territories that in 1840 belonged to other nations, and the meaning of "Manifest Destiny," the slogan used to describe the ethos of conquering the continent west of the Mississippi River. Second, we explore the nature of life on the western farming, mining, and urban frontiers. Next, the chapter examines responses of Native Americans and Hispanic-Americans to expansion and illuminates the clash between cultures, a tragic part of the westward movement.

## PROBING THE TRANS-MISSISSIPPI WEST

Until the 1840s, except for small populations in Missouri, Arkansas, and Louisiana, most Americans lived east of the Mississippi. The admission of new states between 1815 and 1840 bore witness to the steady settlement of the eastern half of the continent. As frontier log cabins gave way to brick and clapboard houses, farmers cleared and planted land that earlier settlers had ignored. Roads replaced tracks, and new churches, schools, stores, and banks attested to the march of civilization toward the Mississippi. By 1860, some 4.3 million Americans had moved west of the great river.

### Foreign Claims and Possessions

With the exception of the Louisiana Territory, most of the trans-Mississippi region belonged to Spain in 1815. That country's vast empire stretched south to Mexico and west to the Pacific and included present-day Texas, Arizona, New Mexico, Nevada, Utah, western Colorado,

small parts of Wyoming, Kansas, and Oklahoma, and California. When Mexico won its independence from Spain in 1821, it inherited these lands and the 75,000 Spanish-speaking inhabitants and Indian tribes living there.

To the north of California was the Oregon country, a vaguely defined area extending from California to Alaska. Both Great Britain and the United States claimed the Oregon country on the basis of explorations in the late eighteenth century and fur trading in the early nineteenth century. Joint occupation, agreed upon in the Convention of 1818 and the Occupation Treaty of 1827, temporarily avoided settling the boundary question.

### Removing the Five "Civilized Nations"

As they occupied lands east of the Mississippi, white farmers forced Indian tribes from the South and Old Northwest to resettle west of the river. Thus eastern Indian tribes became the first to migrate in large numbers to the trans-Mississippi West in this period. Their grim experiences prefigured what would become the typical pattern of race relations in the new territories.

In 1788, five southern tribes (the Cherokee, Choctaw, Chickasaw, Seminole, and Creek) possessed huge tracts of land in Florida, the Carolinas, Georgia, Tennessee, Alabama, and Mississippi. Land-hungry whites relentlessly pressured these tribes to cede their lands, and they largely succeeded. Cherokee tribal hold-

*Moving west in the 1820s usually meant crossing the Appalachians; a generation later it meant crossing the Mississippi and usually the Rockies.*

### Expanding Boundaries: The United States in 1853

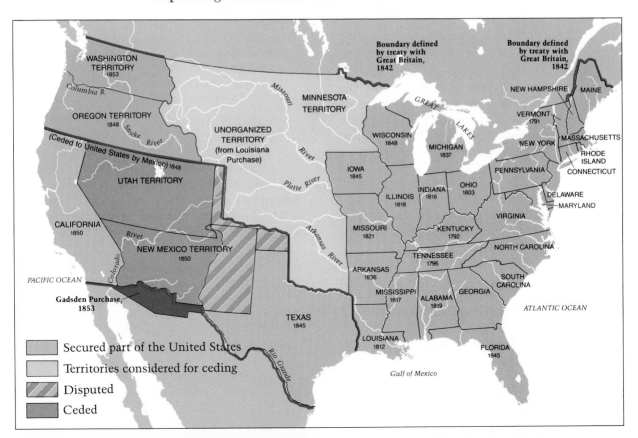

ings, exceeding 50 million acres in 1802, had dwindled to only 9 million 20 years later. Recognizing that their survival was threatened, the tribes acted to end the deadly pattern. By 1825, the Creek, Cherokee, and Chickasaw had each resolved to restrict land sales to government agents. The Cherokee, who had already assimilated many elements of white culture including white clothing, agricultural practices, and slaveholding (see Chapter 10), established a police force to prevent local leaders from selling off tribal land piecemeal.

Tribal determination to resist pressure confronted white resolve to gain these southern lands for cotton planting and mining. Jackson's election in 1828 reinforced the whites wishing to relocate the tribes west of the Mississippi. Like Jefferson before him, Jackson believed that the Indians must flee from the contamination of white settlement. In his first annual message to Congress, the former Indian fighter announced that Indian tribes had no permanent rights to the soil. Overlooking tribal adaptation to white culture, he ominously warned Native Americans either to move west "so they could learn the arts of civilization" or to abandon tribal rules in favor of state laws.

With the president's position clear, the crisis soon came to a head in Georgia. In 1829, the Georgia legislature declared the Cherokee tribal council illegal and its laws null and void in Cherokee territories and announced that the state had jurisdiction over both the tribe and its lands. In the following year, the Cherokee were forbidden to defend their interests by bringing suits against whites into the Georgia courts or even by testifying in such cases. Without legal recourse on the state level, the Cherokee carried their protest to the Supreme Court. In 1832, Chief Justice Marshall supported their position in *Worcester* v. *Georgia*, holding that Georgia laws did not apply to the Cherokee nation.

Legal victory could not, however, suppress white land hunger. Georgia, with Jackson's blessing, defied the Court ruling. By 1835, harassment, intimidation, and bribery had persuaded a minority of chiefs to sign a removal treaty. That year, Jackson informed the Cherokee, "I am sincerely desirous to promote your welfare. Listen to me therefore while I tell you

you cannot remain where you are. Circumstances . . . render it impossible that you can flourish in the midst of a civilized community." Despite the president's pronouncement and the treaty, the Cherokee refused to leave their lands. Therefore, in 1837 and 1838, the United States Army herded them west to the "Great American Desert." The removal, whose $6 million cost was deducted from the $9 million awarded the tribe for their eastern lands, brought death to perhaps a quarter of the 15,000 who set out. Other southern and some northwestern tribes between 1821 and 1840 shared a similar fate. The Cherokee remember this event as *Nuna-da-ut-sun'y*—"The Trail Where They Cried," or "The Trail of Tears."

Not all white Americans applauded these dark deeds. Memorials opposing removal poured into Congress from New England and the East. Religious groups that supported Indian missionaries claimed that Native Americans had a right to their tribal lands. Political foes of Jackson decried his position. One who sympathized with the southern tribes described their devastating experience in these words:

> Many a warrior and squaw died on the road from exhaustion and the maladies engendered by their treatment; and their relations and friends could do nothing more for them than fold them in their blankets and cover them with boughs and bushes, to keep off the vultures, which followed their route by thousands and soared over their heads.

## Traders, Trappers, and Cotton Farmers

Americans were familiar with the lands in the trans-Mississippi West long before the great migrations of the 1840s and 1850s. As early as 1811, Americans engaged in the fur trade in Oregon, and within ten years, fur trappers and traders were actively exploiting the Rocky Mountain region. Their trade, which flourished for almost 20 years, was based on the rendezvous system. Each summer traders from St. Louis, the center of the fur trade, met with mountain men and Indians at a selected site in the wilderness to exchange their goods for beaver pelts trapped the preceding year. When the wiles of the trappers almost exterminated the beaver, the Rocky

Mountain system disintegrated. But a commerce in bison robes prepared by the Plains tribes continued to flourish in the area around the upper Missouri River and its tributaries until after 1860.

Freed from the yoke of Spain in 1821, the Southwest opened to American traders. Each year caravans from "the States" followed the Santa Fe Trail over the plains and mountains, loaded with weapons, tools, and brightly colored calicoes. The 40,000 inhabitants of Santa Fe proved to be eager buyers, exchanging precious metals and furs for the manufactured goods. Eventually, some of the "Anglos" settled there. Their economic activities helped to prepare the way for military conquest later.

To the south, in Texas, land for cotton rather than trade attracted settlers and squatters in the 1820s. The lure of cheap land drew more Americans to the area than to any other. By 1835, almost 30,000 Americans were living in Texas, the largest group of Americans living outside the nation's boundaries at that time.

On the Pacific, a handful of New England traders carrying sea-otter skins to China anchored in the harbors of Spanish California in the early nineteenth century. By the 1830s, as the near extermination of the animals ruined this trade, a commerce based on California cowhides and tallow developed. New England ships tied up for months in California ports while hides were collected from local ranches in exchange for clothes, boots, hardware, and furniture manufactured in the East.

The fact that much of the trans-Mississippi West lay outside of U.S. boundaries did little to deter American activities there. By the 1840s, a keen interest in these western territories had emerged, nourished by the growing amount of information available. Government reports by explorers like Zebulon Pike and John C. Frémont provided detailed information about the interior, while routes that fur trappers like Jim Bridger, Kit Carson, and Jedediah Smith had mapped out reached the reading public in guidebooks and news articles. General guides like Lansford Hastings's *Emigrants' Guide to Oregon and California* (1845) not only provided practical instructions but urged Americans to migrate west.

In his guide, Hastings implied that Mexican and British sovereignty presented only minor obstacles to American expansion. He conceded that California, as a Mexican possession, was a problem. But not so Oregon. "So far from having any valid claim to any portion of it," Hastings argued, Great Britain "had not right even to occupy it." The clinching argument was that American settlers were already trickling into the Pacific Northwest, bringing progress with them. Surely the day could not be far distant, he wrote, "when genuine Republicanism and unsophisticated Democracy shall be reared up . . . upon the now wild shores, of the great Pacific," to replace the "ignorance, superstition, and despotism" that reigned there.

Hastings's belief that Americans would obtain rights to foreign holdings in the West came true within a decade. In the course of the 1840s, the United States, through war and diplomacy, acquired Mexico's territories in the Southwest and on the Pacific (1,193,061 square miles) as well as title to the Oregon country up to the 49th parallel (another 285,000 square miles). Later, with the Gadsden Purchase in 1853, the country rounded out its continental holdings with an additional 29,640 square miles of Mexican territory.

### Manifest Destiny

What explained the fervid urge to expand? Bursts of florid rhetoric accompanied territorial growth, and Americans used the slogan "Manifest Destiny" to justify and account for it. The phrase, coined in 1845 by John L. O'Sullivan, editor of the *Democratic Review*, referred to the conviction that the superiority of American institutions and white culture gave Americans a God-given right, even an obligation, to spread their civilization across the entire continent. Lewis Cass, the Gibsons, Lansford Hastings, and many other Americans agreed.

This sense of uniqueness and mission was a legacy of early Puritan utopianism and the millennial republicanism of the Revolutionary era. By the 1840s, however, an argument for territorial expansion had joined the belief that the United States possessed a unique civilization. The successful absorption of the Louisiana Territory, rapid population growth, and advances in transportation and communication bolstered the idea of national superiority and the notion that the United States could successfully absorb new territories. Publicists of Manifest Destiny proclaimed that the nation must.

## WINNING THE TRANS-MISSISSIPPI WEST

Manifest Destiny was an ideology that justified expansion but did not actually cause it. Concrete events in Texas triggered the national government's determination to acquire territories west of the Mississippi River.

The Texas question originated in the years when Spain held most of the Southwest. Although some settlements such as Santa Fe were as old as Jamestown, the Southwest, primarily considered by the Spanish as a buffer zone for Mexico, was sparsely populated and only slightly developed. The main centers of Spanish settlement, in coastal California, southern Arizona, New Mexico, the Rio Grande basin, and the San Antonio River valley, were geographically distant from one another and thousands of miles from Mexico City. Even though these northern borderlands constituted a weak link in the defensive perimeter of the Spanish Empire, their international status was strengthened in 1819. In the negotiations for the Transcontinental Treaty with Spain, the United States accepted a southern border excluding Texas, to which the Americans had made vague claims stemming from the Louisiana Purchase.

### Annexing Texas

By the time the treaty was ratified in 1821, Mexico had won its independence from Spain. The new nation of Mexico inherited the borderlands, its people, and its problems. Mexicans soon had reason to wonder whether the American disavowal of any claim to Texas included in the Transcontinental Treaty would last, for political leaders like Henry Clay began to call for "reannexation." Fear about American expansionism, fueled by several attempts to buy Texas and by continuing aggressive American statements, permeated Mexican politics.

In 1823, the Mexican government decided to strengthen the border areas by increasing settle-

ment. To attract emigrants, it offered land in return for token payments and pledges to become Roman Catholics and Mexican citizens. Stephen F. Austin, who gained rights to bring 300 families into Texas, was among the first of the American *empresarios*, or contractors, to take advantage of this opportunity. His call for settlers brought an enthusiastic response, as Mary Austin Holley recalled. "I was a young thing then, but 5 months married, my husband . . . failed in Tennessee, proposed to commence business in New Orleans. I ready to go anywhere . . . freely consented. Just then Stephen Austin and Joe Hawkins were crying up Texas—beautiful country, land for nothing etc.—Texas fever rose then . . . there we must go. There without much reflection, we did go." Like the Holleys, most of the American settlers came from the South, and some brought slaves. By the end of the decade, some 15,000 white Americans and 1,000 slaves lived in Texas, far outnumbering the 5,000 Mexican inhabitants.

Mexican officials soon began to question the wisdom of their invitation. Few American settlers became Catholics, and they remained more American than Mexican. A minority of the settlers were malcontents. They disliked being deprived of American laws and customs and resented limitations on their economic and commercial opportunities. In late 1826, a small group of them raised the flag of rebellion and declared the Republic of Fredonia. Although settlers like Austin assisted in putting down the brief uprising, American newspapers hailed the rebels as "apostles of democracy" and called Mexico "an alien civilization."

Mexican anxiety grew apace. Secretary of Foreign Relations Lucas Aláman accused American settlers of being advance agents of the United States. "They commence by introducing themselves into the territory which they covet," he told the Mexican Congress, "grow, multiply, become the predominant party in the population. . . . These pioneers excite . . . movements which disturb the political state of the country . . . and then follow discontents and dissatisfaction."

In 1829, the Mexican government altered its Texas policy. Determined to curb American influence, the government abolished slavery in Texas. The next year, it forbade further emigration from the United States, and officials began to collect customs duties on goods crossing the Louisiana border. But little changed in Texas. American slave owners freed their slaves and then forced them to sign life indenture contracts. Emigrants still crossed the border and continued to outnumber Mexicans.

Tensions escalated to the brink of war. In October 1835, a skirmish between the colonial militia and the Mexican forces signaled the beginning of hostilities. Sam Houston, one-time governor of Tennessee and army officer, became commander in chief of the Texas forces. Although Texans called the war with Mexico a revolution, a Vermont soldier perhaps more accurately observed, "It is in fact a rebellion."

Mexican dictator and general Antonio López de Santa Anna, hurried north to crush the rebellion with an army of 6,000 conscripts. Although he had a numerical advantage, many of his soldiers were Mayan Indians who had been drafted unwillingly, spoke no Spanish, and were exhausted by the long march. Supply lines were spread thin. Nevertheless, Santa Anna and his men won the initial engagements of the war: the Alamo at San Antonio, which has become an American legend, fell to him, taking Davy Crockett and Jim Bowie with it. So too did the fortress of Goliad, to the southeast.

As he pursued Sam Houston and the Texans towards the San Jacinto River, carelessness proved Santa Anna's undoing. Although fully anticipating an American attack, the Mexican general and his men settled down to their usual siesta on April 21, 1836, without posting an adequate guard. As the Mexicans dozed, the Americans attacked. With cries of "Remember the Alamo! Remember Goliad!" the Texans overcame the army, captured its commander in his slippers, and won the war within 20 minutes. Their casualties numbered only two, while 630 Mexicans lay dead.

With the victory at San Jacinto, Texas gained its independence. Threatened with lynching, Santa Anna saw little choice but to

## The Evolution of Texas

sign the treaty of independence setting the republic's boundary at the Rio Grande. When news of the disastrous events reached Mexico City, however, the Mexican Congress repudiated "an agreement carried out under the threat of death." Mexico maintained that Texas was still part of Mexico.

The new republic started off shakily enough. It was financially unstable, unrecognized by its enemy, rejected by its friends. Although Texans immediately sought admission to the Union, their request failed. Jackson, whose agent in Texas had reported that the republic was so weak that "her future security must depend more upon the weakness and imbecility of her enemy than upon her own strength," was reluctant to act quickly. Strong opposition to annexation of another slave state came from many northerners. The Union was precariously balanced, with 13 free and 13 slave states. Texas would upset that equilibrium in favor of the South. Petitions poured into Congress in 1837 opposing annexation, and John Quincy Adams made repeated speechs denouncing the idea. Annexation was too explosive a political issue to pursue; debate finally died down and then disappeared.

For the next few years, the Lone Star Republic led a precarious existence. Mexico still refused to recognize its independence but could send only an occasional raiding party across the border. Texans skirmished with Mexican bands, did their share of border raiding, and suffered an ignominious defeat in an ill-conceived attempt to capture Santa Fe in 1841. Diplomatic maneuvering in European capitals for financial aid and recognition were only moderately successful. Financial ties with the United States increased, however, as trade grew and many Americans invested in Texas bonds and lands.

Texas became headline news again in 1844. "It is the greatest question of the age," an Alabama expansionist declared, "and I predict will agitate the country more than all the other public questions ever have." He was right. Although President John Tyler reopened the question of annexation, hoping that Texas would ensure his reelection, the issue literally exploded. It brought to life powerful sectional, national, and political tensions. Southern Dem-

ocrats insisted that the future of the South hinged on the annexation of Texas. "Now is the time to vindicate and save our institutions," John C. Calhoun proclaimed. His supporters hoped that by exploiting the Texas issue, Calhoun would win the White House.

Other wings of the Democratic party capitalized more successfully on the issue, however. Lewis Cass, Stephen Douglas of Illinois, and Robert Walker of Mississippi vigorously supported annexation, not because it would expand slavery, a topic they were eager to avoid, but because it would spread the benefits of American civilization. Their arguments, classic examples of the basic tenets of Manifest Destiny, put the question into a national context of expanding American freedom. So powerfully did they link Texas to Manifest Destiny and avoid sec-

*James K. Polk, elected by a narrow margin in 1844, was a staunch expansionist. Though his lame duck predecessor annexed Texas before he took office, it was Polk who fought against Mexico to retain and expand the territory claimed.*

tional problems that their candidate, James Polk of Tennessee, secured the party's nomination at the Democratic convention in Baltimore in 1844. His platform called for "the reannexation of Texas at the earliest practicable period" and the occupation of the Oregon Territory. Manifest Destiny had come of age.

Whigs tended to oppose annexation, fearing slavery's expansion and the growth of southern power with the addition of another slave state. Democrats were exploiting Manifest Destiny, they insisted, more as a means of securing office than of bringing freedom to Texas.

The Whigs were right that annexation would bring victory to the Democrats. Polk won a close election in 1844. But by the time he took the oath of office in March 1845, Tyler had resolved the question of annexation. In his last months in office, Tyler pushed through Congress a joint resolution admitting Texas to the Union. Unlike a treaty, which required the approval of two-thirds of the Senate and which Tyler had failed to win in 1844, a joint resolution needed only majority support. Nine years after its revolution, Texas finally became part of the Union.

### War with Mexico

When Mexico heard the news of annexation, it immediately severed diplomatic ties with the United States. It was easy for Mexicans to interpret the events from the 1820s on as part of a gigantic American plot with Texas as its object. During the war for Texas independence, American papers, especially those in the South, had enthusiastically hailed the efforts of the rebels, while southern money and volunteers had aided the Texans in their struggle. Now that the Americans had gained Texas, would they want still more?

In his inaugural address in 1845, President Polk pointed out "that our system may easily be extended to the utmost bounds of our territorial limits, and that as it shall be extended the bonds of our Union, so far from being weakened will become stronger." What were those territorial limits? Did they extend into the territory the Mexican government considered as its own?

James Polk, along with many other Ameri-

cans, failed to appreciate how humiliated Mexicans felt over the annexation of Texas or the pressures on its government to respond belligerently. Knowing the extent of Mexican weakness, the president anticipated that Mexico would grant what he wanted. As the Mexicans feared, he had grandiose plans. Polk supported a Texas boundary at the Rio Grande rather than the Nueces River, 150 miles farther north. He was also determined to have California and New Mexico.

Even before the Texans had time to accept the long-awaited invitation to join the Union, rumors were afloat that Mexico planned to invade Texas. As a precautionary move, Polk ordered General Zachary Taylor to move "on or near the Rio Grande." By October 1845, Taylor and 3,500 American troops had reached the Nueces River. The positioning of an American army in Texas did not mean that Polk actually expected war. Rather, he hoped that a show of military force, coupled with secret diplomacy, would bring the desired concessions. In November, the president sent his secret agent, John L. Slidell, to Mexico City with instructions to secure the Rio Grande border and to buy Upper California and New Mexico. When the Mexican government refused to receive Slidell, an angry Polk decided to force Mexico into accepting American terms. He ordered Taylor south to the Rio Grande. To the Mexicans their presence was an act of war since Mexico insisted that the Nueces River was the legitimate boundary. Democratic newspapers and expansionists enthusiastically hailed Polk's provocative decision.

It was only a matter of time before an incident occurred to serve as the American justification for hostilities. In late April, the Mexican government declared a state of defensive war. Two days later, a skirmish broke out between Mexican and American troops. When Polk received Taylor's report, he quickly drafted a war message and presented it to Congress. The President claimed that Mexico had "passed the boundary of the United States . . . invaded our territory and shed American blood upon American soil." "War exists," he claimed, and, he added untruthfully, "notwithstanding all our efforts to avoid it, exists by act of Mexico."

Although Congress passed a declaration of war, the conflict bitterly divided Americans. Many, including Abraham Lincoln, questioned Polk's initial account. Debate continued as American troops swept into Mexico and advanced toward the capital. Although the Mexicans were also fighting Indian tribes on their northern borders, the government refused to admit defeat and negotiate an end to the hostilities. The war dragged on and on. The *American Review*, a Whig paper, proclaimed that the conflict was a "crime over which angels may weep." As Philadelphian Joseph Sill wrote in his diary in October 1847, "There is a widely spread conviction . . . that it is a wicked & disgraceful war."

Yet Polk enjoyed the enthusiastic support of expansionists. Thomas Gibson's men, like all the other soldiers, were eager volunteers. Some expansionists even urged permanent occupation of Mexico. Illinois Democratic senator Sidney Breese told the Senate, "The avowed objects of the war . . . [were] to obtain redress of wrongs, a permanent and honorable peace, and indemnity for the past and security for the future." To secure these goals, Breese could even contemplate permanent occupation with "great ultimate good" to the United States, to Mexico, "and to humanity."

Despite inflated rhetoric, the military stalemate continued. In the end, chance helped draw hostilities to a close. Mexican moderates ap-

## The Mexican War

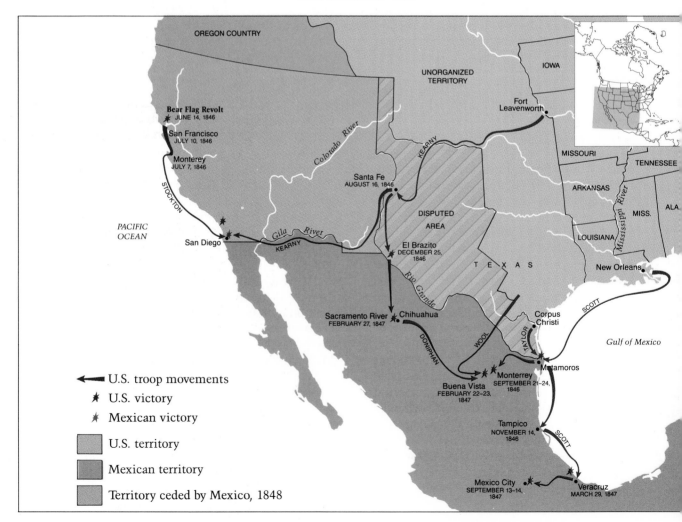

proached Polk's diplomatic representative, Nicholas Trist, who was with the American army in Mexico. In Trist's baggage were detailed, though out-of-date, instructions outlining Polk's requirements: the Rio Grande boundary, Upper California, and New Mexico. Although the president had lost confidence in Trist and had ordered him home, Trist stayed in Mexico to negotiate an end to the war. Having obtained most of Polk's objectives, Trist returned to Washington to an ungrateful president. Apparently Polk had wanted more territory from Mexico for less money. Firing him from his job at the State Department, Polk denounced Trist as an "impudent and unqualified scoundrel."

## California and New Mexico

Although Texas and Mexico dominated the headlines, Polk made it clear from the early days of his presidency that California and New Mexico were part of any resolution of the Mexico crisis. Serious American interest in California dated only from the late 1830s. A few Americans, mostly traders and shopkeepers, had settled in California during the 1820s and 1830s, but they constituted only a small part of the population. Many had married into Californio families and taken Mexican citizenship. But

*Public opinion was divided over Polk's war for Mexican territory. This Currier & Ives print gloats over the U.S. victory at Buena Vista, but many Americans felt the United States had no right to the lands it was fighting for.*

gradual recognition of California's fine harbors, its favorable position for the China trade, and the suspicion that other countries, especially Great Britain, had designs on the region nourished the conviction that it must become part of the United States.

In 1842, a comic dress rehearsal of rebellion occurred when a United States naval commodore, Thomas Catsby Jones, believing that war had broken out with Mexico, sailed into Monterey, forced the Mexican commander to surrender, and proclaimed California's annexation. This "annexation" was more farcical than real. When Jones learned of his error, he apologized and watched the Mexican flag hoisted once more. Yet the arrival of 1,500 American overland emigrants in a three-year period intensified the friction. These newcomers had little interest in blending into Californio society. They and their families wanted an American California. As one resident understood, "Once let the tide of emigration flow toward California, and the American population will soon be sufficiently numerous to play the Texas game."

In 1845, Polk appointed Thomas Larkin, a successful American merchant in Monterey, as his confidential agent. Larkin had clear instructions should Californians decide to break with Mexico. "While the President will make no effort and use no influence to induce California to become one of the free and independent states of the Union," wrote Polk's secretary of state, James Buchanan, to Larkin, "yet if the people should desire to unite their destiny with ours, they would be received as brethren." Polk's efforts to purchase California suggested, however, that he was sensitive to the fragility of American claims to the region. But Santa Anna, who bore the burden of having lost Texas, was in no position to sell. Thus in 1846, California settlers seized the initiative and rose up against Mexican "tyranny." Within a short time, the shabby rebellion of the "exiles from civilization" had succeeded.

New Mexico, bounded by the Louisiana Purchase on the east, Texas on the south, and the Mojave Desert on the west, was also on Polk's list. The area had maintained ties with the United States since the 1820s, when American traders began to bring their goods to Santa Fe.

Economic profits stimulated American territorial appetites. As the oldest and largest Hispanic group in North America (60,000 out of 75,000), however, New Mexicans had little desire for annexation. The unsuccessful attempt by the Texans to capture Santa Fe in 1841 and border clashes the two following years did not enhance the attractiveness of their Anglo neighbors. But standing awkwardly in the path of westward expansion and further isolated from Mexico by the annexation of Texas in 1846, New Mexico's future as a Mexican province was uncertain.

In June 1846, shortly after war with Mexico was declared, the Army of the West, led by Colonel Stephen W. Kearney, left Fort Leavenworth, Kansas, headed for New Mexico. Kearney's orders were to occupy Mexico's northern provinces and to protect the lucrative Santa Fe trade. Two months later, the army took Santa Fe without a shot. The takeover was deceptively easy. Believing that he had secured New Mexico, Kearney set out for California that September. Resistance erupted in New Mexico and California, however. Kearney himself was wounded. In the end, however, superior American military strength won the day. By January 1847, both California and New Mexico were firmly in American hands.

### The Treaty of Guadalupe Hidalgo

Negotiated by Trist and signed on February 2, 1848, the Treaty of Guadalupe Hidalgo dictated the fate of most people living in the Southwest. The United States absorbed the region's 75,000 Spanish-speaking inhabitants and its 150,000 Native Americans and increased its territory by one million square miles. Mexico received $15 million and in 1853 would receive another $10 million for large tracts of land in southern Arizona and New Mexico (the Gadsden Purchase). In the treaty, the United States guaranteed the civil and political rights of former Mexican citizens and their rights to land and also agreed to take care of all American claims against Mexico.

If the territorial gains were immense, some costs were equally huge: 13,000 American lives snuffed out, mostly by diseases like measles and dysentery, and $97 million expended for military operations. But the war was over, and the Americans had won.

### The Oregon Question

Belligerence and war secured vast areas of the Southwest and California for the United States. In the Pacific Northwest, American acquisitiveness faced not a crisis-ridden Mexican government but mighty Great Britain. There diplomacy became the means for territorial gains.

Despite the disputed nature of claims to the Oregon Territory, Polk told the crowd huddled under umbrellas on his inauguration day that "our title to the country of Oregon is 'clear and unquestionable,' . . . already our people are preparing to perfect that title by occupying it with their wives and children." Polk's words reflected American confidence that settlement carried the presumption of possession. But the British did not agree. Although Polk's final address was far less offensive than the first draft of his speech, the British responded angrily. As the London *Times* warned, "Ill regulated, overbearing, and aggressive . . . [Polk's] pretensions amount, if acted upon, to the clearest *causa belli*

*Despite Britain's longstanding claim to the Oregon Territory, thousands of U.S. citizens settled there in the 1840s. By 1857, when this photo of Oregon City was taken, the border with Canada was well defined, and many more thousands of Americans lived in the territory.*

which has yet arisen between Great Britain and the American Union."

Though many in Great Britain judged the president's speech belligerent, Polk correctly identified an American presence in Oregon Territory. Like emigrants to Texas and California, Americans had not hesitated to settle disputed territories in the Northwest. Between 1842 and 1845, the number of Americans in Oregon grew from 400 to over 5,000. Most located south of the Columbia River in the Willamette Valley. By 1843, these settlers had written a constitution and soon after elected a legislature. At the same time, the stage was set for an eventual compromise. British interests in the area were declining as the fur trade dwindled. Attractive commercial opportunities elsewhere were opening up; colonies like New Zealand lured English settlers away from the Pacific Northwest.

The flamboyance of Polk's posture and the expansive nature of American claims made mediation difficult, however. The Democratic platform and the slogan that had helped elect Polk laid claim to a boundary of 54°40′. In fact, Polk was not willing to go to war with Great Britain for Oregon. Privately, he considered reasonable a boundary at the 49th parallel, which would extend the existing Canadian-American border to the Pacific and secure the harbors of the Puget Sound for the United States. But Polk could hardly admit this to his Democratic supporters, who had so enthusiastically shouted "Fifty-four forty or fight" during the recent campaign.

Not long after his inaugural, Polk offered his compromise to Great Britain. But his tone was so offensive that the British minister rejected the offer at once. Polk compounded his error by gracelessly withdrawing the suggestion. In his year-end address to Congress in 1845, the president created more diplomatic difficulties. Urging the protection of American settlers in Oregon, the president again publicly claimed that Oregon belonged to the United States. In addition, he asked Congress to give Britain the one-year notice required by previous agreements to terminate joint occupation there.

Discussions about Oregon occupied Congress for months in early 1846. Debate, however, gradually revealed deep divisions about Oregon and the possibility of war with Great Britain. It was evident that despite slogans, most Americans did not want to fight for all of Oregon and preferred to resolve the crisis diplomatically. As war with Mexico loomed, this task became more urgent.

The British, too, were eager to settle the issue. In June 1846, the British agreed to accept the 49th-parallel boundary if Vancouver Island remained in British hands. Polk took the unorthodox step of forwarding this proposal to the Senate for a preliminary response. Within days, the Senate overwhelmingly approved the compromise. Escaping some of the responsibility for retreating from slogans by sharing it with the Senate, Polk ended the crisis just a few weeks before the declaration of war with Mexico.

As these events show, Manifest Destiny was an idea that supported and justified expansionist policies. It corresponded, at the most basic level, to what Americans believed, that expansion was both necessary and right. As early as 1816, American geography books pictured the nation's western boundary at the Pacific and included Texas. Poems, essays, and stories about winning the West, enlivened with illustrations of covered wagons and Indian fighters, were standard reading fare. Popular literature typically described

### The Oregon Country

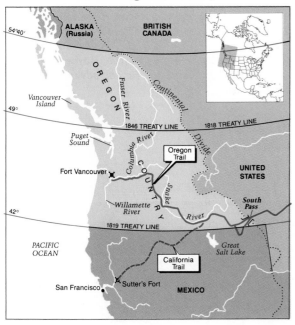

Indians as a dying race that had failed in the basic tasks of cultivating the soil and conquering the wilderness. Mexicans were tossed off as "unjust and injurious neighbor[s]." Only whites could make the wilderness flower. Thus, as lands east of the Mississippi filled up, Americans automatically called upon familiar ideas to justify expansion.

## GOING WEST

After diplomacy and war clarified the status of the western territories, Americans lost little time in moving there. What had been a trickle of emigrants became a flood. During the 1840s, 1850s, and 1860s, thousands of Americans left their homes for the frontier. By 1860, California alone had 380,000 settlers.

Some chose to migrate by sea. Although the trip was expensive, one could sail from Atlantic or Gulf Coast ports around South America to the West Coast or take ship for Panama, cross the isthmus by land, and then continue by sea. Most emigrants, however, chose land routes. In 1843, the first large party succeeded in crossing the plains and mountains to Oregon. More followed. Between 1841 and 1867, some 350,000 traveled over the Overland trails to California or to Oregon, while others trekked part of the way to intermediate points like Colorado and Utah.

### The Emigrants

Most of the emmigrants headed for the Far West, where slavery was prohibited, were white and American-born. They came from the Midwest and Upper South. A few free blacks made the trip to the West Coast as well. Pioneer Margaret Frink remembered seeing "a Negro woman . . . tramping along through the heat and dust, carrying a cast iron black stove on her head, with her provisions and a blanket piled on top . . . bravely pushing on for California." Emigrants from the Deep South usually selected Arkansas or Texas as their destination, and many brought their slaves with them. By 1840, over 11,000 slaves toiled in Texas and 20,000 in Arkansas.

The many pioneers who kept journals during the five- to six-month overland trip captured the human dimension of emigrating. Their journals, usually their only contribution to the his-

torical record, focused on day-to-day events and expressed some of the thoughts and emotions experienced on the long journey west. One migrant, Lodisa Frizzell, described her feelings at parting in 1852:

> Who is there that does not recollect their first night when started on a long journey, the well known voices of our friends still ring in our ears, the parting kiss feels still warm upon our lips, and that last separating word FAREWELL! sinks deeply into the heart. It may be the last we ever hear from some or all of them, and to those who start . . . there can be no more solemn scene of parting only at death.

Virgil Pringle's diary entry in 1846 recorded less emotionally the breakaway from a familiar life.

*The belief that white Americans had a right and an obligation to tame the wilderness encouraged many to move west into the newly annexed territories. The hardships of the journey were glorified as sacrifices made for the advancement of civilization.*

"Left Hickory Grove [his farm] this day with my family for Oregon."

Like Pringle and Frizzell, most emigrants traveled with family and relatives. Only during the gold rush years did large numbers of migrants, usually young men, travel independently. Migration was a family experience, mostly involving men and women from their late twenties to early forties. A sizable number of them had recently married. Few of the migrants were old. And for most, migration was a familiar experience. Like other geographically mobile Americans, emigrants to the Far West had earlier moved to other frontiers, often as children or as newlyweds. The difference was the vast distance to this frontier and the seemingly final separation from home.

## Migrants' Motives

What led so many Americans to sell most of their possessions and embark on an unknown future thousands of miles away? Many believed that frontier life would offer rich opportunities.

A popular folksong expressed this widespread conviction:

> Since times has been hard, I'll tell you sweet-
> heart,
> I've a notion to leave off my plow and my cart,
> Away to Californy a journey pursue,
> To double my fortunes as other men do.

The kinds of opportunities emigrants expected varied widely. Thousands sought riches in the form of gold nuggets and gold dust. Others anticipated making their fortune through commerce, since merchants, shopkeepers, and peddlers would all be needed to supply settlers with the goods of civilization. Some emigrants intended to be among the first on the frontier in order to speculate in land. They planned to acquire large blocks of public lands and then sell them later to settlers at a handsome profit. The possibility of professional rewards gained from practicing law or medicine on the frontier attracted still others.

Most migrants dreamed of bettering their

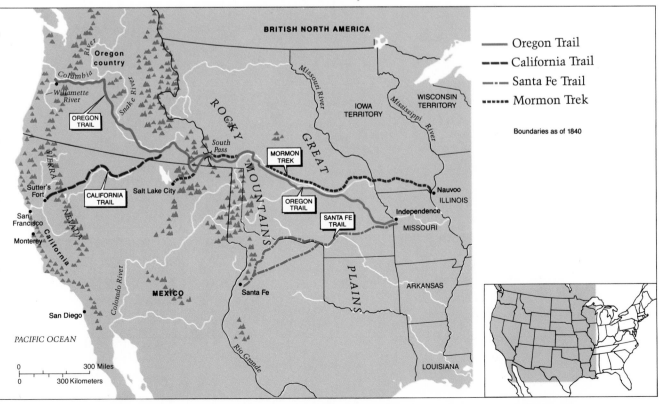

Overland Trails, 1840

# Western Population Advance, 1830–1850

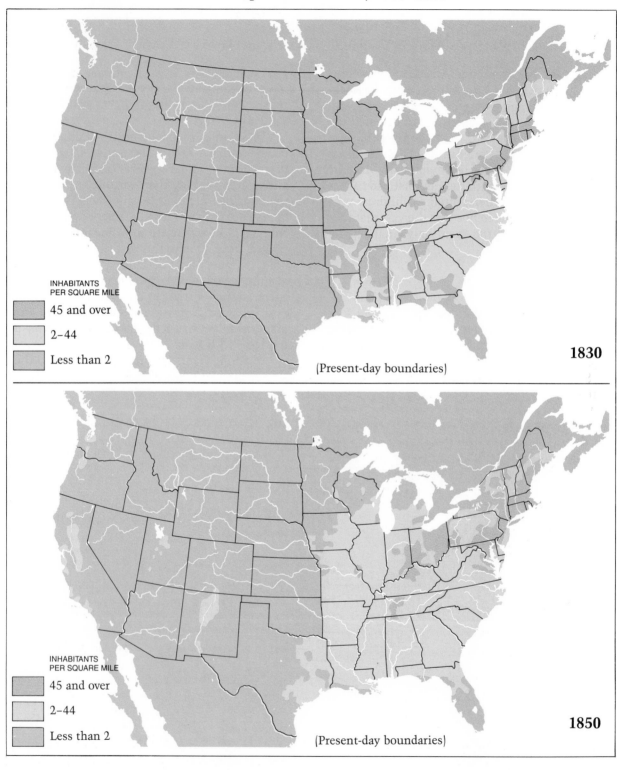

INHABITANTS
PER SQUARE MILE

45 and over

2–44

Less than 2

**1830**

(Present-day boundaries)

INHABITANTS
PER SQUARE MILE

45 and over

2–44

Less than 2

**1850**

(Present-day boundaries)

life by cultivating the land. As one settler explained, "The motive that induced us to part with pleasant associates and dear friends of our childhood days, was to obtain from the government of the United States a grant of land that 'Uncle Sam' had promised." Federal and state land policies made the acquisition of land increasingly alluring. Preemption acts during the 1830s and 1840s gave "squatters" the right to settle public lands before they were offered for sale and then allowed them to purchase these lands at the minimum price once they came on the market. At the same time, the amount of land a family had to buy shrank to only 40 acres. In 1862, the Homestead Act went further by offering 160 acres of government land free to citizens or future citizens over 21 who lived on the property, improved it, and paid a small registration fee. Oregon's land policy, which predated the Homestead Act, was even more generous. It awarded a single man 320 acres of free land and a married man 640 acres provided he occupied his claim for four years and made improvements.

Some emigrants hoped the West would restore them to health. Settlers from the Mississippi valley wished to escape the region's debilitating agues and fevers. Doctors advised those suffering the dreaded tuberculosis that the long out-of-doors trip and the western climate might cure them. Even invalids grasped at the advice offered by one doctor in 1850 who urged them to "attach themselves to the companies of emigrants bound for Oregon or Upper California."

Others pursued religious or cultural missions in the West. As Americans moved to successive frontiers, a lively debate arose, especially among those originally from the Northeast, as to whether expansion would signal the decline of religion and culture. Thus missionary couples like David and Catherine Blaine, who settled in Seattle when it was a frontier outpost, determined to bring Protestantism and education west. Stirred by the stories they had heard of the "deplorable . . . morals" on the frontier, they willingly left the comforts of home to evangelize and educate westerners. Still others, like the Mormons, made the long trek to Utah to establish a society in conformity with their religious beliefs.

Not everyone who dreamed of setting off for the frontier could do so, however. Unlike the moves to earlier frontiers, the trip to the Far West involved considerable expense. The sea route, while probably the most comfortable, was the most costly. Guidebooks estimated that the trip around Cape Horn came to $600 per person. For the same sum, four people could make the overland trip. And if the emigrants sold their wagons and oxen at the journey's end, the final expenses might amount to only $220. Clearly, however, the initial financial outlay was considerable enough to rule out the trip for the very poor. Despite increasingly liberal land policies, migration to the Far West (with the exception of group migration to Utah) was a movement of middle-class Americans.

### The Overland Trails

The trip started for most emigrants in the late spring when they left their homes and headed for starting points in Iowa and Missouri: Council Bluffs, Independence, Westport, St. Joseph. There companies of wagons gathered, and when grass was up for the stock, usually by the middle of May, they set out. Emigrant trains first followed the valley of the Platte River. Making only 15 miles a day, they slowly wound their way through the South Pass of the Rockies heading for destinations in California or Oregon.

Emigrants found the first part of the trip novel and even enjoyable. The scenery, with its spring and early summer flowers, was new. Familiar chores were a challenge out in the open. The traditional division of labor known at home persisted. Generally, men did the "outdoor" work. They drove and repaired the wagons, ferried cattle and wagons across rivers, hunted, and stood guard at night. Women labored at domestic chores, caring for children, cooking meals, and washing clothes. Young children stayed out of the way in wagons, while older brothers and sisters walked and lent a hand to their elders. Many of the children later remembered the trip as an exciting adventure. Sometimes a day off from traveling provided a chance for fun. Trains might stop to observe the Sabbath, allowing men and animals time to rest and the women an opportunity to catch up on the laundry.

Nineteenth-century journals kept by hundreds of ordinary men and women traveling west on the overland trails constitute a rich source for exploring the nature of the westward experience. They are also an excellent example of how private sources can be used to deepen our understanding of the past. Diaries, journals, and letters all provide us with a personal perspective on major happenings. Since these sources tend to focus on the concrete, they convey some sense of the texture of daily life in the nineteenth century, daily routines and amusements, clothing, habits, and interactions with family and friends. They also provide evidence of the varied concerns, attitudes, and prejudices of the writers, thus providing a test of commonly accepted generalizations about individual and group behavior.

Like any historical source, diaries, journals, and letters must be used carefully. If possible, it is important to note the writer's age, sex, class, and regional identification. Although this information may not always be available, some of the writer's background can usually be deduced from what he or she has written. It is also important to consider for what purpose and for whom the document was composed. This information will help to explain the tone or character of the source and what has been included or left out. It is, of course, important to avoid generalizing too much from one or even several similar sources. Only after reading many diaries, letters, and journals is it possible to make valid generalizations about life in the past.

Here we present excerpts from two travel journals of the 1850s. Few of the writers considered their journals to be strictly private. Often they were intended as a family record or as information for friends back home. Therefore, material of a personal nature has often been excluded. Nineteenth-century Americans referred to certain topics, such as pregnancy, only indirectly, or not at all.

The first excerpts come from Mary Bailey's 1852 journal. Mary was 22 when she crossed the plains to California with her 32-year-old doctor husband. Originally a New Englander, Mary had lived in Ohio for six years before moving west. The Baileys were reasonably prosperous and were able to restock necessary supplies on the road west. Robert Robe was 30 when he crossed along the same route a year earlier than the Baileys, headed for Oregon. Robert was a native of Ohio and a Presbyterian minister.

As you read these excerpts, notice what each journal reveals about the trip west. What kinds of challenges did the emigrants face on their journey? Do these correspond to the picture you may have formed from novels, television, and movies? What kinds of work needed to be done, and who did it? Can you see any indication of a division of work based on sex? What kind of interactions appear to have occurred between men and women on the trip? What does the pattern tell us about nineteenth-century society? How does the painting of the "emigrant train" reinforce the journal accounts of men's and women's roles?

Each of these journals should be read in its entirety, but these short excerpts do suggest that men and women, as they traveled west, may have had different concerns and different perspectives on the journey. In what ways do the two accounts differ, and how are they similar?

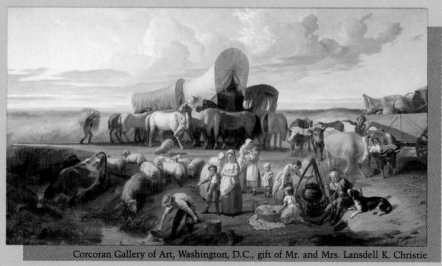

Corcoran Gallery of Art, Washington, D.C., gift of Mr. and Mrs. Lansdell K. Christie

***Benjamin Franklin Reinhart*, The Emigrant Train Bedding Down for the Night, *1867***

## A JOURNAL OF MARY STUART BAILEY

Wednesday, April 13, 1852
Left our hitherto happy home in Sylvania amid the tears and parting kisses of dear friends, many of whom were endeared to me by their kindness shown to me when I was a stranger in a strange land, when sickness and death visited our small family & removed our darling, our only child in a moment, as it were. Such kindness I can never forget. . . .

Friday, 21st [May]
Rained last night. Slept in the tent for the first time. I was Yankee enough to protect myself by pinning up blankets over my head. I am quite at home in my tent.

12:00 Have traveled in the rain all day & we are stuck in the mud. I sit in the wagon writing while the men are at work doubling the teams to draw us out. . . .

Sunday, 23rd.
Walked to the top of the hill where I could be quiet & commune with nature and nature's God. This afternoon I was annoyed by something very unpleasant & shed many tears and felt very unhappy. . . .

Thursday, 4th [June]
Very cold this morning after the shower. . . . We stopped on the banks of the Platte to take dinner. I am sitting on the banks of the Platte with my feet almost in the water. Have been writing to my Mother. How I wish some of my own relations wih me. . . .

Sunday, 4th [July]
Started at 3 o'clock to find feed or know where it was. Had to go 4 or 5 miles off the road. Found water & good grass. Camped on the sand with sage roots for fuel. It is wintery, cold & somewhat inclined to rain, not pleasant. Rather a dreary Independence Day. We speak of our friends at home. We think they are thinking of us. . . .

Monday, 12th.
Stayed in camp another day to get our horse better. He is much improved. It is cold enough. Washed in the morning & had the sick headache in the afternoon. . . .

Thursday, 12th [August]
Very warm. Slept until we stopped to take breakfast. Mr. Patterson starts as soon as light & stops in the heat of the day to rest the animals. We do not have much time to do anything except 4 or 5 hours in the middle of the day. . . .

Friday, 17th [September]
Have been confined ever since Monday with ague in. my face which is very much swollen. Have suffered very much. We are now in Carson Valley. Plenty of trees but the country is very barren.

Saturday, 18th.
Very pleasant, delightful weather. Feel much better today. We are not stirring this afternoon. We have heard of a great deal of suffering, people being thrown out on the desert to die & being picked up & brought to the hospital. . . .

Tuesday, November 8th
Sacramento city has been nearly consumed. The Dr. has had all his instruments & a good deal of clothing burned, loss not exceeding $300. It really seems as though it was not right for us to come to California & lose so much. I do not think that we shall be as well off as at home.

Sandra L. Myres, ed., *Ho for California! Women's Overland Diaries from the Huntington Library* (San Marino, Calif.: The Henry E. Huntington Library, 1980).

## A JOURNAL OF ROBERT ROBE

[May] 19. [1851] A fine day. The first spent in travelling on the plains of the Platte river.

20. Continued our journey up the Platte valley which I would judge to be here some 12 miles wide on this side of the river. The only game seen here are the antelope and wolf beside some wild fowl.

21. A rainy morning started early passed on old Pawnee village in ruins. The houses are constructed by placing timbers in forks and upon these without placing upright poles then rushes bound with [illegible] and finally earth. Chimney in center. Day became more & more rainy and wound up with a storm which beggared description.

22. Bluff approach the river—travelling less monotonous river finely skirted with timber.

23. Roads very muddy in afternoon. Today our waggon severed itself from our former companions & joined a company of Californians.

24. Before starting a trader direct from Ft. Kearney arrived at our camp. He informs us it is yet 25 miles thither. Travelling is by no means dangerous a waggon of provisions passing with only three guards. In the afternoon passed the entrance of the Independence Weston & St. Jo roads. Emigrants became more numerous.

25. Passed Fort Kearney this morning and after a short drive encamped. Having conversed with some of the soldiers I find they consider life very monotonous.

26. Roads heavy—short drive—a storm.

27. High Bluffs on the opposite side of river approach and present a beautiful appearance. At night a fearful storm.

28. Roads heavy nothing singular.

29. Have arrived in the region abounding in Buffalo. At noon a considerable herd came in sight. the first any of us had ever seen. thus now for the chase—the horsemen proved too swift in pursuit and frightened them into the Bluffs without capturing any—the footmen pursued however and killed three pretty good success for the first.

30. Nothing remarkable today.

31. Game being abundant we resolved to rest our stock and hunt today—Started in the morning on foot. Saw probably 1000 Buffalo. Shot at several and killed one. Where ever we found them wolves were prowling around as if to guard them. Their real object is however no doubt to seize the calves as their prey. Saw a town of Prairie dogs, they are nearly as large as a gray squirrel. They bark fiercely when at a little distance but on near approach flee to their holes. Wherever they are we see numerous owls. After a very extensive ramble and having seen a variety of game we returned at sunset with most voracious appetites.

June 1. The Bluffs become beautifully undulating losing their precipitous aspect and the country further back is beautifully rolling prairie.

2. In the evening camped beside our old friends Miller and Dovey. They had met with a great loss this morning their 3 horses having taken fright at a drove of buffalo and ran entirely away. Some of our company killed more buffalo this evening & a company went in the night with teams to bring them in.

3. Spent the forenoon in an unsuccessful search for the above mentioned horses. In the afternoon pursued & caught our company after

4. Crossed the south fork of the Platte at 2 P.M.

*Pacific Northwest Quarterly* 19 (Jan. 1928): 52–63.

As the trip lengthened, difficulties multiplied. Cholera often took a heavy toll. Trouble with Indians, which began to intensify only in the 1850s, made emigrants jumpy during the second half of the trip. (Between 1840 and 1860, about 400 emigrants were killed by Indians, 90 percent of them during the second half of the trip.) Traveling grew more arduous as deserts and mountains replaced rolling prairies.

Since it was imperative to get across the final mountain ranges of the Sierras and Cascades before the first snowfall, there was a pressing need to push ever onward. Animals weakened by constant travel, poor feed, and bad water sickened, collapsed, and often died. As families faced the harsh realities of travel, they had to lighten their wagons by throwing out possessions so lovingly brought from home. Food grew scarce.

The familiar division of responsibilities broke down. Women found themselves driving wagons, loading them, even helping to drag them over rocky mountain trails. Their husbands worked frantically with the animals and the wagons as the time of the first snowfall drew closer. Tempers frayed among tired, overworked, and anxious families. Finally, five or six months after setting out, emigrants arrived, exhausted and often penniless, in Oregon or California. As one wrote on a September day in 1854, her journey had ended "which for care, fatigue, tediousness, perplexities and dangers of various kinds, can not be excelled."

The strains of the trip led some groups to draw up rules and elect officers. This did not prevent dissension, however. Many companies split because of arguments over the pace of travel or the number of rest stops or because some changed their minds about their eventual

*The adventure of the trail turned into a nightmare for many, as the terrain grew rougher and food scarcer in the second half of the journey.*

destination. Family harmony often collapsed under the strain of increased work loads, the irritations of travel, and crises of sickness and even death. Mary Power, who with her husband and three children crossed in 1853, revealed exasperation and depression in her journal: "I felt my courage must fail me, for there we were in a strange land, almost without anything to eat, a team that was not able to pull an empty wagon." In a letter she was even more candid: "I felt as though myself and the little ones were at the mercy of a madman." Men too lost nerve as they confronted the hazards of travel. Oregon-bound John Minto described coming upon a father of four, "lying on his back upon a rock, taking the rain in his face, seemingly given up all thought of manly struggle," while the cry of Indians sent some men in another train into their wagons to hide.

## LIVING ON THE FRONTIER

When emigrants finally arrived at their destinations, their feelings ranged from acute disappointment to buoyant enthusiasm. But whether elated or depressed, they had no choice but to start anew. As they turned toward building a new life in the West, they naturally drew upon

their experiences back east. "Pioneers though we are, and proud of it, we are not content with the wilds . . . with the idleness of the land, the rudely construct[ed] log cabin," one Oregon settler explained. "Pioneers are not that kind of folks."

## The Agricultural Frontier

Pioneer farmers faced the urgent task of establishing their homesteads and beginning agricultural operations. First, the family had to locate a suitable claim. Clearing the land and constructing a crude shelter followed. Only then could crops be planted. Since emigrants had brought few of their possessions west, their work was more difficult. A young Oregon bride who set up housekeeping in the 1840s with only a stew kettle and three knives was not unusual. A letter from Sarah Everett to her sister-in-law in New York State told the tale of hardship. Pleased with the gift of pretty trimmings, Sarah confessed, "I am a very old woman. My face is thin sunken and wrinkled, my hands bony and withered and hard—I shall look strangely I fear with your nice undersleeves and coquettish cherry bows." Sarah was 29 years old.

After months of intense interaction with other travelers, families now found themselves alone on their claims. The typical frontier household consisted of parents with one to four children. No wonder the pioneers often felt lonely and thought longingly of old friends or that women helped men with their work while men assisted their wives in domestic chores like washing.

For several years, this relative isolation was the rule. One pioneer remembered, "We were . . . 'all told,' eleven families within a radius of six or eight miles, widely separated by our holdings and three hundred and twenty acres to each family. In those days anyone residing within twenty miles was considered a neighbor." But the isolation usually ended within a few years as most frontier farming areas attracted new emigrants and old settlers seeking better claims.

As rural communities grew, settlers worked to establish schools, churches, and clubs. These organizations drew together people from different places and backgrounds and helped mold them into a new community. They also served to redefine acceptable forms of behavior and remind members of conventional standards and beliefs.

The determination to reestablish familiar institutions was most apparent in politics and law. In Oregon, for example, the pioneers set up a political system based on eastern models before the status of the territory was resolved. Before permanent schools or churches existed, men resumed the familiar political rituals of voting, electioneering, and talking politics. They were also going to court to resolve controversies and to ensure law and order. Although modern movies and novels suggest that violence was a part of everyday life on the frontier, this was not true on the farming frontier. Courts, rather than rough and ready vigilante groups, usually handled the occasional violence.

Setting up a common school system was more difficult and less urgent in the eyes of many frontier communities than beginning political life. Few settlers initially thought education important enough to tax themselves for permanent public schools. There were some schools, of course. But most operated sporadically and only for students who could pay at least part of the fees.

Various obstacles hindered organized religion. Although settlers often attended early church services no matter what the denomination, community growth proved a mixed blessing. When confirmed believers gathered in their own churches, they often discovered to their dismay that the congregation was not large enough to sustain the new church financially. Nor were converts plentiful, for many settlers had grown out of the habit of regular churchgoing and giving. In early Seattle, Catherine and David Blaine were shocked at their situation. "Observation and experience have taught us since we left home," David remarked, "the unwelcome lesson that separation from gospel influences has rendered them quite indifferent to gospel truth." Catherine believed, "This is an awfully wicked country."

The chronic shortage of cash on the frontier was a factor that retarded the growth of both schools and churches. Until farmers could send their goods to market, the amount of cash they had to spare was limited. Geographic mobility also contributed to institutional instability. Up to three-quarters of the population of a frontier county might vanish within a ten-year period as emigrants left to seek better claims. Some farmed in as many as four different locations until they found a satisfactory claim. Institutions relying on continuing personal and financial support suffered accordingly.

Yet even if their efforts to re-create familiar institutional life often faltered, settlers did not lose sight of their goals. Newspapers, journals, and books, which circulated early on the frontier, reinforced familiar values and norms and kept determination strong. As more and more settlers arrived, the numbers willing to support educational, religious, and cultural institutions grew. In the end, as one pioneer pointed out, "We have a telegraph line from the East, a daily rail road train, daily mail and I am beginning to feel quite civilized. And here ended my pioneer experience." Only 16 years had passed since this emigrant had crossed the Plains.

Although the notion of special economic and social opportunities on the frontier nourished emigration, often the dream was more illusory than real. Western society rapidly acquired a social and economic structure similar to the one in the East. Frontier newspapers referred to leading settlers as the "better" sort, giving voice to an emerging world of social and economic distinctions. The appearance of workers for hire and tenant farmers also pointed to real economic differences and hinted at the difficulties those on the bottom would face as they tried to improve their situation.

Their widespread geographic mobility also indicates that many found it difficult to capitalize on the benefits of homesteading. Census data show that those who moved were generally less successful than the core of stable residents, who became the community's economic and social leaders. Of course, those on the move may have believed that fortune would finally smile on them at their next stop. But one wife was not so hopeful. When her husband announced that they were to move once again, she commented, "Perhaps I was not quite so enthusiastic as he. I seemed to have heard all this before."

### The Mining Frontier

On the mining frontier, rapidly circulating tales of prospectors who had reportedly struck it rich fueled the fantasies of fortune hunters. The news of discovery of gold in 1848 in California swept the country like "wildfire," in the words of one Missouri emigrant. Thousands set out as fast as they could to cash in on the bonanza. Within a year, California's population ballooned from 14,000 to almost 100,000. By 1852, that figure had more than doubled.

Like migrants to the agricultural frontier, the forty-niners were mostly young (in 1850 over half the people in California were in their twenties). Unlike pioneers headed for the rural frontier, however, the gold seekers were unmarried, predominantly male, and heterogeneous. Of those pouring into California in 1849, about 80 percent came from the United States, 8 percent from Mexico, and 5 percent from South America. The rest came from Europe and Asia. Few were as interested in settling the West as they were in extracting its precious metals and returning home rich.

California was the first and most dramatic of the western mining frontiers. But others sprang up. Rumors of gold sent between 25,000 and 30,000 emigrants, many from California, to Brit-

*San Francisco in 1853 had grown from a shantytown to a city with board sidewalks and kerosene streetlamps. The bay, choked with abandoned ships in 1849 when crewmen deserted to go to the goldfields, was partially filled in to make level land for new buildings.*

ish Columbia in Canada in 1858. A year later, the news of gold strikes in Colorado set off another frantic rush for fortune. Precious metals discovered in the Pacific Northwest early in the decade and in Montana and Idaho a few years later kept dreams alive and the prospectors moving. In the mid-1870s, yet another discovery of gold, this time in the Black Hills of North Dakota, attracted hordes of fortune seekers.

The discovery of gold or silver spurred immediate, if usually short-lived, growth. In contrast to the agricultural frontier, where early settlers were isolated and the community expanded gradually, the mining frontier came to life almost overnight with the discovery of gold or silver. Mining camps, ramshackle and often hastily constructed, soon housed hundreds or even thousands of miners and people serving them. Merchants, saloonkeepers, cooks, druggists, gamblers, and prostitutes hurried into new boom areas as fast as prospectors. Usually about half of the residents of any mining camp were there to relieve the miners of their profits, not to prospect themselves.

Given the motivation, character, and ethnic

*Few women settled in early mining camps, but they often found that profitable opportunities awaited them in the predominantly male environment.*

## Western Mining Frontier

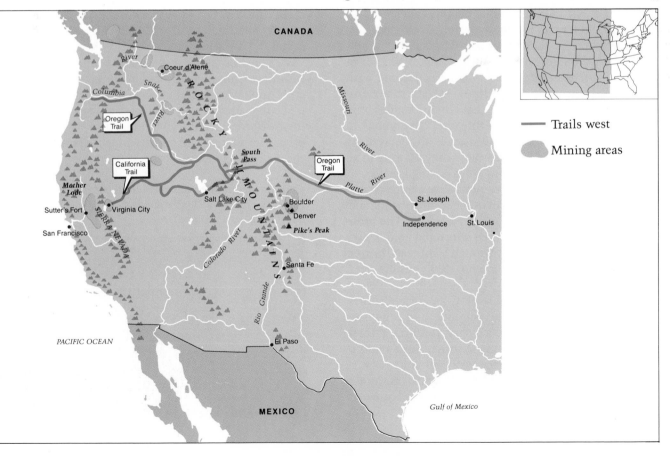

diversity of those flocking to boom towns, and given the feeble attempts to set up local government in what was perceived as a temporary community, it was hardly surprising that mining life was often disorderly. Racial antagonism between American miners and foreigners, whom they labeled "greasers" (Mexicans), "chinks" (Chinese), "keskedees" (Frenchmen), and lesser "breeds," led to ugly riots and lynchings. Fistfights, drunkenness, even murder occurred often enough to become part of the lore of the gold rush. Wrote one woman, "In the short space of twenty four days, we have had murders, fearful accidents, bloody deaths, a mob, whippings, a hanging, an attempt at suicide, and a fatal duel."

If mining life was usually not this violent, it tolerated behavior that would have been unacceptable farther east. Miners were not trying to re-create eastern communities but to get rich. So convinced were they of the raucous and immoral character of mining communities that married men hesitated to bring wives and families west. As one declared, "I would much prefer that a wife of mine should board in a respectable bawd house in the city of New York than live anywhere in the city of San Francisco."

Although the lucky few struck it rich or at least made enough money to return home with pride intact, miners' journals and letters to family and friends reveal that many made only enough to keep going. Wrote one, "Everybody in the States who has friends here is always writing for them to come home. Now they all long to go home . . . But it is hard for a man to leave . . . with nothing . . . I have no pile yet, but you can bet your life I will never come home until I have something more than when I started." The problem was that easily mined silver and gold deposits soon ran out. Although Chinese miners proved adept at finding what early miners overlooked, the remaining rich deposits lay deeply embedded in rock or gravel. Cooperative efforts, capital, technological experience, and expensive machinery all were necessary to extract these metals. Eventually, mining turned into a corporate industrial concern, with miners as wage earners. As early as 1852, the changing nature of mining in California had transformed most of the shaggy miners into wage workers.

Probably 5 percent of early gold rush emigrants to California were women and children. Many of the women also anticipated getting "rich in a hurry." Because there were so few of them, the cooking, nursing, laundry, and hotel services women provided were highly valued. When Luzena Wilson arrived in Sacramento, a miner offered to pay her $10 for a biscuit. That night, Luzena dreamt she saw "crowds of bearded miners striking gold from the earth with every blow of the pick, each one seeming to leave a share for me." Yet it was all very hard work, and some wondered if the money compensated for the exhaustion. As Mary Ballou thought it over, she decided, "I would not advise any Lady to come out here and suffer to toil and fatigue I have suffered for the sake of a little gold." As men's profits shrank, so too did those of the women who served them.

Some of the first women to arrive on the mining frontier were prostitutes. They rejected the hard labor of cooking and washing that "respectable" women performed, hoping that the sex ratio would make their profession especially profitable. Prostitutes may have comprised as much as 20 percent of California's female population in 1850, and they probably vastly outnumbered respectable women in early mining camps. During boom days, they made good money and sometimes won a recognized place in society. But prostitutes always ran risks in a disorderly environment. They were more often the victims of murder and violence than the recipients of courtesy.

*Coming west not to advance civilization but to get rich, miners usually made no pretense of upholding eastern manners.*

The Mexicans, South Americans, Chinese, and small numbers of blacks seeking their fortunes in California soon discovered the unpleasant truth. Though each of these groups made substantial contributions to California's growth, racial discrimination flourished vigorously in the land of golden promise. At first, American miners hoped to force foreigners out of the gold fields altogether. But an attempt to declare mining illegal for all foreigners failed. Next, a tax was imposed on foreign miners. So high was the tax that thousands of Mexicans left the mines, while the Chinese found other jobs in San Francisco and Sacramento. As business stagnated in mining towns, however, white miners had second thoughts about the levy and reduced it. By 1870, when the tax was declared unconstitutional, the Chinese, who had paid 85 percent of it, had "contributed" $5 million to California for the right to prospect. The hostility that led to

*Photographed in the 1870s, the near ghost town of Ophir City, Nevada, attests to the boom-and-bust pattern of the mining frontier. A few individuals continued to prospect, hoping all their lives to strike one rich vein.*

this legislation also fed widespread violence against the Chinese and Mexicans.

American blacks found that their skin color placed them in a situation akin to that of foreigners. Deprived of the vote, forbidden to testify in civil or criminal cases involving whites, excluded from the bounties of the state's homestead law, blacks led a precarious existence. When news arrived of the discovery of gold in British Columbia in the late 1850s, hundreds of blacks as well as thousands of Chinese left the state hoping that the Canadian frontier would be more hospitable than California.

Alluring as the mining frontier was, men's and women's fantasies of dazzling riches rarely came true. The ghost towns of the West testify to the typical pattern: boom, bust, decay, death. The empty streets and rotting buildings stood as symbols of dashed hopes and disappointed dreams.

Yet gold had a tremendous impact on the West as whole. Between 1848 and 1883, California mines supplied two-thirds of the country's gold. This gold transformed San Francisco from a sleepy town into a bustling metropolis. It fueled the agricultural and commercial development of California and Oregon as miners became a market for goods and services. Gold built harbors, railroads, and irrigation systems not only in California and Oregon but all over the West. Though only a few people made large fortunes, both the region and the nation profited from gold.

### The Mormon Frontier

In the decades before 1860, most emigrants headed for the Far West. Along the way, some stopped to rest and buy supplies in Salt Lake City, the heart of the Mormon state of Deseret. There they encountered a society that seemed familiar and orderly, yet foreign and shocking. Visitors admired the attractively laid out town with its irrigation ditches, gardens, and tidy houses. But as they noted the decorous nature of everyday life, they searched for signs of rebellion in the faces of Mormon women and gossiped about polygamy. Emigrants who opposed slavery were fond of equating the position of the black slave with that of the Mormon wife. They were amazed that so few Mormon women seemed interested in escaping from the bonds of plural marriage.

Violent events had driven the Mormons to the arid Great Basin area. Joseph Smith's murder in 1844 marked no end to the persecution of his followers. By the fall of 1846, angry mobs had succeeded in chasing the last of the "Saints" out of Nauvoo, Illinois. As they struggled to join their advance groups at temporary camps in Iowa, Smith's successor, Brigham Young, realized that the survival of his flock of more than 3,000 could best be ensured by fleeing the country altogether. The Saints must create the kingdom of God anew, somewhere in the West, far removed from the United States, that "Babylon" of corruption and injustice.

The Mexican war unexpectedly furthered Mormon plans. At first, most Mormons proba-

*Successor after the murder of Joseph Smith in 1844, Brigham Young led the Mormons to the remote Great Salt Lake Basin, at the time part of Mexico's territory.*

bly agreed with Hosea Stout, who was glad "to learn of the war," hoping it "might never end until the States were entirely destroyed, for they had driven us into the wilderness, and now were laughing at our calamaties [sic]." But Brigham Young realized that war might provide capital needed for the new Mormon kingdom. By raising 500 Mormon young men for Kearney's Army of the West, Young acquired vital resources. The battalion's advance pay bought wagonloads of supplies for starving and sick Mormons strung out along the trail between Missouri and Iowa and helped finance the impending great migration.

Young selected the Great Basin area, technically part of Mexico, as the most likely site for his future kingdom. It was arid and remote, 1,000 miles from its nearest "civilized" neighbors. But if irrigated, Mormon leaders concluded, it might prove as fertile as the fields and vineyards of ancient Israel.

In April 1847, Young led an exploratory expedition of 143 men, 3 women, and 2 children to this promised land. In late July, after reaching Salt Lake, Young exclaimed, "This is the place." Before returning to Iowa to prepare Mormons for the trip to Utah, he announced his land policy. Settlers would receive virtually free land on the basis of a family's size and its ability to cultivate it. After Young left, the expeditionary group followed his directions to construct irrigation ditches and begin planting.

The following months and years tested Young's organizational talents and his followers' cooperative abilities. By September 1847, 566 wagons and 1,500 of the Saints had made the arduous trek to Salt Lake City. Still more Mormons came the next year, inspired by visions of a new Zion in the West. Their trip was also a collective venture, planned and directed by church leaders. By 1850, the Mormon frontier had attracted over 11,000 settlers. Missionary efforts in the United States and abroad, especially in Great Britain and Scandinavia, drew thousands of converts to the Great Basin. The church emigration society and a loan fund facilitated the journey for many who could never have otherwise undertaken the trip. By the end of the decade, over 30,000 Saints lived in Utah, not only in Salt Lake City but also in more than 90 village colonies planned by Young. Though hardship marked these early years, the Mormons thrived. As one early settler remarked, "We have everything around us we could ask."

Non-Mormon or "Gentile" emigrants passing through Utah found much that was recognizable. The government had familiar characteristics. Most Mormons were farmers; many of them came originally from New England and the Midwest and shared many of the same customs and attitudes. But outsiders perceived profound differences, for the heart of Mormon society was not the individual farmer living on his own homestead but the cooperative village.

Years of persecution had nourished a strong sense of group identity and acceptance of church leadership. Organized by the church leaders, who made the essential decisions, farming was a collective enterprise. All farmers were allotted land. All had irrigation rights, for water did not belong to individuals but to the community as a whole. During Sunday services, the local bishop might give farming instructions to his congregation along with his sermon. As Young explained, "I have looked upon the community of Latter-day Saints in a vision and beheld them organized as the great family of heaven, each person performing his several duties in his line of industry, working for the good of the whole more than for individual aggrandizement." In this vast communal effort, every Mormon was expected to work for success, men and women alike. "We do not believe in having any drones in the hive," one woman said tartly.

The church was omnipresent in Utah; in fact, church and state did not exist as distinct entities. Despite familiar governmental forms, church leaders occupied all the important political posts. Brigham Young's Governing Quorum contained the high priests of the church. Together, they made both religious and political decisions.

When it became clear in 1849 that Utah would become a territory, Mormon leaders drew up a constitution. It carefully replicated the familiar divisions of power. But once in place, powers were not separate but overlapping. As one non-Mormon pointed out, "This intimate connection of church and state seems to pervade everything that is done. The supreme power in both being lodged in the hands of the same individuals, it is difficult to separate their two official characters, and to determine whether in any one instance they act as spiritual or merely temporal officers."

The Treaty of Guadalupe Hidalgo officially incorporated Utah into the United States but little affected political and religious arrangements. Brigham Young became territorial governor. Local bishops continued to act as spiritual leaders as well as civil magistrates in Mormon communities. Mormons had come to Utah to establish a kingdom rather than a republic. Their motives dictated the unique politicoreligious nature of the Utah experience.

Other aspects of the Mormon frontier were distinctive. Mormon policy toward the Indians was remarkably enlightened. As one prominent Mormon pointed out, "It has been our habit to shoot Indians with tobacco and bread biscuits rather than with powder and lead, and we are most successful with them." After two expeditions against the Timpanagos and Shoshone Indians in 1850, Mormons concentrated on converting rather than killing Native Americans. Mormon missionaries learned Banock, Ute, Navajo, and Hopi dialects in order to bring the faith to these tribes. They also encouraged Native Americans to become ranchers and farmers.

While most Gentiles could tolerate some of the differences they encountered on the Mormon frontier, few could accept polygamy and the seemingly immoral extended family structure that plural marriage entailed. Although Joseph Smith and other church leaders had secretly practiced polygamy in the early 1840s, Brigham Young only publicly revealed the doctrine in 1852, when the Saints were safely in Utah. Smith believed that the highest or "celestial" form of marriage brought special rewards in the afterlife. Since wives and children contributed to these rewards, polygamy was a means of sanctification. From a practical standpoint, polygamy served to incorporate into Mormon society single female converts who had left their families to come to Utah.

Although most Mormons accepted the doctrine and its religious justification, some found it hard to follow. One woman called it "a great trial of feelings." In actuality, relatively few families were polygamous. During the 40-year period in which Mormons practiced plural marriage, only 10 to 20 percent of Mormon families were polygamous. Few men had more than two wives. Because of the expense of maintaining several families and the personal strains involved, usually only the more successful and visible Mormon leaders practiced polygamy.

Polygamous family life was a far cry from the lascivious arrangement outsiders fantasized. Since jealousy among wives could destroy the institution of plural marriage, Mormon leaders minimized the role of romantic love and sexual attraction in courtship and marriage. Instead, they encouraged marriages founded on mutual attachment, with sex for the purposes of procreation rather than pleasure.

To the shock of outsiders, Mormon women did not consider themselves slaves but rather highly regarded members of the Mormon community. Whether plural wives or not, they saw polygamy as the cutting edge of their society and defended it to the outside world. Polygamy was preferable to monogamy, which left the single woman without the economic and social protections of family life and forced some of them into prostitution, Brenda Pratt explained. "Polygamy . . . tends directly to the chastity of women, and the sound health and morals . . . of their children."

Although they faced obvious difficulties, many plural wives found rewards in polygamy. Without the constant presence of husbands, they had an unusual opportunity for independence. Many treated husbands when they visited as revered friends; their children, not their spouses, provided them with day-to-day emotional satisfaction. Occasionally, plural wives lived together and shared domestic work, becoming close friends. As one such wife put it, "We three . . . loved each more than sisters" and would "go hand in hand together down till eternity."

Although the Mormon frontier seemed alien to outsiders, it succeeded in terms of its numbers, its growing economic prosperity, and its group unity. Long-term threats loomed for this community, however, once the area became part of the United States. Attacks on Brigham

Young's power as well as heated verbal denunciations of polygamy proliferated. Efforts began in Congress to outlaw polygamy. In the years before the Civil War, Mormons were able to withstand these assaults on their way of life. But as Utah became more connected to the rest of the country, the tide would turn against them.

## The Urban Frontier

Many emigrants went west not to claim farmland or to pan for gold but rather to settle in cities like San Francisco, Denver, and Portland. There they hoped to find business and professional opportunities or, perhaps, the chance to make a fortune by speculating in town lots.

Cities were an integral part of frontier life and, in some cases, preceded agricultural settlement. Some communities turned into bustling cities as they catered to the emigrant trade. St. Joseph, Missouri, outfitted families setting out on the overland journey. Salt Lake City offered weary pioneers headed for California an opportunity to rest and restock. Portland was the destination of many emigrants and became a market and supply center for homesteaders.

Some cities grew so rapidly that they have been called "instant cities." San Francisco and Denver were examples of communities that turned into cities almost overnight, reaching populations of 56,802 and 4,749, respectively, by 1860. In each case, the discovery of precious metals sent thousands of miners with diverse demands and desires to and through these places. And once the strike ran out, many miners returned to these cities to make a new start. Still other places supplied frontier farmers and served as their markets. They only gradually acquired urban characteristics.

Commercial life bustled on the urban frontier, offering residents a wide range of occupations and services. As a Portland emigrant remarked in 1852, only a few years after that community's beginning, "In many ways life here . . . was more primitive than it was in the early times in Illinois and Missouri. But in others it was far more advanced. . . . We could get the world's commodities here which could not be had, then, or scarcely at all, in the interior of Illinois or Missouri."

Young, single men seeking their fortunes made up a disproportionate share of the urban population. Frontier Portland had more than three men for every woman. Predictably, urban life was often noisy, rowdy, and occasionally violent. Urban family life could not help but be affected by the presence of so many young men. Mothers worried about their children falling into bad company. Some attempted to reform the atmosphere by pressing for Sunday store closings or prohibition. Other women, of course, enjoyed all the attention that came with the presence of so many young men. As one observed with gusto, "There is plenty of men here. They cast sheeps eyes at Lib and Lucy's girl but have not popt the question yet." Eventually the sex ratio became balanced, but as late as 1880, fully 18 of the 24 largest western cities had more men than women.

Although western cities began with distinctive characters, they soon resembled eastern cities. As a western publication boasted, "Transport a resident of an Eastern city and put him down in the streets of Portland, and he would observe little difference between his new surroundings and those he beheld but a moment before in his native city."

The history of Portland suggests the common pattern of development. In 1845, Portland was only a clearing in the forest, large enough for four streets and 16 blocks. Speculation in town lots was lively. By the early 1850s, Portland had grown into a small trading center with a few rough log structures and muddy tracks for streets. As farmers poured into Oregon, the city became a regional commercial center. More permanent structures were built, giving the city an "eastern" appearance.

The belief that urban life in the West abounded with special opportunities initially drew many young men to Portland and other western cities. Many of them did not find financial success there. Opportunities were greatest for newcomers who brought assets with them. These residents became the elite of the community. By the 1860s, when the city's population had reached 2,874, Portland's Social Club symbolized the emergence of that city's elite. Portland's businessmen, lawyers, and editors controlled an increasing share of the community's wealth and set its social standards. Their elaborate parties, summer trips, and exclusive clubs showed how far Portland had come from its raw frontier beginnings.

## THE CLASH OF CULTURES

Looking at westward expansion through the eyes of white emigrants provides only one view of the frontier experience. An entry from an Oregon Trail journal suggests other perspectives. On May 7, 1864, Mary Warner, a bride of only a few months, described a frightening event. That day, a "fine-looking" Indian had visited the wagon train and tried to buy her. Mary's husband, probably uncertain how to handle the situation, played along, telling the Indian that he would trade his wife for two ponies. The Indian generously offered three. "Then," wrote Mary, "he took hold of my shawl to make me understand to get out [of the wagon]. About this time I got frightened and really was so hysterical [that] I began to cry." Everyone laughed at her, she reported, though surely the Indian found the whole incident no more amusing than had she.

### Indian-White Encounters

This incident starkly reveals the cultural gap between white Americans moving west and the Indian tribes through whose territory they passed. Earlier, both the Spaniards and the Mexicans had attempted to "civilize" the tribes of the Southwest, with mixed results. White Americans were less interested in assimilating Native Americans culturally than in isolating or eliminating them. But to move them thousands of miles away, as the federal government had done in the 1830s with the five southern tribes, was no longer possible with the influx of whites into the trans-Mississippi West.

This was the first time white Americans had come into extensive contact with the powerful Plains tribes, whose culture was different from the eastern Woodlands tribes familiar to white settlers. Probably a quarter million Native Americans occupied the area from the Rocky Mountains to the Missouri River and from the Platte River to New Mexico. Nearest the Missouri and Iowa frontier lived the "border" tribes —the Pawnee, Omaha, Oto, Ponca, and Kansa. These Indians, unlike other Plains tribes, lived in villages and raised crops, though they hunted the buffalo as a supplement to their diet during the summer months. On the Central Plains lived the Brule and Oglala Sioux, the Cheyenne, Shoshoni, and Arapaho, aggressive tribes who followed the buffalo and often raided the border tribes. In the Southwest were the Commanche, Ute, Navajo, and some Apache bands, while the Kiowa, Wichita, Apache, and southern Commanche claimed northern and western Texas as their hunting grounds.

Although there were differences between these tribes, they shared certain characteristics. Most had adopted a nomadic way of life after the introduction of horses in the sixteenth century increased their seasonal mobility from 50 miles to 500 miles. Horses allowed Indian braves to hunt the buffalo with such success that tribes (with the exclusion of the border groups) came to depend on the beasts for food, clothing, fuel, tepee dwellings, and trading purposes. Because women were responsible for processing buffalo products, some men had more than one wife to tan skins for trading.

Mobility also increased tribal contact and conflict. War played a central part in the lives of the Plains tribes. No male became a fully accepted member of his tribe until he had proved himself in battle. But tribal warfare was not like the warfare of white men. Indians sought not to exterminate their enemies nor to claim territory but rather to steal horses and to prove individual

### Indian Tribes and Culture Areas

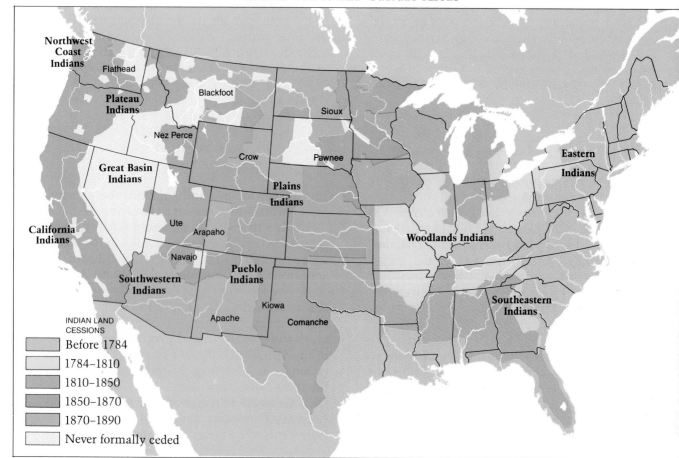

prowess. It was considered braver to touch one's enemy than to kill or scalp him.

This pattern of conflict on the Plains discouraged political unity. Moreover, the tribes themselves were loosely organized. Chiefs enjoyed only limited authority over their followers. As Chief Low Horn, a Blackfoot, explained, chiefs "could not restrain their young men . . . their young men were wild, and ambitious, in their turn to be braves and chiefs. They wanted by some brave act to win the favor of their young women, and bring scalps and horses to show their prowess."

Armed with guns, mounted on fast ponies, and skilled in warfare and raiding, the Plains tribes, though disunified, posed a fearsome obstacle to white expansion. They had signed no treaties with the United States and had few friendly feelings toward whites. Their contact with white society had brought gains through trade in skins, but the trade had also brought alcohol and destructive epidemics of smallpox and scarlet fever.

When the first emigrants drove their wagons across the plains and prairies in the early 1840s, relations between Indians and whites were peaceable. But the intrusion of whites set in motion an environmental cycle that would

*This Tonoccono warrior was painted by John Mix Stanley in 1844 based on the Indians he observed on a trip to central Texas the previous year.*

eventually bring the two groups into conflict. Indian tribes depended on the buffalo but respected this source of life. The Teton Sioux performed rituals to ensure a continuing supply of the animals, while hunters often ritualistically apologized to the Great Unseen Buffalo for slaughtering what the tribe needed.

Whites, however, fed their oxen and horses on the grass needed for both the Indian ponies and the buffalo. And they adopted the "most exciting sport," the buffalo hunt. As the great herds began to shrink, Native American tribes began to battle one another for hunting grounds and food. The powerful Sioux swooped down into the hunting grounds of their enemies and mounted destructive raids against the Pawnee and other smaller tribes. In an 1846 petition to President Polk, the Sioux explained that "for several years past the Emigrants going over the Mountains from the United States, have been the cause that Buffalo have in great measure left our hunting grounds, thereby causing us to go into the Country of Our Enemies to hunt, exposing our lives daily for the necessary subsistence of our wives and Children and getting killed on several occasions." Despite their difficulties, the Sioux had "all along treated the Emigrants in the most friendly manner, giving them free passage through our hunting grounds."

The Sioux requested compensation for damages caused by whites. When their request was denied, they tried to extract taxes from the emigrants passing over their lands. Emigrants were outraged at what they considered Indian effrontery. After all, the United States had won these lands. Frontier newspapers printed letters denouncing the Sioux, demanding adequate protection for travelers and some chastening of the "savages." However, little was done to relieve the suffering of the tribes bearing the brunt of Sioux aggression, the dismay of the Sioux at the white invasion, or the fears of the emigrants themselves.

The discovery of gold in California, which lured over 20,000 across the Plains in 1849 alone, became the catalyst for federal action. The vast numbers of gold seekers and their animals wrought such devastation in the Platte valley that it rapidly became a wasteland for the Indians. The dreaded disease of cholera that whites carried with them spread to the Indians, killing thousands. The source of the disease was clear. The Indians "attribute it to the whites, and they say they brought it amongst them."

To meet the crisis, government officials devised a two-pronged plan. The government would construct a chain of forts to protect emigrants and, simultaneously, call the tribes to a general conference. Officials expected that in return for generous presents, Indians would end tribal warfare and limit their movements to prescribed areas. Tribes were instructed to select chiefs who would speak for them at the conference.

## The Fort Laramie Council

In 1851, the council convened at Fort Laramie. As many as 10,000 Indians, hopeful of ending the destruction to their way of life and eager for the promised presents, gathered at the fort. Tribal animosities were not forgotten, however. Skirmishes occurred on the way to the fort, and the border tribes declined to participate because of their fear of the Sioux. The Comanche, Kiowa, and Apache also refused to come since their enemies, the Sioux and Crow, were to be there.

At the conference, whites told the gathered tribes that times had changed. In the past, "you had plenty of buffalo and game . . . and your Great Father well knows that war has always been your favorite amusement and pursuit. He then left the question of peace and war to yourselves. Now, since the settling of the districts West of you by the white men, your condition has changed." There would be compensation for the destruction of their grass, timber, and buffalo and annual payments of goods and services. But in return, the tribes had to give up their rights of free movement. Tribal boundaries were drawn, and chiefs made promises to stay within them. In most cases, some tribal lands were sold.

The Fort Laramie Treaty was the first agreement between the Plains tribes and the United States government. It expressed the conviction of whites that Indians must stay in clearly defined areas apart from white civilization. The policy of isolation was becoming one of reservations.

But this reservation system and its supposed benefits were still in the future. During the conference, ominous signs appeared that more trouble would precede any "resolution" of Indian-white affairs. Sioux chief Black Hawk told whites, "You have split the country and I do not like it." His powerful tribe refused to be restricted to lands north of the Platte, for south of the river lay their recently conquered lands. "These lands once belonged to the Kiowas and the Crows," one Sioux explained, "but we whipped those nations out of them and in this we did what the white men do when they want the lands of the Indians." The words suggested that Indians, despite agreements, would not willingly abandon their traditional way of life for confinement. In the following years, it would become evident that Americans and Sioux had conflicting interests south of the Platte. Elsewhere in the trans-Mississippi West, other tribes, like the fierce Navajo of New Mexico, also resisted white attempts to confine them.

## Overwhelming the Hispanic-Americans

In the Southwest, in Texas, and in California, Americans had to contend with a Spanish-speaking population. The scornful American attitude toward these people, expressed in Thomas Gibson's letter at the beginning of this chapter, was echoed by expansionist Lewis Cass. Speaking in a congressional debate concerning the annexation of New Mexico, Cass stated, "We do not want the people of Mexico, either as citizens or as subjects. All we want is a portion of territory . . . with a population, which would soon recede, or identify itself with ours." Americans were persuaded that Mexicans were lazy, ignorant, and cunning, the very "dregs of society." Although Mexicans easily recognized such cultural arrogance, they lacked the numbers to fend off American aggression.

The nature of the Anglo-Hispanic interaction differed from place to place. The greatest numbers of Spanish-speaking people lived in New Mexico. Most were of mixed blood, living marginally as ranch hands for rich landowners or as farmers and herdsmen in small villages dominated by a *patron* or headman. As the century wore on, Americans produced legal titles and took over lands long occupied by peasant farmers and stock raisers. Despite economic reversals, there were enough New Mexicans to ensure the survival of their rural culture well into the twentieth century.

The light-skinned upper class of landowners fared better. Even before the conquest, rich New Mexicans had protected their future by establishing contacts with American businessmen and by sending their sons east to American schools. When the United States annexed New Mexico, this substantial and powerful class contracted strategic marriage and business alliances with the Anglo men who slowly trickled into the territory. During the 1850s, they maintained their influence and prestige and their American connections. Only rarely did they bother themselves with the plight of their poor countrymen. Class was more important than ethnic or cultural ties.

In Texas, the Spanish-speaking residents, only 10 percent of the population in 1840, had shrunk to a mere 6 percent by 1860. Although the upper class also intermarried with Americans, they lost most of their power as Germans, Irish, French, and Americans poured into the state. Poor Hispanics, whose dark skins symbolized racial inferiority to whites, clustered in low-paying and largely unskilled jobs.

In California, the discovery of gold radically changed the situation for the Californios. In 1848, there were 7,000 Californios and about 14,000 Anglos. By 1860, the Anglo population had ballooned to 360,000. Hispanic-Americans were hard pressed to cope with the rapid influx of outsiders. At first, Californios and several thousand Mexicans from Sonora joined Anglos and others in the gold fields. But competition there fed antagonism and finally open conflict. Posters warned foreigners out of the gold fields. In Anglo eyes, one Hispanic was much like another, even if one claimed to be a Californio with political rights and another a Sonoran. Taxes and terrorism succeeded finally in forcing most Spanish speakers out of the mines and established the racial contours of the new California.

Other changes were even more disastrous. In 1851, the California legislature passed the Gwinn Land Law, supposedly a measure for validating Spanish and Mexican land titles. In fact, the law forced landowners to defend what was already theirs and encouraged squatters to settle on land in the hopes that the title would prove false. It took an average of 17 years to establish clear title to land. The process was slow and unfamiliar. As one woman explained, her mother had been "totally unprepared for the problems that came with American rule. Not only was the language foreign to her, but also the concept of property taxes, mortgages and land title regulations." Landowners found themselves paying American lawyers large fees, often in land, and borrowing at high interest rates to pay for court proceedings. A victory at court

*Before the annexation of the lands in the Southwest, Mexican culture was well established, though great diversity existed from one locality to another.*

often turned into a defeat when legal expenses forced owners to sell their lands to pay debts. In the south, where Anglos judged land less valuable than in the mining north, the process of dispossession was slower. But by the early 1860s, the ranch class there had also lost most of its extensive holdings.

Many working-class Hispanic-Americans lived marginal existences in California's growing towns and cities. Others became cowboys on American ranches or lived on their own small ranches in the backcountry. For them, the coming of the Anglos represented little in the way of opportunity or advancement. By 1870, the average Hispanic-American worker's property was worth only about a third of its value 20 years earlier. As newspaper editor and champion of the Mexican-American cause Francisco Ramirez pointed out in Los Angeles's *El Clamor Publico* in 1856, "California has fallen into the hands of the ambitious sons of North America who will not stop until they have satisfied their passions, by driving the first occupants of the land out of the country, villifying their religion and disfiguring their customs."

Western movies and novels have played a large role in forming images of the nineteenth-century West. Cowboys, sheriffs, outlaws, and bandits gallop across screens and pages. One of these outlaws, a sombrero-clad rider, merits a closer look in the context of American expansion into the Southwest. As the career of Tiberio Vasquez, a notorious *bandido* in southern California, suggests, some Hispanics felt that they could protest events only through violence:

> My career grew out of the circumstances by which I was surrounded. . . . As I grew to manhood I was in the habit of attending balls and parties given by the native Californians, into which the Americans, then beginning to become numerous, would force themselves and shove the native born men aside, monopolizing the dance and the women. This was about 1852. A spirit of hatred and revenge took possession of me. I had numerous fights in defense of my countrywomen. The officers were continually in pursuit of me. I believed we were unjustly and wrongfully deprived of the social rights that belonged to us.

What Anglos called crime, Tiberio Vasquez called self-defense.

## CONCLUSION: Fruits of Manifest Destiny

Like Lewis Cass, many nineteenth-century Americans saw the West as a valuable territorial acquisition for the nation and were confident of its special opportunities. The expanding nation did, of course, gain vast natural wealth in the trans-Mississippi West in the 1840s and 1850s. But only a small fraction of the hopeful emigrants heading for the frontier realized their dreams of success. And the move west had a seamy side as cultures clashed, as Mexicans, Native Americans, Mormons, and other whites confronted one another to gain or retain the land. The West was a mosaic not only of race and religion but of occupations. Farmers, ranchers, miners, and city dwellers all tried to plunder the West of the treasures they imagined it contained.

During the 1840s and 1850s, however, most Americans were more concerned with another kind of cultural clash, the clash between the northern system of free land and free labor and the southern system of plantation slavery. The relationship of the system of slavery to new lands became a hotly debated political issue in Congress, in the North and the South, and in the territories themselves. Brutal events in Kansas became a preview of war. The movement west was thus an important factor leading to the Civil War. It is to this story that we turn in the following chapter.

## Recommended Reading

Ray Allen Billington gives two overviews of the move west in *America's Frontier Heritage* (1966) and *The Far Western Frontier, 1830–1860* (1965). Gilbert C. Fite treats agriculture in *The Farmer's Frontier, 1865–1900* (1966). The cities of the West are the subject of *The Urban West at the End of the Frontier* (1978) by Lawrence H. Larson.

Frederick Merk explores Manifest Destiny in *Manifest Destiny and Mission in American History* (1963), while Norman A. Graebner presents a collection of documents with a helpful introduction in *Manifest Destiny* (1968). Gene Brack provides the Mexican view of American expansion in *Mexico Views Manifest Destiny, 1821–1846* (1975). The diplomatic maneuvering for control of Oregon is the subject of David Pletcher, *The Diplomacy of Annexation: Texas, Oregon, and the Mexican War* (1973).

Bernard Sheehan discusses Indian removal in *Seeds of Extinction: Jeffersonian Philanthropy and the American Indian* (1973), as does Wilcomb E. Washburn in *The Indian in America* (1975) and Charles Hudson in *The Removal of the Southeastern Indians* (1978). George Pierre Castile treats the clash of cultures in *North American Indians: An Introduction to the Chichimeca* (1979). Robert A. Trennert portrays relations during a crucial period in *Alternative to Extinction: Federal Indian Policy and the Beginnings of the Reservation System, 1846–1851* (1975). Peter Nabakov has edited a collection of Indian responses in *Native American Testimony: An Anthology of Indian and White Relations* (1978).

Julie Roy Jeffrey compensates for the neglect of women in older frontier studies in *Frontier Women: The Trans-Mississippi West, 1840–1880* (1979). Sandra Myres edited women's diaries in *Ho for California! Women's Overland Diaries from the Huntington Library* (1980), while John Mack Faragher provides an interpretation of the trail experience in *Women and Men on the Overland Trail* (1978). Although there were not many blacks on the frontier, William Loren Katz studies them in *The Black West* (1971). As for the Mormons, Wallace Stegner's study, *The Gathering of Zion: The Story of the Mormon Trail* (1964), can serve as an introduction. There are several studies of Hispanics including Leonard Pitt's *The Decline of the Californios: A Social History of the Spanish-Speaking Californians, 1846–1890* (1970); Paul Rodman's essay in John G. Clark, ed., *The Frontier Challenge: Responses to the Trans-Mississippi West* (1971); M. S. Meir and Feliciano Rivera, *The Chicanos: A History of Mexican-Americans* (1972); and Alfredo Mirande and Evangeline Enriquez, *La Chicana: The Mexican-American Woman* (1979).

## TIME LINE

| | |
|---|---|
| 1803–1806 | Lewis and Clark expedition |
| 1818 | Treaty on joint U.S.-British occupation of Oregon |
| 1819 | Spain cedes Spanish territory in United States and sets transcontinental boundary of Louisiana Purchase, excluding Texas |
| 1821 | Mexican independence<br>Opening of Santa Fe Trail<br>Stephen Austin leads American settlement of Texas |
| 1821–1840 | Indian removals |
| 1829 | Georgia revokes Cherokee rights |
| 1830 | Mexico abolishes slavery in Texas |
| 1836 | Texas declares independence<br>Battles of the Alamo and San Jacinto |
| 1840s | Emigrant crossings of Overland Trail |
| 1844 | James Polk elected president |
| 1845 | "Manifest Destiny" coined<br>United States annexes Texas and sends troops to the Rio Grande<br>Americans attempt to buy Upper California and New Mexico |
| 1846 | Mexico declares defensive war<br>United States declares war and takes Santa Fe<br>Resolution of Oregon question |
| 1847 | Attack on Veracruz and Mexico City<br>Mormon migration to Utah begins |
| 1848 | Treaty of Guadalupe Hidalgo |
| 1849 | California gold rush begins |
| 1850 | California admitted to the Union |
| 1851 | Fort Laramie Treaty |
| 1853 | Gadsden Purchase |
| 1862 | Homestead Act |

# CHAPTER 15
## THE UNION IN PERIL

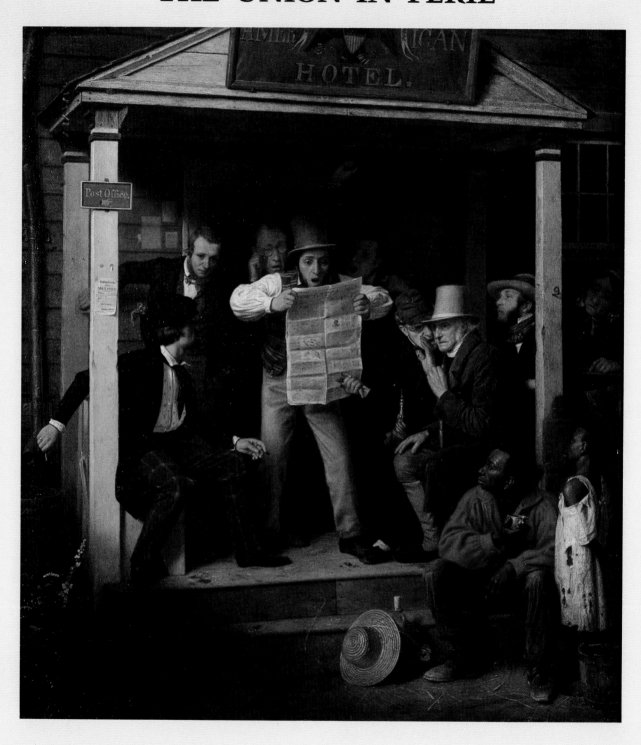

The autumn of 1860 was a time of ominous rumors and expectations. The election was held on November 6 in an atmosphere of crisis. In Springfield, Illinois, Abraham Lincoln, taking coffee and sandwiches prepared by "the ladies of Springfield," waited as the telegraph brought in the returns. By one A.M. victory was certain. He reported later, "I went home, but not to get much sleep, for I then felt, as I never had before, the responsibility that was upon me." And with good cause. He and the American people faced the most serious crisis since the founding of the Republic.

Lincoln won an unusual four-party election, receiving only 39 percent of the popular vote. He had appealed almost exclusively to northern voters in a blatantly sectional campaign, defeating his three opponents by carrying every free state except New Jersey. Alone among the candidates, Illinois senator Stephen Douglas campaigned actively in every section of the country. For his efforts he received the second highest number of votes. Douglas's appeal, especially in the closing days of the campaign, was "on behalf of the Union," which he feared—correctly—was in imminent danger of splitting apart.

Other Americans sensed the mood of crisis that fall and faced their own fears and responsibilities. A month before the election, plantation owner Robert Allston wrote his oldest son, Benjamin, that "disastrous consequences" would follow from a Lincoln victory. Although his letter mentioned the possibility of secession, he dealt mostly with plantation concerns: a new horse, the mood of the slaves, ordering supplies from the city, instructions for making trousers on a sewing machine. After Lincoln's election, Allston corresponded with a southern colleague about the need for "an effective military organization" in order to resist "Northern and Federal aggression." In this shift from sewing machines to military ones, Robert Allston prepared for what he called the "impending crisis."

Frederick Douglass, however, greeted the election with characteristic optimism. Not only was this an opportunity to "educate . . . the people in their moral and political duties," he said, but "slaveholders know that the day of their power is over when a Republican President is elected." But no sooner had Lincoln's victory been determined than Douglass's hopes turned sour. He noted that Republican leaders, in their desire to keep southern border states from seceding, sounded more anti-abolitionist than antislavery. They vowed not to touch slavery in areas where it already existed, which included the District of Columbia, and they promised to enforce the hated Fugitive Slave Act and to put down slave rebellions. Slavery would in fact, Douglass bitterly concluded, "be as safe, and safer" with Lincoln than with a Democratic president.

Michael Luark, an Iowa farmer, was not so sure. Born in Virginia, Luark was a typically mobile nineteenth-century American. After growing up in Indiana, he followed the mining booms of the 1850s to Colorado and California before returning to the Midwest to farm. Luark searched for a good living and resented all the furor over slavery. He could not, however, avoid the issue. Writing in his diary on the last day of 1860, Luark looked ahead to 1861 with a deep sense of fear. "Startling" political changes would occur, he predicted, perhaps even the "Dissolution of the Union and Civil War with all its train of horrors." He blamed abolitionist agitators, perhaps reflecting his Virginia origins. On New Year's Day, he expressed his fears that Lincoln would let the "most ultra sectional and Abolition" men disturb the "vexed Slavery question" even further, as Frederick Douglass wanted. But if this happened, Luark warned, "then farewell to our beloved Union of States."

Within four months of this diary entry, the guns of the Confederate States of America fired on a federal fort in South Carolina, and the Civil War began. Luark's fears, Douglass's hopes, and Lincoln's and Allston's preparations for responsibility all became realities. The explanation of the peril and dissolution of the Union forms the theme of this chapter.

471

For so calamitous an event there were numerous causes, large and small. The reactions of Allston, Douglass, and Luark to Lincoln's election suggest some of them: moral duties, sectional politics, growing apprehensions over emotional agitators, and a concern for freedom and independence on the part of blacks, white southerners, and western farmers. But as Douglass understood, by 1860 it was clear that "slavery is the real issue, the single bone of contention between all parties and sections. It is the one disturbing force, and explains the confused and irregular motion of our political machine."

This chapter analyzes how the momentous issue of slavery disrupted the political system and eventually the Union itself. We will look at how four major developments between 1848 and 1861 contributed to the Civil War: first, a sectional dispute over the extension of slavery into the western territories; second, the breakdown of the political party system; third, growing cultural differences in the views and life styles of southerners and northerners; and fourth, intensifying polarization between the two regions over losing freedom and sacred republican rights at the hands of the other. A preview of civil war, bringing all four causes together, occurred in 1855–1856 in Kansas. Eventually, emotional events, mistrust, and irreconcilable differences made conflict inevitable. The election of Lincoln was the precipitating spark that touched off the conflagration of civil war, with all its "train of horrors."

## SLAVERY IN THE TERRITORIES

Senator Lewis Cass's confident proclamations (Chapter 14) that the western territories were areas of individual freedom where civilization would advance and political and social harmony would prevail were premature. As countless westward migrants discovered, personal costs attended the American march into the West. For Native Americans and Mexicans whose land stood in the way, the consequences for both culture and livelihood were much worse. Still another cultural collison would occur in the western territories, this one involving Yankees and slaveholders.

For some 60 years after the Constitutional Convention, the North and the South had managed to settle their differences over issues concerning slavery. Political compromise had successfully resolved the question of the slave trade and counting slaves for congressional representation in 1787. The Missouri Compromise in 1820 had established a workable principle of balancing the admission of free and slave states to the Union and had also defined a geographic line (36°30′) in the Louisiana Territory to determine future decisions. In 1832 and 1833,

compromise had defused South Carolina's nullification of the tariff. The gag rule in 1836 had kept divisive abolitionist petitions to end slavery off the floor of Congress.

The key to these successful compromises was the existence of a two-party system with intersectional membership. Whigs and Democrats lived on both sides of the Mason-Dixon line. The party system encouraged developing party loyalties as an "antidote," as Van Buren put it, to sectional allegiance. Whigs and Democrats expressed their differences over cultural and economic issues, sometimes passionately, but the volatile issue of slavery was largely kept out of political campaigns and congressional debates. This changed in the late 1840s.

### Free Soil and the Wilmot Proviso

As the Mexican War broke out in 1846, it seemed likely that the United States would acquire new territories in the Southwest. Would they be slave or free? To an appropriations bill to pay for the war, David Wilmot, a freshman congressman from Pennsylvania, added a short amendment declaring that "neither slavery nor involuntary servitude shall ever exist" in any territories acquired from Mexico. The debates in Congress over the Wilmot Proviso were significant because legislators voted along sectional rather than party lines. They divided not as Whigs and Democrats but as northerners and southerners.

A Boston newspaper prophetically observed at the time that Wilmot's resolution "brought to a head the great question which is about to divide the American people." As the Mexican War ended, several solutions were presented to deal with this question of slavery in the territories. The first was Wilmot's "free soil" idea of preventing any extensions of slavery. But did Congress have the power or right to do so? Two precedents suggested that it did. One was the Northwest Ordinance, which had prohibited the entry of slaves into states created in the Upper Midwest, and the other was the Missouri Compromise.

Supporters of "free soil" cited both models, making moral, economic, and political arguments for the Wilmot Proviso. For some, slavery was a moral evil to be attacked and destroyed. For free northern farmers who looked to move westward, competition with an expanding system of large-scale slave labor presented an economic threat. Nor did they wish to compete for land with free Negroes either. Other northerners supported the Wilmot Proviso as a means of restraining what seemed to them the growing political power and, in Wilmot's words, the "insufferable . . . arrogance" of the "spirit and demands of the Slave Power." They argued that in defense of slavery, southerners trampled on revered principles of liberty and equality.

Opposed to the free-soil position were the arguments of Senator John C. Calhoun of South Carolina, expressed in several resolutions introduced in the Senate in 1847. Not only did Congress lack the constitutional right to exclude slavery from the territories, Calhoun argued, but it had a positive duty to protect it. The Wilmot Proviso, therefore, was unconstitutional, as was the Missouri Compromise and any other federal act that prevented slaveholders from taking their slave property into the territories of the United States.

Economic, political, and moral considera-

tions stood behind the Calhoun position. Many southerners hungered for new cotton lands in the West and Southwest, even in Central America and the Caribbean. Politically, southerners feared that northerners wanted to trample on *their* liberties, namely, the right to protect their institutions against destructive abolitionists. Southern leaders saw the Wilmot Proviso as a moral issue that raised questions about basic republican principles. One congressman called it "treason to the Constitution," and Senator Robert Toombs of Georgia warned that if the proviso were passed by Congress, he would favor disunion rather than "degradation."

With such divisive potential, it was natural that many Americans sought a compromise solution to keep slavery out of politics. Polk's secretary of state, James Buchanan of Pennsylvania, proposed that the Missouri Compromise line be extended through the lands acquired from Mexico to the Pacific Ocean. This seemed a perfect way of perpetuating the compromise of 1820 that had contained sectional controversy for 30 years. But it was also a way of avoiding thornier questions concerning the morality of slavery and the constitutionality of congressional authority.

Another solution, called "popular sovereignty," was also a way of begging these issues. As promulgated by Lewis Cass, the doctrine of popular sovereignty left the decision whether to permit slavery in a territory to the local territorial legislature. This idea appealed to the American democratic belief in local self-government and popular participation. Few noticed at the time that the important question of when a territorial legislature could decide to permit or forbid slavery (while still in the territorial stage or when applying for statehood) was unclear. Cass deliberately left these subtleties ambiguous, reasoning that both northern and southern politicians would find popular sovereignty appealing because they could each argue that their side would win the territorial vote.

The question of slavery in the territories created an atmosphere of crisis. A few people talked of secession, but without much popular support. Those who argued for compromise and the continuation of intersectional parties prevailed, as the election of 1848 illustrated.

The Democratic party, attracted to the idea

that popular sovereignty could mean all things to all people, nominated its chief spokesman, Lewis Cass. He denounced abolitionists and the Wilmot Proviso but otherwise avoided the issue of slavery. The Democrats, however, recognized the growing importance of sectional feeling by printing two campaign biographies of Cass, one for the South and one for the North.

The Whigs found an even better way to hold the party together by evading the slavery issue. Passing over Henry Clay, they nominated the Mexican War hero, General Zachary Taylor, a Louisiana slaveholder. Taylor compared himself to Washington as a "no party" man who was above politics. This was nearly the only thing he stood for. Southern Whigs supported Taylor because they thought he might understand the burdens of slaveholding, while northern Whigs were pleased that he took no stand on the Wilmot Proviso.

The evasions of the two major parties disappointed Calhoun, who tried to create a new unified southern party. His "Address to the People of the Southern States" rehearsed the history of northern attempts to destroy slavery. Threatening secession, Calhoun called for a united effort against further attempts to interfere with the southern right to extend slavery. But only 48 of 121 southern representatives signed the address, and his effort failed. Calhoun's argument, however, pointed to the future and raised the specter of secession and disunion.

Warnings also issued from the North. A faction of Democrats in New York bolted the party to support Van Buren, a Cass foe for several years, for president. At first, the split had more to do with internal state politics than moral principles, but it soon involved the question of slavery in the territories. Disaffected "conscience" Whigs from Massachusetts, unhappy with a slaveholder as their party standard-bearer, were also interested in a third-party alternative. These groups met in Buffalo, New York, to form the Free-Soil party and nominate Van Buren as president. The platform of the new party, composed of an uneasy mixture of ardent abolitionists and racist opponents of free black mobility into western lands, pledged to fight for "free soil, free speech, free labor and free men."

General Taylor won the election easily, largely because defections from Cass in New York and Pennsylvania to the Free-Soilers cost the Democrats the electoral votes from those states. Still, the two-party system survived, and purely sectional parties were prevented. Both major parties essentially retained the popular votes they had received in 1844. The Free-Soilers, though doing some damage, carried only about 10 percent of the popular vote, and no states.

## The Compromise of 1850

Taylor won the election by avoiding slavery issues, but as president he could no longer do so. As he was inaugurated in 1849, a number of compelling questions faced the nation. The rush of some 80,000 unruly gold miners to California qualified that territory for admission to the Union. But California's entry as a free state would upset the balance between slave and free states in the Senate that had prevailed since 1820.

The unresolved status of the Mexican cession in the Southwest posed a second problem. The longer the area was left unorganized, the louder local inhabitants called for an application of either the Wilmot Proviso or the Calhoun doctrine of protecting the extension of slavery. The boundary between Texas and the New Mexico Territory was also in dispute, with Texas claiming lands all the way to Santa Fe. This increased northern fears that Texas might be divided into five or six slave states.

The existence of slavery and one of the largest slave markets in North America in the nation's capital was another problem, especially to abolitionists. Southerners, in turn, resented the lax federal enforcement of the Fugitive Slave Act of 1793. They called for a stronger act and particularly wanted to end the protection that northerners gave runaway slaves as they fled along the underground railroad to Canada.

Although Taylor was a newcomer to politics (he had never even voted in a presidential election before 1848), he tried to tackle these problems in a statesmanlike manner. He thought he could sidestep the conflict over slavery in the territories by inviting California and New Mexico to apply immediately for statehood, presumably as free states. Calhoun and other southerners felt betrayed. Because Taylor believed he had been elected by a broad coalition of voters, he made nonpartisan appointments. This irritated traditional Whig leaders like Clay and Webster, who resented the new president's attempt to change and weaken their party.

Early in 1850, therefore, the old compromiser, Henry Clay, sought to regain control of the Whig party by proposing solutions to the divisive issues before the nation. Having secured Webster's support, Clay introduced a series of resolutions intended to settle these issues once and for all. The stormy debates, great speeches, and political maneuvering that followed provided one of the crucial and dramatic moments of American history. By early summer, despite some 70 speeches on behalf of his compromise, Clay's Omnibus Bill was defeated in the Senate, one resolution after another. As new bills were proposed, a tired and disheartened 73-year-old Henry Clay left Washington, hoping to regain his strength. He never did. But the moment of apparent defeat turned out to be an opportunity for success. A new compromiser emerged, Stephen Douglas of Illinois. Under Douglas's leadership, and with the support of Millard Fillmore, who succeeded to the presidency upon Taylor's

untimely death in midsummer, a series of bills was finally passed.

Although slightly altered, the Compromise of 1850 put into law essentially the same package introduced by Clay nine months earlier. California entered the Union as a free state, upsetting the balance of free and slave states, 16 to 15. The territorial governments of New Mexico and Utah were organized by letting the people of those territories decide for themselves whether to permit slavery. The Texas–New Mexico border was settled in a compromise that denied Texas the disputed area. In turn, the federal government compensated Texas with $10 million to pay off debts owed to Mexico. The slave trade, but not slavery itself, was abolished in the District of Columbia.

The most controversial part of the compromise was the Fugitive Slave Act, which contained many provisions that northerners found offensive. One denied a jury trial to the alleged fugitive, establishing special commissioners to decide special cases. (A commissioner received $5 for setting a fugitive free but $10 for returning a fugitive to his or her owner.) Another provision compelled all northern citizens to assist in the

## The Compromise of 1850

# RECOVERING THE PAST

The history of average, anonymous Americans can be recovered in letters, diaries, folktales, and other non-traditional sources. But in times of political conflict with enormous implications for all Americans, as in the years before the Civil War, historians turn to more conventional sources such as congressional speeches. Recorded in the *Congressional Globe*, these speeches are a revealing means of recovering the substance, tone, and drama of political debate.

Despite the cynical view of American politics held by some European visitors, the mid-nineteenth century was an era of giants in the United States Senate: Daniel Webster, Henry Clay, Thomas Hart Benton, John C. Calhoun, William Seward, and Stephen Douglas. When Congress debated a major issue, such as the tariff, nullification, or the extension of slavery, large crowds would pack the Senate galleries. The speeches would then be quickly printed and widely distributed. These spectacular oratorical encounters provided mass entertainment and political instruction. Such was the case with the Senate speeches over the Compromise of 1850. The three principal figures early in the debates were Clay (Kentucky), Calhoun (South Carolina), and Webster (Massachusetts), each of whom delivered a great address crowning a long, distinguished career.

Born within five years of each other as the American Revolution was ending (1777–1782), each man began his political career in the House of Representatives in the War of 1812 era. Each served a term as secretary of state; in addition, Clay was speaker of the House and Calhoun secretary of war and vice-president. Each served for over a decade in the Senate (Clay, 13 years; Calhoun, 15 years; Webster, 19 years). Each was a party leader, Clay and Webster of the Whigs and Calhoun of the Democrats. During their 40 years of public service, they represented strong nationalistic positions as well as their various states and sections. All three were candidates for president between 1824 and 1844. All three spent most of their careers in the political shadow of Andrew Jackson, and all three had serious conflicts with him.

Many years of political and ideological conflict with each other not only sharpened their oratorical skills but also led to mutual respect. Webster said of Calhoun that he was "the ablest man in the Senate. He could have demolished Newton, Calvin, or even John Locke as a logician." Calhoun said of Clay, "He is a bad man, but by God, I love him." And "Old Man Eloquent" himself, John Quincy Adams, said of Webster that he was "the most consummate orator of modern times."

It was therefore a momentous event when they each prepared speeches and met for one last encounter

## HENRY CLAY
### February 5–6, 1850

I have seen many periods of great anxiety, of peril, and of danger in this country, and I have never before risen to address any assemblage so oppressed, so appalled, and so anxious; and sir, I hope it will not be out of place to do here, what again and again I have done in my private chamber, to implore of Him who holds the destinies of nations and individuals in His hands, to bestow upon our country His blessing, to calm the violence and rage of party, to still passion, to allow reason once more to resume its empire. . . .

Mr. President, it is passion, passion-party, party, and intemperance—that is all I dread in the adjustment of the great questions which unhappily at this time divide our distracted country. Sir, at this moment we have in the legislative bodies of this Capitol and in the States, twenty old furnaces in full blast, emitting heat, and passion, and intemperance, and diffusing them throughout the whole extent of this broad land. Two months ago all was calm in comparison to the present moment. All now is uproar, confusion, and menace to the existence of the Union, and to the happiness and safety of this people. . . .

Sir, when I came to consider this subject, there were two or three general purposes which it seemed to me to be most desirable, if possible, to accomplish. The one was, to settle all the controverted questions arising out of the subject of slavery. . . . I therefore turned my attention to every subject connected with the institution of slavery, and out of which controverted questions had sprung, to see if it were possible or practicable to accommodate and adjust the whole of them. . . .

We are told now, and it is rung throughout this entire country, that the Union is threatened with subversion and destruction. Well, the first question which naturally rises is, supposing the Union to be dissolved,—having all the causes of grievance which are complained of,—How far will a dissolution furnish a remedy for those grievances? If the Union is to be dissolved for any existing causes, it will be dissolved because slavery is interdicted or not allowed to be introduced into the ceded territories; because slavery is threatened to be abolished in the District of Columbia, and because fugitive slaves are not returned, as in my opinion they ought to be, and restored to their masters. These, I believe, will be the causes; if there be any causes, which can lead to the direful event to which I have referred. . . .

Mr. President, I am directly opposed to any purpose of secession, of separation. I am for staying within the Union, and defying any portion of this Union to expel or drive me out of the Union.

early in 1850. Clay was over 70 years old and in failing health, but he came out of retirement to try to keep the Union together. He defended his compromise proposals in a four-hour speech spread over two days, February 5 and 6. The Senate galleries were so packed

# SENATE SPEECHES

## JOHN C. CALHOUN
### March 4, 1850

Having now, Senators, explained what it is that endangers the Union, and traced it to its cause, and explained its nature and character, the question again recurs—How can the Union be saved? To this I answer, there is but one way by which it can be—and that is—by adopting such measures as will satisfy the States belonging to the Southern section, that they can remain in the Union consistently with their honor and their safety. . . .

But can this be done? Yes, easily; not by the weaker party, for it can of itself do nothing—not even protect itself—but by the stronger. The North has only to will it to accomplish it—to do justice by conceding to the South an equal right in the acquired territory, and to do her duty by causing the stipulations relative to fugitive slaves to be faithfully fulfilled—to cease the agitation of the slave question, and to provide for the insertion of a provision in the Constitution, by an amendment, which will restore to the South, in substance, the power she possessed of protecting herself, before the equilibrium between the sections was destroyed by the action of this Government. . . .

But will the North agree to this? It is for her to answer the question. But, I will say, she cannot refuse, if she has half the love of the Union which she professes to have, or without justly exposing herself to the charge that her love of power and aggrandizement is far greater than her love of the Union. At all events, the responsibility of saving the Union rests on the North, and not on the South. . . . If the question is not now settled, it is uncertain whether it ever can hereafter be; and we, as the representatives of the States of this Union, regarded as governments, should come to a distinct understanding as to our respective views, in order to ascertain whether the great questions at issue can be settled or not. If you, who represent the stronger portion, cannot agree to settle them on the broad principle of justice and duty, say so; and let the States we both represent agree to separate and part in peace. If you are unwilling we should part in peace, tell us so, and we shall know what to do.

## DANIEL WEBSTER
### March 7, 1850

MR. PRESIDENT: I wish to speak to-day, not as a Massachusetts man, nor as a Northern man, but as an American, and a member of the Senate of the United States. It is fortunate that there is a Senate of the United States; a body not yet moved from its propriety, not lost to a just sense of its own dignity and its own high responsibilities, and a body to which the country looks, with confidence, for wise, moderate, patriotic, and healing counsels. It is not to be denied that we live in the midst of strong agitations, and are surrounded by very considerable dangers to our institutions and government. The imprisoned winds are let loose. . . .

I speak to-day for the preservation of the Union. "Hear me for my cause." I speak to-day, out of a solicitous and anxious heart, for the restoration to the country of that quiet and that harmony which make the blessing of this Union so rich, and so dear to us all. . . . I shall bestow a little attention, Sir, upon these various grievances existing on the one side and on the other. I begin with complaints of the South. . . . and especially to one which has in my opinion just foundation; and that is, that there has been found at the North, among individuals and among legislators, a disinclination to perform fully their constitutional duties in regard to the return of persons bound to service who have escaped into the free States. In that respect, the South, in my judgment, is right, and the North is wrong. Every member of every Northern legislature is bound by oath, like every other officer in the country, to support the Constitution of the United States; and the article of the Constitution which says to these States they shall deliver up fugitives from service is as binding in honor and conscience as any other article. . . .

Peaceable secession! Peaceable secession! The concurrent agreement of all the members of this great republic to separate! A voluntary separation, with alimony on one side and on the other. Why, what would be the result? Where is the line to be drawn? What States are to secede? What is to remain American? What am I to be? An American no longer? Am I to become a sectional man, a local man, a separatist, with no country in common with the gentlemen who sit around me here, or who fill the other house of Congress? Heaven forbid! Where is the flag of the republic to remain? Where is the eagle still to tower? or is he to cower, and shrink, and fall to the ground?

that listeners were pushed into hallways and even into the rotunda of the Capitol. Copies of his speech were in such demand that over 100,000 were printed.

A month later, on March 7, the scene was repeated as Webster rose to join Clay in defending the compromise. Three days earlier, although too ill to deliver the speech himself, Calhoun had "tottered into the Senate" on the arm of a friend to hear James Mason of Virginia read his rejection of the compromise. Within a month, Calhoun was dead. Clay and Webster followed him to the grave two years later, and Senate leadership passed on to Seward, Douglas, and a new generation of Senate giants.

As you read the brief selections from each speech, try to imagine yourself sitting in the gallery overlooking the Senate floor, listening to each man, and absorbing the drama of the moment. How do the oratorical styles differ? Which specific passages make the best substantive points in support of each man's argument? Which passages convey the most emotional power? Which speaker is most persuasive to you? Why? To what extent do they agree on the fugitive slave issue? What can you infer about the personality of these men from their speeches?

enforcement of the act, which called upon them to hunt down and turn in runaway slaves.

## Consequences of Compromise

The Compromise of 1850 was the last attempt to keep slavery out of politics. How well it succeeded in doing so is debatable. The intersectional party system was severely tested, but for a while was preserved. Voting behavior on the several bills varied, with legislators following sectional lines on some issues and party lines on others. Douglas had good reason to feel pleased, celebrating the acts of 1850 as a "final settlement" of the slavery question.

The Compromise of 1850, however, was only an armistice that delayed more serious sectional conflict. Two new ingredients were added to American politics. The first hinted at the realignment of parties along sectional lines. Political leaders as different as Calhoun, Webster, Van Buren, and New York senator William Seward all either flirted with or committed themselves to new parties. Second, although repudiated by most ordinary citizens, ideas like secessionism, disunion, and a "higher law" than the Constitution entered more and more political discussions. Some people wondered whether the question of slavery in the territories could be compromised away the next time it arose.

Others were immediately upset. The new fugitive slave law angered many northerners because it brought the evils of slavery right into their midst. The owners of runaway slaves hired agents, labeled "kidnappers" in the North, to hunt down fugitives. In a few dramatic episodes, most notably in Boston, literary and religious intellectuals led mass protests to resist slave hunters' efforts to return alleged fugitives to the South. When Senator Webster supported the law, he was denounced by New England abolitionists as "indescribably base and wicked." Theodore Parker called the act itself "a hateful statute of kidnappers," and Ralph Waldo Emerson said it was "a filthy law" that he would not obey.

Frederick Douglass would not obey it either. As a runaway slave himself, he was threatened with arrest and return to the South until friends overcame his objections and purchased his freedom. Douglass still risked harm by his strong defiance of the Fugitive Slave Act. Arguing the "rightfulness of forcible resistance," he urged free blacks to arm themselves and even wondered whether it was not justifiable to kill kidnappers. "The only way to make the Fugitive Slave Law a dead letter," he said in Pittsburgh in 1853, "is to make a half dozen or more dead kidnappers." Douglass raised money for black fugitives, hid runaways in his home, and helped hundreds escape to Canada.

Other northerners, white as well as black, increased their work for the underground railroad in response to the fugitive slave law. Several states passed "personal liberty laws" that prohibited the use of state officials and institutions in the recovery of fugitive slaves. But most

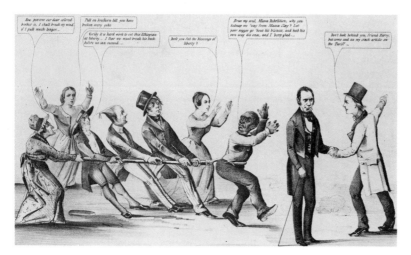

*The hypocrisy of the 1850 Fugitive Slave law is pointed out in this cartoon, where white citizens preach liberty at a black man they are catching. Henry Clay stands with his back to them while talking to a northerner about another subject.*

northerners complied with the law. Of some 200 blacks arrested in the first six years of the law, only 15 were rescued, and only 3 of these by force. Failed rescues, in fact, had more emotional impact than successful ones. In two cases in the early 1850s (Thomas Sims in 1851 and Anthony Burns in 1854), angry mobs of abolitionists in Boston, reminiscent of the pre-Revolutionary days of the Tea Party, failed to prevent the forcible return of blacks to the South. These celebrated cases aroused the antislavery emotions of more northerners than the abolitionists had been able to do in a thousand tracts and speeches.

But the spoken and written word also fueled emotions over slavery in the aftermath of 1850. In an Independence Day speech in 1852, Douglass wondered, "What, to the American slave, is your 4th of July?" It was, he said, the day that revealed to the slave "the gross injustice and cruelty to which he is the constant victim." To a slave the American claims of national greatness were vain and empty; the "shouts of liberty and equality" were "hollow mockery . . . mere bombast, fraud, deception, impiety, and hypocrisy." Douglass's speeches, like those of another exslave, Sojourner Truth, took on an increasingly strident tone in the early 1850s.

At a women's rights convention in Akron, Ohio, in 1851, Truth made one of the decade's boldest statements for minority rights. The convention was attended by clergymen, who kept interrupting the proceedings to heckle female speakers. Up stood Sojourner Truth. She pointed to her many years of childbearing and hard, backbreaking work as a slave, crying out in a repetitive refrain, "And ain't I a woman?" Referring to Jesus, she asked where he came from: "From God and a woman: Man had nothing to do with Him." Referring to Eve, she concluded, "If the first woman God ever made was strong enough to turn the world upside down all alone, these women together ought to be able to turn it back, and get it right side up again! And now they is asking to do it, the men better let them." Her brief speech silenced the hecklers.

As Truth spoke, another American woman, Harriet Beecher Stowe, was finishing a novel, *Uncle Tom's Cabin*, that would go far toward turning the world upside down and trying to right it again. As politicians were hoping the American people would forget slavery, Stowe's novel brought it to the attention of thousands. She gave readers an absorbing indictment of the horrors of slavery and its immoral impact on both northerners and southerners. Published initially in serial form, each month's chapter ended at a nail-biting dramatic moment. Readers throughout the North cheered Eliza's daring escape across the ice floes on the Ohio River, cried over Uncle Tom's humanity and Little Eva's death, and suffered under the lash of Simon Legree.

When published in full in 1852, *Uncle Tom's Cabin* became one of the all-time best-sellers in American history. In the first year, over 300,000 copies were printed, and Stowe's novel was eventually published in 20 languages. When President Lincoln met Stowe in 1863, he is reported to have said to her, with a twinkle in his eye, "So you're the little woman who wrote the book that made this great war!"

## POLITICAL DISINTEGRATION

The response to *Uncle Tom's Cabin* and the Fugitive Slave Act indicated that politicians had congratulated themselves too soon for saving the Republic in 1850. Already occurring were other developments, not all dealing with slavery, that would weaken the ability of political parties—and ultimately the nation—to withstand the passions aroused by slavery.

### The Apathetic Election of 1852

Political parties, then and now, thrive on their ability to convince voters that their party stands for moral values and economic policies crucially different from those of the opposition. In the period between 1850 and 1854, these differences were blurred, thereby undermining party loyalty. First, both parties scrambled to convince voters that they had favored the Compromise of 1850, which becalmed the nettlesome slavery issue. In addition, several states rewrote their constitutions and remodeled their laws in the early 1850s, standardizing many political and economic procedures. One effect of these changes was to reduce the number of patronage jobs available for party victors to dispense. Another effect was to regularize the process, begun in the 1830s, for securing a banking, railroad, or other corporate charter, removing the role formerly played by the legislature. Both of these weakened the importance of the party in citizens' lives.

The third development that weakened parties was economic. For almost a quarter of a century, Whigs and Democrats had disagreed over such issues as the tariff, money and banking systems, and government support for internal improvements. But economic conditions improved markedly in the early 1850s. In a time of prosperity, party distinctions over economic policies seemed less important. An ample money supply made the revenues of a high tariff less necessary. Moreover, in the rush for railroad charters during the boom of the early fifties, local connections were more important than national party politics.

Economic issues continued to exist, but these battles were fought at the local rather than national level. Thus Georgia voters in 1851 disagreed over commercial banking laws, taxes for internal improvements, and, as an Augusta newspaper put it, "the jealousies of the poor who owned no slaves, against the rich slaveholder." In Indiana, where Congressman George Julian observed that people "hate the Negro with a perfect if not a supreme hatred," legislators rewrote the state constitution in 1851, depriving blacks of the rights to vote, attend white schools, and make contracts. Those who could not post a $500 bond were expelled from the state, and an 1852 law made it a crime for blacks to settle in Indiana. In Massachusetts, temperance reform and a law limiting the working day to ten hours were hot issues. Fleeting political alliances developed around particular issues and local personalities. As a Baltimore businessman said, "The two old parties are fast melting away."

The lessening significance of political parties was illustrated by the election of 1852. The Whigs nominated General Winfield Scott, another Mexican War hero, whom they hoped would repeat the success of Taylor four years earlier. With Clay and Webster both dead, party leadership had passed to William Seward, who wanted a president he could influence more successfully than the prosouthern Fillmore. Still, it took 52 ballots to nominate Scott over Fillmore, with serious costs in the party allegiance of southern Whigs. Democrats had their own problems deciding on a candidate. After 49 ballots, in which Cass, Douglas, and Buchanan each held the lead for a time, the party turned to the lackluster Franklin Pierce of New Hampshire as a compromise candidate.

The two parties offered little choice. Both played down issues in order not to widen intraparty divisions. Voter interest diminished. "Genl. Apathy is the strongest candidate out here," was the report from Ohio, while in Baltimore the *Sun* remarked that "there is no issue that much interests the people." Democratic prospects were aided by thousands of new Catholic immigrants from Ireland and Germany. Eligible for naturalization and, therefore, the right to vote after only three years, they were influenced by party officials, usually Democrats, who bought their votes with bribes and drinks. The Whigs, on the other hand, were seriously weakened by internal conflicts and defections. Pierce won easily, 254 to 42 electoral votes.

### The Kansas-Nebraska Act

The date of the Whig party's final disintegration can be pinpointed to a February day in 1854 when southern Whigs stood to support Stephen Douglas's Nebraska bill, thus choosing to be more southern than Whig. Many reasons caused the Illinois senator to introduce a bill organizing the Nebraska Territory (which included Kansas as well). As an ardent nationalist and chairman of the Committee on Territories, he was concerned for the continuing development of the West. As an Illinoisan in a period of explosive railroad building, he wanted the eastern terminus for a transcontinental railroad in Chicago rather than in rival St. Louis. This meant organizing the lands west of Iowa and Missouri.

Political reasons also played a role. Douglas wanted to recapture the party leadership he had held when he led the fight to pass the Compromise of 1850. He also harbored presidential ambitions. Although he had replaced Cass as the great advocate of popular sovereignty, which won him favor among northern Democrats, he needed the support of southern Democrats. Many southerners, especially slaveholders from Missouri, just east of the Nebraska Territory, opposed the organization of the territory unless it were open to slavery. The problem, as Douglas knew well, was that the entire Nebraska Territory lay north of the line where slavery had been prohibited by the Missouri Compromise.

Douglas's bill, introduced early in 1854, recommended using the principle of popular sovereignty in organizing the Kansas and Nebraska territories. This meant that the inhabitants could vote slavery in, thereby violating the Missouri Compromise. Douglas reasoned, however, that the climate and soil of the prairies in Kansas and Nebraska would never support a slavery-based agriculture, and the people would decide to be a free state. Therefore, he could win the votes he needed for the railroad without also getting slavery. His bill, then, ignored the Missouri Compromise, simply stating that the state or states created out of the Nebraska Territory would enter the Union "with or without slavery, as their constitution may prescribe at the time of their admission."

Douglas miscalculated. Northerners from his own party immediately attacked him and his bill as a "criminal betrayal of precious rights" and as part of a plot promoting Douglas's presidential ambitions by turning free Nebraska over to "slavery despotism." The outrage among Whigs and abolitionists was even greater. Frederick Douglass branded the act a "hateful" attempt to extend slavery, the result of the "audacious villainy of the slave power." He went to Douglas's own state of Illinois to confront, as he put it, "my distinguished namesake," calling him a man of the people who had gone wrong by ranging himself "on the side of oppressors."

But Stephen Douglas was a fighter. The more he was attacked as a "Judas" and a "Benedict Arnold," the harder he fought. Eventually his bill passed, but not without seriously damaging the political party system. What began as a railroad measure ended in reopening the question of slavery in the territories that Douglas and others had thought finally settled in 1850. What began as a way of avoiding conflict ended up in violence over whether Kansas would enter the Union slave or free. What began as a way of strengthening party lines over issues ended up destroying one party (the Whigs), planting deep, irreconcilable divisions in another (the Democrats), and creating two new ones (Know-Nothings and Republicans).

## Expansionist "Young America"

The Democratic party was weakened in the early 1850s not only by the Kansas-Nebraska

*Stephen Douglas's 1854 bill to allow Kansas and Nebraska to decide the slavery question for themselves sparked violent controversy and led to the death of the Whig party.*

Act but also by an ebullient, expansive energy that led Americans to adventures far beyond Kansas. As republican revolutions erupted in Europe in 1848, Americans greeted them as evidence that the American model of free republican institutions was the wave of the future. Those dedicated to the idea of this continuing national mission, which ironically included the spread of slavery, were called "Young America." An early expression of the spirit of Young America was the enthusiastic reception given the exiled Hungarian revolutionary Louis Kossuth while on a tour of the United States in 1851. At a dinner in Kossuth's honor, Daniel Webster announced that "we shall rejoice to see our American model upon the Lower Danube and on the mountains of Hungary." Webster was an old man at the time, with but a year to live, but he captured the mood of many Americans at midcentury.

Pierce's platform in 1852 recalled the successful expansionism of the Polk years, declaring that the Mexican War had been "just and necessary." Many Democrats took their overwhelming victory as a mandate to continue adding territory to the Republic. A Philadelphia newspaper in 1853 described the United States as a nation bound on the "East by sunrise, West by sunset, North by the Arctic Expedition, and South as far as we darn please." It was southward expansion into Latin America that looked most attractive.

Many of Pierce's diplomatic appointments were southerners interested in adding new cotton-growing lands to the national domain. As ambassador to Mexico, for example, Pierce sent James Gadsden, a railroad man from South Carolina. Almost immediately, Gadsden negotiated with Mexican president Santa Anna for the acquisition of large parts of northern Mexico, including all of Lower California (the Baja Peninsula). Gadsden failed to get all the land he wanted, but he did manage to purchase a strip of desert along the southwest border in order to build a trans-continental railroad linking the Deep South with the Pacific Coast.

The failure to acquire more territory from Mexico legally did not discourage expansionist Americans from pursuing illegal means.

During the 1850s, Texans and Californians staged dozens of raids (called "filibusters") into Mexico. The most daring adventurer of the era was William Walker, a slight 100-pound Tennesseean with a zest for danger and power. After migrating to southern California, Walker made plans to add slave lands to the country. In 1853, he invaded Lower California with less than 300 men and declared himself president of the independent Republic of Sonora. Although eventually arrested and tried in the United States, he was acquitted after eight minutes of deliberation.

Back Walker went, invading Nicaragua two years later. He overthrew the government, proclaimed himself to have been elected dictator, and issued a decree legalizing slavery. When the Nicaraguans, with British help, acted to regain control of their country, the United States Navy rescued Walker. After a triumphant tour in the South, he tried twice more to conquer Nicaragua. Walker came to a fitting end in 1860 when he was captured and shot by a Honduran firing squad after invading that country.

Undaunted by failures in the Southwest, the Pierce administration looked more seriously to the acquisition of Cuba, a Spanish colony many Americans thought destined to be a part of their country. One expansionist even suggested that Cuba physically belonged to the United States because it had been formed by alluvial deposits from the Mississippi River. "What God has joined together let no man put asunder," he said. The acquisition of Cuba was necessary, many maintained, as an extension of America's Manifest Destiny and as an ideal place for expanding the slave-based economy of the southern states. Senator Albert Gallatin Brown of Mississippi baldly said, "I want Cuba . . . and one or two Mexican States . . . and a foothold in Central America . . . for the spread of slavery."

A decade earlier, the Polk administration had offered Spain $10 million for Cuba, but the offer had been refused. Unsuccessful efforts were then made to foment a revolution among Cuban sugar planters, who would then request annexation by the United States. One Latin adventurer organized an invasion of Cuba, launched from New Orleans in 1850. When his attempt failed, he was executed, and hundreds of captured comrades were sent to Spain. The citizens of New Orleans rioted in protest, storming the Spanish consulate, which forced an embarrassed Congress to pay an indemnity. A few years later, the former governor of Mississippi, with the support of his friend, Secretary of War Jefferson Davis, made plans to raise $1 million and 50,000 troops to invade the island. The proposed expedition, which would conclude by carving Cuba into several new slave states, was aborted.

Although President Pierce did not support these illegal efforts, his administration did want Cuba. Secretary of State William Marcy instructed the emissary to Spain, Pierre Soulé, to offer $130 million for Cuba. If that failed, Marcy suggested stronger measures. In 1854, the secretary arranged for Soulé and the American ministers to France and England to meet in Belgium to consider options. The result was the Ostend Manifesto, a document intended to pressure Spain to sell Cuba to the United States. It also provides a fascinating glimpse of American expansionist attitudes.

The manifesto cited several reasons why Cuba "belongs naturally" to the United States. Both geographically and economically, the ministers argued, the fortunes and interests of Cubans and southerners were so "blended" that they were "one people with one destiny." Trade and commerce in the hemisphere would "never be secure" until Cuba was part of the United States. Moreover, southern slaveholders feared that a slave rebellion would "Africanize" Cuba, like Haiti, suggesting all kinds of "horrors to the white race" in the nearby southern United States. The American acquisition of Cuba was necessary, therefore, to "preserve our rectitude and self-respect."

If Spain refused to sell the island, the ministers threatened a Cuban revolution in which the Americans would "support . . . their neighbors and friends." If that should fail, the manifesto warned, "we should be justified in wresting it from Spain." Even Secretary Marcy was shocked when he received the document from Belgium, and he quickly rejected it. Like the Kansas-Nebraska Act, the Ostend Manifesto was urged most by those in the Democratic party who advocated the expansion of slavery. The out-

raged reaction of northerners in both cases divided and weakened the Democratic party.

## Nativism, Know-Nothings, and Republicans

Foreign immigration (see Chapter 11) damaged an already enfeebled Whig party and created concern among many native-born Americans. To the average, hardworking Protestant American, the foreigners pouring into the cities and following the railroads westward spoke unfamiliar languages, wore funny clothes, drank alcohol freely in grogshops, and increased crime and pauperism. Still worse, they attended Catholic churches, where the Latin mass and eucharistic rituals offended those used to Protestant worship, and sent children to their own schools. Furthermore, they seemed content with a lower standard of living and would work for lower wages in worse conditions than American workers, thus threatening their jobs. Perhaps worst of all, many said, the new immigrants corrupted American politics.

Catholic immigrants preferred the Democratic party out of traditional loyalties and because Whigs were more inclined than Democrats to interfere with religion, schooling, drinking, and other aspects of personal behavior. It was mostly former Whigs, therefore, who founded a new national party in 1854, the American party, to oppose the new immigrants. Members wanted a longer period of naturalization in order to guarantee the "vital principles of Republican Government" and pledged themselves never to vote for Irish Catholics for public office since it was assumed that their highest loyalty was to the pope in Rome. They also agreed to keep information about their order secret. If asked, they would say, "I know nothing." Hence, they were dubbed the Know-Nothing party.

The Know-Nothings were overwhelmingly a party of the middle and lower classes, workers who worried about their jobs and wages and farmers and small-town Americans who worried about disruptive new forces in their lives. As one New Yorker put it in 1854, "Roman Catholicism is feared more than American slavery." It was widely believed that Catholics slavishly obeyed the orders of their priests, who represented a church that had long been associated with European despotism. The opposition of the Catholic church to the revolutionary movements of 1848 in Europe intensified the fears of many Protestant Americans that a mass of Catholic voters deeply threatened their democratic order. In the 1854 and 1855 elections, the Know-Nothings gave anti-Catholicism a national political focus for the first time. They did so well that they even appeared to replace the Whigs as the second major party.

Although the nativists argued that it was papism that most threatened to subvert freedom and other republican values, others maintained that the slavepower of the South was the chief danger. No sooner had the debates over Nebraska ended than a group of ex-Whigs and Free-Soilers met and formed the nucleus of another new party, called the Republican party.

*In this 1852 American party cartoon, a poor immigrant is accosted by Webster, Houston, Douglas, and Scott, each seeking his vote. Partly to prevent such blatant political hucksptering, the Know-Nothings emerged urging tighter restrictions on immigration and citizenship.*

## Immigration: Volume and Sources, 1840–1860

*Source:* U.S. Bureau of the Census.

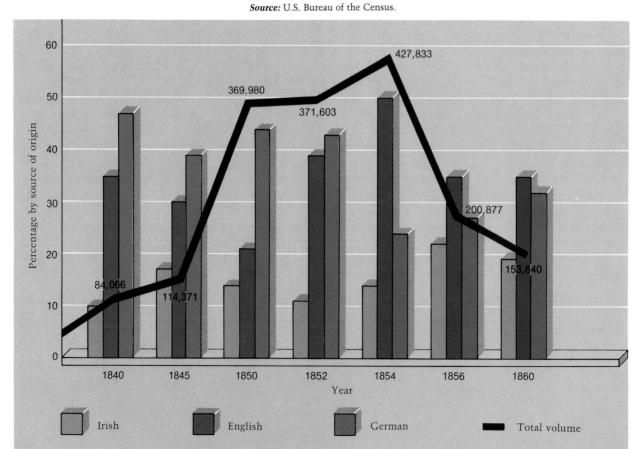

Composed almost entirely of northerners, the Republican party combined four main elements. The first group, led by Seward, Senators Charles Sumner of Massachusetts and Salmon P. Chase of Ohio, and Representative George Julian of Indiana, were ardent abolitionists determined to prohibit slavery in the territories. They also sought to divorce the federal government from the support of slavery by freeing slaves in the District of Columbia, repealing the Fugitive Slave Act, and eliminating the internal slave trade. There were, however, limits to the idealism of most Republicans. A more moderate and larger group, typified by Abraham Lincoln of Illinois, opposed slavery in the western territories only but would not interfere with it where it already existed. This group also indicated that it would not support efforts to achieve equal rights for northern free blacks.

Republicans were anti-Catholic as well as antislavery. This third element of the party, reflecting the traditional Whig reformist impulse, felt responsible for cleansing America of its sins of intemperance, impiety, parochial schooling, and other forms of immorality. Another sin included voting for Democrats, who were accused of catering to "the grog shops, foreign vote, and Catholic brethren" by combining "the forces of Jesuitism and Slavery." The fourth element of the Republican party, a Whig legacy from the American System of Henry Clay, included those who wanted the federal government to promote commercial and industrial development and the dignity of labor. This meant advocating a protective tariff for industry, generous federal land grants for railroads, and cheap homesteading lands for free farmers.

The chief test of the strengths of the Republican and Know-Nothing (American) parties came in 1856. Which party could best oppose the Democrats? The American party nominated Fillmore, who had strong support in the Upper South and border states. The Republicans chose John C. Frémont, a Free-Soiler from Missouri with virtually no political experience. The Democrats nominated James Buchanan of Pennsylvania, commonly known as "a northern man with southern principles." Frémont's strength in the North helped him carry several free states, while Fillmore won only Maryland. Buchanan, taking advantage of the divided opposition, won the election, but with only 45 percent of the popular vote.

After 1856, the Know-Nothings died out as a party, largely because of the Republican party's broad appeal but also because their secrecy, intense hatreds, and occasional violent attacks on Catholic voters damaged their image. Such behavior was as threatening to republican values as popery itself. But the Know-Nothings represented a powerful current in American politics that would return again and again in American history when the nation seeemed threatened by social and economic changes. It became convenient for many to label others "un-American" and seek to root them out. Although the Know-Nothing party disappeared after 1856, nativism did not.

## Changing Political Party Systems and Leaders

| *First Party System: 1790s–1820s* | |
|---|---|
| Republican* | Federalist |
| Jefferson | Hamilton |
| Madison | John Adams |
| Monroe | |
| *Transition: 1824 and 1828* | |
| Democrat-Republican | National Republican |
| Jackson | J. Q. Adams |
| *Second Party System: 1830s–1850s* | |
| Democrat | Whig |
| Jackson | Clay |
| Van Buren | Webster |
| Calhoun | W. H. Harrison |
| Polk | |
| *Third Party System: 1856–1890s* | |
| Democrat | Republican* |
| Douglas | Lincoln |
| Pierce | Seward |
| Buchanan | |

*Note that the REPUBLICAN party label begins in one tradition and ends up in the other.

# KANSAS AND THE TWO CULTURES

However appealing nativist issues were for many Americans, the problem of slavery was the issue that would not disappear. As Democrats sought ways of expanding slavery and other American institutions westward across the Plains and south into Cuba in the mid-1850s, Republicans wanted to halt the advance of slavery to prove to the world, as Seward said, that the American "experiment in self-government" still worked. In 1854, Lincoln worried that it was slavery that "deprives our republican example of its just influence in the world." The specific cause of his concern was the likelihood that slavery might be extended into Kansas as a result of the passage that year of Stephen Douglas's Kansas-Nebraska Act.

### Competing for Kansas

During the congressional debates over the Kansas-Nebraska bill, Seward had accepted the challenge of slave-state senators to "engage in competition for the virgin soil of Kansas." Speaking for "the cause of freedom," the New York senator pronounced that God would "give the victory to the side which is stronger in numbers than it is in right." The passage of the Kansas-Nebraska Act in 1854 opened the way for proslavery and antislavery forces to meet physically and to compete with each other, both in numbers and in righteousness, over whether Kansas would become a slave or free state.

No sooner had the bill passed Congress than Eli Thayer founded the Massachusetts Emigrant Aid Society to recruit free-soil settlers to go to Kansas. From New York, Frederick Douglass called for "companies of emigrants from the free states . . . to possess the goodly land." By the summer of 1855, about 1,200 New England colonists had migrated to Kansas.

One of the migrants was Julia Louisa Lovejoy, a minister's wife from Vermont. As a Mississippi riverboat carried her into a slave state for the first time, she described the dilapidated plantation homes of the monotonous Missouri shore as reflecting "the blighting mildew of slavery." By the time Julia and her husband arrived in the Kansas Territory, she had concluded that "the inhabitants and morals" of slaveholding Missourians who had moved into Kansas were of "an *undescribably repulsive* and undesirable character." To Julia Lovejoy, northerners came to bring the "energetic Yankee" virtues of morality and economic enterprise to the drunken, unclean slaveholders of the Southwest.

Perhaps she had in mind David Atchison, Democratic senator from Missouri. Atchison believed that Congress had an obligation to protect slavery in the territories, thereby permitting Missouri slaveholders to move into Kansas. As early as 1853, he pledged himself "to extend the institutions of Missouri over the Territory at whatever sacrifice of blood or treasure." He described New England migrants as "negro thieves" and "abolition tyrants." He recommended to fellow Missourians that they defend their property and interests "with the *bayonet* and with *blood*" and, if need be, "to kill every God-damned abolitionist in the district."

Under Atchison's inflammatory leadership, secret societies sprang up in the Missouri counties adjacent to Kansas. They vowed to combat the evil influence of the Free-Soilers. One editor exclaimed that northerners came to Kansas "for the express purpose of stealing, running off and hiding runaway negroes from Missouri [and] taking to their own bed . . . a stinking negro wench." It was not slaveholders but New Englanders, he said, who were immoral, uncivilized, and hypocritical. Rumors of 20,000 such Massachusetts migrants spurred Missourians to action. Thousands poured across the border late in 1854 to vote in the first territorial election. Twice as many ballots were cast as the number of registered voters, and in one polling place only 20 of over 600 voters were legal residents.

The proslavery forces overreacted to their fear of the New England migrants and their intentions. The permanent population of Kansas was composed primarily of migrants from Missouri and other border states who were more concerned with land titles than slavery. They were opposed to any blacks—slave or free—

moving into their state. As one clergyman put it, "I kem to Kansas to live in a free state and I don't want niggers a-trampin' over my grave."

In March 1855, a second election was held to select a territorial legislature. The pattern of border crossings, intimidation, and illegal voting repeated itself. Atchison himself, drinking "considerable whiskey" along the way, led a band of armed men across the state line to vote and frighten would-be Free-Soil voters away. Not surprisingly, a small minority of eligible voters elected a proslavery territorial legislature. Free-Soilers, meanwhile, staged their own constitutional convention in Lawrence and created a Free-Soil government at Topeka. It banned blacks from the state. The proslavery legislature settled first in Shawnee Mission and then in Lecompton, giving Kansas two governments.

The struggle shifted to Washington, where President Pierce, who could have nullified the illegal election, did nothing. Congress debated the wrongs in Kansas and sent an investigating committee, which further inflamed passions. Throughout 1855, the call to arms grew more strident. One proslavery newspaper invited southerners to bring their weapons and "send the scoundrels" from the North "back to whence they came, or . . . to hell, it matters not which." Robert Allston heard the call in South Carolina. He wrote his son Benjamin that he was "raising men and money . . . to counteract the effect of the Northern hordes. . . . We are disposed to fight the battle of our rights . . . on the field of Kansas."

Both sides saw Kansas as a holy battleground for their version of moral right. An Alabaman, Colonel Jefferson Buford, even sold his slaves to raise money to hire an army of 300 men to fight for slavery in Kansas, promising free land to his recruits. Both a Baptist and a Methodist minister blessed their departure from Montgomery. The Baptist promised them God's favor and gave each man a Bible. Northern Christians responded in kind. At Yale University, the noted minister, Henry Ward Beecher, presented 25 Bibles and 25 Sharps rifles to young men who would go fight for the Lord in Kansas. "There are times," he said, "when self-defense is a religious duty. If that duty was ever imperative it is now, and in Kansas." Beecher suggested that rifles would be of greater use and "moral agency" than Bibles. Missourians dubbed them "Beecher's Bibles" and vowed, as one newspaper put it, "Blood for Blood! . . . for each drop spilled, we shall require one hundred fold!"

### "Bleeding Kansas"

As civil war threatened in Kansas, a Brooklyn poet, Walt Whitman, heralded American democracy in his epic poem, *Leaves of Grass* (1855). Whitman identified himself as the embodiment of average Americans "of every hue and caste, . . . of every rank and religion." Ebulliently, Whitman embraced urban mechanics, southern woodcutters, planter's sons, runaway slaves, mining-camp prostitutes, and a catalog of others in his poetic celebration of "the word Democratic, the word En-Masse." At the same time, Whitman's faith in the American masses was shaken in the mid-1850s. He worried that a knife would be plunged into "the breast" of the Union, thus bringing on "the red blood of civil war."

Inevitably, as Whitman feared, blood flowed in Kansas. In May 1856, with the support of a prosouthern federal marshall, a mob entered Lawrence, smashed the offices and presses of a Free-Soil newspaper, fired several cannonballs into the Free State Hotel, and destroyed homes and shops. Three nights later, motivated by vengeance and a feeling that he was doing God's will, a crazed John Brown led a small New England band, including four of his sons, to a proslavery settlement near Pottawatomie Creek. There they dragged five men out of their cabins and, despite the terrified entreaties of their wives, hacked them to death with swords.

Violence also entered the halls of Congress in Washington. That same week, abolitionist senator Charles Sumner delivered a tirade that became known as "The Crime Against Kansas." He lashed out against the "murderous robbers" and "incredible atrocities of the Assassins and . . . Thugs" from the South. With nasty invective, he accused proslavery Senate leaders, especially Atchison and Andrew Butler of South Carolina, of cavorting with "the harlot, Slavery." Two days later, Butler's nephew, Congressman Preston Brooks, avenged the honor of his colleague by beating Sumner senseless with his cane as he sat at his Senate desk.

The sack of Lawrence, the massacre at Pottawatomie Creek, and the caning of Sumner set off a minor civil war, which historians have called "Bleeding Kansas." It lasted throughout the summer. Crops were burned, homes destroyed, fights broke out in saloons and streets, and night raiders tortured and murdered their enemies. For those like Charles Lines, who just wanted to farm his land in peace, it was impossible to remain neutral. Lines hoped his neighbors near Lawrence would avoid "involving themselves in trouble." But when a "mild man" in the community much like himself was tortured by proslavery forces, tied up, and left to die, Lines finally took up arms and joined the battle. He wrote to a friend that "blood must end in the triumph of the right."

Even before the bleeding of Kansas began, the New York *Tribune* warned, "We are two peoples. We are a people for Freedom and a people for Slavery. Between the two, conflict is inevitable." The moral rhetoric and violence in Kansas demonstrated that what was at stake was the competing visions of two separate cultures for the future destiny of the United States.

*A preview of the Civil War occurred in Kansas. When a proslavery mob sacked Lawrence, leveling the Free State Hotel, a summer of violence followed, later known as "Bleeding Kansas."*

Despite many similarities between the North and the South, as well as tremendous variations within each section, the stereotyped gap between the two sides widened as the hostilities of the 1850s increased.

## Northern Views and Visions

The North saw itself, as Julia Lovejoy suggested, as a prosperous land of bustling commerce, vigorous enterprise, and expanding, independent agriculture. Northern farmers and workers were self-made free men who believed in individualism and democracy. In the "free labor system" of the North, as both Seward and Lincoln often said, there was equality of opportunity and upward mobility. Both generated more wealth. Although the North contained many growing cities, northerners revered the values of the small towns that spread from New England across the Upper Midwest. These values included a respect for the rights of the people

### "Bleeding Kansas"

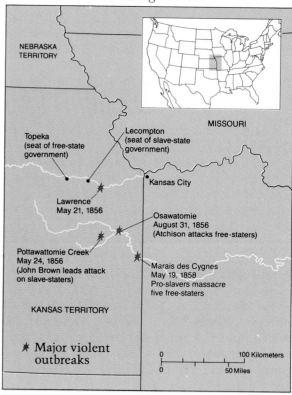

tempered by the rule of law, individual enterprise balanced by a concern for one's neighbors, and a fierce morality rooted in Calvinist Protestantism. Northerners would regulate morality—by persuasion if possible but by legislation if necessary—to remove the sins of irreligion, illiteracy, and intemperance from American society. It was no accident that the ideas of universal public education and laws against the sale and consumption of alcohol both began in New England.

Northerners valued the kind of republican government that guaranteed the rights of free men, enabling them to achieve economic progress. Specifically, this meant supporting government action to promote free labor, industrial growth, immigration, foreign trade (protected by tariffs), and the development of railroads and free farm homesteads westward across the continent. Energetic mobility both westward and upward would dissolve state, regional, and class loyalties and increase the sense of nationhood. A strong Union could achieve national, and even international, greatness. These were the conditions, befitting a chosen people, that would, as Seward put it, spread American institutions around the world and "renovate the condition of mankind."

Only free men could achieve economic progress and a moral society. Therefore, the worst sin in the northerner's view was the loss of one's freedom. Slavery was the root of all evil. It was, Seward said, "incompatible with all . . . the elements of the security, welfare, and greatness of nations." The South, then, represented the antithesis of everything that northerners saw as good. Southerners were seen as unfree, backward, economically stagnant, uneducated, lawless, immoral, and out of harmony with the values and ideals of the nineteenth century. Julia Lovejoy's denunciation of slaveholding Missourians was mild. Her fellow migrants to Kansas described southerners as subhuman, unclean, and uncivilized. They were, as one put it, "drunken ourang-outans," "wild beasts" who drank whiskey, ate dirt, uttered oaths, raped slave women, and fought or dueled at the slightest excuse. In the popular language of the day, they were known as "Pukes."

## The Southern Perspective

If in the North the values of economic enterprise were most important, southerners revered social values most. Like the English gentry they sought to emulate, they saw themselves as courteous, refined, hospitable, and chivalrous. By contrast, they saw northerners as coarse, ill-mannered, aggressive, and materialistic "Yankees." In a society where one person in three was a black slave, racial distinctions and paternalistic relationships were crucial in maintaining order and white supremacy. Fear of slave revolt was ever present. The South had five times more military schools than the North. Northerners educated the many for economic utility, but southerners educated the few for grace and character. In short, the South saw itself as a genteel, ordered society guided by the aristocratic code of the gentleman planter.

Southerners agreed with northerners that sovereignty in a republic rested in the people, who created a government of laws to protect life, liberty, and property. But unlike people in the North, southerners believed that the democratic principle of self-government was best preserved in local political units such as the state. Southerners were ready to fight to defend their sacred rights against any tyrannical encroachment on their liberty, as they had in 1776. They saw themselves, in fact, as true revolutionary patriots. Like northerners, southerners cherished the Union. But they preferred the loose confederacy of the Jeffersonian past to the centralized nationalism Seward kept invoking.

To southerners, Yankees were in too much of a hurry—to make money, to reform the behavior of others, to put dreamy theories (like racial equality) into practice. Two images dominated the South's view of northerners: either they were stingy, hypocritical, moralizing Puritans, or they were grubby, slum-dwelling, Catholic immigrants. A Georgia paper combined both images in an 1856 editorial: "Free society! we sicken at the name. What is it but a conglomeration of greasy mechanics, filthy operatives, small-fisted farmers, and moon-struck theorists?" These northerners, the paper said, "are devoid of society fitted for well-bred gentlemen."

*These scenes illustrate the contrasting socioeconomic cultures of the antebellum North and South. Rochester in 1860 was a bustling industrial city, delivering manufactured goods to northern markets by canalboats and railroads, while the vital unit of southern commerce was the genteel individual plantation, with steamboats carrying cotton to port cities for trade with Europe.*

Each side, then, saw the other threatening its freedom and infringing upon its view of a proper republican society. Each saw the other imposing barriers to their vision for America's future, which included the economic systems described in Chapters 11 and 12. As hostilities increased, the views each section had of the other grew steadily more rigid and conspiratorial. Northerners saw the South as a "slave power," determined to foist the slave system on free labor throughout the land. Southerners saw the North as full of "black Republicanism," determined to destroy the southern way of life.

## POLARIZATION AND THE ROAD TO WAR

Since the beginning of national parties, these cultural stereotypes and conspiratorial accusations had been held in check. But after Kansas, with the Whigs already replaced by the Republicans, only the Democrats remained a national party. The Nebraska bill, the Ostend Manifesto, and the violence in Kansas, however, had weakened the Democrats. Further events, still involving the question of slavery in the territories, soon split the Democratic party irrevocably into sectional halves: the Dred Scott decision of the Supreme Court (1857), the Lecompton constitutional crisis in Kansas (1857), the Lincoln-Douglas debates in Illinois (1858), John Brown's raid in Virginia (1859), and, finally, Lincoln's election in 1860. These incidents further polarized the negative images each culture held of the other, and set the nation on the final road to civil war.

### The Dred Scott Case

The events of 1857 reinforced the arguments of those who believed in a slave power conspiracy. Two days after James Buchanan's inauguration, the Supreme Court finally ruled in *Dred Scott* v. *Sanford*. The case had been pending before the Court for nearly three years, but the slave family of Dred Scott had been waiting longer for the decision. In 1846, Dred and Harriet Scott had filed suit in Missouri for their freedom. They argued that their master had taken them into Minnesota, Wisconsin, and other territories where the Missouri Compromise prohibited slavery, and therefore they should be freed. By the time the case reached the Supreme Court, the issue of slavery in the territories had become a heated political issue.

When the Court, which had a majority of

southern judges, issued its decision (by a vote of 7 to 2), it made three rulings. First, since blacks were, as Chief Justice Roger Taney put it, "beings of an inferior order [who] had no rights which white men were bound to respect," Dred Scott was not a citizen and had no right to sue in federal courts. Justice Daniel of Virginia was even more indelicate in his consenting opinion, saying that "the African Negro race" did not belong "to the family of nations" but rather was a subject for "commerce or traffic," "slaves," "property." The second ruling stated that the Missouri Compromise was unconstitutional because Congress did not have the power to ban slavery in a territory. And third, the fact that the Scotts had been taken in and out of free states did not affect their status. Despite two eloquent dissenting opinions, Dred and Harriet Scott remained slaves.

These decisions had implications that went far beyond the Scotts' personal freedom. Although the Kansas-Nebraska Act had already nullified the Missouri Compromise in effect, the formal repeal of that compromise in the Dred Scott case was the first time in U.S. history that the Supreme Court had declared a major act of Congress unconstitutional. The arguments about black citizenship insulted and infuriated many northerners. Frederick Douglass called the ruling "a most scandalous and devilish perversion of the Constitution, and a brazen misstatement of the facts of history." Many worried about the few rights free blacks still held.

Even more troublesome was the possibility hinted at in the decision that slavery might be permitted in the free states of the North, where it had long been banned. People who suspected a conspiracy were not calmed when Buchanan endorsed the Dred Scott decision as a final settlement of the right of citizens to take their "property of any kind, including slaves, into the common Territories . . . and to have it protected there under the Federal Constitution." One issue, however, remained unresolved by the Court. Could a territorial legislature write a constitution that permitted the introduction of new slaves? Rather than settling the political issue of slavery in the territories, as Buchanan had hoped, the Dred Scott decision threw it back into American politics. It opened up new questions and increased sectional hostilities.

## Douglas and the Democrats

The Dred Scott decision and Buchanan's endorsement fed northern suspicions of a "slave power" conspiracy to impose slavery everywhere. Events in Kansas, which still had two governments, heightened these fears. In the summer of 1857, Kansas had still another election, with so many irregularities that only 2,000 out of a possible 24,000 voters participated. They elected a proslavery slate of delegates to a constitutional convention meeting at Lecompton as a preparation for statehood. The convention decided to exclude free blacks from the state, to guarantee the property rights of the few slaveholders in Kansas, and to ask voters to decide in a referendum whether to permit more slaves.

The proslavery Lecompton constitution,

*The decision in 1857 to deny Dred Scott's suit for freedom was alarming even to those who took a moderate stance on the issue of slavery.*

which was clearly unrepresentative of the wishes of the majority of the people of Kansas, was sent to Congress for approval. Anxious not to lose the support of southern Democrats, Buchanan endorsed it. Stephen Douglas challenged the president's power and jeopardized his own standing with southern Democrats by opposing it. Facing reelection to the Senate from Illinois in 1858, he needed to hold the support of the northern wing of his party. Congress sent the Lecompton constitution back to the people of Kansas for another referendum. This time they defeated it, which meant that Kansas remained a territory rather than becoming a slave state. As Kansas was left in an uncertain status, the larger political effect of the struggle was to split the Democratic party almost beyond repair.

No sooner had Douglas settled the Lecompton question than he faced reelection in Illinois. Douglas's heroic opposition to the Lecompton constitution had restored his prestige in the North as an opponent of the slave power. This cut some ground out from under the Republican party claim that it was the only force capable of stopping the spread of southern power. As Buchanan rallied southern Democrats against Douglas, some eastern Republicans suggested that the party ought not to oppose his reelection. However, western party leaders had a candidate who understood the need to reestablish Republican moral and political distinctions.

### Lincoln and the Illinois Debates

Although he was relatively unknown nationally and had not held elected office in several years, by 1858, Abraham Lincoln of Illinois had emerged to challenge William Seward for leadership of the Republican party. Lincoln's character was shaped on the midwestern frontier, where he had educated himself, developed mild abolitionist views, and dreamed of America's greatness.

Since Douglas was clearly the leading Democrat, the Senate election in Illinois appeared to be a preview of the presidential election of 1860. The other Douglass, Frederick, had observed that "the slave power idea was the ideological glue of the Republican party." It was Lincoln's handling of this idea that would be crucial in distinguishing him from Stephen Douglas. The

Illinois campaign featured a series of seven debates between Lincoln and Douglas in different cities. With a national as well as a local audience, the debates provided a remarkable opportunity for the two men to state their views on the heated racial issues before the nation.

Lincoln set a solemn tone when he accepted the Republican senatorial nomination in Chicago in June. The American nation, he said, was in a "crisis" and building toward a worse one. "A House divided against itself cannot stand. I believe this government cannot endure, permanently half *slave* and half *free*." Lincoln said he did not expect the Union "to be dissolved" or "the house to fall" but rather that "it will become *all* one thing, or *all* the other." Then he rehearsed the history of the South's growing influence over national policy since the Kansas-Nebraska Act, which he blamed on Douglas. Lincoln stated his firm opposition to the Dred Scott decision, which he believed part of a conspiracy involving Pierce, Buchanan, Taney, and Douglas. People like himself, who opposed this conspiracy, wished to place slavery, he said, on a "course of ultimate extinction."

In the ensuing debates with Douglas, Lincoln reiterated these themes, especially the controversial phrase about "ultimate extinction." He also expressed his views on race and slavery, formed from a blend of experience, principle, and politics. Although far from a radical abolitionist, in these debates Lincoln skillfully staked out a moral position not only in advance of Douglas but well ahead of his time.

Lincoln was also very much a part of his time. He believed that whites were superior to blacks. He did not favor equal rights for free blacks—not the vote, nor jury service, nor intermarriage. He believed, furthermore, that the physical and moral differences between whites and blacks would "forever forbid the two races from living together on terms of social and political equality." He worried about the long-term implications and even considered "separation" and colonization in Liberia or Central America.

Where Lincoln differed from most contemporaries was in the sincere depth of his commitment to the humane principles of the equality and essential dignity of all human beings, including blacks. Douglas, on the other hand, arguing against race mixing in a blatant bid for votes, continually made racial slurs. Lincoln not only believed that blacks were "entitled to all the natural rights . . . in the Declaration of Independence" but also that they had many specific economic rights as well, like "the right to put into his mouth the bread that his own hands have earned." In these rights, blacks were, Lincoln said, *my equal and the equal of Judge Douglas, and the equal of every living man."*

Unlike Douglas, Lincoln hated slavery. At Galesburg, he said, "I contemplate slavery as a moral, social, and political evil." In Quincy, he said that the difference between a Republican and a Democrat was quite simply whether one thought slavery wrong or right. Douglas was more equivocal and dodged the issue in Freeport by pointing out that slavery would not exist if it were not supported by favorable local legislation. Douglas's moral indifference to slavery was clear in his admission that he did not care if a territorial legislature voted it "up or down." Republicans did care, Lincoln affirmed, sounding a warning that the course toward "ultimate extinction" had begun. Although barred by the Constitution from doing anything about slavery where it already existed, Lincoln said that since Republicans believed slavery to be wrong, "we propose a course of policy that shall deal with it as a wrong."

What Lincoln meant by "policy" was not yet clear, even to himself. However, in the debates he did succeed in affirming that the Republican party was the only moral and political force capable of stopping the slave power. It seems ironic now, though it did not at the time, that Douglas won the election. When he and Lincoln met again two years later, the order of their finish would be reversed. Elsewhere in 1858, however, Democrats did poorly, losing 18 congressional seats to the Republicans.

## John Brown's Raid

Unlike Lincoln, John Brown was again prepared to act decisively against slavery. On October 16, 1859, he led a band of 22 men in an assault on a federal arsenal at Harpers Ferry, Virginia (now West Virginia). He hoped that the attack might signal a general uprising of slaves throughout the Upper South or at least provide the arms by which slaves could make their way to freedom. Although he seized the arsenal, he was soon overcome by federal troops. Nearly half his men were killed, including two sons. Brown himself was captured, tried, and hanged for treason. So ended a lifetime of failures.

In death, however, he was not a failure. Brown's daring if foolhardy raid, and his impressively dignified behavior during his trial and speedy execution, unleashed powerful passions, further widening the gap between North and South. Northerners responded to his death with an outpouring of admiration and sympathy, both for the man and his cause. Memorial rallies, parades, and prayer meetings were held. Admirers wrote poems, songs, and speeches in his honor. Thoreau compared Brown to Christ and called him "an angel of light." Abolitionist William Lloyd Garrison, though a pacifist, was moved to wish "success to every slave insurrection" in the South. Ministers called slave revolt a "divine weapon" and glorified Brown's treason as "holy." Frederick Douglass had consulted with Brown before the raid. What he did, Douglass pointed out, was to show that the use of reason was "in vain" as a way to end slavery and that "a system of brute force . . . must be met with its own weapons."

What Brown also did, Douglass said, was to fill southerners with "dread and terror." His raid stimulated a wave of fear of slave revolts, led by hundreds of imaginary Nat Turners, throughout the South. This atmosphere of suspicion eroded freedom of thought and expression. A North Carolinian described a "spirit of terror, mobs, arrests, and violence" in his state. Twelve families in Berea, Kentucky, were evicted from the state for their mild abolitionist sentiments. A Texas minister who criticized the treatment of slaves in a sermon was given 70 lashes.

In response to the Brown raid, southerners also became more convinced, as the governor of South Carolina put it, that a "black Republican" plot in the North was "arrayed against the slaveholders." In this atmosphere of mistrust, southern Unionists lost their influence, and power became concentrated in the hands of those who most favored secession. Only one step remained to complete the southern sense of having become a permanent minority within the United States: withdrawing to form a new nation. Senator Robert Toombs of Georgia, insistent that northern "enemies" were plotting the South's ruin, warned fellow southerners late in 1859, "Never permit this Federal government to pass into the traitorous hands of the black Republican party."

## The Election of 1860

The conflict between Buchanan and Douglas took its toll on the Democratic party. When the nominating convention convened in Charleston, South Carolina, a hotbed of secessionist sentiments, it met for a record ten days without being able to name a presidential candidate. The convention went through 59 ballots, was disrupted twice by the withdrawal of southern delegates, and then adjourned for six weeks. Meeting again, this time in Baltimore, the Dem-

*In the aftermath of John Brown's raid, passions fed by fear were unleashed throughout the South against northern sympathizers, and vice versa. A year later, the editor of a Massachusetts newspaper that expressed southern sympathies found himself the victim of the time-honored mob punishment of tarring and feathering.*

ocrats acknowledged their irreparable division by naming two candidates in two separate conventions. Douglas represented northern Democrats, and John C. Breckenridge, Buchanan's vice-president, carried the banner of the proslavery South. The Constitutional Union party, made up of former southern Whigs and border-state nativists, claimed the middle ground of compromise and nominated John Bell, a slaveholder from Tennessee with mild views.

With Democrats split in two and a new party in contention, the Republican strategy aimed at keeping the states carried by Frémont in 1856 and adding Pennsylvania, Illinois, and Indiana. Seward, the leading candidate for the nomination, had been tempering his antislavery views in order to appear more electable. So had Abraham Lincoln, who seemed more likely than Seward to carry those key states. With some shrewd political maneuvering emphasizing Lincoln's "availability" as a moderate with widespread appeal, he was nominated by his party.

The Republican platform also reflected moderation, reducing attacks on slavery to oppose only its extension. Most of the platform spoke to the concerns of the several elements of the party: tariff protection, subsidized internal improvements, free labor, and a homestead bill. Above all, the Republicans, like southern Democrats, defended their view of what republican values meant for America's future. It did not include the kind of society of equal rights envisioned by Frederick Douglass. An English traveler in 1860 observed that in America "we see, in effect, two nations—one white and another black—growing up together within the same political circle, but never mingling on a principle of equality."

The Republican moderate strategy for electoral victory worked exactly as planned, as Lincoln swept the entire Northeast and Midwest. Although receiving less than 40 percent of the popular vote nationwide, his triumph in the North was decisive. Even a united Democratic party could not have defeated him. With victory assured, Lincoln finished his sandwich and coffee on election night in Springfield and prepared for the consequences and awesome responsibilities of his election. They came even before his inauguration.

### Presidential Elections, 1848–1860

| YEAR | CANDIDATES | PARTY | POPULAR VOTE | ELECTORAL VOTE |
|------|------------|-------|--------------|----------------|
| 1848 | Z. TAYLOR | Whig | 1,360,101 (47%) | 163 |
| | L. Cass | Democrat | 1,220,544 (43%) | 127 |
| | M. Van Buren | Free Soil | 291,263 (10%) | 0 |
| 1852 | F. PIERCE | Democrat | 1,601,474 (51%) | 254 |
| | W. Scott | Whig | 1,386,578 (44%) | 42 |
| | J. Hale | Free-Soil | 156,149 (5%) | 0 |
| 1856 | J. BUCHANAN | Democrat | 1,838,169 (45%) | 174 |
| | J. Frémont | Republican | 1,335,264 (33%) | 114 |
| | M. Fillmore | Know-Nothing | 874,534 (22%) | 8 |
| 1860 | A. LINCOLN | Republican | 1,866,352 (40%) | 180 |
| | S. Douglas | Democrat | 1,375,157 (29%) | 12 |
| | J. Breckinridge | Democrat | 847,953 (18%) | 72 |
| | J. Bell | Constitutional Union | 589,581 (13%) | 39 |

*Note:* Winner's name is in capital letters.

## THE DIVIDED HOUSE FALLS

The Republicans overestimated the extent of Unionist sentiment in the South. They could not believe that the secessionists would prevail after Lincoln's victory. A year earlier, some southern congressmen had walked out in protest of the selection of an antislavery speaker of the House. A Republican leader, Carl Schurz, recalling this act, said that the southerners had taken a drink and then come back. After Lincoln's election, Schurz predicted, they would walk out, take two drinks, and come back again. He was wrong.

### Secession and Uncertainty

On December 20, 1860, South Carolina seceded from the Union, declaring the "experiment" of putting people with "different pursuits and institutions" under one government a failure. By February 1, the other six Deep South states (Mississippi, Florida, Alabama, Georgia, Louisiana, and Texas) had seceded. A week later, delegates met in Montgomery, Alabama, created the Confederate States of America, adopted a constitution, and elected Jefferson Davis its provisional president. The divided house had fallen, as Lincoln had predicted it would. What was not

yet certain, though, was whether the house could be put back together or whether disunion necessarily meant civil war.

The government in Washington had three options. The first was compromise, but the emotions of the time ruled out that possibility. Most proposed compromises were really concessions to the secessionist states. The second option, suggested by Horace Greeley, editor of the New York *Tribune*, was to let the seven states "go in peace," taking care not to lose the border states. But this was opposed by northern businessmen, who would lose profitable economic ties with the South, and by those who believed in an indissoluble Union. The third option was to compel secessionist states to return, which probably meant war.

Republican hopes that southern Unionism would assert itself and make none of these options necessary seemed possible in February 1861. The momentum toward disunion slowed, and no more southern states seceded. The nation waited and watched, wondering what Virginia and the border states would do, what outgoing President Buchanan would do, and what the Congress would do. Prosouthern and determined not to start a civil war in the last

## Major Causes and Events Leading to the Civil War

| DATE | EVENT | IMPACT OR EFFECT AS CAUSE OF CIVIL WAR |
| --- | --- | --- |
| 1600s–1860s | Slavery in the South | Major underlying pervasive cause |
| 1700s–1860s | Development of two distinct socioeconomic systems and cultures | Further reinforced slavery as fundamental socioeconomic, cultural, moral issue |
| 1787–1860s | States' rights, nullification doctrine | Ongoing political issue, less fundamental as cause |
| 1820 | Missouri Compromise (36°30′) | Background for conflict over slavery in territories |
| 1828–1833 | South Carolina tariff nullification crisis | Background for secession leadership in South Carolina |
| 1831–1860s | Antislavery movements, southern justification | 30 years of emotional preparation for conflict |
| 1846–1848 | Mexican War (Wilmot Proviso, Calhoun, and Popular Sovereignty) | Options for slavery in territories issue |
| 1850 | Compromise of 1850 | Temporary and unsatisfactory "settlement" of divisive issue |
| 1851–1854 | Fugitive slaves returned and rescued in North; personal liberty laws passed in North; Harriet Beecher Stowe's *Uncle Tom's Cabin* | Heightened northern emotional reactions against the South and slavery |
| 1852–1856 | Breakdown of Whig party and national Democratic party; creation of a new party system with sectional basis | Made national politics an arena where sectional and cultural differences over slavery were fought |
| 1854 | Ostend Manifesto and other expansionist efforts in Central America | Reinforced image of Democratic party as favoring slavery |
| | Formation of Republican party | Major party identified as opposing the expansion of slavery |
| | Kansas-Nebraska Act | Reopened "settled" issue of slavery in the territories |
| 1856 | "Bleeding Kansas"; Senator Sumner physically attacked in Senate | Foretaste of civil war (200 killed, $2 million in property lost) inflamed emotions and polarized North and South |
| 1857 | Dred Scott decision; proslavery Lecompton constitution in Kansas | Made North fear a "slave power conspiracy," supported by President Buchanan and the Supreme Court |
| 1858 | Lincoln-Douglas debates in Illinois; Democrats lose 18 seats in Congress | Set stage for election of 1860 |
| 1859 | John Brown's raid and reactions in North and South | Made South fear a "black Republican" plot against slavery; further polarization and irrationality |
| 1860 | Democratic party splits in half; Lincoln elected president; South Carolina secedes from Union | Final breakdown of national parties and election of "northern" president; no more compromises |
| 1861 | Six more southern states secede by February 1; Confederate Constitution adopted February 4; Lincoln inaugurated March 4; Fort Sumter attacked April 12 | Civil War begins |

weeks of his already dismal administration, Buchanan did nothing. Congress made some feeble efforts to pass compromise legislation, waiting in vain for the support of the president-elect. And Virginia and the border states, like the entire nation, waited to see what Abraham Lincoln would do.

Frederick Douglass waited too, without much hope. He wanted nothing less than "the complete and universal *abolition* of the whole slave system," as well as equal suffrage and other rights for free blacks. His momentary expectation during the presidential campaign, that Lincoln and the Republicans had the will to do this, had been thoroughly dashed. In November, the voters of New York State had defeated a referendum for equal Negro suffrage by more votes than a similar measure 14 years earlier. Moreover, Douglass saw northern politicians and businessmen "granting the most demoralizing concessions to the Slave Power."

In his despair, Douglass began to explore possibilities for emigration and colonization in Haiti, an idea he had long opposed. In order to achieve full freedom and citizenship in the United States for all blacks, he said in January 1861, he would "welcome the hardships consequent upon a dissolution of the Union." In February, Douglass said, "Let the conflict come." He opposed all compromises, hoping that with Lincoln's inauguration it would "be decided, and decided forever, which of the two, Freedom or Slavery, shall give law to this Republic."

## Lincoln and Fort Sumter

As Douglass penned these thoughts, Lincoln began a long, slow train ride from Springfield, Illinois, to Washington. Along the way he wrote and rewrote his inaugural address, moderating the more coercive first drafts, under Seward's advice. Lincoln's quietness in the period between his election and inauguration had led many to wonder if he were not weak and indecisive. He was not. Lincoln was firmly opposed to secession and to any compromises with the principle of stopping the extension of slavery. He would neither conciliate secessionist southern states nor force their return.

But Lincoln believed in his constitutional responsibility to uphold the laws of the land, and on this significant point he made no changes. The focus of his attention was a federal fort in the harbor of Charleston, South Carolina. Major Robert Anderson, the commander of Fort Sumter, was running out of provisions and had requested new supplies from Washington. Lincoln would enforce the laws and protect federal property at Fort Sumter.

As the new president rose to deliver his inaugural address on March 4, he faced a tense and divided nation. Federal troops, fearing a Confederate attack on the nation's capital, were everywhere. Lincoln asserted his unequivocal intention to enforce the laws of the land, arguing that the Union was constitutionally "perpetual" and indissoluble. He reminded the nation that the "only substantial dispute" at issue was that "one section of our country believes slavery is *right,* and ought to be extended, while the other believes it is *wrong,* and ought not to be extended." Lincoln also indicated that he would make no attempts to interfere with existing slavery or the law to return fugitive slaves.

Nearing the end of his address, Lincoln urged against rash actions and put the burden of

*After winning the presidency in November 1860, Abraham Lincoln had several months in which to agonize about the message he should give the people of a disintegrating union at his inauguration in March 1861.*

initiating a civil war on those "dissatisfied fellow-countrymen" who had seceded. As if aware of the horrible events that might follow, he said in an eloquent conclusion:

> I am loath to close. We are not enemies, but friends. We must not be enemies. Though passion may have strained, it must not break our bonds of affection. The mystic chords of memory, stretching from every battlefield, and patriot grave, to every living heart and hearthstone, all over this broad land, will yet swell the chorus of the Union, when again touched, as surely they will be, by the better angels of our nature.

Frederick Douglass was not impressed with Lincoln's "honied phrases" and accused him of "weakness, timidity and conciliation." Also unmoved, Robert Allston wrote his son from Charleston, where he was watching the developing crisis over Fort Sumter, that the Confederacy's "advantage" was in having a "much better president than they have."

On April 6, Lincoln notified the governor of South Carolina that he was sending "provisions only" to Fort Sumter. No effort would be made "to throw in men, arms, or ammunition" unless the fort were attacked. On April 10, Davis directed General P. G. T. Beauregard to demand the surrender of Fort Sumter. Davis told Beauregard to reduce the fort if Major Anderson refused.

On April 12, as Lincoln's relief expedition neared Charleston, Beauregard's batteries began shelling Fort Sumter, and the Civil War began. Frederick Douglass was about to leave for Haiti when he heard the news. He immediately changed his plans: "This is no time . . . to leave the country." He announced his readiness to help end the war by aiding the Union to organize freed slaves "into a liberating army" to "make war upon . . . the savage barbarism of slavery." The Allstons had changed places, and it was Benjamin who described the events in Charleston harbor to his father. On April 14 Benjamin reported exuberantly "the glorious, and astonishing news that Sumter has fallen." With it fell America's divided house.

## CONCLUSION: The "Irrepressible Conflict"

Lincoln had been right. The nation could no longer endure half slave and half free. The collison between North and South, William Seward said, was not an "accidental, unnecessary" event but "an irrepressible conflict between opposing and enduring forces." Those forces had been at work for many decades but developed with increasing intensity in the years after the introduction of the Wilmot Proviso in 1846. Although economic, cultural, political, constitutional, and emotional forces all contributed to the developing opposition between North and South, slavery was the fundamental, enduring force that underlay all others, causing what Walt Whitman called "the red blood of civil war."

### Recommended Reading

Easily the finest overall account of the political history of the 1850s is David Potter's superb narrative, *The Impending Crisis, 1848–1861* (1976), completed by Donald Fehrenbacher after Potter's death. The classic detailed account is Allen Nevins, *Ordeal of the Union*, 4 vols. (1947–1950). Two recent studies, the first from a British point of view, are Bruce Collins, *The Origins of America's Civil War* (1981) and James McPherson's *Ordeal by Fire: The Civil War and Reconstruction* (1982). Three collections of stimulating essays on recent Civil War scholarship are Eric Foner, ed., *Politics and Ideology in the Age of the Civil War* (1980); Robert Swierenga, ed., *Beyond the Civil War Synthesis* (1975); and Kenneth Stampp, *The Imperiled Union: Essays on the Background of the Civil War* (1980). Stampp has also compiled the most useful combination of primary and secondary sources representing differences of opinion, *The Causes of the Civil War*, rev. ed. (1974), a good book in which to explore various historical interpretations.

Michael Holt's *The Political Crisis of the 1850s* (1978) is the best overall work of "new politics" showing the breakdown of political parties as a major cause of the Civil War. An indispensable work on the ideas of the Republican party is Eric Foner, *Free Soil, Free Labor, Free Men: The Ideology of the Republican Party Before the Civil War* (1970). On ethnic and religious politics and the effects of nativism on political behavior, see Paul Kleppner, *The Third Electoral System, 1853–1892: Parties, Voters, and Political Cultures* (1979); Ronald Formisano, *The Birth of Mass Political Parties: Michigan, 1827–1861* (1971); and Michael Holt, *Forging a Majority: The Formation of the Republican Party in Pittsburgh, 1848–1860* (1969). Specialized works on the effects of the issue of slavery in the territories on sectional rivalry and political parties are Hamilton Holman, *Prologue to Conflict: The Crisis and Compromise of 1850* (1964); Thomas Alexander, *Sectional Stress and Party Strength* (1967); William J. Cooper, *The South and the Politics of Slavery* (1978); and Richard Sewell, *Ballots for Freedom: Antislavery Politics in the United States, 1837–1865* (1976).

On racism in the West, see Eugene Berwanger, *The Frontier Against Slavery: Western Anti-Negro Prejudice and the Slavery Extension Controversy* (1967) and James Rawley, *Race and Politics: "Bleeding Kansas" and the Coming of the Civil War* (1969). The definitive work on the Dred Scott case is Donald Fehrenbacher, *Slavery, Law, and Politics: The Dred Scott Case in Historical Perspective* (1981). On the Buchanan administration and the Lincoln-Douglas debates, see Roy Nichols's classic, *The Disruption of American Democracy* (1948), and Harry Jaffa, *Crisis of the House Divided: An Interpretation of the Lincoln-Douglas Debates* (1959). The final road to war after Lincoln's election in 1860 is detailed in Kenneth Stampp, *And the War Came* (1950); William Barney, *The Road to Secession* (1972); and Steven Channing, *Crisis of Fear: Secession in South Carolina* (1970).

Reading biographies of major figures is an enjoyable and useful way to absorb the political and emotional crises of the 1850s. See Robert Johannsen, *Stephen Douglas* (1973); Stephen Oates, *To Purge This Land with Blood: A Biography of John Brown* (1970) and *With Malice Toward None: The Life of Abraham Lincoln* (1982). A brilliant study of Lincoln's masterful prose is T. Harry Williams, ed., *Abraham Lincoln: Selected Speeches, Messages, and Letters* (1957). The emotional flavor of the decade is captured in Harriet Beecher Stowe's novel, *Uncle Tom's Cabin* (1852), and Walt Whitman's poetry in *Leaves of Grass* (any edition).

## TIME LINE

|  |  |
|---|---|
| 1832 | Nullification crisis |
| 1835–1840 | Intensification of abolitionist attacks on slavery<br>Violent retaliatory attacks on abolitionists |
| 1840 | Liberty party formed |
| 1846 | Wilmot Proviso |
| 1848 | Free-Soil party founded<br>Zachary Taylor elected president |
| 1850 | Compromise of 1850, including Fugitive Slave Act |
| 1850–1854 | "Young America" movement |
| 1851 | Women's rights convention in Akron, Ohio |
| 1852 | Harriet Beecher Stowe publishes *Uncle Tom's Cabin*<br>Franklin Pierce elected president |
| 1854 | Ostend Manifesto<br>Kansas-Nebraska Act nullifies Missouri Compromise<br>Republican and Know-Nothing parties formed |
| 1855 | Walt Whitman publishes *Leaves of Grass* |
| 1855–1856 | Thousands pour into Kansas, creating months of turmoil and violence |
| 1856 | John Brown's massacre<br>Sumner-Brooks incident in Washington<br>James Buchanan elected president |
| 1857 | Dred Scott decision legalizes slavery in territories<br>Lecompton constitution in Kansas |
| 1858 | Lincoln-Douglas debates |
| 1859 | John Brown's raid at Harpers Ferry |
| 1860 | Democratic party splits<br>Four-party campaign<br>Abraham Lincoln elected president |
| 1860–1861 | Seven southern states secede |
| 1861 | Attack on Fort Sumter begins Civil War<br>Confederate States of America founded |

# CHAPTER 16
## SEVERING THE BONDS OF UNION

We cannot escape history," Abraham Lincoln reminded Congress in 1862. "We of this Congress and this administration will be remembered in spite of ourselves. No personal significance, or insignificance, can spare . . . us. The fiery trial through which we pass, will light us down, in honor or dishonor, to the latest generation." Lincoln's conviction that Americans would long remember him and other major actors of the Civil War was correct. Jefferson Davis, Robert E. Lee, Ulysses S. Grant—these are the men whose characters, actions, and decisions have been the subject of continuing discussion and analysis, whose statues and memorials dot the American countryside and grace urban squares. Whether seen as heroes or villains, great men have dominated the story of the Civil War.

Yet from the earliest days, the war touched the lives of even the most uncelebrated Americans. From Indianapolis, 20-year-old Arthur Carpenter wrote to his parents in Massachusetts begging for permission to enlist in the volunteer army: "I have always longed for the time to come when I could enter the army and be a military man, and when this war broke out, I thought the time had come, but you would not permit me to enter the service . . . now I make one more appeal to you." The plea worked, and Carpenter enlisted, spending most of the war fighting in Kentucky and Tennessee.

In that same year, in Tennessee, George and Ethie Eagleton faced anguishing decisions. Though not an abolitionist, George, a 30-year-old Presbyterian preacher, was unsympathetic to slavery and opposed to secession. But when his native state left the Union, George felt compelled to follow and enlisted in the 44th Tennessee Infantry. Ethie, his 26-year-old wife, despaired over the war, George's decision, and her own forlorn situation.

> Mr. Eagleton's school dismissed—and what for? O my God, must I write it? He has enlisted in the service of his country—to war—the most unrighteous war that ever was brought on any nation that ever lived. Pres. Lincoln has done what no other Pres. ever dared to do—he has divided these once peaceful and happy United States. And Oh! the dreadful dark cloud that is now hanging over our country—'tis enough to sicken the heart of any one . . . Mr. E. is gone . . . What will become of me, left here without a home and relatives, a babe just nine months old and no George.

Both Carpenter and the Eagletons survived the war, but the conflict transformed each of their lives. Carpenter had difficulty settling down. The Eagletons, filled with bitter memories of the war years in Tennessee, moved to Arkansas. Ordinary people such as Carpenter and the Eagletons are historically anonymous. Yet their actions on the battlefield and behind the lines helped to shape the course of events, as their leaders realized, even if today we tend to remember only the famous and influential.

For thousands of Americans, from Lincoln and Davis to Carpenter and the Eagletons, war was both a profoundly personal and a major national event. Its impact stretched far beyond the four years of hostilities. The war that was fought to conserve two political, social, and economic visions ended by changing familiar ways of life in both North and South. War was a transforming force, both destructive and creative in its impact on the structure and social dynamics of society and on the lives of ordinary people. This theme underlies the following analysis of the war's three stages: the initial months of preparation, the years of military stalemate between 1861 and 1865, and, finally, resolution.

## ORGANIZING TO FIGHT THE WAR

After the Confederate bombardment of Fort Sumter on April 12, 1861, and the surrender of Union troops the next day, the uncertainty of the secession winter ended. The North's response to Fort Sumter was a virtual declaration of war as President Lincoln called for state militia volunteers to crush southern "insurrection." His action pushed several slave states (Virginia, North Carolina, Tennessee, Arkansas) off the fence and into the southern camp. Other states (Maryland, Kentucky, and Missouri) agonizingly debated which way they should go. The War Between the States was now a reality.

Many were unenthusiastic about the course of events. Southerners like George Eagleton only reluctantly followed Tennessee out of the Union. When he enlisted, he complained of "the disgraceful cowardice of many who were last winter for secession and war . . . but are now refusing self and means for the prosecution of war." Robert E. Lee of Virginia was equally hesitant to resign his federal commission but finally decided that he could not "raise [a] hand against . . . relatives . . . children . . . home." Whites living in the southern uplands (where there were few blacks), yeomen farmers in the Deep South (who owned no slaves), and many residents of border states were dismayed at secession and war.

In the North, large numbers had neither supported the Republican party nor voted for Lincoln. Irish immigrants who feared the competition of free black labor and southerners now living in Illinois, Indiana, and Ohio harbored misgivings about the war. Indeed, northern Democrats at first blamed Lincoln and the Republicans almost as much as the southern secessionists for the nation's crisis.

Nevertheless, the days following Fort Sumter and Lincoln's call for troops saw an outpouring of support on both sides, fueled in part by relief at decisive action, in part by patriotism and love of adventure, in part by unemployment. Northern blacks and even some southern freedman proclaimed themselves "ready to go forth and do battle," while whites like Carpenter enthusiastically flocked to enlist. Sisters, wives, and mothers set to work making uniforms. A New Yorker, Jane Woolsey, described the drama of those early days "of terrible excitement . . . Outside the parlor windows the city is gay and brilliant with excited crowds, the incessant movement and music of marching regiments and all the thousands of flags, big and little, which suddenly came fluttering out of every window and door." "In our little circle of friends," she wrote, "one mother has just sent away an idolized son; another, two; another, four. . . . One sweet young wife is packing a regulation valise for her husband today, and doesn't let him see her cry."

The war fever produced so many volunteers that neither northern nor southern officials could handle the throng. Northern authorities turned aside offers from blacks to serve. Both sides sent thousands of white would-be soldiers home. The eagerness to enlist was fueled by the conviction that the conflict would rapidly come to a glorious conclusion. "We really did not think that there was going to be an actual war," remembered Mary Ward, a young Georgia woman. "We had an idea that when our soldiers got upon the ground and showed, unmistakably that they were really ready and willing to fight . . . the whole trouble would be declared at an end." Lincoln's call for 75,000 state militiamen for only 90 days of service and a similar enlistment term for Confederate soldiers supported the notion that the war would be short.

## The Balance of Resources

Despite the bands, parades, cheers, and confidence, the outcome of the approaching civil conflict was much in doubt. Statistics of population and industrial development suggested that the North would win. But Great Britain had also enjoyed enormous statistical advantages in 1775 and yet had lost the War of American Independence. Many of the North's assets would become effective only with time. The military stalemate in 1861 and 1862 proved that, in the short term, North and South were evenly matched.

In the North, the small federal army of 16,000 was soon supplemented by state militia volunteers called up in April 1861. Probably a quarter of the regular army officers, however, had followed Lee's example and resigned. The

*The first Michigan Regiment, mustering in Detroit to board trains to Washington, received an enthusiastic farewell.*

Confederate army, authorized in March 1861, could count on the service of able military men like Robert E. Lee, Joseph E. Johnston, and Albert Sidney Johnston. Its president, Jefferson Davis, was an 1828 graduate of West Point.

The North's white population greatly exceeded that of the South, giving the appearance of a military advantage. Yet in the early days of war, the armies were not so unevenly matched. Almost 187,000 Union troops bore arms in July 1861, while just over 112,000 men marched under Confederate colors. Even if numerically inferior, southerners believed that their population would prove the superior fighting force because it was more accustomed to an outdoor life and the use of firearms. Whether this was true or not, slaves could carry on vital work behind the lines, freeing most adult white males to serve the Confederacy. Slavery, southerners thought, would prove to be "a tower of strength . . . at the present crisis."

The Union also enjoyed impressive economic advantages. In the North, 1 million workers in 110,000 manufacturing concerns produced goods valued at $1.5 billion, while 110,000 southern workers in 18,000 manufacturing concerns produced goods valued at only $155 million a year. The North had one factory for every southern industrial worker and 70 percent of the nation's railroad tracks were in the North. Producing 17 times as much cotton cloth and woolen goods, 32 times as many firearms, and 20 times as much pig iron as the South, the North could clothe and arm troops and move them and their supplies on a scale that the South could not match. But to be effective, northern industrial resources had to be mobilized for war. That would take time, especially since the government did not intend to direct production. Furthermore, the depleted northern Treasury made the government's first task the raising of funds to pay for military necessities.

The South traditionally depended on imported manufactured goods from the North and from Europe. If Lincoln cut off that trade, the South would face the enormous task of creating its industry almost from scratch. Moreover, its railroad system was organized to move cotton, not armies and supplies. Yet the agricultural South did have important resources of food, draft animals, and, of course, cotton, which southerners believed would secure British and French support. Finally, in choosing to wage a defensive war, the South could tap regional loyalty and would enjoy protected lines of supply and support. Union forces, embarked on an expensive war of conquest, their extended supply lines always vulnerable to attack, would be less mobile and secure than southern troops. The Union had to win a war of conquest and occupation. The South merely had to survive until its enemy tired and gave up.

### The Border States

The uncertainty of the war's outcome and divided loyalties resulted in indecision in the border states. When the seven states of the Deep South seceded during the winter of 1860–1861, the border states adopted a wait-and-see attitude. Of these, Delaware almost certainly identified with the Union camp. But the others vacillated. Their decisions were of critical importance to both North and South.

The states of the Upper South could provide natural borders for the Confederacy along the Ohio River, access to its river traffic, and vital resources, wealth, and population. The major railroad link to the West ran through Maryland and western Virginia. Virginia boasted the South's largest ironworks, while Tennessee was the region's principal source of grain. Missouri provided the road to Kansas and the West and was strategically placed to control Mississippi River traffic. It was difficult to imagine the long- or short-term success of the Confederacy without the border states.

For the North, every border state electing to remain loyal was a psychological triumph for the idea of Union. Nor was the North indifferent

## Resources: North versus South

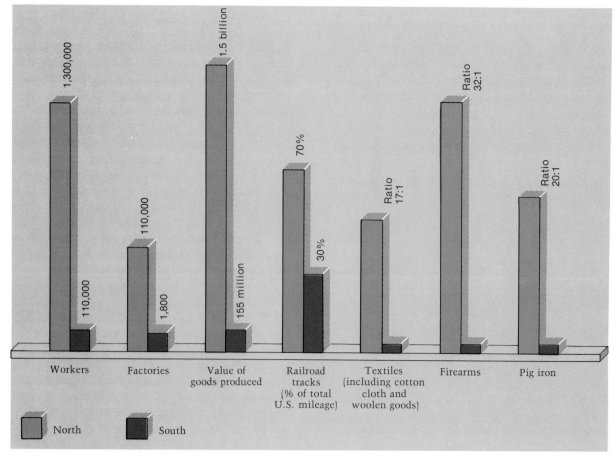

to the economic and strategic advantages of keeping the border states with the Union. Lincoln's call for troops precipitated decisions in several states, however. Between April 17 and May 20, Virginia, Arkansas, Tennessee, and North Carolina joined the Confederacy.

The significance of border-state loyalty was soon dramatized in Maryland. Slave-owning tobacco and wheat planters from the state's southern counties and eastern shore favored secession. Confederate enthusiasts abounded in Baltimore. But in the western and northern parts of the state, small farmers, often of German background, opposed slavery and supported the Union cause.

On the morning of April 19, the 6th Massachusetts Regiment arrived in Baltimore headed for Washington. Because the regiment had to change railroad lines, the soldiers set out across the city on foot and in horsecars. As they marched through the streets, a mob of some 10,000 southern sympathizers, flying Confederate flags, attacked them with paving stones, then bayonets and bullets. Finally, as a contemporary explained, "the patience of their commander was . . . exhausted. He cried out in a voice, which was heard even above the yells of the mob, 'Fire!' . . . A scene of bloody confusion followed." In the commotion, would-be seces-

sionists burned the railroad bridges connecting Baltimore to the North and to the South. Washington found itself cut off from the rest of the Union, an island in the middle of hostile territory.

Lincoln took stern measures to secure Maryland. The president agreed temporarily to route troops around Baltimore. In return, the governor called the state legislature into session at Frederick, a center of Union sentiment in western Maryland. This action and Lincoln's swift violation of civil rights dampened secessionist enthusiasm. Hundreds of southern sympathizers, including 19 state legislators and Baltimore's mayor, were arrested and languished in prison without trial. Although the Chief Justice of the Supreme Court, Roger B. Taney, challenged the legality of the president's action and issued a writ of habeas corpus for the release of John Merryman, a southern supporter, Lincoln ignored him. A month later, Taney ruled in *Ex Parte Merryman* that if the public's safety was endangered, only Congress had the right to suspend the writ of habeas corpus. By then, Lincoln had secured Maryland for the Union.

Though Lincoln's quick and harsh response ensured Maryland's loyalty, he was more cautious elsewhere. Above all, he had to deal with slavery prudently, for any hasty action would

## Secession of the Southern States

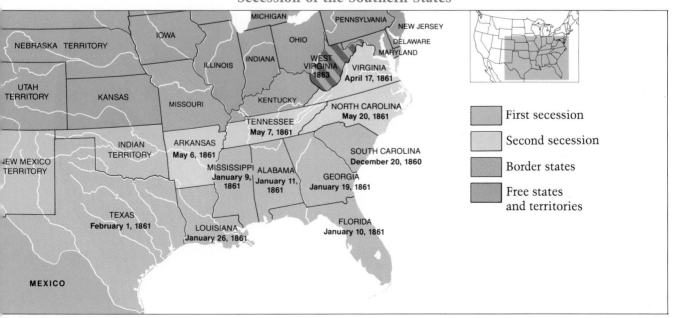

push border states into the waiting arms of the Confederacy. Thus when General John C. Frémont, in a burst of enthusiasm, issued an unauthorized declaration of emancipation in Missouri in August 1861, Lincoln revoked the order and recalled the general. As the president explained, he expected a chain reaction if certain key states left the Union. "I think to lose Kentucky is nearly the same as to lose the whole game. Kentucky gone, we cannot hold Missouri, nor, as I think, Maryland. These all against us, and the job on our hands is too large for us." In the end, after some fighting and much maneuvering, Kentucky and Missouri, like Maryland, stayed in the Union.

### Challenges of War

The tense weeks after Fort Sumter spilled over with unexpected challenges. Neither North nor South could handle the floods of volunteers. Both faced enormous organizational problems as they readied for war. In the South, a nation-state had to be created and its apparatus set in motion. Everything from a constitution and governmental departments to a flag and postage stamps had to be devised. As one onlooker observed, "The whole country was new. Everything was to be done—and to be made."

In February 1861, the original seceding states sent delegates to Montgomery, Alabama, to begin work on a provisional framework and to select a provisional president and vice-president. The delegates swiftly wrote a constitution, much like the federal constitution of 1787 except in its emphasis on the "sovereign and independent character" of the states and its explicit recognition of slavery. The provisional president, Jefferson Davis of Mississippi, tried to put together a geographically and politically balanced cabinet with a moderate face for the outside world. He succeeded in creating a balanced cabinet, but it had few of his friends or, more serious, men of political stature. As time passed, it turned out to be unstable as well. In a four-year period, 14 men held six positions.

Davis's cabinet appointees faced the formidable challenge of creating government departments from scratch. They had to hire employees and initiate administrative procedures with woefully inadequate resources. The president's office was in a hotel parlor. The Confederate Treasury Department was housed in a room in an Alabama bank "without furniture of any kind; empty . . . of desks, tables, chairs or other appliances for the conduct of business." Treasury Secretary Christopher G. Memminger bought furniture with his own money; operations lurched forward in fits and starts. In those early days, when an army captain came to the Treasury with a warrant from Davis for blankets, he found only one clerk. After reading the warrant, the clerk offered the captain a few dollars of his own, explaining, "This, Captain, is all the money that I will certify as being in the Confederate Treasury at this moment." Other departments faced similar difficulties.

Inheriting the federal government, Lincoln never had to set up a postal system or decide whether laws passed before 1861 were valid. Without administrative experience, however,

*Jefferson Davis, named provisional president of the Confederacy in 1861, faced the difficulties of setting up a new government while countering the Union army's advances.*

the new president, like his Confederate counterpart, faced organizational problems. Military officers and government clerks daily left the capital for the South. The Treasury was empty. The Republicans had won their first presidential election, and floods of office seekers who had worked for Lincoln now thronged into the White House looking for rewards.

Nor could Lincoln, who did not know many of "the prominent men of the day," easily select a cabinet. Finally, he appointed important Republicans from different factions of the party to cabinet posts whether they agreed with him or not. Most were almost strangers to the president. Several scorned him as a bumbling backwoods politician. Treasury Secretary Salmon P. Chase actually hoped to replace Lincoln as president in four years' time. Soon after the inauguration, Secretary of State William Seward sent Lincoln a memo condescendingly offering to oversee the formulation of presidential policy.

### Lincoln and Davis

A number of Lincoln's early actions illustrated that he was no malleable backcountry bumbler. As his Illinois law partner, William Herndon, pointed out, Lincoln's "mind was tough—solid—knotty—gnarly, more or less like his body." In his reply to Seward's memo, the president firmly indicated that he intended to run his own administration. After Sumter, he swiftly called up the state militias, expanded the navy, and suspended habeas corpus. He ordered a naval blockade of the South and approved the expenditure of funds for military purposes, all wihout congressional sanction, since Congress was not in session. As Lincoln told legislators later, "The dogmas of the quiet past are inadequate to the stormy present. . . . As our case is new, so must we think anew, and act anew . . .

and then we shall save our country." This willingness to "think anew" was a valuable personal asset, even though some called his expansion of presidential power despotic.

By coincidence, Lincoln and his rival, Jefferson Davis, were born only 100 miles apart in Kentucky. However, the course of their lives diverged radically. Lincoln's father had migrated north and eked out a simple existence as a farmer in Indiana and Illinois. Abraham had only a rudimentary formal education and was largely self-taught. Davis's family, however, had moved South to Mississippi and become cotton planters. Davis grew up in comfortable circumstances, went to Transylvania University and West Point, and fought in the Mexican War before his election to the U.S. Senate. In recognition of his social, political, and economic prominence, Davis served as secretary of war under Franklin Pierce (1853–1857). Tall and distinguished-looking, he appeared every inch the aristocratic southerner.

Although Davis had not been eager to accept the presidency, he had loyally responded to the call of the provisional congress in 1861 and worked tirelessly as the chief executive of the Confederacy until the war's end. His wife, Varina, observed that "the President hardly takes time to eat his meals and works late at night." Some contemporaries suggested that Davis's inability to let subordinates handle details explained this schedule. Others observed that he was sickly, reserved, humorless, too sensitive to criticism, and hard to get along with. But Davis, like Lincoln, found it necessary to "think anew." He reassured southerners in his inaugural address that his aims were conservative, "to preserve the Government of our fathers in spirit." Yet under the pressure of events, he moved toward creating a new kind of South.

## CLASHING ON THE BATTLEFIELD, 1861–1862

The Civil War was the most brutal and destructive conflict in American history. Much of the bloodshed resulted from the application of the theories of Henri Jomini, a French military his-

torian, to the battlefield. Jomini's ideas were enshrined in the curriculum of West Point, where many of the Union and Confederate officers had studied the art of war.

Jomini argued that an army seized victory by concentrating its infantry attack at the weakest point in the enemy's defenses. At the time Jomini wrote, this offensive strategy made military sense. The artillery, stationed well outside the range of enemy fire, could prepare the way for the infantry attack by bombarding enemy lines. By 1861, however, the range of rifles had increased from 100 yards to 500 yards. It was no longer possible to position the artillery close enough to the enemy to allow it to soften up the opposing line in preparation for the infantry charge. During the Civil War, then, enemy fire mowed down attacking infantry soldiers as they ran the 500 fatal yards to the front lines. Battles based on Jomini's theories produced a ghastly crop of dead men.

### War in the East

The war's brutal character would reveal itself only gradually, however, The two armies did not meet until July 1861. The Union commanding general, 70-year-old Winfield Scott, at first pressed for a cautious, long-term strategy, known as the Anaconda Plan. Scott proposed weakening the South gradually through blockades on land and at sea until the northern army was strong enough for the kill. The excited public, however, hungered for action and quick victory. So did Lincoln, who knew that the longer the war lasted, the more embittered the South and the North would both become, making reunion ever more difficult. Under the cry of "Forward to Richmond!" 35,000 partially trained men led by General Irvin McDowell headed out from Washington in sweltering July weather.

**Battle of Bull Run (Manassas Creek)**   Only 25 miles from the capital at Manassas Creek, or Bull Run, as it is also called, northern troops confronted 25,000 raw Confederate soldiers commanded by Brigadier General P. G. T. Beauregard, a West Point classmate of McDowell's. Although sightseers, journalists, and politicians had accompanied the Union troops, expecting only a Sunday outing, the encounter at Bull Run was no picnic. The course of battle swayed back and forth before the arrival of 2,300 fresh Con-

federate troops from the Shendandoah valley decided the day. Union soldiers fled toward Washington in terror and confusion. In a frenzy to reach safety, sightseers mixed with soldiers. An English journalist, William Russell, portrayed the frantic retreat. As troops poured into Washington on July 22, he reported:

> I saw a steady stream of men covered with mud, soaked through with rain . . . pouring irregularly, without any semblance of order, up Pennsylvania Avenue toward the Capitol. . . . I perceived they belonged to different regiments . . . mingled pell-mell together. . . . Hastily [I] . . . ran downstairs and asked an officer . . . a pale young man who looked exhausted to death and who had lost his sword . . . where the men were coming from. "Where from? Well, sir, I guess we're all coming out of Virginny as far as we can, and pretty well whipped too. . . . I know I'm going home. I've had enough of fighting to last my lifetime."

"Pretty well whipped" the Union forces certainly were. Yet the Confederates had lost their chance to turn the rout into the quick and decisive victory they sought. Inexperience was the problem. As General Joseph E. Johnston

*Realizing the benefits of an early victory, Lincoln (center) urged his generals to move into action as soon as troops had received the most basic training.*

pointed out, his men were disorganized, confused by victory, and not well enough supplied with food to chase the Union army back toward Washington.

In many ways, the Battle of Bull Run was prophetic. Victory would be neither quick nor easy. As the disorganization and confusion of both sides suggested, the armies were unprofessional. And it was becoming obvious that bravado would not win the war. Then, too, both sides faced problems with short-term enlistments. Finally, logistic problems connected with mass armies plagued both sides. The Civil War put more men in the field than any previous American engagement. Supplying and moving so many men and ensuring adequate communication, especially during battle, were tasks of an unprecedented kind. It was hardly surprising that the armies floundered trying to meet these logistic challenges.

Robert Allston, a prominent South Carolina rice planter, viewed the battlefield at Bull Run and decided it had been a "glorious tho bloody"

day. For the Union, however, the loss at Bull Run was sobering. Replacing McDowell with 34-year-old General George McClellan, Lincoln began the search for a northern commander capable of winning the war. Seven commanders would serve in the next two years. McClellan, formerly an army engineer, began the task of transforming the Army of the Potomac into a fighting force. Short-term militias went home. When Scott retired in the fall of 1861, McClellan became general in chief of the Union armies.

McClelland had considerable organizational ability but was not a daring leader on the battlefield. Indeed, he had no wish for boldness. Convinced that the North must combine military victory with efforts to persuade the South to return to the Union, McClellan sought to avoid unnecessary and embittering loss of life and property. As he explained, he intended to win the war "by maneuvering rather than fighting."

In March 1862, pushed by an impatient Lincoln, McClellan finally led his army of 130,000 toward Richmond, now the Confederate

## Eastern Theater of the Civil War, 1861–1862

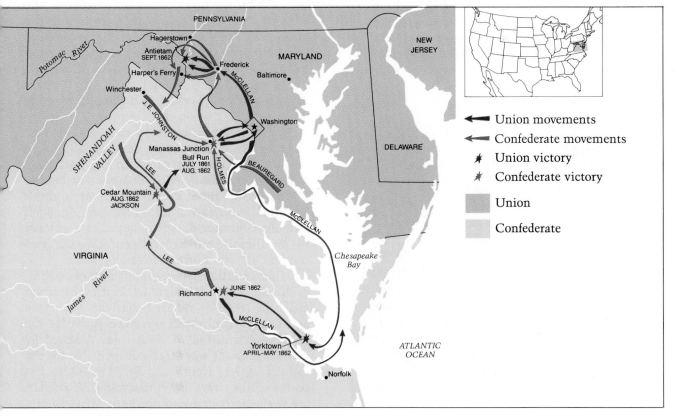

capital. By taking the city without excessive casualties, McClellan hoped the enemy would abandon a war it could never win. By late June, his army was close enough to Richmond to hear its church bells pealing. But just as it seemed that victory was within grasp, Lee counterattacked and slowly drove the Union forces away from Richmond. Losses were heavy on both sides. Finally, orders came from Washington: Abandon the Peninsula campaign.

**Battle of Antietam**   Other Union defeats followed in 1862 as commanders came and went. In September, the South abandoned the defensive with a bold invasion of Maryland. But after a costly defeat at Antietam, in which more than 5,000 soldiers were slaughtered, Lee withdrew his army to Virginia. Victory eluded both sides. The war in the East was stalemated.

### War in the West

The early struggle in the East focused on Richmond, the Confederacy's capital and one of the South's most important railroad, industrial,

*General Lee's 1862 invasion of Maryland ended with the battle of Antietam. Here the horse of a Confederate officer, stripped of saddle and bridle, lies dead on the battlefield.*

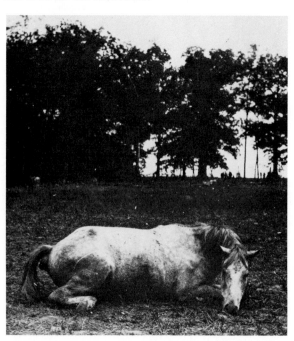

and munitions centers. But the East was only one of three theaters of actions. Between the Appalachian Mountains and the Mississippi lay the western theater, comprising the states of Kentucky, Tennessee, Mississippi, and Alabama. At its edge lay the Mississippi, with its vital river trade and its great port, New Orleans. Here both George Eagleton and Arthur Carpenter served. Beyond lay the trans-Mississippi West—Louisiana, Arkansas, Missouri, Texas, and the Great Plains—where Native American tribes joined the conflict on both sides.

In the western theater, the Union had two strategic objectives: the domination of Kentucky and eastern Tennessee, the avenues to the South and West, and control of the Mississippi River. If Union forces managed to dominate the Mississippi River, they would split the South in two. Major campaigns sought strategic points along rivers and railroads.

Southern forces were determined to hold the 400-mile line stretching from the Appalachian Mountains to the Mississippi. But the western commander, Albert S. Johnston, was hampered by inadequate supplies (many of his men had flintlock muskets, which would not fire in wet weather) and insufficiently trained troops. The weakness of this southern line reflected Davis's belief that the western theater was not so vital to the Confederacy as the Virginia hills.

In the western theater, Ulysses S. Grant came to the fore. Working in his family's leather store in Illinois when the war broke out, Grant had lackluster military credentials. Although he had attended West Point and served creditably in the Mexican War, his career in the peacetime army was undistinguished. Perhaps boredom on frontier posts drove the young Grant to drink and finally to resign from the service. But soon after Fort Sumter, Grant enlisted as a colonel in an Illinois militia regiment. Within two months, he was a brigadier general.

Grant's military genius consisted of an ability to see beyond individual battles to larger goals. In 1862, he realized that the Tennessee and Cumberland rivers were the paths for the successful invasion of Tennessee. Assisted by gunboats, Grant was largely responsible for the capture of Fort Henry and Fort Donelson, key points on the rivers, in February 1862. Confederate troops retreated into northern Mississippi.

**Battle of Shiloh Church (Pittsburgh Landing)**
The two forces clashed again on a rainy April day at Shiloh Church (also called Pittsburgh Landing) in Tennessee. Never had there been a battle of this size on American soil. Albert Johnston commanded 40,000 troops; Grant also had 40,000 men and expected reinforcements of 25,000 more. The battle tilted first toward the Confederacy. But during the first day, General Johnston was hit in the leg. The wound need not have been fatal, but the General stayed in the saddle and bled to death. The arrival of fresh Union troops won the day for the North.

Technically a northern victory, the Battle of Shiloh Church proved to be another costly engagement. The Union suffered over 13,000 casualties, while 10,000 Confederates lay dead. Untreated wounds caused many of the deaths. A full day after the battle had ended, nine-tenths of the wounded still lay in the rain. Many died of exposure; others drowned in the downpour. Though more successful than efforts in the East, such devastating Union campaigns failed to bring decisive results. Western plans were never coordinated with eastern military activities. Victories there did not force the South to its knees.

*Water from a canteen was often the only aid available to wounded or sick soldiers of both armies.*

**The Trans-Mississippi Campaign**   The war in the trans-Mississippi West was a sporadic, far-flung struggle for the control of the manpower and natural resources of this vast area. New Mexico was the scene of an unsuccessful Confederate campaign in early 1862. Missouri and Arkansas saw bitter fighting in 1861 and 1862. The prize both sought was the Missouri River, which flowed into the Mississippi River, bordered Illinois, and affected military campaigns in Kentucky and Tennessee.

In 1861, Confederate forces led by General Sterling Price and General Ben McCulloch, a former Texas Ranger, won a series of bloody

### Trans-Mississippi Campaign of the Civil War

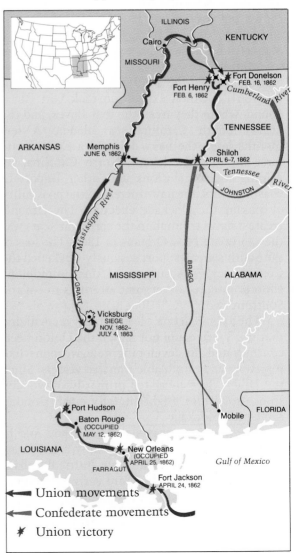

victories. In March 1862, at Pea Ridge in north-western Arkansas, however, the tide turned. There a Confederate army of 16,000, which included a brigade of Native Americans from the Five Civilized Nations, fell before the Union army led by General Samuel Curtis. This defeat put Missouri in the Union camp for the first time in the war, although fierce guerrilla warfare continued in the region.

## Naval Warfare

At the beginning of the war, Lincoln had decided to strangle the South with a naval block-ade. But an effective blockade proved difficult to maintain. With no more than 33 ships, the Union navy tried to close up 189 ports along a 3,500-mile coastline. In 1861, the navy inter-cepted only about one blockade runner in ten and in 1862 one in eight. In the short run, the blockade did little damage to the South.

More successful were operations to gain footholds along the southern coast. In Novem-ber 1861, a Union expedition took Port Royal Sound, where they freed the first slaves, and the nearby South Carolina sea islands. A few months later, the navy defeated a Confederate force on Roanoke Island, North Carolina. By gaining fueling stations and other important coastal points, the navy increased the possibility of making the blockade effective. The Union's greatest naval triumph in the early war years was the capture of New Orleans in 1862. The loss of the South's greatest port seriously weakened the Confederacy. The success of this amphibious effort stimulated other joint attempts to cut the South in two.

The Confederate leadership, recognizing that the South could not match the Union fleet, concentrated on developing new weapons like torpedoes and formidable ironclad vessels. Since the Union fleet consisted primarily of wooden ships, iron ships might literally crash through the Union blockade.

The *Merrimac* was slated for a key role in southern naval strategy. Originally a U.S. war-ship sunk as the federal navy hurriedly aban-doned the Norfolk Navy Yard early in the war, the Confederates raised the vessel and covered it with heavy iron armor. Rechristened the *Virgin-*

*ia*, the ship steamed out of Norfolk in March 1862, heading directly for the Union ships blocking the harbor. Using its 1,500-pound ram and guns, the *Virginia* drove a third of the ships aground and destroyed the squadron's largest ships. Engine trouble forced the *Virginia* to retire for the day, but on the next it was back to finish off the work. Awaiting it, however, was the *Monitor*, a newly completed Union iron vessel. The *Virginia* withdrew after an inconclu-sive duel and was burned when Norfolk was evacuated in May. Southern attempts to buy ironclad ships abroad faded. Thus died southern hopes of penetrating the northern noose.

While technological innovation failed to break the blockade, the Confederate navy was more successful in its policy of harming north-ern commerce. Confederate raiders, many of them built in England, preyed on northern ship-ping and wreaked havoc. In its two-year career, the raider *Alabama*, launched in Liverpool in 1862, destroyed 69 Union merchant vessels val-ued at more than $6 million. But while such blows were costly to the North, they did not seriously damage its overall war effort.

Throughout the first two years of conflict, both sides achieved victories, but the war re-mained deadlocked. Although the South was far

*Iron ships were an innovation used by both navies. Here the Confederate* Virginia *(stubbornly called the* Merrimac *by northerners) confronts the* Union Monitor.

from being defeated, the North was as far from giving up and accepting southern independence. The costs of war, in manpower and supplies, far exceeded what either side had anticipated. The need to replace lost men and supplies thus loomed ever more serious at the end of 1862.

## Cotton Diplomacy

In a civil war that pitted Americans against one another, both sides realized that the attitude of Europe could be critical. If European nations recognized the Confederacy's diplomatic existence, the South's claim of independence stood to gain immense credibility in the eyes of the rest of the world. Furthermore, European loans and assistance might bring the South victory just as French and Dutch aid had helped the American colonies win their independence. If the European nations refused to recognize the South, however, the fiction of the Union was kept alive, undermining Confederate chances for long-term survival. The European powers, of course, consulted their own national interests. Neither England nor France, the two most important nations, wished to back the losing side. Nor did they wish to upset Europe's delicate balance of power by hasty intervention in American affairs. One by one, therefore, the European states declared a policy of neutrality.

Southerners were sure that cotton would be their trump card. English and French textile mills needed cotton, and southerners believed that their owners would eventually force government recognition of the Confederacy and an end to the North's blockade. But a glut of cotton in 1860 and 1861 left foreign mill owners oversupplied. As stockpiles dwindled, European industrialists found cotton in India and Egypt. The conviction that cotton was "the king who can shake the jewels in the crown of Queen Victoria" proved false.

Union Secretary of State Seward sought above all else to prevent diplomatic recognition of the Confederacy. Since the North had its own economic ties with Europe, the Union was not as disadvantaged as southerners thought. Seward daringly threatened Great Britain with war if it interfered in what he insisted was only an internal matter. Some called his boldness reckless,

even mad. Nevertheless, his policy succeeded. Even though England allowed the construction of Confederate raiders in its ports, it did not intervene in American affairs in 1861 or 1862. Nor did the other European powers. Unless the military situation changed dramatically, the Europeans were willing to sit on the sidelines.

## Common Problems, Novel Solutions

As the conflict dragged on into 1863, unanticipated problems appeared in both the Union and the Confederacy, and novel approaches were devised to solve them. War acted as a catalyst for changes that no one could have imagined in those heady spring days of 1861.

The problem of fighting a long war was partly a monetary one. Both Treasuries had been empty initially, and the war proved extraordinarily expensive. Neither side considered trying to finance the war by imposing direct taxes. Such an approach ran counter to custom and risked alienating support. Nevertheless, each side was so starved for funds that it initiated taxation on a small scale. Ultimately taxes financed 21 percent of the North's war expenses (but only 1 percent of southern expenses). Both Treasuries also tried borrowing. Northerners bought over $2 billion worth of bonds, but southerners proved reluctant to buy their government's bonds.

As in the American Revolution, the unwelcome solution was to print paper money. In August 1861, the Confederacy put into circulation $100 million in crudely engraved bills. Millions more followed the next year. Five months later, the Union issued $150 million in paper money, soon nicknamed "greenbacks" because of their color. Although financing the war with paper money was unexpected, the resulting inflation was not.

Both sides confronted similar manpower problems as initial enthusiasm for the war evaporated. In October 1861, a Louisiana man wrote his brother-in-law, "Jord you spoke as if you had some notion of volunteering. I advise you to stay at home." Fighting, it turned out, was nothing like the militia parades and outings familiar to most American adult males. Those in the service longed to go home. The swarm of volun-

*Private Edwin Jennison of Georgia probably posed for this tintype before going to the front. He was killed at Malvern Hill, Virginia.*

teers disappeared. Rather than fill their military quotas from within, rich northern communities began offering bounties ranging between $800 and $1,000 to outsiders who would join up.

Arthur Carpenter's letters give a good picture of life in the ranks and a young man's growing disillusionment with the war. As Carpenter's regiment moved into Kentucky and Tennessee in the winter of 1862, his enthusiasm for army life evaporated. "Soldiering in Kentucky and Tennessee," he complained, "is not so pretty as it was in Indianapolis. . . . We have been half starved, half frozen, and half drowned. The mud in Kentucky is awful." Soldiering often meant marching without enough food, water, or supplies with 50 or 60 pounds of equipment over rutted roads. One blanket was not enough in the winter. In the summer, stifling woolen uniforms attracted lice and other vermin. Poor food, bugs, inadequate sanitation, and exposure spelled disease for many of the men. Carpenter marched

through Tennessee suffering from diarrhea and then fever. His regiment left him behind in a convalescent barracks in Louisville, which he fled as soon as he could. He feared the hospital at least as much as the sickness. "99 Surgeons out of a hundred," he wrote his parents, "would not know whether his patient had the horse distemper, lame toe, or any other disease."

Confederate soldiers, even less well supplied than their northern counterparts, complained similarly. In 1862, a Virginia captain described what General Lee called the best army "the world ever saw":

> During our forced marches and hard fights, the soldiers have been compelled to throw away their knapsacks and there is scarcely a private in the army who has a change of clothing of any kind. Hundreds of men are perfectly barefooted and there is no telling when they can be supplied with shoes.

In such circumstances, desertion was common. An estimated one of every nine men enlisting in the Confederate armies and one of every seven in the Union armies deserted.

As the manpower problems became critical, both governments resorted to the draft. Despite the sacrosanct notion of states' rights, the Confederate Congress passed the first conscription act in American history in March 1862. Four months later, the Union Congress also approved a draft measure. Both laws sought to encourage men already in the army to reenlist and to

## Men Present for Duty in the Civil War

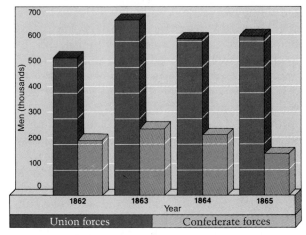

stimulate volunteers rather than to force men to serve. Ultimately, over 30 percent of the Confederate army and 6 percent of the Union forces were drafted.

The Confederacy had to rely more heavily on the draft than did the Union because the North's initial manpower pool was larger and growing. During the war, 180,000 foreigners of military age poured into the northern states. Some came specifically to claim bounties and fight. Immigrants made up at least 20 percent of the Union army.

Necessary though they were, draft laws were very unpopular. The first Confederate conscription declared all able-bodied men between 18 and 35 eligible for military service but allowed numerous exemptions and the purchase of substitutes. Critics claimed that the provision entitling every planter with more than 20 slaves to one exemption from military service favored rich slave owners. Certainly the legislation fed class tension in the South and encouraged disloyalty and desertion among the poorer classes. The advice one woman shouted after her husband as he was dragged off to the army was hardly unique. "You desert again, quick as you kin. . . . Desert, Jake!" The law, as one southerner pointed out, "aroused a spirit of rebellion."

Northern legislation was neither more popular nor fair. The 1863 draft allowed the hiring of substitutes, and $300 bought an exemption from military service. Widespread draft resistance and riots reflected how deeply working-class northerners resented the ease with which monied citizens could avoid army duty. The most serious riot, breaking out in New York City in 1863, lasted three days. Mobs of Irish workers attacked draft officers and the police, then plundered the houses of the rich and looted jewelry stores. Blacks, whom the Irish hated as economic competitors and the cause of the war, were hunted down ferociously. More than 70 people died in the violence. There was much truth in the accusation that the war on both sides was a rich man's war but a poor man's fight.

## Political Dissension

As the war continued, rumbles of dissension grew louder. On February 24, 1862, the Rich-

mond *Examiner* summarized many southerners' frustration. "The Confederacy has had everything that was required for success but one, and that one thing it was and is supposed to possess more than anything else, namely Talent." As victory proved elusive, necessitating unpopular measures like the draft, criticism of Confederate leaders mounted. Jefferson Davis's vice-president, Alexander Stephens of Georgia, became one of the administration's bitterest accusers. Public criticism reflected private disapproval. Wrote one southerner to a friend, "Impeach Jeff Davis for incompetency & call a convention of the States. . . . West Point is death to us & sick Presidents & Generals are equally fatal."

Because the South had no party system, dissatisfaction with Davis and his handling of the war tended to be factional, petty, and often personal in nature. No party mechanism existed to channel or curb irresponsible criticism. Detractors rarely felt it necessary to offer programs in place of Davis's policies. Davis suffered personally from the carping comments of his detractors. More important, the Confederacy suffered. Without a party leader's traditional weapons and rewards, Davis had no mechanism to generate enthusiasm for his war policies.

Although Lincoln has since become a folk hero, at the time many northerners derided his performance and eagerly looked forward to a new president in 1864. Democrats supporting the war effort found Lincoln arbitrary and tyrannical. Fearing his expansion of presidential power, they also worried that extreme Republicans would push Lincoln into making the war a crusade for the abolition of slavery. Some Republicans judged Lincoln indecisive and inept. William Herndon, his former law partner, was one of the many who lashed out against the president. "Does he suppose he can crush—squelch out this huge rebellion by pop guns filled with rose water?" he asked indignantly. "He ought to hang somebody and get up a name for will or decision."

Republicans split gradually into two factions. The moderates favored a cautious approach toward winning the war. They feared the possible consequences of emancipating the slaves, confiscating Confederate property, or arming blacks. The radicals, however, urged

Lincoln to make emancipation a wartime objective. They hoped for a victory that would revolutionize southern social and racial arrangements. The reduction of the congressional Republican majority in the fall elections of 1862 made it imperative that Lincoln not only listen to both factions but also to the Democratic opposition.

## THE TIDE TURNS, 1863–1865

Hard political realities as well as Lincoln's sense of the public's mood help explain why he delayed an emancipation proclamation until 1863. Like congressional Democrats, many northerners supported a war for the Union but not one for emancipation. Not only did many, if not most, whites see blacks as inferior, but they also suspected that emancipation would trigger a massive influx of former slaves who would steal white men's jobs and political rights. Race riots in New York, Brooklyn, Philadelphia, and Buffalo dramatized white attitudes. In Cincinnati, Irish dockworkers attacked blacks who were offering to work for less pay with the cry, "Let's clear out the niggers." Arthur Carpenter's evaluation of blacks was typical of many northern soldiers confronting blacks for the first time. In December 1861, he wrote to his parents:

> No on who has ever seen the nigger in all its glory on the southern plantations . . . will ever vote for emancipation. . . . If emancipation is to be the policy of the war (and I think it will not) I do not care how quick the country goes to pot. The negro never was intended to be equal with the white man. . . . They . . . lie and steal and will not work unless they are made to.

### The Emancipation Proclamation

If the president moved too fast on emancipation, he risked losing the allegiance of people like Carpenter, offending the border states, and increasing the Democrats' chances for political victory. Moreover, he had at first hoped that pro-Union sentiment would emerge in the South and compel its leaders to abandon their rebellion. But if Lincoln did not move at all, he would alienate abolitionists and lose the support of radical Republicans, which he could ill afford.

For these reasons, Lincoln proceeded cautiously. At first, he hoped the border states would take the initiative. In the early spring of 1862, he urged Congress to pass a joint resolution offering federal compensation to states beginning a "gradual abolishment of slavery." Border-state opposition killed the idea and suggested their reluctance to believe, as did Lincoln, that the "friction and abrasion" of war would finally end slavery. Abolitionists and northern blacks, however, greeted Lincoln's proposal with "a thrill of joy."

That summer Lincoln told his cabinet he intended to emancipate the slaves. Secretary of State Seward urged the president to delay any general proclamation until the North won a decisive military victory. Otherwise, he warned, Lincoln would appear to be urging racial insurrection behind the Confederate lines to compensate for northern military bungling.

Lincoln followed Seward's advice, using that summer and fall to prepare the North for the shift in the war's purpose. To counteract white racial fears of free blacks, he promoted various schemes for establishing free black colonies in Haiti and Panama. Seizing unexpected opportunities, he lay the groundwork for the proclamation itself. In August, Horace Greeley, the influential abolitionist editor of the New York *Tribune*, printed an open letter to Lincoln attacking him for failing to act on slavery. In his reply, Lincoln linked the idea of emancipation to military necessity. His primary goal was to save the Union, he wrote.

> If I could save the Union without freeing any slave, I would do it; and if I could save it by freeing all the slaves, I would do it; and if I could do it by freeing some and leaving others alone, I would also do that. What I do about Slavery and the colored race, I do because I believe it helps to save this Union.

If Lincoln attacked slavery, then, it would only be because emancipation would save white lives, preserve the democratic process, and win the conflict for the Union.

In September 1862, the important victory at Antietam in Maryland gave Lincoln the opportunity to issue a preliminary emancipation proclamation. It stated that unless rebellious states (or parts of states in rebellion) returned to the Union by January 1, 1863, the president would declare their slaves "forever free." Although supposedly aimed at bringing the southern states back into the Union, Lincoln never expected the South to lay down arms after two years of bloodshed. Rather, he was preparing northerners to accept the eventuality of emancipation on the grounds of necessity. Frederick Douglass greeted the president's action with jubilation. "We shout for joy," he wrote, "that we live to record this righteous decree."

Not all northerners shared Douglass's joy. In fact, the September proclamation probably harmed Lincoln's party in the fall elections. As one Democratic ditty put it:

"De Union!" used to be de cry—
For dat we want it strong;
But now de motto seems to be,
"De nigger, right or wrong."

Although the elections of 1862 weakened the Republicans' grasp on the national government, they did not destroy it. Still, cautious cabinet members begged Lincoln to forget about emancipation. His refusal demonstrated his vision and humanity, as did his efforts to reduce racial fears. "Is it dreaded that the freed people will swarm forth and cover the whole land," he asked. "Are they not already in the land? Will liberation make them any more numerous? Equally distributed among the whites of the whole country, and there would be but one colored to seven whites. Could the one, in any way, greatly disturb the other?"

Finally, on New Year's Day, 1863, Lincoln issued the final Emancipation Proclamation as he had promised. It was "an act of justice, warranted by the Constitution upon military necessity." Thus what had started as a war to save the Union now also became a struggle that, if victorious, would free the slaves. Yet the proclamation had no immediate impact on slavery. It affected only slaves living in the unconquered portions of the Confederacy. It was silent about slaves in the border states and in parts of the South already in northern hands. These limitations led Elizabeth Cady Stanton and Susan B. Anthony to establish the Woman's Loyal National League to lobby Congress to emancipate all southern slaves.

Though the Emancipation Proclamation did not immediately liberate southern slaves from their masters, it had a tremendous symbolic importance. On New Year's Day, blacks gathered outside the White House to cheer the president and tell him that if he would "come out of that palace, they would hug him to death." They realized that the proclamation had significantly changed the nature of the war. For the first time, the government had committed itself to freeing slaves. Jubilant blacks could only believe that the president's action heralded a "new era" for their race. More immediately, the proclamation sanctioned the policy of accepting blacks as soldiers into the army. Blacks also hoped that the news would reach southern slaves, encouraging them either to flee to Union lines or to subvert the southern war effort by refusing to work for their masters.

Diplomatic concerns also lay behind the Emancipation Proclamation. Lincoln and his advisers anticipated that the commitment to abolish slavery would favorably impress foreign powers. European statesmen, however, did not at once abandon their cautious stance toward the Union. The English prime minister called the proclamation "trash." But important segments of the English public who opposed slavery now came to regard any attempt to help the South as "immoral." Foreigners could better understand and sympathize with a war to free the slaves than they could with a war to save the Union. In diplomacy, where image is so important, Lincoln had created a more attractive picture of the North. The Emancipation Proclamation became the North's symbolic call for human freedom.

## Unanticipated Consequences of War

The Emancipation Proclamation was but another example of the war's surprising consequences. Innovation was necessary for victory. In the final two years of war, both North and South experimented on the battlefields and behind the lines in desperate efforts to conclude the conflict successfully.

One of the Union's experiments involved using black troops for combat duty. Blacks had offered themselves as soldiers in 1861 but had been turned away. They were serving as cooks, laborers, teamsters, and carpenters in the army, however, and composed as much as a quarter of the navy. But as white casualties mounted, so did the interest in black service on the battlefield. One piece of doggerel reflected changing attitudes:

> Some tell us 'tis a burnin' shame
> To make the naygers fight;
> And that the thrade of bein' kilt
> Belongs but to the white:
> But as for me, upon my soul!
> So liberal are we here.
> I'll let Sambo be murthered instead of myself
> On every day in the year.

Other forces beyond white self-interest also lay behind the new policy: the promises of the Emancipation Proclamation and the desire to prove blacks' value to the Union. Black leaders like Frederick Douglass pressed for military service. "Once let the black man get upon his person the brass letter, U. S., let him get an eagle on his button, and a musket on his shoulder and bullets in his pocket," Douglass believed, "there is no power on earth that can deny that he has earned the right to citizenship." By the war's end, 186,000 blacks (10 percent of the army) had served the Union cause, 134,111 of them escapees from slave states.

Enrolling blacks in the Union army was an important step toward citizenship and acceptance of blacks by white society. But the black experience in the army highlighted some of the obstacles to racial acceptance. Black soldiers, usually led by white officers, were second-class soldiers for most of the war, receiving lower pay ($10 a month as compared to $13), poorer food, often more menial work, and fewer benefits than whites. "If we are good enough to fill up white men's places and fight, we should be treated then, in all respects, the same as the white man," one black soldier protested. Yet even whites who were working to equalize black and white pay often considered blacks inferior.

The army's racial experiment had mixed results. But the faithful and courageous service of black troops helped modify some of the most demeaning white racial stereotypes of blacks. The black soldiers, many of them former slaves, who conquered the South felt a sense of pride and dignity as they performed their duties. Wrote one, "We march through these fine thoroughfares where once the slave was forbid being out after nine P.M. . . . Negro soldiers!—with banners floating."

The faith in Jomini's military tactics was another wartime casualty. The infantry charge, so valued at the war's beginning, resulted in horrible carnage. As skepticism in the value of the charge increased, military leaders realized the importance of the strong defensive position. Although Confederate soldiers criticized General Lee as "King of Spades" when he first ordered

*Black soldiers, some from southern states, were accepted for combat duty in the Union army as the war progressed. Here the First Carolina Volunteers gather to celebrate emancipation on January 1, 1863.*

them to construct earthworks, the term evolved into one of affection as it became obvious that earthworks saved lives. Union commanders followed suit. By the end of 1862, both armies dug defensive earthworks and trenches whenever they interrupted their march.

Gone, too, was the courtly idea that war involved only armies. In the first years of war, many officers tried to protect civilians and their property. In his campaign against Richmond, General McClellan actually posted guards to prevent stealing. Such careful concern for rebel property soon vanished, and along with it went chickens, corn, livestock, and, as George Eagleton noted with disgust, even the furnishings of churches, down to the binding of the Bible in the pulpit. Southern troops, on the few occasions when they came North, also lived off the land. War touched all of society, not just the battlefield participants.

**Battle of Chancellorsville**   In the early war years, the South's military strategy combined defense with selective maneuvers. Until the summer of 1863, the strategy seemed to be succeeding, at least in the eastern theater. A Union attempt in December 1862 to take Richmond failed. In May 1863, the northern army returned. But at Chancellorsville, Lee and Stonewall Jackson inflicted a bloody defeat on an army more than twice their size. Stonewall Jackson, mistakenly shot by his own men, was a casualty of that battle. Despite his loss, Chancellorsville was a great Confederate victory. Yet once again, the triumph did not change the course of the war. Realizing this, Lee reviewed his strategy and concluded, "There is nothing to be gained by this army remaining quietly on the defensive." Unless the South won victories in the North, he believed, it could not gain the peace it so desperately needed.

### Changing Military Strategies

In the summer of 1863, Lee led the Confederate Army of Northern Virginia across the Potomac into Maryland and southern Pennsylvania. His goal was a victory that would threaten both

## The Tide Turns, 1863–1865

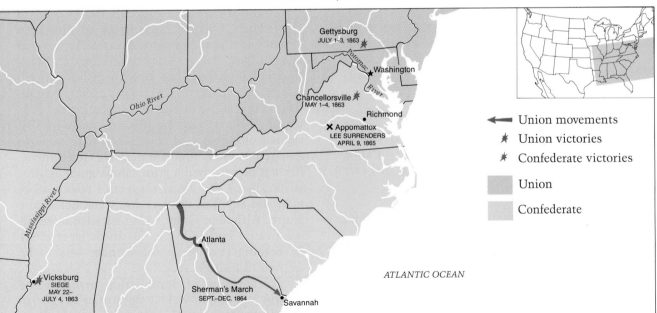

Philadelphia and Washington. He even dreamed of capturing a northern city. Such spectacular feats would surely bring diplomatic recognition and might even force the North to sue for peace. Yet he risked much. The fertile Pennsylvania farmlands would allow his army to live off the land, but since long supply lines stretched far back into Virginia, the enemy could disrupt the flow of military supplies.

**Battle of Gettysburg**  At Gettysburg on a hot and humid July 1, Lee came abruptly face to face with a Union army led by General George Meade. Much hung on the battle's outcome. During the three days of fighting, Lee attacked again and again. The fatal obsession with the infantry charge returned as the general ordered frontal assaults on Union forces positioned along a series of ridges. These costly assaults probably lost him the battle. On July 3, Lee sent three divisions, about 15,000 men in all, against the Union center. The assault, known as Pickett's Charge, was as gallant as it was futile. At 700 yards, the Union artillery opened fire. One southern officer described the scene: "Pickett's division just seemed to melt away in the blue musketry smoke which now covered the hill. Nothing but stragglers came back."

Lee's dreams of victory died that hot week, with grave consequences for the southern cause. A few days before Gettysburg, a southern soldier named William Christian had written to his wife, predicting that

> a defeat here would be ruinous. . . . If we can come out of this country triumphant and victorious, having established a peace, we will bring back to our own land the greatest joy that ever crowned a people.

Fighting in the eastern theater dragged on for another year and a half, but Lee's Gettysburg losses were so heavy that he could never mount another southern offensive. Instead, the Confederacy committed itself to a desperate defensive struggle. Gettysburg marked the turn of the military tide in the East.

**Battle of Vicksburg**  Despite the Gettysburg victory, Lincon was dissatisfied with Gen-

eral Meade, who had failed to finish off Lee's demoralized and exhausted army as it retreated. His disappointment soon faded with news of a great victory at Vicksburg in the western theater. The commander, Ulysses S. Grant, would soon solve Lincoln's leadership problem. His July 4 triumph at Vicksburg was thus doubly significant. Vicksburg represented the completion of the Union campaign to gain control of the Mississippi River and to divide the South. The successful capture of the city illustrated Grant's boldness and flexibility and his ability to think beyond particular engagements to long-term plans for victory. No northern commander in the East could match him.

By the summer of 1863, the military situation finally looked promising for the North. The Union controlled much of Arkansas, Louisiana, Mississippi, Missouri, Kentucky, and Tennessee. In March 1864, Lincoln recognized Grant as the commander to conclude the war and appointed him general in chief of the Union armies. Grant planned for victory within a year. "The art of war is simple enough," he reasoned. "Find out where your enemy is. Get at him as soon as you can. Strike at him as hard as you can, and keep moving on."

Grant intended to destroy the two main Confederate armies, Lee's Army of Northern Virginia and Joe Johnston's Army of Tennessee. Lee, still faithful to some conventional military theories, hoped for one great, decisive victory. Grant, an outsider to the prewar military establishment, had no difficulty in rejecting conventional military wisdom. "If men make war in slavish observance of rules, they will fail," he asserted. He sought no one decisive engagement. Rather, he proposed a grim campaign of annihilation, using the North's superior resources of men and supplies to wear down and defeat the South. Although Grant's plan entailed large casualties on both sides, he justified the strategy by arguing that "now the carnage was to be limited to a single year."

A campaign of annihilation involved the destruction not only of enemy armies but also of the resources that fueled the southern war effort. Although the idea of cutting the enemy off from needed supplies was implicit in the naval blockade, economic or "total" warfare was a relatively new and shocking idea. Grant, however, "regarded it as humane to both sides to protect the persons of those found at their homes, but to consume everything that could be used to support or supply armies." Grant followed this policy as he set out after Lee's army in Virginia. General William Tecumseh Sherman, who pursued General Johnston from Tennessee toward Atlanta, further refined this plan.

The war, Sherman believed, must also be waged in the minds of civilians. His desire was to make southerners "fear and dread" their foes. Therefore, his campaign to Atlanta and his march to Savannah spread destruction and terror. Ordered to forage "liberally" on the land, his army left desolation in its wake. A Georgia woman described in her diary the impact of Sherman's passage:

There was hardly a fence left standing all the way from Sparta to Gordon. The fields were trampled down and the road was lined with carcasses of horses, hogs and cattle that the invaders, unable either to consume or to carry away with them, had wantonly shot down, to starve out the people. . . . The dwellings that were standing all showed signs of pillage, and on every plantation we saw . . . charred remains.

This destruction, with its goal of total victory, showed once more how conflict produced the unexpected. The war that both North and South had hoped would be quick and relatively painless was ending after four long years with great cost to both sides. Moreover, the bitter nature of warfare during that final year threatened Lincoln's hopes for reconciliation.

## CHANGES WROUGHT BY WAR

As bold new tactics emerged both on and off the battlefield, each government took steps that changed their societies in surprising ways. Of the two, the South, which had left the Union to conserve a traditional way of life, experienced the most radical transformation.

### A New South

The expansion of the central government's power in the South, starting with the passage of the 1862 Conscription Act, continued in the last years of the war. Secession grew out of the concept of states' rights, but, ironically, winning the war depended on central direction and control. Recognizing the need for the central government to take the lead, Davis was denounced by many southerners as a tyrant and despot. Despite the accusations, the Confederate Congress cooperated with him and established important precedents. In 1863, they enacted a comprehensive tax law and an impressment act that allowed government agents to requisition and pay for food, horses, wagons, and other necessary war materials, often for only about half their market price. These were prime examples of the central government's power to interfere with private property. Government impressment of slaves for war work in 1863 affected the very form of private property that had originally driven the South from the Union.

The Conscription Act of 1862 did not solve the Confederate army's manpower problems. By 1864, the southern armies were only a third the size of the Union forces. Hence in February 1864, an expanded conscription measure made all white males between the ages 17 and 50 subject to the draft. By 1865, the necessities of war had led to the unthinkable: arming slaves as soldiers. Black companies were recruited in Richmond and other southern towns. However, because the war soon ended, no blacks actually fought for the Confederacy. In a message sent to Congress in November 1864, Davis speculated on some of the issues involved in arming slaves. "Should a slave who had served his country" be retained in servitude, he wondered, "or should his emancipation be held out to him as a reward for faithful service, or should it be granted at once on the promise of such service . . . ?" The war fought by the South to preserve slavery ended in the contemplation of emancipation.

Southern agriculture also changed under the pressure of war. Earlier, the South had imported

# RECOVERING THE PAST

The invention of photography in 1839 expanded the visual and imaginative world of nineteenth-century Americans. For the first time, Americans could visually record events in their own lives and see the images of people and incidents far away from familiar environments. Photographs, of course, also expand the boundaries of the historian's world. As photographic techniques became simpler, more and more visual information about the nineteenth century was captured. Historians can use photographs to discover what nineteenth-century Americans wore, how they celebrated weddings and funerals, and what their families, houses, and cities looked like. Pictures of election campaigns, parades, strikes, and wars show the texture of public life. But historians can also study photographs, as they do paintings, to glean information about attitudes and norms. The choice of subjects, the way in which people and objects are arranged and grouped, and the relationships between people in photographs are all clues to the social and cultural values of nineteenth-century Americans.

Some knowledge of the early history of photography helps to place the visual evidence in the proper perspective. The earliest type of photograph, the daguerreotype, was not a print but the negative itself on a sheet of silver-plated copper. The first daguerreotypes required between 15 and 30 minutes for the proper exposure. This accounts for the stiff and formal quality of many of these photographs. Glass ambrotypes (negatives on glass) and tintypes (negatives on gray iron bases), developed after the daguerreotype, were easier and cheaper to produce. But both techniques produced only one picture and required what to us would seem an interminable time for exposure.

A major breakthrough came in the 1850s with the development of the wet-plate process. In this process, the photographer coated a glass negative with a sensitive solution, exposed the negative (that is, took the picture), then quickly developed it. The new procedure required a relatively short exposure time of perhaps five seconds out of doors and one minute inside. Action shots, however, were still not feasible. The entire process tied the photographer to the darkroom. Traveling photographers carried their darkrooms with them. The advantage of the wet-plate process was that it was possible to make numerous paper prints from one negative, opening new commercial vistas for professional photographers.

Mathew Brady, a fashionable Washington photographer, realizing that the camera was "the eye of history," asked Lincoln for permission to record the

National Archives, Washington, D.C.

**Mathew Brady, Confederate Captives, Gettysburg**

519a

# PHOTOGRAPHY

war with his camera. He and his team of photographers left about 8,000 glass negatives, currently stored in the Library of Congress and the National Archives, as their record of the Civil War. Shown here are two photographs, one of three Confederate soldiers captured at Gettysburg, the other of the battlefield of Cold Harbor in Virginia.

In the first photograph, study and describe the three soldiers. How are they posed? What kind of clothes are they wearing? What about their equipment? What seems to be their physical condition? Using this photograph as evidence, what might you conclude about the southern soldier—his equipment, uniforms, shoes? How well fed do the men in the picture appear? What attitudes are conveyed through their facial expressions and poses? Finally, what kind of mood was the northern photographer trying to create? What might a northern viewer conclude about the South's war effort after looking at this picture?

The second picture was taken in April, 1865,

about a year after the battle at Cold Harbor. In the background, you can see two Union soldiers digging graves. In the foreground are the grisly remains of the battle as shot by the photographer. What do you think is the intent of the photograph? The choice of subject matter shows clearly that photography reveals attitudes as well as facts. What attitude toward war and death is conveyed in this picture? Why is the burial party taking place a full year after the battle? What does this tell us about the nature of civil warfare? Notice that the soldiers are black, as was customary. What might this scene suggest about the experience of black soldiers in the Union army?

These photographs just begin to suggest what can be discovered from old photographs. Your local historical society and library probably have photograph collections available to you. In addition, at home or in a relative's attic you may find visual records of your own family and its history.

National Archives, Washington, D.C.

***Mathew Brady,*** **Burial Party at Cold Harbor**

food from the North and had concentrated on the production of staples such as cotton and tobacco for market. Now, more and more land was turned over to food crops. As one Georgia planter explained, "Every bushel of corn and blade of grass will be greatly needed . . . [by] our armies." Some farmers voluntarily shifted crops, but others responded only to state laws reducing the acreage permitted for cotton and tobacco cultivation. These measures never succeeded in raising enough food to feed southerners adequately. But they contributed to a dramatic decline in the production of cotton, from 4.5 million bales in 1861 to 300,000 bales in 1864.

The South had always depended on importing manufactured goods. Even though some blockade runners were able to evade the Union ships, fewer and fewer slipped through the noose after 1862. The Confederacy could not, in any case, rely on blockade runners to arm and equip the army. Thus war triggered the expansion of military-related industries in the South. Here, too, the government played a crucial role. The war and navy offices directed industrial development, awarding contracts to some private manufacturing firms like Richmond's Tredegar Iron Works and operating other factories themselves. The number of southerners working in industry rose dramatically. In 1861, the Tredegar Iron Works employed 700 workers; two years later, it employed 2,500, more than half of them black. The head of the Army Ordnance Bureau reflected on the amazing transformation. "Where three years ago we were not making a gun, pistol nor a sabre, no shot nor shell . . . we now make all these in quantities to meet the demands of our large armies." At the end of the war, the soldiers were better supplied with arms and munitions than they were with food.

Although the war did not transform the southern class structure, relations between the classes began to change. The solidarity of whites based on racism and their supposed political equality was disintegrating under the pressures of the struggle. Draft resistance and desertion were examples of the growing alienation of common people from a war they saw serving only the interests of upper-class plantation owners. More and more yeoman families also found themselves struggling with grinding poverty as

the men went off to war and as government officials and armies requisitioned needed resources. A poor farmer from Georgia, Harlan Fuller, explained his family's situation in the spring of 1864. Harlan was 50 but now eligible for the draft. "I am liable at any time to be taken away from my little crops leaving my family almost without provisions & no hope of making any crop atal. I have sent six sons to the war & now the seventh enrolled he being the last I have no help left atal." This new poverty was an ominous hint of the decline of the yeoman farming class in postwar years.

### The Victorious North

Although changes in the South were more noticeable, the Union's government and economy also responded to the demands of war. Like Davis, Lincoln was accused by some northerners of being a dictator. Although he rarely tried to control Congress, veto its legislation, or direct government departments, Lincoln did use executive power freely. He violated the writ of habeas corpus by suspending the civil rights of over 13,000 northerners, who languished in prison without trials, curbed the freedom of the press because of supposedly disloyal and inflammatory articles, established conscription, issued the Emancipation Proclamation, and removed army generals. Lincoln argued that this vast extension of presidental power was temporarily justified because, as president, he was responsible for defending and preserving the Constitution.

Many of the wartime changes in government proved more permanent than Lincoln had imagined. The financial necessities of war helped to revolutionize the country's banking system. Ever since Andrew Jackson's destruction of the Bank of the United States, state banks had served American financial needs. Treasury Secretary Chase found this banking system both inadequate and chaotic and proposed to replace it. In 1863 and 1864, Congress passed banking acts that established a national currency issued by federally chartered banks and backed by government bonds. The country had a federal banking system once again.

The northern economy also responded to the demands of wartime. The need to feed soldiers and civilians stimulated the expansion of agriculture and new investment in farm machinery. With so many men off soldiering, farmers were at first short of labor. A McCormick reaper, however, performed the work of four to six men, and farmers began to buy them. During the war, McCormick sold 165,000 of his machines. Northern farming, especially in the Midwest, was well on the way to becoming mechanized. Farmers not only succeeded in growing enough grain to feed civilians and soldiers but gathered a surplus to export as well.

The war also selectively stimulated manufacturing. Although it is easy to imagine that northern industry as a whole expanded during the Civil War, in fact the war retarded overall economic growth. War consumed rather than generated wealth. Between 1860 and 1870, the annual rate of increase in real manufacturing value added was only 2.3 percent, as contrasted to 7.8 percent for the years between 1840 and 1860 and 6 percent for the period 1870 to 1900. Some important prewar industries, like cotton textiles, languished without a supply of southern cotton.

Industries that produced for the war machine, especially those with the advantages of scale, expanded and made large profits, however. Each year, the Union army required 1.5 million uniforms and 3 million pairs of shoes; the woolen and leather industries grew accordingly. Meatpackers and producers of iron, steel, and pocket watches all profited from opportunities provided by the war. Cincinnati was one city that flourished from supplying soldiers with everything from pork to soap and candles.

## On the Home Front

In numerous, less tangible ways, northern and southern society changed under the impact of war. The very fact of conflict established a new perspective for most civilians. War news vied with local events for their attention. They read newspapers and national weekly magazines with a new eagerness. The use of the mails increased dramatically as they corresponded with faraway relatives and friends. As one North Carolina woman wrote, "I never liked to write letters before, but it is a pleasure as well as a relief now." Distant events became almost as real and as vivid as those at home. The war helped to make Americans less parochial and integrated them into the larger world.

For some Americans, like John D. Rockefeller and Andrew Carnegie, war brought army contracts and unanticipated riches. The New

*Newspaper engravings were among the only visual depictions of the war available to civilians. These colored lithographs by Currier & Ives were produced a generation after the war but are very much like the journalistic images of the time. Left: A black regiment, the 54th Massachusetts, storms Fort Wagner, South Carolina. Right: Stonewall Jackson is fatally wounded by his own men at Chancellorsville.*

York *Herald* reported that New York City, had never been "so gay . . . so crowded, so prosperous," as it was in March 1864. Residents of Cincinnati noted people who "became suddenly immensely wealthy, and in their fine equipages, with liveried servants, rolled in magnificence along the city streets." In the South, blockade runners made fortunes slipping luxury goods past Union ships.

For the majority of Americans, however, war meant deprivation. The war effort gobbled up a large part of each side's resources, and ultimately ordinary people suffered. To be sure, the demand for workers ended unemployment and changed employment patterns. Large numbers of women and blacks entered the work force, a phenomenon that would be repeated in all future American wars. But while work was easy to get and wages appeared to increase, real income actually declined. Inflation, especially destructive in the South, was partly to blame. By 1864, the price for eggs in Richmond was $6 a dozen; butter sold for $25 a pound.

Low wages compounded the problem of declining income and particularly harmed women workers. Often forced into the labor market because husbands could save little or nothing from small army stipends, army wives and other women took what pay they could get. As more women entered the work force, employers saw the opportunity to cut costs by slashing wages. In 1861, the Union government paid Philadelphia seamstresses 17 cents for each shirt they made. At the height of inflation, three years later, the government reduced the piecework rate to 15 cents. Private employers paid even less, about 8 cents a shirt. Working women in the South were treated no better by their government or private employers. While war brought prosperity to a few, for most it meant trying to survive on an inadequate income.

Economic dislocation caused by the war reduced the standard of living for civilians. Shortages and hardships were the most severe in the South, which bore the brunt of the fighting. Although some lucky white southerners suffered little during the war, most did without food, manufactured goods, and medicine. Farming families who had no slaves to help with work in the fields fared poorly. As one Georgia woman explained, "I can't manage a farm well enough [alone] to make a suporte." Conditions were most dismal in cities where carts brought in vital supplies since trains were reserved for military use. Hunger was rampant. Food riots erupted in Richmond and other cities; mobs of hungry whites broke into stores to steal food. The very cleanliness of southern cities pointed to urban hunger. As one Richmond resident noted, everything was so "cleanly consumed that no garbage or filth can accumulate."

Thousands of southerners who fled as Union armies advanced suddenly found themselves homeless. "The country for miles around is filled with refugees," noted an army officer in 1862. "Every house is crowded and hundreds are living in churches, in barns and tents." Caught up in the effort of mere survival, worried about what had happened to homes and possessions left behind and whether there would be anything left when they returned, these southerners must have wondered if the cause was worth their sacrifices. Life was probably just as agonizing for those who chose to stay put when Union troops arrived. Virginia Gray, an Arkansas woman, wrote in her diary of her fear of the "feds" and the turmoil they caused when they suddenly appeared and then disappeared.

Slave life was also disrupted by the disappearance of overseers, masters, and mistresses and by the flight of family members. Even the arrival of Union forces could prove a mixed blessing. White soldiers were unknown quantities and, as Carpenter's letter suggested, they might be hostile to blacks, whom they were supposedly liberating. One slave described the upsetting arrival of the Yankees at his plantation in Arkansas: "Them folks stood round there all day. Killed hogs . . . killed cows . . . Took all kinds of sugar and preserves . . . Tore all the feathers out of the mattresses looking for money. Then they put Old Miss and her daughter in the kitchen to cooking." So frightened was this slave's mother that she hid in her bed, only to be roused by the lieutenant who told her, "We ain't a-going to do you no hurt. . . . We are freeing you." But the next day, the Yanks were gone and the confederates back. "Pa was 'fraid of both" and resolved the problem by hiding out in the cotton patch.

## Wartime Race Relations

The journal kept by Emily Harris in South Carolina conveys some of the character of life behind the lines. She revealed not only the predictable story of shortages, hardships, and the psychological burdens of those at home but also the subtle social changes the war stimulated. Emily and her husband David lived on a 500-acre farm with their seven young children and ten slaves. When David went to war, Emily had to manage the farm, even though David worried that she would be "much at a loss with the . . . farm and the negroes."

Emily's early entries establish two themes that persist for the years she kept her diary. She was worried about how David would survive the "privation and hardships" of army life and was also anxious about her own "load of responsibilities." Her December 1862 entry provides a poignant picture of a wife's thoughts. "All going well as far as I can judge but tonight it is raining and cold and a soldier's wife cannot be happy in bad weather and during a battle." The dozens of tasks she had to do depressed her. "I shall never get used to being left as the head of affairs," she wrote in January 1863. "I am not an independent woman nor ever shall be." As time passed, and the war went badly, the dismal news and mounting list of casualties heightened her concern about David's safety.

The changing nature of her relations with her slaves compounded Emily's problems. As so many southerners discovered, war transformed the master-slave relationship. Because Emily could not be the master David had been, her slaves gradually began to take unaccustomed liberties. At Christmas in 1864, several left the farm without her permission, and others stayed away longer than she said they might. "Old Will" boldly requested his freedom. Worse yet, she discovered that her slaves had helped three Yankees who had escaped from prison camp.

The master-slave relationship was crumbling, and Emily reported in her journal the consequences for whites. "It seems people are getting afraid of negroes." Although she did not admit to fear, she did reveal that she could no longer control the blacks, who were increasingly unwilling to play a subservient role.

Understanding what was at stake, slaves, in their own way, often worked for their freedom. Said one later, "Us slaves worked den when we felt like it, which wasn't often." Emily's journal entry for February 22 confessed "a painful necessity." "I am reduced," she said, "to the use of a stick but the negroes are becoming so impudent and disrespectful that I cannot bear it." A mere two weeks later she added, "The Negroes are all expecting to be set free very soon and it causes them to be very troublesom."

The scenes on the Harris farm were repeated throughout the South. Insubordination, refusal to work, even refusal to accept punishment marked the behavior of black slaves, especially those who worked as fieldhands. The thousands of blacks (probably 20 percent of all slaves) who fled toward Union lines after the early months of the war were proof of the changing nature of race relations and the harm slaves could do to the southern cause.

## Women and the War

If Emily Harris's journal reveals that she was sometimes overwhelmed by her responsibilities and shocked by the gradual changes in her dealings with her slaves, it also illustrates how the war affected women's lives. Nineteenth-century ideology promoted women's domestic role and minimized their economic importance. But the war made it impossible for many women to live according to conventional norms of behavior. So many men on both sides had gone off to fight that women had to find jobs and had to carry on farming operations. During the war years, southern women who had no slaves to help with the farmwork, and northern farm wives who labored without the assistance of husbands or sons, carried new physical and emotional burdens.

Women also participated in numerous war-related activities. For many of them the work was new. In both North and South they entered government service in large numbers. In the North, hundreds of women became military nurses. Under the supervision of Drs. Emily and Elizabeth Blackwell, of Dorothea Dix, superintendent of army nurses, and of Clara Barton, northern women nursed the wounded and dying for low pay or even for none at all. They also attempted to improve hospital conditions by attacking red tape and bureaucracy. The diary of a volunteer, Harriet Whetten, revealed the activist attitude of many others:

> I have never seen such a dirty disorganized place as the Hospital. The neglect of cleanliness is inexcusable. All sorts of filth, standing water, and the embalming house near the Hospital . . . No time had to be lost. Miss Gill and I set the contrabands at work making beds & cleaning.

Although men largely staffed southern military hospitals, Confederate women also played an important part in caring for the sick and wounded in their own homes and in makeshift hospitals behind the battle lines. Grim though the work was, many women felt as if they were participating in the real world for the first time in their lives.

Women moved outside the domestic sphere in other forms of volunteer war work. Some women gained administrative experience in soldiers' aid societies and in the United States Sanitary Commission. Many others made bandages and clothes, put together packages for soldiers at the front, and helped army wives and disabled soldiers find jobs. Fund-raising activities realized substantial sums. By the end of the war, the Sanitary Commission had raised $50 million for medical supplies, nurses' salaries, and other wartime necessities.

Many of the changes women experienced during the war years ended once the war was over. Jobs in industry and government disappeared when the men came to reclaim them. Women turned over the operation of farms to returning husbands. But for those women who were widowed or whose men came home maimed, the work had not ended. Nor had the discrimination. Trying to pick up the threads of their former lives, they found it impossible to forget what they had done to help the war effort. At least some of them were sure they had equaled their men in courage and commitment.

## The Election of 1864

In the North, the election of 1864 brought into the political arena some of the transformations of wartime. The Democrats sought to regain power by capitalizing on war weariness and nominated General George McClellan as their presidential candidate. The party proclaimed the war a failure and demanded an armistice with the South. During the campaign, Democrats accused Lincoln of arbitrarily expanding executive power and denounced sweeping economic measures such as the banking bills. Arguing that the president had transformed the war from one for Union into one for emancipation, they tried to inflame racial passions by insinuating that if the Republicans won, the fusion of blacks and whites would result.

Although Lincoln easily gained the Republican renomination because of his tight control over party machinery and patronage, his party did not unite behind him. Lincoln seemed to please no one. His veto of the radical reconstruction plan for the South, the Wade-Davis bill, led to cries of "usurpation." Conservatives were still disgruntled with the Emancipation Proclamation. In August 1864, a gloomy Lincoln told his cabinet that he expected to lose the election. As late as September, some actually hoped to reconvene the Republican convention and select another candidate.

Sherman's capture of Atlanta in September 1864 and the march through Georgia to Savannah helped swing voters to Lincoln. In the end, Republicans had no desire to see the Democrats oust their party. Lincoln won 55 percent of the popular vote and swept the electoral college.

## Why the North Won

In the months after Lincoln's reelection, the war drew to an agonizing conclusion. Sherman moved north from Atlanta into South Carolina and North Carolina while Grant pummeled Lee's forces in Virginia. The losses Grant was prepared to sustain were staggering: 18,000 in the Battle of the Wilderness, over 8,000 at Spotsylvania, and another 12,000 at Cold Harbor. New recruits stepped forward to replace the dead. On April 9, 1865, Grant accepted Lee's surrender at Appomattox. Southern soldiers and officers were allowed to return home with their personal equipment after promising to remain there peaceably. The war was finally over.

The war was, of course, technically won on the battlefield and at sea. But Grant's military strategy succeeded because the Union's manpower and economic resources could survive staggering losses of men and equipment whereas the Confederacy's could not. As Union armies pushed back the borders of the Confederacy, the South lost control of territories essential for their war effort. Finally, naval strategy eventually paid off because the North could build enough ships to make its blockade work. By 1863, it was beginning to hurt the South. In 1861, fully 90 percent of the blockade runners were slipping through the naval cordon. By the war's end, only half made it.

The South had taken tremendous steps toward meeting war needs. But despite the impressive growth of manufacturing and the increasing acreage devoted to foodstuffs, the southern army and the southern people were poorly fed and poorly clothed. As one civilian realized, "The question of bread and meat . . . is beginning to be regarded as a more serious one even than that of War." Women working alone or with disgruntled slaves on farms could not produce enough food. Worn-out farm equipment was not replaced. The government's impressment of slaves and animals harmed production. The half million blacks who fled to Union lines also played their part in pulling the South down in defeat.

New industries could not meet the extraordinary demands of wartime, and advancing

*Damage to southern railroads, whether due to battle, sabotage, or simple wear and tear, could not be repaired. The transportation breakdown led to food riots in southern cities.*

Union forces destroyed many of them. A Confederate officer in northern Virginia observed the military impact of inadequate production. "Many of our soldiers are thinly clothed and without shoes and in addition to this, very few of the infantry have tents. With this freezing weather, their sufferings are indescribable." Skimpy rations, only a third of a pound of meat for each soldier a day by 1864, weakened the Confederate force, whose trail was "traceable by the deposit of dysenteric stool" it left behind. By that time, the Union armies were so well supplied that soldiers often threw away heavy blankets and coats as they advanced.

The South's woefully inadequate transportation system also contributed to defeat. Primitive roads deteriorated and became all but impassable without needed repairs. The railroad system, geared to the needs of cotton, not war, was inefficient. During the war years, tracks wore out or were destroyed. They were not replaced. Rails were too heavy for blockade runners to bother with. And as the Confederate railroad coordinator observed in 1865, "Not a single bar of railroad iron has been rolled in the Confederacy since the war, nor can we hope to do better." Thus food intended for the army rotted awaiting shipment. Supplies were tied up in bottlenecks, and soldiers did without. Food riots in southern cities pointed to the hunger, anger, and growing demoralization of civilians.

Measures taken by the Confederacy to win the war ironically undermined the southern war effort. Conscription, impressment, and taxes all contributed to resentment and sometimes open resistance. They fueled class tensions already strained by the poverty war brought to many yeoman farmers and led some of them to assist the invaders or to join the Union army. The many southern governors who refused to contribute men, money, and supplies on the scale Davis requested implicitly condoned disloyalty to the cause. The belief in states' rights and the sanctity of private property that gave birth to the Confederacy also helped kill it.

It is tempting to compare Lincoln and Davis as war leaders. There is no doubt that Lincoln's humanity, his awareness of the terrible costs of war, his determination to save the Union, and his eloquence set him apart as one of this country's most extraordinary presidents. Yet the personal characteristics of Lincoln and Davis were probably less important than the differences between the political and social systems of the two regions. Without the support of a party behind him, Davis was crippled in efforts to generate enthusiasm and loyalty. Even though the Republicans rarely united behind Lincoln, they uniformly wanted to keep the Democrats from office. Despite all the squabbles, Republicans tended to support Lincoln's policies in Congress and back in their home districts. With considerable resources of patronage at his command, Lincoln was able to line up federal, state, and local officials behind his party and administration.

Just as the northern political system provided Lincoln with more flexibility and support, its social system also proved more able to meet the war's extraordinary demands. Although, as we have seen, both societies adopted innovations in an effort to secure victory, northerners were more cooperative, disciplined, and aggressive in meeting the organizational and production challenges of wartime. In the southern states, old attitudes, habits, and values impeded the war effort. Southern governors, wedded to states' rights, refused to cooperate with the Confederate government. North Carolina, the center of the southern textile industry, actually kept back most uniforms for its own regiments. At the war's end, 92,000 uniforms and thousands of blankets, shoes, and tents still lay in its warehouses. When Sherman approached Atlanta, Georgia's governor would not turn over the 10,000 men in the state army to Confederate commanders. Even slaveholders whose property had been the cause for secession resisted the impressment of their slaves for war work.

In the end, the Confederacy collapsed, exhausted and bleeding. Hungry soldiers received letters from their families revealing desperate situations at home. They worried and then slipped away. By December 1864, the Confederate desertion rate had passed 50 percent. Replacements could not be found. Farmers hid livestock and produce from tax collectors. Many southerners felt their cause was lost and resigned themselves to defeat. But some fought on

till the end. One northerner described them as they surrendered at Appomattox:

> Before us in proud humiliation stood the embodiment of manhood: men whom neither toils and sufferings, nor the fact of death, nor disaster, nor hopelessness could bend from their resolve; standing before us now, thin, worn, and famished, but erect, and with eyes looking level into ours, waking memories that bound us together as no other bond.

### The Costs of War

The long war was over, but the memories of that event would fester for many years to come. About 3 million American men, a third of all free males between the ages of 15 and 59, had served in the army. Each would remember his own personal history of the war. For George Eagleton, who had worked in army field hospitals, the history was one of "Death and destruction! Blood! Blood! Agony! Death! Gaping flesh wounds, broken bones, amputations, bullet and bomb fragment extractions." Of all wars Americans have fought, none has been more deadly. About 360,000 Union soldiers and another 278,000 Confederate soldiers died, about a third of them because their wounds were either improperly treated or not treated at all. Despite the efforts of men like Eagleton and the women army nurses, hospitals could not handle the scores of wounded and dying. "Glory is not for

### War Casualties

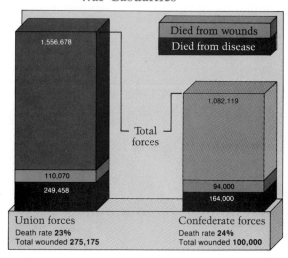

| | |
|---|---|
| Died from wounds | |
| Died from disease | |
| 1,556,678 | 1,082,119 |
| Total forces | |
| 110,070 | 94,000 |
| 249,458 | 164,000 |
| Union forces | Confederate forces |
| Death rate **23%** | Death rate **24%** |
| Total wounded **275,175** | Total wounded **100,000** |

the private soldier, such as die in the hospitals," reflected one Tennessee soldier, "being eat up with the deadly gangrene, and being imperfectly waited on."

Thousands upon thousands of men would be reminded of the human costs of war by the injuries they carried with them to the grave, by the missing limbs that marked them as Civil War veterans. About 275,000 on each side were maimed. Another 410,000 (195,000 northerners and 215,000 southerners) would recall their time in wretchedly overcrowded and unsanitary prison camps. The lucky ones would remember only the dullness and boredom. The worst memory was of those who rotted in prison camps, such as Andersonville in Georgia, where 31,000 Union soldiers were confined. At the war's end, over 12,000 graves were counted there.

Some Americans found it hard to throw off wartime experiences and adjust to peace. As Arthur Carpenter's letters suggest, he gradually grew accustomed to army life. War provided him with a sense of direction and purpose. When it was over, he felt aimless. A full year after the war's end, he wrote, "Camp life agrees with me better than any other." Many others had difficulty in returning to civilian routines and finding a new focus for life. Even those who adjusted successfully discovered that they looked at life from a different perspective. The experience of fighting, of mixing with all sorts of people from many places, of traveling far from home had lifted former soldiers out of their familiar local world and widened their vision. Fighting the war made the concept of national union real.

## An Uncertain Future

What, then, had the war accomplished? On the one hand, death and destruction. Physically, the South had been devastated. Historians have estimated a 43 percent decline in southern wealth during the war years, exclusive of the value of slaves. Great cities like Atlanta, Columbia, and Richmond lay in ruins. Fields lay weed-choked and uncultivated. Tools were worn out. A third or more of the South's stock of mules, horses, and swine had disappeared. Two-thirds of the railroads had been destroyed. Thousands were hungry, homeless, and bitter about their four years of what now appeared a useless sacrifice. Over 3 million slaves, a vast financial investment, were free.

On the other hand, the war had resolved the question of union and ended the debate over the relationship of the states to the federal government. During the war, Republicans seized the opportunity to pass legislation that would foster national union and economic growth: the Pacific Railroad Act of 1862, which set aside huge tracts of public land to finance the transcontinental railroad; the Homestead Act of 1862, which was

*Readjustment to civilian life after years on the march was difficult for nearly every soldier, however eagerly he may have wished for the homecoming.*

*Ruined buildings and women in mourning were common sights in Richmond as the war came to an end.*

to provide the yeoman farmer cheaper and easier across to the public domain; the Morrill Act of 1862, which established support for agricultural (land-grant) colleges; and the banking acts of 1863 and 1864.

The war had also ended by resolving the issue of slavery, that thorny problem that had so long plagued American life. Yet uncertainties outnumbered certainties. What would happen to the former slaves? When blacks had fled to Union lines during the war, commanders had not known what to do with them. Now the problem became even more pressing. Were blacks to have the same civil and political rights as whites? In the Union army, they had been second-class soldiers. The behavior of Union forces toward liberated blacks in the South showed how deep the strain of racism went. One white soldier, caught stealing a quilt by a former slave, shouted, "I'm fighting for $14 a month and the Union"—not to end slavery. Would blacks be given land, the means for economic independence? What would be their relations with their former owners?

What, indeed, would be the status of the conquered South in the nation? Should it be punished for the rebellion? Some people thought so. Should southerners keep their property? Some people thought not. There were clues to Lincoln's intentions. As early as December 1863, the president had announced a generous plan of reconciliation. He was willing to recognize the government of former Confederate states established by a group of citizens equal to 10 percent of those voting in 1860, as long as the group swore to support the Constitution and to accept the abolition of slavery. Not all northerners had agreed with his lenient suggestion, and the debate had continued.

In his 1865 inaugural address, Lincoln urged Americans to harbor "malice towards none . . . and charity for all." "Let us strive," he urged, "to finish the work we are in; to bind up the nation's wounds . . . to do all which may achieve a just and lasting peace." Privately, the president said the same thing. Generosity and goodwill would pave the way for reconciliation. On April 14, he pressed the point home to his cabinet. His wish was to avoid persecution and bloodshed.

That same evening, only five days after the surrender at Appomattox, the president attended a play at Ford's Theater. There, as one horrified eyewitness reported,

> a pistol was heard and a man . . . dressed in a black suit of clothes leaped onto the stage apparently from the President's box. He held in his right hand a dagger whose blade appeared about 10 inches long. . . . Every one leaped to his feet, and the cry of 'the President is assassinated' was heard—Getting where I could see into the President's box, I saw Mrs. Lincoln . . . in apparent anguish.

John Wilkes Booth, a southern sympathizer, had killed the president.

## CONCLUSION: Union Triumphant

As the war ended, many Americans grieved for the man whose decisions had so marked their lives for five years. "Strong men have wept tonight & the nation will mourn tomorrow," wrote one eyewitness to the assassination. Many more wept for friends and relations who had not survived the war but whose actions had, in one way or another, contributed to its outcome. Perhaps not all Americans realized how drastically the war had altered their lives, their futures, their nation. It was only as time passed that the war's impact became clear to them. And it was only with time that they recognized how many problems the war had left unsolved. It is to these years of Reconstruction that we turn next.

## Recommended Reading

Two good general introductions are Peter J. Parish, *The American Civil War* (1975) and David Donald, *Liberty and Union* (1978). Careful studies of the Confederacy during the war include Clement Eaton, *A History of the Southern Confederacy* (1954); Emory M. Thomas, *The Confederate Nation, 1861–1865* (1979); and Paul D. Escott, *After Secession: Jefferson Davis and the Failure of Confederate Nationalism* (1978).

The military aspects of the war can be found in John T. Hubbell, ed., *Battles Lost and Won* (1975) and Russell F. Weigley, *The American Way of War: A History of U.S. Military Strategy and Policy* (1973). Michael Barton has analyzed soldiers' diaries in *Goodmen: The Character of Civil War Soldiers* (1981). Other views of the war from the soldier's perspective include Bell Wiley's two volumes, *The Life of Johnny Reb* (1943) and *The Life of Billy Yank* (1952), and Henry S. Commager, ed., *The Blue and the Gray: The Story of the Civil War as Told by Participants*, 2 vols. (1950).

Eric Foner's essays, collected in *Politics and Ideology in the Age of Civil War* (1980) are invaluable for understanding the political context of the Civil War. Also helpful are David Donald, *Lincoln Reconsidered* (1966 ed.) and James Rawley, *The Politics of Union: Northern Politics During the Civil War* (1974). Cullom Davis and colleagues have edited a series of provocative essays on the Union's complex president, *The Public and Private Lincoln: Contemporary Perspectives* (1979).

Benjamin Quarles studies southern blacks in *The Negro in the Civil War* (1968 ed.), while Leon F. Litwack illuminates changing race relations in *Been in the Storm So Long: The Aftermath of Slavery* (1979). A good primary source is James M. McPherson, ed., *The Negro's Civil War* (1965). The strength of white racism is suggested in George M. Frederickson, *The Black Image in the White Mind* (1971) and in C. Vann Woodward, *American Counterpoint: Slavery and Racism in the North-South Dialogue* (1971).

The experience of women is treated in Mary E. Massey's *Bonnet Brigades* (1966). Although Mary Boykin Chesnut's diary was actually written after the war, her vivid account, *Mary Chesnut's Civil War* (1981) is well worth consulting.

Novels about the Civil War include Stephen Crane's *The Red Badge of Courage* (1966 ed.) and MacKinlay Kantor's *Andersonville* (1955).

## TIME LINE

| | |
|---|---|
| 1861 | Lincoln calls up state militia and suspends habeas corpus |
| | First Battle of Bull Run |
| | Union blockades the South |
| 1862 | Battles at Shiloh, Bull Run, and Antietam |
| | *Monitor* and *Virginia* battle |
| | First black regiment authorized by Union |
| | Union issues greenbacks |
| | South institutes military draft |
| 1863 | Lincoln issues Emancipation Proclamation |
| | Congress adopts military draft |
| | Battles of Gettysburg and Vicksburg |
| | Union Banking Act |
| | Southern tax laws and impressment act |
| | New York draft riots, southern food riots |
| 1864 | Sherman's march through Georgia |
| | Lincoln reelected |
| | Union Banking Act |
| 1865 | Lee surrenders at Appomattox |
| | Lincoln assassinated; Andrew Johnson becomes president |
| | Congress passes Thirteenth Amendment, abolishing slavery |

# PORTFOLIO THREE

## THE ART OF
## AN EXPANDING PEOPLE

### 1820 – 1877

As American explorers and settlers pushed westward in the years before the Civil War, they were constantly fascinated by the diversity of the terrain. Artists and later photographers recorded and interpreted the American countryside. Landscape painting became one of the dominant forms of American art by midcentury as both professional and amateur artists tried to make sense out of the vast continent.

For many artists, just as for writers like Ralph Waldo Emerson, studying nature not only revealed the special meaning of America but was closely related to religion and universal truth. "In the woods, we return to reason and faith," Emerson wrote. "Standing on the bare ground,—my head bathed by the blithe air and uplifted into infinite space,—all mean egotism vanishes. I become a transparent eyeball; I am nothing; I see all; the currents of the Universal Being circulate through me; I am part and parcel of God."

Many of the early landscape paintings were allegorical in nature and patterned after European masterpieces. Then about 1830, a group of American artists, sometimes called the Hudson River school, led by Thomas Cole (1801–1848) and Asher Durand (1796–1886), began to paint American scenes. Their pictures of the wilderness showed romantic landscapes in the Hudson valley, the Adirondacks, and the White Mountains. Other artists, like Albert Bierstadt (1830–1902), discovered the more spectacular scenery in the Rockies, while George Caleb Bingham (1811–1879) and others depicted life in the more settled regions of the Midwest.

Ironically, just as landscape paintings depicting wilderness scenes became popular, more and more wilderness was being destroyed and replaced by farmland and booming towns and cities. In many mid-nineteenth-century landscape paintings, a train can be seen in the distance. The train and the industrialism it brought with it represented progress to many Americans, but it also meant the destruction of the natural landscape that was the very essence of American uniqueness.

The United States was a land of contrasts and contradictions in the period from 1820 to 1865, and painting and the decorative arts expressed some of that uncertainty and ambivalence.

George Caleb Bingham, *The Jolly Flatboatmen in Port*, 1857.
St. Louis Art Museum.

**Both George Caleb Bingham and William Sidney Mount were genre painters who recorded the sights and feel of a particular time and place with great skill and sensitivity. Bingham, who was born in Virginia, spent most of his life in Missouri. He achieved national fame when the National Art Union distributed a print of his *Jolly Flatboatmen* to over 10,000 subscribers. Mount spent most of his life on Long Island, where he recorded the rural scene depicted here.**

William Sidney Mount, *Dancing on the Barn Floor*, 1831.
The Museum at Stony Brook, New York. Gift of Mr. and Mrs. Ward Melville.

Albert Bierstadt, *Yosemite Valley,*
*Glacier Point Trail,* 1875–1880.
Yale University Art Gallery.
Gift of Mrs. Vincenzo Ardenghi.

Albert Bierstadt, born in Germany but
raised in Massachusetts, studied abroad
but then returned to the United States,
where he accompanied several expeditions to the West. On one of them he
explored the spectacular scenery in the
Yosemite valley in California.

Asher Durand was trained as an en-
graver before he turned to landscape painting. His *Kindred Spirits,* probably the
most famous of all American landscape
paintings, is dedicated to the memory of
Thomas Cole. It shows the artist and the
poet William Cullen Bryant conversing in
the midst of a highly romanticized wilderness scene. But it is a scene that has its
realistic elements, for Durand was one of
the first to sketch his scenes outdoors.

Asher Durand, *Kindred Spirits,* 1849.
New York Public Library, Art Division.

George Inness, *The Lackawanna Valley*, 1855.
National Gallery of Art, Washington. Gift of Mrs. Huttleston Rogers.

George Inness's painting features tall, graceful trees and a reclining figure contemplating the pastoral scene. In many respects the picture is much like other landscape paintings, but there is a difference: an industrial town looms in the background, and a train cuts through the heart of the picture. The tree stumps in the foreground represent not destruction of the wilderness so much as progress. For many Americans in the middle of the nineteenth century, industrialism and wilderness seemed to go naturally together. Popular print makers such as Currier & Ives were even more blatant in representing the train as the agent of civilization, as in the second picture, which contains nearly every symbol and cliché possible.

Currier & Ives,
*Across the Continent*,
after Frances Flora Palmer,
1868.
Thomas Gilcrease Institute of
American History and Art,
Tulsa, Oklahoma.

These two rooms and their furnishings illustrate some of the contrasts and contradictions in American life in the decades before the Civil War. The first room is filled with plush, ornate Victorian furniture. The family portraits in elaborate frames, the gas chandelier, the red drapes and carpet speak of the taste and the growing wealth of many of the urban upper class, but it was also a style imitated in the small towns of America.

Parlor, Col. Robert J. Milligan house, Saratoga Springs, New York, built 1853.
Brooklyn Museum. Gift of Sarah Milligan Rand, Kate Milligan Brill, and the Dick S. Ramsay Fund.

The second room is filled with furniture designed by the Shakers, a utopian and celibate sect that reached its peak membership of about 8,000 in 1850. The Shaker craftsmen transferred their ideas about a simple life into undecorated but beautifully designed furniture. They took ordinary rural forms and perfected them. Both Victorian and Shaker furniture are popular today among collectors.

Shaker living room.
Hancock Shaker Village, near Pittsfield, Massachusetts.

# CHAPTER 17
## RECONSTRUCTING AMERICA

In April 1864, one year before Lincoln's assassination, Robert Allston died of pneumonia. His daughter, Elizabeth, was left with a "sense of terrible desolation and sorrow" as the Civil War raged around her, and she and her mother took over the affairs of their many rice plantations. With Yankee troops moving through coastal South Carolina in the late winter of 1864–1865, Elizabeth's sorrow turned to "terror" as Union soldiers arrived in search of liquor, firearms, and hidden valuables. The Allston women survived an insulting search and then fled. In a later raid, Yankee troops encouraged the somewhat reluctant Allston slaves to take furniture and other household goods from the Big Houses, some of which the blacks returned when the Yankees were gone. But before they left, the Union soldiers, in their role as liberators, gave the key to the crop barns to the semifree slaves.

When the war was over, Adele Allston took an oath of allegiance to the United States and secured a written order commanding the blacks to relinquish the keys to the barns. She and Elizabeth made plans to return in the early summer of 1865 to resume control of the family plantations, thereby reestablishing white authority. She was assured that although the blacks had guns and were determined to have the means to a livelihood, "no outrage has been committed against the whites except in the matter of property." Possession of the keys to the barns, Elizabeth wrote, would be the "test case" of whose rights were most important and who was in control.

Not without some fear, Adele and Elizabeth Allston rode up in a carriage to their former home, Nightingale Hall, to confront their former slaves. To their surprise, a pleasant reunion took place. The Allston women greeted the blacks by name, inquired after their children, and caught up on the affairs of those with whom they had lived closely for many years. A trusted black foreman handed over the keys to the barns. This harmonious scene was repeated elsewhere.

But at Guendalos, a plantation owned by an Allston son absent during most of the war fighting with the Confederate army, the women met a very different situation. As their carriage arrived and moved slowly toward the barn, a defiant group of armed ex-slaves lined both sides of the road, following the carriage after it passed by. The tension grew as the carriage stopped by the barn. There the former black driver, Uncle Jacob, was unsure whether to yield the keys to the barns full of rice and corn, put there by black labor. But Mrs. Allston insisted. As Uncle Jacob hesitantly began to hand the keys to her, an angry young man shouted out: "Ef yu gie up de key, blood'll flow." Uncle Jacob slowly slipped the keys back into his pocket.

The tension increased as the blacks sang freedom songs and brandished hoes, pitchforks, and guns in an effort to discourage anyone from going to town for help. Two blacks, however, left the plantation to find some Union military officers to come settle the issue of the keys, most likely on the side of the Allstons. As Adele and Elizabeth waited, word finally arrived that the Union officers, who were difficult to locate, would no doubt be found the next day and would come to Guendalos. The Allstons spent the night restlessly but safely in their house. Early the next morning, they were awakened by a knock at the unlocked front door. Adele slowly opened the door, and there stood Uncle Jacob. Without a word, he handed over the keys to Guendalos.

Most of the essential human ingredients of the Reconstruction era are found in this story. Despite defeat on the battlefields and surrender at Appomattox, southern whites were determined to resume control of both land and labor. Rebellion aside, the law, property titles, and federal enforcement were all on the side of the original owners of the land. The Allston women were friendly to the blacks in a genuine but maternal way and insisted on the restoration of the deferential relationships that existed before the war. Adele and Elizabeth, in short, both feared and cared for their former slaves.

The black freedmen likewise revealed mixed feelings toward their former owners. At different plantations they demonstrated a variety of emotions: anger, loyalty, love, resentment, and pride. Respect was paid to the person of the Allstons but not to their property and crops. The action of the blacks indicated that what they wanted was not revenge but economic independence and freedom.

In this encounter between former slaves and their mistresses, the role of the northern federal officials is most revealing. The Union soldiers, literally and symbolically, gave the keys of freedom to the blacks but did not remain long enough to guarantee that freedom. Although encouraging the freedmen to plunder the master's house and take possession of the crops, when the crucial encounter occurred, the northern officials had disappeared. It is clear that had they been found they would have upheld the land titles of the Allstons. Knowing that, Uncle Jacob handed the keys to land and liberty back to his former owner. The blacks at Guendalos knew that if they wanted to ensure their freedom, they had to do it themselves. Northern help was limited and short-lived.

The goals of each group at the Allston plantations were in conflict with each other. What happened to various human dreams and needs as people sought to form new relationships during Reconstruction is the theme of this chapter. Amid the devastating destruction and countless casualties at the end of a bloody civil war, the survivors sought to put their lives back together again. Victorious but variously motivated northern officials, defeated but defiant southern planters, and impoverished but hopeful freed blacks—all had needs and dreams. In no way could each group fulfill its conflicting goals, yet each had to try. This guaranteed that the Reconstruction era would be a deeply divided one.

## THE BITTERSWEET AFTERMATH OF WAR

"There are sad changes in store for both races," the daughter of a Georgia planter wrote in her diary early in the summer of 1865, adding, "I wonder the Yankees do not shudder to behold their work." In order to understand the bittersweet nature of Reconstruction, one must look at the state of the nation in the spring of 1865, shortly after the assassination of President Lincoln.

### The United States in 1865

The "Union" was in a state of constitutional crisis in April 1865. The status of the 11 states of the former Confederate States of America was unclear. They had claimed the right to secede, were successful for a time, but finally had failed. The North had denied the South's constitutional right to secede but needed four years of Civil

# Conflicting Goals During Reconstruction

| VICTORIOUS NORTHERN ("RADICAL") REPUBLICANS | NORTHERN MODERATES —REPUBLICANS AND DEMOCRATS | OLD SOUTHERN PLANTER ARISTOCRACY (EX-CONFEDERATES) | NEW "OTHER SOUTH" —YEOMAN FARMERS AND EX-WHIGS (UNIONISTS) | BLACK FREEDMEN |
|---|---|---|---|---|
| • Justify the costs of war by remaking southern society in the image of the North<br>• Political but not physical or economic punishment of Confederate leaders<br>• Continue programs of economic progress begun during the war: high tariffs, railroad subsidies, national banking<br>• Maintain the Republican party in power in the nation<br>• Help the freedmen make the transition to full freedom by providing them with the tools of citizenship (suffrage) and equal economic opportunity<br>• Governmental role in achieving these idealistic commitments to justice, equality, and morality | • Speedy establishment of peace and order, reconciliation between North and South<br>• Leniency, amnesty, and merciful readmission of southern states to the Union<br>• Perpetuate the primacy of land ownership, free labor, market competition, and other capitalist values of nineteenth-century American life<br>• Local self-determination of economic and social issues, limited interference by the national government<br>• Limited support for black suffrage<br>• Restraint on efforts to remake social and racial relationships; skeptical of crusades | • Celebrate the noble "lost cause" by defiantly asserting the old ways<br>• Protection from possibilities of northern or black uprising and revenge<br>• Amnesty, pardon, and restoration of confiscated lands<br>• Restore traditional plantation-based market-crop economy with blacks as cheap labor force<br>• Restore traditional political leaders in the states<br>• Restore traditional paternalistic race relations as basis of social order | • Speedy establishment of peace and order, reconciliation between North and South<br>• Recognition of loyal role and economic value of upcountry small yeoman farmers<br>• Create greater diversity in southern economy: capital investments in railroads, factories, and the diversification of agriculture<br>• Displace the planter aristocracy with new political leaders drawn from loyal Unionists and new economic interests<br>• Limited rights and powers to freedmen; suffrage granted only to the educated few | • Physical protection from abuse and terror by local whites<br>• Economic independence through land of one's own (40 acres and a mule) and equal access to trades<br>• Political participation through the right to vote<br>• Equal civil rights and protection under the laws, especially rights of mobility and testimony in court<br>• Educational opportunity and the development of family and cultural bonds |

War and over 600,000 deaths to win the point. Were the 11 states part of the Union or not? Lincoln's official position had been that the southern states had never left the Union, which was "constitutionally indestructible." As a result of their rebellion, they were only "out of their proper relation" with the United States. The president, therefore, as commander in chief, had the authority to decide on the basis for setting relations right and proper again.

Congressional opponents of Lincoln argued that by declaring war on the Union, the Confederate states had broken their constitutional ties and had reverted to a kind of prestatehood status like territories or "conquered provinces." Congress, therefore, which decided on the admission of new states, should resolve the constitutional issues and assert its authority over the reconstruction process. Hidden in this conflict between Congress and the president was a powerful struggle between two branches of the national government. As has happened during nearly every war, the executive branch took on broad powers necessary for rapid mobilization of resources and domestic security. Many people believed, however, that Lincoln went far beyond his constitutional authority. As soon as the war was over, Congress sought to reassert its authority, as it would do after every subsequent war.

In April 1865, the Republican party ruled victorious, and virtually alone. Although less than a dozen years old, the Republicans had made immense achievements in the eyes of the northern public. They had won the war, preserved the Union, and freed the slaves. Moreover, they had enacted most of the old Federalist-Whig economic programs on behalf of free labor and free enterprise: a high protective tariff, a national banking system, broad use of the power to tax and to borrow and print money, generous federal appropriations for internal improvements, the Homestead Act for western farmers, and an act to establish land-grant colleges to teach agricultural and mechanical skills. Alexander Hamilton, John Quincy Adams, and Henry Clay might all have applauded. Despite these achievements, the Republican party was still an uneasy grouping of former Whigs, Know-Nothings, Democrats, and antislavery forces.

The Democratic party, by contrast, was in shambles. Republicans depicted southern Democrats as rebels, murderers, and traitors, northern Democrats as weak-willed, disloyal, and opposed to economic growth and progress. Nevertheless, it had been politically important in 1864 for the Republicans to show that the war was a bipartisan effort. A Jacksonian Democrat and Unionist from Tennessee, Andrew Johnson, had therefore been nominated as Lincoln's vice-president. In April 1865, he sat at the head of the government.

The United States in the spring of 1865 was a picture of stark economic contrasts. Northern cities hummed with productive activity while southern cities lay in ruins. Northern factory chimneys poured forth flames and smoke that gave evidence of the production of railroad tracks and engines, steel, textiles, farm implements, and building materials. Southern chimneys were often all that stood, puncturing the skyline in stony silence above the rubble of devastation. Northern railroad tracks laced the land, while in the South railroads and roads lay in ruins. Southern financial institutions were bankrupt, while in the North they flourished. Northern farms, under increasing mechanization, were more productive than ever before, and free farmers took pride that they had amply fed the Union army and urban workers throughout the war. They saw the Union victory as evidence of the superiority of free over slave labor. By contrast, southern farms and plantations, especially those that had lain in the path of Sherman's march, were like a "howling waste." As one observer described it, the countryside " looked for many miles like a broad black streak of ruin and desolation." Said one resident, "The Yankees came through . . . and just tore up everything."

Although there were pockets of relative wealth in some areas, the South was largely devastated as the soldiers demobilized and returned home in April 1865. There was scarcely a family, North as well as South, that had not suffered a serious casualty in the war. Crippled by amputated limbs and suffering from hunger (a half million southern whites faced starvation), the ragtag remains of the Confederate army suffered widespread sickness, destruction, and social disorder as they traveled home. Yet, as a later southern writer, Wilbur Cash, explained, "If this war had smashed the Southern world, it had left the essential Southern mind and will . . . entirely unshaken." Many southerners wanted nothing less than to resist Reconstruction and restore their old world. Others, the minority who had remained quietly loyal to the Union throughout the war, dreamed of a postwar period not of defiance and restoration of the old order but of reconciliation and development of a new one.

Whatever the extremes of southern white attitudes, the dominant social reality in the spring of 1865 was that nearly 4 million former slaves were on their own, facing the challenges of freedom. After an initial reaction of joy and celebration, expressed in jubilee songs, the freedmen quickly became aware of their continuing dependence on former owners. A Mississippi woman stated the uncertainty of her new status this way: "I used to think if I could be free I should be the happiest of anybody in the world. But when my master come to me, and says— Lizzie, you is free! it seems like I was in a kind of daze. And when I would wake up in the morning I would think to myself, Is I free? Hasn't I got to get up before day light and go into the field of work?" For Lizzie and 4 million other blacks, everything—and nothing—had changed.

## Hopes Among Freedmen

Throughout the South in the summer of 1865, there were optimistic expectations in the old slave quarters. As Union soldiers marched through Richmond, prisoners in slave-trade jails were heard to chant: "Slavery chain done broke at last! Gonna praise God till I die!" The slavery chain, however, was not broken all at once, but link by link. After Union soldiers swept through an area, Confederate troops might follow, or master and overseer would return, and the slaves learned not to rejoice too quickly or openly. Often the return of the master meant severe whippings, worse treatment, and even death for helping Yankee soldiers loot the house.

### The United States in 1865: Crisis at the End of the Civil War

Military casualties
  350,000 Union soldiers dead
  <u>275,000</u> Confederate soldiers dead

  625,000 Total dead

  <u>275,000</u> seriously wounded and maimed
  900,000 casualties nationwide in a total male population of 15 million (nearly 1 in 15)
Physical/Economic crisis
  The South devastated, its railroads, industry, and some major cities in ruins; its fields and livestock wasted
Constitutional crisis
  Eleven ex-Confederate states not a part of the Union, their status unclear and uncertain
Political crisis
  Republican party (entirely of the North) dominant in Congress; a former Democratic slaveholder from Tennessee, Andrew Johnson, in the presidency
Social crisis
  Nearly 4 million black freedmen throughout the South face challenges of survival and freedom, along with thousands of hungry demobilized white southern soldiers and displaced white families
Psychological crisis
  Incalculable resentment, bitterness, anger, and despair throughout North and South

*Both white southerners and their former slaves suffered in the immediate aftermath of the Civil War, as illustrated by this engraving from* **Frank Leslie's Illustrated Newspaper.**

"Every time a bunch of No'thern sojers would come through," recalled one slave, "they would tell us we was free and we'd begin celebratin'. Before we would get through somebody else would tell us to go back to work, and we would go." Another slave recalled celebrating emancipation "about twelve times" in one North Carolina county. So former slaves became cautious about what freedom meant.

Gradually, the freedmen began to express a vision of what life beyond bondage and the plantation might be like. The first thing they did to test the reality of freedom was to leave the plantation, if only for a few hours or days. "If I stay here I'll never know I am free," a South Carolina woman said, and off she went to work as a cook in a nearby town. Some former slaves cut their ties entirely, leaving cruel and kindly masters alike. Some returned to an earlier master, but large numbers of them went to towns and cities for work and to find schools, churches, and association with other blacks, where they would be safe from whippings and retaliation.

Many freedmen left the plantation in search of members of their families. The quest for a missing spouse, parent, or child, sold away years before, was a powerful force in the first few months of emancipation. Black newspapers were filled with advertisements detailing these sorrowful searches. For those who found a spouse or who had been living together in slave marriages, freedom meant getting married legally. Mass wedding ceremonies, sometimes involving many couples, were common sights in the first months of emancipation. Legal marriage was important morally, but it also served such practical purposes as establishing the legitimacy of children and gaining access to land titles and other economic opportunities. Marriage also meant special burdens for black women, who almost immediately assumed a double role as keeper of the house, with all the usual domestic duties performed by women, white or black, and as a producer of income by work outside her home.

Another way in which freedmen demonstrated their new status was by choosing surnames: Lincoln, Grant, and Washington were common. As an indication of the mixed feelings the freedmen had toward their former masters, some would adopt their master's name, while others would pick "any big name 'ceptin' their master's." Often as a symbol of historical identity and family pride, the former slaves selected the name of a first master, "the one my daddy and mammy had."

Emancipation changed black manners around whites as well. Many blacks, even if they were still working on the same plantation, simply behaved differently in order to express what freedom meant. The masks were dropped and the old expressions of humility—tipping a hat, stepping aside, feigning happiness, addressing whites with titles of deference—were discarded. For the blacks, these were necessary symbolic expressions of selfhood; they proved that things were now different. To whites, these behaviors were seen as acts of "insolence," "insubordination," and "puttin' on airs."

However important were choosing names, dropping masks, moving around, getting married, and testing new rights, the primary goal for most freedmen was the acquisition of their own land. "All I want is to git to own fo' or five acres ob land, dat I can build me a little house on and call my home," a Mississippi black said. Only through economic independence, a traditional American goal, could former slaves prove to themselves that emancipation was real.

*Many freed blacks, like these young people photographed in Richmond, Virginia, gravitated to urban centers.*

During the war, some Union generals had placed liberated slaves in charge of confiscated and abandoned lands. In the Sea Islands off the coast of South Carolina and Georgia, blacks had been working 40-acre plots of land and harvesting their own crops for several years. Some had even been given titles of possession to these lands, while others had been organized by northern philanthropists into growing cotton for the Treasury Department in order to prove the superiority of free labor over slavery. In the Davis Bend section of Mississippi, thousands of ex-slaves worked 40-acre tracts on leased lands formerly owned by Jefferson Davis. In this highly successful experiment, they made profits sufficient to repay the government for initial costs, then lost the land to Davis's brother. A more typical situation, however, was one like the Allston plantations, where in the absence of former owners the blacks simply continued familiar agricultural work.

Many freedmen expected a new economic order as fair payment for their years of involuntary work on the land. "It's de white man's turn ter labor now," a black preacher in Florida told a group of fieldhands. Whites would no longer own all the land, he went on, "fur de Guverment is gwine ter gie ter ev'ry Nigger forty acres of lan' an' a mule." Other freedmen were willing to settle for less: One in Virginia offered to take only one acre of land—"Ef you make it de acre dat Marsa's house sets on." Another was more guarded, aware of how easy the power could shift back to white planters: "Gib us our own land and we take care ourselves; but widout land, de ole massas can hire us or starve us, as dey please." However cautiously expressed, the freedmen had every expectation, fed by the intensity of their dreams, that the promised "forty acres and a mule" was forthcoming. Once land, family unity, and education were achieved, they looked forward to civil rights and the vote.

## The White South's Fearful Response

White southerners had equally mixed goals and high expectations at the end of the Civil War. Yeoman farmers and poor whites stood side by side with rich planters in bread lines as together they looked forward to the restoration of their land and livelihood. Suffering from "extreme want and destitution," as a Cherokee County, Georgia, resident put it, white southerners responded with feelings of outrage, loss, and injustice. "I tell you it is mighty hard," said one man, "for my pa paid his own money for our niggers; and that's not all they've robbed us of. They have taken our horses and cattle and sheep *and everything*." Others felt the loss more personally, as former slaves they thought were faithful or for whom they felt great affection suddenly left. "Something dreadful has happened dear Diary," a Florida woman wrote in May 1865. "My dear black mammy has left us . . . I feel lost, I feel as if someone is dead in the house. Whatever will I do without my Mammy?"

A more dominant emotion than sorrow, however, was fear. The entire structure of southern society was shaken, and the semblance of racial peace and order that slavery had provided was shattered. Many white southerners could hardly imagine a society without blacks in bondage. It was the basis not only of social order but of a life style the larger slaveholders, at least, had long regarded as the perfect model of gentility and civilization. Having lost control of all that was familiar and revered, large planters and small farmers alike feared all kinds of inconveniences and horrors.

The mildest of their fears was having to do various jobs and chores they had rarely done

---

### The Promise of Land: 40 Acres

To All Whom It May Concern

Edisto Island, August 15th, 1865

George Owens, having selected for settlement forty acres of Land, on Theodore Belab's Place, pursuant to Special Field Orders, No. 15, Headquarters Military Division of the Mississippi, Savannah, Ga., Jan. 16, 1865; he has permission to hold and occupy the said Tract, subject to such regulations as may be established by proper authority; and all persons are prohibited from interfering with him in his possession of the same.

By command of
 R. SAXTON
　　Brev't Maj. Gen.,
　　Ass't. Comm.
　　S. C., Ga., and Fla.

before, like housework. A Georgia woman, Eliza Andrews, complained that it seemed to her "a waste of time for people who are capable of doing something better to spend their time sweeping and dusting while scores of lazy negroes that are fit for nothing else are lying around idle." Worse yet was the "impudent and presumin'" new manners of former slaves, as a North Carolinian put it. Many worried that the rude behavior meant that blacks wanted social equality. Some distressing signs of equality were already apparent. As the freedmen moved about the cities and countryside looking for relatives and work, they rode on streetcars, railroad trains, and steamboats, thus putting whites into the embarrassing position of boarding a train to find that they must sit down next to a former slave.

The worst fears of southern whites were rape and revenge. Impudence and pretensions of social equality, some thought, would lead to intermarriage, which in turn would produce mulattoes, "Africanization," and the destruction of the purity of the white race. Fears of violence were touched off by the presence of black soldiers. Although demobilization occurred rapidly after Appomattox, a few black militia units remained in uniform, parading with guns in southern cities. This stirred fears of black revenge in the hearts of southern whites. Acts of violence by black soldiers against whites in the early years of Reconstruction, however, were very rare.

Believing that their world was turned upside down, the former planter aristocracy tried to set it right again. Their goal was to restore the old plantation order and appropriate racial relationships. The key to reestablishing white dominance were the "black codes" passed by state legislatures in the first year after the end of the war. Many of the codes granted freedmen the right to marry, sue and be sued, testify in court, and hold property. But these rights were qualified. Complicated passages in the codes explained under exactly what circumstances blacks could testify against whites or own property (mostly they could not) or exercise other rights of free persons. Some rights were denied. Racial intermarriage headed the list, but it also included the right to bear arms, possess alcohol-

ic beverages, sit on trains and other public conveyances except in baggage compartments, enter city limits or be on the streets at night, or congregate in large groups.

Many of the alleged rights guaranteed by the black codes—testimony in court, for example— were passed in order to induce the federal government to withdraw its remaining troops from the South. This was a crucial issue, for freedmen were being assaulted, beaten, and terrorized by marauding groups of whites in the aftermath of Appomattox and needed protection. Countless reported and unreported cases of savage and brutal violence were committed against virtually defenseless blacks in the early years of Reconstruction. In one small district of Kentucky, for example, a government agent reported in 1865:

> Twenty-three cases of severe and inhuman beating and whipping of men; four of beating and shooting; two of robbing and shooting; three of robbing; five men shot and killed; two shot and wounded; four beaten to death; one beaten and roasted; three women assaulted and ravished; four women beaten; two women tied up and whipped until insensible; two men and their families beaten and driven from their homes, and their property destroyed; two instances of burning of dwellings, and one of the inmates shot.

No wonder blacks and their white sympathizers wanted protection and the right to testify in court against whites.

For white planters, the violence was another sign of social disorder that could be eased only by restoring a plantation-based society. Moreover, they needed the freedmen's labor. The crucial provisions of the black codes were thus intended to regulate the freedmen's economic status. "Vagrancy" laws provided that any blacks not lawfully employed, which usually meant by a white employer, could be arrested, jailed, fined, or hired out to a man who would assume responsibility for their debts and future behavior. These arrangements struck some as indistinguishable from slavery. The codes regulated the work contracts by which black laborers worked in the fields for white landowners, including severe penalties for leaving before the yearly contract was fulfilled and rules for behavior, attitude, and manners. Thus southern leaders sought to reestablish their dominance. In a scene often repeated, the slaves on a Louisiana plantation listened to a departing Union officer inform them that they were now free, only to be told by the wife of their former master, "Ten years from today I'll have you all back 'gain."

## NATIONAL RECONSTRUCTION

The intention of this Louisiana plantation mistress and other planters to control the lives of freedmen was thoroughly supported by the black codes passed by southern legislatures. But what kinds of actions would be taken by the government in Washington? The first statements of the new president were far from reassuring to worried southerners. Johnson took a stern stand against the defeated Confederates, telling congressional Republicans he believed that "treason is a crime and crime must be punished." The freedmen might be free of their former owners after all.

### Promised Land Restored to Whites

Richard H. Jenkins, an applicant for the restoration of his plantation on Wadmalaw Island, S. C., called "Rackett Hall," the same having been unoccupied during the past year and up to the 1st of Jan. 1866, except by one freedman who planted no crop, and being held by the Bureau of Refugees, Freedmen and Abandoned Lands, having conformed to the requirements of Circular No. 15 of said Bureau, dated Washington, D. C., Sept. 12, 1865, the aforesaid property is hereby restored to his possession.

. . . The Undersigned, Richard H. Jenkins, does hereby solemnly promise and engage, that he will secure to the Refugees and Freedmen now resident on his Wadmalaw Island Estate, the crops of the past year, harvested or unharvested; also, that the said Refugees and Freedmen shall be allowed to remain at their present houses or other homes on the island, so long as the responsible Refugees and Freedmen (embracing parents, guardians, and other natural protectors) shall enter into contracts, by leases or for wages, in terms satisfactory to the Supervising Board.

Also, that the undersigned will take the proper steps to enter into contracts with the above described responsible Refugees and Freedmen, the latter being required on their part to enter into said contracts on or before the 15th day of February, 1866, or surrender their right to remain on the said estate, it being understood that if they are unwilling to contract after the expiration of said period, the Supervising Board is to aid in getting them homes and employment elsewhere.

### The Presidential Plan

President Johnson's initial toughness, however, soon gave way to leniency. On May 29, 1865, he issued two proclamations setting forth his reconstruction program. Like Lincoln, he maintained that the southern states had never left the Union. His first proclamation continued Lincoln's policies by offering "amnesty and pardon, with restoration of all rights of property" to all former Confederates who would take an oath of allegiance to the Constitution and the Union of the United States. There were exceptions: ex-Confederate government leaders and rich rebels whose taxable property was valued at over $20,000. In this latter exception Johnson revealed his old Jacksonian hostility to wealthy aristocratic planters and his preference for leadership by self-made yeoman farmers like himself. Any southerners not covered by the amnesty proclamation could, however, apply for special individual pardons, which Johnson granted to nearly all who applied. By the fall of 1865, only a handful remained unpardoned.

Johnson's second proclamation accepted the reconstructed government of North Carolina and laid out the steps by which other southern states could reestablish state governments. First, the president would appoint a provisional governor, who would call a state convention representing "that portion of the people of said State who are loyal to the United States." This included those who took the oath of allegiance or were otherwise pardoned. The convention should ratify the Thirteenth Amendment, which abolished slavery, void secession, repudiate all Confederate debts, and then elect new state officials and members of Congress.

Under this lenient plan, each of the southern states successfully completed reconstruction and sent newly elected members to the Congress that convened in December 1865. Southern voters indicated their defiant attitude by electing dozens of former officers and legislators of the Confederacy, including a few not yet pardoned. Some state conventions refused to ratify the Thirteenth Amendment, and those that did asserted their right to compensation for the loss of slave property. No state convention provided for black suffrage, and most did nothing to guarantee civil rights, schooling, or economic protection for the freedmen.

By the end of 1865, many questions had presumably been answered. The southern states had formed new governments and had elected new representatives to Congress. The freedmen were going back to work for their former masters under annual contracts. The new president seemed firmly in charge. The reconstruction of the southern states, less than eight months earlier engaged in bloody battle against the Union, seemed to be over. But northern Republicans were far from satisfied when they looked at President Johnson's efforts. Georges Clemenceau, a young French newspaper reporter covering the war, wondered if the North, having paid so many "painful sacrifices," would "let itself be tricked out of what it had spent so much trouble and perseverance to win."

## The Congressional Plan

As they looked at the situation late in 1865, northern leaders painfully saw that almost none of their postwar goals—moral, political, or psychological—were being fulfilled. The South seemed far from reconstructed and was taking advantage of the president's program to restore the power of the prewar planter aristocracy. The freedmen were receiving neither equal citizenship nor economic independence. And the Republicans were not likely to maintain their political power and stay in office. Would the Democratic party and the South gain by postwar elections what they had been unable to achieve by civil war?

A song popular in the North in 1866 posed the question: "Who shall rule this American Nation?" Would those who had betrayed their country and "murder the innocent freedmen" rule, or those "loyal millions" who had shed their "blood in battle"? The answer was obvious. Congressional Republicans, led by Congressman Thaddeus Stevens of Pennsylvania and Senator Charles Sumner of Massachusetts, thus asserted their own policies for reconstructing the nation. Many southerners believed that the

*Widespread violence against blacks in the wake of emancipation, especially following President Johnson's veto of the Civil Rights Bill, gave rise to the sardonic question, "Slavery is Dead?"*

Republican Congress wanted to transform the South in the North's image and to punish it by providing numerous political and economic rights for the freedmen. Although some congressional leaders did indeed have strong punitive and political motivations, as well as a strong sense of responsibility to set the freedmen on their feet, the vast majority of Republicans were moderates. Although branded as "radicals," only for a brief period in 1866 and 1867 did a restrained "radical" rule prevail.

Rejecting Johnson's notion that the South had already been reconstructed, Congress asserted its constitutional authority to decide on its own membership and refused seats to the newly elected senators and representatives from the old Confederate states. Congress then established the Joint Committee on Reconstruction to investigate conditions in the South. Its report documented disorder and resistance and the appalling treatment and conditions of the freedmen. Even before the report was made final in 1866, Congress passed a civil rights bill to protect the fragile rights of the blacks and extended for two more years the Freedmen's Bureau, an agen-

*A white mob burned this freedmen's school during the Memphis riot of May 1866.*

cy providing emergency assistance at the end of the war. President Johnson vetoed both bills, arguing that they were unconstitutional and calling his congressional opponents "traitors."

Johnson's growing anger forced moderates into the radical camp, and Congress passed both bills over his veto. Both, however, were watered down by weakening the power of enforcement. Southern civil courts, therefore, regularly disallowed black testimony against whites, acquitted whites charged with violence against blacks, sentenced blacks to compulsory labor, and generally made discriminatory sentences for the same crimes. In this judicial climate, racial violence erupted with discouraging frequency.

In Memphis, for example, a race riot occurred in May 1866 that typified race relations during the Reconstruction period and followed the pattern of most urban race riots in America from the colonial era to the 1960s. In the months prior to the riot, there were many cases of unprovoked brutality by local Irish policemen against black Union soldiers stationed at nearby Fort Pickering. A Memphis newspaper suggested that "the negro can do the country more good in the cotton field than in the camp" and criticized what it called "the dirty, fanatical, nigger-loving Radicals of this city" who thought otherwise.

In this inflamed atmosphere, the riot began in a street brawl between the police and some recently discharged but armed black soldiers who forcibly interfered with the arrest of a friend charged with disorderly conduct. After some fighting and an exchange of gunfire, the soldiers went back to their fort. That night, white mobs, led by prominent local officials (one of whom urged the mob to "go ahead and kill the last damned one of the nigger race"), invaded the black section of the city. With the encouragement of the Memphis police, the mobs engaged in over 40 hours of terror, killing, beating, robbing, and raping virtually helpless residents and burning houses, schools, and churches. When it was over, 48 persons, all but two of them black, had died in the riot. The local Union army commander took his time intervening to restore order, arguing that his troops had "a large amount of public property to guard [and] hated Negroes too." A congressional inquiry found that in Memphis, blacks had "no protection from the law whatever."

A month later, Congress proposed to the states the ratification of the Fourteenth Amendment, the single most significant act of the Reconstruction era. The first section of the amendment sought to provide permanent constitutional protection of the civil rights of the freedmen by defining them as citizens. States were prohibited from depriving "any person of life, liberty, or property, without due process of law," and all persons were guaranteed "the equal protection of the laws." In section 2, Congress granted black male suffrage in the South by making blacks whole persons eligible to vote (thus canceling the Constitution's "three-fifths" clause). States that denied this right would have their "basis of representation reduced" proportionally. Other sections of the amendment denied leaders of the Confederacy the right to hold national or state political office (except by act of Congress), repudiated the Confederate debt, and denied claims of compensation by former slave owners for their lost property.

President Johnson urged the southern states not to ratify the Fourteenth Amendment, and ten states immediately rejected it. Johnson then went on the campaign trail in the midterm election of 1866 to ask voters to throw out the radical Republicans. This first campaign since the end of the war was marked by vicious displays of name calling and other low forms of electioneering. The president exchanged insults with hecklers and lashed out against his political opponents. Democrats in both the South and the North appealed openly to racial prejudice in calling for the defeat of those who had passed the Fourteenth Amendment. The nation would be "Africanized," they charged, with black equality threatening both the marketplace and the bedroom.

Republican campaigners, in turn, called Johnson a drunkard and a traitor. Bitter Civil War memories were revived as Republicans "waved the bloody shirt" in telling voters that Democrats were traitorous rebels or draft dodgers, while Republicans were patriotic saviors of the Union and courageous soldiers. Governor Oliver P. Morton of Indiana described the Democratic party as "a common sewer and loathsome receptacle, into which is emptied every element of treason . . . inhumanity and barbar-

ism which has dishonored the age." Although the electorate was moved more by self-interest on other issues than by the persuasive power of these speeches, the result of the election was an overwhelming victory for the Republicans. The mandate was clear that the presidential plan of reconstruction in the seceded states had not worked and that Congress must suggest another.

Therefore, early in 1867, three Reconstruction Acts were passed. The first divided the southern states into five military districts in which military commanders had broad powers to maintain order and protect the rights of property and persons. Congress also defined a new process by which a state could be readmitted to the Union. Qualified voters, which included blacks and excluded unreconstructed rebels, would elect delegates to state constitutional conventions, which then would write new constitutions guaranteeing black suffrage. After the constitutions were ratified by the new voters of the states, elections would be held to choose governors and state legislatures. When a state ratified the Fourteenth Amendment, its representatives to Congress would be accepted, thus completing readmission to the Union.

At the same time as it passed the Reconstruction Acts, Congress also approved a series of bills to restrict the powers of the president and to establish the dominance of the legislative branch over the executive. The Tenure of Office Act, designed to protect the outspoken secretary of war, Edwin Stanton, from removal by Johnson, limited the president's appointment powers. Other measures restricted his power as commander in chief. Johnson behaved exactly as congressional Republicans thought he would, vetoing the Reconstruction Acts, issuing orders to limit the military commanders in the South, and removing cabinet and other government officials sympathetic to Congress's program. The House Judiciary Committee investigated, charging the president with "usurpations of power" and of acting in the "interests of the great criminals" who had led the southern rebellion. It was evident, however, that Johnson was guilty only of holding principles, policies, and prejudices different from congressional leaders, and the House, led by moderate Republicans, rejected the impeachment resolutions.

In August 1867, Johnson finally dismissed Stanton and asked for Senate consent. When this was not forthcoming, the president ordered Stanton to surrender his office, which he refused, barricading himself inside. This time the House rushed impeachment resolutions to a vote, charging the president with "a high misdemeanor" while in office. As constitutionally provided, a trial was held in the Senate, presided over by Chief Justice Salmon P. Chase of the Supreme Court. The evidence seemed clear that Johnson had questionable judgment but had committed no crime that would justify his removal. Yet the passions of the hour made the vote close. With seven Republicans joining Democrats against conviction, the vote was 35 for conviction and 19 against. The effort to find the president guilty as charged fell short of the two-thirds majority required by a single vote. Not for another 100 years would a president, Richard Nixon, again face removal from office through impeachment.

## Congressional Moderation

The impeachment crisis revealed that most Republicans were more interested in protecting themselves than the freedmen and in punishing Johnson rather than the South. Congress's political battle against the president was not matched by an idealistic resolve on behalf of the rights and welfare of the freedmen. As early as the state and local elections of 1867, it was clear that voters preferred moderate reconstruction policies. It is important to look not only at what Congress did during Reconstruction but also at what it did not do.

With the exception of Jefferson Davis, Congress did not put leaders of the Confederacy in prison, and only one person, the commander of the infamous Andersonville prison camp, was put to death. Congress did not insist on a long-term probationary period for the southern states before they could be readmitted to the Union. It did not reorganize southern local governments. It did not mandate a national program of education for the 4 million ex-slaves. It did not confiscate and redistribute land to the freedmen, nor did it prevent President Johnson from taking land away from freedmen who had gained possessory titles during the war. It did not, except indirectly, provide economic help to black citizens.

What Congress did do, and that only reluctantly, was grant citizenship and suffrage to the freedmen. At the end of the Civil War, northerners were no more prepared than southerners to make blacks equal citizens. The Fourteenth Amendment required black suffrage in southern states but not in the North. Senate Republicans rejected a general suffrage amendment in 1866, as did a party convention two years later. Between 1865 and 1869, several states in the North and West held referendums proposing black suffrage. Voters in Kansas, Ohio, Michigan, Missouri, Wisconsin, Connecticut, New York, and the District of Columbia (by a vote of 6,521 to 35!) all turned the proposals down. Only in Iowa and Minnesota (on the third try, and then only by devious wording) did northern whites grant the vote to blacks.

Black suffrage gained support, however, after the election of 1868, when General Grant, a military hero regarded as invincible, barely won the popular vote in several states. Congressional Republicans, therefore, took a second look at the importance of a suffrage amendment as a way of adding grateful black votes to party totals. After a bitterly contested fight, repeated in several state ratification contests, the Fifteenth Amendment, forbidding all states to deny the vote to anyone "on account of race, color, or previous condition of servitude," became part of the Constitution in 1870. A black preacher from Pittsburgh observed that "the Republican party had done the Negro good, but they were doing themselves good at the same time."

For political reasons, therefore, Congress gave blacks the vote but not the land, the opposite priority of what the freedmen wanted. Almost alone, Thaddeus Stevens argued that "forty acres . . . and a hut would be more valuable . . . than the . . . right to vote." He had a plan to confiscate the land of the "chief rebels" and to give a small portion of it, divided into 40-acre plots, to the freedmen. But Congress never considered the measure seriously, for it went against deeply held beliefs of the Republican party and the American people in the sacredness of private property. Moreover, northern business interests concerned with the development of southern industry and with investing in southern land were attracted by the idea of a large propertyless class of cheap black laborers.

Although most Americans, in the North as well as the South, opposed confiscation and did not want blacks to become independent landowners, Congress passed an alternative measure. Proposed by George Julian of Indiana, the Southern Homestead Act of 1866 made public lands available to blacks and loyal whites in five southern states. But the land was of poor quality and inaccessible. No transportation, tools, or seed were provided, and most blacks who might have wanted to take advantage of the offer had only until January 1, 1867, to claim their land. But that was nearly impossible for most because they were under contract with white employers until that date. Only about 4,000 black families even applied for the Homestead Act lands, and less than 20 percent of those saw their claims completed. The record of white claimants was not much better. Congressional moderation, therefore, left the freedmen economically weak as they faced the challenges of freedom.

### Women and the Reconstruction Amendments

One casualty of the Fourteenth and Fifteenth amendments was the goodwill of the women who had been petitioning and campaigning for suffrage for two decades. They had hoped that their support for the Union effort during the war and the suspension of their own demands in the interests of the more immediate concerns of preserving the Union, nursing the wounded, and emancipating the slaves would be recognized by grateful male legislators. During the war, for example, the Woman's Loyal League, headed by Elizabeth Cady Stanton and Susan B. Anthony, gathered nearly 400,000 signatures on petitions asking Congress to pass the Thirteenth Amendment. They were therefore shocked to see the wording of the Fourteenth Amendment, which for the first time inserted the word *male* in the Constitution in referring to a citizen's right to vote.

Stanton and Anthony campaigned actively against the Fourteenth Amendment, despite the pleas of those who, like Frederick Douglass, had long supported woman suffrage, and who also declared that this was "the Negro's hour." When the Fifteenth Amendment was proposed, they wondered why the word *sex* could not have been added to the "conditions" no longer a basis for denial of the vote. Largely abandoned by radical reconstructionists and abolitionist activists, they had few champions in Congress, however, and that battle was lost too.

Disappointment over the suffrage issue was one of several reasons that led to a split in the

### Reconstruction Amendments

| AMENDMENT | SUBSTANCE | DATE OF CONGRESSIONAL PASSAGE | OUTCOME OF RATIFICATION PROCESS |
|---|---|---|---|
| Thirteenth | Prohibited slavery in the United States | January 1865 | Ratified by 27 states, including 8 southern states, by December 1865 |
| Fourteenth | I. Defined equal national citizenship II. Reduced state representation in Congress proportional to number of disfranchised voters III. Denied former Confederates the right to hold office | June 1866 | Rejected by 12 southern and border states by February 1867; radicals made readmission depend on ratification; ratified in July 1868 |
| Fifteenth | Prohibited denial of vote because of race, color, or previous servitude | February 1869 | Ratification by Virginia, Texas, Mississippi, and Georgia required for readmission; ratified in March 1870 |

women's movement in 1869. Anthony and Stanton continued their fight for a national amendment for woman suffrage and other gains, but other women abandoned hope for this and concentrated on securing their rights on a state-by-state basis.

# LIFE AFTER SLAVERY

Union army major George Reynolds boasted to a friend late in 1865 that in the area of Mississippi under his command he had "kept the negroes at work, and in a good state of discipline." Clinton Fisk, a well-meaning white who helped to found a black college in Tennessee, told freedmen in 1866 that they could be "as free and as happy" working again for their "old master . . . as any where else in the world." For many blacks such pronouncements sounded familiar, reminding them of white preachers' exhortations during slavery to work hard and obey their masters. Ironically, though, both Fisk and Reynolds were agents of the Freedmen's Bureau, the crucial agency intended to ease the transition from slavery to freedom for the 4 million ex-slaves.

## The Freedmen's Bureau

Never in American history has one small agency—underfinanced, understaffed, and undersupported—been given a harder task than was the Bureau of Freedmen, Refugees and Abandoned Lands. Its purposes and mixed successes symbolize, as well as those of any other institution, the tortuous course of Reconstruction.

The purposes of the Freedmen's Bureau included issuing emergency rations of food and providing clothing and shelter to the homeless, hungry victims of the war; establishing medical care and hospital facilities; providing funds for transportation for the thousands of freedmen and white refugees dislocated by the war; helping blacks search for and put their families back together; and arranging for legal marriage ceremonies. The bureau also served as a friend in local civil courts to ensure that the freedmen got fair trials. Although not initially empowered to do so, the agency was responsible for the education of the ex-slaves. To bureau schools came many idealistic teachers from various northern Freedmen's Aid societies.

In addition to these many purposes, the largest task of the Freedmen's Bureau was to serve as an employment agency, tending to the economic well-being of the blacks. This included settling them on abandoned lands and getting them started with tools, seed, and draft animals, as well as arranging work contracts with white landowners. It was in the area of work contracts, as we shall see, that the Freedmen's Bureau served more to "reenslave" the freedmen as impoverished fieldworkers rather than to set them on their way as independent farmers.

Although some agents were idealistic young New Englanders eager to help slaves make the difficult adjustment to freedom, others were Union army officers more concerned with social order than social transformation. Working in the midst of a postwar climate of resentment and violence, Freedmen's Bureau agents were constantly accused of partisan Republican politics,

*The Freedmen's Bureau had fewer resources in relation to its purpose than any agency in the nation's history.* Harper's Weekly *published this engraving of freedmen lining up for aid in Memphis in 1866.*

corruption, and partiality to blacks by local white residents. But even the best-intentioned agents would have agreed with General O. O. Howard, commissioner of the bureau, in a belief in the traditional nineteenth-century American values of self-help, minimal government interference in the marketplace, the sanctity of private property, contractual obligations, and white superiority. The bureau's work served to uphold these values.

On a typical day, these overworked and underpaid agents would visit courts and schools in their district, supervise the signing of work contracts, and handle numerous complaints, most involving contract violations between whites and blacks or property and domestic disputes among blacks. One agent sent a man, who had complained of a severe beating, back to work with the advice, "Don't be sassy [and] don't be lazy when you've got work to do." Another, reflecting his growing frustrations, complained that the freedmen were "disrespectful and greatly in need of instruction." Although helpful in finding work for the freedmen, more often than not the agents found themselves defending white landowners by telling the blacks to obey orders, to trust their employers, and to sign and live by disadvantageous contracts.

Despite mounting pressures to support white landowners, personal frustrations, and even threats on their lives, the agents accomplished a great deal. In little more than two years, the Freedmen's Bureau issued 20 million rations (nearly one-third to poor whites), reunited families and resettled some 30,000 displaced war refugees, treated some 450,000 cases of illness and injury, built 40 hospitals and hundreds of schools, provided books, tools, and furnishings —and even some land—to the freedmen, and occasionally protected their economic and civil rights. Black historian W. E. B. Du Bois wrote an epitaph for the bureau that might stand for the whole of Reconstruction: "In a time of perfect calm, amid willing neighbors and streaming wealth," he wrote, it "would have been a herculean task" for the bureau to fulfill its many purposes. But in the midst of hunger, sorrow, spite, suspicion, hate, and cruelty, "the work of any instrument of social regeneration was . . . foredoomed to failure."

## New Economic Dependency

The economic failures of the Freedmen's Bureau, symbolic of the entire congressional program, forced the freedmen into a new economic dependency on their former masters. Although the planter class did not lose its economic and social power in the postwar years, the character of southern agriculture went through some major changes. First, a land-intensive system replaced the labor intensity of slavery. Land ownership was concentrated into fewer and even larger holdings than before the Civil War. From South Carolina to Louisiana, the wealthiest tenth of the population owned about 60 percent of the real estate in the 1870s. Second, these large planters increasingly concentrated on one crop, usually cotton and were tied into the international market. This resulted in a steady drop in food production (both grains and livestock) in the postwar period. And third, reliance on one-crop farming meant that a new credit system emerged in which most farmers, black and white, were dependent on local merchants (often in competition with large landowners) for renting seed, farm implements and animals, provisions, housing, and land itself. These changes affected race relations and class tensions among whites.

This new system, however, took a few years to develop after emancipation. At first, most freedmen signed contracts with white landowners and worked in gangs in the fields as farm laborers very much like during slavery. Watched over by superintendents, who still used the lash to enforce hard toil, they worked from sunrise to sunset. They were paid a meager wage and were issued a monthly allotment of bacon and meal. All members of the family had to work to receive their rations. The freedmen resented this new form of semiservitude, preferring small plots of land of their own to grow vegetables and grains. Moreover, they wanted to be able to send their children to school and insisted on "no more outdoor work" for women.

What the freedmen wanted, a Georgia planter correctly observed, was "to get away from all overseers, to hire or purchase land, and work for themselves." Many blacks, therefore, broke contracts, ran away, engaged in work slowdowns or outright strikes, and otherwise expressed their displeasure with the contract labor system. The former slaves of Adele Allston refused to sign their contracts, even when offered livestock and other favors, and she eventually had to sell much of her land. Another white landowner expressed his frustration over having "to bargain and haggle with our servants about wages." The insistence of blacks on a degree of autonomy and land of their own was the major impetus for the change from the contract system to tenancy and sharecropping. As a South Carolina freedmen put it, "If a man got to go crost de riber, and he can't git a boat, he take a log. If I can't own de land, I'll hire or lease land, but I won't contract."

And so the freedmen became sharecroppers, hiring or leasing small plots of land to work. Families would hitch a team of mules to their old slave cabin to drag it to their assigned plot, as far away from the Big House as possible. The sharecroppers were given seed, fertilizer, farm implements, and all necessary food and clothing to take care of their families. In return, the landlord (or a local merchant) told them what to grow and how much and took a share—usually half—of the harvest. The half retained by the cropper, however, was usually needed to pay for goods bought on credit (at huge interest rates) at the landlord's store. Thus the sharecroppers

---

### A Freedmen's Work Contract

STATE OF SOUTH CAROLINA
*Darlington District*
ARTICLES OF AGREEMENT

This Agreement entered into between Mrs. Adele Allston Exect of the one part, and the Freedmen and Women of The Upper Quarters plantation of the other part *Witnesseth:*

That the latter agree, for the remainder of the present year, to reside upon and devote their labor to the cultivation of the Plantation of the former. And they further agree, that they will in all respects, conform to such reasonable and necessary plantation rules and regulations as Mrs. Allston's Agent may prescribe; that they will not keep any gun, pistol, or other offensive weapon, or leave the plantation without permission from their employer; that in all things connected with their duties as laborers on said plantation, they will yield prompt obedience to all orders from Mrs. Allston or his [*sic*] agent; that they will be orderly and quiet in their conduct, avoiding drunkenness and other gross vices; that they will not misuse any of the Plantation Tools, or Agricultural Implements, or any Animals entrusted to their care, or any Boats, Flats, Carts or Wagons; that they will give up at the expiration of this Contract, all Tools & c., belonging to the Plantation, and in case any property, of any description belonging to the Plantation shall be willfully or through negligence destroyed or injured, the value of the Articles so destroyed, shall be deducted from the portion of the Crops which the person or persons, so offending, shall be entitled to receive under this Contract.

Any deviations from the condition of the foregoing Contract may, upon sufficient proof, be punished with dismissal from the Plantation, or in such other manner as may be determined by the Provost Court; and the person or persons so dismissed, shall forfeit the whole, or a part of his, her or their portion of the crop, as the Court may decide.

In consideration of the foregoing Services duly performed, Mrs. Allston agrees, after deducting Seventy five bushels of Corn for each work Animal, exclusively used in cultivating the Crops for the present year; to turn over to the said Freedmen and Women, one half of the remaining Corn, Peas, Potatoes, made this season. He [*sic*] further agrees to furnish the usual rations until the Contract is performed.

All Cotton Seed Produced on the Plantation is to be reserved for the use of the Plantation. The Freedmen, Women and Children are to be treated in a manner consistent with their freedom. Necessary medical attention will be furnished as heretofore.

Any deviation from the conditions of this Contract upon the part of the said Mrs. Allston or her Agent or Agents shall be punished in such manner as may be determined by a Provost Court, or a Military Commission. This agreement to continue till the first day of January 1866.

Witness our hand at The Upper Quarters this 28th day of July 1865.

*Sharecroppers and tenant farmers, though more autonomous than contract laborers, remained dependent on the landlord for their survival.*

were semiautonomous but remained tied to the landlord's will for economic survival.

Under the tenant system, farmers had only slightly more independence. In advance of the harvest, a tenant farmer promised to sell his crop to a local merchant in return for renting land, tools, and other necessities. He also was obligated to purchase goods on credit against the harvest from the merchant's store. At "settling up" time, the income from the sale of the crop was matched with debts accumulated at the store. It was possible, especially after an unusually bountiful season, to come out ahead and eventually to own one's own land. In fact, however, tenants seemed rarely to do so; they remained in debt at the end of each year and were

## Changes on the Barrow Plantation, 1860–1881

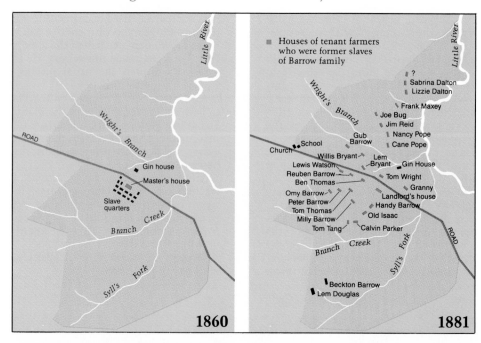

then compelled to pledge the next year's crop. Thus a system of debt peonage replaced slavery, ensuring a continuing cheap labor supply to grow cotton and other staples in the South. Only a very few blacks were able to become independent landowners—about 2 to 5 percent by 1880, but closer to 20 percent in some states by 1900.

These changes in southern agriculture affected yeoman and poor white farmers as well as the freedmen. This raised the threat, always troubling to the planter class, of a coalition between poor black and pro-Unionist white farmers. As a yeoman farmer in Georgia said in 1865, "We should tuk the land, as we did the niggers, and split it, and giv part to the niggers and part to me and t'other Union fellers." But confiscation and redistribution of land was no more likely for white farmers than for the freedmen. Whites, too, were forced to concentrate on growing staples, to pledge their crops against high-interest credit from local merchants, and to face the inevitability of perpetual indebtedness. In the upcountry piedmont area of Georgia, for example, the number of whites who worked their own land dropped from nine in ten before the Civil War to seven in ten by 1880. During the same period, the production of cotton doubled. Reliance on cotton by larger planters meant fewer food crops, which necessitated greater dependence on local merchants for provisions. In 1884, Jephta Dickson of Jackson County, Georgia, purchased over $50 worth of flour, meal, meat, syrup, and peas and corn from a local store, an almost unthinkable situation 25 years earlier, when he would have needed to buy almost no food to supplement his homegrown fare.

In the worn-out flatlands and barren mountainous regions of the South, poor whites found little hope in the era of Reconstruction. Their antebellum heritage of poverty, ill health, and isolation worsened in the years after the war. A Freedmen's Bureau agent in South Carolina described the poor whites in his area as "gaunt and ragged, ungainly, stooping and clumsy in build." They lived a marginal existence, hunting, fishing, and growing corn and potato crops that, as a North Carolinian put it, "come up *puny*, grow *puny*, and mature *puny*." Many poor white farmers, in fact, were even less productive than black sharecroppers. Some became farmhands, earning $6 a month (with board) from other farmers. Other fled to low-paying jobs in urban cotton mills, where they would not have to compete against blacks.

## Sharecropping in the South, 1880

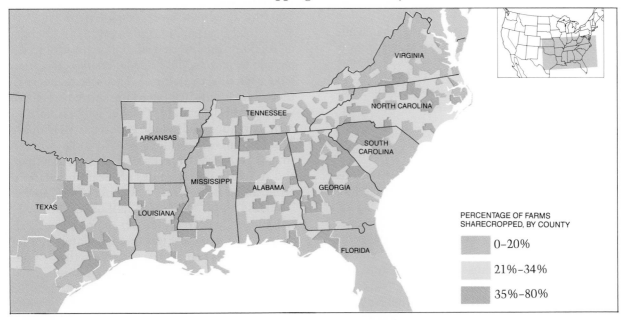

The cultural life of poor southern whites reflected both their lowly position and their pride. Their religion was emotional and revivalistic, centering on the camp meeting. Music and folklore often focused on debt and chain gangs, as well as on deeds of drinking prowess. In backwoods clearings and bleak pine barrens, men and women told tall tales of superhuman feats and exchanged folk remedies for bad health. In Alabama, there were over 90 superstitious sayings for calling rain. Aesthetic expression, in quilt making and house construction, for example, reflected a marginal culture in which everything was saved and put to use.

In part because their lives were so hard, poor whites persisted in their belief in white superiority. As a federal officer reported in 1866, "The poorer classes of white people . . . have a most intense hatred of the Negro, and swear he shall never be reckoned as part of the population." Many poor whites, therefore, joined the Ku Klux Klan and other southern white terror groups that emerged between 1866 and 1868. But however hard life was for poor whites, blacks were far more often sentenced to chain gangs for the slightest crimes and were bound to a life of debt, degradation, and dependency. The high hopes with which the freedmen had greeted emancipation turned slowly to resignation and disillusionment. Felix Haywood, a former Texas slave, recalled:

> We thought we was goin' to be richer than white folks, 'cause we was stronger and knowed how to work, and the whites . . . didn't have us to work for them anymore. But it didn't turn out that way. We soon found out that freedom could make folks proud but it didn't make 'em rich.

## Black Self-Help Institutions

Felix Haywood understood the limitations of government programs and efforts on behalf of the freedmen. It was clear to many black leaders, therefore, that self-help was more reliable. If white institutions were unable to fulfill the promises of emancipation, black freedmen would have to do it themselves. Fortunately, the tradition of black community self-help survived in the organized churches and schools of the antebellum free Negro communities and in the "invisible" cultural institutions of the slave quarters. Religion, as usual, was vital. Emancipation brought an explosion in the growth of membership in black churches. The Negro Baptist church grew from 150,000 members in 1850 to 500,000 in 1870. The various branches of the African Methodist Episcopal church increased fourfold in the decade after the Civil War, from 100,000 to over 400,000 members.

Black ministers continued their tradition as community leaders. Many led efforts to oppose discrimination, some by entering politics. Over one-fifth of the black officeholders in South Carolina were ministers. Most preachers, however, focused on traditional religious themes of sin, conversion, and salvation. An English visitor to the South in 1867 and 1868, after observing a revivalist preacher in Savannah arouse nearly 1,000 people to "sway, and cry, and groan," noted the intensity of black "devoutness." Despite some efforts to restrain the emotionalism characteristic of black worship, most congregations preferred to stay with traditional forms of religious expression. One black woman, when urged to pray more quietly, complained: "We make noise 'bout ebery ting else . . . I want ter go ter Heaben in de good ole way."

The freedmen's desire for education was as strong as for religion. A school official in Virginia echoed the observation of many when he said that the freedmen were "down right crazy to learn." A Mississippi farmer vowed, "If I nebber does do nothing more, I shall give my children a chance to go to school, for I consider education next best ting to liberty." The first teachers of these black children were unmarried northern women, the legendary "Yankee schoolmarms." Sent by groups such as the American Missionary Association, these idealistic young women sought to convert blacks to Congregationalism and to white moral values of cleanliness, discipline, and dutiful work. In October 1865, Esther Douglass found "120 dirty, half naked, perfectly wild black children" in her schoolroom near Savannah, Georgia. Eight months later, she reported to her northern superiors that "their progress was wonderful." They could read, sing hymns, and repeat Bible verses and had learned "about right conduct which they tried to practice."

Glowing reports like this one changed as white teachers grew frustrated with crowded facilities, limited resources, local opposition, and the absenteeism that resulted from the demands of work in the fields. In Georgia, for example, only 5 percent of black children went to school for part of any one year between 1865 and 1870; this contrasted with 20 percent of white children. Furthermore, blacks increasingly preferred their own teachers, who could better understand former slaves. To ensure the training of black preachers and teachers, northern philanthropists founded Howard, Atlanta, Fisk, Morehouse, and other black universities in the South between 1865 and 1867.

Black schools, like churches, became community centers. They published newspapers, provided training in trades and farming, and promoted political participation and land ownership. A black farmer in Mississippi founded both a school and a society to facilitate land acquisition and better agricultural methods. These efforts made black schools objects of local white hostility. A Virginia freedman told a congressional committee that in his county, anyone starting a school would be killed and that blacks were "afraid to be caught with a book." In 1869, in Tennessee alone, 37 black schools were burned to the ground.

White opposition to black education and land ownership stimulated the rise of black nationalism and separatism. In the late 1860s, Benjamin "Pap" Singleton, a former Tennessee slave who had escaped to Canada, returned home. Observing that "whites had the lands and . . . blacks had nothing but their freedom," Singleton urged them to abandon politics and migrate westward. He organized a land company in 1869, purchased public property in Kansas, and in the early 1870s took several groups from Tennessee and Kentucky to that prairie state to establish separate black towns. In following years, thousands of "exodusters" from the Lower South bought some 10,000 acres of unfertile land in Kansas. There they faced both natural and human obstacles to their efforts to develop self-sufficient communities. Most were forced eventually by climate and hostile neighbors to disband and seek relief.

Despairing of ever finding economic independence in the United States, Singleton and other nationalists urged emigration to Canada and Liberia in the 1880s. One of the leaders of the late-nineteenth-century back-to-Africa movement was the Reverend Henry M. Turner. Like Singleton, Turner believed that the only hope for self-respect and freedom for blacks was in Africa. He too condemned politics, calling the Constitution a "dirty . . . lie" that should be "spit upon by every Negro in the land." Other black leaders, most notably Frederick Douglass, disagreed, asserting that suffrage would eventually lead to full citizenship rights within the United States.

*Enthusiasm for education clashed with limited facilities and white values in the early freedmen's schools.*

## RECONSTRUCTION IN THE STATES

Douglass's confidence in the power of the ballot seemed warranted in the enthusiastic early months under the Reconstruction Acts of 1867. With President Johnson neutralized, national Republican leaders were finally in a position to accomplish their political goals. Local Republicans, taking advantage of the inability or refusal of many southern whites to vote, overwhelmingly elected their delegates to state constitutional conventions in the fall of 1867. With guarded optimism and a sense of the "sacred importance" of their work, black and white Republicans turned to the business of setting up the new state governments.

### Republican Rule

Many misconceptions grew about the southern state governments under Republican rule. They were not dominated by illiterate black majorities intent on "Africanizing" the South by passing compulsory racial intermarriage laws, as many whites feared. Nor were these governments unusually corrupt and financially extravagant. Nor did they use massive numbers of federal troops to uphold their will. By 1869, only 1,100 federal soldiers remained in Virginia, and most federal troops in Texas guarded the frontier against Mexico and hostile Indians. Without the support of a strong military presence, then, these new state governments tried to do their work in a climate of economic distress and increasingly violent harassment.

The new governments elected under congressional Reconstruction were made up of a diverse combination of political groups. Labeled the "black and tan" governments by their opponents to suggest that they were dominated by former slaves and mulattoes, they were actually predominantly white, with the one exception of the lower house of the South Carolina legislature. One part of the new leadership consisted of an old Whiggish elite class of bankers, industrialists, and others interested far more in economic growth and sectional reconciliation than in radical social reforms. A second group consisted of northern Republicans who headed south out of motives similar to those that prompt the migration southward in our own time. These included capitalists seeking economic investment in land, railroads, and new industries; retired Union veterans seeking a warmer climate for health purposes; and missionaries and teachers pursuing an outlet for their idealism in the Freedmen's Bureau schools. Such people were unfairly stuck with the label "carpetbaggers."

A third group participating in the Republican state governments was the blacks. A large percentage of black officeholders were mulattoes, many of them well-educated free blacks who came down from the North as preachers,

*Despite threats of white reprisals, black freedmen proudly voted in Republican state governments under the Congressional Reconstruction Plan of 1867.*

teachers, and soldiers. Others, such as John Lynch of Mississippi, were self-educated tradesmen or representatives of the small landed class of southern blacks. In South Carolina, for example, of some 255 black state and federal officials elected between 1868 and 1876, two-thirds were literate and one-third owned real estate. Only 15 percent owned no property at all.

This elite class of black leaders was surprisingly moderate, fashioning its political goals squarely in the American republican tradition. Black leaders reminded whites that they, too, were southerners and Americans, attached both to the land of the South and to the white families they had lived with for generations: "The dust of our fathers mingle with yours in the same grave yards. . . . This is your country, but it is ours too." Because of these intermingled pasts, blacks sought no revenge or reversal of power, only respect and equal opportunity as Americans. As the eloquent petition of a black convention in 1865 explained:

> We simply ask that we shall be recognized as *men*; . . . that the same laws which govern *white men* shall govern *black men*; that we have a right of trial by a jury of our peers; that schools be established for the education of *colored children* as well as *white*, and that the advantages of both colors shall, in this respect, be *equal*; that no impediments be put in the way of our acquiring homesteads for ourselves and our people; that, in short, we be dealt with as others are—in equity and justice.

The primary accomplishments of Republican rule in the South consisted of attempts to bring equity and justice to political, economic, and social opportunity, thus elminating the undemocratic features of earlier state constitutions. All states provided universal manhood suffrage and loosened requirements for holding office. The basis of state representation was made fairer by apportioning more legislative seats to the interior regions of southern states. Social legislation included the abolition of automatic imprisonment for debt and laws for the relief of poverty and care of the handicapped. The first divorce laws in many southern states were passed, as were laws granting property rights to married women. Penal laws were mod-

ernized by reducing the list of crimes punishable by death, in one state from 26 to 5.

Under these governments, the task of financially and physically reconstructing the South was undertaken. Tax systems were overhauled, and generous railroad and other capital investment bonds were approved. Harbors, roads, and bridges were rebuilt. Hospitals, asylums, and other state institutions were established. Most important, the Republican governments provided for a state-supported system of public schools, absent before in most of the South. As in the North, these schools were largely segregated, but for the first time education was made available to rich and poor, black and white alike. As a result, black school attendance increased from 5 to over 40 percent and white from 20 to over 60 percent by the 1880s. All of this cost money, and the Republicans did indeed greatly increase tax rates and state debts. All in all, the Republican governments "dragged the South, screaming and crying, into the modern world."

These considerable accomplishments were achieved in the midst of opposition like that expressed in a convention of Louisiana planters, which labeled the Republican leaders "the lowest and most corrupt body of men ever assembled in the South." There was some corruption, to be sure, but mostly in land sales, fraudulent railway bonds, and construction contracts, the kind of graft that had become a way of life in American politics, South and North, in the aftermath of the Civil War. Given their lack of experience with politics, the black role was remarkable. As Du Bois put it, "There was one thing that the white South feared more than negro dishonesty, ignorance, and incompetence, and that was negro honesty, knowledge, and efficiency."

Despite its effectiveness in modernizing southern state governments, the Republican coalition did not last very long. In fact, as the map indicates, Republican rule lasted for different periods of time in different states. In some states, Virginia, for example, the Republicans ruled hardly at all. Situated in the shadow of Washington, conservatives in Virginia professed their agreement with Congress's Reconstruction guidelines while doing as they pleased. As one of the states most devastated by the war, Virginia looked almost immediately to northern investors to rebuild its cities and to develop industry. Blacks and whites alike flocked to the cities for work. The blacks, however, were denied any but low-paying menial jobs and were herded into overcrowded, disease-ridden ghettos called "Little Africas."

Republican rule lasted the longest in the black-belt states of the Deep South, where the black population was equal to or greater than the white. In Louisiana, Reconstruction began with General Ben Butler's occupation of New Orleans in 1862. Although he insisted on granting civil rights to blacks, he was quickly replaced by a succession of Republican governors in the late 1860s more interested in graft, election laws, and staying in office than in the rights and welfare of black Louisianans. Alabama received a flood of northern capital to develop the rich coal, iron-ore, and timber resources of the northern third of the state. Republican rule in Alabama, as in other states, involved a greater role for towns and merchants, the endorsement of generous railroad bonds, and struggles between the old planter aristocracy and a new industrial one.

The return of Democrats to power did not alter either the tensions caused by the emergent new class structure or traditional race relations. In fact, racial violence, intimidation, and coercion played a major role in replacing Republican governments with a restoration of white Democratic rule. As one southern editor put it, "We must render this either a white man's government, or convert the land into a Negro man's cemetery." The Ku Klux Klan was only one of several secret organizations that used force and violence against black and white Republicans to drive them from power. The cases of North Carolina and Mississippi are representative in showing how conservative Democrats were able to regain control.

After losing a close election in North Carolina in 1868, conservatives waged a concentrated campaign of terror in several counties in the piedmont area of the state. If the Democrats could win these counties in 1870, they would most likely win statewide. In the year prior to the election, several prominent Republicans were killed, including a white state senator, whose throat was cut, and a leading black Union League organizer, who was hanged in the courthouse square with a sign pinned to his breast: "Bewar, ye guilty, both white and black." Scores of citizens were flogged, tortured, fired from their jobs, or forced to flee in the middle of the night from burning homes and barns. The courts consistently refused to prosecute anyone for these crimes. Local papers, in fact, charged that they had been committed "by disgusting ne-

## Return to the Union During Reconstruction

VIRGINIA
1870/1869

NORTH CAROLINA
1868/1870

TENNESSEE
1866/1869

ARKANSAS
1868/1874

MISSISSIPPI
1870/1876

SOUTH CAROLINA
1868/1876

GEORGIA
1870/1871

ALABAMA
1868/1874

TEXAS
1870/1873

LOUISIANA
1868/1877

FLORIDA
1868/1877

1870 Date readmitted to the Union

1870 Date of reestablishment of conservative government

groes and white Radicals." The conservative campaign worked. In the election of 1870, some 12,000 fewer Republicans voted in the two crucial counties than had voted two years earlier, and the Democrats swept back into power.

In the state election in Mississippi in 1875, Democrats used similar tactics, openly announcing that "the thieves . . . , robbers, and scoundrels, white and black," who were in power "deserve death and ought to be killed." In what was called the Mississippi Plan, local Democratic clubs organized themselves into armed militias, marching defiantly through black areas, breaking up Republican meetings, and provoking riots to justify the killing of hundreds of blacks. Armed men were posted during voter registration to intimidate Republicans. At the election itself, anyone still bold enough to attempt to vote was either helped by gun-toting whites to cast a Democratic ballot or driven away from the polls with cannon and clubs. Counties that had earlier given Republican candidates majorities in the thousands, in 1875 managed a total of less than a dozen votes!

Democrats called their victory "redemption." As conservative Democratic administrations resumed control of each state government, Reconstruction came to an end. Redemption

*This lithograph, highlighting the Ku Klux Klan's intimidation through violence, was probably produced for popular sale.*

was the result of a combination of the persistence of white southern resistance, including violence and other coercive measures, and a loss of will to persist in the North. Albion Tourgée summed up the Reconstruction era in his novel *A Fool's Errand* (1879): "The spirit of the dead Confederacy was stronger than the mandate of the nation to which it had succumbed in battle."

## Reconstruction, Northern Style

Congress and President Grant did not totally ignore the violence in the South. Three Force Acts were passed in 1870 and 1871, giving the president strong powers to use federal supervisors to make sure that citizens were not prevented by force or fraud from voting. The third act, known as the Ku Klux Klan Act, declared secret organizations that used disguise and coercion to deprive others of equal protection of the laws illegal. Congress created a joint committee to investigate Klan violence, which reported in 1872 in 13 huge volumes of horrifying testimony. Grant who had supported these measures, delivered special messages to Congress proclaiming the importance of the right to vote, issued proclamations condemning lawlessness, and sent some additional troops to South Carolina. But he refused to send troops to Mississippi to guarantee a safe election in 1875, declaring instead that he and the nation were "tired of these annual autumnal outbreaks."

The success of the Mississippi Plan in 1875, imitated a year later in South Carolina and Louisiana, indicated that congressional reports and presidential proclamations did little to stop the reign of terror against black and white Republicans throughout the South. The Force Acts were wholly inadequate and were themselves weakly enforced. Although there were hundreds of arrests, all-white juries were reluctant to find their fellow citizens guilty of crimes against blacks. They were backed by the United States Supreme Court. In two decisions in 1874, the Court threw out cases against whites found guilty of preventing blacks from voting and held key parts of the Force Acts unconstitutional. In Hamburg, South Carolina, in 1876, several blacks were killed in a riot started in a courtroom when a white mob came to provide its own

We usually read novels, short stories, and other forms of fiction for pleasure, for the enjoyment of plot, style, symbolism, and character development. "Classic" novels such as *Moby Dick*, *Huckleberry Finn*, *The Great Gatsby*, and *The Invisible Man*, to name a few American examples, are not only written well but also explore timeless questions of good and evil, of innocence and knowledge, or of noble dreams fulfilled and shattered. Often we enjoy novels because we find ourselves identifying with one of the major characters. Through that person's problems, joys, relationships, and search for identity we gain insights about our own.

We can also read novels as historical sources, for they reveal much about the attitudes, dreams, fears, life styles, and ordinary everyday experiences of human beings in a particular historical period. They also show how people reacted to and felt about the major events of that era. We must be careful, however, to note the date when a novel was written, especially if different from the period written about. The novelist, like the historian, is a product of time and place and has an interpretive point of view.

Consider, for example, the two novels about Reconstruction quoted here. Neither is considered to have great literary merit, yet each reveals much about different interpretations and diversely impassioned attitudes Americans have always had about the post–Civil War era. The novels are *A Fool's Errand* by Albion Tourgée, a northerner, and *The Clansman* by Thomas Dixon, Jr., a southerner.

Tourgée was a young northern teacher and lawyer who fought with the Union army at several major battles during the Civil War. After the war, he moved to North Carolina, partly for health reasons and partly to begin a legal career. He became a judge and was an active Republican, supporting black suffrage and helping to shape the new state constitution and the codification of North Carolina laws in 1868. With jurisdiction over eight counties, Tourgée earned a reputation as one of the fairest judges in the state. Because he boldly criticized the Ku Klux Klan for its campaign of terror against blacks, his life was threatened many times. When the fearless judge finally left North Carolina in 1879, he published an autobiographical novel about his experiences.

The "fool's errand" in the novel is that of the northern veteran, Comfort Servosse, who like Tourgée seeks to fulfill humane goals on behalf of both blacks and whites in post–Civil War North Carolina.

## A FOOL'S ERRAND

### ALBION TOURGEE (1879)

When the second Christmas came, Metta wrote again to her sister:

"The feeling is terribly bitter against Comfort on account of his course towards the colored people. There is quite a village of them on the lower end of the plantation. They have a church, a sabbath school, and are to have next year a school. You can not imagine how kind they have been to us, and how much they are attached to Comfort. . . . I got Comfort to go with me to one of their prayer-meetings a few nights ago. I had heard a great deal about them, but had never attended one before. It was strangely weird. There were, perhaps, fifty present, mostly middle-aged men and women. They were singing in a soft, low monotone, interspersed with prolonged exclamatory notes, a sort of rude hymn, which I was surprised to know was one of their old songs in slave times. How the chorus came to be endured in those days I can not imagine. It was—

'Free! free! free, my Lord, free!
An' we walks de hebben-ly way!'

"A few looked around as we came in and seated ourselves; and Uncle Jerry, the saint of the settlement, came forward on his staves, and said, in his soft voice,

"'Ev'nin', Kunnel! Sarvant, Missus! Will you walk up, an' hev seats in front?'

"We told him we had just looked in, and might go in a short time; so we would stay in the back part of the audience.

"Uncle Jerry can not read nor write; but he is a man of strange intelligence and power. Unable to do work of any account, he is the faithful friend, monitor, and director of others. He has a house and piece of land, all paid for, a good horse and cow, and, with the aid of his wife and two boys, made a fine crop this season. He is one of the most promising colored men in the settlement: so Comfort says, at least. Everybody seems to have great respect for his character. I don't know how many people I have heard speak of his religion. Mr. Savage used to say he had rather hear him pray than any other man on earth. He was much prized by his master, even after he was disabled, on account of his faithfulness and character."

His efforts are thwarted, however, by threats, intimidation, a campaign of violent "outrages" against Republican leaders in the county, and a lack of support from the so-called wise men in Congress. Historians have verified the accuracy, down to the smallest

# NOVELS

## THE CLANSMAN

### Thomas Dixon, Jr. (1905)

At noon Ben and Phil strolled to the polling-place to watch the progress of the first election under Negro rule. The Square was jammed with shouting, jostling, perspiring negroes, men, women, and children. The day was warm, and the African odour was supreme even in the open air. . . .

Phil and Ben passed on nearer the polling-place, around which stood a cordon of soldiers with a line of negro voters two hundred yards in length extending back into the crowd.

The negro Leagues came in armed battallions and voted in droves, carrying their muskets in their hands. Less than a dozen white men were to be seen about the place.

The negroes, under the drill of the League and the Freedman's Bureau, protected by the bayonet, were voting to enfranchise themselves, disfranchise their former masters, ratify a new constitution, and elect a legislature to do their will. Old Aleck was a candidate for the House, chief poll-holder, and seemed to be in charge of the movements of the voters outside the booth as well as inside. He appeared to be omnipresent, and his self-importance was a sight Phil had never dreamed. He could not keep his eyes off him. . . .

[Aleck] was a born African orator, undoubtedly descended from a long line of savage spell-binders, whose eloquence in the palaver houses of the jungle had made them native leaders. His thin spindle-shanks supported an oblong, protruding stomach, resembling an elderly monkey's, which seemed so heavy it swayed his back to carry it.

The animal vivacity of his small eyes and the flexibility of his eyebrows, which he worked up and down rapidly with every change of countenance, expressed his eager desires.

He had laid aside his new shoes, which hurt him, and went barefooted to facilitate his movements on the great occasion. His heels projected and his foot was so flat that what should have been the hollow of it made a hole in the dirt where he left his track.

He was already mellow with liquor, and was dressed in an old army uniform and cap, with two horse-pistols buckled around his waist. On a strap hanging from his shoulder were strung a half-dozen tin canteens filled with whiskey.

details, of the events in Tourgée's novel. While exposing the brutality of the Klan, Tourgée includes loyal southern Unionists, respectable planters ashamed of Klan violence, and even guilt-ridden poor white klansmen who try to protect or warn intended vic-

tims. In the end, his analysis of the ultimate failure of Reconstruction blames the shortsightedness and incompleteness of the northern congressional program even more than southern violent resistance.

In the year of Tourgée's death, 1905, another North Carolinian published a novel, yet with a very different analysis of Reconstruction and its fate. Thomas Dixon was born during the Civil War. He was a lawyer, North Carolina state legislator, Baptist minister, lecturer, and novelist. *The Clansman*, subtitled "A Historical Romance of the Ku Klux Klan," reflects turn-of-the-century attitudes most white southerners still had about Republican rule during Reconstruction. According to Dixon, once the "Great Heart" Lincoln was gone, a power-crazed, vindictive radical Congress, led by scheming Austin Stoneman (Thaddeus Stevens), sought to impose corrupt carpetbagger and brutal black rule by bayonet on a helpless South. Only through the inspired leadership and redemptive role of the Ku Klux Klan was the South saved from the horrors of rape and revenge.

Dixon dedicated *The Clansman* to his uncle, a Grand Titan of the Klan in North Carolina during the time when two crucial counties were being transformed from Republican to Democratic majorities through intimidation and terror. No such violence shows up in Dixon's novel. Although *The Clansman* clearly twisted the truth of many historical events, it is an accurate and faithful representation of a dominant attitude southerners—and northerners as well—had about those events. When the novel was made the basis of D. W. Griffith's film classic, *Birth of a Nation*, in 1915, these attitudes were firmly imprinted on the twentieth-century American mind.

Both novels convey the events and attitudes of the era by creating clearly defined heroes and villains. Both include exciting chase scenes, narrow escapes, daring rescues, and tragic, heart-throbbing deaths. Both include romantic subplots in which a young white southern man falls in love with a young white northern woman. In each novel, however, the author's primary purpose was to convey his views of the politics of Reconstruction. The romantic elements were added, like sugarcoating around a pill, to make readers enjoy the medicine the novelist wanted them to take. The following are two brief excerpts from each novel, a poor substitute for reading them in their entirety. Notice the obvious differences of style and attitude in the descriptions of Uncle Jerry and Old Aleck.

form of "justice" to some black militiamen who had been arrested for parading on Independence Day. Although the Ku Klux Klan's power was officially ended, the attitudes (and tactics) of Klansmen were not.

The American people, like their leaders, were tired of the battles over the freedmen and were shifting their attention to other matters than fulfilling idealistic principles. Frustrated with the difficulties of trying to transform an unwilling South and seemingly ungrateful blacks, the easiest course was to give blacks their citizenship and the vote and move on to something else. After the interruptions of civil war and its aftermath, most Americans were primarily interested in starting families, finding work, and making money. This meant firing furnaces in the new steel plant in Wheeling, West Virginia, pounding in railroad ties for the Central Pacific in the Nevada desert, struggling to teach in a one-room schoolhouse in Vermont for $23 a month, or battling heat, locusts, and railroad rates on a family homestead in Kansas.

There was "reconstruction" going on in the North as well as the South—an accelerating economic revolution of enormous proportions. As Klansmen met in dark forests to plan their next raid in North Carolina in 1869, the Central Pacific and Union Pacific railroads met at Promontory Point, Utah, completing the transcontinental railroad. As black farmers were "haggling" over work contracts with white landowners in Georgia, the National Labor Union and Knights of Labor were being organized by white workers in Pennsylvania. As southern white tenant farmers found themselves more alienated from rich landowners and merchants, midwestern farmers were organizing the National Grange of the Patrons of Husbandry. And as economic relationships changed, so did the Republican party.

Heralded by the tone of moderation in the state election of 1867 and the national election of Grant in 1868, the Republicans had changed from the party of moral reform to one of material interest. In the continuing struggle in American politics between "virtue and commerce," commerce was again winning. No longer willing to support an agency like the Freedmen's Bureau, Republican politicians had no difficulty supporting huge grants of money and land to the

*To most northerners, the Civil War's end meant renewing family ties and resuming the routine of life at home, as shown in this 1868 Currier & Ives print.*

railroads. As blacks were told to go to work and help themselves, the Union Pacific was being given subsidies of between $16,000 and $48,000 for each mile of track laid across western plains and mountains. As Susan B. Anthony and others were tramping through the snows of upstate New York with petitions for rights of suffrage and citizenship, Boss Tweed and others were defrauding the citizen-taxpayers of New York of millions of dollars by construction and other boondoggles. The fraudulent railroad bonds in southern states were minor crimes compared to the extent of official graft in northern cities and state governments, as well as at the federal level.

A sordid grasping for wealth and power emerged in the nation around 1869, the year financier Jay Gould almost succeeded in cornering the gold market. Henry Adams, the descendant of two presidents, was a young man living in Washington, D.C., during this era. As he wrote later in his autobiography, *The Education of Henry Adams* (1907), he had high expectations in 1869 that Grant, like another "great soldier" and president, George Washington, would restore the moral order and peace that the nation needed. But when Grant announced the members of his cabinet, a group of Army cronies and rich friends to whom he owed favors, Adams felt betrayed, complaining that "a great soldier might be a baby politician."

Ulysses Grant himself was an honest man,

but his judgment of integrity in others was flawed. During his administration occurred a series of scandals that touched several cabinet officers and relatives and even two vice-presidents. Under Grant's appointments, outright graft, as well as loose prosecution and generally negligent administration, flourished in a half dozen departments. Most scandals involved large sums of public money. The Whiskey Ring affair, for example, cost the public millions of dollars in lost tax revenues siphoned off to government officials. Gould's gold scam received the unwitting aid of Grant's Treasury Department and the knowing help of his brother-in-law.

Nor was Congress pure in these various schemes. The Crédit Mobilier was the largest of several scandals in which construction companies for transcontinental railroads (in this case a dummy company) received generous bonds and work contracts in exchange for giving congressmen gifts of money, stocks, and railroad lands. An Ohio congressmen described the House of Representatives in 1873 as "an auction room where more valuable considerations were disposed of under the speaker's hammer than any place on earth." Henry Adams spoke for many Americans when he said that Grant's administration "outraged every rule of decency."

In a novel written about Washington life during this period called *Democracy* (1880), Adams's main character, Mrs. Madeleine Lee, sought to uncover "the heart of the great American mystery of democracy and government." What she found were corrupt legislators and lobbyists in an unprincipled pursuit of power and wealth. "Surely something can be done to check corruption?" Mrs. Lee asked her friend one evening. "Are we forever to be at the mercy of thieves and ruffians? Is a respectable government impossible in a democracy?" The answer she heard was hardly reassuring: "No responsible government can long be much better or much worse than the society it represents."

Was the whole postwar society at fault, then, for this decline in public morality? What had become of the ideals and humanitarian efforts of an earlier generation of Americans? For the time being, at least, they were replaced by attention to the further development of industry, the

making of inventions, the building of transcontinental railroads, and the settlement of the western agricultural, cattle, and mining frontiers. Throughout the land, it was an age of materialistic "go-getters" (see Chapters 18 and 19).

The election of 1872 marked the decline of public interest in moral issues. A "liberal" faction of the Republican party, unable to dislodge Grant, broke off and nominated Horace Greeley, editor of the New York *Tribune*, for president. The liberal Republicans advocated free trade, which meant lower tariffs and fewer grants to railroads, and honest, limited government, which meant civil service reform and noninterference in southern race relations. Democrats, lacking notable presidential candidates, also nominated Greeley, even though he had spent much of his earlier career assailing Democrats as "rascals." Despite his wretched record, Grant easily won a second term. Greeley was beaten so badly, he said, that "I hardly knew whether I was running for the Presidency or the Penitentiary." He died three weeks later.

### The End of Reconstruction

Soon after Grant's second inauguration, a financial panic, caused by overconstruction of railroads and the collapse of some crucial eastern banks, created a terrible depression that lasted throughout the mid-1870s. In times of economic hardship, economic issues dominated politics, further pulling attention away from the plight of the freedmen. As Democrats took control of the House of Representatives in 1874 and looked toward winning the White House in 1876, politicians talked about such issues as new scandals in the Grant administration, General Custer's shocking defeat in the Big Horn Mountains of Montana, unemployment and various proposals for public works expenditures for relief, the availability of silver and greenback dollars, and high tariffs.

No one, it seemed, talked much about the rights and conditions of southern freedmen. Senator Charles Sumner's civil rights bill, intended to put teeth into the Fourteenth Amendment, was passed in 1875 by a guilty Congress largely out of respect for Sumner's death during the debates. But the act was not enforced and was declared unconstitutional by the Supreme Court eight years later. Congressional Reconstruction, long dormant, had ended. The election of 1876 sealed the conclusion.

As their nominee for president in 1876, the Republicans turned to a former governor of Ohio, Rutherford B. Hayes, partly because of his reputation for honesty, partly because he had been an officer in the Union army (a necessity for post–Civil War candidates), and partly because, as Henry Adams put it, he was "obnoxious to no one." The Democrats chose Governor Samuel J. Tilden of New York, who achieved national recognition as a civil service reformer in breaking up the corrupt Tweed Ring.

Tilden won a majority of the popular vote and appeared to have enough electoral votes for victory. Twenty more electoral votes were disputed, all but one in the Deep South states of Louisiana, South Carolina, and Florida, where some federal troops still remained on duty and where Republicans still controlled the voting apparatus. Democrats, however, had applied various versions of the Mississippi Plan to intimidate voters. As one astute reporter put it, the Republican party in the South was "dead as a doornail." How to resolve the disputed electoral votes? Congress created a special electoral commission consisting of five senators, five representatives, and five Supreme Court justices, seven of whom were Democrats and eight Republicans. The vote in each disputed case was 8 to 7 along party lines. Hayes was given all 20 votes, enough to win, 185 to 184.

The Democrats were furious and threatened to stop the Senate from officially counting the electoral votes and thus prevent Hayes's inauguration. The country was in a state of crisis, and some wondered if civil war might start again. But unlike the 1850s, when passions over slavery were aroused, this time compromise was possible on a basis of mutual interests between northerners and southerners interested in modernization of the southern economy through capital investments. They focused on a Pacific railroad linking New Orleans with the West Coast. Southerners wanted northern dollars but not northern political influence. This meant no social agencies, no federal enforcement of the Fourteenth and Fifteenth amendments, and no military occupation, not even the small symbolic presence left in 1876.

As the inauguration date approached, and as newspapers echoed outgoing President Grant's call for "peace at any price," the forces of mutual self-interest concluded "the compromise of 1877." The Democrats agreed to suspend their resistance to the counting of the electoral votes, and on March 2, Rutherford B. Hayes was declared president. In exchange for the presidency, Hayes ordered the last remaining troops out of the South, appointed a former Confederate general to his cabinet, supported federal aid to bolster economic and railroad development in the South, and announced his intentions to let southerners handle race relations themselves. He then went on a goodwill trip to the South, where he told blacks in an Atlanta speech that "your rights and interests would be safer if this great mass of intelligent white men were let alone by the general government." The message was clear: Hayes would not enforce the Fourteenth and Fifteenth amendments, thus initiating a pattern of executive inaction not broken until the middle of the twentieth century. But the immediate crisis was averted, officially ending the era of Reconstruction.

## CONCLUSION: The Price of Peace

The compromise of 1877 cemented the reunion of South and North. In blustery speeches, American statesmen boasted about the opportunities for economic development based on the reconciliation between the formerly estranged sections. Republican party dominance in the White House, though not in Congress, was preserved, with three exceptions, until 1932. In the 12 years between Appomattox and Hayes's inauguration, the diverse dreams of victorious northern Republicans, defeated white southerners, and hopeful black freedmen had conflicted with each other. There was little chance that all could be fulfilled. The peace of 1877 was preserved "at any price," and the price was paid by the freedmen.

In 1880, Frederick Douglass summarized the tragedy of Reconstruction for the freedmen:

> Our Reconstruction measures were radically defective. . . . To the freedmen was given the machinery of liberty, but here was denied to them the steam to put it in motion. They were given the uniform of soldiers, but no arms; they were called citizens, but left subjects; they were called free, but left almost slaves. The old master class . . . retained the power to starve them to death, and wherever this power is held there is the power of slavery.

Douglass went on to say, however, that as he examined the great strides blacks had made in economic survival and education, it was a wonder to him "not that freedmen have made so little progress, but, rather, that they have made so much; not that they have been standing still, but that they have been able to stand at all."

A few years later, W. E. B. Du Bois wrote a short story about two boyhood playmates, one black and one white, from the fictional town of Altamaha, Georgia. Both young men were named John and both were sent north to school to prepare for leadership of their respective communities, the black John as a teacher and the white John as a judge and possible governor of the state. While they were away, the black and white people of Altamaha, each race thinking of its own John and not of the other, except with "a vague unrest," waited for "the coming of two young men, and dreamed . . . of new things that would be done and new thoughts that all would think."

After several years, both Johns returned to Altamaha, but the hopes and dreams of a new era of racial justice and harmony were shattered by a series of tragic events. Neither John understood the people of the town, and each was in turn misunderstood. Black John's school was closed because he was teaching ideals of liberty. Heartbroken and discouraged as he walked through the forest near town, he surprised the white John in an attempted rape of his sister. Without a word, black John picked up a fallen limb and with "all the pent-up hatred of his great black arm" smashed his boyhood playmate to death. Within hours he was lynched.

Du Bois's story capsulizes the human cost of the Reconstruction era. The black scholar's hope for reconciliation by "a union of intelligence and sympathy across the color-line" was smashed in the tragic encounter between the two Johns. Both young men, each once filled with glorious dreams, lay dead under the pines of the Georgia forest. Dying with them were hopes that interracial harmony, intersectional trust, and humane, just, equal opportunities and rights for the freedmen might be the legacies of Reconstruction. Conspicuously absent in the forest scene was the influence of the victorious northerners. They had turned their attention to other, less noble causes.

## Recommended Reading

The two best brief overviews of the Reconstruction era are John Hope Franklin, *Reconstruction After the Civil War* (1961) and Kenneth Stampp, *The Era of Reconstruction, 1865–1877* (1965). A recent collection of essays on the issues of the era can be found in Morgan Kousser and James M. McPherson, eds., *Region, Race, and Reconstruction: Essays in Honor of C. Vann Woodward* (1982). For a controversial but brilliantly insightful analysis of Reconstruction from a black perspective, see W. E. B. Du Bois, *Black Reconstruction* (1935) and *The Souls of Black Folk* (1903).

The fullest, most moving account of the black experience in the transition from slavery to freedom is Leon Litwack's massive and sensitive work, *Been in the Storm So Long: The Aftermath of Slavery* (1980). See also Willie Lee Rose, *Rehearsal for Reconstruction* (1964), an account of the earliest adjustments to freedom in the Sea Islands. The southern white response to emancipation is described in James Roark, *Masters Without Slaves: Southern Planters in the Civil War and Reconstruction* (1977).

The economy of the South and the freedmen's experience with land are described in Roger Ransom and Richard Sutch, *One Kind of Freedom: The Economic Consequencs of Emancipation* (1977). A more optimistic view is in Robert Higgs, *Competition and Coercion: Blacks in the American Economy, 1865–1914* (1977). An excellent new work showing the white experience with tenancy in the changing economy of the South is Stephen Hahn, *The Roots of Southern Populism* (1983). For an excellent view of the New South, see C. Vann Woodward, *Origins of the New South, 1877–1913* (1951). The Freedmen's Bureau has been the subject of several studies, the best of which are Peter Kolchin, *First Freedom* (1972); Claude

Oubré, *Forty Acres and a Mule: The Freedmen's Bureau and Black Land Ownership* (1978); and Donald Nieman, *To Set the Law in Motion: The Freedmen's Bureau and the Legal Rights of Blacks, 1865–1868* (1979). Continuing racial prejudice in the South and North is the subject of C. Vann Woodward, *The Strange Career of Jim Crow*, 3d rev. ed. (1974) and Rayford Logan, *The Betrayal of the Negro*, rev. ed (1965).

Northern politics during Reconstruction have been widely discussed. See LaWanda Cox and John Cox, *Politics, Principles, and Prejudice, 1865–1866* (1963); Eric McKitrick, *Andrew Johnson and Reconstruction* (1960); David Donald, *The Politics of Reconstruction* (1965); and Michael Les Benedict, *A Compromise of Principle: Congressional Republicans and Reconstruction, 1863–1869* (1974). Grant's presidency and the abandonment of the freedmen by northern Republicans can be traced in William McFeeley, *Grant: A Biography* (1981) and William Gillette, *Retreat from Reconstruction, 1869–1879* (1979). The campaign of violence that ended the Republican governments in the South is told with gripping horror in Allen Trelease, *White Terror: The Ku Klux Klan Conspiracy and Southern Reconstruction* (1971). The end of Reconstruction is the subject of C. Vann Woodward's classic little book *Reunion and Reaction* (1956).

Five novels written at different times and representing different interpretations of the story of Reconstruction are Albion Tourgée, *A Fool's Errand* (1879); Thomas Dixon, *The Clansman* (1905); W. E. B. Du Bois, *The Quest of the Silver Fleece* (1911); Howard Fast, *Freedom Road* (1944); and Ernest Gaines, *The Autobiography of Miss Jane Pittman* (1971).

## TIME LINE

| | |
|---|---|
| 1865 | Civil War ends<br>Lincoln assassinated; Andrew Johnson becomes president<br>Johnson proposes general amnesty and reconstruction plan<br>Racial confusion, widespread hunger, and demobilization<br>Thirteenth Amendment ratified<br>Freedmen's Bureau established |
| 1865–1866 | Black codes<br>Repossession of land by whites and freedmen's contracts |
| 1866 | Freedmen's Bureau renewed and Civil Rights Act passed over Johnson's veto<br>Southern Homestead Act<br>Ku Klux Klan formed<br>Tennessee readmitted to Union |
| 1867 | Reconstruction Acts passed over Johnson's veto<br>Impeachment controversy<br>Freedmen's Bureau ends |
| 1868 | Fourteenth Amendment ratified<br>Impeachment of Johnson fails<br>Ulysses Grant elected president |
| 1868–1870 | Ten states readmitted under congressional plan |
| 1869 | Georgia and Virginia reestablish Democratic party control |
| 1870 | Fifteenth Amendment ratified |
| 1870s–1880s | Black "exodusters" migrate to Kansas |
| 1870–1871 | Force Acts<br>North Carolina and Georgia reestablish Democratic control |
| 1872 | General Amnesty Act<br>Grant reelected president |
| 1873 | Crédit Mobilier scandal<br>Panic causes depression |
| 1874 | Alabama and Arkansas reestablish Democratic control |
| 1875 | Civil Rights Act<br>Mississippi reestablishes Democratic control |
| 1876 | Hayes-Tilden election |
| 1876–1877 | South Carolina, Louisiana, and Florida reestablish Democratic control |
| 1877 | Compromise of 1877; Rutherford B. Hayes assumes presidency and ends Reconstruction |
| 1880s | Tenancy and sharecropping prevail in the South<br>Disfranchisement and segregation of southern blacks begins |

# PART FOUR
# AN INDUSTRIALIZING PEOPLE

# 1865–1900

In the last half of the nineteenth century, Americans rapidly left the problems of the Civil War era behind and turned their energies toward transforming their society from one based on agriculture to one based on heavy industry. This economic and social transition was neither smooth nor steady. But by 1900, the United States had emerged as one of the world's great industrial powers.

Chapters 18, 19, and 20 form a unit. Chapter 18, "The Farmer's World," examines the ways in which American farmers modernized and vastly expanded production after the Civil War. Even though agriculture provided the basis for urban industrial development, many farmers did not win the rewards they had anticipated. The South remained backward despite efforts to modernize. Rural protest publicized farmers' complaints and contributed to the formation of a powerful third party. While the postwar period was difficult for some farmers, it was disastrous for Native Americans. By 1900, the power of the Plains Indians had been broken and the reservation system finally set in place.

Chapter 19, "The Rise of Smokestack America," focuses on the character of industrial progress and urban expansion. We explore the growing diversity of the American work force and its various experiences in and responses to the new world of industry. The labor conflicts of the period indicate the difficulty of these years for most working-class Americans.

In Chapter 20, "Politics and Protest," we turn to middle-class Americans, the first to benefit from industrial progress. Despite their many comforts and opportunities, however, middle-class Americans had concerns that led them to play an increasing role in urban, state, and national politics. Usually they worked for moderate reform, which they hoped would bring about human betterment and social harmony.

Chapter 21, "The United States Becomes a World Power," demonstrates the international consequences of the country's successful industrialization. Like other world powers, the United States nourished imperial ambitions in the 1890s and acquired its own colonies. But expansionism brought difficult dilemmas in America's relationship with the rest of the world. After 1900, the United States continued to play a more active role in international affairs but stood aside from the race for colonies.

# PARALLEL EVENTS

| | 1865 | 1870 | 1875 | 1880 | 1 |

## CULTURAL and TECHNOLOGICAL

1860s  Bessemer and open-hearth steel processes introduced

1865  Vassar College founded
1866  Atlantic Cable laid
1867  First Horatio Alger novels published
First elevated railway in New York City
1869  First transcontinental railroad link completed

1870  Thomas Edison invents stock ticker
1870s  Expansion of public schools and higher education begins

1873  Mark Twain and Charles Dudley Warner coin the expression "Gilded Age"
1874  Barbed wire patented
First electric streetcar runs in New York City

1875  Wellesley College founded
First running of the Kentucky Derby
1876  Centennial Exposition in Philadelphia
Alexander Graham Bell invents telephone
First major baseball league formed
1877  Mark Twain, *Adventures of Tom Sawyer*
C. H. Hines begins making root beer

1879  Henry George, *Progress and Poverty*
Light bulb perfected

1880s  Social Darwinism and Social Gospel

1881  Tuskegee Institute founded

1883  Brooklyn Bridge
1884  W. D. Howells, *The Rise of Silas Lapham*

## SOCIAL and ECONOMIC

1866  National Labor Union founded
1867  National Grange founded
1868  Eight-hour day for federal employees
1869  Prohibition party formed
Knights of Labor formed

1870  Wyoming Territory grants suffrage to women
1870s  J. D. Rockefeller forms Standard Oil of Ohio
Tweed Ring exposed
1872  Chicago fire
Yellowstone National Park established
Montgomery Ward, first mail-order house, opens
1873  Bethlehem Steel begins production
1873–1879  Depression
1874  Women's Christian Temperance Union founded
Greenback party formed

1875–1876  Indian Wars in Black Hills

1877  Nez Percé Indian uprisings
Black exodusters to Kansas
Railroad strikes

1880s  "New South"

1882  Standard Oil Trust established
1883–1885  Depression
1884  Southern Farmers' Alliance founded

## POLITICAL

1867  Alaska purchased
1868–1874  "Granger" Laws

1871  Indian Appropriation Act
Army suppresses Apache

1875  Specie Resumption Act
United States–Hawaii commercial treaty

1877  Rutherford B. Hayes becomes president
*Munn v. Illinois*
1878  Bland-Allison Act

1880  James A. Garfield elected
1880s  Bossism and urban reform
1881  Garfield assassinated; Chester A. Arthur becomes president
1882  Chinese Exclusion Act
1883  Pendleton Civil Service Act
1884  Grover Cleveland elected

| 1865 | 1870 | 1875 | 1880 | 18 |

# 1865–1900

## CULTURAL and TECHNOLOGICAL

- 1888 Edward Bellamy, *Looking Backward*
- 1889 Andrew Carnegie, "The Gospel of Wealth"
- 1890s Electric trolleys
- 1890 Alfred Thayer Mahan, *Influence of Sea Power upon History*
- 1891 Hamlin Garland, *Main-Travelled Roads*
- 1893 Stephen Crane, *Maggie: A Girl of the Streets*
  World's Exposition in Chicago
  City Beautiful movement
- 1895 Elizabeth Cady Stanton, *Woman's Bible*
- 1896 Charles Sheldon, *In His Steps*
- 1898 Charlotte Perkin Gilman, *Women and Economics*
- 1899 John Dewey, *School and Society*
- 1900 Theodore Dreiser, *Sister Carrie*

## SOCIAL and ECONOMIC

- 1885 "New Immigration"
- 1886 AFL founded
  Haymarket Riot
- 1887 College Settlement House Association founded
- 1888 Colored Farmers' Alliance established
- 1889 Hull House founded
- 1889–1890 Ghost Dance
  Battle of Wounded Knee
- 1890 General Federation of Women's Clubs founded
  National American Women Suffrage Association formed
- 1892 Homestead strike
- 1893 Anti-Saloon League founded
- 1893–1897 Depression
- 1894 Pullman strike
  Coxey's march
- 1895 Atlanta Compromise speech

## POLITICAL

- 1887 Dawes Act
  Interstate Commerce Act
- 1888 Benjamin Harrison elected
- 1890 Sherman Anti-Trust Act
  Sherman Silver Purchase Act
  McKinley Tariff
- 1890s Jim Crow laws and disfranchisement attempts in the South
- 1892 Populist Party formed
  Cleveland elected to second term
- 1893 Hawaiian coup by American sugar growers
- 1895 Cuban Revolution
  *United States v. E. C. Knight*
- 1896 William McKinley elected
  *Plessy v. Ferguson*
- 1898 Sinking of the *Maine*
  Spanish-American War
  Treaty of Paris
  Annexation of Hawaii and the Philippines
- 1899–1900 Open Door notes
- 1899–1902 Philippine-American War
- 1900 Boxer Rebellion in China
- 1901 McKinley assassinated; Theodore Roosevelt becomes president
- 1902 Platt Amendment
- 1904 Roosevelt Corollary

# CHAPTER 18
## THE FARMER'S WORLD

In 1873, Milton Leeper, his wife Hattie, and their baby Anna climbed into a wagon piled high with their possessions and set out to homestead in Boone County, Nebraska. Once on the claim, the Leepers confidently dreamed of their future. Wrote Hattie to her sister in Iowa, "I like our place the best of any around here." "When we get a fine house and 100 acres under cultivation," she added, "I wouldn't trade with any one." But Milton had broken in only 13 acres when disaster struck. Hordes of grasshoppers appeared, and the Leepers fled their claim and took refuge in the nearby town of Fremont.

There they stayed for two years. Milton worked first at a store, then hired out to other farmers. Hattie sewed, kept a boarder, and cared for chickens and a milk cow. The family lived on the brink of poverty but never gave up hope. "Times are hard and we have had bad luck," Hattie acknowledged, but "I am going to hold that claim . . . there will [be] one gal that won't be out of a home." In 1876, the Leepers triumphantly returned to their claim with a modest sum of $27 to help them start over.

The grasshoppers were gone, there was enough rain, and preaching was only half a mile away. The Leepers, like others, began to prosper. Two more daughters were born and cared for in the comfortable sod house, "homely" on the outside but plastered and cozy within. As Hattie explained, the homesteaders lived "just as civilized as they would in Chicago."

Their luck did not last. Hattie, pregnant again, fell ill and died in childbirth along with her infant son. Heartbroken, Milton buried his wife and child and left the claim. The last frontier had momentarily defeated him, although he would try farming in at least four other locations before his death in 1905.

The Leepers' failure to establish a successful homestead reflected some of the constraints of rural life in the late nineteenth century. Another farmer described the paradoxical rewards of bountiful crops. "We were told two years ago to go to work and raise a big crop; that was all we needed. We went to work and plowed and planted; the rains fell, the sun shone, nature smiled, and we raised the big crop they told us to; and what came of it? Eight cent corn, ten cent oats, two cent beef and no price at all for butter and eggs—that's what came of it." Still a third perspective on the agricultural frontier comes from Red Cloud, a Sioux, who told railroad surveyors in Wyoming, "We do not want you here. You are scaring away the buffalo."

This chapter focuses on the experiences of red, white, and black rural Americans in the late nineteenth century. During these years, farmers joined the modern industrial world. With the help of machinery, they enormously expanded land under cultivation, produced bumper crops, and shipped them by railroad to markets. They hoped to profit from the country's economic transformation at the same time that they contributed to it by providing cheap food for industrial workers. Yet all too frequently, farmers felt cheated by the unpredictable and often meager rewards they received. Their anguish did not match that of the Native Americans, who were robbed of their land, nor of American black farmers mired in debt peonage. But their pain was sharp enough to turn some into critics of American life and to push others into politics.

## THE MODERNIZATION OF AGRICULTURE

Between 1865 and 1900, the nation's farms more than doubled in number as Americans pushed into the vast areas west of the Mississippi and broke virgin land. In both newly settled and older areas, farmers raised specialized crops with the aid of modern machinery and relied on the expanding railroad system to send them to market (see Chapter 19). The character of agriculture became increasingly capitalistic. Farmers, as one New Englander pointed out, "must understand farming as a business; if they do not it will go hard with them."

### Rural Myth and Reality

The number of Americans who still farmed the land testified to the continuing vitality of the rural tradition. In the late eighteenth century, Benjamin Franklin praised "industrious frugal farmers," who populated the country's interior, while Thomas Jefferson viewed them as the "deposit for substantial and genuine virtue" and fundamental to the health of the republic.

The notion that the farmer and farm life symbolized the essence of America persisted as the United States industrialized. The popularity of inexpensive Currier and Ives prints, depicting idyllic rural scenes, suggests how captivated Americans were by the idealized view of country life. Healthy, well-dressed, vigorous farmers are the sturdy yeomen of Jefferson's imagination. Farm wives appear robust and attractive, apparently satisfied with the rhythms of country life. Rural children amuse themselves in pleasant diversions—skating, fishing, riding on wagons, gathering fruit. They live in solid, cozy houses. All is well in the countryside.

Another set of Currier and Ives prints implied that there need be no conflict between the new technological industrial world and rural America. Trains, representing the new, chug peacefully through farmlands, while cheering children and trusting adults look on. Railroads bring progress but not the destruction of the land or the livelihood of those on it.

The prints were nostalgic wishful thinking. However much Americans wanted to believe that no tension existed between technological

## Average Farm Acreage, 1860–1900

| REGION | 1860 | 1870 | 1880 | 1890 | 1900 |
|---|---|---|---|---|---|
| *Land in Farms (1,000 acres)* | | | | | |
| United States | 407,213 | 407,735 | 536,082 | 623,219 | 841,202 |
| North Central | 107,900 | 139,215 | 206,982 | 256,587 | 317,349 |
| South | 225,514 | 189,556 | 234,920 | 256,606 | 362,036 |
| West | 12,718 | 16,219 | 26,194 | 47,282 | 96,407 |
| Northeast | 61,082 | 62,744 | 67,986 | 62,744 | 65,409 |
| *Average Acreage per Farm (acres)* | | | | | |
| United States | 199 | 153 | 134 | 137 | 147 |
| North Central | 140 | 124 | 122 | 133 | 145 |
| South | 335 | 214 | 153 | 140 | 138 |
| West | 367 | 336 | 313 | 324 | 393 |
| Northeast | 108 | 104 | 98 | 95 | 97 |

**Source:** U.S. Bureau of the Census.

## Agriculture in the 1880s

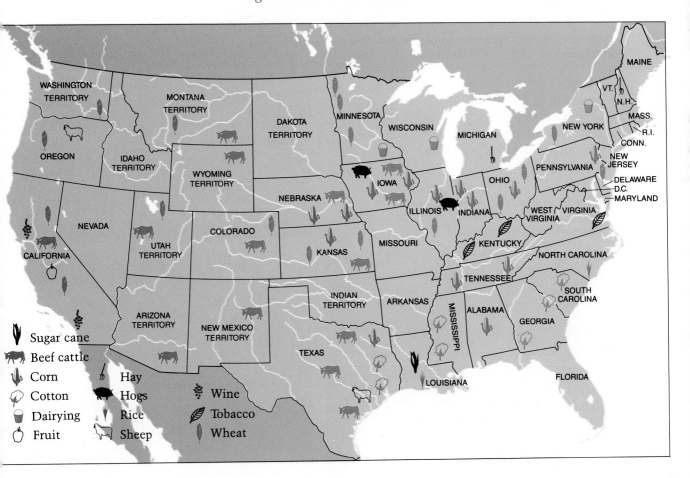

Sugar cane
Beef cattle
Corn          Hay
Cotton        Hogs        Wine
Dairying      Rice        Tobacco
Fruit         Sheep       Wheat

progress and agriculture, it did. Farmers were no longer the backbone of the work force. In 1860, they represented almost 60 percent of the labor force; by 1900, less than 37 percent of employed Americans were farmers. At the same time, farmers' contribution to the nation's wealth declined from a third to a quarter.

Nor were farmers the independent yeomen of the rural myth. They were increasingly entangled with the industrial and urban world. Reliable, cheap transportation allowed them to specialize in the market crop most suited to their location. Farmers on the Great Plains now grew most of the country's wheat, while those in the Midwest replaced that crop with corn, which they used as feed for their hogs and cattle. Eastern farmers turned to vegetable, fruit, and dairy farming. Some, like Milachi Dodge from New Hampshire, gave up farming altogether. As he explained, when his "boys came home" from the Civil War, "they did not want to work on a farm, and I sold my farm out." Cotton continued to dominate the economy of the South, although tobacco, wheat, and rice were also cultivated there. In the Far West, grain, fruits, and vegetables predominated.

As farmers specialized in cash crops for national and international markets, their success depended increasingly on outside forces and demands. Bankers and loan companies provided the necessary capital to expand farm operations, middlemen stored and sometimes sold produce, railroads carried farm goods to market. A prosperous American economy put money into laborers' pockets for food purchases. Even international conditions affected the American farmer. After 1870, exports of wheat, flour, and animal products rose, with wheat becoming the country's chief cash crop. Thus the cultivation of wheat in Russia and Argentina meant fewer foreign buyers for American grain. The decision of several European countries between 1879 and 1883 to ban American pork imports, which they feared were infected with trichinosis, translated into losses for American stock raisers.

Farming had become a modern business.

*The appeal of an idealized view of life helps to explain the popularity of Currier & Ives prints in mid-nineteenth century America.*

"Watch and study the markets and the ways of marketmen . . . learn the art of 'selling well,'" one rural editor advised his readers in 1887. "The work of farming is only half done when the crop is out of the ground." Like other businesses of the post–Civil War era, farming depended more and more on machinery. "It is no longer necessary for the farmer to cut his wheat with sickle or cradle, nor to rake it and bind it by hand; to cut his cornstalks with a knife and shock the stalks by hand; to thresh his grain with a flail," reported one observer. Harvesters, binders, and other new machines, pulled by work animals, performed these tasks for him.

These machines diminished much of the drudgery of farming life and made the production of crops easier, more efficient, and cheaper. Moreover, they allowed a farmer to cultivate far more land than he had been able to do with hand tools, so that by 1900 more than twice as much land was in cultivation as there had been in 1860. But machinery was expensive, and many American farmers had to borrow to buy it. In the decade of the 1880s, mortgage indebtedness grew 2½ times faster than agricultural wealth.

## New Farmers, New Farms

As farmers became dependent on machinery, brought new land into cultivation, raised specialized crops, and sent them to faraway markets, they operated much like other nineteenth-century businessmen. Some even became large-scale entrepreneurs. Small family farms still typified American agriculture, but vast mechanized operations, devoted to the cultivation of one crop, appeared, especially west of the Mississippi River. These farms had a few huge barns for storage of machinery and a handful of other farm buildings but few gardens, trees, or outbuildings. No churches or villages interrupted the monotony of the landscape.

The bonanza farms, established in the late 1870s on the northern plains, symbolized the trend to large-scale agriculture. Thousands of acres in size, these wheat farms required large capital investments (many were, in fact, owned by corporations) and depended on machinery, a hired work force, and efficient managers. The farm that Oliver Dalrymple operated for two Northern Pacific Railroad directors used 200 pairs of harrows and 125 seeders for planting. Harvesting the grain required 155 binders and 26 steam threshers. At peak times, the farm's work force numbered 600 men. The result was a harvest of 600,000 bushels of wheat in 1882. Although bonanza farms were not typical, they highlighted the dramatic agricultural changes that were occurring everywhere on a smaller scale.

*Bonanza farms, a development of the 1870s, foreshadowed the agribusiness concerns of the twentieth century.*

## Agricultural Productivity, 1800–1900

| CROP AND PRODUCTIVITY INDICATOR | 1800 | 1840 | 1880 | 1900 |
|---|---|---|---|---|
| **Wheat** | | | | |
| Worker-hours/acre | 56 | 35 | 20 | 15 |
| Yield/acre (bushels) | 15 | 15 | 13 | 14 |
| Worker-hours/100 bushels | 373 | 233 | 152 | 108 |
| **Corn** | | | | |
| Worker-hours/acre | 86 | 69 | 46 | 38 |
| Yield/acre (bushels) | 25 | 25 | 26 | 26 |
| Worker-hours/100 bushels | 344 | 276 | 180 | 147 |
| **Cotton** | | | | |
| Worker-hours/acre | 185 | 135 | 119 | 112 |
| Yield/acre (pounds of lint) | 147 | 147 | 179 | 191 |
| Worker-hours/bale | 601 | 439 | 318 | 280 |

*Source:* U.S. Bureau of the Census.

## Overproduction and Falling Prices

Farmers so fervently subscribed to the rural myth captured by Currier and Ives that they did not initially realize that the technology they embraced might backfire. Gradually they began to discover unanticipated problems as they cultivated more land with the assistance of machinery. Productivity rose 40 percent between 1869 and 1899. Almost every crop showed impressive statistical gains. The yields for some crops like wheat were so large, however, that the domestic market could not absorb them.

The prices farm products commanded steadily declined. In 1867, corn sold for 78 cents a bushel. By 1873, it had fallen to 31 cents, and by 1889 to 23 cents. Wheat similarly plummeted from about $2 a bushel in 1867 to only 70 cents a bushel in 1889. Cotton profits also spiraled downward, the value of a bale depreciating from $43.60 in 1866 to $30.00 in the 1890s.

This pattern of falling prices did not automatically hurt farmers. The late nineteenth century was a deflationary period. Because paper money was withdrawn gradually after the Civil War and not much silver was coined, the supply of money rose more slowly than productivity. As a result, prices fell by more than half between the end of the Civil War and 1900. Farmers were getting less for their crops but were also paying less for their purchases.

Deflation may have encouraged overproduction, however. To make the same amount of money, it seemed to many farmers that they had to raise larger and larger crops. As they did, prices fell even lower. Furthermore, deflation increased the real value of debts. In 1888, it took 174 bushels of wheat to pay the interest on a $2,000 mortgage at 8 percent. By 1895, it took 320 bushels.

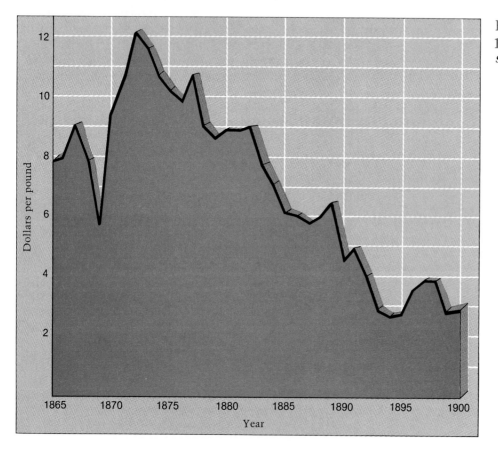

### Price of Wheat Flour, 1865–1900

*Source:* U.S. Bureau of the Census.

## Farming on the Great Plains

Between 1870 and 1900, the acreage devoted to farming tripled west of the Mississippi. The rapid expansion of land under cultivation was closely linked to the opening of the Great Plains (North and South Dakota, Kansas, Nebraska, Oklahoma, and Texas) to agricultural settlement.

In the mid-nineteenth century, farmers had passed over the Plains, regarding them as unsuitable for farming, and continued on to the Far West. Views of the farming potential of the Plains changed after the Civil War, however. Railroads eager for business as they laid down new lines, town boosters eager for inhabitants, and land speculators eager to sell their holdings all undertook major promotional efforts to persuade farmers to settle the Plains. "This is the sole remaining section of paradise in the western world; all the wild romances of the gorgeous orient dwindle into nothing when compared to the everyday realities of Dakota's progress," one newspaper exclaimed. "All that is needed is to plow, plant and attend to the crops properly; the rains are abundant." The rainfall, which was above average for the region in the 1880s, seemed to substantiate the argument regarding adequate moisture.

Industrial innovations of the late nineteenth century also facilitated the expansion of agriculture. At approximately the 98th meridian, the prairies with their tall grasses merged into the short grasses of the Plains. Few trees grew there, and this was one reason why emigrants chose not to stop. Only with a cheap fencing material to replace wood could the Great Plains states be settled and cultivated. The breakthrough occurred in the 1870s, when Joseph Glidden, a visitor to a county fair, noticed an exhibit that featured a strip of wood with protruding points. The device was to hang on fences to keep animals out. Why not, thought Glidden, make fencing wire with protruding barbs? Before long, he and a partner were mass-producing hundreds of miles of barbed wire fencing, as were their eager competitors. The region's unpredictable weather posed another kind of problem, especially at harvest time. Twine binders, which speeded up the grain harvesting, minimized the possibility of crop loss. Water shortages were relieved by the 1890s, when mail-order steel windmills for pumping water from deep underground wells became available.

In the first boom period of settlement, lasting from 1879 to the early 1890s, tens of thousands of eager families like the Leepers moved onto the Great Plains and began farming. Some made claims under the Homestead Act, which granted 160 acres to any family head or adult who lived on the claim for five years or who paid $1.25 an acre after six months of residence. Because homestead land was frequently less desirable than land held by railroads and speculators, however, most settlers bought land outright rather than taking up claims.

The costs of getting started were thus more substantial than the Homestead Act would suggest. Western land was cheap compared to farmland in the East, but an individual farmer was fortunate if he could buy a good quarter section for under $500. The costs of machinery would ultimately reach about $700. Although some farmers thought it made better economic sense to lease rather than to buy land, many had to rent because they lacked the capital to purchase land and set up operations. In 1880, some 20 percent of the Plains farmers were tenants, and this percentage rose over time.

Many of the new settlers were immigrants, making the Great Plains the second most important destination for them. The most numerous arrived from Germany, the British Isles, and Canada. Many Scandinavians, Czechs, and Poles also moved to the new frontier. Unlike the single male immigrants flocking to American cities for work, these newcomers came with their families. From the beginning, they intended to put down roots in the new country and stay.

Life on the Plains frontier often proved to be difficult. Wrote Miriam Peckham, a Kansas homesteader:

> I tell you Auntie no one can depend on farming for a living in this country. Henry is very industrious and this year had in over thirty acres of small grain, 8 acres of corn and about an acre of potatoes. We have sold our small grain . . . and it come to $100; now deduct $27.00 for cutting,

$16.00 for threshing, $19.00 for hired help, say nothing of boarding our help, none of the trouble of drawing 25 miles to market and 25 cts on each head for ferriage over the river and where is your profit. I sometimes think this a God forsaken country, the [grass]hopper hurt our corn and we have 1/2 a crop and utterly destroyed our garden. If one wants trials, let them come to Kansas.

Peckham's letter highlights the uncertainties of frontier life: the costs of machinery, the vagaries of crops and markets, the threat of pests and natural disasters. Her letter also points to the shortage of cash. Unlike earlier emigrants to the Far West, who had to have the means to finance the six-month trip, many Plains pioneers took up their homesteads with only a few dollars in their pockets. Frontier diaries often noted the marginality of early frontier operations, describing loans from family in the East and debts. The phrase "did not pay for it" occurs repeatedly. Survival often depended on how well the family managed to do during the crucial first years. If they succeeded in raising and selling their crops, they might accumulate the capital needed to continue. But if nature was harsh or their luck bad, or if they were unable to adjust to new conditions, the chances of failure were great.

Many settlers found the vast treeless plains depressing and even frightening. One New England visitor explained, "It has been terrible on settlers, on the women especially, for there is no society and they get doleful and feel almost like committing suicide for want of society." This was the point many authors chose to emphasize. O. E. Rolvaag's novel *Giants in the Earth* (1927) shows the wife of a Norwegian immigrant farmer driven to madness and death. Hamlin Garland's *Main-Travelled Roads* (1891) pictures overworked, hopeless women whom the frontier defeats. As Garland explained, he had written his stories in a "mood of resentment" after visiting "my mother on a treeless farm."

Life on the Plains was not always so discouraging as these authors suggest. Willa Cather, who spent her childhood in Nebraska, showed both the harshness and the lure of prairie life in her novels. Alexandra Bergson, the main character of *O Pioneers!* (1913), loves the land: "It

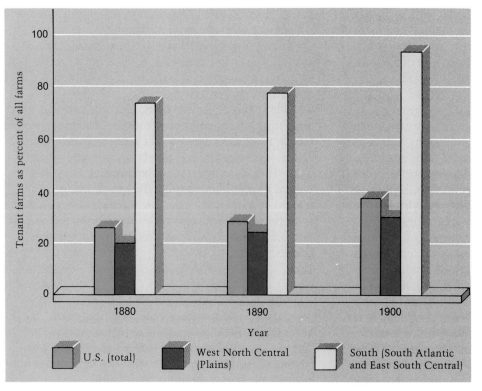

**Percentage of Farms Operated by Tenants, 1880–1900**

***Source:*** U.S. Bureau of the Census.

seemed beautiful to her, rich and strong and glorious." The thousands of letters and diaries that survive from the period also provide a more positive picture of farming life. Elam Bartholemew's diary contains news of visitors, trips, and social events. In 1880, only six years after he had settled in northern Kansas, Elam's journal reveals that 1,081 people stopped at his home. His wife served 783 meals to visitors. Trips to church, parties, sings, and neighborhood get-togethers brightened family life. There were many occasions when the Bartholemews "enjoyed ourselves very much."

The Plains frontier required many adjustments, however. Scarce water and violent changes in temperature called for new modes of behavior and resourcefulness. Without firewood, farmers learned to burn corncobs and twisted wheat for warmth. The log cabin, long the symbol of frontier life, disappeared as inventive settlers discovered how to build houses of sod "bricks." Although from a distance such houses often looked like mounds of earth, "homely old things," as Hattie Leeper described them, they frequently had glass windows, wooden shingles, and even plastered interiors. Dark and gloomy to our eyes, they were comfortable, cozy, and practical for the settlers. Walls, 2 to 3

*Unlike their counterparts farther east, Plains settlers were forced to abandon traditional modes of shelter. The Rawding family lived in a house with a sod roof in Nebraska in 1886.*

feet thick, kept out the scorching summer heat and fierce cold of winter, the moaning winds, and the prairie fires. The solidity of the sod house provided a welcome contrast to the impersonal power and scale of nature.

The first boom on the Great Plains halted abruptly in the late 1880s and early 1890s. Falling agricultural prices reduced profits. Then, the unusual rainfall that had lured farmers to settle semiarid regions disappeared. A devastating drought followed. One farmer reported in 1890 that he had earned $41.48 from his wheat crop, yet his expenses for seed and threshing amounted to $56.00. Many were destitute and survived on boiled weeds, a few potatoes, and a little bread and butter. Although cash was scarce on the frontier, credit had not been. Many farmers had accumulated debts they now could not repay. Thousands lost their farms to creditors. Some stayed on as tenants. Homesteaders like the Leepers gave up. By 1900, two-thirds of homesteaded farms had failed. Many homesteaders fled east. In western Kansas, the population declined by half between 1888 and 1892. The wagons of those who retreated bore the epitaph of their experience: "In God We Trusted: In Kansas We Busted."

## The Early Cattle Frontier

In the mid-1870s, two Plains settlers became embroiled in a conflict that symbolized the meeting of the farming and cattle frontiers. John Duncan was a cattleman and Peter Schmidt a German farmer. Duncan allowed his cattle to roam over the Plains and feed on its grasses. Some wandered onto Schmidt's property, devoured his corn, and destroyed his garden. Schmidt managed to run the cattle off but was outraged at the damage. For many years, such incidents had been rare, for few farmers were living on the Plains. As settlement increased in the 1880s and 1890s, they became more common.

The early cattle frontier was a post–Civil War phenomenon, rooted in Union military strategy. During the war, the North had split the South in two and cut Texas off from Confederate markets. At the end of the war, Texas had 5 million longhorns roaming the range. The postwar burst of railroad construction provided a way of turning cattle into dollars. If the cattle were driven north from Texas to railroad connections where they could then be shipped to slaughtering and packing houses in cities like Chicago and Kansas City, their value would soar. Thus started the first cattle drives, so well known through stories, movies, and television. In the late 1860s, cowboys herded thousands of longhorns north to towns like Abilene, Wichita, and Dodge City.

Some of the cattle were sold to ranchers on the Great Plains, where grasses were ripe for grazing. In the late 1870s and early 1880s, huge ranches appeared in eastern Colorado, Wyoming, and Montana and in western Kansas, Nebraska, and the Dakotas. These ventures, many owned by outside investors, paid off handsomely. Because the cattle could roam at will over the public domain, they cost owners little

*The romantic figure of the cowboy sprang into the popular imagination from books of fiction illustrated by artists such as Frederick Remington.*

as they fattened up. A Texas steer, bought for $7 or $8, could be set out to graze and then sold for $60 or $70. The cowboys (a third of them Mexican and black) who herded the steers, however, earned only meager wages of $25 and $40 a month, just enough to pay for a fling in the saloons, dance halls, and gambling palaces in Dodge City or Abilene when taking the cattle to market.

By the mid-1880s, the first phase of the cattle frontier was coming to an end. As the clash between Peter Schmidt and John Duncan indicated, farmers were moving onto the Plains, buying up public lands once used for grazing, and fencing them in. But the struggle between cattle ranchers and farmers was not the only reason for the cattle frontier's collapse. Eager to make as large a profit as possible, ranchers overstocked their herds in the mid-1880s. Hungry cattle ate everything in sight, then grew weak as grass became scarce. As was so often the case on the Plains, the weather had a part to play. A winter of memorable blizzards followed the very hot summer of 1885. Cattle, usually able to forage for themselves during the winter months, could not dig through the deep snow to the grass and died from starvation. By spring, 90 percent of the cattle were dead. As one cattleman's journal observed, "An overstocked range must bleed when the blizzards sit in judgment." Frantic owners dumped their remaining cattle on the market, getting $8 or even less for each animal.

In the aftermath, those ranchers who remained stock raisers adopted new techniques. Experimenting with new breeds, they began to replace their longhorns, to fence their herds in, and to feed them grain during the winter months. Consumers were hungering for tender beef rather than the tough flesh of animals who roamed the Plains in any case, and these new methods satisfied the market. Ranching, like farming, was becoming more a modern business and less the colorful adventure portrayed in popular culture.

### Cornucopia on the Pacific

When gold was discovered in California, Americans rushed west to find it. But as one father told his eager son, "Plant your lands; these be your best gold fields." He was right; farming eventually proved to be California's greatest asset. But farming in California hardly resembled the rural life Currier and Ives depicted. Nor did it embody the hopes of the framers of the Homestead Act.

Although federal and state land policies supposedly promoted "homes for the homeless," little of California's land was actually homesteaded or developed as small family farms. When California entered the Union, Mexican ranchers held vast tracts of land, which never became part of the public domain. Neither Mexican-Americans nor small farmers profited from the 20 years of confusion over the legitimacy of Mexican land titles. Speculators did, and acquired much of the Californios' land. Consequently, small farmers faced steep prices when they wished to buy land. The costs of starting out in California were substantial. As Charles Reed observed in 1869, "Land which but two years ago could have been bought . . . for from $1 to $1.25 per acre cannot now be bought for less than $10 to $15 per acre."

Generous grants from the public domain (16 percent by 1880) were awarded to the railroads. Railroads encouraged settlers to put down roots, then sold the improved land to the highest bidder. In 1871, reformer Henry George described California as "not a country of farms but a country of plantations and estates. Agriculture is speculation. . . . There is no state in the Union in which settlers have been more persecuted, so robbed as in California."

George accurately observed the large size of California's farms. In 1870, the average California farm was 482 acres, while in the United States at large the average farm was only 153 acres and in the North Central region 124 acres. By 1900, farms of 1,000 acres or more made up two-thirds of the state's farmland.

California's landscape reflected the reality of large-scale farming. As one California visitor reported to the New York *Times* in 1887, "You go through miles and miles of wheat fields, you see the fertility of the land and the beauty of the scenery, but where are the hundreds of farm houses . . . that you would see in Ohio or Iowa?"

Small farmers and ranchers did exist, of course, but they found it difficult to compete with large, mechanized operators using cheap migrant laborers (usually Mexican or Chinese). One wheat farm in the San Joaquin Valley was so vast that workers started plowing in the morning at one end of the 17-mile field, ate lunch at its halfway point, and camped at its end that night before returning the next day.

The value of much of California's agricultural land, especially the southern half of the Central Valley, depended on water. Many gold rush immigrants were stunned by the appearance of the summer landscape. The grasses were brown and yellow; the earth was parched, and in places the temperature rose above 100 degrees Fahrenheit. By the 1870s, however, water, land, and railroad companies were taking on the huge costs of building dams, headgates, and canals and then selling hitherto barren lands along with water rights, passing along the costs to settlers in the form of high prices. By 1890, over a quarter of California's farms benefited from irrigation.

Although grain was initially California's most valuable crop, it faced stiff competition from farmers on the Plains and in other parts of the world. Some argued that "land capable of raising Adriatic figs, Zante currants, French prunes, Malaga raisins, Batavia oranges, Sicily lemons, citrons, limes, dates and olives, and our own incomparable peaches, apricots, nectarines, pears, quinces, plums, pomegranates, apples, English and native walnuts, chestnuts, pecans and almonds, in a climate surpassing that of Italy, is too valuable for the cultivation of simple cereals." But high railroad rates and primitive shipping conditions limited the volume of fresh fruit and vegetables sent to market. When the first shipment of 300 boxes of California oranges went east in 1877, they took a whole month to reach St. Louis. As growers around Los Angeles turned to the cultivation of navel oranges in the late 1870s, however, the Southern Pacific Railroad recognized the profits the fruit might bring to the railroad. In 1881, it halved its rates and entered into a rate war with the newly constructed Santa Fe Railroad. By 1890, benefiting from the lower rates, 4,000 carloads of oranges headed east.

The introduction of refrigerated railroad cars

*By 1900, efficient railroads and refrigerated freight cars made fresh fruit and other products accessible to most of the nation. Note the bananas and other nonlocal products in this Vermont country store.*

in the 1880s also boosted fruit and vegetable production. In June 1888, fresh apricots and cherries successfully survived the trip from California to New York. A few years later, California fruit was being sold in London. Some travelers even began to grumble that the railroads treated produce better than people. Per-

haps the complaint was true. The daily eastern express contained "two sleeping cars, two or three passenger cars, and twenty cars loaded with green fruit." The comments highlighted the fact that successful agriculture in California depended on the railroad system, irrigation, and the use of machinery.

## THE SECOND GREAT REMOVAL

Black Elk, an Ogalala Sioux, recalled an ominous dream:

> A long time ago my father told me what his father told him, that there was once a Lakota [Sioux] holy man, called Drinks Water, who dreamed what was to be; and this was long before the coming of the Wasichus [white men]. He dreamed . . . that a strange race had woven a spider's web all around the Lakotas. And he said: "When this happens, you shall live in square gray houses, in a barren land, and beside those square gray houses you shall starve."

So great was the wise man's sorrow that he died soon thereafter. During Black Elk's lifetime, the nightmarish prophecy came true.

As farmers settled the western frontier and became entangled in a national economy, they clashed with the Indian tribes who lived on the land. In California, disease and violence killed off 90 percent of the Native American population in the 30 years following the gold rush. Elsewhere, the struggle between Native Americans and whites was both prolonged and bitter.

### Background to Hostilities

As pointed out in Chapter 14, the Plains Indians' way of life centered around hunting the buffalo. Increased emigration to California and Oregon in the 1840s and 1850s interrupted tribal pursuits and animal migration patterns. The federal government tried to persuade the Plains tribes to stay far away from white wagon trains and white settlers. Yet this policy was meaningless to Native Americans. As Lone Horn, a Miniconjon chief, explained when American commissioners at the 1851 Fort Laramie Council asked him if he would be satisfied to live on the Missouri River, "When the buffalo comes close to the river, we come close to it. When the buffaloes go off, we go off after them." The concept of land ownership and settled life made little sense to the Plains Indians, just as nomadic life seemed barbarous to whites.

During the Civil War, tribes that President Andrew Jackson had earlier resettled in Oklahoma divided in their support of the Union and the Confederacy. Some of the tribes kept slaves. Most feared that northerners could not be trusted. Thus some of the tribes sided with the Confederacy, while others remained loyal to the Union. After the war, however, all "were treated as traitors." The federal govenment nullified earlier pledges and treaties, leaving Indians defenseless against further incursions on "their" lands. As settlers pushed into Kansas, Indians living in Kansas were shunted into Oklahoma.

## The White Perspective

At the end of the Civil War, a state of war existed between red and white men on the Plains. The shameful massacre of friendly Cheyenne at Sand Creek, Colorado, by the Colorado Volunteers in 1864 sparked widespread hostilities. Although not all whites condoned the slaughter, the deliberations of the congressional commission authorized to make peace on the Plains illustrated the limits of their point of view. The commission, which included the commander of the Army in the West, Civil War hero General William T. Sherman, accepted as fact that "an industrious, thrifty, and enlightened population" of whites would occupy most of the West. All Native Americans, the commission believed, should relocate in one of two areas: the western half of present-day South Dakota, and Oklahoma. There they would learn the ways of white society and receive instruction in agricultural and mechanical arts. The offer of annuities, food, and clothes, it was

thought, would help placate the Indians and ease their transition from a "savage" to a "civilized" life.

At two major conferences in 1867 and 1868, Native American chiefs listened to these proposals. Some agreed with the terms; others did not. As Santanta, a Kiowa chief, explained, "I don't want to settle. I love to roam over the prairies." In any case, the agreements extracted were not binding since none of the chiefs had authority to speak for their tribes. The U.S. Senate dragged its feet in approving the treaties. The Cheyenne, Kiowa, and Comanche took to the warpath. Supplies promised to Indians who settled in the reserved areas failed to materialize, and wildlife proved too sparse to support them. These Indians soon drifted back to their former hunting grounds.

As General Sherman had warned, however, "All who cling to their old hunting ground are hostile and will remain so till killed off." To his brother he had written, "The more we can kill

*Comanche leader Asa-to-yet, photographed c. 1870, demonstrates by his dress the clash between cultures that Native Americans continued to face.*

this year, the less will have to be killed the next war." Sherman entrusted General Philip Sheridan with the duty of dealing with the Indians in 1867. Sheridan introduced a new tactic of winter campaigning. The intent was to seek out the Indians who divided into small groups during the winter and to exterminate them.

The completion of the transcontinental railroad in 1869 added yet another pressure for "solving" the Indian question. Transcontinental railroads wanted rights-of-way through Indian lands and needed white settlers to make their operations profitable. Not only did they carry thousands of hopeful settlers to the West, but miners and hunters as well.

In his 1872 annual report, the commissioner for Indian affairs, Francis Amasa Walker, addressed the two fundamental questions troubling whites: how to prevent Indians from blocking movement and settlement throughout the Great Plains and what to do with them once they had been controlled. Walker wanted to buy the "savages" off since they could, after all, mount 8,000 warriors in the field. With promises of food and gifts, he hoped to lure them onto reservations, where they would be subjected to "a rigid reformatory discipline."

Coercion would be necessary since Indians, according to Walker, were "unused to manual labor, and physically unqualified for it by the habits of the chase . . . without forethought and without self control . . . with strong animal appetites and no intellectual tastes or aspirations to hold those appetites in check." The reservations he described in his proposal for their betterment sounded more like prisons than schools. Indians could not leave the reservation without permission and could be arrested if they tried to do so. Though Walker considered himself to be a "friend of humanity" and wished to save the Indians from destruction, he also thought that their only choice was to "yield or perish."

## The Tribal View

Native Americans did not yield passively to such attacks on their ancient way of life and to the violation of treaties. Black Elk remembered that in 1863, when he was only 3, his father had his leg broken in a fierce battle against the white men. "When I was older," he recalled,

I learned what the fighting was about. . . . Up on the Madison Fork the Wasichus had found much of the yellow metal that they worship and that makes them crazy, and they wanted to have a road up through our country to the place where the yellow metal was; but my people did not want the road. It would scare the bison and make them go away, and also it would let the other Wasichus come in like a river. They told us that they

*The spectacular Native American victory over General Custer's army in 1876 had little effect on the onslaught of white civilization.*

wanted only to use a little land, as much as a wagon would take between the wheels; but our people knew better.

Black Elk's father and many others soon decided that fighting was their only recourse. "There was no other way to keep our country." But "wherever we went, the soldiers came to kill us, and it was all our country."

Broken promises fed Indian resistance. In 1875, the federal govenment allowed gold prospectors to stream into the Black Hills, part of the Sioux reservation and considered a holy place by them. The Sioux, led by Chiefs Sitting Bull, Crazy Horse, and Rain-in-the-Face, took to the warpath. Despite their victory over General George Custer at the Battle of Little Big Horn in 1876, the well-supplied and well-armed U.S. Army finally overwhelmed them. Crazy Horse was murdered. Elsewhere, General Sherman defeated Native American tribes in Texas, while in the Pacific Northwest, Nez Percé Chief Joseph surrendered.

An important ingredient of white victory was the wholesale destruction of the buffalo. The animals were central to the Indian way of life, culture, and religion. As one Pawnee chief explained, "Am afraid when we have no meat to offer, Great Spirit . . . will be angry & punish us." But the herds of buffalo gradually died out as railroads crossed the Plains with settlers, miners, and hunters. Eager sportsmen shot the beasts from train windows. Railroad crews ate the meat. Cattle competed for grass. The demand for buffalo bones for fertilizer and hides for robes and shoes encouraged the destruction.

The slaughter, which had claimed 13 million animals by 1883, is one that many modern wildlife enthusiasts find disgraceful. The Indians considered white men demented. "They just killed and killed because they liked to do that," said one, while when "we hunted the bison . . . [we] killed only what we needed." But the slaughter fitted the plans of those determined to curb the movements of Native Americans. As Secretary of the Interior Columbus Delano explained in 1872, "I cannot regard the rapid disappearance of the game from its former haunts as a matter prejudicial to our management of the Indians." Rather, he said, "as they become convinced that they can no longer rely upon the supply of game for their support, they will return to the more reliable source of subsistence furnished at their agencies."

### The Dawes Act

Changes in federal policy also contributed to the disintegration of Native American culture and life. In 1870, Congress ended the practice, in effect since the 1790s, of treating the tribes as sovereign nations. This attempt to undermine tribal integrity and the prestige of tribal leaders (who would no longer be recognized as speaking for their tribes) was accompanied by other measures. The government urged tribes to establish court systems in place of tribal justice and extended federal jurisdiction to the reservations. Tribes were also warned not to gather for religious ceremonies.

The Dawes Severalty Act of 1887 pulled together the strands of federal Indian policy that emerged after the Civil War and set its course for the rest of the century. The legislation ended the traditional policy of treating individual Indians as members of their tribes. Believing that tribal bonds kept Indians in savagery, reformers intended to destroy them. As Theodore Roosevelt noted approvingly, the bill was "a mighty pulverizing engine to break up the tribal mass." Rather than allotting reservation lands to tribal groups, the legislation declared that each individual family head was eligible for a homestead grant of 160 acres. By holding out this lure, the framers of the bill hoped to encourage Indians to settle in one place and to farm as white men did. Those who accepted allotments would become citizens and presumably forget their tribal identity. Although Indian agents explained that Native Americans opposed the Dawes Act, Congress did not hesitate to legislate on their behalf.

Another motive was also at work. Even if each Indian male claimed 160 acres, millions of "surplus" acres would remain for sale and for white settlement. Within 20 years of the Dawes Act, Native Americans had lost 60 percent of their lands. The federal govenment held the profits from land sales "in trust" and used them for the "civilizing" mission.

Weekly and monthly magazines constitute a rich primary source for the historian, offering a vivid picture of the issues of the day and useful insights into popular tastes and values. With advances in the publishing industry and an increasingly literate population, the number of these journals soared in the years following the Civil War. In 1865, only 700 periodicals were published. Twenty years later there were 3,300. As the *National Magazine* grumbled, "Magazines, magazines, magazines! The news-stands are already groaning under the heavy load, and there are still more coming."

Some of these magazines were aimed at the mass market. *Frank Leslie's Illustrated Newspaper*, established in 1855, was one of the most successful. At its height, circulation reached 100,000. Making skillful use of pictures (sometimes as large as 2 by 3 feet and folded into the magazine), the weekly magazine covered important news of the day as well as music, drama, sports, and books. Although Leslie relied more heavily on graphics and sensationalism than modern news weeklies, his publication was a forerunner of *Newsweek* and *Time*.

Another kind of weekly magazine was aimed primarily at middle- and upper-class readers. Editors like the oft-quoted Edwin Lawrence Godkin of *The Nation*, with a circulation of about 30,000, hoped to influence those in positions of authority and power by providing a forum for the discussion of reform issues. In contrast, *Scribner's* revealed a more conservative, middle-of-the-road point of view. Both magazines, however, exuded a confident, progressive tone characteristic of middle-class Americans.

*Harper's Weekly* was one of the most important magazines designed primarily for middle- and upper-class readers. Established in 1857, this publication continued in print until 1916. The success of *Harper's Weekly*, which called itself a "family newspaper," rested on a combination of its moderate point of view and an exciting use of illustrations and cartoons touching on contemporary events. In this magazine, for example, are found the cartoons of Thomas Nast. In large part because of the use of graphics, in 1872 the circulation of *Harper's Weekly* reached a peak of 160,000.

Illustrated here is a page from the January 16, 1869, issue of *Harper's Weekly*. The layout immediately suggests the importance of graphics. Most of the page is taken up with the three pictures. The top and bottom pictures are wood engravings based on drawings by Theodore R. Davis, one of *Harper's* best known illustrator-reporters. The center picture was derived from a photograph.

The story featured on this page concerns a victory of General George Custer in the war against the Cheyenne tribe. Davis had been a correspondent in the West covering Custer's actions in 1867. But when news of Custer's victory arrived, Davis was back in New York. He thus drew upon his imagination for the two scenes reproduced on this page. What kind of characterization of Native Americans does Davis give in the picture at the top of the page? What view of American soldiers does he suggest? At the bottom of the page, you can see soldiers slaughtering "worthless" horses while Cheyenne tepees burn in the background. Would the average viewer have any sympathy for the plight of the Cheyennes by looking at this picture? This "victory," in fact, involved not only the slaughter of horses but also of all males over age 8.

The editors' decision to insert a picture that had nothing to do with the incident being reported was obviously significant. As you can see, the subject is a white hunter who had been killed and scalped by Indians. What kind of special relationship were the editors suggesting by placing the picture of one dead white hunter in the center of a page that primarily covered a specific conflict between the Indians and the U.S. Army? How might the reader respond to the group of pictures as a whole? How do you? How does the text contribute to the overall view of the Indian–white relationship that the pictures suggest? By considering the choice of graphics and text, you can begin to discover how magazines provide insight, not only into the events of the day but also into the ways magazines shaped the values and perspectives of nineteenth-century men and women.

**Harper's Weekly, *January 16, 1869***

# MAGAZINES

CUSTER'S INDIAN SCOUTS CELEBRATING THE VICTORY OVER BLACK KETTLE.—[SKETCHED BY THEO. R. DAVIS.]

## THE INDIAN WAR.

THE Indian Peace Commission of 1867 accomplished greater harm than benefit. Treaties were entered into with the Cheyennes, Arrapahoes, Kiowas, Comanches, and at the recommendation of the Commission the Powder River country was abandoned. This latter action was construed as the result of timidity on the part of the Government, and immediately the Sioux extended their depredations to the Pacific Railroad, on the Platte, while the Indians south of the Arkansas attempted to drive the whites out of the Smoky Hill country.

Last August the Cheyennes took the war-path, and the valleys of the Saline and Solomon rivers became the theatre of a relentless savage war. It was at first supposed that the Cheyennes were about to attack a hostile tribe, but soon the mask was laid aside, and in less than a month one hundred whites fell victims to the tomahawk and scalping-knife. The chiefs of the Arrapahoes had promised to

. THE SCALPED HUNTER.—[PHOTOGRAPHED BY WM. S. SOULE.]

proceed to Fort Cobb and get their annuities, and thence withdraw to their reservation. Instead of fulfilling their promises, they began a series of depredations on the line between Fort Wallace and Denver, in Colorado Territory. The Kiowas and Comanches about the same time entered into an agreement at Fort Zarah to remain at peace, and left with that impression fixed on the minds of those who represented the Government. The next information was that the Kiowas and Comanches had joined the Cheyennes and Arrapahoes. General SHERIDAN, taking the practical view of the condition of affairs within the limits of his department, at once transferred his head-quarters to the field, and commenced preparations for a determined war. General SULLY'S fight near this point, FORSYTH'S gallant fight on the Arrikaree fork of the Republican, CARPENTER'S and GRAHAM'S fight on the Beaver branch of the Republican, General CARR'S decisive fight in the same vicinity, and General CUS-

CUSTER'S COMMAND SHOOTING DOWN WORTHLESS HORSES.—[SKETCHED BY THEO. R. DAVIS.]

## Ghost Dance

By the 1890s, Native Americans were curbed but not entirely broken. The Ghost Dance movement, which envisioned help from the Great Spirit rather than the Indians themselves, indicated tribal weakness. Based on the promises of the Paiute prophet Wovoka, who told believers that natural disasters would strike down whites while Indians, dancing as ghosts, avoided destruction, the movement spread from tribe to tribe. Believers expressed their faith and hope by rituals of dancing and meditation. The more frequently they danced, the quicker the whites were to vanish.

Although Wovoka prophesied that whites would disappear without the assistance of Indians, American settlers were not so sure. Indian agents tried to prevent the dancing. When the Indians refused, attempts were made to arrest a Sioux medicine man, Sitting Bear. In the confusion of arrest, Sitting Bear was killed. Bands of Sioux left the reservation. The army followed in swift pursuit. Using the most up-to-date machine guns, the army massacred 200 men, women, and children, in the snow at Wounded Knee in 1890.

Thus arose the lament of Black Elk, who saw his people diminished, starving, despairing:

> Once we were happy in our own country and we were seldom hungry, for then the two-leggeds and the four-leggeds lived together like relatives, and there was plenty for them and for us. But then the Wasichus came, and they have made little islands for us and other islands for the four-leggeds, and always these islands are becoming smaller, for around them surges the gnawing flood of the Washichus; and it is dirty with lies and greed.

# THE NEW SOUTH

Of all the nation's agricultural regions, the South was the poorest. In 1880, southerners' yearly earnings were only half the national average. But despite poverty and backwardness, some southerners during the late nineteenth century dreamed of making the agricultural South the rival of the industrial North.

The vision of a modern, progressive, and self-sufficient South had roots in the troubled decade of the 1850s. At that time, southern intellectuals and writers had argued that the South must throw off its dependence on the North and on cotton. "The smoke of the steam engine should begin to float over the cotton fields, and the hum of spindles and the click of looms make music on all our mountain streams," the editor of the New Orleans *Picayune* insisted.

## Southerners Face the Future

But not enough southerners had listened. Now, after the disastrous experience of war and reconstruction, the cry for regional self-sufficiency grew sharper. Publicists of the movement for a "New South" argued that southern backwardness did not stem from the war itself, as so many southerners wished to believe, but from basic conditions in southern life, a rural economy based on cotton foremost among them. The defeat only made clearer the reality of the nineteenth century. Power and wealth came not from cotton but from factories, machines, and cities.

Henry Grady, editor of the Atlanta *Constitution* and the New South's most famous spokesman, dramatized the need for change with his story of a southerner's funeral:

> They buried him in the midst of a marble quarry; they cut through solid marble to make his grave; and yet a little tombstone they put above him was from Vermont. They buried him in the heart of a pine forest, and yet the pine coffin was imported from Cincinnati. They buried him within touch of an iron mine, and yet the nails in his coffin and the iron in the shovel that dug his grave were imported from Pittsburgh. . . . They put him away . . . in a New York coat and a Boston pair of shoes and a pair of breeches from Chicago and a shirt from Cincinnati, leaving him

nothing to carry into the next world with him to remind him of the country in which he lived and for which he fought for four years, but the chill of blood in his veins and the marrow in his bones."

Regional pride and self-interest clearly dictated a new course. As Grady told a Boston audience in 1886, industrial advances would allow the South to match the North in another, more peaceful contest. "We are going to take a noble revenge," he said, "by invading every inch of your territory with iron, as you invaded ours twenty-nine years ago."

In hundreds of speeches, editorials, pamphlets, articles, and books, spokesmen for the New South tried to persuade fellow southerners of the need for change. Southerners must abandon prewar ideals that glorified leisure and gentility and adopt the ethic of hard work. To lure northern bankers and capitalists, New South advocates held out attractive investment possibilities. Since the South was short of capital, northern assistance was as critical to realizing the dream as was southern cooperation. Thus, said one New South advocate persuasively, "the profits to be reaped from investments in the South . . . appear to be fabulous." He confidently predicted that the South would become the "El Dorado of the next half century."

These arguments did not fall on deaf ears. In a bid to attract manufacturers, several southern state governments offered tax exemptions and cheap labor based on leasing state prison convicts. Texas and Florida awarded the railroads land grants, and cities like Atlanta and Louisville mounted huge industrial exhibitions as incentives to industrial progress. Middle-class southerners were impressed and increasingly accepted new entrepreneurial values in place of prewar ideals of leisure and gentility. The most startling example of commitment to the vision of a New South may have come in 1886 when southern railroad companies decided to bring their tracks into line with the "standard" northern gauges. On a Sunday in May, 8,000 men equipped with sledgehammers and crowbars attacked the 2,000 miles of track belonging to the Louisville and Nashville Railroad Company and moved the western rail 3 inches to the east. On that same day, they also adjusted the iron wheels of 300 locomotives and 10,000 pieces of rolling stock to fit the new gauge.

During the late nineteenth century, northern money flowed south as dollars replaced the moral fervor and political involvement of the Civil War and Reconstruction years. In the 1880s, northerners increased their investment in the cotton industry sevenfold and financed the expansion of the southern railroad system. In turn, northern investments stimulated southern cities to embark on an extended period of expansion. By 1900, some 15 percent of all southerners lived in cities, whereas only 7 percent had in 1860. (The national averages for these years were 40 percent and 20 percent, respectively.)

The city of Birmingham, Alabama, became one of the symbols of the New South. In 1870, the site of the future city was a peaceful cornfield. The next year, two northern real estate speculators arrived on the scene, encouraged in their booster schemes by the area's rich iron deposits. Despite a siege of cholera and the depression of the 1870s, Birmingham became within a 30-year period the center of the southern iron and steel industry. By 1890, a total of 38,414 people lived in the city. Coke ovens, blast furnaces, rolling mills, iron foundries, and machine shops belched smoke where once there had only been fields. Millions of dollars of finished goods poured forth from the city's mills and factories and were carried away over eight railroad lines.

Other southern cities flourished as well. Memphis prospered from its lumber industry and the manufacturing of cottonseed products, while Richmond became the country's tobacco capital even as its flour mills and iron and steel foundries continued to produce wealth. Augusta, Georgia, became the "Lowell of the South," a leader in the emerging textile industry that blossomed in Georgia, North and South Carolina, and Alabama. Augusta's eight cotton mills employed about 2,800 workers, many of them women and children.

## The Other Side of Progress

New South leaders, a small group of merchants, industrialists, and planters, bragged about the growth of the iron and textile industries and paraded statistics to prove the success of efforts to modernize. The South, one writer boasted, was "throbbing with industrial and railroad activity." But despite such optimism about matching or even surpassing the North's economic performance, the South made slow progress.

Older values persisted. Indeed, New South spokesmen paradoxically kept older chivalric values alive by romanticizing the recent past. "In the eyes of Southern people," one publication asserted, "all Confederate veterans are heroes." Loyalty to the past impeded full acceptance of a new economic order. It was significant that despite the interest in modernization, the southern school system lagged far behind that of the North.

Although new industries and signs of progress abounded, the South did not better its position relative to the North. Whereas in 1860 the South had 17 percent of the country's manufacturing concerns, by 1904 it had only 15 percent. During the same period, the value of its manufactures grew from 10.3 percent of the total value of manufactures in the United States to only 10.5 percent. Commerce and government work still were responsible for urban growth, as they had been before the Civil War. The South's achievements were not insignificant during a period in which northern industry and cities rapidly expanded, but they were not enough to make the South the equal of the North.

Moreover, the South failed to reap many of the benefits of industrialization. Southern businessmen like Richmond banker and railroad president John Skelton Williams hoped "to see in the South in the not distant future many railroads and business institutions as great as the Pennsylvania Railroad, the Mutual Life Insurance Company, the Carnegie Steel Company or the Standard Oil Company." This was not to happen. As in the antebellum period, the South was an economic vassal of the North.

Southern industrialism did not change that status. There were more and more southern businessmen, but with the exception of the American Tobacco Company, no great southern corporations arose. Instead, southerners worked for northern companies and corporations, which absorbed southern businesses or dominated them financially. By 1900, for example, five corporations directed three-quarters of the railroad mileage in the South (excluding Texas), and northern bankers controlled all five. Northerners also took over the southern steel industry.

As this happened, profits flowed north. "Our capitalists are going into your country," the Lowell *Manufacturers' Record* accurately noted, "because they see a chance to make money there, but you must not think that they will give your people the benefit of the money they make. That will come North and enrich their heirs, or set up public libraries in our country towns." As dollars fled north, so too went the power to make critical decisions. In many cases, northern directors determined that southern mills and factories could handle only the early stages of processing, while northern factories finished the goods. Thus southern cotton mills sent yarn and coarse cloth north for completion. Southern manufacturers who did finish their products, hoping to compete in the marketplace, found that railroad rate discrimination robbed their goods of any competitive edge.

Individual workers in the new industries may have found factory life preferable to sharecropping, but their rewards were meager. The thousands of women and children in factories were silent testimony to the fact their husbands and fathers could not earn sufficient wages to support them at home. As usual, women and children earned lower wages than men. Managers justified these policies toward women and children. The employment of children, claimed one Augusta factory president, was "a matter of charity with us; some of them would starve if they were not given employment. . . . Ours are not overworked. The work we give children is very light." Actually, many children at his factory were doing the same work as adults, for children's pay.

In general, all workers earned lower wages and worked longer hours in the South than elsewhere. Per capita income was the same in 1900 as it had been in 1860—and only half the national average. In North Carolina in the 1890s, workers were paid an average of 50 cents a day and toiled 70 hours a week. Black workers, who made up 6 percent of the southern manufacturing force in 1890 (but who were excluded from textile mills), usually had the worst jobs and lowest wages.

## Cotton Still King

Although New South advocates envisioned the South's transformation from a rural to an industrial society, they always recognized that agriculture had to be transformed as well. "It's time for an agricultural revolution," Grady proclaimed. "When we once decide that southern lands are fit for something else besides cotton, and then go to work in earnest to multiply and diversify our products and industries, independence and wealth will be the certain reward of our intelligent and industrious farmers."

The overdependence on "King Cotton" hobbled southern agriculture by making farmers the victims of faraway market forces and an oppressive credit system. Old cotton plantations must be subdivided into small diversified farms, Grady advised. He was especially impressed by the possibilities of truck farming, which could produce "simply wonderful profits." A good truck farm, he argued, "would give employment throughout the entire season, and at the end of it the fortunate farmer would have before him the assurance that diversified crops and a never-failing market alone afford, with no [fertilizer] . . . bills to settle, and no liens past or to come to disturb his mind."

A new agricultural South with new class and economic arrangements did emerge, but it was not the one Grady and others envisioned. Despite the breakup of some plantations following the Civil War, large landowners proved resourceful in holding on to their property and in dealing with postwar conditions, as Chapter 17 showed. As they adopted new agricultural arrangements, former slaves sank into debt peonage.

White farmers on small and medium-size holdings fared only slightly better in the New South than black tenants and sharecroppers. Immediately after the war, high cotton prices had tempted them to raise as much cotton as they could. Then prices began a disastrous decline (from 11 cents a pound in 1875 to less than 5 cents in 1894). "At the close of the war a 500 lb. bale of cotton would bring $100," a Cherokee County, Georgia, tenant complained in 1891, "and today it will bring $32.50." Yeoman farmers became entangled in debt. Each year, farmers found themselves buying supplies on credit from merchants so that they could plant the

*The predominance of cotton in southern agriculture remained unchallenged in the decades after the Civil War.*

next year's crop and support their families until harvest time. In return, merchants demanded their exclusive business and acquired a lien (or claim) on their crops. But when harvest time came and crops were sold (at declining prices), farmers usually discovered they had not earned enough to settle with the merchant, who had charged dearly for store goods and whose annual interest rates might exceed 100 percent. Each year, thousands of farmers fell further and further behind.

Such was the case of S. R. Simonton, a South Carolina farmer. Between 1887 and 1895, he spent $2,681 at T. G. Patrick's furnishing house. Because he could manage to pay back only $687, he lost his land and became a tenant farmer. Others shared the same fate. The number of tenants slowly crept upward, while the number of small independent farmers fell. By 1900, over half the South's white farmers and three-quarters of its black farmers were tenants. Although tenancy was increasingly all over rural America, nowhere did it rise more rapidly than in the Deep South.

These patterns had baneful results for individual southerners and for the South as a whole. Caught in a cycle of debt and poverty, few farmers could think of improving agricultural techniques or diversifying crops. In their desperate attempt to pay off debts, they concentrated on cotton, despite falling prices. "Cotton brings money, and money pays debt," was the small farmer's slogan. Landowners also pressured tenants to raise a market crop. Far from diversifying, as Grady had hoped, farmers increasingly limited the number of crops they raised. By 1880, the South was not growing enough food to feed its people adequately. Poor nutrition contributed to chronic bad health and sickness.

## The Nadir of Black Life

Grady and other New South advocates painted a picture of a strong, prosperous, and industrialized South, a region that could deal with the troublesome race issue without the interference of any "outside power." Grady had few regrets over the end of slavery, which he thought had contributed to southern economic backwardness. Moreover, since he realized that black labor would be crucial to the transformation he sought, he advocated racial cooperation.

But racial cooperation did not mean equality. Grady assumed that blacks were racially inferior and supported an informal system of segregation. "The negro is entitled to his freedom, his franchise, to full and equal legal rights," Grady wrote in 1883. But "social equality he can never have. He does not have it in the north, or in the east, or in the west. On one pretext or another, he is kept out of hotels, theatres, schools and restaurants."

By the time of Grady's death in 1889, a much harsher perspective on southern race relations was replacing his view. In 1891, at a national assembly of women's clubs in Washington, D.C., a black woman, Frances Ellen Watkins Harper, anticipated efforts to strip the vote from blacks and appealed to the white women at the meeting not to abandon black suffrage. "I deem it a privilege to present the negro," she said, "not as a mere dependent asking for Northern sympathy or Southern compassion, but as a member of the body politic who has a claim upon the nation for justice, simple justice." This claim, she continued, was for "protection to human life," for "the rights of life and liberty," and for relief from charges of ignorance and poverty. These were "conditions which men outgrow." Women, of all people, should understand this and not seek to achieve their own right to vote at the expense of the vote for black men. "Instead of taking the ballot from his hands, teach him how to use it, and add his quota to the progress, strength, and durability of the nation."

The decision by congressional leaders in 1890 to shelve a proposed act for protecting black civil rights and the defeat of the Blair bill providing federal assistance for educational institutions left black Americans vulnerable, as Frances Harper realized. The traditional sponsor of the rights of freedmen, the Republican party, left blacks to fend for themselves as a minority in the white South. The courts also abandoned blacks. In 1878, the Supreme Court declared unconstitutional a Louisiana statute banning discrimination in transportation. In 1882, the Court voided the Ku Klux Klan Act of 1871, deciding that the civil rights protections of the

Fourteenth Amendment applied to states rather than to individuals. In 1883, the provisions of the Civil Rights Act of 1875, which assured blacks of equal rights in public places, were declared unconstitutional.

Neither political nor media leaders in the North opposed these actions. In fact, northerners increasingly resorted to negative stereotypes in discussing blacks. They were pictured as either ignorant, lazy, loyal, childlike fools or as lying, stealing, raping degenerates. Obviously, they could not be left to themselves nor given the same rights and freedoms whites enjoyed. Instead, blacks needed the paternal protection of the superior white race. These stereotypes filled the magazines and newspapers and were perpetuated in cartoons, advertisements, "coon songs," serious art and theater, and the minstrel shows that dominated northern entertainment.

The *Atlantic Monthly* in 1890 anticipated a strong current in the magazine literature when it expressed doubts that this "lowly variety of man" could ever be brought up to the intellectual and moral standards of whites. Other magazines openly opposed suffrage as wasted on those too "ignorant, weak, lazy and incompetent" to make good use of it. *Forum* magazine suggested that "American Negroes" had "too much liberty." When this freedom was combined with natural "race traits" of stealing and hankering after white women, the *Forum* advised in 1893,

*Stereotypes of blacks in the popular media ranged from patronizing to defamatory.*

black crime increased. Only lynching and burning would work to deter the "barbarous" rapist and other "sadly degenerated" Negroes corrupted since the Civil War by independence and too much education. The author concluded that the Negro question was "more vital" than gold, silver, or the tariff. Unrestrained by northern public opinion, and with the blessing of Congress and the Supreme Court, southern citizens and legislatures sought to make blacks permanently second-class members of southern society.

In the political sphere, white southerners amended state constitutions to disenfranchise black voters. By various legal devices—the poll tax, literacy tests, "good character" and "understanding" clauses administered by white voter registrars, and all-white primary elections—blacks lost the right to vote. The most ingenious method was the "grandfather clause," which specified that only citizens whose grandfathers were registered to vote on January 1, 1867, could cast their ballots. This virtually excluded blacks. Beginning with Mississippi in 1890, all 11 former Confederate states changed their constitutions by 1910 to exclude the black vote. The results were dramatic. Louisiana, for example, contained 130,334 registered black voters in 1896. Eight years later, there were only 1,342.

A second tactic in the 1890s was the passage of state and local laws that legalized informal segregation in public facilities. Beginning with railroads and schools, "Jim Crow" laws were extended to libraries, hotels, restaurants, hospitals, asylums, prisons, theaters, parks and playgrounds, cemeteries, toilets, morgues, sidewalks, drinking fountains, and nearly every possible place where blacks and whites might intermingle. The Supreme Court upheld these laws in 1896 in *Plessy* v. *Ferguson* by declaring that "separate but equal" facilities did not violate the equal protection clause of the Fourteenth Amendment. The Court's decision opened the way for as many forms of legal segregation as the imaginations of southern lawmakers could devise.

Political and social discrimination made it ever more possible to keep blacks permanently confined to agricultural and unskilled labor and dependent on whites for their material welfare.

In 1900, nearly 84 percent of black workers nationwide engaged in some form of agricultural labor as farmhands, overseers, sharecroppers, or tenant or independent farmers or in service jobs, primarily domestic service and laundry work. These had been the primary slave occupations. The remaining 16 percent worked in forests, sawmills, mines, and, with northward migration, in northern cities. Gone were the skilled black tradesmen of slavery days. At the end of the Civil War, at least half of all skilled craftsmen in the South had been black. But by the 1890s, the percentage had decreased to less than 10 percent, as whites systematically excluded blacks from the trades. Such factory work as blacks had been doing was also reduced, largely in order to drive a wedge between poor blacks and whites to prevent unionization. In Greensboro, North Carolina, for example, where in 1870 some 30 percent of all blacks worked in skilled trades or factory occupations, by 1910 blacks in the skilled trades had been reduced to 8 percent, and not a single black worked in a Greensboro factory. The exclusion of blacks from industry prevented them from acquiring the skills and habits that would enable them to rise into the middle class as would many European immigrants and their children by the mid-twentieth century.

Blacks did not accept their declining position passively. In the mid-1880s, they enthusiastically joined the mass worker organization, the Knights of Labor (discussed in Chapter 19), first in cities such as Richmond and Atlanta, then in rural areas. As one South Carolina black explained, "We are bo[u]nd to join something what will lead to better rights than we have." Probably blacks made up between half and a third of the Knights' membership in the South. But southern whites grated at the Knights' policies of racial cooperation, fearing that economic cooperation might lead to social equality. "The forcing of a colored man among the white people here had knocked me out of the order," reported one. The Charleston *News and Courier* warned of the dangers of "miscegenation" and claimed that the South would be left "in the possession of . . . mongrels and hybrids." As blacks continued to join it, whites abandoned the order in growing numbers. The flight of whites weakened the organization in the South, and a backlash of white violence finally smashed it.

Against this backdrop, incidents of lawless lynchings and other forms of violence against blacks increased. On February 21, 1891, the New York *Times* reported that in Texarkana, Arkansas, a mob apprehended a 32-year-old black man, Ed Coy, charged with the rape of a white woman, tied him to a stake, and burned him alive. As Coy proclaimed his innocence to a large crowd, his alleged victim herself somewhat hesitatingly put the torch to his oil-soaked body. The *Times* report concluded that only by the "terrible death such as fire . . . can inflict" could other blacks "be deterred from the commission of like crimes." Ed Coy was one of over 1,400 black men lynched or burned alive during the 1890s. About a third were charged with sex crimes. The rest were accused of a variety of "crimes" related to not knowing their place: marrying or insulting a white woman, testifying in court against whites, having "a bad reputation."

## Diverging Black Responses

White discrimination and exploitation nourished new protest tactics and ideologies among blacks. For years, Frederick Douglass had been proclaiming that blacks should remain loyal Americans and count on the promises of the Republican party. But on his deathbed in 1895, his last words were allegedly "Agitate! Agitate! Agitate!"

Among black expressions of protest, one was a woman's. In Memphis, Tennessee, Ida B. Wells, the first woman to become editor of an important newspaper, launched a campaign against lynching in 1892. So hostile was the response from the white community that Wells carried a gun to protect herself. When white citizens finally destroyed the press and threatened her partner, Wells left Memphis to pursue her activism elsewhere.

Other voices called for black separatism within white America. T. Thomas Fortune wrote in the black New York *Freeman* in 1887 that "there will one day be an African Empire." Three years later, he organized the Afro-American League (a precursor of the NAACP), insisting that blacks must join together to fight the rising tide of discrimination. "Let us stand up," he urged, "in our own organization where color will not be a brand of odium." The league encouraged independent voting, opposed segregation and lynching, and urged the establishment of black institutions like banks to support black businesses. As a sympathetic journalist explained, "The solution of the problem is in our own hands. . . . The Negro must preserve his identity."

While some promoted black nationalism, most blacks worked patiently but persistently within white society for equality and social justice. In 1887, J. C. Price formed the Citizens Equal Rights Association, which supported the continuation of various petitions and direct-action campaigns to protest segregation. The Association also called for state laws to guarantee equal rights in the aftermath of the Supreme Court's 1883 ruling. Other blacks boycotted streetcars in southern cities, and Daniel Payne, a Methodist bishop, got off the Jim Crow car on a Florida train and with great ceremony walked to a church conference. Other blacks petitioned Congress, demanding reparations for unpaid labor as slaves.

Effort to escape oppression in the South, like "Pap" Singleton's movement to found black towns in Tennessee and Kansas, continued. In the 1890s, black leaders lobbied to make the Oklahoma Territory, recently opened to white settlement, an all-black state. Blacks founded 25 towns there, as well as in other states and even Mexico. But these attempts, like earlier ones, were short-lived, crippled by limited funds and the hostility of white neighbors. Singleton eventually recommended migration to Canada or Liberia as a final solution, and later black nationalist leaders also looked increasingly to Africa. Bishop Henry McNeal Turner, a former Union soldier and prominent black leader, despaired of ever securing equal rights for blacks in the United States. He described the Constitution as "a dirty rag, a cheat, a libel" and said that it ought to be "spit upon by every Negro in the land." In 1894, he organized the International Migration Society to return blacks to Africa, arguing that "this country owes us forty billions of dollars" to help. He succeeded in sending two boatloads of emigrants to Liberia, but this colonization effort worked no more successfully than those earlier in the century.

As Douglass had long argued, no matter how important African roots might be, blacks had been in the Americas for generations and would have to win justice and equal rights here. W. E. B. Du Bois, the first black to receive a Ph.D. from Harvard, agreed. Yet in 1900, he attended the first Pan-African Conference in London, where he argued that blacks must lead the struggle for liberation both in Africa and in the United States. It was at this conference that Du Bois first made his prophetic comment that "the problem of the Twentieth Century" would be "the problem of the color line."

Despite these vigorous voices of militant anger and nationalistic fervor, most black Americans continued to follow the slow, moderate self-help program of Booker T. Washington, the best-known black leader in America. Born a slave, Washington had risen through hard and obedient work to become the founder (in 1881) and principal of Tuskegee Institute in Alabama, which he personally and dramatically built into the largest and best-known industrial training school in the country. At Tuskegee, young blacks received a highly disciplined education in scientific agricultural techniques and vocational skilled trades. Washington believed that economic self-help and the familiar Puritan virtues of hard work, frugality, cleanliness, and moderation were the way to success. He spent much of his time traveling the North to secure generous gifts to support Tuskegee from northern philanthropists. In time, he became a favorite of the American entrepreneurial elite.

In 1895, Washington was asked to deliver a speech at the Cotton States and International Exposition in Atlanta, celebrating three decades of industrial and agricultural progress since the Civil War. He took advantage of that invitation, a rare honor for the former slave, to make a significant statement about the position of blacks in the South. Without a hint of protest, Washington decided "to say something that would cement the friendship of the races." He therefore proclaimed black loyalty to the economic development of the South while accepting the lowly status of southern blacks. "It is at the bottom of life we must begin, and not at the top," he declared. "In all things that are purely social we can be as separate as the fingers, yet one as the hand in all things essential to mutual progress." Washington also effectively renounced black interest in either the vote or civil rights as well as social equality with whites. Whites throughout the country enthusiastically acclaimed Washington's address, but many blacks called his "Atlanta Compromise" a serious setback in the struggle for black rights.

Washington has often been charged with conceding too quickly that political rights should follow rather than precede economic well-being. In 1903, Du Bois confronted Washington directly in *The Souls of Black Folk*, arguing instead for the "manly assertion" of a program of equal civil rights, suffrage, and high-

er education in the ideals of liberal learning. A trip through the black belt of Dougherty County, Georgia, showed Du Bois the "forlorn and forsaken" condition of southern blacks. The young sociologist saw that most blacks were confined to various forms of dependent agricultural labor, "fighting a hard battle with debt" year after year. Although "here and there a man has raised his head above these murky waters . . . a pall of debt hangs over the beautiful land." Beneath all others was the cotton picker, who, with the help of his wife and children, would have to work from sunup to sundown to pick the 100 pounds of cotton to make 50 cents. The lives of most blacks were still tied to the land of the South. If they were to improve their lives, rural blacks would have to organize.

## PROTESTING FARMERS

During the post–Civil War period, many farmers both black and white, began to realize that only by organizing could they hope to ameliorate the conditions of rural life. Not all were dissatisfied with their lot, however. Midwestern farmers and farmers near city markets successfully adjusted to new economic conditions and had little reason for discontent. As this chapter has pointed out, however, farmers in both the South and the West faced new problems and difficulties. Many of them were ready to join farm organizations.

### The Grange

The earliest effort to organize white farmers came in 1867 when Oliver Kelley founded the National Grange of the Patrons of Husbandry. At first the organization emphasized social and cultural goals. The Grange hoped to encourage "a cordial and social fraternity of the farmers all over the country," Kelly explained. Farmers needed to become progressive—"to read and think, to plant fruit and flowers, [and] beautify their homes."

The social and fraternal goals were shortly joined by other more aggressive ones. Dudley Adams, speaking to an Iowa Grange in 1870,

pointed to the powerlessness of "the immense helpless mob" of farmers who were the victims of "human vampires." Their salvation lay in organization, Adams maintained.

More and more farmers, especially those in the Midwest and the South, agreed with Adams. The depression of the 1870s (discussed in Chapter 19) sharpened discontent. By 1875, an estimated 800,000 had joined the Grange. The "Farmers' Declaration of Independence," read before local granges on July 4, 1873, captured the new activist spirit. The time had come, the declaration announced, for farmers suffering from "oppression and abuse" to rouse themselves and, by "all lawful and peaceful means," to cast off "the tyranny of monopoly." While the declaration clearly expressed rural discontent, it gave few indications that Grangers recognized the complex reasons for their problems.

Grangers were looking for culprits close to home. Middlemen seemed to be obvious examples of the oppressors. They gouged the American farmer by raising the prices of finished goods farmers needed to buy and by lowering the prices they received for their products. Some of the Granger "reforms" attempted to bypass middlemen by establishing buying and selling cooperatives. Although many of the cooperatives failed, they indicated that farmers realized that they could not respond to new conditions on an individual basis but needed to act collectively.

Operators of grain elevators also drew fire. Midwestern farmers claimed that these merchants often misgraded their wheat and corn and paid less than its worth. But the railroads, America's first big business, were the greatest offenders. As the next chapter will show, cutthroat competition among railroad companies generally brought lower rates. But even though rates dropped nationwide, the railroads often set high rates in rural areas. Moreover, railroads awarded discriminatory rebates to large shippers and put small operators at a disadvantage.

Although the Grange was originally nonpolitical, farmers recognized that they had to take political action if they were to confront the mighty railroads. Other groups also wished to see some controls imposed on the railroads.

*Originally a social organization, the Grange soon adopted a political agenda to represent agrarian interests.*

Many western businessmen were victimized by railroad policies that favored large Chicago grain terminals and long-distance shippers over local concerns. Between 1869 and 1874, both businessmen and farmers in Illinois, Iowa, Wisconsin, and Minnesota lobbied for state railroad laws. The resulting Granger Laws (an inaccurate name because the Grangers should not be given complete credit for them) established the maximum rates railroads and grain elevators could charge. Other states passed legislation setting up railroad commissions with power to regulate railroad rates. In some states, railroad pools were declared illegal, as were rebates, passes, and other practices that seemed to represent "unjust discrimination and distortion."

Railroad companies and grain elevators quickly challenged the legality of the new laws. In 1877, the Supreme Court upheld the legislation in *Munn* v. *Illinois.* Even so, it soon became apparent that although state commissions had authority over local rates and fares, they could not control long-haul rates. To make up for the money they lost on local hauls, railroads often raised long-haul charges, thus frustrating the intent of the laws. Other complicated issues involved determining what was a fair rate, who was competent to decide that rate, and what was a justifiable return for the railroad. The tangle of questions that state regulation raised proved difficult to resolve at the local level.

Although the Granger Laws failed to solve the questions involved in attempts to control the railroads, they established an important principle. As the Supreme Court decision made clear, state legislatures had the power to regulate businesses of a public nature like the railroads. But the failure of the Granger Laws led to greater pressure on Congress to continue the struggle against big business.

## Interstate Commerce Act

In 1887, Congress responded to farmers, railroad managers who wished to regulate the fierce competition that threatened to bankrupt their companies, and shippers who objected to transportation rates by passing the Interstate Commerce Act. That legislation required that railroad rates be "reasonable and just" and that rate schedules be made public and declared practices such as rebates illegal. The act also set up the first federal regulatory agency, the Interstate Commerce Commission (ICC). The ICC had the power to investigate and prosecute lawbreakers, but the legislation limited its authority to control over commerce conducted between states.

Like state railroad commissions, the ICC found it difficult to define a reasonable rate. Moreover, thousands of cases overwhelmed the tiny staff in the early months of operation. In the long run, the lack of enforcement power was most serious. The ICC's only recourse was to bring offenders into the federal courts and engage in lengthy legal proceedings. Few railroads worried about defying ICC directions on rates. When they appeared in court four or five years later, they often won their cases from judges suspicious of new federal authority. Between 1887 and 1906, a total of 16 cases made their way to the Supreme Court; 15 of them were decided in the railroads' favor. As one railroad executive candidly admitted, "There is not a road in the country that can be accused of living up to the rules of the Interstate Commerce Law."

## The Southern Farmers' Alliance

The Grange declined in the late 1870s as the nation recovered from depression. But neither farm organizations nor farm protest died. Depression struck farmers once again in the late 1880s and worsened as the 1890s began. Official statistics told the familiar, dismal story of falling prices for cereal crops grown on the plains and prairies. A bushel of wheat that had sold for $1 in 1870 was worth 60 cents in the 1890s. Kansas farmers, in 1889, were selling their corn for a mere 10 cents a bushel. The national currency shortage, which usually reached critical proportions at harvest time, helped to push agricultural prices ever lower. And while prices declined, the load of debt climbed. Mortgage rates ranged between 18 and 36 percent, and shipping rates were high. It sometimes cost a farmer as much as one bushel of corn to send another one to market.

A Kansas farmer's letter reveals some of the human consequences of such statistics:

> At the age of 52 years, after a long life of toil, economy and self-denial, I find myself and family virtually paupers. With hundreds of cattle, hundreds of hogs, scores of good horses, and a farm that rewarded the toil of our hands with 16,000 bushels of golden corn, we are poorer by many dollars than we were years ago. What once seemed a neat little fortune and a house of refuge for our declining years . . . has been rendered valueless.

Under these pressures, farmers turned again to organization, education, and cooperation. The Southern Farmers' Alliance was one of the most important reform organizations. Its roots stretched back to the late 1870s on the Texas frontier. A decade later, the Alliance launched an ambitious organizational drive, sending lecturers throughout the South and onto the western plains. Eventually, Alliance lecturers reached 43 states and territories, bringing their message to 2 million farming families.

Traveling lecturers explained the nature and goals of the Alliance, whipped up enthusiasm, and helped to establish state alliances. In turn, county alliances and local farmers' clubs, each with their own lecturers, were organized to complete a far-reaching agrarian network. Alliance newspapers like the *Progressive Farmer* in North Carolina and the *National Economist*, published in Washington, D.C., reinforced the message Alliance members heard at local, county, and state meetings.

An article in the *National Economist* pointed out some of the Alliance's fundamental beliefs. "The agricultural population of to-day is becoming rapidly aroused to the fact that agriculture, as a class, can only be rendered prosperous by radical changes in the laws governing money, transportation, and land." The economic and social position of farmers had slipped, even though as producers the farming class was critical to national well-being. The farmer's condition was, in the words of an Alliance song, "a sin," the result of the farmer's forgetting that "he's the man that feeds them all." Alliance lecturers proposed various programs that would help realize their slogan: "Equal rights to all, special privileges to none."

On the one hand, the Alliance experimented with buying and selling cooperatives in order to free farmers from the clutches of supply merchants, banks, and other credit agencies. Although these efforts often failed in the long run, they taught the value of cooperation to achieve common goals. On the other hand, the Alliance supported legislative efforts to regulate powerful monopolies and corporations, which they believed gouged the farmer. Many Alliance members also felt that increasing the money supply was critical to improving the position of farmers and supported a national banking system empowered to issue paper money.

The Alliance also called for a variety of measures to improve the quality of rural life: better public schools for rural children, state agricultural colleges, and an improvement in the status of women. "This order has the good sense, magnanimity and moral courage," declared Hattie Huntingdon of Louisiana, "to lay aside deeply-rooted prejudices handed down from the barbaric past and admit women into its fold and proclaim to the world that it believes in equal rights to all."

By 1890, discontent swept over America's farmlands. In the Midwest, where farmers were prospering by raising hogs and cattle on cheap grain, and in the East, where farmers were growing fruit and vegetables for urban markets, discontent was muted. But that summer in Kansas, hundreds of farmers packed their families into wagons to set off for Alliance meetings or to parade in long lines through the streets of nearby towns and villages. Floats garnished with evergreens proclaimed that the farmers' new organization focused on live issues, not the dead ones Congress debated.

Similar scenes occurred throught the West and the South. A farmer's wife, Zenobia Wheeless, captured the hopeful spirit of the protest in her letter to North Carolina Alliance leader Leonidas Polk. "We rode sixteen miles . . . to hear Brother Tracy [an organizer from Texas]— started about sun-up and trotted all the way . . . . Brother Tracy's lecture was very interesting . . . it seemed that all eyes were riv-

eted upon him." Zenobia's enthusiasm led her to write, "Brother Polk, if you will come to some of our appointments in reach of us, I will ride the same distance to hear a lecture from you, if I knew there would not be a single sister to accompany me." Never had there been such a wave of organizational activity in rural America. In 1890, more than a million farmers counted themselves as Alliance members.

The Alliance network also included black farmers. In 1888, black and white organizers established the Colored Farmers' Alliance, headed by a white Baptist minister, R. M. Humphrey. The Colored Farmers' Alliance recognized that black and white farmers faced common economic problems and must cooperate to ameliorate their shared plight. The fact that many southern cotton farmers depended on black labor and had a different perspective from blacks was not immediately recognized as a barrier. In 1891, however, cotton pickers working on plantations near Memphis, Tennessee, went on strike. White posses chased the strikers, lynched 15 of them, and demonstrated that racial tensions simmered just below the surface.

### The Ocala Platform

In December 1890, the National Alliance gathered in Ocala, Florida, to develop an official platform. As delegates deliberated, it became clear that most of them thought the federal government had failed to address the farmers' problems. "Congress must come nearer the people or the people will come nearer the Congress," warned the Alliance's president. Both parties were far too subservient to the "will of corporation and money power." Thus the platform called for the direct election of U.S. senators. Alliance members supported lowering the tariff, a much debated topic in Congress, but their justification, emphasizing the need to reduce prices for "the poor of our land," had a radical ring. Their money plank went far beyond what any national legislator was likely to consider. Rejecting the notion that only gold had value or, indeed, that precious metals had to be the basis for currency, Alliance leaders boldly envisioned a new banking system controlled by the federal govenment. They demanded that the government take an active economic role by increasing the amount of money in circulation in the form of Treasury notes and silver. More money would lead to inflation, higher prices, and a reduction in debt, they believed.

The platform also called for the creation of subtreasuries (federal warehouses) in agricultural regions where farmers could store their produce at low interest rates until market prices favored selling. To tide farmers over until that time, the federal government would loan farmers up to 80 percent of the current local price for their products. Thus the platform plan would free farmers from the twin evils of the credit merchant and depressed prices at harvest time. Other demands included a graduated income tax and support for the regulation of transportation and communication networks. If regulation failed, the government was called upon to take over both networks and run them for the public's benefit.

In the context of late nineteenth-century political life, almost all of these planks were radical. They demanded that the government take aggressive action to assist the country's farmers at a time when the government favored big business (see Chapter 20). Even though a majority of farmers did not belong to the Alliance, many Americans feared that the organization was capable of upsetting political arrangements. The New York *Sun* reported that the Alliance had caused a "panic" in the two major parties. The Alliance's warning that the people would replace their representatives unless they were better represented was already coming true. Although the Alliance was not formally in politics, it had supported sympathetic candidates in the fall elections of 1890. A surprising number of these local and state candidates had won. Alliance victories in the West harmed the Republican party enough to cause President Harrison to refer to "our election disaster."

Having entered politics indirectly, dissatisfied Alliance members pressed for an independent political party. For a short time they hoped that the Democratic party might respond to their concerns, but it soon appeared that legislators who courted Alliance votes conveniently forgot their pledges once elected. Alliance support did not necessarily bring action on issues of interest to farmers, nor even respect. One Texas farmer reported that the chairman of the state Democratic executive committee "calls us all skunks" and observed that "anything that has the scent of the plowhandle smells like a polecat" to the Democrats. On the national level, no one seemed much interested in the Ocala platform. As one North Carolinian observed, "I am not able to perceive any very great difference between the two parties."

Among the first to realize the necessity of forming an independent third party was Georgia's Tom Watson. "We are in the midst of a great crisis," he argued. "We have before us three or four platforms . . . [and] the Ocala platform is the best of all three. It is the only one that breathes the breath of life. . . . Let the Democratic party take warning." Watson also realized that electoral success in the South would depend on unity between white and black farmers.

### The People's Party

In February 1892, the People's, or Populist, party was established, with almost 100 black delegates in attendance. Leonidas Polk, president of the Alliance and promoter of a political coalition between the South and the West, emerged as the natural choice as the party's presidential candidate that fall. "The time has arrived," he thundered, "for the great West, the great South, and the great Northwest, to link their hands and hearts together and march to the ballot box and take possession of the government, restore it to the principles of our fathers, and run it in the interest of the people." But by the time the party met at its convention in July in Omaha, Nebraska, Polk had died. The party nominated James B. Weaver, a Civil War veteran from Iowa, as its presidential candidate, and James G. Field, a former Confederate soldier, for vice-president.

The platform preamble, written by Ignatius Donnelly, a Minnesota farmer, author, and politician, caught much of the urgent spirit of the agrarian protest movement in the 1890s:

We meet in the midst of a nation brought to the verge of moral, political and material ruin. Corruption dominates the ballot box, the legislatures, the Congress, and touches even the ermine of the bench. The people are demoralized. . . . The fruits of the toil of millions are boldly stolen to build up colossal fortunes . . . we breed two great classes—paupers and millionaires.

The charge was clear: "The controlling influences dominating the old political parties have allowed the existing dreadful conditions to develop without serious effort to restrain or prevent them."

The Omaha platform demands, drawn from the Ocala platform of 1890, were greatly expanded. They included more means of direct democracy (direct election of senators, direct primaries, the initiative, referendum, and the secret ballot) and several planks intended to enlist the support of urban labor (eight-hour day, immigration restriction, and condemnation of the use of Pinkerton agents as an "army of mercenaries . . . a menace to our liberties"). The People's party also endorsed a graduated income tax, the free and unlimited coinage of silver at a ratio of 16 to 1 (meaning that the U.S. Mint would have to buy silver for coinage at 1/16 the current official price of the equivalent amount of gold), and, rather than regulation, government ownership of railroads, telephone, and telegraph. "The time has come," the platform said, "when the railroad corporations will either own the people or the people must own the railroads."

The Populist party attempted to widen the nature of the American political debate to promote a new vision of the government's role, and to address the farmers' problems. But the tasks facing the party in its attempt to win power were monumental. Success at the polls meant weaning the South away from the Democratic party, encouraging southern whites to work with blacks, and persuading voters of both parties to abandon familiar political ties. Nor were all Alliance members eager to follow their leaders into the third party. At the most basic level, the Populists had to create the political machinery necessary to function in the 1892 electoral campaign.

Despite these obstacles, the new party pressed forward. Unlike the candidates of the major parties in 1892, Benjamin Harrison and Grover Cleveland, Weaver actively campaigned. In the South, he faced rowdy audiences, rotten eggs, and rocks from hostile Democrats, who disapproved of attempts to form a biracial political coalition. The results of the campaign were mixed. Although Weaver won over a million popular votes (the first third-party candidate to do so), he carried only four states (Kansas, Colorado, Idaho, and Nevada) and parts of two others (Oregon and North Dakota) for a total of 22 electoral votes. The attempt to break the stranglehold of the Democratic party on the South had failed. Democrats raised the cry of "nigger rule" and fanned racial fears. Those white farmers who viewed the alliance with blacks as one of necessity voted Democratic. Intimidation tactics and violence frightened off others. Just as important, Weaver failed to appeal to city workers, who were suspicious of the party's anti-urban tone and its desire for higher agricultural prices (which meant higher food prices); to people living east of the Mississippi; and even to relatively prosperous midwestern farmers, who saw little of value in the Omaha platform.

Although the People's party failed to appeal to a cross section of American voters in 1892, it gained substantial support. Miners and mine owners in states like Montana, Colorado, and New Mexico favored the demand for coinage of silver. Most populists, however, were rural Americans in the South and West who for one reason or another were out of the mainstream of American life. Economic grievances sharpened political discontent. But Populists were often no poorer or more debt-ridden than other farmers. They did tend to lead more isolated lives, however; often their farms were far from towns, villages, and railroads. They felt powerless to affect the workings of their political, social, and economic world. Thus they responded to a party offering to act as their advocate.

Farmers who were better integrated into their world tended to believe they could work through existing political parties. In 1892, when thousands of farmers and others were politically and economically discontented, they voted for Cleveland and the Democrats, not the Populists.

Yet the Populists did not lose heart in 1892, as Chapter 20 will show. Populist governors were elected in Kansas and North Dakota. The party swept Colorado. It was obvious that the showing of the party in the South, where even Tom Watson lost his bid for a congressional seat, stemmed from violent opposition and fraud on the part of the Democrats. Georgia Democrats manipulated black votes to defeat Populists. Returns in Richmond County revealed a Democratic majority of 80 percent in a total vote twice the size of the actual number of legal voters.

## CONCLUSION: The Reality of Agricultural America

The late nineteenth century was a turbulent time in rural America. The Indian "problem," which had plagued Americans for 200 years, was tragically solved for a while, but not without resistance and bloodshed. Few whites were troubled by these events. Most were caught up in the challenge of responding to a fast-changing world. Believing themselves to be the backbone of the nation, white farmers brought the Indian lands into cultivation, modernized their farms, and raised bumper crops. But success and a comfortable competency eluded many of them. Some, like Milton Leeper, never gave up hope or farming. Many were caught in a cycle of poverty and debt. Others fled to the cities, where they joined the industrial work force described in the next chapter. Many turned to collective action and politics. Their actions demonstrate that they did not merely react to events but attempted to shape them.

## Recommended Reading

Gilbert C. Fite provides a detailed study of the last agricultural frontier in *The Farmer's Frontier, 1865–1900* (1966). Henry Nash Smith discusses changing views of the Plains in *Virgin Land: The American West as Symbol and Myth* (1950). J. B. Jackson deals with the transformation of landscape in *American Space: The Centennial Years, 1865–1976* (1972). Annette Kolodny deals with women's perceptions of the West in *The Land Before Her: Fantasy and Experience of the American Frontiers, 1630–1860* (1984). Land policy is the subject of Paul W. Gates, *History of Public Land Law Development* (1978), while Alan G. Bogue discusses farm indebtedness in *Money at Interest: The Farm Mortgage on the Middle Border* (1955). Fred C. Luebke has edited a collection of essays dealing with immigrants on the Plains frontier, *Ethnicity on the Great Plains* (1980). Howard R. Lamar provides a history of the Southwest in *The Far Southwest, 1846–1880* (1963), and Earl Pomeroy covers the Far West in *The Pacific Slope: A History of California, Oregon, Washington, Idaho, Utah, and Nevada* (1965).

R. W. Paul writes of the mining frontier in *Mining Frontiers of the Far West, 1848–1880* (1963). Robert R. Dykstra explores urban development and social ten-

sions on the cattle frontier in *The Cattle Towns: A Social History of the Kansas Cattle Trading Centers* (1970). Joseph B. Frantz and Julian E. Choate focus on the cowboy in *The American Cowboy: The Myth and the Reality* (1968).

On relations between whites and Native Americans, see William T. Hagan, *American Indians* (1979 ed.) and Wilcomb E. Washburn, *The Indian in America* (1975). Also useful are Ronald T. Takaki, *Iron Cages: Race and Culture in Nineteenth-Century America* (1979); Francis P. Prucha, *American Indian Policy in Crisis: Christian Reformers and the Indians* (1976); and Ralph K. Andrist, *The Long Death: The Last Days of the Plains Indians* (1964). John G. Neihardt, *Black Elk Speaks* (1932) is the account of a holy man of the Ogalala Sioux.

For the New South, see C. Vann Woodward, *The Origins of the New South, 1877–1913* (1951) and Paul M. Gaston, *The New South Creed: A Study in Southern Mythmaking* (1970). Also helpful are Robert C. McMath and Orville V. Burton, eds., *Toward a New South: Studies in Post-Civil War Southern Communities* and Blaine A. Brownell and David R. Goldfield, eds., *The City in Southern History* (1977). On race relations, see H. N. Rabinowitz, *Race Relations in the*

Urban South (1978) and Morgan Kousser, *The Shaping of Southern Politics: Suffrage Restriction and the Establishment of the One-Party South* (1974).

Lawrence Goodwyn provides a provocative study of populism in *The Populist Moment: A Short History of the Agrarian Revolt in America* (1978). Other studies include Sheldon Hackney, *Populism to Progressivism in Alabama* (1969); Bruce Palmer, *"Men Over Money": The Southern Populist Critique of American Capitalism* (1980); and Peter H. Argersinger, *Populism and Politics: William Alfred Peffer and the People's Party* (1974). An analysis of the organization that gave birth to populism is to be found in Robert C. McMath, *Populist Vanguard: A History of the Southern Farmers' Alliance* (1975).

Good novels include Willa Cather, *My Ántonia* (1918) and O. E. Rolvaag, *Giants in the Earth* (1927).

## TIME LINE

| | |
|---|---|
| 1860s | Cattle drives from Texas begin |
| 1865–1867 | Sioux Wars on the Great Plains |
| 1867 | National Grange founded |
| 1869 | Transcontinental railroad completed |
| 1869–1874 | Granger Laws |
| 1873 | Financial panic triggers economic depression |
| 1874 | Barbed wire patented |
| 1875 | Black Hills gold rush incites Sioux War |
| 1876 | Custer's last stand at Little Big Horn |
| 1877 | *Munn* v. *Illinois* <br> Bonanza farms in the Great Plains |
| 1880s | "New South" |
| 1881 | Tuskegee Institute founded |
| 1883–1885 | Depression |
| 1884 | Southern Farmers' Alliance founded |
| 1886 | Severe winter ends cattle boom |
| 1887 | Dawes Severalty Act <br> Interstate Commerce Act <br> Farm prices plummet |
| 1888 | Colored Farmers' Alliance founded |
| 1890 | Afro-American League founded <br> Sioux Ghost Dance movement <br> Massacre at Wounded Knee <br> Ocala platform |
| 1890s | Black disenfranchisement in South <br> Jim Crow laws passed in South <br> Declining farm prices |
| 1892 | Populist party formed |
| 1895 | Booker T. Washington's "Atlanta Compromise" address |
| 1896 | *Plessy* v. *Ferguson* |

# CHAPTER 19
## THE RISE OF SMOKESTACK AMERICA

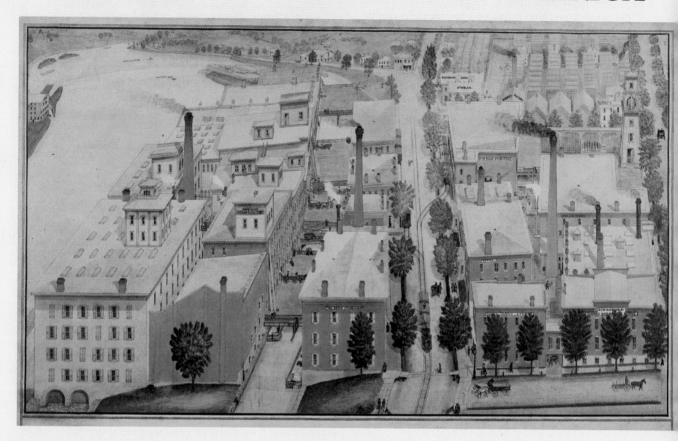

By 1883, Thomas O'Donnell had lived in the United States for over a decade. He was 30 years old, married, with two young children. His third child had died in 1882, and O'Donnell was still in debt over the funeral. Money was scarce, for O'Donnell was a textile worker in Fall River, Massachusetts, and not very well educated. "I went to work when I was young," he explained, "and have been working ever since." However, O'Donnell worked only sporadically at the mill. New machines needed "a good deal of small help," and the mill owners preferred to hire man-and-boy teams. Since O'Donnell's children were only 1 and 3, he often saw others preferred for day work. Once, when he was passed over, he recalled, "I said to the boss . . . what am I to do; I have got two little boys at home . . . how am I to get something for them to eat; I can't get a turn when I come here. . . . I says, 'Have I got to starve; ain't I to have any work?'"

O'Donnell and his family were barely getting by even though he worked with pick and shovel when he could. He estimated that he had earned only $133 over the course of the previous year. Rent came to $72. The family spent $2 for a little coal but depended for heat on driftwood that O'Donnell picked up on the beach. Clams were a major part of the family diet, but there were days when there was nothing to eat at all.

The children "got along very nicely all summer," but it was now November, and they were beginning to "feel quite sickly." It was hardly surprising. "One has one shoe on, a very poor one, and a slipper, that was picked up somewhere. The other has two odd shoes on, with the heel out." His wife was healthy but not ready for winter. She had two dresses, one saved for church, and "an undershirt that she got given to her, and . . . an old wrapper, which is about a mile too big for her; somebody gave it to her."

O'Donnell was describing his family's marginal existence to a Senate committee that was gathering testimony in Boston in 1883 on the relations between labor and capital. As the senators heard the tale, they asked him why he did not go west. "It would not cost you over $1,500," said one senator. The gap between senator and worker could not have been more dramatic. O'Donnell replied, "Well, I never saw over a $20 bill . . . if some one would give me $1,500 I will go." Asked by the senator if O'Donnell had friends who could provide him with the funds, O'Donnell sadly replied no.

The senators, of course, were far better acquainted with the world of comfort and leisure than they were with the poverty of families like the O'Donnells. From their vantage point, they could clearly see the fruits of industrial progress. As the United States became a world industrial leader in the years after the Civil War, its factories poured forth an abundance of ever-cheaper goods ranging from steel rails and farm reapers to mass-produced parlor sets. These were years of tremendous growth and significant economic and social change. Manufacturing replaced agriculture as the leading source of economic growth between 1860 and 1900. By 1890, a majority of the American work force held nonagricultural jobs; over a third lived in cities. A rural nation of farmers was becoming a nation of industrial workers and city dwellers.

As O'Donnell's testimony illustrates, however, change and progress were not synonymous for everyone. Although no nationwide studies of poverty existed, estimates suggest that perhaps half of the American population was too poor to take advantage of the new goods of the age.

This chapter examines America's transformation between 1865 and 1900. During these years, the industrial system expanded and became immensely productive. Big business became the common form of organization, the city the preferred location for manufacturing. New labor needs were met by a growing industrial work force, much of it foreign-born. The chapter's central theme grows out of O'Donnell's story: as the United States built up its railroads, cities, and factories, its production and profit orientation resulted in the maldistribution of wealth and power. Although many were too exhausted by life's daily struggles to protest new inequalities, strikes and other forms of working-class resistance punctuated the period. The social problems that accompanied the country's industrial development would capture the attention of reformers and politicians for decades to come.

## THE CHARACTER OF INDUSTRIAL PROGRESS

When Americans went to war in 1861, agriculture was the country's leading source of economic growth. Forty years later, manufacturing had taken its place. During these years, the production of manufactured goods outpaced the growth of population. By 1900, three times as many goods per person existed as in 1860. Per capita income increased by over 2 percent a year. But these aggregate figures disguise the fact that many people did not win any gains at all.

As the character of American manufacturing shifted, new regions grew to industrial importance. From New England to the Midwest lay the country's industrial heartland. New England was still a center of light industry, and the Midwest continued to process natural resources. Now, however, the production of iron, steel, and transportation equipment joined the older manufacturing operations there. In the Far West, manufacturers concentrated on processing the region's natural resources, but heavy industry made strides as well. In the South, the textile industry put down roots by the 1890s, although the South as a whole was far less industrialized than either the North or the Midwest.

### Rise of Heavy Industry

Although many factors contributed to the dramatic rise in industrial productivity, the changing nature of the industrial sector itself explains many of the gains. Manufacturers before the Civil War had concentrated either on producing textiles, clothing, and leather products or on processing agricultural and natural resources like grain, hogs, or lumber. While these industries continued to be important, heavy industry, which produced goods like steel, iron, petroleum, and machinery, grew rapidly. The manufacturing of "producer's goods" (goods intended for other producers rather than consumers) provided the basis for economic growth.

### Population and Economic Growth, 1855–1919

|  | 1855–1890 | 1889–1919 |
|---|---|---|
| Population | 2.5% | 1.8% |
| Real gross product | 4.0 | 3.9 |
| Real product per capita | 1.5 | 2.1 |
| Total factor input | 3.7 | 2.2 |
| Labor | 3.0 | 1.8 |
| Nonlabor | 4.6 | 3.1 |
| Total factor productivity | 0.3 | 1.7 |
| Real product per unit of |  |  |
| Labor input | 1.0 | 2.0 |
| Nonlabor input | −0.6 | 0.7 |

**Source:** Porter, *Encyclopedia of Economic History*, 1980.

Farmers, who bought machinery for their farms; manufacturers, who installed new equipment in their factories; and railroads, which bought steel rails for their tracks, all contributed to rising productivity figures.

Technological innovations that revolutionized production lay behind the rise of heavy industry. The evolution of the steel industry shows the transforming power of new technology. Before the Civil War, the production of iron was a slow and expensive process. Skilled and highly paid workers provided the backbone of the work force. The introduction of the Bessemer and open-hearth processes in the 1870s made it possible to convert iron ore cheaply and more easily into hard steel. The need for skilled workers declined. Dramatic changes in the steel industry resulted. The industry as a whole expanded, production soared, and prices fell. When Andrew Carnegie introduced the Bessemer process into his plant in the mid-1870s, the price of steel plummeted from $100 a ton to $50. In another two years the price dropped to $40; by 1890, steel cost only $12 a ton.

In turn, the production of a cheaper, stronger, and more durable material than iron created new goods, new demands, and new markets. The railroads had relied on iron rails, which flattened

*New developments in industry and engineering spawned marvels such as the Brooklyn Bridge, hailed as a triumph of our time.*

and split in a few years. Now they consumed 1.5 million tons of hard steel rails a year as they built new lines across the country. Bridge builders soon realized the possibilities of steel-cable suspension designs, and architects such as Louis Sullivan began to use steel for the nation's first high-rise buildings. Countless Americans bought steel in more humble forms: wire, nails, bolts, needles, screws.

New sources of power facilitated the conversion of American industry to mass production. Because steam engines and coal were so expensive, early manufacturers had depended on water power provided by streams and rivers. With the opening of new anthracite coal deposits, however, the cost of this fuel dropped, and American industry rapidly shifted to steam. In 1869, about half of the industrial power used came from water; by 1900, steam engines accounted for 80 percent of the nation's industrial energy supply. Steam freed industry to relocate from riversides, mostly in rural areas, to the cities and thus played a critical role in the growth of factory-filled cities in the late nineteenth century.

The completion of the transportation and communications network after the Civil War was fundamental to economic growth. In 1860, most railroads were located in the East and Midwest. From 1862 on, both national and state governments vigorously promoted railroad construction with land grants from the public domain. Eventually the railroads received over 180 million acres, an area about 1½ times the size of Texas. Similarly, counties and cities donated land for stations and terminals, bought railroad stock, made loans and grants, and gave tax breaks to railroads.

With such incentives, the first transcontinental railroad was completed in 1869. A burst of railroad construction followed. Four additional transcontinental lines and miles of feeder and branch roads were laid down in the 1870s and 1880s. By 1890, trains rumbled across 165,000 miles of tracks. As railroads crisscrossed the country, Western Union lines arose alongside them. Mass production and distribution depended on fast, efficient, and regular transportation. The completion of the national system both encouraged and supported the adoption of mass production and mass marketing.

## Meeting Capital Needs

All these changes demanded huge amounts of capital. The creation of the railroad system alone cost over a billion dollars by 1859, in contrast to the canal system's modest price tag of under $2 million. The completion of the national railroad network required another $10 billion. Reduced opportunities for investments abroad encouraged British, French, and German investors to pour funds into American enterprise. Foreigners contributed a third of the sum needed to complete the railroad system. Americans were also eager to support new ventures, and began to devote an increasing percentage of the national income to investment purposes rather than consumption.

Although savings and commercial banks continued to invest the capital of their depositors, investment banking houses like Morgan & Co. played a new and significant role in matching resources with economic enterprises. Investment bankers marketed investment opportunities. They bought up blocks of corporate bonds (which offered set interest rates and eventually the repayment of principal) at a discount for interested investors and also sold stocks (which paid dividends only if the company made a profit). Because stocks were riskier investments than bonds, buyers were at first cautious. But when John Pierpont Morgan, a respected investment banker, began to market stocks, they became more popular. The market for industrial securities rapidly expanded in the 1880s and 1890s. Although some Americans feared the power of investment bankers, they were integral to the economic expansion of the late nineteenth century.

## Railroads: The First Big Business

As the nature of the American economy changed, big businesses became the characteristic form of economic organization. Big businesses, with large amounts of capital, could afford to build huge factories, buy and install the latest, most efficient machinery, hire hundreds of workers, and use the most up-to-date methods. The result was more goods at lower prices. Machines costing thousands of dollars mass-produced goods costing pennies.

The railroads were the pioneers of big business and a great modernizing force in America. After the Civil War, railroad companies expanded rapidly. In 1865, the typical railroad was only 100 miles long. Twenty years later, it was 1,000. In 1888, a medium-size Boston railroad company had three times as many employees and received six times as much income as the Massachusetts state government.

The size of railroads, the huge costs of construction, maintenance, and repair, and the complexity of operations required unprecedented amounts of capital and new management techniques. No single person could finance a railroad or hope to supervise its operations involving hundreds of miles of track and hundreds of employees. Nor could any one person resolve the thorny issues raised by such a large enterprise. How should the operations and employees be organized? What were the long-term and short-term needs of the railroad? What were proper rates? What should be company policy toward unions? What share of the profits did workers deserve? The creation of large businesses posed these questions and many more.

Unlike small businesses with modest overhead costs, railroads faced high constant costs. Maintaining equipment and roads was expensive. In addition, railroads carried a high burden of debt, incurred to pay for construction and expansion. The necessity of meeting regular interest payments and expenses forced railroads to do as much business and to use their equipment as intensively as possible. If 20 cars were almost as expensive to pull as 25, why not haul 25?

High costs and the need to use equipment intensively encouraged aggressive and competitive business techniques. To attract freight, railroads wooed customers with low rates. Railroad freight charges dropped steadily during the last quarter of the century. When two lines or more competed for the same traffic, railroads often offered lower rates than their rivals or secret rebates (cheaper fares in exchange for all of a company's business). Rate wars helped customers, but they could end in a railroad's bankruptcy. Instability plagued the railroad industry even as it expanded.

In the 1870s, railroad leaders attempted to stabilize conditions by eliminating ruinous and ruthless competition. As George Perkins of the

Chicago, Burlington, and Quincy Railroad explained, "The struggle for existence and the survival of the fittest is a pretty theory, but it is also a law of nature that even the fittest must live as they go along." Railroad leaders established "pools," informal agreements to set uniform rates or to divide up the traffic. Yet pools never completely succeeded in ending competition. Too often, individual companies disregarded their agreements, especially when the business cycle took a downturn.

Railroad leaders were also tempted to control costs and counter the late-nineteenth-century pattern of falling prices by slashing their

*Conveniences such as the dining car meant more complex management problems for railroad administrators.*

INTERIOR OF **DINING CARS** ON THE
**CINCINNATI, HAMILTON & DAYTON R.R.**

workers' wages. Owners justified their strategy by reasoning that they had taken all the business risks. As a result, railroads were plagued by worker unrest, some of which will be described later in this chapter.

The huge scale and complexity of the railroads required new management techniques. In 1854, the directors of the Erie Railroad hired engineer and inventor Daniel McCallum to devise a system to make railroad managers and their employees more accountable. In his report the following year, McCallum highlighted the differences between large and small organizations. In a small organization, one could pay personal attention to all the details of operation. But McCallum argued that, "any system that might be applicable to the business and extent of a short road would be found entirely inadequate to the wants of a long one."

McCallum's system, emphasizing the division of responsibilities and a regular flow of information, attracted widespread interest, and railroads became the pioneers in rationalized administrative practices and management techniques. Their procedures became models for other businesses in decision making, scheduling, and engineering. The behavior the railroads exhibited—their competitiveness, their attempt to underprice one another, their eventual interest in merger, their tendency to cut workers' wages—were also followed by other big businesses in the late nineteenth century as they faced similar economic conditions.

## Growth in Other Industries

By the last quarter of the century, the textile, metal, and machinery industries equaled the railroads in size. In 1870, the typical iron and steel firm employed under 100 workers. Thirty years later, the average work force was four times as large. By 1900, more than 1,000 American factories had giant labor forces ranging between 500 and 1,000. Almost 450 others employed more than 1,000 workers. Big business had come of age.

Business expansion was accomplished in one of two ways (or a combination of both). Some owners like Andrew Carnegie integrated their businesses vertically. Vertical integration meant adding operations either before or after the production process. Even though he had introduced the most up-to-date innovations in his steel mills, Carnegie realized he needed his own sources of pig iron, coal, and coke. This was "backward" integration, away from the consumer, in order to avoid dependence on suppliers. When Carnegie acquired steamships and railroads to transport his finished products, he was integrating "forward," toward the consumer. Companies that integrated vertically frequently achieved economies of scale through more efficient management techniques.

Other companies copied the railroads and integrated horizontally by combining similar businesses. The objective was not to control the various stages of production, as was the case with vertical integration, but rather to gain a monopoly of the market in order to eliminate competition and to stabilize prices. Horizontal integration sometimes resulted in some economies and thus greater profits, but not always. But the control over prices that monopoly provided did boost earnings.

John D. Rockefeller's company, Standard Oil of New Jersey, used the strategy of horizontal integration. By a combination of astute and ruthless techniques, Rockefeller bought or drove out his competitors. Although Standard Oil never achieved a complete monopoly of the market, by 1898 it was refining almost 84 percent of the nation's oil. As Rockefeller concluded, "The day of individual competition [in the oil business] . . . is past and gone."

Rockefeller's remarks accurately characterized new economic conditions. As giant businesses competed intensely, often cutting wages and prices, smaller and weaker producers were driven under or absorbed. Business ownership became increasingly concentrated. In 1870, some 808 American iron and steel firms competed in the marketplace. By 1900, the number had dwindled to less than 70.

Like the railroads, many big businesses chose to incorporate. Although corporations were not new, most manufacturing firms were unincorporated in 1860. By 1900, corporations turned out two-thirds of the country's industrial goods.

Business gained many advantages by incorporating. The sale of stock made it possible to raise sums for large-scale operations. The principle of limited liability protected investors, while the corporation's legal identity ensured its survival after the death of original and subsequent shareholders. Longevity suggested a measure of stability that heightened the attractiveness of the corporation as an investment.

### Increase in Size of Industries, 1860–1900

| INDUSTRY | Average Establishment Size (Workers) | |
| --- | --- | --- |
| | 1860 | 1900 |
| Agricultural implements | 8 | 65 |
| Carpets and rugs | 31 | 214 |
| Cotton goods | 112 | 287 |
| Glass | 81 | 149 |
| Hosiery and knit goods | 46 | 91 |
| Iron and steel | 65 | 333 |
| Leather | 5 | 40 |
| Malt liquors | 5 | 26 |
| Paper and wood pulp | 15 | 65 |
| Shipbuilding | 15 | 42 |
| Silk and silk goods | 39 | 135 |
| Slaughtering and meatpacking | 20 | 61 |
| Tobacco | 30 | 67 |
| Woolen goods | 33 | 67 |

*Source:* U.S. Bureau of the Census.

### The Unpredictable Economic Cycle

The transformation of the economy was neither smooth nor steady. Rockefeller described his years in the oil business as "hazardous" and confessed that he did not know "how we came through them."

Two depressions, one from 1873 to 1879 and the other from 1893 to 1897, were far more severe than economic downturns before the Civil War. Prewar depressions stemmed from collapsing land values, unsound banking practices, and changes in the supply of money. The depressions of the late nineteenth century, when the economy was larger and more interdependent, were industrial in character and far-ranging in impact. Large-scale unemployment, a new phenomenon in American life, accompanied them.

During expansionary years, manufacturers flooded markets with their goods. The pattern of falling prices that characterized the postwar period and the fierce competition between producers may well have combined to encourage overproduction. When the market was finally saturated, sales and profits declined, and the economy spiraled downward. Owners cut back on production and laid workers off. Industrial workers, now an increasing percentage of the American work force, depended solely on wages for their livelihood. As they economized and bought less food, farm prices also plummeted. Farmers, like wage workers, cut back on purchases. Business and trade stagnated, and the railroads were finally affected. Eventually, the cycle bottomed out, but in the meantime, millions had been unemployed, thousands of businesses had gone bankrupt, and many Americans had suffered deprivation and hardship.

## URBAN EXPANSION IN THE INDUSTRIAL AGE

The new industrial age was one of rapid urban expansion. Before the Civil War, manufacturers had relied on water power and chosen rural sites for their factories. Now as they shifted to steam power, they selected urban locations that offered them workers, specialized services, and local markets. Although technological innovations like electric lights (invented in 1879) and telephones (1876) were still not widespread, they further increased the desirability of urban sites. The railroad network provided manufacturers with the necessary links to distant materials and markets. Industry, rather than commerce or finance, was the force behind urban expansion between 1870 and 1900.

Cities of all sizes grew. The population of New York and Philadelphia doubled and tripled. Smaller cities, especially those in the industrial Midwest like Omaha, Duluth, and Minneapolis, boasted impressive growth rates. Southern cities, as we saw in Chapter 18, also shared in the dramatic growth. In the Far West during the 1880s, Spokane exploded from 350 to 20,000 and Tacoma from 1,100 to 36,000. In 1870, some 25 percent of Americans lived in cities; by 1900, fully 40 percent of them did.

### A Growing Population

The American population, as a whole, was growing at a rate of about 2 percent a year, but cities were expanding far more rapidly. What accounted for the dramatic increase in urban population?

Certainly not a high birthrate. Although more people were born than died in American cities, births made only a modest contribution to the urban population explosion. The general pattern of declining family size that had emerged before the Civil War continued. By 1900, the average woman bore only 3.6 children, in contrast to 5.2 in 1860. In cities, moreover, families tended to have fewer children than their rural counterparts. And urban children faced a host of health hazards like tuberculosis, diarrhea, and diphtheria. All city residents were vulnerable, but children especially so. The death rate for infants was twice as high in cities as in the countryside. In the 1880s, half the children born in Chicago would not live to celebrate their fifth birthday.

### Migration from Farms and Towns

The swelling population of late nineteenth-century cities came from the nation's small towns and farms and from abroad. For both

### Ten Largest Cities in the United States, 1850 and 1890

| 1850 | 1890 |
| --- | --- |
| 1. New York | 1. New York |
| 2. Philadelphia | 2. Chicago |
| 3. Baltimore | 3. Philadelphia |
| 4. Boston | 4. St. Louis |
| 5. New Orleans | 5. Boston |
| 6. Cincinnati | 6. Baltimore |
| 7. Brooklyn | 7. Pittsburgh |
| 8. St. Louis | 8. San Francisco |
| 9. Albany | 9. Cincinnati |
| 10. Pittsburgh | 10. Cleveland |

*Source:* U.S. Bureau of the Census.

foreigners and Americans alike, the decision to relocate resulted from a combination of pressures, some encouraging them to abandon their original homes, others attracting them to the urban environment.

For rural Americans, the "push" came from the modernization of agricultural life. Factories poured out farm machines that replaced human hands. By 1896, one man with machinery could harvest 18 times as much wheat as a farmer working with hand tools in 1830. Then, too, rural life was often monotonous and drab.

Work in the industrial city was the prime attraction. Although urban jobs were often dirty, dangerous, and exhausting, so too, was farmwork. Moreover, by 1890, manufacturing workers were earning hundreds of dollars more a year than farm laborers. Some industrial workers, like the miners in the Far West, earned even more. Part of the difference between rural and urban wages was eaten up by the higher cost of living in the city, but not all.

An intangible but important lure was the glitter of city life. The young man who found Kansas City to be a "gilded metropolis" filled with "marvels," a veritable "round of joy," was dazzled by the excitement of urban life, its culture and amusements. Shops, theaters, restaurants, churches, department stores, newspapers, ball games, and the urban throng all amazed young men and women who had grown up on farms and in small towns. Although these pleasures were often out of reach, the fascination remained.

Novelists like Theodore Dreiser and Stephen Crane captured both the glamor and dangers of city life. Writing in a style termed literary realism, they examined social problems and cast their characters in carefully depicted local settings. Dreiser's novel *Sister Carrie* (1900) follows a typical country girl as she comes to Chicago. Carrie dreams of sharing Chicago's amusements and fantasizes a life of wealth, excitement, and ease. She finds, however, that the city's luxuries and pleasures are far from the reach of a mere factory employee. She discovers that by using her sex she can enjoy the city's pleasures. Many readers were shocked to discover that Carrie's "sin" was never punished. The novel ends with a contemplative but not repentant Carrie.

In *Maggie: A Girl of the Streets* (1893), Stephen Crane's heroine meets punishment at the story's end. As a young girl, Maggie retains her purity in the heart of New York's most appalling slums. Eventually, the city's pleasures lead to a loss of innocence. Maggie turns in despair to prostitution, and the reader is left at the novel's conclusion to guess whether Maggie has been murdered or commits suicide. Crane, and others, were as fascinated as they were repelled by the urban environment. Whether Eden or Sodom, the industrial city cast a powerful spell over American writers and American culture.

Southern blacks, often single and young, also fed the migratory stream into the cities. In the West and North, blacks comprised only a tiny part of the population: 3 percent in Denver in the 1880s and 1890s, 2 percent in Boston. In southern cities, however, they were more numerous. About 44 percent of Atlanta's residents in the late nineteenth century were black, and in Nashville, blacks made up about 38 percent of the population. No matter where they were,

*Cities like Chicago offered a variety of sights, sounds, and activities which attracted those raised in rural isolation.*

however, the city offered them few rewards, no glamor, and many dangers.

## Newcomers from Overseas

During the 40 years before the Civil War, 5 million immigrants poured into the United States to seek their fortune. From 1860 to 1900, almost 14 million arrived. Although three-quarters of them stayed in the Northeast, they also could be found in most cities across the nation except in the South. In many of these cities, they outnumbered native-born whites.

As the flow of immigration increased, the national origin of immigrants shifted. Until 1880, three-quarters of the immigrants, often called the "old immigrants," hailed from the British Isles, Germany, and Scandinavia. Irish and Germans were the largest groups. Then the pattern slowly began to change. By 1890, Irish, English, Germans, and Scandinavians made up only 60 percent of all immigrants, while "new immigrants" from southern and eastern Europe

(Italy, Poland, Russia, Austria, Hungary, Greece, Turkey, and Syria) comprised most of the rest. Italian Catholics and eastern European Jews were the most numerous, followed by Slavs. The changing pattern is captured by one comparison. In 1870, probably 90 percent of the country's European immigrants came from Britain, Ireland, or western Europe. In 1900, less than half did.

Cheaper and better transportation made the great tide of migration possible, but dissatisfaction with conditions at home sparked the decision to leave. Overpopulation diminished opportunities. "The first thing I remember is that we lived in a little cabin in the greatest poverty," recalled one new American. Sometimes famine was a driving force, as it was when the Irish potato crop failed in the 1840s. Disease and epidemics forced others from their homelands. "We would have eaten each other had we stayed," claimed one Italian immigrant.

Efforts to modernize European economies also encouraged immigration. New agricultural

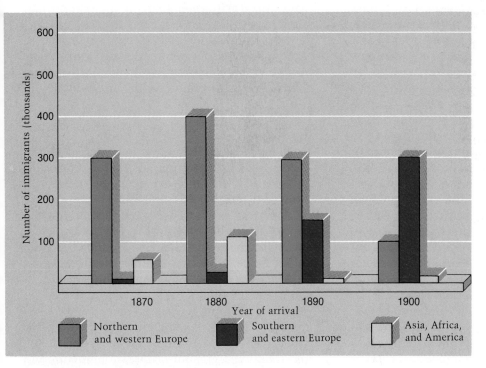

**Immigration:
Source and Volume,
1870–1900**

***Source:*** U.S. Bureau of the Census.

techniques led landlords to consolidate their land, thereby evicting longtime tenants. Artisans and craftsmen whose skills were obsolete with the introduction of machinery pulled up stakes and headed for the United States. Government policies pushed others to leave. In eastern Europe, especially in Russia, the official persecution of minorities and the expansion of the draft for the czar's army led millions of Jewish families and others to emigrate.

Opportunity in the "golden land" of America also detached thousands of immigrants from their homelands. State commissioners of immigration and American railroad and steamship companies, eager for workers and customers, wooed potential immigrants. Friends and relatives in America encouraged others to follow. Their letters described favorable living and working conditions and contained promises of helping newcomers find work. Often passage money was slipped between the pages as well. The ways in which people already in this country helped to facilitate the emigration of those still at home has led to the description of this movement of people as a "chain migration."

Like rural and small-town Americans, Europeans came primarily to work. When times were good in the United States, migration was heavy. When times were bad, numbers fell off. Most immigrants were young single men, who, in contrast to immigrants before the Civil War, had few skills. (Jews, however, came most often in family groups, and women predominated among the Irish.) They hoped to earn enough money in America to realize their ambitions at home. A surprising number, perhaps as many as a third, eventually returned home.

Asian immigrants, the majority of them from southern China, also came to the United States in the late nineteenth century. They too fled overpopulation, depressed conditions, unemployment, and crop failures and hoped for work in the "Land of the Golden Mountains." "We were very very much in debt because of the local warfare," explained one immigrant. "We planted each year, but we were robbed. We had to borrow. When news about the Gold Rush in California was spread by the shippers, my father decided to take the big chance."

Although only 264,000 Chinese came to the

*Possibly coming to join a male family member, these women were photographed as they landed at the Battery in New York City.*

United States between 1860 and 1900, they constituted a significant minority on the West Coast. Most of them were unskilled male contract laborers who had promised to work for a number of years and then return to their homeland. They performed some of the hardest and dirtiest jobs in the West, including railroad and levee construction and mining and factory work. They also often performed work that American men shunned, and they started hundreds of laundries in western communities.

## The Industrial City

This growing and variegated population, the increasing concentration of manufacturing in urban areas, and improvements in transportation led to new physical and social arrangements in American cities. The private sector and the profit motive determined the way cities developed, and the results depressed many observers. James Bryce, a Scottish visitor, discovered that in American cities "monotony haunts one like a nightmare." Slums, which were not new, seemed disturbing because so many people lived in them. Yet these same cities also boasted of grand mansions, handsome business and industrial buildings, grandiose civic monuments, and acres of substantial middle-class homes.

By the last quarter of the nineteenth century, the jumbled arrangements of the antebellum walking city, whose size and configuration had been limited by the necessity of walking to work, disappeared. Where once substantial houses, businesses, and small artisan dwellings had stood side by side, central business districts emerged. Here were banks, shops, theaters, professional firms, and businesses. Few people lived downtown, although many worked or shopped there. Surrounding the business center were areas of light manufacturing and wholesale activity with housing for workers. Beyond these working-class neighborhoods stretched middle-class residential areas. Then came the suburbs, with "pure air, peacefulness, quietude, and natural scenery." Scattered throughout the city were pockets of industrial activity surrounded by crowded working-class housing.

This new pattern, with the poorest city residents clustered near the center, is familiar today. However, it was a reversal of the early-nineteenth-century urban form when at least some of the most desirable housing was to be found in the heart of the city. New living arrangements were also more segregated by race and class than those in the preindustrial walking city. Homogeneous social and economic neighborhoods emerged, and it became more unusual

*Commuting to work from the suburbs became a common pattern as trains and streetcars became larger and faster.*

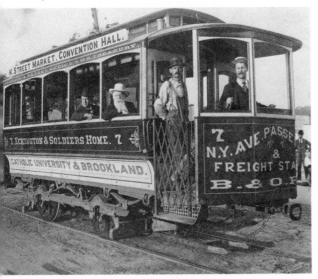

than before for a poor, working-class family to live near a middle- or upper-class family.

The changing urban geography was closely connected to the dense development of the central business district, the rise of heavy industry, and improvements in transportation. Better transportation increasingly allowed middle- and upper-class residents to live away from their work and from grimy industrial districts.

The urban transportation revolution started modestly in the 1820s and 1830s with the horse-drawn omnibus. This slow-moving vehicle accommodated only 10 to 12 passengers. Its expensive fares obliged most people to seek housing within walking distance of their work. In the 1850s, many cities introduced horse railways. Pulling cars over rails with as many as 25 passengers, horses could cover 5 to 6 miles an hour. The horse railways, which radiated from city centers like the spokes of a wheel, allowed the city to expand outward about 4 miles. The cost of a fare limited ridership to the middle and upper classes. The introduction of cable cars, trolley cars, and subways after 1880 further extended city boundaries and broadened residential choices for the middle class.

## Neighborhoods and Neighborhood Life

Working-class neighborhoods clustered near the center of most industrial cities. Here lived newcomers from the American countryside, and since most immigrants settled in cities, crowds of foreigners as well.

Ethnic groups frequently chose to concentrate in particular neighborhoods, often located near industries requiring their labor. In Detroit in 1880, for example, 37 percent of the city's native-born families lived in one area while 40 percent of the Irish inhabited the "Irish West Side." Over half the Germans and almost three-quarters of the Poles lived on the city's east side. Although such neighborhoods often had an ethnic flavor, with small specialty shops and foreign-language signs, they were not ethnic ghettos. Immigrants and native-born Americans often lived in the same neighborhoods, on the same streets, and even in the same houses. Toward the end of the century, when ethnic enclaves emerged, they were just that—enclaves within a neighborhood. Italians might live in one block but Jews on the next.

Working-class neighborhoods were often what would be called slums today. They were crowded, unsanitary, and inadequately provided with public services. Many workers lived in houses once occupied by middle- and upper-class residents, now divided and subdivided to accommodate more people than the original builders had intended. Others lived in tenements, specially constructed to house as many families as possible, or in cheaply built housing for one or more families. Facilities were woefully inadequate. Outdoor privies, often shared by several families, were the rule. Water came from outdoor hydrants and had to be carried inside for cooking, washing, and cleaning. When there were indoor fixtures, they frequently emptied waste directly into unpaved alleys and courts. Adequate sewage systems did not exist. Piles of garbage and waste material stank in the summer and froze in the winter. Even when people kept their own living quarters clean, their outside environment was unsanitary and unhealthy. It was no surprise that urban death rates were so high. Only at the turn of the century did the public health movement begin to make a dent in these living conditions.

Not every working-class family lived in abject circumstances. Skilled workers might rent comfortable quarters, and a few might even own their own houses. A study of 397 working-class families in Massachusetts found the family of one skilled worker living "in a tenement of five rooms in a pleasant and healthy locality, with good surroundings. The apartments are well furnished and parlor carpeted." The family even had a sewing machine. But the unskilled and semiskilled workers were not so fortunate. The Massachusetts survey described the family of an unskilled ironworker crammed into a tenement of four rooms,

in an overcrowded block, to which belong only two privies for about fifty people. When this place was visited the vault had overflowed in the yard and the sink-water was also running in the same place, and created a stench that was really frightful. . . . The house inside, was badly furnished and dirty, and a disgrace to Worcester.

Drab as many working-class neighborhoods were, working families created a community life that helped to alleviate some of the dreariness of their physical surroundings. The expense of moving around the city helped encourage a neighborhood and family focus. So too, paradoxically, did the long hours spent at work. What free time and energy one had were apt to be spent close to home.

A wide range of institutions and associations came to life in urban neighborhoods. Frequently they were based on ethnic ties. They made residents feel at home in the city yet at the same time often separated them from native-born Americans and other ethnic groups. Irish associational life, for example, focused around the Roman Catholic parish church, its Irish priest, and its many clubs and group activities, Irish nationalist organizations, and ward politics. Irish saloons were convivial places for men to meet, socialize, drink, and talk politics. Jews, on the other hand, gathered in their synagogues, Hebrew schools, and Hebrew- and Yiddish-speaking literary groups. Germans had their family saloons and educational and singing societies. While such activities may have slowed assimilation into American society and discouraged intergroup contact, they provided companionship, social life, and a bridge between life in "the old country" and life in America. Working-class men and women were far from being mere victims of their environment. They found the energy, squeezed out the time, and even saved the money to support a network of social ties and associations.

Black Americans faced the most wretched living conditions of any group in the city. In the North, they often lived in segregated black neighborhoods. In southern cities, they could be found scattered in back alleys and small streets. Many could only afford to rent rooms.

Some of the suffering that accompanied life in squalid neighborhoods was tempered by the rich associational life that emerged wherever former slaves gathered in the late nineteenth century. Black churches enjoyed phenomenal growth. The Afro-American Methodist Episcopal Church, with a membership of 20,000 in 1856, established churches in every city and sizable town and by 1900 claimed more than

400,000 members. Often associated with churches were mutual aid societies. By 1880, some 193 had been established in Savannah, Georgia, alone.

Some urban blacks in the late nineteenth century also rose into the middle class and, in spite of the heavy odds against them, created the nucleus of professional and artistic life. Henry Ossawa Tanner gained international recognition as a painter by 1900, black educators such as George Washington Williams wrote some of the first Afro-American histories, and novelists such as Charles W. Chesnutt, William Wells Brown, and Paul Laurence Dunbar produced noteworthy novels and short stories.

Beyond working-class neighborhoods and pockets of black housing lay streets of middle-class houses. Here lived the urban lower middle class: clerks, shopkeepers, bookkeepers, salesmen, and small tradesmen. Their salaries allowed them to buy or rent houses that offered some privacy and comfort. Separate spaces for cooking and laundry work kept hot and often odorous housekeeping tasks away from other living areas. The houses boasted up-to-date features like gas lighting and bathrooms. Outside, the neighborhoods were cleaner and more attractive than those in the inner city. Residents could pay for garbage collection, gaslights, and other improvements.

### Streetcar Suburbs

On the fringes of the city were houses for the substantial middle class and the rich, who either made their money in business, commerce, and the professions or inherited family fortunes. Public transportation sped them downtown to their offices and then back to their families. For example, Robert Work, a modestly successful cap and hat merchant, moved his family to a $5,500 house in West Philadelphia in 1865 and commuted more than 4 miles to work. The 1880 census revealed his family's comfortable life style. The household contained two servants, two boarders, his wife, and their eldest son, who was still in school. The Works' house had running hot and cold water, indoor bathrooms, and other modern conveniences of the age like central heating. Elaborately carved furniture, rugs,

draperies, and lace curtains probably graced the downstairs, where the family entertained and gathered for meals. Upstairs, comfortable bedrooms provided a maximum of privacy for family members. The live-in servants, who did most of the housework, shared little of this space or privacy, however. They were restricted to the kitchen and pantry and to bedrooms in the attic.

### The Social Geography of the Cities

Industrial cities of this era were places where people were sorted out according to class, occupation, and race. The physical distances between upper- and middle-class neighborhoods and working-class neighborhoods meant that city dwellers often had little firsthand knowledge of people who were different from themselves. Ignorance led to distorted views and social disapproval. Middle-class newspapers unsympathetically described laboring men as "loafing in the sunshine" and criticized the "crowds of idlers, who, day and night, infect Main Street." Yet those "crowds of idlers" were often men who could not find work. The comments of a working-class woman to her temperance visitors in 1874 suggest the sharp view from the bottom of society up: "When the rich stopped drinking, it would be time to speak to the poor about it."

*Wealthy citizens, living in luxurious homes in prosperous neighborhoods, had little understanding of the daily lives of the poor.*

# INDUSTRIAL WORK

The presence of so many foreigners affected the character and composition of the urban working class. Immigrants made up a seventh of the population in the late nineteenth century. But because most were young men of working age, they composed a fifth of the labor force and over 40 percent of laborers in the manufacturing and extractive industries. In cities, where they tended to settle, they comprised more than half of the population in general and of the working class in particular. As a Protestant clergyman observed, "Not every foreigner is a working man, but in the cities, at least, it may be said that every working man is a foreigner."

## The Importance of Ethnic Diversity

The fact that more than half of the urban industrial class was foreign, unskilled, and often had only a limited command of English had a tremendous impact on industrial work, urban life, labor protest, and local politics. Eager for the unskilled positions rapidly being created as mechanization and mass production took hold, immigrants often had little in common with native-born workers or even with one another. American working-class society was thus a mosaic of nationalities, cultures, religions, and interests, a patchwork where colors clashed as often as they complemented one another.

The ethnic diversity of the industrial work force helps explain its occupational patterns. Although every city offered somewhat different employment opportunities, generally occupation was related to ethnic background and experience.

At the top of the working-class hierarchy, native-born Protestant whites held a disproportionate share of well-paying skilled jobs. They were the aristocrats of the working class. Their jobs demanded expertise and training, as had been true of skilled industrial workers in the pre–Civil War period. But their occupations bore the mark of late nineteenth-century industrialism. They were machinists, iron puddlers and rollers, engineers, foremen, conductors, carpenters, plumbers, mechanics, and printers.

Beneath native-born whites, skilled northern European immigrants filled most of the positions in the middle ranks of the occupational structure. The Germans, who arrived with training as tailors, bakers, brewers, and shoemakers, moved into similar jobs in this country, while Cornish and Irish miners secured skilled jobs in western mines. The Jews, who had tailoring experience in their homelands, became the backbone of the garment industry (where they faced little competition from American male workers, who considered it unmanly to work on women's clothes).

But Irish peasants and newly arrived Italians, Slavs, and others had no urban-industrial experience. They labored in most of the unskilled, dirty jobs near the bottom of the occupational ladder. They relined blast furnaces in steel mills, carried raw materials or finished products from place to place, or cleaned up after skilled workers. Often they were carmen or day laborers on the docks, ditchdiggers, or construction workers. Hiring was often on a daily basis. Unskilled work provided little in the way of either job stability or income.

At the very bottom, blacks occupied the

*Opportunities for advancement rarely existed for black workers. On this Philadelphia project the hod-carriers were black but the bricklayers were white.*

most marginal positions as janitors, servants, porters, and laborers. Racial discrimination generally excluded them from industrial jobs, even though their occupational background differed little from that of rural white immigrants. Since there were always plenty of whites eager to work, it was not necessary to hire blacks except occasionally as scabs during a labor strike. "It is an exceptional case where you find any colored labor in the factories," observed one white, "except as porters. Neither colored female . . . nor male laborer is engaged in the mechanical arts."

## The Changing Nature of Work

The rise of big business, which relied on mechanization for the mass production of goods,

changed the size and shape of the work force and the nature of work itself. More and more Americans were becoming wage earners rather than independent artisans. The number of manufacturing workers doubled between 1880 and 1900, with the fastest expansion in the unskilled and semiskilled ranks.

But the need for skilled workers remained. New positions, as in steam fitting and structural ironwork, appeared as industries expanded and changed. Older skills became increasingly obsolete, however. Moreover, all skilled workers faced the possibility that technical advances would eliminate their favored status or that employers would eat away at their jobs by having unskilled helpers take over parts of them. In industries as different as shoemaking, cigar making, and iron puddling, new methods of production and organization undermined the position of skilled workers.

## Work Settings and Experience

The workplace could be a dock or cluttered factory yard, a multistoried textile mill, a huge barnlike steel mill with all the latest machinery, or a mine tunnel thousands of feet underground. A majority of American manufacturing workers now labored in factories (rather than the shops of an earlier age), and the numbers of those working in large plants dominated by the unceasing rhythms of machinery increased steadily.

Some Americans, however, still toiled in small shops and sweatshops tucked away in basements, lofts, or immigrant apartments. Even in these smaller settings, the pressure to produce was almost as relentless as in the factory, for volume, not hours, determined pay. When contractors cut wages, workers had to speed up to earn the same pay.

The organization of work divided workers from one another. Those paid by the piece were competing against the speed, agility, and output of other workers. It was hard to feel any bonds with these unknown and unseen competitors. In large factories, workers separated into small work groups and mingled only rarely with the rest of the work force. The clustering of ethnic groups in certain types of work also undermined worker solidarity.

### Labor Force Distribution, 1870–1900

*Source:* U.S. Bureau of the Census.

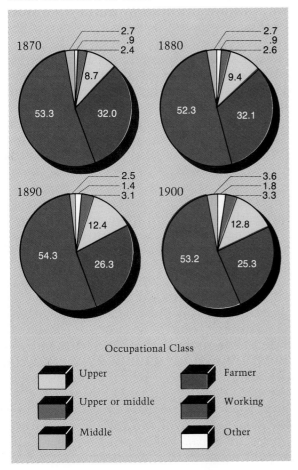

Occupational Class

Upper — Farmer

Upper or middle — Working

Middle — Other

All workers had one thing in common: a very long working day. Although the hours of work had fallen from the 12 hours per day expected in factories before the Civil War, people still spent over half their waking hours on the job—usually ten hours a day, six days a week. Different occupations had specific demands. Bakers worked a 65-hour week, canners toiled for 77. Sweatshop workers might labor far into the night long after factory workers had gone home.

Work was usually unhealthy, dangerous, inconvenient, and comfortless. Although a few states passed laws to regulate work conditions, enforcement was spotty. Few owners paid much attention to the location of toilets, drinking facilities, or washing areas. Nor did they concern themselves with the health or safety of their employees. Women bent over sewing machines developed digestive illnesses and curved spines. New drilling machinery introduced in western mines filled the shafts with tiny stone particles that caused lung disease. Accident rates in the United States far exceeded those of Europe's industrial nations. Each year, 35,000 died from industrial mishaps. Iron and steel mills were the big killers, although railroad casualties alone mounted to 6,000 fatalities a year during the 1890s. Nationwide, nearly one-quarter of the men reaching the age of 20 in 1880 would not reach their forty-fourth birthday (compared to 7 percent today). American business owners had little legal responsibility—and some felt none—for employees' safety or health. The law placed the burden of avoiding accidents on workers, who were expected to quit if they thought conditions were unsafe.

Industrial workers labored at jobs that were also increasingly specialized and monotonous. The size of many firms allowed a kind of specialization that was impossible in a small enterprise. Even skilled workers did not produce a complete product, and the range of their skills was narrowing. "A man never learns the machinist's trade now," one New Yorker grumbled. "The different branches of the trade are divided and subdivided so that one man may make just a particular part of a machine and may not know anything whatever about another part of the same machine." Cabinetmakers found themselves not crafting cabinets but putting together and finishing pieces made by others. It was not surprising that many skilled workers complained that they were being reduced to the status of drudges and wage slaves.

Still, industrial work provided some personal benefits. Large, complex operations with high fixed costs could usually not afford to shut down and wait out hard times. Workers in these firms congratulated themselves for securing jobs in an apparently more stable environment. "The mass of workingmen," said one, "like to feel that their situations are as permanent as possible, and this they cannot do when employed in a small shop."

Other aspects of the new arrangements helped humanize the workplace. Workers who obtained their jobs through family and friends found themselves in the same departments with them. In most industries, the foreman controlled day-to-day activities. It was the foreman who selected workers from the crowds at the gate, fired those who proved unsatisfactory, selected appropriate materials and equipment, and determined the order and pace of production. Since the foreman was himself a member of the working class who had climbed his way up, he

*Factory work was usually uncomfortable and hazardous. Here workers in the Stetson hat factory cut fur for hats to be sewn together by hand.*

might understand and sympathize with subordinates. Yet the foreman could also be authoritarian and harsh, especially if the workers he supervised were unskilled or belonged to another ethnic group.

## The Worker's Share in Industrial Progress

Industrialists like Andrew Carnegie and John D. Rockefeller made huge fortunes during the late nineteenth century. They symbolized the continuing pattern of wealth concentration that had begun in the early period of industrialization. In 1890, the top one percent of American families possessed over a quarter of the wealth, while the share held by the top 10 percent was about 73 percent. Economic growth still benefited those who tried to direct its path, and they claimed the lion's share of the rewards.

But what of the workers who tended the machines that lay at the base of industrial wealth? Working-class Americans made up the largest segment of the labor force (probably around 60 percent), so their experience reveals important facets of the American social and economic system and American values.

Statistics of increasing production, of ever more goods, tell part of the story. Figures on real wages also reveal something important. Industry still needed skilled workers and paid them well. Average real wages rose over 50 percent between 1860 and 1900. Skilled manufacturing workers, who made up about a tenth of the nonagricultural working class in the late nineteenth century, saw their wages rise by about 74 percent. But unskilled wages increased by only 31 percent. The differential was substantial and widened as the century drew to a close.

Taken as a whole, the working class accrued substantial benefits in the late nineteenth century, even if its share of the total wealth did not increase. American workers had more material comforts than their European counterparts. But the general picture conceals the realities of working-class economic life. A U.S. Bureau of Labor study of working-class families in 1889 revealed great disparities of income: a laborer earned $384 a year, while a carpenter took home $686. The carpenter's family lived comfortably in a four-room house. Their breakfast usually included meat or eggs, hotcakes, butter, cake, and coffee. Such hearty fare was out of the question for the laborer's family, however; they ate bread and butter as the main portion of two of their three daily meals.

For workers who could not secure steady employment, rising real wages were meaningless. Workers, especially those who were unskilled, often found work only sporadically. When times were slow or conditions depressed, as they were between 1873 and 1879 and 1893 and 1897, employers, especially those in small firms, laid off both skilled and unskilled workers and reduced wages. Even in a good year like 1890, one out of every five men outside of agriculture had been unemployed at least a month. One-quarter lost four months or more.

Since unemployment insurance did not exist, workers had no cushion against losing their jobs. One woman grimly recalled, "If the factory shuts down without warning, as it did last year for six weeks, we have a growing expense with nothing to counterbalance." Older workers who had no social security or those who had had accidents on the job but no accident insurance had severely reduced incomes. Occasionally, kindhearted employers offered assistance in hard times, but it was rarely enough. The Lawrence Manufacturing Company compensated one of its workers $50 for the loss of a hand and awarded another $66.71 for a severed arm.

Although nineteenth-century ideology pictured men as breadwinners, many working-class married men could not earn enough to support their families alone. A working-class family's standard of living thus often depended on its number of workers. Today, two-income families are common. But in the nineteenth century,

## Unemployment Rates, 1870–1899

| PERIOD | AVERAGE PERCENT UNEMPLOYED | PEAK YEAR | PERCENT UNEMPLOYED IN PEAK YEAR |
|---|---|---|---|
| 1870–1879 | 10% | 1876 | 12–14% |
| 1880–1889 | 4 | 1885 | 6–8 |
| 1890–1899 | 10 | 1894 | 15+ |

married women did not usually take outside employment, although they contributed to family income by taking in sewing, laundry, and boarders. In 1890, only 3.3 percent of married women were to be found in the paid labor force.

### The Family Economy

If married women did not work for pay outside their homes, their children did. The laborer whose annual earnings amounted to only $384 depended on his 13-year-old son, not his wife, to go out and earn the $196 that was so critical to the family's welfare. Sending children into the labor market was an essential survival strategy for many working-class Americans. In 1880, one-fifth of the nation's children between the ages of 10 and 14 held jobs.

Child labor was closely linked to a father's income, which in turn depended on skill, ethnic background, and occupation. Immigrant families more frequently sent their young children out to work (and also had more children) than native-born families. Middle-class reformers who had sentimental views of childhood and who thought all children should be under the care of mothers and teachers were disapproving. As one investigator of working-class life re-

ported, "Father never attended school, and thinks his children will have sufficient schooling before they reach their tenth year, thinks no advantage will be gained from longer attendance at school, so children will be put to work as soon as able." Reformers believed that such fathers condemned their children to future poverty by taking them out of school, whereas sending children to work was actually a means of coping with the immediate threat of poverty.

### Women at Work

By age 14, many more young people were working for wages. Half of all Philadelphia's students had quit school by that age. Daughters as well as sons were expected to take positions, although young women from immigrant families were more likely to be working than young American women. As *Arthur's Home Magazine* for women pointed out, a girl's earnings would help "to relieve her hard-working father of the burden of her support, to supply home with comforts and refinements, to educate a younger brother."

Employed women earned far less than men. An experienced female factory worker might be paid between $5 and $6 a week, while an unskilled male laborer could make about $8. Discrimination, present from women's earliest days in the work force, persisted. Still, factory jobs were desirable because they paid better than other kinds of work open to women.

Employment opportunities for women were narrow, and ethnic taboos and cultural traditions helped to shape choices. About a quarter of working women secured factory jobs. Italian and Jewish women (whose background ruled out domestic work) clustered in the garment industry, while Poles and Slavs went into textiles, food processing, and meatpacking. In some industries, like textiles, women composed an important segment of the work force. But about 40 percent of them, especially those from Irish, Scandinavian, or black families, took jobs as maids, cooks, laundresses, and nurses.

Domestic service meant low wages, unpleasant working conditions, and little free time, usually one evening a week and part of Sunday. A Minneapolis housemaid described her ex-

### Status of Young People (12–20) by Ethnicity in Detroit in 1900

| ETHNIC GROUP | SCHOOL | WORK | HOME |
|---|---|---|---|
| Native white American* | 54.7% | 40.4% | 4.9% |
| | 56.1 | 16.9 | 27.0 |
| Black | 50.0 | 50.0 | 0.0 |
| | 45.5 | 40.9 | 13.6 |
| Irish | 43.2 | 48.6 | 8.1 |
| | 43.2 | 39.8 | 17.0 |
| German | 30.5 | 59.5 | 10.0 |
| | 29.2 | 45.1 | 25.8 |
| Polish | 26.4 | 63.5 | 10.1 |
| | 26.1 | 56.2 | 17.6 |
| Russian | 53.3 | 30.0 | 16.7 |
| | 17.4 | 60.9 | 21.7 |

*Note:* Percentage of boys are indicated in blue; percentage of girls are indicated in red.
*Born in the United States of two American-born parents.
**Source:** Zunz, *The Changing Face of Inequality*, 1982.

hausting routine. "I used to get up at four o'clock every morning and work till ten P.M. every day of the week. Mondays and Tuesdays, when the washing and ironing was to be done, I used to get up at two o'clock and wash or iron until breakfast time." Nor could domestics count on much sympathy from their employers. "Do not think it necessary to give a hired girl as good a room as that used by members of the family," said one lady of the house. "She should sleep near the kitchen and not go up the front stairs or through the front hall to reach her room."

Although a servant received room and board, the pay hovered between $2 and $5 a week. The fact that so many women took domestic work despite the job's disadvantages speaks clearly of their limited opportunities.

The dismal situation facing working women drove some, like Rose Haggerty, into prostitution. Burdened with a widowed and sickly mother and four younger brothers and sisters, Rose went to work at age 14 in a New York paper-bag factory. She earned $10 a month, but $6 went for rent. Her fortunes improved when a friend helped her buy a sewing machine. Rose then sewed shirts at home, often working as long as 14 hours a day. Her earnings supported her family until the piecework rate for shirts was suddenly slashed in half. In desperation, Rose contemplated suicide. But when a sailor offered her money for spending the night with him, she realized she had an alternative. Prostitution meant food, rent, and heat for her family. "Let God Almighty judge who's to blame most," the 20-year-old Rose reflected, "I that was driven, or them that drove me to the pass I'm in."

Prostitution appears to have increased in the late nineteenth century, although there is no way of knowing the actual numbers of women involved. Probably most single women accepted the respectable jobs open to them. They tolerated discrimination and low wages because their families depended on their contributions. They also knew that when they married, they would probably leave the paid work force behind forever.

Marriage hardly ended women's work, however. Like colonial families, late nineteenth-century working-class families operated as economic units. The unpaid domestic labor of working-class wives was critical to family survival. With husbands away for 10 to 11 hours a day, women bore the burden and loneliness of caring for children. They did all the domestic chores. Since working-class families could hard-

*Domestic work was exhausting and underpaid, but for women of some cultures it was the only respectable form of employment.*

ly afford labor-saving conveniences, housework was time-consuming and arduous. Without a refrigerator, a working-class woman spent part of each day shopping for food (more expensive in small quantities). The washing machine, advertised to do the "ordinary washing of a family in only one or two hours," was out of the question with a price tag of $15. Instead, women carried water from outside pumps, heated it up on the stove, washed clothes, rinsed them with fresh water, and hung them up to dry. Ironing was a hot and unpleasant job in small and stuffy quarters. Keeping an apartment or house clean when the atmosphere was grimy and roads unpaved and littered with refuse and horse dung was a challenge.

As managers of family resources, married women had important responsibilities. What American families had once produced for themselves now had to be bought. It was up to the working-class wife to scour secondhand shops to find cheap clothes for her family. She was the one to make all the small domestic economies that were vital to survival. One woman trying to make ends meet said, "In summer and winter alike I must try to buy the food that will sustain us the greatest number of meals at the lowest price."

Women also supplemented family income by taking in work. Jewish and Italian women frequently did piecework and sewing at home. In the Northeast and Midwest, between 10 and 40 percent of all working-class families kept boarders. Immigrant families, in particular, often chose to make ends meet by taking single young countrymen into their homes. The cost was the added burden of work (providing meals and clean laundry), the need to juggle different work schedules, and the sacrifice of privacy. But the advantages of extra income far outweighed the disadvantages for many working-class families.

Black women's working lives again indi-

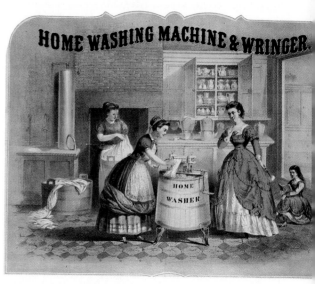

*Popular with those who could afford it, the washing machine appeared after the Civil War but remained out of reach for working-class families.*

cate the great obstacles blacks faced in late nineteenth-century cities. Although few married white women worked outside the home, black women did so both before and after marriage. In southern cities in 1880, about three-quarters of single black women and one-third of married women worked outside the home. This contrasted to percentages for white women of 24 percent and 7 percent. Since industrial employers would not hire black women, most of them had to work as domestics or laundresses. The high percentage of married black women in the labor force reflected the marginal wages their husbands earned. But it also may be explained partially by the lessons black women had derived from slavery, where they had learned that children could thrive without the constant attention of their mothers.

## CONFLICT BETWEEN CAPITAL AND LABOR

Industrial workers did not passively accept their lot in the new industrial America. Although they welcomed the progress the factory made possible, they rejected their employers' claim to most of the profits. Bad pay, poor working conditions, and long hours, they argued, reduced workers to the status of wage slaves. Fashioning their arguments from their republican legacy, workers claimed that the Republic itself was in danger of being undermined as citizen workers were degraded.

## On-the-Job Protests

Many workers staunchly resisted unsatisfactory working conditions such as those described by a Detroit tinner, who complained that bosses treated employees "like any other piece of machinery, to be made to do the maximum amount of work with the minimum expenditure of fuel." Skilled workers, like iron puddlers and window-glass blowers, had indispensable knowledge about the production process and practical experience and were in a key position to direct on-the-job actions. Sometimes their goal was to retain control over critical work decisions. Detroit printers, for example, struggled to hold on to the privilege of distributing headlines and white space (the "fat") rather than letting their bosses hand out the "fat" as a special reward and means of increasing competition among workers. Others hoped to humanize work. Cigar makers clung to their custom of having one worker read to others as they performed their tedious chores. Often workers sought to control the pace of production.

While unlimited production might furnish the owner with large profits, it was likely to harm workers. A glutted market meant massive layoffs, a reduction in the prices paid for piecework, and worsening work conditions. Thus workers established informal production quotas on the job. An experienced worker might whisper to a new hand, "See here, young fellow, you're working too fast. You'll spoil our job for us if you don't go slower."

A newspaper account of a glassblowers' strike in 1884 illustrates the clashing perspectives of capital and labor. With an eye toward increasing profits, the boss tried to speed up production. "He knew if the limit was taken off, the men could work ten or twelve hours every day in the week; that in their thirst for the mighty dollar they would kill themselves with labor; they would 'black sheep' their fellows by doing the labor of two men." But his employees resisted his proposal, refusing to drive themselves to exhaustion for a few dollars more.

Their goal was not riches but a decent pace of work and a respectable reward. Thus, "they thundered out no. They even offered to take a reduction that would average ten percent all around, but they said, 'We will keep the forty-eight box limit.' Threats and curses would not move them."

In attempting to protect themselves and preserve the dignity of their labor, workers devised ways of combating employer attempts to speed up the production process. They denounced fellow workers who refused to honor production codes as "hogs," "runners," "chasers," and "job wreckers"; they ostracized and even injured them. As the banner of the Detroit Coopers' Union proudly proclaimed at a parade in 1880: "Each for himself is the bosses' plea/ [but] Union for all will make you free."

Absenteeism, drunkenness at work, and general inefficiency were other widespread worker practices that contained elements of protest. In three industrial firms in the late nineteenth century, one-quarter of the workers stayed home at least one day a week. Some of these lost days were due to layoffs, but not all. The efforts of employers to impose stiff fines on absent workers were measures of their frustration at workers who refused to cooperate.

To a surprising extent, workers made the final protest by quitting their jobs altogether. Most employers responded by penalizing workers who left without giving sufficient notice—to little avail. A Massachusetts labor study in 1878 found that although two-thirds of them had been in the same occupation for more than ten years, only 15 percent of the workers surveyed were in the same job. A similar rate of turnover occurred in the industrial work force in the early twentieth century. Workers unmistakably and clearly voted with their feet.

## Strike Activity

The most direct and strenuous attempts to change conditions in the workplace came in the form of thousands of strikes punctuating the late nineteenth century. In 1877, railroad workers staged the first nationwide industrial strike. This was the first time the military was called out in force to break a strike; violent clashes

Students of history can discover fascinating materials on nineteenth-century life by exploring the published records of the American political system. The *Congressional Globe*, the proceedings of the Senate and the House, privately published from 1833 to 1873, reveals the nature of congressional deliberations in an era when debate, such as that over the Compromise of 1850 in the Senate, was the focus of the national political process. After 1873, the government published these proceedings in the *Congressional Record*. The *Record* is not a literal transcription of debate, for members can edit their remarks, insert speeches, and add supporting materials. Still, it gives a good sense of the proceedings of both the Senate and the House.

Much of the serious work of government, past and present, takes place in congressional committees. One foreign observer called Congress "not so much a legislative assembly as a huge panel from which committees are selected." The committee system is almost as old as the constitutional system itself and is rooted in the Constitution's granting of the lawmaking power to Congress. From the start, Congress divided into assorted committees to gather information, enabling members to evaluate legislative proposals intelligently.

Two kinds of committees existed in the House and Senate. Standing committees had permanent responsibility for reviewing legislative proposals on a host of financial, judicial, foreign, and other affairs. By 1892, the Senate had 44 standing committees, and the House had 50. Select committees were temporary, often charged with investigating specific problems. In the late nineteenth century, congressional committees investigated such problems as Ku Klux Klan terrorism, the sweatshop system, tenement house conditions, and relations between labor and capital. In each case, extensive hearings were held.

Congressional hearings have become increasingly important sources of historical evidence in recent years. Hearings show the Senate and the House of Representatives in action as they seek to translate popular sentiment into law. But they also reveal public attitudes themselves as they record the voices of Americans testifying in committee halls. Because one function of legislative hearings is to enable diverse groups to express their frustrations and desires, they often contain the testimony of witnesses drawn from many different social and economic backgrounds. Included here is the partial testimony of a Boston laborer, Thomas O'Donnell, who appeared before the Senate Committee on Education and Labor in 1883. Because working-class witnesses like O'Donnell usually left no other record of their experiences or thoughts, committee reports and hearings provide an invaluable insight into the lives and attitudes of ordinary people.

Hearings also reveal the attitudes and social values of committee members. Hence, caution is needed in the use of hearings. Witnesses often have vested interests and are frequently coached and cautious in what they communicate on the stand. Committee members often speak and explore questions for other reasons, usually political, than to illuminate issues.

Despite these limitations, committee hearings are rich sources of information. In this excerpt, what can you learn about the life of the witness testifying before the committee? In what way are the values of the committee members in conflict with those of the witness? Why is the chairman so harsh toward the witness? Is he entirely unsympathetic? Why do you think the questioner overemphasizes the relationship between moral beliefs and economic realities? What kinds of social tensions does the passage reveal?

Have you observed any recent hearings of congressional investigating committees on television? Are moral behavior and hunger still topics of concern for Americans? How is the interaction between modern haves and have-nots similar to and different from those between O'Donnell and the committee members in 1883? Do ethical beliefs and economic realities still separate social classes?

## HEARINGS ON THE RELATIONS BETWEEN LABOR AND CAPITAL

**Q.** You get a dollar a day, wages?—**A.** That is the average pay that men receive. The rents, especially in Somerville, are so high that it is almost impossible for the working men to live in a house.

**Q.** What rent do you pay?—**A.** For the last year I have been paying $10 a month, and most of the men out there have to pay about that amount for a house—$10 a month for rooms.

**Q.** For a full house, or for rooms only?—**A.** For rooms in a house.

**Q.** How many rooms?—**A.** Four or five.

**Q.** How much of your time have you been out of work, or idle, for the last full year, say?—**A.** I have not been out of work more than three weeks altogether, because I have been making a dollar or two peddling or doing something, when I was out of work, in the currying line.

**Q.** Making about the same that you made at your trade?—**A.** Well, I have made at my trade a little more than that, but that is the average.

**Q.** Are you a common drunkard?—**A.** No, sir.

**Q.** Do you smoke a great deal?—**A** Well, yes, sir; I smoke as much as any man.

The **CHAIRMAN.** I want to know how much you have got together in the course of a year, and what you have spent your money for, so that folks can see whether you have had pay enough to get rich on.

The **WITNESS.** A good idea.

The **CHAIRMAN.** That is precisely the sort of idea that people ought to know. How much money do you think you have earned during this last year; has it averaged a dollar a day for three hundred days?

The **WITNESS.** I have averaged more than that; I have averaged $350 or $400, I will say, for the year.

**Q.** You pay $10 a month rent; that makes $120 a year?—**A.** Yes, sir.

The **CHAIRMAN.** I have asked you these questions in this abrupt way because I want to find out whether you have spent much for practices that might have been dispensed with. You say you smoke?

The **WITNESS.** Yes, sir.

**Q.** How much a week do you spend for that?—**A.** I get 20 cents worth of tobacco a week.

**Q.** That is $10.40 a year?—**A.** Yes, sir.

**Q.** And you say you are not a common drunkard?—**A.** No, sir.

**Q.** Do you imagine that you have spent as much more for any form of beer, or ale, or anything of that kind, that you could have got along without?—**A.** No, sir.

**Q.** How much do you think has gone in that way?—**A.** About $1 or $2.

**Q.** During the whole year?—**A.** Yes, sir.

**Q.** That would make $11.40 or $12.40—we will call it $12—gone for wickedness. Now, what else, besides your living, besides the support of your wife and children?—**A.** Well, I don't know as there is anything else.

**Q.** Can you not think of anything else that was wrong?—**A.** No, sir.

**Q.** Twelve dollars have gone for sin and iniquity; and $120 for rent; that makes $132?—**A.** Yes.

**Q.** How many children have you?—**A.** Two.

**Q.** Your family consists of yourself, your wife, and two children?—**A.** Yes.

**Q.** One hundred and thirty-two dollars from $400 leaves you $268, does it not?—**A.** Yes, sir.

**Q.** And with that amount you have furnished your family?—**A.** Yes, sir.

**Q.** You have been as economical as you could, I suppose?—**A.** Yes.

**Q.** How much money have you left?—**A.** Sixty dollars in debt.

**Q.** How did you do that?—**A.** I don't know, sir.

**Q.** Can you not think of something more that you have wasted?—**A.** No, sir.

**Q.** Have you been as careful as you could?—**A.** Yes, sir.

**Q.** And you have come out at the end of the year $60 in debt?—**A.** Yes, sir.

**Q.** Have you been extravagant in your family expenses?—**A.** No, sir; a man can't be very extravagant on that much money. . . .

**Q.** And there are four of you in the family?—**A.** Yes, sir.

**Q.** How many pounds of beefsteak have you had in your family, that you bought for your own home consumption within this year that we have been speaking of?—**A.** I don't think there has been five pounds of beefsteak.

**Q.** You have had a little pork steak?—**A.** We had a half a pound of pork steak yesterday; I don't know when we had any before.

**Q.** What other kinds of meat have you had within a year?—**A.** Well, we have had corn beef twice I think that I can remember this year—on Sunday, for dinner.

**Q.** Twice is all that you can remember within a year?—**A.** Yes—and some cabbage.

**Q.** What have you eaten?—**A.** Well, bread mostly, when we could get it; we sometimes couldn't make out to get that, and have had to go without a meal.

**Q.** Has there been any day in the year that you have had to go without anything to eat?—**A.** Yes, sir, several days.

**Q.** More than one day at a time?—**A.** No.

**Q.** How about the children and your wife—did they go without anything to eat too?—**A.** My wife went out this morning and went to a neighbor's and got a loaf of bread and fetched it home, and when she got home the children were crying for something to eat.

**Q.** Have the children had anything to eat to-day except that, do you think?—**A.** They had that loaf of bread—I don't know what they have had since then, if they have had anything.

**Q.** Did you leave any money at home?—**A.** No, sir.

**Q.** If that loaf is gone, is there anything in the house?—**A.** No, sir; unless my wife goes out and gets something; and I don't know who would mind the children while she goes out.

between strikers, the police, and the military ensued. A wave of confrontations occurred thereafter. Between 1881 and 1905, an unbelievable 36,757 strikes involving over 6 million workers erupted, three times the strike activity in France.

These numbers suggest that far more than the "poorest part" of the workers were involved. Many investigations of this era found evidence of widespread working-class discontent. When Samuel M. Hotchkiss, commissioner of the Connecticut Bureau of Labor Statistics, informally surveyed the state's workers in 1887, he was shocked by the "feeling of bitterness," the "distrust of employers," the "discontent and unrest." These sentiments exploded into strikes, sabotage, and violence, most often linked to demands for higher wages and shorter hours.

Nineteenth-century strike activity underwent important changes, however, as the consciousness of American workers expanded. In the period of early industrialization, discontented laborers rioted in their neighborhoods rather than at their workplaces. The Lowell protests of the 1830s (Chapter 11) were not typical. Between 1845 and the Civil War, however, strikes at the workplace began to replace neighborhood riots. Although workers showed their anger against their employers by turning out and often called for higher wages, they had only a murky sense that they might use the strike as a weapon to force employers to improve working conditions.

As industrialization transformed work and an increasing percentage of the work force entered factories, collective actions at the workplace proliferated. Local and national unions played a more important role in organizing protest, conducting 60 percent of the strikes between 1881 and 1905. As working-class leaders realized more clearly the importance of collective action in dealing with their opponents and perceived how transportation had tightly knit the nation together, they also tried to coordinate local and national efforts. By 1891, more than one-tenth of the strikes called by unionized workers were sympathetic strikes. Coordination between strikers employed by different companies improved as workers tried to order capitalism by making the same wage demands. Finally,

wages among the most highly unionized workers became less of an issue. Workers tried to create more humane conditions. Some tried to end subcontracting and the degradation of skills. Others, like the glassblowers, struggled to enforce work rules. Indeed, by the early 1890s, over one-fifth of strikes involved the rules governing the workplace.

### Labor Organizing

The Civil War experience colored labor organizing in the postwar years. As one working-class song pointed out, workers had borne the brunt of that struggle. "You gave your son to the war / The rich man loaned his gold / And the rich man's son is happy to-day, / And yours is under the mold." Now workers who had fought to save the Union argued that wartime sacrifices justified efforts to gain justice and equality in the workplace.

Labor leaders quickly realized the need for national as well as local organizations to protect the laboring class against "despotic employers." In 1866, several craft unions and reform groups joined in a national federation, the National Labor Union. Claiming 300,000 members by the early 1870s, the organization supported a range of causes including temperance, women's rights, and the establishment of cooperatives to bring the "wealth of the land" into "the hands of those who produce it," thus ending "wage slavery."

The call for an eight-hour day reveals some of the basic assumptions of the organized labor movement. Few workers thought of employers as a hostile class or of the economic system as so flawed that it must be eliminated. But they did believe bosses were often dangerous tyrants. The long hours employers demanded threatened to turn citizens into slaves. But the eight-hour day would curb the power of owners and allow workers the time to cultivate the qualities necessary for republican citizenship.

Many of the NLU's specific goals survived, although the organization did not. An unsuccessful attempt to create a political party and the depression of 1873 decimated the NLU and many local unions as well. Survival and the search for a job took precedence over union causes.

## The Knights of Labor and the AFL

As the depression wound down, a new mass organization, the Noble Order of the Knights of Labor, rose to national importance. Founded as a secret society in 1869, the order became public and national when Terence V. Powderly was elected Grand Master Workman in 1879. The Knights of Labor sought "to secure to the workers the full enjoyment of the wealth they create." Since the industrial system denied workers their fair share as producers, the Knights of Labor proposed to mount a cooperative system of production alongside the existing system. "There is no reason," Powderly believed, "why labor cannot, through cooperation, own and operate mines, factories and railroads." Cooperative efforts would give workers the economic independence necessary for citizenship, while an eight-hour day would provide them with the leisure for moral, intellectual, and political pursuits.

The Knights of Labor opened its ranks to all American producers. By producers the Knights of Labor meant all contributing members of society—skilled and unskilled, black and white, men and women. Only the idle and corrupt (bankers, speculators, lawyers, saloonkeepers, and gamblers) were to be excluded. Membership was even open to sympathetic merchants and manufacturers. In fact, many shopkeepers joined the order and advertised their loyalty as "friend of the workingman."

This inclusive membership policy meant that the Knights potentially had the power of great numbers. They grew in spurts, attracting miners between 1874 and 1879 and skilled urban tradesmen between 1879 and 1885. The great masses of unskilled workers poured in thereafter.

Although Powderly frowned upon using the strike as a labor weapon, the organization reaped the benefits of grass-roots strike activity. Local struggles proliferated after 1883. In 1884, unorganized workers of the Union Pacific Railroad walked off the job when management announced a wage cut. Within two days, the company caved in, and the men joined the Knights of Labor. The next year, a successful strike against the Missouri Pacific Railroad brought in another wave of members. Then, in 1886, the Haymarket Riot in Chicago led to such a growth in labor militancy that in that single year the membership of the Knights of Labor ballooned from 100,000 to 700,000.

The "riot" at Haymarket was, in fact, a peaceful protest meeting connected with a lockout at the McCormick Reaper Works. When the Chicago police arrived to disperse the crowd, a bomb exploded. Seven policemen were killed. Although no one knows who planted the bomb, eight anarchists were tried and convicted. Overheated newspaper accounts put the blame on "long-haired, wild-eyed, bad-smelling, atheistic, reckless foreign wretches, who never did an honest hour's work in their lives."

Labor agitation and turbulence spilled over into politics. In 1884 and 1885, the Knights of Labor lobbied to secure a national contract labor law and state anticonvict labor laws. The organization also pressed successfully for the creation of a federal Department of Labor. As new members poured in, however, direct political action became increasingly attractive. Between 1885 and 1888, the Knights of Labor sponsored candidates in 200 towns and cities in 34 states and 4 territories. They achieved many electoral victories. In Waterloo, Iowa, a bank janitor ousted a successful attorney to become the town's mayor. Despite local successes, no national labor party emerged. But in the 1890s, the Knights cooperated with the Populists in their attempt to reshape American politics and society.

Despite the dramatic surge in membership, the Knights of Labor could not sustain their momentum as the voice for the American laboring people. A strike against Jay Gould's southwestern railroad system in 1886 failed, tarnishing the Knights' reputation. Consumer and producer cooperatives fizzled; the policy of accepting both black and white workers led to strife and discord in the South. The two major parties proved adept at coopting labor politicians. As labor politicians became respectable, they left the rank and file to fend for themselves.

The failure of local leaders was paralleled by the failure of national leadership. Powderly was never able to unify or direct his diverse following. His concern with general reform issues and political action dissatisfied those pressing for better wages and work conditions. Nor could Powderly control the militant elements who opposed him. Local, unauthorized strike actions were often ill-considered and violent. Lawlessness helped neither the organization as a whole nor its members. By 1890, the membership had dropped to 100,000, although the Knights of Labor continued to play a role well into the 1890s.

In the 1890s, the American Federation of Labor, founded in 1886, replaced the Knights of Labor as the nation's dominant union. The history of the Knights indicated the problems of a national union that admitted all who worked for wages but officially rejected strike action in favor of methods like politics and arbitration. The leader of the AFL, Samuel Gompers, had a different notion of effective worker organization. Gompers's experience as head of the Cigarmakers' Union in the 1870s and as a founder of the Federation of Organized Trades and Labor Unions in 1881 convinced him that skilled workers should put their specific occupational interests before the interests of workers as a whole. By so doing, they could control the supply of skilled labor and keep wages up.

Gompers organized his union as a federation of skilled trades—cigar makers, iron molders, ironworkers, carpenters, and others—each one autonomous yet linked through an executive council to work together for prolabor national legislation and mutual support during boycott and strike actions. Gompers was a practical man who believed in "pure and simple unionism." He repudiated the notion of a cooperative commonwealth and dreams of ending the wage system, accepting the fact that workers "are a distinct and practically permanent class of modern society." Thus he focused on immediate, realizable "bread and butter" issues, particularly higher wages, shorter hours, industrial safety, and the right to organize.

Although Gompers rejected direct political action as a means of obtaining labor's goals, he did believe in the value of the strike. He told a congressional hearing in 1899 that unless working people had "the power to enter upon a strike, the improvements will all go to the employer and all the injuries to the employees." He was a shrewd organizer and knew from bitter experi-

ence the importance of dues high enough to sustain a strike fund through a long, tough fight.

Under Gompers's leadership, the AFL grew from 140,000 in 1886 to nearly one million by 1900. Although his notion of a labor organization was elitist, he succeeded in steering his union through a series of crises, fending off challenges from socialists to his left and corporate opposition to strikes from his right. But there was no room in his organization for the unskilled or for blacks, who were judged to be of an "abandoned and reckless disposition."

The AFL made a brief and halfhearted attempt to unionize women in 1892. Hostile male attitudes constituted a major barrier against organizing women. Men resented women as co-workers and preferred them to stay in the home. The AFL stood firmly for the principle that "the man is the provider" and that women who work in factories "bring forth weak children." The Boston Central Labor Union declared in 1897 that "the demand for female labor [is] an insidious assault upon the home . . . it is the knife of the assassin, aimed at the family circle." Change was slow in coming. In 1900, the International Ladies Garment Workers Union (ILGWU) was established. Although women were the backbone of the organization, men dominated the leadership.

## Working-Class Setbacks

Despite the growth of working-class organizations, workers lost many of their battles with management. Some of the more spectacular clashes reveal why working-class activism often ended in defeat and why so many workers lived precariously on the edge of poverty.

In 1892, silver miners in Coeur d'Alene, Idaho, went on strike when their employers installed machine drills in the mines, reduced skilled workers to shovelmen, and announced a wage cut of a dollar a day. The owners, supported by state militiamen and the federal government, successfully broke the strike by using scabs, but not without armed fighting. Several hundred union men were arrested, herded into huge bull pens, and eventually tried and found guilty of a wide variety of charges. Out of the defeat emerged the Western Federation of Miners, founded by "Big Bill" Haywood, whose chief political goal was an eight-hour law for miners. The pattern of struggle in Coeur d'Alene was followed in many subsequent strikes, most notably in the Cripple Creek mining area of Colorado in 1894.

Determined mine owners characteristically met strikes by shutting off credit to unionmen, hiring strikebreakers and armed guards to break the union, and paying spies to infiltrate unions. Violence was frequent, and each confrontation usually ended with the arrival of state militia, the erection of bull pens, incarceration or intimidation of strikers and their local sympathizers, legal action, and elaborate blacklisting systems. In spite of this, the WFM won as many strikes as it lost.

## The Homestead and Pullman Strikes

The most serious setback to labor occurred in 1892 at the Homestead steel mills near Pittsburgh, Pennsylvania. The Homestead plant had been recently purchased by Andrew Carnegie,

*Pinkerton detectives as pictured in* **Harper's** **Weekly,** *1892, leaving the scene of the Homestead steel strike.*

who put Henry Clay Frick in charge. Together they wanted to eliminate the Amalgamated Association of Iron, Steel, and Tin Workers, which threatened to increase its organization of the steel industry. After three months of stalemated negotiations over a new wage contract, Frick issued an ultimatum. Unless the union accepted wage decreases, he would lock them out and replace them with others. As the deadline passed, Frick erected a formidable wood and barbed wire fence around the entire plant, with searchlight and guard stands on it, and hired 300 armed Pinkerton agents to guard the factory. As they arrived on July 6, they engaged armed steelworkers in a daylong gun battle. Several men on both sides were killed, and the Pinkertons were driven off.

Frick telegraphed Pennsylvania's governor, who sent 8,000 troops to crush both the strike and the union. Two and a half weeks later, Alexander Berkman, a New York anarchist who sympathized with the plight of the oppressed Homestead workers, broke into Frick's office and attempted to assassinate him. The events at Homestead dramatized the lengths to which both labor and capital would go to achieve their ends.

Observing these events, Eugene Victor Debs of Terre Haute, Indiana, for many years an ardent organizer of railroad workers, wrote that "if the year 1892 taught the workingmen any lesson worthy of heed, it was that the capitalist class, like a devilfish, had grasped them with its tentacles and was dragging them down to fathomless depths of degradation." Debs saw 1893 as the year in which organized labor would "escape the prehensile clutch of these monsters." But 1893 brought a new depression and even worse challenges and setbacks for labor. Undaunted, Debs succeeded in combining several of the separate railroad brotherhoods into a united American Railway Union (ARU). Within a year, over 150,000 railroadmen were in the ARU, and Debs won a strike against the Great Northern Railroad, which had attempted to slash workers' wages.

Debs faced his toughest crisis at the Pullman Palace Car Company in Chicago. Pullman was planned as a model company town with management controlling all aspects of workers' lives. "We are born in a Pullman house, fed from the Pullman shop, taught in the Pullman school, catechized in the Pullman church, and when we die we shall be buried in the Pullman cemetery and go to the Pullman hell," said one worker wryly.

Late in 1893, as the depression worsened, Pullman cut wages by one-third and laid off many workers but made no reductions in rents or prices in the town stores. Forced to pay in rent what they could not recover in wages, working families struggled to survive the winter. In some cases parents kept their children home from school because they had no shoes or coats and could keep warm only in bed. Those still at work suffered speedups, intimidations, and further wage cuts. Desperate and "without hope," the Pullman workers joined the ARU in the spring of 1894 and went out on strike.

In late June, after Pullman refused to submit the dispute to arbitration, Debs led the ARU into a sympathetic strike in support of the striking Pullman workers. Carefully advising his lieutenants to "use no violence" and "stop no trains," Debs sought to boycott trains handling Pullman cars throughout the West. As the boycott spread, the General Managers Association, which ran the 24 railroads centered in Chicago, came to the support of George Pullman, convinced that "we have got to wipe him [Debs] out." After hiring some 2,500 strikebreakers, they appealed to the state and federal governments for military and judicial support in stopping the strike.

Governor Altgeld of Illinois, sympathizing with the workers and believing that local law enforcement was sufficient, opposed the use of federal troops. But Richard Olney, a former railroad lawyer and President Cleveland's attorney general, persuaded the president that only federal troops could restore law and order. On July 2, Olney obtained a court injunction to end the strike as a "conspiracy in restraint of trade." Two days later, Cleveland ordered federal troops in to support the injunction and crush the strikers.

Violence now escalated rapidly. Local and federal officials hired armed guards, and the railroads paid them to help the troops. Within two days, strikers and guards were engaged in bitter fighting, freight cars were burned, and

over $340,000 worth of railroad property was destroyed. The press described "Unparalleled Scenes of Riot, Terror and Pillage" and "Frenzied Mobs Still Bent on Death and Destruction." As troops continued to pour into Chicago, the violence worsened, leaving scores of workers dead.

Debs's resources were near an end unless he could enlist wider labor support. "Capital has combined to enslave labor," he warned other labor groups. "We must all stand together or go down in hopeless defeat." When Samuel Gompers refused his support, the strike ended. Debs and several other leaders were arrested for contempt of the court injunction of July 2 and found guilty. A lifelong Democrat, Debs soon became a confirmed socialist. His arrest and the defeat of the Pullman strike provided a deathblow to the American Railway Union. In 1895, the Supreme Court upheld the legality of using an injunction to stop a strike and provided management with a powerful weapon to use against unions in subsequent years. The labor movement emerged from the 1890s with a distinct disadvantage in its conflicts with organized capital.

Although in smaller communities strikes against outside owners might receive support from the local middle class, these labor conflicts illustrate the widespread conviction among the American middle and upper class that unions and their demands were un-American. Many claimed to accept the idea of a worker organization. But they would not concede that unions should participate in making economic or work decisions. Most employers violently resisted union demands as infringements of their rights to hire and fire, to lock workers out, to hire scabs, or to reduce wages in times of depression. However, the sharp competition of the late nineteenth century combined with a pattern of falling prices stiffened employers' resistance to workers' demands. State and local governments and the courts frequently supported them in their battles to curb worker activism.

The severe depressions of the 1870s and 1890s also undermined working-class activism. Workers could not focus on union issues when survival itself was in question. They could not afford union dues nor turn down offers of work, even at wages below union standards. Many unions collapsed during hard times. Of the 30 national unions in 1873, fewer than 10 managed to survive the depression.

A far more serious problem was the reluctance of most workers to organize even in favorable times. In 1870, less than one-tenth of the industrial work force belonged to unions, about the same as on the eve of the Civil War. Thirty years later, despite the expansion of the work force, only 8.4 percent (mostly skilled workers) were union members.

Why were workers so slow to join unions? Certainly, diverse work settings made it difficult for workers to recognize common bonds. Moreover, many unskilled workers sensed that labor aristocrats did not have their interest at heart. Said one Cleveland Pole, "The [union] committee gets the money, 'Bricky' Flannigan [a prominent Irish striker] gets the whiskey, and the Polack gets nothing."

Moreover, many native-born Americans still clung to the tradition of individualism. "The sooner working-people get rid of the idea that somebody or something is going to help them," one Massachusetts shoemaker declared, "the better it will be for them." Others continued to nourish dreams of escaping from the working class and entering the ranks of the middle class. The number of workers who started their own small businesses attests to the power of that ideal, which prevented an identification with working-class causes.

The ethnic and religious diversity of the work force also made it difficult to forge a common front. No other industrial country depended so heavily on immigrants for its manufacturing labor force. The lack of common cultural traditions and goals created friction and misunderstandings. In addition, immigrants clustered in certain jobs and were insulated from other workers, both foreign-born and American. Ethnic and related skill differences also clouded common class concerns.

The perspective of immigrant workers contributed to their indifference to unions and to tension with native-born Americans. Many foreigners planned to return to their homeland and had limited interest in changing conditions in the United States. Moreover, since their goal was to work, they took jobs as scabs. Much of

the violence that accompanied working-class actions erupted when owners brought in strikebreakers. To some Americans, immigrants were to blame for both low wages and failed worker actions. Divisions among workers were often as bitter as those between strikers and employers. When workers divided, employers benefited.

The tension within laboring ranks was most dramatically displayed in the anti-Chinese campaign of the 1870s. In that decade, white workers in the West began to blame the Chinese for the economic hardships whites suffered. A meeting of San Francisco workers in 1877 in favor of the eight-hour day exploded into a rampage against the Chinese. The destruction of 25 laundries marked the beginning of months of anti-Chinese activities in the West. Angry mobs killed Chinese workers in Tacoma, Seattle, Denver, and Rock Springs, Wyoming. "The Chinese must go! They are stealing our jobs!" became a rallying cry for American workers.

Hostility was expressed at the national level with the Chinese Exclusion Act of 1882. The law prohibited the immigration of both skilled and unskilled Chinese workers for a ten-year period. It was extended in 1892 and made permanent in 1902. While both middle- and working-class Americans supported sporadic efforts to cut off immigration, working-class interest illuminated the deep divisions that undermined worker unity.

At the same time, many immigrants, especially those who were skilled, did support unions and cooperate with native-born Americans. In 1886, immigrants made up two-thirds of Illinois's union membership. Moreover, ethnic bonds could serve labor causes by tying members to one another and to the community at large. For example, in the 1860s and 1870s, as the Molders' Union in Troy, New York, battled with manufacturers, its Irish membership won sympathy and support from the Irish-dominated police force, the Roman Catholic church, fraternal orders, and public officials.

The importance of workers' organizations and of their informal actions on the job lies not so much in their successful outcomes as in the implicit criticism they offered of American society. Using the language of republicanism, many workers lashed out at an economic order that robbed them of their dignity and humanity. As producers of wealth, they protested that so little of it was theirs. As members of the working class, they rejected the middle-class belief in individualism and social mobility.

## The Balance Sheet

Except for skilled workers, most laboring people found it impossible to earn much of a share in the material bounty created by industrialization. Newly arrived immigrants especially suffered from low pay and economic uncertainty. Long hours on the job and the necessity of walking to and from work left workers little free time. Family budgets could include, at best, only small amounts for reading material and recreation. Even a baseball game ticket was a luxury.

Yet this view of the harshness of working-class life is partly determined by our own standards of what is acceptable today. Since so few working-class men or women recorded their thoughts and reactions, it is hard to know just what they expected or how they viewed their experiences. But their perspectives were influenced by their cultural heritages and backgrounds. The family tenement, one Polish immigrant remarked, "seemed quite advanced when compared with our home in Khelm [Chelm]." American poverty was preferable to

Russian pogroms. A ten-hour factory job might be an improvement over farmwork that started at dawn and ended at dusk.

Studies of several cities show that nineteenth-century workers achieved limited but very real occupational mobility. A few, one in five in Los Angeles and Atlanta during the 1890s, for example, managed to climb into the middle class. Most immigrant workers were stuck in ill-paid, insecure jobs, but their children ended up doing somewhat better. The son of an unskilled laborer might move on to become a semiskilled or skilled worker as new immigrants took the jobs at the bottom.

Mobility, like occupation, was related to background. Native-born whites, Jews, and Germans rose more swiftly and fell less often than Irish, Italians, or Poles. Cultural attitudes, family size, education, and group leadership all contributed to different ethnic mobility patterns. Jews, for example, valued education and sacrificed to keep children in school. By 1915, Jews represented 85 percent of the free City College student body in New York City, 20 percent of New York University's student body, and one-sixth of those studying at Columbia University. With an education, they moved upward. The Slavs, however, who valued a steady income over mobility and education, took their children out of school and sent them to work at an early

## Two Nineteenth-Century Budgets

| Monthly budget of a laborer, his wife, and child in 1891; his income is $23.67. | | Monthly budget of a married bank accountant with no children in 1892; his income about $66.50. | |
|---|---|---|---|
| Food | $6.51 | Food | $13.22 |
| Rent | 9.02 | Rent | 9.88 |
| Furniture | 3.61 | Taxes and insurance | 7.11 |
| Taxes and insurance | 3.32 | Utilities | 4.99 |
| Utilities | 2.94 | Dry goods | 2.45 |
| Sundries | 1.09 | Sundries | 2.10 |
| Tobacco | .66 | Transportation | 1.71 |
| Medicine | .29 | Reading material | .53 |
| Clothes | .21 | Liquor and tobacco | .42 |
| Dry goods | .16 | Furniture | .30 |
| Postage | .10 | Medicine | .27 |
| Transportation | .08 | Clothes | .19 |
| | $28.01 | | $43.17 |

Source: Zunz, *The Changing Face of Inequality,* 1982.

age. This course of action, they believed, not only helped out the family but gave the child a head start in securing reliable, stable employment. Italians valued family above individual success and heeded the southern Italian proverb, "Do not make your child better than you are." Differing attitudes and values led to different aspirations and career patterns.

The one group that enjoyed no mobility at all was Afro-Americans. They were largely excluded from the industrial occupational structure and restricted to unskilled jobs. Unlike immigrant industrial workers, they did not have the opportunity to move to better jobs as new unskilled workers took the positions at the bottom.

Although occupational mobility was limited for immigrants, there were often other kinds of rewards that compensated for the lack of success at the workplace. The Irish, for example, did not move as rapidly into better occupations as some other groups, but they did manage to buy their own houses. Coming from a country where home ownership had been all but impossible, the acquisition of a house may well have loomed as a great achievement. Home ownership allowed a family to earn extra income by taking in boarders; in addition, it provided some protection against the uncertainties of industrial life and the coming of old age. The Irish also proved adept politicians and came to dominate big-city government in the late nineteenth century.

Their political success opened up city jobs, particularly in the police force, to the Irish. In 1886, one-third of Chicago's police force was Irish-born; many more were second-generation Irish-Americans. Moreover, the Irish dominated the hierarchy of the Catholic church. Members of the group who did not share in this mobility could benefit from ethnic connections and take pride in their group's achievements.

Likewise, participation in social clubs and fraternal orders partially compensated for lack of advancement at work. Ethnic associations, parades, and holidays provided a sense of identity and security that offset the limitations of the job world.

Moreover, a few rags-to-riches stories always encouraged the masses who struggled. The family of John Kearney, in Poughkeepsie, New York, for example, achieved modest success. After 20 years as a laborer, John managed to start his own business as a junk dealer. He became his own boss and even bought a simple house. His sons started off in better jobs than their father. One became a grocery-store clerk, later a baker, a policeman, and finally, at the age of 40, an inspector at the waterworks. Another was an iron molder, while the third son was a post-office clerk and eventually the superintendent of city streets. This was success, even if not on the scale of the industrial giants like Andrew Carnegie and John D. Rockefeller. It was enough to keep the American dream alive.

## CONCLUSION: The Complexity of Industrial Capitalism

The late nineteenth century was a period of rapid growth as the United States became one of the world's industrial giants. Many factors contributed to the "wonderful accomplishments" of the age. They ranged from sympathetic government policies to the rise of big business and the emergence of a cheap industrial work force. But it was also a turbulent period. Many Americans benefited only marginally from the new wealth. Some of them protested by joining unions, by walking out on strike, or by on-the-job actions. Most lived their lives more quietly and never had the opportunity that Thomas O'Donnell did of telling their story to others. But as the next chapter shows, middle-class Americans began to wonder about the O'Donnells of the country. It is to their concerns, worries, and aspirations that we now turn.

# Recommended Reading

The late nineteenth-century industrial world has been the subject of lively historical investigation. A helpful overview of economic change is provided by Stuart Bruchey, *Growth of the Modern American Economy* (1975); Alfred W. Niemi, *U.S. Economic History: A Survey of the Major Issues* (1975); and Robert L. Heilbroner, *The Economic Transformation of America* (1977). Samuel P. Hays gives a useful analysis in *The Response to Industrialism, 1885–1914* (1957), while Robert Weibe investigates one preoccupation of the age in *The Search for Order, 1877–1920* (1967).

On big business, see Glenn Porter, *The Rise of Big Business, 1860–1910* (1973) and Alfred D. Chandler, Jr., *The Visible Hand: The Managerial Revolution in American Business* (1977). Edward C. Kirkland illuminates the business mind in *Dream and Thought in the Business Community, 1860–1900* (1964), while his *Industry Comes of Age: Business, Labor, and Public Policy, 1860–1900* (1961) gives a general survey of business in the late nineteenth century.

Zane Miller's *The Urbanization of America* (1973) is one of several good introductions to city growth in the late nineteenth century; see also Sam Bass Warner, Jr., *Streetcar Suburbs: The Process of Growth in Boston, 1870–1900* (1962). Gunther Barth examines urban culture in *The Rise of Modern City Culture in Nineteenth-Century America* (1980). James Borchert explores black life in *Alley Life in Washington: Family, Community, Religion, and Folklife in the City, 1850–1970* (1980).

For the immigrant experience, begin with Thomas J. Archdeacon, *Becoming American: An Ethnic History* (1983) and consult Stephan Thernstrom, ed., *The Harvard Encyclopedia of American Ethnic Groups* (1980). Alan M. Kraut brings together varied material on immigrants in *The Huddled Masses: The Immigrant in American Society, 1880–1921* (1982), while *Ethnic Chicago* (1981), edited by Peter Jones and Melvin G. Holli, deals with different immigrant groups in that city.

Studies of working-class life and work include Herbert G. Gutman, *Work, Culture, and Society in Industrializing America* (1976); David M. Gordon, Richard Edwards, and Michael Reich, *Segmented Work, Divided Workers: The Historical Transforma-*

tion of Labor in the United States (1982); Daniel Nelson, *Managers and Workers: Origins of the New Factory System in the United States, 1880–1920* (1975); Daniel T. Rodgers, *The Work Ethic in Industrial America* (1978); David Montgomery, *Workers' Control in America: Studies in the History of Work, Technology, and Labor Struggles* (1970); Daniel J. Walkowitz, *Worker City, Company Town: Iron and Cotton-Worker Protest in Troy and Cohoes, New York, 1855–84* (1978); and Theodore Hershberg, ed., *Philadelphia: Work, Space, Family, and Group Experience in the Nineteenth Century* (1981).

Labor conflicts are the focus of Robert V. Bruce's *1877: Year of Violence* (1959). Leon Fink explores the Knights of Labor in several communities in *Workingmen's Democracy: The Knights of Labor and American Politics* (1983).

Women and work are the subject of Alice Kessler-Harris, *Out to Work: A History of Wage-Earning Women in the United States* (1982); Julie Matthaei, *An Economic History of Women in America: Women's Work, the Sexual Division of Labor, and the Development of Capitalism* (1982); and David M. Katzman, *Seven Days a Week: Women and Domestic Service in Industrializing America* (1978).

Irvin G. Wyllie investigates the idea that hard work would result in upward mobility in *The Self-Made Man in America: The Myth of Rags to Riches* (1954). The realities of mobility and assimilation are studied by Stephan Thernstrom in *Poverty and Progress: Social Mobility in a 19th Century City* (1964) and in *The Other Bostonians: Poverty and Progress in the American Metropolis, 1880–1970* (1973). Similar works include Clyde and Sally Griffen, *Natives and Newcomers: The Ordering of Opportunity in Mid-Nineteenth-Century Poughkeepsie* (1978); Michael P. Weber, *Social Change in an Industrial Town: Patterns of Progress in Warren, Pennsylvania, from Civil War to World War I* (1976); and Thomas Kessner, *The Golden Door: Italian and Jewish Immigrant Mobility in New York City, 1880–1915* (1977).

Novels of the period include Theodore Dreiser, *Sister Carrie* (1900); Stephen Crane, *Maggie: A Girl of the Streets* (1893); Abraham Cahan, *The Rise of David Levinsky* (1917); and Thomas Bell, *Out of This Furnace* (1976 edition).

## TIME LINE

| | |
|---|---|
| 1843–1884 | "Old immigration" |
| 1844 | Telegraph invented |
| 1850s | Steam power widely used in manufacturing |
| 1859 | Value of U.S. industrial production exceeds value of agricultural production |
| 1866 | National Labor Union founded |
| 1869 | Transcontinental railroad completed Knights of Labor organized |
| 1870 | Standard Oil of Ohio formed |
| 1870s–1880s | Consolidation of continental railroad network |
| 1873 | Bethlehem Steel begins using Bessemer process |
| 1873–1879 | Depression |
| 1876 | Alexander G. Bell invents telephone |
| 1877 | Railroad workers hold first nationwide industrial strike |
| 1879 | Thomas Edison invents incandescent light |
| 1882 | Chinese Exclusion Act |
| 1885–1914 | "New immigration" |
| 1886 | American Federation of Labor founded Haymarket Riot in Chicago |
| 1887 | Interstate Commerce Act |
| 1890 | Sherman Anti-Trust Act |
| 1892 | Standard Oil of New Jersey formed Coeur d'Alene strike Homestead steelworkers strike |
| 1893 | Chicago World's Fair |
| 1893–1897 | Depression |
| 1894 | Pullman railroad workers strike |
| 1900 | International Ladies' Garment Workers Union founded Corporations responsible for two-thirds of U.S. manufacturing |

# CHAPTER 20
## POLITICS AND PROTEST

In his best-selling utopian novel *Looking Backward* (1888), Edward Bellamy likened the American society of his day to a huge stagecoach. Dragging the coach along sandy roads and over steep hills were "the masses of humanity." While they strained desperately "under the pitiless lashing of hunger" to pull the coach, at the top sat the favored few, riding well out of the dust in breezy comfort. The fortunate few, however, were constantly fearful that they might lose their seats from a sudden jolt, fall to the ground, and have to pull the coach themselves.

Bellamy's famous coach allegory introduced a utopian novel in which the class divisions and pitiless competition of the nineteenth century were replaced by a classless, caring, cooperative new world. Economic anxieties and hardships were supplanted by satisfying labor and leisure. In place of the coach, all citizens in the year 2000 walked together in equal comfort and security under a huge umbrella over the sidewalks of the city. Bellamy's outlook on American life was a middle-class reformist one. His book had an enormous appeal not only because of his humane economic analysis but also because he clothed it in the form of a novel, complete with futuristic technological wonders, a double-dream trick ending, and a romantic love story.

As the novel opens, it is 1887. The hero, Julian West, a wealthy Bostonian, falls asleep worrying about the effect local labor struggles might have on his upcoming wedding. When he wakes up, it is the year 2000. The new society he discovers through his genial guide, Dr. Leete, is one in which all citizens live in material comfort and happiness. The utopia had come about peacefully through the development of one gigantic trust, owned and operated by the national government. All citizens between 21 and 45 work in an industrial army with equalized pay and work difficulty. Retirement after age 45 is devoted to hobbies, reading, culture, and such minimal political and judicial leadership as is needed in a society without crime, poverty, graft, vice, or war.

Bellamy's treatment of the role of women in the world of 2000 reflected his own era's struggle with changing relationships. On the one hand, new labor-saving gadgets relieved women of housework, and they served, like men, in the industrial army. Women married not for dependence but for love and could even initiate romantic relationships. On the other hand, the women Bellamy portrayed were still primarily responsible for shopping, supervision of domestic and aesthetic matters, and nurturing the young. In a special women's division of the industrial army, they worked shorter hours in "lighter occupations." The purpose of equality of the sexes and more leisure, the novel made clear, was to enable women to cultivate their "beauty and grace." Moreover, "their power of giving happiness to men," Dr. Leete said, "has been of course increased."

Bellamy's book was immensely popular. Educated middle-class Americans were attracted by his vision of a society in which humans were both morally good and materially well off. Readers were intrigued not only by all that was new but also by how much of the old society was preserved. The traditional male view of woman's place and purpose was one example. But Bellamy also retained such familiar values as individual taste and incentive, private property, and rags-to-riches presidents. Like most middle-class Americans of his day, he disapproved of European socialism. Although the collectivist features of Bellamy's utopia were socialistic, he and his admirers called his system "nationalism" and looked to conventional politics to implement it. In the early 1890s, with Americans buying nearly 10,000 copies of *Looking Backward* every week, over 160 Nationalist clubs were formed to crusade for the adoption of Bellamy's ideas.

In the transformation of industrial, urban, and agrarian life in the United States in the late nineteenth century, the dreams and aspirations of many Americans went unfulfilled, as we have seen. The wealthiest 10 percent, who rode high on the social coach, dominated politics. Except for token expressions of support, they ignored the cries of factory workers, immigrants, farmers, blacks, and other victims of change. But as the century drew to a close, the call for political reform was heard more often, not just from these victims but also from middle-class Americans like Bellamy. They were motivated both by fears of a general disruption and by a genuine humane commitment to help the less fortunate.

This chapter describes, first, conventional American politics at the national and local level from Reconstruction to the early 1890s, and second, the world of the comfortable classes, including the dilemmas and burdens of middle-class women and men and their protests against the corrosive problems of urban industrial life. The chapter concludes with an account of the Populist revolt in the 1890s, culminating in the election of 1896.

## POLITICS IN THE GILDED AGE

American government in the 1870s and 1880s supported the interests of those who rode at the top of the coach. Although some modern observers think the national government should have tackled problems like poverty, unemployment, and trusts, few nineteenth-century Americans would have agreed. They mistrusted organized power and believed in laissez-faire, a doctrine by which government largely kept its hands off economic problems. After the traumas of the Civil War era, when a strong, centralized state pursued high moral causes, late nineteenth-century political leaders favored a period of governmental passivity. This would permit the continuing pursuit of industrial expansion and wealth. As Republican leader Roscoe Conkling explained, the primary role of government was "to clear the way of impediments and dangers, and leave every class and every individual free and safe in the exertions and pursuits of life."

What followed, Henry Adams observed, was the most "thoroughly ordinary" period in American politics since Columbus. Ordinary politics, however, did not necessarily mean honest politics, as he knew well: "One might search the whole list of Congress, Judiciary, and Executive during the twenty-five years 1870–95 and find little but damaged reputation." Few eras of American government were as corrupt as this one, and Adams was especially sensitive to this

*Starry-eyed Edward Bellamy captured the imagination of millions with his futuristic* Looking Backward.

decline in the quality of democratic politics. His autobiography, *The Education of Henry Adams* (1907), contrasted the low political tone of his own age with the exalted political morality of the days of grandfather John Quincy Adams and great-grandfather John Adams.

## Politicians, Parties, and Presidents

In a satirical book in 1873, Mark Twain, with Charles Dudley Warner, coined the expression "Gilded Age" as a synonym for political corruption during Grant's presidency. The expression, with its suggestion of shallow glitter, has come to characterize social and political life in the last quarter of the nineteenth century. In these years, the dominant branch of government was Congress, and the moral quality of legislative leadership was typified by men such as James G. Blaine and Roscoe Conkling. Despite a scandal in which he was paid for supporting favors to railroads and then lied about it afterwards, Blaine was probably the most popular Republican politician of the era. A man of enormous charm, intelligence, wit, and ability, he served his country as senator from Maine, twice as secretary of state, and was a serious contender for the presidency in every election from 1876 to 1892.

Blaine's intraparty foe, Roscoe Conkling, was even more typical. The New York *Times* described him as "a man by whose career and character the future will judge of the political standards of the present." A stalwart Republican who controlled the rich patronage jobs of the New York customhouse, Conkling spent most of his career in patronage conflicts with fellow Republicans. He quarreled even more with civil service reformers, who believed government jobs should be dispensed for merit rather than party loyalty. Conkling could imagine no other purpose of politics and accused them of wanting the jobs for themselves. "Their real object is office and plunder." Fittingly, his career ended when he resigned from the Senate in a patronage dispute with President Garfield. Though he served in Congress for over two decades, Conkling never drafted a bill. This did not hurt his career, for in the Gilded Age, legislation was not Congress's primary purpose.

In 1879, a student of legislative politics, Woodrow Wilson, expressed his disgust with the degradation of politics in the Gilded Age in eight words: "No leaders, no principles; no principles, no parties." There was little to distinguish the two major parties from each other. They differed not over principles but patronage, not over issues but the spoils of office. At stake in elections were not laws but the thousands of government jobs at the disposal of the winning candidate and his party. In a shrewd analysis of the American political system in the late nineteenth century, an English observer, Lord James Bryce, concluded that the most cohesive force in American politics was "the desire for office and for office as a means of gain." The two parties, like two bottles of liquor, Bryce said, bore different labels, yet "each was empty."

The clear ideological party positions taken during the Civil War and Reconstruction had all but disappeared. The Republican party frequently reminded voters of its role in winning the Civil War and preserving the Union. Republican votes still came from northeastern Yankee industrial interests and from New England migrants across the Upper Midwest. The main support for Democrats still came primarily from southern whites, northern workers, and Irish Catholic and other urban immigrants. For a few years, Civil War and Reconstruction issues generated party differences. But after 1876, on national issues at least, party labels did indeed mark "empty" bottles.

The two parties were evenly matched. In three of the five presidential elections between 1876 and 1892, one percent of the vote separated the two major candidates. In 1880, for example, James Garfield defeated his Democratic opponent by only 7,018 votes. In 1884, Grover Cleveland squeaked by James G. Blaine by a popular vote margin of 48.5 to 48.2 percent. In two elections (1876 and 1888), the electoral vote winner had fewer popular votes. Further evidence of political stalemate was that neither party was able to control the White House and both houses of Congress for long. Although all the presidents in the era except Cleveland were Republicans, the Democrats controlled the House of Representatives in eight of the ten sessions of Congress between 1875 and 1895.

## Presidential Elections, 1872–1892

| YEAR | CANDIDATES | PARTY | POPULAR VOTE | ELECTORAL VOTE |
|------|-----------|-------|--------------|----------------|
| 1872 | U. S. GRANT | Republican | 3,596,745 (56%) | 286 |
|      | H. Greeley | Democrat | 2,843,446 (44%) | 66 |
| 1876 | S. Tilden | Democrat | 4,284,020 (51%) | 184 |
|      | R. B. HAYES | Republican | 4,036,572 (49%) | 185 |
| 1880 | J. GARFIELD | Republican | 4,449,053 (48%) | 214 |
|      | W. S. Hancock | Democrat | 4,442,035 (48%) | 155 |
|      | J. B. Weaver | Greenback-Labor | 308,578 (3%) | 0 |
| 1884 | G. CLEVELAND | Democrat | 4,911,017 (48.5%) | 219 |
|      | J. Blaine | Republican | 4,848,334 (48.2%) | 182 |
|      | Minor parties | | 325,739 (3.3%) | 0 |
| 1888 | G. Cleveland | Democrat | 5,540,050 (48.6%) | 168 |
|      | B. HARRISON | Republican | 5,444,337 (47.9%) | 233 |
|      | Minor parties | | 396,441 (3.5%) | 0 |
| 1892 | G. CLEVELAND | Democrat | 5,554,414 (46%) | 277 |
|      | B. Harrison | Republican | 5,190,802 (43%) | 145 |
|      | J. B. Weaver | Populist | 1,027,329 (9%) | 22 |

*Note:* Winner's name is in capital letters.

Lord Bryce titled one of the chapters of his book on American politics "Why Great Men Are Not Chosen Presidents." Gilded Age presidents were an undistinguished group. They played only a minor role in national life, especially when compared to industrial entrepreneurs like Carnegie, Rockefeller, Swift, and Armour. None of them—Rutherford B. Hayes (1877–1881), James Garfield (1881), Chester A. Arthur (1881–1885), Grover Cleveland (1885–1889 and 1893–1897), and Benjamin Harrison (1889–1893)—served two consecutive terms. None was strongly identified with any particular issue. None has been highly regarded by historians.

*Although the tariff protectionist Harrison defeated Cleveland in 1888 (reversed in 1892), all Gilded Age presidents were essentially "preservers" rather than innovators.*

Although Cleveland was the only Democrat in the group, his positions differed little from those of the Republicans. Upon his election in 1884, financier Jay Gould sent him a telegram stating his confidence that "the vast business interests of the country will be entirely safe in your hands." When Cleveland violated the expectation that presidents should not initiate ideas by devoting his entire annual message in 1887 to a call for a lower tariff, Congress listened politely and did nothing. Voters turned him out of office a year later.

Most Americans expected their presidents to take care of party business by rewarding faithfuls with government positions. The scale of patronage was enormous. Garfield complained of having to dispense thousands of jobs as he took office in 1881, worrying, he said, "whether A or B should be appointed to this or that office." Garfield is remembered primarily for being shot early in his administration by a disappointed office seeker. He achieved heroic stature only by hanging on for 2½ months before he died. His successor, Chester Arthur, was so closely identified with Conkling's patronage operation that when Garfield's shooting was announced, a friend said with shocked disbelief, "My God! Chet Arthur in the White House!"

## National Issues

Arthur surprised his doubters by proving himself a capable and dignified president, responsive to the growing demands for civil service reform. Four issues were important at the national level in the Gilded Age: the tariff, currency, civil service, and government regulation of railroads (see Chapter 18). In confronting these issues, legislators tried to serve both their own self-interest and the national interest of an efficient, productive economy.

The tariff was one issue where party, as well as regional attitudes toward the use of government power, made some difference. Republicans believed in using the state to support business interests and stood for a high protective tariff. A nation demonstrated its "intelligence," one orator said, by using law to promote a "dynamic and progressive" society. The tariff would protect American businessmen as well as wage earners and farmers from the competition and products of foreign labor. By contrast, Democrats stressed that a low tariff exemplified the "economic axiom . . . that the government is best which governs least." High tariffs falsely substituted the aims and actions of the state for those that should come from "individual initiative."

Although Democrats were identified with a low tariff position and Republicans with a high one, in reality there was little consistency in either party's stand. In practice, politicians accommodated local interests each time the tariff was adjusted. Democratic senator Daniel Vorhees of Indiana explained, "I am a protectionist for every interest which I am sent here by my constituents to protect." Other legislators acted similarly on behalf of their states. Those supporting a high protective tariff to shield them from foreign competition represented Pennsylvania iron and steel manufacturers, West Virginia coal miners, and Louisiana beet growers. But New York importers, southern cotton growers, and western farmers and cattle ranchers, who depended on foreign markets, wanted lower tariffs.

Tariff revisions were bewilderingly complex in their accommodation to these many special interests. As one senator knowingly said, "The contest over a revision of the tariff brings to light a selfish strife which is not far from disgusting." Usually, a tariff included a mixture of higher and lower rates that defied understanding. Since the federal government depended on tariffs and excise taxes (primarily on tobacco and liquor) for most of its revenue, there was little chance that the tariff would be abolished or substantially lowered. Moreover, the surpluses produced by the tariff during the Gilded Age helped the parties finance patronage jobs as well as government programs.

The question of money was also complicated. During the Civil War, the federal government had circulated paper money (greenbacks) that could not be exchanged for gold or silver. In the late 1860s and 1870s, politicians debated whether the United States should return to a metallic standard, which would allow paper money to be exchanged for specie. Proponents of a hard-money policy supported either withdrawing all paper money from circulation or making it convertible to specie. They opposed increasing the volume of money because they thought it would lead to higher prices. Greenbackers, who advocated soft money, argued that there was not enough currency in circulation for an expanding economy and urged increasing the supply of paper money. An indequate money supply, they believed, led to falling prices and an increase in interest rates, which harmed farmers, industrial workers, and all those in debt.

Hard-money interests had more power and influence. In 1873, Congress demonetized silver. In 1875, it passed the Specie Resumption Act, gradually retiring greenbacks from circulation and putting the nation firmly on the gold standard. But as large supplies of silver were discovered and mined in the West, pressure was resumed for increasing the money supply by coining silver. Soft-money advocates pushed for the unlimited coinage of silver in addition to gold. A compromise of sorts was reached in 1878 with passage of the Bland-Allison Act requiring the Treasury to buy between $2 million and $4 million of silver each month and to coin it as silver dollars. Despite the increase in money supply, the period was not an inflationary one but a time of falling prices, disappointing the supporters of soft money. Their response was to push for more silver, which continued the controversy into the 1890s.

The third issue of the Gilded Age was civil service reform, "a subject" Henry Adams observed, "almost as dangerous in political conversation in Washington as slavery itself in the old days before the war." The worst feature of the spoils system was that parties financed themselves by assessing holders of patronage jobs, often as much as one percent of their annual salaries. Reformers, most of whom were upper- and middle-class white American-born Protestants, pressed for competitive examinations, allegedly to ensure the creation of a professional, honest, nonpartisan permanent civil service. But what some wanted was to deny the spoils of office to immigrants and their urban political machine bosses.

Civil service reform had first been raised during the Grant administration, but little was accomplished. The assassination of Garfield, however, created enough public support to force Congress to take action. The Pendleton Act of 1883 established a system of merit examinations covering about one-tenth of federal offices. A mighty reform, the Pendleton Act failed to transform American political life. Gradually, more bureaucrats fell under its coverage, but parties became no more honest. As campaign contributions from government employees dried up, parties turned to other financial sources. In 1888, record corporate contributions helped to elect Harrison.

## The Lure of Local Politics

The fact that the major parties did not disagree substantially on issues like money and civil service does not mean that nineteenth-century Americans found politics dull or uninteresting. In fact, far more eligible voters turned out in the late nineteenth century than at any time since. Between 1876 and 1896, some 78.5 percent of those eligible to vote for president did so. By contrast, in the 1984 election, less than 55 percent of eligible Americans voted for president.

What explains such an amazing nineteenth-century turnout? Americans went to the polls in large numbers for many reasons, but the most compelling ones were local. Iowa corn farmers voted for state representatives who favored curbing the power of the railroads to set high grain-shipping rates. While Irish Catholics in New York sought political support for their parochial schools, third-generation middle-class American Protestants from Illinois or Connecticut voted for laws that would compel attendance at public schools. Nashville, Tennessee, whites supported laws that established segregated railroad cars and other public facilities. Milwaukee German brewery workers voted against local temperance laws because they valued both their jobs and their beer. Ohio and Indiana Protestant farmers, on the other hand, believing they were protecting social order and morality against hard-drinking Catholic immigrants, pushed for temperance laws.

The influx of the new immigrants, especially in the mushrooming cities, played a large role in stimulating political participation. As traditional ruling groups, usually native-born, left local government for business, where they found more money and status, urban bosses stepped in. Their power to control city government rested on an ability to deliver the votes of poor, uneducated immigrants. In countless ways, the bosses helped these constituents in return for votes. Bosses like "Big Tim" Sullivan of New York and "Hinky Dink" Kenna of Chicago operated informal welfare systems. They handed out jobs and money for rent, fuel, and bail. Sullivan gave new shoes as birthday presents to all poor children in his district, as well as turkeys to poor families at Thanksgiving. Above all, party bosses provided a personal touch in a strange and forbidding environment. As one boss explained, "I think that there's got to be in every ward somebody that any bloke can come to—no matter what he's done—and get help."

New York City's Tammany Hall boss, George Washington Plunkitt, perfected the relationship of mutual self-interest with his constituents, as the accompanying account shows. The favors he provided in return for votes ranged from attending weddings and funerals to influencing police and the courts. His clients included not only Jewish brides, Italian mourners, and burned-out tenants but also job seekers, store owners, saloonkeepers, and madams, all of whom needed favors. State party leaders were no less effective than urban bosses in mobilizing voters. In 1900, for example, Pennsylvania Republican party leaders were said to have lists of over 800,000 voters, each one annotated with his usual voting behavior. An Indiana Republican state chairman appointed 10,000 district workers in 1884 responsible for discovering the "social and political affiliation" of every single voter.

Party leaders also won votes by making political participation exciting. Nineteenth-century campaigns were punctuated by parades, rallies, and oratory. Campaign buttons, handkerchiefs, songs, and other paraphernalia generated color and excitement in political races where substantive issues were not at stake. In the election of 1884, for example, emotions ran high over the moral lapses of the opposition candidate. The Democrats made much of Blaine's record of dishonesty, chanting in election eve parades and rallies: "Blaine! Blaine! James G.

Blaine! / Continental liar from the state of Maine!" Republicans, in turn, learning of an illegitimate child fathered by Grover Cleveland, answered with their own chant: "Ma! Ma! Where's my pa? / Gone to the White House, Ha! Ha! Ha!" Cleveland won, in part because a Republican clergyman unwisely called the Democrats the party of "Rum, Romanism, and Rebellion" on election eve in New York. The remark backfired, and the Republicans lost both New York, which should have been a safe state, and the election.

The response of voters in New York in 1884 demonstrated that local and ethnocultural issues rather than national and economic questions explained party affiliation and political behavior. If voters were cool toward the tariff and civil service, they expressed strong interest in temperance, anti-Catholicism, compulsory school attendance and Sunday laws, aid to parochial schools, racial issues, restriction of immigration, and "bloody shirt" reminders of the Civil War.

Party membership reflected voter interest in these important cultural, religious, and ethnic questions. Midwestern Scandinavians and Lutherans, for example, tended to be Republicans, as were northerners who belonged to Protestant denominations. These groups believed in positive government action. Since the Republican party had proved its willingness in the past to mobilize the power of the state to reshape society, people who wished to regulate moral and economic life were attracted to it. Catholics and various immigrant groups found the Democratic party more to their liking because it opposed government efforts to regulate morals. Said one Chicago Democrat, "A Republican is a man who wants you t' go t' church every Sunday. A Democrat says if a man wants t' have a glass of beer on Sunday he can have it."

These differences caused spirited local contests, particularly over prohibition. Many Americans considered drinking a serious social problem. By 1880, the annual consumption of brewery beer had risen in 30 years from 2.7 to 17.9 gallons per capita. Although this increase could have been the result of changes in drinking habits, many feared that alcoholism was on the increase. Certainly the number of saloons ballooned. In one city, saloons outnumbered churches 31 to 1. This shocked those who believed that drinking would destroy the American character, corrupt politics, and lead to brutality, crime, and unrestrained sexuality. Women especially supported temperance because they were often the targets of drunken male violence. Rather than trying to persuade individuals to give up drink, as the temperance movement had done earlier in the century, many now sought to make drinking a crime.

The battle in San Jose, California, illustrates the strong passions such efforts aroused. In the 1870s, temperance reformers put on the ballot a local option referendum to ban the sale of liquor in San Jose. Women, using their influence as guardians of morality, erected a temperance tent where they held conspicuous daily meetings. Despite denunciations from some clergymen and heckling from some of the town's drinkers, the women refused to retreat to their homes. On election eve, a large crowd appeared at the temperance tent, but a larger one turned up at a proliquor rally. In the morning, women roamed the streets, urging men to adopt the referendum. Children were marched around to the polls and saloons, singing, "Father, dear father, come home with me now." By afternoon the mood grew ugly, and the women were harassed and threatened by drunken men. The prohibition proposal lost by a vote of 1,430 to 918.

Similarly emotional conflicts occurred in the 1880s at the state level over other issues, especially education. In Iowa, Illinois, and Wisconsin, Republicans sponsored laws mandating that children attend "some public or private day school," defined as schools that provided instruction in English. The intent of these laws was to undermine parochial schools, which taught in the language of the immigrants. In Iowa, where a state prohibition law was passed as well, the Republican slogan was "A schoolhouse on every hill, and no saloon in the valley." Confident in their cause, Protestant Iowa Republicans proclaimed that "Iowa will go Democratic when hell goes Methodist." It went Republican. But in Wisconsin, the Bennett law for compulsory school attendance was so strongly anti-Catholic that it backfired. Many voters, disillusioned with Republican moralism, shifted to the Democratic party. Campaigns like these,

which both reflected and nourished ethnic tension, continued into the 1890s.

## Republican Legislation in the Early 1890s

For many years, the decade of the 1890s was mistakenly called the "gay nineties." The decade is best understood, however, as a time dominated by a terrible depression and by worsening economic and social conflict. The rise in agrarian discontent, lynchings, and violent and repressive labor strikes all testify to this. But even before the onset of depression, Congress began to shift away from laissez-faire toward activism in order to confront national problems.

In the first six months of 1890, Republicans in Congress moved forward with legislation in five areas: pensions for Civil War veterans and their dependents, trusts, the tariff, the money question, and rights for blacks. The Dependent Pensions Act, providing generous support of $160 million a year to Union veterans and their dependents, sailed through Congress and was quickly signed into law by President Harrison.

The Sherman Anti-Trust Act also passed easily, with only one nay vote. The bill declared illegal "every contract, combination . . . or conspiracy in restraint of trade or commerce." Although the bill was vague and not really

*Women, often targets of drunken male violence, campaigned for temperance as well as for equal rights. Here Victoria Claflin Woodhull reads a suffrage proposal to the House Judiciary Committee in 1871.*

intended to break up large corporations, it addressed anxieties many Americans felt about the effect of business combinations on equal opportunity. Five years later, the Supreme Court showed that the Sherman Act would not hurt trusts. In *United States* v. *E. C. Knight*, the Court ruled that the American Sugar Refining Company, which controlled more than 90 percent of the nation's sugar refining capacity, was not in violation of the Sherman Act.

A tariff bill introduced in 1890 by Ohio Republican William McKinley generated more controversy. McKinley's bill, which he said was "made for the American people and American interests," attempted to make good the Republican stance on protection by raising certain tariff rates. Despite heated opposition from agrarian interests, whose products were generally not protected, the bill passed the House. In the Senate, however, nearly 500 amendments extended debates and stimulated rumors of large defections to the Democrats. "The charge against the protective policy which has injured it most," Blaine reflected, "is that its benefits go wholly to the manufacturer and the capitalist, and not at all to the farmer." Republican leaders succeeded in modifying the bill to please some farmers, and the McKinley Tariff scraped by, 33 to 27.

Silver was even trickier. Recognizing the appeal of free silver to agrarian debtors, Republican leaders feared the party might be destroyed by the issue. Senator Sherman proposed a compromise measure that momentarily satisfied almost everyone. The Sherman Silver Purchase Act ordered the Treasury to buy 4.5 million ounces of silver monthly (nearly all the silver produced) and to issue Treasury notes for it. Silverites were pleased by the proposed increase in the money supply. Opponents felt they had averted the worst, free coinage of silver. The gold standard remained secure.

As the party of action, the Republicans were prepared to confront violations of the voting rights of southern blacks in 1890. President Harrison told the editor of the New York *Tribune*, "I feel very strong upon the question of a free ballot." Political considerations paralleled moral ones. Since 1877, the South had become a Democratic stronghold, where party victories could be traced to fraud and intimidation of black Republican voters. "To be a Republican . . . in the South," one Georgian noted, "is to be a foolish martyr." Republican legislation, then, would honor old commitments to the freedmen and improve party fortunes in the South. An elections bill, proposed by Massachusetts senator Henry Cabot Lodge, would protect voter registration and ensure fair elections by setting up mechanisms for investigating charges of bribery and fraud and dealing with contested elections. A storm of disapproval from Democrats greeted the measure, which they labeled the "Force Bill." Cleveland called it "a dark blow at the freedom of the ballot," while the Mobile *Daily Register* claimed that it "would deluge the South in blood." Although House Speaker Reed steered the bill through the House, Senate Democrats delayed action with a filibuster.

Meanwhile, Republicans worried that they could not pass both the elections bill and the McKinley Tariff, which was languishing in the Senate. Pennsylvania senator Matt Quay, who had skillfully directed Harrison's election in 1888, proposed that if the Democrats ceased their delaying tactics so that the tariff could come to a vote, the Republicans would agree to put off consideration of the elections bill. The ploy worked, marking the end of major party efforts to protect black voting rights in the South until the 1960s. In a second setback for black southerners, the Senate defeated a bill to provide federal aid to schools in the South, mostly black, that did not receive their fair share of local and state funds. These two failed measures were the last gasp of the Republican party's commitment to the idealistic principles of Reconstruction. As we saw in Chapter 19, the decade that followed these defeats was one of growing violent oppression of southern blacks and a steady loss of their rights. "The plain truth is," said the New York *Herald*, "the North has got tired of the negro."

The legislative efforts of the summer of 1890, impressive by nineteenth-century standards, fell far short of solving the nation's problems. Trusts grew more rapidly after the Sherman Act than before. Union veterans were pleased by their pensions, but southerners were incensed that Confederate veterans were not covered. Others regarded the pension measure as extravagant and labeled the 51st Congress the "billion-dollar Congress." Despite efforts to please farmers, many still viewed tariff protection as a benefit primarily for eastern manufacturers. Farm prices continued to decline, and gold and silver advocates were only momentarily silenced. Black rights were put off to another time. Nor did Republican legislative activism lead the Republicans to a "permanent tenure of power," as party leaders had hoped. Voters abandoned the GOP in droves in the 1890 congressional elections, dropping the number of Republicans in the House from 168 to 88.

Two years later, Cleveland won a presidential rematch with Harrison. His inaugural address underlined the lesson he drew from the legislative activism of the Republicans in 1890. "The lessons of paternalism ought to be unlearned," he said, "and the better lesson taught that while the people should . . . support their government, its functions do not include the support of the people."

### The Depression of 1893

Cleveland's philosophy of government soon faced a difficult test. No sooner had he taken office than began one of the worst depressions ever to grip the American economy, lasting from 1893 to 1897. As had been true in 1873, the severity of the depression was heightened by the growth of a national economy and economic interdependence.

The depression started in Europe and spread to the United States as overseas buyers cut back on their purchases of American products. Shrinking markets abroad soon crippled American manufacturing. Moreover, many foreign investors, worried about the stability of American currency after passage of the Sherman Silver Purchase Act, dumped some $300 million of their securities in the United States. As gold left the country to pay for these securities, the nation's supply of money declined. At the same time, falling prices hurt farmers, many of whom discovered that it cost more to raise their crops and livestock than they could recover in the market. Workers fared no better, as wages fell faster than the price of food and rent.

The collapse in 1893 was caused not only by overseas economic developments but also by serious overextensions of the economy at home, especially in railroad construction. Farmers,

moreover, troubled by falling prices, planted more and more crops, hoping somehow that the market would pick up. As the realization of overextension spread, confidence faltered, then gave way to financial panic. When the stock market crashed early in 1893, investors frantically sold their shares, companies plunged into bankruptcy, and the cycle of disaster spread. People rushed to exchange paper notes for gold, reducing gold reserves and confidence in the economy even further. Banks called in their loans, which by the end of the year led to 16,000 business bankruptcies and 500 bank failures.

The decrease in available capital and diminished buying power of rural and small-town Americans (still half the population) forced massive factory closings. Within a year, an estimated 3 million Americans, 20 percent of the work force, were unemployed. Suddenly people began to look fearfully at the presence of tramps wandering from city to city looking for work. "There are thousands of homeless and starving men in the streets," one young man reported from Chicago, indicating that he had seen "more misery in this last week than I ever saw in my life before."

As in Bellamy's coach allegory, the misery of the many was not shared by the few, which only increased discontent. While unemployed men groveled in garbage dumps for food, the wealthy gave lavish parties sometimes costing $100,000. At one such affair, diners ate their meal mounted on horses; at another, many guests proudly proclaimed that they had spent over $10,000 on their dresses. While poor families shivered in poorly heated tenements, the very rich built million-dollar summer resorts at Newport, Rhode Island, or grand mansions on New York's Fifth Avenue and Chicago's Gold Coast. While Lithuanian immigrants walked or rode streetcars to Buffalo steel factories to work, wealthy men skimmed across lakes and oceans in huge pleasure yachts. J. P. Morgan owned three, one with a crew of 85 sailors. Amid such inequalities of wealth Supreme Court Justice John Harlan noticed "a deep feeling of unrest" in the nation; agrarian activist "Sockless" Jerry Simpson more bluntly described "a struggle between the robbers and the robbed."

Nowhere were these inequalities more apparent than in Chicago during the World's Columbian Exposition, which opened on May 1, 1893, five days before plummeting prices on the stock market began the depression. The Chicago World's Fair was designed, as President Cleveland said in an opening-day speech, to show off the "stupendous results of American enterprise." When he pushed an ivory telegraph key, he started electric current that unfurled flags, spouted water through gigantic fountains, lit 10,000 electric lights, and powered huge steam

## Major Legislative Activity of the Gilded Age

| *National** | |
|---|---|
| 1871 | Civil Service Commission created |
| 1873 | Coinage Act demonitizes silver |
| | "Salary Grab" Act (increased salaries of Congress and top federal officials) partly repealed |
| 1875 | Specie Resumption Act retires greenback dollars |
| 1878 | Bland-Allison Act permits partial coining of silver |
| 1882 | Chinese Exclusion Act |
| | Federal Immigration Law restricts certain categories of immigrants and requires head tax of all immigrants |
| 1883 | Standard time (four time zones) established for the entire country |
| | Pendleton (Civil Service) Act |
| 1887 | Interstate Commerce Act sets up Interstate Commerce Commission |
| | Dawes Act divides Indian tribal lands into individual allotments |
| 1890 | Dependent Pension Act grants pensions to Union army veterans |
| | Sherman Anti-Trust Act |
| | Sherman Silver Purchase Act has goverment buy more silver |
| | McKinley Tariff sets high protective rates |
| | Federal Elections Bill to protect black voting rights in South fails in Senate |
| | Blair bill to provide support for equal education defeated |
| 1891 | Immigration law gives federal government control of overseas immigration |
| 1893 | Sherman Silver Purchase Act repealed |
| 1894 | Wilson-Gorman Tariff lowers duties slightly |
| 1900 | Currency Act puts United States on gold standard |

| *State and Local** | |
|---|---|
| 1850s–1880s | State and local laws intended to restrict or prohibit consumption of alcoholic beverages |
| 1871 | Illinois Railroad Act sets up railroad commission to fix rates and prohibit discrimination |
| 1874 | Railroad regulatory laws in Wisconsin and Iowa |
| 1881 | Kansas adopts statewide prohibition |
| 1882 | Iowa passes state prohibition amendment |
| 1880s | Massachusetts, Connecticut, Rhode Island, Montana, Michigan, Ohio, and Missouri all pass local laws prohibiting consumption of alcohol |
| 1889 | New Jersey repeals a county-option prohibition law of 1888 |
| | Bennett Law in Wisconsin and Edwards Law in Illinois mandate compulsory attendance of children at schools in which instruction is in English |
| | Kansas, Maine, Michigan and Tennessee pass antitrust laws |
| 1889–1890 | Massachusetts debates compulsory-schooling-in-English bill |
| 1889–1902 | Eleven ex-Confederate states amend state constitutions and pass statutes restricting the voting rights of blacks |
| 1890–1910 | Eleven ex-Confederate states pass segregation laws |
| 1891 | Nebraska passes eight-hour workday law |
| 1893 | Colorado adopts woman suffrage |
| 1894–1896 | Woman suffrage referendums defeated in Kansas and California |

*Note the kinds of laws in question at the different levels.

engines, 37 in one building alone. For six months, some 27 million visitors strolled around the White City designed by Daniel H. Burnham and admired its wide lagoons, white plaster buildings modeled on classical styles, and exhibit halls filled with inventions. Built at a cost of $31 million, the fair celebrated the marvelous mechanical accomplishments of American enterprise. Its elegant design stimulated a "City Beautiful" movement that made many cities more attractive and enjoyable for their residents.

But as well-to-do fairgoers sipped pink champagne, men, women, and children in the immigrant wards of Chicago less than a mile away drank contaminated water, crowded into packed tenements, and looked in vain for jobs. The area around Jane Addams's Hull House was especially disreputable, with saloons, gambling halls, brothels, and pawnshops dotting the neighborhood. "If Christ came to Chicago," a British journalist, W. T. Stead, wrote in a book of that title in 1894, this would be "one of the last precincts into which we should care to take Him." Stead's book showed readers the "ugly sight" of corruption, poverty, and wasted lives

in a city with 200 millionaires and 200,000 unemployed men.

Despite the magnitude of despair during the depression, national politicians and leaders were reluctant to respond. Only mass demonstrations forced city authorities to provide soup kitchens and places for the homeless to sleep. When an army of unemployed led by Jacob Coxey marched into Washington in the spring of 1894 to press for some form of public work relief, its leaders were arrested for stepping on the grass of the Capitol. Cleveland's reputation for callous disregard for citizens suffering from the depression worsened later that summer when he sent federal troops to Chicago to crush the Pullman strike. The president focused his efforts on tariff reform and repeal of the Silver Purchase Act, which he blamed for the depression. Few leaders in either major party, however, thought the federal government was responsible for alleviating the sufferings of the people.

Others, however, came forward with ideas and programs to deal not only with the problems spawned by the depression but also with those stemming from the country's dramatic urban and industrial transformation since the Civil

*Consciousness of the depression-worsened disparity between rich and poor was especially heightened during the World's Columbian Exposition in Chicago in 1893.*

War. Unskilled Slavic workers tending blast furnaces in Steelton, Pennsylvania, railway firemen in Terre Haute, Indiana, and pregnant Italian immigrant women in New Haven, Connecticut, tenements did not need an economic collapse to make them aware of these problems. But for many middle-class Americans, the depression, coming near the end of a century of triumphant progress symbolized by the Chicago exposition, served as a catalyst for the reexamination of the society America had become.

## THE LIFE OF THE MIDDLE CLASS

Americans with middling incomes had reason to be sensitive to the economic polarization and social conflict around them. Middle-class Americans neither dragged the coach in ceaseless toil nor sat at the very top. But this steadily growing group of educated professionals, white-collar clerks and salesmen, corporation managers, and public employees was determined to enjoy a smooth ride. With a relatively comfortable position on the coach, they had much to lose. By the 1890s, the average income for middle-class Americans had risen by about 30 percent since the Civil War. Although the general cost of living rose even faster than income, the difference was met by more members of the family holding jobs and by taking in lodgers in middle-class homes. By 1900, 36 percent of urban families owned their own homes, many of which were made more comfortable by the addition of indoor private bathrooms, iceboxes, and other conveniences.

The progress of American industry had raised the living standard for increasing numbers of Americans, who were better able to purchase consumer products manufactured, packaged, and promoted in an explosion of technological inventions and shrewd marketing techniques. The following familiar products and brands were invented or mass-produced for the first time in the 1890s: Del Monte canned fruits and vegetables, National Biscuit Company (Nabisco) crackers, Van Camp's pork and beans, Wesson oil, Lipton tea, Wrigley's Juicy Fruit chewing gum, Cracker Jacks, Tootsie Rolls, the

*A comfortable well-furnished home represented years of hard work and careful, planning for middle-class Americans from New Mexico to Virginia, as reflected here.*

Historians recover the past, as we have seen, not only through the printed words in books, diaries, magazines, tax lists, and government documents but also through such visual records as paintings, photographs, and buildings. All material objects recovered from the past, in fact, help historians understand how people lived and what they valued and thought. The products of the human experience include everything from tools to toys, farm implements to furniture, and cooking pots to clothes. Historians have learned from anthropologists that every object, no matter how trivial, tells them something about people's lives. We call such objects material culture.

Consider, for example, the mail-order catalog, according to one historian a "characteristically American kind of book." The origins of buying products through the mail can be traced back to Benjamin Franklin's promotion of his stove, the Pennsylvania fireplace, in 1744. But the significance of the mail-order catalog emerged with the spectacular success of the Montgomery Ward and Sears, Roebuck catalogs in the 1880s and 1890s. The tremendous growth of the

*Two pages from the Sears, Roebuck & Co. catalog, 1897*

639a

Sears, Roebuck catalog, the "Farmer's Bible," from a circulation of 318,000 in 1897 to over 3 million by 1907, is not our focus here, nor is the way in which it brought city goods to rural Americans. But for historians seeking to discover how middle-class Americans lived in the late nineteenth century, the mail-order catalog is a gold mine of information. It provides insight into the economics of pricing policies, the aesthetics of advertising, and social aspects of style and taste; and it is also a "paperback museum" of the objects the American people bought and used daily.

Shown here are two pages from the Sears, Roebuck fall catalog of 1897 depicting women's clothing and washing machines. What do these pages reveal about fashions and prices in 1897, the state of technology, and the image and role of women? How do these pages compare with the equivalent items from a contemporary Sears catalog? What changes have occurred and what has not changed since the turn of the century? What other items of material culture do you think would be especially revealing of middle-class life?

Hershey bar, shredded wheat, Aunt Jemima pancake mix, Jello-O, Campbell's soup, Fig Newtons, Canada Dry ginger ale, Coca-Cola, Pepsi-Cola, and Michelob beer. Cooked chopped meat put between two pieces of bread was first sold (for 7 cents) and called a "hamburger" in 1899.

Numerous other familiar items were developed during the last decade of the century: bottle caps, aluminum saucepans, book matches, zippers, Gillette razors, Kodak cameras, the motion picture camera, phonographs and, of course, the gasoline-engine motorcar. The first major amusement park in America, Coney Island, and the first public golf course both opened in the 1890s. Bicycling became a popular middle-class activity, basketball was invented, and professional baseball emerged as America's favorite spectator sport during the decade. In 1897, the first Cheyenne rodeo and the first Boston marathon took place.

More time for recreation and greater access to consumer goods signaled the power of industrialism to transform the lives of middle-class Americans. Once favored with greater buying power, middle-class Americans sought to organize efficient ways of producing, purchasing, and consuming the newfound wealth. American women were both agents of the rise in consumer spending and were themselves often on display as stylish objects of leisure and ostentatious wealth.

Shopping for home furnishings, clothes, and other items became an integral part of many middle-class women's lives. William Dean Howells, an author who believed that literature should realistically reflect life, described the newly rich middle classes in his novel *The Rise of Silas Lapham* (1884). Howells depicted one of Lapham's two daughters, Irene, who spent her abundant leisure in shopping and on her appearance every day. Many of these goods that Irene and others bought so eagerly were to be found in the new department stores that began to appear in the central business districts in the 1870s. These stores fed women's desire for material possessions at the same time as they revolutionized retailing.

Shopping was just one example of middle-class women's new leisure. A plentiful supply of immigrant servant girls relieved urban middle-class wives of many housekeeping chores, and smaller families lessened the burdens of motherhood.

## New Freedoms for Middle-Class Women

At the same time that many middle-class women enjoyed more leisure time and enhanced purchasing power, they won new freedoms. Several states granted women more property rights in marriage, adding to their growing sense of independence. Women, moreover, had finally cast off confining crinolines and bustles. The new dress, a shirtwaist blouse and ankle-length skirt, was more comfortable for working, school, and sports. The *Ladies' Home Journal* recommended bicycling, tennis, golf, gymnastics— even having fewer babies—to women in the early 1890s. This "new woman" was celebrated as *Life* magazine's attractively active, slightly rebellious "Gibson girl."

Women used their new freedom to join organizations of all kinds. Literary societies, charity groups, and reform clubs like the Women's Christian Temperance Union gave women organizational experience, awareness of their talents, and contact with people and problems away from their traditional family roles. The General Federation of Women's Clubs, founded

*Increased leisure time and changing styles of dress led to new freedoms and the popularity of sports for the middle class in the 1890s, as seen in this picture of women bicyclists in Crawfordsville, Indiana.*

in 1890, had one million members by 1920. The depression of 1893 stimulated many women to become socially active investigating slum and factory conditions, but some began this work even earlier. Jane Addams told her graduating classmates at the Rockford, Illinois, Female Seminary in 1881 to lead lives "filled with good works and honest toil," then went off herself to found Hull House, a social settlement that did more than its share of good works.

Job opportunities for these educated middle-class women were generally limited to social service and teaching school. Still regarded as a suitable female occupation, teaching was a highly demanding job as urban schools expanded under the pressure of a burgeoning population. Women teachers, many of them hired only because they accepted lower pay, often faced classes of 40 to 50 children in poorly equipped rooms. In Poughkeepsie, New York, teachers earned the same salaries as school janitors. By the 1890s, the willingness of middle-class women to work for low pay opened up other jobs as office workers, department store clerks, nurses, and service personnel. In San Francisco, for example, the number of clerical jobs doubled between 1852 and 1880. By 1900, nearly 20

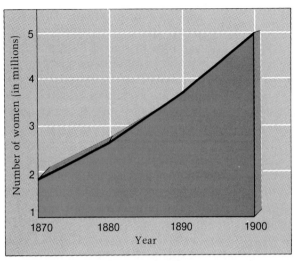

**Growth of Women in the Labor Force, 1870–1900**
*Source:* U.S. Bureau of the Census.

percent of American women were in the labor force, although most were immigrant women in low-paying jobs. Moving up to status jobs was difficult, even for middle-class women.

In the years after the Civil War, educational opportunities for women expanded. New wom-

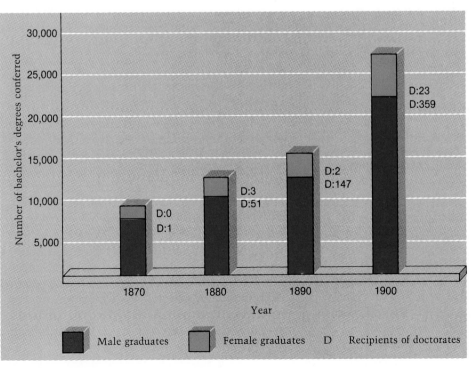

**Increase in Higher Education, 1870–1900**
*Source:* U.S. Department of Commerce.

en's colleges such as Smith, Mount Holyoke, Vassar, Bryn Mawr, and Goucher offered students programs similar to those at competitive men's colleges, while state schools in the Midwest and West dropped prohibitions against women. The numbers of women attending college rose. In 1890, 13 percent of all college graduates were women, a figure that increased to nearly 20 percent by 1900.

Higher education prepared women for conventional female roles as well as for work and public service. A few courageous graduates succeeded in joining the professions, but they had to overcome numerous barriers. Many medical schools refused to accept women students. As a Harvard doctor explained in 1875, a woman's monthly period "unfits her from taking those responsibilities which are to control questions often of life and death." Despite the obstacles, 2,500 women had managed to become physicians and surgeons by 1880 (comprising 2.8 percent of the total). Women were less successful at breaking into the legal world. In 1880, there were fewer than 50 female lawyers in the entire country, and as late as 1920, only 1.4 percent of the nation's lawyers and judges were women. George Washington University did not admit women to law school because mixed classes would be an "injurious diversion of attention of the students." Despite such resistance, by the first years of the twentieth century the number of women professionals (including teachers) was increasing at three times the rate of men.

One reason for the greater independence of American women was that they were having fewer babies (an average of 3.56 in 1900, half as many as in 1800). This was especially true of educated women. In 1900, nearly one in five married women was childless. Decreasing family size and an increase in the divorce rate (one of 12 marriages in 1905) added to men's fears that the family, traditional sex roles, and social order were threatened by the new woman. Theodore Roosevelt called this "race suicide" and argued that the falling white birthrate endangered national self-interest.

Arguments against the new woman intensified as many men reaffirmed Victorian stereotypes of "woman's sphere." Magazine editors and ministers borrowed from biology, sociology, and theology to support the notion that a woman's place was in the home. One male orator in 1896 attacked the new woman's public role because "a woman's brain involves emotions rather than intellect." This fact, he cautioned, "painfully disqualifies her for the sterner duties to be performed by the intellectual faculties. The best wife and mother and sister would make the worse legislator, judge and police."

Many men worried about female independence because it threatened their own masculinity. Male campaigns against prostitution and for sex hygiene, as well as efforts to reinforce traditional sex roles, reflected their deeper fears that female passions might weaken male vigor. The intensity of men's opposition to the new woman put limits on her emerging freedom.

### Struggle for Suffrage

Many women understandably felt pulled between their public and private lives, between their obligations to self, family, and society. This tension was not usually openly expressed. A few women writers, however, began to express the frustrations and dilemmas of middle-class women. Kate Chopin's novel *The Awakening* (1899) portrayed a young woman who, in awakening to her own sexuality and life's possibilities beyond being a "mother-woman," defied conventional expectations of woman's role. Her sexual affair and eventual suicide prompted a St. Louis newspaper to say of the novel that it was "too strong drink for moral babes and should be labeled 'poison.'"

Some middle-class women, Jane Addams, for example, avoided marriage altogether, preferring the supportive, integrative relationships found in the female settlement house community. "Married life looks to me . . . terribly impoverished for women," a Smith College graduate observed, declaring that "most of my deeper friendships have been with women." A few women boldly advocated free love or, less openly, formed lesbian relationships. Although most preferred traditional marriages and chose not to work outside the home, the generation of women that came of age in the 1890s married less—and later—than any other in American history.

One way women reconciled the conflicting pressures between their private and public lives, as well as deflected male criticism, was to see their work as maternal. Addams called Hull House "the great mother breast of our common humanity." The women's clubs took as their motto the intention to "show a more glorious womanhood . . . the mother-women working with all as well as for all." One of the leading female organizers of coal workers was "Mother" Jones, and the fiery feminist anarchist Emma Goldman titled her monthly journal *Mother Earth.* By using maternal, nurturant language to describe their work, women furthered the very arguments used against them. Many, of course, remained economically dependent on men, and all women still lacked the essential rights of citizenship to effect basic change. The struggle to achieve those rights demanded not social but political activism.

In the years after the Seneca Falls Convention in 1848, women's civil and political rights advanced very slowly. Although in several western states they received the right to vote in municipal and school-board elections, only the territory of Wyoming, in 1869, had granted full political equality before 1890. Colorado, Utah, and Idaho enfranchised women in the 1890s, but no other states granted suffrage until 1910. This slow pace was in part the result of an antisuffrage movement led by an odd combination of ministers, saloon interests, and those men who felt threatened in various ways by women's voting rights. "Equal suffrage," said a Texas senator, "is a repudiation of manhood."

In the 1890s, leading suffragists reappraised the situation. The two wings of the women's rights movement, split since 1869, combined in 1890 as the National American Woman Suffrage Association (NAWSA). Although Elizabeth Cady Stanton and Susan B. Anthony continued to head the association, they were both in their seventies, and effective leadership soon passed to younger, more moderate women. The new leaders concentrated on the single issue of the vote rather than dividing their energies among

*Woman's new role as a professional, such as this Red Cross nurse in the Spanish-American War, was often defended and praised in terms of its similarity to the role of a mother in the home.*

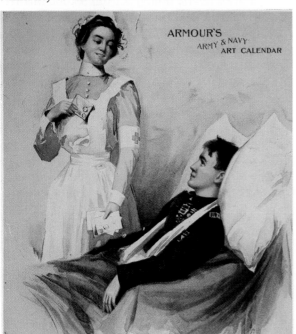

*The young Jane Addams was one of the college-educated women who chose to remain unmarried and pursue a career of social reform serving immigrant families in her Hull House, Chicago neighborhood.*

the many causes Stanton and Anthony had espoused. Moderate leaders were also embarrassed by Stanton's *Woman's Bible* (1895), a devastating attack on the religious argument against women's suffrage. At the NAWSA convention in 1896, despite the pleas of Anthony not to "sit in judgment" on her good friend, a resolution renouncing any connection with Stanton's book passed by a vote of 53 to 41.

Changing leadership meant a shift from principled to expedient arguments for the suffrage. Since 1848, suffragists had made their argument primarily from principle, citing, as Stanton argued at a congressional hearing in 1892, "the individuality of each human soul; our Protestant idea, the right of individual conscience and judgment; our republican idea, individual citizenship." But Stanton's leadership was on the wane, and the younger generation shifted to three expedient arguments. The first was that women needed the vote to pass self-protection laws that would guard them against the hazards peculiar to women presented by rapists, state age-of-consent laws, and industrial work. As Florence Kelley argued, "No disfranchised class of workers can . . . hold its own in competition with enfranchised rivals." The second argument insisted that modern urban life would benefit from women's maternal concern for improved health, living conditions, and morals. Addams called women "urban housekeepers" who would clean up tenements, saloons, factories, and corrupt politics.

The third expedient argument also reflected urban middle-class reformers' prejudice against non-Protestant newcomers to the city. As immigrant men arrived in America, they were almost immediately permitted to vote, a vote often bought by the local machine boss. Suffragists argued that educated, native-born American women should be given the vote to counteract the undesirable influence of ignorant, illiterate, and immoral male immigrants. In a speech in Iowa in 1894, Carrie Chapman Catt, who would succeed Anthony as president of NAWSA in 1900, argued that the "Government is menaced with great danger . . . in the votes possessed by the males in the slums of the cities," a danger that could be averted only by cutting off that vote and giving it instead to women. In the new

century it would be under the leadership of women like Catt that suffrage would finally be secured.

## Male Mobility and the Success Ethic

As women's lives were changing, so also were men's. "What a tremendous question it is—what shall I be?" 20-year-old Charles William Eliot wrote to a friend just before the Civil War. As the postwar economy expanded, many new job opportunities opened up for middle-class men. The growing complexity of census classifications attests to some of them. Where once the census taker had noted only the occupation of "clerk," now were listed "accountant," "salesman," and "shipping clerk." As the lower ranks of the white-collar world became more specialized, the number of middle-class jobs increased.

To prepare for these new careers, Americans required more education. The number of public high schools in the United States increased from 160 in 1870 to 6,000 in 1900. By 1900, 31 states and territories had compulsory school attendance laws.

Higher education also expanded in this period. The number of students in colleges and universities nearly doubled, from 53,000 in 1870 to 101,000 in 1900. Charles Eliot went on to become an outstanding educator, serving as president of Harvard from 1869 to 1909. He led Harvard through a period of dynamic growth, introducing several reforms such as higher faculty salaries and sabbatical leaves as well as the "elective" system of course selection for students. Harvard's growth reflected the rise of the university to a new stature in American life. As the land-grant state universities (made possible by the Morrill Act of 1862) continued to expand, generous gifts from wealthy businessmen helped to found leading research universities such as Stanford, Johns Hopkins, and the University of Chicago.

These developments led to greater specialization and professionalism, opening up still more careers in various fields of education, medicine, law, and business. Before the Civil War, a Swedish pioneer in Wisconsin described a young man he knew, who after "working as a mason . . .

laid aside the trowel, got himself some medical books, and assumed the title of doctor." But by the 1890s, with government licensing and the rise of professional schools, no longer were tradesman likely to read up on medicine and become doctors. In fact, the word *career* did not take on its modern meaning until 1893. In this period, organizations like the American Medical Association and the American Bar Association were regulating and professionalizing membership. The number of law schools doubled in the last quarter of the century, and 86 new medical schools were founded in the same period. Dental schools increased from 9 to 56 between 1875 and 1900.

The need for lawyers, bankers, architects, and insurance agents to serve business and industry expanded career opportunities. Between 1870 and 1900, the number of engineers, chemists, metallurgists, and architects grew rapidly. As large companies formed, many more managerial positions were required. As the public sector expanded, new careers in social service and government opened up as well. Many of these positions were filled by young professional experts emerging from graduate training in the social sciences. The professional disciplines of history, economics, sociology, psychology, and political science all date from the last 20 years of the nineteenth century.

The social ethic of the age stressed that economic rewards were available to anyone who fervently sought them. Many people argued that unlike Europe, where family background and social class determined social rank, in America few barriers held back those of good character and diligent work habits. Those who doubted that this opportunity existed needed only to be reminded of the examples of Benjamin Franklin and Abraham Lincoln. The Great Emancipator himself had said that "if any continue in the condition of a hired laborer for life it is because of a dependent nature which prefers it, or singular folly or improvidence or misfortune." Writers, lecturers, clergymen, and politicians zealously propagated the rags-to-riches tradition of upward mobility. Self-help manuals that outlined the steps to success for self-made men became widely available.

The best-known popularizer of the rags-to-

riches myth was Horatio Alger, Jr. His 119 novels, with titles like *Luck and Pluck*, *Strive and Succeed*, and *Bound to Rise*, were read by millions of American boys. In a typical Alger novel, the story opens with the hero leading the low life of a shoeshine boy in the streets. Dressed in rags, he sleeps in packing crates and unwisely spends what little money he has on tobacco, liquor, gambling, and the theater. A chance opportunity occurs, like diving into the icy waters of the harbor to save the life of the daughter of a local banker, and changes the Alger hero's life. He gives up his slovenly ways to work hard, save his money, and study. Eventually he rises to a prominent position, like vice-president of the bank owned by the rescued girl's father. Although moralists pointed to virtuous habits as crucial in Alger's heroes, success often depended as much on luck as on pluck.

Unlimited and equal opportunity for upward advancement in America has never been as easy as the "bootstraps" ethic maintains. But the persistence of the success myth owes something to the fact that many Americans, particularly those who began well, did rise rapidly. Native-born, middle-class whites tended to have the skills, resources, and connections that opened up the most desirable jobs. Financier Jay Gould overstated the case in maintaining that most of the nation's business and financial leaders were self-made men. "Nearly every one that occupies a prominent position has come up from the ranks," he said. In fact, the typical big businessman was a white, Anglo-Saxon Protestant from a middle- or upper-class family whose father was most likely in business, banking, or commerce.

### The Gospel of Wealth

Ideology supported the importance of winning the race to the top. Ministers preached countless sermons and wrote treatises emphasizing the moral superiority of the wealthy and justifying social class arrangements. Episcopal bishop William Lawrence wrote that it was "God's will that some men should attain great wealth." Philadelphia Baptist preacher Russell Conwell's famous sermon, "Acres of Diamonds," delivered 6,000 times to an estimated audience of 13 million, praised riches as a sure sign of "godliness" and stressed the power of money to "do good."

Industrialist Andrew Carnegie expressed the ethic most clearly. In his article "The Gospel of Wealth" (1889), Carnegie celebrated the benefits of better goods and lower prices that resulted from competition, arguing that "our wonderful material development" outweighed the harsh costs of competition. The concentration of wealth in the hands of a few leading industrialists, he concluded, was "not only beneficial but essential to the future of the race." Those most fit would bring order and efficiency out of the chaos of rapid industrialization. Carnegie's defense of the new economic order in his article and in a book, *Triumphant Democracy* (1886), found as many supporters as Bellamy's *Looking Backward*. Partly this was because Carnegie insisted that the rich were obligated to spend some of their wealth to benefit their "poorer brethren." Carnegie built hundreds of libraries, most still operating in large and small towns throughout the United States. In later years, the philanthropist turned his attentions to other projects, including world peace.

Carnegie's ideas about wealth were drawn from an ideology known as social Darwinism, based on the work of Charles Darwin, whose famous *Origin of Species* was published in 1859. Darwin had concluded that plant and animal species had evolved through a process of natural selection. In the struggle for existence, some species managed to adapt to their environment and survived. Others failed to adapt and perished. Herbert Spencer, an English social philosopher, adopted these notions of the "survival of the fittest" and applied them (as Darwin had not) to human society. Progress, he said, resulted from relentless competition in which the weak failed and were eliminated while the strong climbed to the top. He believed that "the whole effort of nature is to get rid of such as are unfit, to clear the world of them, and make room for better."

When Spencer visited the United States in 1882, leading men of business, science, religion, and politics thronged to honor him with a lavish banquet at Delmonico's restaurant in New York City. Here was the man whose theories justified their amassed fortunes because they were men of "superior ability, foresight, and adaptability." Spencer warned against any interference in the economic world by tampering with the natural laws of selection. The select at the dinner heaped their praise on Spencer as founder of not only a new sociology but also a new religion.

*The luxury of a fashionable home full of ornate fine art was accessible to anyone who worked hard, according to advocates of the Gospel of Wealth and social Darwinism. Successful families like the Vanderbilts, they said, represented humanity's "fittest" element. Contrast this scene with that of the middle- and lower-class families pictured earlier in this chapter.*

Spencer's American followers, like Carnegie and William Graham Sumner, a professor of political economy at Yale, familiarized the American public with the basic ideas of social Darwinism. They emphasized that poverty was the inevitable consequence of the struggle for existence and that attempts to end it were pointless, if not immoral. Although Sumner's emotional hero was the middle-class "forgotten man" like his father, his writings defended the material accumulations of the wealthy. To take power or money away from millionaires, Sumner scoffed, was "like killing off our generals in war." It was "absurd," he wrote, to pass laws permitting society's "worst members" to survive or to "sit down with a slate and pencil to plan out a new social world." Sumner was so consistent in his opposition to government intervention that he also opposed protective tariffs, which led some irritated rich Yale alumni to seek his dismissal.

The scientific vocabulary of social Darwinism, with its insistence on natural law, seemingly injected scientific rationality into what often seemed a baffling economic order. Underlying laws of political economy, like the laws governing the natural world, dictated all economic affairs. Social Darwinists also believed in the superiority of the Anglo-Saxon race, which they argued had reached the highest stage of evolution. Their theories were used to justify race supremacy and imperialism as well as the monopolistic efforts of American businessmen. Railroad magnate James J. Hill said that the absorption of smaller railroads by larger ones was the industrial analogy of the victory in nature of the fit over the unfit. John D. Rockefeller, Jr., told a YMCA class in Cleveland that "the growth of a large business is merely a survival of the fittest." Like the growth of a beauty rose, "the early buds which grow up around it" must be sacrificed. This was, he said, "merely the working out of a law of nature and a law of God."

Others took a less rosy outlook. Brooks Adams, brother of Henry, wrote that social philosophers like Spencer and Sumner were "hired by the comfortable classes to prove that everything was all right." Fading aristocratic families like the Adamses, who were being displaced by a new industrial elite, may have felt a touch of envy and loss of status. They succeeded, however, in suggesting that social change was not as closed as the social Darwinists claimed.

## MIDDLE-CLASS REFORM

In the late 1870s, Henry George observed that wherever the highest degree of "material progress" had been realized, "we find the deepest poverty." George's book, *Progress and Poverty* (1879), was an early statement of the contradictions of American life. With Bellamy's *Looking Backward*, it was one of the most influential books of the age, selling 2 million copies by 1905. Although George admitted that economic growth had produced wonders, he pointed out the social costs and rejected the gloomy social Darwinian notion that nothing could be done about them. His solution was to break up landholding monopolists who profited from the increasing value of their land and rents they collected from those who actually did the work. He proposed, therefore, a "single tax" on the unearned increases in land value received by landlords. His solution may seem overly simple, but George's optimistic faith in the capacity of humans to effect change made him appealing to middle-class intellectual reformers.

### Pragmatism: Underpinning for Reform

The pragmatists, led by two philosophers, John Dewey (see Chapter 22) and William James, established a far more complex foundation for reform efforts than did Henry George. James, a professor at Harvard, argued that while environment was important, so too was human will. What a person wanted or thought could influence the course of human events. "What is the 'cash value' of a thought, idea, or belief?" James asked. What was its result? "The ultimate test for us of what a truth means," he suggested, was in the consequences of a particular idea, in "the conduct it dictates."

In an early study, "Great Men and Their Environment" (1880), James emphasized the role of extraordinary individuals in fostering change. James and other intellectuals, especially many of the young social scientists gathering statistics about American society, rejected the social determinism of Herbert Spencer. They argued that the application of intelligence and human will could change the "survival of the fittest" into the "fitting of as many as possible to survive." Their position encouraged educators, economists, and reformers of every stripe, giving them an intellectual justification to struggle against the misery and inequalities of wealth found in many sectors of their society.

### Settlements and Social Gospel

Jane Addams understood the gap between progress and poverty. She saw it in the misery in the streets of Chicago in the winter of 1893. For some time she had been aware that life in big cities for working-class families was bitter and hard. "The stream of laboring people goes past you," she wrote, and as "you see hard working-men lifting great burdens . . . your heart sinks with a sudden sense of futility." Born in a small rural community in Illinois, Addams found herself attracted on a visit to Europe in the mid-1880s not to art galleries and cathedrals but to urban factories and slums. Such conditions, she knew, existed in the United States as well, and she developed a plan "to aid in the solution of the social and industrial problems which are engendered by the modern conditions of life in a great city."

Vida Scudder, too, "felt the agitating and painful vibrations" of the depression. Like Addams, this young professor of literature at Wellesley College had been influenced by English settlement house models. When she returned from study at Oxford "kindled with the flame of social passion," Scudder was resolved to do something to alleviate the suffering of the poor. She and six other Smith College graduates formed the College Settlements Association, an organization of college women who founded and worked in settlement houses.

Like Addams and Scudder, other middle-class activists worried about social conditions, particularly the degradation of life and labor in America's cities, factories, and farms. They were mostly professionals—lawyers, ministers, teachers, journalists, and academic social scientists. Influenced by European social prophets like Karl Marx, Leo Tolstoy, and Victor Hugo and by Americans such as Emerson, Whitman, and Bellamy, most turned to the ethical teachings of Jesus for inspiration in solving social problems.

The message they began to preach in the 1890s was highly idealistic, ethical, and Christian. They preferred a society marked by cooperation rather than competition, where self-sacrifice rather than self-interest held sway and, as they liked to say, where people were guided by the "golden rule rather than the rule of gold." They meant, in short, to apply the ethics of Jesus to industrial and urban life in order to bring about the kingdom of heaven on earth. Some preferred to put their goals in more secular terms; they spoke of radically transforming American society. Most, however, worked within existing institutions. As middle-class intellectuals, they tended to stress an educational approach to problems. But they were also practi-

*"Your heart sinks with a sudden sense of futility," wrote Jane Addams when she viewed the living conditions of America's urban poor.*

cal, involving themselves in an effort to make immediate, tangible improvements by running for public office, crusading for legislation, mediating labor disputes, and living in poor neighborhoods.

The settlement house movement typified the blend of idealism and practicality characteristic of middle-class reformers in the 1890s. In the fall of 1889, Addams opened Hull House in Chicago and Scudder started Denison House in Boston. A short time later, on New York's Lower East Side, Lillian Wald opened her "house on Henry Street." The primary purpose of the settlement houses was to help immigrant families, especially women, adapt Old World rural styles of childbearing and child care, housekeeping, cooking, and health care to the realities of urban living in America. This meant launching day nurseries, kindergartens, boarding rooms for working women, and classes in sewing, cooking, nutrition, health care, and speaking English. The settlements also frequently organized young people's sports clubs and coffeehouses as a way of keeping them out of the saloons.

A second purpose of the settlement house movement was to provide college-educated

*Many of the settlement houses included public health clinics, like this one at Vida Scudder's Denison House in Boston.*

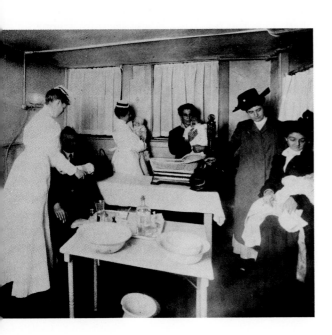

women with meaningful work at a time when they faced professional barriers and to allow them to preserve the strong feelings of sisterhood they had experienced in college. Settlement houseworkers, Scudder wrote, were like the "early Christians" in their renunciation of worldly goods and dedication to a life of service. Living in a settlement was in many ways an extension of woman's traditional role as nurturer of the weak. A third goal was to gather data exposing social misery in order to spur legislative action, such as developing city building codes for tenements, abolishing child labor, and improving safety in factories. Hull House, Addams said, was intended in part "to investigate and improve the conditions in the industrial districts of Chicago."

The settlement house movement, with its dual emphasis on the scientific gathering of facts and spiritual commitment, nourished the new academic study of sociology, first taught in divinity schools. Many organizations were founded to blend Christian belief and academic study in an attempt to change society. One was the American Institute of Christian Sociology, founded in 1893 by Josiah Strong, a Congregational minister, and Richard T. Ely, a University of Wisconsin economist. Similar organizations were the Christian Social Union, the Church Association for the Advancement of the Interests of Labor, and the Society of Christian Socialists.

These organizations viewed the purpose of religion as collective redemption rather than individual salvation. The latter was the prevailing view as presented in the wave of urban revivals led by the portly Dwight Moody in the 1870s. The revivals appealed to lower-class rural folk who were either drawn to the city by expectant opportunities or pushed there by economic ruin. They were supported by businessmen, who felt that religion would make workers and immigrants more docile. Revivalists emphasized the battle against sin through individual conversion. These revivals helped nearly to double Protestant church membership in the last two decades of the century. Although some urban workers drifted into secular faiths like socialism, most remained conventionally religious.

In the 1890s many Protestant ministers immersed themselves in the Social Gospel movement, which tied salvation to social betterment. Like the settlement house workers, these religious leaders sought to make Christianity relevant to industrial and urban problems. In Columbus, Ohio, Congregational minister Washington Gladden advocated collective bargaining and various forms of corporate profit sharing in books such as *Working Men and Their Employers*, *Social Salvation*, and *Applied Christianity*. A young Baptist minister in the notorious Hell's Kitchen area of New York City, Walter Rauschenbusch, raised an even louder voice. Often called upon to conduct funeral services for children killed by the airless, diseased tenements and sweatshops, Rauschenbusch was fired to unleash scathing attacks on the selfishness of capitalism and the irrelevance of a church that preached individual salvation rather than "social redemption." His progressive ideas for social justice and a welfare state were later published in two landmark Social Gospel books, *Christianity and the Social Crisis* (1907) and *Christianizing the Social Order* (1912).

Perhaps the most influential book promoting social Christianity was a best-selling novel, *In His Steps*, published in 1897 by Charles Sheldon. *In His Steps* portrayed the dramatic transformations in business relations, tenement life, and urban politics made possible by the work of a few community leaders who resolved to base all their actions on the single question, What would Jesus do? For a minister, this meant seeking to "bridge the chasm between the church and labor." For the idle rich, it meant settlement house work and reforming prostitutes. For landlords and factory owners, it meant taking action to improve living and working conditions for tenants and laborers. Although streaked with naive sentimentality characteristic of much of the Social Gospel, Sheldon's novel prepared thousands of influential middle-class Americans for progressive civic leadership after the turn of the century.

## Reforming the City

The crucial event in *In His Steps* was a city election pitting moral middle-class reformers against seedy saloon interests and corrupt urban political machines. No late nineteenth-century institution needed reforming as much as urban government. The president of Cornell University described American city governments as "the worst in Christendom—the most expensive, the most inefficient, and the most corrupt." A Philadelphia committee found "inefficiency, waste, badly paved and filthy streets, unwholesome and offensive water, and slovenly and costly management" to have been the rule for years. New York and Chicago were even worse.

Rapid urban growth taxed the abilities of city leaders. Population increase and industrial expansion created new demands for service. Flush toilets, thirsty horses pulling street railways, and industrial users of water, for example, all exhausted the capacity of municipal waterworks built for an earlier age. As city governments struggled to respond to new needs, they raised taxes and incurred vast debts. This combination of rapid growth, indebtedness, and poor services, coupled with the influx of new immigrants, prepared fertile ground for graft and "bossism."

The rise of the boss was intimately connected to the growth of the city. As cities mushroomed, new voters appeared, many of them immigrants. Traditional ruling groups, native-born in most cases, left government for business, where more money and status beckoned. Into the resulting power vacuum stepped the boss. In an age of urban expansion, bosses dispensed patronage jobs in return for votes and contributions to the party machine. They awarded street railway, gas line, and other utility franchises and construction contracts to local businesses in return for kickbacks and other favors. They also passed on tips to friendly real estate men about the location of projected city improvements. Worse yet, the bosses received favors from the owners of saloons, brothels, and gambling clubs in return for their help with police protection, bail, and influence with the courts. These institutions, however unsavory we might think them today, were vital to the urban economy and played an important role in easing the immigrants' way into American life. For many young women, the brothel was a means of economic survival. For men, the saloon was the center of social life, as well as a place for cheap meals and information about work and aid to his family.

"Bossism" deeply offended middle-class urban reformers, who were unkindly dubbed "goo-goos" for their insistence on purity and good government. They opposed not only graft and vice but also the perversion of democracy by the exploitation of ignorant immigrants. As one explained, the immigrants "follow blindly leaders of their own race, are not moved by discussion, and exercise no judgment of their own." Indeed, he concluded, they were "not fit for the suffrage."

The programs of urban reformers were similar in most cities. They not only worked for the "Americanization" of immigrants in public schools (and opposed parochial schooling) but also formed clubs or voters' leagues to discuss the failings of municipal government. They delighted in making spectacular exposures of electoral irregularities and large-scale graft. These discoveries led to strident calls for ousting the mayor, often an Irish Catholic, and replacing

*William Tweed, most famous of the city bosses, is represented as a continuing force long after his death in this cartoon by Thomas Nast.*

BRIBERY & CORRUPTION

NEW YORK

RIGHT UNDER HER NOSE; EVERY DAY IN THE WEEK

him with an honest reform candidate, usually an Anglo-Saxon Protestant.

Clearly implied in the reformers' agenda to strip power from the bosses was a preference for urban political leadership by people like themselves. Most urban reformers could barely hide their distaste for the "city proletariat mob," as one put it. They proposed to replace the bosses with expert city managers, who would bring honest professionalism to city government. They hoped to make government less costly and thereby lower taxes. One effect of their emphasis on cost efficiency was to cut services to the poor. Another was to disenfranchise working-class and ethnic groups, whose political participation depended on the old ward boss system.

Not all urban reformers were elitist, managerial types. Samuel Jones, for example, both opposed the boss system and had a passionate commitment to democratic political participation by the urban immigrant masses. An immigrant himself, Jones was a self-made man in the rags-to-riches mold. Beginning in poverty in the oil fields of Pennsylvania, he worked his way up to the ownership of several oil fields and a factory in Toledo, Ohio. Once successful, however, Jones espoused a different ethic than Carnegie's "Gospel of Wealth." He was, he said, "a Golden Rule man," converted by a combination of firsthand contact with the "piteous appeals" of people put out of work by the depression and by his reading of Emerson, Whitman, Tolstoy, and the New Testament.

In 1894, Jones resolved "to apply the Golden Rule as a rule of conduct" in his factory. He instituted an eight-hour day for his employees, a $2 minimum wage per day (50 to 75 cents higher than the Toledo average for ten hours), a cooperative insurance program, and an annual 5 percent Christmas dividend. He hired ex-criminals and outcasts that no one else would employ and plastered the Golden Rule all over his factory walls. Anticipating various twentieth-century industrial reforms, Jones created a company cafeteria, where he offered a hot lunch for 15 cents, a Golden Rule park for workers and their families, employee music groups, and a Golden Rule Hall, where he regularly invited prominent visionaries, many of them socialists, to speak.

In 1897, declaring that "after three years of a

test I am pleased to say the Golden Rule works," Jones decided to extend his notions of cooperation and brotherhood to city government, much like Hazen Pingree had been doing in nearby Detroit. Running as a maverick Republican, Jones was elected to an unprecedented four terms as mayor of Toledo. Installed by the voters, he advocated municipal ownership of natural gas, street railways, and other utilities; public works jobs and housing for the unemployed; more civic parks and playgrounds; and free municipal baths, pools, skating rinks, sleigh rides, vocational education, and kindergartens.

Few of these reforms were implemented, yet Jones's unorthodox ideas and behavior incurred the wrath of nearly every prominent citizen in Toledo. As a pacifist, he did not believe in violence or coercion of any kind. Therefore, he took away policemen's side arms and heavy clubs. When he sat as judge in police court, he regularly dismissed most cases of petty theft and drunkenness brought before him, charging that the accused were victims of an unjust social order and that only the poor went to jail for such crimes. He refused to advocate closing the saloons or brothels, and when prostitutes were brought before him, he usually dismissed them only after fining every man in the room 10 cents—and himself a dollar—for permitting prostitution to exist. The crime rate in Toledo, a notoriously sinful city, decreased during his tenure, and Jones was adored by the plain people. When he died in 1904, nearly 55,000 persons, "tears streaming down their faces," filed past his coffin.

## THE ELECTION OF 1896

"Golden Rule" Jones was ahead of his time, anticipating many urban reforms of the twentieth century. National politicians, too, struggling to find appropriate measures to end the depression and impress voters in the mid-1890s, initiated some modern political ideas and changed the composition of the two major parties—but not without being pushed by a strong third party, the Populists. The election of 1896 was one of the most critical in American history, for it upset the party equilibrium that had characterized politics since the Civil War.

### A Crucial Election Campaign

Although the People's party had lost its bid to gain control of the national government in 1892 (see Chapter 18), the crisis of the depression of 1893 created new political opportunities. Democratic president Grover Cleveland responded to the depression by repealing the Sherman Silver Purchase Act in an effort to stabilize currency. Wealthy silver mine owners were infuriated. Cleveland's handling of Coxey's march and the Pullman strike also alienated workers. In 1894, large numbers of voters abandoned the Democrats, giving both the Populist and Republican parties high hopes for electoral success in 1896.

As the election approached, Populist leaders focused on the issues of fusion and silver. Populist successes in 1894 had come through the tactic of fusing with one of the major parties by agreeing on a joint ticket. But fusion always required abandoning much of the Populist platform, thus weakening the party's distinctive character. Under the influence of silver mine owners, many Populists became convinced that the hope of the party lay in a single-issue commitment to the free and unlimited coinage of silver. Weaver expected both parties to nominate gold candidates, which would send disappointed silverites to the Populist standard.

The Republicans, holding their convention first, nominated William McKinley on the first ballot. A congressman from 1877 to 1891 and twice governor of Ohio, McKinley was happily identified with the high protective tariff that bore his name. Republicans were quick to cite the familiar argument that prosperity depended on the gold standard and protection and blamed the depression on Cleveland's attempt to lower the tariff. The excitement of the Democratic convention in July contrasted with the staid, smoothly organized Republican one. Cleveland had already been repudiated by his party as state after state elected convention delegates pledged to silver. Gold Democrats, however, had enough power left to wage a close battle for the platform plank on money.

The surprise nominee of the convention was an ardent young silverite, William Jennings Bryan, a 36-year-old congressman from Nebraska. Few saw him as presidential material, but as a member of the Resolutions Committee, Bryan arranged to give the closing argument for a silver plank himself. His dramatic speech swept the convention for silver and ensured his own nomination. "I come to speak to you," Bryan cried out, "in defense of a cause as holy as the cause of liberty—the cause of humanity." At the conclusion of what was to become one of the most famous political speeches in American history, Bryan attacked the goldbugs and promised, "Having behind us the producing masses of this nation . . . and toilers everywhere, we will answer their demand for a gold standard by saying to them: 'You shall not press down upon the brow of labor this crown of thorns, you shall not crucify mankind upon a cross of gold.'" As he spoke, Bryan stretched out his arms as if on a cross, and the convention exploded with applause.

Populist strategy lay in shambles with the

*William Jennings Bryan, surprise nominee at the 1896 Democratic Convention, was a vigorous proponent of "the cause of humanity."*

nomination of a Democratic silver candidate. Some party leaders favored fusion with the entire Democratic ticket. Antifusionists were outraged, in part because the Democratic vice-presidential candidate, Arthur Sewall, was an East Coast banker and hard-money man. An unwise compromise was achieved when the Populist convention nominated Bryan but instead of Sewall chose Populist Tom Watson of Georgia as his running mate. The existence of two silverite slates damaged Bryan's electoral hopes.

During the campaign, McKinley stayed at his home in Canton, Ohio, where some 750,000 admirers came to visit him, helped by low excursion rates offered by the railroads. Republican strategy featured an unprecedented effort to reach voters through a highly sophisticated mass-media campaign, heavily financed by such major corporations as Standard Oil and the railroads. Party leaders hired thousands of speakers to support McKinley and distributed over 200 million pamphlets to a voting population of 15 million. The literature, distributed in 14 languages, was designed to appeal to particular national, ethnic, regional, and occupational groups. To all these people, McKinley was advertised as "the advance agent of prosperity."

From his front porch in Canton, McKinley responded to Bryan's challenge by aiming his appeal not only at the business classes but also at unemployed workers, to whom he promised "a full dinner pail." He also spoke about the money issue, declaring that "our currency today is . . . as good as gold." Free silver, he maintained, would lead to inflation and more economic disaster. Recovery depended not on money but on tariff reform, which would stimulate American industry and provide jobs—"not open mints for the unlimited coinage of the silver of the world," he said, "but open mills for the full and unrestricted labor of American workingmen."

In sharp contrast to the Republican stay-at-home policy, Bryan took his case to the people. Three million people in 27 states heard him speak as he traveled over 18,000 miles, giving as many as 30 speeches a day. Bryan's message was simple. Prosperity would return, with free coinage of silver. Government policies should attend to the needs of the producing classes rather than the vested interests that believed in the gold standard. "That policy is best for this country," Bryan proclaimed, "which brings prosperity first to those who toil." But his rhetoric favored rural toilers. "The great cities rest upon our broad and fertile prairies," he had said in the "Cross of Gold" speech. "Burn down your cities and leave our farms, and your cities will spring up again as if by magic; but destroy our farms and the grass will grow in the streets of every city in the country." Urban workers were little inspired by this rhetoric, nor were immigrants impressed by Bryan's prairie moralizing.

To many people, Bryan's nomination represented a threat to social harmony. Influential East Coast opinion molders overwhelmingly opposed the brash young Nebraskan. Theodore Roosevelt wrote that "this silver craze surpasses belief. Bryan's election would be a great calamity." A Brooklyn minister declared that the Democratic platform was "made in Hell." One newspaper editor said of Bryan that he was just like Nebraska's Platte River: "six inches deep and six miles wide at the mouth." Others branded him a "madman" and an "anarchist." The New York *Mail* wrote that "no wild-eyed and rattle-brained horde of the red flag ever proclaimed a fiercer defiance of law, precedent, order, and government."

With such intense interest in the election, it was predictable that voters would turn out in record numbers. In key states like Illinois, Indiana, and Ohio, 95 percent of those eligible to vote went to the polls. When the voting was over, McKinley had won 271 electoral votes to Bryan's 176. Over 7 million Americans from all segments of society voted for the "advance agent of prosperity." Millionaire Mark Hanna jubilantly wired McKinley: "God's in his heaven, all's right with the world." Bryan had been defeated by the largest majority since Grant trounced Greeley in 1872.

Although Bryan won over 6 million votes (46 percent of the total), more than any previous Democratic winner, he failed to carry the Midwest and lost parts of the South and Far West. Nor could he make large inroads into the votes of the urban middle-classes and industrial masses, who had little confidence that the Democrats could stimulate economic growth or cope with the problems of industrialism. McKinley's promise of a "full dinner pail" was more convincing than the untested formula for free silver. But chance also played a part in Bryan's defeat. Bad wheat harvests in India, Australia, and Ar-

## Election of 1896

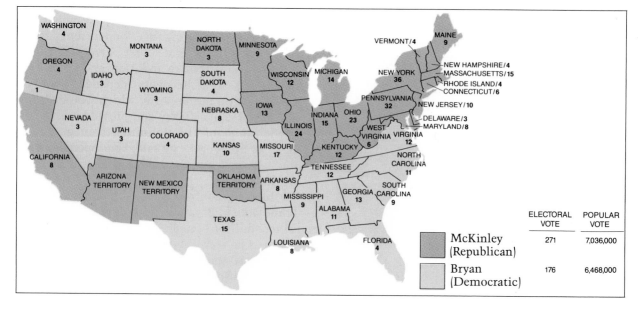

gentina drove up grain prices in the world market. Many of the complaints of American farmers evaporated amid rising farm prices.

## The New Shape of American Politics

The landslide Republican victory marked the end of the political equilibrium and party identifications that had characterized American politics since the end of the Civil War. Republicans assumed a new image as the party of prosperity and lost their identification with the politics of piety. The Democratic party, which would remain under Bryan's leadership until 1912, took on the mantle of reform and moralism. Populists, demoralized by fusion with a losing campaign, fell apart and disappeared. Asked a despondent Populist, Ignatius Donnelly, "Will the sun of triumph never rise? I fear not." His pessimism was premature, for within the next 20 years most Populist issues were taken over and adopted by politicians of the major parties.

Another result of the election of 1896 was a change in the pattern of political participation. After 1896, the Republicans were the dominant party in America for 16 years. They held sway in the North and West, while the Democrats, their rolls diminished by those who abandoned the party in 1896, especially from cities, could dominate political life only in the South. Few states had hotly contested two-party political battles. There seemed less and less reason to continue party activities aimed at bringing out large numbers of voters. Likewise, the individual voter had less and less motivation to cast a ballot, especially since election results were so often a foregone conclusion. Many black voters in the South, moreover, were disfranchised. Thus the high rate of political participation that had characterized the nineteenth century since the Jackson era gradually declined. In the twentieth century, political involvement among poorer Americans lessened considerably, a phenomenon unique among western industrial countries.

McKinley had promised that Republican rule meant prosperity, and no sooner did he take office than the economy recovered. Discoveries of gold in the Yukon and Alaskan Klondike increased the money supply, thus killing the silver mania until the early 1930s. Industrial production returned to full capacity. In a tour of the Midwest in 1898, McKinley spoke to cheering crowds about the hopeful economic picture. "We have gone from industrial depression to industrial activity," he told citizens of Clinton, Iowa. "We have gone from labor seeking employment to employment seeking labor." His audience burst into enthusiastic applause.

McKinley's election marked not only the return of an era of economic health but also the emergence of the executive as the preeminent focus of the American political system. Just as McKinley's campaign set the pattern for the extravagant efforts to win office that have dominated modern times, his conduct as president foreshadowed the nature of the twentieth-century presidency. McKinley rejected traditional views of the president as the passive executor of laws, instead playing an active role in dealing with Congress and the press. His frequent trips away from Washington testified to his respect for public opinion. Some historians regard McKinley as the first of the modern presidents. As we shall see in the next chapter, he transformed the presidency into a potent force not only in domestic life but in world affairs as well.

## CONCLUSION: Looking Forward

The chapter began with Edward Bellamy's imaginary look backward from the year 2000 at the grim economic realities and unresponsive politics of American life in the late nineteenth century. Through the efforts of middle-class reformers like Jane Addams, Walter Rauschenbusch, and "Golden Rule" Jones, as well as through the promise of a new national politics represented by the influence of populism on the major parties, many Americans began to look forward to the kind of cooperative, caring, and cleaner world envisioned in Bellamy's utopian novel.

As the year 1900 approached, people took a predictably intense interest in what the new century would be like. Henry Adams, still the pessimist, saw an ominous future, predicting the explosive and ultimately destructive energy of unrestrained industrial development, symbolized by the "dynamo" and other engines of American power. Such forces, he warned, would overwhelm the gentler, moral forces represented by art, woman, and religious symbols like the Virgin. But others were more optimistic, preferring to place their confidence in America's historic role as an exemplary nation, demonstrating to the world the moral superiority of its economic system, democratic institutions, and middle-class Protestant values. Surely the new century, most thought, would see not only the continued perfection of these values and institutions but also the spread of American influence throughout the world. Such confidence resulted in an outward thrust by the American people even before the old century had ended. We turn to that in the next chapter.

## Recommended Reading

The politics of the Gilded Age is treated usefully in the context of other developments of late nineteenth-century life in H. Wayne Morgan, *From Hayes to McKinley: National Party Politics, 1877–1896* (1969); John A. Garraty, *The New Commonwealth, 1877–1890* (1968); Robert Wiebe, *The Search for Order, 1877–1920* (1967); Samuel P. Hays, *The Response to Industrialism, 1885–1914* (1957); and Morton Keller, *Affairs of State: Public Life in Late Nineteenth Century America* (1977). A recent analysis of politics in the 1890s (and a good example of the "new political history") is R. Hal Williams, *Years of Decision: American Politics in the 1890s* (1978). The new social and political history is well represented by Richard Jensen, *The Winning of the Midwest: Social and Political Conflict, 1888–1896* (1971) and Paul Kleppner, *The Third Electoral System, 1853–1892: Parties, Voters, and Political Cultures* (1979).

The lives of middle-class men and women are understood best by a variety of different approaches. See Peter Filene, *Him/Her/Self: Sex Roles in Modern America* (1974) and the relevant chapters in Mary Ryan's excellent survey, *Womanhood in America*, 3d ed. (1983). An astute study of the battle for the vote is Aileen Kraditor, *The Ideas of the Woman's Suffrage Movement, 1890–1920* (1965). Social Darwinism and the success ethic are covered in Richard Hofstadter, *Social Darwinism in American Thought*, rev. ed. (1955); Irvin G. Wyllie, *The Self-Made Man in America* (1954); and John Cawelti, *Apostles of the Self-Made Man: Changing Concepts of Success in America* (1965).

Novels that capture the flavor of middle-class life in the late nineteenth century include Mark Twain and Charles Dudley Warner, *The Gilded Age* (1873); William Dean Howells, *The Rise of Silas Lapham* (1885) and *A Hazard of New Fortunes* (1889); Kate Chopin, *The Awakening* (1899); and Charles Sheldon, *In His Steps* (1896). Stephen Crane, *Maggie: A Girl of the Streets* (1895); Theodore Dreiser, *Sister Carrie* (1900); and Frank Norris, *The Octopus* (1901) depict a middle-class view of both middle- and lower-class life.

Two classic works on late nineteenth-century reform are Richard Hofstadter, *Age of Reform: From Bryan to F.D.R.* (1955) and John Sproat, *"The Best Men" Liberal Reformers in the Gilded Age* (1968). The best studies of middle-class urban reformers and the bossism they opposed are John Allswang, *Bosses, Machines, and Urban Voters* (1977); Arthur Mann, *Yankee Reformers in an Urban Age: Social Reform in Boston, 1880–1900* (1954); and Allen F. Davis, *Spearheads for Reform: The Social Settlements and the Progressive Movement, 1890–1914* (1967). See also William Riordon's delightful recovery of the words of a typical boss, *Plunkitt of Tammany Hall* (1963, originally published in 1905). One can understand the personal views and feelings of the urban reformers by reading about their lives, either through a biographical study of ten reformers, Peter

Frederick, *Knights of the Golden Rule: The Intellectual as Christian Social Reformer in the 1890s* (1976), or through two revealing autobiographies, Jane Addams, *Twenty Years at Hull House* (1910) and Vida Scudder, *On Journey* (1937).

The profound impact of the depression of 1893 is seen in Charles Hoffman, *The Depression of the Nineties: An Economic History* (1970) and David P. Thelen, *The New Citizenship: Origins of Progressivism in Wisconsin, 1885–1900* (1972). Populism and the election of 1896 are covered in a straightforward account by Paul Glad, *McKinley, Bryan and the People* (1964) and the titles listed in Chapter 18.

## TIME LINE

| | |
|---|---|
| 1873 | Congress demonetizes silver |
| 1875 | Specie Resumption Act |
| 1877 | Rutherford B. Hayes becomes president |
| 1878 | Bland-Allison Act |
| 1879 | Henry George, *Progress and Poverty* |
| 1880 | James A. Garfield elected president |
| 1881 | Garfield assassinated; Chester A. Arthur succeeds to presidency |
| 1883 | Pendleton Civil Service Act |
| 1884 | Grover Cleveland elected president<br>W. D. Howells, *The Rise of Silas Lapham* |
| 1887 | College Settlement House Association founded |
| 1888 | Edward Bellamy, *Looking Backward*<br>Benjamin Harrison elected president |
| 1889 | Jane Addams establishes Hull House<br>Andrew Carnegie promulgates "The Gospel of Wealth" |
| 1890 | General Federation of Women's Clubs founded<br>Sherman Anti-Trust Act<br>Sherman Silver Purchase Act<br>McKinley Tariff<br>Elections bill defeated |
| 1890s | Wyoming, Colorado, Utah, and Idaho grant woman suffrage |
| 1892 | Cleveland elected president for the second time; Populist party wins over a million votes<br>Homestead steel strike |
| 1893 | World's Columbian Exposition, Chicago |
| 1893–1897 | Financial panic and depression |
| 1894 | Pullman strike<br>Coxey's march on Washington |
| 1895 | *United States* v. *E. C. Knight* |
| 1896 | Charles Sheldon publishes *In His Steps*<br>Populist party fuses with Democrats<br>William McKinley elected president |
| 1897 | "Golden Rule" Jones elected mayor of Toledo, Ohio<br>Economic recovery begins |

# CHAPTER 21
## THE UNITED STATES BECOMES
## A WORLD POWER

In January 1899, as the United States Senate was locked in a dramatic debate over whether to ratify the Treaty of Paris concluding the recent war with Spain over Cuban independence, American soldiers uneasily faced Filipino rebels across a neutral zone around the outskirts of Manila, capital city of the Philippines. Until recently, the Americans and Filipinos had been allies, together defeating the Spanish to accomplish the liberation of the Philippines. The American fleet under Commodore George Dewey had destroyed the Spanish naval squadron in Manila Bay on May 1, 1898. Three weeks later, an American ship personally delivered from exile the native Filipino insurrectionary leader, Emilio Aguinaldo, to lead rebel forces on land while the Americans patrolled the seas and waited for reinforcements.

At first the Filipinos looked on the Americans as liberators. Although the United States' intentions were never clear, Aguinaldo believed that as in Cuba, the Americans had no territorial ambitions. They would simply drive the Spanish out and then leave themselves. In June, therefore, Aguinaldo declared the independence of the Philippines and began setting up a constitutional form of government. American officials pointedly ignored the independence ceremonies. When the armistice ended the war in August, American troops denied Filipino soldiers the right to liberate and occupy Manila and shunted them off to the suburbs. The armistice agreement recognized American rights to "the harbor, city, and bay of Manila." Later that fall, the Treaty of Paris gave the United States the entire Philippine Island archipelago.

Consequently, tension mounted in the streets of Manila and along 14 miles of trenches separating American and Filipino soldiers. Taunts, obscenities, and racial epithets were shouted across the neutral zone. Barroom skirmishes and knifings punctuated the city at night; American soldiers searched houses without warrants and took goods from stores without paying for them. Their behavior was not unlike that of English soldiers in Boston in 1775.

On the night of February 4, 1899, Private William Grayson and Private Miller of Company B, 1st Nebraska Volunteers, were on patrol by their regimental outpost in Santa Mesa, a Manila suburb surrounded on three sides by insurgent trenches. The Americans had orders to shoot any Filipino soldiers found in the neutral area. As the two Americans cautiously worked their way to an advanced point near a bridge over the San Juan River, they heard a Filipino signal-whistle up ahead, answered by another. Then a red lantern flashed from a nearby blockhouse. The two froze as four Filipinos emerged from the darkness on the road ahead. "Halt!" Grayson shouted. The native lieutenant in charge answered, "Halto!" either mockingly or because he had similar orders. Standing less than 15 feet apart, the two men repeated their commands. After a moment's hesitation, Grayson fired, killing his opponent with one bullet. As the other Filipinos jumped out at them, Grayson and Miller killed two more. Then they turned and ran back to their own lines, shouting warnings of attack. A full-scale battle followed.

The next day, Commodore Dewey cabled Washington that the "insurgents have inaugurated general engagement" and promised a hasty suppression of the insurrection. The outbreak of hostilities marked the end of the Senate debates. On February 6, the Senate ratified the Treaty of Paris, thus formally annexing the Philippines.

The Filipino-American War lasted two years longer than the Spanish-American War that caused it and involved several times more troops and casualties. In what came to be a guerrilla war with some similarities to those fought later in the twentieth century in Asia and Central America, native nationalists tried to undermine the American will to fight by hit-and-run attacks. American soldiers, meanwhile, remained in heavily garrisoned cities, foraying out on search-and-destroy missions intended to root out rebels and pacify the countryside.

Costs to both sides were high. In all, nearly 200,000 American troops were sent to that distant Asian land; 4,234 were buried there, and 2,800 more were wounded. The cost was $400 million. Filipino casualties were much greater. In addition to the 18,000 killed in combat, an estimated 200,000 Filipinos (20 percent of the population) died of famine and disease because U.S. soldiers burned villages and destroyed crops and livestock to disrupt the economy and deny rebel fighters their food supply. Atrocities on both sides increased with the frustrations of a lengthening war. Although Aguinaldo was captured in 1901, the war did not end until July 1902.

*Clustered in trenches against Filipino nationalists, the presence of American soldiers in the faraway Philippine Islands in 1899 was a harbinger of twentieth-century wars to come.*

How did all this happen? What brought Private Grayson to "shoot my first nigger," as he put it, halfway around the world in distant Asia? For the first time in history, regular American soldiers found themselves fighting outside North America. The "champion of oppressed nations," as Aguinaldo said, had turned into an oppressor nation itself, actively expanding the American way of life and American institutions to faraway peoples against their will.

The war in the Philippines marked a critical transformation in America's role in the world. Within a few years at the turn of the century, the United States acquired an empire, however small by European standards, and established itself as a world power. This chapter will review the historical dilemmas of America's role in the world, especially those of the expansionist nineteenth century. Then we will examine the motivations for the intensified expansionism of the 1890s and how they were manifested in Cuba, the Philippines, and elsewhere. Finally, we will look at how the fundamental patterns of modern American foreign policy were established for Latin America, Asia, and Europe in the early twentieth century.

## STEPS TOWARD EMPIRE

The forces that brought Privates Grayson and Miller far from home in Nebraska to the Philippines lay deep in American history. As early as the Puritan migration from England to Massachusetts Bay in the seventeenth century, Americans faced a dilemma of how to do good in a world that does wrong. John Winthrop sought to set up a "city on a hill" in the New World, a model community of righteous living for others in the world to behold and imitate. "Let the eyes of the world be upon us," Winthrop said, and that wish, reaffirmed during the American Revolution, became a permanent goal of American policy toward the outside world.

### America as a Model Society

Americans in the nineteenth century continued to believe in the idea of the nation's special mission. The Monroe Doctrine in 1823 pointed out moral differences between the monarchical, arbitrary governments of Europe and the free republican institutions of the New World. As the American Revolutionary model was followed in the Spanish colonies in South and Central America, Monroe warned Europe to stay out. In succeeding decades, a number of distinguished European visitors (discussed in Chapter 13) came to study "democracy in America" to see for themselves "the great social revolution" at work. They found widespread democracy, representative and responsive political and legal institutions, a religious commitment to the notion of human perfectibility, unlimited energy, and the ability to utilize unregulated economic activity and inventive genius to produce more things for more people.

Who could resist such a model? In a world that was evil, the American people believed that they stood as a transforming force for good. Many others agreed. The problem was how a nation committed to isolationism was to do the transforming. One way was to encourage other nations to observe and imitate the good example set by the United States. But often other nations preferred their own society or were attracted to other models of modernization, as has frequently happened in the twentieth century. This implied a more aggressive foreign policy.

Indeed, assertive self-interest and internationalism as well as selfless idealism and isolationism have guided the American rise to power in the world. Americans have rarely simply focused on perfecting the good example at home, waiting for others to copy it. This requires patience and passivity, two traits not prevalent in Americans. Rather, throughout history, the American people have actively and sometimes

# United States Territorial Expansion

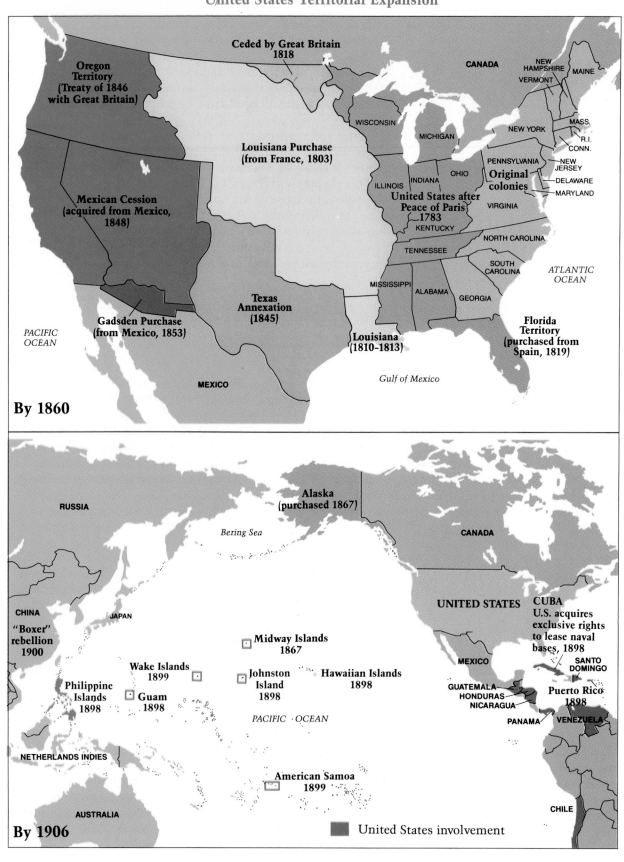

**By 1860**

Oregon Territory (Treaty of 1846 with Great Britain)

Ceded by Great Britain 1818

CANADA

NEW HAMPSHIRE
VERMONT
MAINE

WISCONSIN

MICHIGAN

NEW YORK

MASS.
R.I.
CONN.

Louisiana Purchase (from France, 1803)

PENNSYLVANIA

NEW JERSEY
DELAWARE
MARYLAND

Mexican Cession (acquired from Mexico, 1848)

ILLINOIS

INDIANA

OHIO

Original colonies

United States after Peace of Paris 1783

VIRGINIA

KENTUCKY

NORTH CAROLINA

TENNESSEE

SOUTH CAROLINA

*ATLANTIC OCEAN*

Gadsden Purchase (from Mexico, 1853)

Texas Annexation (1845)

MISSISSIPPI

ALABAMA

GEORGIA

Florida Territory (purchased from Spain, 1819)

*PACIFIC OCEAN*

Louisiana (1810–1813)

MEXICO

*Gulf of Mexico*

**By 1906**

RUSSIA

Alaska (purchased 1867)

*Bering Sea*

CANADA

CHINA

JAPAN

UNITED STATES

CUBA
U.S. acquires exclusive rights to lease naval bases, 1898

"Boxer" rebellion 1900

Midway Islands 1867

MEXICO

SANTO DOMINGO

Wake Islands 1899

Johnston Island 1898

Hawaiian Islands 1898

GUATEMALA
HONDURAS
NICARAGUA

Puerto Rico 1898

Philippine Islands 1898

Guam 1898

PANAMA

VENEZUELA

*PACIFIC OCEAN*

NETHERLANDS INDIES

American Samoa 1899

AUSTRALIA

CHILE

United States involvement

forcefully imposed their ideas and institutions on others. The international crusades of the United States, well intentioned if not always well received, have usually been motivated by a mixture of idealism and self-interest. Hence the effort to spread the exemplary American model to an imperfect world has been both a blessing and a burden, both for others and for the American people themselves.

The first century of American independence was marked by a continuous and consistent expression of continental expansionism. Jefferson's purchase of the Louisiana Territory in 1803 and the grasping for Florida and Canada by War Hawks in 1812 signaled an intense American interest in territorial growth. Although the United States remained "unentangled" in European affairs for most of the century, as both Washington and Jefferson had advised, the American government and people were very much entangled elsewhere. To the Cherokee, Seminole, Sioux, Nez Percé, Navajo, and other Native American nations, the United States was far from isolationist. Nor did the Canadians, the Spanish in Florida, or the Mexicans in Texas and California consider the Americans nonexpansionist. Until midcentury, the United States pursued its "Manifest Destiny" (see Chapter 14) by expanding across the North American continent. But in the 1850s, Americans began to look outward beyond their own continent. This trend was marked most significantly by Commodore Perry's visit to Japan, the expansion of the China trade, and the various expeditions into the Caribbean in search of more cotton lands and a canal connecting the two oceans.

## Expansion After Seward

These outward thrusts were accelerated under the influence of Lincoln's secretary of state, William Seward. During the Civil War, Seward was preoccupied with preventing the Confederacy from receiving foreign aid and diplomatic recognition. But once the war ended, he revived his vision of an America that would hold a "commanding sway in the world." Although restrained in his territorial ambitions, Seward believed that the United States was destined to exert commercial domination "on the Pacific ocean, and its islands and continents." His goal was that from markets, raw materials, and trade would come the "regeneration of . . . the East."

Toward this end, Seward purchased Alaska from Russia in 1867 for $7.2 million. He also acquired a coaling station in the Midway Islands in the mid-Pacific and paved the way for American commercial expansion in Korea, Japan, and China. Moreover, he advocated the annexation of Cuba and other islands of the West Indies and tried to negotiate a treaty securing an American-built canal through the isthmus of Panama. Seward dreamed of "possession" of the whole North and Central American continent and ultimately of "control of the world." Although his larger dreams went unrealized, his interest in expansion into the Caribbean persisted among business interests and politicians after Cuba's attempted revolt against Spain in 1868.

Urged on by friends two years later, President Grant tried to force the Senate to annex Santo Domingo (Hispaniola), an island near Cuba. Supporters cited the strategic importance of the Caribbean and made forceful arguments for the economic value of raw materials and markets that the addition of Santo Domingo would bring. Senatorial opponents argued that expansionism violated the American principle of self-determination and government by the consent of the governed. They pointed out, moreover, that the native peoples of the Caribbean were brown-skinned, culturally inferior, non-English-speaking, and therefore unassimilable. Finally, they argued that expansionism would be likely to involve foreign entanglements, necessitating a large, expensive navy, growth in the size of government, and higher taxes. The Senate rejected the treaty to annex Santo Domingo.

Although reluctant to add territory outright, American interests in Latin America and Asia, fed by Seward's hunger for commercial dominance, continued. A number of statesmen asserted the United States' unmistakable influence in these areas. President Hayes said in 1880 that despite a treaty with England pledging joint construction and control of a canal across either Panama or Nicaragua, he was certain that if such a canal were built, it would be "under American control" and would be considered "virtually a part of the coast line of the United States." But nothing came of diplomatic efforts with Nicaragua to smooth the way for an American-built canal except Nicaraguan suspicions of U.S. intentions.

In 1881, Secretary of State James G. Blaine sought to convene a conference of American nations to promote hemispheric peace and trade. Although motivated mostly by his presidential ambitions, his effort nevertheless led to the first Pan-American Conference eight years later. The Latin Americans may have wondered what Blaine intended, for in 1881 he intervened in three separate border disputes in Central and South America, in each case at the cost of goodwill and trust, especially from Chile and Mexico.

Ten years later, relations with Chile were harmed again when several American sailors on shore leave were involved in a barroom brawl in Valparaiso. Two Americans were killed and several others injured. American pride was also injured, and President Benjamin Harrison sent

an ultimatum calling for a "prompt and full reparation." After threats of war, Chile complied.

Similar incidents occurred as American expansionists pursued Seward's goals in the Pacific. In the mid-1870s, American sugar-growing interests in the Hawaiian Islands were strong enough to place whites in positions of influence over the native monarchy. In 1875, they succeeded in obtaining a reciprocity treaty admitting Hawaiian sugar duty free to the United States. When the treaty was renewed two years later, the United States also gained rights to a naval base at Pearl Harbor on the island of Oahu.

Native Hawaiians resented the growing influence of American sugar interests, especially as they contracted to bring in large numbers of Japanese immigrant workers. In 1891, the strongly nationalist Queen Liliuokalani assumed the throne in Hawaii and promptly abolished the constitution, seeking to establish control over whites in the name of "Hawaii for the Hawaiians." In 1893, with the help of U.S.

*Iolani Palace, former home of Queen Liliuokalani, was the scene of annexation ceremonies in 1898, when Hawaii became a U.S. territory.*

gunboats and marines, the whites staged a palace coup (a revolution later called one "of sugar, by sugar, for sugar") and sought formal annexation by the friendly Harrison administration. But before final Senate ratification could be achieved, Grover Cleveland, who opposed imperial expansion, returned to the presidency for his second term and stopped the move. He was, however, unable to remove the white sugar growers from power in Hawaii. They waited patiently for a more desirable time for annexation, which came in the midst of the war in 1898.

Moving ever-closer toward the fabled markets of the Far East, the United States acquired a naval station at Pago Pago in the Samoan Islands in 1878. However, it had to share the port with Great Britain and Germany. In an incident in 1889, American and German naval forces almost engaged each other, but a typhoon wiped out both navies and ended the crisis. Troubles in the Pacific also occurred in the late 1880s over the American seizure of several Canadian ships in fur seal–fishing disputes in the Bering Sea. This issue was settled only by the British threat of naval action and with the ruling of an international arbitration commission, which ordered the United States to pay damages.

The United States confronted the English closer to home as it sought to replace Britain as the most influential nation in Central American affairs. In 1895, a boundary dispute between Venezuela and British Guiana threatened to bring British intervention against the Venezuelans. President Cleveland, in need of a popular political issue because of the depression, discovered the political value of a tough foreign policy by defending a weak sister American republic against the British bully. He asked Secretary of State Richard Olney to send a message to Great Britain. Olney's note, which was stronger than Cleveland had intended, invoked the Monroe Doctrine, declared the United States as "practically sovereign on this continent" and demanded British acceptance of international arbitration to settle the dispute. The British ignored the note, and war threatened. Although England was the chief rival of the United States for economic influence in the Caribbean, both sides eventually realized that war between them would be "an absurdity." The dispute was settled by agreeing to an impartial American commission to settle the boundary.

These increasing conflicts in the Caribbean and Pacific signaled the rise of an American presence beyond the borders of the United States. Yet as of 1895, the nation had neither the means nor a consistent policy for enlarging its role in the world. The diplomatic service was small, inexperienced, and unprofessional. Around the world, American emissaries kept sloppy records, issued illegal passports, involved themselves in petty local issues and frauds, and exhibited insensitive behavior toward native cultures. It was not until the 1930s that a high embassy official in Peking spoke Chinese. The U.S. Army, numbering about 28,000 men in the mid-1890s, ranked thirteenth in the world, behind that of Bulgaria. The navy, which had been dismantled after the Civil War and partially rebuilt under President Arthur, ranked no higher than tenth and included too many ships powered by dangerously outdated boilers. These limited and backward instruments of foreign policy were inadequate to support the aspirations of an emerging world power, especially one whose rise to power had come so quickly.

## EXPANSIONIST MOTIVES IN THE 1890s

In 1893, the historian Frederick Jackson Turner wrote that for three centuries "the dominant fact in American life has been expansion." Turner observed that the "extension of American influence to outlying islands and adjoining countries" indicated that expansionism would continue. Although not himself an imperialist, Turner's observations struck a responsive chord in a country that had always been restless, mobile, and optimistic. With the western American frontier closed, Americans would surely look for new frontiers, for mobility and markets as well as for morality and missionary activity. The motivations for the expansionist impulse of the late 1890s were similar to those that had prompted people to settle the New World in the first place: greed, glory, and God. We will examine these impulses under the categories of profits, patriotism, piety (defined broadly as moral mission), and politics.

## Searching for Overseas Markets

Albert Beveridge of Indiana bragged in 1898 that "American factories are making more than the American people can use; American soil is producing more than they can consume. Fate has written our policy for us; the trade of the world must and shall be ours." Americans like Beveridge believed in the dream of Seward, Blaine, and others to establish a commercial empire in the islands and adjoining countries of the Caribbean Sea and the Pacific Ocean. With a strong belief in free enterprise and open markets for investing capital and selling products, American businessmen saw potentially huge profits in the heavily populated areas of Latin America and Asia. They also viewed it as essential to get their share of these markets in order to stay competitive with European countries. The attraction was enhanced by the availability in those lands of abundant raw materials such as sugar, coffee, fruits, oil, rubber, and minerals.

An increase in commerce necessitated the support of a stronger navy and the existence of coaling stations and colonies. Business interests, which were supplanting agricultural interests in the political arena, began to shape diplomatic and military strategy. As Senator Orville Platt of Connecticut said in 1893, "A policy of isolation did well enough when we were an embryo nation, but today things are different. . . . We are sixty-five million of people, the most advanced and powerful on earth, and regard to our future welfare demands an abandonment of the doctrines of isolation." By 1901, the economic adviser for the State Department described overseas commercial expansion as "a natural law of economic and race development."

Not all businessmen in the 1890s agreed that commercial expansion backed by a vigorous foreign policy was an unmixed good. Some saw

it as dangerous and costly, preferring traditional trade with Canada and Europe rather than risky new ventures in Asia and Latin America. Securing colonies and developing markets and investment opportunities far from the American mainland not only would require initially high expenses but also might involve the United States in wars with commercial rivals or native peoples in distant places. Some businessmen, furthermore, thought it more important in 1897 to secure the recovery from the depression than to secure little islands in Asia.

But the decrease in domestic consumption during the depression also encouraged businessmen to expand into new markets to sell surplus goods. The tremendous growth of American industrial and agricultural production in the post–Civil War years made expansionism an attractive alternative to drowning in overproduction. For many businessmen, new markets were preferable to cutting prices, which would redistribute wealth by allowing the lower classes to buy excess goods, or laying off workers, which would increase social unrest. Thus many reasons, not least the fear of overproduction and a desire to remain competitive in international markets, convinced hesitant businessmen to expand. They were led by the newly formed National Association of Manufacturers, which emphasized foreign trade in 8 of 14 purposes outlined in 1896: "The trade centres of Central and South America are natural markets for American products."

Despite the depression of the 1890s, these products appeared at a staggering rate. The United States moved from fourth in the world in manufacturing in 1870 to first in 1900, doubling the number of factories and tripling the value of farm output, mainly cotton, corn, and wheat. The United States led the world not only in railroad construction (206,631 miles of tracks in 1900, four times more than in 1870) but also in agricultural machinery and mass-produced technological products such as sewing machines, electrical implements, telephones, cash registers, elevators, and cameras. Manufactured goods grew nearly fivefold between 1895 and 1914.

Not surprisingly, the total value of American exports tripled, jumping from $434 million in 1866 to nearly $1.5 billion in 1900. By 1914, exports had risen to $2.5 billion, a 67 percent increase over 1900. The increased trade continued to go mainly to Europe rather than Asia. In 1900, for example, only 3 to 4 percent of U.S. exports went to China and Japan. Nevertheless, interest in Asian markets grew, especially as agricultural production continued to increase and prices remained low. Farmers dreamed of selling their surplus wheat to China. They were supported in this case by James J. Hill of the Great Northern Railroad, who printed wheat cookbooks in various Asian languages and distributed them in the Far East, hoping to fill his westward-bound boxcars and merchant ships with wheat and other grains.

Investment interest and activity followed a similar pattern. American direct investments abroad increased from an estimated $634 million to $2.6 billion between 1897 and 1914. Although investments were largest in Britain, Canada, and Mexico, the potential of Asia and Central America received the most attention. Central American investment increased from $21 million in 1897 to $93 million by the eve of World War I, mainly in mines, railroads, and banana and coffee plantations. At the turn of the century came the formation and growth of America's biggest multinational corporations—the United Fruit Company, Alcoa Aluminum,

Amalgamated Copper, Du Pont, American Tobacco, and others. Although slow to respond to investment and market opportunities abroad, these companies soon supported an aggressive foreign policy and the expansion of America's role in the world.

## Patriotism and the Foreign Policy Elite

American interest in investments, markets, and raw materials abroad reflected a determination not to be left out of the international competition among European powers and Japan for commercial spheres of influence and colonies in Asia, Africa, and Latin America. England, France, and Germany were frequently on the verge of war with one another as they scrambled for colonies as a measure of economic worth and national glory. In 1898, a State Department memorandum stated that the "enlargement of foreign consumption of the products of our mills and workshops has . . . become a serious problem of statesmanship as well as commerce." The memo went on to note that "we can no longer afford to disregard international rivalries now that we ourselves have become a competitor in the world-wide struggle for trade." The national state, then, recognized its role in supporting commercial interests, and politicians were eager to be of service.

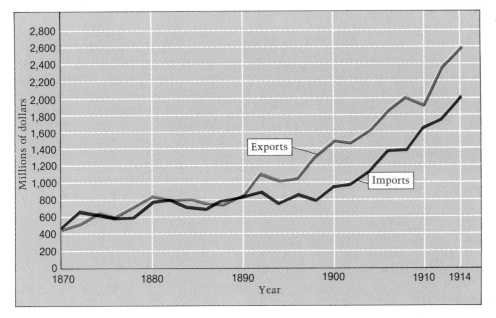

**American Foreign Trade, 1870–1914**

Some people, however, saw national glory and greatness itself as a legitimate motivation for expansionism. In the late 1890s, a small group of men centered around Assistant Secretary of the Navy Theodore Roosevelt and Senator Henry Cabot Lodge of Massachusetts emerged as highly influential leaders of a changing American foreign policy. These vigorous and intensely nationalistic young men wanted a shift in official policy from "continentalism" to what Lodge called the "large policy." They were successful. By 1899, Assistant Secretary of State John Bassett Moore wrote that the United States had finally moved "into the position of what is commonly called a world power. . . . Where formerly we had only commercial interests, we now have territorial and political interests as well." Roosevelt agreed that economic interests should take second place to questions of what he called "national honor."

The new foreign policy elite was much influenced by the writings of Alfred Thayer Mahan, a naval strategist and author of several books on the importance of sea power to national greatness. Mahan had captained a warship sent to protect American property in Central America in 1885. His study of history argued that in a world of Darwinian struggle for survival, national power depended on naval supremacy, control of sea lanes, and vigorous development of domestic resources and foreign markets. He advocated colonies in both the Caribbean and the Pacific, linked by a canal built and controlled by the United States. Strong nations, Mahan wrote, had a special responsibility to dominate weak ones. In a world of constant "strife," where "everywhere nation is arrayed against nation," it was imperative that Americans begin "to look outward." National pride and glory would surely follow.

## The Missionary Impulse

As Mahan's and Roosevelt's statements suggest, a strong sense of duty and the missionary ideal of doing good for others also motivated expansionism. A statesman once boasted that "with God's help, we will lift Shanghai up and up, ever up, until it is just like Kansas City." Richard Olney agreed, saying in 1898 that "the mission of this country is . . . to forego no fitting opportunity to further the progress of civilization." Motivated by America's sense of itself as a model nation, such statements sometimes rationalized the exploitation and oppression of weaker peoples. Although the European countries had their own justifications for imperialism, Americans such as Roosevelt, Lodge, and Mahan all would have agreed with the following paraphrase of popular expansionist beliefs:

*Advocates of expansionism urged enlarging the size of the U.S. Navy, part of which is pictured here in 1892. The armored warship Maine, soon to figure in the outbreak of the Spanish-American War, is shown in the middle foreground.*

Certain nations are more civilized than others. These nations are peopled by those who are white, Anglo-Saxon, Protestant, and English-speaking. They enjoy free enterprise and republican political institutions, meaning representative government, shared power, and the rule of law. Further evidence of the civilized nature of such nations includes their advanced technological and industrial development, large middle classes, and high degree of education and literacy. The prime examples in the world are England, Germany, and the United States.

In the natural struggle for existence, the races and nations that survive and prosper, such as these, prove their fitness and superiority over others. The United States, as a matter of history, geographic location, and political genius, is so favored and fit that God has chosen it to take care of and uplift less favored peoples. This responsibility cannot be avoided. It is a national duty, or burden—the "white man's burden"—that civilized nations undertake to bring peace, progressive values, and ordered liberty to the world.

These ideas, widespread in popular thought, described America's providential sense of itself. As a missionary put it in 1885, "The Christian nations are subduing the world in order to make mankind free." Josiah Strong, a Congregational minister, was one of the most ardent advocates of American missionary expansionism. Although his book *Our Country* (1885) was concerned primarily with internal threats to American social order, in a long chapter titled "The Future of the Anglo-Saxon Race" Strong made his case for an outward thrust. He argued that in the struggle for survival among nations, the United States had emerged as the center of Anglo-Saxonism and was "divinely commissioned" to spread the blessings of political liberty, Protestant Christianity, and civilized values over the earth. "This powerful race," he wrote, "will move down upon Mexico, down upon Central and South America, out upon the islands of the sea, over upon Africa and beyond." In a cruder statement of the same idea, Albert Beveridge said in 1899 that God had prepared English-speaking Anglo-Saxons to become "the master organizers of the world to establish and administer governments among savages and senile peoples."

If not so crudely, missionaries carried similar Western values to non-Christian lands around the world. China was a favorite target. The number of American Protestant missionaries in China increased from only 436 in 1874 to 5,462 in 1914. The largest increase came in the 1890s. Although the missionaries were not as effective as they had hoped to be, the estimated number of Christian converts in China jumped from 5,000 in 1870 to nearly 100,000 in 1900. This number, a small fraction of the Chinese population, included many young reformist intellectuals who absorbed Western ideas in Christian mission colleges and went on to lead the Revolution of 1912 that brought an end to the Manchu dynasty. Economic relations between China and the United States increased at approximately the same rate as missionary activity. The number of American firms in China grew from 50 to 550 between 1870 and 1930, while trade increased 15-fold.

## Politics and Public Opinion

These figures suggest how economic, religious, moral, and nationalistic motivations became interwoven in American expansionism in the late 1890s. Although less significant than the other motives, politics also played a role. For the first time in American history, public opinion over international issues loomed large in presidential politics. The psychological tensions and economic hardships of the depression of the 1890s jarred national self-confidence. Foreign adventures and the glories of expansionism provided an emotional release from domestic turmoil and promised to restore patriotic pride—and maybe even win votes.

This process was helped by the rise of a highly competitive popular press, the penny daily newspaper, which brought international issues before ordinary citizens. When several newspapers in New York City, most notably William Randolph Hearst's *Journal* and Joseph Pulitzer's *World,* competed to see which could stir up more public support for the Cuban rebels in their struggle for independence from Spain, politicians ignored the public outcry at their peril. The daily reports of Spanish atrocities in 1896 and 1897 kept public moral outrage constantly before President McKinley as he considered his course of action. His Democratic opponent, William Jennings Bryan, entered the fray. Although in principle a pacifist, he too advocated United States intervention in Cuba on moral grounds of a holy war to help the oppressed. Bryan even raised a regiment of Nebraska volunteers to go off to the war, but the Republican administration kept him far from battle and therefore far from the headlines.

Politics, then, in addition to profits, patriotism, and piety, was a motivating factor in the expansionist impulse of the 1890s. These four motivations interacted to influence the Spanish-American War, the annexation of the Philippine Islands, and the foreign policy of President Theodore Roosevelt.

*Support for the military became fashionable with the help of the popular press. Here officers of the Massachusetts State Militia pose with their wives who have come to visit them at summer encampment.*

## CUBA AND THE PHILIPPINES

Lying 90 miles off the southern tip of Florida, Cuba had been the object of intense American interest for a half century. Although successful in thwarting American adventurism in Cuba in the 1850s, Spain was unable to halt the continuing struggle of the Cuban people for relief from exploitive slave labor in the sugar plantations and for independence.

### The Road to War

When the Cuban revolt flared up anew in 1895, the Madrid government again failed to implement reforms but instead sent General "Butcher" Weyler with 50,000 troops to quell the disturbance. When Weyler began herding rural Cuban citizens into "reconcentration" camps, Americans were outraged. An outpouring of sympathy swept the nation, especially as reports came back of the miserable conditions and horrible suffering in the camps. Sensational-

ist newspapers in the United States, competing for readers, stirred up sentiment with pages of bloody stories of atrocities. "The old, the young, the weak, the crippled—all are butchered without mercy," wrote the New York *World*.

The Cuban struggle appealed to a country convinced of its role as protector of the weak and defender of the right of self-determination. One editorial deplored Spanish "injustice, oppression, extortion, and demoralization" while describing the Cubans as heroic freedom fighters "largely inspired by our glorious example of beneficent free institutions and successful self-government." Motivated by genuine humanitarian concern and a sense of duty, many Americans held Cuba rallies to raise money and food for famine relief. They called for land reforms, and some advocated armed intervention, but neither President Cleveland nor President McKinley wanted a war over Cuba.

Self-interested motives also played a role.

For many years, Americans had looked with great interest on the profitable resources and strategic location of the island. American companies had invested extensively in Cuban sugar plantations. By 1897, trade with Cuba had reached $27 million per year. Appeals for reform had much to do with ensuring a stable environment for further investments, as well as for the protection of sugar fields against the ravages of civil war.

The election of 1896 diverted attention from Cuba to the issues of free silver and jobs, but only temporarily. A new government in Madrid recalled Weyler and seemed ready to bring about some reforms, even promising a degree of self-government to the Cubans. But these concessions were halfhearted. Conditions worsened in the reconcentration camps, and the American press kept the plight of the Cuban people before the public. McKinley, anxious not to take any action that might upset business recovery from the depression, skillfully resisted the pressure for war. But his skill could not control Spanish misrule or Cuban aspirations for freedom. The fundamental causes of the war—Spanish intransigence in the face of persistent Cuban rebellion and American sugar interests and sympathies for the underdog—were seemingly unstoppable.

Events early in 1898 sparked the outbreak of war. Rioting in Havana intensified both Spanish repression and American outrage. As pressures for war increased, a letter from the Spanish minister to the United States, Depuy de Lôme, calling McKinley a "weak" hypocritical politician, was intercepted by spies and made public. The American populace was inflamed as Hearst's New York *Journal* called De Lôme's letter "the worst insult to the United States in its history."

A second event was more serious. When the rioting broke out, the U.S. battleship *Maine* was sent to Havana harbor to protect American citizens. Early in the evening on February 15, a tremendous explosion blew up the *Maine*, killing 262 men. American advocates of war, who assumed Spanish responsibility, called immediately for intervention. Newspaper publishers offered rewards for discovery of the perpetrators of the crime and broadcast slogans like "Remember the *Maine!* To hell with *Spain!*"

Assistant Secretary of State Theodore Roosevelt, who had been preparing for war for some time, said that he believed the *Maine* had been sunk "by an act of dirty treachery on the part of the Spaniards" and that he would "give anything if President McKinley would order the fleet to Havana tomorrow." When the president did not, Roosevelt privately declared that McKinley had "no more backbone than a chocolate éclair" and continued to ready the navy for action. Although an official board of inquiry concluded that an external submarine mine caused the explosion, to this day no one is certain of the source. Probably a faulty boiler or some other internal problem set off the explosion, a possibility even Roosevelt later conceded.

After the sinking of the *Maine*, Roosevelt took advantage of Secretary of the Navy John D. Long's absence from the office one day to send a cable to Commodore George Dewey, commander of the United States Pacific fleet at Hong Kong. Roosevelt's message ordered Dewey to fill his ships with coal and, "in the event" of a declaration of war with Spain, to sail to the

*Remembering the* Maine, *citizens decorated its mast in observance of the second anniversary of its sinking in Havana Harbor.*

Philippines and make sure "the Spanish squadron does not leave the Asiatic coast." Roosevelt wrote in his diary that night that "the Secretary is away and I am having immense fun running the Navy." When Long returned to work and discovered his assistant's action, he wrote that "Roosevelt has come very near causing more of an explosion than happened to the *Maine.*"

Roosevelt's act was not impetuous, as Long thought, but consistent with naval policies he had been urging upon his more cautious superior for more than a year. As early as 1895, the navy had formulated plans for attacking the Philippines. Influenced by Mahan and Lodge, Roosevelt advocated the continuing creation of a large, modern navy, which had been suspended in the mid-1890s. He also believed that the United States should construct an interoceanic canal, acquire the Danish West Indies (the Virgin Islands), annex Hawaii outright, and oust Spain from Cuba. As Roosevelt told McKinley late in 1897, he was putting the navy in "the best possible shape" for "when war began." His order to Dewey, then, reflected a well-thought-out strategy to implement the "large policy" necessary for the advance of civilization.

The public outcry over the *Maine* drowned out McKinley's efforts to calm the populace and avoid war. The issues had become highly political, especially with midterm elections in the fall and a presidential race only two years away. Fellow Republican Senator Lodge warned McKinley that "if war in Cuba drags on through the summer with nothing done we shall go down to the greatest defeat ever known." McKinley hoped that the Madrid government would make the necessary concessions in Cuba and sent some tough demands in March. But the Spanish response was delayed and inadequate, refusing to grant full independence to the Cubans.

On April 11, 1898, President McKinley sent an ambiguous message to Congress that seemed to call for war. Two weeks later, Congress authorized the use of troops against Spain and passed a resolution recognizing Cuban independence, actions amounting to a declaration of war. In a significant additional resolution, the Teller Amendment, Congress stated that the United States had no intentions of annexing Cuba, guaranteeing the Cubans the right to determine their own destiny. Senator George F. Hoar of Massachusetts, who later assailed the United States for its war against the Filipinos, declared that the intervention in Cuba would be "the most honorable single war in all history," undertaken without "the slightest thought or desire of foreign conquest or of national gain or advantage."

### "A Splendid Little War"

As soon as war was declared, Theodore Roosevelt resigned his post in the Navy Department and cabled Brooks Brothers to rush a "lieutenant-colonel's uniform" to him. Black regiments as well as white headed to Tampa, Florida, with Roosevelt to be shipped to Cuba. One black soldier, noting the stark differences in the southern reception of the segregated regiments, commented, "I am sorry that we were

*Although accused of weakness, McKinley was a wise, vigorous, and far-seeing president in an expansionist era.*

not treated with much courtesy while coming through the South." Blacks were especially sympathetic to the Cuban people's independence because of a common heritage. As one soldier wrote in his journal, "Oh, God! at last we have taken up the sword to enforce the divine rights of a people who have been unjustly treated." As the four-month war neared its end in August, John Hay wrote Roosevelt that "it has been a splendid little war; begun with the highest motives, carried on with magnificent intelligence and spirit." It was a good feeling, a very American one, selflessly rescuing the oppressed and helping them achieve self-rule. As one soldier wrote home, describing his arrival in Puerto Rico: "It's a wonderful sight how the natives respect us. They take off their hats and say Viva Americana."

It was a "splendid" war also because compared to the long, bloody Civil War or even the British fight with the Boers in South Africa going on at the same time, the war with Spain was short and relatively easy. Naval battles were won almost without return fire. At both major naval engagements, Manila Bay and Santiago Bay, only two Americans died, one of them from heat prostration while stoking coal. The islands of Guam and Puerto Rico were taken virtually without a shot. Only 385 men died from Spanish

bullets, but over 5,000 succumbed to tropical diseases.

The Spanish-American War was splendid in other ways, as letters from American soldiers suggest. One young man wrote that his comrades were all "in good spirits" because oranges and coconuts were so plentiful and "every trooper has his canteen full of lemonade all the time." Another wrote his mother that he found Cuba not only cooler but better than Texas in many ways: "Our money is worth twice as much as Spanish money. We do not want for anything." And another wrote his brother that he was having "a lot of fun chasing Spaniards."

But for many men, the war was anything but splendid. One soldier wrote that "words are inadequate to express the feeling of pain and sickness when one has the fever. For about a week every bone in my body ached and I did not care much whether I lived or not." Another wrote, "One of the worst things I saw was a man shot while loading his gun. The Spanish Mauser bullet struck the magazine of his carbine, and . . . the bullet was split, a part of it going through his scalp and a part through his neck. . . . He was a mass of blood."

The "power of joy in battle" that Teddy Roosevelt felt "when the wolf rises in the heart" was not a feeling shared by all American sol-

## The Spanish-American War

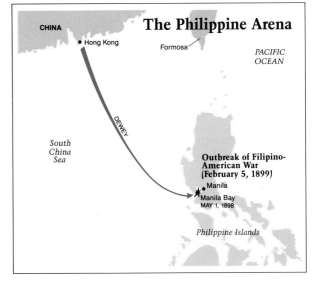

*The celebrated charge of "Teddy's Rough Riders" up San Juan Hill, which so greatly helped Roosevelt's political career, was protected by black troops like these from the Ninth U.S. Calvary (on right).*

diers. Roosevelt's brush with death at Las Guásimas and his celebrated charge up San Juan Hill near Santiago, his flank protected by black troops, made 3-inch headlines and propelled him toward the New York governor's mansion in Albany. "I would rather have led that charge," he said later, "than served three terms in the U.S. Senate." Nonetheless, no one did as much during the war as Roosevelt to advance not only his political career but also the cause of expansion and national glory.

### The Philippines Debates

Roosevelt's act of ordering Dewey to Manila initiated the chain of events that led to the annexation of the Philippines. The most crucial battle of the Spanish-American War took place on May 1, 1898, when Dewey totally destroyed the Spanish fleet in Manila Bay and cabled McKinley for additional troops. The president said later that upon receiving Dewey's cable he was not even sure "within two thousand miles" where "those darned islands were." Actually, McKinley had approved Roosevelt's policies and knew what course of action to pursue. He sent twice as many troops as Dewey had asked for and began the process of shaping American

public opinion to accept the "political, commercial [and] humanitarian" reasons for annexing all 7,000 Philippine islands. The Treaty of Paris gave the United States all of them in exchange for a $20 million payment to Spain.

The treaty was sent to the Senate for ratification during the winter of 1898–1899. Senators for and against annexation hurled arguments at each other across the floor of the Senate as American soldiers hurled oaths and taunts across the neutral zone at Aguinaldo's insurgents near Manila. Private Grayson's encounter in February, marked the passage of the treaty in the Senate and began the Filipino-American War. The treaty barely received the necessary two-thirds majority, primarily because the Republicans made an effective case and because they had Democratic support.

The debates over the Philippines took place in a wider arena than the Senate. The entire nation joined in, as the issues loomed much larger than the islands in question. At stake were two very different views of foreign policy and of America's vision of itself. Although he spent several months quietly seeking advice, listening to public opinion, and acting as if he were unsure what to do, McKinley finally recommended annexation.

Many Democrats supported the president out of fear of being labeled disloyal, as had happened in the 1860s. Fellow Republicans confirmed McKinley's arguments for annexation, adding even more racist ones. Filipinos were described as childlike, savage, stunted in size, dirty, and backward. Comparisons were made with blacks and Native Americans, and policies were proposed befitting the inferior condition in which white Americans saw the Filipinos. Roosevelt called Aguinaldo "a renegade Pawnee" and said that the Filipinos had no right "to administer the country which they happen to be occupying." The attitudes favoring annexation, therefore, asserted Filipino inferiority and incapacity for self-rule while also reflecting America's proud sense of itself in 1900 as a nation of civilized order and progress.

## McKinley's Annexation Argument

In a speech to a group of expansionist Methodist ministers and missionaries in 1900, President McKinley explained his reasons for recommending annexation of the Philippines. His statement summarizes most of the reasons for expansionism. It also offers a fascinating glimpse into the inner process of presidential decision making (or at least of how a President later sought to justify a decision).

The truth is I didn't want the Philippines and when they came to us as a gift from the gods, I did not know what to do about them. . . . And one night it came to me this way—(1) that we could not give them back to Spain—that would be cowardly and dishonorable; (2) that we could not turn them over to France or Germany—our commercial rivals in the Orient—that would be bad business and discreditable; (3) that we could not leave them to themselves—they were unfit for self-government—and they would soon have anarchy and misrule over there worse than Spain's was; and (4) that there was nothing left for us to do but to take them all, and to educate the Filipinos, and uplift and civilize and Christianize them, and by God's grace do the very best we could by them, as our fellowmen for whom Christ also died. And then I went to bed, and went to sleep, and slept soundly, and the next morning I sent for the chief engineer of the War Department (our map-maker), and I told him to put the Philippines on the map of the United States, and there they are, and there they will stay while I am President!

Other Americans were not so positive about such "progress." A small but vocal group organized in the Anti-Imperialist League vigorously opposed both the war and annexation. Many of them represented a fading elite, feeling displaced by the younger generation of modern expansionists. By attacking imperialism, the anti-imperialists struck out against the forces of modernism that they felt threatened their social position. They included a cross section of American dignitaries: ex-presidents Harrison and Cleveland, Samuel Gompers and Andrew Carnegie, William James, Jane Addams, Mark Twain, and many others.

The major anti-imperialist arguments pointed out how imperialism in general and annexation in particular contradicted American ideals. First, the annexation of territory without immediate or planned steps toward statehood was unprecedented and unconstitutional. Second, to occupy and govern a foreign people without their consent was a violation of the ideals of the Declaration of Independence. In one of the strongest anti-imperialist statements, Senator Hoar, who had called the war in Cuba "honorable," described the war in the Philippines in the following way:

> We changed the Monroe Doctrine from a doctrine of eternal righteousness and justice, resting on the consent of the governed, to a doctrine of brutal selfishness looking only to our own advantage. We crushed the only republic in Asia. We made war on the only Christian people in the East. We converted a war of glory to a war of shame. We vulgarized the American flag. We introduced perfidy into the practice of war. We inflicted torture on unarmed men to extort confession. We put children to death. We devastated provinces. We baffled the aspirations of a people for liberty.

A third argument was that social reforms needed at home demanded American energies and money before foreign expansionism. "Before we attempt to teach house-keeping to the world," one writer put it, we needed "to set our own house in order."

Not all anti-imperialist arguments were so noble. Some were practical or downright racist. One position alleged that since the Filipinos were nonwhite, Catholic, and inferior in size and intelligence, they were unassimilable. Annexation would lead to miscegenation and contamination of Anglo-Saxon blood. Senator Ben Tillman of South Carolina argued that although it was permissible to "walk on the necks of every colored race" whites came into contact with, he still opposed "incorporating any more colored men into the body politic." The practical argument suggested that once in possession of the Philippines, the United States would have to defend them, possibly even acquiring more territories. This would require higher taxes and bigger government in order to build and support the navy that holding such possessions demanded. Some saw the Philippines as a burden that would require American troops to fight distant Asian wars.

The last argument became fact when Private Grayson's encounter started the Filipino-American War. As U.S. treatment of the Filipinos during the war became more and more like Spanish mistreatment of the Cubans, the hypocrisy of American behavior became even more evident. This was especially true for black American soldiers who fought in the Philippines. They identified with the dark-skinned insurgents, whom they saw as tied to the land, burdened by debt, and pressed by poverty like themselves. They were also called "nigger" from morning to night. "I feel sorry for these people," a sergeant in the 24th Infantry wrote. "You have no idea the way these people are treated by the Americans here."

The war starkly exposed the hypocrisies of shouldering the white man's burden. Upon reading a report that 8,000 Filipinos had been killed in the first year of the war, Carnegie wrote a letter, dripping with sarcasm, congratulating McKinley for "civilizing the Filipinos. . . . About 8000 of them have been completely civilized and sent to Heaven. I hope you like it." Another writer penned a devastating one-liner: "Dewey took Manila with the loss of one man—and all our institutions." One of the most active anti-imperialists, Ernest Howard Crosby, wrote a parody of Rudyard Kipling's "White Man's Burden," which he titled "The Real 'White Man's Burden'":

Take up the White Man's burden.
  Send forth your sturdy kin,
And load them down with Bibles
  And cannon-balls and gin.
Throw in a few diseases
  To spread the tropic climes,
For there the healthy niggers
  Are quite behind the times.

They need our labor question, too,
  And politics and fraud—
We've made a pretty mess at home,
  Let's make a mess abroad.

The efforts of Crosby and other anti-imperialists were unsuccessful, failing either to prevent annexation or to interfere with the war effort. However prestigious and sincere, they had little or no political power. They were seen as an older, conservative, elite group of Americans opposed to the kind of dynamic progress represented by Teddy Roosevelt and other expansionists. They were out of tune with the period of exuberant national pride, prosperity, and promise.

## Expansionism Triumphant

By 1900, Americans had ample reason to be patriotic. Within a year, the United States had

*Bringing "civilization" to the Filipinos, American soldiers stand guard over captured guerrillas in 1899.*

acquired several island territories, thereby joining the other great powers of the world. But several questions arose over what to do with the new territories. What was their status? Were they colonies? Would they be granted statehood or would they develop gradually from colonies to constitutional parts of the United States? Moreover, did the native peoples of Hawaii, Puerto Rico, Guam, and the Philippines have the same rights as American citizens on the mainland? Were they protected by the U.S. Constitution? The answers to these difficult questions emerged in a series of Supreme Court cases, congressional acts, and presidential decisions.

Although slightly different governing systems were worked out for each new territory, the solution in each was to define its status somewhere between subject colony and candidate for statehood. Territorial status came closest. The native people were usually allowed to elect their own legislature for internal lawmaking but had governors and other judicial and administrative officials appointed by the American president. William Howard Taft, for example, was McKinley's appointee as the first civilian governor in the Philippines, where he was effective in moving the Filipinos toward self-government. Final independence did not come until 1946, however, and elsewhere the process was equally slow. The question of constitutional rights was resolved by deciding that Hawaiians and Puerto Ricans, for example, would be treated differently from Texans and Oregonians. In the "insular cases" of 1901, the Supreme Court ruled that these people would achieve citizenship and constitutional rights only when Congress said they were ready. To the question, Does the Constitution follow the flag?, the answer, as Secretary of State Elihu Root put it, was, "Ye-es, as near as I can make out the Constitution follows the flag—but doesn't quite catch up with it."

The optimistic, nationalistic spirit of the American people was revealed most clearly in the election of 1900, when McKinley defeated Bryan more resoundingly than in 1896. Bryan's intentions to make imperialism the "paramount issue" of the campaign failed, in part because the debates on the Philippines question had ended long before the campaign began, the issue settled in favor of annexation. The Philippine-American War was actually popular, and it was politically unwise to risk being branded a traitor by opposing it. In the closing weeks of the campaign, Bryan and the Democrats shied away from imperialism and the war as a "paramount issue" and focused more on economic issues—trusts, labor question, and (again) free silver.

But Bryan fared no better on those issues. The discovery of gold in Alaska had returned prosperity to American workers. Cries for reform fell on deaf ears. The McKinley forces rightly claimed that under four years of Republican rule more money, jobs, thriving factories, and manufactured goods had been created. Moreoever, McKinley pointed to the tremendous growth in American prestige abroad. Spain had been kicked out of Cuba, and the American flag flew in many places around the globe. It had been a triumphant four years. As a disappointed Tom Watson put it, noting the end of the Populist revolt with the war fervor over Cuba, "The Spanish war finished us. The blare of the bugle drowned out the voice of the reformer."

He was more right than he knew. Within one year, the active expansionist, Theodore Roosevelt, went from assistant secretary of the navy

## Presidential Elections, 1896–1900

| YEAR | CANDIDATES | PARTY | POPULAR VOTE | ELECTORAL VOTE |
|------|------------|-------|--------------|----------------|
| 1896 | W. McKINLEY | Republican | 7,035,638 (51%) | 271 |
| | W. J. Bryan | Democrat/Populist | 6,467,946 (47%) | 176 |
| 1900 | W. McKINLEY | Republican | 7,219,530 (52%) | 292 |
| | W. J. Bryan | Democrat | 6,358,071 (46%) | 155 |

*Note:* Winner's name is in capital letters.

to colonel of the Rough Riders to governor of New York. For some Republican politicos, who thought he was too vigorous, unorthodox, and independent, this quick rise to prominence as a potential rival to McKinley came too fast. One way to eliminate Roosevelt politically, or at least slow him down, they thought, was to make him vice-president, which they did at the Republican convention in 1900. But six months into McKinley's second term, while attending an exposition in Buffalo, McKinley was shot and killed by an anarchist, the third presidential assassination in less than 40 years. "Now look," exclaimed party boss Mark Hanna, who had opposed putting Roosevelt on the ticket; "that damned cowboy is President of the United States!"

## ROOSEVELT'S ENERGETIC DIPLOMACY

At a White House dinner party in 1905, a guest told a story about his visit to the Roosevelt home when Teddy had been a baby. "You were in your bassinet, making a good deal of fuss and noise," the guest reported, "and your father lifted you out and asked me to hold you." Secretary of State Elihu Root looked up from his plate and asked, "Was he hard to hold?" Whether true or not, the story reveals much about President Roosevelt's principles and policies on foreign affairs. As president from 1901 to 1909, and as the most dominating American personality for the 15 years between 1897 and 1912, Roosevelt made much fuss and noise about the activist role he thought the United States should play in the world. As he implemented his policies, it often seemed as if he was "hard to hold." Roosevelt's energetic foreign policy in Latin America, Asia, and Europe paved the way for the vital role of the United States as a world power.

### Foreign Policy as Darwinian Struggle

Roosevelt's personal principles and presidential policies went together. He was an advocate of both individual physical fitness and collective national strength. As an undersized, weak young boy who suffered humiliating drubbings by schoolmates, he undertook a rigorous program of strengthening his body through boxing and other exercise. During summers spent on his ranch in the North Dakota Badlands, Roosevelt learned to value "the strenuous life" of the cowboy. He read Darwin and understood that life among humans, as in nature, was a constant struggle for survival.

Roosevelt extended his beliefs about strenuous struggle from individuals to nations. His ideal was "a nation of men, not weaklings." To be militarily prepared and to fight well were, for Roosevelt, the tests of racial superiority and national greatness. "All the great masterful races," he said, "have been fighting races." Although he believed in Anglo-Saxon superiority, he admired—and feared—the military prowess of the Japanese. Powerful nations, like individuals, Roosevelt believed, had a duty to cultivate qualities of vigor, strength, courage, and moral commitment to civilized values. In practical terms this meant developing natural resources, building large navies, and being constantly prepared to fight. "I never take a step in foreign policy," he wrote, "unless I am assured that I shall be able eventually to carry out my will by force."

Although known for his advice to "speak softly and carry a big stick," Roosevelt often not only wielded a large stick but spoke loudly as well. In one speech in 1897 he used the word *war* 62 times, saying that "no triumph of peace is quite so great as the supreme triumphs of war." But despite his bluster, Roosevelt was usually restrained in the exercise of force. For helping to end the Russo-Japanese War, he was awarded the Nobel Peace Prize in 1906. The purpose of the big stick and the loud talk was to preserve order and peace in the world. "To be prepared for war," he said, "is the most effectual means to promote peace."

Roosevelt divided the world into civilized and uncivilized nations, the former usually defined as Anglo-Saxon and English-speaking. The civilized nations had a responsibility to "police" the uncivilized, not only maintaining order but also spreading superior values and institutions. This "international police power," as Roosevelt called it, was the "white man's burden." As part of this burden, civilized nations sometimes had to fight wars against the uncivilized, as the British did against the Boers in South Africa and the Americans did in the Philippines. These wars were justified because the blessings of culture and racial superiority were passed on to the vanquished by the victors.

A war between two civilized nations, however, such as between Germany and England, was wasteful and foolish, upsetting order in the world. Above all, Roosevelt believed in the balance of power. Strong, advanced nations had a duty to use their power to preserve order and peace. This included the United States after 1898, especially after the annexation of the Philippines. The United States had "no choice," Roosevelt said, but to "play a great part in the world." Americans could no longer "avoid responsibilities" that followed from "the fact that on the east and west we look across the waters at Europe and Asia."

As Roosevelt looked across the oceans, he developed a highly personal style of diplomacy. Rather than relying on the Department of State, he preferred face-to-face contact and personal exchange of letters with foreign ambassadors, ministers, and heads of state. Under Roosevelt, foreign policy was made while horseback-riding with the German ambassador or while discussing history with the ambassador from France. A British emissary observed that Roosevelt had a "powerful personality" and a commanding knowledge of the world. As a result, ministries from London to Tokyo respected both the president and the power of the United States.

When threat of force was inadequate to accomplish his goals, Roosevelt used direct personal intervention as a third-party mediator. "In a crisis the duty of a leader is to lead," he said. Congress was too slow and deliberate to play a significant role in foreign affairs. When he wanted Panama, Roosevelt bragged later, "I took the Canal Zone" rather than submitting a long "dignified State Paper" for congressional debate on an appropriate policy. And while Congress debated the appropriateness of his actions, he was fond of pointing out, the building of the canal across Panama began. Roosevelt's energetic executive activism in foreign policy set a pattern followed by nearly every twentieth-century American president.

*The "big stick" came to be a memorable image in American diplomacy as Teddy Roosevelt sought to make the United States a policeman not only of the Caribbean basin, but also of the whole world.*

One of the most enjoyable ways of recovering the values and attitudes of the past is through political cartoons. Ralph Waldo Emerson once said, "Caricatures are often the truest history of the times." A deft drawing of a popular or unpopular politician can freeze ideas and events in time, conveying more effectively than columns of type the central issues of the day and creating an immediate response in the viewer. It is this freshness that makes caricatures such a valuable source when attempting to recover the past. Cartoonists are often at their best when they are critical, exaggerating a physical feature of a political figure or capsuling public sentiment against the government.

The history of political cartoons in the United States goes back to Benjamin Franklin's "Join or Die" cartoon calling for colonial cooperation against the French in 1754. But political cartoons were rare until Andrew Jackson's presidency. Even after such cartoons as "King Andrew the First" in the 1830s, they did not gain notoriety until the advent of Thomas

Nast's cartoons in *Harper's Weekly* in the 1870s. Nast drew scathing cartoons exposing the corruption of William "Boss" Tweed's Tammany Hall, depicting Tweed and his men as vultures and smiling deceivers. "Stop them damn pictures," Tweed ordered. "I don't care so much what the papers write about me. My constitutents can't read. But, damn it, they can see pictures." Tweed sent some of his men to Nast with an offer of $100,000 to "study art" in Europe. The $5,000-a-year artist negotiated up to a half million dollars before refusing Tweed's offer. "I made up my mind not long ago to put some of those fellows behind bars," Nast said, "and I'm going to put them there." His cartoons helped drive Tweed out of office.

The emergence of the United States as a world power and the rise of Theodore Roosevelt gave cartoonists plenty to draw about. An impetus to political cartoons was given by the rise of cheap newspapers such as William Randolph Hearst's *Journal* and Joseph Pulitzer's *World*. When the Spanish-American War broke out, newspapers whipped up public sentiment

**"The Spanish Brute Adds Mutilation to Murder,"
by Grant Hamilton, in** Judge, *July 9, 1898*

**"Liberty Halts American Butchery
in the Philippines," from** Life, *1899*

by having artists draw fake pictures of Spaniards stripping American women at sea and encouraging cartoonists to depict the "Spanish brute." Hearst used these tactics to increase his paper's daily circulation to one million copies. But by the time of the Philippines debates, many cartoonists took an anti-imperialist stance, pointing out American hypocrisy. Within a year cartoonists shifted from depicting "The Spanish Brute Adds Mutilation to Murder" (1898) to "Liberty Halts American Butchery in the Philippines" (1899). The cartoons are very similar in condemning "butchery" of native populations, but the target has of course changed. Although Uncle Sam as a killer is not nearly as menacing as the figure of Spain as an ugly gorilla, in both cartoons there is a similarity of stance, the blood-soaked swords, and a trail of bodies behind.

When Theodore Roosevelt rose to the presidency, cartoonists rejoiced. His physical appearance and personality made him instantly recognizable, a key factor in the success of a political cartoon. His broad grin, eyeglasses, and walrus mustache were the kind of features that fueled the cartoonist's imagination. A man of great energy, Roosevelt's style was as distinctive as his look. Other factors, such as the "Rough Rider" nickname, the symbol of the "big stick," and policies like "gunboat diplomacy" made Teddy the perfect target for political cartoons.

To understand and appreciate the meaning of any cartoon, certain facts must be ascertained, such as the date, artist, and source of the cartoon, the particular historical characters, events, and context depicted in it, the significance of the caption, and the master symbols employed by the cartoonist. The two remaining cartoons, "Panama or Bust" (1903) and "For President!" (1904), were both printed in American daily newspapers. Aside from the context and meaning of each cartoon, which should be obvious, note how the cartoonists use familiar symbols from Roosevelt's life and American history to underline the ironic power of their point. How many can you identify, and how are they used?

*"Panama or Bust," from* The New York Times, *1903*

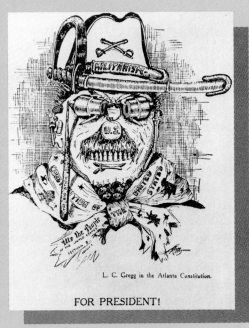

FOR PRESIDENT!

*"For President," by L. C. Gregg,
in the Atlanta* Constitution, *1904*

## Policeman of the Caribbean

As late as 1901, the Monroe Doctrine was still regarded, according to Roosevelt, as the "equivalent to an open door in South America." To the United States this meant that although no nation had a right "to get territorial possessions," all nations had equal commercial rights in the Western Hemisphere south of the Rio Grande. But as American investments poured into Central America and Caribbean islands, that policy changed to one of the primary right of the United States to dominant influence in the lands of the Caribbean basin. Order was indispensable for profitable economic activity.

This change was demonstrated in 1902, when Germany and Great Britain seized several Venezuelan gunboats and blockaded its ports in order to force the Venezuelan government to pay defaulted debts. Roosevelt was especially worried that German influence would replace the British. He insisted that the European powers accept arbitration of the disputed financial claims and threatened to "move Dewey's ships" to the Venezuelan coast to enforce his intentions. The crisis passed, largely for other reasons, but Roosevelt's threat of force made the paramount presence and self-interest of the United States in the Caribbean very clear.

After the Spanish were expelled from Cuba, the United States supervised the island under Military Governor General Leonard Wood until 1902, when the Cubans elected their own congress and president. The United States honored Cuban independence, as it had promised to do in the Teller Amendment. But through the Platt Amendment, which Cubans reluctantly attached to their constitution in 1901, the United States obtained many economic rights in Cuba, a naval base at Guantanamo Bay, and the right of intervention if Cuban sovereignty were ever threatened. Newspapers in Havana assailed this violation of their newfound independence. One cartoon, titled "The Cuban Calvary," showed a figure representing "the Cuban people" crucified between two thieves, represented as Wood and McKinley.

American policy intended to make Cuba a model of how a newly independent nation could achieve orderly self-government with only minimal guidance. Cuban self-government, however, was shaky. By 1906, an internal political crisis between rival factions threatened to plunge the infant nation into civil war. Roosevelt was disappointed, if not downright furious, with "that infernal little Cuban republic." At Cuba's request, he sent warships to patrol the coastline and special commissioners and troops "to restore order and peace and public confidence." As he left office in 1909, Roosevelt proudly proclaimed that "we have done our best to put Cuba on the road to stable and orderly government." The road was paved with sugar. U.S. trade with Cuba increased from $27 million in the year before 1898 to an average of $43 million per year during the following decade. Along with economic development, American political and even military involvement in Cuban affairs continued throughout the century.

The pattern repeated itself on other Caribbean islands. The Dominican Republic, for example, suffered from unstable governments and economic ill health. In 1904, as a revolt erupted, European creditors pressured the Dominican government for payment of $40 million in defaulted bonds. With the presence of U.S. warships to discourage European intervention, the United States took over the collection of customs in the republic. Two years later, the United States intervened to settle a disruptive conflict between two Central American strongmen in Guatemala and Nicaragua, where American bankers controlled nearly 50 percent of all trade.

Roosevelt's policy that civilized nations should "insist on the proper policing of the world" was clarified in 1904 in his annual message. The goal of the United States, he said, was to have "stable, orderly and prosperous neighbors." A country that paid its debts and kept order "need fear no interference from the United States." A country that did not, but rather committed "chronic wrong-doing" and loosened the "ties of civilized society," would require the United States to intervene as "an international police power." This doctrine became known as the Roosevelt Corollary to the Monroe Doctrine. Whereas Monroe's doctrine had warned European nations not to intervene in the Western Hemisphere, Roosevelt's corollary justified American intervention. Starting with a desire to protect property, loans, and investments, the United States often interceded in these countries to maintain order. This meant supporting the brutal regimes of small elites who owned most of the land, suppressed social unrest, and acted as surrogates of American policy. As the St. Louis *Post-Dispatch* commented, the Monroe Doctrine now could be understood to mean "you mind your business and we'll mind yours."

After 1904, the Roosevelt Corollary was invoked in several Caribbean countries. Intervention usually required the landing of U.S. Marines to counter the threat posed by political instability and bankruptcy to American economic interests: railroads, mines, and the production of sugar, bananas, and coffee. Occupying the capital and major seaports, American marines, bankers, and customs officials usually remained for several years, until they were satisfied that stability had been reestablished. Roosevelt's successors, William Howard Taft and Woodrow Wilson, pursued the same interventionist policy. Later presidents, most recently Ronald Reagan, would do likewise.

### Taking the Panama Canal

In justifying the intervention of 2,600 American troops in Honduras and Nicaragua, Philander Knox, secretary of state from 1909 to 1913,

said that "we are in the eyes of the world, and because of the Monroe Doctrine, held responsible for the order of Central America, and its proximity to the Canal makes the preservation of peace in that neighborhood particularly necessary." The building of the Panama Canal was not yet finished when Knox spoke, but it had already become a vital cornerstone of United States policy in the region. Three problems had to be surmounted in order to fulfill the long-sought goal of an interoceanic connection. First, an 1850 treaty bound the United States to build a canal jointly with Great Britain. But in 1901, John Hay, secretary of state between 1901 and 1905, convinced the British to cancel the treaty in exchange for an American guarantee that the canal, once built, would be "free and open to the vessels of commerce and of war of all nations." A second problem was where to build the canal. After considering a lengthy but technically easy route through Nicaragua, American engineers settled on the shorter but more rugged path across the isthmus of Panama, where a French firm, the New Panama Company, had already begun work.

The third problem was that Panama was a province of Colombia and thus could not negotiate with the United States. The Colombian government was unimpressed with the share of a likely settlement the Americans would provide in buying up the New Panama Canal Company's $40 million in assets. Indeed, in 1903, the

*Despite protests from the Panamanian government, in 1903 the United States acquired the right to build and operate a canal across the isthmus. An enormous engineering undertaking, the Panama Canal was completed in 1914.*

Colombian senate rejected a treaty negotiated by Hay, but mostly on nationalistic, not financial, grounds. Roosevelt, angered by this rebuff, called the Colombians "Dagoes" and "foolish and homicidal corruptionists" who, like highway robbers, he thought, tried to "hold us up."

Aware of Roosevelt's fury, encouraged by hints of American support, and eager for the economic benefits the building of a canal would bring, Panamanian nationalists in 1903 staged a revolution led by several rich families and a Frenchman, Philippe Bunau-Varilla of the New Panama Canal Company. The Colombian army, dispatched to quell the revolt, was deterred by the presence of an American warship; local troops were separated from their officers, who were bought off. The bloodless revolution occurred on November 3; the next day, Panama declared its independence. On November 6, the United States officially recognized the new government in Panama. Although Roosevelt did not formally encourage the revolution, it would not have occurred without American money and support.

On November 18, Hay and Bunau-Varilla signed a treaty establishing the American right to build and operate a canal through Panama and to exercise "titular sovereignty" over the 10-mile-wide Canal Zone for 99 years. The Panamanian government protested the treaty, to no avail, and a later government called it "the treaty that no Panamanian signed." Roosevelt, boasting later that he "took the canal," claimed that his diplomatic and engineering achievement, completed in 1914, would "rank . . . with the Louisiana Purchase and the acquisition of Texas."

## Opening the Door to China

Throughout the nineteenth century, American relations with China were restricted to a small but profitable trade. The British, in competition with France, Germany, and Russia, took advantage of the weak, crumbling Manchu dynasty by making trade treaties with China. These gave access to treaty ports and most-favored-nation trading privileges in various spheres of influence throughout the country. After 1898, Americans with dreams of exploit-

ing the seemingly unlimited markets of China wanted to join the competition and enlarge their share. The United States, too, wanted favorable commercial rights and a place to sell surplus goods. Moral interests, however, including many missionaries, reminded Americans of their revolutionary tradition against European imperialism. They made clear their opposition to crass U.S. commercial exploitation of a weak nation and supported the preservation of China's political integrity against continuing interference by the European powers.

American attitudes toward the Chinese people reflected this confusion of motives. Some Americans held an idealized view of China as the center of Eastern wisdom and saw a "special relationship" between the two nations. But the dominant American attitude viewed the Chinese as heathen, exotic, backward, and immoral. This negative stereotype was reflected in the

*European and American forces cooperated in quelling China's Boxer Rebellion in 1900. Here a European count makes his entrance at Peking's Sacred Gate, escorted by Bengal Lancers subject to the British crown.*

Exclusion Act of 1882 and the riots in western states against Chinese workers in the 1870s and 1880s. The Chinese, in turn, regarded the United States with a mixture of curiosity, resentment, suspicion, and disdain, as well as with admiration for a potential, if arrogant, guardian.

The annexation of Hawaii, Samoa, and the Philippines in 1898 and 1899 convinced Secretary of State Hay that the United States should announce its own policy for China. The result was the Open Door notes of 1899–1900, which became the cornerstone of U.S. policy in Asia for much of the twentieth century. The first note, focusing on customs-collection issues, opened a door for American trade by declaring the principle of equal access to commercial rights in China by all nations. The second note, addressing Russian movement into Manchuria, called upon all countries to respect the "territorial and administrative integrity" of China. This second principle opened the way for a larger American role in Asia, offering China protection from foreign invasions and preserving a balance of power in the Far East.

An early test of this new role came during the Boxer Rebellion in 1900. The Boxers were a society of young traditionalist Chinese in revolt against both the Manchu dynasty and the growing Western presence and influence in China. During the summer of 1900, fanatical Boxers killed some 242 missionaries and other foreigners and besieged the western quarter of Peking. Eventually, an international military force of 19,000 troops, including some 3,000 Americans sent from the Philippines, marched on Peking to end the siege.

The American relationship with China was plagued by the exclusionist immigration policy. Despite the barriers and riots, Chinese workers kept coming to the United States, entering illegally from Mexico and British Columbia. In 1905, Chinese nationalists at home boycotted American goods and called for a change in immigration policy. Roosevelt, who had a low opinion of the Chinese as a "backward" people, bristled with resentment and sent troops to the Philippines as a threat. Halfheartedly, he also asked Congress for a modified immigration bill, but nothing came of it.

A year later, he faced a similar crisis with Japan. The San Francisco school board, claiming that Japanese children were "crowding the whites out of the schools," segregated them into separate schools and asked Roosevelt to persuade Japan to stop the emigration of its people. Though the Japanese were insulted, they agreed to limit the migration of unskilled workers to the United States in a gentleman's agreement signed in 1907. In return, the segregation law was repealed, but not without disturbing the harmonious relations between the two nations.

Despite exclusion and insults, the idea that the United States had a unique guardian relationship with China persisted into the twentieth century. Since Japan had ambitions in China, this created a rivalry between Japan and the United States, testing the American commitment to preserve the Open Door in China and the balance of power in Asia. Economic motives in Asia, however, proved to be less significant. Investments there developed very slowly, as did the dream of the "great China market" for American grains and textiles. Although textile exports to China increased from $7 million to nearly $24 million in a decade, the China trade always remained larger in imagination than in reality.

### Japan and the Balance of Power

Roosevelt relied on the skillful use of diplomacy and negotiation rather than American military intervention to balance one Asian power against another. The Boxer Rebellion of 1900 left Russia, with 50,000 troops in Manchuria, the strongest nation in eastern Asia. Roosevelt's admiration for the Japanese as a "fighting" people and a valuable factor in "the civilization of the future" contrasted with his low respect for the Russians, whom he described as "corrupt," "treacherous," and "incompetent." As Japan moved into Korea and Russia into Manchuria, Roosevelt hoped that each would check the growing power of the other.

Because of increasing Russian strength, Roosevelt welcomed news in 1904 that Japan had launched a successful surprise attack on Port Arthur in Manchuria, beginning the Russo-Japanese War. He was "well pleased with the

Japanese victory," he told his son, "for Japan is playing our game." But when Japanese victories continued, on sea and on land, many Americans worried that Japan might play the game too well, shutting the United States out of Far Eastern markets. Roosevelt shifted his support toward Russia. When the Japanese expressed interest in an end to the war, the American president was pleased to exert his influence.

Roosevelt's role in bringing the two foes to the conference table won him the Nobel Peace Prize. His goal was to achieve peace and leave a balanced situation. "It is best," he wrote, that Russia be left "face to face with Japan so that each may have a moderative action on the other." The negotiations and resulting treaty were carried out in the summer of 1905 near Portsmouth, New Hampshire. No single act better symbolizes the new posture of American power and presence in the world than the signing of a peace treaty ending a war in Manchuria between Russia and Japan halfway around the globe in New Hampshire!

The Treaty of Portsmouth actually left Japan dominant in Manchuria and established the United States as the major balance to Japan's power. Almost immediately, the Japanese developed a naval base at Port Arthur, built railroads, and sought exclusive rights of investment and control in the Chinese province. In part because of his lack of respect for the Chinese, Roosevelt willingly recognized Japan's "dominance in Manchuria," as well as its control in Korea. But in return, in the Root-Takahira Agreement of 1908, he received Japan's promise to honor U.S. control in the Philippines and to make no further encroachments into China.

These agreements over territorial divisions barely covered up the tensions in Japanese-American relations. Some Japanese were angry that they had not received in the Portsmouth Treaty the indemnities they had wanted from Russia, and they blamed Roosevelt. American insensitivity to the immigration issue also left bad feelings. In Manchuria, U.S. Consul General Willard Straight aggressively pushed an anti-Japanese program of financing capital investment projects in banking and railroads. This policy, later known as "dollar diplomacy" under

Roosevelt's successor, William Howard Taft, like the pursuit of markets, was larger in prospect than results. Nevertheless, the United States was in Japan's way, and rumors of war circulated in the world press.

It was clearly time for Roosevelt's version of the "big stick." In 1907, he told Secretary of State Root that he was "more concerned over the Japanese situation than almost any other. Thank Heaven we have the navy in good shape." Although the naval buildup had begun over a decade earlier, under Roosevelt the U.S. Navy had developed into a formidable force. From 1900 to 1905, outlays to the navy more than doubled, from $56 million to $117 million. Such a naval spending binge was without peacetime precedent. In 1907, to make it clear that "the Pacific was as much our home waters as the Atlantic," Roosevelt sent his new, modernized "Great White Fleet" on a goodwill tour around the world. The first stop was the Japanese port of Yokohama. Although American sailors were greeted warmly, the act may have stimulated navalism in Japan, which came back to haunt the United States in 1941. But for the time being, the balance of power in Asia was preserved.

## Preventing War in Europe

The United States was willing to stretch the meaning of the Monroe Doctrine to justify sending marines and engineers to Latin America and the navy and dollars to Asia. Treaties, agreements, and the protection of territories and interests entangled the United States with foreign nations from Panama and the Dominican Republic to the Philippines and Manchuria. Toward Europe, however, the traditional policies of neutrality and nonentanglement continued. Neither the moral civilizing of unregenerate natives nor American self-interest seemed appropriate in Europe. Still, there was an American role to be played even there, and Roosevelt was anxious to play it.

The most powerful nations of the world were European. Roosevelt therefore believed that the most serious threats to world peace and civilized order lay in relationships among Germany, Great Britain, and France. He established two fundamental policies toward Europe that with only minor variations would define the U.S. role throughout the century. The first was to make friendship with Great Britain the cornerstone of U.S. policy. As Roosevelt told King Edward VII in 1905, "In the long run the English people are more apt to be friendly to us than any other." Second, the crucial goal of a neutral power like the United States was to prevent the outbreak of a general war in Europe among strong nations. Toward this end Roosevelt depended on his personal negotiating skills and began the practice of summit diplomacy.

It is difficult now to think of England as anything other than the most loyal friend of the United States outside of North America. Yet throughout most of the nineteenth century, England was America's chief enemy and commercial rival. From the War of 1812 to the Venezuelan border crisis of 1895, conflict with Great Britain developed in squabbles over old debts and trade barriers, disputes over Canadian borders and fishing jurisdictions, and British interference in the American Civil War.

The Venezuelan crisis and a number of other events at the turn of the century shocked the United States and England into an awareness of their mutual interests. Both nations appreciated the neutrality of the other in their respective wars shouldering the "white man's burden" against the Filipinos and the Boers. Roosevelt

## United States Involvement in Asia, 1898–1909

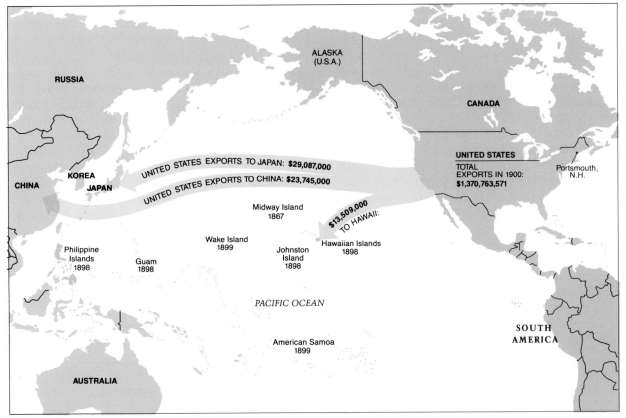

| Japanese-American relations: | 1904–1905 | Russo-Japanese War; Peace Treaty signed in Portsmouth, N.H. | 1906 | San Francisco School Affair |
| | 1905 | Taft-Katsura Agreement | 1907 | Gentlemen's Agreement |
| | | | 1908 | Root-Takahira Agreement |
| | | | 1907–1909 | Great White Fleet |

supported British imperialism because he favored the dominance of "the English-speaking race" and because he believed that England was "fighting the battle of civilization." Furthermore, both nations were concerned about the growth of German power in Europe, Africa, and the Far East. As German naval power increased, England had to bring its fleet closer to home. Friendly allies were needed to police parts of the world formerly patrolled by the British navy. England therefore concluded a mutual-protection treaty with Japan in 1902 and willingly let the Americans police Central America and the Caribbean Sea.

Similarities of language and cultural traditions, as well as strategic self-interest, drew the two countries together. Roosevelt's personal style furthered the connection. He was clearly and unashamedly pro-British, and his most intimate circle of friends included many Englishmen. Although Roosevelt sometimes made blustery speeches critical of English policies, his British bias was never in doubt. He knew, as he wrote Lodge in 1901, that the United States had "not the least particle of danger to fear" from England and that the major menace to peace in Europe would come from German ambitions and militarism. As Roosevelt left the presidency in 1909, one of his final acts was to proclaim the special American friendship with Great Britain.

German Kaiser Wilhelm II often underestimated the solidity of the Anglo-American friendship and thought that Roosevelt was really pro-German, an error the American president skillfully used. He cultivated the kaiser to make him think they were friends sharing mutual interests. Wilhelm therefore sought Roosevelt's support on several diplomatic issues between 1905 and 1909. In each case Roosevelt was able to flatter the kaiser while politely rejecting his overtures. The relationship gave Roosevelt a unique advantage in influencing affairs in Europe in order to prevent an outbreak of war.

The Moroccan crisis in 1905 and 1906 is illustrative. European powers competed for colonies and spheres of influence in Africa as well as in Asia. Germany in particular resented French dominance along the North African coast in Morocco and feared the recent Anglo-French

entente. The kaiser precipitated a crisis in the summer of 1905 by delivering a bellicose speech in Casablanca, Morocco, intended to split the British and French and to force an opening of commercial doors in Morocco. In this endeavor he sought help from Roosevelt. The French were outraged at Wilhelm's boldness, and war threatened.

Roosevelt intervened, arranging a conference in Algeciras, Spain, to prevent war and settle the issues of commerce and police administration in Morocco. Although he sent an experienced diplomat and close friend to represent the United States at Algeciras, the critical negotiations occurred in the correspondence between Wilhelm and Roosevelt. In the spring of 1906 a treaty was signed that displeased the kaiser. The French secured "exclusive" administration of Morocco, and the Germans suffered a humiliating defeat. As Roosevelt explained his own role, "I was most suave and pleasant with the Kaiser, yet when it became necessary . . . I stood him on his head with great decision."

Roosevelt's successful countering of meddlesome German policies continued, as did his efforts in preventing war. At the Hague conference on disarmament in 1907, the kaiser sought an agreement to reduce British naval supremacy, a superiority Roosevelt thought "quite proper." The German emperor also tried to promote a German-Chinese-American entente to balance the Anglo-Japanese Treaty in Asia. Roosevelt rebuffed all these efforts. While on a European tour in 1910, the retired American president was warmly entertained and celebrated by Wilhelm, who continued to misunderstand him. Roosevelt, meanwhile, kept on urging his English friends to counter the German naval buildup in order to maintain peace in Europe.

In 1911, Roosevelt wrote that there would be nothing worse than that "Germany should ever overthrow England and establish the supremacy in Europe she aims at." German interest "to try her hand in America," he thought, would surely follow. To avert such horrors, Roosevelt's policy for Europe included cementing friendship with England and, while maintaining official neutrality, using diplomacy to prevent hostilities among European powers. The relationship between Great Britain and Germany continued to deteriorate, however, and by 1914 a new American president, Woodrow Wilson, would face the terrible reality that Roosevelt had so skillfully helped to prevent. When World War I finally broke out, no American was more eager to fight on the British side against the Germans than the hero of San Juan Hill.

## CONCLUSION: The Responsibilities of Power

Since the earliest settlements in Massachusetts Bay, Americans had struggled with the dilemma of how to do good in a world that did wrong. The realities of power in the 1890s brought increasing international responsibilities. Roosevelt said in 1910 that because of "strength and geographical situation" the United States had itself become "more and more the balance of power of the whole world." This ominous responsibility was also an opportunity to extend American economic, political, and moral influence around the globe.

As president in the first decade of the twentieth century, Roosevelt established the basic policies of the United States toward the rest of the world. Americans dominated and policed Central America and the Caribbean Sea to maintain order, protect investments and other economic interests, and keep European influence out. In the Far East, Americans marched through Hay's Open Door with treaties, troops, navies, and dollars to protect the newly annexed Philippine Islands, to develop markets and investments, and to preserve the balance of power in Asia. In Europe, the United States sought both to remain neutral and uninvolved in European affairs and at the same time to cement Anglo-American friendship and prevent "civilized" nations from going to war with one another.

How well these policies worked would be seen later in the twentieth century. Whatever the particular judgment, the fundamental ambivalence of America's sense of itself as a model "city on a hill," an example to others, remained. As widening involvements around the world—the Philippine-American War, for example—painfully demonstrated, it was difficult for the United States to be both responsible and good, both powerful and loved. The American people thus learned to experience both the satisfactions and burdens of the missionary role.

## Recommended Reading

The best overviews of the emergence of America as a world power in the late nineteenth century, each emphasizing different motives for expansion, are Walter La Feber, *The New Empire: An Interpretation of American Expansion, 1860–1898* (1963); Milton Plesur, *America's Outward Thrust, 1865–1890* (1971); Robert Beisner, *From the Old Diplomacy to the New, 1865–1900* (1975); and Charles Campbell, *The Transformation of American Foreign Relations, 1865–1900* (1976).

On the immediate causes of expansionism in the 1890s and the war with Spain, see Ernest May, *Imperial Democracy: The Emergence of America as a Great Power* (1961); H. Wayne Morgan, *America's Road to Empire: The War with Spain and Overseas Expansion* (1965); and David Healy, *U.S. Expansion: Imperialist Urge in the 1890s* (1970). Particular aspects of American expansion are discussed in Rubin Weston, *Racism in U.S. Imperialism: The Influence of Racial Assumptions on American Foreign Policy,*

1893–1946 (1972); William Widenor, *Henry Cabot Lodge and the Search for an American Foreign Policy* (1980); and Emily Rosenberg, *Spreading the American Dream: American Economic and Cultural Expansion, 1890–1945* (1982). McKinley's leadership is covered in Lewis Gould, *The Presidency of William McKinley* (1980).

On the Spanish-American War see Frank Freidel, *The Splendid Little War* (1958). More recent works are David Trask, *The War with Spain in 1898* (1981), and a fascinating account of the war experiences of black soldiers, Willard Gatewood, Jr., *"Smoked Yankees" and the Struggle for Empire: Letters from Negro Soldiers, 1898–1902* (1971). The brutal suppression of the Philippine rebels is described in Leon Wolff, *Little Brown Brother: How the United States Purchased and Pacified the Philippine Islands at the Century's Turn* (1961) and Richard Welch, *Response to Imperialism: The United States and the Philippine-American War, 1899–1902* (1979). Some anti-imperialists are treated in Robert Beisner, *Twelve Against Empire: The Anti-Imperialists, 1898–1900* (1975). Gerald Linderman discusses the war at home in *The Mirror of War: American Society and the Spanish-American War* (1974).

The standard work on Roosevelt's foreign policy is Howard Beale, *Theodore Roosevelt and the Rise of America to World Power* (1956). Newer interpretations can be found in Raymond Esthus, *Theodore Roosevelt and the International Rivalries* (1970) and Frederick Marks II, *Velvet on Iron: The Diplomacy of Theodore Roosevelt* (1979). Charles E. Neu, *An Uncertain Friendship: Theodore Roosevelt and Japan, 1906–1909* (1967) traces that relationship, and Dana Munro, *Intervention and Dollar Diplomacy in the Caribbean, 1900–1920* (1964) discusses the Roosevelt Corollary. A lengthy but readable story of the Panama Canal is David McCollough, *The Path Between the Seas: The Creation of the Panama Canal, 1870–1914* (1977). Walter La Feber has documented how thoroughly American interests have dominated Central America in *The Panama Canal* (1978) and *Inevitable Revolutions: The United States in Central America* (1983).

## TIME LINE

| | |
|---|---|
| 1823 | Monroe Doctrine |
| 1857 | Trade opens with Japan |
| 1867 | Alaska purchased from Russia |
| 1870 | Failure to annex Santo Domingo (Hispaniola) |
| 1875 | Sugar reciprocity treaty with Hawaii |
| 1877 | United States acquires naval base at Pearl Harbor |
| 1878 | United States acquires naval station in Samoa |
| 1882 | Chinese Exclusion Act |
| 1889 | First Pan-American conference |
| 1890 | Alfred Mahan publishes *Influence of Sea Power upon History* |
| 1893 | Hawaiian coup by American sugar growers |
| 1895 | Renewed outbreak of Cuban revolt against Spanish<br>Venezuelan boundary dispute |
| 1896 | Weyler's reconcentration policy in Cuba<br>McKinley-Bryan presidential campaign |
| 1897 | Theodore Roosevelt's speech at Naval War College |

| 1898 | | |
|---|---|---|
| | January | De Lôme letter |
| | February | Sinking of the battleship *Maine* |
| | April | Spanish-American War; Teller Amendment |
| | May | Dewey takes Manila Bay |
| | July | Annexation of Hawaiian Islands |
| | August | Americans liberate Manila; war ends |
| | December | Treaty of Paris; annexation of the Philippines |

| | |
|---|---|
| 1899 | Senate ratifies Treaty of Paris<br>Philippine-American War begins<br>American Samoa acquired |
| 1899–1900 | Open Door notes |
| 1900 | Boxer rebellion in China<br>William McKinley reelected president |
| 1901 | Supreme Court insular cases<br>McKinley assassinated; Theodore Roosevelt becomes president |
| 1902 | Philippine-American War ends<br>U.S. military occupation of Cuba ends<br>Platt Amendment<br>Venezuela debt crisis |
| 1903 | Panamanian revolt and independence<br>Hay–Bunau-Varilla Treaty |
| 1904 | Roosevelt Corollary |
| 1904–1905 | Russo-Japanese War ended by treaty signed at Portsmouth, New Hampshire |
| 1904–1906 | United States intervenes in Nicaragua, Guatemala, Cuba |
| 1905–1906 | Moroccan crisis |
| 1906 | Roosevelt receives Nobel Peace Prize |
| 1907 | Gentleman's agreement with Japan |
| 1908 | Root-Takahira Agreement |
| 1909 | U.S. Navy ("Great White Fleet") sails around the world |
| 1911 | U.S. intervenes in Nicaragua |
| 1914 | Opening of the Panama Canal<br>World War I begins |
| 1916 | Partial home rule granted to the Philippines |

# PORTFOLIO FOUR

# THE ART OF
# AN INDUSTRIALIZING PEOPLE

## 1 8 6 5 – 1 9 0 0

The time from the Civil War to the turn of the century has been called the Gilded Age. But the period is also referred to as the American Renaissance because so many neoclassical public and private buildings were constructed during these years and so many artists, collectors, and architects identified with the period of the Renaissance in Europe. It was also an age of opulence, when great fortunes were made and the very wealthy could afford to build summer "cottages" that looked like European palaces in Newport, Rhode Island; the Berkshires; and elsewhere. But usually when they filled their houses with art, it was to Europe that they looked, for American painting had little prestige next to the great masters. Many American artists, at least those who could afford it, trained in Europe, and many remained there. Europe seemed more supportive of artists than did the United States, where the machine was rapidly replacing the craftsman and the emphasis seemed to be on business success rather than artistic excellence.

Yet all was not bleak. The years from 1865 to 1900 witnessed a great burst of creative energy in America. It was during this period that many American cities built museums and libraries. Stimulated in part by the Centennial Exposition in Philadelphia in 1876, but even more by the World Columbian Exposition in Chicago in 1893, many American cities founded new cultural institutions. These new museums contained little American art in the beginning, and they were always closed on Sundays, making it impossible for the working class to visit them. Eventually, however, they would help to create a cultural renaissance in America.

Architects contributed to the new era by designing impressive new urban structures. Henry Hobson Richardson (1838–1886) popularized buildings patterned after the Romanesque style, while others experimented with a more utilitarian approach. Louis Sullivan (1856–1924), the most prominent architect of the Chicago school, argued that "form follows function." His business buildings and skyscrapers, even with their organic decorations, seemed revolutionary in much of the country, where architects continued to adapt European styles for their clients.

American artists also experimented with new forms during this time of industrial expansion and ostentatious display. Despite the heavy hand of European tradition, American artists such as Winslow Homer and Thomas Eakins established their own style. Eakins used the camera and new scientific studies of light and anatomy to create an authentic American realistic style. He also helped to train a new generation of American artists in Philadelphia, Chicago, New York, and other cities.

Another kind of American art flourished in this period as well. Far removed from and untouched by the formal study of art on either continent, thousands of American folk artists, untrained but talented, created enduring symbols for a growing nation. Whether the result was a carefully designed quilt, painted furniture, a wall mural, or a weather vane crafted by a farmer in his spare time, the art of the people sometimes seemed to have more vitality than the art of the museums.

Mary Cassatt, *Baby Reaching for an Apple*, 1893.
Virginia Museum, Richmond. Anonymous gift.

Mary Cassatt (1844–1926) was one of the outstanding artists of her generation and the most important American impressionist. She was the only American to exhibit her work alongside that of Degas, Renoir, and Monet. Although her father opposed her becoming an artist, she studied at the Pennsylvania Academy of Fine Arts in Philadelphia before going to Europe, where she spent most of her life. Even though she was already well known in Europe when she returned to Philadelphia for a visit in 1898, the Philadelphia *Ledger* reported: "Mary Cassatt, sister of Mr. Cassatt, President of the Pennsylvania Railroad, returned from Europe yesterday. She has been studying painting in France and owns the smallest Pekingese dog in the world." One French critic had called her one of the two most important living American artists, but in America she was important for owning a small dog.

Winslow Homer, *Snap the Whip*, 1872.
Butler Institute of American Art, Youngstown, Ohio.

Winslow Homer (1836–1910) is best known for his paintings of life near the sea, but here he depicts a rural scene of boys playing a favorite game. Like many nineteenth-century painters, Homer made his living for years by doing engravings to illustrate magazine articles. He documented American life in the last decades of the nineteenth century, but he was always more than an illustrator. He was concerned with light, order, and organization. Some of his later paintings, in fact, move toward an abstract design.

Thomas Eakins, *Max Schmitt in a Single Scull*, 1871.
Metropolitan Museum of Art, New York. Alfred N. Punnett Fund and gift of George D. Pratt.

**Thomas Eakins (1844–1916) spent most of his life in Philadelphia, though he studied for a time in Europe. As a painter, he depended on science as a means of understanding reality. He studied anatomy in order to understand the human body. He also studied engineering and photography and was one of the first artists to use stop-motion photographs to perfect his paintings. In *Max Schmitt* it is possible to tell exactly the time of day and the season of the year. The iron bridge in the background reminds us that Eakins painted in an age being transformed by industrialism. Sometimes his attempts to be faithful to the real world got him into trouble. The art jury at the Centennial Exposition rejected his picture *The Gross Clinic* as "distasteful and not art." In 1886, he resigned from his position at the Pennsylvania Academy of Fine Arts because the directors censured him for allowing young women to paint a nude male model.**

Thomas Pollock Anshutz, *Cabbages*, 1879.
Metropolitan Museum of Art, New York. Morris K. Jesup Fund.

Among Eakins's many students were Henry O. Tanner (1859–1937), the nineteenth century's most distinguished Afro-American artist, and Thomas Pollock Anshutz (1851–1912), born in Kentucky and trained in New York and Paris. Upon Eakins's resignation from the Academy, Anshutz assumed his post and perpetuated his style. Glimpses of lower-class life such as *Ironworkers Noontime* characterize Anshutz's work. In *Cabbages*, he forthrightly depicts the poverty of this black family, yet portays them with grace and dignity.

The quilt was made by Harriet Powers, a black woman born a slave in Atlanta, Georgia, in 1837. An example of the beauty and usefulness of folk art created by women of all backgrounds, the quilt interprets biblical history in a sincere yet imaginative manner. The upper left panel depicts Eve being tempted by a tiger-striped (and footed) serpent, while at center left we see the bloody murder of Abel by his brother Cain. The far right panel in the bottom row depicts Joseph, Mary, and the baby Jesus accompanied by symbolic crosses and the star of Bethlehem.

Harriet Powers,
*Bible Quilt*, c. 1885.
National Museum of American
History, Smithsonian Institution,
Washington.

C. Graham, *The Ferris Wheel*,
World's Columbian Exposition, 1893.
Chicago Historical Society.

**William Morris Hunt (1827–1895) was one of the most popular architects of his day. He specialized in designing homes patterned after European mansions for the very rich. The ornate and elaborate decoration of this dining room contrasts with the spare and simple steel Ferris wheel designed by George Washington Gales for the Chicago World's Columbian Exposition in 1893. Made of the same steel that made skyscrapers possible, the Ferris wheel was 250 feet in diameter and fascinated a generation just getting accustomed to the beauty and power of the machine.**

Dining room, William Vanderbilt's Marble House,
completed 1892.
Preservation Society of Newport County, Rhode Island.
Photo Richard Cheek.

# PART FIVE
# A MODERNIZING PEOPLE

# 1900–1945

In the first half of the twentieth century, the powerful and populous society that Americans had built was faced with repeated challenges. Two costly world wars and the greatest economic depression the modern world has known occurred within the lifetime of most Americans born in the late nineteenth century. But the United States emerged in 1945, at the end of World War II, with its political and economic system intact and indeed strengthened, though American society was considerably altered in the process.

Chapter 22, "The Progressives Confront Industrial America," explores the greatest outburst of reformist thought and activity since the antebellum period. It explains how the progressives, while accepting the basic structure of the capitalist system, attempted to bring moral vision and scientific expertise to bear on the problems created by rapid industrialization, urbanization, and immigration after the Civil War. Chapter 23, "America in the Great War," addresses the transforming power of extended military conflict on business, government, labor, race relations, the role of women, and American foreign policy.

The era between World War I and World War II is the subject of Chapters 24 and 25. In Chapter 24, "Affluence and Anxiety," the so-called Roaring Twenties are revealed as an era of paradox, filled with prosperity mixed with poverty, optimism alongside disillusionment, inventiveness combined with intolerance, and flamboyant heroism countered by fallen idols. Chapter 25, "The Great Depression and the New Deal," probes the causes and effects of the Great Depression of 1929–1939 and analyzes the attempts of Franklin Roosevelt's New Deal to repair the economic and social damage it caused.

Although the New Deal introduced key elements of the modern capitalist welfare state and greatly increased the regulatory power of the federal government, it never proved able to lift the country from economic depression. That, ironically, came about only with American involvement in World War II. Chapter 26, "The American People and World War II," presents this devastating conflict as both a momentous military struggle between Allied and Axis powers and as a powerful engine of social change within American society. It also shows how the war spawned a complex diplomatic contest between the Eastern and Western blocs of the Allied Powers, led by the United States and the Soviet Union, for ascendancy in the postwar age.

# PARALLEL EVENTS

**1900    1905    1910    1915    1920**

## CULTURAL and TECHNOLOGICAL

1901  Frank Norris, *The Octopus*
1903  Wright brothers make first heavier-than-air flight
1906  Upton Sinclair, *The Jungle*
1908  Frank Lloyd Wright designs Robie House in Chicago
1909  First Model T Ford produced
1910  Jane Addams, *Twenty Years at Hull House*
1911  Frederick Winslow Taylor, *The Principles of Scientific Management*
1913  First assembly line at Ford Motor Company Armory Show, New York
1914  Panama Canal completed
1915  D. W. Griffith produces *The Birth of a Nation*
1916  Margaret Sanger organizes New York Birth Control League
1920  First commercial radio broadcast, WWJ Detroit

## SOCIAL and ECONOMIC

1901  United States Steel Corporation organized
1902  Anthracite coal strike
1903–1910  Muckrakers attack social evils and corruption
1905  Industrial Workers of the World (IWW) organized
1907  Panic caused by business failures
Gentleman's agreement stops emigration of Japanese laborers to United States
1908  *Muller v. Oregon* upholds Oregon law limiting hours of work for women
1909  National Association for the Advancement of Colored People (NAACP) organized
1911  Triangle fire in New York kills 146 textile workers
1913  Federal Reserve System organized Department of Labor organized
1914  Clayton Act strengthens antitrust legislation
1917  Literacy test for new immigrants established
1917–1918  Espionage Act and Sedition Act passed
1918–1919  Influenza epidemic kills 500,000 people in United States
1919  United States becomes creditor nation for the first time.
1921  Immigration limited to 3 percent of each

## POLITICAL

1900  William McKinley reelected president
1901  McKinley assassinated; Theodore Roosevelt becomes president
Socialist Party of America formed
1904  Roosevelt reelected
1906  Hepburn Act
Pure Food and Drug Act
Meat Inspection Act
1908  William Howard Taft elected president
1910  Mann-Elkins Act
1912  Woodrow Wilson elected president
1913  Sixteenth Amendment provides for an income tax
Seventeenth Amendment provides for direct election of senators
1914  World War I begins in Europe
1915  *Lusitania* sunk
1916  Wilson reelected
1917  United States declares war on Germany and Austria–Hungary
1918  War ends in Europe
1919  Senate defeats League of Nations treaty
Eighteenth Amendment establishes prohibition
National Prohibition Enforcement Act
1920  Warren G. Harding elected president
Nineteenth Amendment provides for woman suffrage
1921–1922  Washington conference to limit naval

**1900    1905    1910    1915    1920**

# 1900–1945

| | 1925 | 1930 | 1935 | 1940 | 1945 |
|---|---|---|---|---|---|

## CULTURAL and TECHNOLOGICAL

- 1925 John Scopes convicted of illegally teaching theory of evolution in Tennessee
- 1926 Langston Hughes, *Weary Blues*
- 1927 Charles Lindbergh flies alone to Paris
  Sacco and Vanzetti executed
  *The Jazz Singer*, first feature-length talking movie
- 1929 William Faulkner, *The Sound and the Fury*
- 1934–1938 Radar developed by Army Signal Corps and U.S. Navy
- 1935 Walt Disney releases *Flowers and Trees*, first movie in color
- 1935–1943 WPA artists' and writers' projects
- 1938 Nylon and fiberglass developed
- 1939 John Steinbeck, *The Grapes of Wrath*
  New York World's Fair
  First scheduled television broadcast
- 1941 Penicillin, one of the first "miracle drugs," developed
- 1942 Jet plane first tested in United States
- 1943 Wendell Willkie, *One World*
- 1944 First electronic calculator developed
  Serviceman's Readjustment Act ("GI Bill")
- 1945 First atomic bomb exploded in New Mexico

## SOCIAL and ECONOMIC

- 1924 Immigration limited to 2 percent of nationality in country in 1890
- 1925 A & W Root Beer becomes first fast-food franchise
- 1929 Stock market crash
- 1934 Indian Reorganization Act
- 1935 Committee for Industrial Organization (CIO) formed
- 1936 United Auto Workers hold sit-down strike at General Motors plant in Flint, Michigan
- 1938 Fair Labor Standards Act
- 1941 President Roosevelt issues Executive Order 8802 outlawing discrimination in defense industries
- 1942 Congress of Racial Equality (CORE) founded
- 1944 Bretton Woods Conference sets up World Bank and International Monetary Fund

## POLITICAL

- president
  Teapot Dome scandal
  Coolidge reelected
- 1924
- 1928 Herbert Hoover elected president
- 1932 Franklin Roosevelt elected president
- 1933 TVA, CCC, NIRA, AAA, and other New Deal acts passed
- 1935 Social Security, WPA, and other New Deal legislation passed
- 1936 Roosevelt reelected
- 1937 National Housing Act passed
- 1939 World War II begins in Europe
- 1940 Roosevelt reelected for third term
- 1941 Japanese attack Pearl Harbor; Japan and Germany declare war on United States
- 1942 United States defeats Japanese in Battle of Midway
  Allies invade North Africa
- 1944 Invasion of Normandy
  Roosevelt reelected for fourth term
- 1945 United States drops atomic bomb on Hiroshima and Nagasaki
  World War II ends
  Roosevelt dies; Harry S. Truman becomes president

| 1925 | 1930 | 1935 | 1940 | 1945 |
|---|---|---|---|---|

# CHAPTER 22
## THE PROGRESSIVES CONFRONT
## INDUSTRIAL AMERICA

Frances Kellor, a young woman who grew up in Ohio and Michigan, received her law degree in 1897 from Cornell University and became one of the small but growing group of professionally trained women. Deciding that she was more interested in solving the nation's social problems than in practicing law, she moved to Chicago, studied sociology, and trained herself as a social reformer. Kellor believed passionately that poverty and inequality could be eliminated in America. She also had the progressive faith that if Americans could only hear the truth about the millions of people living in urban slums, they would rise up and make changes. She was one of the experts who provided the evidence to document what was wrong in industrial America.

Like many progressives, Kellor believed that environment was more important than heredity in determining ability, prosperity, and happiness. Better schools and better housing, she thought, would produce better citizens. Even criminals, she argued, were simply victims of environment. Kellor demonstrated that poor health and deprived childhoods explained the only differences between the criminals and the college students. If it were impossible to define a criminal type, then it must be possible to reduce crime by improving the environment.

Kellor was an efficient professional. Like the majority of the professional women of her generation, she never married but devoted her life to social research and social reform. She lived for a time at Hull House in Chicago and at the College Settlement in New York, centers not only of social research and reform but also of lively community. For many young people, the settlement, with its sense of commitment and its exciting conversation around the dinner table, provided an alternative to the nuclear family or the single apartment.

While staying at the College Settlement, Kellor researched and wrote a muckraking study of employment agencies, published in 1904 as *Out of Work*. She revealed how employment agencies exploited immigrants, blacks, and other recent arrivals in the city. Kellor's book, like the writing of most progressives, spilled over with moral outrage. But Kellor went beyond the moralism to suggest corrective legislation at the state and national levels.

Kellor became one of the leaders of the movement to Americanize the immigrants pouring into the country in unprecedented numbers. Between 1899 and 1910, over 8 million immigrants came to the United States, most from southern and eastern Europe. Many people feared that this flood of immigrants threatened the very basis of American democracy. Kellor and her co-workers represented the side of progressivism that sought state and federal laws to protect the new arrivals from exploitation and to establish agencies and facilities to educate and Americanize them. Another group of progressives, often allied with organized labor, tried to pass laws to restrict immigration. Kellor did not entirely escape the racism that was a part of her generation's world view, but she did maintain that all immigrants could be made into useful citizens.

Convinced of the need for a national movement to push for reform legislation, Kellor helped to found the National Committee for Immigrants in America, which tried to promote a national policy "to make all these people Americans," and a federal bureau to organize the campaign. Eventually she helped establish the Division of Immigrant Education within the Department of Education. But it was a political movement led by Theodore Roosevelt that excited her most.

Kellor, more than almost any other single person, had been responsible for alerting Roosevelt to the problems the immigrants faced in American cities. When Roosevelt formed the new Progressive party in 1912, she was one of the many social workers and social researchers who joined him. She campaigned for Roosevelt and directed the Progressive Service Organization, to educate voters in all areas of social justice and welfare after the election. After Roosevelt's defeat and the collapse of the Progressive party in 1914, Kellor continued to work for Americanization. She spent the rest of her life promoting justice, order, and efficiency and trying to find ways for resolving industrial and international disputes.

Frances Kellor personified the two most important aspects of progressivism, the first nationwide reform movement of the modern era: one, commitment to social justice under industrial capitalism, and two, a search for order and efficiency in a world made more complex by rapid industrialization, immigration, and spectacular urban growth. This chapter traces some of the most important aspects of progressivism, a broad but sometimes internally divided movement that influenced almost all aspects of American life. It will look at the social justice movement that sought to promote reform among the poor and to improve life for the victims of an industrial civilization. It surveys life among the workers in the progressive era, a group that reformers sometimes helped but often misunderstood. Then it traces the reform movements in the cities and the states. Finally, it examines progressivism at the national level during the administrations of Theodore Roosevelt and Woodrow Wilson.

## THE SOCIAL JUSTICE MOVEMENT

The social justice movement in its broadest sense tried to humanize the industrial city. The leaders, many of them women, were most often middle-class social workers, ministers, intellectuals, and writers. Many had been shocked by reading books like Henry George's *Progress and Poverty* (1879) and Edward Bellamy's *Looking Backward* (1888) and by the 1893 depression (see Chapter 20). They hoped to improve housing, build better schools, abolish child labor, and limit the hours of work for both men and women. They wanted parks and playgrounds and a better life for the poor and the recent immigrants. Sometimes, however, they seemed more interested in controlling the threat of the poor and foreign-born than in promoting reform, and they quite consciously tried to teach middle-class values. But like all progressives, they believed that by altering the environment they could reconstruct society and eliminate poverty. Combining optimism with moral idealism, they had no intention of abandoning corporate capitalism or dramatically altering the American system of government. They did not always agree among themselves over tactics or even about the reform agenda, but all knew that change was necessary if American democracy was to survive in an urban industrial age.

### The Muckrakers

The publicists of the progressives' concerns were a group of writers, labeled the muckrakers, who exposed corruption and other evils in American society. Theodore Roosevelt gave the muckrakers their name when, in a speech in 1906, he compared some of the writers to the man with the muckrake in John Bunyan's *Pilgrim's Progress*. He was so busy raking the dirt that he never looked up or tried to do anything about it.

In part the muckrakers were a product of a revolution in journalism that had begun in the 1890s. Nineteenth-century magazines, like *Atlantic*, *Century*, and *Scribner's*, had small circulations and appealed only to a highly educated audience. The new magazines, like *American*, *McClure's*, and *Cosmopolitan*, had slick formats, carried more advertising, and sold more widely. Several had circulations of more than a half million in 1910. Competing with each other for readers, editors eagerly published the articles of a new generation of investigative reporters who wanted to let the public know about what was wrong in American society.

Lincoln Steffens, a young California journalist, wrote a series of articles for *McClure's* exposing the connections between respectable urban businessmen and corrupt politicians. When published in 1904 as *The Shame of the Cities*, Steffens's account became a battle cry for people determined to clean up the graft in city government. Ida Tarbell, a teacher turned journalist, had grown up near Titusville in western Pennsylvania, almost next door to the first oil well in the United States. She published several successful books, including biographies of Napoleon and Lincoln, before turning her attention to the Standard Oil Company and John D. Rockefeller. Her exposé, based on years of research, did not try to hide her outrage at Rockefeller's ruthless ways and unfair business practices.

After Steffens and Tarbell achieved popular success with their articles and books, many others followed. Ray Stannard Baker exposed the railroads; David Graham Phillips showed how politics and business were allied at the highest level in *The Treason of the Senate* (1906). Robert Hunter, a young settlement worker, shocked the American people in 1904 with his book *Poverty*. Setting the minimum annual income at $460 for a family of five, he found 10 million people living below that level. Realistic fiction also mirrored such concerns. Upton Sinclair's novel *The Jungle* (1906) described the horrors of the Chicago meatpacking industry, while Frank Norris in *The Octopus* (1901) dramatized the railroad's stranglehold on the farmers.

## Working Women and Children

Nothing disturbed the social justice progressives more than the sight of children, sometimes

*Child labor was one of the first evils the progressives sought to abolish. These boys, employees in a Pennsylvania mine, were photographed in 1911 by Lewis Hine for the Child Labor Committee.*

as young as 8 or 10, working long hours in dangerous and depressing factories. Young people had worked in factories since the beginning of the industrial revolution, but that did not make the practice any less horrible to the reformers. "Children are put into industry very much as we put in raw material," Jane Addams objected, "and the product we look for is not better men and women, but better manufactured goods."

The social justice reformers documented horrible tales about bootblacks, newspaper boys, and the army of young factory workers of both sexes who risked their health and ruined their lives for a few pennies. "Annie Chihlar, a delicate-looking little girl, was found working at 144 West Taylor Street," one report from Chicago began. Annie, it turned out, was only 12 and underweight with a bad curvature of the spine. But her employer produced a doctor's certificate saying she was in perfect health, and her mother insisted that she needed her daughter's income to help support the family's younger children. The reformers sometimes appeared to have little sympathy for the families like Annie's who depended on the wages of their children. Instead they focused on the human resources being wasted and tried to pass laws to protect the child in industrial America.

Florence Kelley was one of the most important leaders in the crusade against child labor. Kelley had grown up in an upper-class Philadelphia family and graduated from Cornell in 1882. Like Addams and Kellor, she was a member of the first generation of college women. When the University of Pennsylvania refused her admission as a graduate student because she was a woman, she went to the University of Zurich in Switzerland. There she married a Polish physician and was converted to socialism. But the marriage failed. Some years later, Kelley moved to Chicago with her three children, became a Hull House resident, and poured her energies into the campaign against child labor. Energetic and outgoing, she was called by one of her friends "explosive, hot-tempered, determined . . . a smoking volcano that at any moment would burst into flames." When she could find no attorney in Chicago who would argue a child labor case against some of the prominent corporations, she went to law school, passed the bar exam, and argued the cases herself.

Although Kelley and the other child labor reformers won a few cases, they quickly realized that they needed state laws if they were going to have any real influence. Marshaling their evidence about the tragic effects on growing children of long working hours in dark and damp factories, they successfully pressured the Illinois state legislature to pass an anti–child labor law. A few years later, however, the state supreme court declared the law unconstitutional.

Child labor was an emotional issue, not only because many businesses made large profits by employing children but also because many legislators and government officials, remembering their own rural childhoods, argued that it was good for the children's character to work hard and take responsibility.

In the first decade of the twentieth century, the reformers moved to the national level. Florence Kelley again led the charge. In 1899, she had become secretary of the National Consumers League, an organization that enlisted consumers in a campaign to pressure elected officials and corporations to ensure that products were produced under safe and sanitary conditions. It was not Kelley, however, but Edgar Gardner Murphy, an Alabama clergyman, who suggested the formation of the National Child Labor Committee. Like many other Social Gospel ministers, Murphy believed that the church had a responsibility to reform society as well as to save souls. He was appalled by the number of young children who worked in the textile mills in the South, where they were exposed to great danger and condemned to "compulsory ignorance."

The National Child Labor Committee, with headquarters in New York, drew up a model state child labor law, encouraged state and city campaigns, and coordinated the movement around the country. Two-thirds of the states passed some form of child labor law between 1905 and 1907, but many laws had loopholes and exempted a large number of children, including newsboys and youngsters who worked in the theater. The committee also supported a national bill introduced in Congress by Indiana senator Albert Beveridge in 1906 "to prevent the employment of children in factories and mines." The bill went down to defeat. However, the child labor reformers convinced Congress in 1912 to establish a children's bureau in the Department of Labor. Despite these efforts, compulsory school attendance laws did more to reduce the number of children who worked than federal and state laws, which proved difficult to pass and even more difficult to enforce.

The crusade against child labor was a typical social justice reform effort. Its origins lay in the moral indignation middle-class reformers felt at the sight of little children and adolescents ruining their lives in factories. But the reform effort did not stop at moral outrage. The reformers gathered statistics, took photographs documenting the abuse of children, and marshaled their evidence to lobby for legislation first on the local level, then in the states, and eventually in Washington. Like other progressive reform efforts, the battle against child labor was only partly successful.

The reformers were especially concerned for the young people who got into trouble with the law, often for pranks that in rural areas would have seemed harmless. They feared for young people tried by adult courts and thrown into jail with hardened criminals. Almost simultaneously in Denver and Chicago, reformers organized juvenile courts. The judges in these courts had the authority to put the delinquent youths on probation, take them from their families and make them wards of the state, or assign them to an institution. The juvenile court did work in many cases and often helped prevent young delinquents from adopting a life of crime. Yet the juvenile offender was frequently deprived of all rights of due process, a fact that the Supreme Court finally recognized in 1967, when it ruled that children were entitled to procedural rights when accused of a crime.

Closely connected with the anti–child labor movement was the effort to limit the hours of work for women. It seemed inconsistent at best to protect a girl until she was 16 and then give her the "right to work from 8 A.M. to 10 P.M., thirteen hours a day, seventy-eight hours a week for $6." Florence Kelley and the National Consumers League led the campaign. It was foolish and unpatriotic, they argued, to allow "the mothers of future generations" to work long hours in dangerous industries. As a Pennsylvania superior court stated, "Adult females are a class as distinct as minors separated by natural conditions from all other laborers, and are so constituted as to be unable to endure physical exertion and exposure. . . ."

The most important court case, however, came before the Supreme Court in 1908. Josephine Goldmark, a friend and co-worker of Kelley's at the Consumers League, wrote the brief for *Muller* v. *Oregon* that her brother-in-law, Louis Brandeis, used when he argued the case. The Court upheld the Oregon ten-hour law largely because of Goldmark's sociological argument, which detailed the danger and disease that factory women faced. After the Supreme Court decision, most states fell into line and passed protective legislation for women, though many companies found ways to circumvent the laws. Even the work permitted by the law seemed too long to some women. "I think ten hours is too much for a woman," one factory worker stated. "I have four children and have to work hard at home. Make me awful tired. I would like nine hours. I get up at 5:30. When I wash, I have to stay up till one or two o'clock."

By contending that "women are fundamentally weaker than men in all that makes for endurance: in muscular strength, in nervous energy, in the powers of persistent attention and application," the reformers won some protection for women workers. But their arguments that women were weaker than men would eventually be turned around and used to reinforce gender segregation of the work force for the next half century.

In addition to working for protective legislation for working women, the social justice progressives also campaigned for woman suffrage. Unlike some supporters who argued that middle-class women would offset the ignorant and corrupt votes of immigrant men, these social reformers supported votes for all women. Addams argued that urban women not only could vote intelligently but also needed the vote to protect, clothe, and feed their families. Women in an urban age, she suggested, needed to be municipal housekeepers. Through the suffrage they would ensure that elected officials provided adequate services—pure water, uncontaminated food, proper sanitation, and police protection. The progressive insistence that all women needed the vote helped to push woman suffrage toward the victory that would come during World War I.

## Home and School

The social justice progressives, who had imbibed much of the philosophy of pragmatism, believed that if they could only provide better housing and education, they would alter the lives of the poor and create a better world. Books such as Jacob Riis's *How the Other Half Lives* (1890) horrified them. With vivid language and haunting photographs, Riis, a Danish immigrant turned reformer, documented the overcrowded tenements, the damp, dark alleys, and the sickness and despair that affected people who lived in New York's slums. Reformers had been trying to improve housing for the poor for years. They had constructed model tenements and other housing projects, often called "philanthropy plus 5 percent" because investors promised to take only a limited return on their money. They sent "friendly visitors" into these projects to collect the rent and to teach the immigrants how to live like the middle class. Riis led a movement in New York to replace the worst slums with parks and playgrounds. In the first decade of the twentieth century, the progressives took a new approach toward the housing problems. They collected statistics, conducted surveys, organized committees, and constructed exhibits to demonstrate the effect of urban overcrowding. Then they set out to pass tenement house laws.

New York City, which had some of the worst tenement housing, took the lead. Lawrence Veiller, a short, stocky, bearded graduate of City College of New York, realized the need for reform during the depression of 1893. An expert on all aspects of housing, Veiller organized an exhibition with photographs, maps, and statistical studies to demonstrate the need for change and then drafted a model tenement house bill. It passed the New York legislature in 1901 and was soon copied by other states. The New York law required fire escapes, a window for each room, and a water closet for each apartment. But the new laws were often evaded or modified. They did not solve the problems of slum housing, but the progressives kept up the fight. In 1910, they organized the National Housing Association, and some of them looked ahead to federal laws and even to government-subsidized housing.

The housing reformers combined a moral sense of what needed to be done to create a more just society with practical ability to organize public opinion and get laws passed. They also had a paternalistic view toward the poor. Many reformers were depressed by the clutter and lack of privacy in immigrant tenements. One reformer's guide, *How to Furnish and Keep House in a Tenement Flat,* recommended "wood-stained and uncluttered furniture surfaces, iron beds with mattresses, and un-upholstered chairs. . . . Walls must be painted not papered . . . screens provide privacy in the bedrooms; a few good pictures should grace the walls. . . ." But often immigrant family ideals and values differed from those of the middle-class reformers. The immigrants actually preferred clutter and did not mind the lack of privacy. Despite the reformers' efforts to separate life's functions into separate rooms, most immigrants still crowded into the

*New York's tenement house bill of 1901 sent inspectors into the slums to cite violations. Yet landlords often found ways to avoid complying with the new standards.*

kitchen and hung religious objects rather than "good pictures" on the walls.

Ironically, many middle-class women reformers who tried to teach the working-class families how to live in their tenement flats had never organized their own homes. Often they lived in settlement houses, where they ate in a dining hall and never had to worry about cleaning, cooking, or doing laundry. Some of them, however, began to realize that the domestic tasks expected of women of all classes kept many of them from taking their full place in society. Charlotte Perkins Gilman, author of *Women and Economics* (1898), dismantled the traditional view of "woman's sphere" and sketched an alternative. Suggesting that entrepreneurs ought to build apartment houses designed to allow women to combine motherhood with careers, she advocated shared kitchen facilities and a common dining room, a laundry run by efficient workers, and a roof-garden day nursery run by a professional teacher.

Gilman, who criticized private homes as "bloated buildings, filled with a thousand superfluities," was joined by a few radicals in promoting new living arrangements. Most Americans, however, of all political persuasions continued to view the home as sacred space where the mother ruled supreme and created an atmosphere of domestic tranquility for the husband and children.

Next to better housing, the progressives stressed better schools as a way to produce better citizens. As they existed, public school systems were often rigid and corrupt. Far from producing citizens who would help to transform society, the schools seemed to reinforce the conservative habits that blocked change. A reporter who traveled around the country in 1892 discovered mindless teachers who drilled pupils through repetitive and rote learning. A Chicago teacher advised her students, "Don't stop to think, tell me what you know." When asked why the students were not allowed to move their heads, a New York teacher replied, "Why should they look behind when the teacher is in front of them?"

Progressive education, like many other aspects of progressivism, revolted against the rigid and the formal in favor of flexibility and change.

Progressive education had many roots. One was the kindergarten movement imported from Germany in the mid-nineteenth century. The kindergarten sought to help children learn through creative play. If the very young could learn through joyous and experimental participation in art and music, why could not that spirit be used for students at other levels of education? The social settlements provided another source for progressive education. At Hull House in Chicago, the Henry Street Settlement in New York, and other centers, social workers discovered that they needed new methods to interest immigrant adults. Trying to teach grown men and women how to read English by using children's books with poems like "I am a yellow bird, I can sing. I can fly, I can sing to you" seemed not only ridiculous but also impractical. Other sources of progressive education were the vocational schools in the city and the agricultural schools in the country, both of which tried to teach practical skills and relate education to the real world.

John Dewey, a practitioner of the pragmatic approach to social change, was the key philosopher of progressive education. Growing up in Burlington, Vermont, he tried throughout his life to create a sense of the small rural community in the city. In his laboratory school at the University of Chicago, he experimented with new educational methods. He replaced the school desks, which were bolted down and always faced the front, with seats that could be moved into circles and arranged in small groups. The movable seat, in fact, became one of the symbols of the progressive education movement.

Dewey insisted that the schools be child-centered, not subject-oriented. Teachers should teach children rather than teach history or mathematics. Dewey did not mean that history and math should not be taught but that those subjects should be related to the students' experience. Students should learn by doing. They should actually build a house, not just study how others constructed houses. Students should not just learn about democracy; the school itself should operate like a democracy. Dewey also maintained, somewhat controversially, that the schools should become instruments for social

reform. But like most progressives, Dewey was never quite clear whether he wanted the schools to help the students adjust to the existing world or whether he wanted the schools to turn out graduates who would change the world. Although he wavered on that point, the spirit of progressive education, like the spirit of progressivism in general, was optimistic. The schools could create more flexible, better-educated, more understanding adults who would go out to improve society.

## Crusades Against Saloons, Brothels, and Movie Houses

Given their faith in the reforming potential of healthy and educated citizens, it was logical that most social justice progressives opposed the sale of alcohol. Some came from Protestant homes where the consumption of any liquor was considered a sin, but most favored prohibition for the same reasons they opposed child labor and favored housing reform. They saw eliminating the sale of alcohol as part of the process of reforming the city and conserving human resources.

Americans did drink great quantities of beer, wine, and hard liquor, and the amount they consumed rose rapidly after 1900, peaking between 1911 and 1915. An earlier temperance movement had achieved some success in the 1840s and 1850s (see Chapter 12), but only three states still had prohibition laws in force. The modern antiliquor movement began in the 1890s with a concerted effort on the part of the Women's Christian Temperance Union, the Anti-Saloon League, and a coalition of religious leaders and social reformers. During the progressive era, temperance forces had considerable success in influencing legislation. Seven states passed temperance laws between 1906 and 1912.

The reformers were appalled to see young children going into saloons to bring home a pail of beer for the family. They were horrified by tales of alcoholic fathers beating wives and children. But most often progressives focused on the saloon and its social life. Drug traffic, prostitution, and political corruption all seemed somehow related to the saloon. "Why should the community have any more sympathy for the

# RECOVERING THE PAST

As we saw in Chapter 16, photographs are a revealing way of recovering the past visually. But when looking at a photograph, especially an old one, it is easy to assume that it is an accurate representation of the past. Photographers, however, like novelists and historians, have a point of view. They take their pictures for a reason, and often to prove a point. As one photographer remarked, "Photographs don't lie, but liars take photographs."

To document the need for reform in the cities, progressives collected statistics, made surveys, described settlement house life, and even wrote novels. But they discovered that the photograph was often more effective than words. Jacob Riis, the Danish-born author of *How the Other Half Lives* (1890), a devastating exposure of conditions in New York City tenement house slums, was also a pioneer in urban photography. Others had taken pictures of dank alleys and street urchins before, but Riis was the first to photograph slum conditions with the express purpose

of promoting reform. At first he hired photographers, but then he bought a camera and taught himself how to use it. He even tried a new German flash powder to illuminate dark alleys and tenement rooms in order to record the horror of slum life.

Riis made many of his photographs into lantern slides and used them to illustrate his lectures on the need for housing reform. Although he was a creative and innovative photographer, his pictures were often far from objective. His equipment was awkward, his film slow. He had to set up and prepare carefully before snapping the shutter. His views of tenement ghetto streets, and poor children now seem almost like clichés, but they were designed to make Americans angry, thus arousing them to reform.

Another important progressive photographer was Lewis Hine. Trained as a sociologist, like Riis he taught himself photography. Hine used his camera to illustrate his lectures at the Ethical Culture School in New York. In 1908, he was hired as a full-time

International Museum of Photography at George Eastman House, Rochester, New York

***Lewis Hine,*** **Carolina Cotton Mill,** *1908*

697a

investigator by the National Child Labor Committee. His haunting photographs of children in factories helped to convince many Americans of the need to abolish child labor. Hine's children were appealing human beings. He showed them eating, running, working, and staring wistfully out factory windows. His photographs avoided the pathos that Riis was so fond of recording, but just as surely they documented the need for reform.

Another technique that the reform photographer used was the before-and-after shot. The two photographs shown here of a one-room apartment in Philadelphia early in the century illustrate how progressive reformers tried to teach immigrants to imitate middle-class manners. The "before" photograph shows a room cluttered with washtubs, laundry, cooking utensils, clothes, tools, even an old Christmas decoration. In the "after" picture, much of the clutter has been cleaned up. A window has been installed to let in light and fresh air. The wallpaper, presumably a

haven for hidden bugs and germs, has been torn off. The cooking utensils and laundry have been put away. The woodwork has been stained, and some ceremonial objects have been gathered on a shelf.

What else can you find that has been changed? How well do you think the message of photographic combinations like this one worked? Would the immigrant family be happy with the new look and condition of their room? Could anyone live in one room and keep it so neat?

As you look at these, or any photographs, ask yourself, What is the photographer's purpose and point of view? Why did he take the picture at this particular angle? Why does he center on these people or these objects? What does the photographer reveal about his or her purpose? What does the photograph reveal unintentionally? How have fast film and new camera styles changed photography? What subjects do reform-minded photographers train their cameras on today?

*Anonymous before and after photographs of an immigrant family in Philadelphia*

saloon . . . than . . . for a typhoid-breeding pool of filthy water . . . a swarm of deadly mosquitoes, or . . . a nest of rats infected with bubonic plague?" an irate reformer asked.

Although they never quite understood the role alcohol played in the social life of many ethnic groups, Jane Addams and other settlement workers appreciated the role of the saloon as a neighborhood social center. Addams started a coffeehouse at Hull House in an attempt to lure the neighbors away from the evils of the saloon. In his study *Substitutes for the Saloon*, Raymond Caulkins, a young social worker, suggested parks, playgrounds, municipal theaters, and temperance bars as replacements for the saloons, where so many men gathered after work.

The progressives never found an adequate replacement for the saloon, but they set to work to pass local and state prohibition laws. As in many other progressive efforts, they joined forces with diverse groups to push for change. Their combined efforts led to victory on December 22, 1917, when Congress sent to the states for ratification a constitutional amendment prohibiting the sale, manufacturing, or importing of intoxicating liquor within the United States. The spirit of sacrifice for the war effort facilitated its rapid ratification.

In addition to the saloon, the progressives saw the urban dance hall and the movie theater as threats to the morals and well-being of young people, especially young women. The motion picture, which had been invented in 1889, developed as an important form of entertainment only during the first decade of the twentieth century. At first, the "nickelodeons," as the early movie theaters were called, appealed mainly to a lower-class and largely ethnic audience. In 1902, New York City had 50 theaters; by 1908, there were over 400 showing 30-minute dramas and romances.

It was not until just before World War I, when D. W. Griffith produced long epics such as *The Birth of a Nation*, that the movies began to attract a middle-class audience. Many early films were imported from France, Italy, and Germany; because they were silent, it was easy to use subtitles in any language. But one did not need to know the language, or even be able to

read, to enjoy the action. That was part of the attraction of the early films. Many had plots that depicted premarital sex, adultery, and violence, and, unlike later films, many attacked authority and had tragic endings. The *Candidate* (1907) showed an upper-class reform candidate who gets dirt thrown at him for his efforts to clean up the town. The film *Down With Women* (1907) showed well-dressed men denouncing woman suffrage and the incompetence of the weaker sex, but throughout the film only strong women are depicted. In the end, when the hero is arrested, a woman lawyer defends him.

Some of the films stressed slapstick humor or romance and adventure; others bordered on pornography. The reformers objected not only to the plots and content of the films but also to the location of the theaters, near saloons and burlesque houses, and to their dark interiors. "In the dim auditorium which seems to float on the world of dreams . . . an American woman may spend her afternoon alone," one critic wrote. "She can let her fantasies slip through the darkened atmosphere to the screen where they drift in rhapsodic amours with handsome stars." It was these fantasies, in addition to the other things they imagined were going on in the dark, that disturbed the reformers. But for young immigrant women, who made up the bulk of the

*Reformers objected to films such as* Tess of the Storm Country, *which dealt with the subject of unwed motherhood. Nevertheless, some immigrant women found these films appealing.*

audience at most of the early movie theaters, the films provided some of the few exciting moments in their lives. One daughter of strict Italian parents remarked, "The one place I was allowed to go by myself was the movies. I went to the movies for fun. My parents wouldn't let me go anywhere else, even when I was twenty-four."

The saloons, dance halls, and movie theaters all seemed dangerous to progressives interested in improving life in the city because they all appeared to be somehow connected with the worst evil of all, prostitution. Campaigns against prostitution had been waged since the early nineteenth century, but they were nothing compared with the progressives' crusade to wipe out what they called "the social evil." All major cities and many smaller ones appointed vice commissions and made elaborate studies of prostitution. The reports, which often ran to several thick volumes, were typical progressive documents. Compiled by experts, they were filled with elaborate statistical studies and laced with moral outrage.

The progressive antivice crusade attracted many kinds of people, for often contradictory reasons. There were racists and immigration restrictionists who maintained that it was always the inferior people, blacks and recent immigrants, especially those from southern and eastern Europe, who became prostitutes and pimps. There were some connected with the social hygiene movement who denounced prostitution as part of their campaign to fight ignorance and prudity about sex. A number of women reformers joined the campaign and ar-

gued for a single sexual standard. They wanted men to be as chaste and as pure as women. Others worried about prostitutes spreading venereal disease to unfaithful husbands, who would pass it on to unsuspecting wives and unborn babies, leading eventually to race suicide. Most progressives, however, stressed the environmental causes of vice. They viewed prostitution, along with child labor and poor housing, as evils that could be eliminated through education and reform.

Most of the progressive antivice reformers stressed the economic causes of prostitution. "Is it any wonder," the Chicago Vice Commission asked, "that a tempted girl who receives only six dollars per week working with her hands sells her body for twenty-five dollars per week when she learns there is a demand for it and men are willing to pay the price?" "Do you suppose I am going back to earn five or six dollars a week in a factory," one prostitute asked an investigator, "when I can earn that amount any night and often much more?"

Despite all their reports and all the publicity, the progressives failed to end prostitution and did virtually nothing to address its roots in poverty. They wiped out a few red-light districts, closed a number of brothels, and managed to push a bill through Congress (the Mann-Elkins Act of 1910) that prohibited the interstate traffic of women for immoral purposes. Perhaps more important, in several states they got the age of consent for women raised, and in 20 states they made the Wassermann test for venereal disease mandatory for both men and women before a marriage license could be issued.

## THE WORKER IN THE PROGRESSIVE ERA

The progressive reformers sympathized with industrial workers who struggled to earn a living for themselves and their families. But often they had little understanding of what it was like to sell one's strength by the hour. Middle-class reformers and working-class leaders occasionally cooperated during the progressive era, but often their goals were as divergent as their experiences.

### Adjusting to Industrial Labor

John Mekras arrived in New York from Greece in 1912 and traveled immediately to Manchester, New Hampshire, where he found a job in the giant Amoskeag textile mill. He did not speak a word of English. "So they took me to the employment office," he later remembered, "and I went there, and the man who hands out the jobs sent me to the spinning room. There I don't know anything about the spinning. I'm a farmer. I don't know anybody when I get in there. Just like a lost sheep I feel there. Everybody, especially the women, they talk to me nice but I don't know what the boss is talking about." Mekras didn't last long at the mill. He was one of the many industrial workers who had difficulty adjusting to factory work in the early twentieth century.

Many workers, whether they were from Greece, from eastern Europe, from rural Vermont, or from Michigan, confronted a bewildering world based on order and routine. Like the young women who went to the textile factories in Lowell in the 1820s and 1830s, they faced difficult adjustments (see Chapter 11). On the farm, in small towns, or in craft shops, workers had engaged in task-oriented work. They decided when and how the job was to be done. They organized their own time. Often on a festival day, a nice day in summer, or a bad day in the winter, they did not work. But in the factory, the clock, the bell tower, and the boss

*Immigrants accustomed to rural life found American cities bewildering. These Jews, immigrating to Texas from St. Petersburg, experienced the same difficulty in reverse.*

dominated life. They were ordered to work at 6 A.M., told when to break for lunch and when to quit at night. Often the boss stood over them to make sure they did their job right. As had been true earlier, many workers resented the pressure and routine of factory work. They resisted the routine by staying home on a festival day or taking unauthorized breaks. Often they got fired or quit. In the woolen industry, the annual turnover of workers between 1907 and 1910 was more than 100 percent. In New York needle shops in 1912 and 1913, the turnover rate was over 250 percent. Overall in American industry, one-third of the workers stayed at their jobs less than a year.

This industrial work force, still composed largely of immigrants, had a fluid character. Many migrants, especially those from southern and eastern Europe, expected to stay only for a short time and then return to their homeland. "Italians come to America with the sole intention of accumulating money," one Italian-American writer complained in 1905. "Their dreams, their only care is the bundle of money . . . which will give them, after 20 years of deprivation, the possibility of having a mediocre standard of living in their native country." Many men came alone—70 percent in some years. They saved money by living in a boarding-house. In 1910, two-thirds of the workers in Pittsburgh made less than $12 a week, but by lodging in boarding houses and paying $2.50 a month for a bed, they could save perhaps one-third of their pay. "Here in America one must work for three horses," one immigrant wrote home. "The work is very heavy, but I don't mind it," another wrote; "let it be heavy, but may it last without interruption."

About 40 percent of those who immigrated to America in the first decade of the twentieth century returned home, according to one estimate. In the years of economic downturn, such as 1908, more Italians and Austro-Hungarians left the United States than entered it. For many immigrants, the American dream never materialized. But these reluctant immigrants provided the mass of unskilled labor that American industry exploited and sometimes consumed much the way other Americans exploited the land and the forests. The great pool of immigrant workers meant profits for American industry.

The nature of work continued to change in the early twentieth century as industrialists extended late-nineteenth-century efforts to make their factories and their work forces more efficient and productive. In some industries, the invention of new machines revolutionized work and eliminated skilled jobs. Glassblowing machines invented about 1900, for example, replaced thousands of glassblowers or reduced them from craftsmen to workers. Power-driven machines, better-organized operations, and, finally, the moving assembly line, first perfected by Henry Ford, transformed the nature of work and turned most laborers into unskilled tenders of machines.

John Brophy, a coal miner and labor official, remembered how much pride his father had in his work as a miner. "The skill with which you undercut the vein, the judgment in drilling the coal after it has been undercut and placing the exact amount of explosive so that it would do an effective job of breaking the coal from the solid . . . indicated the quality of his work." But by the beginning of the twentieth century, undercutting machines and the mechanization of most mining operations robbed the miners of any pride in their work.

It was more than machines, however, that changed the nature of industrial work. The principles of scientific management, which set out new rules for organizing work, were just as important. The key figure was Frederick Taylor, the son of a prominent Philadelphia family. Taylor had a nervous breakdown while at a private school. When his physicians prescribed manual labor as a cure, he went to work as a laborer at the Midvale Steel Company in Philadelphia. Working his way up rapidly while studying engineering at night, he became chief engineer at the factory in 1880s. Later he used this experience to rethink the organization of industry.

Taylor was obsessed with efficiency. He proved that a worker with a short-handled shovel could do more work than one with a long-handled shovel. Most of all he studied all kinds of workers and timed the various components of their jobs with a stopwatch. "The work of every workman is fully planned out by the management at least one day in advance," Taylor wrote in 1898, "and each man receives in most cases complete written instructions, describing in detail the task which he is to accomplish, as well as the means to be used in doing the work."

Many owners enthusiastically adopted Taylor's concepts of scientific management, seeing an opportunity to make their factories more profitable. But in most cases the workers resented the drive for efficiency. Foremen disliked taking orders from college men who had never run a machine. The workers hated the stopwatch, the demand for more speed in each operation, and the tighter managerial control. "We don't want to work as fast as we are able to," one machinist remarked. "We want to work as fast as we think it comfortable for us to work."

## Union Organizing

Samuel Gompers, the ex-cigar maker and head of the American Federation of Labor, attacked Taylorism, realizing that it would reduce workers to "mere machines." "The heart of the workingman is sound," Gompers claimed as he defended the American labor union member against Taylor's charge that he loafed and worked inefficiently. Gompers never found an effective way to counter Taylor's charges, but the AFL prospered during the progressive era. Between 1897 and 1904, union membership grew from 447,000 to over 2 million, with three out of every four union members claimed by the AFL. By 1914, the AFL alone had over 2 million members. The "pure and simple unionism" preached by Gompers was most successful among coal miners, railroad workers, and the building trades. Gompers, as we saw in Chapter 19, ignored the growing army of unskilled and immigrant workers and concentrated on a strategy of raising the wages and improving the working conditions of the skilled craftsmen who were members of unions affiliated with the AFL.

For a time Gompers's strategy seemed to work. Several industries negotiated with the AFL as a way of avoiding disruptive strikes. The National Civic Federation, formed in 1905, was made up of business leaders, labor organizers, and representatives of the community. It supported conservative unionism and condemned the twin evils of socialism on the one hand and antiunion employers on the other. But the cooperation was short-lived. Labor unions were defeated in a number of disastrous strikes, and the National Association of Manufacturers launched an aggressive counterattack. "Organized labor . . . does not place its reliance upon reason and justice," the NAM president charged. "It is in all essential features a mob knowing no master except its own will. Its history is stained with blood and ruin." The tactics used were familiar ones. The NAM and other employer associations provided strikebreakers, used industrial spies, and blacklisted union members to prevent them from obtaining other jobs.

The Supreme Court came down squarely on management's side, ruling in the *Danbury Hatters* case in 1908 that trade unions were subject to the Sherman Anti-Trust Act. Thus union members themselves could be held personally liable for money lost by a business during a strike. The courts at all levels usually sided with employers. They often declared strikes illegal and were quick to issue restraining orders, making it impossible for workers to interfere with the operation of a business.

Many of the social justice progressives sym-

## Union Membership, 1900–1920

*Source:* U.S. Bureau of the Census.

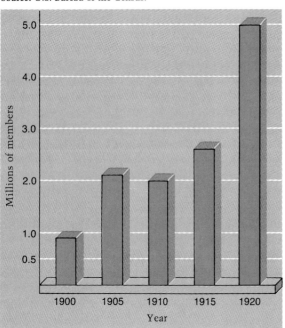

pathized with the working class but spent more time promoting protective legislation than in strengthening organized labor. They also found themselves cast in the role of mediators during industrial disputes. Often it was difficult for the upper- and middle-class reformers to comprehend what life was really like for those who had to work six days a week.

Working women and their problems aroused more sympathy among progressive reformers than did the plight of working men. The number of women working outside the home increased steadily during the progressive era, from over 5 million in 1900 to nearly 8.5 million in 1920. But few belonged to unions, only a little over 3 percent in 1900, and the percentage declined by half by 1910 before increasing a little after that date with aggressive organizing in the textile industry and the clothing trades.

Although the AFL had hired Mary Kenney as an organizer in the 1890s and accepted a few women's unions into affiliation, as a general rule the policy of Gompers and the other leaders was to oppose organizing women workers (see Chapter 19). "The demand for female labor," one labor leader announced, "is an insidious assault upon the home . . . it is the knife of the assassin, aimed at the family circle."

Yet of necessity women continued to work to support themselves and their families. Many upper-class women reformers tried to help these working women in a variety of ways. The settlement houses organized day-care centers, clubs, and classes, and many reformers tried to pass protective legislation. Tension and misunderstanding often cropped up between the reformers and the working women, but one organization in which there was genuine cooperation was the Women's Trade Union League. Founded in 1903, the League was organized by Mary Kenney and William English Walling, a socialist and reformer, but it also drew local leaders from the working class, such as Rose Schneiderman, a Jewish immigrant cap maker, and Leonora O'Reilly, a collar maker. The league established branches in most of the large eastern and midwestern cities and served for more than a decade as an important force in helping to organize women into unions. The league forced the AFL to pay more attention to women, helped out in time of strikes, put up bail money for those arrested, and publicized the plight of working women.

## Garment Workers and the Triangle Fire

Thousands of young women, most of them Jewish and Italian, were employed in the garment industry in New York City. Most were between 16 and 25; some lived with their families, and others lived alone or with a roommate. They worked a 56-hour, six-day week and made about $6 for their efforts. New York was the center of the garment industry, with over 600 shirtwaist (blouse) and dress factories employing more than 30,000 workers. Like other industries, garment manufacturing had changed in the first decade of the twentieth century. Once conducted in thousands of dark and dingy tenement rooms, now all the operations were centralized in large loft buildings in lower Manhattan. These buildings were an improvement over the sweating labor of the tenements, but many were overcrowded, and they had few fire escapes or safety features. In addition, the owners applied scientific management techniques in order to increase their profits, and that made life miserable for the workers. Most of the

*The fire at the Triangle Shirtwaist Company in 1911 killed scores of women workers and launched a statewide investigation of working conditions.*

women had to rent their own sewing machines and even had to pay for the electricity they used. They were penalized for mistakes or for talking too loudly. They were usually supervised by a male contractor who badgered them and sometimes even asked for sexual favors.

In 1909, some of the women went out on strike to protest the working conditions. The International Ladies' Garment Workers Union (ILGWU) and the Women's Trade Union League supported them. But strikers were beaten and sometimes arrested by unsympathetic policemen and by strikebreakers on the picket lines. At a mass meeting held at Cooper Union in New York on November 22, 1909, Clara Lemlich, a young shirtwaist worker who had been injured on the picket line and was angered by the long speeches and lack of action, rose and in an emotional speech in Yiddish demanded a general strike. The entire audience pledged its agreement. The next day all over the city, the shirtwaist workers went out on strike. "The uprising of the twenty thousand," as the strike was called, startled the nation. One young worker wrote in her diary, "It is a good thing, that strike is. It makes you feel like a grown-up person." The Jews learned a little Italian and the Italians a little Yiddish so that they could communicate. Many social reformers, ministers, priests, and rabbis urged the strikers on. Mary Dreier, an upper-class reformer and president of the New York branch of the Womens' Trade Union League, was arrested for marching with the strikers. A young state legislator, Fiorello La Guardia, later to become a congressman and mayor of New York, was one of many public officials to aid the strikers.

The shirtwaist strikers won, but the victory was limited. Over 300 companies accepted the union's terms, but others refused to go along. The young women went back to work amid still oppressive and unsafe conditions. That became dramatically obvious on Saturday, March 25, 1911, when, near closing time, a fire broke out on the eighth floor of the ten-story loft building housing the Triangle Shirtwaist Company near Washington Square in New York. There had been several small fires in the factory in previous weeks, so no one thought much about another one. But this one was different. Within minutes, the top three floors of the factory were a raging inferno. Many exit doors were locked. The elevators broke down. There were no fire escapes. Forty-six women jumped to their deaths, some of them in groups of three and four holding hands. Over 100 died in the flames.

Shocked by the Triangle fire, the state legislature appointed a commission to investigate working conditions in the state. One investigator for the commission was a young social worker, Frances Perkins, who in the 1930s would become secretary of labor. She led the politicians through the dark lofts, filthy tenements, and unsafe factories around the state to show them the conditions under which young women worked. The result was the passage of bills in the state legislature limiting the work of women to 54 hours, abolishing labor by children under 14, and improving safety regulations in factories. One of those who helped pass the legislation in Albany was a young state senator named Franklin Delano Roosevelt.

The investigative commission was a favorite progressive tactic. When there was a problem, reformers often got a city council, a state legislature, or the federal government to appoint a commission. If they could not find a government body to give them a mandate, they made their own studies. They brought in experts, compiled statistics, and published reports.

The federal Industrial Relations Commission, created in 1912 to study the causes of industrial unrest and violence, conducted one of the most important investigations. As it turned out, the commission spent most of its time investigating a dramatic and tragic incident of labor-management conflict in Colorado, known as the Ludlow Massacre. A strike broke out in the fall of 1913 in the vast mineral-rich area of southern Colorado, much of it controlled by the Colorado Fuel and Iron Industry, a company largely owned by the Rockefeller family. It was a paternalistic empire where workers lived in company towns and sometimes in tent colonies. They were paid in company scrip and forced to shop at the company store. When the workers, supported by the United Mine Workers, went on strike demanding an eight-hour day, better safety precautions, and the removal of armed guards, the company refused to negotiate. The strike

turned violent, and in the spring of 1914, strikebreakers and national guardsmen fired on the workers. Eleven children and two women were killed in an attack on a tent city near Ludlow, Colorado.

The Industrial Relations Commission called John D. Rockefeller, Jr., to testify and implied that he was personally guilty of the murders. The commission decided in its report that violent class conflict could be avoided only by limiting the use of armed guards and detectives, by restricting monopoly, by protecting the right of the workers to organize, and, most dramatically, by redistributing wealth through taxation. The commission's report, not surprisingly, fell on deaf ears. Most progressives denied the commission's conclusion that class conflict was inevitable.

### Radical Labor

Not everyone accepted the progressives' faith in investigations and protective labor legislation. Nor did everyone approve of Samuel Gompers's conservative tactics or his emphasis on getting better pay for skilled workers. A group of about 200 radicals met in Chicago in 1905 to form a new union as an alternative to the AFL. They called it the Industrial Workers of the World and talked of one big union. Like the Knights of Labor in the 1880s, the IWW would welcome all workers: the unskilled and even the unemployed, women, blacks, Asians, and all other ethnic groups. Daniel De Leon of the Socialist Labor party attended the organizational meeting, and so did Eugene Debs. Debs, who had been converted to socialism after the Pullman strike of 1894, had already emerged by 1905 as one of the outstanding radical leaders in the country. Also attending, was Mary Harris Jones, who dressed like a society matron but attacked labor leaders "who sit on velvet chairs in conferences with labor's oppressors." In her sixties at the time, everyone called her "Mother" Jones. She had been a dressmaker, a Populist, and a member of the Knights of Labor. During the 1890s, she had marched with miners' wives on the picket line in western Pennsylvania. She was imprisoned and denounced, but by 1905 she was already a legend.

Presiding at the Chicago meeting was "Big Bill" Haywood. He had been a cowboy, a miner, and a prospector. Somewhere along the way he had lost an eye and mangled a hand, but he had a booming voice and a passionate commitment to the American working class. "We are here to confederate the workers of this country into a working-class movement that shall have for its purpose the emancipation of the working class from the slave bondage of capitalism." Denouncing Gompers and the AFL, he talked of class conflict. "The purpose of the IWW," he proclaimed, "is to bring the workers of this country into the possession of the full value of the product of their toil."

The IWW remained a small organization, troubled by internal squabbles and disagreements. Debs and De Leon left after a few years. Haywood remained the dominant figure in the movement, which played an important role in organizing the militant strike of textile workers in Lawrence, Massachusetts, in 1912 and the following year in Paterson, New Jersey, and Akron, Ohio. But the IWW had its greatest success organizing itinerant lumbermen and migratory workers in the Northwest.

Many American workers still did not feel, as did European workers, that they were engaged in a perpetual class struggle with their capitalist employers. Some immigrant workers, intent on earning enough money to go back home, had no time to join the conflict. Most of those who stayed in the United States were consoled by the promises of the American dream. Thinking they might secure a better job or move up into the middle class, they avoided labor militancy. They knew that even if they failed, their sons and daughters would profit from the American way. The AFL, not the IWW, became the dominant American labor movement. But for a few the IWW represented a dream of what might have been. For others its presence, even though it was small and largely ineffective, meant that perhaps someday a European-style working-class movement might develop in America.

## REFORM IN THE CITIES AND STATES

The reform movements of the progressive era usually started at the local level, then moved to the state level and finally to the nation's capital. Progressivism in the cities and states had roots in the depression and discontent of the 1890s. The reform banners called for more democracy, more power for the people, and for legislation regulating railroads and other businesses. Yet the professional and business classes were the movement's leaders. They intended to bring order out of chaos and to modernize the city and the state during a time of rapid growth.

### Municipal Reformers

Americans have always seen their cities as places of sin, avarice, and corruption rather than as centers of civilization. William Jennings Bryan expressed some of this antiurban feeling in his famous "Cross of Gold" speech, when he stressed the superiority of the farms over the cities. There seemed something almost un-American about the American city: "If a man stayed in the city long enough he would almost inevitably lose those qualities that made him an American," David Graham Phillips, a muckraking journalist and novelist, had one of his characters in *The Golden Fleece* announce.

American cities grew rapidly in the last part of the nineteenth and the first part of the twentieth centuries. New York, which had a population of 1.2 million in 1880, grew to 3.4 million by 1900 and to 5.6 million in 1920. Chicago expanded even more dramatically, from 500,000 in 1880 to 1.7 million in 1900 and to 2.7 million in 1920. Cleveland's population doubled between 1880 and 1900 and doubled again before 1920. Even in the South, where urbanization was slower, Birmingham increased from 38,000 in 1900 to 178,000 in 1920. In California, Los Angeles was a town of 11,000 in 1880 but multiplied ten times by 1900, and then increased by five times, to more than a half million, by 1920.

The spectacular and continuing growth of the cities caused massive problems and created a

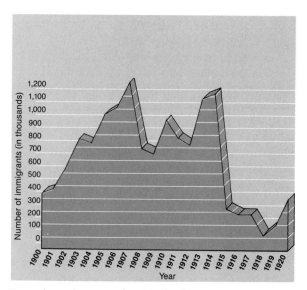

**Immigration to the United States, 1900–1920**

*Source:* U.S. Bureau of the Census.

need for housing, transportation, and municipal services. But it was the kind of people who were moving into the cities that worried many observers. Americans from the small towns and farms continued to be attracted to the urban centers, as they had throughout the nineteenth century. But the greatest surge in population was caused by immigration. Fully 40 percent of New York's population and 36 percent of Chicago's was foreign-born in 1910, and if one added the children of the immigrants, the percentage approached 80 percent in some cities. Huge sections of the cities in the Northeast and the Midwest were filled with sights, sounds, and smells that seemed strange and threatening to the native-born Americans who ventured there. They might as well have been in Naples or Warsaw. These new immigrants from eastern and western Europe, according to Francis Walker, the president of MIT, were "beaten men from beaten races, representing the worst failures in the struggle for existence." They seemed to threaten the American way of life and the very tenets of democracy.

The municipal reform movements of the progressive era were motivated in part by a fear of the city and its new inhabitants. But they also were an extension of the many efforts to clean

up the cities in the late nineteenth century. They built on the reform campaigns of "Golden Rule" Jones and Hazen Pingree (see Chapter 20). But there was a greater sense of urgency, perhaps because urban problems seemed to have reached a crisis stage.

The twentieth-century reformers, mostly middle-class citizens like those in the nineteenth, wanted to regulate and control the sprawling metropolis, restore democracy, reduce corruption, and limit the power of the political bosses and their immigrant allies. They formed committees and appointed commissions. There were committees of 15 and committees of 100; there were bureaus of municipal research, civic clubs, voters' leagues, and good government associations. Usually these organizations were composed of businessmen and professionals, often allied with settlement workers, ministers, and experts from the universities.

When these reformers talked of restoring power to the people, they usually meant their

*This famous photograph by Alfred Stieglitz captures the spirit of those who crowded into steerage to emigrate to America.*

*Cities grew so rapidly that they became not only unmanageable, but so crowded as to make movement difficult. This 1909 photograph shows Dearborn Street, looking south from Randolph Street, in Chicago.*

kind of people. One Rhode Island reformer put it bluntly:

> It stands to reason that a man paying $5,000 taxes in a town is more interested in the well-being and development of his town than the man who pays no taxes. . . . It equally stands to reason that the man of the $5,000 tax should be assured a representation in the committee which lays the tax and spends the money which he contributes. . . . Shall we be truly democratic and give the property owners a fair share or shall we develop a tyranny of ignorance which shall crush him?

Not all reformers were so candid, and the municipal reform movements in most cities did try to make the urban scene more livable for all kinds of people. But the chief aim of municipal reform was to make the city more organized and efficient for the business and professional classes.

Municipal reform movements varied from city to city. In Boston, the reformers tried to strengthen the power of the mayor, to break the hold of the city council, and to eliminate the corruption associated with the council. The reformers succeeded in removing all party designations from city election ballots, and they extended the term of the mayor from two to four years. But to their chagrin, in the election of 1910 the reform candidate was defeated by a foe of reform, the Irish Politician John Fitzgerald (the grandfather of John F. Kennedy), who was elected for the longer term. In other cities, the reformers used different tactics, but they almost always did elaborate studies and carried on campaigns to reduce corruption.

The most dramatic innovation was the commission form of government that replaced both mayor and council with nonpartisan administrators. This innovation began quite accidentally when a hurricane devastated Galveston, Texas, in September 1900. In one of the worst natural disasters in the nation's history, over 6,000 people were killed and more than half the city wiped out. The existing government was helpless to deal with the crisis, so the state legislature appointed five commissioners to run the city during the emergency. The idea spread to Houston, Dallas, and Austin and to many other cities in other states. It proved most popular in small to medium-sized cities in the Midwest and Pacific Northwest. By the time of World War I, more than 400 cities had adopted the commission form. Dayton, Ohio, went one step further: After a disastrous flood in 1913, the city hired a city manager to run the city and to report to the elected council. Government by experts was the perfect symbol of what most progressive municipal reformers had in mind.

The commission and the expert manager did not replace the mayor in most large cities. One of the most flamboyant and successful of the progressive mayors was Tom Johnson of Cleveland. Johnson had made a fortune by investing in utility and railroad franchises before he was 40. But he read Henry George's *Progress and Poverty* and was so influenced by it that he began a second career as a reformer. After serving in Congress, he was elected mayor of Cleveland in 1901. During his two terms in city hall he managed to reduce transit fares and to build parks and municipal bath houses throughout the city. Johnson also broke the connection between the police and prostitution in the city by promising the madams and the brothel owners that he would not bother them if they would be orderly and not steal from their customers or pay off the police. His most controversial move, however, was to push for city ownership of the street railroads and utilities (sometimes called municipal socialism). "Only through municipal ownership," he argued, "can the gulf which divides the community into a small dominant class on one side and the unorganized people on the other be bridged." Johnson was defeated in 1909 in part because he alienated so many powerful business interests, but one of his lieutenants, Newton D. Baker, was elected mayor in 1911 and carried on many of his programs.

### The City Beautiful

In Cleveland, both Tom Johnson and Newton Baker promoted the arts, music, and adult education. They also supervised the construction of a civic center, a library, and a museum. Most other American cities during the progressive era set out to beautify and to bring culture to the metropolitan centers. They were influenced at least in part by the great, classical white city constructed for the Chicago World's Fair of 1893 and by the grand European boulevards such as the Champs Élysées in Paris. The architects of the "city beautiful movement" preferred the impressive and ceremonial architecture of Rome or of the Renaissance for libraries, museums, railroad stations, and other public buildings. The huge Pennsylvania Station in New York was modeled after the imperial Roman baths of Caracalla, while the Free Library in Philadelphia was an almost exact copy of a building in Paris. The city beautiful leaders tried to make the city more attractive and meaningful for the middle and upper classes. The museums and the libraries were closed on Sundays, the only day the working class could possibly visit them.

Another group of progressives, especially those connected with the social settlements, were more concerned with neighborhood parks and playgrounds than with the ceremonial boulevards and grand buildings. Hull House established the first public playground in Chicago. Jacob Riis, the housing reformer, and Lillian Wald of the Henry Street Settlement campaigned in New York for small parks and for the opening of schoolyards on weekends. Some progressives, including many settlement workers, looked back nostalgically to their rural childhoods and desperately tried to get urban children out of the city in the summertime to rural camps. But they also tried to make the city more livable as well as more beautiful.

Most progressives had an ambivalent attitude toward the city. They feared it, and they loved it. Some saw the great urban areas filled with immigrants as a threat to American democracy, but one of Tom Johnson's young assistants, Frederic C. Howe, wrote a book called *The City: The Hope of Democracy* (1905). Hope or threat, the progressives realized that the United States had become an urban nation and that the problems of the city had to be faced one way or another.

### Reform in the States

The progressive movements in the states had many roots and took many forms. In some states, especially in the West, progressive attempts to regulate railroads and utilities were simply an extension of populism. In other states, the reform drive bubbled up from reform efforts in the cities. Most states passed laws during the progressive era designed to extend democracy and give more authority to the people. Initiative and referendum laws allowed citizens to originate legislation and to overturn laws passed by the legislature, while recall laws gave the people a way to remove elected officials. Most of these "democratic" laws worked better in theory than in practice, but the passage of the laws in many states did represent a genuine effort to remove special privilege from government.

Much of the state legislation was concerned with the aspect of progressivism that sought order and efficiency, but many states passed social justice measures as well. Maryland enacted the first workmen's compensation law in 1902, giving employees pay for days missed because of job-related injuries. Illinois approved a law giving aid to mothers with dependent children. Several states passed anti-child labor bills, and Oregon's ten-hour law restricting women's labor became a model for other states.

The states with the most successful reform movements elected strong and aggressive governors: Charles Evans Hughes in New York, Hoke Smith in Georgia, Hiram Johnson in California,

Woodrow Wilson in New Jersey, and Robert La Follette in Wisconsin. Next to Wilson, La Follette was the most famous and in many ways the model progressive governor. Born in a small town in Wisconsin, he graduated from the University of Wisconsin in 1879 and was admitted to the bar. Practicing law during the 1890s in Madison, the state capital, he received a large retainer from the Milwaukee Railroad, and he defended the railroad against both riders and laborers who sued the company.

But Wisconsin, like most of the rest of the country, was hard hit by the depression of 1893. More than a third of the citizens in the state were out of work; farmers lost their farms, and many small businesses went bankrupt. At the same time, the rich seemed to be getting richer. "Men are rightly feeling that a social order like the present, with its enormous wealth side by side with appalling poverty . . . cannot be the final form of human society," a Milwaukee minister announced. As grass-roots discontent spread across the state, a group of municipal reformers in Milwaukee attacked the giant corporations and the street railways. Several newspapers joined the battle and denounced special privilege and corruption wherever they found it. Everyone could agree on the need for tax reform, for railroad regulation, and for more participation of the people in government.

La Follette, who had been little interested in reform in his early career, took advantage of the general mood of discontent to win the governorship in 1901. "Now his face was calm—now a thundercloud—now full of sorrow," one newspaper reported. It seemed ironic that La Follette, who had once taken a retainer from a railroad, now was elected governor by attacking the railroads, but La Follette was a shrewd politician. He used professors from the University of Wisconsin, just across town from the capital building, to prepare reports and do statistical studies. Then he worked with the legislature to pass a state primary law and an act regulating the railroads. "Go back to the first principles of democracy, go back to the people" was his battle cry. The "Wisconsin idea" attracted the attention of journalists like Lincoln Steffens and Ray Stannard Baker, and they helped to popularize the "laboratory of democracy" around the country. La Follette became a national figure and was elected to the Senate in 1906.

The progressive movement did improve government and make it more responsible to the people in states like Wisconsin. For example, the railroads were brought under the control of a railroad commission. But by 1910, the railroads no longer complained about the new taxes and restrictions. They had discovered that it was to their advantage to make their operations more efficient, and often they were able to convince the commission that they should raise rates or abandon the operation of unprofitable lines. Progressivism in the states, like progressivism everywhere, had mixed results. But the spirit of reform that swept through the country was real, and progressive movements on the local level did eventually have an impact on Washington, especially during the administrations of Theodore Roosevelt and Woodrow Wilson.

## THEODORE ROOSEVELT AND THE SQUARE DEAL

President William McKinley was shot in Buffalo, New York, on September 6, 1901, by Leon Czolgosz, an anarchist. He died eight days later, making Theodore Roosevelt, at 42, the youngest man ever to become president. The nation mourned its fallen leader, while in many cities anarchists and other radicals were rounded up for questioning. McKinley had not been a great president, but he had looked dignified and was respected by the American people.

No one knew what to expect from Roosevelt. Mark Hanna, a senator from Ohio and a conservative Republican leader, protested when Roosevelt had been nominated for vice-president, "Don't you realize that there's only one life between that madman and the White House?" But some of the social justice progressives remembered that Roosevelt had suggested that the soldiers ought to fire on the strikers during the Pullman strike in 1894. Roosevelt was controversial when he took office, and he remained controversial when he left the White

House 7½ years later. But even his enemies could agree that he was a dominant force in American life.

## A Strong and Controversial President

Roosevelt, though young, came to the presidency with considerable experience. He had run unsuccessfully for mayor of New York, served a term in the New York state assembly, spent four years as a United States civil service commissioner, and served two years as the police commissioner of New York City. His exploits in the Spanish-American War brought him to the public's attention, but he had also been an effective assistant secretary of the navy and a reform governor of New York. While police commissioner and governor, he had been influenced by a number of progressives. Jacob Riis, the housing reformer, became one of his friends and led him on nighttime explorations of the slums of New York City. He had also impressed a group of New York settlement workers with his genuine concern for human misery, his ability to talk to all kinds of people, and his willingness to learn about social problems. But no one was sure how Roosevelt would act as president. He came from an upper-class family and had associated with the important and the powerful all over the world. He had published a number of books and was one of the most intellectual presidents since

*Young and energetic, Theodore Roosevelt was a dynamic though controversial president.*

Thomas Jefferson. But none of these things assured that he would be a progressive in office.

Roosevelt loved being president. He called the office a "bully pulpit," and he enjoyed talking to the people and the press. His high-pitched voice might have been a handicap, but he made up for it with great enthusiasm and exuberance. With an appealing personality and a sense of humor, he made a good subject for the new mass-market newspapers and magazines. The American people quickly adopted him as their favorite. They called him "Teddy" and named a stuffed bear after him. According to one Englishman, he was second only to Niagara Falls as an American phenomenon. Sometimes his exuberance got a little out of hand. On one occasion he took a foreign diplomat on a nude swim in the Potomac River. You have to understand, another observer remarked, that "the president is really only six years old."

Roosevelt was much more than an exuberant 6-year-old. He was the strongest president since Lincoln. By reorganizing and revitalizing the executive branch, reorganizing the army command structure, and modernizing the consular service, he made many aspects of the federal government more efficient. He established the Bureau of Corporations, appointed independent commissions staffed with experts, and enlisted talented and well-trained men to work for the government. "TR," as he became known, called a White House conference on the care of dependent children, and in 1905 he even summoned college presidents and football coaches to the White House to discuss ways to limit violence in football. He angered many social justice progressives by not going far enough. In fact, on one occasion Florence Kelley was so furious with him that she walked out of the oval office and slammed the door. But he was the first president to listen to the pleas of the progressives and to invite them to the White House. Learning from experts like Frances Kellor, he became more concerned with social justice as time went on.

## Dealing with the Trusts

One of Roosevelt's first actions as president was to attempt to control the large industrial corporations. He took office in the middle of an unprecedented movement of business consolidation. Between 1897 and 1904, some 4,227 companies combined to form 257 large corporations. U.S. Steel, the first billion-dollar corporation, was formed in 1901 by joining Carnegie Steel with its eight principal competitors. In one stroke the new company controlled two-thirds of the market, and J. P. Morgan made $7 million for supervising the operation. The Sherman Anti-Trust Act of 1890 had been virtually useless in controlling the trusts, but a new outcry from muckrakers and progressives called for regulation. Some even demanded the return to the age of small business. Roosevelt was not opposed to bigness, nor to the right of businessmen to make money. "Our aim is not to do away with corporations," he remarked in 1902; "on the contrary, these big aggregations are the inevitable development of modern industrialism." But he thought some businessmen were arrogant, greedy, and irresponsible. "We draw the line against misconduct, not against wealth," he said.

To the shock of much of the business community, he directed his attorney general to file suit to dissolve the Northern Securities Company, a giant railroad monopoly put together by James J. Hill and financier J. P. Morgan. Morgan came to the White House to tell Roosevelt, "If we have done anything wrong, send your man to my man and they can fix it up." Roosevelt was furious, and he was determined to let Morgan and other businessmen know that they could not deal with the president of the United States as just another tycoon.

The government won its case and proceeded to prosecute some of the largest corporations, including Standard Oil of New Jersey and the American Tobacco Company. However, Roosevelt's antitrust policy did not end the power of the giant corporations or even alter their methods of doing business. More disturbing to consumers, it did not force down the price of kerosene, cigars, or railroad tickets. But it did breathe some life into the Sherman Anti-Trust Act, and it increased the role of the federal government as regulator.

Roosevelt sought to strengthen the regulatory powers of the federal government in other ways. He steered the Elkins Act through Congress in 1903 and the Hepburn Act in 1906, which together strengthened the power of the Interstate Commerce Commission (ICC). The first act eliminated the use of rebates by railroads, a way that many large corporations had used to get favored treatment. The second act broadened the power of the ICC and gave it the right to investigate and enforce rates. Both bills,

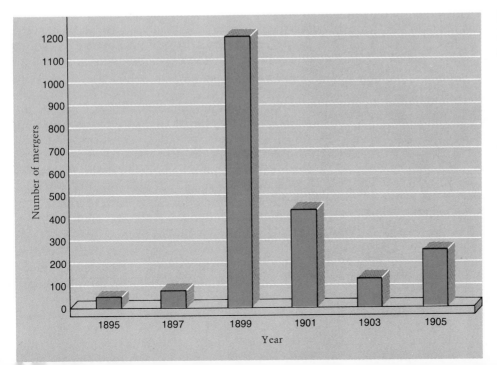

**Business Mergers, 1895–1905**

**Source:** U.S. Bureau of the Census.

however, were watered down by congressional opposition, and they did not end the abuses or satisfy the farmers and small businessmen who had always been the railroads' chief critics.

Roosevelt was a firm believer in corporate capitalism. He detested socialism and felt much more comfortable around business executives than labor leaders. Yet he saw his role as mediator and regulator. His view of the power of the presidency was illustrated in 1902 during the anthracite coal strike. Led by John Mitchell of the United Mine Workers, the coal miners went on strike to protest low wages, long hours, and unsafe working conditions. In 1901, a total of 513 coal miners had been killed. The mine owners, who often were also railroad owners, refused to talk to the miners. They hired strikebreakers and used private security forces to threaten and intimidate the miners. The employer's position in its extreme form was articulated by George F. Baer of the Reading Railroad.

*Before the Pure Food and Drug Act of 1906, patent medicines routinely contained addictive and dangerous drugs. By 1912, though the problem persisted, public awareness had increased dramatically.*

He argued that workingmen had no right to strike or to say anything about working conditions: "The rights and interests of the laboring man will be protected and cared for, not by the labor agitators, but by the Christian man to whom God in His infinite wisdom has given the control of the property interests of the country, and upon the successful management of which so much depends."

Although Roosevelt had no particular sympathy for labor, he certainly would not have gone as far as Baer. In the fall of 1902, however, schools began closing for lack of coal, and it looked like many citizens would suffer through the winter. Coal that usually sold for $5 a ton rose to $14. Roosevelt called the owners and representatives of the union to the White House even though the businessmen protested that they would not deal with "outlaws." Finally, the president appointed a commission that included representatives of the union as well as the community. Within weeks, the miners went back to work with a 10 percent raise.

### Meat Inspection and Pure Food and Drugs

Roosevelt's first major legislative reform began almost accidently in 1904 when Upton Sinclair, a 26-year-old muckraking journalist, started to collect information and to do research on the conditions in the Chicago stockyards. Born in Baltimore, Sinclair had grown up in New York, where he wrote dime novels to pay his tuition at City College. He was converted to socialism by his reading and by his association with a group of idealistic young writers in New York. Though he knew little about Chicago, he was driven by a desire to expose the exploitation of the poor and oppressed in America. He was impressed with the data the settlement workers had collected on all aspects of urban problems. Sinclair boarded at the University of Chicago settlement while he did research, conducted interviews, and wrote the story that would be published in 1906 as *The Jungle*.

Sinclair's novel told the story of the Rudkus family, who emigrated from Lithuania to Chicago filled with ambition and hope. But the American dream failed for them. Sinclair documented exploitation in his fictional account, but it was his description of contaminated meat that received most of the attention. He described spoiled hams treated with formaldehyde and sausages made from rotten meat scraps, rats, and other refuse. Hoping to convert his readers to socialism, what Sinclair did instead was to turn their stomachs and cause a public outcry for better regulation of the meatpacking industry.

Selling 25,000 copies in its first six weeks, *The Jungle* disturbed many people including Roosevelt, who, it was reported, could no longer enjoy his breakfast sausage. Roosevelt ordered a study of conditions in the meatpacking industry and then used the report to pressure Congress and the meatpackers to accept a bill introduced by Albert Beveridge, the progressive senator from Indiana.

In the end, the Meat Inspection Act of 1906 was a compromise. It enforced some federal inspection and mandated sanitary conditions in all companies selling meat in interstate commerce. The meatpackers defeated a provision that would have required the dating of all meat. Some of the large meatpackers supported the compromise bill because it gave them an advantage in their battle with the smaller firms. Yet the bill was a beginning. It illustrates how muckrakers, social justice progressives, and public outcry eventually led to reform legislation. It also shows how Roosevelt used the public mood and manipulated the political process to get a bill through Congress. Many of the progressive reformers were disappointed with the final result, but Roosevelt was always willing to settle for half a loaf rather than none at all. Ironically, the Meat Inspection Act helped restore the public's confidence in the meat industry and aided the industry increase its profits.

Taking advantage of the publicity that circulated around *The Jungle*, a group of reformers, writers, and government officials pushed for legislation to regulate the sale of food and drugs. Americans consumed an enormous quantity of patent medicines, which they purchased through the mail, from traveling salesmen, and from local stores. One article pointed out in 1905:

> Gullible Americans will spend this year some seventy-five million dollars in the purchase of patent medicines. In consideration of this sum it will swallow huge quantities of alcohol, an appalling amount of opiates and narcotics, a wide assortment of varied drugs ranging from powerful and dangerous heart depressants to insidious liver stimulants; and, far in excess of all other ingredients, undiluted fraud. For fraud exploited by the skillfulest of advertising bunco men is the basis of the trade.

Many packaged and canned foods contained dangerous chemicals and impurities. One popular remedy, Hosteter's Stomach Bitters, was revealed on analysis to contain 44 percent alcohol. Coca-Cola, a popular soft drink, actually contained cocaine for a few years, and many medicines were laced with opium. Many people, including women and children, became alcoholics or drug addicts in their search to feel better. The Pure Food and Drug Act that passed Congress on the same day in 1906 as the Meat Inspection Act was not a perfect bill by any means, but it was a beginning. It prevented some of the worst abuses, including eliminating the cocaine from Coca-Cola.

## Conservation

Although Roosevelt was pleased with the new legislation for regulating the food and drug industries, he always considered his conservation program his most important domestic achievement. An outdoorsman, hunter, and amateur naturalist since his youth, he was also a close friend of Gifford Pinchot, who had been educated in France and Germany in the scientific management of forests. For more than a century it appeared that American natural resources were inexhaustible, but by 1900 it became obvious to Pinchot and Roosevelt that much of the forests had been destroyed, the rivers polluted and filled with silt, the land eroded, and other resources exploited for private gain. Roosevelt called a conservation conference in 1908. The conservation pioneers, who were usually scientists and experts from the East, talked of planned uses of natural resources. But lumbermen, ranchers, miners, and all who thought they could make a profit out of the land opposed any attempt to turn land over to federal control. Another group, however, led by men like John Muir, a naturalist, thought the land should be preserved in its wild state. Muir helped organize the Sierra Club in 1892 and also led the successful campaign to create Yosemite National Park in California.

As usual, Roosevelt took a middle course, siding with Pinchot and his followers. But during his administration, over 150 million acres were set aside as public land, three times the area of federal lands when he took office.

## Progressivism for Whites Only

Like most of his generation, Roosevelt thought in stereotyped racial terms. He believed that blacks and Asians were inferior, and he feared that the Anglo-Saxon race was being threatened in America by massive migrations from southern and eastern Europe. Yet Roosevelt was a politician, and he made gestures of goodwill to most groups. He even invited Booker T. Washington to the White House in 1901, though he was viciously attacked by many in the South for this break in etiquette. He also appointed several qualified blacks to minor federal posts, most notably Dr. William D. Crum to head the Charleston, South Carolina, customs house in 1905. But at other times he seemed insensitive to the needs and feelings of black Americans. This was especially true in his handling of the Brownsville, Texas, riot of 1906. Members of a black army unit stationed there, angered by discrimination against them, rioted one hot August night. Exactly what happened no one was sure, but one white man was killed and several wounded. Waiting until after the midterm elections of 1906, Roosevelt ordered all 167 members of three companies dishonorably discharged. It was an unjust punishment for an unproved crime, and 66 years later the secretary of the army granted honorable discharges to the men, most of them by that time dead.

The progressive era coincided with the years of greatest segregation in the South, but even the most advanced progressives seldom included blacks in their reform schemes. Hull House, like most social settlements, was segregated, although Jane Addams more than most progressives struggled to overcome the racist attitudes of her day. She helped found a settlement that served a black neighborhood in Chicago, and she

spoke out repeatedly against lynching. Addams also supported the founding of the National Association for the Advancement of Colored People in 1909, the most important progressive-era organization aimed at promoting equality and justice for black people. Actually it was the work of three other settlement workers and the cooperation of W. E. B. Du Bois that led to the formation of the NAACP.

William English Walling and his wife Anna Strunsky were lecturing in the Midwest in 1908 on the plight of the Russian peasant when they heard of a race riot in Springfield, Illinois. Suddenly the problems of blacks in Abraham Lincoln's hometown seemed more pressing than the difficulties of Russian peasants. Walling wrote an angry article on the black problem, which was read by Mary White Ovington, a New York settlement worker whose book, *Half a Man* (1911), was, next to Du Bois's study, *The Philadelphia Negro* (1899), the best study of the way blacks lived in northern cities. Ovington and Walling involved Henry Moskowitz, another settlement worker and reformer, and together they gained the support of a number of prominent citizens, including Oswald Garrison Villard, grandson of abolitionist William Lloyd Garrison.

The white social reformers enlisted the help of Du Bois, who had moved further away from

*Tuskegee Institute followed Booker T. Washington's philosophy of black advancement through accommodation to the white status quo.*

the conservative and accommodationist policies of Booker T. Washington. Incensed by the increase in lynching, the disenfranchisement of blacks in most southern states, and the race riots in Springfield, Atlanta, and other cities, Du Bois had called a conference of young and militant blacks in 1905. They met in Canada, not far from Niagara Falls, and issued an angry statement. The Niagara Movement, as it came to be called, was small but distinctly different from Washington's approach. "We want to *pull down* nothing but we don't propose to be pulled down . . . ," the platform announced. "We believe in *taking what we can get* but we don't believe in being satisfied with it and in permitting anybody for a moment to imagine we're satisfied." When the Niagara movement combined with the NAACP, Du Bois became editor of its journal, *The Crisis*. He toned down his rhetoric, but he tried to promote equality for all blacks. The NAACP was a typical progressive organization, seeking to work within the American system to promote reform. But to Roosevelt and to many others who called themselves progressives, the NAACP seemed dangerously radical.

### William Howard Taft

After two terms as president, Roosevelt decided to step down. "I believe in a strong executive," he remarked in 1908. "I believe in power, but I believe that responsibility should go with power, and that it is not well that the strong executive should be a perpetual executive." But he apparently regretted his decision even before he left the presidency. He was only 50 years old and at the peak of his popularity and power. Since the United States system of government provides little creative function for former presidents, Roosevelt decided to travel and to go big-game hunting in Africa. But before he left he handpicked his successor.

William Howard Taft, Roosevelt's personal choice for the Republican nomination in 1908, was a distinguished lawyer, federal judge, and public servant. Born in Cincinnati, he had been the first civil governor of the Philippines and secretary of war under Roosevelt. After defeating William Jennings Bryan for the presidency in

1908, he quickly ran into difficulties. In some ways he seemed more progressive than Roosevelt. His administration instituted more suits against monopolies in one term than Roosevelt had in two. He supported the eight-hour day and legislation to make mining safer and urged the passage of the Mann-Elkins Act in 1910, which strengthened the ICC by giving it more power to set railroad rates and extending its jurisdiction over telephone and telegraph companies. Taft also encouraged the process that eventually led to the passage of the federal income tax, which was authorized under the Sixteenth Amendment, ratified in 1913. It probably did more to transform the relationship of the government to the people than all other progressive measures combined.

Taft's biggest problem was his style and personality. He was a huge man, weighing over 300 pounds. Rumors circulated that he found it necessary to have a special oversized bathtub installed in the White House. Easily made fun of, the president had a ponderous prose and a dull speaking style that failed to inspire the public. He also lacked Roosevelt's political skills and angered many of the progressives in the Republican party, especially the midwestern insurgents led by Senator Robert La Follette of Wisconsin. Many progressives were annoyed when he signed the Payne-Aldrich Tariff, which midwesterners thought left rates on cotton and wool cloth and other items too high and played into the hands of the eastern industrial interests. Even Roosevelt was infuriated when his successor reversed many of his conservation policies and fired Chief Forester Gifford Pinchot, who had attacked Secretary of the Interior Richard A. Ballinger for giving away rich coal lands in Alaska to mining interests. Roosevelt broke with Taft, letting it be known that he was willing to run again for president. This set up one of the most exciting and significant elections in American history.

### The Election of 1912

Woodrow Wilson won the Democratic nomination for president in 1912. Born two years before Roosevelt, Wilson came from a very different background and would be cast in opposition to the former president during most of his political career. Yet the two had much in common. Both made important contributions to progressivism and to the development of liberalism in America.

Wilson was the son and grandson of Presbyterian ministers. Growing up in a comfortable and intellectual household, he very early seemed more interested in politics than in religion. After graduating from Princeton University in 1879, he studied law at the University of Virginia and practiced law briefly in Atlanta before entering graduate school at The Johns Hopkins University in Baltimore. Soon after receiving his Ph.D. he published a book, *Congressional Government* (1885), that established his reputation as a shrewd analyst of American politics. He taught history briefly at Bryn Mawr College near Philadelphia and at Wesleyan in Connecticut before moving to Princeton. Less flamboyant than Roosevelt, he was an excellent public speaker with the power to convince people with his words.

In 1902, Wilson was elected president of Princeton University, and during the next few years he established a national reputation as an educational leader. His greatest success was the preceptorial system, which brought undergraduates together with young instructors in small groups. A few years later, however, he failed in his attempt to eliminate the elite eating clubs and to make the graduate school the center of the university. Wilson had never lost interest in politics, however, so when offered a chance by the Democratic machine to run for governor of New Jersey, he took it eagerly. In his two years as governor he showed courage as he quickly alienated some of the conservatives who had helped to elect him. Building a coalition of reformers, he worked with them to pass a direct primary law and a workmen's compensation law. He also created a commission to regulate transportation and public utility companies. By 1912, Wilson was not only an expert on government and politics but had also acquired the reputation of a progressive.

Roosevelt, who had been speaking out on a variety of issues since 1910, competed with Taft for the Republican nomination, but Taft, as the incumbent president and party leader, was able

to win it. Roosevelt, however, startled the nation by walking out of the convention and forming a new political party, the Progressive party. The new party would not have been formed without Roosevelt, but the party was always more than Roosevelt. It appealed to progressives from all over the country who had become frustrated with the conservative leadership in both parties.

Many social workers and social justice progressives supported the Progressive party because of its platform, which contained provisions they had been advocating for years. The Progressives supported an eight-hour day, a six-day week, the abolition of child labor under age 16, and a federal system of accident, old age, and unemployment insurance. Unlike the Democrats, the Progressives also endorsed woman suffrage. "Just think of having all the world listen to our story of social and industrial injustice and have them told that it can be righted," one social worker exclaimed.

Most of those who supported the Progressives in 1912 did not realistically think they could win, but they were convinced that they could organize a new political movement that would replace the Republican party, just as the Republicans had replaced the Whigs after 1856. To this end, Progressive leaders, led by Kellor, set up the Progressive Service, designed to apply the principles of social research to educating voters between elections.

The Progressive convention in Chicago seemed to many observers more like a religious revival meeting than a political gathering; others thought it seemed like a social work conference. The delegates sang "Onward Christian Soldiers," "The Battle Hymn of the Republic," and "Roosevelt, Oh Roosevelt" (to the tune of "Maryland, My Maryland"). They waved their bandannas, and when Jane Addams rose to second Roosevelt's nomination, a large group of women marched around the auditorium with a banner that read "Votes for Women." The Progressive cause "is based on the eternal principles of righteousness," Roosevelt announced. "In the end the cause itself shall triumph."

The enthusiasm for Roosevelt and the Progressive party was misleading, for behind the unified facade there were many disagreements.

Roosevelt had become more progressive on many issues since leaving the presidency. He even attacked the financiers "to whom the acquisition of untold millions is the supreme goal of life, and who are too often utterly indifferent as to how these millions are obtained." But he was not as committed to social reform in many areas as were some of the delegates. Perhaps the most divisive issue was the controversy over seating black delegates from several southern states. A number of social justice progressives fought hard to include a plank in the platform supporting equality for blacks and for seating the black delegation. Roosevelt, however, thought he had a realistic chance to carry several southern states, and he was not convinced that black equality was an important progressive issue. In the end, no blacks sat with the southern delegates, and the platform made no mention of black equality.

The political campaign in 1912 became a contest primarily between Roosevelt and Wilson, with Taft, the Republican candidate, ignored by most reporters who covered the campaign. On one level the campaign became a debate over political philosophy, concerning the proper relationship of government to society in a modern industrial age. Roosevelt borrowed

some of his ideas from a book, *The Promise of American Life* (1909), written by Herbert Croly, a young journalist. But he had also been working out his own philosophy of government. He spoke of the "new nationalism." In a modern industrial society, he argued, large corporations were "inevitable and necessary." What was needed was not the breakup of the trusts but increased power in the hands of the federal government to regulate business and industry and to ensure the rights of labor, women and children, and other groups. He argued for using Hamiltonian means to assure Jeffersonian ends, for using strong central government to guarantee the rights of the people.

Wilson responded with a slogan and program of his own. Using the writings of Louis Brandeis, Wilson talked of the "new freedom." He sought to restore the old forms of economic competition and equality of opportunity and argued against too much federal power. "Free men need no guardians," he argued and suggested that big government would inevitably lead to benefits for big business. "What I fear . . . is a government of experts," Wilson declared, as he attacked Roosevelt's programs as simply "regulated monopoly."

The level of debate during the campaign was

## Major Parties in the Presidential Election of 1912

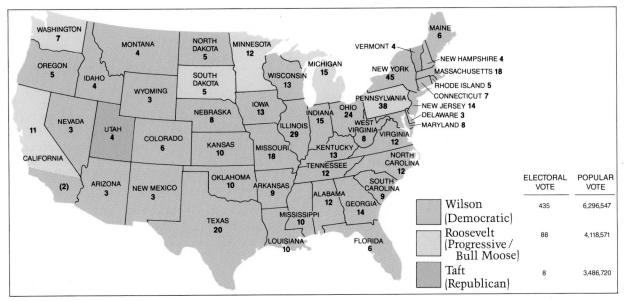

impressive, making this one of the few elections in American history when important ideas were actually discussed. But it is easy to exaggerate the differences between Roosevelt and Wilson. There was some truth in the charge of William Allen White, the editor of the Emporia *Gazette* in Kansas, when he remarked, "Between the New Nationalism and the New Freedom was that fantastic imaginary gulf that always had existed between Tweedle-dum and Tweedle-dee." Certainly in the end the things that Roosevelt and Wilson could agree on were more important than the issues that divided them. Both Roosevelt and Wilson urged reform within the American system. Both defended corporate capitalism and both opposed socialism and radical labor organizations such as the IWW. Both wanted to promote more democracy and strengthen conservative labor unions. Both were very different in style and substance from the fourth candidate, Eugene Debs, who ran on the Socialist party ticket in 1912.

Debs, in 1912, was the most important socialist leader in the country. The socialists, unlike the progressives, argued for fundamental change in the American system. Socialism was always a minority movement in the United States, but it had its greatest success in the first decade of the twentieth century. Thirty-three cities including Milwaukee, Wisconsin; Reading, Pennsylvania; Butte, Montana; Jackson,

Michigan; and Berkeley, California, chose socialist mayors. Socialists Victor Berger from Wisconsin and Meyer London from New York were elected to Congress. The most important socialist periodical, *Appeal to Reason*, published in Girard, Kansas, increased its circulation from about 30,000 in 1900 to nearly 300,000 in 1906. Socialism appealed to a diverse group. Some reformers, such as Florence Kelley and William English Walling, joined the party because of their frustration with the slow progress of reform, but the party also attracted many recent immigrants.

A tremendously appealing figure and a great orator, Debs had run for president in 1900, 1904, and 1908, but in 1912 he reached much wider audiences in many parts of the country. His message differed radically from that of Wilson or Roosevelt. The Socialist party is "organized and financed by the workers themselves," he announced, "as a means of wresting control of government and industry from the capitalists and making the working class the ruling class of the nation and the world." Debs polled almost 900,000 votes in 1912 (6 percent of the popular vote), the greatest vote ever achieved by a socialist in the United States. Wilson received 6.3 million votes, Roosevelt a little more than 4 million, and Taft 3.5 million. But Wilson garnered 435 electoral votes, Roosevelt 88, and Taft only 8.

## WOODROW WILSON AND THE NEW FREEDOM

Wilson was elected largely because Roosevelt and the Progressive party split the Republican vote. But once elected, Wilson became a vigorous and aggressive chief executive who set out to translate his ideas about progressive government into legislation. Wilson was the first southerner elected president since Zachary Taylor in 1848 and only the second Democrat since the Civil War. Wilson, like Roosevelt, had to work with his party, and that restricted how progressive he could be. But he was also constrained by his own background and inclinations. Still, like Roosevelt, Wilson became more progressive during his presidency.

### Tariff and Banking Reform

Wilson was not as charismatic as Roosevelt. No one called him "Woody." He had a more difficult time relating to people in small groups, but he was an excellent public speaker who dominated through the force of his intellect. He probably had an exaggerated belief in his ability to persuade and a tendency to trust his own intuition too much. Ironically, his early success in getting his legislative agenda through Congress probably contributed to the overconfidence that would get him into difficulty later in foreign affairs. But his ability to push his legislative program through Congress during his first two years in office was matched only by Franklin Roosevelt during the first months of the New Deal and by Lyndon Johnson in 1965.

Within a month of his inauguration, Wilson went before a joint session of Congress to outline his legislative program. He recommended reducing the tariff to eliminate favoritism, freeing the banking system from Wall Street control, and restoring competition in industry. By appearing in person before Congress, he broke a precedent established by Thomas Jefferson. First on his agenda was tariff reform. The Underwood Tariff passed in 1913 was not a free-trade bill, but it did reduce the schedule for the first time in many years.

Attached to the Underwood Tariff bill was a provision for a small and slightly graduated income tax, which had been made possible by the passage of the Sixteenth Amendment. It imposed a modest rate of 1 percent on income over $4,000 (thus exempting a large proportion of the population), with a surtax rising to 6 percent on high incomes. The income tax was enacted to replace the money lost from lowering the tariff. Wilson seemed to have no interest in using it to redistribute wealth in America.

The next item on Wilson's agenda was re-

*Many progressives were disappointed in Wilson for his refusal to support a constitutional amendment granting women the right to vote.*

form of the banking system. The financial panic of 1907 had revealed the need for a central bank, but few people could agree on the exact nature of the reforms. The progressive faction of the Democratic party, armed with the findings of the Pujo Committee's investigation of the money trust, argued for a banking system and a currency controlled by the federal government. The congressional committee, led by Arsène Pujo of Louisiana, had revealed a massive consolidation of banks and trust companies and a system of interlocking directorates and informal arrangements that concentrated resources and power in the hands of a few firms such as the J. P. Morgan company. But talk of banking reform raised the specter among conservative Democrats and the business community of socialism, populism, and the monetary ideas of William Jennings Bryan.

The bill that passed Congress was a compromise. In creating the Federal Reserve System, it was the first reorganization of the banking system since the Civil War. The bill provided for 12 Federal Reserve Banks and a Federal Reserve Board appointed by the president. The bill also created a flexible currency, based on the federal reserve notes, that could be expanded or contracted as the situation required. The Federal Reserve System was not without its flaws, as later developments would show, and it did not end the power of the large eastern banks; but it was an improvement, and it appealed to the part of the progressive movement that sought order and control.

Despite these reform measures, Wilson was not very progressive in some of his actions during his first two years in office. In the spring of 1914, he failed to support a bill that would have provided long-term rural credit financed by the federal government. He refused to support a woman suffrage amendment, arguing that the states should decide who could vote. He also failed to support an anti–child labor bill after it had passed the House. But most distressing to some progressives, he permitted the segregation of blacks in several federal departments.

Booker T. Washington had remarked on Wilson's election, "Mr. Wilson is in favor of the things which tend toward the uplift, improvement, and advancement of my people, and at his hands we have nothing to fear." But when southern Democrats, suddenly in control in many departments, began dismissing black federal officeholders, especially those "who boss white girls," Wilson did nothing. When the NAACP complained that the shops, offices, rest rooms, and lunchrooms of the Post Office and Treasury Departments and the Bureau of Engraving were segregated, Wilson replied, "I sincerely believe it to be in their [the blacks'] best interest."

## Moving Closer to a New Nationalism

How to control the great corporations in America was a question much debated by Wilson and Roosevelt during the campaign. Wilson's solution was the Clayton Act, submitted to Congress in 1914. The bill prohibited a number of unfair trading practices, outlawed the interlocking directorate, and made it illegal for corporations to purchase stock in other corporations if this tended to reduce competition. It was not clear how the government would enforce these provisions and ensure the competition that Wilson's New Freedom doctrine called for, but the bill became controversial for another reason. Labor leaders protested that the bill had no provision exempting labor organizations

from prosecution under the Sherman Anti-Trust Act. When a section was added exempting both labor and agricultural organizations, Samuel Gompers hailed it as labor's Magna Charta. It was hardly that because the courts interpreted the provision so that labor unions remained subject to court injunctions during strikes despite the Clayton Act.

More important than the Clayton Act, which both supporters and opponents realized was too vague to be enforced, was the creation of the Federal Trade Commission (FTC), modeled after the ICC, with enough power to move directly against corporations accused of restricting competition. The FTC was the idea of Louis Brandeis, but it was accepted by Wilson even though it seemed to move him more toward the philosophy of New Nationalism.

The Federal Trade Commission and the Clayton Act did not end monopoly, and the courts in the next two decades did not increase the government's power to regulate business. Yet during Wilson's first two years, more power had been centered in the federal government and in the executive branch. Like Roosevelt, Wilson had not satisfied the advanced progressives, but the outbreak of war in Europe and the need to win the election of 1916 would influence him in becoming more progressive in the next years.

### Presidential Elections of the Progressive Era

| YEAR | CANDIDATES | PARTY | POPULAR VOTE | ELECTORAL VOTE |
|------|-----------|-------|--------------|----------------|
| 1904 | THEODORE ROOSEVELT | Republican | 7,628,834 (56.4%) | 336 |
|      | Alton B. Parker | Democratic | 5,084,401 (37.6%) | 140 |
|      | Eugene V. Debs | Socialist | 402,460 (3.0%) | 0 |
| 1908 | WILLIAM H. TAFT | Republican | 7,679,006 (51.6%) | 321 |
|      | William J. Bryan | Democratic | 6,409,106 (43.1%) | 162 |
|      | Eugene V. Debs | Socialist | 420,820 (2.8%) | 0 |
| 1912 | WOODROW WILSON | Democratic | 6,286,820 (41.8%) | 435 |
|      | Theodore Roosevelt | Progressive | 4,126,020 (27.4%) | 88 |
|      | William H. Taft | Republican | 3,483,922 (23.2%) | 8 |
|      | Eugene V. Debs | Socialist | 897,011 (6.0%) | 0 |
| 1916 | WOODROW WILSON | Democratic | 9,129,606 (49.3%) | 277 |
|      | Charles E. Hughes | Republican | 8,538,221 (46.1%) | 254 |

*Note:* Winners' names appear in capital letters.

## CONCLUSION: The Limits of Progressivism

The progressive era was a time when many Americans set out to promote reform because they saw poverty, despair, and disorder in the country transformed by immigration, urbanism, and industrialism. The progressives, unlike the socialists, however, saw nothing fundamentally wrong with the American system. Progressivism was largely a middle-class movement that sought to help the poor, the immigrants, and the working class. Yet the poor were rarely consulted about policy, and many groups, especially blacks, were almost entirely left out of reform plans. Progressives had an optimistic view of human nature and an exaggerated faith in statistics, commissions, and committees. They talked of the need for more democracy, but they often succeeded in promoting a government run by experts. They believed there was a need to regulate business, promote efficiency, and spread social justice, but these were often contradictory goals. In the end, their regulatory laws tended to aid business and to strengthen corporate capitalism, while social justice and equal opportunity remained difficult to achieve.

Progressivism was a broad, diverse, and sometimes contradictory movement that had its roots in the 1890s and came to a climax in the early twentieth century. It began with many local movements and moved to the

### Key Progressive Era Legislation

| YEAR | LEGISLATION | PROVISIONS |
| --- | --- | --- |
| 1901 | New York State Tenement House Law | Prohibited the worst tenement houses; required fire escapes, lights in dark hallways, a window for each room, etc. (Soon copied by other states.) |
| 1902 | Maryland Workmen's Compensation Law | Paid workers benefits for injuries on the job. |
| 1902 | Wisconsin Direct Primary Law | Allowed voters rather than politicians to select candidates. |
| 1902 | Oregon initiative and referendum laws | Gave voters power to initiate legislation and vote on important issues. |
| 1902 | National Reclamation Act (Newlands Act) | Set aside proceeds from sale of public lands to promote irrigation projects in the West. |
| 1903 | Oregon women's labor law | Limited work for women in industry to ten hours a day. |
| 1903 | Elkins Act | Strengthened Interstate Commerce Act by eliminating rebates. |
| 1906 | Hepburn Act | Authorized ICC to fix maximum railroad rates. |
| 1906 | Pure Food and Drug Act | Prohibited sale and transportation of adulterated or fraudulently labeled foods and drugs. |
| 1906 | Meat Inspection Act | Enforced sanitary conditions in meatpacking plants. |
| 1910 | Mann Act | Prohibited interstate transportation of women for immoral purposes. |
| 1913 | Sixteenth Amendment | Authorized federal income tax. |
| 1915 | La Follette Seaman's Act | Regulated conditions of employment of maritime workers. |
| 1916 | Federal Farm Loan Act | Provided farmers with low-interest long-term loans. |
| 1916 | Federal Child Labor Law | Barred products produced by children from interstate commerce. (Declared unconstitutional in 1918.) |
| 1919 | Eighteenth Amendment | Prohibited sale and production of intoxicating liquors. |
| 1920 | Nineteenth Amendment | Gave women the right to vote. |

state and finally to the national level. Neither Theodore Roosevelt nor Woodrow Wilson was an advanced progressive, but during both administrations, progressivism achieved some success. Both presidents strengthened the power of the presidency, and both promoted the idea that the federal government had the responsibility to regulate and control and to promote social justice. Progressivism would be altered by World War I, but it survived, with its strengths and weaknesses, to have an impact on American society through most of the twentieth century.

## Recommended Reading

A good starting point for an exploration of the progressive movement is Arthur S. Link and Richard L. McCormick, *Progressivism* (1983). Robert H. Wiebe, *The Search for Order* (1967) emphasizes the middle-class nature of the movement as well as the drive for efficiency and professionalization. Gabriel Kolko, *The Triumph of Conservatism* (1963) sees most of the campaigns for progressive legislation as led by businessmen for their own advantage. Paul Boyer, *Urban Masses and Moral Order in America, 1820–1920* (1978) finds a continuity of the reform impulse across a century and rates fear of immigrants and the city and a desire for social control as the most important ingredients of progressivism.

Allen F. Davis, *Spearheads for Reform* (1967) and Roy Lubove, *The Progressives and the Slums* (1962) emphasize the social justice movement. Lawrence Cremin, *The Transformation of the School* (1951) is the best book on progressive education. Ruth Rosen, *The Lost Sisterhood* (1982) tells the fascinating story of the crusade against prostitution. David P. Thelen,

*The New Citizenship* (1972) describes the origins of progressivism in Wisconsin, the state where it reached its greatest triumphs, while Dewey W. Grantham, *Southern Progressivism* (1983) details the impact of progressivism on a region often thought to have been little influenced by the movement. David Brody, *Workers in Industrial America* (1980) and Alice Kessler-Harris, *Out to Work* (1982) both have perceptive chapters on the impact of progressivism on industrial workers.

John Morton Blum, *The Progressive Presidents* (1980) and John Milton Cooper, Jr., *The Warrior and the Priest* (1983) give interesting interpretations of Roosevelt and Wilson. Nick Salvatore, *Eugene V. Debs* (1982) is the best biography of America's most important radical.

Novels include Upton Sinclair's *The Jungle* (1906), a classic muckraking novel about the meatpacking industry, and Charlotte Perkins Gilman's *Her Land* (1915), a story of a female utopia.

## TIME LINE

| | |
|---|---|
| 1901 | McKinley assassinated; Theodore Roosevelt becomes president<br>Robert La Follette elected governor of Wisconsin<br>Tom Johnson elected mayor of Cleveland<br>Model tenement house bill passed in New York<br>Formation of U.S. Steel |
| 1902 | Anthracite coal strike |
| 1903 | Women's Trade Union League founded<br>Elkins Act |
| 1904 | Roosevelt reelected<br>Lincoln Steffens publishes *The Shame of the Cities* |
| 1905 | Frederic C. Howe writes *The City: The Hope of Democracy*<br>Industrial Workers of the World formed |
| 1906 | Upton Sinclair publishes *The Jungle*<br>Hepburn Act<br>Meat Inspection Act<br>Pure Food and Drug Act |
| 1907 | Financial panic |
| 1908 | *Muller* v. *Oregon*<br>*Danbury Hatters* case<br>William Howard Taft elected president |

| | |
|---|---|
| 1909 | Herbert Croly publishes *The Promise of American Life*<br>NAACP founded |
| 1910 | Ballinger-Pinchot controversy<br>Mann-Elkins Act |
| 1911 | Frederick Taylor publishes *The Principles of Scientific Management*<br>Triangle Shirtwaist Company fire |
| 1912 | Progressive party founded by Theodore Roosevelt<br>Woodrow Wilson elected president<br>Children's Bureau established in Department of Labor<br>Industrial Relations Commission founded |
| 1913 | Sixteenth Amendment (income tax) ratified<br>Underwood Tariff<br>Federal Reserve System established<br>Seventeenth Amendment (direct election of senators) passed |
| 1914 | Clayton Act<br>Federal Trade Commission Act<br>AFL has over 2 million members<br>Ludlow (Colorado) Massacre |

# CHAPTER 23
## AMERICA IN THE GREAT WAR

On April 7, 1917, the day after the United States officially declared war on Germany, Edmund P. Arpin, Jr., a young man of 22 from Grand Rapids, Wisconsin, decided to enlist in the army. The war seemed to provide a solution for his aimless drifting. It was not patriotism that led him to join the army but his craving for adventure and excitement. A month later, he was at Fort Sheridan, Illinois, along with hundreds of other eager young men, preparing to become an army officer. He felt a certain pride and sense of purpose, and especially a feeling of comradeship with the other men, but the war was a long way off.

Arpin finally arrived with his unit in Liverpool on December 23, 1917, aboard the *Leviathan*, a German luxury liner that the United States had interned when war was declared and pressed into service as a troop transport. In England, he discovered that American troops were not greeted as saviors. Hostility against the Americans simmered partly because of the previous unit's drunken brawls. Despite the efforts of the United States government to protect its soldiers from the sins of Europe, drinking seems to have been a preoccupation of the soldiers in Arpin's outfit. Arpin also learned something about French wine and women, but he spent most of the endless waiting time learning to play contract bridge.

Arpin saw some of the horror of war when he went to the front with a French regiment as an observer, but his own unit did not engage in combat until October 1918, when the war was almost over. He took part in the bloody Meuse-Argonne offensive, which helped end the war. But he discovered that war was not the heroic struggle of carefully planned campaigns that newspapers and books described. War was filled with misfired weapons, mixups, and erroneous attacks. Wounded in the leg in an assault on an unnamed hill and awarded a Distinguished Service Cross for his bravery, Arpin later learned that the order to attack had been recalled, but the word had not reached him in time.

When the armistice came, Arpin was recovering in a field hospital. He was disappointed that the war had ended so soon, but he was well enough to go to Paris to take part in the victory celebration and to explore some of the famous Paris restaurants and nightclubs. In many ways the highlight of his war experiences was not a battle or his medal but his adventure after the war was over. With a friend he went absent without leave and set out to explore Germany. They avoided the military police, traveled on a train illegally, and had many narrow escapes, but they made it back to the hospital without being arrested.

Edward Arpin was in the army for two years. He was one of 4,791,172 Americans who served in the army, navy, or marines. He was one of the 2 million who got overseas, and one of the 230,074 who were wounded. Some of his friends were among the 48,909 who were killed. When he was mustered out of the army in March 1919, he felt lost and confused. Being a civilian was not nearly as exciting as being in the army and visiting new and exotic places.

Arpin eventually settled down. He became a successful businessman, married, and raised a family. A member of the American Legion, he periodically went to conventions and reminisced with men from his division about their escapades in France. Although the war changed their lives in many ways, most would never again feel the same sense of common purpose and adventure. "I don't suppose any of us felt, before or since, so necessary to God and man," one veteran recalled.

This chapter will explore some of the ways the Great War (as Arpin's generation called it) altered the lives of ordinary Americans and also how it influenced the larger forces of history. We will look at the twisted path that led the United States into the war and at the wartime experiences of the men who went overseas as well as those who stayed at home. For some, the war was a great adventure; for others, it led to tragedy and despair. For most, the war was a patriotic crusade, and those opposed to the government's policies were often treated as traitors. The United States continued its rise during the war as a major world power, but the Russian Revolution of 1917 abruptly changed the nature of diplomacy and altered the international agenda. In 1919 and 1920, the Senate rejected membership in the League of Nations, yet the United States could not remain isolated from international problems. In some ways, the war years marked the triumph of progressive reform. In other ways, hate and intolerance characterized the period.

## THE EARLY YEARS OF THE WAR

Few Americans expected the Great War that erupted in Europe in the summer of 1914 to affect their lives or alter their comfortable world. When a Serbian student terrorist assassinated Archduke Franz Ferdinand of Austria-Hungary in Sarajevo, the capital of Bosnia, a country most Americans had never heard of, it precipitated a series of events leading to the most destructive war the world had ever known.

Despite Theodore Roosevelt's successful peacekeeping attempts in the first decade of the century (see Chapter 21), relationships among the European powers had not improved in any fundamental way. As European nations built up their military forces, they created a complex series of treaties with one another. Austria-Hungary and Germany (the Central Powers) became military allies, while Britain, France, Italy, and Russia (the Allied Powers) agreed to assist one another in case of attack. Americans stood by in disbelief as the assassination ultimately pulled all the major European powers into the vortex of war.

Education, science, social reform, and negotiation had supposedly replaced all-out war as a way of solving international disputes. "It looks as though we are going to be the age of treaties rather than the age of wars, the century of reason rather than the century of force," a leader of the American peace movement had declared only two years before. But as news of the German invasion of Belgium and reports of the first bloody battles began to reach the United States in late summer, it seemed to most Americans that madness had replaced reason. Europeans "have reverted to the condition of savage tribes roaming the forests and falling upon each other in a fury of blood and carnage," the New York Times announced.

The American sense that the nation would never succumb to the barbarism of war, combined with the knowledge that the Atlantic Ocean separated Europe from the United States, contributed to a great sense of relief after the first shock of the war began to wear off. The belief that the United States had no major stake in the outcome of the war and would stay uninvolved was reinforced by Woodrow Wilson's official proclamation of neutrality on August 4, 1914. The president was preoccupied with his own personal tragedy. His wife, Ellen Axson Wilson, died of Bright's disease, at the age of 54, the day after his proclamation. Two weeks later, still engulfed by his own grief, he urged all Americans to "be neutral in fact as well as in name . . . impartial in thought as well as in action." The United States, he argued, must preserve itself "fit and free" in order to do what "is honest and disinterested . . . for the peace of the world." But it was obvious that it was going to be difficult to stay uninvolved, at least emotionally, with the battlefields of Europe.

## American Reactions

Many social reformers who had devoted their lives to eliminating poverty and suffering despaired when they heard the news from Europe. Even during its first months, the war seemed to deflect energy away from reform. "We are three thousand miles away from the smoke and flames of combat, and have not a single regiment or battleship involved," remarked John Haynes Holmes, a liberal New York minister. "Yet who in the United States is thinking of recreation centers, improved housing or the minimum wage?" Settlement worker Lillian Wald responded to the threat of war by helping to lead a "woman's peace" parade down Fifth Avenue. Fifteen hundred women, all dressed in black, marched to protest the war. Jane Addams of Hull House helped to organize the Woman's Peace party. Drawing upon traditional conceptions of female character, she argued that women had a special responsibility to work for peace and to speak out against the blasphemy of war because women and children suffered most in any war, especially in a modern war where civilians as well as soldiers became targets.

While many people worked to promote an international plan to end the war through mediation, others could hardly wait to take part in the great adventure. Hundreds of young American men, most of them students or recent college graduates, volunteered to join ambulance

### European Alignments in 1914

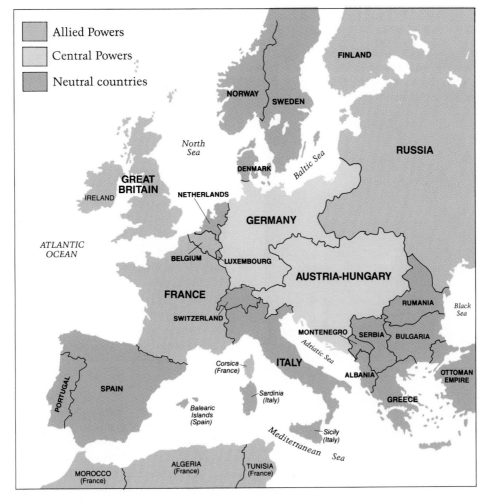

units, to take part in the war effort without actually fighting. Among the most famous of them were Ernest Hemingway, John Dos Passos, and E. E. Cummings, who later turned their wartime adventures into literary masterpieces. Others volunteered for service with the French Foreign Legion or joined the Lafayette Escadrille, a unit of pilots made up of well-to-do American volunteers attached to the French army. Many of these young men were inspired by an older generation who pictured war as a romantic and manly adventure. One college president talked of the chastening and purifying effect of armed conflict, and Theodore Roosevelt preached the virtues of the strenuous life and projected an image of war that was something like a football game where red-blooded American men could test their idealism and manhood.

Alan Seeger, a graduate of Harvard in 1910, was one of those who believed in the romantic and noble purpose of the war. He had been living

*The war in Europe appealed to the sense of adventure in many young American men. However, as in all wars, the women they left behind found it hard to say goodbye.*

in Paris since 1912, and when the war broke out, he quickly joined the French Foreign Legion. For the next two years, he wrote sentimental poetry, articles, and letters describing his adventures. "You have no idea how beautiful it is to see the troops undulating along the road . . . with the captains and lieutenants on horse back at the head of the companies," he wrote his mother. When Seeger was killed in 1916, he became an instant hero. Some called him "America's Rupert Brooke," after the gallant British poet who died early in the war.

Many Americans visualized war as a romantic struggle for honor and glory because the only conflict they remembered was the "splendid little war" of 1898. For them war meant Theodore Roosevelt charging up San Juan Hill and Commodore Dewey destroying the Spanish fleet in Manila harbor without the loss of an American life. Many older Americans recalled the Civil War, but the horrors of those years had faded, and only the memory of heroic triumphs remained. As Oliver Wendell Holmes, the Supreme Court justice who had been wounded in the Civil War, remarked, "War, when you are at it, is horrible and dull. It is only when time has passed that you see that its message was divine."

The reports from the battlefields, even during the first months of the war, should have indicated that the message was anything but divine, but most Americans ignored that. The fighting soon bogged down to a costly and bloody routine. Soldiers on both sides dug miles of trenches and strung out barbed wire to protect them. Thousands were killed in offenses that gained only a few yards or nothing at all. Jane Addams was troubled by other aspects of the struggle. When she returned from Europe in 1915, she reported the stories she had heard, that the young men were tired of war and that the troops were given alcohol and drugs to get into the spirit of the bayonet charge. But she was denounced as a silly old maid who knew nothing of the military and foolishly diminished the bravery and the honor of the soldiers.

Theodore Roosevelt was one of those who attacked Addams. Along with his friend Leonard Wood, the army chief of staff, he led a movement to prepare American men for war. Wood was determined that upper-class and college-educated men be ready to lead the nation into battle. In 1913, he established a camp for college men at Plattsburg, New York, to give them some experience with military life, with order, discipline, and command. By 1915, thousands had crowded into the Plattsburg Training Camp; even the mayor of New York enrolled. The young men learned to shoot rifles and to endure long marches and field exercises. But most of all, they associated with one another. Gathered around the campfire at night, they heard Wood and other veterans tell of winning glory and honor on the battlefield. In their minds at least, they were already leading a bayonet charge against the enemy, and the enemy was Germany.

## Difficulties of Neutrality

Despite Wilson's efforts to promote neutrality, most Americans favored the Allied cause. Some 8 million Austrian- and German-Americans lived in the United States, and some of them naturally supported the cause of the Central Powers. Yet most were so thoroughly Americanized that they had no particular interest in the war. The hatred of some of the Irish against the British led them to take sides not so much for Germany as against England. A few Swedish-Americans distrusted Russia so vehemently that they had difficulty in supporting the Allies. A number of American scholars, physicians, and intellectuals had fond memories of studying in Germany. To them, Germany meant great universities and cathedrals, music and culture. It also represented social planning, health insurance, unemployment compensation, and many of the programs for which the progressives had been fighting.

For most Americans, however, the ties of language and culture tipped the balance toward the Allies. After all, did not the English-speaking people of the world have special bonds and special responsibilities to promote civilization and ensure justice in the world? American connections with the French were not so close, but they were even more sentimental. The French, everyone remembered, had supported the American Revolution, and the French people had given the Statue of Liberty, the very symbol of American opportunity and democracy, to the United States.

Other reasons made real neutrality nearly impossible. Trade, both exports and imports, between the United States and the Allies was much more important than with the Central Powers, and people who controlled trade and ran the great financial institutions favored the Allies. Wilson's advisers, especially Robert Lansing and Edward House, openly supported the French and the British. Most of the newspapers in the country were also owned and edited by people with close ethnic, cultural, and sometimes economic ties to the British and the French. The newspapers were quick to picture the Germans as barbaric Huns and to accept and embellish the atrocity stories that came from the front, some of them planted by British propaganda experts. Gradually for Wilson, and probably for most Americans, the idea that all Europeans were barbaric and decadent was replaced with the perception that England and France were fighting for civilization and culture against the forces of Prussian evil. That did not mean, however, that the American people were willing to go to war to preserve the civilization. They were willing to let France and England do that.

Woodrow Wilson also sympathized with the Allies for practical and idealistic reasons. He wanted to keep the United States out of the war, but he had no objection to using force to promote diplomatic ends. "When men take up arms to set other men free, there is something sacred and holy in the warfare," he had written. Moreover, Wilson believed that by keeping the United States out of the war, he might control the peace. The war, he hoped, would show the futility of imperialism and of empires and would usher in a world where there would be free trade in products and in ideas. The United States had a special role to play in this new world and in leading toward an orderly international society. "We are the mediating nation of the world [and] we are therefore able to understand all nations."

To remain neutral while maintaining trade with the belligerents became increasingly difficult. To remain neutral while having something to say about the peace eventually became impossible. It was the need to trade and the desire to control the peace that finally led the United States into the Great War.

## World Trade and Neutrality Rights

The United States was part of an international economic community in 1914 in a way that it had not been a hundred years earlier during the last great world war, the Napoleonic Wars. The outbreak of war in Europe in the summer of 1914 caused an immediate economic panic in the United States. On July 31, 1914, the Wilson administration closed the stock exchange to prevent an unloading of European securities and a panic of selling. It also adopted a policy discouraging loans by American banks to belligerent nations. Most difficult was the matter of neutral trade. Wilson insisted on the rights of Americans to trade with both the Allies and the Central Powers, but Great Britain instituted an effective naval blockade, mined the North Sea, and began seizing American ships, even those carrying food and raw materials to Italy, the Netherlands, and other neutral nations. The first crisis that Wilson faced was whether or not to accept the British blockade, which went far beyond traditional international law. To do so would be to surrender one of the rights he believed in most ardently, the right of free trade.

Wilson eventually backed down and accepted British control of the sea. His conviction that the destinies of the United States and Great Britain were intertwined outweighed his idealistic belief in free trade. Consequently, American trade with the Central Powers declined between 1914 and 1916 from $169 million to just over $1 million and with the Allies increased during the same period from $825 million to over $3 billion. At the same time, the United States government eased the restrictions on private loans to belligerents. In March 1915, the House of Morgan loaned the French government $50 million, and in the fall of 1915, the French and British obtained an unsecured loan of $500 million from American banks. With dollars as well as sentiments, the United States gradually ceased to be neutral.

Germany retaliated against British control of the seas with submarine warfare. The new weapon, the U-boat (*Unterseeboot*), created un-

precedented problems. According to nineteenth-century international law, a belligerent warship was obligated to warn a passenger or merchant ship before attacking, but the chief advantage of the submarine was surprise. Rising to the surface to issue a warning would have meant being blown out of the water by an armed merchant ship.

On February 4, 1915, Germany announced a submarine blockade of the British Isles. Until Britain gave up its campaign to starve the German population, the Germans would sink even neutral ships. Wilson warned Germany that it would be held to "strict accountability" for illegal destruction of American ships or lives.

In March 1915, a British liner en route to Africa was sunk, with the loss of 103 lives, one of them an American. How should the United States respond? Wilson's advisers could not agree. Robert Lansing, a legal counsel at the State Department, urged the president to issue a strong protest, charging a breach of international

*The sinking of the Lusitania shocked Americans and illustrated the complexity and horror of modern warfare.*

law. William Jennings Bryan, the secretary of state, on the other hand argued that an American traveling on a British ship was guilty of "contributory negligence" and urged Wilson to prohibit all Americans from traveling on belligerent ships in the war zone. Wilson never did settle the dispute, for on May 7, 1915, a greater crisis erupted. A German U-boat torpedoed the British luxury liner *Lusitania* off the Irish coast. The liner, which was not armed but was carrying war supplies, sank within 18 minutes. Nearly 1,200 people, including many women and children, drowned. Among the dead were 128 Americans. Suddenly Americans were introduced to the horror of total war fought with modern weapons, a war that killed civilians, including women and children, just as easily as it killed soldiers.

The tragedy horrified most Americans. Newspapers denounced the act as "mass murder." One writer called the Germans "wild beasts." Some even called for a declaration of war. Wilson and most Americans had no idea of going to war in the spring of 1915, but the president refused to take Bryan's advice and prevent further loss of American lives by simply prohibiting all Americans from traveling on belligerent ships. Instead, he sent a series of protest notes demanding reparation for the loss of American lives and a pledge from Germany that it would cease attacking ocean liners without warning. Bryan resigned as secretary of state over the tone of the notes and charged that the United States was not being truly neutral. Some denounced Bryan as a traitor, but others charged that if the United States really wanted to stay out of the war, Bryan's position was more logical, consistent, and humane than Wilson's. The president replaced Bryan with Robert Lansing, who was much more eager than Bryan to oppose Germany, even at the risk of war.

The tense situation was eased late in 1915, when the German ambassador radioed from the battleship *Arabic* his promise (the *Arabic* pledge) that Germany would not attack ocean liners without warning. But the *Lusitania* crisis caused an outpouring of books and articles urging the nation to prepare for war. The National Security League, the most effective of the preparedness groups, called for a bigger army and

navy, a system of universal military training, and "patriotic education and national sentiment and service among the people of the United States."

Organizing on the other side were a group of progressive reformers and social workers who formed the American Union Against Militarism. They feared that those urging preparedness were deliberately setting out to destroy liberal social reform at home and to promote imperialism abroad.

But Wilson sympathized with the preparedness groups to the extent of asking Congress on November 4, 1915, for an enlarged and reorganized army. The bill met great opposition, especially from southern and western congressmen, but the Army Reorganization Bill that Wilson signed in June 1916 increased the regular army to just over 200,000 and integrated the National Guard into the defense structure. Few Americans, however, expected those young men to go to war. One of the most popular songs of 1916 was "I Didn't Raise My Boy to Be a Soldier." Even before American soldiers arrived in France, however, Wilson used the army and the marines in Mexico and Central America.

### Intervening in Mexico and Central America

Woodrow Wilson came to office in 1913 with a plan to promote liberal and humanitarian ends, not only in domestic policies but also in foreign affairs. Wilson had a vision of a world purged of imperialism, a world of free trade, but a world where American ideas and American products would find their way. Combining the zeal of a Christian missionary with the conviction of a college professor, he spoke of "releasing the intelligence of America for the service of mankind" and of enriching the commerce of the United States and the world "with the products of our mines, our farms, and our factories, with the creations of our thought and the fruits of our character." With his secretary of state, William Jennings Bryan, Wilson denounced the "big stick" and "dollar diplomacy" of the Roosevelt and Taft years. Yet in the end, his administration used force more systematically than those of his predecessors. The rhetoric was different, yet just as much as Roosevelt, Wilson was concerned with maintaining order and stability in the countries to the south in order to promote American economic and strategic interests.

At first Wilson's foreign policy seemed to be reversing some of the most callous aspects of dollar diplomacy in Central America. Bryan signed a treaty with Colombia in 1913 that agreed to pay $5 million for the loss of Panama and virtually apologized for the way the Roosevelt administration had treated Colombia. The Senate, not so willing to admit that the United States had been wrong, refused to ratify the treaty. But a new spirit permeated foreign policy.

The change in spirit proved illusory. After a disastrous civil war in the Dominican Republic, the United States offered in 1915 to take over the country's finances and police force. But when the Dominican leaders rejected a treaty making their country virtually a protectorate of the

*Although Wilson's intervention in Mexico drew criticism from many, others felt he was not forceful enough with the Huerta government.*

United States, Wilson ordered in the marines. They took control of the government in May 1916. Although the Americans built roads, schools, and hospitals, many people resented the American presence. In neighboring Haiti, the situation was somewhat different, but the results were similar. The marines landed at Port-au-Prince in the summer of 1915 to prop up a pro-American regime. In Nicaragua, the Wilson administration kept the marines sent by Taft in 1912 to keep the pro-American regime of Aldolfo Díaz in place and acquired the right, through treaty, to intervene at any time to preserve order and protect American property. Except for a brief period in the mid-1920s, the marines remained until 1933.

Wilson's policy of intervention ran into greatest difficulty in Mexico, a country that had been ruled for more than 40 years by Porfirio Díaz, a dictator who kept order and welcomed American investors. Indeed, by 1910, more than 40,000 American citizens lived in Mexico, and more than a billion dollars of American money was invested in the country. Americans controlled 75 percent of the mines, 70 percent of the rubber, and 60 percent of the oil. In 1911, however, Francisco Madero, a reformer who wanted to destroy the privileges of the upper classes, overthrew Díaz. Two years later, he was deposed and murdered by order of Victoriano Huerta, the head of the army. This was the situation when Wilson became president.

To the shock of many diplomats and businessmen, Wilson refused to recognize the Huerta government. Everyone admitted that Huerta was a ruthless dictator, but diplomatic recognition, the exchange of ambassadors, and the regulation of trade and communication had never meant approval. In the world of business and diplomacy, it merely meant that a particular government was in power. But Wilson, to the great concern of American businessmen, set out to remove what he called a "government of butchers." "The United States Government intends not merely to force Huerta from power," he wrote to a British diplomat, "but also to exert every influence it can to secure Mexico a better government under which all contracts and business concessions will be safer than they have ever been."

At first Wilson applied diplomatic pressure. Then, using a minor incident as an excuse, he asked Congress for power to involve American troops if necessary. Few Mexicans liked Huerta, but they liked even less the idea that a *Norte Americano* was interfering in their affairs. Hence they rallied around the dictator. As they had in 1847, the United States landed troops at Veracruz. Angry Mexican mobs destroyed American property wherever they could find it. Many Europeans and Latin Americans as well as Americans were outraged by Wilson's action.

Wilson's military intervention succeeded in forcing Huerta out of power, but a civil war between forces led by Venustiano Carranza and those led by General Francisco "Pancho" Villa ensued. When Villa made a raid on Columbus, New Mexico, in March 1916, Wilson sent an expedition led by Brigadier General John Pershing to track down Villa and his men. The strange and comic scene developed of an American army charging 300 miles into Mexico unable to catch the retreating villain. Not surprisingly,

given the history of Mexican-American relations, the Mexicans feared that Pershing's army was planning to occupy northern Mexico. Carranza shot off a bitter note to Wilson accusing him of threatening war, but Wilson refused to withdraw the troops. Tensions rose. An American patrol attacked a Mexican garrison, with loss of life on both sides. Just as war seemed inevitable, Wilson agreed to call the troops home and to recognize the Carranza government. But this was in January 1917, and if it had not been for the growing crisis in Europe, it is likely that war would have resulted.

The tragedy was that Wilson, who idealistically wanted the best for the people of Mexico and Central America and who thought he knew exactly what they needed, managed to intervene too often and too blatantly to protect the strategic and economic interests of the United States. In the process, his policy alienated one-time friends of the United States. His policies would contribute to future difficulties in both Latin America and Europe.

## United States Involvement in the Caribbean

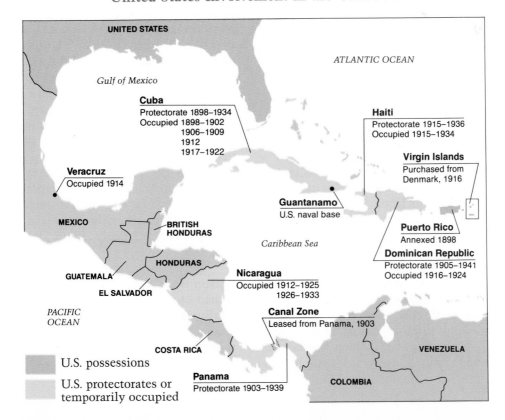

## THE UNITED STATES ENTERS THE WAR

America's decision to go to war in 1917 was opposed by a significant minority, and the decision would remain controversial when it was reexamined in the 1930s. But once involved, the government and the American people made the war into a patriotic crusade that touched on all aspects of American life.

### The Election of 1916

American political campaigns do not stop even in times of international crisis. As 1915 turned to 1916, Wilson had to think of reelection as well as of preparedness, submarine warfare, and the Mexican campaign. At first glance, the president's chances of reelection seemed poor. He had won in 1912 only because Theodore Roosevelt and the Progressive party had split the Republican vote. If those who had supported the Progressives in 1912 returned to the Republican fold, Wilson's chances were slim indeed. Because the Progressive party had done very badly in the 1914 congressional elections, Roosevelt gave signs that he would seek the Republican nomination rather than be a third-party candidate.

Wilson was aware that he had to win over those who had voted for Roosevelt in 1912. In January 1916, he appointed Louis D. Brandeis to the Supreme Court. The first Jew ever to sit on the highest court, Brandeis was confirmed over the strong opposition of many legal organizations. His appointment pleased the social justice progressives because he had always championed reform causes. They made it clear to Wilson that the real test for them was whether or not he supported the anti-child labor and workmen's compensation bills pending in Congress.

In August, Wilson put heavy pressure on Congress and obtained passage of the Workmen's Compensation Bill, which gave some protection to federal employees, and the Keatings-Owen Child Labor Bill, which prohibited the shipment in interstate commerce of goods produced by children under 14 and in some cases under 16. This bill, which was later declared unconstitutional, was a far-reaching proposal that for the first time used federal control over interstate commerce to dictate the conditions under which businessmen could manufacture products.

To attract farm support, Wilson pushed for passage of the Federal Farm Loan Act, which created 12 Federal Farm Loan Banks to extend long-term credit to farmers. Urged on by organized labor as well as by many progressives, he supported the Adamson Act, which established an eight-hour day for all interstate railway workers. Within a few months, Wilson reversed the New Freedom doctrines he had earlier supported and brought the force of the federal government into play on the side of reform. The flurry of legislation early in 1916 provided one climax to the progressive movement. The strategy seemed to work, for progressives of all kinds enthusiastically endorsed the president.

The election of 1916, however, turned as much on foreign affairs as on domestic policy. The Republicans ignored Theodore Roosevelt and nominated instead the staid and respectable Charles Evans Hughes, a former governor of New York and Supreme Court justice. Their platform called for "straight and honest neutrality" and "adequate preparedness." In a bitter campaign, Hughes attacked Wilson for not more vigorously promoting American rights in Mexico and for giving in to the unreasonable demands of labor. Wilson, on his part, implied that the election of Hughes would mean war with both Mexico and Germany and that his opponents were somehow not "100 percent Americans." As the campaign progressed, the peace issue became more and more important, and the cry "He kept us out of war" echoed through every Democratic rally. It was a slogan that would seem strangely ironic in only a few months.

The election was extremely close. In fact, Wilson went to bed on election night thinking he had lost the presidency. The election was not finally decided until it was learned that California had gone Democratic (by less than 4,000 votes). Wilson won by carrying the West as well as the South.

## Deciding for War

Wilson's victory in 1916 was generally interpreted as a mandate for staying out of the European war. But the campaign rhetoric made the president nervous. He had tried to emphasize Americanism, not neutrality. As he told one of his advisers, "I can't keep the country out of war. They talk of me as though I were a god. Any little German lieutenant can put us into war at any time by some calculated outrage."

People who supported Wilson as a peace candidate applauded in January 1917 when he went before the Senate to clarify the American position on a negotiated settlement of the war. The German government had earlier indicated that it might be willing to go to the conference table. Wilson outlined a plan for a negotiated settlement before either side had achieved victory. It would be a peace among equals, "a peace without victory," a peace without indemnities and annexations. The peace settlement Wilson outlined contained his idealistic vision of the postwar world as an open marketplace, and it could have worked only if Germany and the Allies were willing to settle for a draw instead of victory.

The German government refused to accept a peace without victory, probably because early in 1917 the German leaders thought they could win. On January 31, 1917, the Germans announced that they would sink on sight any ship, belligerent or neutral, sailing toward England or France. A few days later, in retaliation, the United States broke diplomatic relations with Germany. But Wilson—and probably most Americans—still hoped to avert war without shutting off American trade. As goods began to pile up in warehouses and American ships stayed idly in port, however, pressure mounted to arm American merchant ships. An intercepted telegram from the German foreign secretary, Arthur Zimmermann, to the German minister in Mexico increased anti-German feeling. If war broke out, the German minister was to offer Mexico the territory it had lost in Texas, New Mexico, and Arizona in 1848. In return, Mexico would join Germany in a war against the United States. When this telegram was released to the press on March 1, 1917, many Americans demanded war against Germany. Wilson still hesitated.

As the country waited on the brink of war, news of revolution in Russia reached Washington. That event would prove as important as the war itself. The March 1917 revolution in Russia was a spontaneous uprising of the workers, housewives, and soldiers against the czarist government because of the intolerable conditions that the war had brought. The army had suffered staggering losses at the front. The civilian population was in desperate condition. Food was scarce, and the railroads and industry had nearly collapsed. The rebels overthrew Czar Nicholas II and established a republic led by Alexander Kerensky. At first Wilson and other Americans were enthusiastic. The overthrow of the feudal aristocracy seemed in the spirit of the American Revolution. Wilson hoped the new regime would fight the war more vigorously against Germany and then join in organizing a world free of imperialism and dictatorship. But within months, the revolution took a more extreme turn. Lenin (whose real name was Vladimir Ilyich Ulyanov) returned from exile in Switzerland and led the radical Bolsheviks to victory over the Kerensky regime in November 1917.

Lenin, a brilliant lawyer and revolutionary tactician, was a follower of Karl Marx (1818–1883). Marx, a German intellectual and radical philosopher, had described the alienation of the working class under capitalism and predicted a growing split between the proletariat (the unpropertied workers) and the capitalists. Lenin extended Marx's ideas and argued that capitalist nations would eventually be forced to go to war over raw materials and markets. Believing that capitalism and imperialism went hand in hand, Lenin, unlike Wilson, argued that the only way to end imperialism was to end capitalism. It was the new Soviet Union, not the United States, that was the model for the rest of the world to follow; communism, Lenin predicted, would eventually dominate the globe. The Russian Revolution posed a threat to Wilson's vision of the world and to his plan to bring the United States into the war "to make the world safe for democracy."

More disturbing than the first news of revolution in Russia, however, was the situation in the North Atlantic, where German U-boats sank five American ships between March 12 and March 21, 1917. Wilson no longer hesitated. On April 2, he urged Congress to declare war. His words conveyed a sense of mission about the United States' entry into the war, but Wilson's voice was low and somber. "It is a fearful thing," he concluded, "to lead this great, peaceful people into war, into the most terrible and disastrous of all wars. . . ." The war resolution swept the Senate 82 to 6 and the House of Representatives 373 to 50.

Once war was declared, most Americans forgot their doubts and joined the glorious cause. Young men rushed to enlist; women volun-

teered to become nurses or to serve in other ways. Towns were united by patriotism.

### A Patriotic Crusade

The declaration of war did not unite everyone in the country behind the war effort. Some pacifists and socialists opposed the war, while a black newspaper, *The Messenger*, decried the conflict. "The real enemy is War rather than Imperial Germany," wrote Randolph Bourne, a young New York intellectual. "We are for peace," Morris Hillquit, a socialist leader, announced. "We are unalterably opposed to the killing of our manhood and the draining of our resources in a bewildering pursuit of an incomprehensible 'democracy' . . . a pursuit which begins by suppressing the freedom of speech and press and public assemblage, and by stifling legitimate political criticism." "To whom does war bring prosperity . . . ?" Senator George Norris of Nebraska asked on the Senate floor. "Not to the soldier . . . not to the broken hearted widow . . . not to the mother who weeps at the death of her brave boy. . . . War brings no prosperity to the great mass of common patriotic citizens. We are going into war upon the command of gold. . . . I feel that we are about to put the dollar sign on the American flag."

For most Americans in the spring of 1917, the war seemed remote. A few days after the war was declared, a Senate committee listened to a member of the War Department staff list the vast quantities of materials needed to supply an American army in France. One of the senators, jolted awake, exclaimed, "Good Lord! You're not going to send soldiers over there, are you?"

To convince senators and citizens alike that the war was real and that American participation was just, Wilson appointed a Committee on Public Information, headed by George Creel, a muckraking journalist from Denver. The Creel Committee launched a gigantic propaganda campaign to persuade the American public that the United States had gone to war to promote the cause of freedom and democracy and to prevent the barbarous hordes from overrunning Europe and eventually the Western Hemisphere. The committee organized a national network of "four-minute men," local citizens with the proper political views who could be used to

*The declaration of war gave Americans a sense of purpose and adventure that was created in part by recruiting posters and government propaganda.*

whip up a crowd to a frenzy of patriotic enthusiasm. These local rallies, enlivened by bands and parades, urged people of all ages to support the war effort and to buy war bonds. The Creel Committee also produced literature for the schools, much of it prepared by college professors who volunteered their services. One pamphlet, titled *Why America Fights Germany*, described in lurid detail a possible German invasion of the United States. The committee also prepared short propaganda movies.

The patriotic crusade soon became stridently anti-German and anti-immigrant. Most school districts banned the teaching of German. In the words of the California Board of Education, German was "a language that disseminates the ideals of autocracy, brutality and hatred." Anything German became suspect. Sauerkraut was renamed "liberty cabbage," and German measles became "liberty measles." Music by German composers was often banned from symphony concerts. Many German-Americans lost their jobs and were ostracized by their neighbors. South Dakota prohibited the use of German on the telephone, and in Iowa a state official announced, "If their language is disloyal, they should be imprisoned. If their acts are disloyal, they should be shot." Occasionally the patriotic fever led to violence. The most notorious incident happened in St. Louis, which had a large German population. Robert Prager, a young German-American, was seized by a mob in April 1918, stripped of his clothes, dressed in an American flag, marched through the streets, and lynched. The eventual trial led to the acquittal of the ringleaders on the grounds that the lynching was a "patriotic murder."

The Wilson administration, of course, did not condone violence and murder, but war always leads to extremist behavior. Not only German-Americans were suspect, but also radicals, pacifists, or anyone who raised doubts about the American war efforts or the government's policies. In New York, the black editors of *The Messenger* were given 2½-year jail sentences for the paper's article "Pro-Germanism Among Negroes." In Wisconsin, Senator Robert La Follette, who had voted against the war resolution, was burned in effigy and censored by the faculty of the University of Wisconsin. At a number of universities, professors were dismissed, sometimes for as little as questioning the morality or the necessity of America's participation in the war. James M. Cattell, one of the country's leading psychologists, lost his job at Columbia University for mildly criticizing American policies and for being a nonconformist. Heated patriotism, as it often does, led to fear of subversion and irrational hate.

On June 15, 1917, Congress, at Wilson's behest, passed the Espionage Act, which provided imprisonment of up to 20 years or a fine of up to $10,000 (or both) for persons who incited rebellion, made false reports to help the enemy, or tried to obstruct the recruiting operation or the draft. The act also allowed the postmaster general to prohibit from the mails any matter he thought advocated treason or forcible resistance to United States laws. The act was used to stamp out dissent, even to discipline anyone who questioned the administration's policies. Using the act, Postmaster General Albert S. Burleson banned the magazines *American Socialist* and *The Masses* from the mails.

Congress later added the Trading with the Enemy Act and a Sedition Act. The latter prohibited disloyal, profane, scurrilous, or abusive remarks about the form of government, flag, or uniform of the United States. It even prohibited citizens from opposing the purchase of war bonds. In the most famous case tried under the act, Eugene Debs was sentenced to ten years in prison for opposing the war. In 1919, the Supreme Court upheld the conviction, even though Debs had not explicitly urged the violation of the draft laws. Not all Americans agreed with the decision, for while still in prison Debs polled close to one million votes in the presidential election of 1920. In the end, 2,168 persons were prosecuted and 1,055 were convicted under the Espionage and Sedition acts. But these figures do not include the thousands informally persecuted and deprived of their liberties and their right of free speech by Americans who succumbed to the fear brought on by wartime hysteria.

A group of amateur loyalty enforcers, called the American Protective League, cooperated with the Justice Department. They often reported nonconformists and anyone who did not appear 100 percent loyal. People were arrested for criticizing the Red Cross or a government agency. One woman was sent to prison for writing, "I am for the people and the government is for the profiteers." Ricardo Flores Magon, a leading Mexican-American labor organizer in the Southwest, was sentenced to 20 years in prison for criticizing Wilson's Mexican policy. In Cincinnati, a pacifist minister, Herbert S. Bigelow, was dragged from the stage where he was about to give a speech, taken to a wooded area by a mob, bound and gagged, and whipped. The attorney general of the United States, speaking of those who opposed the government policies, said, "May God have mercy on them for they need expect none from an outraged people and an avenging government."

The Civil Liberties Bureau, an outgrowth of the American Union Against Militarism, protested the blatant abridgment of freedom of speech during the war, but the protests fell on deaf ears at the Justice Department and in the White House. Rights and freedoms have been reduced or suspended during all wars, but the massive disregard for basic rights was greater during World War I than during the Civil War. This was ironic because Wilson had often written and spoken of the need to preserve freedom of speech and civil liberties. During the war, however, he tolerated the vigilante tactics of his own Justice Department, offering no more than feeble protest. Wilson was so convinced his cause was just that he ignored the rights of those who opposed him.

### Raising an Army

How should a democracy recruit an army in time of war? The debate over a volunteer army versus the draft had been going on for several years before the United States entered the war. People who favored some form of universal military service argued that college graduates, farmers, and young men from the slums of eastern cities could learn from one another as they trained together. The opponents of a draft pointed out that people making such claims were most often the college graduates, who assumed they would command the boys from the slums. The draft was not democratic, they

argued, but the tool of an imperialist power bent on ending dissent. "Back of the cry that America must have compulsory service or perish," one of the opponents charged, "is a clearly thought out and heavily backed project to mold the United States into an efficient, orderly nation, economically and politically controlled by those who know what is good for the people." Memories of massive draft riots during the Civil War also led some to fear a draft.

Wilson and his secretary of war, Newton Baker, both initially opposed the draft. Baker, formerly a progressive mayor of Cleveland, was rumored to be a pacifist. In the end, both Wilson and Baker concluded that the draft was the most efficient way to organize military manpower. Ironically, it was Theodore Roosevelt who tipped Wilson in favor of the draft. Even though his health was failing and he was blind in one eye, the old Rough Rider was determined to recruit a volunteer division and lead it personally against the Germans. The officers would be Ivy League graduates and men trained at the Plattsburg camp, with some places reserved for the descendants of prominent Civil War generals and a few French officers, in memory of Lafayette. There would be a German-American regiment and a black regiment (led by white officers). Roosevelt pictured himself leading this mixed but brave and virile group to France to restore the morale of the Allied troops and win the war.

The thought of his old enemy Theodore Roosevelt blustering about Europe so frightened Wilson that he gave his support to the Selective Service Act in part, at least, to prevent such volunteer outfits as Roosevelt planned. Yet controversy filled Congress over the bill, and the House finally insisted that the minimum age for draftees should be 21, not 18. On June 5, 1917, some 9.5 million men between the ages of 21 and 31 registered, with little protest. In August 1918, the act was extended to men between the ages of 18 and 45. In all, over 24 million men registered and over 2.8 million were inducted, making up over 75 percent of those who served in the war.

The draft worked well, but it was not quite the perfect system that Wilson claimed. Most Americans took seriously their obligation of "service" during time of war, but there were flaws in the system. Because so much of the control was vested in the local draft boards, favoritism and political influence allowed some to stay at home. Draft protests erupted in a few places, the largest in Oklahoma, where a group of tenant farmers planned a march on Washington to take over the government and end the "rich man's war." The Green Corn Rebellion, as it came to be called, died before it got started. A local posse arrested about 900 rebels and took them off to jail.

Some men escaped the draft. Some were deferred because of war-related jobs, while oth-ers resisted by claiming exemption for reasons of conscience. The Selective Service Act did exempt men who belonged to religious groups that forbade members from engaging in war, but religious motivation was often difficult to define, and nonreligious conscientious objection was even more complicated. Thousands of conscientious objectors were inducted. Some served in noncombat positions; others went to prison. Roger Baldwin, a leading pacifist, was jailed for refusing military service. But Norman Thomas, a socialist, urged young men to register for the draft and to express their dissent within the democratic process.

## THE MILITARY EXPERIENCE

Family albums in millions of American homes contain photographs of young men in uniform, some of them stiff and formal, some of them candid shots of soldiers on leave in Paris or Washington or Chicago. These photographs testify to the importance of the war to a generation of Americans. For years afterward, the men and women who lived through the war sang "Tipperary," "There's a Long, Long Trail," and "Pack Up Your Troubles" and remembered rather sentimentally what the war had meant to them. For some, the war was a tragic event. But for others it was a liberating experience and the most exciting period in their lives.

### The American Doughboy

The typical soldier, according to the Medical Department, stood 5 feet 7½ inches tall, weighed 141½ pounds, and was about 22 years old. He was given a physical exam, an intelligence test, and a psychological test, and he probably watched a movie called *Fit to Fight,* which warned him about the dangers of venereal disease. The majority of the American soldiers had not attended high school. The median amount of education for native whites was 6.9 years and for immigrants 4.7 years but was only 2.6 years for southern blacks. As many as 31 percent of the recruits were declared illiterate, but the tests were so primitive that they proba-bly tested social class more than anything else. More than half the recent immigrants from eastern Europe ranked in the "inferior" category. Fully 29 percent of the recruits were rejected as physically unfit for service, which shocked the health experts.

Most World War I soldiers were ill-educated and unsophisticated young men, quite different from Ernest Hemingway's heroes or even from Edmund Arpin. They came from the farms, small towns, and urban neighborhoods. They came from all social classes and ethnic groups, yet most were transformed into soldiers. In the beginning, however, they didn't look the part because uniforms and equipment were in short supply. Many men had to wear their civilian clothes for months, and they often wore out their shoes before they were issued army boots. "It was about two months or so before I looked really like a soldier," one recruit remembered.

The military experience changed the lives and often the attitudes of many young men. Women also served with the army. Some went overseas as nurses and telephone operators. Others volunteered for a tour of duty with the Red Cross, the Salvation Army, or the YMCA. Yet the military experience in World War I was predominantly male. Even going to training camp was a new and often frightening experience. A leave in Paris or London, or even in New York or New Orleans, was an adventure to

*Many American women served overseas as nurses with the Red Cross or Salvation Army. They also worked in field kitchens.*

remember for a lifetime. Even those who never got overseas or who never saw a battle would recall their wartime experiences with growing fondness as the years went by. They joined the American Legion, whose purpose was "to preserve the memories and incidents of our associates in the great war . . . to consecrate and sanctify our comradeship." They also experienced more subtle changes. Many soldiers saw their first movie in the army or had their first contact with trucks and cars. Military service changed the shaving habits of a generation because the new safety razor was standard issue. The war also led to the growing popularity of the cigarette rather than the pipe or cigar because a pack of cigarettes fitted comfortably into a shirt pocket and a cigarette could be smoked during a short break. The war experience also caused many men to abandon the pocket watch for the more convenient wristwatch, which had been considered effeminate before the war.

### The Black Soldier

Shortly after the United States entered the war, W. E. B. Du Bois, the black leader and editor of *The Crisis,* urged blacks to close ranks and support the war. Although Du Bois did not speak

for all blacks, he and others predicted that the war experience would cause the "walls of prejudice" to crumble gradually before "the onslaught of common sense." The walls did not crumble, and the black soldier was never treated equally or with fairness during the war. But many blacks served with distinction, and many had their own perceptions changed by the army experience. Blacks had served in all American wars, and many fought valiantly in the Civil War and the Spanish-American War. Yet black soldiers had most often been assigned to menial tasks and kept in segregated units. Black leaders hoped it would be different this time.

The Selective Service Act made no mention of race, and blacks in most cases registered without protest. But many whites, especially in the South, feared having too many blacks trained in the use of arms. This fear was increased in August 1917, when racial violence erupted in Houston, Texas, involving soldiers from the regular army's all-black 24th Infantry Division. Harassed by the Jim Crow laws, which had been tightened for their benefit, a group of soldiers went on a rampage, killing 17 white civilians. Over 100 soldiers were court martialed; 13 were condemned to death. Those

*Assigned to segregated units, black soldiers were also excluded from white recreation facilities. Here black women in Newark, New Jersey, aided by white social workers, sponsored a club to entertain "their men in the service."*

convicted were hanged three days later before any appeals could be filed.

This violence, coming only a month after a race riot in East St. Louis, Illinois, brought on in part by the migration of blacks from the South to the area, caused great concern about the handling of black soldiers. Secretary of War Baker made it clear that the army had no intention of upsetting the status quo, but the appointment of Emmett J. Scott, secretary of Tuskegee Institute, as a special assistant to Baker reassured some blacks. Yet the basic government policy was of complete segregation and careful distribution of black units throughout the country.

Some blacks were trained as junior officers and were assigned to the all-black 92nd Division, where the high-ranking officers remained white. But a staff report decided that "the mass of colored drafted men cannot be used for combatant troops." Most of the black soldiers, including about 80 percent of those sent to France, were used as stevedores and common laborers. Usually they were supervised by white noncommissioned officers. "Everyone who has handled colored labor knows that the gang bosses must be white if any work is to be done," remarked Lieutenant Colonel U. S. Grant, the grandson of the Civil War general. Other black soldiers were used as servants, drivers, and porters for the white officers. It was a demeaning and ironic policy for a government that advertised itself as standing for justice, honor, and democracy.

## Over There

The war that Wilson declared the war to make the world safe for democracy was at once a traditional and a revolutionary struggle. It was the last time that cavalry played any important part in battle and the first to dramatize the significance of technology to victory. As the British cavalry charged German lines with sabers aloft, machine guns mowed them down, just as machine guns slaughtered the thousands of soldiers who leaped from their trenches in vain efforts to win a few yards of enemy territory. Airplanes, used early in the war only for observation, by 1918 were creating terror below with their bombs. Tanks made their first appear-

ance in 1916. Chemical warfare in the form of poison gas introduced a whole new dimension to warfare and dramatized that the day of chivalry had ended.

To this ghastly war, in which both attackers and defenders suffered huge numbers of casualties, Americans made important contributions. In fact, without their help, the Allies might have lost. But the American contribution was most significant only in the war's final months. When the United States entered the conflict in the spring of 1917, the fighting had dragged on for nearly three years. After a few rapid advances and retreats, the war in western Europe had settled down to a tactical and bloody stalemate. The human costs of trench warfare were horrifying. In one battle in 1916, a total of 60,000 British soldiers were killed or wounded in a single day, yet the battle lines did not move an inch. By the spring of 1917, the British and French armies were down to their last reserves. Italy's army had nearly collapsed. In the east, the Russians were engaged in a bitter internal struggle, and in November the Bolshevik Revolution would cause them to sue for a separate peace, freeing the German divisions on the eastern front to join in one final assault in the west.

*World War I was incredibly costly in lives lost and property destroyed.*

Historians have discovered that movies, if carefully studied, reveal dress and hairstyles, customs, social attitudes, and other aspects of life during the period in which they were made. Even more revealing in some ways are films designed explicitly to educate and indoctrinate. Most of the early films were made simply to entertain, but very quickly government officials, businessmen, and others realized the power of the new medium. Thomas Edison made propaganda films about the dangers of tuberculosis as early as 1910, and by the time of World War I, others were making short films to show the public how to prevent everything from typhoid fever to tooth decay.

After the United States entered World War I, the Commission on Training Camp Activities made a film called *Fit to Fight* that was shown to almost all male servicemen. It was an hourlong drama following the careers of five young recruits. Four of them, by associating with the wrong people and through lack of willpower, caught venereal disease. The film interspersed a simplistic plot with grotesque shots of men with various kinds of venereal disease. The film also glorified athletics, especially football and boxing, as a substitute for sex. It emphasized the importance of patriotism and purity for America's fighting force. In one scene, Bill Hale, the only soldier in the film to remain pure, breaks up a peace rally and beats up the speaker. "It serves you right," the pacifist's sister remarks; "I'm glad Billy punched you."

*Fit to Fight* was so successful that the government commissioned another film, *The End of the Road*, to be shown to women who lived near military bases. The film is the story of Vera and Mary. Although still reflecting progressive attitudes, the film's message is somewhat different from *Fit to Fight*. Vera's strict mother tells her daughter that sex is dirty, leaving Vera to pick up "distorted and obscene" information about sex on the street. She falls victim to the first man who comes along and contracts a venereal disease. Mary, on the other hand, has an enlightened mother who explains where babies come from. When Mary grows up, she rejects marriage and becomes a professional woman, a nurse. In the end, she falls in love with a doctor and gets married. *The End of the Road* has a number of subplots and many frightening shots of syphilitic sores. Several illustrations show the dangers of indiscriminate sex. Among

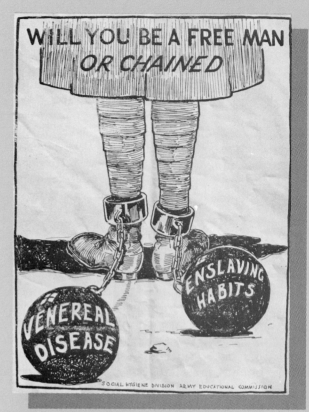

*Social hygiene poster issued by the U.S. Commission on Training Camps during World War I*

other things, the film preached the importance of science, sex education, and the need for self-control. A quotation from the description of *The End of the Road* provided by the government for those who used the film is reprinted here.

What do the anti-VD films tell us about the attitudes, ideas, and prejudices of the World War I period? What images do they project about men, women, and sex roles? Would you find the same kind of moralism, patriotism, and fear of VD today? Have attitudes toward sex changed? Were you shown sex education films in school? Were they like these? Who sponsored them? What can historians learn from such films? How do other movies—popular feature films as well as documentaries—reflect American culture and American values today?

*Scenes from the War Department Commission on Training Camps' film* Fit to Fight

## THE END OF THE ROAD

This is an extraordinary motion picture prepared by the War Department Commission on Training Camp Activities as a part of the Social Hygiene campaign of the United States Government. It handles certain social and sex problems in their relation to women with a frank treatment which is a direct consequence of a new attitude engendered by the war.

These problems have been made at once more acute and more complex by the war. War conditions have disturbed the emotional equilibrium of the people and have tended to multiply the intricacies of sex reactions, particularly among young girls brought into social contact with the soldier. The film is intended to stimulate and strengthen the efforts being made to teach the womanhood and girlhood of our country the vital need of right social adjustments. . . .

Inasmuch as one of the most terrible and socially vital results of sexual misconduct is venereal infection, this has been advisedly stressed, though not accentuated. Throughout, the effort has been to make disease appear to be, as it actually is in life, the often inevitable price of loose living, ignorance, thoughtlessness, and irresponsibility. Realism of the most striking sort is used in this picture. Some clinical cases shown, for example, were photographed in the women's wards, Blackwell's Island, New York.

The fundamental idea of the film is educational, but, quite inevitably, it contains a definite trend throughout towards the moral inspiration which follows any exposition of fine examples and standards of living contrasted with those of opposite stamp.

The film may with propriety be shown to mixed audiences, whether of boys and girls, or adults, though it was designed primarily for girls and women. It presents a valuable lesson to boys and men, for it tellingly illustrates the tragedies resulting from the so-called double standard. Parents, especially mothers, will find in the film the answer to many of their questions and doubts.

The Allies desperately needed fresh American troops, but those troops had to be trained, equipped, and transported to the front. That took time.

A few token American regiments arrived in France in the summer of 1917 under the command of General John J. "Black Jack" Pershing, a tall, serious, Missouri-born graduate of West Point. He had fought in the Spanish-American War and led the Mexican expedition in 1916. When the first troops marched in a parade in Paris on July 4, 1917, the emotional French crowd shouted, "Vive les Américains," and showered them with flowers, hugs, and kisses. But the American commanders were worried that many of their soldiers were so inexperienced that they did not even know how to march, let alone fight. The first Americans saw action near Verdun in October 1917. By March 1918, over 300,000 American soldiers had

reached France, and by November 1918, more than 2 million.

One reason that the United States forces were slow to see actual combat was Pershing's insistence that they be kept separate from the French and British divisions. An exception was made for four regiments of black soldiers who were assigned to the French army. Despite the American warning to the French that they should not overpraise the black troops or "spoil the Negroes" by allowing them to mix with the French civilian population, these soldiers fought so well that the French later awarded three of the regiments the Croix de Guerre, their highest unit citation.

In the spring of 1918, with Russia out of the war and with the British blockade becoming more and more effective, the Germans launched an all-out, desperate offensive to win the war before full American military and industrial

## The Western Front of the Great War in 1918

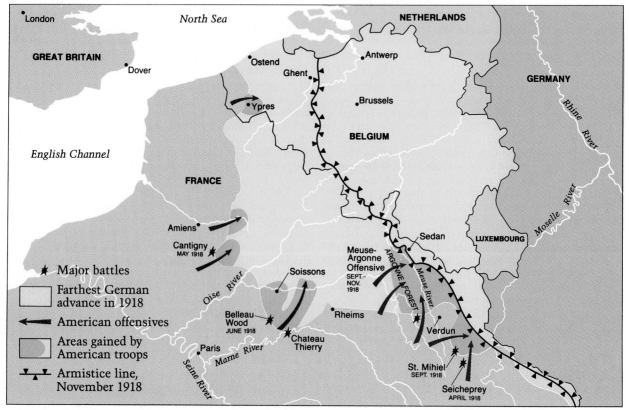

power became a factor in the contest. By late May, the Germans had pushed to within 50 miles of Paris. American troops were thrown into the line and helped stem the German advance at Château-Thierry, Belleau Wood, and Cantigny, place names that would later be endowed with almost sacred significance by the proud survivors. Americans also took part in the Allied offensive led by General Ferdinand Foch of France in the summer of 1918.

In September, over one-half million American troops were involved in the first distinctly American offensive action near St. Mihiel. One enlisted man remembered how he "saw a sight which I shall never forget. It was zero hour and in one instant the entire front as far as the eye could reach in either direction was a sheet of flame, while the heavy artillery made the earth quake." The Americans suffered over 7,000 casualties, but they captured more than 16,000 German soldiers. The victory, even if it came against exhausted and retreating German troops, seemed to vindicate Pershing's insistence on a separate American army. The British and French commanders were critical of what they considered the disorganized, inexperienced, and ill-equipped American forces. They especially denounced the quality of the American high-ranking officers. One French report in the summer of 1918 suggested that it would take at least a year before the American army could become a "serious fighting force."

In a few months more, the war would be over. Over a million American soldiers took part in the final Allied offensive near the Meuse River and the Argonne forest. It was in this battle that Edmund Arpin was wounded. Many of the men were inexperienced, and some, who had been rushed through training as "90-day wonders," had never handled a rifle before arriving in France. There were many disastrous mistakes and bungled situations. The most famous blunder was the "lost battalion." An American unit advanced beyond its support and was cut off and surrounded. The battalion suffered 70 percent casualties before it could be rescued.

The performance of the all-black 92nd Division was also controversial. The 92nd had been deliberately dispersed around the United States and had never trained as a unit. Its higher

officers were white and constantly asked to be transferred. Many of its men were only partly trained and poorly equipped, and they were constantly being called away from their military duties to work as stevedores and common laborers. At the last minute during the Meuse-Argonne offensive, the 92nd was assigned to a particularly difficult position on the line. They had no maps and no wire-cutting equipment. Battalion commanders lost contact with their men, and on several occasions the men broke and ran in the face of enemy fire. The whole division was withdrawn in disgrace, and this incident was used for years to argue that black soldiers would never make good fighting men. Those who made this argument forgot the difficulties under which the 92nd fought and the valor and courage shown by those troops assigned to the French army.

With few exceptions, the Americans fought hard and well. The French and British criticized American inexperience and disarray, but they admired their exuberance, their "pep," and marveled at their extravagance. The ability to move huge numbers of men and equipment efficiently was a major American achievement. One British officer, surveying the abundance of American men and materiel, remarked, "For any particular work they seem to have about five times as much of both as we do." They suffered over 120,000 casualties in the Meuse-Argonne campaign alone. Sometimes it seemed that they simply overwhelmed the enemy with their numbers. One officer estimated that he lost ten soldiers for every German his men killed in the final offensive. Despite the worldwide influenza epidemic of 1918, which eventually killed more American soldiers than did German bullets, the American Expeditionary Force was probably the healthiest army ever assembled. The American army lost 15 of every 1,000 soldiers per year to disease, compared to 65 per 1,000 in the Civil War.

The war produced a few American heroes. Sergeant Alvin York, a former conscientious objector from Tennessee, was probably the most famous. Using only his rifle and pistol, he single-handedly killed or captured 160 Germans. The press made him into a celebrity, but his heroics were not typical. The war was finally won with artillery and the machine gun and, near the end, by the tank, the truck, and the airplane. "To be shelled when you are in the open is one of the most terrible of human experiences," one American soldier wrote. "You hear this rushing, tearing sound as the thing comes toward you, and then the huge explosion as it strikes, and infinitely worse, you see its hideous work as men stagger, fall, struggle, or lie quiet and unrecognizable."

The United States entered the war late but still lost more than 48,000 men and had many more wounded. But the British lost 900,000 men, the French 1.4 million, and the Russians 1.7 million. American units fired French artillery pieces; American soldiers were usually transported in British ships and wore helmets and other equipment modeled after the British. The United States purchased clothing and blankets, even horses, in Europe. American fliers, including heroes like Eddie Rickenbacker, flew French and British planes. The United States contributed huge amounts of men and supplies in the last months of the war, and that finally tipped the balance. But they had entered late and sacrificed little compared to France and England. That would influence the peace settlement.

## DOMESTIC IMPACT OF THE WAR

For at least 30 years before the United States entered the Great War, a debate raged over the proper role of the federal government in regulating industry and protecting people who could not protect themselves. Controversy also centered on the question of how much power the federal government should have to tax and control individuals and corporations, and over the proper relation of the federal government to state and local governments. There had been little agreement, even within the Wilson administration, over the proper role of the federal government. In fact, Wilson had only recently moved away from what he defined in 1912 as the New Freedom. But the war and the problems it raised increased the power of the federal government in a variety of ways. The debate did not end, but the United States emerged from the war a more modern nation, with more power residing in Washington.

### Financing the War

The war by one calculation cost the United States over $33 billion, though if one adds interest and veterans benefits, the total reaches nearly $112 billion. Early in the war, when an economist suggested that the war might cost the United States $10 billion, everyone laughed. Yet many in the Wilson administration knew the war was going to be expensive, and they set out to raise the money by borrowing and by increasing taxes.

Secretary of the Treasury William McAdoo, who had grown up in Georgia and Tennessee but had built a successful career on Wall Street, shouldered the task of financing the war. He studied the policies that Treasury Secretary Salmon Chase had followed during the Civil War. He decided that Chase had made a mistake in not appealing to the emotions of the people. A war must be "a kind of crusade," he remarked. His campaign to sell war bonds or liberty bonds to ordinary American citizens at a very low interest rate called forth patriotic sentiment. "Lick a Stamp and Lick the Kaiser," one poster urged. Celebrities such as film stars Mary Pickford and Douglas Fairbanks promoted the bonds, and McAdoo employed the Boy Scouts to sell them. "Every Scout to Save a Soldier" was the slogan. He even implied that people who did not buy bonds were traitors. "A man who can't lend his government $1.25 per week at the rate of 4% interest is not entitled to be an American citizen," he announced. A banner flew over the main street in Gary, Indiana, which made the point of the campaign clear: "ARE YOU WORTHY TO BE FOUGHT AND DIED FOR? BUY LIBERTY BONDS."

The public responded enthusiastically, but they discovered after the war that their bonds had dropped to about 80 percent of their face value. Because the interest on the bonds was tax-exempt, well-to-do citizens profited more from buying the bonds than did ordinary men, women, and children who joined the bond drives. But the wealthy were not as pleased with McAdoo's other plan to finance the war by raising taxes. The War Revenue Act of 1917 boosted the tax rate sharply, levied an excess profits tax, and increased estate taxes. Another bill the next year raised the tax on the largest incomes to 77 percent. The wealthy protested, but a number of progressives were just as unhappy with the bill, for they wanted to confiscate all income over $100,000 a year. Despite taxes and liberty bonds, however, World War I, like the Civil War, was financed in large part by inflation. Food prices, for example, nearly doubled between 1917 and 1919.

### Increasing Federal Power

At first Wilson tried to work through a variety of state agencies to mobilize the nation's resources. It was quickly apparent, however, that more central control and authority was needed, so he created a series of federal agencies to deal with the war emergency. The first crisis was food. Poor grain crops for two years and an increasing demand for American food in Europe resulted in shortages. To solve the problem, Wilson appointed Herbert Hoover, a young engineer who had won great prestige as head of the Commission for Relief of Belgium, to head the Food Administration. Hoover set out to meet the crisis not so much through government regulation as through an appeal to the patriotism of farmers and consumers alike. He instituted a series of "wheatless" and "meatless" days and urged housewives to cooperate. In Philadelphia, a large sign announced, "FOOD WILL WIN THE WAR; DON'T WASTE IT."

Women emerged during the war as the most important group of consumers. They were urged to save, just as later they would be urged to buy. The *Ladies' Home Journal* announced, "To lose the war because we were unwilling to make the necessary efforts and the required sacrifices in regard to the food supply would be one of the most humiliating spectacles in history."

The Wilson administration used the power of the federal government to organize the re-

*Increased taxes and the sale of Liberty Bonds were not enough to finance the war effort; inflation made up the difference.*

sources of the country in the war effort. The War Industries Board, led by Bernard Baruch, a shrewd Wall Street broker, used the power of the government to control scarce materials and, on occasion, to set prices and priorities. The government itself went into the shipbuilding business. At the largest shipyard, at Hog Island, near Philadelphia, as many as 35,000 men were employed, but the yard did not launch its first ship until the late summer of 1918. For all the efforts of the Emergency Fleet Corporation, American ships could not be produced quickly enough to affect the outcome of the war.

The government also got into the business of running the railroads. When a severe winter and a lack of coordination brought the rail system to near collapse in December 1917, Wilson put all the nation's railroads under the control of the United Railway Administration. The government spent more than $500 million to improve the rails and equipment, and during the 1918 the railroads did run more efficiently than they had under private control. Some businessmen complained of "war socialism," and they resented the way government agencies forced them to comply with rules and regulations. But most came to agree with Baruch that business had much to gain from a close working relationship with government. They could improve the quality of their products, promote efficiency, and increase profits.

### War Workers

The Wilson administration sought to protect and extend the rights of organized labor during the war, while at the same time mobilizing the manpower necessary to keep the factories running. The National War Labor Board insisted on adequate wages and reduced hours, and it tried to prevent the exploitation of women and children working under government contracts. On one occasion, when a munitions plant refused to accept the War Labor Board's decision, the government simply took over the factory. At the same time, when workers threatened to strike, the board often ruled that they could work or be drafted into the army.

The Wilson administration, however, favored the conservative labor movement of Samuel Gompers and the AFL; at the same time, the Justice Department proceeded to put the radical Industrial Workers of the World "out of business." Beginning in September 1917, federal agents conducted massive raids on IWW offices and arrested most of the leaders. The government tolerated the ruthless activity of vigilante groups around the country. In Bisbee, Arizona, the local sheriff, with 2,000 deputies, rounded up 1,200 striking workers and transported them by boxcar to New Mexico. They spent two days in the desert heat without food or water before being rescued. In Butte, Montana, six masked men brutally murdered Frank Little, an IWW organizer. "Had he been arrested and put in jail for his seditious and incendiary talks," Senator H. L. Meyers of Montana suggested, "he would not have been lynched."

Samuel Gompers took advantage of the crisis to strengthen the AFL's position to speak for labor. He lent his approval to administration policies by making clear that he opposed the IWW and the socialists and communists as well. Convincing Wilson that it was important to protect the rights of organized labor during wartime, he announced that "no other policy is compatible with the spirit and methods of democracy." As the AFL won a voice in homefront policy, its membership increased from 2.7 million in 1916 to over 4 million in 1917. Organized labor's wartime gains, however, would prove only temporary.

The war opened up industrial employment opportunities for black men. With 4 million men in the armed forces and the flow of immigrants interrupted by the war, American manufacturers for the first time hired blacks in large numbers. In Chicago before the war, only 3,000 black men held factory jobs. In 1920, more than 15,000 did. Many were doing work that had once been reserved for whites.

The hope of finding an industrial job in a northern city encouraged black families to leave the South, where most blacks had remained after the Civil War. This movement north, often called the Great Migration, continued in the postwar decades. It was the beginning of a significant change in the character of the black community.

The war also created new employment opportunities for women. Posters and patriotic speeches urged women to do their duty for the war effort. "Not Just Hats Off to the Flag, but Sleeves Up for It," one poster announced. Another showed a woman at her typewriter, the shadow of a soldier in the background, with the message: "Stenographers, Washington Needs You."

Women responded to these appeals out of patriotism, as well as out of a need to increase their earnings and to make up for inflation, which diminished real wages. "I used to go to work when my man was sick," one woman reported, "but this is the first time I ever had to go to work to get enough money to feed the kids, when he was working regular." Women went into every kind of industry. They labored in brickyards and in heavy industry, became conductors on the railroad, and turned out shells in munition plants. They even organized the Woman's Land Army to mobilize female labor for the farms. They demonstrated that women could do any kind of job, whatever the physical or intellectual demands. "It was not until our men were called overseas," one woman banking executive reported, "that we made any real onslaught on the realm of finance, and became tellers, managers of departments, and junior and senior officers." One black woman who gave up her position as a live-in servant to work in a paperbox factory declared, "I'll never work in nobody's kitchen but my own any more. No indeed, that's the one thing that makes me stick to this job, but when you're working in anybody's kitchen, well you out of luck. You almost have to eat on the run; you never get any time off." As black women moved out of domestic service, they took jobs in textile mills or even in the stockyards. Racial discrimination, however, even in the North, prevented them from moving too far up the occupational ladder.

Even though women demonstrated that they could take over jobs once thought suitable only for men, their progress during the war proved temporary. Only about 5 percent of the women employed during the war were new to the work force, and almost all of them were unmarried. For most it meant a shift of occupations or a move up to a better-paying position. Moreover,

*The absence of able-bodied men brought women into heavy industry and other formerly male occupations. However, the war did not change the idea that women's place was in the home.*

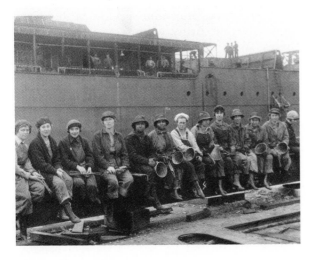

war accelerated trends already under way. It increased the need for telephone operators, sales personnel, secretaries, and other white-collar jobs, and in these occupations women soon became a majority. Telephone operator, for example, became an almost exclusively female job. There were 15,000 operators in 1900 but 80,000 in 1910, and by 1917 women represented 99 percent of all operators as the telephone network spanned the nation. In the end, the war provided limited opportunities for some women, but it did not change the dominant perception that a woman's place was in the home. And after the war was over, the men returned, and the gains made by women almost disappeared. There were 8 million women in the work force in 1910, and only 8.5 million in 1920.

## The Climax of Progressivism

Many of the progressives, especially the social justice progressives, opposed the United States' entry into the war until a few months before the United States declared war. But after April 1917, many began to see the "social possibilities of war." They deplored the death and destruction, the abridgment of freedom of speech, and the patriotic spirit that accompanied the war. But they applauded the social planning stimulated by the conflict. They approved the Wilson administration's support of collective bargaining, the eight-hour day, and protection for women and children in industry. They applauded Secretary of War Baker when he announced, "We cannot afford, when we are losing boys in France, to lose children in the United States at the same time." They welcomed the experiments with government-owned housing projects, and they applauded the wartime successes of woman suffrage and prohibition. Many endorsed the government takeover of the railroads and control of business during the war.

For many social justice progressives who had fought hard, long, and frustrating battles trying to humanize the industrial city, the very fact that suddenly people in high places were listening and approving programs was stimulating. "Enthusiasm for social service is epidemic," one social worker wrote in the summer of 1917; "a luxuriant crop of new agencies is springing up.

We scurry back and forth to the national capital; we stock offices with typewriters and new letterheads; we telephone feverishly regardless of expense, and resort to all the devices of efficient 'publicity work.' . . . It is all very exhilarating, stimulating, intoxicating."

One of the best examples of the influence of the progressives on wartime activities was the Commission on Training Camp Activities, set up early in the war to solve the problem of mobilizing, entertaining, and protecting American servicemen at home and abroad. Chairman of the commission was Raymond Fosdick, a former settlement worker and expert on European and American police systems. He appointed a number of experts from the Playground Association, the YMCA, and social work agencies. They set out to organize community singing and baseball, establish post exchanges and theaters, and even provide university extension lectures to educate and protect the servicemen. The overriding assumption was that the military experience would help produce better citizens, people who would be ready to vote for social reform once they returned to civilian life.

The Commission on Training Camp Activities also incorporated the progressive crusades against alcohol and prostitution. The Military Draft Act prohibited the sale of liquor to men in uniform and gave the president power to establish zones around all military bases where prostitution and alcohol would be prohibited. Some military commanders protested, and at least one city official argued that prostitutes were "God-provided means for the prevention of the violation of innocent girls, by men who are exercising their 'God-given passions.'" Yet the commission, with the full cooperation of the Wilson administration, set out to wipe out sin, or at least to put it out of the reach of servicemen. "Fit to fight" became the motto. "Men must live straight if they would shoot straight," one official announced. It was a typical progressive effort combining moral indignation with the use of the latest scientific prophylaxis. The commissioners prided themselves on having eliminated by 1918 all the red-light districts near the training camps and producing what one person called "the cleanest army since Cromwell's day." When the boys go to France, the secretary of war

remarked, "I want them to have invisible armour to take with them. I want them to have armour made up of a set of social habits replacing those of their homes and communities."

France tested the "invisible armour." The government, despite hundreds of letters of protest from American mothers, decided that it could not prevent the soldiers from drinking wine in France, but it could forbid them to buy or accept as gifts anything but light wine and beer. If Arpin's outfit is typical, the soldiers often ignored the rules. Sex was even more difficult to regulate in France than liquor. Both the British and the French armies had tried to solve the problem of venereal disease by licensing and inspecting prostitutes. Clemenceau, the French premier, found it difficult to comprehend the American attitude toward prostitution, and on one occasion he accused the Americans of spreading disease throughout the French civilian population and graciously offered to provide the Americans with licensed prostitutes. General Pershing considered the letter containing the offer "too hot to handle." So he gave it to Fosdick, who showed it to Baker, who remarked, "For God's sake, Raymond, don't show this to the President or he'll stop the war." The Americans never accepted Clemenceau's offer, and he continued to be baffled by the American progressive mentality.

### Suffrage for Women

In the fall of 1918, while American soldiers were mobilizing for the final offensive in France and hundreds of thousands of women were working in factories and serving as Red Cross and Salvation Army volunteers near the army bases, Woodrow Wilson spoke before the Senate to ask its support of woman suffrage, which he maintained was "vital to the winning of the war." Wilson had earlier opposed the vote for women. His positive statement at this late date was not important, but his voice was a welcome addition to a rising chorus of support for an amendment to the Constitution that would permit the female half of the population to vote.

Not everyone favored woman suffrage. Many people still argued that the vote would make women less feminine, more worldly, and less able to perform their primary tasks as wives and mothers. The National Association Opposed to Woman Suffrage argued that it was only radicals who wanted the vote and declared that woman suffrage, socialism, and feminism were "three branches of the same Social Revolution."

Carrie Chapman Catt, an efficient administrator and tireless organizer, devised the strategy that finally secured the vote for women. Catt, who grew up in Iowa, joined the Iowa Woman Suffrage Association as a young woman of 28 shortly after her first husband died. Before remarrying, she insisted on a legal agreement giving her four months a year away from her husband to work for the suffrage cause. In 1915, she became president of the National American Woman Suffrage Association (NAWSA), the organization founded by Elizabeth Cady Stanton and Susan B. Anthony in 1869.

Catt coordinated the state campaigns with the work in Washington, directing a growing army of dedicated workers. The Washington headquarters sent precise information to the states on ways to pressure congressmen in local districts. In Washington, they maintained a file on each congressman and senator. "There were facts supplied by our members in the states about his personal, political, business and religious affiliations; there were reports of interviews . . . there was everything that could be discovered about his stand on woman suffrage. . . ."

The careful planning began to produce results, but a group of more militant reformers were impatient with the slow progress and broke off from NAWSA to form the National Women's Party (NWP) in 1916. This group was led by Alice Paul, a Quaker from New Jersey, who had participated in some of the suffrage battles in England. Paul and her group picketed the White House, chained themselves to the fence, and blocked the streets. They carried banners that asked, "MR. PRESIDENT, HOW LONG MUST WOMEN WAIT FOR LIBERTY?" In the summer of 1917, the government arrested over 200 women and charged them with "obstructing the sidewalk." It was just the kind of publicity the militant group sought, and they made the most of it. Wilson, fearing even more embarrassment, began to cooperate with the more moderate reformers.

The careful organizing of the NAWSA and the more militant tactics of the NWP both contributed to the final success of the woman suffrage crusade. The war did not cause the passage of the Nineteenth Amendment, but it did accelerate the process. Fourteen state legislatures petitioned Congress in 1917 and 26 in 1919, urging the enactment of the amendment. Early in 1919, the House of Representatives passed the suffrage amendment 304 to 90, and the Senate approved by a vote of 56 to 25. Fourteen months later, the required 36 states had ratified the amendment, and women at last had the vote. "We are no longer petitioners," Catt announced in celebration. "We are not wards of the nation, but free and equal citizens." "This is the woman's age," declared Margaret Dreier Robins of the Woman's Trade Union League. "At last after centuries of disabilities and discriminations, women are coming into the labor and festival of life on equal terms with men."

## PLANNING FOR PEACE

Woodrow Wilson turned the participation of the United States in the war into a religious crusade to change the nature of international relations. It was a war to make the world safe for democracy—and more. On January 8, 1918, in part to counteract the Bolshevik charge that the war was merely a struggle among imperialist powers, he announced his plan to organize the peace. Called the Fourteen Points, it argued for "open covenants of peace openly arrived at," freedom of the seas, equality of trade, the self-determination of all peoples. But his most important point, the fourteenth, called for an international organization, a "league of nations," to preserve peace.

## The Paris Peace Conference

Late in 1918, Wilson announced that he would break precedent and become the first president to leave the country while in office in order to head the American delegation in Paris. Wilson was determined to go to Paris, believing that he alone could overcome the forces of greed and imperialism in Europe and bring peace to the world. Wilson and his entourage of college professors, technical experts, and advisers set sail for Paris on the *George Washington* on December 4, 1918. Lansing, House, and a number of other able men were there. Conspicuously missing, however, was Henry Cabot Lodge or any other Republican senator.

This would prove a serious blunder, for the Senate would have to approve any treaty negotiated at Paris. In the congressional elections of 1918, the Republicans had gained control of both houses of Congress. It is difficult to explain Wilson's lack of political shrewdness, except that he disliked Lodge intensely and hated the process of political bargaining and compromise. Preferring to announce great principles, he had supreme confidence in his ability to persuade and to get his way by appealing to the people.

Wilson's self-confidence grew during a triumphant tour through Europe before the conference. The ordinary people greeted him like a savior who had brought the tragic war to an end. The American president had greater difficulty convincing the political leaders at the peace conference of his genius or his special grace. At Paris, he faced the reality of European power politics and the personalities of David Lloyd George of Great Britain, Vittorio Orlando of Italy, and Georges Clemenceau of France. John Maynard Keynes, the young British economist who was an observer at the peace conference, described Wilson as a "blind and deaf Don Quixote" and pictured him as an impractical idealist trapped and manipulated by the shrewd European diplomats.

Wilson was more naive and more idealistic than his European counterparts, but despite being ill part of the time, he was a clever negotiator who won many concessions at the peace table, sometimes by threatening to go home if his counterparts would not compromise. The European leaders were determined to punish Germany and enlarge their empires. Wilson, however, believed that he could create a new kind of international relations based on his Fourteen Points. He achieved limited acceptance of the idea of the self-determination of people, his dream that each national group could have its own country and that the people should decide in what country they wanted to live.

The peacemakers carved the new countries of Austria, Hungary, and Yugoslavia out of what had been the Austro-Hungarian Empire. In addition, they created Poland, Czechoslovakia, Finland, Estonia, Latvia, and Lithuania, in part to help contain the threat of bolshevism in eastern Europe. France was allowed to occupy the industrial Saar region of Germany for only 15 years with a plebiscite at the end of that time to determine whether the people wanted to become a part of Germany or France. Italy gained the port city of Trieste but was denied the neighboring city of Fiume with its largely Italian-speaking population. Dividing up the map of Europe was difficult at best, but perhaps the biggest mistake that Wilson and other major leaders made was to give the small nations little power at the negotiating table to exclude Soviet Russia entirely.

Wilson won some points at the peace negotiations, but he also had to make major concessions. He was forced to agree that Germany should pay reparations (later set at $33 billion), lose much of its oil- and coal-rich territory, and

*The "Big Four" in December 1919: Italy's Orlando, Britain's Lloyd George, France's Clemenceau, and the U.S. President Wilson.*

admit to its war guilt. He accepted a mandate system, to be supervised by the League of Nations, that allowed France and Britain to take over portions of the Middle East and allowed Japan to occupy Germany's colonies in the Pacific. This was not a "peace without victory," and the sense of betrayal felt by the German people would later have grave repercussions. Wilson also did not win approval for freedom of the seas or the abolition of trade barriers as he wished, but he did gain endorsement for the League of Nations, the organization he hoped would prevent all future wars. The League consisted of a council of the five great powers, elected delegates from the smaller countries, and a World Court to settle disputes. But the key to collective security was contained in Article 10 of the League covenant, which pledged all members "to respect and preserve as against external aggression the territorial integrity" of all other members.

### Women for Peace

While the statesmen met at Versailles to sign the peace treaty hammered out in Paris and to divide up Europe, a group of prominent and successful women, lawyers, physicians, administrators, and writers from all over the world, including many from the Central Powers, met in Zurich, Switzerland. The American delegation was led by Jane Addams and included Florence Kelley of the National Consumers League; Alice Hamilton, a professor at Harvard Medical School; and Jeanette Rankin. As congresswoman from Montana (one of the few states where women could vote), Rankin had voted against the war resolution in 1917. Some of the women who gathered at Zurich had met in 1915 at The Hague, in the Netherlands, to propose an end to the war through mediation. Now they met amid the devastation of war to promote a peace that would last. At their conference they formed the Women's International League for Peace and Freedom. Electing Addams president of the new organization, they denounced the harsh peace terms, which called for disarmament of only one side and exacted great economic penalties against the Central Powers. Prophetically, they predicted that the peace treaty would result in the spread of hatred and anarchy and "create all over Europe discords and animosities which can only lead to future wars."

Hate and intolerance were legacies of the war. They were present at the Versailles peace conference, where Clemenceau especially wanted to humiliate Germany for the destruction of French lives and property. Also hanging over the conference was the Bolshevik success in Russia. Lenin's vision of a communist world order, led by workers, conflicted sharply with Wilson's dream of an anti-imperialist, free trade, capitalist world. The threat of revolution seemed so great that Wilson and the Allies sent American and Japanese troops into Russia in 1919 to attempt to defeat the Bolsheviks and create a moderate republic. But by 1920, the troops had failed in their mission. They withdrew, but Russians never forgot the event, and the threat of bolshevism remained.

### Wilson's Failed Dream

Probably most Americans supported the concept of the League of Nations in the summer of 1919. A few, like former senator Albert Beveridge of Indiana, an ardent nationalist, denounced the League as the work of "amiable old male grannies who, over their afternoon tea, are planning to denationalize America and denationalize the nation's manhood." But 33 governors endorsed the plan. Yet in the end, the Senate refused to accept American membership in the League. The League of Nations treaty, one commentator has suggested, was killed by its friends and not by its enemies.

First there was Lodge, who had earlier endorsed the idea of some kind of international peacekeeping organization but who objected to Article 10, claiming that it would force Americans to fight the wars of foreigners. Chairman of the Senate Foreign Relations Committee, Lodge came from a distinguished Massachusetts family. Like Wilson, he was a lawyer and a scholar as well as a politician. But in background and personality, he was very different from Wilson. A Republican senator since 1893, he had great faith in the power and prestige of the Senate. He disliked all Democrats, especially Wilson, whose idealism and missionary zeal infuriated him.

Then there was Wilson, whose only hope of

passage of the treaty in the Senate was a compromise to bring moderate senators to his side. But Wilson refused to compromise or to modify Article 10 to allow Congress the opportunity to decide whether or not the United States would support the League in time of crisis. Angry at his opponents, who were exploiting the disagreement for political advantage, he stumped the country to convince the American people of the rightness of his plan. The people did not need to be convinced. They greeted Wilson much the way the people of France had. Traveling by train, he gave 37 speeches in 29 cities in the space of three weeks. When he described the graves of American soldiers in France and announced that American boys would never again die in a foreign war, the people responded with applause.

After one dramatic speech in Pueblo, Colorado, Wilson collapsed. His health had been failing for some months, and the strain of the trip was too much. He was rushed back to Washington, where a few days later he suffered a massive stroke. For the next year and a half, the president was incapable of running the government. Protected by his wife and his closest advisers, Wilson became irritable and depressed and unable to lead a fight for the League. For a year and a half the country limped along without a president.

After many votes and much maneuvering, the Senate finally killed the League treaty in March 1920. Had the United States joined the League of Nations, it probably would have made little difference in the international events of the 1920s and 1930s. Nor would American participation have prevented World War II. The United States did not resign from the world of diplomacy or trade, nor did the United States with that single act become isolated from the rest of the world. But the rejection of the League treaty was symbolic of the refusal of many Americans to admit that the world and America's place in it had changed dramatically since 1914.

## CONCLUSION: The Divided Legacy of the Great War

For Edmund Arpin and many of his friends, who left small towns and urban neighborhoods to join the military forces, the war was a great adventure. For the next decades, at American Legion conventions and Armistice Day parades, they continued to celebrate their days of glory. For others who served, the war's results were more tragic. Many died. Some came home injured, disabled by poison gas, or unable to cope with the complex world that had opened up to them.

In a larger sense, the war was both a triumph and a tragedy for the American people. The war created opportunities for blacks who migrated to the North, for women who found more rewarding jobs, and for farmers who suddenly discovered a demand for their products. But much of the promise and the hope proved temporary.

The war provided a certain climax to the progressive movement. The passage of the woman suffrage amendment and the use of federal power in a variety of ways to promote justice and order pleased reformers, who had been working toward these ends for many decades. But the results were often disappointing. Much federal legislation was dismantled or reduced in effectiveness after the war, and votes for women had little initial impact on social legislation.

The Great War marked the coming of age of the United States as a world power, but the country seemed reluctant to accept the new responsibility. The war stimulated patriotism and pride in the country, but it also increased intolerance. With this mixed legacy from the war, the country entered the new era of the 1920s.

## Recommended Reading

Two excellent books featuring different points of view on Woodrow Wilson's foreign policy and the United States' entry into the war are N. Gordon Levin, Jr., *Woodrow Wilson and World Politics* (1968) and Ernest R. May, *The World and American Isolation* (1966). Also see Arthur S. Link, *Woodrow Wilson: Revolution, War, and Peace* (1979). The response of the peace advocates is detailed in C. Roland Marchand, *The American Peace Movement and Social Reform* (1973).

The best general account of the American military involvement in the Great War is Edward M. Coffman, *The War to End All Wars* (1968). Arthur D. Barbeau and Florette Henri, *The Unknown Soldiers: Black American Troops in World War I* (1974) describes the experience of blacks in the military. David M. Kennedy, *Over Here* (1980) is the most comprehensive survey of the impact of the war on American society.

More specialized studies include Donald Johnson, *The Challenge to America's Freedoms* (1963), on civil liberties during the war, and Carol S. Gruber, *Mars and Minerva* (1975), on the impact of the war on higher education. Maurine W. Greenwald, *Women, War, and Work* (1980) describes the influence of the war on women workers. Frederick C. Luebke, *Bonds of Loyalty* (1974) details the experience of German-Americans. Rodolfo Acuna, *Occupied America* (1981) has a section on Mexican-Americans and the war. Christopher Lasch, *The American Liberals and the Russian Revolution* (1962) describes the impact of the Russian Revolution on American policy and attitudes. See also John L. Gaddis, *Russia, the Soviet Union, and the United States* (1978).

Aileen S. Kraditor, *The Ideas of the Women Suffrage Movement* (1965) describes the campaign to win votes for women, which reached a climax during the war. Stanley Cooperman, *World War I and the American Novel* (1970) traces the literary impact of the war. Paul Fussell, *The Great War and Modern Memory* (1975) focuses primarily on the British experience but is indispensable for understanding the importance of the war for the generation that lived through it.

There are many novels focusing on the war. Erich Remarque highlights the horror of war from the European point of view in *All Quiet on the Western Front* (1929). John Dos Passos shows war as a bitter experience in *Three Soldiers* (1921), and Ernest Hemingway portrays its futility in *A Farewell to Arms* (1929).

## TIME LINE

|  |  |
|---|---|
| 1914 | Archduke Ferdinand assassinated; World War I begins |
| | United States declares neutrality |
| | American troops invade Mexico and occupy Veracruz |
| 1915 | Germany announces submarine blockade of Great Britain |
| | *Lusitania* sunk |
| | *Arabic* pledge |
| | Marines land in Haiti |
| 1916 | Army Reorganization Bill |
| | Expedition into Mexico |
| | Wilson reelected |
| | Workmen's Compensation Bill |
| | Keatings–Owen Child Labor Bill |
| | Federal Farm Loan Act |
| | National Women's Party founded |
| 1917 | Germans resume unrestricted submarine warfare |
| | United States breaks relations with Germany |
| | Zimmermann telegram |
| | Russian Revolution |
| | United States declares war on Germany |
| | War Revenue Act |
| | Espionage Act |
| | Committee on Public Information established |
| | Trading with the Enemy Act |
| | Selective Service Act |
| | War Industries Board formed |
| 1918 | Sedition Act |
| | Flu epidemic sweeps nation |
| | Wilson's Fourteen Points |
| | American troops intervene in Russian Revolution |
| 1919 | Paris peace conference |
| | Eighteenth Amendment prohibits alcoholic beverages |
| | Senate rejects Treaty of Versailles |
| 1920 | Nineteenth Amendment grants woman suffrage |

# CHAPTER 24
## AFFLUENCE AND ANXIETY

John and Lizzie Parker were black sharecroppers who lived in a "stubborn, ageless hut squatted on a little hill" in central Alabama. They had two daughters, one age 6, the other already married. The whole family worked hard in the cotton fields, but they had little to show for their labor. One day in 1917, she straightened her shoulders and declared, "I'm through. I've picked my last sack of cotton. I've cleared my last field."

Like many southern blacks, the Parkers sought opportunity and a better life in the North. World War I cut off the flow of immigrants from Europe, and suddenly there was a shortage of workers. Some companies sent special trains into the South to recruit blacks. John Parker signed up with a mining company in West Virginia. The company offered free transportation for his family. "You will be allowed to get your food at the company store and there are houses awaiting for you," the agent promised.

The sound of the train whistle seemed to promise better days ahead for her family as Lizzie gathered her possessions and headed north. But it turned out that the houses in the company town in West Virginia were little better than those they left in Alabama. After deducting for rent and for supplies from the company store, almost nothing was left at the end of the week. John hated the dirty and dangerous work in the mine and realized that he would never get ahead by staying there. Instead of venting his anger on his white boss, he ran away, leaving his family in West Virginia.

John drifted to Detroit, where he got a job with the American Car and Foundry Company. It was 1918, and the pay was good, more than he had ever made before. After a few weeks, he rented an apartment and sent for his family. For the first time Lizzie had a gas stove and an indoor toilet, and Sally, who was now 7, started school. It seemed as if their dream had come true. John had always believed that if he worked hard and treated his fellow man fairly, he would succeed.

Detroit was not quite the dream, however. It was crowded with all kinds of migrants, attracted by the wartime jobs at the Ford Motor Company and other factories. The new arrivals increased the racial tension already present in the city. Sally was beaten up by a gang of white youths at school. Even in their neighborhood, which had been solidly Jewish, the shopkeeper and the old residents made it clear they did not like blacks moving into their community. The Ku Klux Klan, which gained many new members in Detroit, also made life uncomfortable for the blacks who had moved north to seek jobs and opportunity.

Suddenly the war ended, and almost immediately John lost his job. Then the landlord raised the rent, and the Parkers were forced to leave their apartment for housing in a section just outside the city near Eight Mile Road. While the surrounding suburbs had paved streets, wide lawns, and elegant houses, this black ghetto had dirt streets and shacks that reminded the Parkers of the company town where they had lived in West Virginia. Lizzie had to get along without her bathroom. Here there was no indoor plumbing and no electricity, only a pump in the yard and an outhouse.

The recession winter of 1921–1922 was particularly difficult. The auto industry and the other companies laid off most of their workers. John could find only part-time employment, while Lizzie worked as a domestic servant for white families. Because no bus route connected the black community to surrounding suburbs, she often had to trek miles through the snow. The shack they called home was often freezing cold, and it was cramped because their married daughter and her husband had joined them in Detroit.

Lizzie did not give up her dream, however. With strength, determination, and a sense of humor, she kept the family together. In 1924, Sally entered high school. By the end of the decade, Sally had graduated from high school, and the Parkers finally had electricity and indoor plumbing in the house, though the streets were still unpaved. Those unpaved streets stood as a symbol of their unfulfilled dream. The Parkers, like most of the blacks who moved north in the decade after World War I, had improved their lot, but they still lived outside Detroit—and, in many ways, outside America.

Like most Americans in the 1920s, the Parkers, Alabama sharecroppers who moved north, pursued the American dream of success. For them, a comfortable house and a steady job, a new bathroom, and an education for their daughter constituted that dream. For others during the decade, the symbol of success was a new automobile, a new suburban house, or perhaps making a killing on the stock market. The twenties were a time of prosperity when most Americans had a sense of living in an era of technology, an era in which new, modern products made life easier and more exciting. Yet many, like the Parkers, found their dream just out of reach.

This chapter traces some of the conflicting trends of an exciting decade. We will explore the currents of intolerance that influenced almost all the events and social movements of the time. We will also explore some of the developments in technology, especially the automobile, which changed life for almost everyone during the twenties. We will examine a number of groups—women, blacks, industrial workers, and farmers—who had their hopes raised but not always fulfilled during the decade. Finally, we will look at the way business, politics, and foreign policy were intertwined during the age of Harding, Coolidge, and Hoover.

## POSTWAR PROBLEMS

The enthusiasm for social progress that marked the war years evaporated in 1919. Public housing, social insurance, government ownership of the railroads, and many other experiments quickly ended. The sense of progress and purpose that the war had fostered withered. The year following the end of the war was marked by strikes and violence, by fear that Bolsheviks, blacks, foreigners, and others were destroying the American way. Some of the fear and intolerance resulted from wartime patriotism, some from the postwar economic and political turmoil that forced Americans to deal with new and immensely troubling situations.

### Red Scare

Americans in the past had feared radicals and other groups that seemed to be conspiring to overthrow the American way. Catholics, Mormons, Populists, and immigrants of many political views had all been attacked as dangerous and "un-American." But before 1917, anarchists seemed to pose the worst threat. The Russian Revolution changed that. *Bolshevik* suddenly became the most dangerous and devious radical, while *communist* was transformed from one who was a member of a utopian community to a

dreaded, threatening subversive. For some Americans, Bolshevik and German became somehow mixed together, especially after the Treaty of Brest-Litovsk in 1918 removed the new Soviet state from the war. In the spring of 1919, with the Russian announcement of a policy of worldwide revolution and with Communist uprisings in Hungary and Bavaria, many Americans feared that the Communists planned to take over the United States. There were a few American Communists, but they never posed a real threat to the United States or to the American way of life.

The war had badly splintered the Socialist party. Some Socialists, like Eugene Debs, opposed American participation, while others, like William English Walling and Edward Russell, left the party and supported the American war effort. In some cases the dilemma of how to deal with the war split families. This happened to the Stokes family. J. G. Phelps Stokes, a tall, slender graduate of Yale whose father had made a fortune in Manhattan real estate became a socialist when as a settlement worker he saw the contrast between the way his family lived and the way new immigrants struggled on New York's Lower East Side. In one of the biggest weddings of 1905, Stokes married Rose Pastor, a poet, writer, and native of Russia. When the war came, Stokes resigned from the Socialist party and joined the army, but Rose opposed the war and eventually became one of the first American Communists.

Rose Pastor Stokes, John Reed, and a few other American idealists were inspired by developments in Russia. Reed, the son of a wealthy businessman, was born in Portland, Oregon, and went east to private school and then to Harvard. He was a cheerleader for the football team and dabbled at writing, but he spent most of his time in college having a good time. After graduation he traveled and then drifted to Greenwich Village, where he joined his classmate Walter Lippmann and Max Eastman, Mabel Dodge, and other intellectuals and radicals. Reed was converted to socialism by this group, who made him understand that "my happiness is built on the misery of others." Reed was in Europe shortly after the war began and was horrified by the carnage in what he considered a capitalistic war. The news of the Russian czar's abdication in 1917 brought him to Russia just in time to witness the bloody Bolshevik takeover. His eyewitness account, *Ten Days That Shook the World*, optimistically predicted a worldwide revolution. When he saw how little hope there was for that revolution in postwar America, he returned to the Soviet Union. The authoritarian nature of the new regime, which seemed to contradict some of its idealistic rhetoric, shook Reed's faith before his death from typhus in 1920, however.

### Working-Class Protest

Reed was one of the romantic American intellectuals who saw great hope for the future in the Russian Revolution. His mentor Lincoln Steffens, the muckraking journalist, remarked after a visit to the Soviet Union a few years later, "I have been over into the future and it works." But relatively few Americans, even among those who had been socialists, and fewer still among the workers, joined the Communist party. Perhaps in all there were 25,000 to 40,000, and those were split into two groups, the American Communist Party and the Communist Labor Party. The threat to the American system of government was very slight. But in 1919, the Communists seemed to be a threat, particularly

as a series of devastating strikes erupted across the country. Workers in the United States had suffered from wartime inflation, which had almost doubled prices between 1914 and 1919, while most wages remained the same. During 1919, about 4 million workers took part in 4,000 strikes. Few wanted to overthrow the government; they simply wanted higher wages and, in some cases, shorter hours.

On January 21, 1919, some 35,000 shipyard workers went on strike in Seattle, Washington. Within a few days, a general strike paralyzed the city; transportation and business stopped. The mayor of Seattle called for federal troops to put down the strike. Within five days, using strong-arm tactics, the mayor put down the strike and was hailed across the country as a "red-blooded patriot."

Yet the strikes continued elsewhere. In September 1919, all 343,000 employees of U.S. Steel walked out in an attempt to win an eight-hour day and "an American living wage." The average workweek in the steel industry in 1919 was 68.7 hours; the unskilled worker averaged $1,400 per year, while the minimum subsistence for a family of five that the same year was estimated at $1,575. Within days, the strike spread to Bethlehem Steel. From the beginning, the owners blamed the strikes on the Bolsheviks. They put ads in the newspapers urging the workers, "Stand By America, Show Up the Red Agitator." They also imported strikebreakers, provoked riots, broke up union meetings, and finally used police and soldiers to end the strike. Eighteen strikers were killed. Because most people believed the Communists had inspired the strike, the issue of long hours and poor pay got lost, and eventually the union surrendered.

While the steel strike was still in progress, the police in Boston went on strike. Like most other workers, the police were struggling to survive on prewar salaries in inflationary times. The Boston newspapers blamed the strike on Communist influence, but one writer warned that the strike could not succeed because "behind Boston in this skirmish with Bolshevism stands Massachusetts, and behind Massachusetts stands America." College students and army veterans volunteered to replace the police and prevent looting in the city. The president of

Harvard assured the students that their grades would not suffer. The strike was quickly broken, and the striking policemen were dismissed. When Samuel Gompers urged Governor Calvin Coolidge to ask the Boston authorities to reinstate them, Coolidge responded with the laconic statement that made him famous and eventually helped him win the presidency: "There is no right to strike against the public safety by anybody, anywhere, anytime."

Strikes were bad enough, especially strikes that seemed inspired by dangerous radicals, but bombs were even worse. The "bomb-throwing radical" had become almost a cliché, probably stemming from the hysteria over the Haymarket Riot of 1886. On April 28, 1919, a bomb was discovered in a small package delivered to the home of the mayor of Seattle. The next day, the maid of a former senator from Georgia opened a package, and a bomb blew her hands off. In June, other bombings occurred, including one that shattered the front part of the home of Attorney General A. Mitchell Palmer in Washington. The bombings seem to have been the work of misguided radicals who thought they might start a genuine revolution in America. But their effect was to provide substantial evidence that revolution was around the corner, even though most American workingmen wanted only shorter hours, better working conditions, and a chance to realize the American dream.

The strikes and bombs, combined with the general postwar mood of distrust and suspicion, persuaded many people that there was a real and immediate threat to the nation. No one was more convinced than A. Mitchell Palmer. From a Quaker family in a small Pennsylvania town, he had graduated with highest honors from Swarthmore College and had been admitted to the Pennsylvania bar in 1893 at the age of 21. After serving for three terms as a congressman, he helped swing the Pennsylvania delegation to Wilson at the 1912 convention. Wilson offered him the post of secretary of war, but Palmer turned it down because of his Quaker pacifism. He did support the United States' entry into the war, however, and served as alien property custodian, a job created by the Trading with the Enemy Act. It was this position that apparently convinced him of the danger of radical subversive activities in America. The bombing of his

home when he was attorney general intensified his fears, and in the summer of 1919, he determined to find and destroy the Red network. He organized a special antiradical division within the Justice Department and put a young man named J. Edgar Hoover in charge of coordinating all information on domestic radical activities.

As he became more and more obsessed with the "Red menace," Palmer instituted a series of raids, beginning in November 1919. Simultaneously, in several cities, his men rounded up 250 members of the Union of Russian Workers, many of whom were beaten and roughed up in the process. In December, 249 aliens, including the famous anarchist Emma Goldman, were deported, although very few were Communists and even fewer had any desire to overthrow the government of the United States. Palmer's men raided private homes, meeting halls, and organization offices. In Detroit, 500 people were arrested on false charges and forced to sleep or stand in a corridor of a building for 25 hours before they were released. In Boston, 800 people were rounded up, marched in chains, then held in an unheated prison on an island in the harbor.

The Palmer raids, which probably constituted the most massive violation of civil liberties in America history to this date, found few dangerous radicals but did fan the flames of fear and intolerance in the country. In Indiana, a jury quickly acquitted a man who had killed an alien for yelling, "To hell with the United States." In Everett, Washington, a member of the IWW was dragged from his jail cell, castrated, and hanged from a railroad bridge. Billy Sunday, the Christian evangelist, suggested that the best solution was to shoot aliens rather than to deport them.

Palmer became a national hero for ferreting out Communists, even though saner minds protested his tactics. Assistant Secretary of State Louis Post insisted that the arrested aliens be given legal rights, and in the end only about 600 were deported, out of the more than 5,000 arrested. The worst of the "Red Scare" was over by the end of 1920, but the fear of radicals and the emotional patriotism survived throughout the decade to color almost every aspect of politics, daily life, and social legislation.

The Red Scare promoted many patriotic organizations and societies, which took as their task the elimination of communism from American life. These organizations made little distinction among socialists, Communists, liberals, and progressives, and they found Bolsheviks everywhere. The best-known organization was the American Legion, but there was also the American Defense Society, the Sentinels of the Republic (whose motto was "Every Citizen a Sentinel, Every Home a Sentry Box"), the National Association for Constitutional Government, the United States Flag Association, and the Daughters of the American Revolution. Such groups provided a sense of purpose and a feeling of belonging in a rapidly changing America. But often what united their efforts was an obsessive fear of Communists and radicals.

Some of the organizations made special targets of women social reformers. One group attacked the "Hot-House, Hull House Variety of Parlor Bolshevists," and during the 1920s circulated a number of "spider-web charts" that purported to connect liberals and progressives, especially progressive women, to Communist organizations. In one such chart, even the Needlework Guild and the Sunshine Society were accused of being influenced by Communists. The connections were made only through the use of half truths, innuendos, and outright lies. To protest their charges did little good, for those who made the charges knew the truth and would not be deflected from their purpose of exterminating dangerous radicals. As late as 1926, *Scabbard and Blade,* the publication of the Reserve Officers Training Corps, denounced Jane Addams as the head of an international conspiracy and the "most dangerous woman in America."

### Ku Klux Klan

The superpatriotic societies exploited the fear that the American way of life was being subverted from within by radicals and Bolsheviks. The Ku Klux Klan built on similar fears but added anti-Catholicism, anti-Semitism, and antiblack attitudes to promote its own version of "100 percent Americanism." The Klan was organized in Georgia by William J. Simmons, a lay preacher, salesman, and member of many fraternal organizations. He immediately appointed himself the Imperial Wizard. Simmons took the name of the old antiblack Reconstruc-

tion organization that was glorified in 1915 by an immensely popular feature film called *The Birth of a Nation.* The new Klan adopted the white-sheet uniform from the old Klan and admitted only white gentile Americans.

Unlike the original organization, which took almost anyone who was white, the new Klan was thoroughly Protestant and explicitly anti-foreign, anti-Semitic, and anti-Catholic. The Klan declared that "America is Protestant and so it must remain." It opposed the teaching of evolution; glorified old-time religion; supported immigration restriction; denounced short skirts, petting, and "demon rum"; and upheld patriotism and the purity of women. The Klan grew slowly until after the war. In some places, returning veterans could join the Klan and the American Legion at the same table. The Klan added over 100,000 new members in 1920 alone. It grew rapidly because of some aggressive recruiting but also because of the fear and confusion of the postwar period.

The Klan was strong in many small towns and rural areas in the South, where it set out to keep the returning black soldiers in their proper

*Modeled on the Reconstruction anti-black organization, the new Ku Klux Klan opposed Jews, Catholics, and liberals as well as blacks.*

place, but the Klan also spread through all sections of the country, and at least half the members came from urban areas. The Klan was especially strong in the working-class neighborhoods of Detroit, Indianapolis, Atlanta, and Chicago, where fear of everything un-American was increased by the migration of blacks and other ethnic groups to the next street or the next block. The Klan opposed Catholic schools, declared that the Bible should be read in every school every day, and opposed the League of Nations and the World Court. At the peak of its power, the Klan had perhaps 2 million members, and in some states, especially Indiana, Oklahoma, Louisiana, and Texas, the Klan influenced politics and determined some elections. The Klan's power declined after 1924, but widespread fear of Catholicism and everything un-American remained.

### The Sacco-Vanzetti Case

One result of the Red Scare and of the unreasoned fear of foreigners and radicals, which dragged on through much of the decade, was the conviction and sentencing of two Italian anarchists, Nicola Sacco and Bartolomeo Vanzetti. Arrested May 5, 1920, for allegedly murdering a guard during a robbery of the shoe factory in South Braintree, Massachusetts, the two were convicted and sentenced to die in the summer of 1921 on what many liberals considered circumstantial and flimsy evidence. Indeed, it seemed to many that the two Italians, who spoke in broken English and were admitted anarchists, were punished because of their radicalism and their foreign appearance.

It is not clear, even to this day, whether or not Sacco and Vanzetti were guilty of the crime, but the case took on symbolic significance as many intellectuals in Europe and America rallied to their defense and to the defense of civil liberties. Appeal after appeal failed, but finally the governor of Massachusetts appointed a commission to reexamine the evidence in the case. The commission reaffirmed the verdict, and the two were executed in the electric chair on August 23, 1927. But the case and the cause would not die. On the fiftieth anniversary of their deaths in 1977, the governor of Massachusetts exonerated Sacco and Vanzetti and cleared their names.

*Bartolomeo Vanzetti and Nicola Sacco, memorialized in a series of paintings by Ben Shahn, may have been innocent of the murder for which they were executed.*

## THE BENEFITS OF PROSPERITY

Although the decade after World War I was a time of intolerance and anxiety, it was also a time of industrial expansion and unprecedented prosperity. Fueled by new technology, more efficient manufacturing methods, and innovative advertising, industrial production almost doubled during the decade, while the gross national product rose by an astonishing 40 percent. A construction boom created new suburbs around American cities, and the cities themselves were transformed by a new generation of skyscrapers. Everywhere there were signs of prosperity and expansion. After recovering from a postwar depression in 1921 and 1922, the economy took off. The number of telephones installed nearly doubled between 1915 and 1930. Plastics, rayon, and cellophane altered the habits of millions of Americans, while new products, such as cigarette lighters, reinforced concrete, dry ice, and Pyrex glass, created new demands unheard of a decade before.

Perhaps the most tangible sign of the new prosperity was the modern American bathroom. For years, the various functions we associate with the bathroom were separated. There was an outhouse or privy, a portable tin bathtub filled with water heated on the kitchen stove, and a pitcher and washbasin in the bedroom. Hotels and the urban upper class began to install cast-iron bathtubs and primitive flush toilets in the late nineteenth century, but it was not until the early twenties that the enameled tub, toilet, and washbasin became standard. By 1925, American factories turned out 5 million enameled bathroom fixtures annually. The bathroom, with unlimited hot water, privacy, and clean white fixtures, symbolized American affluence.

## Electrification

The 1920s marked the climax of the "second industrial revolution." During the first industrial revolution in the nineteenth century, American industry had primarily manufactured goods intended for other producers. In the first quarter of the twentieth century, as some older industries like coal, textiles, and steel stabilized or declined, new manufacturing concerns that produced rubber, synthetic fabrics, chemicals, and petroleum arose. They focused on goods for consumers, such as silk stockings, washing machines, and cars.

Powering the second industrial revolution was electricity—a form of energy that rapidly replaced steam power after 1900. In the previous two decades, inventors such as Thomas A. Edison and George Westinghouse had developed generators for producing electric current and methods for transmitting it and using it to drive machinery. Edison's illuminating company opened the first commercial power station in New York in 1882; by the end of the century, more than 3,000 stations were supplying businesses and homes with electricity. Meanwhile, Edison's most famous invention, the electric light bulb, was rapidly replacing gas lanterns in homes and on streets.

Between 1900 and 1920, the replacement of steam power by electricity worked as profound a change as had the substitution of steam power for water power after the Civil War. In 1902, electricity supplied a mere 2 percent of all industrial power; by 1929, fully 80 percent derived from electrical generators. Less than one of every ten American homes was supplied with electricity in 1907, but more than two-thirds were by 1929. Powered by electricity, American industries reached new heights of productivity. By 1929, the work force was turning out twice as many goods as had a similarly sized work force ten years before.

Electricity brought dozens of gadgets and labor-saving devices into the home. Washing machines and electric irons gradually reduced the drudgery of washday for women, and vacuum cleaners, electric toasters, and sewing machines lightened housework. But the new machines still needed human direction and did not reduce the time the average housewife spent doing housework. For many poor urban and rural women, the traditional female tasks of carrying water, pushing, pulling, and lifting went on as they had for centuries.

## Automobility

Automobile manufacturing, like electrification, underwent spectacular growth in the 1920s. The automobile was one major factor in the postwar economic boom. It stimulated and transformed the petroleum, steel, and rubber industries. The auto forced the construction and improvement of streets and highways and caused the spending of millions of dollars on labor and concrete. In 1925, the secretary of agriculture approved the first uniform numbering system for the nation's highways, but it was still an adventure to drive from one city to another. The auto created new suburbs and allowed families to live many miles from their work. The filling station, the diner, and the tourist court became familiar and eventually standardized objects on the American landscape. Traffic lights, stop signs, billboards, and parking lots appeared. Hitching posts and watering troughs became rarer, and gradually the garage replaced the livery stable.

The auto changed American life in a variety of ways. It led to the decline of the small crossroads store as well as many small churches because the rural family could now drive to the larger city or town. The tractor changed methods of farming. Trucks replaced the horse and wagon and altered the way farm products were marketed. Buses began to eliminate the one-room school, because it was now possible to transport students to larger schools. The automobile allowed young people for the first time to escape the chaperoning of parents. It was hardly the "house of prostitution on wheels" that one judge called it, but it did change courting habits in all parts of the country. Gradually, as the decade progressed, the automobile became not just transportation but a status symbol. Advertising helped create the impression that it was the symbol of the good life, of sex, freedom, and speed. The auto in turn transformed advertising and design. It even altered the way products were purchased. By 1926, three-fourths of the cars purchased were bought on some kind of deferred-payment plan. Installment credit, first tried by a group of businessmen in Toledo, Ohio, in 1915 to sell more autos, was soon used to sell sewing machines, refrigerators, and other consumer products. "Buy now, pay later" became the American way.

The United States had a love affair with the auto from the beginning. There were 8,000 motor vehicles registered in the country in 1900, and nearly a million in 1912. Only in the twenties did the auto come within the reach of middle-class consumers. In 1929, 4.5 million cars were sold, and by the end of that year, nearly 27 million were registered. Automobile culture was a mass movement.

The auto industry, like most American businesses, went through a period of consolidation in the 1920s. In 1908, over 250 separate companies were producing automobiles in the United States. By 1929, only 44 remained. In other sectors of business, nearly 6,000 mergers occurred between 1925 and 1931. As a result, the 100 largest companies increased their share of total corporate assets from 35.6 percent to almost 44 percent.

A great many men contributed to the development and production of the auto—William Durant, who organized General Motors; Charles Kettering, an engineering genius who developed the electric self-starter; and Ransom E. Olds, who built the first mass-produced moderately priced light car. But above all the others loomed a name that would become synonymous with the automobile itself—Henry Ford.

Ford had the reputation of being a progressive industrial leader and a champion of the common people. Like all men and women who take on symbolic significance, the truth is less dramatic than the stories. Ford is often credited with inventing the assembly line. In actuality it was the work of a team of engineers. But the Ford Motor Company was the first organization

*A major factor in the postwar economic boom was the automobile, which became affordable for middle-class consumers. In the 1920s, Sunday afternoon outings by auto, as here in Louisville, Kentucky, became popular.*

### Motor Vehicle Registration and Sales, 1900–1930

| YEAR | MOTER VECHICLE REGISTRATION | FACTORY SALES |
|---|---|---|
| 1900 | 8,000 | 4,100 |
| 1905 | 78,800 | 24,200 |
| 1910 | 468,500 | 181,000 |
| 1915 | 2,490,000 | 895,900 |
| 1920 | 9,239,100 | 1,905,500 |
| 1925 | 20,068,500 | 3,735,100 |
| 1930 | 26,749,800 | 2,787,400 |

to perfect the moving assembly line and mass-production technology. Introduced in 1913, the new method reduced the time it took to produce a car from 14 hours to an hour and a half. It was the perfect application of Frederick Taylor's system of breaking down each operation into its components, applying careful timing, and integrating the laborer with the machine. The product of the carefully planned system was the Model T, the prototype of the inexpensive family car.

In 1914, Ford startled the country by announcing that he was increasing the minimum pay of the Ford assembly-line worker to $5 a day (almost twice the national average pay for factory workers). Ford was not a humanitarian. He wanted a dependable work force, and he was one of the first to appreciate that the worker was a consumer as well as a producer and that the workers might buy Model T Fords. But work in the Ford factory had its disadvantages. By 1925, the daily wage at Ford dipped below the average in the industry. When the line closed down, as it did periodically, the workers were released without compensation. Moreover, the work on the assembly line was repetitive and numbing.

Henry Ford was not easy to work for. One newspaper account in 1928 called him "an industrial fascist—the Mussolini of Detroit." He was ruthless at applying pressure on his dealers and used them to bail him out of difficult financial situations. Instead of borrowing money from a bank, he forced dealers to buy extra cars, trucks, and tractors. He used spies on the assembly lines and fired workers and executives at the least provocation. But he did produce a car that transformed America.

The Model T, which cost $600 in 1912, was reduced gradually in price until it sold for only $290 in 1924. The "Tin Lizzie," as it was affectionately called, was light and easily repaired. Some owners claimed all one needed was a pair of pliers and some baling wire to keep it running. If it got stuck on bad roads, as it often did, it could be lifted out by a reasonably healthy man. Replacement parts were standardized and widely available. The Model T did not change from year to year, and it did not deviate from its one color, black. Except for adding a self-starter, offering a closed model, and making a few minor face-lift changes, Ford kept the Model T in 1927 much as he had introduced it in 1913. By that time, its popularity had declined as many people traded up to a sleeker, more colorful, and, they thought, more prestigious autos put out by one of Ford's competitors. The Model A, introduced in 1927, was never as popular or as successful as the Model T. The Chevrolet, rather than the Ford, was America's car by the end of the twenties. In 1929, American manufacturers produced 5.3 million cars, a figure not approached again until the 1950s.

### The Exploding Metropolis

The automobile caused American cities to expand into the countryside. In the late nineteenth century, railroads and streetcars had created suburbs near the major cities, but the great expansion of suburban population occurred in the 1920s. Shaker Heights, a Cleveland suburb, was in some ways a typical development. Built on the site of a former Shaker community, the new suburb was planned and developed by two businessmen. They controlled the size and the style of the homes and restricted buyers. No blacks were allowed. Curving roads led off the main auto boulevards, while landscaping and natural areas contributed to a parklike atmosphere. The suburb increased in population from 1,700 in 1919 to over 15,000 in 1929, and the price of lots multiplied by 10 during the decade. Other suburbs grew in an equally spectacular manner. Beverly Hills, near Los Angeles, increased in population by 2,485 percent during the decade. Grosse Pointe Park, near Detroit, grew by 725 percent, and Elmwood Park, near Chicago, by 716 percent. The automobile also allowed industry to move to the suburbs. Employees in manufacturing establishments in the suburbs of the 11 largest cities increased from 365,000 in 1919 to 1.2 million in 1937.

The biggest land boom of all occurred in Florida, where the city of Miami mushroomed from 30,000 in 1920 to 75,000 in 1925. One plot of land in West Palm Beach sold for $800,000 in 1923 and two years later was worth $4 million. A hurricane in 1926 ended the Florida land boom temporarily, but most cities and their suburbs continued to grow during the decade.

The census of 1920 indicated that for the first time, more than half the population of the United States lived in "urban areas" of more than 2,500. The census designation of an urban area was a little misleading because a town of 5,000 could still be more rural than urban. A more significant concept was the metropolitan area of at least 100,000 people. There were only 52 of these areas in 1900, but in 1930 there were 115.

Every city was transformed by the automobile, but the most spectacular growth of all took place in two cities that the car practically created. Detroit grew from 300,000 in 1900 to 1,837,000 in 1930, while Los Angeles expanded from 114,000 in 1900 to 778,000 in 1930. With sprawling subdivisions and shopping centers connected by a growing network of roads, Los Angeles was the city of the future.

While cities expanded horizontally during the 1920s, sprawling into the countryside, city centers grew vertically. A building boom that peaked near the end of the decade created new skylines for most urban centers. Even cities such as Tulsa, Dallas, Kansas City, Memphis, and Syracuse built skyscrapers. By 1929, there were 377 buildings of over 20 stories in American cities. Many were started just before the stock market crash ended the building boom, and the empty offices stood as a stark reminder of the limits of expansion. The most famous skyscraper of all, the Empire State Building in New York, which towered 102 stories in the air, was finished in 1931 but not completely occupied until after World War II.

## A Communications Revolution

Changing communications altered the way many Americans lived as well as the way business was conducted. The telephone was first demonstrated in 1876. By 1899, there were already more than a million phones in operation. During the twenties, the number of homes with phones increased from 9 to 13 million. Still, by the end of the decade, more than half of American homes were without phones.

The radio even more than the telephone symbolized the technological and communicational changes of the 1920s. The first station to begin commercial broadcasting was WWJ in Detroit in the summer of 1920. When WWJ and WKDA, in Pittsburgh, broadcast the World Series in the fall of 1921, they began the process that would transform baseball and eventually football and basketball as well. Five hundred stations took to the air waves in 1922 alone, many of them sponsored by department stores and others by newspapers and colleges. In Chicago, KYW began broadcasting with the city's Civic Opera in the fall of 1921.

Much of the early broadcasting was classical music, but soon there was news analysis and coverage of presidential inaugurals and important events. Some stations produced live dramas, but it was the serials such as "Amos 'n' Andy" that more than any other programs made radio a national medium. Millions of people scattered across the country could sit in their living rooms (and after 1927, in their cars) listening to the same program. Radio advertising be-

## Ten Largest Cities, 1900–1930

| 1900 | 1930 |
| --- | --- |
| 1. New York—4,023,000 | 1. New York—9,423,000 |
| 2. Chicago—1,768,000 | 2. Chicago—3,870,000 |
| 3. Philadelphia—1,458,000 | 3. Philadelphia—2,399,000 |
| 4. Boston—905,000 | 4. Detroit—1,837,000 |
| 5. Pittsburgh—622,000 | 5. Los Angeles—1,778,000 |
| 6. St. Louis—612,000 | 6. Boston—1,545,000 |
| 7. Baltimore—543,000 | 7. Pittsburgh—1,312,000 |
| 8. San Francisco—444,000 | 8. San Francisco—1,104,000 |
| 9. Cincinnati—414,000 | 9. St. Louis—1,094,000 |
| 10. Cleveland—402,000 | 10. Cleveland—1,048,000 |

*Note:* Figures are for the entire metropolitan areas, including suburbs.
**Source:** U.S. Bureau of the Census.

came an important factor in influencing consumer tastes and in creating demand for products. Sixty thousand households owned radios in 1922; by 1929, the number had increased to 10 million. Actors and announcers became celebrities. The music, voice, and noise of the radio, added to the sound of the automobile, marked the end of silence and, to a certain extent, the end of privacy.

Even more dramatic was the phenomenon of the movies. Forty million viewers a week went to the movies in 1922, and by 1929, that had increased to over 100 million. Men, women, and children flocked to small theaters in the towns and to movie palaces in the cities, where they could dream of romance or adventure and be transported to another world. Charlie Chaplin, Rudolph Valentino, Lillian Gish, and Greta Garbo were more famous and more important to millions of Americans than were most government officials. The motion pictures, which before the war had attracted mostly the working class, now seemed to appeal across class, regional, and generational lines.

The movies had the power to influence attitudes and ideas. Some people had worried that films like *The Birth of a Nation*, the great D. W. Griffith epic on the Civil War and Reconstruction, would influence attitudes toward race and region, but in the twenties many parents worried that the movies would dictate ideas about sex and life. One young college woman remembered, "One day I went to see Viola Dana in *The Five Dollar Baby*. The scenes which showed her as a baby fascinated me so that I stayed to see it over four times. I forgot home, dinner and everything. About eight o'clock mother came after me." She also admitted that the movies taught her how to smoke and in some of the movies "there were some lovely scenes which just got me all hot 'n' bothered."

Not only movie stars became celebrities in the 1920s. Sports figures such as Babe Ruth, Bobby Jones, Jack Dempsey, and Red Grange were just as famous. The great spectator sports of the decade owed much to the increase of leisure time and to the automobile, the radio, and the mass-circulation newspaper. Thousands drove automobiles to college towns to watch football heroes perform.

One writer in 1924 called this era "the age of play." He might better have called it "the age of the spectator." The popularity of sports, like the movies and radio, was in part the product of technology.

The year 1927 seemed to mark the beginning of the new age of mechanization and progress. That was the year Henry Ford produced his fifty-millionth car and introduced the Model A. During that year, radio-telephone service was

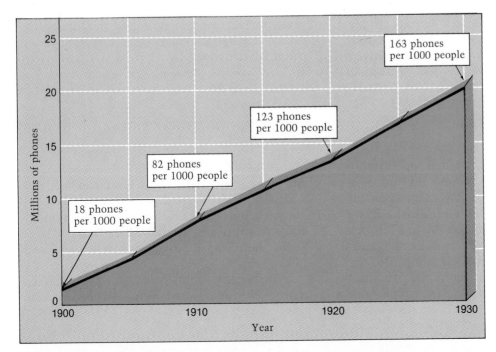

18 phones per 1000 people

82 phones per 1000 people

123 phones per 1000 people

163 phones per 1000 people

Millions of phones

Year

**Telephones in Use, 1900–1930**

*Source:* U.S. Bureau of the Census.

*Sports figures like Jack Dempsey, depicted here by artist George Bellows in a match against Luis Firpo, became celebrities largely through advances in communication and travel.*

*Charles Lindbergh carried the mail for the United States government before he became famous for flying alone across the Atlantic.*

established between San Francisco and Manila. The first radio network was organized (CBS), and the first talking movie was released *(The Jazz Singer)*. In 1927, the Holland Tunnel, the first underwater vehicular tunnel, was opened between New York and New Jersey. It was also the year that Charles Lindbergh flew from New York to Paris in his single-engine plane in 33½ hours. Lindbergh was not the first to fly the Atlantic, but he was the first to fly it alone, an accomplishment that won him $25,000 in prize money and captured the world's imagination. He was young and handsome, and his feat seemed to represent not only the triumph of an individual but also the triumph of the machine. Lindbergh never talked of his accomplishments in the first person; he always said "we," meaning his airplane as well. He was greeted by 4 million people when he returned to New York for a triumphant ticker-tape parade. When they cheered Lindbergh, Americans were reaffirming their faith in American youth and the American character. Lindbergh symbolized their inventive genius, and his plane signified the progress made through technology.

## HOPES RAISED, PROMISES DEFERRED

The 1920s were a time when opportunity seemed to be everywhere. "Don't envy successful salesmen—be one!" one advertisement screamed. Invest in land. Invest in stocks. Buy a car. Build a house. Start a career. Make a fortune. The magazines and newspapers, the radio, business leaders, even the ministers bombarded the nation's citizens with the traditional American message of success. Work hard, save your money, be sober and industrious, believe in God, and you can succeed. "There has never been any necessity in the United States for any healthy human being to remain in a condition of poverty and subordination," wrote Elbert Gary of U.S. Steel. "Families poor in one decade loom leaders in the next."

The benefits of prosperity, however, were no more evenly distributed during that decade than they had been in the past. The income of workers employed in industry increased by only 11 percent from 1923 to 1929, and the real income of farmers declined. On the other hand, corporate profits shot up by 62 percent. The total income of the 12 million American families who made $1,500 a year or less (nearly half of the total) was matched by the income of the 36,000 wealthiest families in the country. Yet there were new benefits for ordinary Americans. Some took advantage of expanding educational opportunities. In 1900, only one in ten young people of high school age remained in school. By 1930, that number had increased to six in ten, and much of the improvement came in the 1920s. In 1900, only one in 33 college-age young people was attending an institution of higher education, but by 1930 the ratio was one in seven. Over a million people were enrolled in the nation's colleges.

In sharp contrast to the nineteenth century, Americans had more leisure time. Persistent efforts by labor unions had gradually reduced the 60-hour workweek of the late nineteenth century to a 45-hour week. Paid vacations, unheard of in the nineteenth century, also became prevalent. In 1916, only 16 of 389 establishments studied had provided paid vacations; by 1926, some 40 percent of 250 companies gave their workers at least one week of vacation with pay.

The American diet also improved during the decade. The consumption of cornmeal and potatoes declined, while the sale of fresh vegetables increased by 45 percent. Health improved and life expectancy increased. But the advantages of better health and more leisure were not equally shared. A white male born in 1900 had a life expectancy of 48 years and a white female of 51 years. By 1930, these figures had increased to 59 and 63 years, respectively. For a black male born in 1900, however, the life expectancy was only 33 years, and for the black female, 35 years. These figures increased to 48 and 47 by 1930, but the discrepancy remained.

## Clash of Values

During the 1920s, new inventions and technological and scientific breakthroughs, together with bolshevism, relativism, Freudianism, bibli-

cal criticism, and other new ideas, seemed to threaten old values. A trial over the teaching of evolutionary ideas in a high school in the little town of Dayton, Tennessee, symbolized the clash of the old versus the new, the traditional versus the modern, the city versus the country.

The scientific community and educated people had long accepted the basic concepts of evolution, if not all the details of Darwin's theories. But many Christians, especially those in the rural South, continued to believe the biblical story of creation as the literal truth. In several states, legislators introduced bills forbidding the teaching of evolution. But it was the Tennessee law enacted in 1925 that became famous, for it made it illegal "for any teacher in any of the universities, normal and all other public schools of the state to teach any theory that denies the story of the divine creation of man as taught in the Bible and to teach instead that man has descended from a lower order of animals."

John Scopes, a young biology teacher (who later went to graduate school at the University of Chicago), decided to test the law. For teaching evolutionary theory to his class, he was arrested and brought to trial. Clarence Darrow, perhaps the country's most famous defense lawyer, was hired to defend Scopes, while the World Christian Fundamentalist Association hired William Jennings Bryan, former presidential candidate and secretary of state, to assist the prosecution. Bryan was old and tired (he died only a few days after the trial), but he was still an eloquent and deeply religious man. In cross-examination, Darrow reduced Bryan's statements to intellectual rubble and revealed also that Bryan was at a loss to explain much of the Bible. He could not explain how Eve was created from Adam's rib, nor where Cain got his wife. Nevertheless, Scopes was declared guilty, for he had clearly broken the law. But the press from all over the country covered the trial and upheld science and academic freedom. Journalists like H. L. Mencken had a field day poking fun at Bryan and the fundamentalists. "Heave an egg out a Pullman window," Mencken wrote, "and you will hit a Fundamentalist almost anywhere in the United States today. . . . They are everywhere where learning is too heavy a burden for mortal minds

Have you ever noticed that television commercials can often be more interesting and creative than the programs? One authority has suggested that the best way for a foreign visitor to understand the American character and popular culture is to study TV commercials. Television advertising, the thesis goes, appeals to basic cultural assumptions. The nature of advertising not only reveals for historians the prejudices, fears, values, and aspirations of a people but also makes an impact on historical development itself, influencing patterns of taste and purchasing habits. One modern critic calls advertising a "peculiarly American force that now compares with such long-standing institutions as the school and the church in the magnitude of its social impact."

As long as manufacturing was local and limited, there was no need to advertise. Before the Civil War, for example, the local area could usually absorb all that was produced; therefore, a simple announcement in a local paper was sufficient to let people know that a particular product was available. But when factories began producing more than the local market could ordinarily consume, advertising came into play to create a larger demand.

Although national advertising began with the emergence of "name brands" in the late nineteenth century, it did not achieve the importance it now holds until the 1920s. In 1918, the total gross advertising revenue in magazines was $58.5 million. By 1920, it had more than doubled to $129.5 million, and by 1929, it was nearly $200 million. These figures should not be surprising in a decade that often equated advertising with religion. The biblical Moses was called "the ad-writer for Deity," and in a best-selling book, Bruce Barton, a Madison Avenue advertiser, reinterpreted Jesus, the "man nobody knows," as a master salesman. Wrote Barton: "He would be a national advertiser today."

The designers of ads began to study psychology to determine what motives, conscious or unconscious, influenced consumers. One psychologist concluded that the appeal to the human instinct for "gaining social prestige" would sell the most goods. Another

## "...and Jane, dear... Jack just raved about my teeth."

"I just smiled my prettiest smile... and let him rave. I could have said 'Of course I have beautiful teeth... I've used Colgate's all my life'. But I didn't want Jack to think I was a living advertisement for Colgate's tooth paste."

*   *   *   *   *

Beautiful teeth glisten gloriously. They compel the admiration of all who see them. And there is health as well as beauty in gleaming teeth, for when they are scrupulously kept clean, germs and poisons of decay can't lurk and breed around them.

### Remove Those Causes of Decay

Save yourself the embarrassment so often caused by poor teeth. Fight the germs of tooth decay.

Colgate's will keep your teeth scrupulously clean. It reaches all the hard-to-get-at places between the teeth and around the edges of the gums, and so *removes causes* of tooth decay. It is the dependable tooth paste for you to use.

### Washes—Polishes—Protects

The principal ingredients of Colgate's are mild soap and fine chalk, the two

things that dental authorities say a safe dental cream should contain. The combined action of these ingredients washes, polishes and protects the delicate enamel of your teeth.

### Use Colgate's Regularly

Just remember that beautiful, healthy teeth are more a matter of good care than of good luck. Use Colgate's after meals and at bedtime. It will keep your teeth clean and gloriously attractive.

And you'll like its taste... even children love to use it regularly.

Priced right too! Large tube 25c.

*Colgate's*
Established 1806

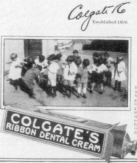

COLGATE'S
RIBBON DENTAL CREAM

*Toothpaste advertisement*

way to sell products, many learned, was to create anxiety in the mind of the consumer over body odor, bad breath, oily hair, dandruff, pimples, and other embarrassing ailments. In 1921, the Lambert Company used the term *halitosis* for bad breath in an ad for Listerine. Within six years, the sale of Listerine had increased from a little over 100,000 bottles a year to more than 4 million. The appeal to sex also sold products, advertisers soon found, as did the desire for

the latest style or invention. But perhaps the most important thing advertisers marketed was youth. "We are going to sell every artificial thing there is," a cosmetic salesman wrote in 1926, "and above all things it is going to be young-young-young! We make women feel young."

Look at the accompanying advertisements carefully. What do they tell you about American culture in the 1920s? What do they suggest about attitudes toward women? Do they reveal any special anxieties? How are they similar to and different from advertising today?

By permission of Leeming Division, Pfizer, Inc.

**Shaving cream advertisement**

**Automobile advertisement (1929)**

to carry." Yet religious fundamentalism and people who held to old values and traditional beliefs continued to survive in a world fast becoming urban, modern, and sophisticated.

## Immigration and Migration

The flow of immigrants from abroad had been reduced to a trickle during the war, and partly because of the wartime situation, many Americans wondered about the advisability of open borders. A movement to restrict immigration had existed for decades. Many feared that the entry of too many foreigners, especially from Asia and from southern and eastern Europe, would dilute the American racial stock. Some labor leaders had argued for restriction in order to raise wages, and a few liberals and social workers had concluded that some restriction was necessary to care adequately for the immigrants already in the country. An act passed in 1882 prohibited the entry of criminals, paupers, and the insane, and special agreements between 1880 and 1908 restricted both Chinese and Japanese immigration. But it was the fear and intolerance of the war years and the period right after the war that led to the passage of the first major restrictive legislation.

The first strongly restrictive immigration law passed in 1917 over President Wilson's veto. It provided for a literacy test for the first time (an immigrant had to read a passage in one of a number of languages). The bill, which also prohibited the immigration of certain political radicals, was inspired by a growing fear that immigrants would flood to American shores after the war. The literacy test did not stop the more than a million immigrants who poured into the country in 1920 and 1921, however. American diplomats abroad warned that millions more were planning to come. Editorial writers pictured vast hordes of "unassimilable" eastern European Jews and other foreigners arriving to threaten the American way of life. The climate was right for the passage of more restrictive legislation.

The resulting law, which passed Congress in 1921, limited European immigration in any one year to 3 percent of the number of each nationality present in the country in 1910. When even

this did not prove restrictive enough, Congress changed the quota in 1924 to 2 percent of those in the country in 1890, in order to limit immigration from southern and eastern Europe and ban all immigration from Asia. The National Origins Act of 1927 set an overall limit of 150,000 European immigrants a year, with more than 60 percent coming from Great Britain and Germany but less than 4 percent from Italy.

The immigration acts of 1921, 1924, and 1927, in sharply limiting European immigration and virtually banning Asian immigrants, cut off the streams of cheap labor that had provided muscle for an industrializing country since the early nineteenth century. At the same time, by exempting immigrants from the Western Hemisphere from the restrictions, the new laws opened the country to Mexican laborers. Hereafter, this would become the largest immigrant group. The need for farm and mine laborers in California and the Southwest encouraged this immigration, as did widespread poverty in Mexico.

Mexican immigrants came in ever larger numbers in the 1920s, though they never matched the flood of eastern and southern Europeans who entered the country before World War I. Nearly half a million arrived in the 1920s, in contrast to only 31,000 in the first decade of the century. Mexican farm workers often lived in primitive camps, where conditions were unsanitary and health care nonexistent. "When they have finished harvesting my crops I will kick them out on the country road," one employer announced. "My obligation is ended."

Mexicans also migrated to industrial cities such as Detroit, St. Louis, and Kansas City. Often they were recruited, their transportation paid by northern companies. The Bethlehem Steel Corporation brought 1,000 Mexicans into its Pennsylvania plant in 1923, and U.S. Steel imported 1,500 as strikebreakers to Lorain, Ohio, about the same time. During the 1920s, El Paso, Texas, became more than half Mexican, San Antonio a little less than half. The Mexican population in California reached 368,000 in 1929, and Los Angeles was about 20 percent Mexican. Like black Americans, the Mexicans found opportunity by migrating, but they did not escape prejudice or hardship.

Blacks migrated north in great numbers in the period from 1915 to 1920. Reduced European immigration and industrial growth caused many northern companies to recruit southern blacks actively. Trains stopped at the depots in small southern towns, sometimes picking up hundreds of blacks in a single day. Lured by editorials and advertisements placed by industries in northern black newspapers such as the *Chicago Defender* and driven out of the South by an agricultural depression, many blacks eagerly headed north.

One young black man wrote to the *Chicago Defender* from Texas that he would prefer to go to Chicago or Philadelphia, but "I don't care where so long as I go where a man is a man." It was the young who tended to move. "Young folks just aren't satisfied to see so little and stay around on the farm all their lives like old folks did," one older man from South Carolina pointed out. Most black migrants were unskilled. They found work in the huge meat-packing plants of Chicago, East St. Louis, Omaha, and Kansas City and in the shipyards and steel mills. Only 50 blacks worked for the Ford Motor Company in 1916, but there were 2,500 working there in 1920 and 10,000 in 1926. The black population of Chicago increased from 44,000 in 1910 to 234,000 by 1930. Cleveland's black population grew from about 8,500 in 1910 to nearly 68,000 at the end of the 1920s.

Blacks unquestionably improved their lives by moving north. But most were like the Parkers, their dreams only partly fulfilled. In most cases they were crowded into segregated housing, and they faced prejudice and hate. "Black men stay South," the *Chicago Tribune* advised, and offered to pay the transportation for any who would return. In one section of Chicago, a group of white residents, fearing the encroachment of blacks, stretched across the street a banner that read: "They Shall Not Pass." Often the young black men moved first and only later brought their wives and children, putting great pressure on many black families. Some young men, like John Parker, restrained their anger, but others, like Richard Wright's fictional Bigger Thomas, portrayed movingly in *Native Son* (1940), struck out violently against white society. The presence of more blacks in the industrial cities of the North led to the development of black ghettos and increased the racial tension that occasionally flared into violence.

One of the worst race riots took place in Chicago in 1919. The riot began at a beach on a hot July day. A black youth drowned in a white swimming area. Blacks claimed he had been hit by stones, but the police refused to arrest any of the white men. A group of blacks attacked the police, and the riot was on. It lasted four days. Blacks were attacked in all parts of the city by white youths who drove through the black sections shooting from car windows. Blacks returned the fire. Several dozen were killed, and hundreds were wounded. The tension between the races did not die when the riot was over.

Race riots broke out in other places as well. There had been a major riot in East St. Louis, Illinois, in 1917, but in the early 1920s, few cities escaped racial tension and violence. Riots exploded in Knoxville, Tennessee, and Omaha, Nebraska. There was even racial conflict in Tulsa and Elaine, Oklahoma, demonstrating that even the rural Southwest was not immune. In Elaine, a group of black tenant farmers organized to try to end their debt slavery and virtual peonage. A group of local sheriffs broke up one of their meetings and killed several blacks. The blacks retaliated. Before the violence ended, 200 blacks and 40 whites lay dead. Seventy-nine blacks were tried for murder, and 13 were sentenced to death, although their sentences were later commuted. One southerner urged blacks in both North and South to be "real niggers, not fools." But in the 1920s, many blacks were no longer content to be second-class citizens. They wanted to share the American dream.

### Marcus Garvey: Black Messiah

A flamboyant black from Jamaica fed a growing sense of black pride in the postwar years. Marcus Garvey arrived in New York at the age of 29. Largely self-taught, he was an admirer of Booker T. Washington. Although he never abandoned Washington's philosophy of self-help, he thoroughly transformed it. Unlike Washington, he had no intention of compromising with white society. In Jamaica, Garvey had founded the United Negro Improvement Associ-

*Marcus Garvey, founder of the United Negro Improvement Association, transformed Booker T. Washington's philosophy into one of black pride and separatism.*

ation. By 1919, he had established 30 branches in the United States, mostly in northern cities. He also set up the newspaper *The Negro World*, the Universal Black Cross Nurses, and a chain of grocery stores and restaurants. He even started an airline, but his biggest project was the Black Star Line, a steamship company, to be owned and operated by blacks. Advocating the return of blacks to Africa, he declared himself the provisional president of an African empire. He glorified the African past and preached that God and Jesus were black.

Garvey won converts, mostly among lower-class blacks, through the force of his oratory and the power of his personality, but especially through his message that blacks should be proud of being black. "Up you mighty race, you can accomplish what you will," he thundered. Thousands of blacks cheered as his African Legion dressed in blue and red uniforms marched by. They waved the black, green, and red flag and sang "Ethiopia, the Land of Our

Fathers," and thousands invested their money in the Black Star Line. The line collapsed before it got started, however, in part because white entrepreneurs sold Garvey inferior ships and equipment. Garvey was arrested for using the mails to defraud shareholders and was sentenced to five years in prison. President Coolidge commuted the sentence but ordered him deported as an undesirable alien.

Garvey's failures were as spectacular as his successes. He was criticized and attacked for his impractical schemes and for his back-to-Africa movement by other black leaders, especially W. E. B. Du Bois. But despite the exotic and romantic nature of Garvey's crusade, he convinced thousands of American blacks, especially the poor and discouraged, that they could join together and accomplish something and that they should feel pride in their heritage and their future.

## Harlem Renaissance and the Lost Generation

A group of black writers, artists, and intellectuals who settled in Harlem after the war led a movement related in some ways to Garvey's black nationalism crusade. It was less flamboyant but in the end more important. They studied anthropology, art, history, and music, and they wrote novels and poetry that explored the ambivalent role of blacks in America. Like Garvey, they expressed their pride in being black and sought their African roots and the folk tradition of blacks in America. But unlike Garvey, they had no desire to go back to Africa. They sought a way to be both black and American.

Alain Locke, a dapper professor of philosophy at Howard University and the first black Rhodes scholar, was in one sense the father of the renaissance. His collection of essays and art, *The New Negro* (1925), announced the movement to the outside world and outlined black contributions to American culture and civilization. Langston Hughes, a poet and novelist born in Missouri, went to high school in Cleveland, lived in Mexico, and traveled in Europe and Africa before settling in Harlem. He wrote bitter but laughing poems, using black vernacular to describe the pathos and the pride of American blacks. In *Weary Blues*, he adapted the rhythm and beat of black jazz and the blues to his poetry. Jazz was an important force in Harlem in the 1920s, and many prosperous whites came from downtown to listen to the music and go to the clubs. The promise of expressing primitive emotions, the erotic atmosphere, the music, and the illegal sex, drugs, and liquor made Harlem an intriguing place for many brought up in a Victorian white America.

The Jamaican Claude McKay, who came to Harlem by way of Tuskegee and Kansas, wrote about the underside of life in Harlem in *Home to Harlem* (1925), one of the most popular of the "new Negro" novels. McKay portrayed two black men, one, Jake, who has deserted the white man's army and finds a life of simple and erotic pleasure in Harlem's cabaret life, the other an intellectual who is unable to make such an easy choice. "My damned white education has robbed me of much of the primitive vitality, the pure stamina, the simple unwaggering strength of the Jakes of the negro race," he laments.

This was the dilemma of many of the Harlem writers: how to be both black and intellectual. They worried that they were dependent on their white patrons, who introduced them to writers and artists in Greenwich Village and made contacts for them at New York publishing houses. Jean Toomer, more self-consciously *avant-garde* than many of the other black writers, came from Washington, D.C., to Harlem, but he moved easily in literary circles in Europe and America. He wrote haunting poems trying to explore the difficulty of black identity, and in a novel, *Cane* (1923), he sketched characters who are maladjusted, almost grotesque figures who shared some of the alienation that many writers felt in the 1920s.

Many of the black writers felt alienated from American society. They tried living in Paris or in Greenwich Village, but most felt drawn to Harlem, which in the 1920s was rapidly becoming the center of black population in New York City. Over 117,000 white people left the neighborhood during the decade, while over 87,000 blacks moved in. Countee Cullen, the only writer in the group actually born in New York, remarked, "In spite of myself I find that I am activated by a strong sense of race consciousness." So was Zora Neale Hurston, born in Florida, who came to New York to study at Barnard College, earned an advanced degree in anthropology from Columbia University, and used her interest in folklore to write stories of robust and passionate blacks. Much of the work of the Harlem writers was read by very small numbers, but they would be rediscovered by another generation of young black intellectuals in the 1960s still struggling with the dilemma of how to be both black and American.

One did not need to be black to be disillusioned with society. Many white intellectuals, writers, and artists also felt alienated from what they perceived as the materialism, comformity, and provincial prejudice that dominated American life. Many writers, including F. Scott Fitzgerald, Ernest Hemingway, E. E. Cummings, and T. S. Eliot, moved to Europe. They wanted to divorce themselves from the country they pretended to detest, but cheap rents and inexpensive food in Paris also influenced their decisions. Many of those who gathered at European cafés, drinking the wine that was illegal in the United States, wrote novels, plays, and poems about America. Like so many American intellectuals in all periods, they had a love-hate relationship with their country.

For many writers, the disillusionment began with the war itself. Hemingway eagerly volunteered to go to Europe as an ambulance driver. But when he was wounded on the Italian front, he reevaluated the purpose of the war and the meaning of all the slaughter. His novel *The Sun Also Rises* (1926) is the story of the purposeless wandering of a group of Americans throughout Europe. But it is also the story of Jake Barnes, made impotent by a war injury. His "unreasonable wound" is a symbol of the futility of life in the postwar period.

F. Scott Fitzgerald, who was married to a beautiful woman and loved to frequent the cafés and the parties in Paris, became a celebrity during the 1920s. He was sometimes confused, even in his own mind, with the dashing heroes he wrote about. He epitomized some of the feelings of despair of his generation, which had "grown up to find all Gods dead, all wars fought, all faiths in man shaken." His best novel, *The Great Gatsby* (1925), was a critique of the American success myth. The book describes the elaborate parties given by a mysterious businessman, who, it turns out, has made his money illegally as a bootlegger. Gatsby hopes to win back a beautiful woman who has forsaken him for another man. But wealth won't buy happiness, and Gatsby's life ends tragically, as so many lives seemed to end in the novels written during the decade.

Paris was the place to which many American writers flocked, but it was not necessary to live in France to be critical of American society. Sherwood Anderson, born in Camden, Ohio, created a fictional midwestern town in *Winesburg, Ohio* (1919) to describe the dull, narrow, warped lives that seemed to provide a metaphor for American culture. Sinclair Lewis, another midwesterner, created scathing parodies of middle-class, small-town life in *Main Street* (1920) and *Babbitt* (1922). The "hero" of the latter novel is a salesman from the town of Zenith. He is a "he-man," a "regular guy" who distrusts "red professors," foreign-born people, and anyone from New York. He lives in a world of gadgets and booster clubs and seems to be the worst product of a standardized civilization. But no one had more fun laughing at the American middle class than H. L. Mencken, who sat in Baltimore, where he edited the *American Mercury* and denounced those he called "the booboisie." He labeled Woodrow Wilson "a self-bamboozled presbyterian" and poked fun at Warren Harding's prose, which he said reminded him of "a string of wet sponges, . . . of stale bean soup, of college yells, of dogs barking idiotically through endless nights. . . ."

Ironically, while intellectuals voiced their despair about the nature of American society and complained that art could not survive in a business-dominated civilization, literature flourished during the decade. The novels of Hemingway, Fitzgerald, Lewis, William Faulkner, and Gertrude Stein, the plays of Eugene O'Neill and Maxwell Anderson, the poetry of T. S. Eliot, Hart Crane, E. E. Cummings, and Marianne Moore, and the work of many black writers marked the 1920s as one of the most creative decades in American literature.

## Women Struggle for Equality

Any mention of the role of women in the 1920s brings to mind the image of the flapper—a young woman with a short skirt, bobbed hair, and boyish figure doing the Charleston, smoking, drinking, and being very casual about sex. F. Scott Fitzgerald's heroines in novels like *This Side of Paradise* (1920) and *The Great Gatsby* (1925) provided the role models for young people to imitate, and movie stars such as Clara Bow and Gloria Swanson, who were openly and aggressively seductive on the screen, supplied even more dramatic examples of flirtatious and provocative behavior.

Without question, many young women acquired more sexual freedom in the 1920s. "None of the Victorian mothers had any idea how casually their daughters were accustomed to being kissed," F. Scott Fitzgerald wrote. However, it is difficult, if not impossible, to know how accustomed those daughters (and their mothers) were to kissing and enjoying other sexual activity. Contraceptives, especially the diaphragm, became more readily available during the decade, and Margaret Sanger, who had been indicted for sending birth control information through the mail in 1914, organized the first American birth control conference in 1921. Still, most states made the selling or prescribing of birth control devices illegal, and federal laws prohibited sending literature discussing birth control through the mail.

Family size declined during the decade (from 3.6 births in 1900 to 2.5 in 1930), and young people were apparently more inclined to marry for love than for security. More women expected sexual satisfaction in marriage (nearly 60 percent in one poll) and felt that divorce was the best solution for an unhappy marriage. Nearly 85 percent in another poll approved of sexual intercourse as an expression of love and affection and not simply for procreation. But the polls were hardly scientific and tended to be biased toward the attitudes of the urban middle class. Despite more freedom for women, the double standard still persisted. "When lovely woman stoops to folly, she can always find someone to stoop with her," one male writer announced, "but not always someone to lift her up again to the level where she belongs."

Women's lives were shaped by other innovations of the 1920s. Electricity, running water, washing machines, vacuum cleaners, and other labor-saving devices made housework easier for

*Conveniences such as electricity and washing machines remained out of reach for many rural and working-class women.*

the middle class. Yet large numbers of rural and urban working-class women were little affected by these developments. Even middle-class women discovered that the new appliances did not reduce the time spent doing housework. Standards of cleanliness rose, and women were urged to make their houses more spotless than any nineteenth-century housekeeper would have felt necessary. At the same time, magazines and newspapers bombarded women with advertising urging them to buy products to make themselves better housekeepers, yet still beautiful. It must have been frustrating for those who could not afford the magic new products or whose hands and teeth and skin failed to look youthful despite all their efforts. The ads also promoted new dress styles, shorter skirts, no corsets. The young at least adopted them quickly, and they also learned to swim (and to display more of their bodies on the beach), to play tennis (but only if they belonged to a tennis club), and to ride a bicycle.

More women worked outside the home. Whereas in 1890, 17 percent of women were employed in the work force, by 1933, 22 percent were. But their share of manufacturing jobs fell from 19 to 16 percent between 1900 and 1930. The greatest expansion of jobs was in white-collar occupations that were being feminized—secretary, bookkeeper, clerk, telephone operator. In 1930, 96 percent of the stenographers were women. Although more married women had jobs (an increase of 25 percent during the decade), most of them worked at low-paying jobs, and most single women assumed that marriage would terminate their employment. For some working women—secretaries and teachers, for example—marriage often led automatically to dismissal. "A married woman's attitude toward men who come to the office is not the same as that of an unmarried woman," one employment agency decided. Married women are "very unstable in their work; their first claim is to home and children," concluded a businessman. If women could not work after their wedding day (and in one poll of college men, only one in nine said he would *allow* his wife to work after marriage), a job as a secretary could be good preparation for marriage. A business office was a good place to meet eligible men, but more than that, a secretary learned endurance, self-effacement, and obedience, traits that would make her a good wife. Considering these attitudes, it is not surprising that the disparity between male

## Women in the Labor Force, 1900–1930

| YEAR | WOMEN IN LABOR FORCE | PERCENT OF WOMEN IN TOTAL LABOR FORCE | WOMEN IN LABOR FORCE AS PERCENT OF TOTAL WOMEN OF WORKING AGE | *Percent of Women in Labor Force* | | |
|---|---|---|---|---|---|---|
| | | | | SINGLE | MARRIED | WIDOWED OR DIVORCED |
| 1900 | 4,997,000 | 18.1 | 20.6 | 66.2 | 15.4 | 18.4 |
| 1910[a] | 7,640,000 | N.A. | 25.4 | 60.2 | 24.7 | 15.0 |
| 1920 | 8,347,000 | 20.4 | 23.7 | 77.0[b] | 23.0 | —[b] |
| 1930 | 10,632,000 | 21.9 | 24.8 | 53.9 | 28.9 | 17.2 |

[a] Data not comparable with other censuses due to a difference in the basis of enumeration.
[b] Single includes widowed and divorced.
**Source:** U.S. Bureau of the Census.

and female wages widened during the decade. By 1930, women earned only 57 percent of what men were paid.

The image of the flapper in the 1920s promised more freedom and equality for women than they actually achieved. The flapper was young, white, slender, and upper-class (Fitzgerald fixed her ideal age at 19), and most women did not fit those categories. The flapper was frivolous and daring, not professional and competent. Although the proportion of women lawyers and bankers increased slightly during the decade, the rate of growth declined, and the number of women doctors and scientists dropped. In the 1920s, women acquired some sexual freedom and a limited amount of opportunity outside the home, but the promise of the prewar feminist movement and the hopes that accompanied the suffrage amendment were left largely unfulfilled.

Winning the vote for women did not assure equality. In most states, a woman's service belonged to her husband. Women could vote, but often they could not serve on juries. In some states, women could not hold office, enter a business, or sign contracts without their husbands' permission. Women were usually held responsible for an illegitimate birth, and divorce laws almost always favored men. Many women leaders were disappointed in the small turnout of women in the presidential election of 1920. To educate women in the reality of politics, they organized the National League of Women Voters to "Finish the Fight." A nonpartisan organization, it became an important educational organization for middle-class women, but it did little to eliminate inequality.

Alice Paul, who had led the militant National Women's Party in 1916, chained herself to the White House fence once again to promote an equal rights amendment to the Constitution. The amendment got support in Wisconsin and several other states, but it was opposed vigorously by progressive women on the grounds that such an amendment would cancel the special legislation that protected women in industry that had taken so long to enact in the two decades before. Feminists disagreed in the 1920s on the proper way to promote equality and rights for women, but the political and social climate was not conducive to feminist causes.

*More women began to hold white-collar jobs such as telephone operator, though marriage often resulted in automatic dismissal.*

## Rural America in the 1920s

Farmers were among those who did not profit from the prosperity of the twenties. Responding to worldwide demands and rising prices for wheat, cotton, and other products, many farmers invested in more land, tractors, and farm equipment during the war. Then prices tumbled. By 1921, the price of wheat had dropped 40 percent, that of corn 32 percent, and hogs 50 percent. Total farm income fell from $10 million to $4 million in the postwar depression. Many farmers could not make payments on their tractors. Because the value of land fell, they often lost both mortgage and land and still owed the bank money. One Iowa farmer remembered, "We gave the land back to the mortgage holder, and then we're sued for the remainder—the deficiency judgment—which we have to pay."

The nature of farming was changing, and that was part of the problem. The use of chemical fertilizers and new hybrid seeds, some developed by government experiment stations and land-grant colleges, increased the yield per acre. By 1930, some 920,000 tractors and 900,000 trucks were in use on American farms. They not only made farming more efficient, but they also released for cash crops land formerly used to raise feed for horses and mules. Production increased at the very time that worldwide demand for American farm products declined. The United States shipped abroad in 1929 only one-third the wheat it had exported in 1919, and only one-ninth the meat.

Not all farmers suffered. During the twenties, the farming class separated into those who were barely getting by or not making it at all and those who earned large profits. Large commercial operations, using mechanized equipment, produced most of the cash crops. At the same time, many small farmers found themselves unable to compete with agribusiness. Some of them, along with many farm laborers, solved the problem of declining rural profitability by leaving the farms. In 1900, fully 40 percent of the labor force worked on farms; by 1930, only 21 percent earned their living from the land.

Farmers received 16 percent of the national income in 1919 but only 9 percent in 1929. While many middle-class urban families were more prosperous than they had ever been, buying new cars, new radios, and new bathrooms, only about one in ten farm families had electricity in the 1920s. The lot of the farm wife was similar to what it had been for centuries. She ran a domestic factory, did all the household chores, and helped on the farm as well. One farm woman on Maryland's Eastern Shore recalled that she heard a neighbor brag about making $1,000 on his cows. "But I saw his wife pumping water for the cows to drink; she always went into the barn to help milk, washed the buckets, helped bottle the milk, and the little boy peddled it before school. The farmer made one thousand dollars, but he had not figured feed or help or interest; that was his 'gross amount.'"

As they had done in the nineteenth century, farmers tried to act collectively in the 1920s through a variety of farm organizations. Congressmen from the farm states began to promote legislation, but they accomplished little during the decade. Most of their effort was spent in supporting the McNary-Haugen Farm Relief Bill, which provided for government support for key agricultural products. The idea was for the government to buy wheat, cotton, and other crops at a "fair exchange value" and then market the excess on the world market at a lower price, thus isolating and protecting the American farmer from the worldwide swing in prices. The bill passed Congress in February 1927, only to be vetoed by President Coolidge. It passed again in revised form the next year, and again the president vetoed it. But farm organizations in all parts of the country learned during the decades how to cooperate and how to influence Congress. That would have important ramifications for the future.

## The Workers' Share of Prosperity

Hundreds of thousands of workers improved their standard of living in the 1920s, but inequality grew. The richest 5 percent of the population increased their share of the wealth from a quarter to a third, and the wealthiest one percent controlled a whopping 19 percent of all income. Workers' real wages rose only slightly between 1923 and 1929, and there was also a great disparity among workers. Those employed on the auto assembly lines or in the new factories producing radios saw their wages go up, and many saw their hours decline. Yet the majority of American working-class families did not earn enough to move them much beyond the subsistence level. One study suggested that a family needed $2,000 to $2,400 in 1924 to maintain an "American standard of living." But in that year, 16 million families earned under $2,000. For the chambermaids in New York hotels who worked seven days a week or the itinerant Mexican migrant laborers in the Southwest, labor was so exhausting that at the end of the day, it was impossible to take advantage of new consumer products and modern life styles, even if they had the money.

While some workers prospered in the 1920s, organized labor fell on hard times. Labor union membership fell from about 5 million in 1921 to less than 3.5 million in 1929. Although a majority of American workers had never supported unions, unions now faced competition from employers' new policies. A number of large employers lured workers away from unions with promises that seemed to equal union benefits: profit-sharing plans, pensions, and their own company unions. The National Manufacturing Association and individual businesses carried on a vigorous campaign to restore the open shop. The leadership of the AFL became increasingly conservative during the decade and had little interest in launching movements to organize the large industries.

The more aggressive unions like the United Mine Workers, led by John L. Lewis, also encountered difficulties. The union's attempt to organize the mines in West Virginia had led to violent clashes between union members and imported guards. President Harding called out troops in 1921 to put down an "army organized by the strikers." The next year, Lewis called the greatest coal strike in history, and further violence erupted, especially in Williamson County, Illinois. Internal strife also weakened the union, and Lewis had to accept wage reductions in the negotiations of 1927.

Organized labor, like so many other groups, struggled desperately during the decade to take advantage of the prosperity. It won some victories, and it made some progress. But American affluence was beyond the reach of many groups during the decade. Eventually the inequality would lead to disaster.

## THE BUSINESS OF POLITICS

"Among the nations of the earth today America stands for one idea: *Business*," a popular writer announced in 1921. "Through business, properly conceived, managed and conducted, the human race is finally to be redeemed." Bruce Barton, the head of the largest advertising firm in the country, was the author of one of the most popular nonfiction books of the decade. In *The Man Nobody Knows* (1925) he depicted Christ as "the founder of modern business." He took 12 men from the bottom ranks of society and forged them into a successful organization. "All work is worship; all useful service prayer," Barton argued. If the businessman would just copy Christ, he could become a supersalesman.

Business, especially big business, prospered in the twenties, and the image of businessmen, enhanced by their important role in World War I, rose further. The government reduced regulation, lowered taxes, and cooperated to aid business expansion at home and abroad. Business and politics, always intertwined, were especially allied during the decade. Wealthy financiers such as Andrew Mellon and Charles Dawes played important roles in formulating both domestic and foreign policy. Even more significant, a new kind of businessman was elected president in 1928. Herbert Hoover, international engineer and efficiency expert, was the very symbol of the modern techniques and practices that many people confidently expected to transform the United States and the world.

### Harding and Coolidge

The Republicans, almost assured of victory in 1920 because of the bitter reaction against Woodrow Wilson, might have preferred to have nominated their old standard-bearer, Theodore Roosevelt, but he had died the year before. Warren G. Harding, a former newspaper editor from Ohio, captured the nomination after meeting late at night with some of the party's most

*Warren G. Harding (left) and his successor, Calvin Coolidge, were extremely popular presidents.*

powerful men in a hotel room in Chicago. What Harding promised no one ever discovered, but the meeting in the "smoke-filled room" became legendary. To balance the ticket, the Republicans chose as their vice-presidential candidate Calvin Coolidge of Massachusetts, who had gained attention by his firm stand during the Boston police strike. The Democrats seemed equally unimaginative. After 44 roll calls, they finally nominated Governor James Cox of Ohio and picked Franklin D. Roosevelt, a young politician from New York, as vice-president. Roosevelt had been the assistant secretary of the navy but otherwise had not distinguished himself.

Harding won in a landslide. His 61 percent of the vote was the widest margin in a presidential election yet recorded. Perhaps of more significance, barely 50 percent of the eligible voters went to the polls. The newly enfranchised women, especially in working-class neighborhoods, stayed away from the voting booths in large numbers. For many people, it did not seem to matter who was president of the United States.

In contrast to the reform-minded Presidents Roosevelt and Wilson, Harding reflected the conservatism of the 1920s. He was a jovial, fun-loving man who brought many Ohio friends to Washington and placed them in positions of power. A visitor to the White House described Harding and his cohorts discussing the problems of the day, with "the air heavy with tobacco smoke, trays with bottles containing every imaginable brand of whiskey" near at hand. At a little house a few blocks from the White House on K Street, Harry Daugherty, Harding's attorney general and longtime associate, held forth with a group of friends. Amid bootleg liquor and the atmosphere of a brothel, they did a brisk business in selling favors, taking bribes, and organizing illegal schemes. Harding was not personally corrupt, and the nation's leading businessmen approved of his policies of higher tariffs and lower taxes. Nor did he spend all his time drinking with his cronies. He called a conference on disarmament and another to deal with the problems of unemployment, and he pardoned Eugene Debs, who had been in prison since the war. Harding once remarked that he could never be considered one of the great presi-

dents, but he thought perhaps he might be "one of the best loved." He was probably right. When he died suddenly in August 1923, the American people genuinely mourned him.

Only after Calvin Coolidge became president did the full extent of the corruption and scandals of the Harding administration come to light. A Senate committee discovered that the secretary of the interior, Albert Fall, had illegally leased government-owned oil reserves in the Teapot Dome section of Wyoming to private business interests in return for over $300,000 in bribes. Illegal activities were also discovered in the Veterans Administration and elsewhere in government. Harding's attorney general resigned in disgrace, the secretary of the navy barely avoided prison, two of Harding's advisers committed suicide, and the secretary of the interior was sentenced to jail.

Coolidge was somewhat dour and taciturn, but honest. There was no hint of scandal about his administration or his personal life. Born in a little town in Vermont, he was sworn in as president by his father, a justice of the peace, in a ceremony conducted by the light of kerosene lamps at his ancestral home. To many, Coolidge represented old-fashioned rural values, simple religious faith, and personal integrity. In fact, he seemed to represent a world that was fast disappearing in the 1920s. Coolidge, however, was uncomfortable playing the role of rural yokel. He was visibly ill at ease as he posed for photographers holding a pitchfork or sitting on a hay rig; he was much more comfortable around corporate executives.

Coolidge ran for reelection in 1924 with the financier Charles Dawes as his running mate. There was little question that he would win. The Democrats nominated John Davis, an affable, able corporate lawyer with little national following. A group of dissidents, mostly representing the farmers and the laborers dissatisfied with both nominees, formed a new Progressive party. They adopted the name, but little else, from Theodore Roosevelt's party of 1912. Nominating Robert La Follette of Wisconsin for president, they drafted a platform calling for government ownership of railroads and ratification of the child labor amendment. La Follette attacked "the control of government and industry by private monopoly." He managed to get nearly 5 million votes, only 3.5 million short of Davis's total. But Coolidge and prosperity won easily.

Like Harding, Coolidge was a popular president. The symbol of his administration was his secretary of the Treasury, Andrew Mellon, one of the wealthiest men in America. He had served under Harding as well, and he set out to lower individual and corporate taxes. In 1922, Congress, with Mellon's endorsement, had repealed the wartime excess profits tax. Although it raised some taxes slightly, it exempted most families from any tax at all by giving everyone a $2,500 exemption, plus $400 for each dependent. In 1926, the rate was lowered to 5 percent and the maximum surtax to 40 percent. Only families with $3,500 income paid any taxes at all. In 1928, Congress reduced taxes further, removed most excise taxes, and lowered the corporate tax rate. The 200 largest corporations increased their assets during the decade from $43 billion to $81 billion.

"The chief business of the American people is business," Coolidge announced. "The man who builds a factory," he said, "builds a temple. . . . The man who works there worships there." Coolidge's idea of the proper role of the federal government was to have as little as possible to do with the functioning of business and the lives of the people. Not everyone approved of his policies, or his personality. "No other president in my time slept so much," a White House usher remembered. But most Americans approved of his inactivity.

### Herbert Hoover

One bright light in the lackluster Harding and Coolidge administrations was Herbert Hoover, who served as secretary of commerce under both presidents. Hoover had made a fortune as an international mining engineer before 1914 and then earned the reputation as a great humanitarian for his work managing the Belgian Relief Committee and directing the Food Administration. His name was mentioned as a candidate for president in 1920, when he had the support of such progressives as Jane Addams, Louis Brandeis, and Walter Lippmann. Even a young Democrat, Franklin Roosevelt, viewed him as a potential presidential candidate until it was clear that he was a Republican and not a Democrat.

Hoover was a dynamo of energy and efficiency. He expanded his department to control and regulate the airlines, radio, and other new industries. By directing the Bureau of Standards to work with the trade associations and with individual businesses, Hoover managed to standardize the size of almost everything manufactured in the United States, from nuts and bolts and bottles to automobile tires, mattresses, and electric fixtures. He supported zoning codes, the eight-hour day in major industries, better nutrition for children, and the conservation of national resources. He pushed through the Pollution Act of 1924, the first preliminary effort to control oil pollution along the coastline.

While secretary of commerce, Hoover used the force of the federal government to regulate, stimulate, and promote, but he believed first of all in American free enterprise and local volunteer action to solve problems. In 1921, he convinced Harding of the need to do something about the problem of unemployment during the postwar recession. The president's conference on unemployment, convened in September 1921, marked the first time any administration had admitted that the national government had any responsibility to the unemployed. The result of the conference (the first of many on a variety of topics that Hoover was to organize) was a flood of publicity, pamphlets, and advice from experts. Most of all, the conference urged state and local governments and businesses to cooperate on a volunteer basis to solve the problem. The primary responsibility of the federal government, Hoover believed, was to educate and promote. With all his activity and his organizing, Hoover got the reputation during the Harding and Coolidge years as an efficient and progressive administrator and he became one of the most popular figures in government service.

### Foreign Policy in the 1920s

The decade of the 1920s is often remembered as a time of isolation, when the United States rejected the League of Nations treaty and turned its back on the rest of the world. It is true that many Americans had little interest in what was going on in Paris, Moscow, or Rio de Janeiro, and it is also true that a bloc of congressmen was determined that the United States would never again enter another European war. But the United States remained involved—indeed, increased its involvement—in international affairs during the decade. Although the United States never joined the League of Nations, and a few dedicated isolationists, led by Senator William Borah, blocked United States membership in the World Court, the United States cooperated with a variety of League agencies and conferences and took the lead in trying to reduce naval armaments and to solve the problems of international finance caused in part by the war.

Indeed, it was business, trade, and finance that marked the decade as one of international expansion. The United States was transformed from a debtor to a creditor nation, and American corporate investments overseas grew sevenfold during the decade. The continued involvement of the United States in the affairs of South American and Central American countries also indicated that the country had little interest in hiding behind its national boundaries. Yet the United States took up its role of international power reluctantly and with a number of contradictory and disastrous results.

"We seek no part in directing the destiny of the world," Harding announced in his inaugural address; but even Harding discovered that international problems would not disappear, and one of those that required immediate attention was the naval arms race. Although there was sentiment among moderates in Japan and Great Britain to restrict the production of battleships, it was the United States, urged on by men like William Borah, that took the lead and called the first international conference to discuss disarmament.

At the Washington Conference on Naval Disarmament, which convened in November 1921, Secretary of State Charles Evans Hughes startled the delegates by proposing a ten-year "holiday" on the construction of warships and by offering to sink or scrap 845,000 tons of American ships, including 30 battleships. He urged Britain and Japan to do the same. Hughes's speech was greeted with enthusiastic cheering and applause, and the delegates set about the task of sinking more ships than the admirals of all their countries had managed to do in a century.

The delegates ultimately reached an agreement fixing the tonnage of capital ships at a ratio of the United States and Great Britain, 5; Japan, 3; and France and Italy, 1.67. Japan agreed only reluctantly, but when the United States promised not to fortify its Pacific island possessions, the Japanese yielded. Retrospectively, in the light of what happened in 1941, the Washington Naval Conference has often been criticized, but in 1921 it was appropriately hailed as the first time in history that the major nations of the world had agreed to disarm. The conference did not cause World War II; neither, as it turned out, did it prevent it. But it was a creative beginning to reducing tensions and to meeting the challenges of the modern arms race. And it was the United States which took the lead by offering to be the first to scrap its battleships.

American foreign policy in the 1920s tried to reduce the risk of international conflict, resist revolution, and make the world safe for trade and investment. Nobody in the Republican administrations of the 1920s even suggested that the United States should remain isolated from Latin America. While American diplomats argued for an open door to trade in China, in Latin America the United States had always assumed a special and distinct role. Throughout the decade, American investment in agriculture, minerals, petroleum, and manufacturing increased in the countries to the south. The United States bought nearly 60 percent of Latin American exports and sold them nearly 50 percent of their imports. "We are seeking to establish a Pax Americana maintained not by arms but by mutual agreement and good will," Hughes maintained. But the United States continued the process of intervention begun earlier. By the end of the decade, the United States controlled the financial affairs of ten Latin American nations. The marines were withdrawn from the Dominican Republic in 1924, but that country remained a virtual protectorate of the United States, until 1941. The marines were ordered from Nicaragua in 1925 but returned the next year when a liberal insurrection threatened the conservative government.

Mexico frightened American businessmen in the mid-1920s by beginning a process of nationalizing foreign holdings in oil and mineral rights. But it was the businessmen and bankers, fearing that further military activity would "injure American interests," who urged Coolidge not to send marines but to negotiate instead. Coolidge appointed Dwight W. Morrow of the J. P. Morgan Company as ambassador, and his conciliatory attitude led to agreements protecting American investments. But it was not until 1928, when Herbert Hoover, as president-elect, made a tour of Latin America, that American policy seemed to change from intervention to cooperation.

The United States' policy of promoting peace, stability, and trade was not always consistent or carefully thought out, and this was especially true in its relationships with Europe. At the end of the war, European countries owed the United States over $10 billion, with Great Britain and France responsible for about three-fourths of that amount. Both countries, caught in the middle of postwar economic problems, suggested that the United States forgive the debts, arguing that they had paid for the war in lives and property destroyed. But the United States, although adjusting the interest and the payment schedule, refused to forget the debt. "They hired the money, didn't they?" Coolidge was supposed to have remarked.

But international debt was not the same as money borrowed at the neighborhood bank; it influenced trade and investment, which the United States wanted to promote. About the only way European nations could repay the United States was by exporting products, but in a series of tariff acts, especially the Fordney-McCumber Tariff of 1922, the United States erected a protective barrier to trade. This act also gave the president power to lower or raise individual rates; both Harding and Coolidge used the power, in almost every case, to raise them. Finally, in 1930, the Hawley-Smoot Tariff raised rates even further, despite the protests of many economists and 35 countries. American policy of high tariffs (a counterproductive policy for a creditor nation) caused retaliation and restrictions on American trade, which American corporations were trying to increase.

The inability of the European countries to export products to the United States and to repay their loans was intertwined with the reparation agreement made with Germany. Germany's economy was in complete disarray in the years after the war, with inflation raging and its industrial plant throttled by the peace treaty. By 1921, Germany was defaulting on its payments. The United States, which believed that a healthy Germany was important to the stability of Europe and of world trade, instituted a plan engineered by Charles Dawes whereby the German debt would be renegotiated and spread over a longer period. In the meantime, American bankers and the American government loaned hundreds of millions of dollars to Germany. In the end, the United States loaned money to Germany so it could make payments to Britain and France so that those countries could continue their payments to the United States.

The United States had replaced Great Britain as the dominant force in international finance, but the nation in the 1920s was a reluctant and inconsistent world leader. The United States had stayed out of the League of Nations and was hesitant to get involved in multinational agreements. However, some agreements seemed proper to sign, and the most idealistic of all was the Kellogg-Briand pact to outlaw war. The French foreign minister, Aristide Briand, suggested a treaty between the United States and France in large part to commemorate long years of friendship between the two countries, but Secretary of State Frank B. Kellogg in 1928 expanded the idea to a multinational treaty to outlaw war. Fourteen nations agreed to sign the treaty, and eventually 62 nations signed, but the only power behind the treaty was moral force rather than economic or military sanctions.

## The Survival of Progressivism

The decade of the 1920s was a time of reaction against reform, but progressivism did not simply die with the end of the war. It survived in many forms through the period that Jane Addams called a time of "political and social sag." Progressives who sought efficiency and order were perhaps happier during the 1920s than those who tried to promote social justice, but even the fight against poverty and for better housing and the various campaigns to protect children persisted throughout the decade. In a sense, the reformers went underground, but they did not disappear or give up the fight. Child labor reformers worked through the Women's Trade Union League, the Consumers League, and other organizations to promote a child labor amendment to the Constitution after the 1919 law was declared unconstitutional in 1922.

The greatest success of the social justice movement was the passage in 1921 of the Sheppard-Towner Maternity Act. This was among the first of federal social welfare legislation, and it was passed during the Harding presidency. This bill, which gave limited benefits to protect the health of women and children, was the product of long progressive agitation. A study conducted by the Children's Bureau discovered that more than 3,000 mothers died in childbirth in 1918 and that more than 250,000 infants also died. The United States ranked eighteenth out of 20 countries in maternal mortality and eleventh in infant deaths. Josephine Baker, the pioneer physician and founder of the American Child Health Association, was not being ironic when she remarked, "It's six times safer to be a soldier in the trenches in France than to be born a baby in the United States."

The maternity bill, introduced by Senator Morris Sheppard of Texas and Representative Horace Towner of Iowa, was suggested by the Children's Bureau. It called for a million dollars a year to aid the states in providing medical aid, consultation centers, and visiting nurses to teach expectant mothers how to care for themselves and their babies. The bill was controversial from the beginning. The American Medical Association, which had supported pure food and drug legislation and laws to protect against health quacks and to enforce standards for medical schools, attacked this bill as leading to socialism and interfering with the relationship between doctor and patient and with the "fee for service" system. Others, especially those who had opposed woman suffrage, argued that it was put forward by extreme feminists, that it was

"inspired by foreign experiments in Communism and backed by radical forces in the country," that it "strikes at the heart of American Civilization," and that it would lead to socializing medicine and radicalizing the children.

Despite the opposition, the bill passed Congress and was signed by President Harding in 1921. The appropriation for the bill was only for six years, and the opposition, again raising the specter of a feminist-socialist-Communist plot, succeeded in repealing the law in 1929. Yet the Sheppard-Towner Act, promoted and fought for by a group of progressive women, indicated that concern for social justice was not dead in the age of Harding and Coolidge.

## Temperance Triumphant

For one large group of progressives, prohibition, like child labor reform and maternity benefits, was an important effort to conserve human resources. At first they argued for local option whereby states, countries, or cities could decide whether or not to make the sale of alcohol illegal. Then, after 1913, they pressed for an amendment to the Constitution. The modern

*People who wanted to drink during the "Noble Experiment" found a way. Here Detroit police raid a basement brewery.*

prohibition movement had more success than the earlier movement in translating the reformers' zeal into the passage of laws.

By 1918, over three-fourths of the people in the country lived in dry states or dry counties, but it was the war that allowed the antisaloon advocates to associate prohibition with patriotism. At first the beer manufacturers supported limited prohibition, but in the end the sale of beer and wine was also prohibited in a patriotic fervor. "We have German enemies across the water," one prohibitionist announced. "We have German enemies in this country too. And the worst of all our German enemies, the most treacherous, the most menacing are Pabst, Schlitz, Blatz and Miller." In 1919, Congress passed the Volstead Act banning the brewing and selling of beverages containing more than one half of one percent alcohol. The thirty-sixth state ratified the Eighteenth Amendment in June 1919, but the country had, for all practical purposes, been dry since 1917. One social worker confidently predicted that the Eighteenth Amendment would reduce poverty, nearly wipe out prostitution and crime, improve labor, and "substantially increase our national resources by setting free vast suppressed human potentialities."

The prohibition experiment probably did reduce the total consumption of alcohol in the country, especially in the rural areas and the urban working-class neighborhoods. There were fewer arrests for drunkenness, and deaths from alcoholism declined. But the legislation showed the difficulty of using law to promote moral reform. Most people who wanted to drink during the "noble experiment" found a way. Speakeasies replaced saloons, and people consumed bathtub gin, home brew, and many strange and dangerous concoctions. The cocktail was invented to disguise the poor quality of much of the liquor being served, and women, at least middle- and upper-class women, began to drink in public for the first time. Prohibition also created great bootlegging rings, which were tied to organized crime in many cities. Al Capone of Chicago was the most famous underworld figure whose power and wealth were based on the sale of illegal alcohol. His organization alone is supposed to have grossed over $60 million in 1927;

ironically, most of the profit came from distributing beer. Many of those who had supported prohibition slowly came to favor its repeal, some because it reduced the power of the states, others because it stimulated too much illegal activity and because it did not seem to be worth the social and political costs.

## The Election of 1928

On August 2, 1927, President Coolidge announced simply, "I do not choose to run for President in 1928." In the following months, Coolidge refused to say whether he could be persuaded to run, but with the announcement, Hoover immediately became the logical candidate. Hoover and Coolidge were not especially close. Coolidge resented what he considered Hoover's spendthrift ways. "That man has offered me unsolicited advice for six years, all of it bad," Coolidge once remarked. Despite the lack of an enthusiastic endorsement from the president and the opposition of some Republicans who thought him too progressive, Hoover easily won the Republican nomination. In a year when the country was buoyant with optimism and when prosperity seemed as if it would go on forever, few doubted that Hoover would be elected.

The Democrats nominated Alfred Smith, a Catholic Irish-American from New York. With his New York accent, his opposition to prohibition, and his flamboyant style, he stood in contrast to the more sedate Hoover. On one level it was a bitter contest between Protestant "drys" and Catholic "wets," between the urban, ethnic Tammany politician and former governor of New York against the rural-born but sophisticated secretary of commerce. Racial and religious prejudice played a role in the campaign, as it often had on American politics. But looked at more closely, the two candidates differed little. Both were self-made men, both were "progressives." Social workers and social justice reformers campaigned for each candidate. Both candidates made an effort to attract women voters, both were favorable to organized labor, both defended capitalism, and both had millionaires and corporate executives among their advisers.

## Presidential Elections, 1920–1928

| YEAR | CANDIDATES | PARTY | POPULAR VOTE | ELECTORAL VOTE |
|------|-----------|-------|--------------|----------------|
| 1920 | WARREN G. HARDING | Republican | 16,152,200 (61.0%) | 404 |
|      | James M. Cox | Democratic | 9,147,353 (34.6%) | 127 |
|      | Eugene V. Debs | Socialist | 919,799 (3.5%) | 0 |
| 1924 | CALVIN COOLIDGE | Republican | 15,725,016 (54.1%) | 382 |
|      | John W. Davis | Democratic | 8,385,586 (28.8%) | 136 |
|      | Robert M. La Follette | Progressive | 4,822,856 (16.6%) | 13 |
| 1928 | HERBERT C. HOOVER | Republican | 21,392,190 (58.2%) | 444 |
|      | Alfred E. Smith | Democratic | 15,016,443 (40.8%) | 87 |

*Note:* Winners' names appear in capital letters.

Hoover won in a landslide, 444 electoral votes to 87 for Smith, who carried only Massachusetts outside the Deep South. But the 1928 campaign revitalized the Democratic party. Smith polled nearly twice as many votes as the Democratic candidate in 1924, and for the first time the Democrats carried the 12 largest cities.

## Stock Market Crash

Hoover, as it turned out, had only six months to apply his progressive and efficient methods to running the country because in the fall of 1929, the prosperity that seemed as if it might go on forever suddenly came to a halt. In 1928 and 1929, speculation had been rampant, and the stock market had boomed. Money could be made everywhere—in real estate and business ventures, but especially in the stock market. "Everybody ought to be Rich," Al Smith's campaign manager argued in an article in the *Ladies' Home Journal* early in 1929. Just save $15 a month and buy good common stock with it, and that money would turn into $80,000 in 20 years (a considerable fortune in 1929). Good common stock seemed to be easy to find in 1929.

Only a small percentage of the American people invested in the stock market, for many had no way of saving even $15 a month. But a large number got into the game in the late 1920s because it seemed a safe and sure way to make money. For many, the stock market came to represent the American economy, and the economy was booming. The New York Times index of 25 industrial stocks reached 100 in 1924, moved up to 181 in 1925, dropped a bit in 1926, and rose again to 245 by the end of 1927.

Then the orgy started. During 1928, the market rose to 331. Many investors and speculators began to buy on margin (borrowing in order to invest). Businessmen and others began to invest money in the market that would ordinarily have gone into houses, cars, and other goods. Yet even at the peak of the boom, probably only about 1.5 million Americans owned stock.

In early September 1929, the New York Times index peaked at 452 and then began to drift downward. On October 23, the market lost 31 points. The next day ("Black Thursday"), it first seemed that everyone was trying to sell, but at the end of the day the panic appeared to be over. It was not. By mid-November, the market had plummeted to 224, about half what it had been two months before. This represented a loss on paper of over $26 billion. Still, a month later, the chairman of the board of Bethlehem Steel could announce, "Never before has American business been as firmly entrenched for prosperity as it is today." Some businessmen even got back into the market, thinking that it had reached its low point. But it continued to go down. Tens of thousands of investors lost everything they owned. Those who had bought on margin had to keep coming up with money to pay off their loans as the value of their holdings declined. There was panic and despair, but the legendary stories of executives jumping out of windows were grossly exaggerated.

## CONCLUSION: A New Era of Prosperity and Problems

The stock market crash ended the decade of prosperity. The crash did not cause the Depression, but the stock market debacle revealed the weakness of the economy. The fruits of economic expansion had been unevenly distributed. There were not enough people to buy the autos, refrigerators, and other products pouring from American factories. The prosperity had been built on a shaky foundation. When that foundation crumbled in 1929, the nation slid into a major depression.

Looking back from the vantage point of the 1930s or from the time of World War II, the 1920s seemed like a golden era—an age of flappers, bootleg gin, constant parties, literary masterpieces, sports heroes, and easy wealth. The truth is much more complicated. More than most decades, the 1920s were a time of paradox and contradictions.

The 1920s were a time of prosperity, yet a great many people, including farmers, blacks, and other ordinary Americans, did not prosper. It was a time of modernization, but only about 10 percent of rural families had electricity. It was a time when women achieved more sexual freedom, but the feminist movement declined. It was a time of prohibition, but many Americans increased their consumption of alcohol. It was a time of reaction against reform, yet progressivism survived. It was a time when intellectuals felt disillusioned with America, yet it was one of the most creative and innovative periods for American writers. It was a time of flamboyant heroes, yet the American people elected the lackluster Harding and Coolidge as their presidents. It was a time of progress, when almost every year saw a new technological breakthrough, but it was also a decade of hate and intolerance. The complex and contradictory legacy of the 1920s continues to fascinate and to influence our own time.

## Recommended Reading

One place to start reading about the twenties is Frederick Lewis Allen, *Only Yesterday* (1931), written shortly after the decade ended and the book that first defined the period as a golden era. Much more serious and better balanced, however, is William E. Leuchtenburg, *The Perils of Prosperity* (1958).

Robert K. Murray, *Red Scare* (1955) is the best place to begin a study of the hate and intolerance that erupted after the war, but John Higham, *Strangers in the Land* (1955) should also be consulted, especially for the Ku Klux Klan and the immigration restriction movement. Andrew Sinclair, *Prohibition* (1962) describes one of the social justice movements after the war. William H. Chafe, *The American Woman: Her Changing Economic and Political Roles* (1972) should also be consulted for the role of women during the decade. Paula Fass, *The Damned and Beautiful* (1977) describes the lifestyles of college youth during the twenties.

Nathan Huggins, *Harlem Renaissance* (1971) and Frederick Hoffman, *The Twenties* (1955) are indispensable for the study of the literary trends during this innovative decade. Robert Sklar, *Movie-Made America* (1976) is excellent on Hollywood and the film industry. James J. Flink, *The Car Culture* (1975) tells the story of the impact of the auto.

Andrew Sinclair, *The Available Man* (1965); Donald R. McCoy, *Calvin Coolidge* (1967); Oscar Handlin, *Al Smith and His America* (1958); and Joan Hoff Wilson, *Herbert Hoover: The Forgotten Progressive* (1975) chart the lives and activities of some of the political leaders. John Kenneth Galbraith, *The Great Crash, 1929* (1954) explains how the twenties came to a tragic end.

Ernest Hemingway's novel *The Sun Also Rises* (1926) is a classic tale of disillusionment and despair in the 1920s. F. Scott Fitzgerald gives a picture of the life of the rich in *The Great Gatsby* (1925). Claude McKay's novel *Home to Harlem* (1928) is one of the best to come out of the Harlem renaissance.

## TIME LINE

| | |
|---|---|
| 1900–1930 | Electricity powers the "second industrial revolution" |
| 1917 | Race riot in East St. Louis, Illinois |
| 1918 | World War I ends |
| 1919 | Treaty of Versailles<br>Strikes in Seattle, Boston, and elsewhere<br>Red Scare and Palmer raids<br>Race riots in Chicago and other cities<br>Marcus Garvey's United Negro Improvement Association spreads |
| 1920 | Warren Harding elected president<br>Women vote in national elections<br>Sacco and Vanzetti arrested<br>Sinclair Lewis publishes *Main Street* |
| 1921 | World Series broadcast on radio<br>Immigration Quota Law<br>Disarmament Conference<br>First birth control conference<br>Sheppard-Towner Maternity Act |
| 1921–1922 | Postwar depression |
| 1922 | Fordney-McCumber Tariff<br>Sinclair Lewis, *Babbitt* |
| 1923 | Harding dies; Coolidge becomes president<br>Teapot Dome scandal |
| 1924 | Coolidge reelected president<br>Peak of Ku Klux Klan activity<br>Immigration Quota Law |
| 1925 | Scopes trial in Dayton, Tennessee<br>F. Scott Fitzgerald, *The Great Gatsby*<br>Bruce Barton, *The Man Nobody Knows*<br>Alain Locke, *The New Negro*<br>Claude McKay, *Home to Harlem*<br>5 million enameled bathroom fixtures produced |
| 1926 | Ernest Hemingway, *The Sun Also Rises* |
| 1927 | National Origins Act<br>McNary-Haugen Farm Relief Bill<br>Execution of Sacco and Vanzetti<br>Lindbergh flies solo, New York to Paris<br>First talking movie, *The Jazz Singer*<br>Henry Ford produces fifty-millionth car |
| 1928 | Herbert Hoover elected president<br>Kellogg-Briand Treaty<br>Stock market soars |
| 1929 | 27 million registered cars in country<br>10 million households own radios<br>100 million people attend movies<br>Stock market crashes |

# CHAPTER 25
## THE GREAT DEPRESSION
## AND THE NEW DEAL

Diana Morgan grew up in a small North Carolina town, the daughter of a prosperous cotton merchant. She lived the life of a "southern belle," oblivious to the country's social and political problems, but the Depression changed her life. She came home from college for Christmas vacation during her junior year to discover that the telephone had been disconnected. Her world suddenly fell apart. Her father's business had failed, her family didn't have a cook or a cleaning woman anymore, and their house was being sold for back taxes. She was confused and embarrassed. Sometimes it was the little things that were the hardest. Friends would come from out of town, and there would be no ice because her family did not own an electric refrigerator and they could not afford to buy ice. "There were those frantic arrangements of running out to the drug store to get Coca-Cola with crushed ice, and there'd be this embarrassing delay, and I can remember how hot my face was."

Like many Americans, Diana Morgan and her family blamed themselves for what happened during the Depression. Americans had been taught to believe that if they worked hard, saved their money, and lived upright and moral lives, they could succeed. Success was an individual matter for Americans. When so many failed during the Depression, they blamed themselves rather than society or larger forces for their plight. The shame and the guilt affected people at all levels of society. The businessman who lost his business, the farmer who watched his farm being sold at auction, the worker who was suddenly unemployed and felt his manhood stripped away because he could not provide for his family were all devastated by the Depression.

Diana Morgan had never intended to get a job; she expected to get married and let her husband support her. But the failure of her father's business forced her to join the growing number of women who worked outside the home in the 1930s. She finally found a position with the Civil Works Administration, a New Deal agency where at first she had to ask humiliating questions of the people applying for assistance to make sure they were destitute. "Do you own a car?" "Does anyone in the family work?" Diana was appalled at the conditions she saw when she traveled around the county to corroborate their stories. She found dilapidated houses, a dirty, "almost paralyzed-looking mother," and a drunken father, together with malnourished children. She felt helpless that all she could do was write out a food order. One day a woman who had formerly cooked for her family came in to apply for help. Each was embarrassed to see the other in changed circumstances.

She had to defend the New Deal programs to many of her friends, who accused her of being sentimental and told her that the poor, especially the poor blacks, did not know any better than to live in squalor. "If you give them coal, they'd put it in the bathtub," was a charge she often heard. But she knew "they didn't have bathtubs to put coal in. So how did anybody know that's what they'd do with coal if they had it?"

Diana Morgan's experience working for a New Deal agency influenced her life and her attitudes; it made her more of a social activist. Her Depression experience gave her a greater appreciation for the struggles of the country's poor and unlucky. Although she prospered in the years after the Depression, the sense of guilt and the fear that the telephone might again be cut off never left her.

This chapter explores some of the causes and consequences of the Great Depression. We will look at Herbert Hoover and his efforts to combat the Depression and then turn to Franklin Roosevelt, the dominant personality of the 1930s. We examine, the New Deal, Roosevelt's program to bring relief, recovery, and reform to the nation. But this chapter also portrays the other side of the 1930s, for the decade did not consist only of the unemployed and New Deal agencies. It was also a time when the radio, the movies, and the automobile had a large impact on the lives of most Americans.

## THE GREAT DEPRESSION

The Great Depression changed Diana Morgan's life as it changed the lives of all Americans who lived through it. The Depression experience also separated her generation from the one that followed. An exaggerated need for security, the fear of failure, a nagging sense of guilt, worry about shattered dreams, and a real sense that it might happen all over again separated the Depression generation from those born after 1940.

### Black Thursday

Few people anticipated the stock market crash in the fall of 1929; prosperity seemed to be a permanent American fixture. But even after the collapse of the stock market, few expected the entire economy to go into a tailspin. General Electric stock, selling for 396 in 1929, fell to 34 in 1932; U.S. Steel declined from 261 to 21. By 1932, the median income had plunged to half what it had been in 1929. Construction spending fell to one-sixth of the 1929 level. By 1932, at least one of every four American breadwinners was out of work, and industrial production had almost ground to a halt.

Why did the nation sink deeper and deeper into depression? After all, only about 2 percent of the population owned stock of any kind. The answer is complex, but the prosperity of the 1920s, it appears in retrospect, was a superficial and shallow prosperity. Farmers and coal and textile workers had suffered all through the 1920s from low prices, and the farmers were the first group in the 1930s to plunge into depression. But other aspects of the economy also lurched out of balance. Two percent of the population received about 28 percent of the national income, while the lower 60 percent only got 24 percent. Businesses increased profits while holding down wages and the prices of raw materials. This pattern had a depressing effect on consumer purchasing power. American workers, like American farmers, did not have the money to buy the goods they helped to produce. There was a relative decline in purchasing power in the late twenties, unemployment was high in some industries, and the housing and automobile industries were already beginning to slacken before the crash.

Well-to-do Americans were speculating a significant portion of their money in the stock market. Their illusion of permanent prosperity helped fire the boom of the 1920s, just as their pessimism and lack of confidence helped exaggerate the depression in 1931 and 1932.

Other factors were also involved. The stock market crash revealed serious structural weaknesses in the financial and banking systems (7,000 banks had failed during the 1920s). Economic relations with Europe contributed to deepening depression. High American tariffs during the 1920s had reduced trade. When American investment in Europe declined in 1928 and 1929, European economies declined. As the European financial situation worsened, the American economy spiraled downward.

The federal government might have prevented the stock market crash and the Depression by more careful regulation of business and the stock market. More central planning might have assured a more equitable distribution of income. But that kind of policy would have taken more foresight than most people had in the 1920s. It certainly would have required different people in power, and it is unlikely that the Democrats, if they had been in control, would have altered the government's policies in fundamental ways.

## Hoover and the Depression

The first reaction to the stock market crash on the part of businessmen and those in government was one of optimism. "I see nothing in the present situation that is either menacing or warranting pessimism," Andrew Mellon announced in December 1929. "All the evidence indicates that the worst effects of the crash upon unemployment will have been passed during the next sixty days," Herbert Hoover reported. Hoover, the great planner and progressive efficiency expert, did not sit idly by and watch the country drift toward disorder. His first statements of optimism were calculated to prevent further panic. In his inaugural address, only a few months before, he had promised to eliminate pockets of poverty, reduce special privilege, aid the farmers, and help all Americans who were old or ill or needy. However, his farm bill was

*Herbert Hoover, photographed on a visit to Yellowstone National Park, agreed with the many analysts who predicted no serious repercussions from the stock market crash.*

the only part of his program enacted by Congress before he had to turn his attention from fine-tuning the economy to trying desperately to save it.

The Agricultural Marketing Act of 1929 set up a $500 million revolving fund to help farmers organize cooperative marketing associations and achieve more efficient production. An amendment tacked on by Congress allowed the Farm Board to attempt to stabilize market fluctuations in the market by establishing minimum prices. The Federal Farm Board was a good example of Hoover's approach to national problems. The Farm Board would loan money to the farmers and help them get organized. Then the government would withdraw, leaving the farmers in control of their life and labor after they had paid the loans back. The Farm Board sought to provide the farmer with equal opportunity through cooperation (a key word for Hoover). As it turned out, the Agricultural Marketing Act of 1929 became the first recovery measure, although it was not intended as such. But as agricultural prices plummeted and banks foreclosed on farm mortgages, the available funds proved inadequate. The Farm Board was helpless to aid the farmer who could not meet his mortgage payments because the price of grain had fallen so rapidly. The Farm Board could not help the Arkansas woman who served lunch to those who came to the auction at her farm and stood weeping in the window as her possessions, including the cows, which all had names, were sold one by one.

Hoover acted aggressively to stem the economic collapse. More than any president before him, he used the power of the federal government and the office of the president to deal with an economic crisis. Nobody called it a depression for the first year at least, for the economic problems seemed very much like other cyclic recessions in the American past. Hoover called conferences of businessmen and labor leaders. He urged cooperation and obtained pledges that businessmen would avoid strikes and keep employment, wages, and production levels from falling. He met with mayors and governors and encouraged them to speed up public works projects. He created agencies and boards, such as the National Credit Corporation and the Emergency

Committee for Employment, to obtain voluntary action to solve the problem.

Hoover even supported a drastic tax cut, which Congress enacted in December 1929. The legislation cut taxes by more than half at the lower end of the scale, to less than one percent for people making less than $5,000. But no laborers made as much as $5,000, and the cuts for most people were so small that the tax reduction did little to stimulate spending. Hoover also went on the radio, though he never felt comfortable with the new medium. He spoke frequently at conferences and launched a massive psychological campaign to convince the American people that the fundamental structure of the economy was sound.

## The Collapsing Economy

Voluntary action and psychological campaigns proved inadequate to stop the Depression. The stock market, after appearing to bottom out in the winter of 1930–1931, continued its decline, responding in part to the European economic collapse that threatened international finance and trade. Of course, not everyone lost money in the market. William Danforth, founder of Ralston Purina, and Joseph Kennedy, film magnate, entrepreneur, and the father of a future president, were among those who made millions of dollars by selling short as the market went down.

But more than a collapsing market afflicted the economy. Over 1,300 additional banks failed in 1930. Despite Hoover's pleas, many factories cut back on production, and some simply closed. U.S. Steel announced a 10 percent wage cut in 1931. As the auto industry laid off workers, the unemployment rate rose to over 40 percent in Detroit. Over 4 million Americans were out of work in 1930, and that increased to at least 12 million by 1932. Foreclosures and evictions created thousands of personal tragedies. There were 200,000 evictions in New York City alone in 1930. While the middle class watched in horror as their life savings and their dreams disappeared, the rich were increasingly concerned as the price of government bonds (the symbol of safety and security) dropped. They began to hoard gold and to fear revolution.

There was never any real danger of revolution. Some farmers organized to dump their milk to protest low prices, and when a neighbor's farm was sold, they gathered to hold a penny auction, bidding only a few cents for equipment and returning it to their dispossessed neighbor. But everywhere people despaired as the Depression deepened in 1931 and 1932. For unemployed blacks and for many tenant farmers, the Depression had little immediate effect because their lives were already so depressed. Most Americans (the 98 percent who did not own stock) did not really notice the stock market crash; for them the Depression meant the loss of a job, a bank foreclosure, or another event. For Diana Morgan it was the discovery that the telephone had been cut off; for some farmers it was burning corn rather than coal because the price of corn had fallen so low it was not worth marketing.

For some in the cities, the Depression meant not having enough money to feed the children. "Have you ever heard a hungry child cry?" asked Lillian Wald of the Henry Street Settlement. "Have you seen the uncontrollable trembling of parents who have gone half starved for weeks so that the children may have food?" In Chicago, children fought with men and women over the garbage dumped by the city trucks. "We have

*Losing his identity as family breadwinner was sometimes as devastating for a man as the financial crisis of unemployment.*

been eating wild greens," a coal miner wrote from Harlan County, Kentucky, "such as Polk salad, violet tops, wild onions . . . and such weeds as cows eat." In Toledo, when municipal and private charity funds were running low, as they did in all cities, those granted assistance were given only 2.14 cents per meal per person. In another city, a social worker noticed that the children were playing a game called "Eviction." "Sometimes they play 'Relief,'" she remarked, "but 'Eviction' has more action and all of them know how to play."

Not everyone went hungry during the Depression or stood in breadlines or lost jobs, but almost everyone was affected in one way or another, and many of the victims tended to blame themselves. A businessman who lost his job and had to stand in a relief line remembered years later how he would bend his head low so nobody would recognize him. A 28-year-old teacher in New Orleans was released because of a cut in funds, and in desperation she took a job as a domestic servant. "If with all the advantages I've had," she remarked, "I can't make a living, I'm just no good, I guess. I've given up ever amounting to anything. It's no use. . . ."

Women's lives were probably disrupted less by the Depression than were those of men. "When hard times hit, it didn't seem to bother mother as much as it did father," one woman remembered. There were many exceptions, of course, but when men lost their jobs, their identity as the family breadwinner was shattered. They wandered around aimlessly with no sense of purpose. Some helped out with family chores, but usually with a sense of bitterness and resentment. For women, however, even when money was short there was still cooking, cleaning, and mending to do, and women were still in command of their homes. Yet many women were forced to do extra work. They took in laundry, found room for a boarder, and made the clothes they formerly would have bought. Women also bore the psychological burden of unemployed husbands, hungry children, and unpaid bills. The Depression altered patterns of family life, and many families were forced to move in with relatives. The marriage rate, the divorce rate, and the birthrate all dropped during the decade. College attendance declined. Many

of these changes created tension and despair that statistics cannot capture.

Hoover reacted to growing despair by urging more voluntary action. "We are going through a period," he announced in February 1931, "when character and courage are on trial, and where the very faith that is within us is under test." He continued to insist on maintaining the gold standard, believing it to be the only responsible currency, and a balanced budget, but so did almost everyone else. Congress was nearly unanimous in supporting those ideals, and Governor Franklin Roosevelt of New York accused Hoover of endangering the country by spending too much. Hoover increasingly blamed the Depression on international economic problems, and he was not entirely mistaken. The world was gripped by depression but, as it deepened, Americans began to blame him for some of the disaster. Hoover became isolated and bitter. The shanties that grew near all the large cities were called "Hoovervilles," and the privies, "Hoover villas." Unable to admit mistakes and to take a new tack, he could not communicate a personal empathy for the poor and the unemployed.

Yet Hoover did try innovative schemes. More public works projects were built during his administration than in the previous 30 years. In the summer of 1931, he attempted to organize a pool of private money to rescue banks and businesses that were near failure. When the private effort failed, he turned reluctantly to Congress, which passed a bill early in 1932 authorizing the Reconstruction Finance Corporation. The RFC was capitalized at $500 million, but a short time later that was increased to $3 billion. It was authorized to make loans to banks, insurance companies, farm mortgage companies, and railroads. Some critics charged that it was simply another trickle-down measure whereby businessmen and bankers would be given aid and the unemployed be ignored. Hoover, however, correctly understood the immense costs to individuals and to communities when a bank or mortgage company failed. The RFC did help shore up a number of shaky financial institutions and remained the major government finance agency until World War II. But it became much more effective under Roosevelt because it loaned directly to industry.

Hoover also asked Congress for a Home Financing Corporation to make mortgages more readily available. The Federal Home Loan Bank Act of 1932 became the basis for the Federal Housing Administration of the New Deal years. He also pushed the passage of the Glass-Steagall Banking Act of 1932, which expanded credit in order to make more loans available to businesses and individuals. Hoover failed to suggest any new farm legislation, even though members of the Farm Board insisted that the only answer to the agricultural crisis was for the federal government to step in and restrict production. Hoover believed that was too much federal intervention. He maintained that the federal government should play an active role, that it should promote cooperation and even create public works. But he firmly believed in loans, not direct subsidies, and he thought it was the responsibility of state and local governments, as well as of private charity, to provide direct relief to the unemployed and the needy.

### The Bonus Army

Many World War I veterans lost their jobs during the Depression, and beginning in 1930, they lobbied for the payment of their veterans' bonuses, not due until 1945. A bill passed Congress in 1931, over Hoover's veto, allowing them to borrow up to 50 percent of the bonus due them, but this concession did not satisfy the destitute veterans or their leaders. In May 1932, about 17,000 veterans marched on Washington. Some took up residence in a shantytown, called Bonus City, in the Anacostia flats outside the city.

In mid-June, the Senate defeated the bonus bill, and most of the veterans, disappointed but resigned, accepted a free railroad ticket home. Several thousand remained, however, along with some wives and children, in the unsanitary shacks during the steaming summer heat. Among them were a small group of committed Communists and other radicals. Hoover exaggerated the subversive elements of those still camped out in Washington, refused to talk to the leaders, and finally called out the U.S. Army.

However, it was General Douglas Mac-

Arthur, the army chief of staff, who ordered the army to disperse the veterans. He described the Bonus Marchers as "a mob . . . animated by the essence of revolution." With tanks, guns, and tear gas the army routed veterans who 15 years before had worn the same uniform as their attackers. Two Bonus Marchers were killed, and several others were injured. "What a pitiful spectacle is that of the great American Government, mightiest in the world, chasing unarmed men, women and children with Army tanks," commented a Washington newspaper. "If the Army must be called out to make war on unarmed citizens, this is no longer America." The army was not attacking revolutionaries in the streets of Washington but was routing bewildered, confused, unemployed men who had seen their American dream collapse.

The Bonus Army fiasco, bread lines, and Hoovervilles would become the symbols of Hoover's presidency. He deserved better because he tried to use the power of the federal government to solve looming economic problems. But in the end his personality and background limited him. He could not understand why army veterans marched on Washington to ask for a handout when he thought they should all be back home working hard, practicing self-reliance, and cooperating "to avert the terrible situation in which we are today." He believed that the greatest

*The Capitol stands serenely in the background as the Bonus Army's shacks burn down, 1932.*

problem besetting Americans was a lack of confidence. But he could not communicate with these people or inspire their confidence. Willing to use the federal government to support business, he could not accept federal aid for the unemployed. He feared an unbalanced budget and a large federal bureaucracy that would interfere with "the American way." Ironically, his actions and his inactions led in the next years to a massive increase in federal power and in the federal bureaucracy.

## ROOSEVELT AND THE FIRST NEW DEAL

The first New Deal, lasting from 1933 to early 1935, focused mainly on recovery from the Depression and relief for the poor and unemployed. Congress passed legislation to aid business, the farmers, and labor and authorized public works projects and massive spending to put Americans back to work. Some of the programs were borrowed from the Hoover administration, and some had their origin in the progressive period. Others were inspired by the nation's experiences in mobilizing for World War I. No single ideological position united all the programs, for Roosevelt was a pragmatist who was willing to try a variety of programs. More than Hoover, he believed in economic planning and in government spending to help the poor.

Roosevelt's caution and conservatism shaped the first New Deal. He did not promote socialism or suggest nationalizing the banks. He was even careful in authorizing public works projects to stimulate the economy. The New Deal was based on the assumption that it was possible to create a just society by superimposing a welfare state on the capitalistic system, leaving the profit motive undisturbed. During the first New Deal, Roosevelt believed he would achieve his goals through cooperation with the business community. Later he would move more toward reform, but at first his primary concern was simply relief and recovery.

The Republicans nominated Herbert Hoover for a second term, but in the summer of 1932 the Depression and Hoover's unpopularity opened the way for the Democrats. After a shrewd campaign, Franklin D. Roosevelt, governor of New York, emerged from the pack and won the nomination. Walter Lippmann's comment during the campaign that Roosevelt was "a pleasant man, who without any important qualifications for office, would like very much to be President" was exaggerated at the time and seemed absurd later. Yet Roosevelt, despite two reasonably successful terms as governor of the nation's most populous state, was not especially well known by the general public in 1932.

As New York's governor, Roosevelt had promoted cheaper electric power, conservation, and old age pensions. Urged on by social workers Frances Perkins and Harry Hopkins, he became the first governor to support state aid for the

*Governor of New York for two terms, Franklin D. Roosevelt was nonetheless a relative stranger to the general public in 1932. As president he inherited the worst national crisis since the Civil War.*

unemployed, "not as a matter of charity, but as a matter of social duty." But it was difficult to tell during the presidential campaign exactly what he stood for. He did announce that the government must do something for the "forgotten man at the bottom of the economic pyramid," and he struck out at the small group of men who "make huge profits from lending money and the marketing of securities." Yet he also mentioned the need for balancing the budget and maintaining the gold standard. Ambiguity was probably the best strategy in 1932, but the truth was that Roosevelt did not have a master plan to save the country. Yet he won overwhelmingly, carrying more than 57 percent of the popular vote.

During the campaign, Roosevelt had promised a "new deal for the American people." But after his victory, the New Deal had to wait for four months because the Constitution provided that the new president be inaugurated on March 4 (this was changed to January 20 by the Twentieth Amendment, ratified in 1933). During the long interregnum, the state of the nation deteriorated badly. The banking system seemed near collapse, and the hardship of depression increased. Despite his bitter defeat, Hoover tried to cooperate with the president-elect and with a hostile Congress. But he could accomplish little. Everyone waited for the new president to take office and to act.

In his inaugural address, Roosevelt announced confidently, "The only thing we have to fear is fear itself." This of course was not true, for the country faced the worse crisis since the Civil War, but Roosevelt's confidence and his ability to communicate with ordinary Americans was obvious early in his presidency. He had a group of clever speech writers, a sense of pace and rhythm in his speeches, and an ability, when he spoke on the radio, to convince listeners that he was speaking directly to them. He instituted a series of radio "fireside chats" to explain to the American people what he was doing to solve the nation's problems. When he said "my friends," millions believed that he meant it, and they wrote letters to him in unprecedented numbers to explain their needs.

During the interregnum, Roosevelt surrounded himself with intelligent and innovative advisers. Some, like James A. Farley, a former New York State boxing commissioner with a genius for remembering names, and Louis Howe, Roosevelt's secretary and confidant since 1912, had helped plan his successful campaign. His cabinet was made up of a mixture of people from different backgrounds who often did not agree with one another. Harold Ickes, the secretary of the interior, was a Republican lawyer from Chicago who had been an ardent supporter of Theodore Roosevelt. Another Republican,

## The Presidential Election of 1932

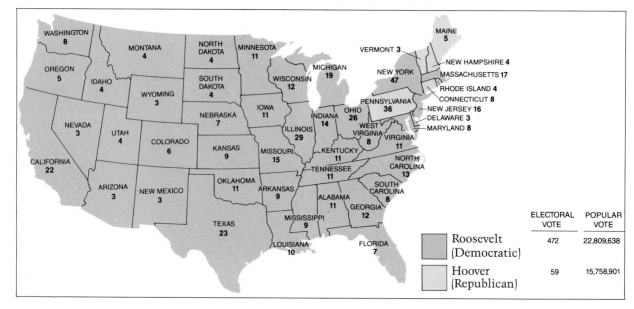

| | ELECTORAL VOTE | POPULAR VOTE |
|---|---|---|
| Roosevelt (Democratic) | 472 | 22,809,638 |
| Hoover (Republican) | 59 | 15,758,901 |

Henry Wallace of Iowa, a plant geneticist and agricultural statistician, became the secretary of agriculture. Frances Perkins, the first woman ever appointed to a cabinet post, had been a New York social worker, secretary of the New York Consumers League, and an adviser to Al Smith.

In addition to the formal cabinet, Roosevelt appointed an informal "Brain Trust," including Adolph Berle, Jr., a young expert on corporation law, and Rexford Tugwell, a Columbia University authority on agricultural economics and a committed national planner. Roosevelt also appointed Raymond Moley, another Columbia professor, who later became one of the president's severest critics, and Harry Hopkins, a nervous, energetic man who loved to bet on horse races and had left Iowa to be a social worker on the Lower East Side of New York. Hopkins's passionate concern for the poor and unemployed would play a large role in formulating New Deal policy.

Then there was Eleanor Roosevelt, the president's wife, who became the most active and controversial first lady. She wrote a newspaper column, made radio broadcasts, traveled widely, and was constantly giving speeches and listening to the concerns of women, minorities, and ordinary Americans all over the country. Attacked by critics who thought she had too much power and mocked for her protruding front teeth, her awkward ways, and her upper-class accent, she courageously took stands on issues of social justice and civil rights. She helped push the president toward social reform.

Roosevelt proved to be an adept politician. He was not particularly well read, especially on economic matters, but he had the ability to learn from his advisers and yet not to be dominated by them. Refusing to work within traditional channels, he continually frustrated subordinates. He took ideas, plans, and suggestions from conflicting sources and somehow combined them. He had "a flypaper mind," one of his advisers decided. There was no overall plan, no master strategy. An improviser and an opportunist who once likened himself to a football quarterback who called one play and if it did not work called a different one, Roosevelt was an optimist by nature. And he believed in action.

## ONE HUNDRED DAYS

Roosevelt took office in the middle of a major crisis, and he had a cooperative Congress willing to pass almost any legislation that he put before it. In three months, a bewildering number of bills were rushed through Congress. Some of them were hastily drafted and not well thought out, and some contradicted other legislation. But many of the laws passed during Roosevelt's first hundred days would have far-reaching implications for the relationship of government to society. Roosevelt was an opportunist, but unlike Hoover, he was willing to use direct government action to solve the problems of depression and unemployment. As it turned out, none of the bills passed during the first hundred days cured the Depression, but taken together the legislation constituted one of the most innovative periods in American political history.

The most immediate problem facing Roosevelt was the condition of the banks. Many had closed, and American citizens, no longer trusting the financial institutions, were hoarding money and putting their assets into gold. Using a forgotten provision of a World War I law, Roosevelt immediately declared a four-day bank holiday. He closed all the banks, savings and loan associations, and credit unions. Three days later, an emergency session of Congress approved his action and within a few hours passed the Emergency Banking Relief Act. The bill gave the president broad powers over financial transactions, prohibited the hoarding of gold, and allowed for the reopening of sound banks, sometimes with loans from the Reconstruction Finance Corporation. Within the next few years, Congress passed additional legislation that gave the federal government more regulatory power over the stock market and over the process by which corporations issued stock. It also passed the Banking Act of 1933, which strengthened the Federal Reserve System, established the Federal Deposit Insurance Corporation, and insured individual deposits up to $5,000. Although the American Bankers Association opposed the plan as "unsound, unscientific, unjust and dangerous," banks were soon attracting depositors by advertising that they were protected by government insurance.

The Democratic platform in 1932 called for reduced government spending and an end to prohibition. Roosevelt moved quickly to accomplish both. The Economy Act, which passed Congress easily, called for a 15 percent reduction in government salaries as well as a reorganization of federal agencies in order to save money. The bill also cut veterans' pensions. The Economy Act did save some money, but the small savings were dwarfed by other bills passed the same week, which called for increased spending. The Beer-Wine Revenue Act legalized 3.2 beer and light wines and levied a tax on both. The Twenty-first Amendment, which was ratified December 5, 1933, repealed the Eighteenth Amendment and ended the prohibition experiment. The veterans, who opposed reduced pensions, and the antiliquor forces, two of the strongest lobbying groups in the nation, were both overwhelmed by a Congress that appeared ready to pass any bill that came to it from the president's office.

Congress gave Roosevelt great power to devalue the dollar and to reduce inflation. Senator Burton K. Wheeler of Montana argued for the old Populist solution of free and unlimited coinage of silver, while others called for issuing billions of dollars in paper currency. The bankers and businessmen feared inflation, but farmers and all who were in debt favored an inflationary policy as a way to raise prices and put more money in their pockets. "I have always favored sound money," Roosevelt announced, "and I do now, but it is 'too darned sound' when it takes so much of farm products to buy a dollar." He rejected the more extreme inflationary plans supported by many congressmen from the agricultural states, but he did take the country off the gold standard. No longer would paper currency be redeemable in gold. The action terrified some conservative businessmen, who argued that it would lead to "uncontrolled inflation and

complete chaos." Even Roosevelt's director of the budget announced solemnly that going off the gold standard "meant the end of Western Civilization."

Devaluation did not end Western civilization, but neither did it lead to instant recovery. After experimenting for a time with pushing the price of gold up by buying it in the open market, Roosevelt and his advisers fixed the price at $35.00 an ounce in January 1934 (against the old price of $20.63). This inflated the dollar by about 40 percent. Roosevelt also tried briefly to induce inflation through the purchase of silver, but then the country settled down to a slightly inflated currency and a dollar based on both gold and silver. Some still believed that gold represented fiscal responsibility, even morality, and others still cried for more inflation.

### Relief Measures

Roosevelt believed in economy in government and in a balanced budget, but he also wanted to help the unemployed and the homeless. It was estimated in 1933 that 1.5 million Americans were homeless. One man with a wife and six children from Latrobe, Pennsylvania, who was being evicted wrote, "I have 10 days to get another house, no job, no means of paying rent, can you advise me as to which would be the most humane way to dispose of myself and family, as this is about the only thing that I see left to do."

Roosevelt's answer was the Federal Emergency Relief Administration (FERA), which Congress authorized with an appropriation of $500 million in direct grants to cities and states. A few months later, Congress created a Civil Works Administration (CWA) to put more than 4 million people to work on various state, municipal, and federal projects. Hopkins, who ran both agencies, had experimented with work relief programs in New York. Like most social workers, he believed it was much better to pay people for some work done than to give them money for clothes and food. A woman with two daughters from Houston, Texas, wrote and asked, "Why don't they give us materials and let us make our children's clothes . . . you've no idea how children hate wearing relief clothes." An accountant working on a road project said, "I'd rather stay out here in that ditch the rest of my life than take one cent of direct relief."

There were many charges of political favoritism and corruption in the CWA, and it was not until the Works Progress Administration was organized in 1935 that work relief became a major part of the plan to relieve the suffering and restore the morale of the unemployed. But the CWA did hire many who had been unemployed. In just over a year, the agency built or restored a half million miles of roads, constructed 40,000 schools and 1,000 airports. It hired 50,000 teachers to keep rural schools open and others to teach adult education courses in the cities. In many ways the CWA helped millions of people get through the bitterly cold winter of 1933–1934. It also put over a billion dollars of purchasing power into the economy. Roosevelt, who later would be accused of deficit spending, feared that the program was costing too much and might create a permanent class of relief recipients. In the spring of 1934, he ordered the CWA closed down.

The Public Works Administration (PWA), directed by Harold Ickes, in some respects overlapped the work of the CWA, but it lasted longer. Between 1933 and 1939, the PWA built hospitals, courthouses, and school buildings. It helped construct structures as diverse as the port of Brownsville, Texas, a bridge that linked Key West to the Florida mainland, and the library at the University of New Mexico. It built the aircraft carriers *Yorktown* and *Enterprise*, planes for the Army Air Corps, and low-cost housing for slum dwellers. One purpose of the PWA was economic pump priming—the stimulation of the economy and consumer spending through the investment of government funds. In the beginning, Ickes was so afraid that there might be scandals in the agency that he spent money slowly and carefully. There were no scandals, but during the first years, PWA projects did little to stimulate the economy.

## Agricultural Adjustment Act

In 1933, farmers were desperate as mounting surpluses and falling prices drastically cut their incomes. Some in the Midwest talked of open rebellion, even of revolution, but many observers saw only hopelessness. Lorena Hickok, a journalist friend of Eleanor Roosevelt who traveled around the country reporting on conditions for Harry Hopkins, described a farmhouse in North Dakota:

No repairs have been made in years. The kitchen floor was all patched up with pieces of tin, a wash boiler cover, tin can lids, some old automobile

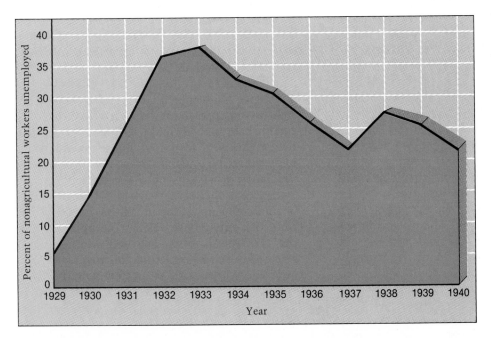

**Unemployment Rate, 1929–1940**

***Source:*** U.S. Bureau of the Census.

license plates. You could see daylight through the crack under the door. Great patches of plaster had fallen from the walls . . . and in the house two little boys . . . were running about without a stitch on save some ragged overalls.

To deal with the agricultural crisis, Congress passed a number of bills in 1933 and 1934. They included the Emergency Farm Mortgage Act, designed to prevent more farm foreclosures and evictions. But the New Deal's principal solution to the farm problem was the Agricultural Adjustment Act (AAA), which sought to control the overproduction of basic commodities so that farmers might regain the same relative purchasing power they had had before World War I. To guarantee these "parity prices" (the average prices in the years 1909–1914), the production of major agricultural staples—wheat, cotton, corn, hogs, rice, tobacco, and milk— would be controlled by paying the farmers to reduce their acreage under cultivation. The AAA levied a tax at the processing stage to pay for the program.

The act aroused great disagreement among farm leaders and economists, but the controversy was nothing compared to the outcry from the public over the initial action of the AAA in the summer of 1933. To prevent a glut on the cotton and pork markets, the agency ordered 10 million acres of cotton plowed up and 6 million little pigs slaughtered. It seemed strange and unnatural, even immoral, to kill pigs and plow up cotton when millions of people were underfed and in need of clothes. The story circulated that in the South, mules trained for many years to walk between the rows of cotton now refused to walk on the cotton plants. Some suggested that those mules were more intelligent than the government bureaucrats who had ordered the action.

The Agricultural Adjustment Act did raise the prices of some agricultural products. But it helped the larger farmers more than the small operators, and it was often disastrous for the tenant farmers and sharecroppers, whom crop reduction made expendable. There were provisions in the act to help marginal farmers, but little trickled down to them. Many were simply cast out on the road with a few possessions and nowhere to go. As for the large farmers, they cultivated their fewer acres more intensely, so that the total crop was not altered very much. In the end, the prolonged drought that hit the farm belt in 1934 did more than the AAA to limit production and raise agricultural prices. But the most important long-range significance of the AAA, which was later declared unconstitutional, was the establishment of the idea that the farmer should be subsidized for limiting his production.

## Industrial Recovery

The flurry of legislation during the first days of the Roosevelt administration contained something for almost every group. The National Industrial Recovery Act (NIRA) was designed to help business, raise prices, control production, and put people back to work. The act established the National Recovery Administration (NRA) with the power to set fair competition codes in all industries. For a time, everyone forgot about antitrust laws and talked of cooperation and planning rather than competition. To run the NRA, Roosevelt appointed Hugh Johnson, who had helped organize the World War I draft and served on the War Industries Board. Johnson used some of his wartime experiences and the enthusiasm of the bond drives to rally the country around the NRA and, implicitly, around all New Deal measures. There were parades and rallies, even a postage stamp, and industries that cooperated could display a blue eagle, the symbol of the NRA. "We Do Our Part," the posters and banners proclaimed, but the results were somewhat less than the promise.

Section 7a of the NIRA, included at the insistence of organized labor, guaranteed labor's right to organize and to bargain collectively and established the National Labor Board to see that their rights were respected. But the board, usually dominated by businessmen, often interpreted the labor provisions of the contracts loosely. Still, it was the labor provisions that explained business disenchantment with the NIRA. In addition, small businessmen complained that the NIRA was unfair to their interests. Any attempt to set prices led to controversy.

Many consumers suspected that the codes and contracts were raising prices, while others feared the return of monopoly in some industries. One woman wrote the president that she was taking down her blue eagle because she had lost her job; another wrote from Tennessee to denounce the NIRA as a joke because it helped only the chain stores. Johnson's booster campaign backfired in the end because anyone with a complaint about a New Deal agency seemed to take it out on the symbol of the blue eagle. Johnson himself was widely disliked, so when the Supreme Court declared the NIRA unconstitutional in 1935, not too many people were sorry. Still, the NIRA was an ambitious attempt to bring some order into a confused business situation, and the labor provisions of the act were picked up later by the National Labor Relations Act.

## Civilian Conservation Corps

One of the most popular and successful of the New Deal programs, the Civilian Conservation Corps (CCC) combined work relief with the preservation of natural resources. It put young unemployed men between the ages of 18 and 25 to work on reforestation, road and park construction, flood control, and other projects. The men lived in work camps (there were over 1,500

in all) and were paid $30 a month, $25 of which had to be sent home to their families. Some complained that the CCC camps, run by the U.S. Army, were unduly military in operation, and one woman wrote from Minnesota to point out that all the best young men were at CCC camps when they ought to be home looking for real jobs and finding brides. Others complained that the CCC did nothing for unemployed young women, so a few special camps were organized for them, but only 8,000 were included in a program that by 1941 had seen 2.5 million men participate. Overall, the CCC was one of the most successful and least controversial of all the New Deal programs.

## Tennessee Valley Authority

Roosevelt, like his Republican namesake, believed in conservation. He promoted flood control projects and added many millions of acres to the country's national forests, wildlife refuges, and fish and game sanctuaries. But the most important New Deal conservation project, the Tennessee Valley Authority (TVA), owed more to Republican George Norris, a progressive senator from Nebraska, than to Roosevelt. During World War I, the federal government had

### The Tennessee Valley Authority

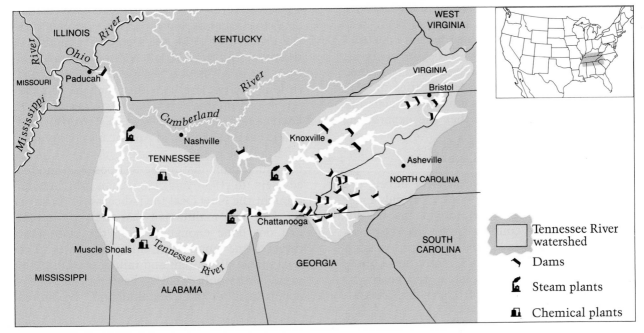

built a hydroelectric plant and two munitions factories at Muscle Shoals, on the Tennessee River in Alabama. The government tried unsuccessfully to sell these facilities to private industry, but all through the 1920s, Norris waged a campaign to have the federal government operate them for the benefit of the people who lived in the valley. Twice Republican presidents vetoed bills that would have allowed federal operation, but Roosevelt endorsed Norris's idea and expanded it to include a regional development plan.

Congress authorized the TVA as an independent public corporation with the power to sell electricity and fertilizer and to promote flood control and land reclamation. Nine major dams and many minor ones were built between 1933 and 1944, and the TVA affected parts of Virginia, North Carolina, Georgia, Alabama, Mississippi, Tennessee, and Kentucky. Some private utility companies claimed that TVA offered unfair competition to private industry, but altogether it was an imaginative experiment in regional planning. It promoted everything from flood control to library bookmobiles. For those who lived in the valley, it meant cheaper electricity. For many, it involved a change in life style. One man from a small town remarked, "I put in an electric hot water heater some time ago, but I have never been about to use it because it cost too much. But now with this new rate I can." For others in the valley, TVA meant radios, electric irons, washing machines, and other appliances for the first time. The largest federal construction project ever launched, it also created jobs for many thousands who helped build the dams. But the regional planning possibilities of TVA were always blunted by government officials and businessmen who feared that the experiment would lead to socialism.

### Critics of the New Deal

The furious legislative activity during the first hundred days of the New Deal did something to alleviate the pessimism and despair hanging over the country. Stock market prices rose slightly, and industrial production was up 11 percent at the end of 1933. Still, the country remained locked in depression, and nearly 12 million Americans were without jobs. Yet Roosevelt captured the imagination of ordinary Americans everywhere. Hundreds of thousands of letters poured into the White House, so many that eventually 50 people had to be hired to answer them. "I've always thought of F.D.R. as my personal friend," a man wrote from Georgia. "I feel very grateful to you for all the good you have already done for all of us," another added from Missouri. "If ever there was a saint, he is one," declared a Wisconsin woman.

But conservatives were not so sure that Roosevelt was a savior; in fact, many businessmen, after being impressed with Roosevelt's early economy measures and approving programs such as the NIRA, began to fear that the president was leading the country toward socialism. Appalled by work relief programs, by regional planning such as the TVA, and by the abandonment of the gold standard, many businessmen were also annoyed by the style of the president, whom they called "that man in the White House."

The conservative revolt against Roosevelt surfaced in the summer of 1934 as the congressional elections approached. A group of disgruntled politicians and businessmen formed the Liberty League. Led by Alfred E. Smith and John W. Davis, two unsuccessful Democratic presidential candidates, the league stood for states' rights, free enterprise, and "the American system of the open shop." The league supported conservative or at least anti–New Deal candidates for Congress, but it had little influence. In the election of 1934, the Democrats increased their majority from 310 to 319 in the House and from 60 to 69 in the Senate (only the second time in the twentieth century that the party in power had increased its control of Congress). A few people were learning to hate Roosevelt, but it was obvious that most Americans approved of what he was doing.

Much more disturbing to Roosevelt and his advisers in 1934 and 1935 than people who thought the New Deal too radical were those on the left who maintained that the government had not done enough to help the poor. One threat came from the Communist party. The widespread discontent and talk of the failure of capitalism would seem to have provided great opportunity for the Communists in the United

States. But except for a few college students and a small number of disillusioned intellectuals and writers, the Communist party attracted few converts. The party particularly failed to win many recruits among the working class in America, even during their time of great despair.

Much more important were other movements promising easy solutions to the problems of poverty and unemployment. In Minnesota, Governor Floyd Olson, elected on a Farm-Labor ticket, accused capitalism of causing the Depression and startled some when he thundered, "I hope the present system of government goes right down to hell." In California, Upton Sinclair, the muckraking socialist and author of *The Jungle,* ran for governor on the platform "End Poverty in California." He promised to pay everyone over 60 years of age a pension of $50 a month and to finance the program with higher income and inheritance taxes. He won in the primary but lost the election, and his EPIC program collapsed.

California also produced Dr. Francis E. Townsend, who claimed he had a national following of over 5 million. His supporters backed the Townsend Old Age Revolving Pension Plan, which promised $200 a month to all unemployed citizens over 60 on the condition that they spent it in the same month they received it. Economists laughed at the utopian scheme, but thousands of Townsend Pension Clubs were organized across the country. As one Minnesota woman wrote to Eleanor Roosevelt, "The old folks who have paid taxes all their lives and built this country up will live in comfort." The plan "will banish crime, give the young a chance to work, pay off the national debt which is mounting every day."

More threatening to Roosevelt and the New Deal than Townsend and Sinclair were the protest movements led by Father Charles E. Coughlin and Senator Huey P. Long of Louisiana.

Father Coughlin, a Roman Catholic priest from the Detroit suburb of Royal Oak, attracted an audience of 30 to 45 million to his national radio show. At first he supported Roosevelt's policies, but then he savagely attacked the New Deal as excessively probusiness. Mixing his religious commentary with visions of a society operating without bankers and big businessmen, he roused his audience with blatantly anti-Semitic appeals. The 1930s was a decade in which anti-Semitism peaked in the United States, and Jews, rather than Catholics, bore the brunt of nativist fury. Groups like the Silver Shirts and the German-American Bund lashed out against Jews. To these and to many other Americans, Father Coughlin's attacks made sense. Most often the "evil" bankers he described were Jewish—the Rothschilds, Warburgs, and Kuhn-Loebs. His message was immensely appealing, especially to the urban lower-middle class.

Huey Long, like Coughlin, had a kind of charisma that won him support from the millions still trying to survive in a country where the continuing depression made day-to-day existence a struggle. Elected governor of Louisiana in 1928, he promoted a "Share the Wealth" program. He taxed the oil refineries and built hospitals, schools, and thousands of miles of new highways. By 1934, he was the virtual dictator of his state, personally controlling the police and the state courts. He threatened to run for president in 1936. Long talked about a guaranteed $2,000 to $3,000 income for all American families (18.3 million families earned less than $1,000 per year in 1936) and promised pensions for the elderly and college educations for the young. He would pay for these programs by taxing the rich and liquidating the great fortunes. Had not an assassin's bullet cut Long down in September 1935, he might have mounted a third-party challenge to Roosevelt.

## THE SECOND NEW DEAL

Responding in part to the discontent of the lower middle class and to the threat of various utopian schemes, Roosevelt moved his programs in 1935 more toward the goals of social reform and social justice. At the same time, he departed from any attempt to cooperate with the business community. "We find our population suffering from old inequalities," Roosevelt announced in his annual message to Congress in January 1935. "In spite of our efforts and in spite of our talk, we have not weeded out the over-privileged and we have not effectively lifted up the underprivileged."

### Work Relief and Social Security

The Works Progress Administration (WPA), authorized by Congress in April 1935, was the first massive attempt to deal with unemployment and its demoralizing effect on millions of Americans. The WPA employed about 3 million people a year on a variety of socially useful projects. The WPA workers, who earned wages lower than private industry paid, built bridges, airports, libraries, roads, and golf courses. Nearly 85 percent of the funds went directly into salaries and wages. A minor but important part of the WPA funding supported writers, artists, actors, and musicians. Richard Wright, Jack Conroy, and Saul Bellow were among the 10,000

*Millions of workers participated in the WPA: here a city street is widened and modernized.*

writers who were paid less than $100 a month. Experimental theater, innovative and well-written guides to all the states, murals painted on the walls of post offices and other public buildings, and the Historical Records Survey were among the long-lasting results of these projects.

Only one member of a family could qualify for a WPA job, and first choice always went to the man in the family. A woman could qualify only if she was head of the household. But eventually more than 13 percent of the people who worked for the WPA were women, although their most common employment was in the sewing room, where old clothes were made over. "For unskilled men we have the shovel. For unskilled women we have only the needle," one official remarked.

The WPA was controversial from the beginning. There were charges that Communists had been hired to paint murals or work on the state guides. For some, a lazy good-for-nothing leaning on a shovel symbolized the WPA. Others who were employed resented the make-work aspects of many of the projects. The initials WPA, some charged, stood for "We Pay for All" or "We Putter Around." Yet for all the criticism, the WPA did useful work; the program built nearly 6,000 schools, more than 2,500 hospitals, and 13,000 playgrounds. More important, it gave millions of unemployed Americans a sense that

### Distribution of Income, 1935–1936

*Source:* U.S. Bureau of the Census.

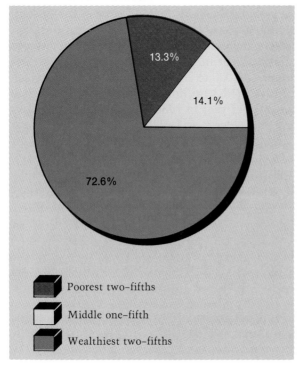

13.3%

14.1%

72.6%

- ■ Poorest two-fifths
- □ Middle one-fifth
- ▨ Wealthiest two-fifths

they were working and bringing in a paycheck to support their families.

The National Youth Administration (NYA) supplemented the work of the WPA and assisted young men and women between the ages of 16 and 25, many of them students. A young law student named Richard Nixon earned 35 cents an hour working for the NYA while he was at Duke University, and Lyndon Johnson began his political career as director of the Texas NYA.

Since the progressive period, a number of social workers and reformers had been arguing for a national system of health insurance, old age pensions, and unemployment insurance. By the 1930s, the United States remained the only major industrial country without such programs. Within the Roosevelt circle, it was Frances Perkins who argued most strongly for social insurance, but the popularity of the Townsend Plan and other schemes to aid the elderly helped convince Roosevelt of the need to act. The number of people over 65 in the country increased from 5.7 million in 1925 to 7.8 million in 1935, and that group demanded action.

The Social Security Act that Congress finally passed in 1935 was a compromise. The plan for federal health insurance was quickly dropped because of opposition from the medical profession. The best-known provision of the act was old age and survivor insurance to be paid for by a tax of one percent on both employers and employees. The benefits initially ranged from $10 to $85 a month. The act also established a cooperative federal-state system of unemployment compensation. Other provisions authorized federal grants to the states to assist in caring for the crippled and the blind. The Social Security Act also provided some aid to dependent children, which would eventually expand to become the largest federal welfare program.

The National Association of Manufacturers denounced social security as a program that would regiment the people and destroy individual self-reliance. In reality it was a conservative and, in some ways, an inept system. In no other country was social insurance paid for in part by a regressive tax on the workers' wages. "We put those payroll contributions there so as to give the contributors a legal, moral, and political right to collect their pensions and unemploy-

ment benefits," Roosevelt later explained. "With those taxes in there, no damn politician can ever scrap my social security program." But the law also excluded large numbers of people, including those who needed it most, such as farm laborers and domestic servants. It discriminated against married women wage earners, and it failed to protect against sickness. Yet for all its weaknesses, it was one of the most important New Deal measures. A landmark in American social legislation, it signified government's acceptance of some responsibility to care for its citizens.

### Aiding the Farmers

The Social Security Act and the Works Progress Administration were the most important, but certainly not the only, signs of Roosevelt's greater concern for social reform. The flurry of legislation in 1935 and early 1936, often called the "second New Deal," also included an effort to help American farmers. Over 1.7 million farm families had incomes of under $500 annually in 1935, and 42 percent of all those who lived on farms were tenants. The Resettlement Administration (RA), motivated in part by a Jeffersonian dream of yeoman farmers working their own land, set out to relocate tenant farmers on land purchased by the government. Lack of funds and

*Mexican workers, actively recruited in the 1920s, found themselves excluded from jobs during the Depression and were often deported back to Mexico.*

fears that the Roosevelt administration was trying to establish collective farms patterned after those in Russia limited the effectiveness of the Resettlement Administration program.

Much more important in making life easier for farm families was the Rural Electrification Administration (REA), which was authorized in 1935 to loan money to cooperatives to generate and distribute electricity in isolated rural areas not served by private utilities. Only 10 percent of the nation's farms had electricity in 1936. When the REA's lines were finally attached, they dramatically changed the lives of millions of farm families who had only been able to dream about the radios, washing machines, and farm equipment advertised in magazines.

In the hill country west of Austin, Texas, for example, there was no electricity until the end of the 1930s. Life went on in the small towns and on the ranches much as it had for decades. Houses were illuminated by kerosene lamps whose wicks had to be trimmed just right or the lamp smoked or went out, but even with perfect adjustment it was difficult to read by them. There were no bathrooms because bathrooms required running water, and running water depended on an electric pump. "Yes, we had running water," one woman remembered. "I always said we had running water because I grabbed those two buckets up and ran the two hundred yards to the house with them."

Women and children hauled water constantly—for infrequent baths, for continuous canning (because without a refrigerator, fruits and vegetables had to be put up almost immediately or they spoiled), and for washday. Washday, always Monday, meant scrubbing clothes by hand with harsh soap on a washboard; it meant boiling clothes in a large copper vat over a wood stove and stirring them with a wooden fork. It was a hot and backbreaking job, especially in summer. Then the women had to lift the hot, heavy clothes into a rinsing tub. After the clothes were thoroughly mixed with bluing (to make them white), they had to be wrung out by hand, then carried to the lines, where they were hung to dry. Tuesday was for ironing, and even in summer a wood fire was needed to heat the irons. It was a rare ironing day when a woman's hand did not slip and cause an ugly burn. And when irons got dirty on the stove, as could so easily happen, dirt got on a white shirt or blouse, and it had to be washed all over again.

It was memory of life in the hill country and personal knowledge of how hard his mother and grandmother toiled that inspired a young congressman from Texas, Lyndon Johnson, to work hard to bring rural electrification to the area. In November 1939, the lights finally came on in the hill country, connecting the area to the twentieth century.

### Controlling Corporate Power and Taxing the Wealthy

In the summer of 1935, Roosevelt also moved to control the large corporations, and he even toyed with radical plans to tax the well-to-do heavily and redistribute wealth in the United States. The Public Utility Holding Company Act, which passed Congress in 1935, was aimed at restricting the power of the giant utility companies, the 12 largest of which controlled more than half the power produced in the country. The act gave various government commissions the authority to regulate and control the power companies and included a "death sentence" clause that gave each company five years to demonstrate that its services were efficient. If it could not demonstrate this, the government could dissolve the company. This was one of the most radical attempts to control corporate power in American history.

In his message to Congress in 1935, Roosevelt also pointed out that the federal revenue laws had "done little to prevent an unjust concentration of wealth and economic power." He suggested steeper income taxes for high-income groups and a much larger inheritance tax. When Congress dropped the stiff inheritance tax provision, however, Roosevelt did not fight to have it restored. Even the weakened bill, increasing estate and gift taxes and raising the income tax rates at the top, angered many in the business community who thought that Roosevelt had sold out to Huey Long's "Share the Wealth" scheme.

### The New Deal for Labor

The increasingly prolabor stance of the Roosevelt administration in 1935 fed the fear of the business leaders and other conservatives. Like many reformers of the progressive period, Roosevelt was more interested in improving the lot of the workingman by passing social legislation than by strengthening the bargaining position of organized labor. He had escaped the antilabor bias of most of those of his background and class, but he had no particular understanding or sympathy for organized labor. Yet he saw labor as an important balance to the power of industry, and he listened to his advisers, especially to Frances Perkins and to Senator Robert Wagner of New York, who persistently presented the needs of organized labor to him.

Even before the Supreme Court declared the NIRA, with its strong labor provisions, unconstitutional in 1935, Wagner had been working hard in Congress for a bill that would replace and extend Section 7a. At first Roosevelt was only mildly interested. But a series of strikes in San Francisco, Minneapolis, and Toledo, some bitter and violent, convinced him of the need for action. Belatedly he supported the Wagner Act, officially called the National Labor Relations Act, which outlawed blacklisting and a number of other practices and reasserted labor's right to organize and to bargain collectively. The act also established a Labor Relations Board with the power to certify a properly elected bargaining unit. The act did not require workers to join unions, but it made the federal government a regulator, or at least a neutral force, in management-labor relations. That alone made the National Labor Relations Act one of the most important of the New Deal reform measures.

The Roosevelt administration's friendly attitude toward organized labor helped to increase union membership from under 3 million in 1933 to 4.5 million by 1935. Many groups, however, were left out, including farm laborers, unskilled workers, and women. Approximately 10 million women worked for wages in the 1930s, and the percentage of women in the work force increased slightly during the decade. Yet only about 3 percent of the women who worked belonged to unions, and women were paid only about 60 percent of the wages paid to men for equivalent work. Because women labored at occupations less affected by the economic downturn, fewer women than men lost their jobs during the thirties (there were fewer women employed in heavy industry, for example). Many families survived only because of the woman's paycheck.

Still, many people resented the fact that women were employed at all, and there was a growing assumption, even stronger than in the 1920s, that a woman's place was in the home. The Brotherhood of Railway and Steamship Clerks ruled that no married woman whose husband could support her was eligible for a job. One writer had a perfect solution for the unemployment problem. "There are approximately 10,000,000 people out of work in the United States today," he wrote; "there are also 10,000,000 or more women, married and single, who are jobholders. Simply fire the women, who shouldn't be working anyway, and hire the men. Presto! No unemployment. No relief rolls. No Depression." Women remained underpaid, underunionized, and underrepresented in many "male" occupations. But during a decade when popular culture insisted that women belonged at home, many women had to work for wages.

The American Federation of Labor had little interest in organizing the army of unskilled workers, but a new group of committed and militant labor leaders emerged in the 1930s to take up that task. John L. Lewis, the eloquent head of the United Mine Workers who had won union recognition from the soft coal industry,

*Frances Perkins, a former social worker, served as Roosevelt's Secretary of Labor.*

was the most aggressive, but he was joined by David Dubinsky of the International Ladies Garment Workers and Sidney Hillman, president of the Amalgamated Clothing Workers. Dubinsky was born in Poland, Hillman in Lithuania. Both were socialists who believed in economic planning, but both had worked closely with social justice progressives. Hillman had even lived for a time at Hull House in Chicago. These new progressive labor leaders formed the Committee of Industrial Organization (CIO) within the AFL and set out to organize workers in the steel, auto, and rubber industries. They organized everyone into an industrywide union much the way the Knights of Labor had done in the 1880s, rather than separating workers by skill or craft as the AFL preferred.

Many young and militant workers, including many blacks, joined the CIO. They were angry at their poor pay and the way management controlled their lives. In 1936, the workers at three rubber plants in Akron, Ohio, went on strike without permission from the leaders. Instead of picketing outside the factory, they occupied the buildings and took them over. The "sit-down strike" became a new protest technique. A strike against a General Motors factory in Atlanta, Georgia, spread to Flint, Michigan. When management tried to cut off the delivery of food to the workers barricaded inside the factories, the workers drove off the police with a barrage of auto door hinges, bolts, stones, bottles, and coffee cups. The police retaliated with tear gas and rifles but were finally driven off by high-powered water hoses that the workers discovered in the factory. Fourteen of the pickets and spectators were wounded, and several policemen were injured by flying objects.

At one point in the struggle, which became known as the "Battle of Running Bulls," a young woman in the crowd grabbed a microphone and urged all the women spectators to join the pickets. Other women organized an emergency brigade to bring food and water to the strikers. "We had not asked for it," Bob Travis, one of the organizers of the strike recalled. "We had been content to allow reason and common sense to rule in our relationship with the company. But when pressed . . . we had to answer blow with blow to convince General Motors of our rights under the law." It took six weeks, but General

Motors finally accepted the United Auto Workers as their employees' bargaining unit.

The General Motors strike was the most important event in a critical period of labor upheaval. A group of workers using disorderly but largely nonviolent tactics (as the civil rights advocates would in the mid-1950s) demanded their rights under the law. They helped to make labor's voice heard in the decision-making process in major industries where labor had long been denied any role. They also helped to raise the status of organized labor in the eyes of many Americans.

"Labor does not seek industrial strife," Lewis announced. "It wants peace, but a peace with justice." As the sit-down tactic spread, justice was often accompanied by violence. Chrysler capitulated without much difficulty. But the Ford Motor Company used hired gunmen to discourage the strikes. A bloody struggle ensued before Ford finally agreed to accept the UAW as the bargaining agent. Even U.S. Steel, which had been militantly antiunion, signed an agreement with the Steel Workers Organizing Committee calling for a 40-hour week and an eight-hour day. But other steel companies refused to go along. In Chicago on Memorial Day in 1937, a confrontation between the police and peaceful pickets at the Republic Steel plant resulted in ten deaths. In the "Memorial Day Massacre," as it came to be called, the police fired without provocation into a crowd of workers and their families, who had gathered near the plant in a holiday mood. All ten of the dead were shot in the back.

Despite the violence and management's use of undercover agents within unions, the CIO gained many members. William Green and the leadership of the AFL were horrified at the aggressive tactics of the new labor leaders. They expelled the CIO leaders from the AFL only to see them form a separate Congress of Industrial Organization (the initials stayed the same). By the end of the decade, the CIO had infused the labor movement with a new spirit. Accepting unskilled workers, blacks, and others who had never belonged to a union before, they won increased pay, better working conditions, and the right to bargain collectively in most of the basic American industries. Jim Cole, a black butcher at one of the meatpacking plants in

Chicago, tried to join the Amalgamated Butchers and Meat Cutters, an AFL union, but they turned him away because he was black. He remembered when the CIO came. "Well, I tell you, we Negroes was glad to see it come. Sometimes the bosses or the company stooges try to keep the white boys from joining the union. They say, 'You don't want to belong to a black man's organization. That's all the CIO is.' Don't fool nobody, but they got to lie, spread lying words around."

## America's Minorities in the 1930s

A half million blacks became union members through the CIO during the 1930s, and many blacks were aided by various New Deal agencies. Yet the familiar pattern of discrimination, low-paying jobs, and intimidation through violence persisted. Lynchings in the South actually increased in the New Deal years, rising from 8 in 1932 to 28 in 1933 and 20 in 1935. An NAACP representative investigating the lynching of a young black man in Florida in 1933 decided that the alleged charge of rape was only the surface cause; the more basic reason was economic. "The lynching had two objects; first to intimidate and threaten white employers of Negro labor, and secondly to scare and terrorize Negroes so they would leave the country and their jobs could be taken over by white men."

The migration of blacks to northern cities, which had started during World War I, continued during the 1930s. Lynchings and the threat of violence caused many blacks to migrate. The collapse of cotton prices also forced black farmers and farm laborers to flee north in order to survive. But since most were poorly educated, they discovered that they soon became trapped in northern ghettoes, where they were eligible for only the most menial jobs. The black unemployment rate was triple that of whites, and blacks often received less per person in welfare payments.

Black leaders attacked the Roosevelt administration for supporting or allowing segregation in government-sponsored facilities. The TVA model town of Norris, Tennessee, was off limits for blacks, and AAA policies actually drove blacks off the land in the South. The CCC segregated black and white workers, and the PWA financed segregated housing projects. Some charged that NRA stood for "Negroes Rarely Allowed." Many blacks wrote in broken English to the president or to Eleanor Roosevelt to protest discrimination in New Deal agencies. As one woman from Georgia put it, "I can't sign my name Mr. President they will beat me up and run me away from here and this is my home." Blacks ought to realize, a writer in The Crisis warned in 1935, "that the powers-that-be in the Roosevelt administration have nothing for them."

Roosevelt, dependent on the vote of the solid South and fearing that he might antagonize southern congressmen whose backing he needed, refused to support the two major civil rights bills of the era, an antilynching bill and a bill to abolish the poll tax. Yet Harold Ickes and Harry Hopkins worked hard to make sure that blacks were given opportunities in the CCC, the WPA, and other agencies. By 1941, there were 150,000 black federal employees, more than three times the number during the Hoover administration. Although most of them worked in the lower ranks, there were also lawyers, architects, office managers, and engineers.

Partly responsible for the presence of more black employees was the "black cabinet," a group of over 50 young blacks who had appointments in almost every government department and New Deal agency. The group met on many Friday evenings at the home of Mary McLeod Bethune to discuss problems and plan strategy. The daughter of a sharecropper and one of 17 children, Bethune had worked her way through the Moody Bible Institute in Chicago. She had founded a black primary school in Florida and then transformed it into Bethune-Cookman College. In the 1920s, she had organized the National Council of Negro Women. In 1934, Harry Hopkins, following the advice of Eleanor Roosevelt, appointed her to the advisory committee of the National Youth Administration. Mary Bethune had a large impact on New Deal policy and on the black cabinet. She spoke out forcefully, she picketed and protested, and she intervened shrewdly to obtain civil rights and more jobs for black Americans.

Although Roosevelt appointed a number of blacks to government positions, he was never particularly committed to civil rights. That was not true of Eleanor Roosevelt, who was educated in part by Mary McLeod Bethune. In 1939, when the Daughters of the American Revolution refused to allow Marian Anderson, a black concert singer, to use their stage, Mrs. Roosevelt publicly protested and resigned her membership in the DAR. She also arranged for Anderson to sing from the steps of the Lincoln Memorial, where 75,000 people gathered to listen and to support civil rights for all black citizens.

Many Mexicans who had been actively recruited for working American farms and in American businesses in the 1920s discovered that they were not needed in the Depression decade. Hundreds of thousands lost their jobs and drifted from the urban barrios to small towns and farms in the Southwest looking for work. By one estimate, there were 400,000 Mexican migrants in Texas alone. The competition for jobs increased the ethnic prejudice. Signs inscribed "Only White Labor Employed" and "No Niggers, Mexicans, or Dogs Allowed" expressed the hate and fear that the Mexicans faced everywhere.

Some New Deal agencies helped destitute Mexicans. A few worked for the CCC and the WPA, but to be employed, an applicant had to qualify for state relief, and that automatically eliminated most migrants. The primary solution was not to provide aid for the Mexicans but to ship them back to Mexico. The Southern Pacific Railroad offered to return the migrants to Mexico for $14.70 a head. A trainload of repatriates left Los Angeles every month during 1933, and thousands were deported from other cities. One estimate placed the number sent back in 1932 at 200,000.

Not all the Mexicans were repatriated, however, and some who remained became militant in their efforts to obtain fair treatment. Mexican strawberry pickers went on strike in El Monte, California, and 18,000 cotton pickers walked away from their jobs in the San Joaquin Valley in 1933. In Gallup, New Mexico, several thousand Mexican coal miners walked out on strike. They constructed a village of shacks and planned to wait out the strike. Even though the miners were aided by some writers and artists from Santa Fe and Taos, the strikers were evicted from their village. Their leader, Jesus Pallares, was arrested and, like so many other Mexican labor leaders, deported to Mexico.

During the Depression, Native Americans also experienced hunger, disease, and despair, and their plight was compounded by years of exploitation. Since the Dawes Act of 1887 (described in Chapter 18), government policy had sought to make the Indian into a property-owning farmer and to limit tribal rights. Native Americans lost over 60 percent of their original 138 million acres through the sale of land declared surplus or by selling their own land, while

*A staunch advocate of equal rights, Eleanor Roosevelt met in 1937, with the National Youth Administration's executive director, Aubrey Williams, and its director of Negro Activities, Mary McLeod Bethume.*

another 20 percent had been parceled out in lots of 160 acres to heads of Native American families who "adopted the habits of civilized life." Few Native Americans profited from this system, but many whites did. Just as other progressives sought the quick assimilation of immigrants, the progressive-era Indian commissioners speeded up the allotment process to increase Indian detribalization. But many Native Americans who remained on the reservations were not even citizens. Finally, in 1924, Congress granted citizenship to all Indians born in the United States. The original Americans became United States citizens, but that did not end their suffering.

Franklin Roosevelt brought a new spirit to Indian policy by appointing John Collier as commissioner of Indian affairs. Collier, who had worked with the immigrant poor in New York, discovered among the Pueblo tribe near Taos, New Mexico, the sense of community and culture he missed in urban, industrial America. He had reorganized the American Indian Defense Association in 1923. As commissioner, he was primarily responsible for the passage of the Indian Reorganization Act of 1934, which sought to restore the political independence of the tribes and to end the allotment policy of the Dawes Act. "Even where a tribal group is split into factions, where leadership has broken down, where Indians clamor to distribute the tribal property, even there deep forces of cohesion persist and can be evoked," Collier wrote.

The bill also sought to promote "the study of Indian civilization" and to "preserve and develop the special cultural contributions and achievements of such civilization, including Indian arts, crafts, skills and traditions." Not all Indians agreed with the new policies. Some chose to become members of the dominant culture, and the Navajos voted to reject the Reorganization Act. Some Americans charged that the act was inspired by communism. Others argued that its principal result would be to increase government bureaucracy, while missionaries claimed that the government was promoting paganism by allowing the Indians to practice their native religions. Still, thanks to the Indian Reorganization Act and a more concerned attitude during the New Deal, there was a reversal of land policy, a revival of interest in tribal identity, and a recognition of the importance of Indian culture, language, and ritual.

## Women and the New Deal

Women made some gains during the 1930s, and more women were appointed to high government positions than in any previous administration. Besides Frances Perkins, the secretary of labor, there was Molly Dewson, a social worker who had worked for the Massachusetts Girls Parole Department and the National Consumers League before becoming head of the Women's Division of the Democratic Committee and then an adviser to Roosevelt. Working closely with Eleanor Roosevelt to promote women's causes, she helped to achieve a number of firsts: two women appointed ambassadors, a judge on the U.S. Court of Appeals, the director of the mint, and many women in government agencies. Katharine Lenroot, director of the Children's Bureau, and Mary Anderson, head of the Women's Bureau, selected many other women to serve in their agencies. Some of these women had worked together as social workers and now joined government bureaus to continue the fight for social justice. But they were usually located in offices where they did not threaten male prerogatives.

Despite the number of women working for the government, feminism declined in the 1930s. Instead of fighting for the absolute right of women to work, it became necessary to argue for married women's rights to support their families. The older feminists died or retired, and they were not replaced by younger women. Women role models in the 1930s seemed to come from Hollywood rather than from Hull House. One committed feminist who did cause a great stir in the thirties was Amelia Earhart, a former social worker who became fascinated with flying. She was attractive and daring and made good copy. She flew across the Atlantic alone and from Newark to Mexico City, but it was her disappearance somewhere over the Pacific in 1937 that garnered the most attention. Despite some dramatic exceptions, the image of woman's proper role in the 1930s continued to be housewife and mother.

## THE END OF THE NEW DEAL

The New Deal was not a consistent or well-organized effort to end the Depression and restructure society. A considerable amount of contradiction riddled the measures passed by Congress. Roosevelt was a politician and a pragmatist, not one who was concerned about ideological consistency. The first New Deal in 1933 and 1934 was basically concerned with relief and recovery, while the legislation passed in 1935 and 1936 was more involved with social reform. In many ways the election of 1936 marked the high point of Roosevelt's power and influence. After 1937, in part because of the growing threat of war but also because of increasing opposition in Congress, the pace of social legislation slowed. Yet several measures passed in 1937 and 1938 had far-reaching significance. Among them were bills that provided for a minimum wage and for housing reform.

### The Election of 1936

The Republicans in 1936 nominated Governor Alfred Landon of Kansas, a moderate who had supported Theodore Roosevelt in 1912. Although he attacked the New Deal at every opportunity, charging that new government programs were wasteful and created a dangerous federal bureaucracy, he did not offer to change much. He only promised to do the same thing more cheaply and efficiently. Two-thirds of the newspapers in the country supported Landon, and the *Literary Digest,* on the basis of a "scientific" poll, predicted his victory.

Roosevelt, helped by signs that the economy was recovering and supported by a coalition of the Democratic South, organized labor, the farmers, and urban voters, won easily. A majority of black Americans for the first time deserted the party of Abraham Lincoln, not because of Roosevelt's interest in civil rights for blacks but because New Deal relief programs assisted many blacks, who made up a large part of the country's poor. A viable candidate to the left of the New Deal failed to materialize. In fact, the Socialist party candidate, Norman Thomas, polled less than 200,000 votes. Roosevelt won by over 10 million votes and carried every state except Maine and Vermont. Even the traditionally Republican states of Pennsylvania, Delaware, and Connecticut, which had voted Republican in every election since 1856, went for Roosevelt. "To some generations much is given," Roosevelt announced in his acceptance speech; "of other generations much is expected. This generation has a rendezvous with destiny." Now he had a mandate to continue his New Deal social and economic reforms.

"I see one-third of a nation ill-housed, ill-clad, ill-nourished," Roosevelt declared in his second inaugural address, and he vowed to alter that situation. But the president's first action in 1937 did not call for legislation to alleviate poverty. Instead he announced a plan to reform

### FDR's Successful Presidential Campaigns, 1932–1944

| YEAR | CANDIDATES | PARTY | POPULAR VOTE | ELECTORAL VOTE |
|------|------------|-------|--------------|----------------|
| 1932 | FRANKLIN D. ROOSEVELT | Democratic | 22,809,638 (57.3%) | 472 |
|      | Herbert C. Hoover | Republican | 15,758,901 (39.6%) | 59 |
|      | Norman Thomas | Socialist | 881,951 (2.2%) | 0 |
| 1936 | FRANKLIN D. ROOSEVELT | Democratic | 27,751,612 (60.7%) | 523 |
|      | Alfred M. Landon | Republican | 16,681,913 (36.4%) | 8 |
|      | William Lemke | Union | 891,858 (1.9%) | 0 |
| 1940 | FRANKLIN D. ROOSEVELT | Democratic | 27,243,466 (54.7%) | 449 |
|      | Wendell L. Willkie | Republican | 22,304,755 (44.8%) | 82 |
| 1944 | FRANKLIN D. ROOSEVELT | Democratic | 25,602,505 (52.8%) | 432 |
|      | Thomas E. Dewey | Republican | 22,006,278 (44.5%) | 99 |

the Supreme Court and the judicial system. The Court had not only invalidated a number of New Deal measures—including, most importantly, the NIRA and the AAA—but other measures as well. Increasingly angry at the "nine old men" who seemed to be blocking progress, Roosevelt hoped to gain power to appoint an extra justice for each justice over 70 years of age, of whom there were six. His plan also called for modernizing the court system at all levels, but that plan got lost in the public outcry over the "court-packing" scheme.

Roosevelt's plan was aimed at nullifying the influence of some of the older and more reactionary justices, but he miscalculated badly. Republicans accused him of being a dictator and of subverting the Constitution. Many congressmen from his own party refused to support him. After months of controversy, he finally withdrew the legislation and admitted defeat. He had perhaps misunderstood his mandate, and he certainly underestimated the respect, even the reverence, that most Americans felt for the Supreme Court. Even in times of economic catastrophe, Americans proved themselves fundamentally conservative toward their institutions, in stark contrast to Europeans, who experimented radically with their governments.

Ironically, though he lost the battle of the Supreme Court, Roosevelt won the war in the end. By the spring of 1937, the Court began to reverse its position and in a 5–4 decision upheld the National Labor Relations Act. Then on July 1, Justice Willis Van Devanter retired, allowing Roosevelt to make his first Supreme Court appointment. This assured at least a shaky liberal majority on the Court. But Roosevelt triumphed

at great cost. His attempt to reorganize the Court dissipated a lot of energy and caused a loss of momentum in his legislative program. The most unpopular action he took as president, it made him vulnerable to criticism from opponents of one or another aspect of the New Deal.

In late 1936 and early 1937, it appeared that the country was finally recovering from the long depression; employment was up, and even the stock market had recovered some of its losses. But in August, the fragile prosperity collapsed. Unemployment shot back up nearly to the peak levels of 1934, industrial production fell, and the stock market plummeted. Roosevelt had probably helped to cause the recession by assuming that the prosperity of 1936 was permanent. He cut federal spending and reduced outlays for relief. He had always believed in balanced budgets and limited government spending, but now, in the face of an embarrassing economic slump that caused many to charge that the New Deal had been a failure, he gave in to those of his advisers who were followers of John Maynard Keynes, the British economist.

Keynes argued that to get out of a depression, the government must spend massive amounts of money on goods and services. This would increase purchasing power and revive production. For the first time, the administration consciously practiced deficit spending, by increasing the money spent on the WPA and other agencies in order to stimulate the economy. It was not a well-planned or well-coordinated effort, however. The economy responded slowly but never fully recovered until wartime expenditures, beginning in 1941, finally eliminated unemployment and ended the Depression.

*Roosevelt's popularity was affirmed with his election to a second term in 1936.*

## Social Reform Continues

Despite an increasingly hostile Congress, a number of important bills passed during 1937 and 1938 completed the New Deal reform legislation. The Bankhead-Jones Farm Tenancy Act of 1937 created the Farm Security Administration to solve the problem of farm tenants, sharecroppers, and people who had lost their farms. More than a million men, women, and children were drifting aimlessly and hopelessly looking for work. Their plight was worsened by the drought that had created a "dust bowl" in the Southwest. It was these conditions that John Steinbeck captured in *The Grapes of Wrath* (1939) in his description of the Joad family and their desperate condition as they migrated in an ancient Hudson from Oklahoma to California. The Farm Security Administration, which provided loans to grain collectives, also set up camps for migratory workers. Some people saw such policies as the first step toward Communist collectives, but the FSA, in fact, never had enough money to make a real difference.

A new Agricultural Adjustment Act, passed in 1938, attempted to meet the problem of farm surpluses, which still existed even after hundreds of thousands of farmers had lost their farms. The new act replaced the processing tax, which had been declared unconstitutional, with direct payments from the federal Treasury to farmers, added a soil conservation program, and provided for marketing of surplus crops. Like its predecessor, it tried to stabilize farm prices by controlling production. But only the outbreak of World War II would end the problem of farm surplus, and then only temporarily.

One of the dreams of progressive reformers was to provide better housing for the urban poor. They believed that a better home environment would help produce better citizens. They had campaigned for city ordinances and state laws. They had built model tenements, but the first experiment with federal housing occurred during World War I. That brief experience encouraged a number of social reformers, who later became advisers to Roosevelt. They convinced him that federal low-cost housing should be part of New Deal reform.

The Reconstruction Finance Corporation made low-interest loans to housing projects, and a few housing projects were constructed by the Public Works Administration. But it was not until the Wagner-Steagall Housing Act of 1937 that Roosevelt and his advisers tried to develop a comprehensive housing policy for the poor. The act provided federal funds for slum-clearance projects and for the construction of low-cost housing. By 1939, however, only 117,000 units had been built. Many of these housing projects were bleak and boxlike, and many of them soon became problems rather than solutions. Though it made the first effort, the New Deal did not meet the challenge of providing decent housing for millions of American citizens.

In the long run, New Deal housing legislation had a greater impact on middle-class housing policies and patterns. During the first hundred days of the New Deal, Congress passed a bill at Roosevelt's urging creating the Home Owners Loan Corporation (HOLC), which over the next two years made over $3 billion in low-interest loans and helped more than a million people save their homes from foreclosure. The HOLC also had a wide impact on housing policy. It introduced the long-term fixed-rate mortgage for the first time. Formerly, all mortgages were for periods of no more than five years and were subject to frequent renegotiation. The HOLC also introduced a uniform system of real estate appraisal that tended to undervalue urban property, especially in neighborhoods that were old, crowded, and ethnically mixed. The system gave the highest ratings to suburban developments where there had been no "infiltration of Jews" or other undesirable groups. This was the beginning of the practice later called "redlining" that made it difficult if not impossible for prospective homeowners to obtain a mortgage in many urban areas.

The Federal Housing Administration (FHA), created in 1934 by the National Housing Act, expanded and extended many of these HOLC policies. The FHA insured mortgages, many of them for 25 or 30 years, reduced the initial down payment required from 30 percent to under 10 percent, and thus made it possible for over 11 million families to buy homes between 1934 and 1972. The system, however, tended to favor the purchase of new suburban homes rather than the repair of older urban residences. New Deal housing policies helped to make the suburban home with the long FHA mortgage part of the American way of life, but the policies also contributed to the decline of many urban neighborhoods.

Just as important as housing legislation was the Fair Labor Standards Act, which passed Congress in June 1938. Roosevelt's bill proposed for all industries engaged in interstate commerce a minimum wage of 25 cents an hour, to rise in two years to 40 cents an hour, and a maximum workweek of 44 hours, to be reduced to 40 hours. The legislation was much amended by Congress, and many groups, including farm laborers and domestic servants, were exempted from the law. Yet when it went into effect, three-quarters of a million workers immediately

## Key New Deal Legislation

| YEAR | LEGISLATION | PROVISIONS |
|---|---|---|
| 1932 | Reconstruction Finance Corporation (RFC) | Granted emergency loans to banks, life insurance companies, and railroads. (Passed during Hoover administration.) |
| 1933 | Civilian Conservation Corps (CCC) | Employed young men (and a few women) in reforestation, road construction, and flood control projects. |
| 1933 | Agricultural Adjustment Act (AAA) | Granted farmers direct payments for reducing production of certain products. Funds for payments provided by a processing tax, which was later declared unconstitutional. |
| 1933 | Tennessee Valley Authority (TVA) | Created independent public corporation to construct dams and power projects and to develop the economy of a nine-state area in the Tennessee River valley. |
| 1933 | National Industrial Recovery Act (NIRA) | Sought to revive business through a series of fair-competition codes. Section 7a guaranteed labor's right to organize. (Later declared unconstitutional.) |
| 1933 | Public Works Administration (PWA) | Sought to increase employment and business activity through construction of roads, buildings, and other projects. |
| 1934 | National Housing Act creates Federal Housing Administration (FHA) | Insured loans made by banks for construction of new homes and repair of old homes. |
| 1935 | Emergency Relief Appropriation Act creates Works Progress Administration (WPA) | Employed over 8 million people to repair roads, build bridges, and work on other projects; also hired artists and writers. |
| 1935 | Social Security Act | Established unemployment compensation and old age and survivors' insurance paid for by a joint tax on employers and employees. |
| 1935 | National Labor Relations Act (Wagner-Connery Act) | Recognized the right of employees to join labor unions and to bargain collectively; created a new National Labor Relations Board to supervise elections and to prevent unfair labor practices. |
| 1935 | Public Utility Holding Company Act | Outlawed pyramiding of gas and electricity companies through the use of holding companies and restricted these companies to activity in one area; a "death sentence" clause gave companies five years to prove local, useful, and efficient operation or be dissolved. |
| 1937 | National Housing Act (Wagner-Steagall Act) | Authorized low-rent public housing projects. |
| 1938 | Agricultural Adjustment Act (AAA) | Continued price supports and payments to farmers to limit production, as in 1933 act, but replaced processing tax with direct federal payment. |
| 1938 | Fair Labor Standards Act | Established minimum wage of 40 cents an hour and maximum workweek of 40 hours in enterprises engaged in interstate commerce. |

received pay raises, and by 1940, some 12 million had had their pay increased. The law also prohibited child labor in interstate commerce, making it the first permanent federal law to prohibit youngsters under 16 from working. And without emphasizing the matter, the law made no distinction between men and women, thus diminishing, if not completely ending, the need for special legislation for women and undercutting the argument of reformers who had opposed an equal-rights amendment to the Constitution.

## THE OTHER SIDE OF THE THIRTIES

The Great Depression and the New Deal so dominate the history of the 1930s that it is easy to conclude that nothing else happened, that there were only bread lines and relief agencies. But there is another side of the decade. A communications revolution changed the lives of middle-class Americans. The sale of radios and attendance at movies increased during the thirties, and literature flourished. Americans were fascinated by technology, especially automobiles. Many people traveled during the decade; they stayed in motor courts and looked ahead to a brighter future dominated by streamlined appliances and gadgets that would mean an easier life.

### Taking to the Road

"People give up everything in the world but their car," a banker in Muncie, Indiana, remarked during the Depression, and that seems to have been true in all sections of the country. Although automobile production dropped off after 1929 and did not recover until the end of the thirties, the number of motor vehicles registered, which declined from 26.7 million in 1930 to just over 24 million in 1933, increased to over 32 million by 1940. If many people could not afford a new car, they drove a used one. Even the "Okies" fleeing the dust bowl of the Southwest traveled in cars. They were secondhand, rundown cars to be sure, but the fact that even many poor Americans owned cars shocked visitors from Europe, where the automobile was still only for the rich. The American middle class traveled at an increasing rate after the low point of 1932 and 1933. In 1938, the tourist industry was the third largest in the United States, behind only steel and automobile production. Over 4 million Americans traveled every year, and four out of five went by car. Many dragged a trailer to sleep in or stopped at the growing number of tourist courts and overnight cabins. In these predecessors of the motel there were no doormen, no bellhops, no register to sign. At the tourist court, all the owner wanted was the automobile license number.

### The Electric Home

If the 1920s were the age of the bathroom, the 1930s were the era of the modern kitchen. The sale of electrical appliances increased throughout the decade, and refrigerators led the way. In 1930, the number of refrigerators produced exceeded the number of iceboxes for the first time. Refrigerator production continued to rise throughout the thirties, reaching a peak of 2.3 million in 1937. At first, the refrigerator was boxy and looked very much like an icebox with a motor sitting awkwardly on top. In 1935, however, the refrigerator, like most other appliances, became streamlined. Sears, Roebuck advertised "The New 1935 Super Six Coldspot . . . Stunning in Its Streamlined Beauty." The Coldspot, which quickly influenced the look of all other models, was designed by Raymond Loewy, one of a group of industrial designers who emphasized sweeping horizontal lines, rounded corners, and a slick modern look. They hoped modern design would stimulate an optimistic attitude and, of course, increase sales.

Replacing an icebox with an electrical refrigerator, as many middle-class families did in the 1930s, altered more than the appearance of the kitchen. It changed habits and life styles, especially for women. An icebox was part of a culture that included icemen, ice wagons (or ice trucks), ice picks, ice tongs, and a pan that had to be emptied continually. The streamlined refrigerator, like the streamlined automobile, became a symbol of progress and modern civilization in the 1930s.

Other appliances signaled changes in life styles. The electric washing machine and electric iron altered the nature of washday. But even with labor-saving machines, most women continued to do their wash on Monday and their ironing on Tuesday, and women spent just as much time at housework. In fact, a great many middle-class families maintained their standard of living during the 1930s only because the women in the family learned to stretch and save and make do. Yet packaged and canned goods became more widely available during the decade. Many women discovered that it was easier, and in some cases cheaper, to serve Kellogg's Corn Flakes or Nabisco Shredded Wheat than to make oatmeal, to serve Van Camp's pork and beans or Heinz spaghetti from a can than to prepare a meal, or to use commercially baked bread than to bake their own.

## Household Appliance Production, 1929–1939

**Source:** U.S. Bureau of the Census.

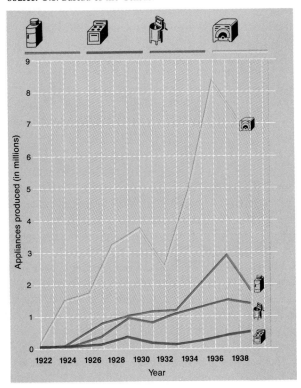

Although most women worked out of dire necessity, some took jobs outside the home to maintain their level of consumption. There was an increase of 50 percent in the number of married women who worked during the decade. At the same time, many rural women, like those in the hill country of Texas and other remote areas, and many wives of the unemployed made do with what was available. Many continued to cook, clean, and sew the way their ancestors had for generations.

### The Age of Leisure

It is ironic that the age of the Depression was also a time when many people worried about how to spend leisure time. The 1920s were a time of spectator sports, of football and baseball heroes, of huge crowds that turned out to see boxing matches. Those sports continued during the Depression decade, although attendance suffered. Softball and miniature golf, which were cheap forms of entertainment and did not require expensive travel, also became popular. But the 1930s were a time when leisure became a problem to be analyzed and to be written about by professionals. During the decade, 450 new books on the subject appeared. Leisure was mechanized; millions put their nickels in a slot and listened to a record played on a jukebox. Millions more played a pinball machine, a mechanized device that had no practical use other than entertainment and could end the game with one word: *tilt*. Many of the popular games of the period had elaborate rules and directions. Contract bridge swept the country during the decade, and Monopoly was the most popular game of all. Produced by Parker Brothers, Monopoly was a fantasy of real estate speculation in which chance, luck, and the roll of the dice determined the winner. But one still had to obey the rules: "Go Directly to Jail. Do Not Pass Go. Do Not Collect $200." During a depression brought on in part by frenzied speculation, Americans were fascinated by a game whose purpose was to obtain real estate and utility monopolies and drive one's opponents into bankruptcy.

The 1930s were also a time of fads and of instant celebrities, created by radio, newsreels, and businessmen ready to turn almost anything to commercial advantage. The leading movie box-office attraction between 1935 and 1938 was Shirley Temple, a blond and adorable child movie star. She inspired Shirley Temple dolls, dishes, books, and clothes. Even stranger was the excitement created by the birth of five identical girl babies to a couple in northern Ontario in 1934. The Dionne quintuplets appeared on dozens of magazine covers and endorsed every imaginable product. Millions waited eagerly for the latest news and the latest article about the babies, and over 3 million made the long trek to see their home in Canada. Both Shirley Temple and the Dionne quintuplet craze were products of the new technology, especially radio and the movies.

### Literary Reflections of the 1930s

Though much of the serious literature of the 1930s reflected the decade's troubled currents,

*More than a source of entertainment, the family radio was a vital link with the world. Here relatives of a crew member on a disabled submarine anxiously await news of the ship's fate.*

reading continued to be a popular and cheap form of entertainment. John Steinbeck, whose later novel *The Grapes of Wrath* (1939) followed the fortunes of the Joad family, described the plight of Mexican migrant workers in *Tortilla Flat* (1935). His novels expressed his belief that there was in American life a "crime . . . that goes beyond denunciation." "In the eyes of the hungry there is a growing wrath," he warned his readers.

Other writers questioned the American dream. John Dos Passos's trilogy *U.S.A.* (1930–1936) conveyed a deep pessimism about American capitalism, a pessimism that many other intellectuals shared. Less political were the novels of Thomas Wolfe and William Faulkner, who more sympathetically portrayed Americans caught up in the web of local life and facing the complex problems of the modern era. Faulkner's fictional Yoknapatawpha County, brought to life in *The Sound and the Fury, As I Lay Dying, Sanctuary,* and *Light in August* (1929–1932), documented the South's racial problems and its poverty as well as its stubborn pride. But the book about the South that became one of the decade's best-sellers was far more optimistic and far less complex than Faulkner's work— Margaret Mitchell's *Gone with the Wind* (1936). Its success suggested that many Americans used reading as an escape, not as an exploration of their problems.

### Radio's Finest Hour

The number of radio sets purchased increased steadily during the decade. In 1929, slightly more than 10 million households owned radios; by 1939, fully 27.5 million households had radio sets. The radio was not just something to turn on for music and news but a piece of furniture that dominated the living room. In many homes the top of the radio became the symbolic mantel where family photos were displayed. Families gathered around the radio at night to listen to and laugh at Jack Benny or Edgar Bergen and Charlie McCarthy or to try to solve a murder mystery with Mr. and Mrs. North. "The Lone Ranger," another popular program, had 20 million listeners by 1939.

During the day there were soap operas, which James Thurber described as "a kind of sandwich, whose recipe is simple enough, although it took years to compound. Between thick slices of advertising, spread twelve minutes of dialogue, add predicament, villainy, and female suffering in equal measure, throw in a dash of nobility, sprinkle with tears, season with organ music, cover with a rich announcer sauce and serve five times a week." After school, teenagers and younger children argued over whether to listen to "Jack Armstrong, the All-American Boy" and "Captain Midnight" or "Stella Dallas" and "The Young Widder Brown."

Most families had only one radio, but everyone could join in the contests or send away for magic rings or secret decoders. The reception was sometimes poor, especially in rural areas and small towns. Voices faded in and out and disappeared completely during storms. But the magic of radio allowed many people to feel connected to distant places and to believe they knew the radio performers personally. Radio was also responsible for one of the biggest hoaxes of all time. On October 31, 1938, Orson Welles broadcast "The War of the Worlds" so realistically that thousands of listeners really believed that Martians had landed in New Jersey. If anyone needed proof, that single program demonstrated the power of the radio.

### The Silver Screen

The 1930s were the golden years of the movies. Between 60 and 90 million Americans went to the movies every week during the decade. The movies were not entirely depression-proof. But talking films had replaced the silent variety in the late twenties, and this drove attendance up. Though it fell off slightly in the early 1930s, by 1934 attendance was climbing again. For many families, even in the depth of the Depression, movie money was just as important as food money.

In the cities one could go to one of the elaborate movie palaces and live in a fantasy world far removed from the reality of Depression America. In small towns across the country, for 25 cents (10 cents under age 12) one could go to at least four movies during the week. There was a Sunday-Monday feature film (except in communities where the churches had prevented Sunday movies), a different feature of somewhat lesser prominence on Tuesday-Wednesday, and another on Thursday-Friday. On Saturday there was a cowboy movie, or perhaps one featuring a detective. Sometimes a double feature played, and always there were short subjects, a cartoon, and a newsreel. On Saturday there was usually a serial that left the heroine or hero in such a dire predicament that you just had to come back the next week to see how she or he survived.

The movies were a place to take a date, to go with friends, or to go as a family. Movies could be talked about for days. Young women tried to speak like Greta Garbo or to hold a cigarette like Joan Crawford. Jean Harlow and Mae West so

*Four movies in one week were commonly billed by small-town theaters during Hollywood's "golden years."*

Cultural historians have often looked at recreation—how a people use their leisure time to have fun—as a way to take the pulse of a nation. Fairs and celebrations can help to explain something about a country's spirit and aspirations. The 1876 Centennial Exposition held in Philadelphia attracted millions of Americans, who came to admire the Corless engine, the telephone, and other technological marvels. They looked forward to a time when American industry would make life better for everyone. The World Columbian Exposition, held in Chicago in 1893, featured the Great White City, a planned and ordered array of classical buildings that contrasted sharply with the chaos and unplanned nature of the real Chicago. During the Bicentennial celebration of 1976, there was no giant fair but instead thousands of smaller celebrations. In the aftermath of Vietnam and Watergate, these local affairs tended to idealize the American past rather than celebrate the present and future. The American people have always, in fact, looked both nostalgically back to "better days" as well as optimistically ahead to a glorious future.

Like the combination of Frontierland and Tomorrowland at Walt Disney World, American fairs usually reflect this double vision. County and state fairs, for example, have a rural, agrarian tone, reflecting their nineteenth-century origins as occasions to show off prizewinning heifers, horses, and sows, giant vegetables and melons, and rhubarb pies and other baked delicacies. These fairs also serve to relieve the boredom of rural life by offering country people the amusements, crowds of people, and other attractions of the fair. In addition to livestock exhibits and other contests, country fairs inevitably include carnival rides and games, shooting galleries, candy and ice cream booths, sideshow freaks, dancing girls, trotting races, and other diversions. What would a historian learn about the American people from the study of local fairs? How do they remind us of earlier days, and what do they suggest about enduring values as well as current events?

In 1939, for example, with the country still in the grip of depression and the world on the brink of war, the United States paused to create a world's fair out of Long Island swampland near New York City. The theme of the fair was a glorious streamlined future. The most conspicuous symbols of the fair were the 700-foot Trylon, a three-sided needle representing "the Fair's lofty purpose," and the Perisphere, 200 feet in diameter. One feature of the fair was a giant

Library of Congress, Washington, D.C.

*Jack Delano*, **County Fair**

Democracity, a model of "a perfectly integrated, futuristic metropolis." Future citizens would spend their time playing in structured parks and recreation facilities, not wasting their time in "dissipated idleness or carousing." Many visitors to the fair saw a demonstration of television for the first time. They also observed a model of a rocket ship advertised as capable of shooting a projectile from New York to London.

But the most popular building at the fair was the General Motors exhibit, which created the future world of 1960. This world was planned, streamlined, and ordered, and it featured skyscrapers and superhighways. It stood in contrast to the chaotic, terrifying world of 1939. Visitors were given a 15-minute simulated airplane ride over the United States of 1960. There they observed a scientific orchard with

Both photos from the Bel Geddes Collection, University of Texas, Austin; by permission of Edith Lutyens Bel Geddes, executrix

*New York World's Fair of 1939–1940. (Above) General Motors building with the Trylon and Perisphere in the background; (right) Armchair Visitors' City of 1960 (Futurama), designed by Norman Bel Geddes*

trees under glass, a futuristic amusement park, a superhighway system, and a modern metropolis with widely spaced quarter-mile-high skyscrapers, separated by parks and smaller buildings.

What does the New York World's Fair tell us about the United States at the end of the 1930s? Why do Americans show such faith in technology, inventions, science fiction, and the future, especially during times of crisis? Or are world's fairs more concerned with selling products than with expressing the nation's hopes and fears? Have you ever been to a world's fair, one of the Disney parks, or some other national fair? What did the exhibits, theme areas, and rides tell you about the attitudes, concerns, spirit, and values of the American people? How do they differ from county and state fairs?

popularized blonde hair that the sale of peroxide shot up. Young men tried to emulate Clark Gable or Cary Grant, and one young man admitted that it was "directly through the movies that I learned to kiss a girl on her ears, neck, and cheeks, as well as on the mouth."

Walt Disney, one of the true geniuses of the movie industry, made his animated cartoons so popular that Mickey Mouse was probably more famous and familiar than most real celebrities. In May 1933, right in the middle of Roosevelt's hundred days, Disney released *The Three Little Pigs*, whose theme song "Who's Afraid of the Big Bad Wolf?" became a national hit overnight. Some felt it had as much to do with raising the nation's morale as did the New Deal legislation. One critic suggested that the moral of the story, as retold by Disney, was that the little pig survived because he was conservative, diligent, and hardworking; others felt that it was the pig who used modern tools and planned ahead who won out.

## CONCLUSION: The Ambivalent Character of the Great Depression

The New Deal, despite a great variety of legislation, did not end the Depression, nor did it solve the problem of unemployment. For many Americans looking back on the decade, the most vivid memory was the shame and guilt of being unemployed, the despair and fear that came from losing a business or being evicted from a home or an apartment. Parents who lived through the decade urged their children to find a secure job, to get married, and to settle down. "Every time I've encountered the Depression it has been used as a barrier and a club," one daughter of Depression parents remembered; "older people use it to explain to me that I can't understand *anything:* I didn't live through the Depression."

New Deal legislation did not solve all the country's problems, but the New Deal did strengthen the power of the federal government, the presidency, and the executive branch. Federal agencies like the Federal Deposit Insurance Corporation and programs like social security influenced the daily lives of most Americans, and rural electrification, the WPA, and the CCC changed the lives of millions. It also established the principle of federal responsibility for the health of the economy and initiated the concept of the welfare state. Federally subsidized housing, minimum-wage laws, and a policy for paying farmers to limit production, all aspects of these principles, had far-reaching implications.

The New Deal was as important for what it did not do as for what it did. It did not promote socialism or cause the redistribution of income or property. It promoted social justice and social reform, but it provided little for people at the bottom of American society. The New Deal did not prevent business consolidation, and, in the end, it probably strengthened corporate capitalism.

Roosevelt, with his colorful personality and his dramatic response to the nation's crisis, dominated his times in a way few presidents have done. Yet there was another side to the 1930s. For some people who lived through the decade, it was not Roosevelt or bread lines but a new streamlined refrigerator or a Walt Disney movie that symbolized the Depression decade.

## Recommended Reading

Lester V. Chandler, *America's Greatest Depression* (1970) discusses the economic impact of the Depression and the government's response to it. Robert S. McElvaine, ed., *Down and Out in the Great Depression* (1983) uses letters written to Eleanor and Franklin Roosevelt to describe the reaction of ordinary Americans. Studs Terkel, *Hard Times* (1970) uses interviews to accomplish the same purpose.

William E. Leuchtenburg, *Franklin Roosevelt and the New Deal* (1963) is a balanced and well-written account. Paul K. Conkin, *The New Deal* (1967) is more critical. Arthur M. Schlesinger, Jr., *The Age of Roosevelt*, 3 vols. (1957–1960) is favorable and fascinating. James MacGregor Burns, *Roosevelt: The Lion and the Fox* (1956) is still the best one-volume biography, but Joseph Lash, *Eleanor and Franklin* (1971) is a lively tale of two lives.

There are a great many specialized studies of the Depression and the New Deal; the following are among the most useful and interesting. Harvard Sitkoff, *A New Deal for Blacks* (1978) discusses the limited attention given to blacks during the decade. Mark Reisler, *By the Sweat of Their Brow* (1976) describes the plight of Mexican-Americans. Lois Scharf, *To Work and to Wed* (1980) and Susan Ware, *Beyond Suffrage* (1981) depict the lot of women during the New Deal era. Irving Bernstein, *Turbulent Years* (1969) discusses the American worker and organized labor. Jerre Mangione, *The Dream and the Deal* (1972) is about the Federal Writer's Project. Richard Pells, *Radical Visions and American Dreams* (1973) describes social thought. Alan Brinkley, *Voices of Protest* (1982) tells the story of Father Coughlin and Huey Long. The other side of the thirties can be followed in Warren Sussman, ed., *Culture and Commitment* (1973) and Siegfreid Giedion, *Mechanization Takes Command* (1948).

John Steinbeck shows Okies trying to escape the dust bowl in his novel, *The Grapes of Wrath* (1939). James Farrell describes growing up in Depression Chicago in *Studs Lonigan* (1932–1935). Richard Wright details the trials of a young black man in *Native Son* (1940).

## TIME LINE

|  |  |
|------|--------|
| 1929 | Stock market crashes<br>Agricultural Marketing Act |
| 1930 | Depression worsens<br>Hawley-Smoot Tariff |
| 1932 | Reconstruction Finance Corporation established<br>Federal Home Loan Bank Act<br>Glass-Steagall Banking Act<br>Federal Emergency Relief Act<br>Bonus March on Washington<br>Franklin D. Roosevelt elected president |
| 1933 | Emergency Banking Relief Act<br>Home Owners Loan Corporation<br>Twenty-first Amendment repeals Eighteenth, ending prohibition<br>Agricultural Adjustment Act<br>National Industrial Recovery Act<br>Civilian Conservation Corps<br>Tennessee Valley Authority established<br>Public Works Administration established |
| 1934 | Unemployment peaks<br>Federal Housing Administration established<br>Indian Reorganization Act |
| 1935 | Second New Deal begins<br>Works Progress Administration established<br>Social Security Act<br>Rural Electrification Act<br>Wagner Act<br>Committee for Industrial Organization (CIO) formed |
| 1936 | United Auto Workers hold sit-down strikes against General Motors<br>Roosevelt reelected president<br>Economy begins rebound |
| 1937 | Attempt to reform the Supreme Court<br>Economic collapse<br>Farm Security Administration established<br>Wagner-Steagall Housing Act |
| 1938 | Fair Labor Standards Act<br>Agricultural Adjustment Act |

# CHAPTER 26
## THE AMERICAN PEOPLE AND WORLD WAR II

N Scott Momaday, a Kiowa Indian born at Lawton, Oklahoma, in 1934, was only 11 when World War II ended, yet the war changed his life. Shortly after the United States entered the war, Momaday's parents moved to Hobbs, New Mexico, where his father got a job with an oil company and his mother worked in the civilian personnel office at an Army Air Force base. Like many couples, they had struggled through the hard times of the Depression. The war meant jobs.

Momaday's best friend was Billy Don Johnson, "a reddish, robust boy of great good humor and intense loyalty." Together they played war, digging trenches and dragging themselves through imaginary mine fields. They hurled grenades and fired endless rounds from their imaginary machine guns, pausing only to drink Kool-Aid from their canteens. At school they were taught history and math, but also how to hate the enemy and be proud of America. They recited the Pledge of Allegiance to the flag and sang "God Bless America," "The Star-Spangled Banner," and "Remember Pearl Harbor."

Momaday's only difficulty was that his Native American face was often mistaken for that of an Asian. Almost every day on the playground, someone would yell, "Hi ya, Jap," and a fight was on. Billy Don always came to his friend's defense, but it was disconcerting, to say the least, to be taken for the enemy. His father read old Kiowa tales to Momaday, who was proud to be an Indian but prouder still to be an American. On Saturday he and his friends would go to the local theater, where they would cheer as they watched a Japanese Zero or a German Me-109 go down in flames. They pretended that they were P-40 pilots. "The whole field of vision shuddered with our fire: the 50-caliber tracers curved out, fixing brilliant arcs upon the span, and struck; then there was a black burst of smoke, and the target went spinning down to death."

Near the end of the war, his family moved again, as so many families did, in order that his father might get a better job. This time they lived right next door to an air force base, and Scott fell in love with the B-17 "Flying Fortress," the bomber that military strategists thought would win the war in the Pacific and in Europe. He felt a real sense of resentment and loss when the B-17 was replaced by the larger but not nearly so glamorous B-29.

Looking back on his early years, Momaday reflected on the importance of the war in his growing up. "I see now that one experiences easily the ordinary things of life," he decided, "the things which cast familiar shadows upon the sheer, transparent panels of time, and he perceives his experience in the only way he can, according to his age." Momaday's life during the war differed from the lives of boys old enough to join the forces, but the war was no less real for him than for those who were older. His youth was influenced by the fact that he was male, but not much by being an Indian or by living in the Southwest. Yet his parents, like all Native Americans in New Mexico and Arizona, could not vote. The Momadays fared better than most Native Americans, who found prejudice against them undiminished and jobs, even in wartime, hard to find. Returning servicemen discovered that they were still treated like "Indians." They were prohibited from buying liquor in many states, and those who returned to the reservations learned that they were ineligible for veterans' benefits.

This chapter traces the gradual involvement of the United States in the international events during the 1930s that finally led to America's participation in the most devastating war the world had seen. We recount the diplomatic and military struggles of the war and the search for a secure peace. We also seek to explain the impact of the war on ordinary people and on American attitudes about the world, as well as its effect on patriotism and the American way of life. The war brought prosperity to some as it brought death to others. It left the American people the most affluent in the world and the United States the most powerful nation.

## THE TWISTING ROAD TO WAR

Looking back on the events between 1933 and 1941, which eventually led to American involvement in World War II, it is easy either to be critical of decisions made or actions not taken or to see everything that happened as inevitable. Historical events are never inevitable, and leaders who must make decisions never have the advantage of retrospective vision; they have to deal with the situation as they find it, and they never have all the facts.

### Foreign Policy in the 1930s

In March 1933, Roosevelt not only faced an overwhelming domestic crisis but also confronted an international crisis. The worldwide depression had caused near financial disaster in Europe. Germany had defaulted on its reparations installments, and most European countries were unable to keep up the payments on their debts to the United States. Hoover had agreed to a brief moratorium on the war debts in 1931 and had pledged American participation in an international economic conference to be held in London in June 1933.

Roosevelt had no master plan in foreign policy, just as he had none in the domestic sphere. In the first days of his administration, he gave conflicting signals as he groped to find a response to the international situation. At first it seemed that the president would cooperate in some kind of international economic agreement on tariffs and currency. But then he undercut the American delegation in London by refusing to go along with any international agreement. Solving the American domestic economic crisis seemed more important to Roosevelt in 1933 than inter-

national economic cooperation. His actions signaled a decision to go it alone in foreign policy in the 1930s.

Roosevelt did, however, alter some of the foreign policy decisions of previous administrations. For example, he pushed for the recognition of the Soviet government in Russia. There were many reasons why the United States had not recognized the Soviet Union during the 1920s. The new regime had failed to accept the debts of the czar's government, but more important, Americans feared communism and believed that recognition meant approval. In reversing this nonrecognition policy, Roosevelt hoped to gain a market for surplus American grain. Although the expected trade bonanza never materialized, the Soviet Union did agree to pay the old debts and to extend rights to American citizens living in the Soviet Union. Diplomatic recognition opened communications between the two emerging world powers.

Led by Cordell Hull, his secretary of state, Roosevelt's administration also reversed the earlier policy of intervention in South America. The United States continued to support dictators, especially in Central America, because they promised to promote stability and preserve American economic interests. But Roosevelt completed the removal of American military forces from Haiti and Nicaragua in 1934, and, in a series of pan-American conferences, he joined in pledging that no country in the hemisphere would intervene in the "internal or external affairs" of any other. The United States still had economic and trade interests in Latin America, however, and with many of the Latin American economies in disarray because of the Depression, there were pressures to resume the policy of intervention.

The first test case came in Cuba, where a revolution threatened American investments of more than a billion dollars. But the United States did not intervene. Instead Roosevelt sent special envoys to work out a conciliatory agreement with the revolutionary government. A short time later, when a coup led by Fulgencio Batista overthrew the revolutionary government, the United States not only recognized the Batista government but also offered a large loan and agreed to abrogate the Platt Amendment (which made Cuba a virtual protectorate of the United States) in return for the rights to a naval base.

The Trade Agreements Act of 1934 gave the president power to lower tariff rates by up to 50 percent and took the tariff away from the pressure of special-interest groups in Congress. Using this act, the Roosevelt administration negotiated a series of agreements that improved trade. By 1935, half of American cotton exports and a good proportion of other products were going to Latin America. So the Good Neighbor policy was also good business for the United States. But increased trade did not solve the economic problems either for the United States or for Latin America.

Another test for Latin American policy came in 1938 when Mexico nationalized the property of a number of American oil companies. Instead of intervening, as many businessmen urged, the State Department patiently worked out an agreement that included some compensation for the companies. The American government might have acted differently, however, if the threat of war in Europe in 1938 had not created a fear that all the Western Hemisphere nations would have to cooperate to resist the growing power of Germany and Italy. At a pan-American conference held in that year, the United States and most Latin American countries agreed to resist all foreign intervention in the hemisphere.

### Neutrality in Europe

About the same time that Roosevelt was elected president in the United States, Adolf Hitler came to power in Germany. Hitler, born in Austria in 1889, had served as a corporal in the German army during World War I. Like many other Germans, he was angered by the Treaty of Versailles. But he blamed the Communists and Jews for Germany's defeat. Hitler had a checkered life after the war. He became the leader of a Fascist group, the Brown Shirts, and in 1923, after leading an unsuccessful coup, was sentenced to prison. While in jail he wrote *Mein Kampf* ("My Struggle"), a long, rambling book spelling out his theories of racial purity, his hopes for Germany, and his venomous hatred of the Jews. After his release from prison, Hitler's following grew. He had a charismatic style and a plan. On January 30, 1933, he became chancellor of Germany, and within a few months he made himself the *Führer* (leader) and absolute dictator.

*Elected chancellor in 1933, Adolf Hitler quickly assumed dictatorial powers and implemented a massive rearmament plan.*

He intended to conquer Europe and to make the Third Reich the center of a new civilization.

In 1934, Hitler announced a program of German rearmament, violating the Versailles Treaty of 1919. Meanwhile, in Italy, a Fascist dictator, Benito Mussolini, was building a powerful military force, and in 1934, he threatened to invade the East African country of Ethiopia. These ominous rumblings in Europe frightened some Americans at the very time they were reexamining American entry into the Great War and vowing that they would never again get involved in a European conflict.

Senator Gerald P. Nye of North Dakota, a conscientious and determined man who had helped expose the Teapot Dome scandal in 1924, turned his attention to investigating the connection between corporate profits and American participation in World War I. His Senate committee held public hearings that revealed that many American businessmen had close relationships with the War Department. Businesses that had produced war materials had made huge profits. Though the committee failed to prove a conspiracy, it was easy to conclude, as many people did, that the United States had been tricked into going to war by the people who profited most from it.

On many college campuses, students demonstrated against war. On April 13, 1934, a day of protest around the country, students at Smith College placed white crosses on the campus as a memorial to the people killed in the Great War and for those who would die in the next one. The next year, even more students went on strike for a day. Students joined organizations like Veterans of Future Wars and Future Gold Star Mothers and protested the presence of the Reserve Office Training Corps on their campuses. One college president, who supported the peace movement, announced. "We will be called cowards . . . [but] I say that war must be banished from civilized society if democratic civilization and culture are to be perpetuated." Not all students supported the peace movement, but in the mid-1930s, a great many young people as well as adults joined peace societies such as the Fellowship of Reconciliation and the Women's International League for Peace and Freedom. They were determined never again to support a foreign war. But in Europe, Asia, and Africa, there were already rumblings of another great international conflict.

### Ethiopia and Spain

In May 1935, Italy invaded Ethiopia after rejecting the League of Nations' offer to mediate the difficulties between the two countries. Italian dive bombers and machine guns made quick work of the small and poorly equipped Ethiopian army. The Ethiopian war, remote as it seemed to most Americans, frightened Congress, which passed a Neutrality Act authorizing the president to prohibit all arms shipments to belligerent nations and to advise all United States citizens not to travel on belligerent ships except at their own risk. Remembering the process that led the United States into World War I, Congress was determined that it would not happen again. Roosevelt used the authority of the Neutrality Act of 1935 to impose an arms embargo. The League of Nations condemned Italy as the aggressor in the war, and Great Britain moved its fleet to the Mediterranean. But neither Britain nor the United States wanted to stop shipments of oil to Italy or to commit its own soldiers to the fight. The embargo on arms had little impact on Italy, but it was disastrous for the poor African nation. Italy quickly defeated Ethiopia, and by 1936, Mussolini had joined forces with Germany to form the Rome-Berlin Axis.

"We shun political commitments which might entangle us in foreign war," Roosevelt announced in 1936. "We are not isolationist except in so far as we seek to isolate ourselves completely from war." But isolation became more difficult when a civil war broke out in Spain in 1936. General Francisco Franco, supported by the Catholic church and large landowners, revolted against the Republican government. Germany and Italy aided Franco, sending planes and other weapons, while the Soviet Union came to the support of the Spanish Republic (the Loyalists).

Great Britain and France, like the United States, tried to remain neutral. But the war split the United States. Most Catholics and many who feared communism sided with Franco. But many American radicals, even those opposed to all war a few months before, found the Loyalist cause worth fighting and dying for. Over 3,000 Americans joined the Abraham Lincoln Brigade, and hundreds were killed fighting against fascism in Spain. "If this were a Spanish matter, I'd let it alone," Sam Levenger, a student at Ohio State, wrote. "But the rebellion would not last a week if it weren't for the Germans and the Italians. And if Hitler and Mussolini can send troops to Spain to attack the government elected by the people, why can't they do so in France? And after France?" Levenger was killed in Spain in 1937 at the age of 20.

Not everyone thought the moral issues in Spain were worth dying for. The United States government tried to stay neutral and to ship arms and equipment to neither side. The Neutrality Act, extended in 1936, technically did not apply to civil wars, but the State Department imposed a moral embargo. However, when an American businessman disregarded it and attempted to send 400 used airplane engines to the Loyalists, Roosevelt asked Congress to extend the arms embargo to Spain. While the United States, along with Britain and France, carefully protected its neutrality, Franco consolidated his dictatorship with the active aid of Germany and Italy. Meanwhile, Congress in 1937 passed another Neutrality Act, this time making it illegal for American citizens to travel on belligerent ships. The act extended the embargo on arms and made even nonmilitary items available to belligerents only on a cash-and-carry basis.

In a variety of ways, the United States tried to make sure that it did not repeat the mistakes that had led it into World War I. Unfortunately, World War II, which moved closer each day, would be a different kind of war, and the lessons of World War I would be of little use.

## War in Europe

Roosevelt had no carefully planned strategy to deal with the rising tide of war in Europe in the late 1930s. He was by no means an isolationist, but on the other hand, he wanted to keep the United States out of the European conflagration. When he announced, "I hate war," he was expressing a deep personal belief that wars solve few problems. Unlike his cousin Theodore Roosevelt, he did not view war as dashing and romantic or a place to prove one's manhood. In foreign policy, just as in domestic affairs, he responded to events, but he moved reluctantly (and with agonizing slowness, from the point of view of many of his critics) toward more and more American involvement in the war.

In March 1938, Hitler's Germany annexed Austria and then in September, as a result of the Munich Conference, occupied the Sudetenland, a part of Czechoslovakia. Within six months, Hitler's armies had overrun the rest of Czechoslovakia. There was little protest from the United States. Most Americans sympathized with the victims of Hitler's aggression and were horrified at the reports of the internment and murder of hundreds of thousands of Jews. But they hoped somehow that compromises could be worked out and that Europe could settle its own problems. Then on August 23, 1939, American leaders were shocked by the news of a Nazi-Soviet pact. Fascism and communism were political philosophies supposedly in deadly opposition. Many Americans had secretly hoped that Nazi Germany and Soviet Russia would fight it out, neutralizing each other. Now they were allies. A week later, Hitler's army attacked Poland. The invasion of Poland marked the official beginning of World War II. Britain and France honored their treaties and came to Poland's defense. "This nation will remain a neutral nation," Roosevelt announced, "but I cannot ask that every American remain neutral in thought as well."

Roosevelt asked for a repeal of the embargo section of the Neutrality Act and for the approval of the sale of arms on a cash-and-carry basis to France and Britain. The United States would help the Allies, but not at the risk of entering the war or even at the threat of disrupting the civilian economy. Yet Roosevelt did take some secret risks. In August 1939, Albert Einstein, a Jewish refugee from Nazi Germany, and some other distinguished scientists warned the president that German scientists were at work on an atomic bomb. Fearing the consequences of a powerful new weapon in Hitler's hands, Roosevelt authorized funds for a top-secret project to try to build an American bomb first. Only a few advisers and key members of Congress knew of the project, which was officially organized in 1941 and would ultimately change the course of human history.

The war in Poland ended quickly. With Germany attacking from the west and the Soviet Union from the east, the fighting was over within a month. The fall of Poland in September 1939 brought a lull in the fighting. A number of Americans, including the American ambassador to Great Britain, Joseph Kennedy, who feared Communist Russia more than Fascist Germany, urged the United States to take the lead in negotiating a peace settlement that would recognize the German and Russian occupation of Poland. The British and French, however, were not interested in such a solution, and neither was Roosevelt.

The interlude, sometimes called the "phony war," came to a dramatic end on April 9, 1940, when Germany attacked Norway and Denmark with a furious air and sea assault. A few weeks later, using armed vehicles supported by massive air strikes, the German *Blitzkrieg* swept through Belgium, Luxembourg, and the Netherlands. A week later, the Germans stormed into France. The famed Maginot line, a system of fortifications designed to repulse a German invasion, was useless as German mechanized forces swept around the end of the line and attacked from the rear. The French guns, solidly fixed in concrete and pointing toward Germany, were never fired. The Maginot line, which would have been an effective defensive weapon in World War I, was useless in the new kind of war of the 1940s. France surrendered in June as the British army fled across the English Channel from Dunkirk.

How should the United States respond to the new and desperate situation in Europe? William Allen White, journalist and editor, and other concerned Americans organized the Committee to Defend America by Aiding the Allies, but others, including Robert Wood of Sears, Roebuck and Charles Lindbergh, the hero of the 1920s, supported a group called America First. They argued that the United States should forget about England and concentrate on defending America. Roosevelt steered a cautious course. He approved the shipment to Britain of 50 over-age American destroyers. In return, the United States received the right to establish naval and air bases on British territory from Newfoundland to Bermuda and British Guiana.

Winston Churchill, prime minister of Great Britain, asked for much more, but Roosevelt hesitated. In July 1940, he did sign a measure authorizing $4 billion to increase the number of American naval warships. In September, Congress passed the Selective Service Act, which provided for the first peacetime draft in the history of the United States. Over a million men were to serve in the army for one year, but they were authorized to serve only in the Western Hemisphere. As the war in Europe reached a crisis in the fall of 1940, the American people were still undecided about the proper response.

## The Election of 1940

Part of Roosevelt's reluctance to aid Great Britain more energetically came from his genuine desire to keep the United States out of the war, but it was also related to the presidential campaign waged during the crisis months of the summer and fall of 1940. Roosevelt, breaking a long tradition by seeking a third term, was opposed by Wendell Willkie of Indiana, a corporation president who won the Republican nomination over more experienced and more isolationist candidates. Despite his big-business ties, Willkie approved most New Deal legislation and supported aid to Great Britain. Energetic and attractive, Willkie was the most persuasive and exciting Republican candidate since Theodore Roosevelt, and he appealed to many who distrusted or disliked Roosevelt. Yet in an atmosphere of international crisis, most voters chose to stay with Roosevelt. He won, 27 million to 22 million, and carried 38 of 48 states.

## Lend-Lease

After the election, Roosevelt invented a scheme whereby he could send aid to Britain without demanding payment. He called it "lend-lease." He compared the situation to loaning a garden hose to a neighbor whose house was on fire. Senator Robert Taft of Ohio, however, thought the idea of loaning military equipment and expecting it back was absurd. He decided it was more like loaning chewing gum to a friend: "Once it had been used you did not want it back." Others were even more critical. Senator

Burton K. Wheeler, an extreme isolationist, branded lend-lease "Roosevelt's triple A foreign policy" because it was designed to "plow under every fourth American boy."

The Lend-Lease Act, which passed Congress in March 1941, destroyed the fiction of neutrality. By that time, German submarines were sinking a half million tons of ships each month in the Atlantic. In June, Roosevelt proclaimed a national emergency and ordered the closing of German and Italian consulates in the United States. On June 22, Germany suddenly attacked the Soviet Union. It was one of Hitler's biggest blunders of the war, for now his armies had to fight on two fronts.

The surprise attack, however, created a dilemma for the United States. Suddenly the great Communist "enemy" had become America's friend and ally. When Roosevelt extended lend-lease aid to Russia in November 1941, many Americans were shocked. Charles Lindbergh said he would prefer an alliance with Nazi Germany with all its faults than with the "godlessness and barbarism that exist in the Soviet Union." But most Americans made a quick transition from viewing the Soviet Union as an enemy to treating it like a friend.

By the autumn of 1941, the United States was virtually at war with Germany in the Atlantic. On September 11, Roosevelt issued a "shoot on sight" order for all American ships operating in the Atlantic, and on October 30, a German submarine sank an American destroyer off the coast of Iceland. The war in the Atlantic, however, was undeclared and opposed by many Americans. Eventually the sinking of enough American ships or another crisis would probably have provided the excuse for a formal declaration of war against Germany. It was not Germany, however, but Japan that provided the dramatic incident that catapulted the United States into World War II.

### The Path to Pearl Harbor

Japan, controlled by ambitious military leaders, was the aggressor in the Far East as Hitler's Germany was in Europe. Its master plan was to replace the white "imperialist" regimes in China, the Philippines, Malaya, Burma, and all of Southeast Asia. Japan invaded Manchuria

in 1931 and launched an all-out assault on China in 1937. The Japanese leaders assumed that at some point the United States would oppose their advance. Certainly the United States would go to war if Japan tried to take the Philippines, but the Japanese attempted to delay that moment as long as possible by diplomatic means. For its part, the United States feared the possibility of a two-front war and was willing to delay the confrontation with Japan until it had dealt with the German threat. Thus between 1938 and 1941, the United States and Japan engaged in a kind of diplomatic shadow boxing.

The United States did exert economic pressure on Japan. In July 1939, the United States gave the required six-months' notice regarding cancellation of the 1911 commercial agreement between the two countries. The next year, the Roosevelt administration forbade the shipment of airplane fuel and scrap metal to Japan, although it permitted the export of some petroleum and other products, hoping that this could avert a crisis. In the spring of 1941, Japan opened negotiations with the United States. But there was little to discuss. Japan would not withdraw from China as the United States demanded. Indeed, Japan, taking advantage of the situation in Europe, occupied French Indochina in 1940 and 1941. In July 1941, Roosevelt froze all Japanese assets in the United States, effectively embargoing trade with Japan.

*Japan's surprise attack on Pearl Harbor on December 7, 1941, united the country behind the war effort.*

Roosevelt had an advantage in the negotiations with Japan, for the United States had broken the Japanese diplomatic code. The American strategy was to avoid crisis. But after General Hideki Tojo became prime minister in October 1941, the Japanese decided to strike at the United States sometime after November 1941 unless the United States offered real concessions. The strike came at Pearl Harbor, the main American Pacific naval base, in Hawaii.

On the morning of December 7, 1941, Japanese airplanes launched from aircraft carriers attacked the United States fleet at Pearl Harbor. The surprise attack destroyed 19 ships (including 5 battleships) and 150 planes and killed 2,335 soldiers and sailors and 68 civilians. On the same day, the Japanese launched attacks on the Philippines, Guam, and the Midway Islands, as well as on the British colonies of Hong Kong and the Malaya Peninsula. The next day, with only one dissenting vote, Congress declared war on Japan. Jeannette Rankin, a member of Congress from Montana who had voted against the war resolution in 1917, voted no again in 1941. She recalled that in 1917, after a week of tense debate, 50 voted against going to war. "This time I stood alone."

Corporal John J. ("Ted") Kohl, a 25-year-old from Springfield, Ohio, was standing guard that Sunday morning near an ammunition warehouse at Hickam Field, near Pearl Harbor. He had joined the army two years before when his marriage failed and he could not find work. A Japanese bomb hit nearby, and Ted Kohl blew up with the warehouse. It was not until Wednesday evening, December 10, that the telegram arrived in Springfield. "The Secretary of War desires to express his deep regrets that your son Cpl. John J. Kohl was killed in action in defense of his country." Ted's younger brothers cried when they heard the news. There would be hundreds of thousands of telegrams and even more tears before the war was over.

December 7, 1941, was a day that "would live in infamy," in the words of Franklin Roosevelt. But it was a day that would have far-reaching implications for American foreign policy and for American attitudes toward the world. The surprise attack united the country in

a way that nothing else could have done. Even the isolationists and those who argued for "America first" quickly became patriots supporting the war effort.

After the shock and anger subsided, Americans searched for a villain. Someone must have blundered, someone must have betrayed the country to have allowed the "inferior" Japanese to have carried out such a successful and devastating attack. A myth persists to this day that the villain was Roosevelt, who, the story goes, knew the Japanese were going to attack but failed to warn the military commanders so that the American people might unite behind the war effort. But Roosevelt did not know. There was no specific warning that the attack was coming against Pearl Harbor, and the American ability to read the Japanese coded messages was no help because the fleet kept radio silence.

The ironic fact was that the Americans, partly because of racial prejudice against the Japanese, underestimated their ability. They ignored many warning signals because they did not believe that the Japanese were capable of launching an attack on a target as far away as Hawaii. Most of the experts, including Roosevelt, expected the Japanese to attack the Philippines or perhaps the Dutch East Indies. Many people blundered and made mistakes, but there was no conspiracy on the part of Roosevelt and his advisers to get the United States into the war.

Even more important in the long run than the way the attack on Pearl Harbor united the American people was its effect on a generation of military and political leaders. Pearl Harbor became the symbol of unpreparedness. For a generation that experienced the anger and frustration of the attack on Pearl Harbor by an unscrupulous enemy, the lesson was to be prepared and ready to stop an aggressor before it had a chance to strike at the United States. The smoldering remains of the sinking battleships at Pearl Harbor on the morning of December 7, 1941, and the history lesson learned there would influence American policy not only during World War II but also in Korea, Vietnam, and the international confrontations of the 1980s.

## THE HOME FRONT DURING THE WAR

Too often wars are described in terms of presidents and generals, emperors and kings, in terms of grand strategy and elaborate campaigns. But wars affect the lives of all people; the soldiers who fight and the women and children and men of all ages who stay home. World War II especially had an impact on all aspects of society—on the economy, on the movies and the radio, even on attitudes toward the proper place for women and blacks. For many people, the war meant opportunity and the end of depression. For others, the excitement of faraway places meant that they could never return home again. For still others, the war left lasting scars.

### Mobilizing for War

Converting American industry to war production was a complex task. Many corporate executives refused to admit that there was an emergency. Shortly after Pearl Harbor, Roosevelt created the War Production Board (WPB) and appointed Donald Nelson, the executive vice president of Sears, Roebuck, to mobilize the nation's resources for an all-out war effort. The WPB offered businesses cost-plus contracts,

*Full employment was one long-awaited change for the better that the war brought. These workers are changing shifts at an aviation plant in Inglewood, California, 1942.*

guaranteeing a fixed and generous profit, and often the government also financed the cost of new plants and equipment. Secretary of War Henry Stimson remarked, "If you . . . go to war . . . in a capitalist country, you have to let business make money out of the process or business won't work." Roosevelt seemed to agree.

The Roosevelt administration leaned over backward to gain the cooperation of businessmen, many of whom had been alienated by New Deal policies. He appointed many business executives to key positions, some of whom, like Nelson, served for a dollar a year. He also abandoned antitrust actions in all industries that were remotely war related. The probusiness policies angered some of the old New Dealers. "The New Dealers are a vanishing tribe," one reformer remarked, "and the moneychangers who were driven from the temple are now quietly established in government offices."•

The policy worked, however. Industrial production increased by 96 percent, and net corporate profits doubled during the war. Large commercial farmers also profited from the war. With many members of Congress supporting their demands, the farmers exacted high support prices for basic commodities. The war years accelerated the mechanization of the farm. A million more tractors joined those already in use in agriculture between 1940 and 1945. At the same time, the farm population declined by 17 percent. But the consolidation of small farms into large ones and the dramatic increase in the use of fertilizer made farms more productive and farming more profitable for the large operators.

In addition to the War Production Board, there were many other government agencies charged with running the war effort efficiently. The Office of Price Administration (OPA), eventually placed under the direction of Chester Bowles, an advertising executive, set prices on thousands of items in an attempt to control inflation. The OPA also rationed scarce products. Because the OPA's decisions affected what people wore and ate and whether they had gasoline, many regarded it as a symbol of unnecessary oppression. The National War Labor Board (NWLB) had the authority to set wages and hours and to monitor working conditions, and it had the right, under the president's wartime emergency powers, to seize industrial plants whose owners refused to cooperate.

Membership in labor unions, despite business opposition, grew rapidly during the war, from a total of 10.5 million in 1941 to 14.7 million in 1945. Labor leaders, however, complained that wage controls coupled with wartime inflation were unfair. The NWLB finally allowed a 15 percent cost-of-living increase on some contracts, but that did not apply to overtime pay, which helped drive up wages in some industries during the war by about 70 percent. Labor leaders were often not content with the raises. In the most famous incident, John L. Lewis broke the no-strike pledge of organized labor by calling a nationwide coal strike in 1943. Lewis sought to raise the average compensation of the mine workers. When Roosevelt ordered the secretary of the interior to take over the mines, Lewis called off the strike. But this bold protest did help raise miners' wages.

In addition to wage and price controls and rationing, the government tried to reduce inflation by selling war bonds and by increasing taxes. The Revenue Act of 1942 raised tax rates, broadened the tax base, increased corporate taxes to 40 percent, and raised the excess-profits tax to 90 percent. In addition, the government initiated a payroll deduction for income taxes. The war made the income tax a reality for most Americans for the first time.

Despite some unfairness and much confusion, the American economy responded to the wartime crisis and turned out the equipment and supplies that eventually won the war. The aviation and auto industries built 300,000 airplanes, 88,140 tanks, and 3,000 merchant ships. In 1944 alone, American factories produced 800,000 tons of synthetic rubber to make up for the supply of natural rubber captured by the Japanese. Although the national debt grew from about $143 billion in 1943 to $260 billion in 1945, the government policy of taxation paid for about 40 percent of the war's cost. In a limited way, the tax policy also helped to redistribute wealth, which the New Deal had failed to do. The top 5 percent income bracket, which controlled 23 percent of the disposable income in 1939, held only 17 percent in 1945. Yet full employment and the increase of two-income families, together with forced savings, would help provide capital for postwar expansion.

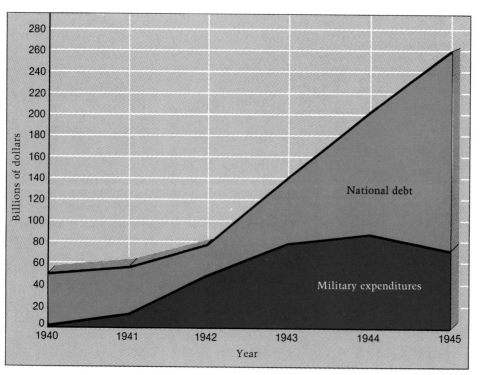

**Military Expenditures and the National Debt, 1940–1945**

*Source:* U.S. Bureau of the Census.

The war stimulated the growth of the federal bureaucracy and accelerated the trend, begun during World War I and extended in the 1930s, toward the government's central role in the economy. The war also increased the cooperation between industry and government, creating what would later be called a military-industrial complex. But for most Americans, despite anger at the OPA and the income tax, the war meant the end of the Depression.

## Patriotic Fervor

In European and Asian cities, the horror and destruction of war were everywhere. But in the United States, the war was remote. Thousands of American families felt the tragedy of war directly with the arrival of an official telegram telling of a son or husband killed in action. For most Americans, however, the war was a foreign war, far removed from the reality of daily life.

The government tried to keep the war alive in the minds of Americans and to keep the country united behind the war effort. The Office of War Information, staffed by writers and advertising executives, controlled the news the American public received about the war. It promoted patriotism and presented the American war effort in the best possible light.

The government also tried to sell everyone war bonds, not only to help pay for the war and reduce inflation but also to sell the war to the American people. As had been true during World War I, movie stars and other celebrities appeared at war bond rallies. Dorothy Lamour, one of Hollywood's glamorous actresses, was credited with selling $350 million worth of bonds, and the popular Carole Lombard was killed in a plane crash while taking part in a bond tour. Schoolchildren purchased war stamps and faithfully pasted them in an album until they had accumulated stamps worth $18.75, enough to buy a $25 bond (redeemable ten years later). Their bonds, they were told, would purchase bullets or a part for an airplane to kill Japs and Germans and defend the American way of life. "For Freedom's Sake, Buy War Bonds," one poster announced. Working men and women purchased bonds through payroll-deduction plans and looked forward to spending the money on consumer goods after the war. In the end, the government sold over $135 billion in war bonds. While the bond drives did help control inflation, they were most important in making millions of

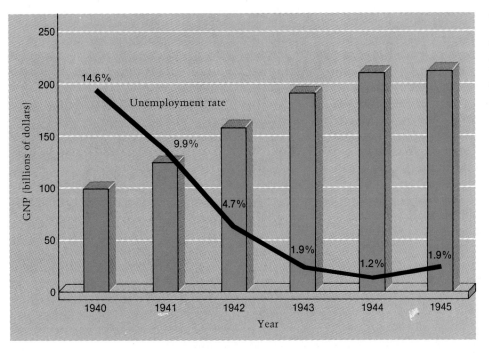

**Gross National Product and Unemployment, 1940–1945**

*Source:* U.S. Bureau of the Census.

Americans feel they were contributing to the war effort.

Those too old or too young to join the armed forces served in other ways. Thousands became air-raid wardens or civilian defense and Red Cross volunteers. They raised victory gardens and took part in scrap drives. Even small children could join the war effort by collecting old rubber, waste paper, and kitchen fats. Boys dived into lakes and rivers to recover old tires and even ripped down iron fences to aid their towns and neighborhoods in meeting their scrap quota. Some items, including gasoline, sugar, butter, and meat, were rationed, but few people complained. Even horsemeat hamburgers seemed edible if they helped win the war. Everything, even the most ordinary act, was interpreted by newspaper and magazine advertising as speeding victory or delaying the war effort. "Hoarders are the same as spies," one ad announced. "Everytime you decide *not* to buy something you help win the war."

## Internment of Japanese-Americans

Cooperating with the war effort fostered a sense of pride, a feeling of community. But wartime campaigns not only stimulated patriotism; they also promoted hate for the enemy. The Nazis, especially Hitler and his Gestapo, had become synonymous with evil even before 1941. But at the beginning of the war there was little animosity toward the German people. "You and I don't hate the Nazis because they are Germans. We hate the Germans because they are Nazis," announced a character in one of Helen MacInnes's novels. But before long most Americans made few distinctions. All Germans seemed evil, although the anti-German hysteria that had swept the country during World War I never developed.

The Japanese were easier to hate than the Germans. The attack on Pearl Harbor created a special animosity toward the Japanese, but the depiction of the Japanese as warlike and subhuman owed something to a long tradition of fear of the so called "yellow peril" and a distrust of all Asians.

The movies, magazine articles, cartoons, and posters added to the image of the Japanese

soldier or pilot with a toothy grin murdering innocent women and children or shooting down helpless Americans. Two weeks after Pearl Harbor, *Time* magazine explained to Americans how they could distinguish our Asian friends the Chinese "from the Japs." "Virtually all Japanese are short, Japanese are seldom fat; they often dry up with age," *Time* declared. "Most Chinese avoid horn-rimmed spectacles. Japanese walk stiffly erect, hard-heeled. Chinese, more relaxed, have an easy gait. The Chinese expression is likely to be more kindly, placid, open; the Japanese more positive, dogmatic, arrogant. Japanese are hesitant, nervous in conversation, laugh loudly at the wrong time."

The racial stereotype of the Japanese played a role in the special treatment of Japanese-Americans during the war. There was some prejudice shown against German- and Italian-Americans, but the Japanese-Americans were

*In the greatest abridgement of civil liberties in the nation's history, over 100,000 Japanese-American civilians were forcibly evacuated to "relocation centers" in remote areas of the Southwest.*

the only group rounded up and put in concentration camps in the greatest mass abridgment of civil liberties in American history.

At the time of Pearl Harbor, about 127,000 Japanese-Americans lived in the United States, most on the West Coast. About 80,000 were nisei (Japanese born in the United States and holding American citizenship) and sansei (the sons and daughters of nisei); the rest were issei (aliens born in Japan who were ineligible for U.S. citizenship). The Japanese had long suffered from racial discrimination and prejudice in the United States. They were barred from intermarriage with other groups and excluded from many clubs, restaurants, and recreation facilities. Many were employed as tenant farmers, as fishermen, or in small businesses. But there was a small professional class of lawyers, teachers, and doctors and a large number of landowning farmers.

Although many retained cultural and linguistic ties to Japan, they posed no more threat to the country than did the much larger groups of Italian-Americans and German-Americans. But their racial characteristics made them stand out as Italian-Americans and German-Americans did not. After Pearl Harbor, an anti-Japanese panic set in on the West Coast. A Los Angeles newspaper reported that armed Japanese were in Lower California ready to attack. Rumors suggested that Japanese fishermen were preparing to sow mines in the harbor, blow up tunnels, and poison the water supply.

West Coast politicians and ordinary citizens urged the War Department and the president to evacuate the Japanese. The president capitulated and issued Executive Order 9066 authorizing the evacuation in February 1942. "The continued pressure of a largely unassimilated, tightly knit racial group, bound to an enemy nation by strong ties of race, culture, custom and religion, constituted a menace which had to be dealt with," General John De Witt argued, justifying the removal on military grounds. But it was racial fear and animosity, not military necessity, that stood behind the order.

Eventually the government built the "relocation centers" in remote, often arid, sections of the West. "The Japs live like rats, breed like rats and act like rats. We don't want them," the

governor of Idaho announced. The camps were primitive and unattractive. "When I first entered our room, I became sick to my stomach," a Japanese-American woman remembered. "There were seven beds in the room and no furniture nor any partitions to separate the males and the females of the family. I just sat on the bed, staring at the bare wall."

About 110,000 Japanese were evacuated. Those who were forced to leave their homes, farms, and businesses lost almost all their property and possessions. Farmers left their crops to be harvested by their American neighbors. Store owners sold out for a small percentage of what their goods were worth. No personal items or household goods could be transported. The Japanese-Americans lost their worldly possessions, but they lost something more—their pride and respect. One 6-year-old kept asking his mother to "take him back to America." He thought his relocation center was in Japan.

The evacuation of the Japanese-Americans appears in retrospect to have been unjustified. Even in Hawaii, where a much larger Japanese population existed, no evacuation was attempted, and there was no sabotage and little disloyalty. "We believe that the German people bear a common political responsibility for outrages secretly committed by the Gestapo and the SS," one American official wrote in 1945. "What are we to think of our own part in a program which violates every democratic social value, yet has been approved by the Congress, the President and the Supreme Court?"

### Black and Hispanic Americans at War

The United States in 1941, even in much of the North, remained a segregated society. Blacks could not live, eat, travel, work, or go to school with the same freedom enjoyed by whites. Blacks profited little from the revival of prosperity and the expansion of jobs early in the war. When blacks joined the military, they were usually assigned to menial jobs as cooks or laborers and were always assigned to segregated units in which the high-ranking officers were white. The myth that black soldiers had failed to perform well in World War I persisted. "Leadership is not imbedded in the negro race yet,"

Secretary of War Henry Stimson wrote, "and to try to make commissioned officers to lead men into battle—colored men—is only to work a disaster to both."

It seemed especially ironic to some black leaders that as the country prepared to fight Hitler and his racist policies, the United States persisted in its own brand of racism. "A jim crow Army cannot fight for a free world," announced *The Crisis,* the journal of the NAACP. But it was A. Philip Randolph who decided to act rather than talk. The son of a Methodist minister, Randolph migrated from Florida to New York at the age of 22. He attended City College and became a socialist for a time, working with the first wave of blacks migrating from the South to the northern cities during and just after World War I. Randolph spent years trying "to carry the gospel of unionism to the colored world." He organized and led the Brotherhood of Sleeping Car Porters, and in 1937, he finally won grudging recognition of the union from the Pullman Company.

Respected and admired by black leaders of all political persuasions, Randolph convinced many of them in 1941 to join him in a march on Washington to demand equal rights. "Dear fellow Negro Americans," Randolph wrote, "be not dismayed in these terrible times. You possess power, great power. Our problem is to harness and hitch it up for action on the broadest, daring and most gigantic scale."

The threat of as many as 100,000 blacks marching in protest in the nation's capital alarmed Roosevelt. At first he sent his assistants, including his wife Eleanor, who was greatly admired in the black community, to dissuade Randolph from such drastic action. But finally he talked to Randolph in person on June 18, 1941. Randolph and Roosevelt struck a bargain. Roosevelt refused to desegregate the armed forces; but in return for Randolph's calling off the march, the president issued Executive Order 8802, which stated that it was the policy of the United States that "there shall be no discrimination in the employment of workers in defense industries or government because of race, creed, color or national origin." He also established the Committee on Fair Employment Practices (FEPC) to enforce the order.

By threatening militant action, the black leaders wrested a major concession from the president. But the executive order did not end prejudice, and the FEPC, which its chairman described as the "most hated agency in Washington," had only limited success in erasing the color line. Many black soldiers were angered and humiliated throughout the war by being made to sit in the back of buses and being barred from hotels and restaurants. Years later, one former black soldier recalled being refused service in a restaurant in Salina, Kansas, while the same restaurant served German prisoners who were in a camp nearby. "We continued to stare," he recalled. "This was really happening. . . . The people of Salina would serve these enemy soldiers and turn away black American G.I.'s."

Many black Americans improved their economic conditions during the war by taking jobs in war industries. Continuing the migration that had begun during World War I, three-quarters of a million blacks moved out of the South into northern and western cities in search of economic opportunity. Some became skilled workers and a few became professionals, but most did the "hard, hot, and heavy" tasks. Those who moved north were often crowded into segregated housing. The racial tension and prejudice were

*Blacks and other minorities also benefited from wartime job opportunities. Even before the United States entered the war, black families like this one moved to the North to work in the defense industry.*

increased by the presence of many white southerners who had also followed the path of opportunity north.

It was not just southerners who wanted to keep black Americans in their place. In Detroit, where a major race riot broke out in the summer of 1943, Polish-Americans had protested a public housing development that promised to bring blacks into their neighborhood. In one year, more than 50,000 blacks moved into that city, already overcrowded with many others seeking wartime jobs. The new arrivals increased the pressure on housing and on other facilities, and the war accentuated the tension among the various groups.

The riot broke out on a hot, steamy day at a municipal park where a series of incidents led to fights between black and white young people and then to looting in the black community. Before federal and state troops restored order, 34 had been killed (25 blacks and 9 whites) and more than $2 million worth of property had been destroyed. Groups of whites roamed the city attacking blacks, overturning cars, setting fires, and sometimes killing wantonly. A group of young men murdered a 58-year-old black "just for the hell of it." "We didn't know him," one of the boys admitted. "He wasn't bothering us. But other people were fighting and killing and we felt like it too." Other riots broke out in Mobile, Los Angeles, New York, and Beaumont, Texas. In all these cities, and in many others where the tension did not lead to open violence, the legacy of bitterness and hate lasted long after the war.

Mexican-Americans, like most minority groups, profited during the war from the increased job opportunities provided by wartime industry. Many left their villages for the first time. Women broke away from their traditional roles and worked outside the home. Mexican-Americans labored in factories in Texas and California and replaced many of the dust-bowl migrants in the fields. They joined the armed forces in unprecedented numbers and found jobs in the oil fields. On one occasion, the Fair Employment Practice Commission ordered the Shell Oil Company to promote three Mexican-Americans who had been the victims of company discrimination. Although there were other attempts during the war to end unfair treatment, prejudice and discrimination were not easy to eliminate.

In California, and in many parts of the Southwest, Mexicans could not use public swimming pools. Often lumped together with blacks, they were excluded from certain restaurants. Usually they were limited to menial jobs and were constantly harassed by the police, picked up for minor offenses, and jailed on the smallest excuse. It was in Los Angeles that the anti-Mexican prejudice flared into violence. The increased migration of Mexicans into the city and old hatreds created a volatile situation. Most of the hostility and anger focused on Mexican gang members or pachucos, especially those wearing zoot suits. The suits consisted of long, loose coats with padded shoulders, ballooned pants, pegged at the ankles, and a wide-brimmed hat. A watch chain and a ducktail haircut completed the uniform. The zoot suit had originated in the black sections of northern cities and became a national craze during the war. It was a way some teenage males could call attention to themselves and shock conventional society.

The zoot-suiters seemed especially to anger soldiers and sailors who were stationed or on leave in Los Angeles. After a number of provocative incidents, violence broke out between the Mexican-American youths and the servicemen in the spring of 1943. The violence reached a peak on June 7 when gangs of servicemen, often in taxicabs, combed the city, attacking all the young zoot-suiters they could find or anyone who looked Mexican. The servicemen, joined by others, beat up the Mexicans, stripped them of their offensive clothes, and then gave them a haircut. The police, both civilian and military, looked the other way, and when they did move in, they arrested the victims rather than their attackers. The local press and the Chamber of Commerce hotly denied that race was a factor in the riots, but *Time* magazine was probably closer to the truth when it called the riots "the ugliest brand of mob action since the coolie race riots of the 1870s."

# SOCIAL IMPACT OF THE WAR

Modern wars have been incredibly destructive of human lives and property, but wars have social results as well. The Civil War ended slavery, ensured the triumph of the industrial North for years to come; it left a legacy of bitterness and transformed the race question from a sectional to a national problem. World War I assured the success of woman suffrage and prohibition, caused a migration of blacks to northern cities, and ushered in a time of intolerance. World War II also had many social results. It altered patterns of work, leisure, education, and family life, caused a massive migration of people, created jobs, and changed life styles. It is difficult to overemphasize the impact of the war on the generation that lived through it.

## Wartime Opportunities

More than 15 million American civilians moved during the war. Like the Momadays, many left home to find better jobs. Americans moved off the farms and away from the small towns; they flocked to cities, where defense jobs were readily available. They moved west: California alone gained more than 2 million people during the war. But they also moved out of the South into the northern cities, while others moved from the North to the South. Late in the war, when there was a shortage of farm labor, some reversed the trend and moved back onto the farms. But a great many people moved somewhere. One observer, noticing the heavily packed cars heading west, decided that it was just like *The Grapes of Wrath*, minus the poverty and the hopelessness.

The World War II migrants poured into industrial centers; 200,000 came to the Detroit area, nearly a half million to Los Angeles, and about 100,000 to Mobile, Alabama. They put pressure on the schools, housing, and other services. Often they were forced to live in new Hoovervilles, trailer parks, or temporary housing. In San Pablo, California, a family of four adults and seven children lived in an 8-by-10-foot shack. In Los Angeles, Mrs. Colin Kelley, the widow of a war hero, could find no place to live until a local newspaper publicized her plight. Bill Mauldin, the war cartoonist, showed a young couple with a child buying tickets for a movie with the caption: "Matinee, heck—we want to register for a week."

The overcrowded conditions, the sense of being away from home, the volatile mixture of people from different backgrounds living close together, and the wartime situation often created tension and sometimes open conflict. Some migrants had never lived in a city and were homesick. On one occasion in a Willow Grove, Michigan, school, the children were all instructed to sing "Michigan, My Michigan"; no one knew the words because they all came from other states. One of the most popular country songs of the period, when thousands had left their mountain homes to find work in the city, was "I Wanna Go Back to West Virginia."

For the first time in years, many families had money to spend, but they had nothing to spend it on. The last new car rolled off the assembly line in February 1942. There were no washing machines, refrigerators, or radios in the stores. There was no gasoline and no tires to permit weekend trips. Even when people had time off, they tended to stay at home or in the neighborhood. Some of the new housing developments had the atmosphere of a mining camp, with drinking, prostitution, and barroom brawls a part of the scene.

The war required major adjustments in American family life. With several million men in the service and others far away working at defense jobs, the number of households headed by a woman increased dramatically. The number of marriages also increased. Early in the war, a young man could be deferred if he had a dependent, and a wife qualified as a dependent. Later many servicemen got married, often to women they barely knew, because they wanted a little excitement and perhaps something to come home to. The birthrate also began to rise in 1940, reversing a long decline since the colonial period as young couples started a family as fast as they could. Some of these were "good-bye babies," conceived just before the husband left to join the military or to go overseas. The illegitimacy rate also went up, and from the outset of the war, the divorce rate began to climb sharply. Yet most of the wartime marriages survived, and many of the women left at home looked ahead to a time after the war when they could settle down to a normal life.

## Women Workers for Victory

Thousands of women took jobs in heavy industry that formerly would have been considered unladylike. They built tanks, planes, and ships, but they still earned less than men. At first, additional women were rarely employed because as the war in Europe pulled American industry out of the long Depression, unemployed men snapped up the newly available positions. In the face of this male labor pool, one government official remarked that we should "give the women something to do to keep their hands busy as we did in the last war, then maybe they won't bother us."

But by 1943, with many men drafted into the service and male unemployment virtually nonexistent, the government was quick to suggest that it was women's patriotic duty to take their place on the assembly line. A government poster showed a woman worker and her uniformed husband standing in front of an American flag with the caption: "I'm proud . . . my husband *wants* me to do my part." The government tried to convince women that if they could run a vacuum cleaner or a sewing machine or drive a car, they could operate power machinery in a factory. Advertisers in women's magazines joined the campaign by showing fashion models in work clothes. A popular song was "Rosie the Riveter," who was "making history working for victory." She also helped her marine boyfriend by "working overtime on the riveting machine."

There were 19.5 million women in the work force at the end of the war, but three-fourths of that number had been working before the conflict, and some of the additional ones might have sought work in normal times. The new women war workers tended to be older, and they were more often married than single. Some worked for patriotic reasons. "Everytime I test a batch of rubber, I know it's going to help bring my three

sons home quicker," a woman worker in a rubber plant remarked. But others went to work for the money or to have something useful to do. Yet in 1944, women's weekly wages averaged $31.21, compared to $54.65 for men, reflecting women's more menial tasks and their low seniority as well as outright discrimination. Still, many women enjoyed factory work. "Boy have the men been getting away with murder all these years," exclaimed a Pittsburgh housewife. "Why I worked twice as hard selling in a department store and got half the pay."

Black women faced the most difficult situation during the war and often were told when they applied for work such things as "We have not yet installed separate toilet facilities" or "We can't put a Negro in the front office." It was not until 1944 that the telephone company in New York City hired a black telephone operator. Still, some black women moved during the war from domestic jobs to higher-paying factory work. Married women with young children also found it difficult to find work. They found few

*Women were encouraged to take jobs in industry as the war progressed.*

day-care facilities and were often told that they should be home taking care of their children.

Women workers often had to endure catcalls, whistles, and more overt sexual harassment on the job. Still, most persisted, and they tried to look feminine despite the heavy work clothes. In one Boston factory, a woman was hooted at for carrying a lunch box. Only men it seemed carried lunch boxes; women brought their lunch in a paper bag.

Many women war workers quickly left their jobs after the war was over. Some left by choice, but dismissals ran twice as high for women as for men. The war had barely shaken the notion that a woman's place was at home. Some women who learned what an extra paycheck meant for the family's standard of living would have preferred to keep working. But most women, and an even larger percentage of men, agreed at the end of the war that women did not deserve "an equal chance with men" for jobs. War work altered individual lives and attitudes, but it did not change dramatically either women's or men's perception of women's proper role. The stereotype of women as weak and dependent persisted in many wartime movies and radio soap operas.

### Entertaining the People

According to one survey, Americans listened to the radio an average of 4½ hours a day during the war. The major networks increased their news programs from less than 4 percent to nearly 30 percent of broadcasting time. Americans heard Edward R. Murrow broadcasting from London during the German air blitz with the sound of the air raid sirens in the background. They listened to Eric Sevareid cover the battle of Burma and describe the sensation of jumping out of an airplane. For the first time, news reporters recorded their comments; the recordings were flown to the nearest studio and broadcast back to the United States. There was a delay, but the broadcast had drama and an immediacy never possible before.

Even more than the reporters, the commentators became celebrities on whom the American people depended to explain what was going on around the world. Millions listened to the clipped, authoritative voice of H. V. Kaltenborn or to Gabriel Heatter, whose trademark was "Ah, there's good news tonight." But the war also intruded on almost all other programming. Even the advertising, which took up more and more air time, reminded listeners that there was a war on. Lucky Strike cigarettes, which changed the color of its package from green to white, presumably because there was a shortage of green paint, made "Lucky Strike Green Has Gone to War" almost as famous as "Remember Pearl Harbor."

The serials, the standard fare of daytime radio, also adopted wartime themes. Dick Tracy tracked down spies, while Captain Midnight fought against the enemy on remote jungle islands. Superman outwitted Nazi agents, while Stella Dallas took a job in a defense plant.

Music, which took up a large proportion of radio programming, also conveyed a war theme. There was "Goodby Momma, I'm Off to Yokohama" and "Praise the Lord and Pass the Ammunition." But more numerous were songs of romance and love, songs about separation and hope for a better time after the war. The danceable tunes of Glenn Miller and Tommy Dorsey became just as much a part of wartime memories as ration books and far-off battlefields.

For many Americans, the motion picture was the most important leisure activity and a part of their fantasy life during the war. Attendance at the movies averaged about 100 million individuals a week. There might not be gasoline for weekend trips or Sunday drives, but the whole family could go to the movies; and then, like Scott Momaday, they could replay them in their imaginations. Even those in the military service could watch American movies on board ship or at a remote outpost. "Pinup" photographs of Hollywood stars decorated the barracks and even the tanks and planes wherever American troops were stationed.

Musical comedies, cowboy movies, and historical romances remained popular during the war, but the conflict intruded even on Hollywood. Most movies were preceded by a newsreel that offered a visual synopsis of the war news, always with an upbeat message and a touch of human interest. The theme was that the Americans were winning the war, even if early in the conflict there was little evidence to argue the case. Many feature films also had a wartime theme, picturing the war in the Pacific complete with grinning, vicious Japanese villains (usually played by Chinese or Korean character actors). In the beginning of these films the Japanese were always victorious, but in the end they always got "what they deserved."

The movies set in Europe differed somewhat from those depicting the Far Eastern war. Here British and Americans, sometimes spies, sometimes downed airmen, could dress up like Germans and get away with it. They outwitted the Germans at every turn, sabotaging important installations and finally escaping in a captured plane.

A number of Hollywood actors went into the service, and some even became heroes. But most, like Ronald Reagan, were employed to produce, narrate, or act in government films. The Office of War Information produced short subjects and documentaries, some of them distinguished, like John Huston's *The Battle of San Pietro*, a realistic depiction of war on the Italian front. More typical were propaganda films meant to indoctrinate American soldiers into the reasons why they were fighting the war. *Letter From Bataan*, a short film made in 1942, portrayed a wounded GI who wrote home asking his brother-in-law to save his razor blades because "it takes twelve thousand razor blades to make one two-thousand-pound bomb." The film ended with the announcement that the soldier had died in the hospital.

### The GIs' War

GI, an abbreviation that stood for "government issue," became the affectionate designation for the ordinary soldier in World War II. The GIs came from every background and ethnic group. Some served reluctantly, some eagerly. A few became genuine heroes. All were turned into heroes by the press and the public, who seemed to believe that one American could easily defeat at least 20 Japanese or Germans. Ernest Pyle, one of the war correspondents who chronicled the authentic story of the ordinary soldier, wrote:

In the magazines war seemed romantic and exciting, full of heroics and vitality. . . . But when I sat down to write, I saw instead men suffering and wishing they were somewhere else. . . . All of them desperately hungry for somebody to talk to besides themselves, no women to be heroes in front of, damn little wine to drink, precious little song, cold and fairly dirty, just toiling from day to day in a world full of insecurity, discomfort, homesickness and a dulled sense of danger.

Bill Mauldin, another correspondent, told the story of the ordinary soldier in a series of cartoons featuring two tired and resigned infantrymen, Willie and Joe. Joe tries to explain what the war is about, "when they run we try to ketch 'em, when we ketch 'em we try to make 'em run." In another cartoon, Willie says, "Joe, yestiddy ya saved my life an' I swore I'd pay you back. Here's my last pair of dry socks." For the soldier in the front line, the big strategies were irrelevant. The war seemed a constant mix-up; much more important were the little comforts and staying alive.

For those in the middle of a battle, the war was no fun, but only one out of eight who served ever saw combat, and even for many of those the war was a great adventure (just as World War I had been). "When World War II broke out I was delighted," Mario Puzo, author of *The Godfather*, remembered. "There is no other word, terrible as it may sound. My country called. I was delivered from my mother, my family, the girl I was loving passionately but did not love. And delivered *without guilt*. Heroically my country called, ordered me to defend it." World War II catapulted young men and women out of their small towns and urban neighborhoods into exotic places where they met new people and did new things.

The war was important for Mexican-Americans, who were drafted and volunteered in great numbers. A third of a million served in all branches of the military, a larger percentage than for many other ethnic groups. Although they encountered prejudice, they probably found less in the armed forces than they had at home, and many returned to civilian life with new ambitions and a new sense of self-esteem.

# RECOVERING THE PAST

World War II was one of those events that in some significant way influenced every family. For those who lost sons, husbands, or fathers, the war was tragic. But for others it meant jobs, travel, adventure, and romance. The Second World War is still the subject of many movies and books, and there are thousands who collect World War II weapons, model planes, and other memorabilia. The generation that lived through the war is inclined to look back nostalgically and to recall the war as a wonderful period in their lives, unlike those who look back at the Vietnam War. In fact, almost as many Americans landed in France in June 1984 to celebrate the fortieth anniversary of D day as invaded Normandy on June 6, 1944. Taking former soldiers and their families back to World War II battlegrounds has become a major tourist industry in Europe.

How did the war influence your family? The study of the family, "humanity's most fundamental and most durable institution," is as important for historians as the study of wars, elections, depressions,

and social currents. One's own family, in fact, is a part of these events. By interviewing family members and writing about their lives, which is called oral history, the past is made both more vivid and more personal. Oral history goes beyond names and dates to the rich immediate texture of people's recollections of personal experiences and feelings. Investigating family members is an opportunity not only to "put your own family into history" but also to develop deeper relations and understanding. As such, it is an act requiring a high degree of respect and responsibility.

You can become an oral historian by asking members of your family about their World War II experience, recovering a partial history of both your family and the war. Talk to your father and mother, your grandparents, and other older relatives. Who in your family served in the armed forces? Who went overseas? Did anyone work in a war industry? Was there a "Rosie the Riveter" in your family? Did your family move during the war? For many people the war meant jobs and the end of depression. Was that true

Library of Congress, Washington, D.C.

**War effort on the home front**

LIFE Magazine, (c) Time Inc.

**Alfred Eisenstadt**, Soldier's Farewell,
Penn Station, 1944

## REMEMBERING THE GOOD WAR

I was nine years old when the war started. It was a typical Chicago working-class neighborhood. It was predominantly Slavic, Polish. There were some Irish, some Germans. When you're a kid, the borders of the world are the few blocks of two-flats, bungalows, cottages, with a lot of little stores in between. My father had a tavern. In those days they put out extras. I remember the night the newsboys came through the neighborhood. Skid-row kind of guys, hawking the papers. Germany had invaded Poland: '39. It was the middle of the night, my mother and father waking. People were going out in the streets in their bathrobes to buy the papers. In our neighborhood with a lot of Poles, it was a tremendous story.

Suddenly you had a flagpole. And a marker. Names went on the marker, guys from the neighborhood who were killed. Our neighborhood was decimated. There were only kids, older guys, and women.

Suddenly I saw something I hadn't seen before. My sister became Rosie the Riveter. She put a bandanna on her head every day and went down to this organ company that had been converted to war work. There was my sister in slacks. It became more than work. There was a sense of mission about it. Her husband was Over There. . . .

There was the constant idea that you had to be doing something to help. It did filter down to the neighborhood: home-front mobilization. We had a block captain. . . .

We'd listen to the radio every night. My father would turn it on to find out what was happening. The way a kid's mind could be shaped by those dulcet voices. The world was very simple. I saw Hitler and Mussolini and Tojo: those were the villains. We were the good guys. And the Russians were the good guys too. The war was always being talked about in the bar. Everybody was a military strategist.

The big event was my brother-in-law coming home, my sister's husband. He had been a combat soldier all the way through. He had all his ribbons and medals on. He was the family hero.

Mike Royko, in Studs Terkel, *"The Good War": An Oral History of World War Two.* Copyright © 1984 by Studs Terkel. Reprinted by permission of Pantheon Books, a Division of Random House, Inc.

for your family? Many young people met their future spouses during the war. Was that true in your family?

Can anyone in your family remember rationing, scrap drives, blackouts, victory gardens? Did anyone eat horsemeat or mix yellow dye with oleomargarine? Can anyone recall the big bands, the movie stars, the newsreels? Although there was widespread support for the war, and patriotism was popular, prejudice and hate still remained. In what ways did your family share in the patriotism or participate in the prejudice? Whether in battles abroad or on the home front, how does the war as recalled by your family differ from the war as described in this chapter?

Look around your home. Are there any surviving memorabilia from the war—old photographs or uniforms, discharge papers, ration books, war stamps, souvenirs, magazines, or other things from the war years? Go to your library and look at a few issues of *Life* or *Look* for the 1940s. What do you notice about the advertisements and the news stories? How do they differ from magazine advertising and reporting today? What happened to the automotive industry and to professional baseball and college football during the war? What do you notice about women's dress styles? What do the two photographs shown here tell you about the American people in World War II?

Did the war mean tragedy or opportunity for your family? "World War II was a holy war and FDR a saint," one writer has remarked. Does your family agree? World War II may have been the last time the country was really united; those who lived through it have inevitably looked at recent events through the perspective of the war years. How did "the Good War," as Studs Terkel called it, influence the political and social views of those in your family old enough to remember it? How do their attitudes about World War II compare with their feelings about more recent American wars?

If the experience of World War II is too distant for the recollections of members of your family, ask them instead about either the Korean War or the Vietnam War. Similar questions are appropriate: ask those who went abroad to describe what the war was like and how they felt about it, and ask those who stayed at home how the war affected or changed their lives.

The accompanying brief excerpt from Studs Terkel's *"The Good War": An Oral History of World War Two* illustrates how the world transformed the family and neighborhood of young Mike Royko, now a Chicago journalist.

Many Native Americans also served. In fact, many Indians were recruited for special service in the Marine Signal Corps. One group of Navajos completely befuddled the Japanese with a code based on their native language. "Were it not for the Navajos, the Marines would never have taken Iwo Jima," one Signal Corps officer declared. But the Navajo code talkers and all other Indians who chose to return to the reservations after the war were ineligible for veterans' loans, hospitalization, and other benefits. They lived on federal land, and that, according to the law, canceled all the advantages that other veterans enjoyed after the war.

For black Americans, who served throughout the war in segregated units and faced prejudice wherever they went, the military experience also had much to teach. Fewer blacks were sent overseas (about 79,000 of 504,000 blacks in the service in 1943), and fewer were in

*About 322,000 American servicemen died in the war, but the government tried to protect the public from the real cost of the battles. This photograph published in 1943 was the first to show dead American soldiers.*

combat outfits, so the percentage of killed and wounded was low among blacks. Many illiterate blacks, especially from the South, learned to read and write in the service. Blacks who were sent overseas began to realize that not everyone viewed them as inferior. One black army officer said, "What the hell do we want to fight the Japs for anyhow? They couldn't possibly treat us any worse than these 'crackers' right here at home." Most realized the paradox of fighting for freedom when the black had little freedom; they hoped things would improve after the war.

Because the war lasted longer than World War I, its impact was greater. In all, over 16 million men and women served in one branch or another of the military service. About 322,000 were killed in the war, and more than 800,000 were wounded. Some 12,000 listed as missing just disappeared. The war claimed many more lives than World War I, and was the nation's costliest after the Civil War. But because of penicillin, blood plasma, sulfa drugs, and rapid battlefield evacuation, the wounded in World War II were twice as likely to survive as in World War I. Penicillin also minimized the threat of venereal disease, but all men who served saw an anti-VD film, just as their counterparts had in World War I.

### Women in Uniform

Women had served in all wars as nurses and cooks and in other support capacities, and during World War II many continued in these traditional roles. A few nurses landed in France just days after the invasion. Nurses served with the army and the marines in the Pacific. They dug their own foxholes and treated men under enemy fire. Sixty-six nurses spent the entire war in the Philippines, most of it as prisoners of the Japanese.

Though nobody objected to women serving as nurses, it was not until April 1943 that women physicians won the right to join the Army and Navy Medical Corps. Some questioned whether it was right for women to serve in other capacities. But Congress authorized full military participation for women (except for combat) because of the military emergency and the argument that women could free men for combat duty. World War II thus became the first war in which women were given regular military status. About 350,000 women joined up, most in the Womens' Army Corps (WACS) and the women's branch of the navy (WAVES). For many of the women who spoke in support of the bill, it was not so much the military situation as the need to assert women's rights to full citizenship, with all its responsibilities, that influenced their support of military service for women.

Many of the recruiting posters suggested that the services needed women "for the precision work at which women are so adept," or to work in hospitals to comfort and attend to the wounded "as only women can do." And most women served in traditional womanly roles, doing office work, cooking, and cleaning. But others were engineers and pilots. Still, men and women were not treated equally. Men were informed about contraceptives and encouraged to use them, but information about birth control was explicitly prohibited for women. Persistent rumors charged many women with drunkenness and sexual promiscuity. On one occasion the secretary of war defended the morality and the loyalty of the women in the service, but the rumors continued. Another delicate problem concerned whether a man should take an order from a woman. The marine corps solved the difficult situation by ruling that a woman officer could command enlisted men if the order originated with a male superior. Despite difficulties, women played important roles during the war, and when they left the service (unlike the women who had served in other wars), they had the same rights and privileges as the male veterans. The women in the service did not permanently alter the military or the public's perception of women's proper role, but they did change a few minds, and many of the women who served had their lives changed and their horizons raised.

## A WAR OF DIPLOMATS AND GENERALS

Pearl Harbor catapulted the country into war with Japan, and on December 11, 1941, Hitler declared war on the United States. Why he did so has never been fully explained; he was perhaps impressed by the apparent weakness of America as demonstrated at Pearl Harbor. He was not required by his treaty with Japan to go to war with the United States, and without his declaration the United States might have concentrated on the war against Japan. But with Hitler's declaration the United States was finally at war against the Axis powers in both Europe and Asia.

### War Aims

Why was the United States fighting the war? What did it hope to accomplish in a peace settlement once the war was over? Roosevelt and the other American leaders never really decided. In a speech before Congress in January 1941, Roosevelt had mentioned the four freedoms: freedom of speech and expression, freedom of worship, freedom from want, and freedom from fear. For many Americans, especially after Norman Rockwell expressed those freedoms in four sentimental paintings, this was what they were fighting for. Roosevelt, who spoke vaguely of the need to extend democracy and to establish a peacekeeping organization, never spelled out in any detail the political purposes for fighting. The only American policy was to end the war as quickly as possible and to solve the political problems created by it when the time came. That policy, or lack of policy, would have important ramifications.

Roosevelt and his advisers, realizing that it would be impossible to mount an all-out war against both Japan and Germany, decided to fight a holding action in the Pacific at first while concentrating their efforts against Hitler in Europe, where the immediate danger seemed greater. But the United States was not fighting alone. It joined the Soviet Union and Great Britain in what became a difficult, but in the end an effective, alliance to defeat Nazi Germany. Churchill and Roosevelt got along well, although they often disagreed on strategy and tactics. Roosevelt's relationship with Stalin was much more strained, but often he agreed with the Russian leader about the way to fight the war. Stalin, a ruthless leader who had maintained his position of power only after eliminating hundreds of thousands of opponents, distrusted both the British and the Americans, but he needed them, just as they depended on him. Without the tremendous sacrifices of the Russian army and the Russian people in 1941 and 1942, Germany would have won the war before the vast American military and industrial might could be mobilized.

## 1942: Year of Disaster

Despite the potential of the American-British-Soviet alliance, almost all the war news in the first half of 1942 was disastrous for the Allied cause. In the Pacific, the Japanese captured the Dutch East Indies with its vast riches in rubber, oil, and other resources. They swept into Burma, took Wake Island and Guam, and invaded the Aleutian Islands of Alaska. They pushed the American garrison on the Philippines onto the Bataan peninsula and finally onto the tiny island of Corregidor, where General Jonathan Wainwright surrendered more than 11,000 men to the Japanese. American reporters tried their best to play down the disasters and to concentrate their stories on the few American victories—and to tell the tales of American heroism against overwhelming odds. One of the soldiers on a Pacific island picked up an American broadcast one night. "The news commentators in the States had us all winning the war," he discovered, "their buoyant cheerful voices talking of victory. We were out here where we would see these victories. They were all Japanese."

In Europe, the Germans pushed deep into Russia, threatening to capture all the industrial centers and the valuable oil fields. For a time it appeared that they would even overrun Moscow. In North Africa, General Erwin Rommel and his mechanized divisions, the Afrika Korps, drove the British forces almost to Cairo in Egypt and threatened the Suez Canal. In the Atlantic, German submarines sank British and American ships more rapidly than they could be replaced.

For a few dark months in 1942 it seemed that the Berlin-Tokyo Axis would win the war before the United States got itself ready to fight.

The Allies could not agree on the proper military strategy in Europe. Churchill advocated tightening the ring around Germany, using bombing raids to weaken the enemy and encouraging resistance among the occupied countries but avoiding any direct assault on the continent until success was assured. He remembered the vast loss of British lives during World War I and was determined to avoid similar casualties in this conflict. Stalin, on the other hand, demanded a second front, an invasion of Europe in 1942, to relieve the pressure on the Russian army, which faced 200 German divisions along a 2,000-mile front. Roosevelt agreed to an offensive in 1942. But in the end, the invasion in 1942 came not in France but in North Africa. The decision was probably right from a military point of view, but it created Russian distrust of Britain and the United States. The delay in opening the second front probably contributed indirectly to the Cold War after 1945.

Attacking in North Africa in November 1942, American and British troops tried to link up with a beleaguered British army. The American army, enthusiastic but inexperienced, met little resistance in the beginning, but at Kasserine Pass in Tunisia, the Germans counterattacked and destroyed a large American force, inflicting 5,000 casualties. Roosevelt, who launched the invasion in part to give the American people a victory to relieve the dreary news from the Far East, learned that victories often came with long casualty lists.

He also learned the necessity of political compromise. In order to gain a cease-fire in conquered French territory in North Africa, the United States recognized Admiral Jean Darlan as head of its provisional government. Darlan persecuted the Jews, exploited the Arabs, imprisoned his opponents, and collaborated with the Nazis. He seemed diametrically opposed to the principles the Americans said they were fighting for. Did the Darlan deal mean the United States would negotiate with Mussolini? Or with Hitler? The Darlan compromise reinforced Soviet distrust of the Americans, but it also angered many Americans as well.

Roosevelt never compromised or made a deal with Hitler, but he did aid General Francisco Franco, the Fascist dictator in Spain, in return for safe passage of American shipping into the Mediterranean. But the United States did not aid only right-wing dictators. They also supplied arms to the left-wing resistance in France, to the Communist Tito in Yugoslavia, and to Ho Chi Minh, the anti-French resistance leader in Indochina. Roosevelt also authorized large-scale lend-lease aid to the Soviet Union. Although criticized by liberals for his support of dictators, Roosevelt was willing to do almost anything to

win the war. Military expediency often dictated his political decisions.

Even on one of the most sensitive issues of the war, the plight of the Jews in occupied Europe, Roosevelt's solution was to win the war as quickly as possible. By November 1942, confirmed information had reached the United States that the Nazis were systematically exterminating Jews. Yet the Roosevelt administration did nothing for more than a year, and even then did scandalously little to rescue European Jews from the gas chambers. Only 21,000 refugees were allowed to enter the United States over a

## World War II: Pacific Theater

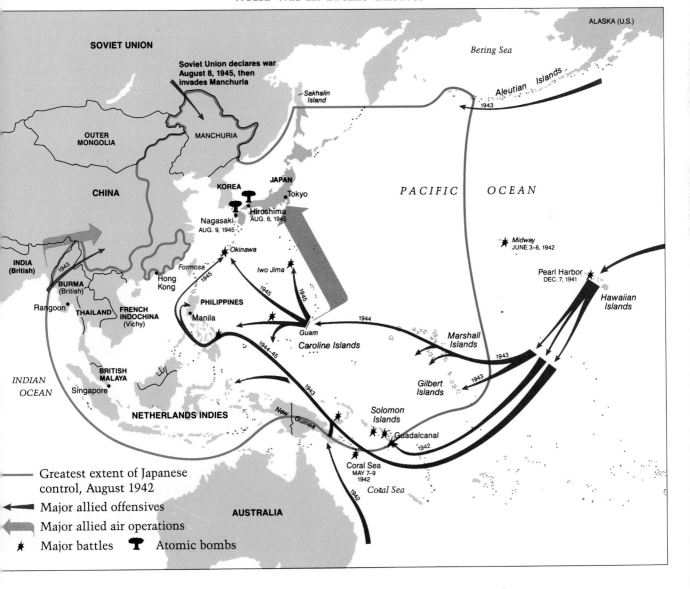

period of 3½ years, just 10 percent of those who could have been admitted under existing immigration quotas. The U.S. War Department rejected suggestions that the Auschwitz gas chambers be bombed, and government officials turned down many rescue schemes. Widespread anti-Semitic feelings in the United States in the 1940s and the fear of massive Jewish immigration help to explain the failure of the Roosevelt administration to act. The fact that the mass media, Christian leaders, and even American Jews failed to mount effective pressure on the government does not excuse the President for his shameful indifference to the systematic murder of millions of people. Roosevelt could not have prevented the Holocaust, but vigorous action on his part could have saved many thousands of lives during the war.

Roosevelt was not always right, nor was he even consistent, but people who assumed he had a master strategy or a fixed ideological position misunderstood the American president.

## A Strategy for Ending the War

The commanding general of the Allied armies in the North African campaign emerged as a genuine leader. Born in Texas, Dwight D. Eisenhower spent his boyhood in Abilene, Kansas. His small-town, rural background made it easy for biographers and newspaper reporters to make him into an American hero. Eisenhower, however, had not come to his hero status easily. He saw no action in World War I; he spent that war training soldiers in Texas. Even though he served as assistant to General Douglas MacArthur in the 1930s in the Philippines, he was only a lieutenant colonel when World War II erupted. General George Marshall had discovered Eisenhower's talents even before the war began. He was quickly promoted to general and achieved a reputation as an expert planner and organizer. Gregarious and outgoing, he had a broad smile that made most people instantly like him. He was not a brilliant field commander and made many mistakes in the African campaign. But he had the ability to get diverse people to work together, which was crucial where British and American units had to cooperate.

The American army moved slowly across North Africa, linked up with the British, invaded Sicily in July 1943, and finally stormed ashore in Italy in September. The Italian campaign proved long and bitter. Despite the fact that the Italians overthrew Mussolini and surrendered in September 1943, the Germans occupied the peninsula and gave ground only after bloody fighting. The whole American army seemed to be bogged down for months. One soldier described the "slushy mud that reaches almost up to your knees, . . . making the roads dangerously slippery." The Allies did not reach Rome until June 1944, and they never controlled all of Italy before the war in Europe ended.

Despite the decision to make the war in Europe the first priority, American ships and planes halted the Japanese advance in the spring of 1942. In the Battle of Coral Sea in May 1942, American carrier-based planes inflicted heavy damage on the Japanese fleet and prevented the invasion of the southern tip of New Guinea and probably of Australia as well. It was the first naval battle in history in which no guns were fired from one surface ship against another; all the damage was caused by airplanes. In World War II, the aircraft carrier would be more important than the battleship. A month later, at the

*President Roosevelt inspects General Eisenhower's troops on Sicily before returning home from the Cairo-Teheran Conference, 1943.*

Battle of Midway, American planes sank four Japanese aircraft carriers and destroyed nearly 300 planes. This was the first major Japanese defeat; it restored some balance of power in the Pacific and ended the threat to Hawaii.

In 1943, the American sea and land forces leapfrogged from island to island, gradually retaking territory from the Japanese and building bases to attack the Philippines and eventually Japan itself. Progress often had terrible costs, however. In November 1943, about 5,000 marines landed on the coral beaches of the tiny island of Tarawa. Despite heavy naval bombardment and the support of hundreds of planes, the

marines met heavy opposition. The four-day battle left more than 1,000 Americans dead and over 3,000 wounded. One marine general thought it was all wasted effort. He thought the island should have been bypassed. Others disagreed. No one asked the marines who stormed the beaches. Less than 50 percent of the first wave survived.

## The Invasion of Europe

Operation Overlord, the code name for the largest amphibious invasion in history, the invasion Stalin had wanted in 1942, began only on

## World War II: European and North African Theaters

*Source:* U.S. Bureau of the Census.

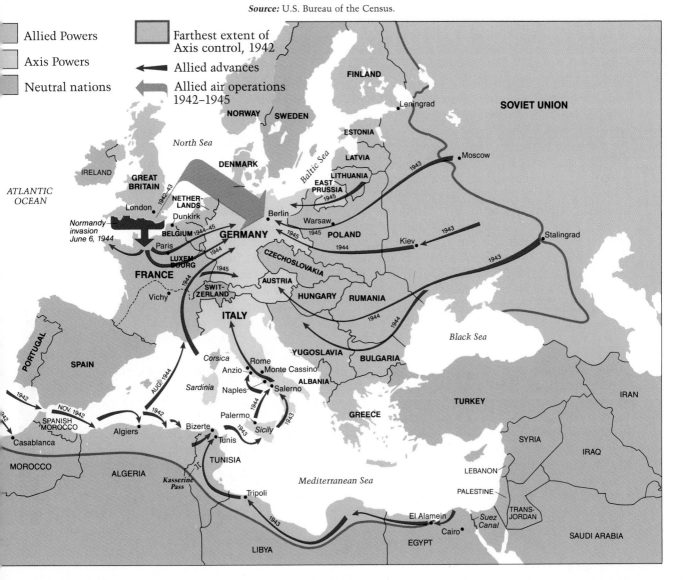

June 6, 1944. It was, according to Churchill, "the most difficult and complicated operation that has ever taken place." The initial assault along a 60-mile stretch of the Normandy coast was conducted with 175,000 men supported by 600 warships and 11,000 planes. Within a month, over a million troops and more than 170,000 vehicles had landed. Such an invasion would have been impossible during World War I.

Eisenhower, now bearing the title Supreme Commander of the Allied Expeditionary Force in Western Europe, coordinated and planned the operation. British and American forces, with some units from other countries, worked together, but Overlord was made possible by American industry, which, by the war's end, was turning out an astonishing 50 percent of all the world's goods. During the first few hours of the invasion, there seemed to be too many supplies. "Everything was confusing," one soldier remembered. It cost 2,245 killed and 1,670 wounded to secure the beachhead. "It was much lighter than anybody expected," one observer remarked. "But if you saw faces instead of numbers on the casualty list, it wasn't light at all."

For months before the invasion, American and British planes had bombed German transportation lines, industrial plants, and even cities. In all, over 1.5 million tons of bombs were dropped on Europe. The massive bombing raids helped make the invasion a success, but evidence gathered after the war suggests that the bombs did not disrupt German war production as seriously as Allied strategists believed at the time. Often a factory or a rail center would be back in operation within a matter of days, sometimes within hours, after an attack. In the end, the bombing of the cities may have strengthened the resolve of the German people to fight to the bitter end rather than destroying their morale.

The most destructive bombing raid of the war, carried out against Dresden on the night of February 13–14, 1945, had no strategic purpose. It was launched by the British and Americans to help demonstrate to Stalin that they were aiding the Russian offensive. Dresden, a city of 630,000, was not an industrial but a communications center. Three waves of planes dropped 650,000 incendiary bombs, creating a firestorm that swept over 8 square miles, destroyed every-thing in its path and killing 135,000 men, women, and children. One of the American pilots remarked, "For the first time I felt sorry for the population below."

With the dashing and eccentric General George Patton and the more staid General Omar Bradley in command, the American army broke out of the Normandy beachhead in July 1944. Led by the tank battalions, it swept across France. It was the American productive capacity and the ability to supply a mobile and motorized army that eventually brought victory. But not all American equipment was superior. The United States was far behind Germany in the development of rockets, but that was not as important in the actual fighting as the inability of the United States, until the end of the war, to develop a tank that could compete in armament or firepower with the German tanks. The American army made up for the deficiency of its tanks in part by having superior artillery. Perhaps even more important, most of the American soldiers had grown up tinkering with cars and radios. Children of the machine age, they managed to make repairs and to keep tanks, trucks, and guns functioning under difficult circumstances. They helped give the American army the superior mobility that eventually led to the defeat of Germany.

Just before Christmas in 1944, when the war in Europe seemed almost over, the Germans launched a massive counterattack along an 80-mile front, much of it held by thinly dispersed and inexperienced American troops. The Germans drove 50 miles inside the American lines before they were checked. During the Battle of the Bulge, as it was called, Eisenhower was so desperate for additional infantry that he offered to pardon any of the military prisoners in Europe if they would take up a rifle and go into battle. Most of the prisoners, who were serving short sentences, declined the opportunity to clear their record. Eisenhower also promised any black soldiers in the service and supply outfits an opportunity to become infantrymen in the white units, though usually with a lower rank. However, Walter Bedell Smith, his chief of staff, pointed out that this was against War Department regulations and was "the most dangerous thing I have seen in regard to race relations."

Eisenhower recanted, not wishing to start a social revolution. Those black soldiers who did volunteer to join the battle fought in segregated platoons with white officers in command.

## The Politics of Victory

As the American and British armies raced across France into Germany in the winter and spring of 1945, the political and diplomatic aspects of the war began to overshadow military concerns. It became a matter not only of defeating Germany but also of determining who was going to control Germany and the rest of Europe once Hitler's armies were defeated. The relationship between the Soviet Union and the other Allies had been badly strained during the war; with victory in sight, the tension became even greater. While the American press pictured Stalin as a wise and democratic leader and the

*As Allied troops closed in on Berlin, the horror of Nazi concentration camps was revealed to the world.*

Russian people as quaint and heroic, a number of high-level American diplomats and presidential advisers distrusted the Russians and looked ahead to a confrontation with Soviet Communism after the war. These men urged Roosevelt to make military decisions with the postwar political situation in mind.

The main issue in the spring of 1945 concerned who would capture Berlin. The British wanted to beat the Russians to the capital city. Eisenhower, however, fearing that the Germans might barricade themselves in the Austrian Alps and hold out indefinitely, ordered the armies south rather than toward Berlin. He also wanted to avoid unnecessary American casualties, and he planned to meet the Russian army at an easily marked spot in order to avoid any unfortunate incidents. The British and American forces could probably not have arrived in Berlin before the Russians in any case, but Eisenhower's decision generated controversy after the war. Russian and American troops met on April 25, 1945, at the Elbe River. On May 2, Berlin fell to the Russians. Hitler committed suicide. The long war in Europe finally came to an end on May 8, 1945. But the political problems remained.

In 1944, the United States continued to tighten the noose on Japan. American long-range B-29 bombers began sustained strikes on the Japanese mainland in June 1944, and by November they were dropping firebombs on Tokyo. In a series of naval and air engagements, especially at the Battle of Leyte Gulf, American planes destroyed most of the remaining Japanese navy. By the end of 1944 an American victory in the Pacific was all but assured. American forces recaptured the Philippines early the next year, yet the American forces had barely touched Japan itself. It might take years to conquer the Japanese on their home islands.

While the military campaigns reached a critical stage in both Europe and the Pacific, Roosevelt took time off to run for an unprecedented fourth term. To appease members of his own party, he agreed to drop Vice-President Henry Wallace from the ticket because some thought him too radical and impetuous. To replace him, the Democratic convention selected a relatively unknown senator from Missouri, Harry S Truman, after passing over several well-known political leaders. Truman, a World War I veteran, had been a judge in Kansas City before being elected to the Senate in 1934. His only fame came when, as chairman of the Senate Committee to Investigate the National Defense Program, he had insisted on honesty and efficiency in war contracts. He got some publicity for saving the taxpayers' dollars. The Republicans nominated Thomas Dewey, the colorless and politically moderate governor of New York, who had a difficult time criticizing Roosevelt without appearing unpatriotic. Roosevelt, who seemed haggard and ill during much of the campaign, still managed to display a sense of humor. Although he won the election easily in 1944, Roosevelt would need more than a sense of humor to deal with the difficult political problems of ending the war and constructing a peace settlement.

### The Big Three at Yalta

Roosevelt, Churchill, and Stalin, together with many of their advisers, met at Yalta in the Crimea in February 1945 to discuss the problems of the peace settlements. Most of the agreements reached at Yalta were secret, and in the atmosphere of the subsequent Cold War, many would become controversial. Roosevelt wanted the help of the Soviet Union in ending the war in the Pacific so as to avoid the needless slaughter of American men in an invasion of the Japanese mainland. In return for a promise to enter the war within three months after the war in Europe was over, the Soviet Union was granted the Kurile Islands, the southern half of Sakhalin, and railroads and port facilities in North Korea, Manchuria, and Outer Mongolia. Later that seemed like a heavy price to pay for the promise, but realistically the Soviet Union controlled most of this territory and could not have been dislodged short of going to war.

When the provisions of the secret treaties were revealed much later, many people would accuse Roosevelt of trusting the Russians too much. But Roosevelt wanted to retain a working relationship with the Soviet Union. If the peace was to be preserved, the major powers of the Grand Alliance would have to work together. Moreover, Roosevelt hoped to get the Soviet

Union's agreement to cooperate with a new peace-preserving United Nations organization after the war.

The European section of the Yalta agreement proved even more controversial than its Far Eastern provisions. Here it was decided to partition Germany and to divide the city of Berlin. But it was the Polish agreements that were most difficult for many to swallow, in part because it had been the invasion of Poland in 1939 that had precipitated the war. The Polish government in exile in London was militantly anti-Communist and looked forward to returning to Poland after the war. Stalin, however, demanded that the eastern half of Poland be given to the Soviet Union to protect its western border. Churchill and Roosevelt finally agreed to the Russian demands with the proviso that Poland be compensated with German territory on its western border. Stalin also agreed to include some members of the London-based Polish group in the new Polish government. He also promised to carry out "free and unfettered elections as soon as possible." The Polish settlement would prove divisive after the war, and it became quickly clear that what the British and Americans wanted in eastern Europe contrasted with what the Soviet Union intended. Yet at the time it seemed imperative that Russia enter the war in the Pacific, and the reality was that in 1945 the Soviet army occupied most of eastern Europe.

The most potentially valuable accomplishment at Yalta was agreement on the need to construct a United Nations, an organization for preserving peace and fostering the postwar reconstruction of battered and underdeveloped countries. In 1942, a total of 26 Allied nations had subscribed to the Atlantic Charter, drafted by Churchill and Roosevelt, which laid down several principles for a lasting peace. Discussions among the Allied powers continued during the war, and at Yalta Stalin agreed with Roosevelt and Churchill to call a conference in San Francisco in April 1945 to draft a United Nations charter.

Spirited debate occurred in San Francisco when the representatives of 50 nations gathered for this task. As finally accepted, amid optimism about a quick end to the war, the charter provided for a General Assembly in which every member nation had a seat. However, this General Assembly was designed mainly as a forum for discussing international problems. The responsibility for keeping global peace was lodged in the Security Council, composed of five permanent members (the United States, the Soviet Union, Great Britain, France, and China) and six other nations elected for two-year terms. It was the Security Council's responsibility to suppress international violence by applying economic, diplomatic, or military sanctions against any nation that all permanent members agreed threatened the peace. In addition, the charter established an International Court of Justice and a number of agencies to promote "collaboration among the nations through education, science, and culture." Among these agencies were the International Monetary Fund, the World Health Organization, and the UN Educational, Scientific, and Cultural Organization (UNESCO).

## The Atomic Age Begins

Two months after Yalta, on April 12, 1945, as the United Nations charter was being drafted, Roosevelt died suddenly of a massive cerebral hemorrhage. The nation was shocked. When an industrial worker in Springfield, Ohio, heard the news, he remarked that he was glad that "the old son of a bitch was gone"; another worker punched him in the face. Roosevelt, both hated and loved to the end, was replaced by Harry Truman, who was both more difficult to hate and harder to love. In the beginning, Truman seemed tentative and unsure of himself. Yet it fell to the new president to make some of the most difficult decisions of all time. The most momentous of all was the decision to drop the atomic bomb.

The Manhattan Project, first organized in 1941, was one of the best-kept secrets of the war. The task of the distinguished group of scientists whose work on the project was centered at Los Alamos, New Mexico, was to manufacture an atomic bomb before Germany did. But by the time the bomb was successfully tested in the New Mexican desert on July 16, 1945, the war in Europe had ended.

The scientists working on the bomb assumed that they were perfecting a military weapon. Yet when they saw the ghastly power of that first bomb, remembered J. Robert Oppenheimer, a leading scientist on the project, "some wept, a few cheered. Most stood silently." Some opposed the military use of the bomb. They realized its revolutionary power and worried about the future reputation of the United States if it unleashed this new force. But a presidential committee made up of scientists, military leaders, and politicians recommended that it be used on a military target in Japan as soon as possible.

"The final decision of where and when to use the atomic bomb was up to me," Truman later remembered. "Let there be no doubt about it. I regarded the bomb as a military weapon and never had any doubt that it should be used." But the decision had both military and political ramifications. Even though Japan had lost most of its empire by the summer of 1945, it still had a military force of several million men and thousands of kamikaze planes that had already wreaked havoc on the American fleet. The kamikaze pilots gave up their own lives to make sure that their planes, heavily laden with bombs, crashed on an American ship. There was little defense against such fanaticism.

Even with the Russian promise to enter the

*The atom bomb's unprecedented destruction is recalled by this 1984 Osaka department store display.*

war, it appeared that an amphibious landing on the Japanese mainland would be necessary to end the war. The monthlong battle for Iwo Jima, only 750 miles from Tokyo, had resulted in over 4,000 American dead and 15,000 wounded, and an invasion of Japan would be much more expensive. The bomb, many thought, could end the war without an invasion. But some of those involved in the decision wanted to pay Japan back for Pearl Harbor, and still others needed to justify spending over $2 billion on the project in the first place. The timing of the first bomb, however, indicates that the decision was intended to impress the Russians and ensure that they had little to do with the peace settlement in the Far East. One British scientist later charged that the decision to drop the bomb on Hiroshima was "the first major operation of the cold diplomatic war with Russia."

On August 6, 1945, two days before the Soviet Union had promised to enter the war against Japan, a B-29 bomber dropped a single atomic bomb over Hiroshima. It killed or severely wounded 160,000 civilians and destroyed 4 square miles of the city. One of the men on board the plane saw the thick cloud of smoke and thought that they had missed their target. "It looked like it had landed on a forest. I didn't see any sign of the city." The Soviet Union entered the war on August 8. When Japan failed to surrender immediately, a second bomb was dropped on the city of Nagasaki on August 9. The Japanese surrendered on August 14, 1945. The war was finally over, but the problems of the atomic age and the postwar world were just beginning.

## CONCLUSION: Peace, Prosperity, and International Responsibilities

The United States emerged from World War II with an enhanced reputation as the world's most powerful industrial and military nation. The demands of the war had finally ended the Great Depression and brought prosperity to most Americans. The war had also ended American isolationism and made the United States into the dominant international power. Of all the nations that fought in the war, the United States had suffered the least. No bombs were dropped on American factories, and no cities were destroyed. Even though more than 300,000 Americans lost their lives, even this carnage seemed minimal when compared to the more than 20 million Russian soldiers and civilians who died or the 6 million Jews and millions of others systematically exterminated by Hitler.

The American people greeted the end of the war with joy and relief. They looked forward to the peace and prosperity for which they had fought. Yet within two years, the peace would be jeopardized by the Cold War, and the United States would be rearming its former enemies, Japan and Germany, in order to oppose its former friend, the Soviet Union. The irony of that situation reduced some of the joy of celebration and made the American people forever more suspicious of their government and its foreign policy.

## Recommended Reading

Many books have been written on the process by which the United States got involved in World War II; the following suggest a variety of approaches. Robert Dallek, *Franklin D. Roosevelt and American Foreign Policy* (1979); Robert A. Divine, *The Reluctant Belligerent* (1979); and Lloyd C. Gardner, *Economic Aspects of New Deal Diplomacy* (1964). For United States policy toward Central America, see Walter La Feber, *Inevitable Revolutions: The United States in Central America* (1983). Gordon W. Prange, *At Dawn We Slept* (1981) is a recent evaluation of the events at Pearl Harbor.

A. Russell Buchanan, *The United States and World War II*, 2 vols. (1965) is a comprehensive account that provides good coverage of the military side of the war. Gaddis Smith, *Diplomacy During the Second World War*, Martin J. Sherwin, *A World Destroyed* (1975), and Gar Alperovitz, *Atomic Diplomacy* (1965) deal with important subjects. Stephen Ambrose, *Eisenhower* (1983) is a well-written account of the most important military commander during the war.

John Morton Blum, *V Was for Victory* (1976), Richard Polenberg, *War and Society* (1972), and Richard R. Lingeman, *Don't You Know There Is a War On?* (1970) are excellent books about the home front. Susan M. Hartmann, *The Home Front and Beyond* (1982) is a fascinating account of women during the war. Richard M. Dalfuime, *Desegregation of the U.S. Armed Forces* (1975) describes segregation in the military during the war. Roger Daniels, *Concentration Camp U.S.A.* (1971) details the depressing story of the relocation of Japanese-Americans during the war.

David S. Wyman, *The Abandonment of the Jews* (1984), tells the story of American policy toward the victims of the Holocaust.

In *The Dollmaker* (1954), Harriette Arnow tells the story of a young woman from Kentucky who finds herself in wartime Detroit. Two other fine novels of the war period are Norman Mailer, *The Naked and the Dead* (1948) and Irwin Shaw, *The Young Lions* (1948).

## TIME LINE

| | |
|---|---|
| 1931–1932 | Japan seizes Manchuria |
| 1933 | Hitler becomes German chancellor<br>United States refuses to join collective sanctions against Germany<br>United States recognizes the Soviet Union<br>Good Neighbor policy announced |
| 1934 | Germany begins rearmament |
| 1935 | Italy invades Ethiopia<br>First Neutrality Act |
| 1936 | Spanish civil war begins<br>Second Neutrality Act |
| 1937 | Hitler annexes Austria, occupies Sudetenland<br>Third Neutrality Act |
| 1938 | German persecution of Jews heightens |
| 1939 | Nazi-Soviet Pact<br>German invasion of Poland; World War II begins |
| 1940 | Roosevelt elected for a third term<br>Selective Service Act |
| 1941 | "Four Freedoms" speech by FDR<br>Lend-Lease Act<br>Germany attacks Russia<br>Japanese assets in United States frozen<br>Japanese attack Pearl Harbor<br>Proposed black march on Washington |
| 1942 | Internment of Japanese-Americans<br>Second Allied front in Africa launched |
| 1943 | Invasion of Sicily<br>Italian campaign<br>United Mine Workers strike<br>Race riots in Detroit and many other cities |
| 1944 | Operation Overlord<br>G.I. Bill passes Congress<br>Roosevelt elected for a fourth term |
| 1945 | Yalta conference<br>Roosevelt dies; Harry Truman becomes president<br>Successful test of atomic bomb<br>Hiroshima and Nagasaki bombed; Japan surrenders |

# PORTFOLIO FIVE

## THE ART OF
## A MODERNIZING PEOPLE

### 1900–1945

Just as the United States gradually became a world power in the period from 1900 to the end of World War II, American art also came of age and emerged as a force to be reckoned with around the world. American architects led by Frank Lloyd Wright had a strong influence in both Europe and Asia, while for many foreign visitors the skyscraper symbolized American vitality and creativity. Two trends dominated American painting during this period: one was the growing popularity of abstract art, the other a continuing concern for documenting the American scene with realistic paintings. Freed by the camera from the need simply to record, a number of European artists, postimpressionists, expressionists, cubists, and others experimented with new forms, and their movements inevitably influenced many artists in America. At the same time, the impulse to paint American subjects in a realistic way remained strong, and this trend was strengthened during the Depression decade as Americans explored the strengths and weaknesses of their civilization through documentaries of all kinds.

In the decade and a half before World War I, a group of young artists who called themselves "the Eight" but whom the critics labeled "the ashcan school" had a large impact on American art. They were called "the ashcan school" not only because they painted ashcans as well as elevated trains, run-down tenements, prostitutes, and other unsavory scenes but also because many of their critics thought their work should be assigned to the ashcan. They painted in different styles and came from many places, but they all eventually settled in New York. Like so many others of the progressive generation, they discovered the city in all its fascinating and appalling details. John Sloan was probably the best known of "the Eight," but George Luks, Maurice Prendergast, and Arthur B. Davies were just as talented. It was Davies who played a large role in organizing the Armory show that opened in New York on February 17, 1913. More than any other single event, this show introduced the American public to modern art and sculpture, both European and American. Many critics were shocked by paintings such as Marcel Duchamp's *Nude Descending a Staircase,* in which the subject was reduced to shapes and lines.

The Armory show marked the acceptance of modern art for sophisticated Americans and inspired Stuart Davis, Georgia O'Keeffe, and many other young artists to join the cubist and abstract movements. Still, the realistic tradition in America remained strong. Edward Hopper, Grant Wood, Thomas Hart Benton, John Curry, and others chose regional subjects and brought vitality to what is sometimes called the "American scene movement." The Depression of the 1930s further stimulated social realism in art, and New Deal programs allowed hundreds of artists to document the look and feel of America.

The great Mexican muralists José Clemente Orozco, Diego Rivera, and David Alfaro Siqueiros influenced many of the murals painted on public buildings during the 1930s under the sponsorship of the Federal Arts Project of the Works Progress Administration. One such American muralist, Marion Greenwood, was born in Brooklyn and studied with John Sloan but traveled to the Southwest to paint the Navajo. From there she went to Mexico, where she depicted Indian and Mexican life in several murals. She was strongly influenced by Siqueiros. Later she returned to the United States and did several murals for the Federal Arts Program including this one for a housing project in Brooklyn. It expressed some of the idealism and faith in the future present in the 1930s, but, in a fate met by many of the New Deal murals, a later generation found it ugly and destroyed it.

Marion Greenwood,
*Planned Community Life (Blueprint for Living)*, 1940.
Photograph Vassar College Art Gallery, Poughkeepsie, New York.
Gift of Patricia Ashley.

Frank Lloyd Wright room, 1914.
Metropolitan Museum of Art, New York. Bequest of Emily Crane Chadbourne.
Installation generosity of Saul P. Steinberg and Reliance Group Holdings, Inc.

Frank Lloyd Wright (1867–1959), a native of Wisconsin, was influenced by Louis Sullivan and by the Arts and Crafts Movement, but he was also an innovative genius who became one of the world's leading architects. He began to build his "prairie houses" in the midwest as early as 1894. Rebelling against the boxes with classical decoration that most Americans lived in, he created one-story structures using natural materials and adapting each house to its site. Wright also opened up the interiors of his houses, as shown in this 1914 example. He used a great many windows, allowed one room to flow into another, and built in most of the furniture. He fought against Victorian clutter and gaudy decoration, preferring natural colors and organic materials. His modern architecture had a wide impact even on the modest ranch houses that millions of Americans lived in after World War II.

Edward Hopper, *Early Sunday Morning*, 1930.
Whitney Museum of American Art, New York.

**Edward Hopper (1882–1967) grew up in Nyack, New York, on the Hudson River just north of New York City. He studied art in New York and was strongly influenced by some of the "ashcan school" painters. After traveling briefly in Europe, he settled down in the United States and spent his life recording the American scene. Although he painted many seascapes and rural scenes, he is most famous for his stark, almost abstract urban scenes. He was fascinated by light but also by the loneliness and isolation he found everywhere in American life.**

John Sloan, *Backyards,
Greenwich Village*, 1914.
Whitney Museum of American Art,
New York.

John Sloan (1871–1951), one of
the leading members of the
Eight, was born in rural Pennsylvania and studied at the
Academy of Fine Arts in Philadelphia. He moved to New York
in 1905 and, like so many other
artists, made his living drawing
illustrations for magazines. His
paintings, like the scene of
Greenwich Village, do not seem
shocking today, but they startled the viewing public in the
first decades of the twentieth
century. Sloan's rebellion, like
so many of the "ashcan" group,
was not so much in form as in
subject. The ordinary and the
mundane became the subjects
of paintings, and that was as
disturbing as the pop artists of
the 1950s painting soup cans
and comic strips.

Marsden Hartley (1877–
1943) shocked the public in
another way. He took a traditional subject and painted it in
an abstract style. Unlike most
of his contemporaries, he was
influenced by Germany rather
than France, and he was there
when the war broke out. This
painting is one of a series he did
in memory of a friend, a young
German officer who died in the
war.

Marsden Hartley,
*Painting, Number 5*, 1914–1915.
Whitney Museum of American Art,
New York. Anonymous gift.

Thomas Hart Benton, *Boom Town*, 1928. Memorial Art Gallery of the University of Rochester, New York. Marion Stratton Gould Fund.

While some artists discovered their subject in the American city, another group, sometimes called the American scene painters or regionalists, found their inspiration in the great American heartland. The most important of these artists were Thomas Hart Benton (1889–1975), Grant Wood (1891–1941), and John Steuart Curry (1897–1946). Benton, who grew up in Missouri, traveled throughout the country and often focused his paintings on the relationship of the workingman to his environment. *Boom Town* is his interpretation of Borger, Texas, "as it was in 1926 in the middle of its rise from a road crossing to an oil city." Despite the realistic subject, there is an abstract air to the picture. Some critics have compared Benton's work to that of El Greco.

Curry grew up in Kansas, and although he lived in New York for a considerable portion of his life, his subject was always the rural life of the Midwest. Even more than Benton, he seemed intent on recording a way of life that was rapidly disappearing in the 1920s and 1930s.

John Steuart Curry, *Baptism in Kansas*, 1928. Whitney Museum of American Art, New York.

# PART SIX
# AN
# ENDURING
# PEOPLE

# 1945–1985

The final section of *The American People* traces the development of our country in recent years. Emerging from World War II as the world's most powerful nation, the United States soon became engaged in a so-called Cold War with the Soviet Union, the world's second most powerful nation. Although this international development worried many Americans, most remained confident in the American way of life, which produced such abundant rewards in the postwar years. But in the 1960s, Cold War policies resulted in a hot war in Vietnam, and the American economy weakened. These changes eroded confidence, caused deep social divisions, and highlighted the limits to progress.

Chapters 27 and 28 are paired. In Chapter 27, "Chills and Fever During the Cold War," we see how the United States moved from an uneasy friendship with the Soviet Union to disillusionment and hostility. The Cold War shaped American foreign policy in all parts of the world and had a domestic impact as well, as Americans faced a second Red Scare in the late 1940s and early 1950s. Chapter 28, "The Dreams of Postwar America," explains how, despite the Cold War, many Americans found the postwar years deeply satisfying. Although not all Americans shared the abundance of the 1950s, the general standard of living rose to unprecedented heights. Some of the people for whom the promises of the American dream failed to materialize began to organize. The 1950s marks the beginnings of the modern civil rights movement.

Chapter 29, "From Self-confidence to Self-doubt," traces the course of a new wave of reformism. As Great Society programs tried to eliminate some of the country's social, economic, and racial problems, blacks, Hispanic-Americans, women, and others organized and struggled to improve their situation. Meanwhile, Cold War policies continued. As the nation became entangled in the Vietnam War, conflict and upheaval undermined the nation's self-confidence.

In Chapter 30, "Illusion and Disillusionment," we trace the Vietnam War to its conclusion and see the government's efforts to contain the social turmoil it helped produce. Political scandals contributed to a continuing mood of disillusionment, as did the declining economic position of the nation. The energy and optimism of reform did not disappear altogether, however, and women, blacks, and others made significant gains during these years. Chapter 31, "Austerity and the American Dream: The United States Since 1976," develops the themes established in Chapter 30 and attempts to set our recent past in perspective.

# PARALLEL EVENTS

| | 1945 | 1950 | 1955 | 1960 | 19 |

## CULTURAL and TECHNOLOGICAL

1946 Benjamin Spock, *Baby and Child Care*
1947 Jackie Robinson becomes first black to play major-league sports
1948 Kinsey publishes first report on human sexuality
     Bell Laboratories develop transistor
1951 J.D. Salinger publishes *The Catcher in the Rye*
1956 Elvis Presley hits No. 1 with "Heartbreak Hotel,"
     Allen Ginsberg, "Howl"
1957 First nuclear power plant opened in Shippingport, Pennsylvania
     Russians launch *Sputnik*
1960s Electronic calculators in office use
      Jet planes used for commercial purposes
1961 Rachel Carson, *Silent Spring*
1962 Bob Dylan gains recognition with "Blowin' in the Wind"
     First American orbits the earth
     Michael Harrington, *The Other America*
1963 Betty Friedan, *The Feminine Mystique*

## SOCIAL and ECONOMIC

1945–1946 Wave of strikes
1947 Report of committee on Civil Rights released
1948 Marshall Plan initiates substantial foreign aid
1952 United States tests first hydrogen bomb
1953 Introduction of "termination" policy to eliminate reservations for Native Americans
1953–1954 Operation Wetback
1955 AFL and CIO merge
     Montgomery bus boycott
1957 Baby boom peaks
     Little Rock school desegregation crisis
1960 Birth control pills made available
     Sit-ins begin
     S.D.S. founded
1960s Wave of mergers in American industry
1961 Freedom Rides to the South
1963 Birmingham demonstration
     March on Washington
1964 Free Speech movement at Berkeley

## POLITICAL

1945 First atomic bombs dropped on Japan; World War II ends
1946 Employment Act
1947 Truman Doctrine
     Taft-Hartley Act
     Truman establishes Federal Loyalty Program
     HUAC probes movie industry
1948 Marshall Plan passed
     Berlin Airlift
     Truman reelected
1949 NATO established
     Truman announces Fair Deal
1950 Alger Hiss convicted
     Korean War begins
     McCarran Internal Security Act
1951 *Denis v. United States*
1952 Dwight D. Eisenhower elected president
1953 Rosenbergs executed for espionage
1954 Army-McCarthy Hearings
     Senate censures Joseph R. McCarthy
     *Brown v. Board of Education* initiates school desegregation
1956 Eisenhower reelected
1957 Civil Rights Act
1960 John F. Kennedy elected
1961 Bay of Pigs invasion
1962 Cuban missile crisis
1963 JFK assassinated; Lyndon B. Johnson becomes president
1964 Civil Rights Act
     War on Poverty launched
     LBJ reelected

| 1945 | 1950 | 1955 | 1960 | 19 |

# 1945–1985

## CULTURAL and TECHNOLOGICAL

- 1965   Ralph Nader, *Unsafe at Any Speed*
- 1966   Masters and Johnson, *Human Sexual Response*
- 1969   Woodstock and Altamont
- 1970s   Electronics transform traditional industries
- 1972   99.8 percent of American households have television sets
- 1972–1973   Development of minicomputers creates new markets
  Introduction of calculators for home use
- 1973   More than one million photocopiers in use
- 1980s   Increasing sales of personal home computers
- 1982   Vietnam Veterans Memorial dedicated
- 1985   17 million VCR's in use; shift of film entertainment into the home
  First space shuttle launched with the sole purpose of gathering military data

## SOCIAL and ECONOMIC

- 1965   Teach-ins begin
  Assassination of Malcolm X
- 1966   "Black Power"
- 1967   Antiwar demonstrations
  Urban riots
- 1968   Martin Luther King assassinated
  AIM established
- 1970   Kent State and Jackson State incidents
- 1971–1975   Busing controversies
- 1971   *Pentagon Papers* published
- 1972   *Ms.* magazine founded
  Title 9 of the Educational Amendments provides funding for women's athletics
- 1973   Battle of Wounded Knee
- 1974   OPEC price increase
- 1977   Department of Energy created
  U.S. trade deficit $26.72 billion
- 1979   Three Mile Island accident
- 1984   Antiabortion campaign receives extensive media coverage; continued bombing of family planning clinics
  Strong U.S. dollar abroad contributes to growing trade deficit

## POLITICAL

- 1965   Voting Rights Act
  Escalation of U.S. involvement in Vietnam
- 1968   Robert F. Kennedy assassinated
  Richard M. Nixon elected president
- 1969   Nixon Doctrine
- 1970   Environmental Protection Agency created
- 1972   Nixon visits China
  Salt 1 agreement
  Watergate break-in
  Nixon reelected
- 1973   United States withdraws from Vietnam
  *Roe v. Wade* strikes down antiabortion laws
- 1974   Nixon resigns as a result of Watergate affair; Gerald Ford becomes president
  Runaway and Homeless Youth Act
- 1976   Jimmy Carter elected president
- 1977   Panama Canal Treaties
- 1978   California passes Proposition 13, cutting property taxes
  *Bakke* decision upholds affirmative action but prohibits fixed quotas
- 1979   SALT II agreement
- 1979–1981   Iranian hostage crisis
- 1980   Ronald Reagan elected president
- 1981   Sandra Day O'Connor becomes first woman Supreme Court justice
- 1984   Geraldine Ferraro nominated as Democratic vice-presidential candidate
  Reagan reelected
- 1985   Reagan's budget proposes deep cuts in domestic spending
  Tax reform debate

# CHAPTER 27
## CHILLS AND FEVER
## DURING THE COLD WAR

Val Lorwin was in Paris in November 1950 when word of the charges against him arrived. A State Department employee, on leave of absence after 15 years of government service, he was in France working on a book. Now he had to return to the United States to defend himself against the accusation that he was a member of the Communist party and thus a loyalty and security risk.

The accusation surprised Lorwin. It almost seemed like a tasteless joke. Yet it was no joke but a grim consequence of the Cold War. Suspicions of the Soviet Union escalated after 1945, and a wave of paranoia swept through the United States. The threat of communism was no laughing matter at home.

Lorwin was an unlikely candidate to be caught up in the fallout of the Cold War. He began to work for the government in 1935, serving in a number of New Deal agencies, then in the Labor Department and on the War Production Board before he was drafted during World War II. While in the army he was assigned to the Office of Strategic Services, an early intelligence agency, and he was frequently granted security clearances in the United States and abroad.

Lorwin, however, did have a left-wing past as an active Socialist in the 1930s. His social life then had revolved around Socialist party causes, particularly the unionization of southern tenant farmers and the provision of aid to the unemployed. He and his wife Madge drafted statements or stuffed envelopes to support their goals. But that activity was wholly open and legal, and Lorwin had from the start been aggressively anti-Communist in political affairs.

Suddenly, Lorwin, like others in the period, faced the nightmare of secret charges against which the burden of proof was entirely on him and the chance of clearing his name slim. Despite his spotless record, Lorwin was told that an unnamed accuser had identified him as a Communist. He was entitled to a hearing if he chose, or he could resign.

Lorwin requested a hearing, held late in 1950. Still struck by the absurdity of the situation, he refuted all accusations but made little effort to cite his own positive achievements. At the conclusion, he was informed that the government no longer doubted his loyalty but considered him a security risk, still grounds nonetheless for dismissal from his job.

When he appealed the judgment, Lorwin was again denied access to the identity of his accuser. This time, however, he thoroughly prepared his defense. At the hearing, a total of 97 witnesses either spoke under oath on Lorwin's behalf or left sworn written depositions testifying to his good character and meritorious service.

The issues in the hearings might have been considered comic in view of Lorwin's record, had not a man's reputation been at stake. The accuser had once lived with the Lorwins in Washington, D.C. Fifteen years later he claimed that in 1935, Lorwin had revealed that he was holding a Communist party meeting in his home and had even shown him a Party card.

Lorwin proved all the charges were groundless. He also showed that in 1935 the Socialist party card was red, the color the accuser reported seeing, while the Communist party card was black. In March 1952, Lorwin was finally cleared for both loyalty and security.

Though he thought he had weathered the storm, Lorwin's troubles were not yet over. His name appeared on one of the lists waved by Senator Joseph McCarthy of Wisconsin, the most aggressive anti-Communist of the era, and Lorwin was again victimized. The next year, he was indicted for making false statements to the State Department Loyalty-Security Board. The charges this time proved as specious as before. Finally, in May 1954, admitting that its special prosecutor had deliberately lied to the grand jury and had no legitimate case, the Justice Department asked for dismissal of the indictment. Lorwin was cleared at last and went on to a distinguished career as a labor historian.

orwin was more fortunate than some victims of the anti-Communist crusade. People rallied around him and gave him valuable support. Despite considerable emotional cost, he survived the witch-hunt of the early 1950s, but his case still reflected vividly the ugly domestic consequences of the breakdown in relations between the Soviet Union and the United States.

The Cold War, which unfolded soon after the end of World War II, powerfully affected all aspects of American life. This chapter describes the worsening relations between the United States and the Soviet Union, the world's two strongest nations, that culminated in a bitter conflict after 1945. It shows how the Cold War, conducted not with bullets but with words and diplomatic maneuvers, colored all foreign policy decisions in the United States. It also reveals its domestic implications, best reflected in the attempt to wipe out all traces of communism at home.

## ORIGINS OF THE SOVIET-AMERICAN CONFRONTATION

The Cold War was rooted in longstanding disagreements between the major powers that had been papered over during the Second World War. Though they had different dreams for the shape of the postwar world, the United States and the Soviet Union avoided conflict with each other in the bitter struggle against a common foe. At the war's end, however, their differences became painfully obvious. The Cold War was the unfortunate result.

### The American View of the USSR

American policymakers in the Cold War period drew on the hopes that had guided the nation during World War II. They envisioned a world that would be stable and secure after victory. In ideological terms, they hoped to spread the values that provided the underpinning of the American dream—liberty, equality, and democracy—around the globe. At the same time, however, they envisioned a world open to American enterprise. They sought a world characterized by peace and prosperity, free trade, and business expansion.

Government leaders wanted to eliminate trade barriers and economic restraints in order to provide worldwide markets for American farm commodities and industrial products. Recollections of the Depression decade haunted them. "We've got to export three times as much as we exported just before the war if we want to keep our industry running at somewhere near capacity," Under Secretary of State William L. Clayton told a congressional committee in March 1945.

Policymaking officials also anticipated a world in which the United States played a central role. Their sense of purpose dated back to the first days of settlement, when Americans had been guided by a sense of mission. Postwar planners shared the patriotic fervor that promoted expansion, imperialism, and finally involvement in the First and Second World Wars. Proud of the American system, they hoped to share their principles and ideals and to prevent future wars.

### American Leadership in the Cold War

Harry Truman led the nation in the first years of the Cold War. The new president was an unpretentious man who took a straightforward approach to public affairs. He was, however, ill prepared for the office he assumed in the final months of World War II. His three months as vice-president had done little to school him in the complexity of postwar issues. Nor had Franklin Roosevelt confided in Truman. No wonder that the new president felt insecure from the start. The day after he became president, he told reporters, "I don't know whether you fellows ever had a load of hay fall on you, but when they told me yesterday what had happened, I felt like the moon, the stars and all the planets had fallen on me." To a former colleague in the Senate, he groaned, "I'm not big enough. I'm not big enough for this job." Others agreed. Tennessee Valley Authority director David Lilienthal spoke for many who found it hard to accept the fact that Roosevelt was gone. "The country," he complained, "doesn't deserve to be left this way."

Yet Truman matured rapidly. A feisty politician, he responded ably to new challenges. Impulsive and aggressive, he made a virtue out of rapid response. At his first press conference, he answered questions so quickly that reporters could not record his responses. A sign on the president's White House desk read "The Buck Stops Here," and he was willing to make quick decisions on issues, even though associates sometimes wondered if he understood all the implications. Roosevelt had shown a masterful sense of timing during the New Deal and, on complex issues during the war, had been even more willing to delay. Truman was less inclined to wait before acting. His rapid-fire decisions had important consequences for the Cold War.

Truman served virtually all of the term to which Roosevelt had been elected, then won another for himself in 1948. In 1952, war hero Dwight D. Eisenhower, who won the presidency for the Republican party for the first time in 20 years, succeeded him.

*Truman's down-to-earth directness was a drawback on formal state occasions, but an asset with the public.*

Eisenhower stood in stark contrast to his predecessor. He had a homey, natural manner that made him widely popular. He conveyed a sense of honesty and strength that translated into a captivating appeal. On occasion, in press conferences or other public gatherings, his comments came out convoluted and imprecise. Yet appearances were deceiving, for beneath his casual approach was real shrewdness. At one point, as he prepared for a session with newsmen and his aides briefed him on a delicate matter, he said, "Don't worry. . . . If that question comes up, I'll just confuse them."

Eisenhower had not taken the typical route to the presidency. In fact, he had very little formal political experience. After his World War II success, he served as army chief of staff, president of Columbia University, and then head of the North Atlantic Treaty Organization. Lack of political background notwithstanding, he did have a genuine ability to get people to compromise and to work together. Though he remained aloof from party politics, he may have entertained hopes of holding office after the war. General George Patton commented in 1943 that "Ike wants to be President so badly you can taste it," and his career choices after the war clearly kept him visible and involved in public affairs. Yet he made no move in that direction until he sought the Republican nomination in 1952.

Ike's limited experience with everyday politics conditioned his sense of the presidential role. Whereas Truman was accustomed to political infighting and wanted to take charge, Eisenhower saw things differently. The presidency for him was no "bully pulpit," as it had been for Theodore Roosevelt or even for FDR. "I am not one of those desk-pounding types that likes to stick out his jaw and look like he is bossing the show," he said. "You do not *lead* by hitting people over the head. Any damn fool can do that, but it's usually called 'assault'—not 'leadership.'" Ike's method, Richard Nixon once observed, "was never to take direct action requiring his personal participation where indirect methods would accomplish the same result."

Though the personal styles of Truman and Eisenhower differed, as did their domestic programs (see Chapter 28), they shared a basic view that governed American foreign policy after

World War II. Both subscribed to traditional American attitudes about self-determination and distrusted Soviet ventures during and after the war. Truman's suspicions were obvious even before the United States entered the struggle. He commented in July 1941, "If we see that Germany is winning we ought to help Russia, and if Russia is winning we ought to help Germany." He accepted collaboration as a marriage of necessity, but he became increasingly hostile to Soviet moves as the war drew to an end. It was now time, he said, "to stand up to the Russians."

Like Truman, Eisenhower believed in the notion of a monolithic Communist force struggling for world supremacy, and he thought the Kremlin in Moscow was orchestrating subversive activity around the globe. Like Truman, he viewed the Soviet system as "a tyranny that has brought thousands, millions of people into slave

*Indirect action and a low-key public image characterized Eisenhower's handling of the presidency.*

camps and is attempting to make all humankind its chattel." For both presidents, the issues could be perceived in such black and white terms. As Eisenhower declared in his 1953 inaugural address, "Forces of good and evil are massed and armed and opposed as rarely before in history. Freedom is pitted against slavery, lightness against dark."

## The Soviet View of America

The Soviet Union formulated its own goals after World War II. Devastated by war, the Russians were determined to rebuild and to protect themselves from another such terrible conflict. Unlike the United States, the Soviet Union had seen the destructive struggle unfold on its own soil and had suffered an enormous loss of life.

The Soviets feared they were vulnerable along their western flank. Such anxieties went back at least to the early nineteenth century, when Napoleon had reached the gates of Moscow. Twice in the twentieth century, invasions had come from the west, most recently when Hitler had attacked in 1941. That offensive had finally been repelled, but at a huge cost. Soviet agriculture and industry were in a shambles. Fearful that the Germans would recover quickly after the war to pose a new threat, the Soviets demanded defensible borders and friendly regimes nearby. They insisted on stable, secure governments in eastern Europe receptive to Soviet military and political dictation.

In World War II, the Russians had played down the notion of world revolution and mobilized support for more nationalistic goals. They still feared capitalist encirclement and the penetration of Western ways (as they had since the nineteenth century) but now remained confident that their new system of communism would eventually triumph, just as Marxist-Leninist doctrine had predicted. Yet the message was trumpeted less aggressively than before. As the struggle drew to a close, the Russians talked little of world conquest, emphasizing socialism within the nation itself and in bordering countries. But in those adjoining areas, they intended to prevent any interference in what they viewed as their necessary zone of influence.

*Joseph Stalin's highly autocratic approach in both domestic and foreign affairs was an affront to American sensibilities.*

## Soviet Leadership in the Cold War

The leader of the Soviet Union at the war's end was Joseph Stalin, who had guided his party and state for 20 years. Ruthless and grim in pursuit of both national and personal ends, he had presided over monstrous purges against his opponents in the 1930s. Vain and vindictive, Stalin exercised a power unknown in Western nations. He now spoke in terms that gave the Soviets alone credit for the victory over Hitler and affirmed the superiority of Russian society as he aggressively formulated a set of Soviet demands.

When Stalin died in March 1953, he left a vacuum in Soviet political affairs. His successor, Nikita S. Khrushchev, used his position as party secretary to consolidate his power. Purges of the party bureaucracy took place, and five years after Stalin's death, Khrushchev held the offices of both prime minister and party secretary. A peasant who had risen to the top, Khrushchev was fond of crude jokes and known for rude behavior. On one occasion he pounded a table at the United Nations with his shoe while the British prime minister was speaking. As Khrushchev continued some of Stalin's hard-line policies, he confronted the equally firm stance of the United States. The Cold War was the result.

# THE BEGINNING OF THE COLD WAR

The Cold War developed by degrees. Frictions, existing since 1917, had been temporarily eased during the war but now began to resurface as the struggle wound down. With the Fascist threat defeated, disagreements about the shape of the postwar world brought the Soviet Union and the United States into conflict.

## Disillusionment with the USSR

During the war, Joseph Goulden, a youngster of about 10, saw the Russians as "brave and skilled partisans." To him, "their heroic stand at Stalingrad was equal to the defense of the Alamo." Soon that comforting image began to fade. In September 1945, fully 54 percent of a national sample trusted the Russians to cooperate with the Americans in the postwar years. Two months later, the figure dropped to 44 percent, and by February 1946, to 35 percent.

*Not unlike some of America's most admired presidents, Nikita Khrushchev worked his way from humble beginnings to head the government of a major world power.*

In recent years, historians have used a new source of evidence, the public opinion poll. People have always been concerned with what others think, and leaders have often sought to frame their behavior according to the preferences of the populace. As techniques of assessing the mind of the public have become more sophisticated, the poll has emerged as an integral part of the analysis of social and political life. Polls now measure opinion on many questions—social, cultural, intellectual, political, and diplomatic. Because of their increasing importance, it is useful to know how to use the polls in an effort to understand and recover the past.

The principle of polling is not new. Throughout American history efforts have been made to predict electoral results. In 1824, for example, the Harrisburg *Pennsylvanian* sought to predict the winner of that year's presidential race, and in the 1880s the Boston *Globe* sent reporters to selected precincts on election night to forecast final returns. In 1916, *Literary Digest* began conducting postcard polls to predict politi-

cal results. By the 1930s, Elmo Roper and George Gallup had developed further the field of market research and public opinion polling. Despite an embarrassing mistake by *Literary Digest* in predicting a Landon victory over FDR in 1936, polling had by World War II become a scientific enterprise.

According to Gallup, a poll is not magic but "merely an instrument for gauging public opinion," especially the views of those often unheard. As Elmo Roper said, the poll is "one of the few ways through which the so-called common man can be articulate." Polling, therefore, is a valuable way to recover the attitudes, beliefs, and voices of ordinary people.

Yet certain cautions should be observed. Like all instruments of human activity, polls are imperfect and may even be dangerous. Historians using information from polls need to be aware of how large the samples were, when the interviewing was done, and how opinions might have been molded by the form of the poll itself. Questions can be poorly phrased. Some questions hint at the desirable answer or otherwise

## FOREIGN POLICY POLLS

**DECEMBER 2, 1949—Atom Bomb**
*Now that Russia has the atom bomb, do you think another war is more likely or less likely?*

| | |
|---|---|
| More likely | 45% |
| Less likely | 28 |
| Will make no difference | 17 |
| No opinion | 10 |

**By Education**
*College*

| | |
|---|---|
| More likely | 36% |
| Less likely | 35 |
| Will make no difference | 23 |
| No opinion | 6 |

*High School*

| | |
|---|---|
| More likely | 44% |
| Less likely | 28 |
| Will make no difference | 19 |
| No opinion | 9 |

*Grade School*

| | |
|---|---|
| More likely | 50% |
| Less likely | 26 |
| Will make no difference | 12 |
| No opinion | 12 |

**May 1, 1950—National Defense**
*Do you think United States Government spending on national defense should be increased, decreased, or remain about the same?*

| | |
|---|---|
| Increased | 63% |
| Decreased | 7 |
| Same | 24 |
| No opinion | 6 |

**SEPTEMBER 18, 1953—Indochina**
*The United States is now sending war materials to help the French fight the Communists in Indochina. Would you approve or disapprove of sending United States soldiers to take part in the fighting there?*

| | |
|---|---|
| Approve | 8% |
| Disapprove | 85 |
| No opinion | 7 |

**JANUARY 11, 1950—RUSSIA**
*As you hear and read about Russia these days, do you believe Russia is trying to build herself up to be the ruling power of the world—or is Russia just building up protection against being attacked in another war?*

| | |
|---|---|
| Rule the world | 70% |
| Protect herself | 18 |
| No opinion | 12 |

**By Education**
*College*

| | |
|---|---|
| Rule the world | 73% |
| Protect herself | 21 |
| No opinion | 6 |

*High School*

| | |
|---|---|
| Rule the world | 72% |
| Protect herself | 18 |
| No opinion | 10 |

*Grade School*

| | |
|---|---|
| Rule the world | 67% |
| Protect herself | 17 |
| No opinion | 16 |

**FEBRUARY 12, 1951—ATOMIC WARFARE**
*If the United States gets into an all-out war with Russia, do you think we should drop atom bombs on Russia first—or do you think we should use the atom bomb only if it is used on us?*

| | |
|---|---|
| Drop A-bomb first | 66% |
| Only if used on us | 19 |
| No opinion | 15 |

The greatest difference was between men and women—72% of the men questioned favored our dropping the bomb first, compared to 61% of the women.

George H. Gallup, *The Gallup Poll: Public Opinion, 1935–1971*, vol. 2 (New York: Random House, 1972) © American Institute of Public Opinion.

influence opinions by planting ideas in the persons interviewed. Polls sometimes provide ambiguous responses that can be interpreted many ways. More serious, some critics worry that human freedom itself is threatened by the pollsters' manipulative and increasingly accurate predictive techniques.

Despite these limitations, polls have become an ever-present part of American life. In the late 1940s and early 1950s, Americans were polled frequently about a variety of topics ranging from foreign aid, the United Nations, and the occupation of Germany and Japan to labor legislation, child punishment, and whether women should wear slacks in public (39 percent of men said no, as did 49 percent of women). Such topics as the first use of nuclear arms, presidential popularity, national defense, and U.S. troop intervention in a troubled area of the world (Indochina) remain as pertinent today as they were then.

The polls included here deal with foreign policy during the Cold War in the early 1950s. How did people respond to the Russian nuclear capability?

Other polls questioned public perceptions of Russian intentions and appropriate American responses. How do you analyze the results of these polls? What do you think is the significance of rating responses by levels of education? In what ways are the questions "loaded"? How might these results influence American foreign policy? What do you think is significant about the Indochina poll? These polls show the challenge and response nature of the Cold War that continues to this day. How do you think Americans would respond today to these questions?

Polls also shed light on domestic issues. Consider the poll on professions for young men and women taken in 1950. What does it tell us about the attitudes of the pollster on appropriate careers for men and women? Why do you think both men and women had nearly identical views on this subject? How do you think people today would answer these questions? Would they be presented in the same way? Also observe the poll on women in politics. To what extent have attitudes on this issue changed in the 1980s?

## DOMESTIC POLICY POLLS

**OCTOBER 29, 1949—Women in Politics**
*If the party whose candidate you most often support nominated a woman for President of the United States, would you vote for her if she seemed qualified for the job?*

Yes . . . . . . . . . . . . . . . . . . . . . 48%
No. . . . . . . . . . . . . . . . . . . . . . 48
No opinion . . . . . . . . . . . . . . . 4

### By Sex
#### Men
Yes . . . . . . . . . . . . . . . . . . . . . 45%
No. . . . . . . . . . . . . . . . . . . . . . 50
No opinion . . . . . . . . . . . . . . . 5

#### Women
Yes . . . . . . . . . . . . . . . . . . . . . 51%
No. . . . . . . . . . . . . . . . . . . . . . 46
No opinion . . . . . . . . . . . . . . . 3

### By Political Affiliation
#### Democrats
Yes . . . . . . . . . . . . . . . . . . . . . 50%
No. . . . . . . . . . . . . . . . . . . . . . 48
No opinion . . . . . . . . . . . . . . . 2

#### Republicans
Yes . . . . . . . . . . . . . . . . . . . . . 46%
No. . . . . . . . . . . . . . . . . . . . . . 50
No opinion . . . . . . . . . . . . . . . 4

*Would you vote for a woman for Vice President of the United States if she seemed qualified for the job?*

Yes . . . . . . . . . . . . . . . . . . . . . 53%
No. . . . . . . . . . . . . . . . . . . . . . 43
No opinion . . . . . . . . . . . . . . . 4

**MAY 5, 1950—Most Important Problem**
*What do you think is the most important problem facing the entire country today?*

War, threat of war . . . . . . . . . . 40%
Economic problems, living costs, inflation, taxes. . . . . . . . . . . . . . . . 15
Unemployment . . . . . . . . . . . . . 10
Communism . . . . . . . . . . . . . . 8
Atomic bomb control . . . . . . . . 6
Strikes and labor troubles . . . . . . 4
Corruption in Government. . . . . . 3
Housing . . . . . . . . . . . . . . . . . 3
Others . . . . . . . . . . . . . . . . . . 11

**JULY 12, 1950—Professions**
*Suppose a young man came to you and asked your advice about taking up a profession. Assuming that he was qualified to enter any of these professions, which one of them would you first recommend to him? (on card)*

Doctor of medicine. . . . . . . . . . 29%
Engineer, builder . . . . . . . . . . . 16
Business executive . . . . . . . . . . 8
Clergyman . . . . . . . . . . . . . . . 8
Lawyer. . . . . . . . . . . . . . . . . . 8
Government worker . . . . . . . . . 6

Professor, teacher. . . . . . . . . . . 5
Banker . . . . . . . . . . . . . . . . . . 4
Dentist. . . . . . . . . . . . . . . . . . 4
Veterinarian . . . . . . . . . . . . . . 3
None, don't know . . . . . . . . . . 9

**JULY 15, 1950—Professions**
*Suppose a young girl came to you and asked your advice about taking up a profession. Assuming that she was qualified to enter any of these professions, which one of them would you first recommend?*

#### Choice of Women
Nurse. . . . . . . . . . . . . . . . . . . 33%
Teacher . . . . . . . . . . . . . . . . . 15
Secretary . . . . . . . . . . . . . . . . 8
Social service worker . . . . . . . . 8
Dietician. . . . . . . . . . . . . . . . . 7
Dressmaker. . . . . . . . . . . . . . . 4
Beautician. . . . . . . . . . . . . . . . 4
Airline stewardess . . . . . . . . . . 3
Actress. . . . . . . . . . . . . . . . . . 3
Journalist . . . . . . . . . . . . . . . . 2
Musician. . . . . . . . . . . . . . . . . 2
Model . . . . . . . . . . . . . . . . . . 2
Librarian . . . . . . . . . . . . . . . . 2
Medical, dental technician . . . . . 1
Others . . . . . . . . . . . . . . . . . . 2
Don't know. . . . . . . . . . . . . . . 4

The views of men on this subject were nearly identical with those of women.

George H. Gallup, *The Gallup Poll: Public Opinion, 1935–1971*, vol. 2 (New York: Random House, 1972). © American Institute of Public Opinion.

Americans became increasingly disillusioned with the Soviet political system. In a series of articles in *Harper's, Life,* and *The New Yorker* in 1946, author-editor John Fischer pointed to the single-minded intensity that characterized the Soviet state. In one story he recalled a conversation with a Soviet official who argued that the United States should cease shortwave broadcasts to the Soviet Union but thought Russia should continue to transmit its messages to the American people. When the perplexed Fischer asked about the apparent contradiction, the Soviet bureaucrat responded that it was "a perfect example of reciprocity." "Your laws," he explained, "provide for free speech, and we observe them. Our laws do *not,* and it would be improper for you to disregard them."

Bill Mauldin, a cartoonist whose work affected millions during the war, published a sketch that captured the repressive nature of the Soviet government. Mauldin depicted two Russian bullies approaching a bedraggled man in a dungeon. One, holding a noose, says, "There's nothing to it, excellency. Comrade Popoff and I have committed hundreds of successful suicides."

As Americans soured on Russia, they began to equate the Nazi and Soviet systems. The hatred of Hitler's Germany was now transferred to Communist Russia. Just as they had in the 1930s, authors, journalists, and public officials began to point to similarities between the regimes, some of them quite legitimate. Both states, they contended, maintained total control over communications and could eliminate political opposition whenever they chose. Both states used terror to silence dissidents. Russian labor camps in Siberia were now compared to the horrible German concentration camps. After the American publication in 1949 of George Orwell's frightening novel *Nineteen Eighty-four,* *Life* magazine noted in an editorial that the ominous figure Big Brother was but a "mating" of Hitler and Stalin. Truman spoke for many Americans when he said in 1950 that "there isn't any difference between the totalitarian Russian government and the Hitler government. . . . They are all alike. They are police governments—police state governments."

American fears were heightened by the lingering sense that the nation had not been quick enough to resist totalitarian aggression in the 1930s. Had the United States stopped the Germans, Italians, or Japanese, it might have prevented the long, devastating war. The free world had not responded quickly enough before and was determined never to repeat the same mistake.

## The Polish Question

The first clash between East and West came, even before the war ended, over Poland. Soviet demands for a sympathetic government there clashed with American hopes for a more representative structure. The Yalta Conference of February 1945 attempted to ensure a representative government for the postwar state (see Chapter 26), but the agreement was loosely worded.

When Truman assumed office, the situation was still unresolved. When his advisers urged a harder line than Roosevelt had been willing to take, Truman determined to stand firm. Averell Harriman, the American ambassador to the Soviet Union, warned that the United States faced a "barbarian invasion of Europe" unless the Soviets could be checked. Truman agreed. "We must stand up to the Russians," he said, "and not be easy with them."

Truman's unbending stance appeared in an April 1945 meeting with Soviet foreign minister Vyacheslav Molotov on the question of Poland. Concerned that the Russians were breaking the Yalta agreements, the president wanted a new, not simply a reorganized, government there. Though Molotov appeared conciliatory, Truman insisted that the Russians keep their word. Truman later recalled that when Molotov protested, "I have never been talked to like that in my life," he himself retorted bluntly, "Carry out your agreements and you won't get talked to like that." Such bluntness contributed to the deterioration of Soviet-American relations.

Truman and Stalin met face to face for the first time at the Potsdam Conference in July 1945, the last of the meetings held by the Big Three during the war. There, as they considered the Russian-Polish boundary, the future fate of Germany, and the American desire to obtain an unconditional surrender from Japan, the two leaders sized each other up. It was Truman's first exposure to international diplomacy at the highest level, and it left him confident of his own abilities. When he was informed, during the meeting, of the first successful atomic bomb test in New Mexico, he became even more determined to stand firm.

## Economic Pressure on the USSR

One major source of controversy in the last stage of the Second World War was the question of American aid to its allies. Responding to congressional pressure at home to limit foreign assistance as hostilities ended, Truman acted impulsively. Six days after V-E Day signaled the end of the European war in May 1945, he issued an executive order cutting off lend-lease supplies to the Allies. The struggle against Japan in the Pacific dragged on, and Russia had agreed to assist there, but even so, ship loading in the United States was halted and ships bound for the Soviet Union and elsewhere were ordered to reverse course. Whether the action was a deliberate effort to use economic weapons for diplomatic effect or was simply a bureaucratic blunder, Secretary of State Edward Stettinius felt the action was "particularly untimely" in view of the delicate state of the Grand Alliance. Truman had been warned of the consequences of his actions and later realized that a phased end to shipments would have been preferable. By then it was too late.

The United States hoped to use economic pressure in other ways as well. Russia desperately needed financial assistance to rebuild after the war and, in January 1945, had requested a $6 billion loan. Roosevelt hedged, hoping to win concessions in return. In August, the Russians renewed their application, this time for only $1 billion. The new president dragged his heels. The United States first claimed to have lost the Soviet request, then in March 1946 indicated a willingness to consider the matter—but only if Russia pledged "nondiscrimination in world commerce." In short, the United States tried to use the loan as a lever to gain access to new markets. Stalin refused the offer and launched his own five-year plan instead.

## Declaring the Cold War

As Soviet-American disagreements increased, both sides stepped up their rhetorical attacks. Stalin spoke out first, in 1946, asserting his confidence in the triumph of the Russian system. Capitalism and communism were on a collision course, he argued, and a series of cataclysmic disturbances would tear the capitalist world apart. The Soviet Union was prepared to strengthen its military forces, even if that meant forgoing consumer goods, to ensure its own survival in a world no longer pursuing peace. Stalin's speech was a stark and ominous statement that worried the West. Supreme Court Justice William O. Douglas called it "the declaration of World War III."

The response to Stalin's speech came not from an American but from England's former prime minister, Winston Churchill, long suspicious of the Soviet state. Speaking in Fulton, Missouri, in 1946, with Truman on the platform during the address, Churchill declared that "from Stettin in the Baltic to Trieste in the Adriatic, an iron curtain has descended across the Continent." To counter the threat, he urged that a vigilant association of English-speaking peoples work to contain Soviet designs.

# CONTAINING THE SOVIET THREAT

Containment became the basis of American policy in the postwar years. Troubled by the rise of a Communist superpower that threatened American interests, both political parties became determined to check Soviet expansion. In an increasingly contentious world, the American government formulated policies to maintain the upper hand.

## Containment Defined

George F. Kennan was the man primarily responsible for defining the new policy. Chargé d'affaires at the American embassy in the Soviet Union, he fired off an 8,000-word telegram to the State Department after Stalin's speech in February 1946. Kennan argued that Soviet-American hostility stemmed from "the Kremlin's neurotic view of world affairs," which in turn was rooted in "the traditional and instinctive Russian sense of insecurity." The rigid Soviet stance was not so much a response to American actions as a reflection of the Russian leaders' own efforts to maintain their autocratic rule. Russian fanaticism would not soften, regardless of how accommodating American policy became. Therefore, it had to be opposed at every turn.

When it arrived in Washington, Kennan's analysis struck a resonant chord. It made his diplomatic reputation, led to his assignment to an influential position in the State Department, and encouraged him to publish an important article under the pseudonym "Mr. X" in *Foreign Affairs*. In that essay he extended his former analysis and expressed his reservations about coexistence. The Russians intended to pursue their own ends for as long as they could. "The whole Soviet governmental machine, including the mechanism of diplomacy," he wrote, "moves inexorably along the prescribed path, like a persistent toy automobile wound up and headed in a given direction, stopping only when it meets with some unanswerable force." Many Americans agreed with Kennan that Soviet pressure had to "be contained by the adroit and vigilant application of counter-force at a series of constantly shifting geographical and political points."

The concept of containment provided the philosophical justification for the hard-line stance that Americans, both in and out of government, adopted. During Truman's presidency, containment was viewed as the cornerstone of all diplomatic initiatives in both Europe and Asia. All three secretaries of state—James F. Byrnes, George C. Marshall, and Dean Acheson—firmly supported the concept. Containment created the framework for military and economic assistance around the globe.

## Containment in the Mediterranean

The first major application of containment policy came in 1947 with the development of the Truman Doctrine to meet a challenge in the eastern Mediterranean. The Soviet Union was pressuring Turkey for joint control of the Darda-

nelles, between the Black Sea and the Mediterranean. Meanwhile, though Russia was not directly involved, a civil war in Greece pitted Communist elements against the ruling English-aided right-wing monarchy. Revolutionary pressures threatened to topple the government.

In February 1947, the British ambassador to the United States informed the State Department that his country could no longer give Greece and Turkey economic and military aid. Exhausted after massive efforts in two world wars, Britain could not help other countries. Would the United States now move into the void?

The State Department quickly developed a proposal for American aid when Britain pulled out. But the administration needed to persuade reluctant legislators that the national interest was involved. A conservative Congress was concerned with smaller budgets and taxes rather than massive and expensive aid programs. Meeting with congressional leaders, Dean Acheson, at the time under secretary of state, warned that "like apples in a barrel infected by one rotten one, the corruption of Greece would infect Iran and all to the east." Eager to persuade legislators of the importance of the moment, he warned that a Communist victory would "open three continents to Soviet penetration." The major powers were now "met at Armageddon" as the Soviet Union pressed for whatever advantage it could get. Only the United States had the will and power to resist.

Administration leaders knew that bipartisan support was necessary to accomplish such a major policy shift. Senator Arthur Vandenberg of Michigan was one of the key Republicans whose approval was necessary to gain support of other party members. Vandenberg also warned that the administration had to develop public support for an interventionist policy. Quite literally, Vandenberg said, administration officials had to begin "scaring hell out of the country" if they were serious about a bold new course of containment.

Truman followed Vandenberg's advice. On March 12, 1947, he told Congress, in a statement that came to be known as the Truman Doctrine, "I believe that it must be the policy of the United States to support free peoples who are resisting subjugation by armed minorities or by outside pressures." Unless the United States acted, the free world might not survive. "If we falter in our leadership," Truman said, "we may endanger the peace of the world—and we shall surely endanger the welfare of our own Nation." To avert that calamity, he urged Congress to appropriate $400 million for military and economic aid to Turkey and Greece.

Not everyone approved of Truman's request or of the extreme way in which he described the situation. Autocratic regimes controlled Greece and Turkey, some observed. Others warned that the United States could not by itself stop encroachment in all parts of the world. Nonetheless, Congress passed Truman's foreign aid bill.

The Truman Doctrine was a major step in the advent of the Cold War. Truman's address, observed financier Bernard Baruch, "was tantamount to a declaration of . . . an ideological or religious war." Truman had succeeded in persuading many Americans that there would be no accommodation with communism. A crucial test had been passed.

## The Marshall Plan, NATO, and NSC-68

The next step involved extensive economic aid for postwar recovery in western Europe. At the war's end, most of Europe was economically and politically unstable, thereby offering opportunities to the Communist movement. In France and Italy, large Communist parties grew stronger and refused to cooperate with established governments. In such circumstances, administration officials believed, Russia might easily intervene. Decisive action was needed, for as the new secretary of state, George Marshall, declared, "The patient is sinking while the doctors deliberate."

Marshall revealed the administration's willingness to assist European recovery in June 1947. He asked all troubled European nations to draw up an aid program that the United States could support, a program "directed not against any country or doctrine but against hunger, poverty, desperation, and chaos." Soviet-bloc countries were welcome to participate, Marshall claimed, although their involvement was un-

likely since they would have to disclose economic records to participate.

The proposed program would assist the ravaged nations while benefiting the United States by providing markets for the booming American economy. And it would advance the nation's ideological aims. American aid, Marshall pointed out, would permit the "emergence of political and social conditions in which free institutions can exist." The Marshall Plan and the Truman Doctrine, Truman noted, were "two halves of the same walnut."

Responding quickly to Marshall's invitation, the western European nations worked out the details of massive requests in the summer of 1947. The Soviets attended the first planning meeting but then withdrew, as American policymakers hoped and expected they would. When the multination request was finally hammered out, American officials pared it down but agreed to provide $17 billion over a period of four years to 16 cooperating nations. This support for European recovery was a unique and unprecedentedly generous act in the nation's history.

Not all Americans supported the Marshall Plan. Henry A. Wallace, former vice-president and secretary of agriculture, who had broken with the administration, called the scheme the "Martial Plan" and argued that it was another step toward war. Some members of Congress feared spreading American resources too thin. But in early 1948, Congress committed the nation to funding European economic recovery, and the containment policy moved forward another step.

Closely related to the Marshall Plan was a concerted Western effort to rebuild Germany and to reintegrate it into a reviving Europe. Germany had been the archenemy during World War II. At Yalta, as the European war drew to an end, Allied leaders had agreed on zonal occupation of Germany and on reparations Germany would pay the victors. Four zones, occupied by the Russians, Americans, British, and French, had been established for postwar administration. A year after the end of the war, however, the balance of power in Europe had shifted. With the Soviet Union threatening to dominate eastern Europe, the West moved to fill the vacuum in central Europe. In late 1946, the Americans and

British merged their zones for economic purposes and began to assign administrative duties to Germans themselves. By the middle of 1947, the process of rebuilding West German industry was under way.

Despite French fears, the United States sought to make Germany strong enough to anchor Europe. Secretary Marshall cautiously laid out the connections for Congress: "The restoration of Europe involves the restoration of Germany. Without a revival of German production there can be no revival of Europe's economy. But we must be very careful to see that a revived Germany cannot again threaten the European community."

In mid-1948, the Soviet refusal to allow land access to West Berlin, located in the Russian zone, put the German issue in bold relief. The blockade was countered by a U.S. and Royal Air Force airlift that flew supplies to the beleaguered Berliners. The fliers named it Operation Vittles, and it worked. It delivered more than 2 million tons of supplies to the city. Operation Little Vittles, so named by Lieutenant Carl S. Halverson, provided bags of candy for the children at the same time. "The difficult we do immediately," a Seabee–Air Force boast proclaimed; "the impossible takes a little longer."

*Operation Vittles airlifted badly needed supplies to West Berliners isolated by the Soviet blockade.*

The next major link in the containment strategy came with the creation of a military alliance in Europe to complement the economic program. In mid-1947, the Soviets had rigged elections in Hungary and eliminated anti-Communist opposition. The next year, Soviet troops massed on the Czechoslovakian border to keep that nation within the Russian orbit. In response, in 1949, the United States took the lead in establishing NATO, the North Atlantic Treaty Organization. Twelve nations formed the alliance, in which an attack against any one member would be considered an attack against all, to be met by appropriate armed force.

The Senate, resistant to such military pacts in the past, approved this time, and the United States established its first military treaty ties with Europe since the American Revolution. Congress went further than merely authorizing membership by voting to give military aid to its NATO allies. The Cold War had changed traditional American attitudes and softened the long-standing reluctance to become closely involved with European affairs.

Two events in 1949 led the United States to define its aims still more specifically. The first was the Communist triumph in the Chinese civil war. The second was the Russian detonation of an atomic device that ended the short-lived American nuclear monopoly. Truman responded by asking for a full-fledged review of America's foreign and defense policy. The National Security Council, organized in 1947 to

## Defense Expenditures, 1945–1960

*Source:* U.S. Bureau of the Census.

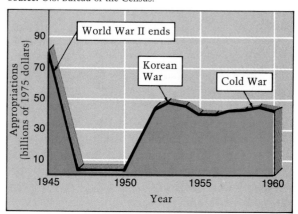

provide policy coordination, undertook the study, with Secretary of State Dean Acheson guiding the effort. The paper that resulted, NSC-68, was an immensely important document that shaped American policy for the next 20 years.

Presented to the National Security Council in 1950, NSC-68 built upon the Cold War rhetoric of the Truman Doctrine, describing America's challenges in cataclysmic terms. "The issues that face us are momentous," the paper said, "involving the fulfillment or destruction not only of this Republic but of civilization itself." Conflict between East and West, the paper assumed, was unavoidable, for amoral Soviet objectives ran totally counter to American aims. Negotiation was useless, for the Sovi-

ets could never be trusted to bargain in good faith.

Having eliminated important options, NSC-68 now laid out the remaining alternatives. The nation could continue on its present course, with relatively limited military budgets, but would fail to achieve its objectives. If the United States hoped to meet the Russian challenge, a far more massive effort was necessary. The nation must increase defense spending from the $13 billion set for 1950 to as much as $50 billion per year and increase the percentage of its budget allotted to defense from 5 to 20 percent. The costs were huge, but if the free world were to survive, the document argued, the United States had to move unilaterally to stem the Communist tide.

## Cold War Europe in 1950

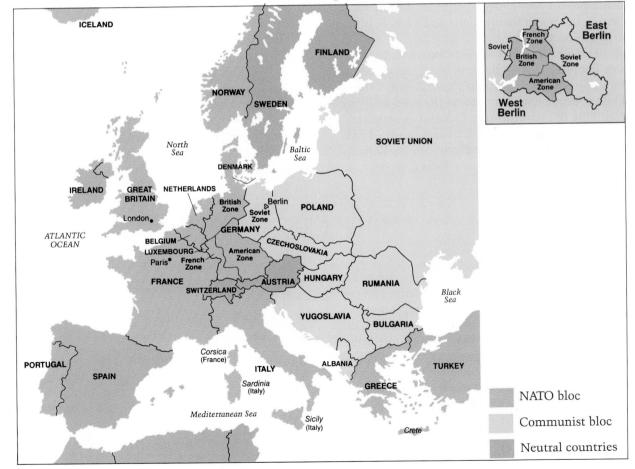

## Containment in the 1950s

Containment, the keystone of American policy throughout the Truman years, was the rationale for the Truman Doctrine, the Marshall Plan, NATO, and NSC-68. In the 1950s, however, under Eisenhower's administration, containment came under attack as too cautious to counter the threat of communism.

For most of Eisenhower's two terms, John Foster Dulles was secretary of state. A devout Presbyterian who hated atheistic communism, he sought to take Truman's policy of containment even further. Responsible for the foreign policy plank in the 1952 Republican platform, which condemned containment as a "negative, futile, and immoral" approach that had lost "countless human beings to a despotism and Godless terrorism," Dulles believed a spiritual offensive was necessary. Instead of advocating containment, the United States should make it "publicly known that it wants and expects liberation to occur."

Though the language was extreme, in practice liberation was difficult to implement. Eisenhower, somewhat more conciliatory than Dulles, knew how remote was the possibility of changing the governments of Russia's satellites. The chance to test the policy came in mid-1953, as East Germans mounted anti-Soviet demonstrations. The United States looked on sympa-

*Secretary of State John Foster Dulles was an outspoken proponent of active measures against Communism.*

thetically but kept its distance. In 1956, when Hungarian "freedom fighters" rose up against Russian domination, the United States again stood back as Soviet forces smashed the rebels. Because Western action could have precipitated a more general conflict, Eisenhower refused to translate rhetoric into action. In the real world of international affairs, liberation was meaningless. Throughout the 1950s, the policy of containment remained in effect.

## AMERICAN POLICY IN ASIA, THE MIDDLE EAST, AND LATIN AMERICA

Although containment resulted from the effort to promote European stability, the United States extended the policy to meet challenges around the globe. The Communist victory in the Chinese civil war in 1949 only underscored the growing threat to order Americans wanted in the postwar world. The Korean War that broke out soon after embroiled the United States in another international conflict barely five years after the end of World War II. Elsewhere in Asia and the Middle East, the United States discovered the tremendous appeal of communism as a social and political system and found that even

greater efforts were necessary to advance American aims.

### The Chinese Revolution

America's commitment to containment became stronger still with the climax of the Chinese Revolution. China, an ally during World War II, had struggled against the conquering Japanese, even as it fought a bitter civil war. The roots of the civil war lay deep in the Chinese past—in widespread poverty, disease, oppression by the landlord class, and national humiliation

*Mao Zedong's effort to reshape China in a Communist mold had begun in the 1920s; in 1949 the People's Republic of China became a reality.*

at the hands of foreign powers. Mao Zedong (Mao Tse-tung*), founder of a branch of the Communist party and of a Marxist study group in the early 1920s, gathered followers who wished to reshape China in a Communist mold. Opposing the Communists were the Nationalists, led by Jiang Jieshi (Chiang Kai-shek). Even though the Communists were forced to retreat in the mid-1930s, Mao persevered. By the early 1940s, Jiang Jieshi's regime was exhausted, hopelessly inefficient, and corrupt. Mao's movement, meanwhile, grew stronger during the Second World War as he opposed the Japanese invaders and won the loyalty of the peasant class.

After the war, the United States hoped for a coalition between Nationalists and Communists, but reconciliation proved impossible. Jiang lost city after city and finally fled in 1949 to the island of Taiwan (Formosa). There he nursed the improbable hope that his was still the rightful government of all China and that he would one day return. Mao's Communist revolution had at last succeeded.

---

*Chinese names are rendered in their modern *pinyin* spelling. At first occurrence, the older but perhaps more familiar Wade-Giles spelling is given in parentheses.

The United States failed to understand the long internal conflict in China. Blinded by the fear of communism, Americans could not recognize Mao's immense popular support. As the Communist army moved toward victory, the New York *Times* termed the group a "nauseous force," a "compact little oligarchy dominated by Moscow's nominees." Mao's proclamation of the People's Republic of China on October 1, 1949, underscored fears of Russian domination, for he had already announced that his regime would support the Soviet Union against the "imperialist" United States.

The Chinese question caused near hysteria in America. Staunch anti-Communists argued that the United States was to blame for Jiang's defeat by failing to provide him with more support. Secretary of State Dean Acheson observed that the result was far beyond American control: "Nothing this country did or could have done within the reasonable limits of its capabilities could have changed that result."

Acheson considered granting diplomatic recognition to the new regime but backed off after the Communists seized American property, harassed American citizens, and openly allied themselves with the Russians. Like other Americans, he viewed the Chinese as Soviet puppets. The new government, Acheson remarked, was "not Chinese" and should not receive American support. At the same time, the United States denied aid to the Nationalists on Taiwan, assuming that the Communists on the mainland would soon conquer that island as well. That position, and the entire American stance, infuriated the largely Republican lobby in the United States, which blamed Truman for having "lost" China.

Tension with China increased during the Korean War and then again in 1954 when Mao's government began shelling Nationalist positions on the offshore islands of Quemoy and Matsu. Eisenhower, now president, was by this time committed to defending the Nationalists on Taiwan from a Communist attack, but he was unwilling to respond in the same way to the shelling of Quemoy and Matsu. By resisting recommendations that the United States plunge into the conflict, he demonstrated once again the limits of containment.

## The War in Korea

The Korean War marked America's growing intervention in Asian affairs. The concern about China and the determination to contain communism led the United States into involvement in a long and bloody struggle in a faraway land. But American objectives were not always clear and were largely unrealized after three years of war.

The conflict in Korea stemmed from tensions lingering after World War II. Korea, long under Japanese control, hoped for independence after Japan's defeat. But the Allies temporarily divided Korea along the 38th parallel when the rapid end to the Pacific struggle allowed Soviet troops to accept Japanese surrender in the north while American forces did the same in the south. The Soviet-American line, initially intended as a matter of military convenience, rigidified after 1945, and in time the Soviets set up a government in the north and the Americans a government in the south. Though the major powers left Korea, they continued to support the regimes they had created. Each hoped to reunify the country on its own terms.

North Korea moved first. On June 25, 1950, North Korean forces invaded South Korea by crossing the 38th parallel. Following Soviet-built tanks, the North Korean troops steadily advanced against the South Korean soldiers. Was the invasion undertaken at Soviet command? Kim Il Sung, the North Korean leader, had visited Moscow earlier and spoken to Stalin about instability in the south. The Russians may have acquiesced in the idea of an attack, but both the planning and timing came at the initiative of the north.

The United States was taken by surprise. Earlier, America had seemed reluctant to defend Korea, but the Communist victory in China had changed the balance of power in Asia. Certain that Russia had masterminded the North Korean offensive and was testing the American policy of containment, Truman was determined to respond vigorously. "In my generation," he announced,

> this was not the first occasion when the strong had attacked the weak. I recalled some earlier instances: Manchuria, Ethiopia, Austria. . . . Each time that the democracies failed to act it had encouraged the aggressors to keep going ahead. . . . If this was allowed to go unchallenged it would mean a third world war, just as similar incidents had brought on the second world war.

Truman readied American naval and air forces and directed General Douglas MacArthur in Japan to provide supplies to South Korea. The United States also went to the United Nations Security Council. With the Soviet Union absent in protest of the UN's refusal to admit the People's Republic of China, the United States secured a unanimous resolution branding North Korea an aggressor, then another resolution calling on members of the organization to assist the

## The Korean War

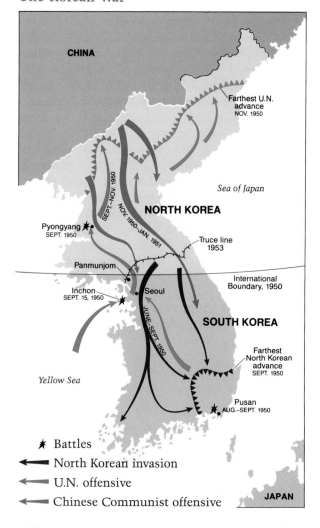

★ Battles

← North Korean invasion

← U.N. offensive

← Chinese Communist offensive

south in repelling aggression and restoring peace.

The president first ordered American air and naval forces into battle south of the 38th parallel, then American ground forces as well. Following a daring amphibious invasion that pushed the North Koreans back to the former boundary line, United Nations troops crossed the 38th parallel, hoping to reunify Korea under an American-backed government. Despite Chinese signals that they regarded this movement toward their border as a threat to their security, the United States pressed on. In October, Chinese troops appeared briefly in battle, then disappeared. The next month, the Chinese mounted a full-fledged counterattack, which pushed the UN forces back below the dividing line again.

Now the war became a brutal stalemate, which provoked a bitter struggle between Douglas MacArthur and his civilian commander in chief. A brilliant but arrogant general, MacArthur called for massive retaliatory air strikes against China. While the administration was most concerned with the containment of communism in Europe, MacArthur argued for

stronger resistance in Asia. Truman was trying to conduct a limited war and to prevent it from becoming a major struggle, but MacArthur wanted to deal the enemy a massive defeat.

MacArthur's public statements, issued from the field, finally went too far. In April 1951, he revealed his views in a letter meant to be made public in the United States. Arguing that the American approach in Korea was wrong, he asserted that "there is no substitute for victory." When the letter appeared, Truman had no choice but to relieve MacArthur for insubordination. The decision outraged many Americans. After the stunning victories of World War II, limited war was frustrating and difficult to understand.

As the furor subsided, Truman pursued more modest goals. After another year of war, the administration was willing to settle for an armistice at the 38th parallel. Peace talks with the North Koreans began while the fighting dragged on. During the campaign of 1952, Eisenhower promised to go to Korea, and three weeks after his election, he did so. When truce talks bogged down again in May 1953, the new administration threatened to use atomic weapons and to launch a massive military campaign. This brought about a resumption of the peace talks.

Although the war was almost over, Anthony Ebron, a marine corporal, noted that "those last

*Korean civilians fled south as American troops marched north toward the disputed 38th parallel.*

*Relieved of his command for insubordination, General Douglas MacArthur returned home to a dignitary's welcome. His wife and son stand next to him in the foreground.*

few days were pretty brutal." At the very end, he said, "we shot off so much artillery [that] the ground shook." Finally, on July 27, 1953, an armistice was signed. The Republican administration had managed to do what the preceding Democratic administration could not. After three long years, the unpopular war had ended.

American involvement carried a heavy price. Despite its limited nature, the Korean War led to 54,000 American deaths and many more wounded. But those figures paled beside the numbers of Korean casualties. As many as 2 million may have died in North and South Korea, and countless others were maimed. A BBC journalist's description of napalm, a highly flammable liquid explosive first used in the war, told at least part of the story:

> In front of us a curious figure was standing, a little crouched, legs straddled, arms held out from his sides. He had no eyes, and the whole of his body, nearly all of which was visible through tatters of burnt rags, was covered with a hard black crust speckled with yellow pus. . . . He had to stand because he was no longer covered with a skin, but with a crust-like crackling which broke easily.

The war also brought significant change in American attitudes and institutions. This was the first war in which United States forces fought in integrated units. Blacks were now integral members of the military service. Military expenditures soared from $13 billion in fiscal 1949–1950 to about $60 billion three years later as the United States rearmed. Military retrenchment came to an end as defense spending followed the guidelines proposed in NSC-68. With more money spent for war and defense, less was available for domestic social programs. The Cold War established new priorities and needs. At home, the buildup caused frustrations for many Americans who could not understand the constraints of limited war. Why, they asked, could they not go in with all the force necessary to end the struggle? Why were American objectives not met?

There were important political effects as well. The Korean War led the United States to sign a peace treaty with Japan in September 1951 and to rely on that nation to maintain the balance of power in the Pacific. At the same time, the struggle poisoned relations with China and ensured a diplomatic standoff that lasted more than 20 years.

## Civil War in Vietnam

Indochina became another Asian battlefield in the Cold War where the United States became deeply entangled. Since the middle of the nineteenth century, France had controlled Indochina, exploiting its supplies of rubber, tin, tungsten, and rice. During World War II, the Japanese occupied the area but allowed French collaborators to continue to direct internal affairs. The Japanese conquest, however, shattered the image of European invincibility and encouraged an independence movement, led by the tireless Communist organizer and revolutionary Ho Chi Minh. Using the American War for Independence as a model, Ho worked through his political organization, the Viet Minh, to expel the Japanese conquerors. In 1945, the Allied powers were faced with the decision of how to deal with Ho and his revolutionary movement.

Franklin Roosevelt, like Woodrow Wilson, believed in self-determination and wanted to end colonialism. Reluctant to allow France to return after the defeat of the Japanese, Roosevelt favored an international trusteeship scheme as a way of preparing for future Vietnamese independence. But France, believing that the nation could "only be a great power so long as our flag continues to fly in all the overseas territory," was determined to regain its colony, and by the time of his death, Roosevelt had backed down.

Ho Chi Minh and the Vietnamese, however, did not abandon national liberation. Guerrilla warfare had won them most of the countryside, and they had established the Democratic Republic of Vietnam in 1945. Although the new government enjoyed widespread support, the United States refused to recognize it. The head of the American Office of Strategic Services mission predicted that if the French returned, the Vietnamese would fight to the death.

A long, bitter struggle between the French and the forces of Ho Chi Minh did break out and became entangled with the larger Cold War.

President Truman was less concerned about ending colonialism than with checking growing Soviet power in Europe and around the world. France was a nation needed to balance Russian strength in Europe, and that meant cooperating with the French in Vietnam.

While the Vietnamese battled the French, the United States watched with alarm. France had been weakened by World War II, and the United States doubted that it could survive a long colonial war. At the same time, the Truman administration was concerned about Vietnam itself. If France was defeated, the West would lose a foothold in a part of the world where a Communist revolution had already succeeded. Worse still, it would face a regime sympathetic to Moscow and the East, for Ho was a confirmed Marxist-Leninist. Though Ho did not, in fact, have close ties to the Soviet state and was committed to his independent nationalist crusade, Truman and his advisers, who saw communism as a monolithic force, assumed that he took orders from Moscow. Hence in 1950, the United States formally recognized the French puppet government in Vietnam. The Vietnamese viewed the Americans as France's colonialist collaborators. The United States in the Truman years did not provide direct military aid to the French, but American economic assistance freed France to use its own resources in the struggle.

After Eisenhower took office, the situation worsened for France. Some 12,000 French troops prepared for a showdown at the fortress of Dien Bien Phu. With a French defeat looming, Eisenhower reviewed American diplomatic options. He believed in the "domino theory," which held that "you have a row of dominos set up, you knock over the first one, and what will happen to the last one is the certainty that it will go over very quickly." At a press conference in April 1954, he warned that Burma, Thailand, and Indonesia would follow if Vietnam fell, and Japan, Taiwan, the Philippines, Australia, and New Zealand might go next. "So the possible consequences of the loss," he said, "are just incalculable to the free world."

At the same time, a cautious Eisenhower was not ready to bolt into Indochina alone. As the price for United States assistance, the French would have to pledge to grant Vietnamese independence at some point. England would have to cooperate in a joint assistance effort. And Congress would have to authorize the necessary support. Eisenhower believed that "only when there is a sudden, unforeseen emergency should the President put us into war without congressional action." Since, as he suspected, none of the conditions was met, the United States refused to intervene directly. Dien Bien Phu finally fell, and an international conference in Geneva divided Vietnam along the 17th parallel, with elections promised in 1956 to unify the country and determine its political fate.

As a result of that division, two new states emerged. Ho Chi Minh held power in the north, while in the south a separate government was formed under Premier Ngo Dinh Diem, a fierce anti-Communist. Intent on taking France's place in Southeast Asia, the United States supported the anti-Communist government in South Vietnam and refused to sign the Geneva agreement. "We must work with these people," Eisenhower said, "and then they themselves will soon find out that we are their friends and that they cannot live without us." Shortly after this, Eisenhower dispatched a CIA unit to conduct secret missions in Vietnam. In 1956, he supported Diem in refusing to hold the national elections in Vietnam called for in the Geneva agreement. In the next few years, American aid increased and military advisers began to assist the South Vietnamese.

### The Middle East

While Cold War attitudes shaped American diplomacy in Southeast Asia, they also influenced responses to events in the Middle East. That part of the world had tremendous strategic importance as the supplier of oil for the industrialized nations. During World War II, the major Allied Powers had occupied Iran, with the provision that they would leave within six months of the war's end. As of early 1946, both Great Britain and the United States had withdrawn, but Russia, which bordered on Iran, remained. Stalin claimed that earlier security agreements had not been honored and, further, demanded oil concessions.

Moving quickly to counter the Soviet threat, the United States took the issue to the newly formed United Nations in March 1946. But the United States was willing to act independently. As Russian tanks neared the Iranian border, Secretary of State Byrnes declared, "Now we'll give it to them with both barrels." The ultimatum threatened vigorous American action and forced the Russians to back down and withdraw.

The Eisenhower administration maintained its interest in Iran. In 1953, the Central Intelligence Agency helped the local army overthrow the government of Mohammed Mossadegh, which had nationalized oil wells formerly under British control, and place the shah of Iran securely on the Peacock Throne. After the coup, British and American companies regained command of the wells, and thereafter the United States government provided military assistance to the shah.

A far more serious episode unfolded west of Iran. In 1948, the United Nations partitioned Palestine into an Arab and a Jewish state. Truman officially recognized the new state of Israel 15 minutes after it was proclaimed. But recognition could not end bitter animosities between Arabs, who felt they had been robbed of their territory, and Jews, who felt they had finally regained their homeland in that region. As Americans looked on, Israel fought its first war against Arab forces from Egypt, Trans-Jordan, Syria, Lebanon, and Iraq.

The United States cultivated close ties with Israel but could not afford to lose the friendship of oil-rich Arab states, nor could it allow them to fall into the Soviet orbit. In Egypt, Arab nationalist General Gamal Abdel Nasser planned a great dam on the Nile River to produce electricity. Nasser proclaimed his country neutral in the Cold War struggle. Dulles offered American financial support for the Aswan project, but Nasser also began discussions with the Soviet Union. The secretary of state furiously withdrew the American offer. Left without funds for the dam, Nasser seized and nationalized the British-controlled Suez Canal in July 1956. At

## The Middle East in 1949

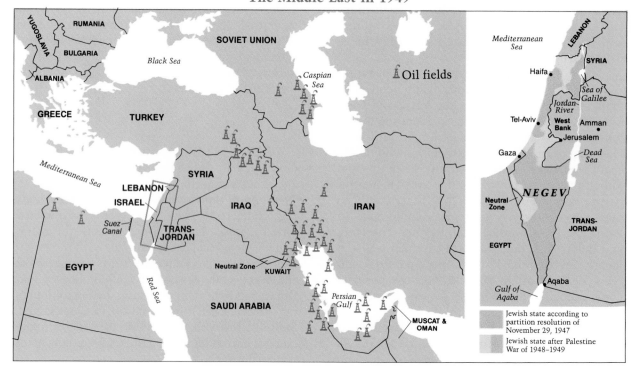

the same time, he closed the canal to Israeli ships. Great Britain, whose citizens owned most of the stock in the canal company, reacted angrily. All of Europe feared that Nasser would disrupt the flow of oil from the Middle East. The United States sought to settle the problem peacefully.

Despite the American stance, Israeli, British, and French military forces invaded Egypt in October and November. Eisenhower, who had not been consulted, was irate. Realizing that the attack might push Nasser into the arms of Moscow, the United States sponsored a UN resolution condemning the attacking nations and cut off oil from England and France. These actions persuaded them to withdraw.

In 1958, the United States again intervened in the Middle East. Concerned about stability there, Eisenhower had declared in the previous year that "the existing vacuum in the Middle East must be filled by the United States before it is filled by Russia." A year later, in line with a congressional resolution that committed the United States to stop Communist aggression, he authorized the landing of 14,000 soldiers in Lebanon to prop up a right-wing government challenged from within.

## Restricting Revolt in Latin America

The Cold War also affected relations with Latin America and provided new reasons for intervention in that region. In 1954, Dulles sniffed Communist activity in Guatemala and ordered CIA support for a coup aimed at overthrowing the elected government of reform-minded Colonel Jacobo Arbenz Guzmán. The right-wing takeover succeeded, restored the property of the United Fruit Company that Arbenz had seized, and demonstrated again the American commitment to stability and private investment, whatever the internal effect or ultimate cost.

The effort in Guatemala fed anti-American feeling throughout Latin America. Many abhorred the interference of their northern neighbor that had pledged a Good Neighbor policy under Franklin Roosevelt. Dulles downplayed hostile sentiment, but when Vice-President Richard Nixon traveled to Venezuela in 1958, he found rabid crowds that stoned his car and almost tipped it over.

The next year, when Fidel Castro overthrew the dictatorial regime of Fulgencio Batista in Cuba, the shortsightedness of American policy became even clearer. Nationalism and the thrust for social reform were powerful forces in Latin America, as in the rest of the Third World. As Milton Eisenhower, Ike's brother and adviser, pointed out: "Revolution is inevitable in Latin America. The people are angry. They are shackled to the past with bonds of ignorance, injustice, and poverty. And they no longer accept as universal or inevitable the oppressive prevailing order." But not all officials shared this perspective. When Castro confiscated American property in Cuba, the Eisenhower administration cut off exports and severed diplomatic ties. In response, Cuba turned to Russia for support.

# ATOMIC WEAPONS AND THE COLD WAR

Throughout the Cold War period, the atomic bomb was a crucial factor in world affairs. Atomic weapons were destructive enough, but when the United States and the Soviet Union both developed hydrogen bombs, an age of overkill began. Americans spoke casually of "massive retaliation" if the Soviet Union ever went too far, but they feared a similar attack on the United States.

## Sharing the Secret of the Bomb

The United States, with British aid, built the first atomic bomb and concealed the project from its wartime ally, the Soviet Union. Soviet spies, however, discovered that the Americans were at work on the bomb. By 1943, a Soviet program to create a Russian atomic bomb was under way.

The question of sharing the atomic secret was pressing in the immediate postwar years. Some felt that Americans should guard their knowledge, arguing that the Russians would take years to duplicate their feat. But nuclear scientists knew that once others saw that the weapon could be made, it would take another nation far less time to do the same thing. Might it not be better to deal with the question of sharing before it was too late? The threat of world destruction was confronted for the first time.

Secretary of War Henry L. Stimson favored cooperating with the Soviet Union. Recognizing the futility of trying to cajole the Russians while "having this weapon ostentatiously on our hip," he suggested that "their suspicions and their distrust of our purposes and motives will increase." International cooperation could be achieved only through mutual accommodation. "The chief lesson I have learned in a long life," Stimson observed, "is the only way you can make a man trustworthy is to trust him, and the surest way you can make a man untrustworthy is to distrust him and to show your distrust."

But the United States never followed Stimson's advice. Truman, increasingly worried about the Soviet presence in eastern Europe, vowed to retain the technological advantage. He resisted a more flexible approach until the creation of a "foolproof method of control" over atomic weapons. Most Americans shared his view.

There was for a time an intent search for a means of international arms control. Realizing by early 1946 that mere possession of the bomb was not making the Russians more malleable, Truman decided to present a plan to the United Nations. Drafted by Dean Acheson and David Lilienthal, the plan proposed an international agency to provide atomic energy control. Bernard Baruch, ambassador to the UN's Atomic Energy Commission, hoping to avoid a Russian veto in the Security Council, modified the plan to establish a system of international inspection and agreement. In fact, as the Russians were quick to point out, this plan allowed American nuclear supremacy until the international agency had gained control of the earth's fissionable material. The Russians called first for destruc-

tion of all atomic weapons, then for a discussion of controls. Negotiations collapsed.

Hence the United States gave up on the process of sharing atomic secrets and moved toward its own internal mechanism of control. The Atomic Energy Act of 1946 established the Atomic Energy Commission to supervise all atomic energy development in the United States and, under the tightest security, to authorize all activity in the nation at large.

## Nuclear Proliferation

As the atomic bomb found its way into popular culture, Americans at first showed more excitement than fear. In Los Angeles, the "Atombomb Dancers" appeared at the Burbank Burlesque Theater. In 1946, the Buchanan Brothers recorded "Atomic Power," which soon appeared on the *Billboard* music charts. A Newport, Arkansas, farmer wrote to the atomic research and development center at Oak Ridge, Tennessee, asking, "I have some stumps in my field that I should like to blow out. Have you got any atomic bombs the right size for the job?"

Yet anxiety lurked beneath exuberance, though it did not surface as long as the United States maintained a nuclear monopoly. Then, in September 1949, reporters were called to the White House and handed a mimeographed announcement. President Truman told the stunned reporters, "We have evidence that within recent weeks an atomic explosion occurred in the U.S.S.R."

The Russians had not publicized their achievement. Rather, over the Labor Day weekend, a U.S. Air Force weather reconnaissance plane on a routine mission had picked up air samples showing higher than normal radioactivity counts. Other samples confirmed this, and scientists soon concluded that Russia had conducted a nuclear test.

The American public was shocked. Suddenly the security of being the world's only atomic power vanished. People wondered whether the Soviet test foreshadowed a nuclear attack. At a meeting of the Joint Committee on Atomic Energy, legislators struggled to comprehend the implications of the news. When a thunderclap filled the air, someone in the room said, "My

God, that must be Number Two!" cutting the tension for the moment. Harold C. Urey, a Nobel Prize–winning scientist, summed up the feelings of many Americans: "There is only one thing worse than one nation having the atomic bomb—that's two nations having it." The atomic genie was out of the bottle, and Americans had to accept the fact that their monopoly had disappeared. An entirely new defense strategy now was necessary.

In early 1950, the arms race picked up speed as Truman authorized the development of a new hydrogen superbomb, potentially far more devastating than the atomic bomb. Edward Teller, a physicist on the Manhattan Project, was intrigued with the novelty of the puzzle. During the war, as other scientists struggled with the problem of fission, he contemplated the possibility that fusion might release energy in even greater amounts. Now he had his chance to proceed.

By 1953, both the United States and the Soviet Union had unlocked the secret of the hydrogen bomb. As kilotons gave way to megatons, the stakes rose. The government remained quiet about MIKE, the first test of a hydrogen device in the Pacific Ocean in 1952, but rumors circulated that it had created a hole in the ocean floor 175 feet deep and a mile wide. A year and a

*Attractive, homey mock-ups were an effective sales tool in encouraging Americans to build private fallout shelters.*

half later, after the 1954 BRAVO test, Lewis Strauss, Atomic Energy Commission chairman, admitted that "an H-bomb can be made . . . large enough to take out a city," even New York. Then, in 1957, Americans learned that the Soviets had fired the first satellite, *Sputnik*, into outer space. The news came shortly after the Soviets had successfully tested their first intercontinental ballistic missile (ICBM). The apparent inferiority of American rocketry and the openness of the country to attack caused great concern.

The discovery of radioactive fallout added another dimension to the nuclear dilemma. Fallout became publicly known after the BRAVO blast, when Japanese fishermen 85 miles away were showered with radioactive dust. They became ill with radiation sickness, and several months later, one of them died. The Japanese, who had earlier seen the effects of atomic weapons at first hand, were outraged and alarmed. Elsewhere people began to realize the terrible impact of the new weapons.

Authors in both the scientific and popular press focused attention on radioactive fallout. Radiation, physicist Ralph Lapp observed, "cannot be felt and possesses all the terror of the unknown. It is something which evokes revulsion and helplessness—like a bubonic plague." Nevil Shute's best-selling 1957 novel *On the Beach*, and the film that followed, also sparked public awareness and fear. The story concerned a war that released so much radioactive waste that all life in the Northern Hemisphere was destroyed, while the Southern Hemisphere was reduced to waiting for the residue to come closer and bring the same deadly end. When *Consumer Reports* warned of the contamination of milk with strontium-90 in 1959, public alarm grew.

One response to growing nuclear stockpiles and the threat of global destruction was the building of bomb shelters. There had been interest in blast shelters in the immediate postwar years, but a national program was prohibitively expensive and never really got under way. With the discovery of fallout, a shelter craze began. Bob Russell, a Michigan sheriff, declared that "to build a new home in this day and age without including such an obvious necessity as a fallout shelter would be like leaving out the bathroom 20 years ago." *Good Housekeeping* magazine carried a full-page editorial in November 1958 that urged the building of family shelters. A cartoon in Pennsylvania's *Harrisburg News* showed the biblical ark, with the caption, "They Laughed at Noah!"

More and more companies advertised ready-made shelters for eager consumers. A firm in Miami reported many inquiries about shelters costing between $1,795 and $3,895, depending on capacity, and planned 900 franchises. *Life* magazine in 1955 featured an "H-Bomb Hideaway" for $3,000. By the end of 1960, the Office of Civil and Defense Mobilization estimated that a million family shelters had been built.

### "Massive Retaliation"

As Americans grappled with the consequences of nuclear weapons, government policy came to depend increasingly on an atomic shield. Truman authorized the development of a nuclear arsenal but also stressed conventional forms of defense. After his election in 1952, Eisenhower found the effort fragmented and wasteful. Concerned with controlling the budget and cutting taxes, Eisenhower and the Republicans decided to rely on atomic weapons as the key to American defense.

Drawing on a new breed of nuclear strategists, like Harvard's Henry Kissinger, who believed that atomic weapons might be used in military confrontations, Dulles argued that the new approach allowed for instant response to Communist aggression "by means and at places of our own choosing." Eisenhower liked the "new look," or policy of "massive retaliation," for it left the enemy uncertain about what the United States might do in a given situation. The policy also allowed troop cutbacks and promised to be cost-effective by giving "more bang for the buck."

Massive retaliation provided for an all-or-nothing response, leaving no middle course. It left no real alternatives between nuclear war and passive retreat. Still, it was wholly consonant with the secretary of state's willingness to use extreme threats to assert the American position in the Cold War. The prospect of direct retaliation, properly used, Dulles felt, could deter Soviet challenges around the world. "The ability to get to the verge without getting into war is the necessary art," he declared. "If you cannot master it you inevitably get into war." Critics called the policy "brinkmanship" and wondered what would happen if the line were crossed in the new atomic age.

## THE COLD WAR AT HOME

The Cold War affected domestic as well as foreign affairs, and its greatest impact came in the creation of an internal loyalty program that produced serious violations of civil liberties. Americans had feared radical subversion before and after the Russian Revolution (See Chapters 18, 23, and 24), but now their fears intensified. The Soviet Union appeared ever more ominous in confrontations around the world. Maps showed half the world colored red to dramatize the spread of the monolithic Communist system. Now Americans began to suspect Communist infiltration at home. It was not enough to meet the challenge abroad; Americans had to root out any traces of communism inside the United States.

### Truman's Loyalty Program

As the Truman administration mobilized support for its containment program in the immediate postwar years, its rhetoric became increasingly shrill. Picturing issues in black and white terms, spokesmen set American virtues against diabolical Russian designs. For Truman, the issue that confronted the world was one of "tyranny or freedom." According to Attorney General J. Howard McGrath, there were "many Communists in America," each bearing "the germ of death for society."

There did seem to be evidence of an internal threat. In February 1945, government agents found some classified government documents in the offices of the allegedly pro-Communist *Amerasia* magazine. A year later, a Canadian commission exposed a number of spy rings and described wartime subversion. Truman responded by appointing a Temporary Commission on Employee Loyalty. Republican gains in the midterm elections of 1946 led him to fear a congressional loyalty probe that could be used for partisan ends, especially since Republicans had accused the Democrats of being "soft on communism." Truman hoped to head off such an investigation by starting his own.

On the basis of the report from his temporary commission, Truman established a new Federal Employee Loyalty Program by executive order in 1947. The FBI was to check its files for evidence of subversive activity, and suspects would then be brought before a new Civil Service Commission Loyalty Review Board. Initially the program included safeguards and assumed that a challenged employee was innocent until guilt had been proved. But those limits did not last long, for as the Loyalty Review Board assumed more and more power, it came to overlook individual rights. Employees about whom there was any doubt, regardless of proof, now found themselves under attack, with little chance to fight back.

The Truman loyalty program examined several million employees and found grounds for dismissing only several hundred. Nonetheless, it bred the largely unwarranted fear of subversion, led to the assumption that absolute loyalty could be achieved, and legitimized investigatory tactics that later became irresponsibly used.

## The Congressional Loyalty Program

While Truman's loyalty probe investigated government employees, Congress embarked on its own program. In the early years of the Cold War, the law became increasingly explicit about what was illegal in the United States. The Smith Act of 1940 made it a crime to advocate or teach the forcible overthrow of the U.S. government. In 1949, Eugene Dennis and ten other Communist leaders were found guilty under its terms. In 1951, in *Dennis* v. *United States,* the Supreme Court upheld the Smith Act, declaring that a real danger of subversion existed in America.

That action cleared the way for the prosecution of other Communist leaders. Nearly 100 were indicted in the early 1950s.

The McCarran Internal Security Act of 1950 further circumscribed Communist activity by declaring that it was illegal to conspire to act in a way that would "substantially contribute" to establishing a totalitarian dictatorship in America. Members of Communist organizations had to register with the attorney general and could not obtain passports or work in areas of national defense. Congress passed the measure over Truman's veto and provided further legal backing for the anti-Communist crusade. The American Communist party, which numbered about 80,000 in 1947, declined to 55,000 in 1950 and 25,000 in 1954.

The investigations of the House Committee on Un-American Activities (HUAC) contributed to that decline. Intent on rooting out subversion, HUAC probed the motion picture industry in 1947 to determine the political inclinations of its members.

When hearings were scheduled, many entertainers and movie stars denounced the procedures. "Say your piece. Write your Congressman a letter! Airmail special!" Frank Sinatra warned, "Once they get the movies throttled, how long will it be before we're told what we can say and cannot say into a radio microphone?"

HUAC pressed on. Protesting its scare tactics, some people the committee summoned refused to testify under oath. They were scapegoated for their stand. The so-called Hollywood Ten, a group of writers, were cited for contempt of court and sent to federal prison. At that, Hollywood knuckled under and blacklisted anyone with even a marginally questionable past. No one on these lists could find jobs at the studios anymore.

Congress made a greater splash with the Hiss-Chambers case. Whittaker Chambers, a former Communist who had broken with the Party in 1938 and had become a successful editor of *Time,* charged that Alger Hiss had been a Communist in the 1930s. Hiss was a distinguished New Dealer who had served in the Agriculture Department before becoming assistant secretary of state. Now out of the government, he was president of the Carnegie

*Accused of spying for the Soviets, Alger Hiss was convicted of perjury and went to prison.*

Endowment for International Peace. He denied Chambers's charge, and the matter might have died there had not freshman congressman Richard Nixon taken up the case. Nixon finally extracted from Hiss an admission that he had once known Chambers. Outside the hearing room, Hiss sued Chambers for libel, whereupon Chambers changed his story and charged that Hiss was a Soviet spy.

With controversial evidence in hand, including several rolls of microfilmed government documents that Chambers contended Hiss had given him to pass to the Russians, HUAC sensed the possibilities of the case. In December 1948, a federal grand jury took the matter a step further. Since the statute of limitations ruled out an espionage indictment, the grand jury indicted Hiss instead for perjury, for lying under oath about his former relationship with Chambers.

The case made front-page news around the nation. Millions of Americans sought to understand what was going on, while also reading about Russia's first atomic explosion and the

final victory of the Communist revolution in China. Chambers appeared unstable and changed his story several times. Yet Hiss, too, seemed contradictory in his testimony and never adequately explained how some copies of stolen State Department documents had been typed on a typewriter he had once owned. The first trial ended in a hung jury; the second trial, in January 1950, sent Hiss to prison for almost four years.

For many Americans, the Hiss case proved the Communist threat in the United States. It "forcibly demonstrated to the American people," Richard Nixon declared, "that domestic Communism was a real and present danger to the security of the nation." It also led people to question the Democratic approach to the problem. After Hiss's conviction but before his appeal, Dean Acheson supported his friend. Regardless of what happened, he said, "I do not intend to turn my back on Alger Hiss." Decent though his affirmation was, it caused the secretary of state political trouble. Truman too was broadly attacked for his comments about the case. Earlier he had called it a "red herring," but the courts had decided otherwise. Critics questioned the strength of Truman's commitment to protect the nation from internal subversion. Ironically, his loyalty program, for all its excesses, faced charges of laxity at home. The dramatic Hiss case helped to discredit the Democrats and to justify the even worse witch-hunt that followed.

## The Second Red Scare

The key anti-Communist warrior in the 1950s was Joseph R. McCarthy. Coming to the Senate from Wisconsin in 1946, McCarthy had an undistinguished career. As he began to contemplate reelection two years hence, he seized on the Communist issue. Truman had carried Wisconsin in 1948, and McCarthy saw in the Communist question a way of mobilizing Republican support. He first gained national attention with a speech before the Wheeling, West Virginia, Women's Club in February 1950, not long after the conviction of Alger Hiss. In that address, McCarthy claimed he had in his hand a list of 205 known Communists in the State

Department. When pressed for details, McCarthy said first that he would release his list only to the president; then he reduced the number of names to 57.

Early reactions to McCarthy were mixed. A subcommittee of the Senate Foreign Relations Committee, after investigating, called his charge a "fraud and a hoax." Even other Republicans like Robert Taft and Richard Nixon questioned his effectiveness. Yet McCarthy persisted, for he found an anxious public primed by the Hiss Case and international events. As his support grew, Republicans realized his partisan value and egged him on. Senator John Bricker of Ohio allegedly told him, "Joe, you're a dirty s.o.b., but there are times when you've got to have an s.o.b. around, and this is one of them." Taft, also from Ohio, provided similar encouragement when he advised, "If one case doesn't work, try another." McCarthy did.

McCarthy selected assorted targets. In the elections of 1950, he attacked Millard Tydings, the Democrat from Maryland who had chaired the subcommittee that dismissed McCarthy's first accusations. A doctored photograph, showing Tydings with deposed American Communist party head Earl Browder, helped bring about Tydings's defeat. McCarthy called Dean Acheson a "pompous diplomat in striped pants, with a phony British accent" and termed him the "Red Dean of the State Department." He slandered George C. Marshall, the architect of victory in World War II and a powerful figure in formulating Far Eastern policy, as "a man steeped in falsehood . . . who has recourse to the lie whenever it suits his convenience."

A demagogue throughout his career, McCarthy gained visibility through extensive press and television coverage. Playing on his tough reputation, he did not mind appearing disheveled, unshaven, and half sober. He used obscenity and vulgarity freely as he spoke of the "vile and scurrilous" objects of his attacks.

McCarthy's tactics worked because the public was alarmed about the Communist threat. The Korean War, which broke out in mid-1950, showed that the Communists were always ready to attack. That same year, the arrest of Julius and Ethel Rosenberg further aroused fears of subversion from within. The Rosenbergs, a seemingly ordinary American couple with two small children, were charged with stealing and transmitting atomic secrets to the Russians. To many Americans, it was inconceivable that the Soviets could have developed the bomb on their own. Only treachery could explain the Soviet explosion of an atomic device.

The next year, the Rosenbergs were found guilty of espionage and sentenced to death. Judge Irving Kauffman expressed the rage of a nation that felt insecure and menaced by the Soviet Union. "Your conduct in putting into the hands of the Russians the A-bomb," he charged, "has already caused, in my opinion, the Communist aggression in Korea . . . and who knows but that millions more of innocent people may pay the price of your treason."

Although some argued, then and today, that hysteria had victimized the Rosenbergs, efforts to prevent their execution failed. In 1953, they were put to death, but anticommunism continued unabated.

When the Republicans won control of the Senate in 1952, McCarthy's power grew. He became chairman of the Government Operations Committee and head of its Permanent Investigations Subcommittee. He now had a stronger base and two dedicated assistants, Roy Cohn and G. David Schine. Together in early 1953, Cohn and Schine went off to Europe on a whirlwind tour of American information cen-

*The Permanent Investigations Subcommittee was headed by Joseph McCarthy (second from left).*

ters, where they briefly inspected books and articles and badgered overseas librarians to begin removing items from the shelves.

As McCarthy's anti-Communist witch-hunt continued, Eisenhower became uneasy. He disliked the senator but, recognizing his popularity, was reluctant to challenge him. Once in office, Ike told associates, when it was suggested that he confront McCarthy directly, "I will not get in the gutter with that guy." At the height of his influence, polls showed that McCarthy had half the public behind him, with far fewer people opposed. With the country so inclined, Eisenhower voiced his disapproval quietly and privately.

With the help of Cohn and Schine, McCarthy pushed on, and finally he pushed too hard. In 1953, the army drafted Schine and then refused to allow the preferential treatment that Cohn insisted his colleague deserved. Angered, McCarthy began to investigate army security and even top-level army leaders themselves. When the army charged that McCarthy was going too far, the Senate began to investigate the complaint.

The Army-McCarthy hearings began in April 1954 and lasted 36 days. Televised to a fascinated nationwide audience, they demonstrated the power of TV to shape people's opinions. Americans saw McCarthy's savage tactics on screen. He came across to viewers as irresponsible and destructive, particularly in contrast to Boston lawyer Joseph Welch, who argued the army's case with quiet eloquence.

When the hearings were over, McCarthy's mystical appeal was shattered. He had been challenged, and the challenger survived. In broad daylight, before a national television audience, his ruthless tactics no longer made sense. The Senate finally summoned the courage to condemn him for his conduct. Conservatives there turned against McCarthy because by attacking Eisenhower and the army, he was no longer limiting his venom to Democrats and liberals. Although McCarthy remained in office, his movement was spent. Three years later, at the age of 48, he died, a broken man.

Yet for a time he had exerted a powerful hold in the United States. "To many Americans," radio commentator Fulton Lewis, Jr., said, "Mc-

Carthyism is Americanism." Seizing upon the frustrations and anxieties of the Cold War, McCarthy struck a resonant chord. As his appeal grew, he put together a following that included both lower-class ethnic groups who responded to the charges against established elites and conservative midwestern Republicans. But his real power base was the Senate, where, particularly after 1952, conservative Republicans saw McCarthy as a means of reasserting their own authority. For the most part, his dominance rested on his colleagues' perception of his strength. Some members of both parties spoke out against him, but most did not. His crusade thus encouraged, McCarthy pressed on until he went too far.

### The Casualties of Fear

As a result of the anti-Communist crusade, a pervasive sense of suspicion permeated American society. In the late 1940s and early 1950s, it no longer seemed safe to dissent. Civil servants, government workers, academics, and actors all came under attack and found that the right of due process often evaporated as the Cold War Red Scare gained ground. Old China hands lost their positions in the diplomatic services, and social justice legislation faltered.

There were countless examples of the impact of this paranoia on American life. In New York, subway workers were fired when they refused to answer questions about their own political actions and beliefs. In Seattle, a fire department officer who denied current membership in the Communist party but refused to speak of his past was dismissed just 40 days before he reached the 25 years of service that would have given him retirement benefits. Navajos in Arizona and New Mexico, facing starvation in the bitter winter of 1947–1948, were denied government relief because of charges that their communal way of life was communistic and therefore un-American. Black artist Paul Robeson, who along with W. E. B. Du Bois criticized American foreign policy, was accused of Communist leanings, found few opportunities to perform, and eventually, like Du Bois, lost his passport.

Then there was Val Lorwin, introduced at

the beginning of the chapter, who suffered through repeated hearings and trials on the basis of malicious and unsubstantiated accusations that threatened to destroy his career. Lorwin was named on one of McCarthy's famous lists, but like so many others, he was really a victim of the larger anti-Communist crusade. He faced the same hurdles others encountered. Denials under oath made no difference. An adequate defense was almost impossible to mount. The charges themselves were often enough to smear a person, regardless of whether they were true or false. Lorwin weathered the storm and was finally vindicated, but others were less lucky. They were the unfortunate victims as the United States became consumed by the passions of the Cold War.

## Major Events of the Cold War

| YEAR | EVENT | EFFECT |
|---|---|---|
| 1946 | Winston Churchill's "Iron Curtain" speech | First Western "declaration" of the Cold War. |
|  | George F. Kennan's long telegram | Spoke of Russian insecurity and the need for containment. |
| 1947 | George F. Kennan's article signed "Mr. X" | Elaborated on arguments in the telegram. |
|  | Truman Doctrine | Provided economic and military aid to Greece and Turkey. |
|  | Federal Employee Loyalty Program | Sought to root out subversion in the U.S. government. |
|  | HUAC investigation of the motion picture industry | Sought to expose Communist influences in the movies. |
| 1948 | Marshall Plan | Provided massive American economic aid in rebuilding postwar Europe. |
|  | Berlin airlift | Brought in supplies when Russia closed off land access to the divided city. |
| 1949 | NATO formed | Created a military alliance to withstand a possible Russian attack. |
|  | First Russian atomic bomb | Ended the American nuclear monopoly. |
|  | Communist victory in China | Made American's fearful of the worldwide spread of communism. |
| 1950 | Alger Hiss convicted | Seemed to bear out Communist danger at home. |
|  | Joseph McCarthy makes first charges | Launched aggressive anti-Communist campaign in the United States. |
|  | NSC-68 | Called for vigilance and increased military spending to counter the Communist threat. |
|  | Outbreak of Korean War | North Korean invasion of South Korea viewed as part of a Russian conspiracy. |
| 1953 | Armistice in Korea | Brought little change after years of bitter fighting. |
| 1954 | Vietnamese victory over French at Dien Bien Phu | Early triumph for nationalism in Southeast Asia. |
|  | Army-McCarthy hearings | Brought downfall of Joseph McCarthy. |

## CONCLUSION: The Cold War in Perspective

The Cold War was the greatest single force affecting American society in the decade and a half after World War II. Tensions grew throughout the postwar years as a bitter standoff between the United States and the Soviet Union emerged. What caused the Cold War? Historians have long differed over the question of where responsibility should be placed. In the early years after the Second World War, policymakers and other commentators justified the American stance as a bold and courageous effort to meet the Communist threat. Later, particularly in the 1960s, as the public started to have doubts about the course of American foreign policy, revisionist historians began to argue that American policy was misguided, insensitive to Soviet needs, and at least a contributing factor to the worsening frictions. As with most historical questions, there are no easy answers, but both sides need to be weighed.

The Cold War stemmed in part from an American vision of the way the world should be. That vision involved peace and prosperity for all, with the United States leading the way. The American view, so eager and hopeful, helped to put the nation on a collision course with nations having a different vision of what the postwar world should be like and with anticolonial movements in Third World countries around the globe. When challenged, Americans proved ready, even eager, to contain communism, just as George Kennan had demanded, to preserve their version of a safe and stable order. The Cold War, with its profound effects at home and abroad, was the unfortunate result.

## Recommended Reading

A number of outstanding books deal with the background and development of the Cold War. Walter La Feber, *America, Russia, and the Cold War, 1945–1980* (4th ed., 1980) is the best brief account of the Cold War from beginning to end. John Lewis Gaddis, *The United States and the Origins of the Cold War, 1941–1947* (1972) is a well-argued and readable examination of the tension that culminated in the breakdown of relations between the United States and the Soviet Union. Thomas G. Patterson, *On Every Front: The Making of the Cold War* (1979) is a perceptive essay on foreign policy in the Cold War years. Thomas H. Etzold and John Lewis Gaddis, *Containment: Documents on American Policy and Strategy, 1945–1950* (1978) is an outstanding collection of the major documents of the early Cold War years.

For foreign policy in the Eisenhower period, the best books are Townsend Hoopes, *The Devil and John Foster Dulles* (1973), a searching examination of the secretary of state, and Robert A. Divine, *Eisenhower and the Cold War* (1981), a brief but sympathetic account of the president's efforts.

On the Korean War, David Rees, *Korea: The Limited War* (1964) gives a good assessment of the major foreign conflict in the 1950s. James A. Michener, *The Bridges at Toko-Ri* (1953) is a contemporary novel that provides a sense of the frustrations during the war.

On the anti-Communist crusade, Richard H. Rovere, *Senator Joe McCarthy* (1960) is a short and readable account of McCarthy and his methods. Robert Griffith, *The Politics of Fear: Joseph R. McCarthy and the Senate* (1970) is a perceptive analysis of McCarthy's position of power in the Senate and the forces that brought him down. Thomas C. Reeves, *The Life and Times of Joe McCarthy: A Biography* (1982) is a full-scale treatment of the anti-Communist leader. David M. Oshinsky, *A Conspiracy So Immense: The World of Joe McCarthy* (1983) is a vivid examination of McCarthy and his times. See also Allen Weinstein, *Perjury: The Hiss-Chambers Case* (1978) and Ronald Radash and Joyce Milton, *The Rosenberg File: A Search For Truth* (1984).

## TIME LINE

| | | | |
|---|---|---|---|
| 1945 | Yalta Conference<br>Roosevelt dies; Harry Truman becomes<br>  president<br>Potsdam Conference | 1950 | *(continued)*<br>McCarran Internal Security Act |
| 1946 | American Plan for control of atomic<br>  energy fails<br>Atomic Energy Act<br>Iran crisis<br>Churchill's "iron curtain" speech | 1950–1953 | Korean War |
| | | 1951 | Japanese-American Treaty<br>*Dennis* v. *United States* |
| 1947 | Truman Doctrine<br>Marshall Plan launched<br>Federal Employee Loyalty Program<br>House Un-American Activities<br>  Committee (HUAC) investigates the<br>  movie industry | 1952 | Dwight D. Eisenhower elected president<br>McCarthy heads Senate Permanent<br>  Investigations Subcommittee |
| | | 1953 | Stalin dies; Krushchev consolidates<br>  power<br>East Germans stage anti-Soviet<br>  demonstrations<br>Shah of Iran returns to power in<br>  CIA-supported coup |
| 1948 | Berlin airlift<br>Israel created by UN<br>Hiss-Chambers case<br>Truman reelected president | 1954 | Fall of Dien Bien Phu ends French<br>  control of Indochina<br>Geneva Conference<br>Guatemalan government overthrown<br>  with CIA help<br>Mao's forces shell Quemoy and Matsu<br>Army-McCarthy hearings |
| 1949 | Soviet Union tests atomic bomb<br>North Atlantic Treaty Organization<br>  (NATO) established<br>George Orwell publishes *Nineteen<br>  Eighty-four*<br>Mao Zedong's forces win Chinese civil<br>  war; Jiang Jieshi flees to Taiwan | | |
| | | 1956 | Suez incident<br>Hungarian "freedom fighters"<br>  suppressed<br>Eisenhower reelected |
| 1950 | Truman authorizes development of the<br>  hydrogen bomb<br>Alger Hiss convicted<br>Joseph McCarthy's Wheeling speech on<br>  subversion | 1957 | Russians launch *Sputnik* satellite |
| | | 1958 | U.S. troops sent to support Lebanese<br>  government |
| | | 1959 | Castro deposes Batista in Cuba |

# CHAPTER 28
## THE DREAMS OF POSTWAR AMERICA

Ray Kroc, an ambitious salesman, headed toward San Bernardino, California, on a business trip in 1954. For more than a decade he had been selling "multimixers"—stainless steel machines that could make six milkshakes at once—to restaurants and other eating establishments around the United States. On this trip he was particularly interested in checking out a hamburger stand run by Richard and Maurice McDonald, who had bought eight of his "contraptions" and could therefore make 48 shakes at the same time.

Always eager to increase sales, Kroc wanted to see the McDonalds' operation for himself. The 52-year-old son of Slavic parents had sold everything from real estate to radio time to paper cups before peddling the multimixers but had enjoyed no stunning success. Yet he was still on the alert for the key to the fortune that was part of the American dream. As he watched the lines of people at the San Bernardino McDonald's, the answer seemed at hand.

The McDonald brothers sold only standard hamburgers and french fries, but they had developed a system that worked exceedingly well. It was fast, efficient, and clean. It drew on the automobile traffic that moved along Route 66. And it was profitable indeed. Sensing the possibilities, Kroc proposed that the two owners open other establishments as well. When they balked, he negotiated a 99-year contract that allowed him to sell the fast-food idea and the name—and their golden arches design—wherever he could.

On April 15, 1955, Kroc opened his first McDonald's in Des Plaines, a suburb of Chicago. Three months later, he sold his first franchise in Fresno, California, and others soon followed. Kroc scouted out new locations, almost always on highway "strips," persuaded people to put up the capital, and provided them with specifications guaranteed to ensure future success. For his efforts, he received a percentage of the gross take.

From the start, Kroc insisted on rigid standardization. Every McDonald's was the same—from the two functional arches supporting the glass enclosure that housed the kitchen and take-out window to the single arch near the road bearing a sign indicating how many 15-cent hamburgers had already been sold. All menus and prices were exactly the same, and Kroc demanded that everything from hamburger size to cooking time be constant. He insisted, too, that the establishments be clean. No pinball games or cigarette machines were permitted; the premium was on a good hamburger, quickly served, at a nice place.

Kroc had tremendous drive. He was fond of Calvin Coolidge's dictum—"Press on. Nothing in the world can take the place of persistence"—and it soon appeared in McDonald's offices everywhere. Kroc was interested in expanding rapidly. He believed that "when you're green, you're growing; when you're ripe, you rot." As far as he was concerned, he had only just begun.

McDonald's, of course, was an enormous success. In 1962, total sales exceeded $76 million. In 1964, before the company had been in operation ten years, it had sold over 400 million hamburgers and 120 million pounds of french fries. By the end of the next year, there were 710 McDonald's stands in 44 states. In 1974, only 20 years after Kroc's vision of the hamburger's future, McDonald's did $2 billion worth of business. When Kroc died in 1984, 45 billion burgers had been sold at 7,500 outlets in 32 countries. Ronald McDonald, the clown who came to represent the company, became known to children around the globe after his Washington, D.C., debut in November 1963. When McDonald's began to advertise, it became the country's first restaurant to buy TV time. Musical slogans like "You deserve a break today" and "We do it all for you" became better known than some popular songs.

The tale of McDonald's is more than the simple success story of one firm. It provides an example of the development of new trends in the 1950s in the United States. Kroc capitalized on the changes of the automobile age. He understood that a restaurant, not in the city but along the highways, where it could draw on heavier traffic, had a better chance of success. The drive-in design, catering to a new and ever-growing clientele, soon became a common pattern.

He understood, too, how the franchise notion provided the key to rapid growth. He was not prepared to open up thousands of stands himself. Instead he sold the idea to eager entrepreneurs who stood to make sizable profits themselves as long as they remained a part of the larger whole. Not simply in the hamburger business but in numerous other industries as well, the franchise method helped create a nationwide web of firms.

Finally, Kroc sensed the importance of standardization and uniformity. He understood the mood of the time, the quiet conformity of Americans searching for success. The McDonald's image may have been monotonous, but that was part of its appeal. Customers always knew just what they would get wherever they found the golden arches. If the atmosphere was "bland", that too was deliberate. As Kroc said, "Our theme is kind of synonymous with Sunday school, the Girl Scouts, and the YMCA. McDonald's is clean and wholesome." It was a symbol of the age.

This chapter describes the changes in American society in the decade and a half after World War II. It shows how, for most Americans, this was a period of material comfort at home. After years of depression and war, they were ready to settle into new homes and cars and jobs, to enjoy all the trappings of the good life. Yet the chapter also shows that while millions of Americans led lives as sunny as McDonald's, the lives of others—blacks, Indians, and Hispanic-Americans—were still defined by the struggle for social justice and economic viability. Their experience suggested the limits of the postwar American dream.

*Americans knew just what they would get wherever the McDonald's golden arches were found.*

# DEMOBILIZATION AND ECONOMIC BOOM

In spite of Cold War anxieties, most Americans found security and stability after 1945. As servicemen came home and resumed their lives, the population grew and the economy boomed. Large corporations increasingly dominated the business world. New products flooded the market. There were affordable gadgets galore. For the growing middle class, the revival of prosperity conveyed the sense that all was well in the United States.

## Returning GIs

When World War II ended, American servicemen wanted to come home as quickly as possible. After peace was declared, politicians were deluged with messages. Families at home applied additional pressure. One serviceman's wife communicated her appeal through the Wyoming *State Tribune:* "He's fat, sway-backed, has several teeth missing and hobbles into age thirty-eight this month. . . . But he has a nice smile —with what teeth he has left—and I love him. So why don't you send him home?" A senator received more than 200 pairs of baby booties carrying notes that said, "I miss my daddy."

With that kind of pressure, the GIs did come home rapidly. The number of servicemen on active duty dropped from 12 million in 1945 to 3 million in mid-1946 to 1.6 million in mid-1947. The influx of ex-servicemen caused competition in the housing and employment markets and complicated the transition to civilian life.

The GI Bill of 1944 eased the process of reentering American society. The package of benefits it provided was far superior to that awarded veterans of any previous war. It gave returning GIs priority for many jobs and allowances while they looked for work. It promised loans so that they could establish small businesses and low-interest mortgages to purchase homes. Most important, it provided education benefits, up to $500 a year for college or trade school tuition and $75 a month for expenses.

Millions of Americans took advantage of the GI benefits. Almost half of 16 million eligible GIs went to school, and this caused the greatest wave of college building in American history. At the same time, the proportion of Americans owning their own homes soared, from 45 percent in 1940 to 65 percent in 1960. The postwar boom was partly a result of the provisions of the GI Bill, and it helped millions of families move into the middle class.

## The Peacetime Economy

Americans in the aftermath of war, realizing that only wartime spending had ended the Depression, feared a postwar collapse. When *Fortune* magazine took a poll of businessmen, it discovered that 58 percent of them anticipated the return of hard times.

Inflation soon caused concern. While Americans wanted to keep prices under control, they also wished to end wartime restrictions. Rationing, imposed by the Office of Price Administration (OPA) during the war, kept price levels stable but was often frustrating. As Sidney W. May, a New York businessman, protested, "My Dear President: With so many automobiles around, how did they gather so many horses asses and put them in the OPA?" With consumer goods initially in short supply, the administration feared that if controls were abandoned too quickly, prices would soar.

In 1946, an increasingly conservative Congress extended the OPA's authority for another year but stripped it of enforcement powers. Truman vetoed the bill and left the country without any control mechanism. Almost immediately, prices rose. Within a month, the cost-of-living index was up 6 points, and consumers began to demand action.

In Princeton, New Jersey, housewives calling themselves the Militant Marketers boycotted stores charging inflated prices. In Detroit, auto workers shut down production lines for a day and congregated in Cadillac Square to protest. Eventually Congress passed a weak bill to stem the tide, but the damage had already been done. A year and a half after the end of the war, the consumer price index was up almost 25 percent. One critic tartly observed that the OPA name and acronym should be changed to the Office for Cessation of Rationing and Priorities, or OCRAP.

Working-class Americans found the transition to a peacetime economy as difficult as they had in the past (see Chapter 23). Massive layoffs left 2.7 million workers without jobs by March 1946. Wage issues were also unresolved. After the wartime years of restraint, workers wanted pay increases they regarded as long overdue. Furthermore, many more of them belonged to unions. The percentage of nonagricultural workers who were union members rose from 13 percent in 1935 to 27 percent in 1940 and to 35 percent by 1945. When wage demands were refused, millions of workers walked out. In 1946, some 4.6 million workers marched on picket lines, more than had turned out ever before in the history of the United States. They struck in the automobile, steel, and electrical industries. The most serious trouble came with the railroads and soft-coal mines.

The railroad problem came to a head in the spring of 1946. When union leaders rejected an arbitrated settlement and set a strike date, Truman told them, "If you think I'm going to sit here and let you tie up this whole country, you're crazy as hell." When that blunt approach failed to work, the president asked Congress for the power to draft strikers into the armed forces if their actions caused a national emergency. Questioned about the constitutionality of his proposal, he said, "We'll draft 'em first and think about the law later." Although a settlement was reached, Truman still pushed for his retaliatory draft. Though the House of Representatives went along, cooler heads in the Senate allowed the plan to die.

The coal miners, led by John L. Lewis, the United Mine Workers' arrogant and defiant head, went out on strike in April 1946, accepted a settlement, then backed out of it. Determined to break the strike, Truman obtained a court injunction, which Lewis defied. Both leader and union were cited for contempt of court. Eventually Lewis was fined $10,000 and the union $3.5 million. The disgruntled workers returned to the mines, but Truman's bold actions alienated many working-class Americans. Labor had been a major segment of the Democratic coalition

under Roosevelt in the 1930s. Now that loyalty began to wane.

The strikers had problems enough of their own. Steve Hutchinson, a semiskilled operator working for U.S. Steel in Pittsburgh, was anxious about giving up a sure wage in the hope of getting a larger paycheck. But he went out in 1946 with the rest of the union. Food was sometimes scarce. His wife would "buy a big old soup bone, something with just a small bit of meat on it, and boil it in a pot of white beans. That was lunch and dinner and maybe lunch the next day. Day-old bread, no sugar in the coffee, hamburger when we had meat, which wasn't often. I even gave up cigarettes, and me a two-pack-a-day man." But it turned out to be worth it when the union won a favorable settlement.

For all the early postwar difficulties, it was a time of hope and high expectations for most Americans. Charles Lehman, a veteran from Missouri, later recalled, "I was a twenty-one-year-old lieutenant with a high school education, and my only prewar experience was as a stock boy in a grocery store. But on V-J day, I *knew* it was only a matter of time before I was rich—or well-off, anyway." In the postwar years, hopes triumphed over fears as the economy boomed.

The statistical evidence of economic success was impressive. The gross national product (GNP) jumped from just over $200 billion in 1940 to around $300 billion in 1950 and by 1960 had climbed above $500 billion. Per capita income rose from $2,100 in 1950 to $2,435 in 1960. Almost 60 percent of all families in the country were now part of the middle class, a dramatic change from the class structure of nineteenth- and early twentieth-century America. With real purchasing power rising by 22 percent between 1946 and 1960, families had far more discretionary income—money to satisfy wants as well as needs—than before. At the end of the Great Depression, fewer than one-quarter of all households had any discretionary income; in 1960, three of every five did.

The United States, which produced half the world's goods, was providing new products that average Americans, unlike their parents, could afford. Higher real wages allowed people across social classes to buy consumer goods, and that consumer power, in contrast to the underconsumption of the 1920s and 1930s, spurred the economy. In the words of one government official, Adolf A. Berle, Jr., Americans were caught up in a spirit of "galloping capitalism."

The automobile industry was a key part of the economic boom. Just as cars and roads transformed America in the 1920s when mass production came of age, so they contributed to the transformation three decades later. Limited to the production of military vehicles during World War II, the auto industry expanded dramatically in the postwar period. Two million cars were made in 1946, four times as many in 1955. Customers now chose from a wide variety of engines, colors, and optional accessories. Fancy grills and tail fins distinguished each year's models.

## Weekly Earnings of Manufacturing Workers

| YEAR | INDEX OF AVERAGE WEEKLY EARNINGS OF WORKERS IN MANUFACTURING | INDEX OF REAL AVERAGE WEEKLY EARNINGS OF WORKERS IN MANUFACTURING |
|------|------|------|
| 1940 | 21.9 | 53.1 |
| 1941 | 25.8 | 59.3 |
| 1942 | 31.9 | 66.3 |
| 1943 | 37.6 | 73.5 |
| 1944 | 40.1 | 77.3 |
| 1945 | 38.6 | 72.8 |
| 1946 | 38.2 | 66.2 |
| 1947 | 43.5 | 66.0 |
| 1948 | 47.1 | 66.4 |
| 1949 | 47.8 | 68.0 |
| 1950 | 51.6 | 72.8 |
| 1951 | 56.3 | 73.5 |
| 1952 | 59.2 | 75.5 |
| 1953 | 62.4 | 79.0 |
| 1954 | 62.6 | 78.9 |
| 1955 | 66.4 | 84.3 |
| 1956 | 69.6 | 86.8 |
| 1957 | 71.7 | 86.4 |
| 1958 | 72.7 | 85.2 |
| 1959 | 76.8 | 89.3 |
| 1960 | 78.1 | 89.5 |

*Note:* 1967 = 100
**Source:** U.S. Bureau of Labor Statistics.

The development of a massive interstate highway system also stimulated auto production. Rather than encourage the growth of a mass transit system, the Eisenhower administration underscored the American commitment to the car. Through the Interstate Highway Act of 1956 it provided $26 billion, the largest public works expenditure in American history, to build over 40,000 miles of federal highways, linking all parts of the United States.

Though highways added to the problem of pollution and triggered urban flight, the interstate complex was hailed as a key to the country's material development. Justified in part on the grounds that it would make evacuation quicker in the event of nuclear attack, the highway system made its proponents proud. In his memoirs, Eisenhower wrote:

> The total pavement of the system would make a parking lot big enough to hold two-thirds of all the automobiles in the United States. The amount of concrete poured to form these roadways would build . . . six sidewalks to the moon. . . . More than any single action by the

*Widening and improvement of existing routes was a small part of the massive interstate highway program funded by Congress in 1956.*

government since the end of the war, this one would change the face of America.

## The Baby Boom

Population growth was one clear indication of prosperity's return. During the Great Depression, the birthrate had dropped to an all-time low of 19 births per 1,000 population as hard times obliged people to delay marriage and parenthood. As the Second World War boosted the economy, the birthrate began to rise again. Some experts questioned whether the trend was a long-term one, and the Census Bureau cautiously claimed that it was at least partly due to "occasional furloughs," but in fact a real shift was under way.

The birthrate soared in the postwar years as millions of Americans began families. The "baby boom" peaked in 1957, with a rate of more than 25 births per 1,000. In that year, 4.3 million babies were born, one every seven seconds. While the population growth of 19 million in the 1940s was double the rise of the decade before, that increase paled against the increase in the 1950s, which totaled 29 million.

The effects of the baby boom were visible everywhere. There was Monroe Park, a community of 95 house trailers for veterans and their families at the University of Wisconsin. It was called the "state's most fertile five acres." In one week alone in 1947, five families had babies.

## Birth and Population Rates, 1900–1960

*Source:* U.S. Bureau of the Census.

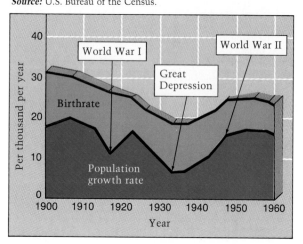

Similar fertility was evident in communities throughout the United States.

The rising birthrate was the dominant factor affecting population growth, but the death rate was also declining. Miracle drugs, such as streptomycin and aureomycin, played a large part in curing illnesses attacking all ages, especially the young. Life expectancy rose: midway through the 1950s, the average was 70 years for whites and 64 for blacks, compared to 55 for whites and 45 for blacks in 1920.

The baby boom had a powerful impact on family patterns and material needs. With the two-child family no longer the norm, growing numbers of youngsters had to be cared for by their parents and by society as a whole. Many women who had taken jobs during the war now left the work force to raise their children and care for their homes. The demand grew for diaper services and baby foods. When they entered school, the members of the baby boom generation strained the educational system. Between 1946 and 1956, enrollment in grades 1 through 8 soared from 20 million to 30 million. Since school construction had slowed during the Depression and had virtually halted during the Second World War, classrooms were needed. Teachers, too, were in short supply.

## Population Shifts and the New Suburbs

As Americans became more populous, they also became more mobile. For many generations, lower-class Americans had been the most likely to move; now geographic mobility spread to the middle class. Each year in the 1950s, over a million farmers left their farms in search of new employment. Other Americans picked up stakes and headed on as well. Some moved to look for better jobs. Others, like Bob Moses of Baltimore, simply wandered a while after returning home from the war and then settled down. Moses, traveling in a 1937 Chevrolet with some high school friends, was going "nowhere in particular, just roaming. We'd see a kink in a river on the map, and head there." After regimented military life, it was good to be free.

The war had produced increasing movement, most of it westward, as people gravitated toward the cities where shipyards, airplane factories, and other industrial plants were located.

After the war, that migration pattern persisted, as the West and the Southwest continued to grow. Sun Belt cities like Houston, Albuquerque, Tucson, and Phoenix underwent phenomenal expansion. The population of Phoenix soared from 65,000 in 1940 to 439,000 in 1960. In the 1950s, Los Angeles pulled ahead of Philadelphia as the third largest city in the United States. One-fifth of all the growth in the period took place in California's promised land. By 1963, California had passed New York as the nation's most populous state.

After the war, another form of movement became even more important in the United States. Although the proportion of Americans defined as residents of metropolitan areas increased from 51 to 63 percent between 1940 and 1960, this disguised another shift. Millions of white Americans fled from the inner city to suburban fringes, intensifying a movement that had begun before the war. Fourteen of the nation's largest cities actually lost population in that decade, including New York, Boston, Chicago, Philadelphia, and Detroit. As central cities became places where poor nonwhites clustered, new urban and racial problems emerged.

For people of means, cities were places to work and then to leave at five o'clock. In Man-

| METROPOLITAN AREAS | YEAR 1920 | 1940 | 1960 | 1980 |
|---|---|---|---|---|
| Los Angeles | 879 | 2,916 | 6,039 | 7,478 |
| San Diego | 74 | 289 | 1,033 | 1,862 |
| Phoenix | 29 | 186 | 664 | 1,509 |
| Tucson | 20 | 37 | 266 | 531 |
| Dallas | 185 | 527 | 1,084 | 2,430 |
| Houston | 168 | 529 | 1,418 | 2,905 |
| San Antonio | 191 | 338 | 716 | 1,072 |
| New Orleans | 398 | 552 | 907 | 1,256 |
| Atlanta | 249 | 559 | 1,017 | 2,030 |
| Miami | 30 | 268 | 935 | 1,626 |

POPULATION (in thousands)

| 0–250 | 250–1,000 | 1,000–3,000 | Over 3,000 |
|---|---|---|---|

**Growth of Sun Belt Cities, 1920–1980**
*Source:* U.S. Bureau of the Census.

**Population Shifts, 1940 to 1950**

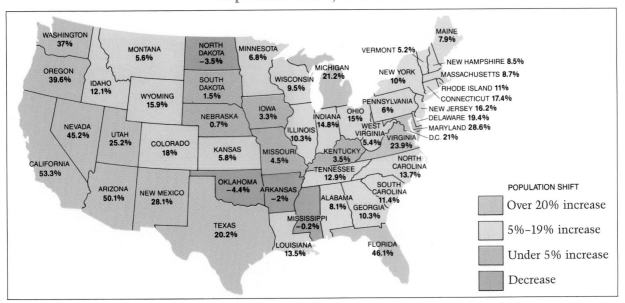

POPULATION SHIFT
Over 20% increase
5%–19% increase
Under 5% increase
Decrease

hattan, south of City Hall, the noontime population of 1.5 million dropped to 2,000 during the night. The outlying regions, writer John Brooks argued, were "draining downtown of its nighttime population, except for night watchmen and derelicts; it was becoming a part-time city, tidally swamped with bustling humanity every weekday morning when the cars and commuter trains arrived, and abandoned again at nightfall when the wave sucked back—left pretty much to thieves, policemen, and rats."

As the cities declined, the suburbs blossomed. If the decade after World War I had witnessed a rural-to-urban shift, the decades after World War II saw a reverse shift to the regions outside the central cities, usually accessible only by car. By the end of the 1950s, a third of all Americans resided in suburbs.

Americans moved to the suburbs to buy homes that would accommodate their larger families. The number of owner-occupied houses rose from 15.2 million in 1940 to 23.5 million ten years later. Often rapidly constructed and overpriced, suburban tract houses provided the appearance of comfort and space and the chance to have at least one part of the American dream, a place of one's own. Set in developments with names like Scarborough Manor, Peppermill Village, and Woodbury Knoll, they seemed safe from the growing troubles of the cities, insulated from the difficulties of the world outside.

A key figure in the suburbanization movement was William J. Levitt, a builder eager to take a gamble and reap the rewards of a growing demand. Levitt, who had erected custom-built homes before, saw the advantages of mass production during World War II, when his firm put up dwellings for war workers. Aware that mortgage money was readily available as a result of the GI Bill, he felt that suburban development was a sure bet. But to cash in, Levitt knew he had to use new methods of construction.

Mass production was the key. Individually designed houses were a thing of the past, he believed. "The reason we have it so good in this country," he said, "is that we can produce lots of things at low prices through mass production." Houses were among them. Working on a careful schedule, Levitt's team brought precut and preassembled materials to each site, put them together, and then moved on to the next location.

As on an assembly line, tasks were broken down into individual steps. Groups of workers performed but a single job, moving from one tract to another.

Levitt proved that his system worked. Construction costs at Levittown, New York, a new community of 17,000 homes built in the late 1940s, were only $10 per square foot, compared to the $12 to $15 that was common elsewhere. The next Levittown appeared in Bucks County, Pennsylvania, several years after the first, and another went up in Willingboro, New Jersey, at the end of the 1950s. Having guessed right, Levitt provided a model for other developers.

Suburbanization changed the landscape of the United States. Huge tracts of land now contained acres of standardized squares, each with a house with a two-car garage and a manicured lawn. Woods disappeared, for it was cheaper to cut down all trees than to work around them. Folksinger Malvina Reynolds described the new developments she saw:

Little boxes on the hillside
Little boxes made of ticky tacky
Little boxes on the hillside
Little boxes all the same.
There's a green one and a pink one
And a blue one and a yellow one

*The step-by-step mass production of Levitt's housing can be seen in this 1957 view of the partially completed Bucks County tract.*

And they're all made out of ticky tacky
And they all look just the same.

As suburbs flourished, businesses followed their customers out of the cities. Shopping centers led the way. At the end of World War II, there were eight, but the number multiplied rapidly in the 1950s. In a single three-month period in 1957, 17 new centers opened; by 1960, there were 3,840 in the United States. Developers like Don M. Casto, who built the Miracle Mile near Columbus, Ohio, understood the importance of location as Americans moved out of the cities. "People have path-habits," he said, "like ants."

Shopping centers catered to the suburban clientele and transformed consumer patterns. They offered easy parking and convenient late-evening hours. Suburban dwellers could remain entirely insulated from the cities if they wished, but their new shopping patterns undermined the downtown department stores.

## Corporate Change

In the years after 1945, the major corporations increased their hold on the American economy. World War II had encouraged the growth of big business. Antitrust activity was suspended in the interest of wartime production, while government contracts encouraged expansion. During the war, two-thirds of all military contracts were awarded to 100 firms, and half of all contracts went to three dozen giants. Tremendous industrial concentration occurred during the war. In 1940, some 100 companies accounted for 30 percent of all manufacturing output in the United States. Three years later, that figure had risen to 70 percent.

Concentration continued after the war. There had been several waves of mergers in the twentieth century. Another wave took place in the 1950s, making oligopoly—domination of a given industry by a few firms—a dominant feature of American capitalism. At the same time, the economy saw the development of conglomerates—firms that diversified with holdings in a variety of industries. That process began in the 1950s and continued thereafter.

Expansion took other forms as well. Even as the major corporations expanded, so too did smaller franchise operations like McDonald's, Kentucky Fried Chicken, and Burger King. Other firms, providing services rather than products, changed the shape of the American work force. Fewer Americans worked in manufacturing jobs, a reversal of a 150-year trend, and the growth of jobs in the service sector also reduced the number of Americans engaged in farming. Offices, hospitals, restaurants, computer companies, and a variety of other firms employed people who performed services increasingly in demand in a highly sophisticated economy.

Huge corporations became even more impersonal than before. In many firms, the bureaucratic style predominated, with white-collar employees seemingly dressing, thinking, and

## Shifts in Population Distribution, 1940–1960

*Source:* U.S. Bureau of the Census.

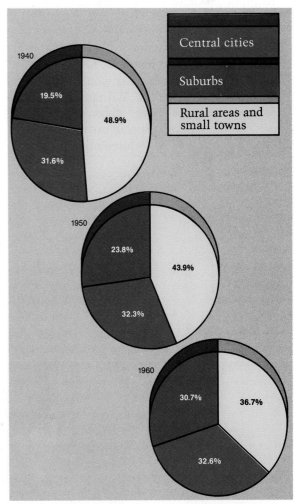

acting the same (as depicted in a popular novel and film of the 1950s, *The Man in the Gray Flannel Suit*). Money and material well-being were the prizes of corporate life. Corporations provided a secure working atmosphere and a comfortable leisure environment. The country clubs built by IBM or the model homes constructed by Richfield Oil were perquisites that kept employees loyal to their firms.

White-collar employees paid a price for the comfort. Corporations, preaching that teamwork was far more important than individuality, indoctrinated employees and conveyed the appropriate standards of conduct. RCA issued company neckties. IBM had training programs to teach employees the company line. Some large firms even set up training programs to show wives how their own behavior could help their husbands' careers. Just as product standardization became increasingly important, individual acceptance of company norms became necessary. "Personal views can cause a lot of trouble," an oil company recruiting pamphlet noted, suggesting that business favored moderate or conservative ideas that would not threaten the system. Author William H. Whyte described young executives whose ultimate goal was "belongingness." Social critic C. Wright Mills observed, "When white-collar people get jobs, they sell not only their time and energy but their personalities as well."

## Technology Supreme

Rapid technological change occurred in the postwar years. Some of the developments—the use of atomic energy, for example—flowed directly from war research. Others emerged from the research and development activities sponsored by big business.

Computers led the way. A German engineer, Konrad Zuse, had devised an electromagnetic computer before the war. Supported by IBM, Howard H. Aiken, a young professor of mathematics at Harvard, was not far behind. The Mark I computer was switched on in 1943. It stood 8 feet high and 55 feet long and contained about a million components.

Other computational machines soon followed. In 1946, the Electronic Numerical Integrator and Calculator, called ENIAC, was built at the University of Pennsylvania. It contained 18,000 electronic tubes and required tremendous amounts of electricity and special cooling. But the machine worked. In an advertised test, it set out to multiply 97,367 by itself 5,000 times. A reporter pushed the necessary button, and the task was completed in less than half a second.

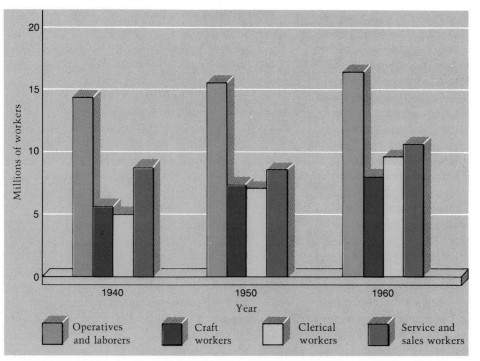

**Occupational Distribution, 1940–1960**

*Source:* U.S. Department of Labor.

Yet even that machine was limited. Its tubes occasionally failed, it had a small memory, and it could perform only one task at a time. Mathematician John Von Neumann's system for storing instructions within the computer itself was the next step. As research continued, IBM, Bell Telephone, and Sperry-Rand all developed computers for business uses. But costs were high and components often unreliable. The computer seemed to be a specialized piece of equipment, intended only for companies with massive needs. The breakthrough came with the development of the transistor. In 1948, three scientists at Bell Laboratories created minuscule solid-state components that ended reliance on electronic tubes. Faster and more reliable, transistors became indispensable in the decade that followed.

The computer transformed American society as surely as industrialization had changed it a century before. It allowed for sophisticated forms of space exploration. Airlines, hotels, and other businesses computerized their reservation systems. Business accounting, inventory control, and even decision making began to rely on computers. Computer programmers and operators were in increasing demand. Computer technology also opened the way for change in other fields. Tiny transistors could power not only radios but miniature hearing aids that could be incorporated into the frame of a pair of eyeglasses. Stereophonic hi-fi sets, using new transistor components, could provide a better sound.

Americans continued their love affair with appliances and gadgets. By the end of the 1950s, most families had at least one automobile, as well as the staple appliances they had begun to purchase before—a refrigerator, a washing machine, a television, and a vacuum cleaner. Dozens of less essential items also became popular. There were electric can openers, electric pencil sharpeners, and electric toothbrushes. There were push-button phones and aerosol bombs, and automatic transmissions to take care of shifting car gears.

## Tempting the Consumer

Americans hungered for the new goods, but if and when demand faltered, a revitalized advertising industry was ready to persuade consumers that their needs were greater than they knew. Advertising had come of age in the 1920s, as businesses persuaded customers that only by buying new products could they attain status and satisfaction. Advertising faltered when the economy collapsed in the 1930s but began to revive during the war as firms sought to keep the public aware of consumer goods, even those in short supply. With the postwar boom, advertisers again began to hawk their wares.

Although marketing staffs of major firms maintained that the customer was supreme and made up his or her own mind, subtle manipulation was involved. Acquisitive desires were encouraged, with the means of gratification spelled out. One researcher for the J. Walter Thompson agency even quoted Benjamin Franklin, that apostle of thrift, to justify purchasing whenever possible: "Is not the hope of being one day able to purchase and enjoy luxuries a great spur to labor and industry? . . . May not luxury therefore produce more than it consumes, if, without such a spur, people would be, as they are naturally enough inclined to be, lazy and indolent?"

Motivational research became more sophisticated, uncovering new ways of persuading people to buy. Taking the place of radio, television played an important part in conveying the spirit of consumption to millions of Americans. Unlike radio, which could only describe new commodities, television could show them to consumers. Shows like "The Price Is Right" stressed consumption in direct ways: Contestants were awarded goods for quoting their correct retail price. Drawing on a talent that was sharpened in the shopping centers and department stores, the show encouraged the acquisition of ever more material goods.

If the appeal often seemed overdone, advertisers had their defenders too. Vance Packard argued in 1957 in his best-selling book *The Hidden Persuaders* that advertisers "fill an important and constructive role in our society. Advertising, for example, not only plays a vital role in promoting our economic growth but is a colorful, diverting aspect of American life; and many of the creations of ad men are tasteful, honest works of artistry." That may have been true of some ads, but others were garish and conveyed a sense of material wealth run amok.

With its emphasis on the benefits of consuming, the United States became, in economist John Kenneth Galbraith's phrase, "the affluent society." Americans had weathered the poverty and unemployment of the 1930s, made sacrifices during a long war, and now intended to enjoy their newfound abundance and leisure time. By 1950, most wage laborers worked a 40-hour week, and 60 percent of nonagricultural workers enjoyed paid vacations, whereas few had in 1930. Most Americans regarded all this as their due, sometimes neglecting to look beyond the immediate objects of their desire. The decade, journalist William Shannon wrote, was one of "self-satisfaction and gross materialism . . . . The loudest sound in the land has been the oink and grunt of private hoggishness . . . . It has been the age of the slob."

*Supermarkets burgeoning with convenience foods were an everyday manifestation of the 1950's consumer revolution.*

## CONSENSUS AND CONFORMITY

As the economy grew, an increasing sense of sameness pervaded middle-class society. This was the great age of conformity, when Americans of all social groups learned to emulate those around them rather than strike out on their own. Even children could not escape the homogenizing tendencies. Sociologist David Riesman pointed out that in the classic nursery rhyme "This Little Pig Went to Market," each pig went his own way. "Today, however, all little pigs go to market; none stay home; all have roast beef, if any do; and all say 'we-we.'"

### The Impact of Television

If stories helped indoctrinate children into society's basic norms, television played an even more important part. Developed commercially in the 1930s, television became a major influence on American life after World War II. In 1946, there were fewer than 17,000 sets; by 1949, some 250,000 a month were being bought; and by 1960, three-quarters of all American families owned at least one set. In 1955, the average American family had the set on four to five hours each day. Some studies predicted that an American student, on graduating from high school, would have spent 11,000 hours in class

and 15,000 hours before the "tube." Viewers were bombarded by the advertising images exposing them to the luxury items needed for the good life, even as they watched the often insipid shows that dominated the medium in its early days.

Young Americans grew up to the strains of "Winky Dink and You," "The Mickey Mouse Club," and "Howdy Doody Time" in the 1950s. Older viewers attended to situation comedies

### Households Owning Radios and Televisions, 1940–1960

*Source:* U.S. Bureau of the Census.

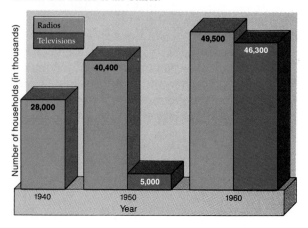

like "I Love Lucy" and "Father Knows Best" and live dramas such as "Playhouse 90." They watched Elvis Presley play his guitar and sing, and they danced to the rock and roll music played on "American Bandstand." Many of the programs aimed at children depicted violence and crime. Hopalong Cassidy was one of America's defenders who became a cult hero in his time. The gunslinging cowboy provided a role model that hundreds of American manufacturing firms capitalized on by making toy guns.

The youth of the 1950s grew up with a common, shared experience that others in the past had not known. Television, far more seductive with its visual imagery than radio, helped shape societal norms. Louis Kronenberger, a cultural critic, pointed out that whereas the automobile in the 1920s had taken Americans away from the home, the television set was bringing them back, but changing the very nature of the home in the process. In the past, he wrote, "where Mother and Father, Jane and John on their treks and travels exchanged pleasantries and ideas, they sit now for hours, side by side, often shoulder to shoulder, scarcely exchanging a glance. Or if they do address one another, they do so crossly, campaigning for this program or that."

## Conformity in School and Religious Life

The willingness to conform to group norms spread to colleges and universities, where students were cautious and sought security. They joined fraternities and sororities and engaged in panty raids and other pranks but took little interest in world affairs. "I observe," Yale President A. Whitney Griswold told a graduating class in 1950, "that you share the prevailing mood of the hour, which in your case consists of bargains privately struck with fate—on fate's terms."

Americans in the postwar years returned to their churches in record numbers. Church membership doubled between 1945 and 1970. In part, church attendance reflected a desire to challenge "godless communism" at the height of the Cold War (see Chapter 29); in part, it resulted from the power of suggestion that led Americans to do

*Billy Graham offered an appealingly traditional philosophy for those who questioned the morality of society's changes.*

what others did. Religion also seemed to reinforce the importance of family life. As one slogan put it, "The family that prays together stays together." Moreover, religion became increasingly appealing. Evangelist Billy Graham, often introduced as "a man with God's message for these crisis days," preached to millions at his revivals. He capitalized on the media, using radio, television, and film to spread his message. By the end of the 1950s, fully 95 percent of all Americans identified with some religious denomination.

Dwight D. Eisenhower reflected the national mood when he observed that "our government makes no sense unless it is founded in a deeply felt religious faith—and I don't care what it is." In 1954, Congress added the words "under God" to the pledge to the flag, and the next year voted to require the phrase "In God We Trust" on all American currency. Yet religion was often devoid of piety and doctrinal understanding. In one public opinion poll, 80 percent of the respondents indicated that the Bible was God's revealed word, but only 35 percent were able to name the four Gospels and over half were unable to name even one.

## Back to the Kitchen

World War II had interrupted traditional patterns of behavior for both men and women. As servicemen went overseas, women left their homes to work. After 1945, there was a period of adjustment as the men returned. In the 1950s, traditional gender roles were reaffirmed although, paradoxically, more women entered the work force than ever before.

Men, of course, were expected to go to school and then find jobs to support their families. Viewing themselves as the primary breadwinners, they expected their jobs to be waiting for them after the war. For women, the situation was more difficult. Many had enjoyed working during the war and were reluctant to retreat to the home, although they were persistently encouraged by the government and their employers to do so. In 1947, *Life* magazine ran a long photo essay called "The American Woman's Dilemma." It argued that women were caught in a conflict between the traditional expectation to stay home and the desire to have a paid job. A 1946 *Fortune* poll also captured the discontent of some women. Asked whether they would prefer to be born again as men or women, 25 percent of the women asked said they would prefer to be men. That dissatisfaction was strongest among white, well-educated, middle-class women, which was understandable since black and lower-class white women were usually required by their families' economic circumstances to continue working outside the home.

By the 1950s, doubts and questions had been mostly suppressed. The baby boom increased average family size and made the decision to remain home easier. The flight to the suburbs gave women more to do, and they settled into the routines of redecorating their homes and gardens and transporting children to and from activities and schools.

In 1956, when *Life* produced a special issue on women, the message differed strikingly from that of nine years earlier. Profiling Marjorie Sutton, the magazine spoke of the "Busy Wife's Achievements" as "Home Manager, Mother, Hostess, and Useful Civic Worker." Married at 16, Marjorie was now busy with the PTA, Campfire Girls, and charity causes. She cooked and sewed for her family, which included four children, supported her husband by entertaining 1,500 guests a year, and worked out on the trampoline "to keep her size 12 figure."

Marjorie Sutton reflected the widespread so-cial emphasis on marriage and home. Many women who went to college did so to find husbands; if this succeeded, they dropped out. Almost two-thirds of the women in college stopped before completing a degree, compared to less than half of the men. Women were expected to marry young, have children early, and support their husbands' careers. "Modern man needs an old-fashioned woman around the house," novelist Sloan Wilson asserted.

Despite the reaffirmation of the old ideology that a woman's place was in the home, the 1950s was a period of unnoticed but important change. Because the supply of single women workers was diminished by the low birthrate of the Depression years and by increased schooling and early marriage, older married women began entering the labor force in large numbers for the first time. In 1940, only 15 percent of American wives had jobs. By 1950, 21 percent were employed, and ten years later, the figure had risen to 30 percent. Moreover, married women now composed over half of all working women, a dramatic reversal of earlier patterns.

Although many working women were poor, divorced, or widowed, many came from the middle class. Their income helped their families acquire the desirable new products that were badges of middle-class status. They stepped into the new jobs created by economic expansion. Women clustered in office, sales, and service positions, occupations already defined as female. They and their employers considered their work subordinate to their primary role as wives and mothers. Comparatively few entered professions where they would have challenged traditional notions of woman's place. As *Life* magazine pointed out in 1956, "Household skills take her into the garment trades; neat and personable, she becomes office worker and sales lady; patient and dextrous, she does well on competitive, detailed factory work; compassionate, she becomes teacher and nurse."

Black women worked as always, but after the war they often lost the jobs they had won during the conflict. As the total percentage of women in the Detroit automobile industry dropped from 25 to 7.5, for example, jobs for black women nearly disappeared. Their median income at the end of the 1940s was less than half that of white women. Nor did they obtain white-collar work so easily as white women. But during the 1950s, they succeeded both in moving into white-collar positions and improving their income. By 1960, more than a third of all black women had clerical, sales, service, or professional jobs, and their paychecks were 70 percent of those of white women.

Despite the mixed character of women's experience, society at large continued to view women in traditional ways. The belief that women's main role was still at home justified paying them low wages and denying them promotions. Adlai Stevenson, Democratic presidential candidate in 1952 and 1956, defined their role in politics by telling a group of women that "the assignment for you, as wives and mothers, you can do in the living room with a baby in your lap or in the kitchen with a can opener in your hand." As in much of the nineteenth century, a woman was "to influence man and boy" in her "humble role of housewife."

Pediatrician Benjamin Spock agreed. In his enormously popular *Baby and Child Care* (1946), responsible more than any other book for the child-rearing patterns of the postwar generation, he advised mothers to stay at home with their children and not to work if they wanted to raise stable and secure youngsters.

Movies seized on popular stereotypes and dramatized them. Doris Day, with her charm and clean appearance, was a favorite heroine. In movie after movie, she showed how an attractive woman who played her cards right could land her man—the assumed goal of every woman.

Sexuality was a troublesome if compelling topic in the postwar years. In 1948, Alfred C. Kinsey's *Sexual Behavior in the Human Male* was published. Kinsey was an Indiana University zoologist who had previously studied the gall wasp. When asked to teach a course on marriage problems, he found little published material about human sexual activity and decided to collect his own. He compiled case histories of 5,300 white males, analyzed their personal backgrounds, and recorded patterns of sexual behavior.

Kinsey shocked the country with his statistics on premarital, extramarital, and otherwise illicit sexual activity. Sixty-seven percent of all males who went to college, he concluded, had engaged in sexual intercourse before marriage; 84 percent of those who went to high school but not beyond had done the same. Thirty-seven percent of the total male population had experienced some kind of overt homosexual activity. One out of every six farm boys in America had copulated with animals. Kinsey published a companion volume, *Sexual Behavior in the Human Female* (1953), that detailed many of the same sexual patterns. Although many denounced the books, both sold widely, for they opened the door to a subject that had previously been considered taboo.

Such interest in sexuality appeared in the fascination with sex goddesses like Marilyn Monroe. With her blonde hair, breathy voice, and raw sexuality, she seemed to personify the

*Sex goddesses of the screen—such as Marilyn Monroe, shown here in* Gentlemen Prefer Blondes*—represented the fantasies of American males in the family-oriented 1950s.*

forbidden side of the good life and became one of Hollywood's most popular stars. The images such film goddesses presented corresponded to male fantasies of women. As for these men's wives, they were expected to manage their suburban homes and to be cheerful and willing objects of their husbands' desire.

## Cultural Rebels

Not all Americans fit the stereotypes of the 1950s. Some were alienated from the culture and rebelled against its values. Even as young people struggled to meet the standards and expectations of their peers, they were intrigued by Holden Caulfield, the main figure in J. D. Salinger's popular novel, *Catcher in the Rye* (1951). Holden, a sensitive student at boarding school, felt surrounded by "phonies" who threatened individuality and independence. Holden's sad and ill-fated effort to preserve his own integrity in the face of pressures to conform aroused readers' sympathy and struck a resonant chord in them.

A group of writers, often called the "beat generation," espoused unconventional values in their stories, poems, and "happenings." Confronting apathy and conformity, they insisted there were alternatives. Stressing spontaneity and spirituality, they claimed that intuition was more important than reason, Eastern mysticism more valuable than Western faith. The "beats" went out of their way to challenge the norms of respectability. They rejected materialism, engaged in overt sexual activity designed to shock, and helped popularize marijuana.

Their literary work reflected their approach to life. Finding conventional academic forms confining, they rejected them. Jack Kerouac typed his best-selling novel *On the Road* (1957), describing freewheeling trips across country, on a 250-foot roll of paper. Lacking conventional punctuation and paragraph structure, the book was a paean to the free life the beats espoused.

Poet Allen Ginsberg, like Kerouac a Columbia University dropout, became equally well known for his poem "Howl." Written during one wild weekend in 1955 while Ginsberg was under the influence of drugs, the poem was a scathing critique of the modern, mechanized culture and its effects.

Reading the poem to a group of poets in San Francisco, Ginsberg bobbed and weaved as he communicated the electric rhythm of his verse. He became a celebrity when "Howl" appeared in print in 1956. The poem developed into a cult piece, particularly after the police seized it on the grounds that it was obscene. When the work survived a court test, national acclaim followed for Ginsberg. He and the other beats would furnish a model for rebellion in the 1960s.

The popularity of Salinger, Kerouac, and Ginsberg owed much to a revolution in book publishing and to the democratization of education that accompanied the program of GI educational benefits. More Americans than ever before acquired a taste for literature, and they found huge numbers of inexpensive books available because of the "paperback revolution." The paperback had been introduced in 1939, but it was not until after World War II that it began to dominate the book market. By 1965, readers could choose among some 25,000 titles, available not only in bookstores but in supermarkets, drugstores, and airplane terminals, and they purchased these cheap volumes at the rate of nearly 7 million copies per week.

The signs of cultural rebellion also appeared in popular music. Parents recoiled as their children flocked to hear a young Tennessee singer named Elvis Presley belt out "rock and roll" songs. Presley's black leather jacket and ducktail haircut became standard dress for rebellious male teenagers.

American painters, shucking off European influences that had shaped American artists for two centuries, also became a part of the cultural rebellion. They were led by Jackson Pollock and his "New York school." This group of artists discarded the easel, laid gigantic canvases on the floor, and then used trowels, putty knives, and sticks to lay on paint, glass shards, sand, and other materials in wild explosions of color. Known as abstract expressionists, these painters regarded the unconscious as the source of their artistic creations. "I am not aware of what is taking place [as I paint]," Pollock explained; "it is only after that I see what I have done." Like much of the literature of rebellion, abstract expressionism reflected the artist's alienation from a world becoming filled with nuclear threats, computerization, and materialism.

# DOMESTIC POLICY UNDER TRUMAN AND EISENHOWER

In the prosperous postwar era, two very different men exercised presidential leadership. Harry S Truman took the same aggressive stance at home as he adopted in foreign affairs. A conservative Congress, however, blocked him at every turn. His successor, Dwight D. Eisenhower, created a very different imprint. Genial and calm, the war hero conveyed to Americans the feeling that everything was all right.

## Postwar Public Policy

Even as he grappled with the immediate problems of postwar reconversion, Truman addressed broader questions. Like his predecessor, Franklin Roosevelt, he believed that the federal government should move toward defined economic and social goals. To that end, less than a week after the end of World War II, Truman called on Congress to pass legislation guaranteeing all Americans jobs, decent housing, educational opportunities, and a variety of other rights. His 21-point program, he contended, would produce stability and security in the postwar era. He wanted full-employment legislation, a higher minimum wage, greater unemployment compensation, and housing assistance. During the next ten weeks, Truman sent blueprints of further proposals to Congress, including health insurance and atomic energy legislation. This liberal program soon ran into fierce political opposition.

The debate surrounding the Employment Act of 1946 hinted at the fate of Truman's proposals. The Employment Act was a deliberate effort to apply the theory of English economist John Maynard Keynes to maintain economic equilibrium and prevent depression. The initial bill committed the government to maintaining full employment by monitoring the economy and taking remedial actions in case of decline. Those actions included tax cuts and spending programs to stimulate the economy and reduce unemployment.

Liberals hailed the measure, but business groups like the National Association of Manufacturers claimed that such government intervention would undermine free enterprise and move the United States one step closer to socialism. Congress cut the proposal to bits. As finally passed, the act created a Council of Economic Advisers to make recommendations to the president, who was to report annually on the state of the economy. But it stopped short of committing the government to using fiscal tools to maintain full employment when economic indicators turned downward. The act was only a modest continuation of New Deal attempts at economic planning.

## Truman Battles a Conservative Congress

As the midterm elections of 1946 approached, Truman and his supporters knew they were vulnerable. Many Democrats still pined for FDR, and when they questioned what Roosevelt would have done had he been alive, the standard retort was, "I wonder what Truman would do if he were alive." Often seeming like a petty, bungling administrator, Truman became the butt of countless political jokes. Support for Truman dropped from 87 percent of those polled after he assumed the presidency to 32 percent in November 1946. Gleeful Republicans asked the voters, "Had enough?"

The voters answered that they had. Republicans won majorities in both houses of Congress for the first time since the 1928 elections, and a majority of the governorships as well. In Atlantic City, New Jersey, a Republican candidate for justice of the peace who had died a week before the election was victorious in the sweep.

After the 1946 election, Truman faced an unsympathetic 80th Congress. Republicans and conservative Democrats, dominating both houses, sought to reverse the liberal policies of the Roosevelt years. Hoping to reestablish congressional authority and cut the power of the executive branch, they insisted on less government intervention in the business world and in private life. Their goals included tax reduction and curtailment of the privileged position they felt labor had come to enjoy.

When the new Congress met, it moved to cut federal spending and reduce taxes. Robert A.

One way to recover the past is through music. Popular songs not only provide insight into attitudes and beliefs but also quickly convey the mood and feelings of an era. Through their lyrics, songwriters express the hopes and fears of a people and the emotional tone of an age. Consider, for example, the powerful message conveyed in the Democratic party adoption of "Happy Days Are Here Again" as a campaign theme during the Great Depression. The decline of pop music and the rise of rock and roll in the 1950s tells historians a great deal about social moods and changes in that decade.

The pop music style of romantic ballads and novelty numbers with smooth singing and a quiet beat dominated the early 1950s. Popular songs such as "I Believe," "Young at Heart," and "Tennessee Waltz," sung by Frankie Laine, Frank Sinatra, and Patti Page, respectively, typified the musical tastes of young adults eager to establish a secure suburban family life in the aftermath of the upheavals of the Depression and World War II. The lyrics in these songs are bland, homey, and overly sentimental.

Contrasting with these syrupy ballads was the rhythm and blues performed by black artists for black audiences. A strong beat and mournful tone were the distinguishing marks of this music. The two styles not only had different beats and rhythms but also treated common themes, like love, in different ways. Pop artists sang of sentimental love, while rhythm and blues singers expressed emotional and physical love.

In the 1950s, the first baby-boom teenagers emerged with a distinctive musical taste and enough discretionary income to influence the growth of the popular music industry. No longer children and not yet adults, these affluent teenagers struggled to define themselves in the Eisenhower age of suburban conformity. At first they were drawn to the beat of rhythm and blues as a rebellion against the mellow pop music of their parents. As the teenage market grew, white groups began to imitate black rhythm-and-blues songs, as in the 1954 song "Sh-Boom," done originally by the Chords and remade by the Crew Cuts.

But teenage listeners became increasingly dissatisfied with these imitations and looked for a livelier type of music. They found it in rock and roll (the name referred to descriptions of sex in black music). One of the first rock hits was "Rock Around the Clock" by Bill Haley and the Comets, from the controversial movie about an urban high school, *Blackboard Jungle* (1955). Parents worried about the

*Paul Schutzer*, **Little Anthony**, *1958*

*Robert Kelley*, **Elvis Presley**, *1956*

influence this music would have on their children. Some thought rock music caused juvenile delinquency, while others worried about its origins in "race music" and its sexual suggestiveness.

It took a truck driver from Memphis, Elvis Presley, to turn rock and roll into virtually a teenage religion, giving it a preeminence in teenage culture it has yet to relinquish. Presley's sexy voice, gyrating hips, and other techniques borrowed from black singers helped make him the undisputed "king of rock." A multimedia blitz of movies, television, and radio helped to make songs like "Heartbreak Hotel," "Don't Be Cruel," and "Hound Dog" smash singles. Eighteen Presley hits sold more than a million copies in the last four years of the 1950s. Almost alone, Presley mobilized a whole new teenage record market, making himself a millionaire in the process. In 1956, teenagers bought 50 percent of all records, and in two years that figure had risen to 70 percent. The popularity of Elvis Presley helped bring black singers like Fats Domino and Chuck Berry into the mainstream of rock music.

Pop music died a rapid death as rock and roll swept the nation. "Your Hit Parade," a popular televison show featuring top pop hits in the early 1950s, was canceled in 1957 because its singers looked ridic-ulous singing rock songs. In that same year, "American Bandstand" attracted teenage viewers with 90 minutes of dancing and rock music every day after school. The clean-looking young host, Dick Clark, gave rock and roll a better image with parents. In addition, many black artists toned down the sexual references and softened the hard beat of their songs in hopes of appealing to the larger white audience.

As rock and roll developed in the late 1950s, it focused on topics that appealed to the teenage market. Favorite themes were dances ("At the Hop"), love ("Why Must I Be a Teenager in Love?"), and the fear of parental punishment for teenage romance ("Wake Up, Little Susie"). Adults, then as now, were slow to understand the appeal of such music, reflecting a wider gap in generational perspective, as the lyrics of the song "Teen-Age Crush" suggest.

The 1950s saw a revolution in music that reflected a larger demographic shift and changing social values in the United States. How did popular music reflect the changes that occurred in the 1960s and 1970s, decades featuring the Beatles, Bob Dylan, the Rolling Stones, Simon and Garfunkel, the Doors, Stevie Wonder, the Eagles, Elton John, Neil Young, Michael Jackson, and others? What changes in the younger generation might account for these continuing musical shifts? What historical forces brought about changes in rock music? What music is popular today, and what does it say about the beliefs, values, and concerns of contemporary American youth?

LIFE Magazine, (c) Time Inc.

**Paul Schutzer, Dick Clark and Dancers, *1958***

### TEEN-AGE CRUSH

They call it a Teen-Age Crush,
They don't know how I feel,
They call it a Teen-Age Crush
They can't believe this is real.

They've forgotten when they were young,
And the way they tried to be free.
All they say is this young generation
Is not just the way it used to be.

I know my own heart,
But you say I'm trying to rush.
Please don't try to keep us apart,
Don't call it a Teen-Age Crush.

Words and music by Joe and Audrey Allison. © 1956 Central Songs, a Division of Beechwood Music Corporation.

Taft, Senate Republican leader, believed that cuts of $5 to $6 billion could be made to bring the budget down to $30 billion. In 1947, Congress twice passed tax-cut measures. Both times Truman vetoed them, but in 1948, another election year, Congress overrode the veto.

Congress also struck at Democratic labor policies. Republicans wanted to keep labor unions in check and were particularly concerned with limiting their right to engage in disruptive strikes as had occurred immediately after the war. Early in Truman's presidency, Congress passed a bill requiring notice for strikes as well as a cooling-off period if a strike occurred. Truman had vetoed that measure. But in 1947, commanding more votes, the Republicans passed the Taft-Hartley Act, which was intended to limit the power of unions by restricting the weapons they could employ. Revising the Wagner Act of 1935, the legislation spelled out unfair labor practices (such as preventing workers from working if they wished) and ruled illegal the closed shop whereby an employee had to join a union before getting a job. States were allowed by the legislation to outlaw the union shop, which forced workers to join the union after they had been hired. The act also allowed the president to call for an 80-day cooling-off period in strikes affecting national security and required union officials to sign non-Communist oaths in order to use governmental machinery designed to protect their rights.

Understandably, union leaders and members were furious. As he vetoed the measure, Truman claimed that it was unworkable and unfair, then went on nationwide radio to seek public approval. He regained some of the support he had earlier lost by his aggressive antistrike position; however, Congress passed the Taft-Hartley measure over the president's veto.

### The Fair Deal and Its Critics

As 1948 approached, Truman determined to win election in his own right. Some Democrats wanted to nominate Eisenhower or William O. Douglas, but that effort failed, leaving Truman with what most people thought was a worthless nomination. Not only was his own popularity waning; the Democratic Party itself seemed to be falling apart.

The civil rights issue—aimed at securing rights for black Americans—led to a Democratic split. Truman hoped to straddle the issue, at least until after the election, to avoid alienating the South. When liberals defeated a moderate platform proposal and pressed for a stronger stand on black civil rights, angry delegates from Mississippi and Alabama stormed out of the convention. They later formed a States' Rights, or Dixiecrat, party. At their own convention, delegates from 13 states nominated Governor J. Strom Thurmond of South Carolina as their candidate for president. They stood for continued racial segregation and wanted no interference with existing customs and practices.

Meanwhile, Henry A. Wallace, for seven years secretary of agriculture, then vice-president during Roosevelt's third term and secretary of commerce after that, was mounting his own challenge. Truman had fired Wallace from his cabinet for supporting a more temperate stand on Soviet relations. Now Wallace became the presidential candidate of the Progressive party. Initially he attracted widespread liberal interest because of his moderate position on Soviet-American affairs, his promotion of desegregation, and his promise to nationalize the railroads and major industries. But as Communists and "fellow travelers" appeared active in his organization, other support dropped off.

In that fragmented state, against the first real third-party challenges since 1912, the Democrats faced the Republicans, who coveted the White House after 16 years out of power. Once again they nominated Thomas E. Dewey, the governor of New York. Egocentric and stiff, Dewey was hardly a charismatic figure. Still, the polls uniformily picked the Republicans to win. Dewey saw little value in brawling with his opponent and conducted his campaign, in the words of one commentator, "with the humorless calculation of a Certified Public Accountant in pursuit of the Holy Grail."

Truman, as the underdog, conducted a vigorous campaign. He sought to appeal to ordinary Americans as an unpretentious man engaged in an uphill fight. Believing that everyone was against him but the people, he addressed the people in terms they could understand. He called the Republicans "a bunch of old mossbacks" out to destroy the New Deal. He attacked the "do nothing" 80th Congress, which he had called into special session in 1948 with instructions to live up to the planks of the Republican platform. Predictably, the legislators failed, providing Truman with handy ammunition. Speaking without a prepared text in his choppy, aggressive style, he warmed to crowds, and they warmed to him. "Give 'em hell, Harry," they yelled. "Pour it on." He did.

All the polls predicted a Republican win. But the pollsters were wrong. On election day, despite the bold headline "Dewey Defeats Truman" in the Chicago *Daily Tribune*, the incumbent president scored one of the most unexpected political upsets in American history, winning a 303–189 margin in the electoral college. Democrats also swept both houses of Congress.

Truman won primarily because he was able to revive the major elements of the Democratic coalition that Franklin Roosevelt had constructed more than a decade before. Despite the rocky days of 1946, Truman managed to hold on to labor, farm, and black votes. The fragmentation of the Democratic party, which had threatened to hurt him severely, helped instead. The splinter parties drew off some votes but allowed Truman to make a more aggressive, direct appeal to the center, and that ultimately accounted for his success.

With the election behind him, Truman pursued his liberal program. In his 1949 State of the Union message, he declared, "Every segment of our population and every individual has a right to expect from our Government a fair deal." Fair Deal became the name for his domestic program, which included the measures he had proposed since 1945.

Some parts of Truman's Fair Deal worked; others did not. The minimum wage was raised, and social security programs were expanded. A housing program brought modest gains but did not really meet housing needs. A farm program, aimed at providing income support to farmers if prices fell, never made it through Congress. Most of his civil rights program failed to win congressional support. The American Medical Association undermined the effort to provide national health insurance, and Congress rejected a measure to provide federal aid to education.

In domestic affairs, Truman often seemed

*In one of America's most remarkable political upsets, Democrats astonished pollsters by winning a sweeping victory in 1948.*

unpragmatic and too ambitious in his confrontations with a conservative and unsympathetic Congress. He frequently appeared most concerned with foreign policy as he strove to secure bipartisan support for his efforts in the Cold War (see Chapter 27). Committed to checking the perceived Soviet threat, he allowed his domestic program to suffer. As defense expenditures mounted, correspondingly less money was available for projects at home.

## The Election of Eisenhower

In 1952, Truman had the support of only 23 percent of the American people, and all indicators pointed to a political shift. The Democrats nominated Adlai Stevenson, Illinois's able and articulate, moderately liberal governor. The Republicans turned to Dwight D. Eisenhower, the World War II hero Americans knew as Ike.

Stevenson approached political issues in intellectual terms. "Let's talk sense to the American people," he said. "Let's tell them the truth." While liberals loved his approach, Stevenson himself anticipated the probable outcome. How, he wondered, could a man named Adlai beat a soldier called Ike?

The Republicans focused on communism, corruption, and Korea as major issues and called the Democrats "soft on communism." They criticized assorted scandals surrounding Truman's cronies and friends. The president himself was blameless, but some of the people near him were not. The Republicans also promised to end the unpopular Korean War.

Throughout the campaign, Eisenhower himself struck a grandfatherly pose, unified the various wings of his party, and went on to win a massive victory at the polls. He received 55 percent of the vote and carried 41 states. The new president took office with a Republican Congress as well and had little difficulty gaining a second term four years later.

### "Modern Republicanism"

Eisenhower believed firmly in limiting the presidential role. Like the Republicans in Congress with whom Truman tangled, he wanted to restore balance in government and to reduce the growth of the federal government. In the process, however, he hoped to preserve gains of the last 20 years that even Republicans accepted. Eisenhower sometimes termed his approach "dynamic conservatism." More often it carried the name "modern Republicanism," which, he explained, meant "conservative when it comes to money, liberal when it comes to human beings."

Above all, economic concerns dominated the Eisenhower years. The president and his chief aides wanted desperately to preserve the value of the dollar, pare down levels of funding, cut taxes, and balance the budget after years of deficit spending.

To achieve those aims, the president appointed George Humphrey, a fiscal conservative, as secretary of the Treasury. Humphrey placed a picture of Andrew Mellon, Calvin Coolidge's ultraconservative Treasury head, in his office and declared, "We have to cut one-third out of the budget and you can't do that just by eliminating waste. This means, whenever necessary, using a meat axe." His words reflected the administration's approach to economic affairs. In times of economic decline, Republican leaders were willing to risk unemployment to keep inflation under control. The business orientation became obvious when Defense Secretary Charles E. Wilson, former president of General Motors, stated his position at confirmation hearings. "What was good for our country was good for General Motors," he declared, "and vice versa."

Eisenhower fulfilled his promise to reduce government's economic role. After support from oil interests in the campaign, the Republican Congress, with a strong endorsement from the president, passed the Submerged Lands Act in 1953. That measure transferred control of about $40 billion worth of oil lands from the federal government to the states. *The New York Times* called it "one of the greatest and surely the most unjustified give-away programs in all the history of the United States."

The administration also sought to reduce federal activity in the electric-power field. Eisenhower favored private rather than public development of power. That sentiment came out clearly in a private comment about the Tennessee Valley Authority, the extensive public power and development project begun during the New Deal. "I'd like to see us *sell* the whole thing," he

### Presidential Elections, 1948–1956

| YEAR | CANDIDATES | PARTY | POPULAR VOTE | ELECTORAL VOTE |
|------|------------|-------|--------------|----------------|
| 1948 | HARRY S. TRUMAN | Democratic | 24,105,812 (49.5%) | 303 |
|      | Thomas E. Dewey | Republican | 21,970,065 (45.1%) | 189 |
|      | J. Strom Thurmond | States' Rights | 1,169,063 (2.4%) | 39 |
|      | Henry A. Wallace | Progressive | 1,157,172 (2.4%) | 0 |
| 1952 | DWIGHT D. EISENHOWER | Republican | 33,936,234 (55.2%) | 442 |
|      | Adlai E. Stevenson | Democratic | 27,314,992 (44.5%) | 89 |
| 1956 | DWIGHT D. EISENHOWER | Republican | 35,590,472 (57.4%) | 457 |
|      | Adlai E. Stevenson | Democratic | 26,022,752 (42.0%) | 73 |

*Note:* Winners' names appears in capital letters.

said, "but I suppose we can't go that far." Still, he opposed a TVA proposal for expansion to provide power to the Atomic Energy Commission and instead authorized a private group, the Dixon-Yates syndicate, to build a plant in Arkansas to meet the need. Later, when charges of scandal arose, the administration canceled the agreement, but the basic preference for private development remained.

Committed to supporting business interests, the administration sometimes saw its program backfire. As a result of its reluctance to stimulate the economy too much, the annual rate of economic growth declined from 4.3 percent between 1947 and 1952 to 2.5 percent between 1953 and 1960. The country suffered three recessions in Eisenhower's eight years. During the slumps, the deficits that Eisenhower so wanted to avoid increased.

Eisenhower's understated approach led to a legislative stalemate, particularly when the Democrats regained control of Congress in 1954. Opponents of the president jibed at Ike's restrained stance and laughed about limited White House leadership. One observed that Eisenhower proved that the country did not "need" a president. Another spoke of the Eisenhower doll —you wound it up and it did nothing at all. Those jokes notwithstanding, Eisenhower remained popular with the voters, who approved of his efforts to cut back on government's role. He left office as highly regarded as he entered it. He was what Americans wanted in prosperous times.

## THE OTHER AMERICA

In the years after World War II, not all Americans enjoyed the prosperity of the growing middle class. While most Americans were unconscious of poverty, it existed in inner cities and rural areas. Nor did all Americans enjoy the same privileges, as became evident when minorities began to press for equal treatment and equal rights. Black Americans and Jews, in the forefront of the civil rights struggle, were joined by Hispanics and Native Americans, who built their protest movements on the model of black protest but moved more slowly than blacks.

### Poverty Amid Affluence

Many people in the "affluent society" lived in poverty. Economic growth favored the upper- and middle classes. Although the popular "trickle-down" theory argued that economic expansion brought benefits to all classes, little, in fact, reached the citizens at the bottom of the ladder. In 1960, according to the Federal Bureau of Labor Statistics, a yearly subsistence-level income for a family of four was $3,000, and for a family of six, $4,000. The Bureau reported that 40 million people (almost a quarter of the population) lived below those levels, and nearly the same number only marginally above the line.

Two million migrant workers labored long hours for a subsistence wage. Many less mobile people were hardly better off. According to the 1960 census, 27 percent of the residential units in the United States were substandard, and even acceptable dwellings were often hopelessly overcrowded in some slums.

Michael Harrington, Socialist author and critic, exposed those conditions in *The Other America*, a devastating account that shocked the country when it appeared in 1962. The poor were everywhere. Harrington described the "economic underworld" in New York City, where "Puerto Ricans and Negroes, alcoholics, drifters, and disturbed people" sought daily positions as "dishwashers and day workers, the fly-by-night jobs" at employment agencies. In the afternoon, "the jobs have all been handed out, yet the people still mill around. Some of them sit on benches in the larger offices. There is no real point to their waiting, yet they have nothing else to do."

Harrington also pictured the rural poor living in what songwriter Woody Guthrie called the "pastures of plenty." The mountain folk of Appalachia, the tenant farmers of Mississippi, and the migrant farmers of Florida, Texas, and California were all caught in the relentless cycle.

## Advent of the Civil Rights Revolution

Between 1945 and 1960, American blacks carried on an energetic campaign to win civil rights. The postwar civil rights movement had many roots. Black leaders had pressed for concessions during World War II and had won some, but not enough to satisfy rising black aspirations; moreover, as the war drew to a close, wars of national liberation inspired American black leaders. The desire for black equality appeared as part of a wider struggle. Adam Clayton Powell, a Harlem preacher (and later congressman), warned that the black man "is ready to throw himself into the struggle to make the dream of America become flesh and blood, bread and butter, freedom and equality. He walks conscious of the fact that he is no longer alone—no longer a minority." Changes in the South also contributed to the new activism. New Deal farm legislation, the popularity of synthetic fabrics, and foreign competition robbed "King Cotton" of his world markets. As cotton farmers turned to less labor-intensive crops like soybeans and peanuts, they ousted their tenants. Between 1930 and 1960, the southern agricultural population declined from 16 million to 6 million. Millions of blacks moved to southern cities, where they found better jobs, better schooling, and freedom from landlord control. Some achieved middle-class status. Still not entirely free, these southern blacks were now ready to attack Jim Crow.

Millions of blacks also headed for northern cities between 1940 and 1960. In the 1950s, Detroit's black population increased from 16 to 29 percent, Chicago's from 14 to 23 percent. Since northern blacks could vote, and usually voted for the Democrats, civil rights became an issue that northern Democratic leaders could not avoid.

During the Truman administration, the racial question was dramatized in 1947 when Jackie Robinson broke the color line and began playing major-league baseball. After four years of preparation by Branch Rickey, general manager of the Brooklyn Dodgers, Robinson was ready to break into white baseball. Sometimes teammates were hostile, sometimes opponents crashed into him with spikes flying high, but Robinson kept his frustrations to himself. A splendid first season helped ease the way, and after Robinson's trailblazing effort, other blacks, formerly confined to the old Negro leagues, started to move into the major leagues, then into professional football and basketball.

The United States found its racial problems caught up with Cold War politics. As leader of the "free world," America appealed for support in Africa and Asia. Discrimination in the United States was an obvious drawback in the struggle to gain new friends. Now there was another compelling reason for whites to confront racial problems at home.

Truman supported the civil rights movement. A moderate on questions of race, he responded to political realities, understanding the growing strength of the black vote. He saw that black interests needed protection and realized that, in urban areas in particular, black support could make the difference between victory and defeat.

Truman first moved in 1946 when the National Emergency Committee Against Mob Violence told him of lynchings and other brutalities still taking place in the South. Disturbed by the account and determined to end such terror, he appointed a Committee on Civil Rights to investigate the problem and make recommendations. Released in October 1947, the report showed that blacks remained second-class citizens in every area of American life. The first such report, it demonstrated unequal treatment in education, housing, and medical care. It was time, the committee vehemently asserted, for the federal government to secure the rights of all Americans, and it set a civil rights agenda for the next two decades.

Though Truman hedged at first, the changing political situation and his own notion of what was just prompted him to action. In February 1948, he sent a ten-point civil rights program to Congress—the first presidential civil rights program since Reconstruction. When the southern wing of the Democratic party bolted later that year, he moved forward even more aggressively. First he issued an executive order barring discrimination in the federal establishment. Then he ordered equality of treatment in the military services. A committee appointed in 1948 oversaw the implementation of the policy and ended military segregation. Equal opportunities for all Americans in the navy, air force, and marine corps were now promised, and, after some resistance, in the army as well. Manpower needs in the Korean War led to the elimination of the last restrictions, particularly when the army found that blacks fought better in integrated than in segregated units.

Elsewhere the administration made small gains. The Justice Department, not previously supportive of NAACP litigation on behalf of equal rights for blacks, entered the battle against segregation and filed briefs challenging the constitutionality of restrictions in housing, education, and interstate transportation. Those helped build the pressure for change that influenced the Supreme Court. Congress, however, did little. Though Truman called for civil rights laws guaranteeing equal rights, southern Democrats like Mississippi senators John Stennis and James Eastland headed subcommittees responsible for considering such legislation. In such circumstances, liberal measures hardly had a chance.

## Integrating the Schools

In the 1950s, as the civil rights struggle gained momentum, the judicial system played a crucial role. The NAACP was determined to overturn the doctrine established in *Plessy* v. *Ferguson* in 1896. In that decision, the Supreme Court had declared that segregation of the black and white races was constitutional if the facilities used by each were "separate but equal." The decree had been used for generations to sanction rigid segregation, primarily in the South, even though separate facilities were seldom, if ever, equal. In attempting to remove this judicial roadblock to black equality, the NAACP had fought many cases over the previous decades.

A direct challenge came in 1951 when Oliver Brown, the father of 8-year-old Linda Brown, sued the school board of Topeka, Kansas, to allow his daughter to attend a school for white children that she passed as she walked to the bus that carried her to a black school farther away. Rebuffed in the local federal court (even though the Kansas judge disagreed with segregation), the plaintiffs appealed, and the case reached the Supreme Court. Justices there were fully aware of the importance of the case. Schools in 21 states and the District of Columbia were segregated at the time, and the Court's ruling would affect them all. Adding other school segregation cases to the one before it, the Court confronted the legal questions.

On May 17, 1954, the Supreme Court released its bombshell ruling in *Brown* v. *Board of Education*. For more than a decade, Supreme Court decisions had gradually expanded black civil rights, and now the Court unanimously decreed that "separate facilities are inherently unequal" and concluded that the "separate but equal" doctrine had no place in public education. A year later, the Court turned to the question of implementation and declared that local school boards, acting with the guidance of lower courts, should move "with all deliberate speed" to desegregate their facilities.

Charged with the ultimate responsibility for executing the law was Dwight D. Eisenhower. Doubting that simple changes in the law could improve race relations, he once observed, "I don't believe you can change the hearts of men with laws or decisions." Privately commenting on the *Brown* ruling, he said, "I personally think the decision was wrong." But he understood that "it makes no difference whether or not I endorse it." Though reluctant to act aggressively, the president knew that according to the Constitution it was his duty to see that the law was carried out.

Eisenhower moved quickly. Even while urging sympathy for the South in its period of transition, he acted immediately to desegregate the Washington, D.C., schools as a model for the rest of the country. He sought to end continuing discrimination in other areas too, mandating desegregation in navy yards and veterans' hospitals.

Even so, the South resisted. In district after district, vicious scenes occurred. White children often echoed the feelings of their parents. One Tennessee teacher heard such taunts as "If you come back to school, I'll cut your guts out." Blacks endured eggs splattered on their books, ink spread on their clothes, and worse.

The crucial confrontation came in Little Rock, Arkansas, in 1957. A desegregation plan, to begin with the token admission of a few black students to Central High School, was ready to go into effect. Then, just before the school year was to begin, Governor Orval Faubus declared on television that it would not be possible to maintain order if integration took place. National Guardsmen, posted by the governor to keep the peace and armed with bayonets, turned away nine black students as they tried to enter the school. After three weeks, a federal court ordered the troops to leave. When the black children entered, the white students, spurred on by the example of their elders, belligerently opposed them, chanting such slogans as "Two, four, six, eight, we ain't gonna integrate." In the face of hostile mobs, the black children left the school.

With the lines drawn, attention focused on the moderate man in the White House. While the Guardsmen were still at the school, the president had met with the Arkansas governor and had taken a cautious stand in the hope that the crisis would dissolve of its own accord. Now, however, he faced a situation in which Little Rock whites were clearly defying the law. As a former military officer, Ike knew that such resistance could not be tolerated. He denounced the "disgraceful occurrence," urged those obstructing the law to "cease and desist," and finally took the one action he had earlier called unthinkable.

For the first time since the end of Reconstruction, an American president called out federal troops to protect the rights of black citizens. Paratroopers converged on Little Rock, and National Guardsmen were placed under federal command. The black children entered the school and attended classes with the military protecting their rights. Under those circumstances, desegregation began.

### Black Gains on Other Fronts

Meanwhile, blacks themselves began to organize in ways that profoundly advanced the civil rights movement. The crucial event occurred in Montgomery, Alabama, in December 1955. Rosa Parks, a 42-year-old black seamstress who was also secretary of the state NAACP, sat down in the front of a bus in a section reserved by custom for whites. Tired from a hard day's work, she refused when ordered to move back. Told she would be arrested, she quietly held her ground. The police were called at the next stop, and Parks was arrested and ordered to stand trial for violating the segregation laws. She had not intended to challenge the law or cause a scene. Modestly, she recalled, "I felt it was just something I had to do."

Black civil rights officials seized the issue.

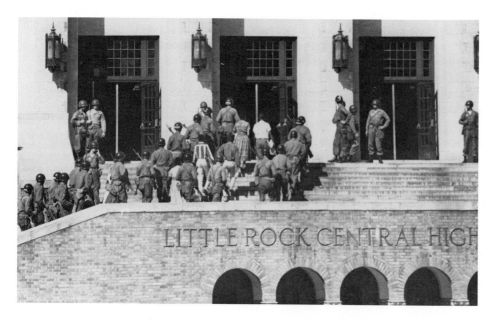

*National Guardsmen and federal troops escorted Little Rock, Arkansas black students to class in 1957 as Eisenhower's desegregation program was enforced.*

*Baptist minister Martin Luther King, Jr., emerged as the spokesman for blacks protesting transit discrimination in Montgomery, Alabama.*

E. D. Nixon, state NAACP president, told Parks, "This is the case we've been looking for. We can break this situation on the bus with your case." Though Parks knew she would lose her job, she agreed to cooperate. The next evening, resistance began. Fifty black leaders met to discuss the case and decided to organize a massive boycott of the bus system. Martin Luther King, Jr., the 27-year-old minister of the Baptist church in which the meeting was held, soon emerged as the most prominent spokesman of the protest. King held a Ph.D. in philosophy in addition to religious credentials. He was an impressive figure and an inspiring speaker. In his moving speeches, he conveyed his concern at the economic and social discrimination suffered by blacks. "There comes a time when people get tired . . . of being kicked about by the brutal feet of oppression," he declared. It was time to be more assertive, to cease being "patient with anything less than freedom and justice." The black clergy was to play a vital role in mobilizing civil rights protesters in the next two decades.

King was arrested, as he was to be many times, but 50,000 blacks in Montgomery walked or formed car pools to avoid the transit system. Their actions cut gross revenue by 65 percent on city buses. Almost a year later, the Supreme Court ruled that bus segregation, like school segregation, violated the Constitution, and the boycott ended. But the mood it fostered continued, and peaceful protest became a way of life for many blacks.

Meanwhile, a concerted effort developed to guarantee black voting rights. The provisions of the Fifteenth Amendment notwithstanding, many states had circumvented the law for decades (see Chapter 19). Some required a poll tax or a literacy test or an examination of constitutional understanding. Blacks often found themselves excluded from the polls.

Eisenhower believed in the right to vote, yet even there he had reservations. To a press conference he declared, "I personally believe if you try to go too far too fast in this delicate field that has involved the emotions of so many millions of Americans, you are making a mistake." As a bill worked its way through Congress, Ike was not much help. He seemed unsure about specific provisions and took a characteristically restrained stance toward congressional actions.

Due largely to the legislative genius of Senate majority leader Lyndon B. Johnson of Texas, the civil rights bill, the first since Reconstruction, moved toward passage. With his eye on the presidency, Johnson wanted to establish his credentials as a man who could look beyond narrow southern interests. Paring the bill down to the provisions he felt would pass, Johnson pushed the measure through.

The Civil Rights Act of 1957 created a Civil Rights Commission and empowered the Justice Department to go to court in cases where blacks were denied the right to vote. The bill was a compromise measure, yet it was the first successful effort to protect civil rights in 82 years.

To plug loopholes and add enforcement mechanisms to the 1957 act, civil rights activists worked for another measure. Johnson again took the lead, and after breaking a filibuster, he helped secure the Civil Rights Act of 1960. It set stiffer punishments for people who interfered with the right to vote, but again stopped short of authorizing federal registrars to register blacks to vote and so was generally ineffective.

The civil rights movement made important

strides during the Eisenhower years, though little of the progress resulted from the president's leadership. Rather, the efforts of blacks themselves and the rulings of the Supreme Court brought significant change. The period of civil rights activities, now launched, would continue in the next decade.

### Mexican Migrant Laborers

In the years after World War II, Spanish-speaking groups in the United States suffered from many of the same problems blacks faced. They came from Cuba, Puerto Rico, Mexico, and Central America. Often unskilled and illiterate, they gravitated to the cities like other less fortunate Americans. Chicanos, or Mexican-Americans, were the most numerous newcomers. Like black Americans, they sought to better their lives, but they were less successful in their quest.

Chicanos faced peculiar difficulties and widespread discrimination. During World War II, as the country faced a labor shortage at home, American farmers sought Mexican braceros (helping hands) to harvest their crops. A program to encourage the seasonal immigration of farm workers continued after the war when the government signed a Migratory Labor Agreement with Mexico. Between 1948 and 1964, some 4.5 million Mexicans were brought to the United States for temporary work. Braceros were expected to return to Mexico at the end of their labor contract, but often they stayed, hoping to better their lives in America. Joining them were millions more who entered the country illegally.

Conditions were harsh for the braceros in the best of times. In periods of economic difficulty, they worsened. During the 1953–1954 recession, the government mounted Operation Wetback to deport illegal entrants and braceros who had illegally remained in the country. Deportations numbered 1.1 million. As immigration officials searched out illegal workers, all Chicanos found themselves vulnerable. They bitterly protested the violations of their rights, to little effect.

Operation Wetback did not end the reliance on Mexican farm laborers. A coalition of south-ern Democrats and conservative Republicans, mostly representing farm states, extended the Migratory Labor Agreement with Mexico. Two years after the massive deportations of 1954, a record 445,000 braceros crossed the border to work on American farms.

The political attacks in the heated days of the Red Scare also brought persecution to Chicanos active in radical causes. Agapito Gómez had lived in the United States for 25 years. He had an American-born wife. Nonetheless, he found himself questioned for past union activities. In the 1930s, he had been part of a Depression-relief organization and had joined the CIO. When he refused to divulge the names of people with whom he had worked, immigration officials took away his alien card. José Noriega found himself in the same position. He had been in the United States for more than 40 years. He too had a union past, as a member of a long-shoremen's association. When questioned in 1952, like Gómez, he refused to cooperate. The government initiated deportation proceedings.

In addition to economic oppression, Chicanos in all walks of life faced discrimination in the schools, uncertain access to public facilities, and occasional exclusion from the governing

*Exclusion from public swimming pools was one form of discrimination faced by Chicanos. These children swam in an irrigation ditch.*

process, which they did not always understand. They protested such restrictions and occasionally met with success. In mid-1946, the Tempe, Arizona, Chamber of Commerce allowed Chicanos entrance to the city's swimming pool as a result of pressure from a Chicano veterans' group. A concerted effort to register new voters in Los Angeles led to the election of Edward Roybal to the Los Angeles City Council in 1949. He was the first person of Mexican descent to serve there since 1881 and later was elected to Congress.

The advances, however, were limited. In the late 1940s, many Chicanos sought official classification as Caucasian in the hope that the change would lead to better treatment. But even when the designation changed, their status did not. They still faced discrimination and police brutality, particularly in the cities with the largest Chicano populations.

Los Angeles, with its large number of Chicanos, was the scene of numerous unsavory racial episodes. In mid-1951, on receiving a complaint about a loud record player, police officers raided a baptismal gathering at the home of Simon Fuentes. Breaking into the house without a warrant, they assaulted the members of the party. At the end of the year, in the "Bloody Christmas" case, officers removed seven Mexican-Americans from jail cells and beat them severely. Chicanos protested such episodes, often through the *Asociación Nacional México-Americana*, an organization founded the year before in New Mexico to protect the human rights of those facing discrimination. Sometimes they achieved recourse; more often they did not.

Yet in the 1950s, Chicano activism was fragmented. Many Mexican-Americans considered their situation hopeless. More effective mobilization had to wait for another day.

### Native Americans

American Indians also acted to defend their own interests, but with even greater difficulties. Not only did they have to fight the forces of cultural change that were eroding tribal tradition, but they also had to resist the federal government's reversal of New Deal Indian policy.

In the postwar years, Indians faced the same technological developments affecting other Americans. As power lines reached the reservations, Indians purchased televisions, refrigerators, washing machines, and automobiles. This inevitably changed old ways of life. Those Indians who gravitated to the cities often had difficulty adjusting to urban life and faced discrimination much like that experienced by Mexican-Americans and blacks.

Just after the end of World War II, Native Americans achieved an important victory when Congress established the Indian Claims Commission. The commission was mandated to review tribal cases pleading that ancestral lands had been illegally taken from them through violation of federal treaties. Hundreds of tribal suits against the government in federal courts were now possible. Many of them would lead to large settlements of cash—a form of reparation for past injustices—and sometimes the return of long-lost lands.

The Eisenhower administration, determined to cut back on federal activity wherever possible, dramatically turned away from the New Deal policy of government support for tribal autonomy. In the Indian Reorganization Act of 1934, the government had stepped in to restore lands to tribal ownership and end their loss or sale to outsiders. In 1953, instead of trying to encourage Native American self-government, the administration adopted a new approach, known as the "termination" policy. The government proposed settling all outstanding claims and eliminating reservations as legitimate political entities. To encourage their assimilation into mainstream society, the government offered small subsidies to families who would leave the reservations and relocate in the cities.

The new policy victimized the Indians. With their lands no longer federally protected and their members deprived of treaty rights, many tribes became unwitting victims of people who wanted to seize their land, just as they had been throughout the nineteenth century. Though promising more freedom, the new policy caused undue disruption and was discontinued in 1961.

Almost all tribes resisted termination, and as they did they began to articulate a new sense of identity to the outside world. A Seminole petition to the president in 1954 summed up a general view. "We do not say that we are superior or inferior to the White Man and we do not say that the White Man is superior or inferior to us," the document said. "We do say that we are not White Men but Indians, do not wish to become White Men but wish to remain Indians, and have an outlook on all things different from the outlook of the White Man."

## CONCLUSION: Qualms Amid Affluence

In general, the United States in the decade and a half after World War II was stable and secure. Recessions occurred periodically, but the economy righted itself after short downturns. For the most part, business boomed. Millions of middle-class Americans joined the ranks of suburban property owners, enjoying the benefits of shopping centers and fast-food establishments and other material manifestations of what they considered the good life.

Some Americans, however, never shared in the prosperity, but they were not visible from the suburbs. Black Americans and other minority groups were beginning to mobilize, yet their protest remained peaceful. Many still believed they could share in the American dream and remained confident that deeply rooted patterns of discrimination could be changed.

Toward the end of the period, after the Soviet Union became the first nation to place a satellite in orbit, a wave of anxiety swept the nation. Some Americans began to criticize the materialism that apparently had caused the nation to fall behind. Critics began to explore questions of national purpose. Raising these questions made them more willing to criticize other shortcomings in American life. It also legitimated challenges by other groups.

Criticisms and anxieties notwithstanding, the United States continued to develop according to Ray Kroc's dreams as he first envisioned McDonald's establishments across the land. The standard of living remained high for many of the nation's citizens. Healthy and comfortable, upper- and middle-class Americans assumed that their society would continue to prosper. But the "other Americans" had begun to make their voices heard, and the echoes would reverberate even more loudly in future years.

## Recommended Reading

A number of good books describe domestic developments in the years between 1945 and 1960. Richard Polenberg, *One Nation Divisible: Class, Race, and Ethnicity in the United States Since 1938* (1980) is a useful survey of recent America that includes a description of the growth of suburbia. William Leuchtenburg, *A Troubled Feast* (1979) is a perceptive assessment of the entire post-1945 period that focuses on the consumer culture that came into prominence after World War II.

Robert J. Donovan, *Conflict and Crisis: The Presidency of Harry S Truman, 1945–1948* (1977) is a detailed overview of Truman's first term. *Tumultuous Years: The Presidency of Harry S Truman* (1982), by the same author, carries the story through the second term. Barton J. Bernstein and Allen J. Matusow, *The Truman Administration: A Documentary History* (1966) is an excellent collection of documents on various facets of policy in Truman's two terms. Harry S Truman, *Memoirs* (2 vols., 1955, 1956) is Truman's own account of his years at the top.

For the Eisenhower period, Charles C. Alexander, *Holding the Line: The Eisenhower Era, 1952–1961* (1975) provides a good general introduction to the American mood and government policy during Ike's years as president. Dwight D. Eisenhower, *Mandate for Change, 1953–1956* (1963) is the first volume of Ike's memoirs of his years in office; *Waging Peace* (1965) is the concluding volume.

Fiction can often give a good sense of period. Sloan Wilson, *The Man in the Gray Flannel Suit* (1955) is a novel that conveys a good sense of the materialism of the affluent 1950s.

On women, William H. Chafe, *The American Woman: Her Changing Social, Economic, and Political Roles, 1920–1970* (1972) is an outstanding survey of women's struggle in the past 50 years, with some particularly pertinent observations on the postwar years. Betty Friedan, *The Feminine Mystique* (1963) is a polemical book describing the stereotypical role of women in the 1950s as they focused on being housewives and mothers.

For further details on civil rights, see Harvard Sitkoff, *The Struggle for Black Equality, 1954–1980* (1981), a readable survey of the movement since the early 1950s. Richard Kluger, *Simple Justice* (1975) tells the full story of the *Brown* v. *Board of Education* decision and its implications.

Several recent books provide useful background on the equality efforts of other minorities in the United States. Rodolfo Acuña, *Occupied America: A History of Chicanos* (1981) gives insight into the Chicanos' struggle in the years after World War II. Alvin M. Josephy, Jr., *Now That the Buffalo's Gone* (1982) details Indian struggles over the past several decades.

## TIME LINE

|  |  |
|------|-------|
| 1943 | Mark I computer developed |
| 1944 | GI Bill passed |
| 1945 | World War II ends<br>Wave of strikes in heavy industries |
| 1946 | Truman vetoes bill extending Office of Price Administration<br>Prices rise by 25 percent in 18 months<br>Union strikes in the auto, coal, steel, and electrical industries<br>Employment Act<br>Dr. Spock's *Baby and Child Care* |
| 1947 | Taft-Hartley Act<br>Jackie Robinson breaks the color line in major-league baseball |
| 1948 | Executive order bars discrimination in federal government<br>Armed forces begin to desegregate<br>"Dixiecrat" party formed<br>Truman defeats Dewey<br>Kinsey Report on human sexuality<br>Transistor developed at Bell Lab |
| 1949 | Truman launches Fair Deal |
| 1950 | Asociación Nacional México-Americana formed |
| 1951 | J. D. Salinger's *Catcher in the Rye* |
| 1952 | Dwight D. Eisenhower elected president |
| 1953 | Submerged Lands Act<br>Rosenbergs executed for espionage |
| 1954 | *Brown* v. *Board of Education* |
| 1955 | Montgomery bus boycott begins<br>First McDonald's opens in Illinois |
| 1956 | Eisenhower reelected<br>Interstate Highway Act<br>Allen Ginsberg's "Howl" |
| 1957 | Little Rock school integration crisis<br>Civil Rights Act<br>"Baby boom" peaks with 4.3 million births<br>*Sputnik* launched by Soviet Union |
| 1959 | One-third of all Americans reside in suburbs |
| 1960 | Three-fourths of all families own a TV<br>Civil Rights Act<br>GNP hits $500 billion<br>John F. Kennedy elected president |

# CHAPTER 29
## FROM SELF-CONFIDENCE
## TO SELF-DOUBT

Ron Kovic was a typical all-American boy. Born in 1946, he grew up on Long Island. Life was secure in the comfortable post–World War II years, as Kovic shared the dreams of millions of others his age.

"I loved baseball more than anything else in the world." Later he recalled "playing catch-a-fly-you're-up for hours with a beat-up old baseball. We played all day long out there, running across that big open field with all our might, diving and sliding face-first into the grass, making one-handed, spectacular catches."

When baseball did not occupy him, television did. "The whole block grew up watching television," he observed. "There was Howdy Doody and Rootie Kazootie, Cisco Kid and Gabby Hayes, Roy Rogers and Dale Evans. The Lone Ranger was on Channel 7. We watched cartoons for hours on Saturdays".

Anxious moments occasionally intervened. Kovic, like others, wondered how the Russians had managed to put a satellite into space before the United States. He grew up fearing "the Communist threat" and even became persuaded that Communists "were infiltrating our schools, trying to take over our classes and control our minds."

Yet that fear was but a reflection of the patriotism of his day. Like most Americans, Kovic had an unquestioning confidence in the "American way." Moreover, he had been born on the Fourth of July and could take the words of "I'm a Yankee Doodle Dandy" to heart as holiday fireworks went off.

Caught up in the spirit of the New Frontier, Kovic was stunned when President John F. Kennedy was shot. "I truly felt I had lost a dear friend," he wrote. "I was deeply hurt. . . . The pain stuck with me for a long time after he died."

Still, life went on, and Kovic remained intent on doing something for his nation. After graduating from high school, Kovic enlisted in the marines. The desire to be a hero drove him on, carried him through basic training, and stayed with him through a first tour of duty in the war in Vietnam. Proud of what he was doing, he signed up for a second tour. Only then did the conflict begin to tear him apart.

Kovic wanted to win medals, to be brave, but instead was increasingly haunted by his conduct in the war. He accidently shot and killed an American corporal and, as if to atone for his deed, plunged on even more aggressively, certain that he was "serving America in this its most critical hour, just like President Kennedy had talked about." Yet that effort, too, ended in disaster when his unit shot at shadowy figures moving in a village hut, only to learn that the wounded and dead were innocent children.

For Kovic the final blow came later. First hit in the foot, he then took a 30-caliber sniper bullet in the spine. The pain in his foot vanished, but so did all sensation below his chest. Suddenly, all he could feel was "the worthlessness of dying right here in this place at this moment for nothing."

Ron Kovic returned from the war paralyzed from the chest down. As he went from hospital to hospital, feeling the muscle tone of his legs disappear, he became overwhelmed by despair, heightened by the growing opposition to the war in the United States. Kovic grew to believe that he had been trapped in a meaningless crusade and then left to dangle on his own. He became one of the many protesters who finally helped bring the war to an end.

Yet he could never forget the price he had paid. "I feel like a big clumsy puppet with all his strings cut," he wrote. Even more poignantly he observed:

> I am the living death
> the memorial day on wheels
> I am your yankee doodle dandy
> your john wayne come home
> your fourth of july firecracker
> exploding in the grave

Ron Kovic's passage through the 1960s reflected that of American society as a whole. Millions of Americans shared his views as the decade began, feeling sure of their nation's destiny. Mostly comfortable and confident, they were nonetheless ready to embrace John Kennedy's New Frontier. They agreed that social reform was necessary at home, a vigilant anti-Communist course needed abroad. Though people were shocked when Kennedy was assassinated in November 1963, they rallied behind Vice-President Lyndon Johnson, who pressed ahead to complete Kennedy's reform program. But when the Johnson administration deepened American involvement in the civil war in faraway Vietnam, the middle-class consensus in the United States began to come apart. The reform movement fell victim to the turbulence of the war and the opposition it raised. And the values of the nation, particularly of its young, began to change. Not all Americans suffered what Ron Kovic went through. But they did experience many of the same transitions, and they too came to question their own actions and those of their nation in troubled times.

This chapter describes the transitions that occurred in the 1960s. It explores the shift from optimistic hope that the nation could solve all problems to pessimistic doubt that it could deal with crises anywhere. And it examines the groups who raised doubts about American values and policies as the decade came to an end.

## THE PRESIDENCY IN THE SIXTIES

As the new decade dawned, fresh political leadership emerged, as men much younger than Dwight Eisenhower vied for the presidency. John Kennedy in particular sought to reaffirm a sense of national purpose, yet both candidates, Kennedy and Richard Nixon, still clung to many of the assumptions that had guided America in the past. Both saw incremental reform and a vigilant foreign policy as the keys to keeping the nation safe and strong.

### The Election of 1960

In 1960, Richard Nixon, vice-president for eight years under Eisenhower, set his sights on the presidency. Incumbency should have served as an advantage, but an economic recession hurt the Republicans, and Eisenhower's own lukewarm support proved damaging. Never close to Nixon, Eisenhower made matters worse when asked what decisions his vice-president had helped make. "If you give me a week, I might think of one," he responded.

In the Democratic party, John Kennedy, an ambitious young senator from Massachusetts who had eyed the presidency for some time, now made his bid. First, however, he had to overcome the Catholic hurdle, for no Roman Catholic had ever been elected president, and conventional wisdom held that none could win in the aftermath of Al Smith's defeat in 1928. Pointed stories injected a hostile note into the campaign. One critic advised voters to join the church of their choice—while there was still time. Despite such attacks, Kennedy managed to defuse the religious issue in the primary campaign. His primary victory in Protestant West Virginia, where opponent Hubert Humphrey had long been friendly with organized labor, showed that religion did not harm his chances for election.

Kennedy and Nixon squared off against each other in the first televised debates ever held between presidential candidates. Television changed the course of the campaign. Both men were articulate, but by projecting a more energetic and dynamic image, Kennedy gained the upper hand. While Nixon challenged points his opponent made, Kennedy looked beyond Nixon and seemed to be addressing the American people at large. Television, increasingly important in shaping American attitudes, had now become a significant part of the political process.

Kennedy's victory was a narrow one. The electoral margin of 303 to 219 concealed the close popular tally, in which he triumphed by less than 120,000 of 68 million votes. Given the curious nature of the electoral college, the actual result was even closer. If but a few thousand people had voted differently in Illinois and Texas, the election would have gone to Nixon.

Kennedy won in 1960 because he carried traditionally Democratic areas and did well in the cities among black and ethnic voters. The debates, too, had an important impact on the outcome. In a survey for CBS, pollster Elmo Roper estimated that 57 percent of the people voting felt that the debates had influenced their choice. Another 6 percent indicated that their final decision resulted from the debates alone. As Kennedy himself concluded after his narrow victory, "It was TV more than anything else that turned the tide."

### JFK and LBJ

Kennedy's style gave a new stamp to the office. At 43, he was the youngest man ever elected to the presidency. Son of a former ambassador to England and grandson of an Irish-American mayor of Boston, he appeared energetic, able, and articulate. He had the capacity to voice his aims in language the average American could understand. During the campaign he had noted "uncharted areas of science and space, unsolved problems of peace and war, unconquered pockets of ignorance and prejudice, unanswered questions of poverty and surplus" that must be confronted, for "the New Frontier is here whether we seek it or not." He made the same point even more eloquently in his inaugural address: "The torch has been passed to a new generation of Americans—born in this century, tempered by war, disciplined by a hard and bitter peace, proud of our ancient heritage." Noting the need to reaffirm American values and to move ahead together, he concluded, "And so, my fellow Americans: Ask not what your country can do for you—ask what you can do for your country."

Kennedy generated confidence, viewing himself as "tough-minded" and "hard-nosed." Unlike Ike, Kennedy believed in strong leadership. He admired the political figures he described in his Pulitzer Prize–winning book *Profiles in Courage*. The president, he believed, "must serve as a catalyst, an energizer," who

## The Confusing 1960 Presidential Election

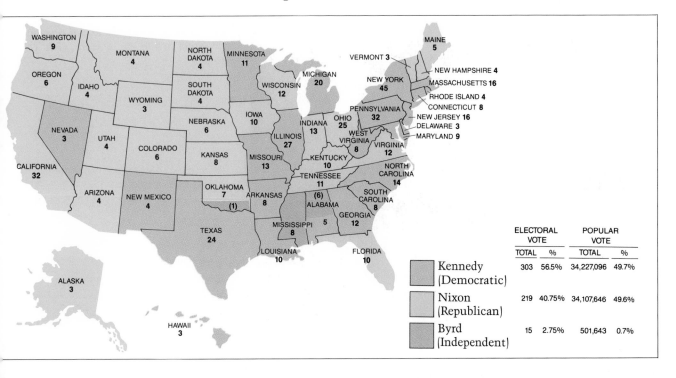

|  | ELECTORAL VOTE | | POPULAR VOTE | |
|---|---|---|---|---|
|  | TOTAL | % | TOTAL | % |
| Kennedy (Democratic) | 303 | 56.5% | 34,227,096 | 49.7% |
| Nixon (Republican) | 219 | 40.75% | 34,107,646 | 49.6% |
| Byrd (Independent) | 15 | 2.75% | 501,643 | 0.7% |

would perform "in the very thick of the fight." Widely read, especially in history, Kennedy sought to follow Franklin Roosevelt's example of keeping power in his own hands and working through problems himself.

Kennedy surrounded himself with talented assistants. On his staff were 15 Rhodes scholars and several famous authors. The secretary of state was Dean Rusk, a former member of the State Department who had then served as president of the Rockefeller Foundation. The secretary of defense was Robert S. McNamara, the president of the Ford Motor Company, who had proved creative in using computer analysis.

Also contributing to the Kennedy style was his glamorous, charming, and graceful wife Jacqueline. Nobel Prize winners came to a special White House dinner; artists and musicians performed before invited guests. The Kennedys and their friends played touch football on the grass and promoted 50-mile hikes. Energy and exuberance filled the air. The administration seemed like the Camelot of King Arthur's day.

When the president was tragically cut down in his prime by an assassin's bullet, his vice-president tried to carry on the dream in his own way. Johnson was a less charismatic figure than Kennedy but a more effective politician. He used his considerable political talents to construct an impressive legislative program.

Schooled in Congress and influenced by FDR, Johnson was the most able legislative leader of the postwar years. As Senate majority leader, he became famous for his ability to get things done. He was an enormously egotistical man and a fountain of energy and force. Ceaseless in his search for information, tireless in his attention to detail, he knew the strengths and weaknesses of everyone he faced. He could flatter and cajole and was famous for the "Johnson treatment": he would confront someone in the hall and bear down until he got his way.

In the 1960s, Kennedy and Johnson, each in turn, sought to remobilize the nation after the placid Eisenhower years. Both used the presidency more aggressively to shape public opinion. Like Theodore Roosevelt, they saw the office as a "bully pulpit," yet with added possibilities, for radio and television had become enormously influential. Kennedy sparked the public imagination and generated a sense of hope; Johnson produced the legislative results that made

*Glamour and grace characterized the Kennedy style. The president and first lady were photographed at a reception in Vienna while on a state visit to Europe.*

change possible. Both shared the vision of a society in which the comforts of life would be more widely shared and poverty eliminated. By the middle of the decade, they had made progress toward these goals. Both had a vision of the nation so dominant and strong in the world that it could impose its will in all parts of the globe. That misperception finally turned their dream into a nightmare at home and abroad.

## THE NEW FRONTIER AND SOCIAL REFORM

In the early 1960s, the Democratic administration addressed questions of domestic reform. While the 1950s had been prosperous for most Americans, segments of the society remained caught in the web of poverty, and minority groups continued to face discrimination. Confident of America's destiny and design, Kennedy and his associates began to consider how to alleviate these problems without challenging the system as a whole.

### The Kennedy Approach

As his presidency progressed, Kennedy realized not only the necessity of maintaining a healthy economic system but also the need to provide welfare programs that went beyond the liberal offerings of the past. In late 1962, Kennedy told one of his advisers, "I want to go beyond the things that have already been accomplished. Give me facts and figures on things we still have to do." As for civil rights, Kennedy knew that blacks were an important part of the Democratic coalition. He had made promises to them during the campaign and now would have to make good. Yet while Kennedy espoused liberal goals and social justice, in reality his policies and programs were limited and restrained. The president spoke out eloquently on occasion, but his close electoral victory limited his mandate to embark on major reform programs. Furthermore, his party lost two seats in the Senate and 22 in the House in 1960. Though they retained majorities in both chambers, the Democrats included many conservative southerners who were often unsympathetic to liberal goals and opposed any changes in race relations.

One of Kennedy's major aims was to end the lingering recession by working with the business community. At the same time, he was determined to keep inflation under control. These two goals conflicted when, in the spring of 1962, steel companies sought what the administration regarded as excessive price increases. Democratic leaders were especially disturbed because the administration had proved its friendship for business by persuading steelworkers to accept a modest contract, assuming that management would show similar restraint in controlling prices. The angry president termed the price increases unreasonable and unjustifiable and went on television, charging that the firms showed "utter contempt" for the interests of 185 million Americans. Determined to force the steel companies to their knees, Kennedy pressed for a congressional investigation. The Justice Department and the Federal Trade Commission moved to examine the possibility that the steel firms were working too closely with one another in making price agreements. The Defense Department threatened to deny contracts to the offending companies.

The large companies backed down and reinstituted the earlier price levels. Although Kennedy won, he paid a price for his victory. Business leaders disliked the heavy-handed approach and decided that this Democratic administration, like all the others, was hostile to business. In late May, six weeks after the steel crisis, the stock market plunged in the greatest drop since the Great Crash of 1929. Kennedy received the blame. "When Eisenhower had a heart attack," Wall Street analysts joked, "the market broke . . . if Kennedy would have a heart attack, the market would go up."

It now seemed doubly pressing to end the economic slump. Earlier a proponent of a balanced budget, Kennedy adopted a Keynesian approach to economic growth. Budget deficits had promoted prosperity during the Second

World War and might work in the same way in peacetime too. In June 1962, the president announced that deficits, properly used, might help the economy. In early 1963, he called for a $13.5 billion cut in corporate taxes over the next three years. While that cut would cause a large deficit, it would also provide capital that could stimulate the economy and ultimately bring added tax revenues.

Opposition mounted on all sides. Conservatives refused to accept the basic premise that deficits would stimulate economic growth and argued, as Eisenhower declared, that "no family, no business, no nation can spend itself into prosperity." In Congress, opponents pigeonholed the proposal in committee, and there it remained.

On other issues Kennedy also encountered resistance. Though he proposed legislation increasing the minimum wage and providing for federal aid for education, medical care for the elderly, housing subsidies, and urban renewal, the legislative results were disappointing. His new minimum-wage measure passed Congress, in pared-down form, but Kennedy did not have the votes in Congress to achieve most of his legislative program.

That became even more evident in the struggle to aid public education. Soon after taking office, Kennedy proposed a $2.3 billion program of grants to the states over a three-year period to help build schools and raise teachers' salaries. Immediately, a series of prickly questions emerged. Was it appropriate to spend large sums of money for social goals? Would federal aid bring federal control of school policies and curriculum? Should assistance go to segregated schools? Should it go to parochial schools? The administration proved willing to allow assistance to segregated schools, thereby easing white southern minds. On the Catholic question, however, it stumbled to a halt. Kennedy at first insisted that he would not allow his religion to influence his actions and opposed aid for parochial schools. As Catholic pressure mounted and the administration realized that Catholic votes were necessary for passage, Kennedy began to reconsider. But in the end, the school aid measure died in the House Rules Committee.

## Black Activism and the Fight for Civil Rights

In the volatile area of civil rights, the administration's efforts also faltered. The movement that had begun to grow in the 1950s became more intense in the next decade, forcing political leaders of all persuasions, including Kennedy, to scramble to keep abreast of events.

The Montgomery bus boycott marked the advent of a mass civil rights movement in the South. While the National Association for the Advancement of Colored People (NAACP) continued to challenge segregation in the courts, activists continued to urge civil disobedience and nonviolent direct action. Sit-in demonstrations began in North Carolina in 1960 when black college students took their places at a segregated Woolworth's lunch counter and deliberately violated southern segregation laws by refusing to leave. The sit-ins captured media attention, and soon thousands of blacks were involved in the campaign. The following year, the sit-ins gave rise to freedom rides, aimed at testing southern transportation facilities, recently desegregated by a Supreme Court decision. Organized initially by the Congress of Racial Equality (CORE) and aided by the Student Nonviolent Coordinating Committee (SNCC), the program sent groups of blacks and whites together on buses heading south and stopping at terminals along the way. The riders, peaceful themselves, anticipated confrontations that would publicize their cause and generate political support.

In North and South alike, consciousness of the need to combat racial discrimination grew. Young people in particular, most of them students, enlisted in the effort to change restrictive patterns deeply rooted in American life. White clergy of all denominations became socially active in ways not seen since the Social Gospel movement of the late ninteenth century (when civil rights was not one of their concerns). The civil rights movement became the most powerful moral campaign since the abolitionist crusade before the Civil War. Often working together, blacks and whites vowed to eliminate racial barriers.

Participants in the movement came from every direction. Anne Moody, who grew up in a small town in Mississippi, personified the awakening of black consciousness that led to action. As a child, she had watched the passivity of blacks in the face of discrimination and struggled to understand just what "the white folks' secret" really was. She saw the murder of friends and acquaintances who had somehow transgressed the limits set for blacks. And she became frustrated at members of her own race for not doing anything about the injustices she saw. "I began to look upon Negro men as cowards," she later wrote. "I could not respect them for smiling in a white man's face, addressing him as Mr. So-and-So, saying yessuh and nossuh when after they were home behind closed doors that same white man was a son of a bitch, a bastard, or any other name more suitable than mister."

Through her own efforts, Moody became the first of her family to go to college. Once there, she found her own place in the civil rights movement. At Tougaloo College in Jackson, Mississippi, she joined the NAACP and also became involved in the activities of SNCC and CORE. Slowly, she noted, "I could feel myself beginning to change. For the first time I began to think something would be done about whites killing, beating, and misusing Negroes. I knew I was going to be a part of whatever happened." She participated in sit-ins where she was thrashed and jailed for her role, but she remained deeply involved. She learned how to protect herself when threatened by angry whites. Though often exhausted and discouraged, she knew that she was part of something important.

Many whites also joined the struggle in the South. Mimi Feingold, a white student at Swarthmore College in Pennsylvania, had been active in northern civil rights protests and antinuclear efforts in the late 1950s, but when the sit-in movement began, she became much more deeply involved. She helped picket Woolworth's in Chester, Pennsylvania, and sought to unionize Swarthmore's black dining hall workers. But she wanted to do still more. In 1961, after her sophomore year, she headed south to join the freedom rides sponsored by CORE.

The civil rights workers she met often got the confrontations they expected. On the freedom rides, they frequently stepped off the buses to face derogatory shouts and brutal assault. Injuries were common as southern whites attacked them with rocks and chains. One bus was pelted with stones, then burned. Feingold's group had a bomb scare in Montgomery, Alabama, and knew that the last such bus to enter the state had been blown up. Like many others, Mimi went to jail as an act of conscience. In Jackson, Mississippi, where she spent a month behind bars, she heard other women screaming in response to the humiliating searches local police conducted. Background made no difference to officials in the South. Yale University chaplain William Sloane Coffin, Jr., was one of many arrested for trying to use facilities in a Montgomery terminal with an integrated group of clergymen.

In 1962, the civil rights movement gained further momentum. James Meredith, a black air force veteran and student at Jackson State College, sought to enter the all-white University of Mississippi, only to be rejected on racial grounds. Suing to gain admission, he carried his case to the Supreme Court, where Justice Hugo Black affirmed his claim. But then Governor Ross Barnett, an adamant racist, asserted that Meredith would not be admitted, whatever the Court decision, and on one occasion personally blocked the way. "We never have trouble with our people," he told Attorney General Robert F. Kennedy, who was supporting Meredith's claim, "but the NAACP, they want to stir up trouble down here." With the issue joined, a major riot began. One angry white southerner's effort to drive a bulldozer into the administration building failed only when the vehicle stalled. Tear gas covered the university grounds, and by the end of the riot, two men were dead and hundreds hurt.

An even more violent confrontation began in April 1963, in Birmingham, Alabama, where Martin Luther King, Jr., decided to launch another attack on southern segregation. Forty percent black, the city was rigidly segregated along racial and class lines. King later explained, "We believed that while a campaign in Birmingham would surely be the toughest fight of our civil rights careers, it could, if successful, break the back of segregation all over the nation."

Though the protests were nonviolent, the responses were not. City officials declared that protest marches violated city regulations against parading without a license, and, over a five-week period, they arrested 2,200 blacks, some of them young school children. Police Commissioner Eugene "Bull" Connor used high-pressure fire hoses, electric cattle prods, and trained police dogs to force the protesters back. Newspaper photographers and television camera operators recorded the events for people around the world to see, and many who saw them were aghast. As newsman Eric Sevareid observed, "A newspaper or television picture of a snarling police dog set upon a human being is recorded in the permanent photo-electric file of every human brain."

### Kennedy's Response

When Kennedy ran for office, he was well aware of the importance of the black vote. During the campaign, he announced that "if the President does not himself wage the struggle for equal rights—if he stands above the battle—then the battle will inevitably be lost." He asserted too that a "stroke of the pen" could end racial segregation in federally funded housing. That approach succeeded in bringing him 70 percent of the black vote, and in some states where the tally had been close, particularly Michigan and Illinois, black support made a crucial difference.

Once in office, however, Kennedy dragged his heels. Reluctant to press white southerners on civil rights when he needed their votes on other issues, Kennedy failed to sponsor any civil rights legislation. Nor did he fulfill his campaign promise to end housing discrimination by presidential order, despite gifts of numerous bottles of ink. Not until November 1962, after the midterm elections, did he take a modest action —an executive order ending segregation in federally financed housing. Under Robert Kennedy the Justice Department worked to end discrimination in interstate transportation and to guarantee blacks the right to register and vote in the South. But to Martin Luther King, Jr., this was hardly enough: "If tokenism were our goal, this

Administration has moved us adroitly towards its accomplishment."

Events finally forced Kennedy to take actions he had hoped to avoid. When James Meredith was refused admission to the University of Mississippi because of his color in 1962, the president, like his predecessor in the Little Rock crisis, had to send federal troops to restore control and to guarantee Meredith's right to attend. The administration also forced the desegregation of the University of Alabama and helped arrange a compromise providing for desegregation of Birmingham's municipal facilities, implementation of more equitable hiring practices, and formation of a biracial committee. And when violence erupted in Birmingham and thousands of blacks abandoned nonviolence and rampaged through the streets, Kennedy readied federal troops to intervene.

The events in Birmingham raised the horrifying possibility of black revolution and helped to push Kennedy toward a bold stance. In a nationally televised address, he called the quest for equal rights "a moral issue" and asserted, "We preach freedom around the world, and we mean it . . . ; but are we to say to the world, and much more importantly, to each other that this is a land of the free except for the Negroes . . . ?" He sent Congress a new civil rights bill, far stronger than the moderate one proposed earlier in the year. The legislation prohibited segregation in public places, banned discrimination wherever federal money was involved, and advanced the process of school integration. Polls showed that 63 percent of the nation supported his stand.

To lobby for passage of that measure, civil rights leaders, pressed from below by black activists, arranged a massive march on Washington in August 1963. Kennedy did not favor the demonstration, for he feared it would alienate Congress and provoke violence in the capital city. After his efforts failed to get the organizers to call it off, however, Kennedy supported the march, which proved to be an almost festive affair. More than 200,000 people gathered from across the country and demonstrated enthusiastically. Celebrities were present: Ralph Bunche, James Baldwin, Sammy Davis, Jr., Harry Belafonte, Jackie Robinson, Lena Horne. The folk-

*Martin Luther King's famous "I have a dream" speech was delivered to the assembled crowd during the 1963 march on Washington.*

music artists of the early 1960s were there as well. Joan Baez, Bob Dylan, and Peter, Paul, and Mary sang songs associated with the movement such as "Blowin' in the Wind" and "We Shall Overcome."

But the high point of the day was the address by Martin Luther King, Jr., who had become the nation's preeminent spokesman for civil rights. For many blacks and whites, he seemed to represent the struggle itself. Long interested in Gandhi's theory of nonviolent protest, he had become committed to nonviolent resistance. Working through his own Southern Christian Leadership Conference, he pressed vigorously for racial change. At the March on Washington, in a powerful address, he proclaimed his faith in the decency of his fellow citizens. With all the power of a southern preacher, he implored his audience to share his faith.

## The Struggle for Equal Rights

| YEAR | EVENT | EFFECT |
|------|-------|--------|
| 1947 | Report of Truman's Committee on Civil Rights | Showed that blacks remained second-class citizens in America. |
| 1948 | Truman issues executive order integrating the armed forces | Opened the way for equal opportunities in the armed forces. |
| 1954 | *Brown* v. *Board of Education* decision | Supreme Court ruled that local school boards should move "with all deliberate speed" to desegregate facilities. |
| 1955 | Montgomery bus boycott | Black solidarity tested local petty segregation laws and customs. |
| 1957 | Little Rock school integration crisis | White resistance to integration of Little Rock's Central High School resulted in Eisenhower's calling in federal troops. |
|      | Civil Rights Act | Created Civil Rights Commission and empowered Justice Department to go to court to guarantee blacks the right to vote. |
| 1960 | Civil Rights Act | Plugged loopholes in Civil Rights Act of 1957. |
|      | Sit-in demonstrations begin | Gained support for desegregation of public facilities. |
| 1961 | Freedom rides begin | Dramatized struggle to desegregate transportation facilities. |
| 1962 | James Meredith attempts to attend University of Mississippi | Required federal intervention to uphold blacks' rights to attend public institutions. |
| 1963 | Effort to desegregate Birmingham, Alabama | Brutal response of police televised, sensitizing entire nation to plight of blacks. |
|      | March on Washington | Gathered support and inspiration for the civil rights movement; scene of Martin Luther King's "I Have a Dream" speech |
| 1964 | Civil Rights Act | Outlawed racial discrimination in public accommodations. |
| 1965 | Voting Rights Act | Allowed federal examiners to register black voters where necessary. |
| 1971 | Busing decision | Supreme Court ruled that court-ordered desegration was constitutional, even if it employed busing. |
| 1978 | *Bakke* decision | Supreme Court declared that affirmative action was constitutional but that firm racial quotas were not. |

"I have a dream," King declared, "that one day this nation will rise up and live out the true meaning of its creed: 'We hold these truths to be self-evident, that all men are created equal.' I have a dream that one day on the red hills of Georgia, the sons of former slaves and the sons of former slave-owners will be able to sit together at the table of brotherhood." It was a fervent appeal, and one to which the crowd responded. Each time King used the refrain "I have a dream," thousands of blacks and whites roared together. King concluded by quoting from an old hymn: "Free at last! Free at last! Thank God almighty, we are free at last!"

Despite the power of the rhetoric, not all listeners were moved. Anne Moody, who had come up from her activist work in Mississippi to attend the event, sat on the grass by the Lincoln Memorial as the speaker's words rang out. "Martin Luther King went on and on talking about his dream," she said. "I sat there thinking that . . . we never had time to sleep, much less dream." Nor was the Congress prompted to do much. Despite large Democratic majorities, strong southern resistance to the cause of civil rights remained, and as of November 1963, Kennedy's bill was still bottled up in committee. Not even the March on Washington had moved it along.

## THE GREAT SOCIETY

Kennedy found that too often he had to bow to political realities. Real movement toward social goals came only when large congressional majorities allowed his successor, Lyndon Johnson, to use his considerable talents to pass programs intended to realize the "Great Society."

### Assassination and Change in Command

Facing reelection in 1964, Kennedy hoped not only to win the presidency for a second term but also to increase Democratic strength in Congress. In November 1963, he traveled to Texas, where he hoped to unite the state's Democratic party for the upcoming election. Dallas, one of the stops on the trip, had a reputation as being less than cordial to the administration. Four weeks before, Adlai Stevenson, ambassador to the United Nations, had been abused there by a conservative mob. Now, on November 22, Kennedy had a chance to see for himself. Arriving at the airport, Henry González, a congressman accompanying the president in Texas, remarked jokingly, "Well, I'm taking my risks. I haven't got my steel vest yet." As the party entered the city in an open car, the president encountered friendly crowds. Suddenly shots rang out, and Kennedy slumped forward. Desperately wounded, he died a short time later at a Dallas hospital. Lee Harvey Oswald, the assassin, was himself shot and killed a few days later in the jail where he was being held.

Without warning, Lyndon Johnson was president of the United States. As vice-president, he had never been comfortable with the Kennedy crowd and had felt stifled in his subordinate role. He was, he knew, a far better legislative leader than JFK, but he was out of Congress in a position where he seemed to have no power.

Despite his own ambivalence about Kenne-

*The assassination of Kennedy thrust Lyndon Johnson into the presidency amid an atmosphere of shocked grief and loss.*

dy, Johnson understood the profound shock gripping the nation. Well aware that millions of Americans regarded him as a pretender to the throne, he embraced Kennedy's goals. Four days after he assumed office, he made his first public address. He began, in a measured tone, with the words, "All I have, I would have given gladly not to be standing here today." He asked members of Congress to work with him, and he underscored the theme "Let us continue" throughout his speech.

Johnson was determined to secure the measures that Kennedy sought but had been unable to extract from Congress. He took the bills to reduce taxes and ensure civil rights as his first and most pressing priorities, but he was interested too in aiding public education, providing medical care for the aged, and eliminating poverty. By the spring of 1964, the outlines of his own expansive vision were taking shape, and he had begun to use the phrase "Great Society" to describe his reform program. After a landslide victory over conservative Republican challenger Barry Goldwater in 1964, in which LBJ received 61 percent of the popular vote and an electoral margin of 486 to 52, he had a far more impressive mandate than Kennedy had ever enjoyed.

### Civil Rights Under Johnson

Civil rights reform was LBJ's first legislative priority, although his own earlier record on the issue was mixed. A southerner from Texas, he first voted against a series of civil rights measures in his years in the House of Representatives, then became more sympathetic as his own career advanced and he recognized a larger constituency. By 1955, when he became Senate majority leader and eyed the White House, he was ready to play a much more active role. He broke with the South when he guided the Civil Rights Acts of 1957 through Congress. His commitment to racial justice was far stronger than Kennedy's. Indeed, Johnson had urged Kennedy to visit the South and to tell whites that segregation was evil and un-Christian.

In 1963, Johnson revived Kennedy's civil rights proposal, which had been sidetracked in Congress. Seizing the opportunity provided by Kennedy's assassination, Johnson told Congress, "No memorial oration or eulogy could more eloquently honor President Kennedy's memory than the earliest possible passage of the civil rights bill." Soon after he took office, he assured black leaders that he would push for the civil rights bill.

Johnson indicated that he would accept no compromise on civil rights. After the House of Representatives passed the bill, the Senate became bogged down in a lengthy filibuster. Johnson responded by persuading his old colleague, minority leader Everett Dirksen, to work for cloture—a two-thirds vote to cut off debate. In June 1964, the Senate for the first time imposed cloture to advance a civil rights measure, and passage soon followed. "No army can withstand the strength of an idea whose time has come," Dirksen commented.

The Civil Rights Act of 1964 outlawed racial discrimination in all public accommodations and authorized the Justice Department to act with greater authority in school and voting matters. In addition, an equal-opportunity provision prohibited discriminatory hiring on grounds of race, gender, religion, or national origin in firms with more than 25 employees. The legislation was one of the great achievements of the 1960s. The system of segregation put in place in the South in the late nineteenth century lost its legal sanctions. Blacks now were promised legal equality as they had been 100 years before.

Johnson realized that the Civil Rights Act of 1964 was a starting point, not the stopping point. Patent discrimination still existed in American society. Despite the voting rights measures of 1957 and 1960, blacks still found it difficult to vote in large areas of the South. Freedom Summer, sponsored by SNCC and other civil rights groups in Mississippi in 1964, focused attention on the problem by sending black and white students south to work for black rights. Early in the summer, two whites, Michael Schwerner and Andrew Goodman, and one black, James Chaney, were murdered. By the end of the summer, 80 workers had been beaten, 1,000 arrests had been made, and 37 churches had been bombed. The following year, Martin Luther King, Jr., proposed another march, this one from Selma to Montgomery, Alabama, to dramatize the situation.

Just a few days before the Selma march,

President Johnson addressed a joint session of Congress, with television cameras carrying the speech nationwide. Pleading for a voting bill that would close the loopholes of the previous two acts, he began by saying, "I speak tonight for the dignity of man and the destiny of democracy. . . . It is wrong . . . to deny any of your fellow Americans the right to vote." Stopping at one point and raising his arms, he slowly repeated the words from the old hymn that had become the marching song of the movement: "And . . . we . . . shall . . . overcome." The members of Congress responded with thunderous applause. Once again using all the pressure he could muster, he helped break a filibuster and signed a second civil rights measure into law.

The Voting Rights Act of 1965, perhaps the most important law of the decade, singled out the South for its restrictive practices and authorized the U.S. attorney general to appoint federal examiners to register voters where local officials were obstructing the registration of blacks. In the year after passage of the act, 400,000 blacks registered to vote in the Deep South; by 1968, the number reached a million.

## The Great Society in Action

Had Johnson achieved nothing more than the two civil rights acts, his administration would have been notable. In fact, he accomplished much more. Under his prodding, Congress responded with the strongest legislative program since the New Deal. The president directed much of the activity. He appointed task forces that included legislators to study problems and suggest solutions, worked with them to draft bills, and maintained close contact with congressional leaders through a sophisticated liaison staff. Not since the Roosevelt years had there been such a coordinated effort to promote legislation.

Action followed in many areas. Following Kennedy's lead, Johnson pressed for a tax cut to stimulate the economy. To gain conservative support, he agreed to hold down spending; the tax bill passed. With the tax cut in hand, the president pressed for the poverty program that Kennedy had begun to plan. For the first time in

American history, the government developed a program specifically directed at ending poverty. As Johnson declared in his 1964 State of the Union message, "This administration today, here and now, declares unconditional war on poverty in America." The center of the effort to eradicate poverty was the Economic Opportunity Act of 1964. It created an Office of Economic Opportunity to provide education and training for unskilled young people trapped in the poverty cycle, VISTA (Volunteers in Service to America) to assist the poor at home, and assorted community-action programs to give the poor themselves a voice in improving housing, health, and education in their own neighborhoods.

The election of 1964 gave Johnson the mandate he needed to enact the rest of his program. Receiving 61 percent of the popular vote, he scored a clear victory over Republican Barry Goldwater with 486 electoral votes. With congressional majorities of 68–32 in the Senate and 295–140 in the House, Johnson broke the conservative Republican–Southern Democratic alignment that had hobbled reform programs in the past.

Aware of the escalating costs of medical care, Johnson proposed a medical assistance plan. Truman had proposed such a measure almost two decades before but had failed to win congressional approval. Nor had Kennedy accomplished anything in this area. Johnson, however, provided the necessary leadership. To head off conservative attacks, the administration tied the Medicare measure to the established social security system and limited the program to the elderly. Medicaid met the needs of the poor below the age of 65 who could not afford private insurance. The Medicare-Medicaid program was the most important extension of federally directed social benefits since the Social Security Act of 1935.

Johnson was similarly successful in his effort to provide aid for elementary and secondary schools. Kennedy had met defeat when Catholics had insisted on assistance to parochial schools. Johnson, a Protestant, was able to deal with that ticklish question without charges of favoritism. He endorsed a measure to give money to the states based on the numbers of children from low-income families. Those funds would then be distributed to public as well as private schools to benefit all needy children.

In LBJ's expansive vision, the federal government would ensure that all shared in the promise of American life. As a result of his prodding, Congress passed a new housing act to provide rent supplements to the poor and created a Department of Housing and Urban Development. It reformed the restrictive immigration policy, which for decades had rested on racial and national quotas, although immigration was still restricted in terms of numbers. It provided legal assistance for the poor. It moved further in funding education, including colleges and universities in its financial grants. Finally, Congress provided artists and scholars with assistance through new National Endowments for the Arts and Humanities. Not since the Works Progress Administration in the New Deal had such groups been granted government aid.

## A Sympathetic Supreme Court

The Supreme Court also supported and promoted social change in the 1960s. Under the leadership of Chief Justice Earl Warren, the Court followed the lead it had taken in 1954 in *Brown* v. *Board of Education*. Several decisions reaffirmed the Court's support of black rights. Having disposed of the issue of school segregation, the Court moved against Jim Crow practices in other public establishments. Providing quick support for the Civil Rights Act of 1964 and the Voting Rights Act of 1965, the justices gave notice that the Court would no longer uphold discriminatory customs.

The Court also supported civil liberties. Where earlier judicial decisions had affirmed restrictions on members of the Communist party and radical groups, now the Court began to protect the rights of individuals who held radical political views. Similarly, the Court sought to protect accused suspects from police harassment. In *Gideon* v. *Wainwright* (1963) the justices decided that poor suspects had the right to free legal counsel. In *Escobedo* v. *Illinois* (1964) they ruled that an offender had to be given access to an attorney during questioning, while in *Miranda* v. *Arizona* (1966) they argued that

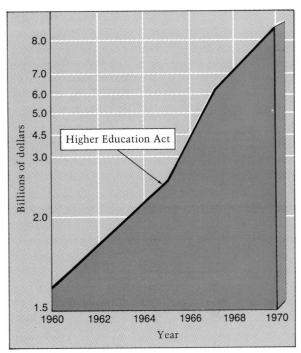

**Federal Aid to Education in the 1960s**
*Source:* U.S. Bureau of the Census.

offenders had to be warned that statements extracted by the police could be used against them and that they could remain silent.

Other decisions also broke new ground. *Baker* v. *Carr* (1962) opened the way to reapportionment of state legislative bodies, according to the standard, in Justice William O. Douglas's words, of "one person, one vote." Meanwhile, the Court ruled that prayer in the public schools was unconstitutional and decided that obscenity laws could no longer restrict allegedly pornographic material that might have some "redeeming social value."

## The Great Society Under Attack

For a few years, the Great Society worked as Johnson had hoped. The tax cut proved effective. After its passage, GNP rose steadily, 7.1 percent in 1964, 8.1 percent in 1965, and 9.5 percent in 1966. At the same time, the budget deficit dropped. Unemployment fell, and inflation remained under control. Medical programs provided a measure of security for the old and the poor. Education flourished as schools were built,

## Major Great Society Programs

| DATE OF PASSAGE | PROGRAM | EFFECT |
| --- | --- | --- |
| January 23, 1964 (ratified) | Twenty-fourth Amendment | Banned poll tax as prerequisite in federal elections. |
| February 26, 1964 | Tax Reduction Act | Lowered federal personal tax rates. |
| July 2, 1964 | Civil Rights Act | Banned discrimination in public accommodations; gave attorney general right to file suit to desegregate schools or other facilities; banned discrimination in employment on basis of race, color, religion, sex, or national origin. |
| July 9, 1964 | Urban Mass Transportation Act | Provided $375 million in financial aid to urban-transit systems. |
| August 30, 1964 | Economic Opportunity Act | Authorized ten separate programs to be conducted by the Office of Economic Opportunity, including Job Corps and VISTA. |
| September 3, 1964 | Wilderness Preservation Act | Designate 9.1 million acres of national forest lands to be safeguarded permanently against commercial use and construction of permanent roads and buildings. |
| April 11, 1965 | Elementary and Secondary Education Act | Provided $1.3 billion in aid to elementary and secondary schools. |
| July 30, 1965 | Medicare | Provided medical care for the aged through the social security system. |
| August 6, 1965 | Voting Rights Act | Suspended literacy tests and other voter tests; authorized federal supervision of registration in states and districts where few voting-age residents had voted earlier. |
| August 10, 1965 | Omnibus Housing Act | Provided rent supplements to low-income families and federal aid to place low-income persons in private housing. |
| September 9, 1965 | Department of Housing and Urban Development | Provided special programs concerned with housing needs, fair-housing opportunities, and the improvement and development of communities. |
| September 9, 1965 | National Foundation of the Arts and Humanities | Provided financial assistance for painters, actors, dancers, musicians, and others in the arts. |
| October 2, 1965 | Water Quality Act | Required states to establish and enforce water quality standards for all interstate waters within their boundaries. |
| October 3, 1965 | Immigration laws | Revision set new quotas. |
| October 20, 1965 | Air Quality Act | Amended earlier laws. |
| October 20, 1965 | Higher Education Act | Provided federal scholarships to undergraduates and others. |
| September 9, 1966 | National Traffic and Motor Vehicle Safety Act | Set federal safety standards. |
| September 9, 1966 | Highway Safety Act | Required states to set up federally approved safety programs. |
| September 23, 1966 | Minimum wage | Raised minimum wage from $1.25 to $1.40 per hour; extended coverage. |
| October 15, 1966 | Department of Transportation | Provided federal agencies to administer policies, in conjunction with state and local officials, regarding highway planning, development, and construction; urban mass transit; railroads; aviation; and safety of waterways, ports, highways; and oil and gas pipelines. |
| November 3, 1966 | Model Cities | Encouraged rehabilitation of slums. |

and salaries increased in response to the influx of federal aid.

Yet the gains proved short-lived. Some programs promised too much, and disillusionment followed when they failed to meet expectations. Often the criticisms that surfaced had been heard from the start. Conservatives were uneasy about centralization of authority as they saw government take over more of the responsibility for defining the national welfare. They also worried about involving the poor themselves, for they argued that recipients of aid often lacked a broad vision of the nation's needs.

More incisive were the criticisms from the left. Radicals claimed that the Great Society was a warmed-over version of the New Deal three decades before. The same middle-class liberal orientation remained, with the real intent of programs to provide the poor with middle-class values. "The welfare state is more machinery than substance," young critic Tom Hayden charged. No real effort had been made to redistribute income. Great Society programs rested on the belief that the American system was basically sound and that economic growth, not the redistribution of wealth, would secure the benefits of the American dream for all. Nor was enough money allocated to the new social programs. Though several billion dollars were spent before the Vietnam War drew off resources and disrupted the economy, even that was not enough to meet the needs of 30 or 40 million disadvantaged people. As Michael Harrington concluded, "What was supposed to be a social war turned out to be a skirmish and, in any case, poverty won."

## Black Power Challenges Liberal Reform

Nowhere were criticisms more pronounced than in the area of civil rights. There as elsewhere, expectations had been raised, but many blacks still saw fundamental inequalities in American life and vociferously declared their unwillingness to wait any longer for reform. The civil rights movement initially had been an integrated, nonviolent campaign with Martin Luther King, Jr., as its acknowledged leader. But now black-white tensions began to appear within organizations, and the dominance of King's nonviolent approach ended. More militant

spokesmen articulated a long-suppressed rage in language that often shocked white liberals.

Anne Moody, the stalwart activist in Mississippi, voiced some of the doubts so many blacks felt about the possibility of real change. Tired and discouraged after months of struggle, on one occasion she boarded a bus taking civil rights workers north to testify about the abuses that still remained. As she listened to the others singing the movement's songs, she could only think of the suffering she had so often seen. "We Shall Overcome" reverberated around her, but all she could think was, "I WONDER. I really WONDER."

One episode that contributed to a black sense of betrayal by white liberals occurred at the Democratic National Convention of 1964 in Atlantic City. SNCC, active in the Freedom Summer project in Mississippi, had founded a Freedom Democratic party as an alternative to the all-white delegation that was to represent the state. Before the credentials committee, black activist Fannie Lou Hamer testified that she had been beaten, jailed, and denied the right to vote. Yet the committee's final compromise was that the white delegation would still be seated, with two members of the protest organization offered seats at large. That response hardly satisfied those who had risked their lives and families to try to vote in Mississippi. As civil rights leader James Forman observed, "Atlantic City was a powerful lesson, not only for the black people from Mississippi, but for all of SNCC. . . . No longer was there any hope . . . that the federal government would change the situation in the Deep South." SNCC, once a religious, integrated organization, began to change into an all-black cadre that could mobilize poor blacks for militant action.

Increasingly, angry blacks argued that something was going to have to give. In *The Fire Next Time* (1962), James Baldwin, a prominent black author, wrote of the "rope, fire, torture, castration, infanticide, rape; death and humiliation; fear by day and night, fear as deep as the marrow of the bone" that were part of the black past. "For the horrors of the American Negro's life," he declared, "there has been almost no language." Unless change came soon, the worst could be expected: "If we do not now dare everything, the fulfillment of that prophecy, recreated from the Bible in song by a slave, is upon us: *God gave Noah the rainbow sign, No more water, the fire next time!"*

Even more responsible for focusing aggressive black sentiment was Malcolm X. Born Malcolm Little and raised in ghettos from Detroit to New York, he became intimately familiar with the sordid side of black urban life. In his preconversion days, he wore a zoot suit, conked his hair, and hustled numbers and prostitutes in the big cities. Only when he was arrested did he begin to question his past. In prison, he became a convert to the Nation of Islam and a disciple of black leader Elijah Muhammad. He began to preach that the white man was responsible for the black man's condition and that blacks had to help themselves.

Malcolm had little use for the moderate civil rights movement represented by SNCC and Martin Luther King. He grew tired of hearing "all of this nonviolent, begging-the-white-man kind of dying . . . all of this sitting-in, sliding-in, wading-in, eating-in, diving-in, and all the rest." The March on Washington he termed the "Farce on Washington." Arguing in favor of black separation from the white race for most of his public career, he urged blacks to take care of themselves. He appealed to blacks to fight racism "by any means necessary" and insisted that the "day of nonviolent resistance is over."

Malcolm's articulate affirmation of blackness and his justification of self-defense struck a resonant chord. With widespread media attention, he became the most dynamic spokesman for poor blacks since Marcus Garvey in the 1920s. Though he was assassinated by a black antagonist in 1965, his perspective helped shape the ongoing struggle against racism.

One man influenced by Malcolm's message was Stokely Carmichael. Born in Trinidad, he came to the United States at the age of 11 and became an American. Because his family remained involved in the black nationalist independence movement in the Caribbean, Carmichael grew up with an interest in political affairs. At the Bronx High School of Science he read voraciously, attended left-wing meetings, became interested in socialism, and gravitated into black protest. Aware of civil rights activity at predominantly black Howard University in Washington, D.C., he went there for college. Soon after arriving at Howard, he and other students took over the Washington chapter of SNCC. He participated in pickets and demonstrations and was beaten and jailed. Frustrated with the strategy of civil disobedience, he urged fieldworkers to carry weapons for self-defense. It was time for blacks to cease depending on whites, he argued, and to make SNCC into a black organization. His election as head of SNCC in 1966 reflected the movement's shifting course.

The split in the black movement became clear in June 1966 when Carmichael's followers challenged those of Martin Luther King at a demonstration. King still adhered to nonviolence and to interracial cooperation. Their movement's song, "We Shall Overcome," was drowned out by Carmichael's followers' song, "We Shall Overrun." The turning point came when Carmichael, just out of jail, jumped onto a flatbed truck to address the group. "This is the twenty-seventh time I have been arrested—and I ain't going to jail no more!" he shouted. "The only way we gonna stop them white men from whippin' us is to take over. We been saying

*"The day of nonviolence is over," proclaimed Malcolm X; many poor blacks listened enthusiastically.*

freedom for six years and we ain't got nothing. What we gonna start saying now is Black Power!" Carmichael had the audience in his hand. As he repeated, "We . . . want . . . Black . . . Power!" the crowd roared back the same words.

Meanwhile, other blacks proposed more drastic action. Huey Newton of the Black Panthers, another militant organization that vowed to eradicate not only racial discrimination but capitalism as well, proclaimed that "political power comes through the barrel of a gun." H. Rap Brown, who followed Carmichael as head of SNCC, became known for his statement that "violence is as American as cherry pie."

Violence accompanied the more militant calls for reform and showed that racial injustice was not a southern problem but an American one. In the North, blacks faced informal segregation, poverty, and inferior housing and schools.

Many were unwilling to wait quietly for their lives to improve. Riots erupted in Rochester, New York City, and several New Jersey cities in 1964. In 1965, in the Watts neighborhood of Los Angeles, a massive uprising lasting five days left 34 dead, more than 1,000 injured, and hundreds of structures burned to the ground. Violence broke out again in other cities in 1966 and again in 1967. Now cries of "Get Whitey" and "Burn, baby, burn" replaced the nonviolence of the earlier civil rights movement. Martin Luther King, Jr., fell before a white assassin's bullet in April 1968. Angry blacks reacted by demonstrating once more in cities around the country. As the National Advisory Commission on Civil Disobedience noted in the Kerner Report of 1968, "The nation is rapidly moving toward two increasingly separate Americas." Black protest highlighted inequities and dramatized the inadequacy of white liberal reform.

## THE RISING CALL FOR REFORM

Blacks were not the only Americans to demand justice and to decry racism. Native Americans and Hispanic-Americans also pressed for change, while women became increasingly militant and better organized in their efforts to eliminate sexism in America.

### Tribal Voices

Native Americans continued to suffer second-class status as the 1960s began. They had endured the termination policy of the Eisenhower years, when the federal government embarked on a program of urban relocation aimed at forcing them to assimilate into mainstream American life. That effort had worked poorly, as thousands of Native Americans traded reservation poverty for urban poverty. In 1961, the United States Commission on Civil Rights observed that for Indians, "poverty and deprivation are common. Social acceptance is not the rule. In addition, Indians seem to suffer more than occasional mistreatment by the instruments of law and order on and off the reservations." Indians, in short, faced obstacles much like those blacks encountered.

As the Indian population grew from 550,000 in 1960 to 790,000 in 1970, Democratic administrations abandoned Eisenhower's termination policy and tried to give Native Americans a greater voice in their own affairs. Many tribes,

*Poverty and discrimination marked the daily lives of most Native Americans, both on reservations and in mainstream urban communities.*

however, still protested what they called the federal government's "colonial rule."

Led by a new generation of leaders, Native Americans tried to protect what was left of their tribal lands. Elders reminded young people, "Once we owned all the land." For generations, federal and state governments had steadily encroached on Native American territory. "Everything is tied to our homeland," D'Arcy McNickle, a Flathead anthropologist, told other Indians in 1961 as they started to organize.

The new activism was apparent on the Seneca Nation's Allegany reservation in New York State. Although the Seneca's right to the land was established by a treaty made in 1794, the federal government had planned since 1928 to build the Kinzua Dam there as part of a flood-control project. Surveys were taken, but for years little was done. In 1956, after hearings to which the Indians were not invited and about which they were not informed, Congress appropriated funds for the project. When court appeals failed to block the scheme, the Seneca turned to President Kennedy in 1961. Kennedy, however, supported the government's right to take the land it had promised not to take in 1794. The dam was eventually built, and although the government belatedly passed a $15 million reparations bill, money did not compensate for the loss of 10,000 acres of land that contained sacred sites, hunting and fishing grounds, and homes.

Native American leaders then brought a wave of lawsuits charging violations of treaty rights. In 1967, in the first of many decisions upholding the Indian side, the U.S. Court of Claims ruled that the government had forced the Seminole in Florida to cede their land in 1823 for an unreasonably low price. The court directed the government to pay additional funds 144 years later. That decision was a source of some satisfaction to the Seminole population, although the compensation had not yet been paid by 1982.

The most dramatic displays of the new Native American militancy began with the founding of the American Indian Movement (AIM) in 1968. Organized by George Mitchell and Dennis Banks, Chippewa living in Minneapolis, AIM sought to help neglected Indians in the city. It managed to get Office of Economic Opportunity funds channeled to Indian-controlled organiza-

tions. It also established patrols to protect drunken Indians from harassment by the police. As its successes became known, chapters formed in other cities.

## César Chávez and the United Farm Workers

Hispanic-Americans also became actively involved in efforts to gain their share of the American dream. Some were Puerto Ricans living in the Northeast; others were Cubans settling mainly in Florida. Many more were Mexican-Americans, who lived in the Southwest and called themselves Chicanos in California and Tejanos in Texas. In these names they expressed more ardently a sense of solidarity and group pride. In 1960, just under 3.5 million people with Spanish surnames lived in the Southwest. Their per capita income was half that of Anglos, and their social and cultural separation was reinforced by inferior education and political weakness.

With Johnson's poverty program, Mexican-Americans hoped for improved opportunities. But they soon found that most efforts were oriented toward black Americans and that bureaucrats were often less sensitive to the problems of equally exploited but less vocal groups. From this they learned the value of pressure politics in a pluralistic society. In the election of 1960, Mexican-Americans supported Kennedy, helping him win Texas. In 1961, Henry B. Gonzàlez was elected to Congress from San Antonio. Three years later, Elizo ("Kika") de la Garza of Texas won election to the House and Joseph Montoya of New Mexico went to the Senate. Chicanos were gaining a political voice and began to anticipate the day when it could help them improve their lives.

More important than political representation, which came only slowly, was direct action. César Chávez, founder of the United Farm Workers, proved what could be done by organizing one of the most exploited and ignored groups of laboring people in the country, the migrant farm workers of the West. Born in Yuma, Arizona, Chávez went to California in the 1940s. There he acquired organizational skills. Two decades later, he established his own union, the United Farm Workers. Concentrating on migrant Mexican fieldhands who worked long hours in the fields for meager pay, he chose a loyal cadre to conduct a door-to-door and field-to-field campaign. By 1965, his organization had recruited 1,700 members and was beginning to attract volunteer help. His intent was to present the farm workers' struggle as part of the larger national struggle for civil rights.

Chávez first took on the grape growers of California. Calling the grape workers out on strike, the union demanded better pay and working conditions as well as the recognition of the union. When the growers did not concede, Chávez launched a nationwide consumer boycott of their products. Although the Schenley Corporation and several wine companies came to terms, others held out. In 1966, the DiGiorgio Corporation agreed to permit a union election but then rigged the results. When California governor Edmund G. Brown launched an investigation that resulted in another election, he became the first major political figure to support the long

*Migrant Mexican field hands were organized by César Chávez who led their fight for better pay and working conditions.*

powerless Chicano fieldhands. This time the United Farm Workers won.

Chávez himself became a national figure. Stories about him ran in the *Wall Street Journal, Life,* and *Time.* Robert Kennedy befriended him and helped rally support by visiting him and his strikers in the fields. When Kennedy was assassinated in 1968, Chicanos believed they had lost their best ally. But Chávez continued to inspire other Mexican-Americans. Soon, militant groups like the Young Citizens for Community Action and the Brown Berets were operating in numerous cities.

## Attacking the Feminine Mystique

The women's movement, like the Mexican-American and Native American movements, had roots in the civil rights activity of the 1950s and 1960s. Women involved in civil rights agitation discovered that men, black and white, held the policy positions, while women were relegated to menial chores when not actually involved in demonstrations or voter drives. Many women also felt sexually exploited by the men with whom they worked. Stokely Carmichael's comment only underscored their point. "The only position for women in SNCC," he said, "is prone." Despite growing dissatisfaction and their awareness of sexual exploitation, the women recognized the importance of militant, well-publicized pressure groups in bringing about change.

Although the civil rights movement supplied some of the impetus behind the women's movement, broad social changes provided the preconditions. During the 1950s and 1960s, increasing numbers of married women entered the labor force, and half of all women worked. Cries for fair treatment arose from some of them. In 1963, the average working woman earned only 63 percent of what a man could expect, in 1973, only 57 percent. Just as important, many more young women were attending college. By 1970, women earned 41 percent of all B.A.'s awarded, in comparison to only 25 percent in 1950. These educated young women held high hopes for themselves. Many found that sexual liberation failed to bring equality. They would find feminism compelling both in its analysis of women's problems and in the solutions it offered.

Just as in the civil rights movement, reform legislation led the effort to end sexual discrimination. Title 7 of the 1964 Civil Rights bill, as originally drafted, prohibited discrimination on the grounds of race. During legislative debate, conservatives opposed to black civil rights proposed an amendment to include discrimination on the basis of gender. In this way, they hoped to defeat the entire bill. But the amendment passed, giving women a legal tool for attacking discrimination. They discovered, however, that the Equal Employment Opportunities Commission regarded women's complaints of discrimination as far less important than those of blacks.

When a small group of women failed to win support from existing women's groups to pressure the commission to change its policies, they decided to form their own civil rights organization. In 1966, 28 professional women, including Betty Friedan, established the National Organization for Women (NOW) "to take action to bring American women into full participation in the mainstream of American society *now*." By full participation the founders not only meant fair pay and equal opportunity but a new, more egalitarian form of marriage. NOW also attacked "the false image of women now prevalent in the media." By 1967, some 1,000 women had joined the organization, and four years later, its membership reached 15,000.

NOW was a political pressure group and did not seem radical enough to some young women. The radical feminists, who had come up through the civil rights movement, felt that NOW's

### Women Working Outside the Home, 1890–1970

*Source:* U.S. Bureau of the Census.

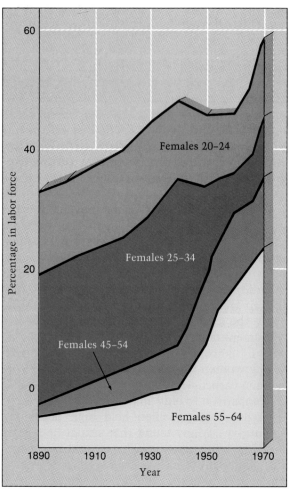

*Awareness of racial discrimination led to women's speaking out against unequal opportunity based on sex, as in this advertisement sponsored by the National Organization for Women.*

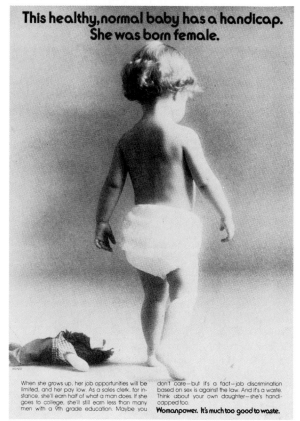

agenda did not adequately confront the problem of gender discrimination. They sought to make women understand the extent of their oppression through the technique of consciousness raising. Soon used by other radical groups, consciousness raising encouraged women to analyze "a women's experience at the hands of men as a *political* phenomenon," as writer Susan Brownmiller explained.

## INTENSIFICATION OF THE COLD WAR

While activists challenged inequities and contradictions in American life, the nation remained locked in confrontation abroad. Kennedy and Johnson both saw the world in Cold War terms, just as their predecessors had, and perceived threats by Communists in near and far corners of the globe. Their responses to overseas Communist actions increased America's web of foreign entanglements and led to war in Vietnam. The opposition to that war helped to shatter the Cold War consensus at home.

John Kennedy entered office interested above all in foreign policy and determined to stand firm in the face of the Russian threat. Despite all the talk about a New Frontier, most of his foreign policy ideas were old. During the campaign, Kennedy declared: "The enemy is the communist system itself—implacable, insatiable, unceasing in its drive for world domination." In his inaugural address, he dramatically described the dangers and challenges the United States faced. "In the long history of the world," he cried out, "only a few generations have been granted the role of defending freedom in its hour of maximum danger." The United States would "Pay any price, bear any burden, meet any hardship, support any friend, oppose any foe, to assure the survival and success of liberty." Under Kennedy, the space program was expanded in an effort to meet Russian challenges in space. In 1962, the first American, John Glenn, orbited the earth. Kennedy promised that within ten years an American would land on the moon. His promise was realized a mere seven years later.

Kennedy's most imaginative approach to the Cold War involved the promotion of "peaceful revolution" in unaligned Third World countries. By providing nonmilitary assistance programs that increased agricultural productivity and built modern transportation and communica-

tions systems, Kennedy hoped to promote stable and pro-Western governments throughout Latin America, Africa, and Asia. The Peace Corps, established in 1961, was a part of this approach. Under its auspices, thousands of idealistic volunteers spent two-year terms as teachers, health workers, sanitation engineers, and agricultural advisers in dozens of developing nations.

Such attempts at "nation building" often brought medical care, schools, and sanitation to isolated villages in Third World countries. Much of the economic aid, however, disappeared in administration costs or ended up in the hands of local elites. Moreover, acceptance of American values and forms of enterprise rarely took hold simply because of the presence of Peace Corps volunteers.

### Confrontations in Cuba and Berlin

While attempts to promote social progress and pro-American governments in developing nations went forward, Kennedy faced direct challenges from the Soviet Union almost from the beginning of his presidency. The first came at the Bay of Pigs in the spring of 1961. Cuban-American relations had been strained since Fidel Castro's revolutionary army had overthrown the dictatorial Fulgencio Batista, a longtime American ally, in 1959. As Castro expropriated private property of major American corporations, which for decades had dominated the Cuban economy, the United States became increasingly concerned. More than simply economic issues were involved. American officials were convinced that a radical regime in Cuba that was leaning toward the Soviet Union provided a model for upheaval elsewhere in Latin America and threatened the venerable Monroe Doctrine.

Just before Kennedy assumed office, the United States broke diplomatic relations with

Cuba. The CIA, meanwhile, was covertly training anti-Castro exiles to storm the Cuban coast at the Bay of Pigs. The American planners assumed the invasion would lead to an uprising of the Cuban people against Castro. When Kennedy learned of the plan, he approved it. The plan was bold and offered the kind of challenge that Kennedy thought would prove his toughness. He overruled the opposition of Senator J. William Fullbright, chairman of the Foreign Relations Committee, who argued that "the Castro regime is a thorn in the flesh; but it is not a dagger in the heart." Nor did he listen to the objection of marine commandant David Shoup, who claimed that Cuba could not be taken easily.

The invasion, on April 17, 1961, was an unmitigated disaster. Castro was able to keep troops from coming ashore, and there was no popular uprising to greet the invaders. The United States stood exposed in the eyes of the world for attempting to overthrow a sovereign government. It had broken agreements not to interfere in the internal affairs of hemispheric neighbors and had intervened clumsily and unsuccessfully.

Although chastened by the debacle at the Bay of Pigs, Kennedy remained determined to deal sternly with the perceived Communist threat. On meeting Soviet leader Nikita Khrushchev in Vienna, in June 1961, he felt cornered on the question of Berlin. The Russians were pressing for a settlement that would reflect the reality of the city's division into eastern and western zones in the aftermath of World War II and prevent the flight of East Germans to the West. Fearful that the Soviet effort signaled designs on the Continent as a whole, Kennedy sought $3 billion more in defense appropriations, more men for the armed forces, and funds for a civil defense fallout shelter program, as if to warn of the possibility of nuclear war. After the Russians erected a wall in Berlin to seal off their section, the crisis eased. But Kennedy felt he had overreacted. Sensitive to his image as world leader, he believed he had come off second-best in the struggle.

## The Cuban Missile Crisis

The next year, Kennedy had a chance to recoup some of his lost prestige, though again at the risk of war. Fearful of American designs on Cuba, Castro had secured Russian assistance. According to American aerial photographs of October 1962, the Soviet Union had begun to place offensive missiles on Cuban soil. The missiles did not change the strategic balance significantly, for the Soviets could still wreak untold damage on American targets from bases farther away, and American missiles stood on the borders of the Soviet Union in Turkey. But with Russian weapons installed just 90 miles from American shores, appearance was more important than strategic balance. Kennedy was determined to confront the Russians (not the Cubans) and win.

Meeting with top staff members, the president went over the alternatives, ruling out an air strike to knock out the missile sites. He moved nonetheless to a position of full alert. Bombers and missiles were fueled, armed with nuclear weapons, and readied to go. The fleet prepared to move, and troops stood set to invade. Kennedy himself went on nationwide TV to tell the American people about the missiles and to demand their removal. He declared that the United States would not shrink from the risk of nuclear war and announced a naval blockade around Cuba to prevent Soviet ships from bringing in additional missiles. He called the move a quarantine, for a blockade was an act of war.

As the Soviet ships steamed toward the blockade, and the nations stood "eyeball to eyeball" at the brink, the American and Russian people held their breath. Americans, on the one hand, applauded the president and accepted the situation in the terms he had defined. On the other hand, they feared a cataclysmic confrontation that could bring the world to an end.

After several days, the tension broke, but only because Khrushchev called the Russian ships back and then sent a long letter to Kennedy pledging to remove the missiles if the United States ended the blockade and promising to stay out of Cuba altogether. A second letter demanded that America remove its missiles from Turkey as well. The United States responded affirmatively to the first letter, ignored the second, and said nothing about its intention, already voiced, of removing its own missiles from Turkey. With that the crisis ended.

The Cuban missile crisis was the most terrifying confrontation of the Cold War. Kennedy had led the world closer to nuclear war than it had ever been. The president emerged from the crisis as a hero who had stood firm. His reputation was enhanced, as was the image of his party in the coming congressional elections. Yet as the relief of the moment began to fade, critics charged that what Kennedy saw as his finest hour was in fact an unnecessary crisis. Though Kennedy had shown some restraint in not authorizing an air attack, he had neglected normal channels of diplomacy and had moved precariously close to the brink. He had avoided disaster only, as Dean Acheson observed, by "plain dumb luck," when the Russians showed restraint. One consequence of the affair was the establishment of a Soviet-American hot line to avoid similar episodes in the future. Another was Russia's determination to increase its nuclear arsenal so that it would never again be exposed as inferior to the United States.

## The Vietnam Quagmire

In another part of the world, neither Kennedy nor his successor proved as fortunate in avoiding armed conflict. In Southeast Asia, the United States almost entered Laos in the spring of 1961 to head off Communist influence. In Vietnam, however, America refused to maintain such neutrality. There, Vietnamese leader Ho Chi Minh continued his struggle to liberate his land in what had become a bitter civil war (see Chapter 27).

Unsympathetic to Ho's regime in North Vietnam, the United States steadily increased its support to South Vietnam. By the time Eisenhower left the presidency in 1961, some 675 American military advisers were assisting the South Vietnamese. After the Bay of Pigs, Kennedy decided to increase that level of assistance. Not only advisers, however, went to South Vietnam. American troops began to be sent there, and by the end of 1963, over 16,000 Americans were engaged in the war.

Despite American backing, South Vietnamese leader Ngo Dinh Diem was rapidly losing support within his own country. Buddhist priests burned themselves alive in the capital of Saigon to dramatize Diem's unpopularity. American officials began to realize that Diem would never reform. After receiving assurances that the United States would not object to an internal coup, South Vietnamese military leaders assassinated Diem and seized the government.

As he considered the situation in Vietnam, Kennedy faced a dilemma. He understood the importance of popular support for the South Vietnamese government if that country were to maintain its independence. But he was reluctant to withdraw and let the Vietnamese solve their own problems. When Kennedy met with a violent death shortly after Diem's assassination, Lyndon Johnson faced a situation in flux in Vietnam.

Johnson shared many of Kennedy's assumptions about the threat of communism. His understanding of the past led him to believe that aggressors had to be stopped or their actions would lead to world war, as had been true in World War II. Like Kennedy, Johnson believed in the domino theory, which held that if one country in a region fell, others were bound to follow.

In office, Johnson was determined to defend American interests from communism. Often

*In an extreme demonstration of disapproval, a Buddhist monk burns himself alive to protest the American-backed Diem government.*

frustrated by what he called those "piddly little pissant" countries, he involved himself in a small crisis in Panama over the question of which flag—the American or the Panamanian—should fly in the Canal Zone. In the Dominican Republic, the issue was more serious. In 1965, he sent 20,000 troops to help buttress a military junta. His flimsy claims about the threat of communism and the importance of protecting American tourists created a wedge between his administration and liberals.

That wedge would widen over the question of Vietnam. Though Kennedy had expanded the American commitment there, Johnson took the Vietnam War and made it his own. Soon after assuming office, he reached a fundamental decision that guided policy for the next four years. South Vietnam was more unstable than ever after the assassination of Diem. Guerrillas, known as Viet Cong, challenged the regime, sometimes covertly, sometimes through the National Liberation Front, their political arm. Aided by Ho Chi Minh and the North Vietnamese, the insurgent Viet Cong slowly gained ground. Henry Cabot Lodge, the American ambassador to South Vietnam, told Johnson that if he wanted to save that country, and indeed the whole region, he had to stand firm. "I am not going to lose Vietnam," Johnson replied. "I am not going to be the President who saw Southeast Asia go the way China went."

In the election campaign of 1964, Johnson posed as a man of peace. "We don't want our American boys to do the fighting for Asian boys," he declared. "We are not going to send American boys nine or ten thousand miles away from home to do what Asian boys ought to be doing for themselves." He criticized those who suggested moving in with American bombs. All the while, however, he was planning to increase American involvement in the war.

In August 1964, Johnson cleverly obtained congressional authorization for the war. North Vietnamese torpedo boats, he announced, had, without provocation, attacked American destroyers in the international waters of the Gulf of Tonkin, 30 miles from North Vietnam. Only later did it become clear that the American ships had violated the territorial waters of North Vietnam by assisting South Vietnamese commando

raids in offshore combat zones. With the details of the attack still unclear, Johnson used the episode to obtain from Congress a resolution giving him authority to "take all necessary measures to repel any armed attack against the forces of the United States and to prevent further aggression." Not aware that the president had been carrying the resolution around for some time, Congress passed it by a vote of 416 to

## The Vietnam War

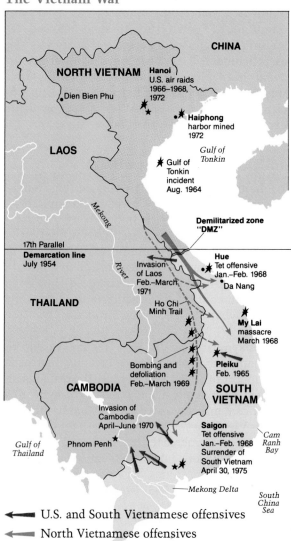

← U.S. and South Vietnamese offensives

← North Vietnamese offensives

←---- Major North Vietnamese supply routes into South Vietnam

✱ Major battles or actions

0 in the House and 88 to 2 in the Senate. It gave Johnson the leverage he sought. As he noted, it was "like grandma's nightshirt—it covered everything."

Military escalation began in earnest in February 1965, after Viet Cong forces killed 7 Americans and wounded 109 in an attack on an American base at Pleiku. Johnson responded by authorizing retaliatory bombing of North Vietnam to cut off the flow of supplies and to ease pressure on South Vietnam. At the same time, the president sent American ground troops into action. Only 25,000 American soldiers were in Vietnam at the start of 1965. By the end of the year, there were 184,000, and the number swelled to 385,000 in 1966, 485,000 in 1967, 500,000 in 1968. "Remember, escalation begets escalation," Senator Mike Mansfield futilely warned the president in mid-1965.

Massive amounts of American supplies and personnel changed the character of the conflict. No longer simply military advisers in Southeast Asia, American forces became direct participants in the fight to prop up a dictatorial regime in faraway South Vietnam. Although a more effective government headed by Nguyen Van Thieu and Nguyen Cao Ky was finally established, the level of violence increased. Saturation bombing of North Vietnam continued. Fragmentation bombs, killing and maiming countless civilians, and napalm, which seared

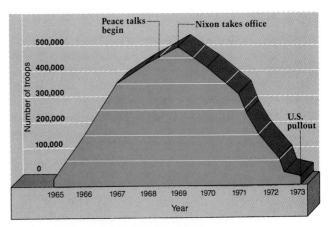

**U.S. Troops in Vietnam, 1965–1973**
*Source:* U.S. Department of Defense.

off human flesh, were used extensively. Similar destruction wracked South Vietnam. Yet the North Vietnamese and their revolutionary allies in South Vietnam pressed on. Like LBJ, they sought not compromise but victory.

In early 1968, the North Vietnamese mounted the massive Tet offensive, attacking provincial capitals and district towns in South Vietnam. In Saigon, they struck the American embassy, Tan Son Nhut air base, and the presidential palace. Though beaten back, they won a psychological victory. American audiences, tuned to the television for nightly reports, came to realize that the war perhaps could not be won.

## UPHEAVAL AT HOME

As the American people became more deeply involved in revolutionary struggles abroad that never brought the promised victories, they also experienced the disruption of their own society. Different groups clamored for greater access to the American dream. Rejecting the stable patterns of affluent life that their parents had forged in the decade before, some young middle-class Americans embraced radical political activity; many more adopted new standards of music and dress. A sexual revolution accompanied a drug revolution, leading some Americans to believe that society itself was collapsing.

### The Roots of Change

The demographic patterns of the post–World War II years lay behind youthful activism and helped explain the generation gap. Members of the baby boom generation came of age in the 1960s, and many more of them, especially from the large middle class, moved on to some form of higher education than in any previous generation. Between 1950 and 1964, the number of students in college more than doubled. By the end of the 1960s, college enrollment was more than four times what it had been in the 1940s.

In the last 30 years, television has played an increasingly important part in American life, providing historians with another source of evidence about American culture and society in the recent past.

Television's popularity by the 1950s was the result of decades of experimentation dating back to the nineteenth century. In the 1930s, NBC installed a television station in the new Empire State Building in New York. With green makeup and purple lipstick to provide better visual contrast, actors began to perform before live cameras in studios. At the end of the decade, "Amos 'n' Andy," a popular radio show, was telecast, and as the 1940s began, Franklin D. Roosevelt became the first president to appear on television. World War II interrupted the development of television as Americans relied on radio to bring them news from abroad. In the aftermath of the war, however, the commercial development of television quickly resumed. Assembly lines that had made electronic implements of war were now converted to consumer production, and thousands of new sets appeared on the market. The opening of Congress could be seen live in 1947; baseball coverage improved that same year due to the adaptation of the zoom lens; children's shows like "Howdy Doody" and "Kukla, Fran, and Ollie" made their debut; and "Meet the Press," a radio interview program, made the transition to television.

Although sports programs, variety shows hosted by Ed Sullivan and Milton Berle, TV dramas, and episodic series ("I Love Lucy" and "Gunsmoke," for example) dominated TV broadcasting in the 1950s, television soon became entwined with politics and public affairs. Americans saw Senator Joseph McCarthy for themselves in the televised Army-McCarthy hearings in 1954; his malevolent behavior on camera contributed to his downfall. The 1948 presidential nominating conventions were the first to be televised, but the use of TV to enhance the public image of politicians was most thoroughly developed by the fatherly Dwight D. Eisenhower and the charismatic John F. Kennedy. Some argue that the televised debate in 1960 between the tanned, handsome Kennedy and a pasty white Richard Nixon helped elect Kennedy.

In 1963, a horrified public watched as officials used snarling police dogs and thunderous fire hoses on peaceful marchers in the Birmingham civil rights demonstrations, thus arousing public opinion against southern resistance. And people throughout the United States shared the tragedy of John Kennedy's assassination in November 1963, sitting stunned before their sets trying to understand the events of his fateful Texas trip. The shock and sorrow of the American people was repeated in the spring of 1968 as

they watched the funerals of Martin Luther King and Robert Kennedy. A year later, a quarter of the world's population watched as Neil Armstrong became the first man to set foot on the moon. Whether depicting tragedies or triumphs, few Americans complained when these television news spectaculars pushed popular series such as "Bonanza," "The Beverly Hillbillies," "I Spy," and "Dr. Kildare" off the screen.

## TELEVISION TONIGHT

6:30—WTTV **4**: Leave It to Beaver. Beaver tries to help a friend who has run away from home. Repeat.

6:30—WLW-I **13**: Cheyenne has a Laramie adventure in which Slim, Jess and Jonesy work on a cattle drive. Repeat.

7:30—WTTV **4**: The Untouchables. Eliot Ness tries to deal with a late gangster's niece who has a record of the murdered hood's career. Repeat.

7:30—WLW-I **13**: Voyage to the Bottom of the Sea presents "Mutiny," in which Admiral Nelson shows signs of a mental breakdown during the search for a giant jellyfish which supposedly consumed a submarine.

7:30—WFBM-TV **6**: Members of the Indianapolis Rotary Club discuss the 1965 business outlook with former U.S. Sen. Homer Capehart.

8:00—WFBM-TV **6**: The Man From UNCLE is in at a new time and night. Thrush agents try to recapture one of their leaders before Napoleon Solo can deliver him to the Central Intelligence Agency. Ralph Taeger is guest star.

8:00—WISH-TV **8**: I've Got a Secret welcomes the panel from To Tell the Truth: Tom Poston, Peggy Cass, Kitty Carlisle and Orson Bean.

8:30—WLW-I **13**: Basketball, I.U. vs. Iowa.

8:30—WISH-TV **8**: Andy Griffith's comedy involves Goober's attempts to fill in at the sheriff's office.

9:00—WFBM-TV **6**: Andy Williams is visited by composer Henry Mancini, Bobby Darin and Vic Damone. Musical selections include "Charade," "Hello Dolly" and "Moon River."

9:00—WTTV **4**: Lloyd Thaxton welcomes vocal group, Herman's Hermits.

9:00—WISH-TV **8**: Lucille Ball is driven to distraction by a secret package she has been instructed not to open.

9:30—WISH-TV **8**: Many Happy Returns. Walter's plan for currying favor with the store's boss hits a snag.

10:00—WFBM-TV **6**: Alfred Hitchcock presents Margaret Leighton as a spinster who goes mad when she cannot cope with the strain of rearing an orphaned niece in "Where the Woodbine Twineth."

10:00—WLW-I **13**: Ben Casey gets help in diagnosing a boy's illness from an Australian veterinarian with terminal leukemia. The vet's knowledge of bats provides the key.

10:00—WISH-TV **8**: "Viet Nam: How We Got In—Can We Get Out?" is the topic of CBS Reports.

*Indianapolis News, January 11, 1965.*

# TELEVISION

This combination of visual entertainment and enlightenment made owning a television set virtually a necessity. By 1970, fully 95 percent of American households owned a TV set, a staggering increase from the 9 percent only 20 years earlier. Fewer families owned refrigerators or indoor toilets.

The implications of the impact of television on American society are of obvious interest to historians. How has television affected other communications and entertainment industries, such as radio, newspapers, and movies? What does the content of TV programming tell us about the values, interests, and tastes of the American people?

Perhaps most significant, what impact has TV had on the course of historical events like presidential campaigns, human relations, and wars? In the late 1960s, for example, television played an important part in shaping impressions of the war in Vietnam. More and more Americans began to understand the nature and impact of the war as TV newscasters brought visual images of burning huts and wounded soldiers into American living rooms every evening. As the combined Viet Cong–North Vietnamese forces attacked Saigon during the Tet offensive of 1968, American TV networks showed scenes of a kind never screened before. One such clip, on NBC News, showed the chief of the South Vietnamese National Police, General Loan, looking at a Viet Cong prisoner, lifting his gun, and calmly blowing out the captive's brains.

The picture you see here is a still snapshot of the execution that appeared on television and later won the Pulitzer Prize for the photographer. The picture makes a powerful impression on its own, but the impact was even stronger when the film clip on TV replayed the actual event for 20 million people.

Examine the image closely. What feelings do you see on the face of the prisoner? What is the mood of General Loan? Now try to imagine seeing this action unfold on the television screen. Following a brief introduction by Chet Huntley, an NBC News correspondent reported on the battle for Saigon. After some background on the struggle, he said that government forces had captured the commander of the Viet Cong commando unit. "He was roughed up badly but refused to talk," the narrator continued, and declared that General Loan "was waiting for him." After that he said no more. On screen, Loan moved to the prisoner's side and shot him in the side of the head. Viewers watched the corpse drop to the ground.

How do you respond to such an image? Knowing that this drama involved real people, how do you think the television audience might have reacted to this segment of the evening news? How vivid does violence need to be to make a strong impression? How might such a scene have helped focus the growing frustration with the war and aid efforts to end it? Reflect on more recent incidents you have seen "live" on TV, and ponder how they have affected the history of events in your lifetime.

*General Loan, Southeast Vietnam's police chief executing a Vietcong suspect in Saigon, a news photo by Eddie Adams, from LIFE Magazine, March 1, 1968*

Wide World Photos

937b

There were far more students than there were farmers, coal miners, or railroad workers. College had become a training ground for industry and corporate life; more important, it gave students time to experiment and grow before they went out into the world to make a living.

In college, some students joined the struggle for civil rights. Hopeful at first, they gradually became discouraged by the limitations of the government's commitment, despite the rhetoric of Kennedy and the New Frontier.

### The Student Movement

Out of that disillusionment arose the radical spirit of the New Left. Civil rights activists were among those who in 1960 organized Students for a Democratic Society (SDS) from the older Student League for Industrial Democracy. In 1962, SDS issued a manifesto, the Port Huron Statement, written largely by Tom Hayden of the University of Michigan. "We are people of this generation, bred in at least modest comfort, housed now in universities, looking uncomfortably at the world we inherit," it began. It went on to deplore the vast social and economic distances separating people from each other and to condemn the isolation and estrangement of modern life. The document called for a better system, one rooted in "self-cultivation, self-direction, self-understanding and creativity." Seeking "a democracy of individual participation," the Port Huron Statement pledged SDS to the creation of a "New Left."

Folksinger Bob Dylan, politically active himself, captured something of the new, more radical mood with a song in 1963:

> Come mothers and fathers
> Throughout the land
> And don't criticize
> What you can't understand
> Your sons and daughters
> Are beyond your command
> There's a battle
> Outside and it's ragin'
> It'll soon shake your windows
> And rattle your walls . . .
> For the times they are a-changin'.

The first blow of the growing student rebellion came at the University of California in Berkeley. There civil rights activists became involved in a confrontation that quickly became known as the free-speech movement. It began in

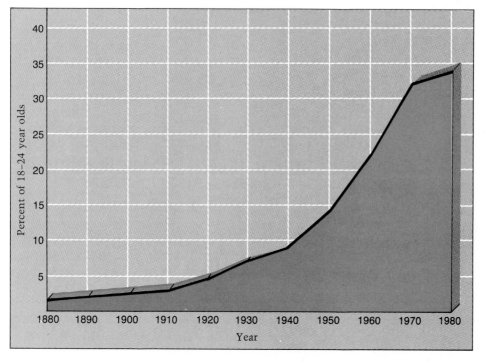

**College Enrollment, 1940–1980**

*Source:* U.S. Department of Commerce.

September 1964 when the university refused to allow students to distribute protest material outside the main campus gate. The students, many of whom had worked in the movement in the South, argued that their tables were off campus and therefore not subject to university restrictions on political activity. Defiantly, they resolved to fight back. When police arrested one of the leaders, students surrounded the police car and kept it from moving all night.

Although the administration eventually sought a compromise, the university regents chose to take disciplinary action against the student leaders. Mario Savio, one who found himself in the spotlight, was charged with biting a policeman on the thigh, and other accusations followed. When the regents refused to drop the charges, the students occupied the administration building. Savio called the university an impersonal machine: "It becomes odious, so we must put our bodies against the gears, against the wheels . . . and make the machine stop until we're free." Joan Baez sang "We Shall Overcome," the marching song of the civil rights movement, and something of the mood of that struggle prevailed. Then, as in the South, police stormed in and arrested the students in the building. A student strike, with faculty aid, mobilized wider support for the right to free speech.

*"Stop the war now!" was a familiar chant as students across America rallied for peace. In 1968 Columbia University protestors barricaded themselves inside the school's main library.*

Though the free-speech movement at Berkeley was the opening blow of the student revolt, it was still basically a plea for traditional liberal reform. Students sought only the reaffirmation of a longstanding right, the right to express themselves as they chose, and they aimed their attacks at the university, not at society as a whole. Later, in other institutions, the attack broadened.

As in the civil rights movement, student protest, once launched, developed and swelled. The ferment at Berkeley spread to other campuses in the spring of 1965 as students questioned methods of college discipline, attacked conservative drinking and visitation rules, sought student involvement in university affairs, argued for curricular reform, and demanded admission of more minority students. Their success in gaining their demands changed the shape of American higher education.

## The New Left Struggles Against the War

The mounting protest against the escalation of the Vietnam War fueled the youth movement and gave it a new focus. Initially the critics were few. As the troop buildup began, 82 percent of the public felt that American forces should stay in Vietnam until the Communist elements withdrew. Then students began to question assumptions about the need to battle communism in every corner of the globe. The first antiwar teach-in took place in March 1965 at the University of Michigan. Other teach-ins followed across the country. Initially both supporters and opponents of the war appeared at the teach-ins, but soon the sessions became more like antiwar rallies than instructional affairs.

SDS seized upon the growing antiwar sentiment. Earlier, the radical student organization had been more interested in the struggle for civil rights and the organization of working-class elements in the cities. But as the antiwar movement grew, SDS recognized the possibilities for increasing its influence and plunged in, campaigning against the draft, attacking ROTC units on campus, and seeking to discredit firms that produced the destructive tools of war. "Make love, not war," slogans proclaimed as more and more students became involved in political demonstrations at dozens of colleges. "Hey, hey, LBJ. How many kids did you kill today?" opponents of the war chanted. In 1967, some 300,000 people marched in New York City. In Washington, D.C., 100,000 tried to close down the Pentagon. By 1968, protest had become almost a way of life. Between January 1 and June 15, hundreds of thousands of students staged 221 major demonstrations at more than 100 educational institutions.

Confrontation became the new tactic of radical students. The most dramatic episode came in April 1968 at Columbia University, where the issues of civil rights and war were tightly interwoven. A strong SDS chapter urged the university to break ties with the Institute of Defense Analysis, which specialized in military research. The Students' Afro-American Society tried to stop the building of a new gymnasium, which it claimed encroached on the Harlem community and disrupted life there. Together the two groups marched on Low Memorial Library. Then the alliance split, as whites occupied one building, blacks another. Finally, the president of the university called in the police, and the uprising was quelled. Hundreds of students were arrested; many were hurt. A student sympathy strike followed, and Columbia closed its doors early that spring.

The New Left became a powerful force in the 1960s. Although activists were never in the majority, radicals did succeed in attracting more and more students to their cause as the decade drew to an end. Together they focused opposition to the Vietnam War, even as they issued new challenges to American society. The impatience and frustration evident in the student protest movement could also be seen in other areas of American life as political upheaval was accompanied by cultural change.

## Challenging Cultural Norms

In the 1960s, many Americans, particularly young people, lost faith in the sanctity of the American system. "There was," observed Joseph Heller, the irreverent author of *Catch-22* (1955), "a general feeling that the platitudes of Americanism were horseshit." The protests exposed the emptiness of some of the old patterns, and many Americans, some politically active, some not, found new ways to assert their individuality and independence. As in the political sphere, the young led the way. Often drawing on the example of the beats of the 1950s, the literary figures who had rejected conventional canons of respectability, they sought new means of expressing themselves.

Surface appearances were most visible and, to older Americans, most troubling. The "hippies" of the 1960s carried themselves in different ways. Men let their hair grow and sprouted beards; men and women both donned jeans, muslin shirts, and other simple garments. Stressing spontaneity above all else, some rejected traditional marital customs and gravitated to communal living groups. Their example, shocking to some, soon found its way into the culture at large. More men grew long hair and discarded ties and jackets. Women threw off confining clothing like girdles and embraced new fashions—miniskirts, longer dresses, slacks and jeans for casual wear.

Sexual norms underwent a revolution as more people separated sex from its traditional ties to family life. A generation of young women came of age with access to "the pill"—an oral contraceptive that was effortless to use and rid sexual experimentation from the threat of pregnancy. Americans of all social classes became more open to exploring, and enjoying, their sexuality. Scholarly findings supported natural inclinations. In 1966, William H. Masters and Virginia E. Johnson published *Human Sexual Response*, based on intensive laboratory observation of couples engaged in sexual activities. Describing the kinds of response that women, as well as men, could experience, they destroyed the myth of the sexually passive woman.

Nora Ephron, author and editor, summed up the sexual changes of the 1960s as she reflected on her own experiences. In 1962, after graduating from Wellesley College, she had moved to New York to work. Wanting a method of regular birth control, she visited the Margaret Sanger Clinic and began taking the pill. Initially she had "a hangover from the whole Fifties virgin thing," she recalled. "The first man I went to bed with, I was in love with and wanted to marry. The second one I was in love with, but I didn't have to marry him. With the third one, I thought I *might* fall in love." For a time she stopped taking the pill whenever she broke up with someone, but that proved inconvenient. As her doctor asked, "Who knows what's coming around the corner?" For many Americans in the 1960s, someone new was rounding the corner all the time.

The arts reflected the sexual revolution. Federal courts ruled that books like D. H. Lawrence's *Lady Chatterley's Lover* were not obscene, as had earlier been determined. Many suppressed works, long available in Europe, now began to appear. Nudity became more common on stage and screen. In *Hair*, a rock musical, one scene featured the disrobing of performers of both sexes in the course of an erotic celebration. What had been unthinkable a decade before now became commonplace in the arts.

Paintings reflected both the mood of dissent and the urge to innovate that were apparent in the larger society. "Op" artists painted sharply defined squares, circles, stripes, and other geometric figures in clear, vibrant colors, starkly different from the flowing, chaotic work of the abstract expressionists. "Pop" artists like Andy Warhol, Roy Lichtenstein, and Jasper Johns made ironic comments on American materialism and taste with the representations of everyday objects like soup cans, comic strips, or pictures of Marilyn Monroe. Their paintings broke with formal artistic conventions. Some used spray guns and fluorescent paints to gain effect. Others even tried to make their pictures look like giant newspaper photographs.

Hallucinogenic drugs also became a part of the counterculture. The beats had experimented with drugs, as had others, but now their use became common. One prophet of "the drug scene" was Timothy Leary, who, with Richard Alpert, was doing scientific research at Harvard University on LSD. Fired from their research posts for violating a pledge to the University Health Service not to experiment with undergraduates, the two men promoted the cause of LSD nationally. As Alpert drifted into a commune in New Mexico, Leary aggressively asserted that drugs were necessary to free the mind. Working through his group, the League for

Spiritual Discovery, he dressed in long robes and preached his message, "tune in, turn on, drop out."

Another apostle of life with drugs was Ken Kesey. Born and raised in Oregon, he had finished college in 1958 and entered Stanford for graduate work. There he wrote his first novel, *One Flew Over the Cuckoo's Nest*, and began participating in medical experiments at a hospital where he was introduced to LSD. With the profits from his novel, Kesey established a commune of "Merry Pranksters" near Palo Alto, California. In 1964, the group headed east in a converted school bus painted in psychedelic Day-Glo colors, wired for sound, and stocked with enough orange juice and acid to sustain the Pranksters across the continent. After a series of outlandish adventures, they returned to California, where many of them were arrested. That only enhanced Kesey's standing in the drug culture.

Drug use was no longer confined to an urban subculture of musicians, artists, and the streetwise. Young professionals began experimenting with cocaine as a stimulant. Taking a "tab" of LSD became part of the coming-of-age ritual for many middle-class college students. But it was marijuana that became phenomenally popular in the 1960s. "Joints" of "grass" were passed around at high school, neighborhood, and college parties as readily as were cans of beer in the previous generation.

Music became intimately connected with these cultural changes. The rock and roll of the 1950s and the gentle strains of folk music gave way to a new kind of rock that swept the country—and the world. The Beatles were the major influence, as they took first England, then the United States, by storm. Other groups enjoyed enormous commercial success while attacking materialism and other bourgeois values. Mick Jagger of the Rolling Stones was an aggressive, sometimes violent showman on stage whose androgynous style showed his contempt for conventional sexual norms. Jim Morrison of the Doors conveyed a raw sexuality in his dialogue with the audience. Janis Joplin, a hard-driving, hard-drinking woman with roots in the blues, reflected the intensity of the new rock world until her early death by drugs.

Though spontaneous and exuberant, the counterculture had a dismal underside. Young people gathered where they could, many in the Haight-Ashbury section of San Francisco, where runaway "flower children" mingled with "burned-out" drug users and radical activists. Many of its heroes, like Jimmy Hendrix, died of drug overdoses. Joan Didion, a perceptive essayist, wrote of American society in 1967: "Adolescents drifted from city to torn city, sloughing off both the past and the future as snakes shed their skins, children who were never taught and would never now learn the games that had held the society together."

## CONCLUSION: The Unraveling of the Affluent Society

The people of the United States had been severely buffeted in the eight years after electing John Kennedy to the presidency. In 1960, there was confidence that the nation, though not without problems, was healthy and strong, able to withstand challenges around the world and protect the American way of life. The New Frontier and the Great Society pushed forward liberal reforms. Yet they had not taken the measure of deep-running cultural shifts that had occurred. Idealistic Americans who joined organizations like the Peace Corps found, as one of them observed, that their experience "forever altered our view of our own country, and more significantly, it altered our perception of ourselves and our responsibilities." Political leaders seemed out of touch with their constituents, particularly the young.

The nation was drifting. The consensus that had bound together successful Americans—and those still hopeful of success—had vanished. Serious problems, at home and abroad, seemed almost beyond solution.

### Recommended Reading

For a good introduction to the basic foreign and domestic policies of the period, see Jim F. Heath, *Decade of Disillusionment: The Kennedy-Johnson Years* (1975). On John Kennedy, Herbert S. Parmet, *JFK: The Presidency of John F. Kennedy* (1983) is a comprehensive account of the White House years. Henry Fairlie, *The Kennedy Promise* (1972) is a scathing assessment of the actual record of the Kennedy administration. Doris Kearns, *Lyndon Johnson and the American Dream* (1976) is a readable analysis of the Johnson presidency by a political scientist and former White House fellow. Allen J. Matusow provides a brilliant analysis of the 1960s in *The Unraveling of America: A History of Liberalism in the 1960s* (1984).

A great deal has been written about the Vietnam War. George C. Herring, *America's Longest War: The United States and Vietnam, 1950–1975* (1979) is the best brief account of American policy in that conflict, particularly in the 1960s and thereafter.

The civil rights movement has also been extensively described. Harvard Sitkoff, *The Struggle for Black Equality, 1954–1980* (1981) is a short but stimulating overview of the civil rights struggle. Clayborne Carson, *In Struggle: SNCC and the Black Awakening of the 1960s* (1981) provides a good treatment of one phase of the movement. Anne Moody, *Coming of Age in Mississippi* (1968) is the eloquent autobiography of a young southern black woman who became involved in the civil rights movement.

On the women's movement, Sara Evans, *Personal Politics: The Roots of Women's Liberation in the Civil Rights Movement and the New Left* (1979) offers a penetrating examination of the links between various reform movements in the 1960s. Sara Davidson, *Loose Change* (1977) is a novel describing the lives of women in the 1960s.

For a good treatment of recent Indian struggles see Alvin M. Josephy, Jr., *Now That the Buffalo's Gone* (1982).

Rodolfo Acuña, *Occupied America: A History of Chicanos* (1981) provides a useful overview of Chicano affairs.

For the growth of the counterculture, see William L. O'Neill, *Coming Apart* (1971). Tom Wolfe, *The Electric Kool-Aid Acid Test* (1968) is a vivid account of Ken Kesey and the drug culture of the 1960s.

## TIME LINE

| | |
|---|---|
| 1960 | John F. Kennedy elected president<br>Sit-ins begin<br>Students for a Democratic Society (SDS) founded |
| 1961 | Freedom rides<br>Bay of Pigs invasion fails<br>Khrushchev and Kennedy meet in Vienna<br>Berlin Wall constructed<br>Michael Harrington publishes *The Other America*; Joseph Heller, *Catch-22*; Ken Kesey, *One Flew Over the Cuckoo's Nest* |
| 1962 | JFK confronts steel companies<br>Meredith crisis at the University of Mississippi<br>Cuban missile crisis<br>SDS's Port Huron Statement |
| 1963 | Birmingham demonstration<br>Civil rights march on Washington<br>Kennedy assassinated; Lyndon B. Johnson becomes president<br>Buddhist demonstrations in Vietnam<br>President Diem assassinated in Vietnam<br>Betty Friedan, *The Feminine Mystique* |
| 1964 | Freedom Democratic party attempts to gain recognition at the Democratic national convention<br>Gulf of Tonkin Resolution<br>Civil Rights Act<br>Economic Opportunity Act initiates War on Poverty<br>Race riots in New York City<br>Free-speech movement, Berkeley<br>Johnson reelected president |

| | |
|---|---|
| 1965 | Vietnam conflict escalates<br>Marines sent to Dominican Republic<br>Martin Luther King leads march from Selma to Montgomery<br>Voting Rights Act<br>United Farm Workers grape strike<br>Teach-ins begin<br>Department of Housing and Urban Development established<br>Elementary and Secondary Education Act<br>Assassination of Malcolm X<br>Watts riot in Los Angeles |
| 1966 | Stokely Carmichael becomes head of SNCC and calls for "black power"<br>Black Panthers founded<br>NOW founded<br>Masters and Johnson, *Human Sexual Response* |
| 1967 | Antiwar demonstrations<br>Urban riots in 22 cities |
| 1968 | Kerner Commission report on urban disorders<br>Martin Luther King, Jr., assassinated<br>Robert F. Kennedy assassinated<br>Antiwar demonstrations increase<br>Tet offensive<br>Student demonstrations at Columbia and elsewhere<br>Chicago Democratic convention riots<br>Richard Nixon elected president |

# CHAPTER 30
## ILLUSION AND DISILLUSIONMENT

Ann Clarke—as she chooses to call herself now—always wanted to go to college. But girls from Italian families rarely did when she was growing up. Her mother, a Sicilian immigrant and widow, asked her brother for advice: "Should Antonina go to college?" "What's the point?" he said. "She's just going to get married."

Life had not been easy for Antonina Rose Rumore. As a child in the 1920s, her Italian-speaking grandmother cared for her while her mother worked to support the family, first in the sweatshops, then as a seamstress. Even as she dreamed, Ann accommodated her culture's demands for dutiful daughters.

Responsive to family needs, Ann finished the high school Commercial Course in three years. She struggled with ethnic prejudice as a legal secretary on Wall Street, but still believed in the American dream and the Puritan work ethic. She was proud of her ability to bring money home to her family.

When World War II began, Ann wanted to join the WACS. "Better you should be a prostitute," her mother said. Ann went off to California instead, where she worked at resorts. When she left California, she vowed to return to this land of freedom and opportunity.

After the war, Ann married Gerard Clarke, a college man with an English background. Her children would grow up accepted with Anglo names. Over the next 15 years, Ann devoted herself to her family. She was a mother above all, and that took all her time. But she waited for her own chance: "I had this hunger to learn, this curiosity."

By the early 1960s, her three children were all in school. Promising her husband to have dinner on the table at six, she enrolled at Pasadena City College. It was not easy. Family still came first. A simple problem was finding time to study. When doing dishes or cleaning house, she memorized lists of dates, historical events, and other material for school.

Holiday time was difficult. Ann occasionally felt compelled to give everything up "to make Christmas." Terminating a whole semester's work two weeks before finals, she sewed nightgowns instead of writing her art history paper.

Her conflict over her studies was intensified by her position as one of the first older women to go back to college. "Sometimes I felt like I wanted to hide in the woodwork," she admitted. Often her teachers were younger than she. It took four years to complete the two-year program. But she was not yet done. She wanted a bachelor's degree. Back she went, this time to California State College at Los Angeles.

As the years passed and the credits piled up, Ann became an honors student. Her children, now in college themselves, were proud and supportive; dinners became arguments over Faulkner and foreign policy. Even so, Ann still felt caught between her worlds at home and outside. Since she was at the top of her class, graduation should have been a special occasion. But she was only embarrassed when a letter from the school invited her parents to attend the final ceremonies. Ann could not bring herself to go.

With a college degree in hand, Ann returned to school for teaching credentials. Receiving her certificate at age 50, she faced the irony of social change. Once denied opportunities, Italians had assimilated into American society. Now she was just another Anglo in Los Angeles, caught in a changing immigration wave; the city now sought Hispanics and other minorities to teach in the schools. Jobs in education were tightening, and she was close to "retirement age," so she became a substitute in Mexican-American areas for the next ten years, specializing in bilingual education.

Meanwhile, Ann was troubled by the Vietnam War. "For every boy that died, one of us should lie down," she told fellow workers. She was not an activist, rather one of the millions of quieter Americans who ultimately helped bring change.

The social adjustments caused by the war affected her. Her son grew long hair and a beard and attended protest rallies. He would antagonize the ladies in Pasadena, she worried. Her daughter came home from college in boots and a leather miniskirt designed to shock. Ann accepted her children's changes as relatively superficial, confident in their fundamental values; "they were good kids." She trusted them, even as she worried.

Ann Clarke's experience paralleled that of millions of women in the 1960s and 1970s. Caught up for years in traditional patterns of family life, these women began to recognize their need for something more. Even as their lives changed, society changed too. New social and political issues compelled some to speak out. And their involvement helped change the political and social dialogue in the United States.

This chapter describes the trials the nation endured between 1968 and 1976. It deals with the changes Ann Rumore Clarke and others experienced as they struggled with their own problems, only to see their communities polarize. It shows how the country responded to war, injustice, and political scandal. And it portrays the efforts of concerned Americans to promote reform on all fronts, even in troubled times.

## REPUBLICAN LEADERSHIP

After eight years of Democratic rule, the ferment sparked by the Vietnam War led to a change in command. Elected president in 1968, Richard Nixon faced deep divisions in the country as he sought to end the war and restore tranquility at home. But his efforts produced a backlash, and his own quest for political power eventually brought him disgrace. He was succeeded by Gerald Ford, a more modest man whose major achievement was to restore some confidence in the United States.

### The Election of 1968

Nixon had long dreamed of the nation's highest office. In 1968, his chances seemed good. The Democratic party, like the country itself, was split by the Vietnam War. Senator Eugene McCarthy of Minnesota opposed further American involvement in the struggle, challenged incumbent Lyndon Johnson in the New Hampshire primary, and almost won. Americans were tired of the drawn-out, expensive war and ready to express their frustration at the polls. His popularity waning, Johnson dramatically announced that he would not seek another term. As McCarthy promoted his candidacy, Robert F. Kennedy, the charismatic brother of the slain president, launched his own bid for the nomination. It ended in his assassination, which shook the country. Inheriting the role of leading contender was Vice-President Hubert H. Humphrey, a longtime advocate of civil rights and social justice but also a firm supporter of the anti-

Communist doctrine of containment that had provided the rationale for involvement in Vietnam.

When the Democratic party convened in Chicago in August 1968, it was severely fragmented. Party regulars wanted to close ranks, while insurgents demanded recognition of their position on the draft and the war. On the radical fringe, some groups adopted confrontation tactics to dramatize their militancy. The National Mobilization to End the War in Vietnam was one such group. More important was the Yippie organization, led by Jerry Rubin and Abbie Hoffman. The Youth International Party sought to merge hippies and radicals and provided guerrilla theater. The group envisioned a "festival of life" to compete with the "convention of death" the Democrats were holding. They spoke of putting LSD into the Chicago water supply, having thousands of people run naked through the streets, and disarming the police. As they anticipated, they came up squarely against the longtime boss of Chicago, Mayor Richard Daley, who determined to use his police force to keep order.

The Chicago police swept demonstrators out of the parks at night. The first confrontations took place soon after the convention began, but the major incident came on the climactic evening when the convention nominated Hubert Humphrey. As thousands of demonstrating Yippies and others massed outside the hotel where the convention was being held, the police, seeking to push them back, lost

control. What occurred was, quite simply, a police riot, in which the forces of order went wild, clubbing not only demonstrators but also newsmen, bystanders, men and women both, all in front of the television cameras recording the incident for the country to see. Inside the hall, Senator Abraham Ribicoff of Connecticut denounced the "Gestapo tactics on the streets of Chicago" as delegate polling took place. Humphrey won the nomination, but by then the prize was badly tarnished.

Complicating the general election was the third-party campaign of Governor George C. Wallace of Alabama, a southern demagogue who exploited racial tensions for his own ends. Broadening his appeal to include northern working-class voters as well as southern whites, Wallace criticized the "left-wing theoreticians, briefcase-totin' bureaucrats, ivory-tower guideline writers, bearded anarchists, smart-aleck editorial writers and pointy-headed professors." Wallace hoped to ride the considerable blue-collar resentment of the radical forces causing upheaval in America into office.

Nixon's nomination by the Republicans was a triumph in a turbulent career. Running for vice-president in 1952, Nixon had almost been dropped from the ticket when charges of a slush fund surfaced. Only his maudlin televised appeal to the American public saved him then. After his loss to Kennedy in 1960 and his defeat in a race for governor of California in 1962, his political career appeared over. He told the press on that latter occasion, "You won't have Nixon to kick around any more because, gentleman, this is my last press conference." But after the Goldwater disaster in 1964, Nixon began to campaign for Republican candidates and reestablished a base of support.

Delighting in the Democratic convention debacle, Nixon worked to add the same constituency Wallace sought to his political base. He demanded law and order in America, claimed he had a plan to end the Vietnam War, and ran a

*The presence of left-wing demonstrators in confrontation with the Chicago police started as a nonviolent protest but turned ugly during the course of the 1968 Democratic Convention.*

*Speaking to the "silent majority," Nixon promised to reinstitute traditional values and restore law and order.*

carefully orchestrated campaign. No longer bitter or shrill, he adopted a stable, even aloof, stance and let his vice-presidential running mate, Governor Spiro Agnew of Maryland, lead the attack. Agnew, much like the Nixon of old, called Hubert Humphrey "squishy soft on Communism" and declared that "if you've seen one city slum, you've seen them all."

Even those comments, however, failed to slow the Republican momentum. As the campaign closed, Johnson halted all bombing of North Vietnam, but that gesture did not help Humphrey. Nixon received 43.4 percent of the popular vote, not quite one percent more than Humphrey, with Wallace capturing the rest, but it was enough to give Nixon a majority in the electoral college. The Democrats won both houses of Congress.

## The Nixon Administration

In and out of office, Nixon was a remote man, lacking humor and grace. As one of his speech writers said, there was "a mean side to his nature" that he strove to conceal. Earlier in his career he was labeled "Tricky Dick." Later he tried to bury that image. But he appeared to be a mechanical man, always calculating his next step.

Nixon embraced political life, but never with the exuberance of Lyndon Johnson. He was most comfortable alone or with a few wealthy friends. Even at work, he insulated himself, preferred written contacts to personal ones, and often retreated to a small room in the executive office building to be alone.

In Nixon's cabinet sat only white, male Republicans. Yet for the most part, Nixon worked around his cabinet, relying on other White House staff appointees. In domestic affairs, Arthur Burns, a former chairman of the Council of Economic Advisers, and Daniel Patrick Moynihan, a Harvard professor of government (and a Democrat) were the most important. In foreign affairs, the major figure was Henry A. Kissinger, another Harvard government professor, even more talented and ambitious, who directed the National Security Council staff and later became secretary of state.

Still another tier of White House officials insulated the president from the outside world and carried out his commands. None had public policy experience, but all shared an intense loyalty to their leader, a quality that Nixon prized. Advertising executive H. R. Haldeman, a tireless Nixon campaigner, became chief of staff. Of his relationships with the president, Haldeman remarked, "I get done what he wants done and I take the heat instead of him."

Working with Haldeman was lawyer John Ehrlichman. Starting as a legal counselor, Ehrlichman rose to the post of chief domestic adviser. Haldeman and Ehrlichman framed issues and narrowed options for Nixon. They came to be known as the "Berlin Wall" for the way they guarded the president's privacy. Finally there was John Mitchell, known as "El Supremo" by the staff, as the "Big Enchilada" by Ehrlichman. A tough, successful bond lawyer from Nixon's New York law office, he became a fast friend and managed the 1968 campaign. In the new administration he assumed the post of attorney general and gave the president daily advice.

## Gerald Ford

Gerald Ford succeeded to the presidency when Richard Nixon and his closest counselors became embroiled in a political scandal following the 1972 reelection campaign. Ford proved to be a very different leader.

From the start, Ford was a reassuring presence, for he was a decent, popular man. In a long congressional career that began after World War II, he became House minority leader and was well liked by his colleagues on Capitol Hill. He was an unassuming, unpretentious man who believed in traditional virtues. Republicans felt a burst of relief when Nixon chose him as vice-president in 1973, after Spiro Agnew resigned in disgrace for accepting bribes. Yet some critics questioned his capacity. Ford himself acknowledged his limitations when he declared, "I am a Ford, not a Lincoln." Those limitations soon became evident. Yet his genial personality quieted some of the fears Americans harbored about their country.

# REPUBLICAN FOREIGN POLICY

When Nixon assumed office in 1969, the nation was deeply divided by the Vietnam War. He understood that he must end the conflict, either by victory or withdrawal. Long fascinated by international relations, he hoped to play a major diplomatic role. "I've always thought this country could run itself domestically without a President," he once observed, implying that such was not the case with foreign affairs.

## The Agony of the Vietnam War

Nixon gave top priority to extricating the country from Vietnam while still finding a way to win the war. For the first time in American history, a president faced huge numbers of people opposed to their government's war policy. In mid-1969, the president announced the Nixon Doctrine, which asserted that the United States would give aid to friends and allies but would not undertake the full burden of troop defense. He thereupon embarked on the policy of Vietnamization, which entailed removing American forces and replacing them with Vietnamese ones. At the same time, Americans launched ferocious air attacks on North Vietnam. "Let's blow the hell out of them," Nixon instructed the Joint Chiefs of Staff. Between 1968 and 1972, American troop strength dropped from 543,000 to 39,000, and the reduction won political support for Nixon at home. Yet as the transition occurred, the South Vietnamese steadily lost ground to the Viet Cong.

War protests multiplied in 1969 and 1970. In November 1969, as a massive protest demonstration took place in Washington, D.C., the first stories surfaced about the massacre of civilians in Vietnam the year before. Journalist Seymour M. Hersh had heard rumors about the My Lai episode and had begun to piece together an account of what had occurred. His efforts provided the American people with horrifying evidence of the war's brutality.

My Lai, a small village in Vietnam, was allegedly harboring 250 members of the enemy Viet Cong. An American infantry company was helicoptered in to clear out the village. C Com-

pany had already had heavy combat losses, but instead of soldiers, this time it found women, children, and old men. Perhaps inured to the random destruction already wrought by the American military, perhaps concerned with the sometimes fuzzy distinction between combatants and civilians in a guerrilla war, the American forces lost control.

Lieutenant William L. Calley, Jr., a mild-mannered officer, first ordered, "Round everybody up," and then said, "Take care of 'em." When Paul Meadlo, a private from a small Indiana farm town, simply guarded the people he had collected, Calley said, "Hey, Meadlo, I said take care of 'em." At that the Americans began mowing down the civilians in cold blood. Later Meadlo recalled:

> We huddled them up. We made them squat down. . . . I poured about four clips into the group. . . . The mothers was hugging their children. . . . Well, we kept right on firing. They was waving their arms and begging. . . . I still dream about it. About the women and children in my sleep. Some days . . . some nights, I can't even sleep.

Americans at home were shocked at stories of the civilian slaughter. Yet once the initial revulsion began to subside, they proved less willing to condemn. Some sympathized with Calley, who, they argued, was simply responding to the demands of war. When Calley was court-martialed, convicted for at "least twenty-two murders" and sentenced to life imprisonment, Nixon realized that many Americans thought the sentence too harsh. He ordered Calley released from prison while the case was under appeal and announced that he would personally review it before any sentence was carried out. As the furor died down, the military reduced his sentence to ten years. Eligible for parole in six months, Calley was soon free.

While the My Lai episode led many to wonder about American conduct of the war, incidents on several college campuses made them question the use of troops at home. A disaster at Kent State University was set in motion by a series of presidential decisions in April 1970. Much as Nixon wanted to defuse opposition to the Vietnam War, like LBJ he was determined not to lose it either. Therefore, as he publicized his Vietnamization policy, he looked for other ways to achieve victory. Realizing that the Vietnamese relied on supplies funneled through Cambodia, Nixon announced that American and Vietnamese troops were invading that country to clear out the Communist enclaves there. The United States, he said, would not stand by as "a pitiful helpless giant" when there were actions it could take to stem the Communist advance.

Nixon's invasion of Cambodia brought renewed demonstrations on college campuses, some with tragic results. At Kent State, in Ohio, the response was fierce. The day after the president announced his moves, disgruntled students gathered downtown. Worried about the crowd, the local police called in sheriff's deputies to disperse the students. The next evening, groups of students collected on college grounds. Assembling around the ROTC building, they began throwing firecrackers and rocks at the structure, which had become a hated symbol of the war. Then they set it on fire and watched it burn to the ground.

The governor of Ohio ordered the National Guard to the university. Tension grew as they set up tents on campus and took over the gym. Finally, it exploded. Loading their guns and donning gas masks, the Guardsmen prepared to disperse the gathering mob. As the students fell back, some threw rocks or empty canisters of gas. Most, however, were so far away that they could not have reached the troops. At midday, the soldiers knelt down and aimed their rifles at the students as if to warn them to stop. Then they rose together, huddled with one another, and finally began to retreat to a different position. At the top of a hill they turned and suddenly began firing in unison at the students below.

When the firing ceased, four students lay dead, nine wounded. Two of the dead had been demonstrators, who were more than 250 feet away when shot. The other two were innocent bystanders, almost 400 feet from the troops.

Students around the country, as well as other Americans, were outraged by the attack. Many were equally disturbed about a similar attack at Jackson State University in Mississippi. Policemen and highway patrolmen poured automatic weapon fire into a women's dormitory without warning. When the shooting stopped, two people were dead, more wounded. The dead there, however, were black students at a black institution, and white America paid less attention to that attack.

In 1971, the Vietnam War made major headlines once more when the New York *Times* began publishing a secret Department of Defense account of American involvement in the war. The so called Pentagon Papers, leaked by Daniel Ellsberg, a defense analyst, gave Americans a firsthand look at the fabrications and faulty assumptions that had guided the steady expansion of the struggle. Even though the study stopped with the Johnson years, the Nixon administration was furious and sought a Supreme Court injunction to halt publication of the series. By a split vote the Court ruled against the government, and readers continued to learn more about the nightmarish war.

Vietnam remained a political football as Nixon ran for reelection in 1972. Negotiations aimed at a settlement were under way, and just before election day, Henry Kissinger announced, "Peace is at hand." When South Vietnam seemed to balk at the proposed settlement, however, the administration responded with the most intensive bombing campaign of the war.

*When Ohio National Guardsmen fired on a crowd of antiwar demonstrators, killing four students, even prowar Americans were shocked.*

Hanoi, the capital of North Vietnam, was hit hard; then the North Vietnamese harbors were mined. Only in the new year was a cease-fire finally signed. Kissinger shared the 1973 Nobel Peace Prize with his North Vietnamese counterpart Le Duc Tho. Tho rejected his part of the prize with the observation that the war between North and South Vietnam was not yet over, even though the American troops were finally going home. Kissinger had no such compunctions and accepted his share of the award.

After Nixon left office, the conflict in Vietnam lingered on into the spring of 1975, yet by that time American troops had been evacuated. When at last the North Vietnamese consolidated their control over the entire country, Gerald Ford called for another $1 billion in aid, even as the South Vietnamese were abandoning arms and supplies in chaotic retreat. Congress refused, leaving the crumbling government of South Vietnam to fend for itself. Republicans hailed Kissinger for having finally freed the United States from the Southeast Asian quagmire. Antiwar critics, on the other hand, condemned him for continuing involvement in the war for so long. *New Republic* wryly observed that Kissinger brought peace to Vietnam in the same way Napoleon brought peace to Europe: by losing.

The conflict was finally over, but the costs were immense. In the longest war in its history, the United States lost almost 58,000 men, with far more wounded or maimed. Blacks and Chicanos suffered more than whites since they were disproportionately represented in the armed forces. Financially, the nation spent over $150 billion in an ultimately unsuccessful war. Domestic reform had slowed, then stopped. American society had been deeply divided. Only time would heal the wounds.

## Détente

If the Republicans' Vietnam policy was a questionable success, in other areas Nixon's accomplishments were impressive. The Red-baiter of the past was able to deal imaginatively and successfully with the Communist powers. In so doing he reversed the direction of American policy since the Second World War. Bypassing Congress, often bypassing his own

Department of State, the president depended most heavily on Kissinger, his national security adviser. Kissinger grasped the complexity of the world situation, understood the tensions within the Communist realm, and exploited them to restore better American relations with both the Soviet Union and China.

Nixon's most dramatic step was opening formal relations with the People's Republic of China. In the two decades since Mao Zedong's victory on the Chinese mainland in 1949, the American position had been that Jiang Jieshi's rump government on Taiwan was the rightful government of the Chinese people; consequently, there had been no diplomatic relations with the Communist regime. In 1971, with an eye on the forthcoming political campaign, the administration began softening its rigid stand. After the Chinese invited an American table-tennis team to visit the mainland, the United States eased some of the trading restrictions in force. Then in August 1971, Nixon announced that he intended to visit China the following year, the first American president ever to do so.

That bold step signified Nixon's understanding that the People's Republic was an established force representing the Chinese people. The president knew that the rest of the world had for years recognized the People's Republic and wanted to seat it in the United Nations.

*Secretary of State Henry Kissinger was instrumental in arranging Nixon's visit to China, which opened the way to American recognition of the Communist state.*

Moreover, he suspected that he could use Chinese friendship as a bargaining chip when he dealt with the Soviet Union. Finally, American leaders officially acknowledged what most nations already knew: Communism was not monolithic. At home, Nixon believed that he could open a dialogue with the Chinese Communists without political harm, for he had long been a vocal critic of communism and could hardly be accused of being "soft" on it. He knew also that the coverage of a dramatic trip could give him a real boost in the press.

Nixon went to China in February 1972. He met with Chinese leaders Mao Zedong and Zou Enlai (Chou En-lai), talked about international problems, exchanged toasts, and saw some of the major sights. Wherever he went, American television cameras followed, helping to introduce the American public to a nation about which they knew little. Though formal relations were not yet restored, détente between the two countries had begun.

Nixon also used his new China policy to seek better ties with the Soviet Union. He and Kissinger hoped to be able to play one Communist state against the other, and by and large, they accomplished their aim. Several months after his trip to China, Nixon visited Russia, where he was also warmly welcomed. After several cordial meetings, the president and Soviet premier Leonid Brezhnev agreed to limit missile stockpiles, work together in space, and ease the longstanding restrictions on trade. Businessmen applauded the new approach, and most Americans approved of détente.

Nixon dealt with the Communist governments with tact and skill. Using his Chinese and Russian initiatives to neutralize opposition to the phased withdrawal of troops in Vietnam, he bought time to pursue Vietnamization on his own terms.

When Gerald Ford assumed office, he followed the policies begun under Nixon. Kissinger remained secretary of state and continued to play an influential role in foreign affairs. In May 1975, an episode in another part of Southeast Asia reflected the difficulties of new policies. Cambodian forces captured the *Mayaguez*, an American merchant ship cruising inside the territorial waters of that country. When American protests went unanswered, the United States sent 350 marines to attack an island where the crew was thought to be held. The operation's cost was 41 American lives. Since the Cambodians were evidently preparing to return both ship and crew, the bloodshed proved unnecessary. Yet in the aftermath of the Vietnamese defeat, Kissinger and Ford were anxious to respond vigorously and to avoid the impression that the United States had been weakened by the war. Their opponents, however, called the raid a case of overkill.

Ford continued the Strategic Arms Limitation Talks (SALT) that provided hope for eventual nuclear disarmament. He also accepted the Helsinki Accords, which defined European security arrangements and underscored basic human rights. He pursued friendly relations with China and elsewhere maintained the spirit of détente, even while rejecting the term. In the mid-1970s, American foreign policy tended to be reactive, yet the country remained at peace, avoided major confrontations, and continued to define a less aggressive role for itself abroad.

*Improved relations with the Soviet Union resulted from Nixon's shrewd foreign policy. In 1972 Brezhnev joined him in a toast on signing the Strategic Arms Limitation Pact.*

## SEARCHING FOR STABILITY

As the Republicans struggled with Vietnam and détente, they faced serious problems as home. The economy suffered a series of shocks. Social fragmentation and polarization were more pronounced than they had ever been in the twentieth century. Nixon hoped that his victory and strong presidential leadership could defuse antiwar protest. But forces were smoldering that even he could not control. And eventually political scandal compounded his difficulties and brought him down.

### The Oil Embargo and the Economy Under Nixon

Nixon inherited an already faltering economy. President Johnson had escalated the war in Vietnam but had been unwilling to raise taxes from 1965 to 1967 to pay for it. As demand generated by war needs rose, so too did prices and the wages employers had to pay their workers. Inflation slowly crept up, from 2.2 percent in 1965 to 4.5 percent in 1968.

Nixon tried to restrain inflation by tightening monetary and fiscal policy. Although parts of the plan worked, a mild recession occurred in 1969–1970, and inflation did not abate. Realizing the political dangers of pursuing his policy

further, Nixon imposed wage and price controls to stop inflation and used monetary and fiscal policies to stimulate the economy. After his reelection, however, he lifted wage and price controls, and inflation began to rise.

Other factors contributed to the spiral of rising prices. Eager to court the farm vote, the administration made a large wheat sale to Russia in 1972. But government officials had miscalculated. With insufficient wheat left for the American market, grain prices shot up. Twenty-five years of grain surpluses suddenly disappeared, and shortages occurred. Other agricultural setbacks like corn blight compounded the problem. Between 1971 and 1974, farm prices rose 66 percent as agricultural inflation accompanied industrial inflation.

The most critical factor in disrupting the economy, however, was the Arab oil embargo. American economic expansion had rested on cheap energy just as American patterns of life had depended on inexpensive gasoline. Although OPEC (the Organization of Petroleum Exporting Countries) had slowly raised oil prices in the early 1970s, the 1973 war between Israel, Egypt, and Syria led Saudi Arabia to impose an embargo on oil shipped to Israel's ally, the United States. Other OPEC nations quadrupled

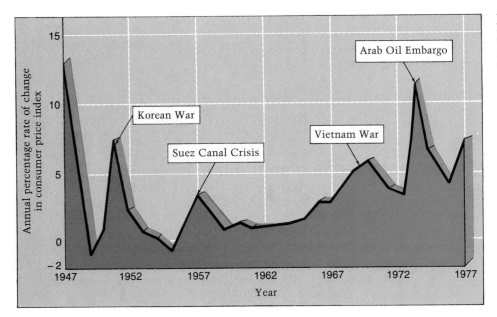

**Rate of Inflation, 1947–1977**

*Source:* U.S. Bureau of Labor Statistics.

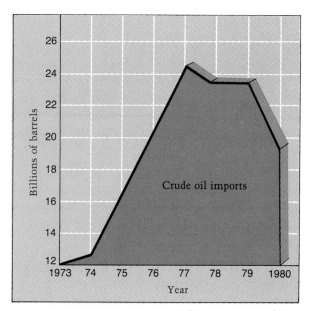
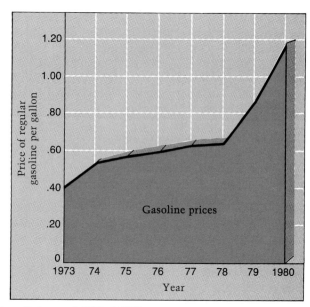

**Oil Imports and Gasoline Prices, 1973–1980**
*Source:* U.S. Energy Information Administration.

their prices. Dependent on imports for one-third of their energy needs, Americans faced shortages and skyrocketing prices. When the embargo ended in 1974, prices remained high.

The oil crisis affected all aspects of American economic life. Manufacturers, farmers, homeowners—all were touched by high energy prices. A loaf of bread that had cost 28 cents in the early 1970s jumped to 89 cents, and automobiles cost 72 percent more in 1978 than they had in 1973. Accustomed to filling up their cars' tanks for only a few dollars, Americans were shocked at paying 65 cents a gallon. In 1974, inflation reached 11 percent. But as higher energy prices encouraged consumers to cut back on their purchases, the nation also entered a recession. Unemployment climbed to 9 percent, the highest level since the 1930s. Inflation and high unemployment were worrisome bedfellows.

As economic growth and stability eluded him, Nixon also tried to reorganize the rapidly expanding welfare programs. As a result of the Great Society programs, the government was spending more, in an effort that critics claimed was inefficient and unnecessary since it discouraged people from seeking work. Nixon faced a dilemma. He recognized the conservative tide growing in the Sun Belt regions of the country

from Florida to Texas to California, where many voters wanted cutbacks in what they viewed as excessive government programs. At the same time, he wanted to win traditionally Democratic blue-collar workers over to his side by reassuring them that the Republicans would not dismantle the parts of the welfare state on which they relied. At the urging of domestic adviser Daniel

**Unemployment Rate, 1940–1982**
*Source:* U.S. Bureau of Labor Statistics.

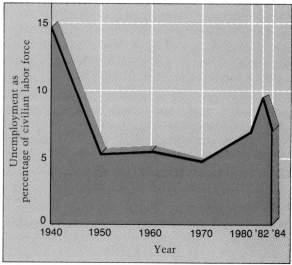

Moynihan, Nixon endorsed an expensive but feasible work-incentive program. The Family Assistance Plan would have guaranteed a minimum yearly stipend of $1,600 to a family of four, with food stamps providing about $800 more. The program, aiming to cut "welfare cheaters" who took unfair advantage of the system, required all participants to register for job training and to accept employment when found. Proponents, who probably exaggerated the number of "welfare cheaters," wanted to make it more profitable to work than to subsist on the public rolls. Though promising, the program died in the Senate, but it indicated what the administration hoped to do.

## Social Polarization

While dealing with economic questions, Nixon also had to confront the deep social divisions engendered by the Vietnam War and the "generation gap" that divided Americans on moral and social issues. In his election victory statement, Nixon declared that his overriding objective was "to bring the American people together. We want to bridge the generation gap. We want to bridge the gap between the races." But the fragmentation continued to grow.

Large numbers of young people, embracing the ethos of the counterculture and profoundly apolitical, were not moved by election campaigns and victory statements. Seven months after Nixon's inauguration, on the weekend of August 15–16, 1969, some 400,000 gathered in a large pasture in upstate New York for the Woodstock rock festival. There, despite intense heat and torrential rain, despite inadequate supplies of water and food, the festival unfolded in a spirit of affection. Some people took off their clothes and paraded in the nude, some engaged in public lovemaking, and most shared whatever they had, particularly the marijuana that seemed endlessly available, while major rock groups provided ear-splitting, around-the-clock entertainment for the assembled throng.

The weekend went off without a hitch. The police chose not to enforce the drug laws and thereby avoided confrontations. The promoters had chartered helicopters to whisk away anyone suffering a drug overdose. For the most part, the gigantic crowd remained under control. Supporters hailed the festival as an example of the new and better world to come.

Other Americans, however, viewed the antics of the young with distaste. They deplored the uninhibited drug use, nudity, and sexuality, all brought into their living rooms on nightly television news shows. No matter how much the proponents hailed the "Woodstock Nation," much of America was appalled. The festival only underscored the generational polarization.

Other aspects of the counterculture became more visible at another festival four months later in Altamont, California. There 300,000 people gathered at a stock-car raceway to attend a rock concert climaxing an American tour by the immensely popular Rolling Stones. Woodstock had been well planned; the Altamont affair was not. In the absence of adequate security, the Stones hired a band of Hell's Angels to maintain control. Those tough motorcyclists, fond of terrorizing the open road, prepared to keep order in their own way.

The spirit at Altamont was different from the start. The peace and joy of Woodstock were replaced by a lurking fear of what could go wrong. "It was a gray day, and the California hills were bare, cold and dead," wrote Greil Marcus, a music critic. The crowd was "ugly, selfish, territorialist, throughout the day." One

*The 1969 rock festival at Woodstock represented the "dawning of the age of Aquarius" for some; for others it was an orgy of illicit and disreputable behavior.*

naked woman made a game of selecting a male, approaching him, and rubbing her body against his. When he began to respond, she screamed and ran away. A fat man bounded onto the stage to dance naked to the music of one of the preliminary groups but clumsily trampled those around him and finally aroused the Hell's Angels, who charged him with weighted pool cues and beat him to the ground. An undercurrent of violence simmered, Marcus observed, as "all day long people . . . speculated on who would be killed, on when the killing would take place. There were few doubts that the Angels would do the job."

With the Stones on stage, the fears were realized. As star Mick Jagger looked on, the Hell's Angels beat a young black man to death. A musician who tried to intervene was knocked senseless. Other beatings occurred, accidents claimed several more lives, and drug-overdosed revelers found no adequate medical support.

Altamont revealed the underside of the counterculture and exposed the worst fears of less sympathetic Americans. *Rolling Stone*, the rock world's journal, deplored the commercial, promotional greed that had inspired the concert. Greil Marcus summed up the contradictions of both the concert and the movement: "A young black man murdered in the midst of a white crowd by white thugs as white men played their version of black music—it was too much to kiss off as a mere unpleasantness." But Altamont represented more than continuing racial tension; it also showed the dark side of the counterculture, its self-indulgent, anarchic nature.

Another episode in Nixon's first year reflected the political, as opposed to cultural, split in the United States. The Weathermen, a militant fringe group of the Students for a Democratic Society (SDS), sought in October 1969 to show that the revolution had arrived with a frontal attack on Chicago, scene of the violent Democratic convention of 1968.

The New Left had been increasingly active in the late 1960s, and as it seized upon the issue of the Vietnam War and broadened its critique of American society, the SDS became a significant force. After a series of factional disputes, the Weathermen (who took their name from a line in a Bob Dylan song, "You don't need a weather-

man to know which way the wind blows") emerged as one of the most radical groups.

Starting on October 8, Weathermen from all over the country converged on Chicago, mobilized themselves, and prepared to attack. In the evening, dressed in hard hats and jackboots, wearing work gloves and other forms of padding, they rampaged through the streets with clubs and pipes, chains and rocks. They ran into the police, as they had expected and hoped, and continued the attack. Some were arrested, others were shot, and the rest withdrew to regroup. For the next two days, they plotted strategy, engaged in minor skirmishes, and prepared for the final thrust. It came on the fourth day, once again pitting aggressive Weathermen against hostile police.

Why had the Weathermen launched their attack? "The status quo meant to us war, poverty, inequality, ignorance, famine and disease in most of the world," Bo Burlingham, a participant from Ohio, reflected. "To accept it was to condone and help perpetuate it. We felt like miners trapped in a terrible poisonous shaft with no light to guide us out. We resolved to destroy the tunnel even if we risked destroying ourselves in the process."

The rationale of the Chicago "national action" may have been clear to the participants, but it convinced few other Americans. There and elsewhere, citizens were infuriated at what they saw. In New York City, when students demonstrated in the Wall Street area in the aftermath of the Kent State affair, angry construction workers on their lunch break attacked them. Carrying signs reading "Don't worry, they don't draft faggots," and "Get the hippie! Get the traitor!" they rushed at the demonstrators with lead pipes and fists. As was so often the case, middle-class and working-class Americans found themselves on different sides.

### Law and Order

Underlying Nixon's hopes of bringing America together was the conviction that this process must begin by restoring law and order. He hoped to exploit the growing backlash as most working-class and many middle-class Americans became increasingly hostile to the protest movements of the 1960s. Crime rates seemed to be rising as drug use spread. Permissive attitudes toward sex flouted old codes. Racial and political disruptions threatened the pursuit of the middle-class American dream. At home, by promising to restore the old values they shared, Nixon intended to cultivate the groups who feltchange had gone too far.

One part of the administration's campaign involved denouncing disruptive elements. Nixon lashed out at demonstrators—he called the students "bums" at one point. More and more, however, he relied on his vice-president to play the part of hatchet man, just as Nixon had done for Eisenhower as his vice-president. Spiro Agnew had a gift for jugular attack. In one campaign speech he told students sympathetic to the SDS, "I know you'd like to overthrow the government, but on November fifth, we'll put a man in office who'll take this country forward without you." In office he was no less vituperative. "Ideological eunuchs" he called students, "parasites of passion." Opposition elements made up an "effete corps of impudent snobs," who did untold damage in the United States, he stated.

Another part of Nixon's effort to promote stability involved attacking the communications industry, which he believed undermined consensus in America. The media, he felt, not only represented the views of the "Eastern establishment" but showed a personal hostility toward him as well. Nixon had long grumbled about his treatment in the press, considering "the influential majority of the news media to be part of my political opposition." Early in his term, he decided to take on the television networks for what he considered biased and distorted coverage of his policies. Again Agnew was directed to spearhead the attack, and he did so with relish.

Most important, however, was the effort of Attorney General John Mitchell to demonstrate that the administration supported the values of citizens upset by domestic upheavals. Mitchell sought enhanced powers for a campaign on crime, sometimes at the expense of individuals' constitutional rights. With little respect for the right of dissent, he intended to send a message to the entire country that the new team in the White House would not tolerate the excesses that had led to violence in the streets.

One part of Mitchell's plan involved reshaping the Supreme Court, which had rendered increasingly liberal decisions on the rights of defendants in the past decade and a half. That shift, Republican leaders argued, had led to moral and ethical looseness in the United States and had encouraged the recent disruptions. In his first term, Nixon had the extraordinary opportunity to name four judges to the Court, and he nominated men who shared his views. His first choice was Warren E. Burger as Chief Justice to replace the liberal Earl Warren, who was retiring. Burger, a moderate, was confirmed quickly. Other appointments, however, were more partisan and reflected Nixon's aggressively conservative approach. Intent on appealing to white southerners, he first selected Clement Haynesworth of South Carolina, then G. Harrold Carswell of Florida. Both men on examination showed such racial biases or limitations that the Senate refused to confirm them. Nixon then appointed Harry Blackmun, Lewis F. Powell, Jr., and William Rehnquist, all able and qualified, and all inclined to tilt the Court in a more conservative way.

Over the next few years, the Court shifted to the right. It narrowed defendants' rights in an attempt to ease the burden of the prosecution in its cases and slowed the process of liberalization by upholding pornography laws if they mirrored community standards. On other questions, however, the Court did not always move as the president had hoped. In the 1973 *Roe* v. *Wade* decision, the Court legalized abortion, stating that women's rights included the right to control their own bodies. This decision was one that the feminists, a group hardly supported by the president, had ardently sought.

## "Southern Strategy" and Showdown on Civil Rights

Nixon's intent was to underscore his allegiance to conservative groups in order to solidify a firm political base. Nowhere was that approach more evident than in the area of civil rights. Nixon felt that he had little to gain by courting blacks, for in 1968 the Republicans had won barely 5 percent of the black vote. Furthermore, an effort to woo the black electorate could endanger the attempt to obtain white southern support. Both the president and the attorney general felt that the civil rights movement had run its course. It was now in their interest to shape government policy to secure the votes of southern whites.

From the start, the administration sought to dampen the federal commitment to civil rights. Nixon himself once declared that "there are those who want instant integration and those who want segregation forever. I believe that we need to have a middle course between those two extremes." Given the continued resistance to racial change in some parts of the country, such a middle course involved very little action at all.

In line with political priorities, the administration moved, at the start of Nixon's first term,

*Busing was mandated to end de facto school segregation in the North, drawing violent opposition from whites in some cities and requiring police protection for those bused.*

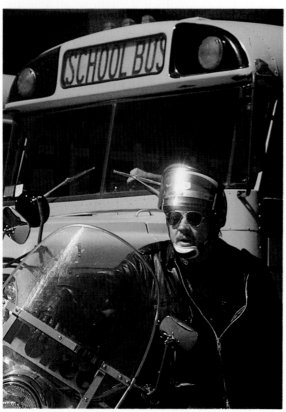

to reduce the appropriation for fair-housing enforcement. Then the Department of Justice tried to prevent extension of the Voting Rights Act of 1965, which had added a million blacks to the voting rolls and led to the election of thousands of black officials, especially in northern cities. Congress approved the extension, but the administration had made clear its position on racial issues. When South Carolina senator Strom Thurmond and others tried to suspend federal school desegregation guidelines, the Justice Department urged a delay in meeting desegregation deadlines in 33 of Mississippi's school districts. The NAACP appealed, and the Supreme Court ruled unanimously that "the obligation of every school system is to terminate dual school systems at once." Publicly disagreeing with the decision, Nixon showed his sympathy with white southern sentiment while at the same time avoiding blame for the integration of Mississippi's schools.

Nixon also faced the growing controversy over busing as a means of desegregation, a highly charged issue in the 1970s. Transporting students from one area to another to attend school was nothing new. A century before, in 1869, Massachusetts had set aside money to send children to and from school in carriages and wagons, and over the next 50 years, public funding for student transport became lawful in all states. Busing, in fact, had usually been viewed by parents as an educational advantage, for their children could be moved from a one-room schoolhouse to a consolidated school. By 1970, over 18 million students, almost 40 percent of those in the United States, rode buses to school. Yet when busing became tangled with the question of integration, it inflamed passions.

The busing question first surfaced in the South. There, in the years before the Supreme Court endorsed integration, busing had long been used to maintain segregated schools. Some black students in Selma, Alabama, for example, traveled 50 miles by bus to an entirely black trade school in Montgomery, even though a similar school for whites stood nearby. Now, however, busing had become a means of breaking down racial barriers.

The issue came to a head in North Carolina, in the Charlotte-Mecklenburg school system.

The 550-square-mile district had over 84,000 students in more than 100 schools. Twenty-nine percent of the pupils were black, and they were concentrated primarily in one section of the region. A desegregation plan involving voluntary transfer was in effect, but there, as elsewhere, many blacks still attended largely segregated schools. A federal judge ruled that the district was not in compliance with the latest Supreme Court decisions, and in 1971, the Supreme Court ruled that district courts had broad authority to order the desegregation of school systems—by busing, if necessary.

Earlier, Nixon had opposed such busing, and the Court decision did not affect his position. The fact that George Wallace had spoken out against busing and won Florida's Democratic primary in March 1972 was not lost on Nixon. The president approached Congress for a moratorium or even a restriction on busing and went on television to denounce it. Although Congress did not accede to his request, southerners knew where the president stood. As more and more southern cities were obliged to establish transportation plans to integrate their schools, however, resistance grew.

As the busing mandate spread to the North, resistance spilled out of the South. In the North, in many of the nation's largest cities, schools were as rigidly segregated as in the South, largely due to residential patterns. This segregation was called *de facto* to differentiate it from the *de jure* or legal segregation that had existed in the South. Mississippi senator John C. Stennis, a bitter foe of busing, hoped to stir up the North by making it subject to the same standards as the South. "Parents," he said, "are not going to permit their children to be boxed up and crated and hauled around the city and the country like common animals." And, he informed Northern colleagues, "if you have to [integrate] in your area, you will see what it means to us." His proposal, adopted in the Senate, required that federal desegregation guidelines be enforced uniformly throughout the nation or not used at all. Court decisions subsequently ordered many northern cities to desegregate their schools.

In Boston, the effort to integrate proved rockier than anywhere else in the North. In 1973, despite a state measure eight years earlier requiring districts to desegregate any schools more than half black, 85 percent of the blacks in Boston attended schools that had a black majority. More than half the black students were in schools that were 90 percent black. In June 1974, a federal judge ordered that busing begin. The first phase, involving 17,000 pupils, was to start in the fall of that year.

Watching the process unfold, Thomas J. Cottle, of the Children's Defense Fund of the Washington Research Project in Boston, closely followed two families, one white, one black. Though he changed their names in a report he presented in the popular press, he captured their sentiments and their words.

Clarence Charles McDonough III, a white parent, was irate when he learned that his son Cassie was to be transferred by bus from the white school he attended to a black school farther away. "They did it to me," he screamed as Cottle visited one day.

> They went and did it to me. . . . I told you they would. I told you there'd be no running from 'em. You lead your life perfect as a pane of glass, go to church, work 40 hours a week at the same job—year in, year out—keep your complaints to yourself, and they still do it to you. They're forcing that boy to go to school miles from here in a dangerous area to a school no one knows a damn thing about, just so they can bring these other kids in, kids who don't belong here.

Black father Ronald Dearborn also had anxieties of his own about what his son Claudell might face in a white area. "It's a long way," he said, "even by car. Let's hope they keep those buses running fine. I'd hate to think what would happen if they broke down some night over there. If white folks don't look kindly at having black folks attending their schools, they sure won't like to see a bunch of black youngsters parked outside their home all night." Unlike Clarence McDonough, however, he supported school desegregation. As Francine, Claudell's mother, pointed out, such steps were necessary, even if bruises were involved, for "when you're black, you know all about falling—and what you don't know this country teaches you mighty fast, even when you go to schools where everyone is black, like we did."

For both Cassie and Claudell, attendance at different elementary schools went smoothly. Reassigned high school students were less fortunate. A white boycott at South Boston High cut attendance from the anticipated 1,500 to less than 100 on the first day. Buses bringing in black students were stoned and some children cut. White working-class South Bostonians felt that they were being asked to carry the burden of middle-class liberals' racial views. Similar resentments and anger triggered racial episodes elsewhere. In many cases, white families either enrolled their children in private schools or fled the city altogether.

Busing became a bitter issue, one that reflected the still volatile nature of the quest for equal rights. Given his own private views and political ends, Nixon hoped to slow down the civil rights movement, and to a degree, he did. Yet he never viewed himself as a racial bigot. Rather he saw himself as a man who would do whatever was practical to assist in racial relations. "I care," he once insisted to James Farmer, a black leader appointed to the post of assistant secretary of health, education, and welfare. "I just hope people will believe that I *do* care." But actions spoke louder than words, and only pressures from others kept the civil rights movement alive.

## Watergate and the 1972 Reelection Campaign

Shortly after taking office, the Nixon administration found itself at a standoff with the legislative branch: Both houses of Congress were solidly Democratic. Nixon was determined to end the legislative stalemate by winning a second term and sweeping Republican majorities into both houses of Congress in 1972.

Nixon's reelection campaign was even better organized than the effort four years before. Sparing no expense, the president relied on aides who were fiercely loyal and prepared to do anything to win. Special counsel Charles W. Colson described himself as a "flag-waving, . . . anti-press, anti-liberal Nixon fanatic." He had earlier played an important part in developing an "enemies list" of prominent figures judged to be unsympathetic to the administration. White House counsel John Dean defined his task as finding a way to "use the available federal machinery to screw our political enemies." Active in carrying out commands were E. Howard Hunt, a former CIA agent and a specialist in "dirty tricks," and G. Gordon Liddy, a one-time member of the FBI, who prided himself on his willingness to do anything without flinching. Hunt and Liddy had earlier been members of the "Plumbers," who tried to plug government leaks after the Pentagon Papers affair.

The Committee to Re-elect the President (CREEP), headed by John Mitchell, who resigned as attorney general to do so, launched a massive fund-raising drive, aimed at collecting as much money as it could before the reporting of contributions became necessary under a new campaign-finance law. That money could be used for any purpose, including payments for the performance of dirty tricks aimed at disrupting the opposition's campaign. Other funds financed an intelligence branch within CREEP that had Liddy at its head and included Hunt.

Early in 1972, Liddy and his lieutenants proposed an elaborate scheme to wiretap the phones of various Democrats and to disrupt their nominating convention. Twice Mitchell refused to go along, arguing that the plan was too risky and expensive. Finally he approved a modified version of the plan to tap the phones of the Democratic National Committee at its headquarters in the Watergate apartment complex in Washington, D.C. Mitchell, formerly the top justice official in the land, had authorized breaking the law.

The wiretapping attempt took place on the evening of June 16 and ended with the arrest of those involved. They carried with them money and documents that could be traced to CREEP and incriminate the reelection campaign. Top officials of the Nixon reelection team had to decide quickly what response to make.

## Cover-up and Catastrophe

Reelection remained the most pressing priority, so Nixon's aides played the matter down and used federal resources to head off the investigation. When the FBI traced the money carried by the burglars to CREEP, the president authorized the CIA to call off the FBI on the grounds that national security was at stake. Though not involved in the planning of the break-in, the president was now party to the cover-up. In the succeeding months, he authorized payment of hush money to silence Hunt and others. Top members of the administration, including Mitchell, perjured themselves in court to shield the higher officials who were involved.

Nixon won the election of 1972 in a landslide, receiving 60.7 percent of the popular vote and trouncing his opponent, George McGovern, a liberal senator from South Dakota, even more soundly in the electoral college. He failed, however, to gain the congressional majorities necessary to support his programs.

Even worse, he had to watch the trial of the Watergate burglars. While the matter seemed closed when the defendants pleaded guilty and were sentenced to jail, it refused to die. Judge John Sirica was not satisfied that justice had been done, asserting that the evidence indicated that others had played a part. Meanwhile, two zealous reporters, Bob Woodward and Carl Bernstein of the Washington *Post*, were following a trail of leads on their own. Slowly they recognized who else was involved. On one occasion, when they reached Mitchell and asked him about a story tying him to Watergate, he turned on them in fury. "All that crap, you're putting in the paper?" he said. "It's all been denied."

Mitchell's irritation notwithstanding, the unraveling of Watergate continued. The Senate Select Committee on Presidential Campaign Activities undertook an investigation, and one of the convicted burglars testified that the White House had been involved in the episode. Newspaper stories provided further leads, and the Senate hearings in turn provided new material for the press. Faced with rumors that the White House was actively involved, Nixon decided that he had to release Haldeman and Ehrlichman, his two closest aides, in an effort to save his own neck. On nationwide TV he declared that he would take the ultimate responsibility for the mistakes of others, for "there can be no whitewash at the White House."

In May 1973, the Senate committee began televised public hearings, reminiscent of the earlier McCarthy hearings of the 1950s. As millions of Americans watched, the drama built. John Dean, seeking to save himself, testified that Nixon knew about the cover-up, and other staffers revealed a host of illegal activities undertaken at the White House: Money had been paid to the burglars to silence them; State Department documents had been forged to smear a previous administration; wiretaps had been used to prevent top-level leaks. The most electrifying moment was the disclosure that the president had in his office a secret taping system that recorded all conversations. Tapes could verify or disprove the growing rumors that Nixon had in fact been party to the cover-up all along.

In an effort to demonstrate his own honesty, Nixon agreed to the appointment of Harvard law professor Archibald Cox as a special prosecutor in the Department of Justice. But when Cox tried to gain access to the tapes, Nixon resisted and finally fired him. Nixon's own popularity had begun to drop, and even the appointment of another special prosecutor, Leon Jaworski, did

### Presidential Elections, 1968 and 1972

| YEAR | CANDIDATES | PARTY | POPULAR VOTE | ELECTORAL VOTES |
|------|-----------|-------|--------------|-----------------|
| 1968 | RICHARD M. NIXON | Republican | 31,783,783 (43.4%) | 301 |
|      | Hubert H. Humphrey | Democratic | 31,271,839 (42.7%) | 191 |
|      | George C. Wallace | Amer. Independent | 9,899,557 (13.5%) | 46 |
| 1972 | RICHARD M. NIXON | Republican | 45,767,218 (60.6%) | 520 |
|      | George S. McGovern | Democratic | 28,357,668 (37.5%) | 17 |

*Note:* Winners' names appears in capital letters.

# RECOVERING THE PAST

In an earlier chapter we looked at political cartoons of Theodore Roosevelt to gain insight into the past through the cartoons found on the editorial pages of newspapers. We saw how cartoonists depend on caricature in distorting the features of a subject, thus making their point at a moment's glance. With sometimes biting humor, they make us laugh in recognition of a political predicament or larger social truth. Some galvanize our emotions to action. The best cartoons hold up a mirror to help us see ourselves as we are, full of human frailties yet touched with nobility.

Editorial cartoons are not the only kind of graphic technique to stir such reactions. Many other forms of humorous cartoons, from Saturday morning television films to comic books and newspaper "funny pages," suggest the issues and moral questions that concern the people of a particular era. Historians, therefore, can sometimes recover the deepest truths about the past by noticing what makes people laugh. We laugh at those aspects of our personalities and culture that matter the most to us.

From 1972 to 1975, no issue mattered more to the American people than the truth about the events associated with "Watergate" and how much President Nixon knew about those affairs. Nixon's combative relationship with the press, coupled with his easily identified features (heavy jowls, pointed nose), made

**Herbert Block, "Tape Job," August 28, 1973**

**Tony Auth, "I cannot tell the truth . . . ," August 8, 1974, from Behind the Lines by Tony Auth**

# CARTOON HUMOR

**Garry Trudeau, "Doonesbury," September 17, 1973**

him a ready target of cartoonists. The mysteriously missing 18½ minutes from the White House tapes and other examples of a presidential cover-up of the truth about Watergate provided clever cartoonists with irresistible opportunities to poke fun. At stake, however, was not just some petty criminal actions, or even the fate of the Nixon presidency, but rather deeper, troublesome questions about justice, liberty, truth, and the nation's faith in the American constitutional system.

The accompanying cartoons, drawn by four of the most incisive cartoonists of recent times, all originated in the Watergate crisis of the 1970s. Tony Auth and Herbert Block (known as Herblock) were then editorial political cartoonists for the Philadelphia *Inquirer* and the Washington *Post*, respectively. Jules Feiffer, like Garry Trudeau ("Doonesbury"), creates comic strips not only on political subjects but on every conceivable aspect of modern culture. Each is syndicated nationally and has published several volumes of his collected cartoons. Each provided wit and insight to help the American people interpret the events of Watergate. Historians, too, can understand some of the emotional power and anguish all Americans, including the president himself, went through during this era by looking at cartoon humor. Like all great cartoons, they speak for themselves.

**Jules Feiffer, "King Kong," from Jules Feiffer's America from Eisenhower to Reagan, 1982**

not help. More and more Americans now believed that the president had had at least some part in the cover-up and should take responsibility for his acts. *Time* magazine ran an editorial headlined "The President Should Resign," and Congress considered impeachment. The first steps, in accordance with constitutional mandate, began in the House of Representatives.

In late July 1974, the House Judiciary Committee, made up of 21 Democrats and 17 Republicans, debated the impeachment case. By sizable tallies, it voted to impeach the president on the grounds of obstruction of justice, abuse of power, and refusal to obey a congressional subpoena to turn over his tapes. A full House of Representatives vote still had to occur, and the Senate would have to preside over a trial before removal could take place. But for Nixon the handwriting was on the wall.

After a brief delay, on August 5 Nixon obeyed a Supreme Court ruling and released the tapes. They contained clear evidence of his complicity in the cover-up. His ultimate resignation became but a matter of time. Four days later, on August 9, 1974, the extraordinary episode came to an end as Nixon became the first American president ever to resign.

### The Ford Interlude

In the aftermath of the Watergate affair, Washington was in a state of turmoil. Americans wondered whether any politician could be trusted to guide public affairs. The new president, Gerald Ford, suddenly found himself thrust into an office he had never planned to hold. As the economy spiraled downward, Ford faced the task of trying to restore national confidence.

Ford worked quickly to restore trust in the government. He emphasized conciliation and compromise, and he promised to cooperate both with Congress and with American citizens. The nation responded gratefully. *Time* magazine pointed to "a mood of good feeling and even exhilaration in Washington that the city had not experienced for many years."

The new president weakened that base of support, however, by pardoning Richard Nixon barely a month after his resignation. Haldeman,

Ehrlichman, Mitchell, Dean, and other Nixon administration officials faced indictment, trial, and imprisonment for their part in the Watergate affair, but their former leader, even before a hearing, was to go free of prosecution for any crimes committed while president of the United States. Ford hoped that his magnanimous gesture would help heal the nation's wounds, but in fact it only raised doubts about his judgment. Now Ford was booed and jeered, just as Johnson and Nixon before him had been, and he too had to leave speaking engagements through back doors to avoid demonstrators angry over the pardon.

On policy questions, Ford followed the direction established during the Nixon years. Staying on as secretary of state, Kissinger maintained continuity in the field of foreign affairs. On the domestic front, the president's decidedly conservative bent often threw him into confrontation with a Democratic Congress. Economic problems proved most pressing in 1974 as inflation, fueled by oil-price increases, rose to 11 percent a year, unemployment stood at 5.3 percent, and gross national product declined. Home construction slackened and interest rates rose, while stock prices fell. Nixon, preoccupied with the Watergate crisis, had been unable to curb

*Gerald Ford's genial, unpretentious personality made him a reassuring presence after the Nixon administration; here he seeks the White House photographer's advice on the use of a camera.*

rising inflation and unemployment. Not since Franklin Roosevelt took office in the depths of the Great Depression had a new president faced economic difficulties so severe.

Like Herbert Hoover 45 years before him, Ford hoped to restore confidence and persuade the public that conditions would improve. His WIN campaign called on Americans to "Whip Inflation Now" and urged them to wear red and white WIN lapel buttons, save rather than spend a part of their income, and plant their own vegetable gardens to challenge rising prices in the stores. The plan had no substantive machinery to back it up, ignored the root causes of the problem, and soon disappeared.

The administration introduced a tight-money policy as a means of curbing inflation. It led to the most severe recession since the Depression, with unemployment peaking at 12 percent in 1975. Congress pushed for an antirecession spending program. Recognizing political reality, Ford endorsed a multibillion-dollar tax cut coupled with higher unemployment benefits. The economy made a modest recovery, although inflation and unemployment remained high, and federal budget deficits soared.

Ford proved unable to develop a successful response to the energy crisis, which played such a crucial role in disrupting the economy. In the civil rights arena, Ford asked his own attorney general, Edward H. Levi, to consider supporting antibusing advocates in a Boston court case, then accepted the advice that the idea be dropped. In the aftermath of the Vietnam War, he proposed an amnesty program for those who had fled the draft. It seemed excessively harsh to those concerned and consequently failed to work; in a six-month period, of 126,900 eligible, only 22,500 applied. The others remained abroad or in hiding, still unable or unwilling to come home.

Throughout his short tenure as president, Ford was often embroiled in conflict with Congress. He vetoed numerous bills, including those creating a consumer-protection agency and expanding programs in education, housing, and health. In response, Congress overrode a higher percentage of vetoes than at any time since the presidency of Franklin Pierce more than a century before. Rather than reviving the country after Watergate, Ford frequently found himself powerless to affect it.

## THE CLIMAX OF SOCIAL REFORM

The turbulent 1960s had spawned an assortment of movements and groups. In the troubled 1970s, they continued to grow, although they were often affected by the uncertain economy.

### Feminism at High Tide

In 1971, Helen Reddy expressed the energy of the woman's movement in a song called "I Am Woman":

I am woman, hear me roar
In numbers too big to ignore
And I know too much to go back and pretend
'Cause I've heard it all before
And I've been down there on the floor,
No one's ever gonna keep me down again.
Oh, yes, I am wise
But it's wisdom born of pain.
Yes, I've paid the price

But look how much I gained.
If I have to
I can do anything.
I am strong,
I am invincible,
I am woman.

Only a few years before, in 1962, a Gallup poll revealed that a majority of women did not believe that American women suffered discrimination. The facts, however, told a different story, for even though more women were working, they did not receive equal pay for equal work. In 1977, the working woman earned 57 percent of what her male counterpart did; in 1939, she had earned 61 percent. Moreover, employers systematically excluded women from many positions. Most still held "female" jobs in the clerical, sales, and service sectors.

The confrontations of the 1960s began to alter that state of affairs as well as the perception of women's role. In the early 1970s, a survey noted that in a two-year period, the number of college students who felt that women were oppressed had doubled, and the numbers continued to rise. Whereas in 1970 a survey of first-year college students showed that men interested in such fields as business, medicine, engineering, and law outnumbered women eight to one, in 1975 the ratio had dropped to three to one. The proportion of women beginning law school quadrupled between 1969 and 1973.

Several publications helped to spread the ideas of the women's movement. Gloria Steinem, author of a regular political column in *New York* magazine, first thought of herself as a professional journalist with no particular interest in women's affairs. "I certainly didn't understand that women were an 'out' group," she noted, "and I would even insist that I wasn't discriminated against as a woman." While working on a story about abortion, however, she began to realize that discrimination took many forms. She realized she "had been unable to get an apartment because, the reasoning was, a single woman wasn't financially responsible—and if she *was* responsible, she was probably a prostitute." Steinem began writing more about

*Our Bodies, Ourselves* **and Ms.** *magazine were among the publications spawned by the women's movement to give women greater control over various aspects of their lives.*

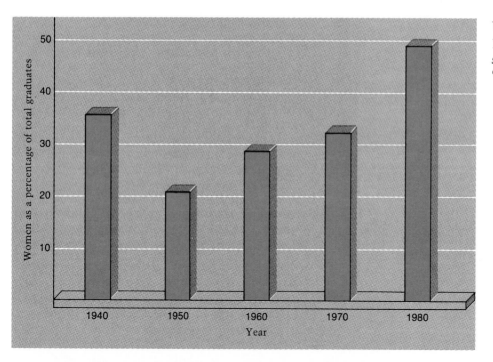

**Women College Gradua**
**1940–1980**

***Source:*** U.S. Department of Commerce.

women, and in 1971 she banded together with several other women to found a new magazine. *Ms.* succeeded beyond their wildest dreams and reached a wide audience of women who were not members of feminist organizations. In the first eight days, the 300,000 copies of the preview issue sold out. By 1973, there were almost 200,000 subscribers. Most of them were under 35, had graduated from college, and were working in professional, managerial, or technical jobs.

Other publications also publicized the issues and concerns of the women's movement. *The New Woman's Survival Catalogue* provided useful advice to women readers. *Our Bodies, Ourselves*, a handbook published by a woman's health collective, encouraged women to understand and control their bodies; it sold 850,000 copies between 1971 and 1976.

These new books and magazines differed radically from older women's magazines like *Good Housekeeping* and *Ladies' Home Journal.* Those publications aimed at women at home and focused on their domestic interests, needs, and sometimes fantasies. *Ms.*, on the other hand, dealt with abortion, and provided a forum for the discussion of important feminist issues.

Despite certain shared interests, women's struggle for equality was decentralized, diffuse, and often internally divided. As *Time* magazine pointed out in 1972, "The aims of the movement range from the modest, sensible amelioration of the female condition to extreme and revolutionary visions." Groups like NOW pressed for equal employment opportunities, child-care centers, and abortion reform. Women both in and out of NOW who were concerned with legal reforms worked for congressional passage, then ratification, of the Equal Rights Amendment (ERA) to the Constitution. Passed by Congress in 1972, it stated simply, "Equality of rights under the law shall not be denied or abridged by the United States or by any State on account of sex." Thirty of the required 38 states quickly ratified it, a few others followed, and for a time final approval seemed imminent.

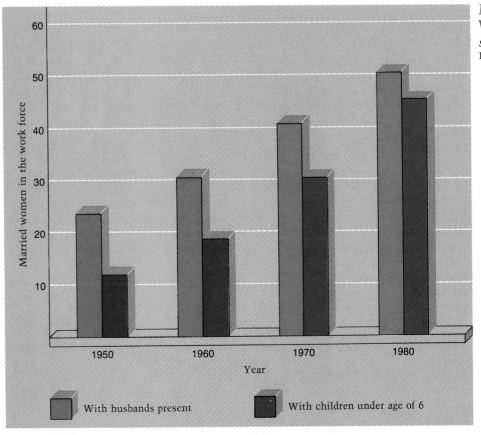

**Married Women in the Work Force, 1950–1980**

*Source:* U.S. Bureau of Labor Statistics.

Other feminist groups adopted more radical positions. Legal changes were not enough, they argued. Fundamental changes in sexual identity were needed to end male domination and social exploitation. Shulamith Firestone, a former member of the New Left, explained in *The Dialectic of Sex* (1970) the necessity of a new society in which women were freed "from the tyranny of their reproductive biology by every means available." Moreover, traditional gender and family roles must be discarded and "the childbearing and childrearing role [diffused] to the society as a whole, men as well as women." Other socialist feminists claimed that it was not enough to strike out at male domination, for capitalist society itself was responsible for women's plight. Only through the process of revolution could women be free.

Moderates and radicals alike generated opposition. Gloria Steinem was often ridiculed. One man, she recalled, approached her on the street and said, "I have ten women employees and I pay them a third of what I pay men, and if I had to pay them more, I'd fire them. What do you think of *that*?" Nixon himself sided with the traditionalists when in 1971 he vetoed an appropriation for day-care centers with the argument that they undermined the sanctity of the family. He insisted that "the vast moral authority of national government . . . must be . . . consciously designed to cement the family in its rightful position as the keystone of our civilization."

Women themselves resisted feminism for many reasons. Many felt the women's movement was contemptuous of women who stayed at home to perform all the tasks that had traditionally been expected of them. Marabel Morgan was one who still insisted that the woman had a place at home by her husband's side. The wife of a Florida attorney, she argued that "it is only when a woman surrenders her life to her husband, reveres and worships him, and is willing to serve him, that she becomes really beautiful to him." In her book *The Total Woman* (1973) she counseled others to follow the 4A approach: accept, admire, adapt, appreciate. She suggested ways of meeting a husband at the door and cited approvingly the case of one woman who "welcomed her husband home in black mesh stockings, high heels, and an apron. That's all." Everything was designed to move from "fizzle to sizzle," and substantial numbers of women wanted to hear the message. As of 1975, some 500,000 copies of the hardcover volume had been sold before a paperback version appeared.

In the realm of politics, Phyllis Schlafly headed a nationwide campaign to block ratification of the ERA. Author of several books, including one strongly supporting the conservative presidential candidate Barry Goldwater a decade before, she was both vigorous and articulate. On the ERA she was adamant: "It won't do anything to help women, and it will take away from women the rights they already have, such as the right of a wife to be supported by her husband, the right of a woman to be exempted from military combat, and the right, if you wanted it, to go to a single-sex college." The ERA, she predicted, would lead to the establishment of coed bathrooms, the elimination of alimony, and the legalization of homosexual marriage. Women, she argued, already had legal backing enough for their rights.

Despite the counterattacks, the women's movement flourished in the 1970s. But like other earlier attempts to change the status of women, it was fueled largely by the grievances of middle-class women. Focusing on issues of interest to them, the movement often ignored the special problems of black and white working-class women. As one black woman told Betty Friedan, "We don't want anything to do with that feminist bag." Most black women found race a far more compelling problem than gender. Black women, Friedan was told, wanted "black men to get ahead." Nor did the feminists' emphasis on the satisfaction of working outside the home make much sense to white working-class women who could only expect dull, monotonous, and poorly paid jobs if they went to work. They preferred to stay at home if they could.

## Hispanics and Native Americans

As women pressed for reform, Native Americans remained intent on voicing their grievances and publicizing their demands. The American Indian Movement (AIM), founded in

1968, gave them a platform and a focus for gaining rights and regaining lost lands.

The new militancy was dramatized in November 1969, when a landing party of 78 Indians seized Alcatraz Island in San Francisco Bay. It was the site of a defunct federal prison, declared surplus property five years before. Pointing to the Fort Laramie Treaty of 1868, which permitted male Indians to file homestead claims on federal lands, the occupiers took over the island to protest symbolically the inability of the Bureau of Indian Affairs to "deal practically" with questions of Indian welfare. They converted the island into a cultural and educational center but in 1971 were removed by federal officials.

In 1972, militants launched the Broken Treaties Caravan to Washington. For six days, insurgents occupied the Bureau of Indian Affairs. In 1973, AIM took over the South Dakota village of Wounded Knee, where in 1890 the U.S. 7th Calvary had massacred the Sioux. The reservation surrounding the town was mired in poverty. Half the families were on welfare, alcoholism was widespread, and 81 percent of the student population had dropped out of school. The occupation was meant to dramatize these conditions and to draw attention to the 371 treaties AIM leaders claimed the government had broken. Federal officials responded by encircling the

*The American Indian Movement's 1973 occupation of Wounded Knee dramatized unfair government treatment of Native Americans.*

area, and, when AIM tried to bring in supplies, killed one Indian and wounded another. The confrontation ended with a government agreement to reexamine the treaty rights of the Indians, although little of substance was subsequently done.

Hispanics in America also adopted more militant tactics. Their population, approximately 9 million in 1970, increased by a third during the decade as a result of growing immigration and a high birthrate. Hispanics constituted the nation's largest minority group after black Americans; Spanish, rather than Italian, became the most commonly spoken foreign language. The Mexican-American population in particular soared, as did a consciousness of its rights.

In the West and Southwest, Mexican-American studies programs flourished. By 1969, at least 50 existed in California alone. They offered degrees, built library collections, and provided Chicanos access to their own past. The campuses also provided a network linking students together and mobilizing them for political action.

Beginning in 1968, Mexican-American students began to protest conditions in the secondary schools. They pointed bitterly to overcrowded and run-down institutions and to the 50 percent dropout rate that came from expulsion, transfer, or failure because students had never been taught to read. In March 1968, some 10,000 Chicano students walked out of five high schools in Los Angeles. Their actions inspired other walkouts in Colorado, Texas, and other parts of California and led to demands for Mexican teachers, counselors, and courses and better facilities.

At the same time, new organizations sprang up. A few years before, teenager David Sánchez and four Chicanos in East Los Angeles had formed a group called Young Citizens for Community Action. Gradually the organization evolved from a service club to a defensive patrol. Now known as Young Chicanos for Community Action, the group adopted a paramilitary stance. Its members became identified as the Brown Berets and formed chapters throughout the Midwest and Southwest.

Other Hispanics began to organize politically. José Angel Gutiérrez was one of those in

Texas who recognized the need for political activism to change conditions that had existed for generations. On one occasion, at a press conference, he gained national attention by exploding, "Kill the *gringo!*" Anglo-Americans were afraid that he meant it literally. Gutiérrez attended a rally in March 1969 at San Félipe del Río to protest the cancellation of a government-funded neighborhood project. Three months later, he and a few others went to his hometown of Crystal City, Texas, to begin organizing Hispanics at the grass-roots level. When students began to protest conditions at the local high school, a citizens' organization led by Gutiérrez stepped in to develop a spirit of solidarity. From that group emerged the La Raza Unida political party, which began to play a major role in the area and successfully promoted Mexican-American candidates for political offices. Throughout the 1970s, it gained strength in the West and Southwest.

Hispanic-Americans also participated in the more general protest against the Vietnam War. Because the draft drew most heavily from the poorer segments of society, the Hispanic casualty rate was far higher than that of the population at large. In 1969, the Brown Berets organized the National Chicano Moratorium Committee and staged antiwar demonstrations. They argued that this was a racial war, with black and brown Americans being used against their Third World compatriots. Some the of rallies ended in confrontations with the police and brought charges of police brutality.

Aware of the growing numbers and growing demands of Hispanic-Americans, the Nixon adminstration sought to defuse their anger and win their support. Recognizing that with 5 percent more of the Mexican-American vote in Texas in 1968, Nixon would have carried the state, political analysts advised an effort to lure Mexican-Americans into the Republican camp. By dangling political positions, government jobs, and promises of better programs for Mexican-Americans they attempted to secure their support. The effort paid off; Nixon received 31 percent of the Hispanic vote in 1972. Rather than reward his Hispanic followers, however, the president moved to cut back the poverty program that had begun under Johnson.

*Chicano pride showed itself in thousands of urban murals, a by-product of the grass-roots Hispanic rights movement of the early 1970s.*

Although disillusioned and discouraged in the mid-1970s, Mexican-Americans could take some comfort from a Supreme Court decision in 1974 that declared that schools had to meet the needs of children with a limited grasp of English. That decision led to federal funding of bilingual education.

They could also take pride in their achievements in the fields. A nationwide consumer boycott of grapes, lettuce, and other products harvested by exploited labor finally ended in success. In 1975, César Chávez's long struggle for farmworkers ended in the successful passage in California of a measure that required growers to bargain collectively with the elected representatives of the workers. Farmworkers had never been covered by the National Labor Relations Board. Now they were guaranteed legitimate elections and the representation they had long sought. This soon brought higher wages and improved working conditions—proof that strenuous organizing could bring results.

### Environmental and Consumer Movements

While women and ethnic minorities pursued their own demands, other groups mobilized for action. The environmental movement, which emerged in the mid-1960s, grew rapidly.

A Gallup poll revealed that while only 17 percent of the public considered air and water pollution to be one of the three major governmental problems in 1965, that figure had risen to 53 percent by 1970.

The modern environmental movement, which revived issues raised during the progressive era, gathered momentum after the publication in 1962 of Rachel Carson's *Silent Spring.* She took aim at chemical pesticides, particularly DDT, which had increased crop yields yet had disastrous side effects. As Americans learned of the pollutants surrounding them, they became increasingly worried about pesticides, the automobile, and industrial wastes that filled the air with smog. Lyndon Johnson, whose vision of the Great Society included "an environment that is pleasing to the senses and healthy to live in," pressed for and won basic legislation to halt the destruction of the country's natural resources.

Public concern mounted further in 1969 when it was discovered that thermal pollution from nuclear power plants was killing fish in both eastern and western rivers. DDT was threatening the very existence of the bald eagle, the nation's emblem. A massive oil spill off the coast of southern California turned white beaches black and wiped out much of the marine life in the immediate area.

Some environmentalists pressed for preservation of unspoiled areas, but far more pressured legislative and administrative bodies to regulate polluters. During Nixon's presidency, Congress passed a Clean Air Act, a Water Quality Improvement Act, and a Resource Recovery Act, and mandated a new Environmental Protection Agency to spearhead the effort to control abuses. Conservation and environmental protection were predominately middle-class concerns and often conflicted with the need of working-class Americans for economic growth and the greater employment opportunities it promised.

Related to the environmental movement was a growing consumer movement dating from the 1960s. Americans throughout the twentieth century, particularly in the 1950s, had become attracted to fashionable clothes, house furnishings, and electrical and electronic gadgets, their appetites whetted by mass advertising. Congress had established a variety of regulatory efforts to protect citizens from unscrupulous sellers. In the 1970s, a strong consumer movement grew, aimed at protecting the interests of the purchasing public and making business more responsible to consumers.

Leading the movement was Ralph Nader. He had become interested in the issue of automobile safety while studying law at Harvard and had pursued that interest as a consultant to the Department of Labor. His book, *Unsafe at Any Speed: The Designed-in Dangers of the American Automobile* (1965), argued that many cars were coffins on wheels. Head-on collisions, even at low speeds, could easily kill, for cosmetic bumpers could not withstand modest shocks. He termed the Corvair "one of the nastiest-handling cars ever built" because of its tendency to roll over in certain situations. His efforts paved the way for the National Traffic and Motor Vehicle Safety Act of 1966.

Nader's efforts attracted scores of volunteers, called "Nader's Raiders." They turned out critiques and reports and, more important, inspired consumer activists at all levels of government—city, state, and national. Consumer-protection offices began to monitor a flood of complaints as ordinary citizens became more aware of their rights.

## Countercurrents of Self

While some Americans worked to change the system through political action, others rejected the idealism of the 1960s and followed their own bent, "doing their own thing," as a popular phrase put it. Social commentator Tom Wolfe termed the 1970s the "Me Decade." Millions of Americans began to look inward rather than outward. Books like Eric Berne's *Games People Play* (1969) popularized transactional analysis, a therapeutic approach focusing on interpersonal relationships. The Esalen Institute in Big Sur, California, offered encounter sessions to those who could afford to come to the center for a week. Participants were encouraged to face their feelings as honestly as they could, and screams and sobs, moans and groans filled the air.

That entire approach, whether through Esalen or a similar group, aimed, in Wolfe's words, at "changing one's personality—remaking, remodeling, elevating, and polishing one's very *self* . . . and observing, studying, and doting on it." People were encouraged to strip away the excess baggage tied on by society or self "in order to find the Real Me." Broken marriages became the norm as more and more couples chose to acknowledge that husband and wife had to go their own way.

While some Americans sought salvation in narcissistic quests, increasing numbers became involved in mystical religious movements that promised internal peace of a different sort. Some embraced transcendental meditation. Others became involved with Zen. Cults proliferated, as the Hare Krishnas, the Unification Church of the Reverend Sun Myung Moon, the Children of God, and a host of other groups drew people, mostly young, into their midst.

Barbara Garson, author of a New Left drama about Lyndon Johnson in the 1960s, observed the personal consequences of the new age. Her husband had assisted her earlier. Now "my husband Marvin forsook everything (me included) to find peace. For three years he wandered without shoes or money or glasses. Now he is in Israel with some glasses and possibly some peace." Like Marvin, many former members of the radical fringe were set adrift. "Some follow a guru," wrote Garson, "some are into Primal Scream, some seek a rest from the diaspora—a home in Zion."

## CONCLUSION: The Struggle for Stability

By 1976, political upheaval had subsided, and the nation, often in private ways, embarked on the struggle for stability. America had finally extricated itself from Vietnam, only to fall into a domestic quagmire—Watergate.

Many Americans tried to escape the shocks by withdrawing to their personal world, but this could not undo the changes that had occurred. Civil rights pressures remained intense. Women like Ann Clarke, met at the start of the chapter, were going back to school in ever-increasing numbers and finding jobs after years of hearing that they should stay at home. Though Richard Nixon had declared that he wanted to draw the nation together, his actions had only split it further apart. The nation was again in pursuit of tranquility and economic health.

## Recommended Reading

A number of books provide good introductions to the 1960s. Milton Viorst, *Fire in the Streets: America in the 1960's* (1979) is a vivid account of the turbulence of the decade that gives a real sense of the participants involved. William L. O'Neill, *Coming Apart: An Informal History of America in the 1960s* (1971) deals largely with the earlier part of the decade but has a good assessment of the latter period as well.

On the Nixon presidency, Rowland Evans, Jr., and Robert D. Novak, *Nixon in the White House* (1972) offers the best assessment of public policy and politics in the first term. Richard Nixon, *RN: The Memoirs of Richard Nixon* (1978) is his own account of his life and achievements.

On Gerald Ford, John Hersey, *The President* (1975) is a perceptive treatment of how Nixon's successor operated in the White House by one of America's best-known authors. Richard Reeves, *A Ford, Not a Lincoln* (1975) is an even more penetrating account of how Ford functioned as president.

For the Watergate affair, J. Anthony Lukas, *Nightmare: The Underside of the Nixon Years* (1976) provides the background necessary to understand the scandal and places that crisis in the proper perspective. Carl Bernstein and Bob Woodward, *All the President's Men* (1974) is the vivid story by two journalists of how they helped unravel the Watergate scandal and implicate the White House in the crisis.

On women's issues, Sara Evans, *Personal Politics: The Roots of Women's Liberation in the Civil Rights Movements and the New Left* (1979) contains some perceptive observations about the state of the women's movement in the 1970s. Peter Gabriel Filene, *Him/Her/Self: Sex Roles in Modern America* (1975) begins with the nineteenth century and has a useful section on the changes and developments of recent years. For more detail on Ann Clarke, see Barbara Clarke Mossberg, *Backstage of the American Dream* (1986).

Rodolfo Acuña, *Occupied America: A History of Chicanos* (1981) is a good account of Chicanos in America, particularly in the modern period.

## TIME LINE

|  |  |
| --- | --- |
| 1966 | National Traffic and Motor Vehicle Act |
| 1968 | Police and protesters clash at Democratic national convention |
| | Chicano student walkouts |
| | Richard Nixon elected president |
| | My Lai massacre |
| | American Indian Movement (AIM) founded |
| 1969 | Nixon Doctrine announced |
| | Moratorium against the Vietnam War |
| | SALT talks begin |
| | Woodstock and Altamont rock festivals |
| | Weathermen's "Days of Rage" in Chicago |
| | Native Americans seize Alcatraz |
| | La Raza Unida founded |
| 1970 | U.S. invasion of Cambodia |
| | Kent State and Jackson State shootings |
| 1971 | New York *Times* publishes Pentagon Papers |
| | *Ms.* magazine founded |
| 1971–1975 | School busing controversies in North and South |
| 1972 | Nixon visits China and the Soviet Union |
| | Watergate break-in |
| | Nixon reelected president |
| | SALT I treaty on nuclear arms |
| | Congress passes Equal Rights Amendment |
| | Broken Treaties Caravan to Washington |
| 1973 | Vietnam cease-fire agreement |
| | Arab oil embargo |
| | Watergate hearings in Congress |
| | *Roe* v. *Wade* |
| | Agnew resigns as vice-president |
| | AIM occupies Wounded Knee |
| 1974 | OPEC price increases |
| | Inflation hits 11 percent |
| | Unemployment reaches 7.1 percent |
| | Nixon resigns; Gerald Ford becomes president |
| | Ford pardons Nixon |
| 1975 | *Mayaguez* incident |
| | South Vietnam falls to the Communists |
| | Farmworkers grape boycott |
| | Unemployment reaches 12 percent |

# CHAPTER 31

## AUSTERITY AND
## THE AMERICAN DREAM:
## THE UNITED STATES SINCE 1976

After 11 years as a baggage handler, Andy Hjelmeland of Maple Plain, Minnesota, found himself out of work in December 1980. Hjelmeland was not immediately concerned, however, for he had never before had trouble finding employment. Like Hjelmeland, Jerry Espinoza of Los Angeles also lost his job in the early 1980s. He had been with the Bethlehem Steel plant in California for 23 years. Now it closed its doors, and he too was faced with finding a new job.

Both Hjelmeland and Espinoza, in their mid-forties, discovered that conditions had changed since they had last sought work. The unemployment rate, which stood at 3.5 percent in 1969, was now almost three times as high. Old industries suffered serious difficulties and could not compete with more vital firms abroad. As they declined, they laid off their employees.

Millions of unemployed Americans pursued every lead for the few jobs available in the early 1980s. Hjelmeland found himself up against 300 applicants when he responded to a local newspaper advertisement calling for a "handyman." Espinoza, facing similar competition, discovered that his search for work was complicated by his Hispanic background.

Although Hjelmeland had a happy marriage and two healthy sons, he found the strains difficult to bear. He continued to fill out applications and to answer ads, but the repeated rejections filled him with dismay. "It was a new experience for me to confront an impenetrable wall," he observed. "I began to feel like a person on a blacklist." After years of paying bills on time, he now faced a growing stack of unpaid bills. A parking ticket lost in the pile was followed by an arrest warrant that added insult to injury.

Espinoza faced similar strains. He had five children to support and mortgage payments due. Unemployment benefits and his wife's paychecks kept the family going. Like Hjelmeland, his problems mounted. After his two decades at Bethlehem, he was worn out. He had hearing problems, a result of running noisy machines without ear protection. His left hand was scarred, and two fingers were numb from an accident on the job. A back injury from work still troubled him. "When I go looking for a job, no one is hiring," Espinoza said. "Or maybe they are hiring but they look at me and maybe I'm too old or maybe it's my nationality, because they still discriminate."

The discrimination rankled most of all. Hispanics had an annual jobless rate of 13.8 percent in 1982, far higher than the Anglo unemployment rate of 8.6 percent. Latinos with jobs worked vigorously for their part of *el sueño americano*, the American dream. But often the doors were closed.

For both Hjelmeland and Espinoza, old attitudes gave way as the months of unemployment grew. Hjelmeland had previously viewed food stamp and welfare recipients as "freeloaders," but now he had to apply for food stamps himself. "My wavering self-esteem plummeted," he confessed. "By my own lights I had officially become a loser." Espinoza was similarly glum. "One day you're OK, the next day you're depressed," he said. "We're just lost souls now, that's what we are, lost souls."

Both Hjelmeland and Espinoza found the administration in Washington insensitive to their fate. When President Ronald Reagan, who took office in early 1981, lashed out at television officials for harping on the continuing economic troubles across the country and asked, "Is it news that some fellow out in South Succotash someplace has just been laid off . . . should be interviewed nationwide?" Hjelmeland was irate. "I wish," he said, "the President could be that unemployed guy in South Succotash for just one month." The administration had an economic recovery program, but to the unemployed it often seemed far too slow or unworkable.

The difficulties of Hjelmeland and Espinoza mirrored those of countless Americans who could not understand what had gone wrong. At a time when people were recovering from the shocks of the Vietnam War and the disillusionment of the Watergate affair, they found their nation mired in the worst economic recession since the dismal days of the Great Depression half a century before. The years of post–World War II abundance had ended. Earlier, in the midst of plenty, some observers had pointed to the pockets of poverty that still existed, but the poor were easily ignored. Now even middle-class citizens found themselves unemployed.

Americans understood that their nation was less competitive in the international arena, but they felt powerless to remedy this. Policymakers discovered that the old economic formulas did not work. Some people, particularly the hardest hit, began to worry about the durability of the capitalist economic system itself.

This chapter describes America's efforts to regain its economic health after 1976. It deals with the program of a Democratic president who never managed to promote the stability he promised in his campaign. It describes the approach of his conservative Republican successor, who sought to roll back the welfare programs of the past and deregulate the economy while embarking on the greatest arms buildup in United States history. This chapter also shows the struggles of ordinary Americans to cope with hard times. Old and new groups, defined by gender, race, and class, sought to advance their own interests. Women continued to press for reform. Ethnic and racial groups likewise remained committed to the goals they had pursued in the past. But they faced more resistance now, particularly as new groups defined goals of their own. American society changed in the late 1970s and early 1980s, but not as much as some Americans demanded. This chapter charts their continuing quest for the American dream.

## THE DISORDERED ECONOMY

From the early 1970s on, the economy reeled under the impact of declining productivity, galloping inflation, oil shortages, and high unemployment. Some people in the middle and higher ranks suffered, but the recession most seriously affected working-class Americans while the middle and upper classes improved their standard of living. Economists disagreed about the reasons for the economic slump and recommended contradictory remedies. None of their remedies succeeded in restoring the growth rate or confidence that the American economy would resume its steady expansion.

### Economic Stagnation

The United States had been the world's technological leader since the late nineteenth century, but by the 1970s it seemed to be losing that position. After 1973, productivity slowed in virtually all American industries; in the early 1970s, economic growth averaged 2.3 percent annually in contrast to its average of 3.2 percent in the 1950s. Thereafter, it dropped to 1.3 percent annually.

The causes of this decline were complex. The oil crisis and rising oil prices (see Chapter 30) played a part, as did government policies aimed at curbing inflation by keeping machines idle and environmental regulations intended to make industries change their methods of operation. The war in Vietnam diverted federal funds from support for research and development at the same time that Japan, Germany, and the Soviet Union were increasing their R&D expenditures.

While American industry became less productive, other industrial nations moved forward. German and Japanese industries, rebuilt after World War II with American aid and aggressively modernized thereafter, reached new heights of efficiency. As a result, the United States began to lose its share of the world market for industrial goods. In 1946, the country had provided the world with 60 percent of its iron and steel. In 1978, it provided a mere 16 percent. Some of this decline was inevitable as other nations rebuilt their economies after World War II. But so efficient and cost-effective were foreign steel producers that the United States found itself importing a fifth of its iron and steel. By 1980, Japanese car manufacturers had also captured nearly a quarter of the American automobile market. The auto industry, which had been a mainstay of economic growth for much of the twentieth century, suffered plant shutdowns and massive layoffs.

Unemployment emerged as the most visible sign of the country's economic problems. In 1975, during the administration of Gerald Ford, it reached a high of 9 percent and then declined to 7.5 percent after Jimmy Carter took office in early 1976. Under Carter the rate hovered between 5.6 and 7.8 percent. During Reagan's first year, the job situation deteriorated badly. By the end of 1982, the unemployment rate had climbed to 10.8 percent, with black unemployment over 20 percent. Nearly a third of America's industrial capacity lay idle, and 12 million Americans were out of work.

Blue-collar workers, now a declining percentage of the work force, were the first to feel

## Share of Total Manufacturing Output of Four Industrial Countries, 1950–1977

*Source:* U.S. Bureau of Labor Statistics.

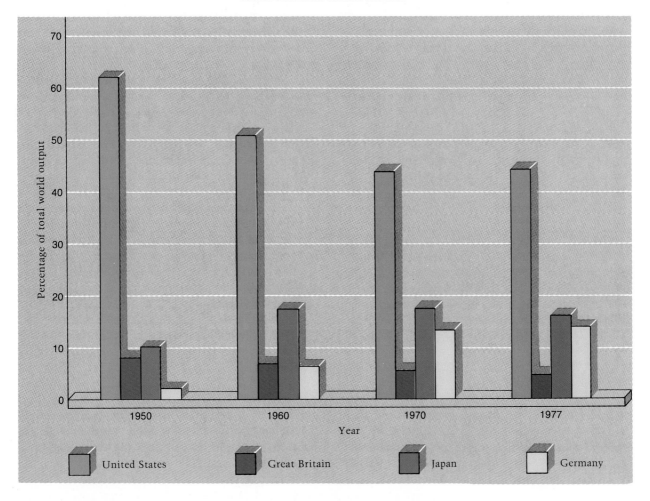

the effects. After World War II, American workers had enjoyed both a rise in real income and a reduction in hours of work. In the disordered economy, wages failed to keep pace with inflation, however, and many industrial workers were laid off.

The ability of blue-collar workers to protect themselves against adversity was hampered by the economic problems of the nation at large and by the faltering position of the trade union movement as a whole. Although unions had emerged from World War II claiming 35 percent of American nonagricultural workers as members, this percentage began to decrease steadily in the mid-1950s. Union membership rose in the public sector, but this increase did not reverse the general decline in membership. In 1956, some 26 percent of nonagricultural workers had belonged to unions. By 1984, only 21 percent did.

This contraction stemmed from several factors—the shift from blue-collar to white-collar work, the growing numbers of women and young people in the work force (groups that have historically been difficult to organize), and the more forceful opposition to unions by managers applying the provisions of the Taft-Hartley Act of 1947. This erosion of membership made un-

*For millions of unemployed, Christmas dinner 1982 was eaten at charity soup kitchens.*

ions less effective in dealing with employers. For example, in Groton, Connecticut, an affiliate of the United Auto Workers called a strike of ship workers in 1983. But after 15 months, workers accepted a "very bad" contract, leaving 43 percent of the strikers unemployed. As union leaders admitted, "No one will attempt . . . to defend the package." This pattern was repeated elsewhere.

White-collar workers were not immune to economic difficulties. Unemployment rose among all groups, and many professionals in their forties who had lost their jobs found it as difficult to find work as Andy Hjelmeland and Jerry Espinoza. Middle-class college graduates who expected professional positions were often "underemployed."

Inflation accompanied widespread unemployment and undermined the purchasing power of people already in difficulty. The rate, which had reached about 12 percent early in Ford's presidency, dropped to 4.8 precent when Carter took office. Soon, however, it spiraled upward again, reaching 12.4 percent in 1980. Under Reagan that rate began to fall, to 8.9 percent in his first year and to about 5 percent during the remainder of his first term.

### The Farmer's Paradox of Plenty

After the mid-1970s, American farmers suffered too. Continuing a trend that began in the early twentieth century, the number of farmers

## Union Membership, 1950–1980

*Source:* U.S. Bureau of Labor Statistics.

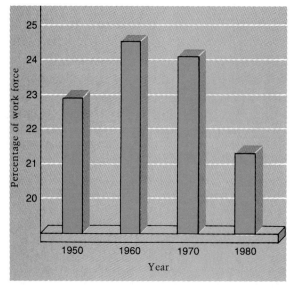

declined steadily. When Franklin Roosevelt took office in 1933, some 6.7 million farms covered the American landscape. Fifty years later, farm families numbered only 2.4 million. Overall, the lot of American farmers improved during this half century, much of the earlier pervasive rural poverty having given way to a decent existence and sometimes considerable wealth. Part of this improvement stemmed from the huge strides that were made in agricultural productivity through the use of chemical fertilizers, irrigation, pesticides, and scientific agricultural management. Equally important were the government's price-support programs, initiated during the New Deal to shield struggling farmers from unstable prices.

Yet, paradoxically, family farms continued to disappear, and farming income became more concentrated in the hands of the largest operators. In 1983, the largest one percent of the nation's farmers produced 30 percent of all farm products; the top 12 percent generated 90 percent of all farm income. The top one percent of America's growers had average annual incomes of $572,000, but most small and medium-size farmers had incomes below the official government poverty line.

The extraordinary productivity of American farmers led to unexpected setbacks in the 1980s.

Farm Indebtedness, 1950–1982

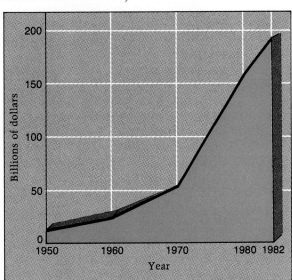

In the 1970s, as food shortages developed in many countries, the United States became the "breadbasket of the world." Farmers increased their output to meet multibillion-bushel grain orders from India, China, Russia, and other countries and profited handsomely from high grain prices caused by global shortages. Often they borrowed heavily to increase production, sometimes at interest rates up to 18 percent. However, the fourfold increase in oil prices beginning in 1973 drove up the cost of running the modern mechanized farm. When a worldwide economic slump began in 1980, overseas demand for American farm products declined sharply, and farm prices fell. Farmers who had borrowed money at high interest rates, when corn sold at $3 to $4 per bushel, now found themselves trying to meet payments on these loans with corn that brought only $2 per bushel.

Thousands of farmers, caught in the cycle of overproduction, heavy indebtedness, and falling prices, watched helplessly as banks and federal agencies foreclosed on their mortgages and drove them out of business. For example, Dale Christensen, an Iowa corn grower, faced foreclosure in 1983 when the Farmers Home Administration called in his overdue payments on debts totaling $300,000. "I am 58 years old," he said. "My whole life has gone into this farm." He was one of many struggling farmers, who, in spite of government crop-support programs that cost more in 1982 than all welfare programs for the poor, had to face leaving behind a livelihood that went back generations in his family.

### Business Failures

The recession of 1980–1983 afflicted every region of the country. Business failures proliferated as large and small businessmen closed their doors and fired their employees. In 1982, business bankruptcies rose 50 percent from the previous year. In one week in June 1982, a total of 548 businesses failed, close to the 1932 weekly record of 612.

No area was immune from the recession. Louisville, Kentucky, had considered itself safe from the threats other areas faced but found it was mistaken in 1982. Despite the hope that people would continue drinking and smoking in bad times as well as good, the Brown & Williamson Tobacco Corporation, manufacturer of Kool, Raleigh, and Viceroy cigarettes, closed down its Louisville branch. Then Joseph E. Seagram & Sons shut its bottling plant. General Electric released almost 10,000 of its 23,000 workers, and International Harvester closed a plant employing 6,500 people.

Detroit was one of the hardest-hit areas in the United States. An industrial city revolving around automobile manufacturing, it suffered from the high interest rates that made car sales plummet. Thousands of workers were left to fend for themselves as assembly lines slowed or stopped altogether. The unemployment rate rose to more than 19 percent. The entire city suffered from the decline. The $357 million Renaissance Center, which included a large hotel surrounded by four modern office buildings, had been expected to revitalize downtown Detroit when it opened in 1977. Instead it wallowed in red ink, and in early 1983 its owners defaulted on a huge mortgage.

The closing of Hudson's department store symbolized Detroit's severe depression. That magnificent block-square centerpiece of the J. L. Hudson Company had served downtown Detroit for 91 years and had become a local institution. With its wood-paneled elevators and brass water fountains, it was Detroit's symbol of elegance. Hudson's replaced women's stockings torn in the store. It provided clerks who spoke 14 languages to assist the immigrant population. Everyone had a favorite memory of the store, which had seemed to represent the vitality of the city. Larry Hanlin remembered shopping excursions with his ten brothers and sisters: "My mother would get all of us dressed in our best, line us up and give us all a spanking, just in case we had any remote thoughts about misbehaving in the store." When he was older, he occasionally skipped school to spend a day there. "It was our big adventure—" he said, "our Disneyland." But then Hudson's, like so many other places, fell upon hard times. It had earned $153 million in 1953, but by 1981 profits had declined to $43 million, with 1982 expected to be even lower. With that, the management decided to maintain the suburban branches but to close the downtown store that had spawned all the rest.

Some areas initially seemed "recession-proof." The Sun Belt—the vast southern region stretching from coast to coast—prospered far more than other parts of the country. Economic growth there was fostered by the availability of cheap, nonunion labor, tax advantages that state governments offered corporations willing to locate plants there, and its favorable climate. Journalist Kirkpatrick Sale described the economic boom there in 1975 in his book *Power Shift: The Rise of the Southern Rim and Its Challenge to the Eastern Establishment*. Newspapers and magazines picked up the theme and ran stories showing how the area was outstripping other parts of the country in winning government grants, attracting modern industries, and enjoying new wealth. To some observers, the Sun Belt, once a relatively backward region, had become the new promised land.

By the early 1980s, however, the Sun Belt also suffered economic problems. Despite an enviable record of growth and prosperity in parts of the region, large areas began to stagnate. The unemployment rate in California in mid-1982 reached the national average of 9.5 percent, while in Texas it was 7 percent, higher than it had been for ten years. There was more joblessness in Greenlee County, Arizona, than anywhere in the country. In Jefferson County,

*Even such prosperous sun-belt states as Texas felt the effects of the recession.*

Mississippi, 67 percent of the population lived below the poverty line.

Millions of Americans, like Andy Hjelmeland and Jerry Espinoza, had to deal with the sudden loss of material comfort and the security they earned through hard work. Struggle became their way of life. Michael Wilk, a 31-year-old auto technician from Hamtramck, Michigan, lost his $18,000-a-year job in 1981. His wife Nydia continued to earn $240 a week as an inspector at the same factory, but that was the family's only income. When Nydia tried to make ends meet by working two full-time jobs, she lost 27 pounds and developed ulcers. Michael initially went out looking for work, but in depressed Detroit few jobs were available, and gasoline became too expensive to waste. Finally he resorted to reading want ads and watching TV. "I go from feeling depressed to not caring about anything and then back again," he said. "Sometimes I'm so paralyzed by it all that I just sit and stare out the window."

Not all Americans suffered, however. With 10 percent of the population unemployed, 90 percent remained at work, and many improved their standard of living. But virtually everyone felt the recession in some way. Everyone had a jobless friend or relative. Nobody could avoid the numerous For Sale signs on the lawns of houses where residents, unable to meet their mortgage payments, had moved out, their faith in the American dream of home ownership badly shaken because losing a home was an attack on the status they had struggled to achieve. Everyone watched tax revenues, and then public services, decline as hard-hit Americans paid fewer taxes than before.

## THE DEMOGRAPHIC TRANSFORMATION

As Americans confronted extraordinary economic problems, basic population patterns continued to develop in unspectacular but significant ways. Urban growth tailed off. The population became older. The number of nontraditional households increased. New immigrants streamed into the country. Such changing demographic contours often brought changes that challenged local, state, and federal governments charged with meeting the needs of their constituents.

### American Society in 1980

The 1980 census revealed that in the previous decade the population of the United States had increased from 203 million to 227 million. That rise of 11.5 percent was the second-lowest rate of growth in the nation's history. In the baby boom decade between 1950 and 1960, population had grown by 19 percent; between 1960 and 1970, it had increased 13.3 percent. Only the growth rate in the Depression decade of 1930–1940 had been lower.

The census highlighted important structural changes that had been occurring. The urban rate of growth, which had been slowing since 1950, leveled off entirely. In 19 states, the rural part of the population actually increased. The age distribution of the population shifted toward the elderly. Between 1960 and 1980, the part of the population under the age of 5 decreased by one fifth, while the part over the age of 65 increased by about 53 percent.

Household composition also changed. Gone was the traditional household headed by a male wage earner with his wife at home. Less than a quarter of all American households fit that description. Another quarter of all households were classified as "nonfamily households," while the proportion of families headed by women who had children under 18 grew from 10 percent to 18 percent in the decade of the 1970s. Among whites, the proportion of families headed by women rose from 8 percent to 13 percent; among blacks it grew from 31 percent to 47 percent.

### The New Pilgrims

Another shift occurred as the United States admitted new immigrants from a variety of foreign nations. A fifth of the decade's population growth stemmed from this immigration,

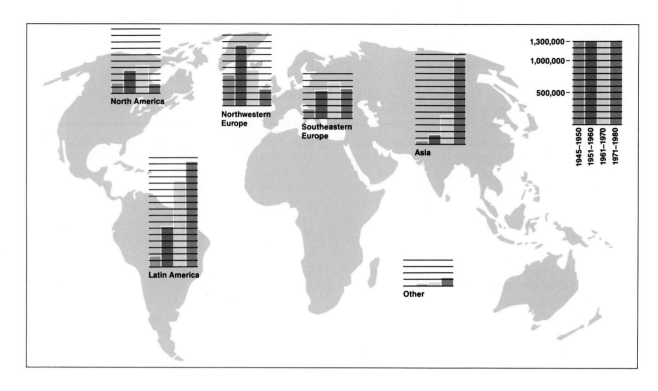

## Immigration: Volume and Sources, 1941–1980

*Source:* U.S. Bureau of the Census.

## Population Shifts, 1970 to 1980

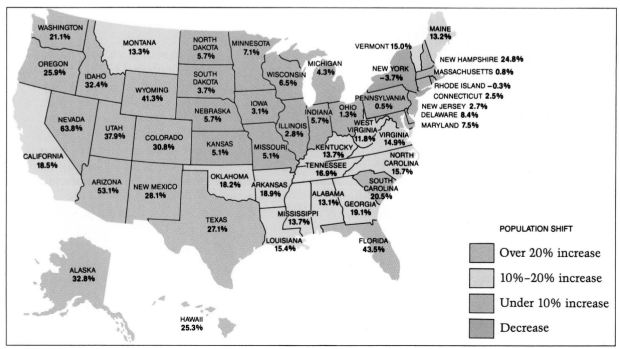

which was spurred by the Immigration and Nationality Act of 1965. Part of Lyndon Johnson's Great Society program, this act authorized the acceptance of immigrants impartially from all parts of the world. Because the national-origins system of the 1920s had favored western Europeans and was therefore frankly racist, most immigrants between 1930 and 1960 had come from Europe or Canada. Between 1977 and 1979, however, only 16 percent came from these areas, while 40 percent came from Asia and another 40 percent from Latin America. Always a nation of immigrants, the United States was once again receiving new ethnic infusions.

As had long been true, the desire for jobs fostered immigration. But foreign crises also fueled the influx. After 1975, the United States accepted more than a half million Vietnam refugees. In 1980, more than 160,000 arrived. That same year, the nation admitted 125,000 Cubans and Haitians to southern Florida. The official total of all immigrants in 1980 was 808,000, the highest in 60 years.

Millions more arrived illegally. As the population of Latin American nations soared and as economic conditions deteriorated, more and more people looked to the United States for relief. In the mid-1970s, Leonard Chapman, commissioner of the Immigration and Naturalization Service, estimated that there might be 12 million foreigners in the nation illegally. While official estimates were lower, Attorney General William French Smith declared in 1983, "Simply put, we've lost control of our own borders."

The United States had once again become a melting pot of people from very different parts of the world. In Los Angeles, Samoans, Taiwanese, Koreans, Vietnamese, and Cambodians competed for jobs and apartments with Mexicans, blacks, and Anglos, just as newcomers from different countries had contended with one another in New York City a hundred years earlier. Throughout the country, in Miami, in Houston, in Brooklyn, the languages heard in the schools and on the streets changed, as did the very complexion of the society.

Each group, each family, had its own story. Nguyen Ninh and Nguyen Viet, two brothers who remained in Vietnam after the victory of the North Vietnamese in 1975, were among the many who finally fled their war-torn country by boat. The boat sank, but they were rescued, only to be shuttled to Kuwait, then Greece, and finally to the United States, where another brother had arrived a few years before. Though they spoke no English, they immediately began to look for work. One became a carpenter's helper; the other, an attendant at a valet-parking firm. With the money they earned, they helped other members of their family emigrate. Slowly they learned English, obtained better jobs, and saved enough money to purchase a home.

*Cuban "boat people," classified as refugees from Castro's Communist regime, were permitted to register for resident status.*

### Growing Up

In the mid-1970s, the birthrate began to rise after 18 years of decline. Demographers viewed the increase as part of a long-term trend. The Census Bureau estimated that there would be 4 million births in 1983, compared to 3.1 million in 1975.

In an era of economic austerity, new children sometimes posed problems for their families. An extra mouth to feed could make a difference to a family on the fringe. The arrival

# RECOVERING THE PAST

As we reach our own time, the historical past most worth recovering, perhaps, is our own. Our own story is as valid a part of the story of American history as Revolutionary War soldiers, frontier women, reform politicians, and immigrant grandparents. In this increasingly computerized and depersonalized age, the person we need to recover and know is ourself, a self that has been formed, at least in part, by the entire American experience we have been studying.

Autobiography is the form of writing in which people tell their own life's history. Although written autobiographies are at least as old as the literature of the early Christians, such as *The Confessions of St. Augustine*, the word itself dates from 1808, shortly after the French and American revolutions. That is no accident. These momentous events represented the triumph of individual liberty and the sovereignty of the self. *The Autobiography of Benjamin Franklin*, written between 1771 and his death in 1790, is a classic celebration of the American success story. Franklin's work set the standard for one autobiographical form, the memoir of one's public achievements and success. The other brief autobiographical excerpt also reflects the tone and range of this tradition.

Not all autobiographies are written late in life to celebrate one's accomplishments. The confessional autobiography, unlike most memoirs explores the author's interior life, acknowledging flaws and failures as well as successes; it may be written at any age. The purpose of this type of autobiography is not just to reconstruct one's past to preserve it for posterity, but rather to find from one's past an identity in order to know better how to live one's future. The story of religious confessions and conversions is an obvious example. This form also includes secular self-examinations such as those by Maxine Hong Kingston in *The Woman Warrior* (1976), Piri Thomas in

## AUTOBIOGRAPHICAL MEMOIRS

### BENJAMIN FRANKLIN

DEAR SON,

I have ever had a pleasure in obtaining any little anecdotes of my ancestors. You may remember the enquiries I made among the remains of my relations when you were with me in England and the journey I undertook for that purpose. Imagining it may be equally agreeable to you to know the circumstances of my life—many of which you are yet unacquainted with—and expecting a week's uninterrupted leisure in my present country retirement, I sit down to write them for you. Besides, there are some other inducements that excite me to this undertaking. From the poverty and obscurity in which I was born and in which I passed my earliest years, I have raised myself to a state of affluence and some degree of celebrity in the world. As constant good fortune has accompanied me even to an advanced period of life, my posterity will perhaps be desirous of learning the means, which I employed, and which, thanks to Providence, so well succeeded with me. They may also deem them fit to be imitated, should any of them find themselves in similar circumstances.

*The Autobiography of Benjamin Franklin* (1771)

### ELIZABETH CADY STANTON

It was 'mid such exhilarating scenes that Miss Anthony and I wrote addresses for temperance, anti-slavery, educational and woman's rights conventions. Here we forged resolutions, protests, appeals, petitions, agricultural reports, and constitutional arguments; for we made it a matter of conscience to accept every invitation to speak on every question, in order to maintain woman's right to do so. To this end we took turns on the domestic watchtowers, directing amusements, settling disputes, protecting the weak against the strong, and trying to secure equal rights to all in the home as well as the nation.

It is often said, by those who know Miss Anthony best, that she has been my good angel, always pushing and goading me to work, and that but for her pertinacity I should never have accomplished the little I have. On the other hand it has been said that I forged the thunderbolts and she fired them. Perhaps all this is, in a measure, true. With the cares of a large family I might, in time, like too many women, have become wholly absorbed in a narrow family selfishness, had not my friend been continually exploring new fields for missionary labors. Her description of a body of men on any platform, complacently deciding questions in which woman had an equal interest, without an equal voice, readily aroused me to a determination to throw a firebrand into the midst of their assembly.

Elizabeth Cady Stanton, *Eighty Years and More: Reminiscences, 1815–1897* (1898)

*Down These Mean Streets* (1967), or by Maya Angelou in a series of five autobiographical sketches beginning with *I Know Why the Caged Bird Sings* (1969). The remaining excerpts are two of the finest examples of confessional autobiography and suggest its variety.

These examples hardly suggest the full range of the autobiographical form or how available to all people is the opportunity to tell the story of one's life. In 1909, William Dean Howells called autobiography the "most democratic province in the republic of letters." A recent critic agrees, pointing out that "to this genre have been drawn public and private figures: poets, philosophers, prizefighters; actresses, artists, political activists; statesmen and penitentiary prisoners; financiers and football players; Quakers and Black Muslims; immigrants and Indians. The range of personality, experience, and profession reflected in the forms of American autobiography is as varied as American life itself."

Your story, too, is a legitimate part of American history. But writing an autobiography, while open to all, is deceptively difficult. Like historians, autobiographers face problems of sources, selection, interpretation, and style. As in the writing of any history, the account of one's past must be objective, not only in the verifiable accuracy of details but also in the honest selection of representative events to be described. Moreover, as in the writing of fiction as well as history, the autobiographer must provide a structured form, an organizing principle, literary merit, and thematic coherence to the story. Many other challenges face the would-be autobiographer, such as finding an appropriate balance between one's external, public life and the internal, private self, or how to handle problems of memory, ego (should one, for example, use the first or third person?), and death.

To get an idea of the difficulties of writing an autobiography, try writing your own. Limit yourself to 1,000 words. Good luck.

## CONFESSIONAL AUTOBIOGRAPHIES

### MALCOLM X

I want to say before I go on that I have never previously told anyone my sordid past in detail. I haven't done it now to sound as though I might be proud of how bad, how evil, I was.

But people are always speculating—why am I as I am? To understand that of any person, his whole life, from birth, must be reviewed. All of our experiences fuse into our personality. Everything that ever happened to us is an ingredient.

Today, when everything that I do has an urgency, I would not spend one hour in the preparation of a book which has the ambition to perhaps titillate some readers. But I am spending many hours because the full story is the best way that I know to have it seen, and understood, that I had sunk to the very bottom of the American white man's society when—soon now, in prison—I found Allah and the religion of Islam and it completely transformed my life.

*The Autobiography of Malcolm X,* with the assistance of Alex Haley (1964)

### BLACK ELK

And so it was all over.

I did not know then how much was ended. When I look back now from this high hill of my old age, I can still see the butchered women and children lying heaped and scattered all along the crooked gulch as plain as when I saw them with eyes still young. And I can see that something else died there in the bloody mud, and was buried in the blizzard. A people's dream died there. It was a beautiful dream.

And I, to whom so great a vision was given in my youth,—you see me now a pitiful old man who has done nothing, for the nation's hoop is broken and scattered. There is no center any longer, and the sacred tree is dead.

*Black Elk Speaks,* as told through John G. Neihardt (1932)

of children often required new decisions about the relationship between family and career. Women entering the work force with long-range employment commitments had to juggle work and home schedules and find adequate child-care facilities.

The rising divorce rate also affected children. By 1980, the divorce rate had reached a historic peak. In that year, the courts granted nearly 1.2 million divorces, the highest total in the nation's history. For each 1,000 marriages, 490 divorces occurred, up from 328 per 1,000 in 1970 and 258 per 1,000 in 1960. Many splits involved fights over the young.

In the past, divorced mothers had almost always gained custody over the children, but now husbands increasingly asserted their parental rights. Sometimes the struggles became angry and intense. In 1977, Diane and James Tilden fought over their 10-year-old son Jimmy. A New York judge gave James custody, except in the summer. When he handed over his son to his ex-wife, James was concerned, and with good reason, for she promptly disappeared. He found her in Florida, but a judge there gave her custody of the boy. James then smuggled his son back to New York and successfully appealed the Florida case. Finally he had complete custody—and $34,000 in legal fees. Jimmy had become a pawn in a larger game.

Runaways also became a problem. According to some estimates, more than a million children between the ages of 10 and 17 were on the run. They left home for various reasons. Some were driven out. Others were victims of physical abuse. Still others fled violent arguments or other recession-induced strains in family life. Many returned home within a few days. Some, however, remained on city streets. In 1974, Congress passed a Runaway and Homeless Youth Act, which established telephone hot lines and temporary shelters. But the shelters served only 45,000 youths a year, leaving countless others without help.

Even more ominous was the rising death rate among the young. The Public Health Service reported in 1982 that the death rate for most Americans had dropped significantly over a 30-year period, but the rate for those between 15 and 24 rose steadily after 1976. Automobile accidents, murders, and suicides caused three out of four deaths for that group.

## Growing Old

As concern with the problems of the young increased, awareness of the plight of the old also grew. Elderly people made up the fastest-growing age group in modern America. Between 1900 and 1980, when the population of the country tripled, the number of people over 65 rose eightfold. In the 1970s alone, Americans over 75 grew by more than 37 percent. Underlying the rapid increase was the steady advance in medical care, which in the twentieth century had increased life expectancy from 47 to 73 years. Americans watched Bob Hope celebrate his eightieth birthday, George Burns, approaching 90, continue to act, and Ronald Reagan, over 70, govern the country. They became aware of what columnist Max Lerner called "the aging revolution," which promised to become the most lasting of all of the twentieth-century social changes.

The elderly raised new issues in a nation suffering economic stagnation. Many wanted to continue working and resented mandatory retirement rules that drove them from their jobs. Pleading their cause was Representative Claude Pepper of Florida, the octogenarian head of the House Select Committee on Aging, who declared, "I am like an old hickory tree. The older I get, the tougher I get." Legislation in 1978 raised the mandatory retirement age from 65 to 70. That helped older workers but decreased employment opportunities for younger workers seeking jobs.

Generational resentment over jobs was compounded by the knotty problems faced by the social security system established a half century before. As more and more Americans retired, the system could not generate sufficient revenue to make the payments due without assistance from the general governmental fund. In the early 1980s, it appeared that the entire system might collapse. A temporary solution, in part involving higher taxes for those still employed and a later age for qualifying for benefits, rescued the fund, but other hard decisions for the future were postponed.

At an intensely personal level, American families faced difficult decisions about how to care for older parents who could no longer care for themselves. In the past, the elderly might naturally have come into their children's homes, but attitudes and family patterns had changed. Children were fewer than in earlier generations, and as women gravitated to jobs outside, they were less able to assist in the home care of an elderly parent. Retirement villages and nursing homes provided two alternatives, but the decision to place a parent under institutional care was often excruciating.

Margaret Stump, an occupational therapist from Tenafly, New Jersey, agonized over such a decision. For six years she flew to Lima, Ohio, every three months to see her mother, who was over 90 years old. Finally she decided to bring her to a New Jersey nursing home. "I felt that she'd be better once she got to a home," Margaret recalled. "But I knew she wanted to be in her own house. It was a very difficult decision. I had to wait until I thought she wouldn't know where she was."

## The New Students

Another group of Americans faced the future more aggressively. College students were more numerous than ever before. After World War II, partly as a result of GI education benefits, higher education became broadly accessible for the first time in American history. College enrollment, which had never exceeded 1.5 million before 1945, rose to nearly 3 million in the early 1960s and reached 12 million in 1981. Women and minority students entered college in unprecedented numbers.

Students in the late 1970s and 1980s became more conservative. Gone was the sense of outrage that had mobilized thousands in the social struggles of the 1960s. Now students were more willing to work within the system. Howard Shapiro, a Yale senior, noted in 1983, "If you want to change things, you have to work with those in power. I see a whole new cycle, with people aiming at the same good goals but in different ways. Instead of having a sit-down strike, students will meet with the administration and try to compromise."

Some students, not sure of themselves or their goals, gravitated toward the various cults that grew up and recruited on campus. The Unification Church of the Reverend Sun Myung Moon grew rapidly, as did The Way International and the International Society for Krishna Consciousness. "I didn't know anything about cults when I got involved," said Heidi Feiwel, a Cornell University student who became part of The Way International. But in her freshman year, "I didn't have that many friends, and this was a source of community." By the end of her second year, her family had become concerned, and her father arranged for "deprogramming" to try to make her understand why she had become so committed to the religious group.

Most students coped with uncertain times by preparing for careers. Large numbers of them chose business or economics courses, while enrollment in the liberal arts dropped sharply. Conscious of the need to repay the loans that often provided their major source of support and of the difficulty of finding good jobs, students made choices reflecting concern for a career in a particular field rather than concern for a broad general education.

## THE CONTINUING STRUGGLE FOR EQUALITY

In the 1970s and 1980s, women, blacks, Hispanic-Americans, and Native Americans continued their struggle for equal opportunity and treatment. But the pace of change slowed as the economic climate made many Americans, convinced that enough had been done already for these groups, less sympathetic to reform.

### Consolidating Feminist Gains

In general, liberals applauded the accomplishments of the women's movement. Betty Friedan, whose book *The Feminine Mystique* (1963) had helped mobilize a pervasive discontent two decades before, admitted in 1983:

I am still awed by the revolution that book helped spark. . . . I keep being surprised, as the changes the women's movement set in motion continue to play themselves out in our lives—the enormous and mundane, subtle and not so subtle, delightful, painful, immediate, far-reaching, paradoxical, inexorable and probably irreversible changes in womens's lives—and in men's.

Changes had indeed occurred. Affirmative action had made jobs for women more accessible. Women made tremendous gains in such diverse fields as coal mining, where the percentage of women rose from 0.001 to 11.4 between 1973 and 1979, and banking, where the percentage increased from 18 to 34 in the ten years after 1970. According to the U.S. Census Bureau, 45 percent of mothers with preschool children held jobs away from home in 1980. That figure was four times greater than it had been 30 years before. More day-care centers existed, although not nearly enough to meet the need; they allowed women greater flexibility in finding work. At the same time, fathers were playing a greater role in their children's lives.

Legal changes brought women more benefits and opportunities. Title 9 of the Education Amendments of 1972, which barred gender bias in federally assisted education activities and programs, stimulated colleges to admit far more women to law, medical, dental, and business schools and to drop nepotism restrictions that kept husbands and wives from teaching at the same schools. The same measure changed the nature of intercollegiate athletics. Big Ten schools, which spent millions of dollars on men's programs, in 1974 spent an average of $3,500 a year on women's sports. That was no longer legal, and while complete equity remained a distant goal, women's athletics benefited. By 1980, 30 percent of the participants in intercollegiate athletics were women, compared to 15 percent before Title 9 had become law.

In politics women also made important strides forward. Jane Byrne succeeded Richard Daley as Chicago's mayor, and women also won mayoral races in Houston, Honolulu, and San Francisco. In 1981, President Ronald Reagan appointed Sandra Day O'Connor as the first woman Supreme Court justice, and in 1984, Geraldine Ferraro, a Democratic member of Congress, became the first woman vice-presidential candidate for a major party. Far more women were elected to state legislatures and to Congress. As women began to win elective office, political analysts noted that women voters began to show distinctive voting behavior. In the election of 1980, analysts observed a "gender gap": For the first time, women were voting significantly differently from men. Men supported Ronald Reagan by a margin of 56 to 36. Women, alarmed by his hard-line foreign policy and opposition to the Equal Rights Amendment, voted for him by a much smaller margin of 46 to 45.

In 1982, a film about a man who dressed as a woman to get a job became one of the major hits

### Changes in Female Employment, 1940–1980
*Percent of all employed women*

|  | 1940 | 1950 | 1960 | 1970 | 1980 |
|---|---|---|---|---|---|
| Professional and technical | 13.2% | 10.8% | 12.4% | 15.3% | 16.7% |
| Managers and administrators | 3.8 | 5.5 | 5.7 | 3.6 | 6.9 |
| Sales | 7.0 | 8.8 | 7.7 | 7.4 | 6.8 |
| Clerical | 21.2 | 26.4 | 30.3 | 34.5 | 35.1 |
| Craft workers | 0.9 | 1.1 | 1.6 | 1.8 | 1.8 |
| Operatives | 18.4 | 18.7 | 15.2 | 15.1 | 10.7 |
| Laborers | 0.8 | 0.4 | 0.4 | 1.0 | 1.3 |
| Service workers | 28.9 | 22.9 | 23.7 | 20.5 | 19.5 |
| Farm workers | 5.8 | 5.4 | 4.4 | 0.8 | 1.2 |

*Source:* Oppenheimer, *The Female Labor Force in the United States,* 1976.

of the season. *Tootsie,* starring Dustin Hoffman, was a funny film with a serious side. Posing as Dorothy Michaels, Michael Dorsey, a rather unpleasant man, challenged sexual harassment, argued with the male chauvinists at work, and became a real battler for women's rights. In the process, Dorothy came across as a much nicer person than Michael had ever been. When he finally reverted to being himself, Betty Friedan noted, "the sensitivity he acquired, sharing woman's experience, made him a much better, stronger, more tender man."

In the tenth anniversary issue of *Ms.* magazine, in 1982, founding editor Gloria Steinem noted the differences a decade had made. "Now, we have words like 'sexual harassment' and 'battered women,'" she wrote. "Ten years ago, it was just called 'life.'" Other examples followed: "Now, rape is defined as a crime of violence— and victims are less likely to be raped again by the law." Perhaps best of all: "Now, we are becoming the men we wanted to marry. Ten years ago, we were trained to marry a doctor, not be one."

Yet old problems persisted. Perhaps the most troubling involved continuing wage differentials between women and men. In 1982, full-time working women earned an average of 62 cents for every dollar earned by men. Though new

*Disappointment and frustration cloud the faces of Chicago mayor Jane Byrne and NOW president Eleanor Smeal as the Illinois state legislature, despite a massive rally, fails to ratify the ERA in 1982.*

opportunities were opening up, most women remained in waitressing, nursing, secretarial, or light industry jobs—the so-called pink-collar positions that paid poorly. Arguments that women should receive equal pay for equal work now led to demands for equal pay for different jobs of similar value. Comparable-worth cases began to work their way through the courts. The issue surfaced, too, in the campaign of 1984, though without any agreement on the question.

The women's rights movement, in its long history, had never been unified, and in the decade 1974 to 1984 women continued to debate their roles and rights. Despite changes in their portrayal by the media, a subtle sex-appeal image remained. Ellen Goodman took exception to an advertisement showing the Maidenform woman as a doctor. "There she was," Goodman wrote, "hair tied back primly, medical chart in her left hand, pen in her right hand, long white jacket over her shoulders, exposing her lacy magenta bra and panties." There she was, according to the caption, "making the rounds in her elegant Delectables." Goodman was disgusted, for, she observed, "I always thought she was a candidate for a cold, not a medical degree." More troubling was the implication that the doctor "is revealed in the flesh, to be—yes, indeed—just another woman insecure about her femininity, just another woman in search of sex appeal, just another woman who needs 'silky satin tricot with antique lace scalloping.'"

Women who applauded when the Supreme Court legalized abortion in 1973 discovered that the question of abortion remained very much alive. The number of abortions increased dramatically in the decade after the decision. By some estimates there were 10 million lawful abortions, or one for every three births. In response, "pro-life" forces mobilized as never before. Nellie Gray organized a march on Washington every January 22 to call attention to the anniversary of the *Roe* v. *Wade* decision. "It's murder, pure and simple," she said. "Abortion means killing babies." Opponents lobbied to cut off federal funds that allowed the poor to obtain the abortions the better off could pay for themselves; they insisted that abortions should be performed in hospitals and not in less expensive clinics; and they worked to reverse the original decision itself. Though the Supreme Court, which included the first woman in its history, reaffirmed its judgment in 1983, the pro-life movement was not deterred.

Agitation over the ERA also became more intense. Ratification of the Equal Rights Amendment had been taken for granted after its favorable vote in Congress in 1972, so much so that no ratification strategy was thought necessary. Within a few years, 35 states had agreed to the measure, but then the momentum disappeared. Even with an extension in the deadline granted in 1979, the amendment could not win the necessary 38-state support. Phyllis Schlafly and others continued their highly effective opposition campaign, gaining the assistance of women who felt threatened by the changes occurring and men, particularly in state legislatures, who had long been uncomfortable with the women's movement. By mid-1982, the ERA was dead.

Although women could savor their gains, some worried that complacency was setting in. Many young women who enjoyed the fruits of the movement avoided the feminist label and shunned involvement in militant campaigns. Others remained active, convinced that only with continued pressure would women achieve full equality.

## The Continuing Significance of Race

Like the women's movement, the black and Hispanic movements found that progress came at a slower pace than in the decade before. Some gains were made, but racial inequality persisted in many areas of American life.

Significant change occurred in politics and education. Black political candidates won mayoral elections in major cities, including Detroit, Los Angeles, Cleveland, and Chicago. In the election of 1982, the number of black representatives in Congress increased from 18 to 21, and in state and local elective offices some 6,000 blacks served their constituents. Federal affirmative-action guidelines brought more blacks into colleges and universities. In 1950, only 83,000 black students were enrolled in college. A decade later, more than one million were working for college degrees. But black enrollment in colleges peaked at 9.3 percent of the population in 1976 and by 1980 dropped to 9.1 percent, just what it had been in 1973.

As many blacks moved into the middle class, they left far behind a much larger and deeply impoverished black lower class, most of it living in urban ghettos. By 1981, fully 34 percent of black families were classified as poor, in contrast to 11 percent of white families. Black poverty was intimately tied to the worsening state of the economy, a changing job market, and remnants of racism. The automobile, steel, rubber, and coal industries, which had traditionally employed many unskilled and semiskilled laborers and had given immigrants their start in America, were shrinking. The new need was for highly trained workers who knew how to operate computers or could qualify for jobs in banks and offices. Many urban blacks lacked the education and training for these jobs. By 1981, the black unemployment rate was twice that of whites, and in almost every major city, the unemployment rate of black teenagers exceeded 40 percent. A troubling phenomenon that con-

### Black Occupational Progress, 1940–1980

|  | 1940 | 1950 | 1960 | 1970 | 1980 |
|---|---|---|---|---|---|
| Black males as percentage of white males employed as professional, technical, managerial, or administrative workers | 18% | 21% | 22% | 32% | 63% |
| Ratio of median black to white family income | .37 | .54 | .55 | .61 | .58 |

*Source:* U.S. Department of Labor.

tributed to black poverty was the dramatic rise in female-headed families. In 1940, only 18 percent of black families had a female head. By 1980, 49 percent did. (By contrast, the figures were 10 and 13 percent for whites.)

Some whites protested that black progress came at their expense and hence was the product of "reverse discrimination." In 1973 and 1974, for example, Allan Bakke, a white, applied to the medical school at the University of California at Davis. Twice rejected, he sued on the grounds that a racial quota reserving 16 of 100 places for minority-group applicants was a form of reverse discrimination that violated the Civil Rights Act of 1964. In 1978, the Supreme Court ordered Bakke's admission to the medical school, but in a complex ruling involving six separate opinions, the Court upheld the consideration of race in admissions policies, even while arguing that quotas could no longer be imposed. The decision received widespread attention and caused many people to fear a white backlash.

Hispanics in the United States, their numbers continuing to grow, began to play an increasingly important role in American affairs. According to the 1980 census, there were 14.6 million Hispanics, up 61 percent from the 9 million a decade before (the figures did not include the millions in the country illegally). Hispanics made up the fastest-growing minority group and promised soon to overtake the blacks as the country's largest minority. A government official pointed out that this means: "Not too far in the future, many areas will have Spanish-speaking majorities, and Latin American culture will make a very deep impression on the mainstream of U.S. society."

Despite population gains, economic conditions remained grim for many Hispanics. While the median family income for white families reached $17,900 in 1978, for Hispanic-Americans it was, though higher than for blacks, only $12,800. And in rural areas, many Mexican-Americans, living in shanties that had no electricity or plumbing, survived on about $4,000 a year.

Language difficulties and other problems of adjustment plagued Hispanic children in the schools. Richard Rodriguez, an articulate Chicano who did graduate work in English at Yale, recalled the boyhood shock of coming to school and coping with a new language. His experience paralleled that of newcomers from virtually all immigrant groups throughout the history of the United States, but that did not make the experience any smoother. "All my classmates certainly must have been uneasy on that first day of school," he wrote. "But I was astonished." For the first time he heard his name in English.

Eventually Rodriguez acquired fluency in English and became caught up in school and Anglo culture. Like other immigrant children, he found himself growing away from his family, using one form of expression with his parents and relatives and another with the world outside. In time he came to understand how "I had been educated away from the culture of my mother and father." Rodriquez's prizewinning book *Hunger of Memory* (1982) poignantly described the experience of Mexican-American youths in this era.

A movement to implement bilingual education in the schools made some progress but was not necessarily helpful for those who wished to move into the English-speaking mainstream. Most Hispanics failed to receive the education necessary for upward mobility in modern America. Only 30 percent of Hispanic high school students graduated, and less than 7 percent completed college.

*Bilingual classrooms in public schools made learning easier for Hispanic students; some argued that such classes slowed assimilation.*

But affirmative-action efforts helped Hispanics as well as blacks, and a growing network of Hispanic educators and programs promised to ease the way for future students. "Ten years ago, there was no national Chicano academic community," declared Arturo Madrid, president of the National Chicano Council on Higher Education, in 1982. "Now we have a professional presence in higher education." A colleague estimated that there were 5,000 Chicano faculty members in 1980, compared to 2,000 a decade before. Chicanos found themselves, like members of other minority groups, moving from the ranks of the "missing persons" to positions as "the onlys," where, Madrid noted, they served as "the only Chicano dean of this or the only Chicano professor of that."

Hispanics slowly extended the political gains they had made in the early 1970s. In San Antonio, Rudy Ortiz was appointed mayor pro tem in 1978, and Henry Cisneros was elected mayor in 1982. In the following year, Colorado state legislator Federico Peña was elected mayor of Denver. In New Mexico, Governor Toney Anaya called himself the nation's highest elected Hispanic and moved to create a national "Hispanic force." In the 1984 election, recognition grew that large concentrations of Hispanics in states like California, Texas, Florida, and New York could make a major difference in the final result. That gave them a political influence they had not enjoyed earlier.

### The First Americans Still Last

In the decade after 1970, the Native American population increased by 72 percent. Although roughly half continued to live on reservations, an educated elite emerged. From the few hundred Indians in college in the early 1960s, the number reached tens of thousands by 1980. That created a network of educated Native Americans in industries and professions and contributed to a determination to press harder for tribal goals.

One major struggle involved the longstanding effort to hold on to a land base. In the 1970s, when New York State tried to condemn a section of Seneca land for a superhighway running through part of the Allegany reservation, the Seneca went to court. In 1981, the state finally agreed to an exchange: state land elsewhere in addition to a cash settlement in return for an easement through the reservation. That decision encouraged tribal efforts in Montana, Wyoming, Utah, New Mexico, and Arizona to resist similar incursions on reservation lands.

Native Americans also vigorously protested a new assault on their long-abused water rights. On the northern plains, large conglomerates, responding to the international oil shortage, vastly extended their coal strip-mining operations. Fierce legal struggles over possession of limited water resources resulted. Litigating tribes had some legal ammunition because a federal court had ruled in 1973 in a landmark case, involving the water rights of the Paiute on the Nevada-California border, that the government must carry out its obligation as trustee to protect Indian property.

Another effort involved the reassertion of fishing rights. In the Northwest, as in other parts of the nation, the Nisquallie, Puyallup, Muckleshoot, Chippewa, and other Indian tribes argued that they had treaty rights to fish where they chose, without worrying about the intrusive regulatory efforts of the states. Despite pressure from other fishermen, a series of court cases provided the tribes with some of the protection they claimed on the basis of old treaty rights and once again showed that aggressive litigation could make a difference.

## THE NEW REFORMERS

Encouraged by the example of the traditional minorities, other groups began to demand equal opportunity and respect. Homosexuals sought the same freedom from discrimination that women and racial minorities claimed. Consumer advocates insisted that the government curb rampant abuses by advertisers and manufacturers of food, cars, and other products. Vietnam veterans asserted their need for material and emotional support after their wartime sacrifices. These new groups cut across gender, race, and class lines and testified to the continuing ferment for reform in the United States.

### Gay Liberation

Homosexuals of both sexes worked openly to end discrimination. There had always been people who accepted the "gay" life style, but American society as a whole was unsympathetic, and many homosexuals kept their preferences to themselves. The climate of the 1970s encouraged gays to become more open. A nightlong riot in response to a police raid on the Stonewall Inn, a homosexual bar in Greenwich Village in New York, in 1969 helped spark a new consciousness and a movement for gay rights.

Throughout the decade, homosexuals made important gains. In 1973, the American Psychiatric Association ruled that homosexuality should no longer be classified as a mental illness, and that decision was overwhelmingly supported in a vote by the membership the next year. In 1975, the U.S. Civil Service Commission lifted its ban on employment of homosexuals.

In the new climate of acceptance, many gays

*"Round up and quarantine AIDS carriers," urges the placard of one marcher in a KKK anti-gay demonstration in Houston, 1985.*

who had hidden or suppressed their sexuality came "out of the closet." In early 1982, Dan Bradley, head of the national Legal Services Corporation, announced his own homosexuality and described the tensions of a life of concealment. "I subscribed to *Playboy* magazine—I must be the only man who subscribed to it but never read it—just to make sure that when people came to my house there was evidence of my straightness," he said. "I'd make up names of women and told people I had a lot of 'dates'—all sheer fabrication, all lies." Though he was single, he wore a wedding ring for seven years. Far more comfortable after his revelation, Bradley left his former job and worked to promote the passage of a gay civil rights bill.

Women also became more open about their sexual preferences and insisted on freedom from discrimination. A lesbian movement developed, sometimes involving women active in the more radical wing of the women's movement.

Many Americans were unsympathetic to anyone who challenged traditional sexual norms. Churches and some religious groups often lashed out against gays. In 1982, James Tinney, a Pentecostal preacher who had announced his homosexuality three years before, was excommunicated from the Church of God in Christ as he prepared a revival meeting for gays in Washington. In Atlanta, the Metropolitan Community Church, part of a gay domination, was burned after a series of attacks by vandals. Throughout the country, Americans, even those unsympathetic to gay rights, became concerned about AIDS (acquired immune deficiency syndrome), a new disease that struck homosexuals with numerous partners more often than any other group.

### Regulating Corporate America

The consumer movement, sparked by Ralph Nader in the 1960s, continued its efforts despite Republican attempts to dismantle the regulatory apparatus. In 1982, Congress rejected a relatively weak Federal Trade Commission rule that would have required used-car dealers to tell prospective buyers of known problems with the automobiles for sale. Opponents of the FTC measure contended that it would raise the price of a used car. But consumer criticism forced Congress slowly to shift course. The Consumer Federation of America proved willing to play politics and endorse candidates, and 77 of the 94 congressional candidates it backed won. In early 1983, pollster Louis Harris announced that the public rejected, by a 55 to 36 percent margin, "the notion that the consumer movement has run out of steam." Indeed, four of every five Americans felt that "unless they keep fighting, consumer groups may begin to lose what they have achieved."

Concern about the deterioration of the environment increased as people learned more about substances they had once taken for granted. In 1978, the public became alarmed about the lethal effects of toxic chemicals dumped in the Love Canal neighborhood of Niagara Falls, New York. A few years later, attention focused on dioxin, one of the poisons permeating from the Love Canal, which now surfaced in other areas in even more concentrated form. Dioxin, a by-product of the manufacture of herbicides, plastics, and wood preservatives, remained active upon being released in the environment and seemed almost to defy control. Thousands of times more potent than cyanide, it was one of the most deadly substances ever made.

Dioxin made national headlines as a result of problems in Times Beach, Missouri. In the early 1970s, this suburb of St. Louis had sprayed its unpaved streets with waste oil to control dust. The oil later proved to be contaminated, and, after floods in 1982, the contamination spread throughout the town. Finally, the Environmental Protection Agency ordered a $33 million buy-out of all homes and businesses in the area. Other sites in Missouri, New Jersey, and California also revealed the presence of dioxin.

Acid rain also threatened the environment. In the eastern United States and southeastern Canada, industrial and automobile emissions had contaminated the atmosphere enough to kill fish, corrode building surfaces, and damage plants and trees. After extensive monitoring of ecological disruptions, the National Academy of Sciences attributed the damage to polluted rain. Only later, in mid-1983, did the Reagan administration acknowledge the problem, but it proposed no solutions.

Environmental activists also campaigned against nuclear power. Once hailed as the solution to America's energy needs, nuclear plants fell on hard times, particularly after an accident at one of the reactors at Three Mile Island, Pennsylvania, in 1979. There a faulty pressure relief valve led to a loss of coolant that was initially undetected by plant operators, who refused to believe indicators showing a serious malfunction. Part of the nuclear core became uncovered, part began to disintegrate, and the surrounding steam and water became highly radioactive. An explosion releasing radioactivity into the atmosphere appeared possible, and thousands of residents of the area fled. The scenario of nuclear disaster depicted in the film *The China Syndrome* (1979) seemed frighteningly real. The worst never occurred, and the period of maximum danger passed, but the plant remained shut down, filled with radioactive debris, a monument to a form of energy now deemed more potentially destructive than any ever known.

The Three Mile Island episode eroded public confidence in nuclear energy. Nuclear power proved both expensive and dangerous. After 1972, a total of 102 projected plants were canceled, and no new plants were ordered after 1978. In 1983, the nuclear industry suffered another jolt. The Washington Public Power Sup-

*Closed down from 1979 to 1985 because of defective operation, Three Mile Island's nuclear plant is a reminder of the hazards of nuclear power.*

ply System, which had sold $2.25 billion in bonds to finance two new reactors as part of a five-reactor complex, found that huge cost overruns made further construction unfeasible. After extensive efforts to maintain financing, the system succumbed in the largest municipal-bond default in history. Two of the plants were mothballed when analysts concluded that the energy to be produced was not needed. Existing nuclear facilities around the country continued to operate, but antinuclear activists had won a major round in their struggle to make society safer in the atomic age.

## Vietnam Veterans

Another group that became more vocal than before was Vietnam veterans. America abandoned the Vietnam War in 1973, but the aftereffects lingered. Increasing numbers of veterans called attention to Agent Orange, a chemical used widely to defoliate trees in Southeast Asia. It contained dioxin, among other substances, and caused contamination that lasted indefinitely. Former soldiers with a variety of medical ailments now demanded compensation and care for the debilitating results of their service.

Other veterans suffered psychological problems. Delayed stress syndrome, a slow-fuse emotional reaction to the trauma of combat,

*Nearly as controversial as the war it commemorates, the Vietnam Memorial was designed and built in the early 1980s, about a decade after the war ended.*

afflicted many. In late 1982, in Ocala, Florida, Stanley Moody, a former Green Beret, dressed in his combat fatigues, armed himself with an assortment of guns, and rushed from his house. He was going to stop the Viet Cong. An hour or so later, after a one-man gun battle with himself, he lay dead, shot in the head. "Stanley wasn't shooting at anything in particular," said the sheriff's investigator. "He was just having his own war." Most veterans were not as severely disturbed, but many suffered continuing traumas.

Veterans complained particularly about having done their duty only to return to a society that seemed to have little but contempt for the struggle and those who had fought in it. Not until almost a decade after the United States had extricated itself from the war did the nation erect a memorial in Washington to the war dead. But even that gesture generated controversy.

Calls for some kind of monument had resulted in a nationwide design competition. Maya Ying Lin, a 22-year-old Yale University student, triumphed over thousands of other entrants. Her design showed two large black granite walls, inscribed with the names of the 57,939 American dead, forming a V. The memorial was simple and stark, so much so that some veterans argued that it was more of a political statement about the conflict than an honor for the dead soldiers. The government's Fine Arts Commission agreed to add a 50-foot flagpole and a larger-than-life statue of three soldiers.

With the monument complete, the Vietnam Veterans Memorial Fund sponsored a five-day tribute in the capital. It began with the reading of the names of the Americans who died in Vietnam, included a parade down Constitution Avenue, and culminated with the dedication of the monument. The parade was a festive affair. Men appeared with beards and ponytails, looking very much like their antiwar contemporaries 15 years before. "Worst-looking bunch I ever saw," said Colonel Max Sullivan, "and I loved every one of them." Some brought their wives, children, and dogs. People wandered in and out of line, embracing old friends. Marching in the nation's capital before vast crowds, they sensed they had finally gained long-overdue recognition.

For Infantry Captain William Harris of Knoxville, Tennessee, the parade satisfied a deep need. He had run a mortar crew abroad, come home wounded, and had trouble piecing his life together again. When he found he could not talk to anyone but other veterans, he dropped out of the University of Tennessee, got divorced, lived in communes, and only later, after entering law school, managed to settle down. For Harris, the parade ended years of emotional difficulty. "It's catharsis for me," he said. "It washes it out, closes the chapter."

### The Moral Majority

Another group seeking to refashion society was the so-called Moral Majority. Convinced that the country was in the midst of a moral decline, members sought to return religion to a central place in their lives and to revive the values they believed had traditionally made the country strong.

The Moral Majority was deeply concerned about social change. Its members pointed particularly to an increase in crime and immorality. Between 1970 and 1980, the murder rate rose 31 percent, the robbery rate 42 percent, the burglary rate 56 percent, the assault rate 79 percent, and the rape rate 99 percent. The use of drugs spread. Marijuana was not simply a fad but an institution for a broad segment of society. Cocaine use also appeared common. In 1982, Don Reese, a football player, confessed in a cover story in *Sports Illustrated* that "cocaine arrived in my life with my first-round draft into the National Football League in 1974. It has dominated my life ever since." He went on to declare that "cocaine can be found in quantity throughout the NFL," and subsequent disclosures substantiated his charge.

Moral Majority members were also dis-

*The Reverend Jerry Falwell, leader of the Moral Majority, stood up for religious fundamentalism and political conservatism.*

turbed by the vocal efforts of other groups to foster their own interests. They feared the increased openness of homosexuality, objected to abortion, and argued that it was time to respond. Led by the Reverend Jerry Falwell of Virginia, the Moral Majority reflected the revival of fundamental Protestantism in the United States. The movement was part of the growing strength of conservatism in American politics. The right had momentarily seized control of the Republican party in 1964. Now the well-organized religious right determined to enter the political arena. Using modern communication and fundraising techniques, its proponents attacked liberals and their programs. In 1980, the movement helped Ronald Reagan and other politicians who shared his views to gain office. Members hoped that the Republican victory would enable them to translate their vision of America into the law of the land.

## THE CARTER AND REAGAN PRESIDENCIES

As Americans put scandal behind them in the mid-1970s, they elected national leaders who seemed to represent traditional American values. Jimmy Carter, a relative unknown from Georgia when he ran for the presidency, tried to take a fresh approach to the office but soon became bogged down in partisan squabbles. He was followed by former actor Ronald Reagan, who shifted America's course in both foreign and domestic affairs.

## The Election of 1976

In the nation's bicentennial year, incumbent Gerald Ford hoped to win for himself the office he had inherited from Richard Nixon. He faced Jimmy Carter, former governor of Georgia, who stressed that he was not from Washington and that, unlike many of those mired in past scandal, he was not a lawyer. Although Carter's initial lead faltered, most elements of the old Democratic coalition held. Carter won a 50 to 48 percent majority of the popular vote and a 297 to 240 margin in the electoral college. He did well with the working class, blacks, and Catholics. He won most of the South, heartening to the Democrats after Nixon's gains there.

## Human Rights Diplomacy

Carter enjoyed his greatest success in foreign policy, though he had had little diplomatic experience when he took office. Trained as a manager and an engineer at the U.S. Naval Academy and an avowed "born-again" Christian, Carter sought to conduct American foreign policy according to the standards that were part of his personal life.

Carter's major achievement came in the Middle East, where Israel and the Arab nations had fought a series of bitter wars. When Anwar el-Sadat of Egypt and Menachem Begin of Israel began to negotiate a peace settlement in 1978, Carter invited the two adversaries to come to Camp David, in the Maryland hills. There his personal diplomacy helped bring about a peace treaty, signed in March 1979. Israel withdrew from the occupied Sinai peninsula in return for Egyptian recognition and normalized relations. After 30 years of hostilities, Israel and Egypt were at peace.

At home, Carter fought for Senate acceptance of two treaties returning the Panama Canal to Panama by the year 2000. The United States had built the canal and long controlled it, but resentment had grown in Panama over the presence of a foreign power and the way in which the United States had acquired the right to build it. In the agreements, accepted by the margin of a single vote, the United States retained certain rights in the event of crisis but otherwise yielded to Panamanian demands.

In Asia, Carter successfully followed Nixon's initiatives by extending diplomatic recognition to the People's Republic of China. Attempting to modernize their economy, the Chinese sought technical assistance from the United States. American wheat farmers and businessmen eyed the Chinese market of nearly a billion people with enthusiasm, and American diplomats were eager to keep China and Russia at odds.

With the Soviet Union, Carter was less successful. Russian-American relations, the major U.S. diplomatic concern since World War II, fluctuated in the Carter years. Taking over with détente at high tide, the new president declared that the United States had finally escaped its "inordinate fear of Communism" and should forge closer ties with the Soviet state. But then American actions and Russian ventures left the conciliatory policy in shreds.

Like Woodrow Wilson, Carter believed morality should guide foreign policy. But his dedication to a policy of human rights complicated his diplomacy and exposed the difficulties of using morality as "the soul of . . . foreign policy." Carter's position that "our commitment to human rights must be absolute" antagonized the Soviets. They charged the American presi-

*Surrounded by aides, secret service, and newsmen, President Carter gives Prime Minister Begin of Israel and President Sadat of Egypt a walking tour of the battlefield at Gettysburg during a recess from the peace talks at Camp David.*

dent with meddling in their internal affairs when he verbally supported Russian dissidents. Consequently, Russian leaders resisted working with Carter on concrete disputes between the two superpowers.

One prickly issue was arms control. Negotiations for a more comprehensive strategic arms limitation treaty than the agreement of 1972 threatened to break down. Misjudging the Russians, the president offered new weapon-reduction proposals that went much farther than the Soviet Union was prepared to accept. When this threw matters into confusion, Carter backed off, patient negotiation succeeded, and the SALT II agreement was reached in June 1979.

The Soviet Invasion of Afghanistan in December 1979 complicated ratification, however. The Russians considered internal agitation there a threat to their security and invaded the country. After a year and a half of watching the bloody involvement, Carter responded by calling the Soviet move the most serious blow to world peace since World War II. He postponed presenting SALT II to the Senate and imposed an American boycott of the 1980 Olympic Games in Moscow. Détente was effectively dead.

Carter also stumbled in his effort to defuse a major crisis with Iran. Americans had long supported the shah of Iran. Overlooking the corruption and abuse in his regime, they viewed him as a reliable supplier of oil and defender of stability in the Persian Gulf region. In January 1979, revolutionary groups drove the shah from power. In his place sat the Ayatollah Ruholla Khomeini, an Islamic priest who returned from exile in Paris to lead a new fundamentalist Islamic regime.

When Carter admitted the shah to the United States for medical treatment in October 1979, angry Iranian students seized the American embassy in Tehran and held 53 Americans hostage. Their capture became a national cause in the United States. Carter broke diplomatic relations and froze Iranian assets, but this did not bring a release of the hostages. Faced with mounting public criticism, Carter finally authorized a commando raid. Its failure cost Carter the frustration and anger of a large part of the public, which blamed the president for the stalemate. An agreement to free the hostages was finally reached in 1981, but not until the very day Carter left office were the Americans finally released.

## Carter's Domestic Program

On the economic front, Carter pursued a policy of deficit spending. When the Federal Reserve Board increased the money supply to help meet mounting deficits, which reached peacetime records under Carter, inflation rose to about 10 percent a year. Seeking to reduce inflation in 1979, Carter slowed down the economy and cut the deficit slightly. Budget cuts fell largely on social programs and distanced Carter from reform-minded Democrats who had supported him three years before. Yet even that effort to arrest growing deficits was not enough. When the budget released in early 1980 still showed high spending levels, the financial community reacted strongly. Bond prices fell, and interest rates rose dramatically.

Carter failed to construct an effective energy policy. OPEC had been increasing oil prices rapidly since 1973 and would not promise restraint in the future. Americans began to resent their dependence on foreign oil—over 40 percent was imported by the end of the decade—and clamored for energy self-sufficiency. Carter responded in April 1977 with a comprehensive energy program, which he called the "moral equivalent of war." Critics seized on the acronym of that expression, MEOW, to describe the plan and had a field day criticizing the president. Never an effective leader in working with the legislative branch, Carter watched his proposals bog down in Congress for 26 months. Eventually the program committed the nation to move from oil dependence to reliance on coal, possibly even on sun and wind, and established a new synthetic-fuel corporation. Nuclear power, another alternative, seemed less attractive as costs rose and accidents, like the one at Three Mile Island, occurred.

Parts of Carter's domestic program worked, but he often provided ineffective leadership. He frequently reversed course and failed to develop consistent policies. His critics charged that he had no legislative strategy at all, no priorities to communicate to Congress. As columnist Tom

Wicker noted at the end of four years, "He never established a politically coherent administration." That was largely because Carter was less comfortable as a politician, more comfortable as a problem solver and engineer. Like Herbert Hoover, he was a technocrat in the White House. As they had in 1932, Americans wanted a president who promised to lead them out of economic hard times.

## The Election of 1980

Although Carter had wanted to reestablish Democratic control of the country, by the end of his term, his disapproval rating reached 77 percent. With Watergate behind them, the Republicans regrouped and called for a return to conservative principles of government.

Carter faced Ronald Reagan, an actor turned politician. Reagan had served as California's governor for eight years and had sought the presidency in 1976. As heir to Barry Goldwater's conservative mantle, he could count on the support of the growing right. Reagan had a pleasing manner and in the campaign proved his skill as a media communicator. Charging the Carter administration with "a litany of broken

*Governor of California for two terms, Ronald Reagan drew on his earlier experience in the movies to project an appealing, if old-fashioned, image to the public.*

promises," he provided a soothing contrast to the incumbent. He showed real wit as he quibbled with Carter over economic definitions. "I'm talking in human terms and he is hiding behind a dictionary," Reagan said. "If he wants a definition, I'll give him one. A recession is when your neighbor loses his job. A depression is when you lose yours. A recovery is when Jimmy Carter loses his."

Reagan started with an enormous lead in the campaign and held it to the end. He scored a landslide victory, gaining a popular margin of 51 to 41 percent and a 489 to 49 electoral college advantage. He also led the Republican party to control of the Senate. Reagan's strength showed in all areas of the country. He split the traditionally Democratic Jewish vote and working-class vote, though blacks supported Carter as before.

## Reviving the Cold War

In foreign affairs, Reagan asserted American interests far more aggressively than Carter. Rooted in the Cold War tradition, he believed in high defense budgets and a militant approach toward the Soviet Union. To assist him in the formulation and conduct of foreign policy, Reagan appointed as secretary of state General Alexander Haig, former chief of staff in the Watergate White House. When Haig proved both contentious and ambitious, George Shultz, secretary of the Treasury under Nixon, took over.

Reagan moved decisively in a number of areas. Though he spoke of economy in government, he proposed unprecedented defense spending for a massive arms buildup. Over a five-year period, the administration sought a military budget of $1.5 trillion dollars. Arguing that the nation was otherwise vulnerable, the president insisted that spending for weapons, both nuclear and conventional, had to increase.

Reagan also argued that a nuclear war could be fought and won. Discounting scientists' studies that showed cataclysmic destruction in the event of nuclear war, he claimed that the nation would survive. T. K. Jones, deputy undersecretary of defense for strategic and theater nuclear forces, even revived the dormant notion of civil defense. "Dig a hole, cover it with a couple of doors, and then throw three feet of dirt on top . . . ," he advised. "It's the dirt that does it . . . if there are enough shovels to go around, everybody's going to make it."

While promoting defense spending and nuclear superiority, the administration abandoned Senate ratification of SALT II, the arms-reduction plan negotiated under Carter, although it observed its restrictions. Instead the administration proposed that Russia destroy certain missiles in return for an American pledge not to deploy new weapons in Europe. The Soviet Union balked at that idea, so different from the careful negotiation accompanying previous arms talks. The arms race escalated, new U.S. missiles were deployed in western Europe, and in both countries military budgets soared.

Seeing Central America as a Cold War battlefield, the administration intervened there frequently in Reagan's first term. The administration openly opposed the left-wing guerrillas of El Salvador who fought against a repressive right-wing regime. Fearful that another nation might follow the Marxist examples of Cuba and Nicaragua, the United States increased its aid to the antirevolutionary El Salvador government, heedless of a similar course followed years before in Vietnam. It also channeled support to exiled Nicaraguans attempting to overthrow the Socialist government in that country.

In foreign affairs, Reagan proved more rigidly ideological than any president since the end of World War II. He took stands that invited confrontation with Russia and often echoed approaches taken in the early Cold War years. Détente, though initiated under Republican leadership a decade before, collapsed.

## Dismantling the Welfare State

Rooted in Middle America, Reagan fervently believed in the American dream. He looked back nostalgically at a world of heroes and heroic deeds, where a person could make a mark through individual effort. He had played by the rules of the system himself and had won. Others should do the same.

Faced with a stagnating economy and a growing federal establishment, Reagan sought to reverse the twentieth-century movement toward what conservatives saw as government management of every aspect of American life. Upon taking office he announced that he in-

tended to reduce government spending by eliminating "waste, fraud, and abuse." Concerned about the federal deficit, he committed himself to a balanced budget before the end of his term. To accomplish this he demanded cuts, particularly in social programs he viewed as unnecessary.

At the heart of his economic recovery program was the theory of supply-side economics, which held that the reduction of taxes would encourage business expansion, which in turn would lead to a larger supply of goods to help stimulate the system as a whole. "Reaganomics," promoted during the campaign, promised a revitalized economy.

To allow for tax reduction and military expansion, the administration proposed huge cuts in social programs. Public service jobs, mandated under the Comprehensive Employment and Training Act, were eliminated. Unemployment compensation was cut back. Medicare patients were required to pay more for treatment. Welfare benefits were lowered, and food stamp allocations were reduced.

While cutting social programs, the administration also pushed through regressive tax reductions. As finally passed, a 5 percent cut went into effect on October 1, 1981, followed by 10 percent cuts in 1982 and 1983. Although all taxpayers enjoyed some savings, the rich benefited far more than middle- and lower-income Americans. As a result of tax cuts and huge defense expenditures, the budget deficit grew even larger—approaching $200 billion in 1983 and 1984. Deficit spending had long been associated with the Democratic party and balanced budgets with the Republicans, but under Reagan the annual deficit reached historic heights.

As a political conservative distrustful of central government, Reagan also yearned to place power in the hands of state and local government and to reduce the ways in which the federal government touched people's lives. He was determined to cut back the federal regulatory apparatus, for he believed government regulations were partially responsible for the weakening performance of the American economy. Safety regulations were deemed "paternalistic." States, he argued, should not have social goals imposed on them by the national government.

The "New Federalism" was Reagan's attempt to shift responsibilities from the federal to the state level. The program never really got off the ground, as critics charged that the proposal was merely a backhanded way of moving programs from one place to another and then eliminating the funds.

Reagan also took a decidedly conservative approach to social issues. He willingly accepted the support of the New Right and spoke out for public prayer in the schools. The first nongovernmental group to receive an audience at the White House was an antiabortion March for Life contingent.

The president was less supportive of minority groups than his recent predecessors. He opposed busing to achieve racial balance, and his attorney general worked to dismantle affirmative-action programs. Initially reluctant to support extension of the enormously successful Voting Rights Acts of 1965, Reagan relented only under severe criticism from Republicans as well as Democrats. He directed the Internal Revenue Service to cease banning tax exemptions for private schools that discriminated against blacks, only to see that move overturned by the Supreme Court in 1983. Blacks were understandably critical of Reagan, as were Native Americans, who charged that his stance toward government affairs in general and Indian problems in particular was undoing the progress of the preceding ten years.

## The Election of 1984

In 1984, Ronald Reagan sought reelection. After a bitter primary campaign that included black activist Jesse Jackson and Colorado senator Gary Hart, the Democrats nominated Walter Mondale, who had served as Jimmy Carter's vice-president. For his running mate, the Democrats selected Geraldine Ferraro, a congresswoman from New York, the first woman ever to receive a major party's nomination on the presidential ticket.

Reagan ran a bouyant, upbeat campaign with a patriotic theme. His appearance sometimes featured fireworks and swarms of tiny parachutes holding miniature American flags. His unofficial campaign song was "I'm Proud to Be an American." To his audiences he declared, "You ain't seen nothing yet."

Mondale hammered away at the huge and growing budget deficit and criticized the president's foreign policy, especially Reagan's seeming disinterest in halting the massive nuclear arms buildup, while contending that he could be every bit as tough toward the Soviet Union. But he appeared colorless and unexciting, and by mid-September, Mondale trailed Reagan in the polls by 18 percentage points.

His campaign enjoyed its only success in early October, in the aftermath of a televised debate. Invoking the image of John F. Kennedy, Mondale appeared more articulate and aggressive. Reagan seemed unsure of himself, tired at the end. Many Americans questioned whether the 73-year-old president was fit for another term. Reagan regained command in the next TV debate, defusing the age issue when he declared with a grin, "I am not going to exploit my opponent's youth and experience, not at all."

On election day, Reagan scored a second landslide victory. He received 59 percent of the popular vote and swamped Mondale in the electoral college, where he lost only Minnesota, his opponent's home state, and the District of Columbia. Though disappointed, the Democrats netted two additional seats in the Senate and

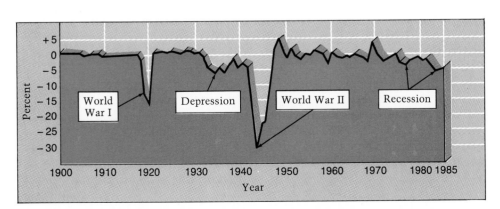

**Federal Budget Surplus or Deficit as Percentage of GNP**

*Sources:* U.S. Bureau of the Census; and Office of Management and Budget.

## Presidential Elections, 1976–1984

| YEAR | CANDIDATES | PARTY | POPULAR VOTE | ELECTORAL VOTE |
|------|-----------|-------|--------------|----------------|
| 1976 | JIMMY CARTER | Democratic | 40,828,657 (50.6%) | 297 |
|      | Gerald R. Ford | Republican | 39,145,520 (48.4%) | 240 |
| 1980 | RONALD REAGAN | Republican | 43,899,248 (51%) | 489 |
|      | Jimmy Carter | Democrat | 36,481,435 (41%) | 49 |
|      | John B. Anderson | Independent | 5,719,437 (6%) | 0 |
| 1984 | RONALD REAGAN | Republican | 53,428,357 (59%) | 525 |
|      | Walter F. Mondale | Democrat | 36,930,923 (41%) | 13 |

*Note:* Winners' names appear in capital letters.

managed to maintain superiority in the House of Representatives.

Reagan's impressive electoral success symbolized not only a personal victory but also an endorsement of the new vision of government that he espoused. Since the New Deal, both Democrats and Republicans had agreed that the national government should monitor the economy and assist the least fortunate. Reagan's 1980 campaign and the efforts of his first administration challenged this vision. By 1984, even the Democrats were hesitant to question the claim that the federal government must curtail its activities. Liberal ideals were in retreat.

The election itself dramatized the collapse of the popular coalition that had sustained the Democratic party since the 1930s. Eighty-five percent of black voters supported Mondale, but only 35 percent of white voters cast their ballot for the national Democratic ticket. Contrary to Democratic party expectations, the nomination of Geraldine Ferraro did not rescue Mondale. The "gender gap" never materialized, and Ferraro's ethnic background failed to win back white ethnic voters.

Analysts offered varying explanations for the apparent collapse of the Democratic coalition and the racial polarization of the voters. Some suggested that whites abandoned the Democrats when blacks pressed for increasing government assistance in the 1960s and 1970s because many of the whites had already profited from government programs. Others pointed out that the economic slowdown of the 1970s had forced Democrats to choose between defense and social programs. Each choice offended some part of the old coalition. Many proclaimed that the election proved that New Deal liberalism was dead, but in 1984 no one could know whether its decline was permanent or temporary. Only time could reveal the full meaning of the election of 1984.

By the time Reagan embarked on his second term, the economy had made a strong recovery. With interest rates and unemployment dropping and economic growth partially restored, the country emerged from the deep recession of the early 1980s. Yet the hardening of the nation's economic arteries had not been completely cured. With unemployment still above 7 percent, millions of disillusioned Americans, like Andy Hjelmeland and Jerry Espinoza, introduced at the beginning of the chapter, wondered if they would ever recapture security and dignity in their lives.

## CONCLUSION: The Recent Past in Perspective

Reagan's second term began with a mixture of hope and fear. His supporters foresaw a new era of conservative government that would foster a less regulated economy, restore older moral codes, continue the steel-ribbed posture toward the Soviet Union, and squelch any Socialist challenges to Western Hemisphere governments aligned with the United States. Reagan's detractors feared that the attacks on the welfare state, which by the beginning of the second term included proposals to cut such programs as Amtrak, subsidies to urban mass-transit systems, legal assistance to the poor, farm-support programs, and student loans, would once again divide the nation into a society of haves and have-nots. Not since the 1930s, when Franklin Roosevelt began his second term, had such wholesale change in government policies centered on the presidency.

Although the assault on the welfare state became dubbed the "Reagan revolution," such programs as social security and Medicare remained securely in place, accepted by all but the most implacable splinter groups. Even the most conservative president in the last half century could not return to a romanticized past of unbridled individualism and puny federal government. The domestic and international challenges facing a modern nation of multiple interest groups—a nation that was incorporated into a worldwide economic and diplomatic system—were far too complex for a government structure on nineteenth-century lines. So, as during many eras of the past, Americans in the 1980s listened to new formulas for facing the future, continued to consult the past for guidance in contemporary problems, argued among themselves on issues ranging from abortion to deficit spending, and for the most part retained a bedrock faith in a national two-party system and their local instruments of government.

## Recommended Reading

There is understandably less published material available for the most recent period than for earlier years. Historians have not yet had a chance to deal in detail with the developments of the immediate past, and fuller descriptions must be found in other sources. The best writing about the years in this chapter appears in the newspapers and magazines of the popular press. But there are a number of useful treatments about selected topics that provide good starting points in various areas.

Andrew Hacker, ed., *U/S: A Statistical Portrait of the American People* (1983) is a helpful compilation of demographic trends based on the 1980 census. Richard Rodriguez, *Hunger of Memory: The Education of Richard Rodriguez* (1982) is a penetrating autobiographical account of a Hispanic boy growing up in the United States. Alvin M. Josephy, Jr., *Now That the Buffalo's Gone* (1982) is a comprehensive survey of recent American Indian struggles. Jimmy Carter, *Keeping Faith: Memories of a President* (1982) is Carter's own story of the White House years. Lou Cannon, *Reagan* (1982) is a veteran reporter's assessment of Reagan's background and early years as president.

### TIME LINE

| | |
|---|---|
| 1976 | Jimmy Carter elected president |
| 1977 | Carter energy program, human rights policy<br>Panama Canal Treaties |
| 1978 | Israeli-Egyptian peace accords at Camp David<br>*Bakke* v. *University of California* |
| 1979 | Three Mile Island nuclear power plant accident<br>Russians invade Afghanistan<br>Iranian revolution overthrows shah<br>SALT II agreement on nuclear arms |
| 1979–1981 | Iranian hostage crisis |
| 1980 | Ronald Reagan elected president |
| 1981 | Sandra Day O'Connor became first woman Supreme Court justice |
| 1981–1983 | Tax cuts; deficit spending increases |
| 1982 | Vietnam Veterans Memorial dedicated<br>Equal Rights Amendment fails |
| 1984 | Geraldine Ferraro nominated for vice-president<br>Reagan reelected |

# PORTFOLIO SIX

## THE ART OF
## AN ENDURING PEOPLE

### 1945 – 1985

The United States emerged from World War II as the most powerful nation in the world. Other countries looked to the United States for help in adjusting to the problems of the postwar world. At the same time, the rest of the world depended on America as a source for vital artistic expression and innovation. New York, not Paris or London, became the artistic capital of the world in the years immediately following the war. Although the 1930s had witnessed an increased migration of artists to New York, other factors also contributed to making the city a vital center for artistic expression. A large group of working artists, the presence of many collectors and galleries, the Museum of Modern Art, and other institutions helped to make New York a stimulating place to work. The New York school of abstract expressionism, as it came to be called, drew strength from many other places in the country, however.

Abstract expressionism included many different styles, each as shocking to the general public as it was exciting to the avant-garde. Jackson Pollock (1912–1956) painted pictures with no apparent focal point, no edge, the paint apparently poured on. Willem de Kooning (1904–) created giant splashes, Mark Rothko (1903–1970) constructed great swaths of color on huge canvases, and others abandoned the square canvas entirely. No sooner had the abstract expressionists reached what seemed the last possible extreme of abstraction, with paintings of a single line or a canvas with only shades of black, when a new group emerged on the scene. Pop art, op art, superrealism, flags, and comic strips all had their day. Artists painted soup cans, geometric designs, and ordinary street scenes, and the critics, if not always the general public, were impressed.

American art remained vital and diverse in the last decades of the twentieth century, and there was not just one center of innovation. Artists from Maine to California, from Texas to Minnesota, in the cities and the towns, took inspiration from their environment. If the ordinary citizens had difficulty understanding the abstract expressionists or appreciating pop art, they could find meaning in the paintings of Andrew Wyeth, who recalled a simpler age and painted in a style that reminded some of Winslow Homer. Folk art and ethnic art took on a new meaning in a postindustrial age when a search for community and family heritage extended to an appreciation of a colorful mural on a city building, a handmade quilt, and simple paintings created by untrained artists.

Willem de Kooning, *Woman*, 1949–1950.
Weatherspoon Art Gallery,
University of North Carolina at Greensboro.
Lena Kernodle McDuffie Memorial Gift.

Both these paintings are of women. The de Kooning has a kind of restless energy about it, as well as a sense of being incomplete. It puts a greater burden on the viewer than does the Wyeth. But Andrew Wyeth has great technical skill and works in a tradition that is familiar and perhaps nonthreatening. Both styles represented in these two paintings existed side by side in the decades after World War II.

Andrew Wyeth, *Christina's World*, 1948.
Museum of Modern Art, New York.

Jasper Johns, *Three Flags*, 1958.
Whitney Museum of American Art,
New York. Fiftieth anniversary gift
of the Gilman Foundation, Inc.,
the Lauder Foundation, A. Alfred
Taubman, an anonymous donor,
and purchase.

The movement called "pop art" burst onto the scene in the late 1950s and early 1960s. Although the name originated in England, the movement itself was very American. A group of talented artists took ordinary objects and symbols from advertising, the newspaper, and everyday life and forced the viewer to look at them in a different way. Jasper Johns (1930–) did a series on the American flag, a symbol so familiar that most people had never really looked at it. In a similar way, Andy Warhol (1928–) isolated commercial products such as Campbell's soup cans, while other artists created sculpture out of ordinary objects.

Andy Warhol, *Campbell's Soup Can
with Peeling Label*, 1962.
Leo Castelli Gallery, New York.

"Joe" chair, 1970.
Designers: De Pas, D'Urbino, and Lonazzi. Manufacturer: Poltronova.
Distributor: Stendig International. Photo courtesy of Stendig
International.

American pop art and other postwar movements had
an enormous influence in Europe and around the
world. One example is the "Joe" chair, a large version
of a baseball glove, created by three Italian designers
in 1970 and named after Yankee star Joe DiMaggio.
   The paintings of Robert Bechtle (1932–), based on
photographs of familiar scenes, are startling for their
detailed photographic realism.

Robert Bechtle, '61 Pontiac, 1968–1969.
Whitney Museum of American Art, New York.
Richard and Dorothy Rodgers Fund.

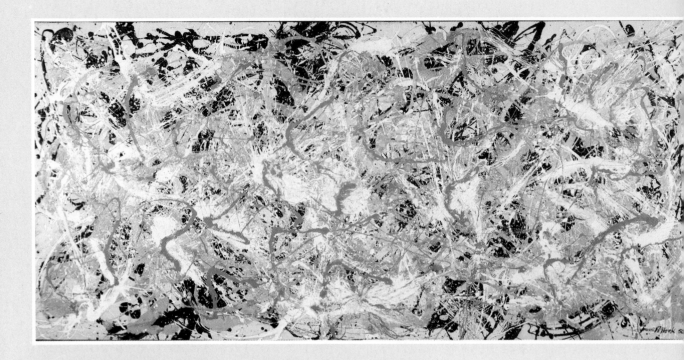

Jackson Pollock, *Number 27*, 1950.
Whitney Museum of American Art, New York.

Jackson Pollock was influenced by the work of Thomas Hart Benton and the murals of José Orozco, but he eliminated the subject matter and simply used color and form. His paintings are sometimes called action paintings. He literally stood in the middle of his paintings when he created them, and he forced his viewer to recapture the creative experience to make any meaning out of his art.

Mark Rothko worked in bright colors and softly edged shapes. "Pictures must be miraculous," he said at one point. After a painting was completed, he maintained, "the intimacy between the creation and the creator is ended. He is an outsider. The picture must be for him, as for anyone experiencing it later, a revelation, an unexpected and unprecedented resolution of an eternally familiar need."

Mark Rothko, *Number 22*, 1949.
Museum of Modern Art, New York.
Gift of the artist.

Oscar Howe,
*Sioux Seed Player*, 1974.
University Art Galleries, University of
South Dakota, Vermillion.

These two paintings exemplify another kind of art that exploded in the years after World War II. Mural art took on new meaning, and a great many young artists sought subjects related to their ethnic and racial heritage as they tried to define their place in America. Oscar Howe (1915–) is a full-blooded Sioux, and in his art, which has been a major influence in the contemporary Indian art movement, he seeks themes from the legends, ceremonies, and traditions of the Sioux people. John Biggers (1924–) was born in North Carolina but in recent years has lived in Houston, Texas, where he has been one of the leaders in a renaissance of black art. His murals are influenced by a long tradition of mural painting, but his subject is the struggle of ordinary black people.

John Biggers,
*The Quilting Party*, 1981.
Music Hall, Houston Civic
Center. Photo Earlie Hudnall
for Artcetera, Houston.

# APPENDIX

# Declaration of Independence in Congress, July 4, 1776

## THE UNANIMOUS DECLARATION OF THE THIRTEEN UNITED STATES OF AMERICA

When, in the course of human events, it becomes necessary for one people to dissolve the political bonds which have connected them with another, and to assume, among the powers of the earth, the separate and equal station to which the laws of nature and of nature's God entitle them, a decent respect to the opinions of mankind requires that they should declare the causes which impel them to the separation.

We hold these truths to be self-evident: That all men are created equal; that they are endowed by their Creator with certain unalienable rights; that among these are life, liberty, and the pursuit of happiness; that, to secure these rights, governments are instituted among men, deriving their just powers from the consent of the governed; that whenever any form of government becomes destructive of these ends, it is the right of the people to alter or to abolish it, and to institute new government, laying its foundation on such principles, and organizing its powers in such form, as to them shall seem most likely to effect their safety and happiness. Prudence, indeed, will dictate that governments long established should not be changed for light and transient causes; and accordingly all experience hath shown that mankind are more disposed to suffer, which evils are sufferable, than to right themselves by abolishing the forms to which they are accustomed. But when a long train of abuses and usurpations, pursuing invariably the same object, evinces a design to reduce them under absolute despotism, it is their right, it is their duty, to throw off such government, and to provide new guards for their future security. Such has been the patient sufferance of these colonies; and such is now the necessity which constrains them to alter their former systems of government. The history of the present King of Great Britain is a history of repeated injuries and usurpations, all having in direct object the establishment of an absolute tyranny over these states. To prove this, let facts be submitted to a candid world.

He has refused his assent to laws, the most wholesome and necessary for the public good.

He has forbidden his governors to pass laws of immediate and pressing importance, unless suspended in their operation till his assent should be obtained; and, when so suspended, he has utterly neglected to attend to them.

He has refused to pass other laws for the accommodation of large districts of people, unless those people would relinquish the right of representation in the legislature, a right inestimable to them, and formidable to tyrants only.

He has called together legislative bodies at places unusual, uncomfortable, and distant from the depository of their public records, for the sole purpose of fatiguing them into compliance with his measures.

He has dissolved representative houses repeatedly, for opposing, with manly firmness, his invasions on the rights of the people.

He has refused for a long time, after such dissolutions, to cause others to be elected; whereby the legislative powers, incapable of annihilation, have returned to the people at large for their exercise; the state remaining, in the mean time, exposed to all the dangers of invasions from without and convulsions within.

He has endeavored to prevent the population of these states; for that purpose obstructing the laws for naturalization of foreigners; refusing to pass others to encourage their migration hither, and raising the conditions of new appropriations of lands.

He has obstructed the administration of justice, by refusing his assent to laws for establishing judiciary powers.

He has made judges dependent on his will alone, for the tenure of their offices, and the amount and payment of their salaries.

He has erected a multitude of new offices, and sent hither swarms of officers to harass our people and eat out their substance.

He has kept among us, in times of peace, standing armies, without the consent of our legislatures.

He has affected to render the military independent of, and superior to, the civil power.

He has combined with others to subject us to a jurisdiction foreign to our constitution, and unacknowledged by our laws, giving his assent to their acts of pretended legislation:

For quartering large bodies of armed troops among us;

For protecting them, by a mock trial, from punishment for any murders which they should commit on the inhabitants of these states;

For cutting off our trade with all parts of the world;

For imposing taxes on us without our consent;

For depriving us, in many cases, of the benefits of trial by jury;

For transporting us beyond seas, to be tried for pretended offenses;

For abolishing the free system of English laws in a neighboring province, establishing therein an arbitrary government, and enlarging its boundaries, so as to render it at once an example and fit instrument for introducing the same absolute rule into these colonies;

For taking away our charters, abolishing our most

valuable laws, and altering fundamentally the forms of our governments.

For suspending our own legislatures, and declaring themselves invested with power to legislate for us in all cases whatsoever.

He has abdicated government here, by declaring us out of his protection and waging war against us.

He has plundered our seas, ravaged our coasts, burned our towns, and destroyed the lives of our people.

He is at this time transporting large armies of foreign mercenaries to complete the works of death, desolation, and tyranny already begun with circumstances of cruelty and perfidy scarcely paralleled in the most barbarous ages, and totally unworthy the head of a civilized nation.

He has constrained our fellow-citizens, taken captive on the high seas, to bear arms against their country, to become the executioners of their friends and brethren, or to fall themselves by their hands.

He has excited domestic insurrection among us, and has endeavored to bring on the inhabitants of our frontiers the merciless Indian savages, whose known rule of warfare is an undistinguished destruction of all ages, sexes, and conditions.

In every stage of these oppressions we have petitioned for redress in the most humble terms; our repeated petitions have been answered only by repeated injury. A prince, whose character is thus marked by every act which may define a tyrant, is unfit to be the ruler of a free people.

Nor have we been wanting in our attentions to our British brethren. We have warned them, from time to time, of attempts by their legislature to extend an unwarrantable jurisdiction over us. We have reminded them of the circumstances of our emigration and settlement here. We have appealed to their native justice and magnanimity; and we have conjured them, by the ties of our common kindred, to disavow these usurpations, which would inevitably interrupt our connections and correspondence. They, too, have been deaf to the voice of justice and of consanguinity. We must, therefore, acquiesce in the necessity which denounces our separation, and hold them, as we hold the rest of mankind, enemies in war, in peace friends.

We, therefore, the representatives of the United States of America, in General Congress assembled, appealing to the Supreme Judge of the world for the rectitude of our intentions, do, in the name and by the authority of the good people of these colonies, solemnly publish and declare, that these United Colonies are, and of right ought to be, FREE AND INDEPENDENT STATES; that they are absolved from all allegiance to the British crown, and that all political connection between them and the state of Great Britain is, and ought to be, totally dissolved; and that, as free and independent states, they have full power to levy war, conclude peace, contract alliances, establish commerce, and do all other acts and things which independent states may of right do. And for the support of this declaration, with a firm reliance on the protection of Divine Providence, we mutually pledge to each other our lives, our fortunes, and our sacred honor.

# Constitution of the United States of America*

## PREAMBLE

We the people of the United States, in order to form a more perfect union, establish justice, insure domestic tranquillity, provide for the common defense, promote the general welfare, and secure the blessings of liberty to ourselves and our posterity, do ordain and establish this Constitution for the United States of America.

## ARTICLE I

**Section 1** All legislative powers herein granted shall be vested in a Congress of the United States, which shall consist of a Senate and a House of Representatives.

**Section 2** The House of Representatives shall be composed of members chosen every second year by the people of the several States, and the electors in each State shall have the qualifications requisite for electors of the most numerous branch of the State Legislature.

No person shall be a Representative who shall not have attained to the age of twenty-five years, and been seven years a citizen of the United States, and who shall not, when elected, be an inhabitant of that State in which he shall be chosen.

Representatives and direct taxes shall be apportioned among the several States which may be included within this Union, according to their respective numbers, *which shall be determined by adding to the whole number of free persons, including those bound to service for a term of years and excluding Indians not taxed, three-fifths of all other persons.* The actual enumeration shall be made within three years after the first meeting of the Congress of the United States, and within every subsequent term of ten years, in such manner as they shall by law direct. The number of Representatives shall not exceed one for every thirty thousand, but each State shall have at least one Representative; *and until such enumeration shall be made, the State of New Hampshire shall be entitled to choose three, Massachusetts eight, Rhode Island and Providence Plantations one, Connecticut five, New York six, New Jersey four, Pennsylvania eight, Delaware one, Maryland six, Virginia ten, North Carolina five, South Carolina five, and Georgia three.*

When vacancies happen in the representation from any State, the Executive authority thereof shall issue writs of election to fill such vacancies.

The House of Representatives shall choose their Speaker and other officers; and shall have the sole power of impeachment.

**Section 3** The Senate of the United States shall be composed of two Senators from each State, *chosen by the legislature thereof,* for six years; and each Senator shall have one vote.

*Immediately after they shall be assembled in consequence of the first election, they shall be divided as equally as may be into three classes. The seats of the Senators of the first class shall be vacated at the expiration of the second year, of the second class at the expiration of the fourth year, and of the third class at the expiration of the sixth year,* so that one-third may be chosen every second year; *and if vacancies happen by resignation or otherwise, during the recess of the legislature of any State, the Executive thereof may make temporary appointments until the next meeting of the legislature, which shall then fill such vacancies.*

No person shall be a Senator who shall not have attained to the age of thirty years, and been nine years a citizen of the United States, and who shall not, when elected, be an inhabitant of that State for which he shall be chosen.

The Vice-President of the United States shall be President of the Senate, but shall have no vote, unless they be equally divided.

The Senate shall choose their other officers, and also a President *pro tempore,* in the absence of the Vice-President, or when he shall exercise the office of President of the United States.

The Senate shall have the sole power to try all impeachments. When sitting for that purpose, they shall be on oath or affirmation. When the President of the United States is tried, the Chief Justice shall preside; and no person shall be convicted without the concurrence of two-thirds of the members present.

Judgment in cases of impeachment shall not extend further than to removal from the office, and disqualification to hold and enjoy any office of honor, trust or profit under the United States: but the party convicted shall nevertheless be liable and subject to indictment, trial, judgment and punishment, according to law.

**Section 4** The times, places and manner of holding elections for Senators and Representatives shall be prescribed in each State by the legislature thereof; but the Congress may at any time by law make or alter such regulations, except as to the places of choosing Senators.

The Congress shall assemble at least once in every year, and such meeting *shall be on the first Monday in December, unless they shall by law appoint a different day.*

---

* The Constitution became effective March 4, 1789.

**Section 5**  Each house shall be the judge of the elections, returns and qualifications of its own members, and a majority of each shall constitute a quorum to do business; but a smaller number may adjourn from day to day, and may be authorized to compel the attendance of absent members, in such manner, and under such penalties, as each house may provide.

Each house may determine the rules of its proceedings, punish its members for disorderly behavior, and with the concurrence of two-thirds, expel a member.

Each house shall keep a journal of its proceedings, and from time to time publish the same, excepting such parts as may in their judgment require secrecy; and the yeas and nays of the members of either house on any question shall, at the desire of one-fifth of those present, be entered on the journal.

Neither house, during the session of Congress, shall, without the consent of the other, adjourn for more than three days, nor to any other place than that in which the two houses shall be sitting.

**Section 6**  The Senators and Representatives shall receive a compensation for their services, to be ascertained by law and paid out of the treasury of the United States. They shall in all cases except treason, felony and breach of the peace be privileged from arrest during their attendance at the session of their respective houses, and in going to and returning from the same; and for any speech or debate in either house, they shall not be questioned in any other place.

No Senator or Representative shall, during the time for which he was elected, be appointed to any civil office under the authority of the United States, which shall have been created, or the emoluments whereof shall have been increased, during such time; and no person holding any office under the United States shall be a member of either house during his continuance in office.

**Section 7**  All bills for raising revenue shall originate in the House of Representatives; but the Senate may propose or concur with amendments as on other bills.

Every bill which shall have passed the House of Representatives and the Senate, shall, before it becomes a law, be presented to the President of the United States; if he approve he shall sign it, but if not he shall return it with objections to that house in which it originated, who shall enter the objections at large on their journal, and proceed to reconsider it. If after such reconsideration two-thirds of that house shall agree to pass the bill, it shall be sent, together with the objections, to the other house, by which it shall likewise be reconsidered, and, if approved by two-thirds of that house, it shall become a law. But in all such cases the votes of both houses shall be determined by yeas and nays, and the names of the persons voting for and against the bill shall be entered on the journal of each house respectively. If any bill shall not be returned by the President within ten days (Sundays excepted) after it shall have been presented to him, the same shall be a law, in like manner as if he had signed it, unless the Congress by their adjournment prevent its return, in which case it shall not be a law.

Every order, resolution, or vote to which the concurrence of the Senate and House of Representatives may be necessary (except on a question of adjournment) shall be presented to the President of the United States; and before the same shall take effect, shall be approved by him, or being disapproved by him, shall be repassed by two-thirds of the Senate and House of Representatives, according to the rules and limitations prescribed in the case of a bill.

**Section 8**  The Congress shall have power:

To lay and collect taxes, duties, imposts, and excises, to pay the debts and provide for the common defense and general welfare of the United States; but all duties, imposts and excises shall be uniform throughout the United States;

To borrow money on the credit of the United States;

To regulate commerce with foreign nations, and among the several States, and with the Indian tribes;

To establish an uniform rule of naturalization, and uniform laws on the subject of bankruptcies throughout the United States;

To coin money, regulate the value thereof, and of foreign coin, and fix the standard of weights and measures;

To provide for the punishment of counterfeiting the securities and current coin of the United States;

To establish post offices and post roads;

To promote the progress of science and useful arts by securing for limited times to authors and inventors the exclusive right to their respective writings and discoveries;

To constitute tribunals inferior to the Supreme Court;

To define and punish piracies and felonies committed on the high seas and offenses against the law of nations;

To declare war, grant letters of marque and reprisal, and make rules concerning captures on land and water;

To raise and support armies, but no appropriation of money to that use shall be for a longer term than two years;

To provide and maintain a navy;

To make rules for the government and regulation of the land and naval forces;

To provide for calling forth the militia to execute the laws of the Union, suppress insurrections, and repel invasions;

To provide for organizing, arming, and disciplining the militia, and for governing such part of them as may be employed in the service of the United States, reserving to the States respectively the appointment of the officers, and the authority of training the militia according to the discipline prescribed by Congress;

To exercise exclusive legislation in all cases whatsoever, over such district (not exceeding ten miles square) as may, by cession of particular States, and the acceptance of Congress, become the seat of government of the United States, and to exercise like authority over all places purchased by the consent of the legislature of the State, in which the same shall be, for erection of forts, magazines, arsenals, dockyards, and other needful buildings;—and

To make all laws which shall be necessary and proper for carrying into execution the foregoing powers, and all other powers vested by this Constitution in the government of the United States, or in any department or officer thereof.

**Section 9** *The migration or importation of such persons as any of the States now existing shall think proper to admit shall not be prohibited by the Congress prior to the year 1808; but a tax or duty may be imposed on such importation, not exceeding $10 for each person.*

The privilege of the writ of habeas corpus shall not be suspended, unless when in cases of rebellion or invasion the public safety may require it.

No bill of attainder or ex post facto law shall be passed.

No capitation or other direct tax shall be laid, unless in proportion to the census or enumeration herein before directed to be taken.

No tax or duty shall be laid on articles exported from any State.

No preference shall be given by any regulation of commerce or revenue to the ports of one State over those of another; nor shall vessels bound to, or from, one State be obliged to enter, clear, or pay duties in another.

No money shall be drawn from the treasury, but in consequence of appropriations made by law; and a regular statement and account of the receipts and expenditures of all public money shall be published from time to time.

No title of nobility shall be granted by the United States: and no person holding any office of profit or trust under them, shall, without the consent of the Congress, accept of any present, emolument, office, or title, of any kind whatever, from any king, prince, or foreign state.

**Section 10** No State shall enter into any treaty, alliance, or confederation; grant letters of marque and reprisal; coin money; emit bills of credit; make anything but gold and silver coin a tender in payment of debts; pass any bill of attainder, ex post facto law, or law impairing the obligation of contracts, or grant any title of nobility.

No States shall, without the consent of Congress, lay any imposts or duties on imports or exports, except what may be absolutely necessary for executing its inspection laws: and the net produce of all duties and imposts, laid by any State on imports or exports, shall be for the use of the treasury of the United States; and all such laws shall be subject to the revision and control of the Congress.

No State shall, without the consent of Congress, lay any duty of tonnage, keep troops or ships of war in time of peace, enter into any agreement or compact with another State, or with a foreign power, or engage in war, unless actually invaded, or in such imminent danger as will not admit of delay.

## ARTICLE II

**Section 1** The executive power shall be vested in a President of the United States of America. He shall hold his office during the term of four years, and, together with the Vice-President, chosen for the same term, be elected as follows:

Each State shall appoint, in such manner as the legislature thereof may direct, a number of electors, equal to the whole number of Senators and Representatives to which the State may be entitled in the Congress; but no Senator or Representative, or person holding an office of trust or profit under the United States, shall be appointed an elector.

*The electors shall meet in their respective States, and vote by ballot for two persons, of whom one at least shall not be an inhabitant of the same State with themselves. And they shall make a list of all the persons voted for, and of the number of votes for each; which list they shall sign and certify, and transmit sealed to the seat of government of the United States, directed to the President of the Senate. The President of the Senate shall, in the presence of the Senate and House of Representatives, open all the certificates, and the votes shall then be counted. The person having the greatest number of votes shall be the President, if such number be a majority of the whole number of electors appointed; and if there be more than one who have such majority, and have an equal number of votes, then the House of Representatives shall immediately choose by ballot one of them for President; and if no person have a majority, then from the five highest on the list said house shall in like manner choose the President. But in choosing the President the votes shall be taken by States, the representation from each State having one vote; a quorum for this purpose shall consist of a member or members from two-thirds of the States, and a majority of all the States shall be necessary to a choice. In every case, after the choice of the President, the person having the greatest number of votes of the electors shall be the Vice-President. But if there should remain two or more who have equal votes, the Senate shall choose from them by ballot the Vice-President.*

The Congress may determine the time of choosing the electors and the day on which they shall give their votes; which day shall be the same throughout the United States.

No person except a natural-born citizen, *or a citizen of the United States at the time of the adoption of this Constitution,* shall be eligible to the office of President; neither shall any person be eligible to that office who shall not have attained to the age of thirty-five years, and been fourteen years a resident within the United States.

In case of the removal of the President from office or of his death, resignation, or inability to discharge the powers and duties of the said office, the same shall devolve on the Vice-President, and the Congress may by law provide for the case of removal, death, resignation, or inability, both of the President and Vice-President, declaring what officer shall then act as President, and such officer shall act accordingly, until the disability be removed, or a President shall be elected.

The President shall, at stated times, receive for his services a compensation, which shall neither be increased nor diminished during the period for which he shall have been elected, and he shall not receive within that period any other emolument from the United States, or any of them.

Before he enter on the execution of his office, he shall take the following oath or affirmation:—"I do solemnly swear (or affirm) that I will faithfully execute the office of the President of the United States, and will to the best of my ability preserve, protect and defend the Constitution of the United States."

**Section 2**   The President shall be commander in chief of the army and navy of the United States, and of the militia of the several States, when called into the actual service of the United States; he may require the opinion, in writing, of the principal officer in each of the executive departments, upon any subject relating to the duties of their respective offices, and he shall have power to grant reprieves and pardons for offenses against the United States, except in cases of impeachment.

He shall have power, by and with the advice and consent of the Senate, to make treaties, provided two-thirds of the Senators present concur; and he shall nominate, and by and with the advice and consent of the Senate, shall appoint ambassadors, other public ministers and consuls, judges of the Supreme Court, and all other officers of the United States, whose appointments are not herein otherwise provided for, and which shall be established by law: but Congress may by law vest the appointment of such inferior officers, as they think proper, in the President alone, in the courts of law, or in the heads of departments.

The President shall have power to fill up all vacancies that may happen during the recess of the Senate, by granting commissions which shall expire at the end of their next session.

**Section 3**   He shall from time to time give to the Congress information of the state of the Union, and recommend to their consideration such measures as he shall judge necessary and expedient; he may, on extraordinary occasions, convene both houses, or either of them, and in case of disagreement between them, with respect to the time of adjournment, he may adjourn them to such time as he shall think proper; he shall receive ambassadors and other public ministers; he shall take care that the laws be faithfully executed, and shall commission all the officers of the United States.

**Section 4**   The President, Vice-President and all civil officers of the United States shall be removed from office on impeachment for, and on conviction of, treason, bribery, or other high crimes and misdemeanors.

### ARTICLE III

**Section 1**   The judicial power of the United States shall be vested in one Supreme Court, and in such inferior courts as the Congress may from time to time ordain and establish. The judges, both of the Supreme and inferior courts, shall hold their offices during good behavior, and shall, at stated times, receive for their services a compensation which shall not be diminished during their continuance in office.

**Section 2**   The judicial power shall extend to all cases, in law and equity, arising under this Constitution, the laws of the United States, and treaties made, or which shall be made, under their authority—to all cases affecting ambassadors, other public ministers and consuls;—to all cases of admiralty and maritime jurisdiction;—to controversies to which the United States shall be a party;—to controversies between two or more States;—*between a State and citizens of another State;*—between citizens of different States; —between citizens of the same State claiming lands under grants of different States, and between a State, or the citizens thereof, and foreign states, citizens or subjects.

In all cases affecting ambassadors, other public ministers and consuls, and those in which a State shall be party, the Supreme Court shall have original jurisdiction. In all the other cases before mentioned, the Supreme Court shall have appellate jurisdiction, both as to law and fact, with such exceptions, and under such regulations, as the Congress shall make.

The trial of all crimes, except in cases of impeachment, shall be by jury; and such trial shall be held in the State where said crimes shall have been committed; but when not committed within any State, the trial shall be at such place or places as the Congress may by law have directed.

**Section 3** Treason against the United States shall consist only in levying war against them, or in adhering to their enemies, giving them aid and comfort. No person shall be convicted of treason unless on the testimony of two witnesses to the same overt act, or on confession in open court.

The Congress shall have power to declare the punishment of treason, but no attainder of treason shall work corruption of blood, or forfeiture except during the life of the person attainted.

### ARTICLE IV

**Section 1** Full faith and credit shall be given in each State to the public acts, records, and judicial proceedings of every other State. And the Congress may by general laws prescribe the manner in which such acts, records, and proceedings shall be proved, and the effect thereof.

**Section 2** The citizens of each State shall be entitled to all privileges and immunities of citizens in the several States.

A person charged in any State with treason, felony, or other crime, who shall flee from justice, and be found in another State, shall on demand of the executive authority of the State from which he fled, be delivered up, to be removed to the State having jurisdiction of the crime.

*No person held to service or labor in one State, under the laws thereof, escaping into another, shall,* *in consequence of any law or regulation therein, be discharged from such service or labor, but shall be delivered up on claim of the party to whom such service or labor may be due.*

**Section 3** New States may be admitted by the Congress into this Union; but no new State shall be formed or erected within the jurisdiction of any other State; nor any State be formed by the junction of two or more States, or parts of States, without the consent of the legislatures of the States concerned as well as of the Congress.

The Congress shall have power to dispose of and make all needful rules and regulations respecting the territory or other property belonging to the United States; and nothing in this Constitution shall be so construed as to prejudice any claims of the United States, or of any particular State.

**Section 4** The United States shall guarantee to every State in this Union a republican form of government, and shall protect each of them against invasion; and on application of the legislature, or of the executive (when the legislature cannot be convened), against domestic violence.

### ARTICLE V

The Congress, whenever two-thirds of both houses shall deem it necessary, shall propose amendments to this Constitution, or, on the application of the legislatures of two-thirds of the several States, shall call a convention for proposing amendments, which, in either case, shall be valid to all intents and purposes, as part of this Constitution, when ratified by the legislatures of three-fourths of the several States, or by conventions in three-fourths thereof, as the one or the other mode of ratification may be proposed by the Congress; provided *that no amendments which may be made prior to the year one thousand eight hundred and eight shall in any manner affect the first and fourth classes in the ninth section of the first article; and* that no State, without its consent, shall be deprived of its equal suffrage in the Senate.

### ARTICLE VI

All debts contracted and engagements entered into, before the adoption of this Constitution, shall be as valid against the United States under this Constitution, as under the Confederation.

This Constitution, and the laws of the United States which shall be made in pursuance thereof; and all treaties made, or which shall be made, under the authority of the United States, shall be the supreme law of the land; and the judges in every State shall be bound thereby, anything in the Constitution or laws of any State to the contrary notwithstanding.

The Senators and Representatives before mentioned, and the members of the several State legislatures, and all executive and judicial officers, both of the United States and of the several States, shall be bound by oath or affirmation to support this Constitution; but no religious test shall ever be required as a qualification to any office or public trust under the United States.

### ARTICLE VII

The ratification of the conventions of nine States shall be sufficient for the establishment of this Constitution between the States so ratifying the same.

Done in Convention by the unanimous consent of the States present, the seventeenth day of September in the year of our Lord one thousand seven hundred and eighty-seven and of the Independence of the United States of America the twelfth. In witness whereof we have hereunto subscribed our names.

# AMENDMENTS TO THE CONSTITUTION*

### AMENDMENT I [1791]

Congress shall make no law respecting an establishment of religion, or prohibiting the free exercise thereof; or abridging the freedom of speech, or of the press; or the right of the people peaceably to assemble, and to petition the government for a redress of grievances.

### AMENDMENT II [1791]

A well-regulated militia being necessary to the security of a free State, the right of the people to keep and bear arms shall not be infringed.

### AMENDMENT III [1791]

No soldier shall, in time of peace, be quartered in any house without the consent of the owner, nor in time of war, but in a manner to be prescribed by law.

### AMENDMENT IV [1791]

The right of the people to be secure in their persons, houses, papers, and effects, against unreasonable searches and seizures, shall not be violated, and no warrants shall issue but upon probable cause, supported by oath or affirmation, and particularly describing the place to be searched, and the persons or things to be seized.

### AMENDMENT V [1791]

No person shall be held to answer for a capital or otherwise infamous crime, unless on a presentment or indictment of a grand jury, except in cases arising in the land or naval forces, or in the militia, when in actual service in time of war or public danger; nor shall any person be subject for the same offense to be twice put in jeopardy of life or limb; nor shall be compelled in any criminal case to be a witness against himself, nor be deprived of life, liberty, or property, without due process of law; nor shall private property be taken for public use without just compensation.

### AMENDMENT VI [1791]

In all criminal prosecutions, the accused shall enjoy the right to a speedy and public trial, by an impartial jury of the State and district wherein the crime shall have been committed, which district shall have been previously ascertained by law, and to be informed of the nature and cause of the accusation; to be confronted with the witnesses against him; to have compulsory process for obtaining witnesses in his favor, and to have the assistance of counsel for his defense.

### AMENDMENT VII [1791]

In suits at common law, where the value in controversy shall exceed twenty dollars, the right of trial by jury shall be preserved, and no fact tried by a jury shall be otherwise reexamined in any court of the United States, than according to the rules of the common law.

### AMENDMENT VIII [1791]

Excessive bail shall not be required, nor excessive fines imposed, nor cruel and unusual punishments inflicted.

---

* The first ten Amendments are known as the Bill of Rights.

## AMENDMENT IX [1791]

The enumeration in the Constitution, of certain rights, shall not be construed to deny or disparage others retained by the people.

## AMENDMENT X [1791]

The powers not delegated to the United States by the Constitution, nor prohibited by it to the States, are reserved to the States respectively, or to the people.

## AMENDMENT XI [1798]

The judicial power of the United States shall not be construed to extend to any suit in law or equity, commenced or prosecuted against one of the United States by citizens of another State, or by citizens or subjects of any foreign state.

## AMENDMENT XII [1804]

The electors shall meet in their respective States, and vote by ballot for President and Vice-President, one of whom, at least, shall not be an inhabitant of the same State with themselves; they shall name in their ballots the person voted for as President, and in distinct ballots the person voted for as Vice-President, and they shall make distinct lists of all persons voted for as President, and of all persons voted for as Vice-President, and of the number of votes for each, which lists they shall sign and certify, and transmit sealed to the seat of government of the United States, directed to the President of the Senate;—the President of the Senate shall, in the presence of the Senate and House of Representatives, open all the certificates and the votes shall then be counted;—the person having the greatest number of votes for President shall be the President, if such number be a majority of the whole number of electors appointed; and if no person have such majority, then from the persons having the highest numbers not exceeding three on the list of those voted for as President, the House of Representatives shall choose immediately, by ballot, the President. But in choosing the President, the votes shall be taken by States, the representation from each State having one vote; a quorum for this purpose shall consist of a member or members from two-thirds of the States, and a majority of all the States shall be necessary to a choice. And if the House of Representatives shall not choose a President whenever the right of choice shall devolve upon them, before *the fourth day of March* next following, then the Vice-President shall act as President, as in the case of the death or other constitutional disability of the President.

The person having the greatest number of votes as Vice-President shall be the Vice-President, if such number be a majority of the whole number of electors appointed; and if no person have a majority, then from the two highest numbers on the list the Senate shall choose the Vice-President; a quorum for the purpose shall consist of two-thirds of the whole number of Senators, and a majority of the whole number shall be necessary to a choice. But no person constitutionally ineligible to the office of President shall be eligible to that of Vice-President of the United States.

## AMENDMENT XIII [1865]

**Section 1** Neither slavery nor involuntary servitude, except as a punishment for crime whereof the party shall have been duly convicted, shall exist within the United States, or any place subject to their jurisdiction.

**Section 2** Congress shall have power to enforce this article by appropriate legislation.

## AMENDMENT XIV [1868]

**Section 1** All persons born or naturalized in the United States, and subject to the jurisdiction thereof, are citizens of the United States and of the State wherein they reside. No State shall make or enforce any law which shall abridge the privileges or immunities of citizens of the United States; nor shall any State deprive any person of life, liberty, or property, wihtout due process of law; nor deny to any person within its jurisdiction the equal protection of the laws.

**Section 2** Representatives shall be apportioned among the several States according to their respective numbers, counting the whole number of persons in each State, excluding Indians not taxed. But when the right to vote at any election for the choice of Electors for President and Vice-President of the United States, Representatives in Congress, the executive and judicial officers of a State, or the members of the legislature thereof, is denied to any of the male inhabitants of such State, being twenty-one years of age and citizens of the United States, or in any way abridged, except for participation in rebellion, or other crime, the basis of representation therein shall be reduced in the proportion which the number of such male citizens shall bear to the whole number of male citizens twenty-one years of age in such State.

**Section 3** No person shall be a Senator or Representative in Congress, or Elector of President and Vice-President, or hold any office, civil or military, under the United States, or under any State, who, having previously taken an oath, as a member of Congress, or as an officer of the United States, or as a member of any State legislature, or as an executive or judicial officer of any State, to support the Constitution of the United States, shall have engaged in insurrection or rebellion against the same, or given aid or comfort to the enemies thereof. Congress may, by a vote of two-thirds of each house, remove such disability.

**Section 4**    The validity of the public debt of the United States, authorized by law, including debts incurred for payment of pensions and bounties for services in suppressing insurrection or rebellion, shall not be questioned. But neither the United States nor any State shall assume or pay any debt or obligation incurred in aid of insurrection or rebellion against the United States, or any claim for the loss of emancipation of any slave; but all such debts, obligations, and claims shall be held illegal and void.

**Section 5**    The Congress shall have power to enforce, by appropriate legislation, the provisions of this article.

### AMENDMENT XV [1870]

**Section 1**    The right of citizens of the United States to vote shall not be denied or abridged by the United States or by any State on account of race, color, or previous condition of servitude.

**Section 2**    The Congress shall have power to enforce this article by appropriate legislation.

### AMENDMENT XVI [1913]

The Congress shall have power to lay and collect taxes on incomes, from whatever source derived, without apportionment among the several States, and without regard to any census or enumeration.

### AMENDMENT XVII [1913]

**Section 1**    The Senate of the United States shall be composed of two Senators from each State, elected by the people thereof, for six years; and each Senator shall have one vote. The electors in each State shall have the qualifications requisite for electors of [voters for] the most numerous branch of the State legislatures.

**Section 2**    When vacancies happen in the representation of any State in the Senate, the executive authority of such State shall issue writs of election to fill such vacancies: Provided that the legislature of any State may empower the executive thereof to make temporary appointments until the people fill

the vacancies by election as the legislature may direct.

**Section 3**    This amendment shall not be so construed as to affect the election or term of any Senator chosen before it becomes valid as part of the Constitution.

### AMENDMENT XVIII [1919]

**Section 1**    After one year from the ratification of this article the manufacture, sale, or transportation of intoxicating liquors within, the importation thereof into, or the exportation thereof from the United States and all territory subject to the jurisdiction thereof, for beverage purposes, is hereby prohibited.

**Section 2**    The Congress and the several States shall have concurrent power to enforce this article by appropriate legislation.

**Section 3**    This article shall be inoperative unless it shall have been ratified as an amendment to the Constitution by the legislatures of the several States, as provided by the Constitution, within seven years from the date of the submission thereof to the States by the Congress.

### AMENDMENT XIX [1920]

**Section 1**    The right of citizens of the United States to vote shall not be denied or abridged by the United States or by any State on account of sex.

**Section 2**    The Congress shall have power to enforce this article by appropriate legislation.

### AMENDMENT XX [1933]

**Section 1**    The terms of the President and Vice-President shall end at noon on the 20th day of January, and the terms of Senators and Representatives at noon on the 3d day of January, of the years in which such terms would have ended if this article had not been ratified; and the terms of their successors shall then begin.

**Section 2**    The Congress shall assemble at least once in every year, and such meeting shall begin at noon on the 3d day of January, unless they shall by law appoint a different day.

**Section 3**    If, at the time fixed for the beginning of the term of the President, the President-elect shall have died, the Vice-President-elect shall become President. If a President shall not have been chosen before the time fixed for the beginning of his term, or if the President-elect shall have failed to qualify, then the President-elect shall act as President until a President shall have qualified; and the Congress may by law provide for the case wherein neither a President-elect nor a Vice-President-elect shall have qualified, declaring who shall then act as President, or the manner in which one who is to act shall be selected, and such persons shall act accordingly until a President or Vice-President shall have qualified.

**Section 4** The Congress may by law provide for the case of the death of any of the persons from whom the House of Representatives may choose a President whenever the right of choice shall have devolved upon them, and for the case of the death of any of the persons from whom the Senate may choose a Vice-President whenever the right of choice shall have devolved upon them.

**Section 5** Sections 1 and 2 shall take effect on the 15th day of October following the ratification of this article.

**Section 6** This article shall be inoperative unless it shall have been ratified as an amendment to the Constitution by the legislatures of three-fourths of the several States within seven years from the date of its submission.

## AMENDMENT XXI [1933]

**Section 1** The eighteenth article of amendment to the Constitution of the United States is hereby repealed.

**Section 2** The transportation or importation into any State, Territory, or Possession of the United States for delivery or use therein of intoxicating liquors, in violation of the laws thereof, is hereby prohibited.

**Section 3** This article shall be inoperative unless it shall have been ratified as an amendment to the Constitution by conventions in the several States, as provided in the Constitution, within seven years from the date of submission thereof to the States by the Congress.

## AMENDMENT XXII [1951]

**Section 1** No person shall be elected to the office of President more than twice, and no person who has held the office of President, or acted as President, for more than two years of a term to which some other person was elected President shall be elected to the office of President more than once. But this article shall not apply to any person holding the office of President when this article was proposed by the Congress, and shall not prevent any person who may be holding the office of President, or acting as President, during the term within which this article becomes operative from holding the office of Presi-

dent or acting as President during the remainder of such term.

**Section 2** This article shall be inoperative unless it shall have been ratified as an amendment to the Constitution by the legislatures of three-fourths of the several States within seven years from the date of its submission to the States by the Congress.

## AMENDMENT XXIII [1961]

**Section 1** The District constituting the seat of Government of the United States shall appoint in such manner as the Congress may direct:

A number of electors of President and Vice-President equal to the whole number of Senators and Representatives in Congress to which the District would be entitled if it were a State, but in no event more than the least populous State; they shall be in addition to those appointed by the States, but they shall be considered for the purposes of the election of President and Vice-President, to be electors appointed by a State; and they shall meet in the District and perform such duties as provided by the twelfth article of amendment.

**Section 2** The Congress shall have the power to enforce this article by appropriate legislation.

## AMENDMENT XXIV [1964]

**Section 1** The right of citizens of the United States to vote in any primary or other election for President or Vice-President, for electors for President or Vice-President, or for Senator or Representative in Congress, shall not be denied or abridged by the United States or any State by reason of failure to pay any poll tax or other tax.

**Section 2** The Congress shall have the power to enforce this article by appropriate legislation.

## AMENDMENT XXV [1967]

**Section 1** In case of the removal of the President from office or of his death or resignation, the Vice-President shall become President.

**Section 2** Whenever there is a vacancy in the office of the Vice-President, the President shall nominate a Vice-President who shall take office upon confirmation by a majority vote of both houses of Congress.

**Section 3** Whenever the President transmits to the President pro tempore of the Senate and the Speaker of the House of Representatives his written declaration that he is unable to discharge the powers and duties of his office, and until he transmits to them a written declaration to the contrary, such powers and duties shall be discharged by the Vice-President as Acting President.

**Section 4**    Whenever the Vice-President and a majority of either the principal officers of the executive departments or of such other body as Congress may by law provide, transmit to the President pro tempore of the Senate and the Speaker of the House of Representatives their written declaration that the President is unable to discharge the powers and duties of his office, the Vice-President shall immediately assume the powers and duties of the office as Acting President.

Thereafer, when the President transmits to the President pro tempore of the Senate and the Speaker of the House of Representatives his written declaration that no inability exists, he shall resume the powers and duties of his office unless the Vice-President and a majority of either the principal officers of the executive department[s] or of such other body as Congress may by law provide, transmit within four days to the President pro tempore of the Senate and the Speaker of the House of Representatives their written declaration that the President is unable to discharge the powers and duties of his office. Thereupon Congress shall decide the issue, assembling within forty-eight hours for that purpose if not in session. If the Congress, within twenty-one days after receipt of the latter written declaration, or, if Congress is not in session, within twenty-one days after Congress is required to assemble, determines by two-thirds vote of both Houses that the President is unable to discharge the powers and duties of his office, the Vice-President shall continue to discharge the same as Acting President; otherwise, the President shall resume the powers and duties of his office.

## AMENDMENT XXVI [1971]

**Section 1**    The right of citizens of the United States, who are eighteen years of age or older, to vote shall not be denied or abridged by the United States or by any State on account of age.

**Section 2**    The Congress shall have power to enforce this article by appropriate legislation.

# States of the United States

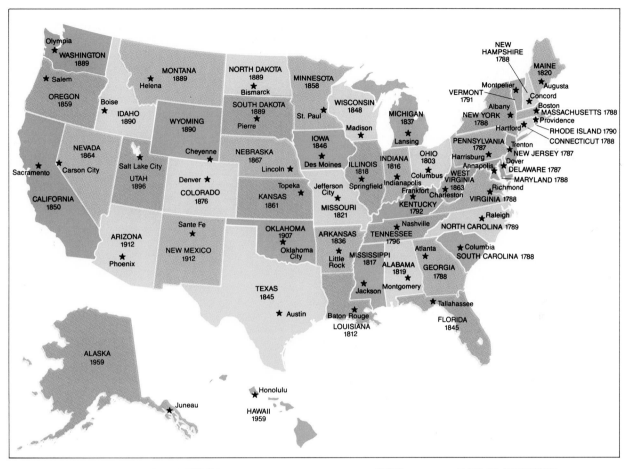

| STATE | DATE OF ADMISSION | STATE | DATE OF ADMISSION |
|---|---|---|---|
| Delaware | December 7, 1787 | Michigan | January 16, 1837 |
| Pennsylvania | December 12, 1787 | Florida | March 3, 1845 |
| New Jersey | December 18, 1787 | Texas | December 29, 1845 |
| Georgia | January 2, 1788 | Iowa | December 28, 1846 |
| Connecticut | January 9, 1788 | Wisconsin | May 29, 1848 |
| Massachusetts | February 6, 1788 | California | September 9, 1850 |
| Maryland | April 28, 1788 | Minnesota | May 11, 1858 |
| South Carolina | May 23, 1788 | Oregon | February 14, 1859 |
| New Hampshire | June 21, 1788 | Kansas | January 29, 1861 |
| Virginia | June 25, 1788 | West Virginia | June 19, 1863 |
| New York | July 26, 1788 | Nevada | October 31, 1864 |
| North Carolina | November 21, 1789 | Nebraska | March 1, 1867 |
| Rhode Island | May 29, 1790 | Colorado | August 1, 1876 |
| Vermont | March 4, 1791 | North Dakota | November 2, 1889 |
| Kentucky | June 1, 1792 | South Dakota | November 2, 1889 |
| Tennessee | June 1, 1796 | Montana | November 8, 1889 |
| Ohio | March 1, 1803 | Washington | November 11, 1889 |
| Louisiana | April 30, 1812 | Idaho | July 3, 1890 |
| Indiana | December 11, 1816 | Wyoming | July 10, 1890 |
| Mississippi | December 10, 1817 | Utah | January 4, 1896 |
| Illinois | December 3, 1818 | Oklahoma | November 16, 1907 |
| Alabama | December 14, 1819 | New Mexico | January 6, 1912 |
| Maine | March 15, 1820 | Arizona | February 14, 1912 |
| Missouri | August 10, 1821 | Alaska | January 3, 1959 |
| Arkansas | June 15, 1836 | Hawaii | August 21, 1959 |

# Territorial Expansion of the United States

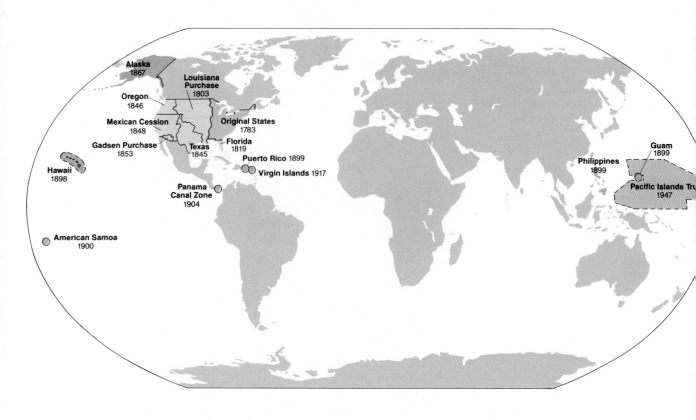

| DATE | TERRITORY | AREA (sq. mi.) | CUMULATIVE TOTAL (sq. mi.) |
|------|-----------|---------------:|---------------------------:|
| 1793 | Original States | 888,685 | 888,685 |
| 1803 | Louisiana Purchase | 827,192 | 1,715,877 |
| 1819 | Florida | 72,003 | 1,787,880 |
| 1845 | Texas | 390,143 | 2,178,023 |
| 1846 | Oregon | 285,580 | 2,463,603 |
| 1848 | Mexican cession | 529,017 | 2,992,620 |
| 1853 | Gadsden Purchase | 29,640 | 3,022,260 |
| 1867 | Alaska | 589,757 | 3,612,017 |
| 1898 | Hawaii | 6,450 | 3,618,467 |
| 1899 | Philippines | 115,600 | 3,734,067 |
| 1899 | Puerto Rico | 3,435 | 3,737,502 |
| 1899 | Guam | 212 | 3,737,714 |
| 1900 | American Samoa | 76 | 3,737,790 |
| 1904 | Panama Canal Zone | 553 | 3,738,343 |
| 1917 | Virgin Islands | 133 | 3,738,476 |
| 1947 | Pacific Islands Trust | 8,489 | 3,746,965 |
|      | All Others | 46 | 3,747,011 |

# Presidential Elections

| YEAR | CANDIDATES | PARTIES | % OF POPULAR VOTE*† | ELECTORAL VOTE‡ | % VOTER PARTICIPATION† |
|---|---|---|---|---|---|
| 1789 | GEORGE WASHINGTON | No party designations | | 69 | |
| | John Adams | | | 34 | |
| | Other candidates | | | 35 | |
| 1792 | GEORGE WASHINGTON | No party designations | | 132 | |
| | John Adams | | | 77 | |
| | George Clinton | | | 50 | |
| | Other candidates | | | 5 | |
| 1796 | JOHN ADAMS | Federalist | | 71 | |
| | Thomas Jefferson | Democratic-Republican | | 68 | |
| | Thomas Pinckney | Federalist | | 59 | |
| | Aaron Burr | Democratic-Republican | | 30 | |
| | Other candidates | | | 48 | |
| 1800 | THOMAS JEFFERSON | Democratic-Republican | | 73 | |
| | Aaron Burr | Democratic-Republican | | 73 | |
| | John Adams | Federalist | | 65 | |
| | Charles C. Pinckney | Federalist | | 64 | |
| | John Jay | Federalist | | 1 | |
| 1804 | THOMAS JEFFERSON | Democratic-Republican | | 162 | |
| | Charles C. Pinckney | Federalist | | 14 | |
| 1808 | JAMES MADISON | Democratic-Republican | | 122 | |
| | Charles C. Pinckney | Federalist | | 47 | |
| | George Clinton | Democratic-Republican | | 6 | |
| 1812 | JAMES MADISON | Democratic-Republican | | 128 | |
| | DeWitt Clinton | Federalist | | 89 | |
| 1816 | JAMES MONROE | Democratic-Republican | | 183 | |
| | Rufus King | Federalist | | 34 | |
| 1820 | JAMES MONROE | Democratic-Republican | | 231 | |
| | John Quincy Adams | Independent Republican | | 1 | |
| 1824 | JOHN QUINCY ADAMS | Democratic-Republican | 30.5 | 84 | 26.9 |
| | Andrew Jackson | Democratic-Republican | 43.1 | 99 | |
| | Henry Clay | Democratic-Republican | 13.2 | 37 | |
| | William H. Crawford | Democratic-Republican | 13.1 | 41 | |
| 1828 | ANDREW JACKSON | Democratic | 56.0 | 178 | 57.6 |
| | John Quincy Adams | National Republican | 44.0 | 83 | |
| 1832 | ANDREW JACKSON | Democratic | 54.5 | 219 | 55.4 |
| | Henry Clay | National Republican | 37.5 | 49 | |
| | William Wirt | Anti-Masonic | 8.0 | 7 | |
| | John Floyd | Democratic | | 11 | |
| 1836 | MARTIN VAN BUREN | Democratic | 50.9 | 170 | 57.8 |
| | William H. Harrison | Whig | | 73 | |
| | Hugh L. White | Whig | | 26 | |
| | Daniel Webster | Whig | 49.1 | 14 | |
| | W. P. Mangum | Whig | | 11 | |
| 1840 | WILLIAM H. HARRISON | Whig | 53.1 | 234 | 80.2 |
| | Martin Van Buren | Democratic | 46.9 | 60 | |
| 1844 | JAMES K. POLK | Democratic | 49.6 | 170 | 78.9 |
| | Henry Clay | Whig | 48.1 | 105 | |
| | James G. Birney | Liberty | 2.3 | | |
| 1848 | ZACHARY TAYLOR | Whig | 47.4 | 163 | 72.7 |
| | Lewis Cass | Democratic | 42.5 | 127 | |
| | Martin Van Buren | Free Soil | 10.1 | | |
| 1852 | FRANKLIN PIERCE | Democratic | 50.9 | 254 | 69.6 |
| | Winfield Scott | Whig | 44.1 | 42 | |
| | John P. Hale | Free Soil | 5.0 | | |
| 1856 | JAMES BUCHANAN | Democratic | 45.3 | 174 | 78.9 |
| | John C. Frémont | Republican | 33.1 | 114 | |
| | Millard Fillmore | American | 21.6 | 8 | |

| YEAR | CANDIDATES | PARTIES | % OF POPULAR VOTE*† | ELECTORAL VOTE‡ | % VOTER PARTICIPATION† |
|---|---|---|---|---|---|
| 1860 | ABRAHAM LINCOLN | Republican | 39.8 | 180 | 81.2 |
| | Stephen A. Douglas | Democratic | 29.5 | 12 | |
| | John C. Breckinridge | Democratic | 18.1 | 72 | |
| | John Bell | Constitutional Union | 12.6 | 39 | |
| 1864 | ABRAHAM LINCOLN | Republican | 55.0 | 212 | 73.8 |
| | George B. McClellan | Democratic | 45.0 | 21 | |
| 1868 | ULYSSES S. GRANT | Republican | 52.7 | 214 | 78.1 |
| | Horatio Seymour | Democratic | 47.3 | 80 | |
| 1872 | ULYSSES S. GRANT | Republican | 55.6 | 286 | 71.3 |
| | Horace Greeley | Democratic | 43.9 | | |
| 1876 | RUTHERFORD B. HAYES | Republican | 48.0 | 185 | 81.8 |
| | Samuel J. Tilden | Democratic | 51.0 | 184 | |
| 1880 | JAMES A. GARFIELD | Republican | 48.5 | 214 | 79.4 |
| | Winfield S. Hancock | Democratic | 48.1 | 155 | |
| | James B. Weaver | Greenback-Labor | 3.4 | | |
| 1884 | GROVER CLEVELAND | Democratic | 48.5 | 219 | 77.5 |
| | James G. Blaine | Republican | 48.2 | 182 | |
| 1888 | BENJAMIN HARRISON | Republican | 47.9 | 233 | 79.3 |
| | Grover Cleveland | Democratic | 48.6 | 168 | |
| 1892 | GROVER CLEVELAND | Democratic | 46.1 | 277 | 74.7 |
| | Benjamin Harrison | Republican | 43.0 | 145 | |
| | James B. Weaver | People's | 8.5 | 22 | |
| 1896 | WILLIAM McKINLEY | Republican | 51.1 | 271 | 79.3 |
| | William J. Bryan | Democratic | 47.7 | 176 | |
| 1900 | WILLIAM McKINLEY | Republican | 51.7 | 292 | 73.2 |
| | William J. Bryan | Democratic; Populist | 45.5 | 155 | |
| 1904 | THEODORE ROOSEVELT | Republican | 57.4 | 336 | 65.2 |
| | Alton B. Parker | Democratic | 37.6 | 140 | |
| | Eugene V. Debs | Socialist | 3.0 | | |
| 1908 | WILLIAM H. TAFT | Republican | 51.6 | 321 | 65.4 |
| | William J. Bryan | Democratic | 43.1 | 162 | |
| | Eugene V. Debs | Socialist | 2.8 | | |
| 1912 | WOODROW WILSON | Democratic | 41.9 | 435 | 58.8 |
| | Theodore Roosevelt | Progressive | 27.4 | 88 | |
| | William H. Taft | Republican | 23.2 | 8 | |
| | Eugene V. Debs | Socialist | 6.0 | | |
| 1916 | WOODROW WILSON | Democratic | 49.4 | 277 | 61.6 |
| | Charles E. Hughes | Republican | 46.2 | 254 | |
| | A. L. Benson | Socialist | 3.2 | | |
| 1920 | WARREN G. HARDING | Republican | 60.4 | 404 | 49.2 |
| | James M. Cox | Democratic | 34.2 | 127 | |
| | Eugene V. Debs | Socialist | 3.4 | | |
| 1924 | CALVIN COOLIDGE | Republican | 54.0 | 382 | 48.9 |
| | John W. Davis | Democratic | 28.8 | 136 | |
| | Robert M. La Follette | Progressive | 16.6 | 13 | |
| 1928 | HERBERT C. HOOVER | Republican | 58.2 | 444 | 56.9 |
| | Alfred E. Smith | Democratic | 40.9 | 87 | |
| 1932 | FRANKLIN D. ROOSEVELT | Democratic | 57.4 | 472 | 56.9 |
| | Herbert C. Hoover | Republican | 39.7 | 59 | |
| 1936 | FRANKLIN D. ROOSEVELT | Democratic | 60.8 | 523 | 61.0 |
| | Alfred M. Landon | Republican | 36.5 | 8 | |
| 1940 | FRANKLIN D. ROOSEVELT | Democratic | 54.8 | 449 | 62.5 |
| | Wendell L. Willkie | Republican | 44.8 | 82 | |
| 1944 | FRANKLIN D. ROOSEVELT | Democratic | 53.5 | 432 | 55.9 |
| | Thomas E. Dewey | Republican | 46.0 | 99 | |
| 1948 | HARRY S TRUMAN | Democratic | 49.6 | 303 | 53.0 |
| | Thomas E. Dewey | Republican | 45.1 | 189 | |

| YEAR | CANDIDATES | PARTIES | % OF POPULAR VOTE*† | ELECTORAL VOTE‡ | % VOTER PARTICIPATION† |
|------|-----------|---------|---------------------|-----------------|------------------------|
| 1952 | DWIGHT D. EISENHOWER | Republican | 55.1 | 442 | 63.3 |
|      | Adlai E. Stevenson | Democratic | 44.4 | 89 | |
| 1956 | DWIGHT D. EISENHOWER | Republican | 57.6 | 457 | 60.6 |
|      | Adlai E. Stevenson | Democratic | 42.1 | 73 | |
| 1960 | JOHN F. KENNEDY | Democratic | 49.7 | 303 | 64.0 |
|      | Richard M. Nixon | Republican | 49.5 | 219 | |
| 1964 | LYNDON B. JOHNSON | Democratic | 61.1 | 486 | 61.7 |
|      | Barry M. Goldwater | Republican | 38.5 | 52 | |
| 1968 | RICHARD M. NIXON | Republican | 43.4 | 301 | 60.6 |
|      | Hubert H. Humphrey | Democratic | 42.7 | 191 | |
|      | George C. Wallace | American Independent | 13.5 | 46 | |
| 1972 | RICHARD M. NIXON | Republican | 60.7 | 520 | 55.5 |
|      | George S. McGovern | Democratic | 37.5 | 17 | |
| 1976 | JIMMY CARTER | Democratic | 50.1 | 297 | 54.3 |
|      | Gerald R. Ford | Republican | 48.0 | 240 | |
| 1980 | RONALD REAGAN | Republican | 50.7 | 489 | 53.0 |
|      | Jimmy Carter | Democratic | 41.0 | 49 | |
|      | John B. Anderson | Independent | 6.6 | 0 | |
| 1984 | RONALD REAGAN | Republican | 58.4 | 525 | 52.9 |
|      | Walter F. Mondale | Democratic | 41.6 | 13 | |

*Candidates receiving less than 2.5 percent of the popular vote have been omitted. Hence the percentage of popular vote may not total 100 percent.

†Prior to 1824, most presidential electors were chosen by state legislators rather than by popular vote.

‡Before the Twelfth Amendment was passed in 1804, the electoral college voted for two presidential candidates; the runner-up became the vice-president.

## Voter Participation

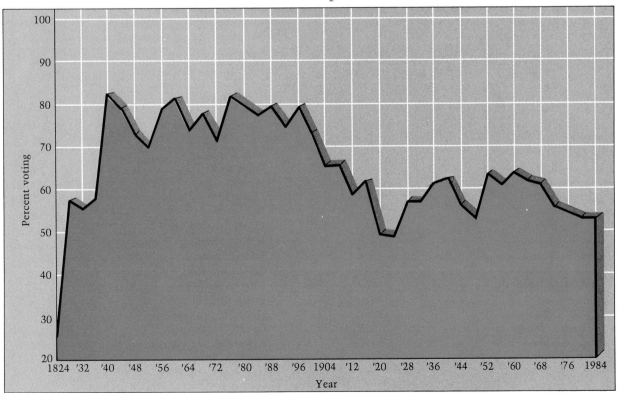

# Vice-Presidents, Cabinet Members, and Justices of the Supreme Court

## VICE-PRESIDENT

| | | | |
|---|---|---|---|
| John Adams | 1789–1797 | Adlai E. Stevenson | 1893–1897 |
| Thomas Jefferson | 1797–1801 | Garret A. Hobart | 1897–1899 |
| Aaron Burr | 1801–1805 | Theodore Roosevelt | 1901 |
| George Clinton | 1805–1812 | Charles W. Fairbanks | 1905–1909 |
| Elbridge Gerry | 1813–1817 | James S. Sherman | 1909–1913 |
| Daniel D. Tompkins | 1817–1825 | Thomas R. Marshall | 1913–1921 |
| John C. Calhoun | 1825–1833 | Calvin Coolidge | 1921–1923 |
| Martin Van Buren | 1833–1837 | Charles G. Dawes | 1925–1929 |
| Richard M. Johnson | 1837–1841 | Charles Curtis | 1929–1933 |
| John Tyler | 1841 | John Nance Garner | 1933–1941 |
| George M. Dallas | 1845–1849 | Henry A. Wallace | 1941–1945 |
| Millard Fillmore | 1849–1850 | Harry S Truman | 1945 |
| William R. King | 1853 | Alben W. Barkley | 1949–1953 |
| John C. Breckinridge | 1857–1861 | Richard M. Nixon | 1953–1961 |
| Hannibal Hamlin | 1861–1865 | Lyndon B. Johnson | 1961–1963 |
| Andrew Johnson | 1865 | Hubert H. Humphrey | 1965–1969 |
| Schuyler Colfax | 1869–1873 | Spiro T. Agnew | 1969–1973 |
| Henry Wilson | 1873–1877 | Gerald R. Ford | 1973–1974 |
| William A. Wheeler | 1877–1881 | Nelson Rockefeller | 1974–1977 |
| Chester A. Arthur | 1881 | Walter F. Mondale | 1977–1981 |
| Thomas A. Hendricks | 1885 | George Bush | 1981– |
| Levi P. Morton | 1889–1893 | | |

## SECRETARY OF STATE (1790–    )

| | | | |
|---|---|---|---|
| Thomas Jefferson | 1790 | Elihu B. Washburne | 1869 |
| Edmund Randolph | 1794 | Hamilton Fish | 1869 |
| Timothy Pickering | 1795 | William M. Evarts | 1877 |
| John Marshall | 1800 | James G. Blaine | 1881 |
| James Madison | 1801 | Frederick T. Frelinghuysen | 1881 |
| Robert Smith | 1809 | Thomas F. Bayard | 1885 |
| James Monroe | 1811 | James G. Blaine | 1889 |
| Richard Rush | 1817 | John W. Foster | 1892 |
| John Q. Adams | 1817 | Walter Q. Gresham | 1893 |
| Henry Clay | 1825 | Richard Olney | 1895 |
| Martin Van Buren | 1829 | John Sherman | 1897 |
| Edward Livingston | 1831 | William R. Day | 1897 |
| Louis McLane | 1833 | John M. Hay | 1898 |
| John Forsyth | 1834 | Elihu Root | 1905 |
| Daniel Webster | 1841 | Robert Bacon | 1909 |
| Hugh S. Legaré | 1843 | Philander C. Knox | 1909 |
| Abel P. Upshur | 1843 | William Jennings Bryan | 1913 |
| John C. Calhoun | 1844 | Robert Lansing | 1915 |
| James Buchanan | 1845 | Bainbridge Colby | 1920 |
| John M. Clayton | 1849 | Charles E. Hughes | 1921 |
| Daniel Webster | 1850 | Frank B. Kellogg | 1925 |
| Edward Everett | 1852 | Henry L. Stimson | 1929 |
| William L. Marcy | 1853 | Cordell Hull | 1933 |
| Lewis Cass | 1857 | Edward R. Stettinius, Jr. | 1944 |
| Jeremiah S. Black | 1860 | James F. Byrnes | 1945 |
| William H. Seward | 1861 | George C. Marshall | 1947 |

## SECRETARY OF STATE *(continued)*

| | | | |
|---|---|---|---|
| Dean G. Acheson | 1949 | Henry A. Kissinger | 1973 |
| John Foster Dulles | 1953 | Cyrus R. Vance | 1977 |
| Christian A. Herter | 1959 | Edmund S. Muskie | 1980 |
| Dean Rusk | 1961 | Alexander M. Haig, Jr. | 1981 |
| William P. Rogers | 1969 | George P. Shultz | 1982 |

## SECRETARY OF THE TREASURY (1789–   )

| | | | |
|---|---|---|---|
| Alexander Hamilton | 1789 | Walter Q. Gresham | 1884 |
| Oliver Wolcott | 1795 | Hugh McCulloch | 1884 |
| Samuel Dexter | 1801 | Daniel Manning | 1885 |
| Albert Gallatin | 1801 | Charles S. Fairchild | 1887 |
| George W. Campbell | 1814 | William Windom | 1889 |
| Alexander J. Dallas | 1814 | Charles Foster | 1891 |
| William H. Crawford | 1816 | John G. Carlisle | 1893 |
| Richard Rush | 1825 | Lyman J. Gage | 1897 |
| Samuel D. Ingham | 1829 | Leslie M. Shaw | 1902 |
| Louis McLane | 1831 | George B. Cortelyou | 1907 |
| William J. Duane | 1833 | Franklin MacVeagh | 1909 |
| Roger B. Taney | 1833 | William G. McAdoo | 1913 |
| Levi Woodbury | 1834 | Carter Glass | 1919 |
| Thomas Ewing | 1841 | David F. Houston | 1919 |
| Walter Forward | 1841 | Andrew W. Mellon | 1921 |
| John C. Spencer | 1843 | Ogden L. Mills | 1932 |
| George M. Bibb | 1844 | William H. Woodin | 1933 |
| Robert J. Walker | 1845 | Henry Morgenthau, Jr. | 1934 |
| William M. Meredith | 1849 | Fred M. Vinson | 1945 |
| Thomas Corwin | 1850 | John W. Snyder | 1946 |
| James Guthrie | 1853 | George M. Humphrey | 1953 |
| Howell Cobb | 1857 | Robert B. Anderson | 1957 |
| Philip F. Thomas | 1860 | C. Douglas Dillon | 1961 |
| John A. Dix | 1861 | Henry H. Fowler | 1965 |
| Salmon P. Chase | 1861 | Joseph W. Barr | 1968 |
| William P. Fessenden | 1864 | David M. Kennedy | 1969 |
| Hugh McCulloch | 1865 | John B. Connally | 1970 |
| George S. Boutwell | 1869 | George P. Shultz | 1972 |
| William A. Richardson | 1873 | William E. Simon | 1974 |
| Benjamin H. Bristow | 1874 | W. Michael Blumenthal | 1977 |
| Lot M. Morrill | 1876 | G. William Miller | 1979 |
| John Sherman | 1877 | Donald T. Regan | 1981 |
| William Windom | 1881 | James A. Baker | 1985 |
| Charles J. Folger | 1881 | | |

## SECRETARY OF WAR (1789–1947)

| | | | |
|---|---|---|---|
| Henry Knox | 1789 | John Armstrong | 1813 |
| Timothy Pickering | 1795 | James Monroe | 1814 |
| James McHenry | 1796 | William H. Crawford | 1815 |
| John Marshall | 1800 | Isaac Shelby | 1817 |
| Samuel Dexter | 1800 | George Graham | 1817 |
| Roger Griswold | 1801 | John C. Calhoun | 1817 |
| Henry Dearborn | 1801 | James Barbour | 1825 |
| William Eustis | 1809 | Peter B. Porter | 1828 |

## SECRETARY OF WAR (continued)

| | | | |
|---|---|---|---|
| John H. Eaton | 1829 | George W. McCrary | 1877 |
| Lewis Cass | 1831 | Alexander Ramsey | 1879 |
| Benjamin F. Butler | 1837 | Robert T. Lincoln | 1881 |
| Joel R. Poinsett | 1837 | William C. Endicott | 1885 |
| John Bell | 1841 | Redfield Proctor | 1889 |
| John McLean | 1841 | Stephen B. Elkins | 1891 |
| John C. Spencer | 1841 | Daniel S. Lamont | 1893 |
| James M. Porter | 1843 | Russell A. Alger | 1897 |
| William Wilkins | 1844 | Elihu Root | 1899 |
| William L. Marcy | 1845 | William H. Taft | 1904 |
| George W. Crawford | 1849 | Luke E. Wright | 1908 |
| Charles M. Conrad | 1850 | Jacob M. Dickinson | 1909 |
| Jefferson Davis | 1853 | Henry L. Stimson | 1911 |
| John B. Floyd | 1857 | Lindley M. Garrison | 1913 |
| Joseph Holt | 1861 | Newton D. Baker | 1916 |
| Simon Cameron | 1861 | John W. Weeks | 1921 |
| Edwin M. Stanton | 1862 | Dwight F. Davis | 1925 |
| Ulysses S. Grant | 1867 | James W. Good | 1929 |
| Lorenzo Thomas | 1868 | Patrick J. Hurley | 1929 |
| John M. Schofield | 1868 | George H. Dern | 1933 |
| John A. Rawlins | 1869 | Harry A. Woodring | 1936 |
| William T. Sherman | 1869 | Henry L. Stimson | 1940 |
| William W. Belknap | 1869 | Robert P. Patterson | 1945 |
| Alphonso Taft | 1876 | Kenneth C. Royall | 1947 |
| James D. Cameron | 1876 | | |

## SECRETARY OF THE NAVY (1798–1947)

| | | | |
|---|---|---|---|
| Benjamin Stoddert | 1798 | Adolph E. Borie | 1869 |
| Robert Smith | 1801 | George M. Robeson | 1869 |
| Paul Hamilton | 1809 | Richard W. Thompson | 1877 |
| William Jones | 1813 | Nathan Goff, Jr. | 1881 |
| Benjamin Williams | | William H. Hunt | 1881 |
| Crowninshield | 1814 | William E. Chandler | 1881 |
| Smith Thompson | 1818 | William C. Whitney | 1885 |
| Samuel L. Southard | 1823 | Benjamin F. Tracy | 1889 |
| John Branch | 1829 | Hilary A. Herbert | 1893 |
| Levi Woodbury | 1831 | John D. Long | 1897 |
| Mahlon Dickerson | 1834 | William H. Moody | 1902 |
| James K. Paulding | 1838 | Paul Morton | 1904 |
| George E. Badger | 1841 | Charles J. Bonaparte | 1905 |
| Abel P. Upshur | 1841 | Victor H. Metcalf | 1907 |
| David Henshaw | 1843 | Truman H. Newberry | 1908 |
| Thomas W. Gilmer | 1844 | George von L. Meyer | 1909 |
| John Y. Mason | 1844 | Josephus Daniels | 1913 |
| George Bancroft | 1845 | Edwin Denby | 1921 |
| John Y. Mason | 1846 | Curtis D. Wilbur | 1924 |
| William B. Preston | 1849 | Charles Francis Adams | 1929 |
| William A. Graham | 1850 | Claude A. Swanson | 1933 |
| John P. Kennedy | 1852 | Charles Edison | 1940 |
| James C. Dobbin | 1853 | Frank Knox | 1940 |
| Isaac Toucey | 1857 | James V. Forrestal | 1945 |
| Gideon Welles | 1861 | | |

## SECRETARY OF DEFENSE (1947–  )

| | | | |
|---|---|---|---|
| James V. Forrestal | 1947 | Clark M. Clifford | 1968 |
| Louis A. Johnson | 1949 | Melvin R. Laird | 1969 |
| George C. Marshall | 1950 | Elliot L. Richardson | 1973 |
| Robert A. Lovett | 1951 | James R. Schlesinger | 1973 |
| Charles E. Wilson | 1953 | Donald H. Rumsfeld | 1975 |
| Neil H. McElroy | 1957 | Harold Brown | 1977 |
| Thomas S. Gates, Jr. | 1959 | Caspar W. Weinberger | 1981 |
| Robert S. McNamara | 1961 | | |

## POSTMASTER GENERAL (1789–1971)

| | | | |
|---|---|---|---|
| Samuel Osgood | 1789 | Walter Q. Gresham | 1883 |
| Timothy Pickering | 1791 | Frank Hatton | 1884 |
| Joseph Habersham | 1795 | William F. Vilas | 1885 |
| Gideon Granger | 1801 | Don M. Dickinson | 1888 |
| Return J. Meigs, Jr. | 1814 | John Wanamaker | 1889 |
| John McLean | 1823 | Wilson S. Bissel | 1893 |
| William T. Barry | 1829 | William L. Wilson | 1895 |
| Amos Kendall | 1835 | James A. Gary | 1897 |
| John M. Niles | 1840 | Charles E. Smith | 1898 |
| Francis Granger | 1841 | Henry C. Payne | 1902 |
| Charles A. Wickliff | 1841 | Robert J. Wynne | 1904 |
| Cave Johnson | 1845 | George B. Cortelyou | 1905 |
| Jacob Collamer | 1849 | George von L. Meyer | 1907 |
| Nathan K. Hall | 1850 | Frank H. Hitchcock | 1909 |
| Samuel D. Hubbard | 1852 | Albert S. Burleson | 1913 |
| James Campbell | 1853 | Will H. Hays | 1921 |
| Aaron V. Brown | 1857 | Hubert Work | 1922 |
| Joseph Holt | 1859 | Harary S. New | 1923 |
| Horatio King | 1861 | Walter F. Brown | 1929 |
| Montgomery Blair | 1861 | James A. Farley | 1933 |
| William Dennison | 1864 | Frank C. Walker | 1940 |
| Alexander W. Randall | 1866 | Robert E. Hannegan | 1945 |
| John A. J. Creswell | 1869 | Jesse M. Donaldson | 1947 |
| James W. Marshall | 1874 | A. E. Summerfield | 1953 |
| Marshall Jewell | 1874 | J. Edward Day | 1961 |
| James N. Tyner | 1876 | John A. Gronouski | 1963 |
| David M. Key | 1877 | Lawrence F. O'Brien | 1965 |
| Horace Maynard | 1880 | W. Marvin Watson | 1968 |
| Thomas L. James | 1881 | Winston M. Blount | 1969 |
| Timothy O. Howe | 1881 | | |

## ATTORNEY GENERAL (1789–  )

| | | | |
|---|---|---|---|
| Edmund Randolph | 1789 | William Wirt | 1817 |
| William Bradford | 1794 | John M. Berrien | 1829 |
| Charles Lee | 1795 | Roger B. Taney | 1831 |
| Theophilus Parsons | 1801 | Benjamin F. Butler | 1833 |
| Levi Lincoln | 1801 | Felix Grundy | 1838 |
| Robert Smith | 1805 | Henry D. Gilpin | 1840 |
| John Breckenridge | 1805 | John J. Crittenden | 1841 |
| Caesar A. Rodney | 1807 | Hugh S. Legaré | 1841 |
| William Pinkney | 1811 | John Nelson | 1843 |
| Richard Rush | 1814 | John Y. Mason | 1845 |

## ATTORNEY GENERAL (continued)

| | | | |
|---|---|---|---|
| Nathan Clifford | 1846 | George W. Wickersham | 1909 |
| Isaac Toucey | 1848 | J. C. McReynolds | 1913 |
| Reverdy Johnson | 1849 | Thomas W. Gregory | 1914 |
| John J. Crittenden | 1850 | A. Mitchell Palmer | 1919 |
| Caleb Cushing | 1853 | Harry M. Daugherty | 1921 |
| Jeremiah S. Black | 1857 | Harlan F. Stone | 1924 |
| Edwin M. Stanton | 1860 | John G. Sargent | 1925 |
| Edward Bates | 1861 | William D. Mitchell | 1929 |
| Titian J. Coffey | 1863 | Homer S. Cummings | 1933 |
| James Speed | 1864 | Frank Murphy | 1939 |
| Henry Stanbery | 1866 | Robert H. Jackson | 1940 |
| William M. Evarts | 1868 | Francis Biddle | 1941 |
| Ebenezer R. Hoar | 1869 | Tom C. Clark | 1945 |
| Amos T. Akerman | 1870 | J. Howard McGrath | 1949 |
| George H. Williams | 1871 | J. P. McGranery | 1952 |
| Edwards Pierrepont | 1875 | Herbert Brownell, Jr. | 1953 |
| Alphonso Taft | 1876 | William P. Rogers | 1957 |
| Charles Devens | 1877 | Robert F. Kennedy | 1961 |
| Wayne MacVeagh | 1881 | Nicholas de B. Katzenbach | 1964 |
| Benjamin H. Brewster | 1881 | Ramsey Clark | 1967 |
| Augustus H. Garland | 1885 | John N. Mitchell | 1969 |
| William H. H. Miller | 1889 | Richard G. Kleindienst | 1972 |
| Richard Olney | 1893 | Elliot L. Richardson | 1973 |
| Judson Harmon | 1895 | William B. Saxbe | 1974 |
| Joseph McKenna | 1897 | Edward H. Levi | 1975 |
| John W. Griggs | 1897 | Griffin B. Bell | 1977 |
| Philander C. Knox | 1901 | Benjamin R. Civiletti | 1979 |
| William H. Moody | 1904 | William French Smith | 1981 |
| Charles J. Bonaparte | 1907 | Edwin Meese | 1985 |

## SECRETARY OF THE INTERIOR (1849–   )

| | | | |
|---|---|---|---|
| Thomas Ewing | 1849 | Richard A. Ballinger | 1909 |
| Thomas M. T. McKennan | 1850 | Walter L. Fisher | 1911 |
| Alexander H. H. Stuart | 1850 | Franklin K. Lane | 1913 |
| Robert McClelland | 1853 | John B. Payne | 1920 |
| Jacob Thompson | 1857 | Albert B. Fall | 1921 |
| Caleb B. Smith | 1861 | Hubert Work | 1923 |
| John P. Usher | 1863 | Roy O. West | 1928 |
| James Harlan | 1865 | Ray L. Wilbur | 1929 |
| Orville H. Browning | 1866 | Harold L. Ickes | 1933 |
| Jacob D. Cox | 1869 | Julius A. Krug | 1946 |
| Columbus Delano | 1870 | Oscar L. Chapman | 1949 |
| Zachariah Chandler | 1875 | Douglas McKay | 1953 |
| Carl Schurz | 1877 | Fred A. Seaton | 1956 |
| Samuel J. Kirkwood | 1881 | Stewart L. Udall | 1961 |
| Henry M. Teller | 1881 | Walter J. Hickel | 1969 |
| Lucius Q. C. Lamar | 1885 | Rogers C. B. Morton | 1971 |
| William F. Vilas | 1888 | Stanley K. Hathaway | 1975 |
| John W. Noble | 1889 | Thomas S. Kleppe | 1975 |
| Hoke Smith | 1893 | Cecil D. Andrus | 1977 |
| David R. Francis | 1896 | James G. Watt | 1981 |
| Cornelius N. Bliss | 1897 | William C. Clark | 1984 |
| Ethan A. Hitchcock | 1899 | Donald Hodel | 1985 |
| James R. Garfield | 1907 | | |

## SECRETARY OF AGRICULTURE (1889– )

| | | | |
|---|---|---|---|
| Norman J. Colman | 1889 | Claude R. Wickard | 1940 |
| Jeremiah M. Rusk | 1889 | Clinton P. Anderson | 1945 |
| J. Sterling Morton | 1893 | Charles F. Brannon | 1948 |
| James Wilson | 1897 | Ezra Taft Benson | 1953 |
| David F. Houston | 1913 | Orville L. Freeman | 1961 |
| Edwin T. Meredith | 1920 | Clifford M. Hardin | 1969 |
| Henry C. Wallace | 1921 | Earl L. Butz | 1971 |
| Howard M. Gore | 1924 | John A. Knebel | 1976 |
| William M. Jardine | 1925 | Bob S. Bergland | 1977 |
| Arthur M. Hyde | 1929 | John R. Block | 1981 |
| Henry A. Wallace | 1933 | | |

## SECRETARY OF COMMERCE AND LABOR (1903–1913)

| | | | |
|---|---|---|---|
| George B. Cortelyou | 1903 | Oscar S. Straus | 1906 |
| Victor H. Metcalf | 1904 | Charles Nagel | 1909 |

## SECRETARY OF COMMERCE (1913– )

| | | | |
|---|---|---|---|
| William C. Redfield | 1913 | Frederick H. Mueller | 1959 |
| Joshua W. Alexander | 1919 | Luther H. Hodges | 1961 |
| Herbert C. Hoover | 1921 | John T. Connor | 1965 |
| William F. Whiting | 1928 | Alex B. Trowbridge | 1967 |
| Robert P. Lamont | 1929 | Cyrus R. Smith | 1968 |
| Roy D. Chapin | 1932 | Maurice H. Stans | 1969 |
| Daniel C. Roper | 1933 | Peter G. Peterson | 1972 |
| Harry L. Hopkins | 1939 | Frederick B. Dent | 1973 |
| Jesse Jones | 1940 | Rogers C. B. Morton | 1975 |
| Henry A. Wallace | 1945 | Elliot L. Richardson | 1976 |
| W. Averell Harriman | 1946 | Juanita M. Kreps | 1977 |
| Charles Sawyer | 1948 | Philip M. Klutznick | 1979 |
| Sinclair Weeks | 1953 | Malcolm Baldrige | 1981 |
| Lewis L. Strauss | 1958 | | |

## SECRETARY OF LABOR (1913– )

| | | | |
|---|---|---|---|
| William B. Wilson | 1913 | W. Willard Wirtz | 1962 |
| James J. Davis | 1921 | George P. Shultz | 1969 |
| William N. Doak | 1930 | James D. Hodgson | 1970 |
| Frances Perkins | 1933 | Peter J. Brennan | 1973 |
| L. B. Schwellenbach | 1945 | John T. Dunlop | 1975 |
| Maurice J. Tobin | 1948 | William J. Usery, Jr. | 1976 |
| Martin P. Durkin | 1953 | F. Ray Marshall | 1977 |
| James P. Mitchell | 1953 | Raymond J. Donovan | 1981 |
| Arthur J. Goldberg | 1961 | William Brock | 1985 |

## SECRETARY OF HEALTH, EDUCATION AND WELFARE (1953–1979)

| | | | |
|---|---|---|---|
| Oveta Culp Hobby | 1953 | Robert H. Finch | 1969 |
| Marion B. Folsom | 1955 | Elliot L. Richardson | 1970 |
| Arthur S. Flemming | 1958 | Caspar W. Weinberger | 1973 |
| Abraham A. Ribicoff | 1961 | Forrest David Matthews | 1975 |
| Anthony J. Celebrezze | 1962 | Joseph A. Califano, Jr. | 1977 |
| John W. Gardner | 1965 | Patricia Roberts Harris | 1979 |
| Wilbur J. Cohen | 1968 | | |

## SECRETARY OF HEALTH AND HUMAN SERVICES (1979– )

| | | | |
|---|---|---|---|
| Patricia Roberts Harris | 1979 | Margaret Heckler | 1983 |
| Richard S. Schweiker | 1981 | | |

## SECRETARY OF EDUCATION (1979– )

| | | | |
|---|---|---|---|
| Shirley Mount Hufstedler | 1979 | William Bennett | 1985 |
| Terrell H. Bell | 1981 | | |

## SECRETARY OF HOUSING AND URBAN DEVELOPMENT (1966–1981)

| | | | |
|---|---|---|---|
| Robert C. Weaver | 1966 | Carla Anderson Hills | 1975 |
| Robert C. Wood | 1969 | Patricia Roberts Harris | 1977 |
| George W. Romney | 1969 | Moon Landrieu | 1979 |
| James T. Lynn | 1973 | Samuel R. Pierce, Jr. | 1981 |

## SECRETARY OF TRANSPORTATION (1966– )

| | | | |
|---|---|---|---|
| Alan S. Boyd | 1966 | Brock Adams | 1977 |
| John A. Volpe | 1969 | Neil E. Goldschmidt | 1979 |
| Claude S. Brinegar | 1973 | Andrew L. Lewis, Jr. | 1981 |
| William T. Coleman, Jr. | 1975 | Elizabeth Dole | 1983 |

## SECRETARY OF ENERGY (1977– )

| | | | |
|---|---|---|---|
| James R. Schlesinger | 1977 | Donald Hodel | 1982 |
| Robert W. Duncan, Jr. | 1979 | John Herrington | 1985 |
| James B. Edwards | 1981 | | |

## JUSTICES OF THE UNITED STATES SUPREME COURT

### Chief Justices

| | | | |
|---|---|---|---|
| John Jay | 1789–1795 | Edward D. White | 1910–1921 |
| John Rutledge | 1795 | William H. Taft | 1921–1930 |
| Oliver Ellsworth | 1796–1799 | Charles E. Hughes | 1930–1941 |
| John Marshall | 1801–1835 | Harlan F. Stone | 1941–1946 |
| Roger B. Taney | 1836–1864 | Frederick M. Vinson | 1946–1953 |
| Salmon P. Chase | 1864–1873 | Earl Warren | 1953–1969 |
| Morrison R. Waite | 1874–1888 | Warren E. Burger | 1969– |
| Melville W. Fuller | 1888–1910 | | |

### Associate Justices

| | | | |
|---|---|---|---|
| John Rutledge | 789–1791 | William Johnson | 1804–1834 |
| William Cushing | 1789–1810 | Henry B. Livingston | 1806–1823 |
| James Wilson | 1789–1798 | Thomas Todd | 1807–1826 |
| John Blair | 1789–1796 | Joseph Story | 1811–1845 |
| James Iredell | 1790–1799 | Gabriel Duval | 1811–1836 |
| Thomas Johnson | 1791–1793 | Smith Thompson | 1823–1843 |
| William Paterson | 1793–1806 | Robert Trimble | 1826–1828 |
| Samuel Chase | 1796–1811 | John McLean | 1829–1861 |
| Bushrod Washington | 1798–1829 | Henry Baldwin | 1830–1844 |
| Alfred Moore | 1799–1804 | James M. Wayne | 1835–1867 |

## ASSOCIATE JUSTICES *(continued)*

| | | | |
|---|---|---|---|
| Philip P. Barbour | 1836–1841 | Joseph R. Lamar | 1911–1916 |
| John Catron | 1837–1865 | Mahlon Pitney | 1912–1922 |
| John McKinley | 1837–1852 | James C. McReynolds | 1914–1941 |
| Peter V. Daniel | 1841–1860 | Louis D. Brandeis | 1916–1939 |
| Samuel Nelson | 1845–1872 | John H. Clarke | 1916–1922 |
| Levi Woodbury | 1845–1851 | George Sutherland | 1922–1938 |
| Robert C. Grier | 1846–1870 | Pierce Butler | 1923–1939 |
| Benjamin R. Curtis | 1851–1857 | Edward T. Sanford | 1923–1930 |
| John A. Campbell | 1853–1861 | Harlan F. Stone | 1925–1941 |
| Nathan Clifford | 1858–1881 | Owen J. Roberts | 1930–1945 |
| Noah H. Swayne | 1862–1881 | Benjamin N. Cardozo | 1932–1938 |
| Samuel F. Miller | 1862–1890 | Hugo L. Black | 1937–1971 |
| David Davis | 1862–1877 | Stanley F. Reed | 1938–1957 |
| Stephen J. Field | 1863–1897 | Felix Frankfurter | 1939–1962 |
| William Strong | 1870–1880 | William O. Douglas | 1939–1975 |
| Joseph P. Bradley | 1870–1892 | Frank Murphy | 1940–1949 |
| Ward Hunt | 1873–1882 | Robert H. Jackson | 1941–1954 |
| John M. Harlan | 1877–1911 | James F. Byrnes | 1941–1942 |
| William B. Woods | 1880–1887 | Wiley B. Rutledge | 1943–1949 |
| Stanley Matthews | 1881–1889 | Harold H. Burton | 1945–1958 |
| Horace Gray | 1882–1902 | Tom C. Clark | 1949–1967 |
| Samuel Blatchford | 1882–1893 | Sherman Minton | 1949–1956 |
| Lucius Q. C. Lamar | 1888–1893 | John Marshall Harlan | 1955–1971 |
| David J. Brewer | 1889–1910 | William J. Brennan, Jr. | 1956– |
| Henry B. Brown | 1890–1906 | Charles E. Whittaker | 1957–1962 |
| George Shiras | 1892–1903 | Potter Stewart | 1958–1981 |
| Howell E. Jackson | 1893–1895 | Byron R. White | 1962– |
| Edward D. White | 1894–1910 | Arthur J. Goldberg | 1962–1965 |
| Rufus W. Peckham | 1896–1909 | Abe Fortas | 1965–1969 |
| Joseph McKenna | 1898–1925 | Thurgood Marshall | 1967– |
| Oliver W. Holmes | 1902–1932 | Harry A. Blackmun | 1970– |
| William R. Day | 1903–1922 | Lewis F. Powell, Jr. | 1972– |
| William H. Moody | 1906–1910 | William H. Rehnquist | 1972– |
| Horace H. Lurton | 1910–1914 | John Paul Stevens | 1975– |
| Charles E. Hughes | 1910–1916 | Sandra Day O'Connor | 1981– |
| Willis Van Devanter | 1910–1937 | | |

# Population of the United States

| YEAR | NUMBER OF STATES | POPULATION | PERCENT INCREASE | POPULATION PER SQUARE MILE |
|------|------------------|------------|------------------|----------------------------|
| 1790 | 13 | 3,929,214 | | 4.5 |
| 1800 | 16 | 5,308,483 | 35.1 | 6.1 |
| 1810 | 17 | 7,239,881 | 36.4 | 4.3 |
| 1820 | 23 | 9,638,453 | 33.1 | 5.5 |
| 1830 | 24 | 12,866,020 | 33.5 | 7.4 |
| 1840 | 26 | 17,069,453 | 32.7 | 9.8 |
| 1850 | 31 | 23,191,876 | 35.9 | 7.9 |
| 1860 | 33 | 31,443,321 | 35.6 | 10.6 |
| 1870 | 37 | 39,818,449 | 26.6 | 13.4 |
| 1880 | 38 | 50,155,783 | 26.0 | 16.9 |
| 1890 | 44 | 62,947,714 | 25.5 | 21.2 |
| 1900 | 45 | 75,994,575 | 20.7 | 25.6 |
| 1910 | 46 | 91,972,266 | 21.0 | 31.0 |
| 1920 | 48 | 105,710,620 | 14.9 | 35.6 |
| 1930 | 48 | 122,775,046 | 16.1 | 41.2 |
| 1940 | 48 | 131,669,275 | 7.2 | 44.2 |
| 1950 | 48 | 150,697,361 | 14.5 | 50.7 |
| 1960 | 50 | 179,323,175 | 19.0 | 50.6 |
| 1970 | 50 | 203,235,298 | 13.3 | 57.5 |
| 1980 | 50 | 226,545,805 | 11.5 | 64.1 |
| 1985 | 50 | 237,839,000 | — | 67.2 |

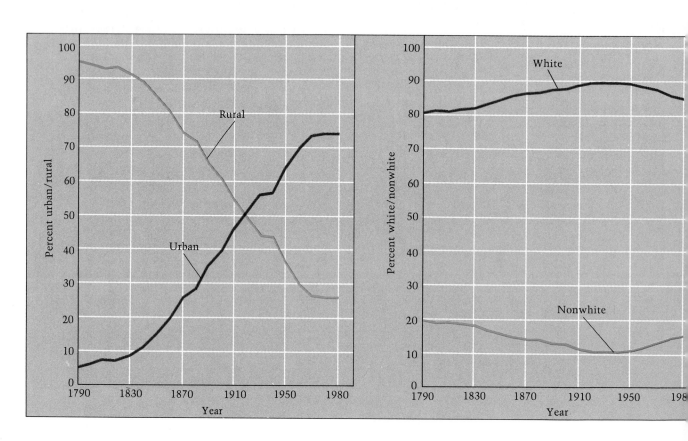

# Demographic Contours of the American People

| YEAR | LIFE EXPECTANCY FROM BIRTH | | AGE AT FIRST MARRIAGE (YEARS) | | NUMBER OF CHILDREN UNDER 5 PER 1000 WOMEN AGE 20–44 | AGE DISTRIBUTION % | | |
|------|-------|-------|------|--------|---------|-------|-------|------|
| | WHITE | BLACK | MALE | FEMALE | | UNDER 15 | 15–59 | OVER 59 |
| 1800 | | | | | 1,342 | | | |
| 1810 | | | | | 1,358 | | | |
| 1820 | | | | | 1,295 | | | |
| 1830 | | | | | 1,145 | | | |
| 1840 | | | | | 1,085 | | | |
| 1850 | | | | | 923 | 41.5 | 54.3 | 4.1 |
| 1860 | | | | | 929 | 40.5 | 55.1 | 4.3 |
| 1870 | | | | | 839 | 39.2 | 55.8 | 5.0 |
| 1880 | | | | | 822 | 38.1 | 56.3 | 5.6 |
| 1890 | | | 26.1 | 22.0 | 716 | 35.5 | 58.0 | 6.2 |
| 1900 | 47.6 | 33.0 | 25.9 | 21.9 | 688 | 34.4 | 59.0 | 6.4 |
| 1910 | 50.3 | 35.6 | 25.1 | 21.6 | 643 | 32.1 | 61.0 | 6.8 |
| 1920 | 54.9 | 45.3 | 24.6 | 21.2 | 604 | 31.8 | 60.6 | 7.5 |
| 1930 | 61.4 | 48.1 | 24.3 | 21.3 | 511 | 29.4 | 62.1 | 8.5 |
| 1940 | 64.2 | 53.1 | 24.3 | 21.5 | 429 | 25.0 | 64.5 | 10.4 |
| 1950 | 69.1 | 60.8 | 22.8 | 20.3 | 589 | 26.9 | 61.0 | 12.2 |
| 1960 | 70.6 | 63.6 | 22.8 | 20.3 | 737 | 31.1 | 55.7 | 13.2 |
| 1970 | 71.7 | 65.3 | 22.5 | 20.6 | 530 | 28.5 | 57.4 | 14.1 |
| 1980 | 74.4 | 69.8 | 23.6 | 21.8 | 440 | 22.6 | 61.6 | 15.7 |

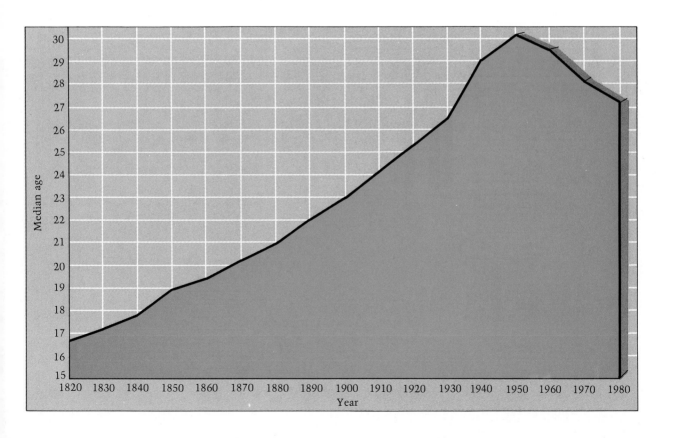

# National Origins of U.S. Immigrants, 1821–1980

| | | | EUROPE | | | | | |
| | | TOTAL EUROPE | NORTH AND WEST | EAST AND CENTRAL | SOUTH AND OTHER | WESTERN HEMI-SPHERE | ASIA | OTHER |
| YEAR | TOTAL IMMIGRANTS | No. % | No. % | No. % | No. % | No. % | No. % | No. % |
|---|---|---|---|---|---|---|---|---|
| 1821–1830 | 144 | 99 (69.2) | 96 (67.1) | —— | 3 ( 2.1) | 12 ( 8.4) | —— | 32 (22.4) |
| 1831–1840 | 599 | 496 (82.8) | 490 (81.8) | —— | 1 ( 1.0) | 33 ( 5.5) | —— | 70 (11.7) |
| 1841–1850 | 1,713 | 1,599 (93.3) | 1,592 (92.9) | 2 ( 0.1) | 5 ( 0.3) | 62 ( 3.6) | —— | 53 ( 3.1) |
| 1851–1860 | 2,598 | 2,453 (94.4) | 2,432 (93.6) | 3 ( 0.1) | 21 ( 0.8) | 75 ( 2.9) | 42 ( 1.6) | 29 ( 1.1) |
| 1861–1870 | 2,315 | 2,065 (89.2) | 2,032 (87.8) | 12 ( 0.5) | 21 ( 0.9) | 167 ( 7.2) | 65 ( 2.8) | 19 ( 0.8) |
| 1871–1880 | 2,812 | 2,272 (80.8) | 2,070 (73.6) | 127 ( 4.5) | 76 ( 2.7) | 405 (14.4) | 124 ( 4.4) | 11 ( 0.4) |
| 1881–1890 | 5,247 | 4,738 (90.3) | 3,778 (72.0) | 624 (11.9) | 331 ( 6.3) | 425 ( 8.1) | 68 ( 1.3) | 16 ( 0.3) |
| 1891–1900 | 3,688 | 3,559 (96.5) | 1,641 (44.5) | 1,210 (32.8) | 704 (19.1) | 41 ( 1.1) | 70 ( 1.9) | 18 ( 0.5) |
| 1901–1910 | 8,795 | 8,136 (92.5) | 1,909 (21.7) | 3,914 (44.5) | 2,313 (26.3) | 361 ( 4.1) | 246 ( 2.8) | 53 ( 0.6) |
| 1911–1920 | 5,736 | 4,376 (76.3) | 998 (17.4) | 1,916 (33.4) | 1,463 (25.5) | 1,141 (19.9) | 195 ( 3.4) | 23 ( 0.4) |
| 1921–1930 | 4,107 | 2,477 (60.3) | 1,302 (31.7) | 591 (14.4) | 587 (14.3) | 1,516 (36.9) | 99 ( 2.4) | 16 ( 0.4) |
| 1931–1940 | 528 | 348 (65.9) | 205 (38.8) | 58 (11.0) | 85 (16.1) | 160 (30.3) | 15 ( 2.8) | 5 ( 0.9) |
| 1941–1950 | 1,035 | 622 (60.1) | 492 (47.5) | 48 ( 4.6) | 82 ( 7.9) | 355 (34.3) | 32 ( 3.1) | 26 ( 2.5) |
| 1951–1960 | 2,516 | 1,328 (52.8) | 445 (17.7) | 611 (24.3) | 272 (10.8) | 996 (39.6) | 151 ( 6.0) | 40 ( 1.6) |
| 1961–1970 | 3,322 | 1,239 (37.3) | 394 (11.9) | 419 (12.6) | 426 (12.8) | 1,579 (47.6) | 445 (13.4) | 58 ( 1.9) |
| 1971–1980 | 4,384 | 801 (18.3) | 188 ( 4.3) | 246 ( 5.6) | 368 ( 8.4) | 1,929 (44.0) | 1,634 (37.3) | 19 ( 0.4) |

*Note:* Numbers are given in thousands.

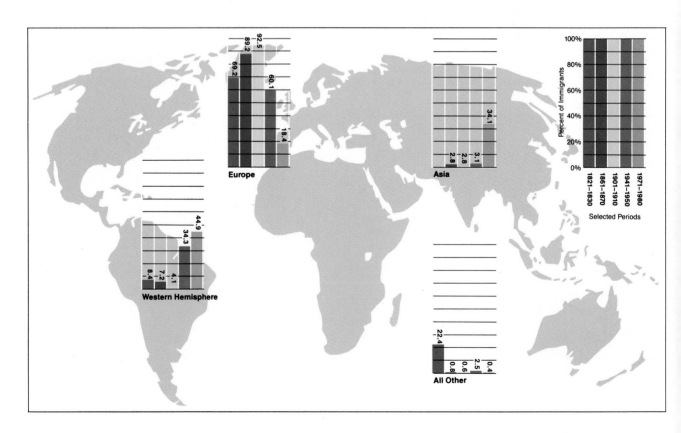

# Characteristics of the American Work Force

| YEAR | TOTAL NUMBER OF WORKERS* (THOUSANDS) | MALE (%) | FEMALE (%) | LABOR UNION MEMBERS (%) |
|---|---|---|---|---|
| 1820 | 3,135 | | | — |
| 1830 | 4,200 | | | — |
| 1840 | 5,660 | | | — |
| 1850 | 8,250 | | | — |
| 1860 | 11,110 | | | — |
| 1870 | 12,930 | 85 | 15 | — |
| 1880 | 17,390 | 85 | 15 | — |
| 1890 | 23,320 | 83 | 17 | — |
| 1900 | 29,070 | 82 | 18 | 3 |
| 1910 | 37,480 | 79 | 21 | 6 |
| 1920 | 41,610 | 79 | 21 | 12 |
| 1930 | 48,830 | 78 | 22 | 7 |
| 1940 | 56,290 | 76 | 24 | 17 |
| 1950 | 65,470 | 72 | 28 | 22 |
| 1960 | 74,060 | 67 | 33 | 24 |
| 1970 | 82,715 | 62 | 38 | 23 |
| 1980 | 104,400 | 58 | 42 | 20 |
| 1984 | 114,464 | 55 | 45 | 18 |

*From 1870 to 1930, military employees are included.

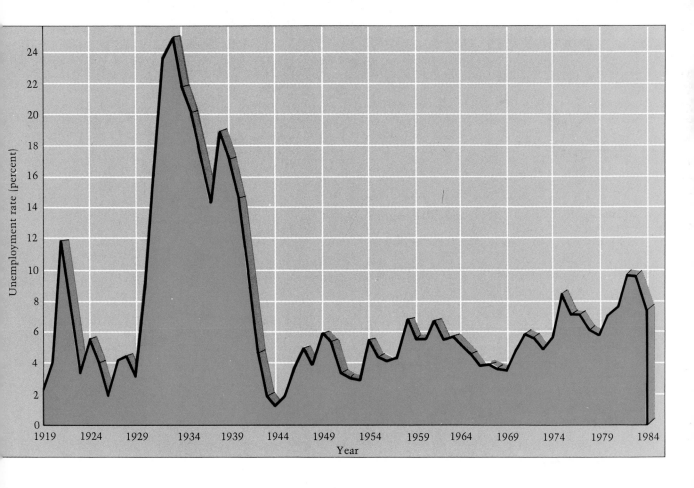

# CREDITS

*Franklin,* 1762. Philadelphia Museum of Art, Mr. and Mrs. Wharton Sinkler Collection. **101** Anonymous American, *The Cheney Family,* 1795. National Gallery of Art, Washington, D. C., gift of Edgar William and Bernice Chrysler Garbisch. **104** Richard J. Stinely, plat of tidewater landscape, from Rhys Isaac, *The Transformation of Virginia* (1983). By permission of University of North Carolina Press. **105** Westover, the mansion of William Byrd II, Charles City County, Va. Library of Congress, Print and Photo Division. Anonymous American, *The Plantation,* c. 1825. Metropolitan Museum of Art, New York, gift of Edgar William and Bernice Chrysler Garbisch. **106** Lithograph of indigo processing. Charleston (S.C.) Library Society. **111** William Russell Birch, *Preparation for War to Defend Commerce,* 1800. Athenaeum of Philadelphia, gift of Mrs. Charles Fearon. **118** John Wollaston, *George Whitefield.* The Bettmann Archive. **121** Anonymous American, *Front View of Yale College and the College Chapel, New Haven,* 1786. Yale University Art Gallery, New Haven, Conn., gift of Jesse Lathrop Moss, B.A. 1869. **124** Henry Dawkins, *The Paxton Expedition.* Library Company of Philadelphia. **134** *Tomochichi and His Nephew,* 1734. National Museum of Natural History, Smithsonian Institution, Washington, D.C. *Mohawk Chief,* c. 1710. Library of Congress, Print and Photo Division. **139** *A View of the Taking of Quebec, September 13th, 1759,* printed for Robert Wilkinson & Bowles & Carver, London. Royal Ontario Museum, Toronto, Canada. **140** Jerry Farnsworth, *Chief Pontiac.* Museum of the American Indian, Heye Foundation, New York. **143** Anonymous American, *Patrick Henry Arguing the "Parson's Cause."* Virginia Historical Society, Richmond, Va. **145** J. W. Barber, New Hampshire Stamp Master in Effigy, from *Interesting Events in the History of the U.S.,* 1829. Metropolitan Museum of Art, New York, bequest of Charles Allen Munn. **152** Title page, Thomas Paine's *Common Sense.* Library of Congress, Print and Photo Division. William Sharp, *Thomas Paine,* engraved after a painting by George Romney, 1793. New-York Historical Society, New York. **155** *To the Delaware Pilots . . . (signed) The Committee for Tarring and Feathering,* Philadelphia, November 27, 1773. New York Public Library, Rare Book Collection. **156** *A Society of Patriotic Ladies, at Edenton in North Carolina,* printed for R. Sayer & J. Bennett, London, 1775. Colonial Williamsburg Foundation, Williamsburg, Va. **158** Tombstone of freedman John Jack. Photo Concord (Mass.) Free Public Library.

**167** Godefroy, *Journée de Lexington.* Daniel Berger, *Das erste Bürger Blut . . . vergossen bey Lexington,* published in Sprengel, *Allgemeines Historisches Taschenbuch . . . ,* 1784. Both, Library of Congress. **170** Joseph Strutt, *America. To those who wish . . . ,* after Robert Edge Pine, 1778. Library of Congress. **172** *Surrender of Earl Cornwallis . . . to General Washington and Count de Rochambeau . . . ,* engraving and etching by Thornton based on a drawing by Hamilton, made for Edward Barnard. Library of Congress. **173** Benjamin West, *American Commissioners of the Preliminary Peace Negotiations with Great Britain,* c. 1783. The Henry Francis du Pont Winterthur Museum, Winterthur, Del. **175** Anonymous, *A Real American Rifle Man,* 1780. Library of Congress. **177** Surgeon's kit, c. 1776. National Museum of American History, Smithsonian Institution, Washington, D.C. **179** François Xav. Habermann, *Représentation de Feu terrible a Nouvelle Yorck . . . ,* 177(?). Library of Congress. **182** *William Jackson,* broadside, Boston, January 1770. Library of Congress. **183** *Now fitting for a Privateer,* broadside, Beverly, Mass., September 17, 1776. American Antiquarian Society; photo Marvin Richmond. **186** Currency of the Continental Congress. American Antiquarian Society; photo Marvin Richmond. **190** J. R. Smith, *Joseph Brant, Mohawk chief,* after G. Romney. New York Public Library, Print and Photograph Division. **191** Newspaper advertisement, Savannah, July 25, 1774. Library of Congress. **195** John Trumbull, The Tory's Day of Judgment, from *M'Fingal.* The Bettmann Archive. **201** *Pennsylvanische Staatsbote,* July 5, 1776. Historical Society of Pennsylvania, Philadelphia. **202** *La Destruction de la Statue Royale a Nouvelle Yorck (Die Zerstörung der Königlichen Bild Saule zu Neu Yorck),* hand-colored etching, Chez Basset, Paris, 177(?). Library of Congress. **204** John Trumbull, New England Town Meeting, from *M'Fingal,* The Bettmann Archive. **206** *Charles W. Peale,* engraving from a broadside, Philadelphia, September 1780. American Antiquar-

ian Society; photo Marvin Richmond. **207** Old State House of Pennsylvania, later called Independence Hall. Independence National Historic Park Collection, Philadelphia. **209** Anonymous portrait, traditionally said to be Abigail Adams. New York State Historical Association, Cooperstown, N.Y. **210** *The Female Patriot,* broadside, New York, May 30, 1770. Library of Congress. **211** Vauthier and Bertrand, *L'Amérique,* 181(?). Library of Congress. **215** Massachusetts State House. The Bostonian Society. **217** I. B. and P. C. Smith, *A Correct View of the Old Methodist Church in John St., New York. The first erected in America. Founded A.D. 1768,* nineteenth century. Metropolitan Museum of Art, New York, Edward W. C. Arnold Collection of New York Prints, Maps, and Pictures, bequest of Edward W. C. Arnold. **225** *Taxation Royal Tyranny,* broadside, Philadelphia, September 22, 1779. Library of Congress. **227** Paul Revere, silver bowl presented to General Wm. Shepard. Yale University Art Gallery, New Haven, Conn., Mabel Brady Garvan Collection. **233** Anonymous, *Constitutional Convention, 1787.* Independence National Historic Park Collection, Philadelphia. **235** First Seal of the United States, 1782. Library of Congress. **241** *President-Elect Washington: The Hero Who Defended the Mothers Will Protect the Daughters,* lithograph. Library of Congress. **242** John Trumbull, *Alexander Hamilton.* Yale University Art Gallery, New Haven, Conn. **244** William Birch and Son, *Bank of the United States, Philadelphia,* 1799. Library of Congress. **245** Jean-Antoine Houdon, *Bust of Thomas Jefferson,* 1789. New-York Historical Society, New York. **247** Frederick Kemmelmeyer, *Washington and His Staff at Fort Cumberland, Maryland, October 18, 1794.* Metropolitan Museum of Art, New York, gift of Edgar William and Bernice Chrysler Garbisch. **251** Joseph Wright, *George Washington,* 1790. Metropolitan Museum of Art, New York. **252** William Winstanley, *John Adams,* 1796. National Park Service, Adams National Historic Site, Quincy, Mass.; photo George Dow. **253** *The Times: A Political Portrait: Triumph Government, Perish All Its Enemies,* c. 1795. New-York Historical Society, New York. **256** Anonymous miniature, *Charles Maurice de Talleyrand-Perigord, Prince de Benevent.* New-York Historical Society, New York. **257** James Van Dyke, *Aaron Burr,* 1834. New-York Historical Society, New York.

**263** William Birch and Son, *Arch Street Ferry, Philadelphia.* New York Public Library, Stokes Collection. **265** Plan of an American New-Cleared Farm, published in P. Campbell, *Travels in North America,* 1793. New York Public Library, Rare Book Division. **268** Benjamin Henry Latrobe, *An Overseer Doing His Duty.* Maryland Historical Society. **270** Anonymous, *At the Loom,* c. 1795. Archives of American Art, Downtown Gallery Papers, Smithsonian Institution, Washington, D.C. **271** William Birch, *Second and Market Streets, Philadelphia,* 1799. New York Public Library, Stokes Collection. **273** Anonymous wood engraving, *Slater Mill, Pawtucket,* c. 1870–1880. Rhode Island Historical Society, Providence, R.I. **278** Strobridge, *Cincinnati, 1800,* after A. J. Swing. Cincinnati (Ohio) Historical Society. **279** George Tattersall, Highways and Byways of the Forest, from *American, Western Sketches,* 1838. Museum of Fine Arts, Boston, M. and M. Karolik Collection. **281** Anonymous, *He that by the plough would thrive . . . ,* c. 1880. Addison Gallery of American Art, Phillips Academy, Andover, Mass., gift of Mrs. Evelyn Roberts. **284** Prudence Punderson, *The First, Second, and Last Scene of Mortality,* late eighteenth century. Connecticut Historical Society, Hartford. **289** Lewis Miller, Ludwig Miller, teacher at the Old Lutheran Schoolhouse in the year 1805, from *Sketches and Chronicles,* 1805. Historical Society of York County, Pa. **291** John Singleton Copley, *Thomas and Sarah (Morris) Mifflin,* 1773. Historical Society of Pennsylvania, Philadelphia. **293** Paul Svinin, *Negro Methodist Meeting.* Metropolitan Museum of Art, New York, Rogers Fund.

**299** Andrew Ellicott, *District of Columbia,* 1792. George I. Parkyns, *View of the Suburbs of the City of Washington,* c. 1800. Both, Library of Congress. **302** Chester Harding, *John Marshall,* 1828. Boston Athenaeum. **306** Boqueto de Woiserie, *View of New Orleans from the Plantation of Marginy, November 1803.* Chicago Historical Society. **313** George Catlin, *Choctaw Eagle Dance.* American Museum of Natural History, New York. **314** *Se-Quo-Yah, Cherokee,* 1838. National Museum of Natural History, Smithsonian Institution, Washington, D.C. **320** George Ropes, *Crowninshield Wharf after the Embargo Act,* c. 1806, commissioned by George Crown-

inshield, Sr. Essex Institute, Salem, Mass. **323** S. W. Fores, *Maddy in Full Flight*, London, 1814. Brown University Library, Providence, R.I., Anne S. K. Brown Military Collection. **324** Ambroise Louis Garneray, *The Battle of Lake Erie*. Chicago Historical Society. **325** Thomas Gimbrede, *John Quincy Adams*, 1826. National Portrait Gallery, Smithsonian Institution, Washington, D.C. **326** Charles Willson Peale, *Self-Portrait of the Artist in His Museum*, 1822. Pennsylvania Academy of the Fine Arts, Philadelphia. **327** Paul Svinin, *Anabaptist Ceremony*. Metropolitan Museum of Art, New York, Rogers Fund.
**337** Mary Keys, *Lockport on the Erie Canal*, 1832. Munson-Williams-Proctor Institute, Museum of Art, Utica, N.Y. **339** Lucius H. Tatham, *Brattleboro and Whitehall Railroad, near Brattleboro, Vermont*, 1860–1870. New-York Historical Society, New York, collection of Mrs. T. K. Boardman, Jr. **342** Southworth and Hawes, *The George Barrell Emerson School in Boston*, c. 1840–1862. Metropolitan Museum of Art, New York, gift of I. N. Phelps Stokes, Edward S. Hawes, Alice Mary Hawes, and Marion Augusta Hawes. **344** The Manchester Print Works, *Gleason's Pictorial*, 1854. Library of Congress. **346** Pendleton, *Lowell, Massachusetts, 1834*. Worcester Art Museum, Worcester, Mass., Goodspeed Collection. **347** Time Table of the Lowell Mills, October 1851. Baker Library, Harvard Business School, Cambridge, Mass. **348** *Drawing In*. Museum of American Textile History, North Andover, Mass. **350** *Ohio River and Cincinnati*, 1858. Public Library of Cincinnati and Hamilton County, Cincinnati, Ohio. **354** Asselineau, *Panoramic View of Philadelphia*, after John Bachman, c. 1855. Historical Society of Pennsylvania, Philadelphia. **357** Erastus Salisbury Field, *Joseph Moore and His Family*, 1839. Museum of Fine Arts, Boston, M. and M. Karolik Collection. **361** Anonymous broadside, *Dreadful Riot on Negro Hill*, July 1827. Library of Congress. **363** N. Currier, *Preparing for Market*, after L. Maurer, 1856. Yale University Art Gallery, New Haven, Conn., Mabel Brady Garvan Collection.
**370** Frederick Douglass, 1855. New York Public Library, Schomburg Center for Research in Black Culture. **376** Black dockworkers, c. 1860. National Archives. **379** Anonymous, *The Quilting Party*, after *Gleason's Pictorial*, October 21, 1854. Abby Aldrich Rockefeller Center for Folk Art, Williamsburg, Va. **381** Adele Petigru Allston and Robert F. W. Allston. South Caroliniana Library, Columbia, S.C. **386** George Fuller, Alabama Interior, January 28, 1858. Private collection. **389** Taylor, *The American Slave Market*, 1852. Chicago Historical Society. **391** Christmas on the Plantation. *Frank Leslie's Illustrated Newspaper*, December 26, 1857. New York Public Library, Astor, Lenox and Tilden Foundations. **393** Black family of five generations, Beaufort, S.C., all born on Plantation of J. J. Smith, photographed by T. H. O'Sullivan, 1862. Library of Congress. **395** George Fuller, Cotton Press and Gin, February 2, 1858. Private Collection. **397** *Horrid Massacre in Virginia*, woodcut, 1831. Library of Congress. **399** Meeting in the African Church, *Frank Leslie's Illustrated Newspaper*, April 30, 1853. Library of Congress. **406** *Symptoms of Indigestion*, 1824. Library Company of Philadelphia. John Neagle, *Pat Lyon at the Forge*, 1829. Pennsylvania Academy of Fine Arts, Philadelphia, gift of the Pat Lyon Family. **409** Cruickshank, *All Creation Going to the White House*, 1829. Library of Congress. **412** Old Hickory, figurehead, 1834. Museum of the City of New York. **415** "A Drop of Hard Cider, or The Tippecanoe Roarer," songbook cover, 1840. Cincinnati Historical Society. **417** J. Maze Burbank, *Religious Camp Meeting*, 1839. The Whaling Museum, New Bedford, Mass. **419** *Portrait of John Humphrey Noyes, Perfectionist*. The Granger Collection, New York. **422** C. C. A. Christensen, *The Nauvoo Temple*, 1844. Brigham Young University Art Museum Collection, Provo, Utah. **423** N. Currier, *The Drunkard's Progress, from the First Glass to the Grave*, 1846. Museum of the City of New York, Harry T. Peters Collection. **425** N. Currier, *Certificate of Marriage*, 1848. Library of Congress. **428** Masthead, *The Liberator*, 1831. The Granger Collection, New York. **431** *Lucy Stone*. Sophia Smith Collection, Smith College, Northampton, Mass. **432** E. Decker, *Elizabeth Cady Stanton; Lucretia Mott*. Both Sophia Smith Collection, Smith College, Northampton, Mass. **439** F. O. C. Darley, *Emigrants Crossing the Plains*. Denver Public Library, Western History Department. **444** Mathew Brady, *James Knox Polk*, 1849. Library of Congress. **447** Currier & Ives, *Flight of the Mexican Army at the Battle of Buena Vista, Feb. 23, 1847*.

Museum of the City of New York. **448** Lorenzo Lorain, *Oregon City*, 1857. Oregon Historical Society. **450** John Russell Bartlett, *Camp in a Snow Storm on Delaware Creek, Texas*. Brown University, Providence, R.I., John Carter Brown Library. **454** *The Rigors of the Trail . . . the End of a Long Day*. Denver Public Library, Western History Department. **456** Anonymous photo of Sacramento Street, San Francisco, 1853. Bancroft Library, University of California at Berkeley. **457** Mining, Auburn Ravine, American River, 1852. California State Library, Sacramento. **458** Charles Nahl, *Saturday Night at the Mines*, 1856. Stanford University Museum of Art, gift of Mrs. Jane L. Stanford. **459** William Henry Jackson, *Ophir City, Nevada*, c. 1875. Denver Public Library, Western History Department. **460** Brigham Young, c. 1850. Utah State Historical Society, Salt Lake City. **465** John Mix Stanley, *Ko-rak-koo-kiss, a Tonoccono Warrior*, 1844. National Museum of American Art, Smithsonian Institution, Washington, D.C. **467** Mission San Fernando Corridors with Gen. Andrés Picos and daughter, by Edward Vischer, 1865. California Historical Society, Ticor Collection of Historical Photographs, Los Angeles.
**476** *The Blessings of Liberty, or How to Hook a "Gentleman ob Color,"* 1851. Library of Congress. **479** Mathew Brady, *Stephen Douglas*, c. 1858. The Bettmann Archive. **482** *Soliciting a Vote*, c. 1852. Library of Congress. **486** *Ruins of the Free State Hotel, Lawrence, Kansas, 1856*, from a daguerrotype taken for Mrs. Sara Robinson. Kansas State Historical Society, Topeka. **488** G. G. Lange, *Rochester, New York, 1860*. Library of Congress. Calvert, *Sunny south*, c. 1850. The Bettmann Archive. **489** Front page, *Frank Leslie's Illustrated Newspaper*, June 27, 1857. New York Public Library: Astor, Lenox and Tilden Foundations. **492** Southern Sympathizer Tarred and Feathered, Haverhill, Massachusetts, *Frank Leslie's Illustrated Newspaper*, August 31, 1861. New York Public Library: Astor, Lenox and Tilden Foundations. **495** Abraham Lincoln, c. 1860. The Bettmann Archive.
**501** First Michigan Regiment musters in Detroit, May 11, 1861, before taking the train to Washington. Detroit Public Library. **504** Jefferson Davis, c. 1857. Museum of the Confederacy, Richmond, Va. **506** President Lincoln with Generals in Camp. Library of Congress. **508** Killed at Antietam: the Horse of a Confederate Officer. Library of Congress. **509** Wounded Zouave Receiving Water. National Archives, Office of the Chief Signal Officer. **510** J. G. Tanner, *Engagement Between the Monitor and the Merrimack*. National Gallery of Art, Smithsonian Institution, Washington, D.C. **512** Pvt. Edwin Jennison of Georgia, killed at Malvern Hill. Library of Congress. **516** Emancipation Day at Smith's plantation, Port Royal Island, S.C., *Frank Leslie's Illustrated Newspaper*, January 24, 1863. New-York Historical Society. **521** Currier & Ives, *The Storming of Fort Wagner, South Carolina . . .*, 1890. Currier & Ives, *Fatal Wounding of Stonewall Jackson . . .*, 1889. Both, Museum of the City of New York. **525** A Relic of Pope's Retreat (Overturned Train). Library of Congress. **527** Currier & Ives, *The Soldier's Dream of Home*. Museum of the City of New York. Ruins of Richmond, May 1865. Library of Congress.
**535** Despairing Southern Family, *Frank Leslie's Illustrated Newspaper*, February 23, 1867. Library of Congress. **536** Freedmen, Richmond, Virginia. Library of Congress. **540** Slavery is Dead? *Harper's Weekly*, January 12, 1867. Library Company of Philadelphia. **541** Burning a Freedmen's School-House, *Harper's Weekly*, May 26, 1866. Library Company of Philadelphia. **545** Waiting for Aid, Freedmen's Bureau, Memphis, *Harper's Weekly*, June 2, 1866. Library of Congress. **548** Negro Home in the South: Sharecroppers. Brown Brothers. **551** Black Schoolchildren. Valentine Museum, Richmond, Va. **552** J. Karst, "I shall discharge every Nigger who votes to adopt this Radical Yankee constitution," from Trowbridge, *A Picture of the Desolated States*, 1868. Library of Congress. **555** *A Visit from the Ku Klux Klan*, 1878. The Granger Collection, New York. **556** Currier & Ives, "Middle Age," from *The Four Seasons of Life*, 1868. Museum of the City of New York.
**566** Currier & Ives: *Winter Morning in the Country*, 1873. Metropolitan Museum of Art, New York, bequest of Adele S. Colgate. *The Pioneer's Home on the Western Frontier*, 1867, The Granger Collection, New York. *The Route to California*, 1871. Metropolitan Museum of Art, New York, gift of George S. Amory. **567** W. A. Raymond, *Oregon Wheat Harvest*, c. 1880. The Bettmann Archive. **571** Solo-

# INDEX

Abolitionism, 97–98
  Emancipation Proclamation in, 514–515
  nineteenth-century, 403, 427–431
    in Northern states, 291, 292–293, 294, 360
    Transcendentalists, 418–419
    Wilmot Proviso, 472–474
    women's rights and, 357, 427, 431–433, 477
  prerevolutionary, 158–159, 191–192
  Quaker, 97–98, 158, 194
  Revolutionary War, 192–195
  underground railroad, 395–396
Abortion, 359, 957, 965, 985–986
Abstract expressionism, 898
Acadia (Nova Scotia), 88. *See also* Nova Scotia
Acheson, Dean, 860, 863, 865, 872, 876, 877
Acid rain, 990
Adams, Abigail, 209
Adams, Brooks, 647
Adams, Charles, 262
Adams, Dudley, 586
Adams, Henry, 556–558, 628–629, 632, 656
Adams, John, 144, 145, 147, 150, 151, 152, 154, 157, 172, 183, 200, 209
  Constitution and, 232, 240
  death of, 331
  Massachusetts state constitution and, 214–215
  presidency of, 252–257, 298
Adams, John Quincy, 255
  presidency of, 330
  presidential campaign of 1828, 407–408
  repeal of gag rule and, 430–431
  as secretary of state under Monroe, 325–326
Adams, Samuel, 125, 141, 146–150, 237
Adamson Act, 734
Addams, Jane, 642–643, 644, 648–649, 695, 698, 716, 727, 728, 759, 780
  Hull House and, 641, 643, 649, 691, 697, 698, 708, 714
  in the Women's International League for Peace and Freedom, 751

Advertising industry, 893–894, 969
Affirmative action
  for blacks, 986
  for Hispanic Americans, 988
  for women, 984
Afghanistan, 994
Africa, 679
  da Gama's voyage around, 15
  ethos of, 11
  gold in, 10–14
  importation of slaves from, 64–66
  Portuguese traders in, 14
  pre-Colombian kingdoms of, 9–11
  return of blacks to, 770
  return of freed slaves to, 428
  Spanish ouster of Moors from, 15
  in World War II, 842, 844
African Methodist Episcopal (AME) church, 390, 550, 606–607
African slaves. *See* Slaves
Afro-American culture, 69
  family life in, 69–70, 72–74, 388–390, 393–394
  Harlem Renaissance, 770–771
  music in, 390, 392–393, 394, 771
  religion in, 390–392, 399, 550, 606–607
Afro-American League, 584–585
Agent Orange, 991
Aging persons, 982–983
Agnew, Spiro, 948, 957
Agricultural Adjustment Act of 1933, 797–798, 807
Agricultural Adjustment Act of 1938, 812
Agricultural Marketing Act of 1929, 789
Agriculture
  agrarian protests, 227
  antebellum period, 362–366, 371–380, 455–456
  Civil War and, 511, 519–520, 521, 525
  colonial
    backcountry, 107
    Carolina colonies, 53–54, 106–107
    Chesapeake Bay colony, 32–39, 104–106
    New England, 46–47, 98–99
  dairy farming, 265, 267, 362
  foreign trade and, 566, 977
  improved transportation methods and, 337–340, 362–363, 365

  migrant workers in, 768, 808, 908–909, 930–931
  modernization of, 564–574, 774–775
    in California, 572–574
    cattle and, 571–572
    equipment in, 569, 573
    falling prices in, 568, 581–582, 588
    farmer protests in, 586–592
    Great Plains, 569–572
    large-scale farms, 567, 573
    myth versus reality in, 564–567
    Southern, 578–579, 581–582, 588–592
  New Deal programs, 797–798, 803–804, 812
  nineteenth-century, 264–269
    Northern, 264–267, 277
    Southern, 267–269, 277
  in the 1920s, 774–775
  in pre-Colombian Africa, 5
  price supports, 775, 798
  Revolutionary War impact on, 183–185
  scientific farming in, 363
  setbacks in the 1970s, 976–977
Aguinaldo, Emilio, 659, 660, 674
AIDS (acquired immune deficiency syndrome), 989
Aiken, Howard H., 892
Airplanes
  Linbergh flight, 766
  in World War I, 741, 744
  in World War II, 844–845
Alabama, 493, 554, 579, 919–920
  civil rights movement in, 906–907
  Reconstruction era, 554
Aláman, Lucas, 442–443
Alamo, 443
Alaska, 4
  gold in, 655
  purchase from Russia, 663
Albany Congress (1754), 138
Albuquerque, New Mexico, 23
Alcohol
  preindustrial consumption of, 283
  repeal of prohibition, 796
  rum, 68, 283
  temperance movements
    nineteenth-century, 423–424, 632, 633–634, 697
    post–World War I, 781–782

Alcohol (*Continued*)
    progressivism and, 697–698,
      781–782
    whiskey, 245, 246–247, 283, 557
    Whiskey Ring affair, 557
    World War I and, 748
Alcott, Bronson, 421
Alger, Horatio, Jr., 645
Algonquin tribe, 3–4
Alien Act of 1798, 254–255, 303
Alien Enemies Act, 254, 303
Allen, Ethan, 151
Allen, Richard, 293, 390
Allston, Adele, 531, 547
Allston, Elizabeth, 531
Allston, Robert Francis Withers,
    380–382, 384, 385, 391, 471,
    485, 496, 507, 531
Almshouses, 286, 288
    eighteenth-century, 113
    nineteenth-century reforms, 426
Alpert, Richard, 941
Altamont, California rock festival,
    955–956
Amalgamated Association of Iron,
    Steel, and Tin Workers, 619
American Anti-Slavery Society, 428,
    429
American Colonizationist Society,
    292–293, 428
American Communist party, 757
*American Dictionary of the English
    Language* (Webster), 327
American Federation of Labor (AFL),
    618, 746
    New Deal era, 805–807
    in the 1920s, 775–776
    scientific management and, 701–
      702
American Fur Company, 312
American Indian Movement (AIM),
    930, 966–967
American Philosophical Society, 116
American Protective League, 737–
    738
American Railway Union (ARU),
    619–620
*American Slavery as It Is* (Weld),
    429
American Temperance Society, 423–
    424
American Union Against Militarism,
    731
Ames, Fisher, 247, 251, 256

Amherst, Jeffrey, 138, 139
Amish, 17
Amory, Jonathan, 182
Anaconda Plan, 506
Anarchy, 81
Anaya, Toney, 988
Anderson, Marian, 808
Anderson, Mary, 809
Anderson, Robert, 495–496
Anderson, Sherwood, 772
Andrews, Eliza, 538
Andros, Edmund, 80–81, 83, 85
Anglicanism, 116
Anne (queen of England), 133
Anthony, Susan B., 515, 544, 545,
    556, 643, 644, 749
Anti-Federalists, 227, 233, 235–240
Antigua, 26
Anti-imperialism, 675–676
Anti-Imperialist League, 675
Anti-Masonic party, 411–412
Antinomianism, 45
Anti-Saloon League, 697
Anti-Semitism
    Nazi, 843–844
    New Deal era, 801
Antitrust legislation, 634–635, 710–
    711, 720
Appalachian Mountains
    as boundary after Revolutionary
      War, 173
    as boundary after Seven Years'
      War, 140
Appliances
    in the 1930s, 814–815
    post-World War II use of, 893
Appomattox, Civil War, 524
Apprenticeship systems, 111
*Arabella* (ship), 262, 263
Aragon, 12, 14
Archaic era, 5
Architecture. *See also* Housing
    Chesapeake Bay colony, 39
    New England colony, 49–50
    skyscrapers, 764
Argentina, 18, 325
Arizona, 23
Armed forces, 731. *See also* Navy;
    specific wars
    blacks in
      Civil War, 516, 519, 526
      Filipino-American War, 676
      Korean War, 868, 905
      Spanish-American War, 673

      World War I, 736, 737, 740–
        741, 742, 743
      World War II, 833–834, 840,
        846–847
    Brownsville, Texas, riot of 1906,
      714
    Cuba and, 934
    Houston, Texas, riot of 1917,
      740–741
    mercenaries in, 88, 168, 174, 180
    National Guard in. *See* National
      Guard
    Native Americans in, 88, 840
    nineteenth-century, 665, 671–
      676, 684
    women in, 739, 840–841
Arms control, 994
Arms race
    nuclear proliferation in, 872–874,
      995–996
    Reagan and, 995–996
Army Reorganization Bill of 1916,
    731
Arnold, Benedict, 178, 179
Arpin, Edmund P., Jr., 725, 743
Arthur, Chester A., 630, 631
Articles of Confederation, 165–167,
    220, 232, 233
Artisans
    in colonial cities, 110–112
    industrialization process and, 350,
      351
    preindustrial manufacturing by,
      271–272
    role in nonimportation agree-
      ments, 147, 155–156
    Seven Years' War and, 140
    use of slaves by, 70, 71
Ashley, William, 273
Assembly
    colonial, 122, 125–126
    postrevolutionary, 213, 216
Assembly line, 701, 762–763
Astor, John Jacob, 264, 312
Asylums, 426
Atchison, David, 484, 485
Atlantic Charter, 848
Atlantic Ocean, 14, 15, 18, 24
Atomic bomb
    development of, 825–826, 849,
      859, 873–874
    Japan and, 849–850
    proliferation, 871–874
    Soviet, 862

Atomic Energy Act of 1946, 872
Atomic Energy Commission, 872–873, 903
Auld, Sophia, 369
Austin, Stephen F., 442
Austria-Hungary, 726, 729, 750, 825
Automation, 701, 762–763
Automobiles, 761–763, 989–990
    in consumer movement, 969
    Japanese, 975
    in the 1930s, 814
    post–World War II boom in, 887–888
*Awakening, The* (Chopin), 642
Aztec empire, 18, 20

*Babbit* (Lewis), 772
*Baby and Child Care* (Spock), 897
Baby boom generation, 888
    colleges and, 937–940
Backcountry, colonial, 107–108, 119–120
Backus, Isaac, 218
Backus, John, 289–290
Bacon, Nathaniel, 76–78, 83
Bacon's Rebellion, 76–78, 83
Baer, George F., 712
Baez, Joan, 939
Baker, Josephine, 781
Baker, Newton D., 708, 738
Baker, Ray Stannard, 693, 709
*Baker* v. *Carr*, 925
Bakke, Allan, 987
Baldwin, James, 927
Baldwin, Luther, 254–255
Ballinger, Richard A., 715
Ballou, Adin, 420
Baltimore, Lord (George Calvert), 37–38
Baltimore, Maryland
    Civil War troops in, 503
    riots of 1812, 323
Bankhead-Jones Farm Tenancy Act of 1937, 812
Banking Act of 1933, 795–796
Bank of North America, 225, 244–245
Bank of the United States, 274
    Second, 328, 340, 411–412
Banks
    Civil War establishment of, 520
    Great Depression and, 788, 790, 791, 792
    national, 225, 244–245, 274, 328, 340, 411–412, 589–590
    New Deal and, 795–796
    panic of 1819 and, 274–275
    state taxes on, 302–303
    Wilson's reforms of, 719
Banks, Dennis, 930
Baptists, 119–120, 122, 217, 218, 550
Barbados, 26, 52, 53, 67, 68
Barbed wire fencing, 569
Barlow, Joel, 327
Barnett, Ross, 919
Barter system, 265, 363
Bartholemew, Elam, 571
Barton, Bruce, 776
Barton, Clara, 523
Bartram, John, 115
Baruch, Bernard, 745, 746, 861
Baseball, 904, 913
Bathrooms, 761
Batista, Fulgencio, 823, 871, 933
Battles. *See* specific wars
Bay of Pigs incident, 933–934
Beat generation, 898
Beatles, 941
Beauregard, P. G. T., 496, 506–508
Beecher, Catherine, 356, 358, 432
Beecher, Henry Ward, 485
Beecher, Lyman, 416, 427
Begin, Menachem, 993
Belcher, Andrew, 90, 115
Bell, John, 492
Bellamy, Edward, 627, 646, 647, 655, 692
Bennett, Richard, 63
Berger, Victor, 718
Beringian epoch, 5
Bering Straits, 4–5
Berkeley, John, 56
Berkeley, William, 77
Berkman, Alexander, 619
Berle, Adolph A., Jr., 795, 887
Berlin Decree, 319
Bermuda, 26
Bernard, Francis, 144, 146
Berne, Eric, 969
Bernstein, Carl, 961
Bethune, Mary McLeod, 807–808
Beveridge, Albert, 666, 669, 694, 713, 751
Bible, 16, 384, 895
Biddle, Nicholas, 341, 411–412
Bigelow, Herbert S., 738
Bilingual education, 968, 987
Bill of Rights, 242, 255
Birmingham, Alabama
    black protests in, 919–920
    as symbol of the New South, 579
Birney, James G., 403, 429
*Birth of a Nation, The,* 759, 765
Black, Hugo, 919
Black codes, 68–69, 538
Black Death, 12
Black Elk, 574, 576, 578
Blackmun, Harry, 957
Black Panthers, 929
Blacks
    in agricultural protest movements, 589
    in the armed forces
        Civil War, 516, 519, 526
        Filipino-American War, 676
        Korean War, 868, 905
        Spanish-American War, 673
        World War I, 736, 737, 740–741, 742, 743
        World War II, 833–834, 840, 846–847
    Christianity of, 293–294, 390–392, 399, 550, 606–607
    civil rights and. *See* Civil rights movement
    community formation by, 293–294
    culture of. *See* Afro-American culture
    debt peonage of, 548–549, 581–582
    discrimination against, 582–586, 833–835, 837, 840, 986–987
    education of, 369, 398, 400, 905–906, 958–960, 986, 997
        antebellum, 361
        Reconstruction, 550–551, 553
    exclusion from postrevolutionary politics, 208–209
    family life of, 536
    free, 293–294, 397–399, 428, 537. *See also* Reconstruction era
    gold rush and, 459
    industrialization process and, 606–607, 608–609, 614
    Ku Klux Klan and, 550, 554, 555–556, 582, 759–760
    movement to cities, 293–294, 359–362, 602–603, 606–607, 834–835, 904

Blacks (*Continued*)
National Association for the Advancement of Colored People, 714–715, 905–907, 918–919
New Deal programs and, 807–808
in the New South, 582–586
occupational mobility of, 623
in Philadelphia riot of 1834, 359–360
population size and growth of, 67, 69, 70, 71, 94, 97–98, 103, 159
post–World War I situation of, 755, 769–772
progressive era and, 714–715
progress of the 1970s and 1980s, 986–987
property rights of Reconstruction era, 537, 538, 543–544, 546–549, 551
in Reconstruction era state governments, 552–553
as slaves. *See* Slaves
as subordinate people, 312, 384, 582, 583
trade union membership of, 806–807
World War I employment of, 746–747
World War II and, 833–835, 837–838, 840, 846–847
Blackwell, Elizabeth, 523
Blackwell, Emily, 523
Blaine, James G., 629, 633, 635, 664
Blair, Francis, 408
Bland-Allison Act of 1878, 632
Bleeding Kansas, 485–486
Bliss, Amos, 290
*Blithedale Romance, The* (Hawthorne), 421
Bodin, Jean, 12
Bolivia, 18, 21
Bolshevik Revolution, 735, 741, 751, 756–757
Bomb shelters, 873–874
Bonds, 598
liberty, 744–745
war, 744–745, 831–832
Bonus Army, 792–793
*Book of Mormon*, 422
Boone, Daniel, 278
Borah, William, 779
Bossism, 633, 650–652

Boston, Massachusetts
British occupation of, 167–168, 178, 180
busing issue in, 959–960
as colonial trade center, 109
Glorious Revolution and, 80–81
Great Awakening revivalism in, 118–119
impact of Seven Years' War on, 141
impressment riot of 1747, 125
"Massacre" of 1770, 147
municipal reform movement in, 707
post–World War I strikes in, 757–758
slaves in, 71
Stamp Act riots in, 131, 144
Tea Party of, 149
Boucher, Jonathan, 205
Bourne, Randolph, 736
Bowdoin, James, 168, 226–227
Bowie, Jim, 443
Bowles, Chester, 829
Boxer Rebellion, 683
Brace, Charles Loring, 426
Braceros, 908
Braddock, James, 138
Bradford, David, 247
Bradford, John, 249
Bradford, William, 42
Bradley, Dan, 989
Bradley, Omar, 846
Brandeis, Louis D., 695, 717, 720, 734
Brant, Joseph, 189–190, 223, 315
Brazil, 18, 19, 20, 22, 72, 396
Breck, Samuel, 344, 353, 356, 412, 413
Breckenridge, John C., 301–302, 492
Breese, Sidney, 446
Brezhnev, Leonid, 952
Briand, Aristede, 780
Bricker, John, 877
Brims (Creek chief), 134–135
Brinckerhoff, Dirck, 199
Brisbane, Albert, 421
Brock, Charles, 380
Bronson, Arthur, 340, 364
Brook Farm, 421
Brooks, John, 890
Brooks, Preston, 485–486
Brophy, John, 701

Brotherhood of Railway and Steamship Clerks, 805
Brotherhood of Sleeping Car Porters, 834
Browder, Earl, 877
Brown, Albert Gallatin, 480
Brown, Charles Brockden, 327
Brown, David, 231, 254
Brown, Edmund G., 931
Brown, H. Rap, 929
Brown, John, 485, 491–492
Brown, Moses, 273
Brown, William Wells, 388, 389, 607
Brown Berets, 967, 968
Brownmiller, Susan, 933
Brownsville, Texas riot of 1906, 714
*Brown* v. *Board of Education*, 905, 925
Bryan, William Jennings, 670, 705, 715, 719, 731–732
election of 1896, 653–655
election of 1900, 677
Scopes trial and, 767
Bryce, James, 604, 629, 630
Buchanan, James, 406, 447, 473, 483, 488–490
Buffalo (animal), 577
Buford, Jefferson, 485
Bunau-Varilla, Philippe, 682
Bureau of Freedmen, Refugees and Abandoned Lands, 541, 545–546
Burger, Warren E., 957
Burgoyne, 170, 174, 178
Burke, Aedanus, 227
Burke, Edmund, 146, 149
Burke, Thomas, 165, 287–288
Burleson, Albert S., 737
Burlingham, Bo, 956
Burnaby, Andrew, 106
Burnham, Daniel H., 638
Burnett, John, 255
Burns, Anthony, 477
Burns, Arthur, 948
Burr, Aaron, 256–257, 308
Bushnell, Horace, 417
Busing, 958–960, 997
Butler, Andrew, 485–486
Butler, Ben, 554
Butler, Charles, 340, 364
Butler, John, 180
Byrd, William, 103, 107
Byrd, William II, 108

Byrne, Jane, 984
Byrnes, James F., 860
Byzantium, 12

Cabot, John (Giovanni Caboto), 24
Cabot, Sebastian, 27
Calhoun, John C., 321, 329, 330,
    384, 405, 407–410, 413, 444,
    473, 474
California, 23, 441, 835, 955–956
    agriculture in, 572–574
    gold rush, 456–459, 465–467, 604
    Hispanic Americans in, 447, 467–
        468, 909, 967, 968
    independence from Mexico, 445,
        447
    Native Americans in, 574–575
    post–World War II growth of, 889
    slavery issue and, 474, 475
Calley, William L., Jr., 949
Calvert, Cecilius, 38
Calvert, George (Lord Baltimore),
    37–38
Calvin, John, 17
Calvinism, 17–18
Cambodia, 950, 952
Campbell, William, 191–192
Canada, 585
    black freedmen in, 551, 585
    escape of black slaves to, 430, 476
    French colonies in, 86–90
    Revolutionary Loyalists in, 196
    during the Revolutionary War,
        168
    Seven Years' War and, 138–139
    War of 1812 and, 321–324
Canal systems, 337, 353, 417
Cane (Toomer), 771
Canning, George, 325
Cannon, James, 156
Cannon, John, 93
Cape Cod, Massachusetts, 41, 42,
    183
Capital, locations of national, 240–
    241, 244, 298
Capital investment
    antebellum, 340
    industrialization process, 598
    preindustrial, 269, 272–273, 340
Capitalism
    bases for American adoption of,
        275–276
    merchant, 269, 272–273
Capone, Al, 782

Caravel, 13
Carey, Mathew, 354
Carmichael, Stokely, 928–929, 931
Carnegie, Andrew, 521, 597, 599–
    600, 619, 646
Carolina colonies, 52–54. See also
        North Carolina colony; South
        Carolina colony
    agriculture in, 53–54
    British occupation of, 170, 171,
        178
    early settlement of, 52–53
    Native Americans and, 53, 57
    slaves in, 52–53, 57, 67, 70, 106
Carpenter, Arthur, 499, 508, 512,
    514, 527
Carpetbaggers, 552
Carroll, Charles, 103
Carson, Rachel, 969
Carswell, G. Harold, 957
Carter, Jimmy
    election of 1976, 993
    presidency of, 993–995
Carter, Landon, 72
Carter, Robert "King," 103
Carteret, George, 56
Cartier, Jacques, 24
Cash, Wilbur, 535
Cass, Lewis, 331, 437, 438, 444, 466,
    472–474
Castile, 12, 14
Castro, Don M., 891
Castro, Fidel, 871, 933–935
Catcher in the Rye (Salinger), 898
Catch-22 (Heller), 940
Cather, Willa, 570–571
Catholicism, 116
    in colonial Maryland, 37–38
    England's westward expansion
        and, 24–25
    Glorious Revolution of 1668 and,
        79–83
    in New France, 86–88
    in the New World, 3, 17, 23
    of nineteenth-century immi-
        grants, 481–483
    Protestant Reformation and, 16–
        17
Catt, Carrie Chapman, 644, 749
Cattell, James M., 737
Cattle, 571–572
Caulkins, Raymond, 698
Cavalry, World War I, 741

Central America, 5. See also specific
        countries
Central Intelligence Agency (CIA),
        870–871
Chain migration, 604
Chambers, Whittaker, 875–876
Chaney, James, 923
Channing, William Ellery, 423
Chapman, Leonard, 981
Charity organizations
    almshouses. See Almshouses
    social reform efforts of, 288–289
    women's role in, 357
Charles I (king of England), 37, 40,
    41, 51
Charles II (king of England), 52, 54,
    56, 79, 80
Charleston, South Carolina, 53
    attack on Fort Sumter, 495–496,
        500
    British occupation of, 170, 171,
        178
Chase, Salmon P., 483, 505, 543,
    744
Chase, Samuel, 231, 302
Chauncy, Elnathan, 101
Chávez, César, 930–931, 968
Chemical warfare, 741
Cherokee tribe, 139, 192
    eighteenth-century cultural
        changes among, 135–136
    nineteenth-century revitalization,
        313–315
    in the Revolutionary War, 188–
        189
    westward movement and, 438–
        440
Chesapeake Bay colonies, 3–4, 76–
    78
    agriculture in, 32–39, 104–106
    daily life, 38–39
    Jamestown, 3, 33–37, 43, 76–78,
        83
    Maryland, 37–38, 69, 78, 82
    Roanoke Island, 26, 32–33
    slaves in, 67, 68, 69–70, 103
Chesapeake (ship), 319
Chesnut, Mary Boykin, 382
Chesnutt, Charles W., 607
Cheves, Langdon, 321
Cheyenne tribe, 575
Chicago, Illinois, 340
    Colombian Exposition of 1893,
        636–638

Chicago, Illinois (*Continued*)
  Democratic convention of 1968
    in, 946–947
  Haymarket Riot of 1886, 617
  riot of 1919 in, 769
  Weathermen in, 956
Chicanos, 908–909. *See also* His-
    panic Americans
Chickasaw tribe, 188, 438–440
  westward movement and, 438–
    440
*Child at Home, The,* 358
Childbirth, 284
Child labor
  Fair Labor Standards Act of 1938,
    814
  Keatings-Owen Child Labor Bill,
    734
  progressivism and, 693–694, 704,
    781
  textile industry, 273, 335, 346,
    349–350, 580
Children
  baby boom generation, 888
  birthrate in 1970s and 1980s, 981–
    982
  in the Great Depression, 790–
    791
  in the industrialization process,
    612
  runaway, 982
  urbanization process impact on,
    358
Chile, 18, 325, 664
China, 15, 33, 183, 441, 447. *See
    also* People's Republic of
    China
  immigrants from, 458–459, 604,
    621, 682–683
  Japanese invasion of, 827
  Korean War and, 866–868
  missionaries in, 669
  Open Door policy, 682–683
  Revolution in, 864–865
  trade with, 667, 682–683
*China Syndrome,* 990
Chinese Exclusion Act of 1882, 621,
    683
Chippewa tribe, 222
Choctaw tribe, 188, 438–440
Cholera, 465–466
Chopin, Kate, 642
Christensen, Dale, 977
Christian, William, 518

Christianity. *See also* Religion; spe-
    cific religions
  as basis of settlement house move-
    ment, 648–649
  of blacks, 293–294, 390–392, 399,
    550
  Catholic-Protestant division
    within, 15–17
  European conflict in, 15–17
  European settlers and, 9, 23
  in international expansionism,
    668–669
  among Native Americans, 3, 313,
    314
  Spanish explorers and, 3
  urban revival movements, 649–
    650
Churchill, Winston, 826, 841–842,
    846, 848, 859
Church of England
  Protestants and, 42
  Puritans and, 40–41
  Quakers and, 54–55
Church of Jesus Christ of Latter Day
    Saints, 422, 459–462
Cincinnati, Ohio
  impact of Civil War on, 521, 522
  nineteenth-century industrializa-
    tion in, 350–352
Cisneros, Henry, 988
Cities. *See also* Urbanization
  automobiles and growth of, 763–
    764
  blacks in, 293–294, 359–362
  colonial, 108–116
    artisans in, 110–112
    as basis for revolutionary agita-
      tion, 143–151, 155–157
    commerce in, 109
    entrepreneurial ethos of, 114–
      115
    intellectual currents in, 115–
      116
    social structure of, 112–114
  disease in, 601, 606
  municipal reform in progressive
    era, 638, 695–696, 705–708
  Native Americans in, 909, 929–
    930
  of the New South, 579
  suburbs of, 607, 763, 888–891
  World War II growth of, 836–837
Citizens Equal Rights Association,
    585

Citizenship
  Native Americans, 809
  naturalization laws, 254, 303
  postrevolutionary limits on, 208–
    211
"City beautiful" movement, 638,
    695–696, 705–708
*City: The Hope of Democracy*
    (Howe), 708
Civilian Conservation Corps (CCC),
    799, 807
Civil liberties
  Japanese-American concentration
    camps and, 833
  World War I and, 737–738
Civil Liberties Bureau, 738
Civil Rights Act of 1875, 583
Civil Rights Act of 1957, 907,
    923
Civil Rights Act of 1960, 907
Civil Rights Act of 1964, 923, 925,
    932, 987
Civil rights movement, 900, 904–
    908
  busing in, 958–960, 997
  development of, 904–905
  Hispanic Americans in, 930–931
  Johnson administration and, 923–
    924, 927–929
  Kennedy administration and, 917,
    918–922, 930
  Native Americans in, 929–930
  New Deal era, 807–808
  nineteenth-century, 582–586
  Nixon administration and, 957–
    958
  protests in, 905–907, 919–922,
    923–924, 928–929
  school integration in, 905–906,
    958–960
  student movement in, 938–940
  voting and, 958
Civil service
  Gilded Age reform of, 632
  loyalty programs, 875
  patronage and, 629, 631, 632,
    650–652
Civil Service Commission Loyalty
    Review Board, 875
Civil War, 499–529, 534, 575. *See
    also* Reconstruction era
  battles of, 505–511, 516–519,
    524–525
    Antietam, 508

Bull Run (Manassas Creek),
506–508
Chancellorsville, 517
Gettysburg, 518
naval, 510–511, 525
Shiloh Church (Pittsburgh
Landing), 509
Trans-Mississippi campaign,
509–510
Vicksburg, 518–519
casualties of, 178
causes of, 472–497
breakdown of political parties,
477–483
cultural differences between
North and South, 484–488
polarization between North and
South, 488–492
precipitating events, 493–496
slavery in the territories, 472–
477
cotton diplomacy in, 511
Emancipation Proclamation and,
514–515, 524
impact of, 519–528, 534
economic, 520–527
in the North, 520–522
on race relations, 522, 523
reasons for Northern victory,
524–526
in the South, 519–520, 521–
522
uncertainty and, 527–528
on women, 522, 523–524
organization for, 500–505
pensions for veterans of, 634,
635
political dissension in, 513–514
problems in fighting of, 511–513,
525–526
surrender at Appomattox, 524
Civil Works Administration (CWA),
796–797
Clark, William, 308
Clarke, Anne, 945
Clarke, Charity, 210–211
Clay, Henry, 321, 325, 329, 330,
410, 413, 474, 475, 483
election of 1828 and, 407–408
election of 1832 and, 411–412
Clayton, William L., 854
Clayton Act, 720
Clemenceau, Georges, 540
*Clermont* (steamboat), 280

Cleveland, Grover, 633
election of, 591
presidency of, 629, 630, 631, 636,
652–653
depression of 1893, 620, 636–
639, 666–667, 709
expansionism in, 665, 670
Cleveland, Ohio
progressive era reforms in, 707–
708
Clinton, De Wit, 285
Clinton, George, 238, 289
Clocks
industrialization and, 345–346
preindustrial use of, 282
Clothing industry, 351
Clymer, George, 246
Coal industry, 597, 712
Coal power, 597
Cocaine, 992
Coffin, William Sloane, Jr., 919
Cohn, Roy, 877–878
Cold War, 853, 854–881
atomic weapons and, 871–874
China and, 864–865
containment in. *See* Containment
Cuba and, 933–935
declaration of, 859
economic aid for Western Europe,
861–862
economic pressure on the Soviet
Union, 859
Korea and, 866–868
Latin America and, 871, 933–935,
936
loyalty programs in, 874–876
Middle East and, 869–871
Poland and, 858–859
under Reagan, 995–996
Red Scare in, 876–879
Soviet view of the United States,
856
Stalin's leadership in, 857
Truman's leadership in, 855–856
United States view of Soviet
Union, 854, 857–858
Vietnam and, 868–869, 935, 936–
937
Cole, Jim, 806–807
Colleges
baby boom generation in, 937–
940
black enrollment, 986
colonial, 120

nineteenth-century growth of,
278, 289, 427, 644
in the 1970s and 1980s,
983
women's, 641–642
College Settlement, 691
Collier, John, 809
Colombia, 18, 22, 325, 681–682,
732
Colonies, English, 3, 27–28, 31–61,
63–91, 131–161. *See also* spe-
cific colonies
backcountry of, 107–108, 119–
120
Carolina. *See* Carolina colonies
Chesapeake Bay. *See* Chesapeake
Bay colonies
daily life in, 38–39
France and, 86–90, 132–141
Holland and, 79
influence of England on, 122–126,
142–147, 148–149
Massachusetts. *See* Massachusetts
colony
New England. *See* New England
colonies
Seven Years' War, 136–141
Colorado, 23
Ludlow Massacre, 704
Sand Creek massacre, 575
Colored Farmers' Alliance, 589
Colson, Charles W., 960
Columbia, 208
Columbus, Christopher, 14, 15, 17,
18, 20, 27
Columbus, Ohio, 891
Comanche tribe, 575
Commercialism
emergence of colonial period,
114–115
growth of nineteenth-century,
262–264
Commission on Training Camp Ac-
tivities, 748
Committee of Fair Employment Prac-
tices (FEPC), 834, 835
Committee of Industrial Organiza-
tion (CIO), 806
Committees of Correspondence,
147–148
Common law, 301
*Common Sense* (Paine), 151, 154,
202

Communication
  newspapers in. *See* Newspapers
  post–World War I growth of, 764–766
  preindustrial, 278–280
  radio in. *See* Radio
  telephone in, 764, 765
  television in. *See* Television
  westward movement and, 456
Communism. *See also* Communist party
  in China, 865, 951–952
  in France, 861
  in Italy, 861
  post–World War I fear of, 756–757
  post–World War I working class protest, 757–759
  in Vietnam, 868–869
Communist Labor party, 757
Communist party, 757. *See also* Cold War
  loyalty programs under Truman and, 874–876
  New Deal programs and, 800–801
  Red Scare movements and, 756–759, 853, 876–878, 908
Communities
  of blacks, 293–294
  preindustrial, 278–286
Compromise of 1850, 475–478
Computers, 892–893
Concentration camps
  Holocaust, 843–844
  Japanese-Americans in, 832–833
Concord, Massachusetts, 151, 157, 167, 175, 176, 180
Condict, John, 209
Confederacy. *See* Confederate States of America
Confederate States of America
  attack on Fort Sumter, 495–496, 500
  border states and, 502–504
  conscription act of, 512–513, 519, 520
  financial concerns, 511, 519
  formation of, 493
  impact of Civil War on, 519–520
  organization to fight Civil War, 500–505
  political dissension in, 513–514
  post–Civil War status of, 532–534, 539–540
  problems of, 525–526

Confederation Congress, 232, 240, 241
  Constitutional Convention and, 232, 234, 235
Confederation of New England, 50
Conformity
  corporations and, 891–892
  education and, 894–895
  in religion, 895
  television and, 894–895
Congregationalists, 218
*Congressional Government* (Wilson), 716
Congress of Industrial Organization, (CIO), 806–807
Congress of Racial Equality (CORE), 918, 919
Conkling, Roscoe, 628–629, 631
Connecticut, 43
  punishment of Loyalists in, 217
  Puritan settlers in, 31–32
  in the Revolutionary War, 179
Connecticut Wits, 327
Connor, Eugene "Bull," 920
Conscription
  Civil War, 512–513, 519, 520
  first laws, 76
  pre–World War II, 826
  Revolutionary War, 176
  during World War I, 738–739
Conscription Act of 1862, 519
Conservation programs, 713–714, 968–969, 990
Constitutional Union party, 492
Constitution(s)
  Federal, 232–240
    amendments to. *See* specific amendments
    electoral process and, 234, 252
    judicial branch powers and, 301–303
    Philadelphia Convention, 232–235, 243
    pre-ratification debate, 235–237
    ratification of, 237–240
    slavery and, 384
  state, 212, 214–216, 218
    Reconstruction era, 539–540, 552–553
    universal white suffrage in, 330–331
Consumer movement, 969, 989–991

Consumer products
  advertising and, 893–894, 969
  appliances, 814–815, 893
  mass production of, 639–640
Containment, 859–861
  China and, 865
  defined, 859–860
  Korea and, 866–868
  in the Mediterranean, 860–861
  military alliance in Europe, 862–863
  in the 1950s, 864
  rebuilding of Germany in, 861–862
Continental Congress, 240
  First, 150, 164
  Second, 150–153, 164–167, 220–228
Contraceptive methods, 358–359, 772, 841, 940–941
  abortion as, 957, 965, 985–986
Contract law, 341
Conwell, Russell, 645–646
Coode, John, 78, 82, 83
Coolidge, Calvin, 758, 883
  election of 1920, 777
  election of 1928, 782
  presidency of, 775, 777–780
Cooper, James Fenimore, 345
Cooperatives, agricultural, 586–587, 589, 798
Corey, Giles, 85
Corn, 566
Corn Laws, 272
Cornwallis, Charles, 164, 170, 171, 172, 174
Coronado, Francisco Vásquez de, 23
Corporations
  advantages of, 600
  antitrust legislation, 634–635, 710–711, 720
  business enterprises as, 264
  consumer movement and, 989–991
  management techniques for, 599, 701–702, 763
  New Deal limits on, 804
  post–World War II changes in, 891–894
  in the recession of 1980–1983, 977–979
  securities of, 598
  Virginia Company, 33–37, 79
Cortés, Hernando, 18, 20

Cosby, William, 127
Cottle, Thomas J., 959
Cotton, 184, 441
  decline of, 904
  Civil War importance of, 511
  modernization of production of, 568
  in the New South, 581–582
  nineteenth-century production of, 268–269, 277
  Reconstruction era importance of, 546, 549
  slaves in production of, 193, 268–269, 277, 371–376
Cotton gin, 268, 372
Coughlin, Charles E., 801
Council of Economic Advisors, 899
Councils, colonial, 122
Counterculture, 940–942, 955–956
Cowboys, 572
Cox, Archibald, 961
Cox, James, 777
Coxey, Jacob, 638
Coy, Ed, 584
Crady, Timothy, 287–288
Crandall, Prudence, 361
Crane, Stephen, 602
Crash of 1929, 783, 788
Crawford, William, 308, 330
Crazy Horse, 576
Credit. *See also* National debt
  debt peonage, 548–549, 581–582
  installment, 762
  national debt, 917–918, 996
  postrevolutionary use of, 225–227
Creek tribe, 134–135, 188, 189, 192
  nineteenth-century armed resistance of, 317, 406
  westward movement and, 438–440
Creel, George, 736
Crockett, David, 317, 443
Croly, Herbert, 717
Crosby, Ernest Howard, 676
Crum, William D., 714
Cuba, 14, 18, 480–481
  Batista in, 823, 871, 933
  Bay of Pigs incident, 933–934
  Castro's takeover, 871, 933–934
  independence from Spain, 669–670, 672
  international expansionism and, 661, 663, 669–674, 680

missile crisis in, 934–935
  self-government of, 680
  Spanish-American War, 672–674
Cullen Countee, 771
Culpeper, John, 78
Currency
  Civil War issuance of, 511, 520
  colonial, 142
  federal reserve notes as basis for, 719
  metallic standard for, 631–632, 635, 636, 652–654, 796
  postrevolutionary, 184, 186–188
  Seven Years' War and, 186
Currency Act of 1764, 142
Curtis, Samuel, 510
Custer, George, 576
Czechoslovakia, 862

Dabney, R. L., 382
Da Gama, Vasco, 15
Dairy farming
  antebellum period, 362
  nineteenth-century, 265, 267
Daley, Richard, 946, 984
Dalrymple, Oliver, 567
*Danbury Hatters* case, 702
Danforth, Thomas, 194, 196
Danforth, William, 790
Dark Ages, 12
Darlan, Jean, 842
Darrow, Clarence, 767–768
*Dartmouth College* v. *Woodward*, 341
Darwin, Charles, 646–647
Daugherty, Harry, 777
Daughters of Liberty, 210
Davenport, James, 119
Davenport, John, 45
Davies, Samuel, 119
Davis, Jefferson, 481, 493, 501, 504, 505, 508, 513, 519, 525–526, 537, 543
Davis, John, 231
Davis, John W., 777, 778, 800
Dawes, Charles, 777, 780
Dawes Severalty Act of 1887, 577, 808–809
Day, Doris, 897
Dean, John, 960, 961
Deane, Silas, 185
DeBow, J. D. B., 377
Debs, Eugene, 619–620, 704, 705, 718, 737, 756, 777

Debt peonage, 548–549, 581–582
Declaration of Causes of Taking-up Arms, 151
Declaration of Independence, 152–153, 168, 200–201
Declaration of Rights and Resolves, 150
Declaration of Sentiments, 433
Declaratory Act of 1766, 145
Deerskin, 53
*Deerslayer, The* (Cooper), 345
Deflation, 568
Delancy, James, 156
Delaney, Martin, 399, 429
Delano, Columbus, 577
Delaware
  as border state in the Civil War, 502–503
  colonial, 98
Delaware tribe, 57, 138, 188, 222
De Leon, Daniel, 704, 705
Democracy, 122, 215
*Democracy* (Adams), 557
Democratic party
  under Carter, 993–995
  characteristics of early, 413, 414
  Chicago convention of 1968, 946–947
  disintegration of, 479–481
  under Eisenhower, 901–903
  election of 1896, 652, 653–654
  election of 1984 impact on, 998
  formation of, 407–408
  under Franklin D. Roosevelt, 793–814
  in the Gilded Age, 629–634, 635
  Jackson presidency and, 408–412
  under Kennedy, 914–917
  under Lyndon Johnson, 922–923
  under Polk, 445–450
  post–Civil War, 534
  Reconstruction era, 554–555
  slavery and, 472–474
  split in, 492
  trade union support of, 426–427
  Van Buren presidency and, 412–415
  under Wilson, 716–720, 734
Democratic-Republican societies, 249–251
Dennis, Eugene, 875
Dennison House, 649
*Dennis* v. *United States*, 875
Denny, William, 126

Department of Labor, 617, 694
Dependent Pensions Act, 634, 635
Depression
    of 1819, 274–275, 286
    of 1837, 412–413
    of 1893, 636–639, 709
        expansion of foreign trade and,
            666–667
        Pullman strike in, 620, 638
    postrevolutionary, 184
Derby, Elias, 182, 264
Descartes, René, 115
*Description of New England*
    (Smith), 41
De Soto, Hernando, 23
Détente, 951–952, 993–994
Detroit, Michigan, 340
    recession of 1980–1983 in, 977–
        979
    riot of 1943, 835
Dewey, George, 659, 671–672
Dewey, John, 647, 697
Dewey, Thomas E., 848, 900–901
De Witt, John, 833
Dewson, Molly, 809
*Dialectic of Sex, The* (Firestone),
    966
Dias, Bartolomeu, 14
Dickinson, John, 165
Dickson, Jephta, 549
Didion, Joan, 942
Diem, Ngo Dinh, 869, 935
Diet
    antebellum period, 362–363
    industrialization process and,
        611
    post–World War I, 767
    preindustrial, 282–283
    of slaves, 386–387, 389
Dionne quintuplets, 816
Dioxin, 990, 991
Diphtheria, 284
Dirksen, Everett, 923
Discrimination
    against blacks, 582–586, 833–835,
        837, 840, 986–987. *See also*
        Civil rights movement
    against Hispanic Americans, 835,
        908–909, 973
    against homosexuals, 989
    in housing, 920
    against women, 348–349, 931–
        933, 963–965, 985. *See also*
        Women's rights movement

Disease(s)
    AIDS (acquired immune defi-
        ciency syndrome), 989
    Black Death, 12
    in cities, 601, 606
    colonial period, 20, 33, 35, 36, 38–
        39, 46, 49, 54
    Native Americans and, 20–21,
        465–466
        preindustrial period, 284–285
        during the Revolutionary War,
            177–178, 180
    during the Seven Years' War, 140
    slave, 387–388
    smallpox, 20, 46, 284
    tuberculosis, 284
    westward movement and, 448,
        453, 454
    in World War I, 743
    yellow fever, 284, 285
Disney, Walt, 818
Divorce, 289–290, 982
Dix, Dorothea, 426, 523
Dixiecrat party, 900
Dodge, Mabel, 757
Dodge, Milachi, 566
Dollar diplomacy, 684
Domesticity, 357–360, 772–773
Dominican Republic, 14, 18, 20,
    291, 306–307, 680, 732, 779,
    936
Dominion of New England, 82
Donne, John, 37
Donnelly, Ignatius, 590, 665
Dorchester, Massachusetts, 31
Dos Passos, John, 816
Douglas, Stephen, 444, 471, 475,
    476, 478–479, 484
    debates with Lincoln, 490–491
    Lecompton Constitution and, 490
Douglas, William O., 859, 900, 925
Douglass, Esther, 550
Douglass, Frederick, 369–370, 385,
    389, 391, 392, 397, 399, 400,
    428–430, 471, 495, 496, 515,
    544, 551, 559, 584, 585
    Compromise of 1850 and, 476,
        477
    Dred Scott case and, 489
    John Brown's raid and, 491
    Kansas-Nebraska Act and, 479,
        484
    on military service by blacks, 516
Draft laws. *See* Conscription

Dragging Canoe (Cherokee chief),
    188–189
Drake, Francis, 25, 35
*Dred Scott* v. *Sanford*, 488–490
Dreier, Mary, 703
Dreiser, Theodore, 602
Drugs, recreational, 898, 941, 955,
    992
Duane, James, 150, 199, 213
Dubinsky, David, 806
Du Bois, W. E. B., 546, 553, 559–
    560, 585, 586, 714–715, 878
    World War I and, 740
Dudley, Thomas, 43
Dulles, John Foster, 864, 870, 871,
    874
Dunbar, Paul Laurence, 607
Duncan, John, 571
Dunkers, 17
Dunmore, Lord, 191–192, 211
Durant, George, 78
Durant, William, 762
Dutch West India Company, 52
Dwight, Timothy, 290, 327
Dyer, Mary, 55
Dylan, Bob, 938, 956

Eagleton, Ethie, 499
Eagleton, George, 499, 508, 517,
    526
Earhart, Amelia, 809
Early, Peter, 292
East India Company, 148–149
East Indies, 15
East Jersey, 56
Eastland, James, 905
Eastman, Max, 757
Ebron, Anthony, 867–868
Economic growth
    antebellum, 336–344
        agriculture in, 362–366, 372–
            373, 377, 380, 455–456
        capital investment in, 340
        education in, 341–343
        government role in, 340–341
        industrialization in. *See* Indus-
            trialization
        innovation in, 341–343
        natural resources and popula-
            tion, 337
        transportation in, 337–340
        urbanization and, 352–354
    industrialization and. *See* Indus-
        trialization

post–World War I
  automobiles in, 761–763
  blacks in, 769–772
  cities in, 763–764
  communications in, 764–766
  electrification in, 761
  immigration and migration in, 768–769
  new values in, 767–768
  rural America in, 774–775
  women in, 772–774
post–World War II, 885–894, 903
preindustrial, 262–270
problems of the early 1970s, 974–979
in the Sun Belt, 978–979
after the War of 1812, 328
Economic Opportunity Act of 1964, 924
Economic policy
  antebellum, 340–341
  of Carter, 994–995
  Cold War, 861–862
  currency in. *See* Currency
  under Ford, 963
  foreign trade in. *See* Foreign trade
  Hamilton's views of, 242–247, 249, 251, 262
  inflation and. *See* Inflation
  under Kennedy, 917–918
  under Lyndon Johnson, 924
  under Madison, 328
  national debt in. *See* National debt
  under Nixon, 953–955
  postrevolutionary, 218–220
  post–World War II, 885–887, 899–903
  of Reagan, 996
  toward the Soviet Union, 859
  tariffs in. *See* Tariffs
  taxes in. *See* Income taxes; Taxes
  unemployment in. *See* Unemployment
Ecuador, 18, 22
Eddis, William, 195
Edison, Thomas A., 761
Education. *See also* Colleges; Schools
  Americanization of, 634, 651
  of baby boom generation, 888, 937–938
  as basis of republican society, 289
  bilingual, 968, 987

of blacks, 369, 398, 400, 905–906, 958–960, 986, 997
  antebellum, 361
  Reconstruction, 550–551, 553
conformity and, 894–895
discrimination in, 905–906, 958–960, 984, 997
economic growth and, 341–343
European views of, 43, 50
of Hispanic Americans, 968, 987–988
importance of, 644–645
industrialization of publishing and, 343, 344–345
integration of schools, 905–906, 958–960
Jewish people and, 622–623
kindergarten movement, 697
of Native Americans, 313, 314
nineteenth-century reforms in, 342, 426
occupational mobility and, 622–623, 644–645
post–World War I growth of, 767
progressivism and, 696–697
public schools, 342, 358, 918
role of women in, 641–642
urbanization process and, 358
of women, 290–291, 641–642, 896, 945, 984
for World War II veterans, 885, 898
*Education of Henry Adams, The* (Adams), 556, 629
Edward VII (king of England), 685
Edwards, Anderson, 392
Edwards, Jonathan, 117, 417
Edwards, Malenda, 335, 347
Edwards, Persis, 335, 346, 347
Egypt, 870, 871, 953–954, 993
Ehrlichman, John, 948, 961
Eighteenth Amendment, 424, 782, 796
Einstein, Albert, 825
Eisenhower, Dwight D.
  election of 1952, 901–902
  presidency of, 855–856, 902–903
    domestic policy, 905–908, 909
    foreign policy, 864, 867–868, 869, 870, 874
    post–World War II adjustment, 895
  in World War II, 844, 846, 847
Eisenhower, Milton, 871

Elderly persons, 982–983
Electoral college, 234
Electoral process, 234, 252
Electric iron, 815
Electricity, 761
  appliances and, 814–815, 893
  in the 1930s, 799–800, 804, 814–815
  reduction of federal activity in, 902–903
  Rural Electrification Administration (REA), 804
  Tennessee Valley Authority and, 799–800, 902–903
Electric washing machine, 815
Electronic Numerical Integrator and Calculator (ENIAC), 892–893
Eliot, Charles William, 644
Eliot, Jaret, 99
Eliot, John, 46, 76
Elizabeth (queen of England), 3, 24–25, 40
Elkins Act of 1903, 711
Ellsberg, Daniel, 950
El Salvador, 996
Elskwatawa (the Prophet), 316
Ely, Richard T., 649
Emancipation Proclamation, 514–515, 524
Embargo Act of 1807, 271, 285, 320–321
Emergency Banking Relief Act of 1933, 795
Emerson, Ralph Waldo, 345, 418–419, 421, 476
*Emigrant's Guide to Oregon and California* (Hastings), 441
Emlen, Anne, 210
Employment Act of 1946, 899
Energy policy, 994
  atomic, 872, 903, 969, 990–991
England, 22, 24–28. *See also* Great Britain
  challenge to Holland, 51–52
  challenge to Spain, 24–25, 88, 132, 133, 135
  Civil War and, 511
  civil war of 1642, 50, 52, 54
  colonies of. *See* Colonies, English
  eighteenth-century neutrality toward, 248–251
  embargo of 1807 and, 320–321
  emergence of nation-state, 12

England (*Continued*)
  *Essex* decision in, 318–319
  explorers in Chesapeake Bay region, 3–4
  Glorious Revolution of 1688. *See* Glorious Revolution of 1688
  Jay's treaty of 1795 with, 251–252
  as model for American culture, 327
  pre-revolutionary fervor and, 153–159
  Puritanism in, 40–41
  Quakers in, 54–55
  Revolutionary War with colonies. *See* Revolutionary War
  slave trade of, 65–66, 67
  struggle with France over New World, 88–90
  taxes on colonies, 142–147, 148–149
  War of 1812 and, 271–272, 321–325
  war with France (1793), 248–249, 262–263
  westward expansion by, 25–27
Enlightenment, 115–116, 155, 289, 305
Entrepreneurs
  colonial cities and, 114–115
  innovation by antebellum, 341–342
  preindustrial, 272–273, 276
Environmental movement, 968–969, 990
Environmental Protection Agency, 990
Ephron, Nora, 940
Episcopalians, 218, 390, 550
Equality
  Jefferson and, 304–306
  in republicanism, 204–205, 287–288
Equal Rights Amendment, 774, 965, 966, 984, 986
Equiano, Olaudah, 66
Ericsson, Leif, 14
Erie Canal, 337, 353, 417
*Escobedo* v. *Illinois*, 925
Eskimos, 27
Espinoza, Jerry, 973, 976, 979
Espionage Act, 737
*Essay on Human Understanding* (Locke), 115
*Essex* decision of 1805, 318–319

Ethiopia, 824
Ethnic diversity, 335. *See also* Immigrants
  antebellum urban tension from, 359–360
  in California gold rush, 457–459
  formation of unions and, 621
  growth of local politics, 632–634, 650–651
  industrialization tensions and, 349–350, 352, 608–609
  of New York colony, 52, 81–82
  in the 1980s, 979–981
  of Pennsylvania colony, 59
  of urban areas, 605–607
Europe, 11–17. *See also* specific countries
  Africa and, 10–11
  emergence from Dark Ages, 12
  expansionistic impulse of, 12–14, 25–27
  first contact with Native Americans, 3–4, 7–9
  outbreak of war in 1793, 248–249, 262–263
Eustis, William, 316
Evangelicalism, 93. *See also* Great Awakening
Everett, Sarah, 455
Evolutionism, 767–768
Excess profits tax, 778
Executive branch
  Civil War and, 534
  McKinley's transformation of, 655
  Reconstruction era, 542–543
Expansionism, international, 659–689
  China and, 682–683
  Cuba and, 661, 663, 669–674, 680
  Hawaiian Islands and, 665
  Japan and, 683–684
  in Latin America, 661, 663–664, 670–674, 679, 680–682
  under McKinley, 670–678
  motives for, 665–670
    financial, 666–667
    missionary activities, 668–669
    patriotism, 667–668
    political, 669–670
  new territories in, 676–678
  Panama and, 679, 681–682
  in the Philippines, 659–660, 674–676

  relationship with Great Britain and, 685–686
  under Seward, 663–664
  under Theodore Roosevelt, 678–687
  United States mission in, 661–663

Factions
  Federalist view of, 236
  political parties as, 216
  in republicanism, 203–204
Factory system. *See* Industrialization; Manufacturing
Fair Deal, 901
Fair Labor Standards Act, 813–814
*Faithful Narrative of the Surprizing Work of God* (Edwards), 117
Fall, Albert, 777
Fallout shelters, 873–874
Falwell, Jerry, 992
Family Assistance Plan, 955
Family life
  African, 11
  birthrate in the 1970s and 1980s, 981–982
  among black slaves, 69–70, 72–74, 388–390, 393–394
  in Chesapeake Bay colonies, 38–39
  industrialization process and, 611–614
  Mormon, 461–462
  Native American, 8–9
  post–World War II, 895–898
  preindustrial communities, 281–282
  Puritan, 46–50, 102–103
  Quaker, 58, 102–103
  of Reconstruction era blacks, 536
  in the Southern colonies, 108
  urbanization process and, 356–359
  westward movement and, 453, 454, 458
  during World War II, 836–837
Farley, James A., 794
Farm Board, 789, 792
Farmer, James, 960
Faubus, Orval, 906
Faulkner, William, 816
Federal Deposit Insurance Corporation (FDIC), 796
Federal Emergency Relief Administration (FERA), 796

Federal Employee Loyalty Program, 875
Federal Farm Loan Act, 734
Federal Home Loan Bank Act of 1932, 792
Federal Housing Administration (FHA), 812–813
*Federalist Papers*, 236
Federalists
  collapse of party system based on, 330
  Constitution and, 232–240
  Jeffersonian Republicans versus, 242, 251, 257–258, 300–304, 305, 307–308, 328–329
  John Adams presidency and, 252–257
  Madison presidency and, 321–325
  organization of, 227–228
  social status and, 287
  Washington presidency and, 240–252
Federal Reserve System, 719, 796
Federal Trade Commission (FTC), 720
Feingold, Mimi, 919
Feiwel, Heidi, 983
Fell, Margaret, 54
Female Moral Reform Society, 432
*Feminine Mystique, The* (Friedan), 983
Feminism. *See* Women's rights movement
Fencing, barbed wire, 569
Fendall, Josias, 78
Ferdinand (king of Aragon/Spain), 12, 14
Ferraro, Geraldine, 984, 997, 998
Feudalism
  in colonial Maryland, 37–38
  European, 12
Field, James G., 590
Fifteenth Amendment, 543, 544, 558, 907
Filipino-American War, 659–660, 671–672, 674–676
Fillmore, Millard, 475, 483
Fink, Mike, 278
Finley, James, 328
Finney, Charles G., 403, 416–417
*Fire Next Time, The* (Baldwin), 927
Firestone, Shulamith, 966
Fischer, John, 858

Fishing, 24, 988
  by French in New World, 86
  Revolutionary War impact on, 183
Fisk, Clinton, 545
Fithian, Philip, 104, 107
Fitzgerald, F. Scott, 771–772
Fitzgerald, John, 707
Fitzhugh, George, 384
Fitzpatrick, Sarah, 391–392
Flintoff, John, 378
Florida
  secession of, 493
  Spanish cessions to the United States, 308
  Spanish settlers in, 23
Foch, Ferdinand, 743
Food Administration, 745
*Fool's Errand, A* (Tourgée), 555
Foot, Samuel, 309
Football, 992
Forbes, John, 138
Force Acts, 555
Force Bill, 410, 635
Ford, Gerald, 948, 951, 952, 962–963, 993
Ford, Henry, 701, 762–763, 765
Ford Motor Company, 762–763, 806
Fordney-McCumber Tariff of 1922, 780
Foreign policy
  under Carter, 993–994
  under Coolidge, 779–780
  under Eisenhower, 864, 867–868, 869, 870, 874
  of expansionism. *See* Expansionism, international
  under Franklin Roosevelt, 822–823
  under Jefferson, 318–326
  under Johnson, 935–937
  under Kennedy, 933–935
  League of Nations and, 751–752, 778–779, 780, 824
  under Madison, 321–325
  under Monroe, 325–326
  in the 1920s, 778–780
  in the 1930s, 822–827
  under Nixon, 949–952
  under Reagan, 995–996
  Social Darwinism and, 678–679
  under Truman, 854–856, 858–863, 866–874

  under Washington, 238–239
  of Wilson in Latin America, 731–733
Foreign trade
  agricultural, 566, 977
  with China, 667, 682–683
  Embargo Act of 1807, 320–321
  European wars and growth of, 262–264
  impact of French Revolution on, 248–249
  with Japan, 667, 683–684, 827–828
  under Jefferson, 318–321
  neutrality during World War I and, 730–731
  nineteenth-century expansionism and, 666–667
  nonimportation agreements in, 147, 155–156, 319
  Revolutionary War impact on, 182–183, 224
  tariffs in. *See* Tariffs
  War of 1812 and, 271–272, 321–325
  West Indies in, 182, 183–184, 318–319, 320
Forman, James, 927
Fort Duquesne, 137–138
Fort Harmar Treaty, 309
Fort Laramie Treaty of 1868, 466, 575, 967
Fort Niagara, 139
Fort Stanwix Treaty, 190, 222, 223
Fort Sumter, 495–496, 500
Fort Ticonderoga, 151
Fortune, T. Thomas, 584
Fosdick, Raymond, 748
Foster, Stephen, 431
Fourier, Charles, 421
Fourteen Points, 749–752
Fourteenth Amendment, 542, 543, 544, 557, 558, 583
Fox, George, 54, 55
France, 19–20, 22, 24
  Civil War and, 511
  Communism in, 861
  Democratic-Republican Societies and, 229–251
  embargo of 1807 and, 320–321
  emergence of nation-state, 12
  John Adams administration and, 253–256
  Louisiana Purchase and, 306–308

France (*Continued*)
   in the Middle East, 871
   Moroccan crisis and, 686
   New World involvement of, 86–
      90, 132–141
   postrevolutionary relations with,
      183, 224, 225
   post–World War I war debt, 780
   in the Revolutionary War, 172–
      173, 174, 225, 243
   Revolution of 1789 and, 248–249,
      305, 318
   Seven Years' War and, 131, 132,
      133, 136–141, 224
   in Vietnam, 868–869
   War of 1812 and, 321–325
   war with England (1793), 248–
      249, 262–263
   in World War I, 726, 729, 730,
      741, 742–743, 744, 750
   in World War II, 825–826, 843,
      846, 847
   XYZ affair and, 253
Franco, Francisco, 824–825, 843
Franklin, Benjamin, 94, 100, 115,
      117–118, 137–138, 141, 151,
      154, 172, 173, 216, 220, 343
   Constitution and, 233, 240
Free blacks, 293–294, 397–399, 428,
      541, 545–546. *See also* Re-
      construction era
Freedmen's Bureau, 541, 545–546
Freedom Democratic party, 927
Freedom Summer, 923, 927
Free soil movement, 472–474
Free-Soil party, 474, 483, 484–485
Frelinghuysen, Theodore, 117
Frémont, John C., 483, 492, 504
French and Indian War. *See* Seven
      Years' War
French Revolution, 248–249, 305,
      318
Frick, Henry Clay, 619
Friedan, Betty, 966, 983–984, 985
Frink, Margaret, 450
Frizzell, Lodisa, 450
Fugitive Slave Act of 1793, 471, 474
Fugitive Slave Act of 1850, 475–
      477
Fugitive slave clause, 234
Fullbright, J. William, 934
Fuller, Harlan, 520
Fuller, Margaret, 421
Fulton, Robert, 280

Furman, Gabriel, 287
Fur trade
   of French in New World, 86
   Native American involvement in,
      135, 312
   Seven Years' War and, 136–138
   westward movement and, 440–
      441

Gadsden, Christopher, 141
Gadsden, James, 480
Gadsden Purchase of 1853, 441, 448,
      480
Gage, Thomas, 149, 150–151, 167
Gag rule, 430–431
Galbraith, John Kenneth, 894
Gallatin, Albert, 252, 303
Galloway, Joseph, 150
*Games People Play* (Berne), 969
Gardiner, John, 290
Gardoqui, Don Diego de, 223
Garfield, James A.
   assassination of, 631, 632
   presidency of, 629, 630, 631
Garland, Hamlin, 570
Garnet, Henry Highland, 429
Garrison, William Lloyd, 388, 427–
      429, 430, 491, 714
Garson, Barbara, 970
Garvey, Marcus, 769–770, 928
Gary, Elbert, 766
Garza, Elizo de la, 930
*Gaspee* (ship), 148
Gates, Horatio, 170
Gayantogogwus, 297
Gay Liberation, 989
General Federation of Women's
      Clubs, 640–641
General Motors, 806
Genêt, Edmund, 249–250, 251
George, Henry, 647, 692, 707
George I (king of England), 133
George II (king of England), 127
George III (king of England), 149,
      168
Georgia
   Cherokee land and, 440
   cotton production in, 193, 268–
      269
   postrevolutionary slavery in, 193
   punishment of Loyalists in, 216–
      217
   ratification of Constitution by,
      237, 238

during the Revolutionary War,
      170–171, 178
   secession of, 493
German Pietists, 420
Germany
   Anglo-American relationship and,
      686–687
   annexation of Austria, 825
   Hitler in, 823–826, 841, 843, 847
   immigrants from, 94–95, 103,
      107, 608, 737, 768
   partition of, 848, 861–862, 934
   post–World War I debt, 780, 822
   Protestant Reformation in, 16–17
   rebuilding of, 861–862
   Revolutionary mercenaries from,
      168, 174, 180
   Samoan Islands incident and, 665
   Soviet feat of, 858
   Spanish Civil War and, 824–825
   in World War I, 726, 729, 730–
      731, 735, 736, 737, 741, 743–
      744, 750–751
   in World War II, 825–827, 841,
      842, 846–847
Gerry, Elbridge, 187, 233, 253
Gest, Erasmus, 364–365
Ghana, 10
Ghent, Treaty of (1814), 323–324
Ghiselin, César, 112
Ghost Dance movement, 578
*Giants of the Earth* (Rolvaag), 570
GI Bill of 1944, 885
Gibson, Thomas, 437, 446, 466
*Gideon* v. *Wainwright*, 925
Gilded Age, 629–639
   civil service reform in, 632
   currency standards in, 631–632,
      635, 636, 652–654
   growth of political participation
      in, 632–634, 650–652
   legislative branch in, 629, 631,
      634–636
   nature of, 629
   presidents of, 629–631
   protective tariffs in, 631, 635–639,
      653
   railroad regulation in, 587–588
   as term, 629
Giles, Alexander, 293
Giles, William Branch, 245, 301,
      302
Gilman, Charlotte Perkins, 696
Ginsberg, Allen, 898

Girard, Stephen, 264
Gladden, Washington, 650
Glass-Steagall Banking Act of 1932, 792
*Gleaner, The* (Murray), 290
Glenn, John, 933
Glidden, Joseph, 569
Glorious Revolution of 1688, 80–85, 122, 124, 126, 132
  in England, 79–80
  Maryland colony and, 82
  Massachusetts colony and, 80–81, 82
  New York colony and, 81–82
  social meaning of, 82–83
  Virginia colony and, 82
Glover, Samuel, 176
*Godey's Lady's Book*, 356
Gold, 21
  in Africa, 10, 12–13, 14
  Alaskan, 655
  as basis for currency
    Gilded Age, 632, 635, 636, 652, 653
    New Deal and, 796
  California gold rush and, 456–459, 465–467, 604
  Seven Cities of Cíbola and, 23
Goldman, Emma, 643, 758
Goldmark, Josephine, 695
Goldwater, Barry, 923, 924, 995
Gómez, Agapito, 908
Gompers, Samuel, 618, 620, 701–702, 704, 705, 720, 746, 758
Gonçalves, Antam, 19
*Gone with the Wind* (Mitchell), 816
González, Henry, 922, 930
Goodell, Moses, 364
Goodman, Andrew, 923
Goodman, Ellen, 985
Good Neighbor policy, 823
Gordon, Thomas, 127
Gordon, William, 208
Gould, Jay, 556–557, 617, 631, 645
Goulden, Joseph, 857
Government
  Cherokee National Council, 314–315
  colonial period, 122–127
    absence of police power, 124–125
    growth of legislative assemblies, 125–126

local politics, 126–127
  Puritan form of, 43, 48
  Quaker, 56
  structuring of, 122–124
  Whig ideology in, 127, 153–155
  constitutions in. *See* Constitution(s)
Governors
  colonial, 122, 125–126
  postrevolutionary power of, 213, 215–216
Grady, Henry, 578–579, 581, 582
Graham, Billy, 895
Graham, Sylvester, 424–425
Granger Laws, 587
Grant, Ulysses S., 508, 518–519, 524
  elections of, 543, 557
  presidency of, 555–558, 629, 632, 663
*Grapes of Wrath, The* (Steinbeck), 812, 816
Gray, Nellie, 985
Gray, Robert, 28
Gray, Virginia, 522
Great American Desert, 440
Great Awakening, 116–122, 205–206, 217
  legacy of, 120–122
  religious apathy prior to, 116–117
  revival movements in, 117–120
  Second, 327–328, 416–418
Great Britain. *See also* England
  immigrants from, 768
  lend-lease program and, 826–827
  Mediterranean states and, 860
  in the Middle East, 869–871
  Oregon and, 438, 441, 448–449
  Panama Canal and, 681
  post–World War I war debt, 780
  United States foreign policy with, 684–687
  Venezuela and, 665, 680, 685
  in World War I, 726, 729, 730, 741, 743, 744
  in World War II, 825–827, 841–842, 844–847
  in the Yalta conference of 1945, 848
Great Compromise, 234
Great Depression, 787–793
  banks in, 788, 790, 791, 792
  Bonus Army fiasco, 792–793
  Crash of 1929 and, 783, 788
  economic collapse in, 790–792

Hoover and, 789–793
  recovery from. *See* New Deal
*Great Gatsby, The* (Fitzgerald), 771–772
Great Lakes
  England and, 318, 325
  Erie Canal and, 337
Great Migration, 746
Great Society program, 923, 924–927, 954–955, 981
Great War. *See* World War I
Greece, 860–861
Greeley, Horace, 413, 493, 514, 557
Green, William, 806
Greenbacks, 631–632
Green Corn Rebellion, 739
Greene, Nathaniel, 170
Greene, William, 275
Green Mountain boys, 151
Grenville, George, 142
Griffith, D. W., 698, 765
Grimké, Angelina, 431
Grimké, Sarah, 431, 433
Griswold, A. Whitney, 895
Gross National Product (GNP)
  under Lyndon Johnson, 925
  post–World War II, 886
Grundy, Felix, 321
Guadelupe Hidalgo, Treaty of, 448, 461
Guam, 673, 677
Guangzhou (Canton), 15
Guatemala, 680, 871
Guiana, 26
Gunsmiths, 185
Gutiérrez, José Angel, 967–968
Gwinn Land Law, 467

Haggerty, Rose, 613
Haig, Alexander, 995
Haiti, 14, 306, 495, 496, 514, 732, 822
Hakluyts, Richard, 25, 26
Haldeman, H. R., 948, 961
Hale, Sarah, 356
*Half a Man* (Ovington), 714
Half-Way Covenant, 116–117
Hallucinogenic drugs, 898, 941, 955, 992
Halverson, Carl, 862
Hamer, Fannie Lou, 927
Hamilton, Alexander, 256–257
  Constitution and, 232, 233, 236, 238

Hamilton, Alexander (*Continued*)
   Federalists and, 227, 308
   as secretary of the treasury under
      Washington, 242–247, 249,
      251, 262
Hamilton, Alice, 751
Hamilton, Andrew, 127
Hammond, James, 380
Hancock, John, 112, 146, 148, 151,
   168
Hancock, Thomas, 112, 140–141
Handsome Lake, 297, 309
Hanlin, Larry, 978
Hanna, Mark, 654, 678, 709
Harding, Warren G.
   election of 1920, 776–777
   presidency of, 777, 779
Harlan, John, 636
Harlem Renaissance, 770–771
Harper, Frances Ellen Watkins, 582
Harpers Ferry, Virginia, 255
   John Brown's raid on, 491–492
Harriman, Averell, 858
Harrington, Michael, 903, 927
Harris, Emily, 523
Harris, William, 992
Harrison, Benjamin, 590, 591
   presidency of, 630, 635, 664–665
Harrison, William Henry, 316, 415
Hart, Gary, 997
Harvard College, 43, 76, 120, 644
Hastings, Leonard, 441
Hawaiian Islands, 677
   attempted annexation of, 664–665
   Pearl Harbor attack, 827–828,
      832–833
Hawley-Smoot Tariff of 1930, 780
Hawthorne, Nathaniel, 345, 421
Hay, John, 673, 681–682, 683
Hayden, Tom, 927, 938
Hayes, Rutherford B., 558, 630
Haymarket Riot of 1886 (Chicago),
   617
Hayne, Robert, 410
Haynesworth, Clement, 957
Haywood, "Big Bill," 618–619, 705
Haywood, Felix, 550
Health. *See also* Disease(s)
   nineteenth-century concern for,
      424–425
   of slaves, 386–388
Hearst, William Randolph, 669
Heller, Joseph, 940
Hell's Angels, 955–956

Helsinki Accords, 952
Hemingway, Ernest, 771
Hendrix, Jimi, 942
Henry, Patrick, 141, 150, 154, 233,
   238, 244
   Stamp Act and, 143–144
Henry Street Settlement, 697, 708
Henry the Navigator (Prince of Por-
   tugal), 13–14
Henry VII (king of England), 12,
   40
Henry VIII (king of England), 24
Hepburn Act of 1906, 711
Herndon, William, 505, 513
Hersh, Seymour M., 949
Hewes, George, 149
Hewes, Joseph, 152
Hickok, Lorena, 797
*Hidden Persuaders* (Packard), 893
Highway system, 280, 304, 887
Hill, James J., 647, 667, 711
Hillman, Sidney, 806
Hillquit, Morris, 736
Hiroshima, atom bomb in, 850
Hispanic Americans
   in California, 447, 467–468
   civil rights movement and, 930–
      931
   discrimination against, 835, 908–
      909, 973
   as migrant workers, 768, 808,
      908–909, 930–931
   New Deal era, 808
   in New Mexico, 447–448, 466–
      467
   progress of the 1970s and 1980s,
      987–988
   protests by, 967–968
   in Texas, 467
   during World War II, 835, 839
Hispaniola (Dominican Republic),
   14, 18, 20, 663
   slave rebellion in, 291, 306–
      307
Hiss, Alger, 875–876
Hitler, Adolf, 823–826, 841, 843,
   847
Hjelmeland, Andy, 973, 976, 979
Hoar, George F., 672, 675
Ho Chi Minh, 843, 868–869, 935,
   936
Hoffman, Abbie, 946
Hoffman, Dustin, 985

Holland, 22. *See also* Netherlands
   English challenge to, 51–52
   New Netherland colony of, 50,
      52, 55–56, 81–82
   slave trade of, 65
   trade of English colonies with, 79
Holland Land Company, 276
Holley, Mary Austin, 442
Hollywood Ten, 875
Holmes, John Haynes, 727
Holmes, Oliver Wendell, 728
Holocaust, 843–844
Holy Alliance, 325
Home Owners Loan Corporation
   (HOLC), 812
Homestead Act of 1862, 453, 527–
   528
Homestead Act of 1866, 544, 569
Homesteaders
   Great Plains, 569–571, 577
   Native American, 577
*Home to Harlem* (McKay), 771
Homosexuals, 989
Hone, Philip, 413
Hooker, Thomas, 45, 47
Hoover, Herbert, 745. *See also* Great
   Depression
   election of 1928, 782–783
   presidency of, 776, 780, 783
   as secretary of commerce, 778
Hoover, J. Edgar, 758
Hoovervilles, 791, 792
Hopedale, Massachusetts, 420
Hopewell culture, 6
Hopi tribe, 6
Hopkins, Harry, 793, 795, 796, 797,
   807
Hopkins, Lemuel, 327
Hopkins, Samuel, 159
Horizontal integration, 600
Hotchkiss, Samuel M., 616
House, Edward, 729
House Committee on Un-American
   Activities (HUAC), 875
House of Representatives, 234
*House of Seven Gables, The* (Hawt-
   horne), 345
Housing
   Chesapeake Bay colony, 39
   discrimination in, 920
   early Great Plains, 571
   fallout shelters in, 873–874
   industrial city, 604–605, 606–607
   mass production of, 890

New Deal programs, 812–813
New England colony, 49–50
    ownership of, 623, 885, 890
    preindustrial, 282
    progressivism and, 695–696
    Puritan, 49–50
    of slaves, 386
    urbanization process and, 355–356
Houston, Sam, 443
Howard, O. O., 546
Howe, Frederic C., 708
Howe, Louis, 794
Howe, Richard, 168
Howe, William, 168, 174
Howells, William Dean, 640
*How the Other Half Lives*, 695
Hudson's Bay, 132
Hughes, Charles Evans, 708, 734, 779
Hughes, Langston, 770–771
Hull, Cordell, 822
Hull House, 641, 643, 649, 691, 697, 698, 708, 714
*Human Sexual Response* (Masters and Johnson), 940
Humphrey, George, 902
Humphrey, Hubert H., 914, 946–947, 948
Humphrey, R. M., 589
Humphries, David, 327
Hundred Years' War (1337–1453), 24
Hungary, 862
*Hunger of Memory* (Rodriguez), 987
Hunt, E. Howard, 960, 961
Hunter, Robert, 693
Hunting. *See also* Fur trade
    in Carolina colony, 53
    Native American, 5, 135, 312
Huntingdon, Hattie, 589
Hurston, Zora Neale, 771
Hutchinson, Anne, 44–45, 55, 102, 144
Hutchinson, Steve, 886
Hutchinson, Thomas, 131, 143, 144, 147, 149
Hydrogen bomb, 873–874
Hydropathy, 424

IBM, 892
Ibn-Battutu, 10
Ibn-Majid, Ahmed, 15

Ice Age, 5
Ickes, Harold, 794, 797, 807
Illinois, 308
Immigrants. *See also* Ethnic diversity
    from China, 604, 621, 682–683
    from Germany, 608, 737, 768
    industrialization and, 603–604, 605–606, 608–609, 621
    from Ireland, 608, 623
    from Italy, 608, 768
    from Japan, 683, 684, 832–833
    from Latin America, 573, 768, 808, 908–909, 930–931, 981
    population of, 979–981
    post–World War I restrictions on, 768–769
Immigration and Nationality Act of 1965, 981
Inca empire, 18, 20
Income taxes, 715, 719
    under Coolidge, 778
    Great Depression and, 790
    New Deal, 804
    post–World War II, 899–900
    under Reagan, 996
    during World War II, 830
Indentured servants
    Chesapeake Bay colony, 35–38
    immigration of, 94, 96–97
    slaves versus, 35–36, 67
India, 15
Indiana, 316, 421
Indian Claims Commission, 909
Indian Reorganization Act of 1934, 809, 909
Indian Ocean, 15
Indians. *See* Native Americans
Indigo, 106, 184
Individualism, 288
    formation of unions versus, 621–622
    Jeffersonian view of, 305
    in occupational mobility, 645
    for women, 290–291
Industrialization, 343–352, 595–625. *See also* Manufacturing; Social justice movement
    capital in, 598
    changing nature of work and, 609
    clocks and, 345–346
    division of wealth in, 605–607, 608, 611–612, 622–623
    economic cycle in, 600–601

factory production methods in, 343–344
    family life and, 611–614
    frontier development of, 350–351
    gospel of wealth and, 645–647
    growth patterns in, 599–600
    heavy industry in, 596–597, 599–600
    immigration and, 603–604, 605–606, 608–609, 621
    impact of, 344–345
    nature of work force in, 699–701
    of the New South, 579–581
    preindustrial era in, 269–276
    publishing industry, 343, 344–345
    railroads in, 597, 598–599
    slaves in, 376
    social status and, 351–352, 376–377
    textile industry, 343–344, 346–350
    urban expansion in. *See* Urbanization
    worker protests in, 614–623. *See also* Trade unions
    workplace environment and, 609–611
Industrial Relations Commission, 704
Industrial securities, 598
Industrial Workers of the World (IWW), 704–705, 746
Inflation
    under Ford, 963
    in the Great Depression, 796
    in the 1970s, 974, 976
    under Nixon, 953–954
    post–Civil War, 522
    postrevolutionary, 186–188, 219
    post–World War II, 885–886
    during World War I, 745, 746–747
    during World War II, 831
*In His Steps* (Sheldon), 650
Installment credit, 762
Intercontinental ballistic missile (ICBM), 873
Intercourse Act of 1790, 309
International Court of Justice, 849
International Ladies' Garment Workers Union (ILGWU), 618, 703
International Migration Society, 585
International Monetary Fund, 849

Interstate Commerce Act of 1887, 587–588
Interstate Commerce Commission (ICC), 588, 711–712, 715
Interstate Highway Act of 1956, 887
Inventions, preindustrial, 268, 341, 372
Investment bankers, 598
Iran, 869–870, 994
Ireland, 16
  English colonization of, 25–26, 27
  immigrants from, 608, 623
    colonial, 94, 95, 103, 107
    racial tensions and, 360, 361
    as textile workers, 349–350
Ironclad ships, 510
Iroquois tribe, 8, 88, 138, 309
  in French-English colonial struggles, 133–134, 137–139
  neutrality pact of, 188
  postrevolutionary land treaties, 190, 222–223
  in the Revolutionary War, 189–191
Isabella (queen of Castile/Spain), 12, 14
Israel, 870, 953–954, 993
Italy
  Communism in, 861
  emergence from Dark Ages, 12
  immigrants from, 608, 768
  invasion of Ethiopia, 824
  peasant uprising in, 83
  Spanish Civil War and, 824–825
  in World War I, 726, 741, 750
  in World War II, 844

Jackson, Andrew, 330, 379, 575
  Creek War and, 317, 406
  early career of, 317, 323, 324, 406–407
  presidency of, 404, 408–412, 430
  War of 1812 and, 323, 324, 406
Jackson, Jesse, 997
Jackson, Rachel, 406, 407, 408, 433
Jackson, Stonewall, 517
Jackson State University, 950
Jagger, Mick, 941, 956
Jamaica, 67
James, William, 647–648
James I (king of England), 33, 35, 37, 40–41
James II (king of England), 63, 79–80, 81

Jamestown, Virginia, 3, 33–37, 43. *See also* Virginia colony
  Bacon's Rebellion in, 76–78, 83
Japan, 14
  atomic bomb in, 849–850
  foreign policy toward, 683–684
  immigrants from, 683, 684, 832–833
  industry of, 975
  peace treaty with, 868
  Pearl Harbor attack by, 827–828, 832–833
  trade with, 667, 683–684, 827–828
  in Vietnam, 868
  in World War II, 841, 842, 844–845, 847, 849–850, 859
Jarratt, Devereaux, 93, 103, 118
Jaworski, Leon, 961–962
Jay, John, 172
  Constitution and, 236, 240
  Federalists and, 227, 228
  negotiation with Spain, 223
  treaty with England, 251–252
Jaworski, Leon, 961–962
Jazz, 771
Jefferson, Thomas, 48, 108, 151, 152, 172, 189, 218, 223, 232, 233, 238, 249
  on blacks, 292
  concept of national bank and, 244, 245
  death of, 331
  embargo of 1807, 271, 285, 320–321
  Kentucky Resolutions and, 255
  presidency of, 298–333
    egalitarian vision in, 304–306
    election of 1800, 256–257, 298–300
    Federalist purge in, 300–304
    foreign policy in, 318–321
    inauguration, 300
    Louisiana Purchase, 304, 306–308, 337, 442
    Native American relations, 309–312, 317
    War of 1812, 271–272
    western exploration in, 308–309
  as secretary of state under Washington, 247, 249, 252
  as vice-president under Adams, 252, 255

Jeffersonian Republicans, 257–258
  collapse of party system based on, 330
  Democratic-Republican societies, 249–251
  Federalists versus, 242, 251, 257–258, 300–304, 305, 307–308, 328–329
  Jefferson's administration and, 298–333
  under John Adams, 253–257
  Madison presidency and, 321–325, 328–329
Jenkins, Robert, 133
Jewish people
  anti-Semitism, 801, 843–844
  education and, 622–623
  industrialization process and, 608
  Nazi extermination of, 843–844
Jiang Jieshi, 865
Johnson, Andrew
  impeachment of, 543
  presidency of, 534, 539–540
Johnson, Anthony, 63
Johnson, Hiram, 708
Johnson, Hugh, 798–799
Johnson, Lyndon, 719, 803, 804, 907, 946, 948, 969
  presidency of, 916, 922–929
    civil rights in, 923–924, 927–929
    foreign policy, 935–937
    Great Society, 923, 924–927, 954–955, 981
  as vice-president, 915–917
Johnson, Richard, 321
Johnson, Tom, 707–708
Johnson, Virginia E., 940
Johnston, Albert Sidney, 501, 508, 509
Johnston, Joseph E., 501, 506–507, 518, 519
Jolliet, Louis, 87
Jomini, Henri, 505–506, 516
Jones, Absalom, 293, 390
Jones, Mary Harris ("Mother Jones"), 643, 704
Jones, Samuel ("Golden Rule"), 651–652, 706
Jones, T. K., 995
Jones, Thomas Catsby, 447
Joplin, Janis, 941
Journalism of the muckrakers, 692–693, 712–713

Judicial branch. *See also* Supreme Court
  Federalists under Jefferson and, 301–303
Judiciary Act of 1801, 301–302
Julian, George, 478, 483, 504, 544
*Jungle, The* (Sinclair), 693, 712–713, 801
Justice Department, 737–738

Kansas-Nebraska Act, 478–479, 484
Kansas Territory, 484–488
Kauffman, Irving, 877
Kearney, John, 623
Kearney, Stephen W., 448
Keatings-Owen Child Labor Bill, 734
Kelley, Abbey, 429, 431–433
Kelley, Florence, 644, 693–695, 710, 718
Kelley, Oliver, 586–587
Kellogg, Frank B., 780
Kellogg-Briand pact, 780
Kellor, Frances, 691, 716
Kemble, Fanny, 379
Kendall, Amos, 408
Kenna, "Hinky Dink," 633
Kennan, George F., 859–860
Kennedy, John F., 707
  assassination, 916, 922
  election of 1960, 914–915
  presidency of, 915–922
    domestic policy, 917–922, 930
    foreign policy, 933–935
    personal characteristics, 915–917
Kennedy, Joseph, 790, 826
Kennedy, Robert F., 919, 931, 946
Kenney, Mary, 702
Kent State University, 949–950
Kentucky, 278, 301
Kentucky Resolutions, 255
Kerouac, Jack, 898
Kesey, Ken, 941
Keteltas, William, 287–288
Kettering, Charles, 742
Keynes, John Maynard, 750, 811, 899
Khomeini, Ayatollah Ruhollah, 994
Khrushchev, Nikita S., 857, 934
Kindergarten movement, 697
King, Martin Luther, Jr., 907, 919, 920, 923, 927, 928, 929
King, Rufus, 233, 321, 330
King George's War, 133

King Philip's War, 75–76
King William's War, 88, 90
Kinsey, Alfred C., 897
Kiowa tribe, 575
Kissinger, Henry, 874
  in the Ford administration, 952, 962
  in the Nixon administration, 948, 950–951
Kithtippecanoe, 316
Knight, Newton, 378, 379
Knights of Labor, 556, 584, 617–618
Knowles, Charles, 125
Know-Nothing party, 481–483
Knox, Henry, 185, 309–310
Knox, John, 17
Knox, Philander, 681
Kohl, John J., 828
Korean War, 865, 866–868, 877
Kossuth, Louis, 480
Kovic, Ron, 913
Kroc, Ray, 883
Kronenberger, Louis, 895
Ku Klux Klan, 550, 554, 759–760
Ku Klux Klan Act, 555–556, 582
Ky, Nguyen Cao, 937

Labor organizations. *See also* Trade unions
  antebellum, 349, 351, 352
  industrialization process and, 615–616
  post–Civil War, 616
  strikes by, 615–616, 617–622
La Follette, Robert, 709, 715, 737, 777–778
La Guardia, Fiorello, 703
Land
  colonial period, 98
    Carolina colonies, 52–53
    Chesapeake Bay colony, 103
    Pennsylvania, 57, 59
    voting rights and, 123–124
  conservation efforts, 713–714, 968–969, 990
  European versus Native American views of, 7–8, 27–28
  expansion of, under Jefferson, 305–309
  federal policy on, 308–312, 314, 315–316, 317, 364–365, 438–440, 453
  for free blacks, 537

  as issue in Articles of Confederation, 165–166
  Native American surrender of, 190, 222–223, 309–317, 439–440, 575–577, 909, 929–930
  nineteenth-century speculation in, 276, 286, 309, 412
  in the Old Northwest, 364–366
  opening of western, 221–223, 308–309, 373–374
  productivity of antebellum, 362–363
  Puritan desire for, 45, 46, 47–48, 50
  of railroads, 573
  settlement of backcountry, 107
  seventeenth-century struggles for, 74–78
  taxes on, 219
Land Act of 1796, 308
Land Act of 1801, 308
Land Act of 1820, 308–309
Landon, Alfred, 810
Lane Seminary, 427
Lansing, John, 233
Lansing, Robert, 729, 730, 731
Laos, 935
Lapp, Ralph, 873
La Raza Unida party, 968
Larkin, Thomas, 447
La Salle, René Robert de, 87
Las Cases, Bartholme, 21
*Last of the Mohicans, The* (Cooper), 345
Latin America. *See also* specific countries
  Cold War and, 871, 933–935, 936
  foreign policy of the 1920s in, 779–780
  Franklin Roosevelt's policy toward, 822–823
  immigrants from, 981
  independence of, 325
  international expansionism and, 661, 663–664, 670–674, 679, 680–682
  Monroe's policy for, 318, 325–326
  slaves in, 291, 306–307, 396
  Wilson's foreign policy in, 731–733
Laud, William, 41
Law enforcement
  in antebellum cities, 359, 360
  colonial period, 124–125

Law enforcement (*Continued*)
Democratic convention of 1968 and, 946–947
National Guard in. *See* National Guard
in student protest movement, 939–940
Lawrence, William, 645
Lawson, Hugh, 380
League of Armed Neutrality, 172
League of Nations, 751–752, 778–779, 780, 824
Leary, Timothy, 941
*Leaves of Grass* (Whitman), 485
Lebanon, 871
Lecompton Constitution (Kansas), 489–490
Lee, Ann, 420
Lee, Richard Bland, 323
Lee, Richard Henry, 150, 152
Lee, Robert E., 500, 501, 508, 512, 516–519, 524
Leeper, Hattie, 563, 571
Leeper, Milton, 563
Leeward Islands, 67
Legislative branch
colonial period
bicameral houses, 122–123
growth of influence, 125–126
Congressional Loyalty Program, 875–876
Constitution and, 234
in the Gilded Age, 629, 631, 634–636
House Committee on Un-American Activities (HUAC), 875
Reconstruction era, 540–545
Lehman, Charles, 886
Leisler, Jacob, 81–82, 83
Lemlich, Clara, 703
Lend-lease, 826–827
L'Enfant, Pierre, 298
Lennox, David, 246
Lenroot, Katherine, 809
*Leopard* (ship), 319
Lesbian movement, 989
*Letters on the Condition of Women and the Equality of the Sexes* (Grimké), 433
Levenger, Sam, 825
Levi, Edward H., 963
Levitt, William J., 890
Levittown, New York, 890
Lewis, Fulton, Jr., 878

Lewis, John L., 776, 805–806, 830, 886
Lewis, Meriwether, 308
Lewis, Sinclair, 772
Lexington, Massachusetts, 151, 167
*Liberator*, 388, 428, 430
Liberia, 551, 585
Liberty
balancing power with 203–204
Jeffersonian view of, 304–306
Liberty bonds, 744–745
Liberty League, 800
Liberty party, 429
Liddy, G. Gordon, 960
Life expectancy
Chesapeake colony, 38
New England colony, 49
post–World War I, 767
post–World War II, 888
preindustrial, 283–284
slave, 387
Lilienthal, David, 855, 872
Lin, Maya Ying, 991
Lincoln, Abraham, 471, 483, 484, 486, 492, 499, 534
assassination of, 528
debates with Douglas, 490–491
election of 1860, 493
inauguration of, 495–496, 528
presidency of, 493–496, 500, 515, 524. *See also* Civil War
Lincoln, Benjamin, 163
Lindbergh, Charles, 766, 826, 827
Lingan, James, 323
Lippmann, Walter, 757, 793
Little, Frank, 746
Little Rock, Arkansas
school desegregation in, 905–906
Livestock, 265, 267, 379
Livingston, Robert, 199, 241
Lloyd, James, 254
Lobbying by farmers, 775
Locke, Alain, 770
Locke, John, 52, 115
Lodge, Henry Cabot, 635, 668, 672, 750, 751, 936
Loewy, Raymond, 814
London, Meyer, 718
London Company, 42
Lone Horn, 575
Long, Huey P., 801, 804
Long, John D., 671–672
Longhorn cattle, 571–572

*Looking Backward* (Bellamy), 627, 646, 647, 692
Lords of Trade, 79
Lorwin, Val, 853, 878–879
Los Angeles, California
Hispanic Americans in, 909
riots of 1943, 835
Louisiana, 438. *See also* New Orleans, Louisiana
cession to England, 139
Reconstruction era, 554, 555
secession of, 493
Louisiana Purchase, 304, 306–308, 337, 442
Louis XI (king of France), 12
Louis XIV (king of France), 86–87, 88
Louis XVI (king of France), 248
Louisville and Nashville Railroad Company, 579
L'Ouverture, Toussaint, 306
Love Canal incident, 990
Lovejoy, Elijah, 430
Lovejoy, Julia Louisa, 484, 486, 487
Lovell, James, 186
Lowell, Francis Cabot, 273, 285
Lowell, Massachusetts, 273
textile industry in, 343, 346–350
Lowell Institute, 341
Loyalists, 167, 168, 170, 173, 174, 178, 179, 194–196
postwar treatment of, 196, 216–217
Loyalty programs, 874–876
LSD, 941
Luark, Michael, 471
Ludlow, Massacre, 704
*Lusitania* disaster, 731
Luther, Martin, 16–17
Luther, Seth, 426
Lutheranism, 16–17
Lynch, John, 553
Lynn, Massachusetts, 272

McAdoo, William, 744–745
MacArthur, Douglas, 792, 844, 866, 867
McCallum, Daniel, 599
McCarran Internal Security Act of 1950, 875
McCarthy, Eugene, 946
McCarthy, Joseph, 853, 876–878
McClellan, George, 507–508, 517, 524

McCoy, Isaac, 313
McCulloch, Ben, 509–510
*McCulloch* v. *Maryland*, 302–303
McDonald's, 883–884
McDougall, Alexander, 145, 147
McDowell, Irvin, 506, 507
McDuffie, George, 331
McGovern, George, 961
McGrath, Howard, 874
MacIntosh, Ebenezer, 131, 132, 138, 144, 147, 148
McKay, Claude, 771
McKinley, William, 635
    assassination of, 678, 709
    election of 1896, 652–655
    presidency of, 655, 670–678
McNamara, Robert S., 916
McNary-Haugen Farm Relief Bill of 1927, 775
McNickle, D'Arcy, 930
Macon's Bill, 321
MacPherson, John, 140
McPherson, William, 247
Madeira, 65
Madison, James
    Constitution and, 233, 236, 238
    Federalists and, 227, 252
    postrevolutionary war debt and, 243, 244
    presidency of, 304, 321–325, 328–329
    Virginia Resolutions and, 255
Madrid, Arturo, 988
Magazines, 692
*Maggie: A Girl of the Streets* (Crane), 602
Magon, Ricardo Flores, 738
Mahan, Alfred Thayer, 668, 672
Maine, 26, 330
*Maine* incident, 671, 672
*Main Street* (Lewis), 772
*Main-Travelled Roads* (Garland), 570
Malcolm X, 928
Mali, 10
Malthus, Thomas, 305
Management techniques, 599, 701–702, 763
Manchuria, 683, 827
Manhattan Project, 849
Manifest Destiny, 441–442, 663. *See also* Westward movement
Manigault, Charles, 285
Mann, Horace, 342, 426

Mann-Elkins Act of 1910, 699, 715
Manning, William, 251
*Man Nobody Knows, The* (Barton), 776
*Mann* v. *Illinois*, 587
Mansfield, Mike, 937
Manufacturing. *See also* Industrialization
    assembly line in, 701, 762–763
    automobile, 762–763, 975
    in the Civil War South, 520, 525
    electrification in, 761
    frontier development of, 350–352
    in the industrialization process, 343–344. *See also* Industrialization
    Japanese, 975
    preindustrial, 268–276
    Revolutionary War impact on, 185–186
    as Union advantage in the Civil War, 501–502, 521, 525
    World War II and, 829–831, 836–838
Manumissions, 292–293, 397, 398
Mao Zedong, 865, 951, 952
*Marbury* v. *Madison*, 302
Marco Polo, 13, 15
Marcus, Greil, 955–956
Marcy, William, 481
Marijuana, 898, 941, 955, 992
Maroons, 395
Marquette, Jacques, 87
Marshall, Andrew, 390
Marshall, George C., 844, 860, 861–862, 877
Marshall, James, 247
Marshall, John, 253, 300, 302, 303, 341, 412, 440
Marshall Plan, 861
Martinique, 139
Marx, Karl, 735
Mary I (queen of England), 24
Maryland, 323
    agrarian protests in, 227
    Articles of Confederation and, 165–166
    as border state in the Civil War, 502–504
    colonial. *See* Maryland colony
    exports of, 184
    slavery in, 193

Maryland colony, 37–38
    Bacon's Rebellion aftermath in, 78
    Glorious Revolution of 1688 and, 82
    slaves in, 69
Masaniello, 83
Mason, George, 233
Mason, John, 31–32, 46
Massachusetts, 183, 272, 420. *See also* Boston, Massachusetts
    battles at Lexington and Concord, 167
    colonial. *See* Massachusetts colony
    Glorious Revolution of 1688 in, 80–81, 82
    land productivity in, 98–99
    nineteenth-century school system, 342
    Pilgrims in, 41–42
    Puritan settlers in, 31
    Quakers in, 55
    religious freedom in, 218
    Shays's Rebellion in, 226–227, 228
    state constitution of, 212, 214–216, 218
    textile industry in, 343, 346–350
Massachusetts colony, 31, 42–50, 75–76. *See also* Concord, Massachusetts
    battles at Lexington and Concord, 151
    English interference with, 147–148
    land productivity in, 98–99
    Pilgrims in, 41–42
    protest of Townshend Acts by, 145–146
    Puritan settlers in, 31
    Quakers in, 55
    struggles with New France, 88–90
    witchcraft in, 83–85
Massive Retaliation, 874
Masters, William H., 940
Mather, Cotton, 99, 102
Matlack, Timothy, 156, 214
Matrilineality
    African, 11
    Native American, 8
Mauldin, Bill, 839, 858
May, Sidney W., 885
*Mayaquez* incident, 952
Mayan empire, 18

*Mayflower,* 42
Mayham, Hezekiah, 227
Meade, George, 518
Meadlo, Paul, 949
Meat Inspection Act of 1906, 713
Meatpacking industry, 350–351
Medicare-Medicaid, 924
Mediterranean region, containment policy in, 860–861
Mekras, John, 699–700
Mellon, Andrew, 778, 789
Melville, Herman, 345
Memminger, Christopher G., 504
Memorial Day Massacre, 806
Memphis, Tennessee
    riot of 1866 in, 541
Mencken, H. L., 772
    Scopes trial and, 767–768
Mennonites, 17
Mercantilism, 275
Merchant capitalists
    shoe industry and, 269, 272
    textile industry and, 269, 272–273
Meredith, James, 919
*Merrimac* (ship), 510
Merryman, John, 503
Metacomet (King Philip), 75–76, 77
Methodists, 217, 392, 417
Mexican Americans. *See* Hispanic Americans
Mexican War, 445–447
    Mormons and, 460
    slavery and, 472–473
Mexico, 18, 20, 21, 22, 325, 585
    annexation of Texas and, 442–445
    California and, 445, 447
    independence of, 438, 442
    migrant laborers from, 573, 768, 808, 908–909, 930–931
    nationalization of oil companies in, 823
    New Mexico and, 445, 447–448
    War of 1846, 445–447, 460, 472–473
    Wilson's foreign policy in, 732–733
    World War I and, 735
Meyers, H. L., 746
Miami tribe, 166, 188
Michigan, 340
Middle class, 639–652
    attitude toward unions, 620
    consumer products and, 639–640

nineteenth-century reforms of, 357, 423–426
    recreational activities of, 640
    sex roles of, 356–359, 640–642, 644–645
    social reforms of, 647–652. *See also* Social reform
    urbanization process and, 355–359, 607, 611
Middle East
    Cold War and, 869–871
    oil embargo of, 953–954
Midway Islands, 663, 845
Midwives, 284
Migrant workers, 573, 768, 808, 908–909, 930–931
Milbourne, Jacob, 82
Military Draft Act, 748
Miller, William, 421–422
Millerites, 421–422
Mills, C. Wright, 892
Mining, 456–459
    gold, 604, 655
    worker strikes in, 618–619
Minto, John, 454
Minutemen, 151, 167
*Miranda* v. *Arizona,* 925
Missionaries
    in international expansionism, 668–669
    for Native Americans, 313, 314
Mississippi
    Reconstruction era, 555
    secession of, 493
Mississippi culture, 7
Mississippi Plan, 555, 558
Mississippi River
    as boundary after Revolutionary War, 173
    French exploration of, 87
    movement west of. *See* Westward movement
    Pike's exploration of, 308
    Spanish closing of, 223, 306
    steamboats on, 280
Missouri
    admission as state, 330
    as border state in the Civil War, 502–503, 504
    slavery and, 484
Missouri Compromise of 1820, 329–330, 472, 473
    Dred Scott case and, 488–490
    nullification of, 478–479

Mitchell, George, 930
Mitchell, John, 712, 861, 948, 957, 960
Mitchell, Margaret, 816
*Moby Dick* (Melville), 345
Model A Fords, 763, 765
Model T Fords, 763
Mohawk tribe, 223
Molasses Act of 1733, 133
Moley, Raymond, 795
Molotov, Vyacheslav, 858
Momaday, N. Scott, 821
Monarchy, 12–14, 122
    American rejection of, 202
Mondale, Walter, 997, 998
*Monitor* (ship), 510
Monroe, James, 292
    Louisiana Purchase and, 306–308
    presidency of, 304, 325–326
Monroe, Marilyn, 897–898
Monroe Doctrine, 318, 326, 661, 680
    Roosevelt Corollary, 580–581
Montezuma, 18
Montgomery, Alabama
    civil rights movement in, 906–907
Montoya, Joseph, 930
Montreal, Quebec
    during the Revolutionary War, 168
    in Seven Years' War, 139
Montserrat, 26
Moody, Anne, 919, 922, 927
Moody, Dwight, 649
Moody, Paul, 273
Moody, Stanley, 991
Moon, Sun Myung, 983
Moore, John Bassett, 668
Moral Majority, 992
Morgan, Daniel, 171
Morgan, Diana, 787, 790
Morgan, John Pierpont, 598, 636, 711, 719
Morgan, Marabel, 966
Mormons
    establishment of, 422
    in Utah, 459–462
Moroccan crisis, 686
Morrill Act of 1862, 528, 644
Morris, Gouverneur, 301
Morris, Lewis, 127
Morris, Robert, 185, 225, 233
Morrison, Jim, 941

Morrow, Dwight W., 780
Morton, Oliver P., 542
Moskowitz, Henry, 714
Mossadegh, Mohammed, 870
Mott, Lucretia, 433
Mound Builders, 6–7
Movies, 765–766
　in the 1930s, 816, 817–818
　post–World War II, 897
　progressivism and, 698–699
　World War II and, 838–839
Moynihan, Daniel Patrick, 948, 954–955
Muckrakers, 692–693, 712–713
Muhammad, Elijah, 928
Miur, John, 713
*Muller* v. *Oregon*, 695
Municipal reform, 638, 695–696, 705–708
Murphy, Edgar Gardner, 694
Murphy, Jeanette Robinson, 392
Murray, Judith Sargent, 290, 291
Murrow, Edward R., 838
Museums, 289, 327
Music
　in Afro-American culture, 771
　black slave, 390, 392–393, 394
　jazz, 771
　of the 1960s, 941
　post–World War II, 898
　rock and roll, 898
Muslims
　in Africa, 10–14
　Europe and, 11–13
　Portuguese oster from East Indies, 15
Mussolini, Benito, 824, 844
Mystic River, Connecticut, 31–32

Nader, Ralph, 969
Nagasaki, atom bomb in, 850
Nairne, Thomas, 67
Napoleon, 305, 318, 319, 321, 323
　Louisiana Purchase and, 306, 307
Narcissism, 969–970
Marragansett tribe, 76
*Narrative of the Life of Frederick Douglass* (Douglass), 400
Nasser, Gamal Abdel, 870–871
National American Woman Suffrage Association (NAWSA), 643–644, 749

National Association for the Advancement of Colored People (NAACP), 714–715, 905–907, 918–919
National Association of Manufacturers, 666, 702
National Child Labor Committee, 694
National Consumers League, 694–695
National debt
　under Jefferson, 304
　under Kennedy, 917–918
　postrevolutionary, 186–187, 224–227, 243–244
　under Reagan, 996
National Grange of the Patrons of Husbandry, 586–587
National Guard, 731. *See also* Law enforcement
　civil rights movement and, 906
　at Kent State University protest, 950
National Housing Association, 696
National Industrial Recovery Act (NIRA) of 1933, 798–799
Nationalists, Chinese, 865
National Labor Relations Act of 1935 (Wagner Act), 805, 900
National Labor Union, 556, 616
National League of Women Voters, 774
National Negro Convention Movement, 430
National Organization for Women (NOW), 932–933, 965
National Origins Act of 1927, 768
National parks, 714
National Republicans, 407, 411. *See also* Whigs
　formation of, 329, 330
National Road, 280, 304
National Security Council, 862–863, 948
National Security League, 731
National Trades Union, 427
National Traffic and Motor Vehicle Safety Act of 1966, 969
National War Labor Board (NWLB), 746, 830
National Women's Party (NWP), 749, 774
National Youth Administration (NYA), 803

Native Americans, 3–9, 309–317. *See also* specific tribes
　American Indian Movement (AIM), 930, 966–967
　armed resistance of nineteenth-century, 315–317, 575–577
　Carolina colonies and, 53, 57
　Chesapeake Bay colonies and, 3, 33–34, 36–37, 76–78
　Christianity among, 3, 313, 314
　in cities, 909, 929–930
　civil rights movement and, 929–930
　in the Civil War, 510, 575
　diseases of, 20–21, 465–466
　early images of, 27–28
　education of, 313, 314
　efforts to assimilate, 312–313, 314
　eighteenth-century cultural changes among, 135–136
　exclusion from postrevolutionary politics, 208
　first contact with Europeans, 3–4, 7–9
　Fort Laramie Council, 466, 575, 967
　in French-English colonial struggles, 88, 133–135
　fur trade by, 135, 312
　as hunters and farmers, 4–7
　as mercenaries, 88
　migration from Asia, 4–5
　Mormons and, 461
　New Deal era, 808–809, 909
　nineteenth-century land policy and, 309–312, 314, 315–316, 317, 438–440, 575–577
　postrevolutionary land treaties of, 190
　post–World War II status, 909–910
　progress of the 1970s and 1980s, 988
　protests by, 575–577, 966–967
　Puritans and, 43, 45–46, 75–76
　Quakers and, 56–57
　revitalization of, 297, 313–314
　in the Revolutionary War, 180, 188–191
　Seven Years' War and, 136–141
　in 1600, 6–7
　as slaves, 20–21, 23, 53, 76, 77
　Spanish conquest and, 18–23
　struggle for land and, 74–78

Native Americans (*Continued*)
  surrender of land by, 190, 222–223, 309–317, 439–440, 909, 930
  twentieth-century land policy and, 909–910, 929–930
  view of land by, 7–8, 27–28
  westward movement and, 463–466, 574–578
  in World War II, 840
*Native Son* (Wright), 769
Nativism, 481–483
Naturalization Act of 1798, 254
Naturalization law, 254, 303
Natural resources, 337
  conservation efforts for, 713–714
  environmental movement, 968–969, 990
Navajo tribe
  in the Marine Signal Corps, 840
Navigation, 13
Navigation Acts, 79, 132, 147
Navy
  Civil War, 510–511, 525
  disarmament conference of 1921, 779
  Great WhiteFleet, 684
  in the Spanish-American War, 673–674
  strengthening of nineteenth-century, 671–672, 684
  submarine warfare, 730–731, 827
  in World War II, 844–846
Navy Department, formation of, 253, 254
Nebraska Territory, 478–479, 484
Negro Baptist church, 550
Nelson, Donald, 829
Nemattenew, 37
Netherlands. *See also* Holland
  Glorious Revolution of 1688 and, 80
  New World involvement of, 50, 52, 55–56
  Protestantism in, 25, 31
  Revolutionary War and, 225, 243
Neutrality
  toward England, 248–251
  of Iroquois tribe, 188
  pre–World War II, 823–826
  of United States in World War I, 729–731
Neutrality Act of 1935, 824–825
Neutrality Proclamation, 250

Neville, John, 246
Newbold, Charles, 267
Newburyport, Massachusetts, 183
New Deal, 787, 904
  first program (1933–1935), 793, 795–801, 810
    Agricultural Adjustment Act of 1933, 797–798, 807
    Civilian Conservation Corps, 799, 807
    criticism, 800–801
    financial institution regulation, 795–796
    National Industrial Recovery Act of 1933, 798–799
    Tennessee Valley Authority, 799–800, 902–903
    work programs, 796–797
  second program (1935–1939), 801–814
    Agricultural Adjustment Act of 1938, 812
    Fair Labor Standards Act of 1938, 813–814
    farm aid, 803–804
    Farm Security Administration, 812
    labor organizations, 804–807
    minority groups in, 807–809
    Reconstruction Finance Corporation, 791, 795, 812
    redistribution of wealth, 804
    Social Security Act, 803, 924
    Supreme Court and, 811
    women in, 802, 809
    Works Progress Administration, 797, 802–803
  World War II mobilization efforts and, 829
New England
  Confederation of, 50
  Dominion of, 80–81, 82
  as term, 41
New England colonies, 98–103. *See also* Massachusetts colony
  agriculture in, 46–47, 98–99
  architecture in, 49–50
  changing values of, 99–100
  Glorious Revolution of 1688 and, 80–82
  maritime activities of, 109
  Native Americans and, 75–76
  New France and, 87–90
  slaves in, 67–68, 70–71

New Federalism, 996–997
Newfoundland, 24, 26, 37, 88, 132, 173
New France, 86–90
  Massachusetts colony struggles with, 88–90
  Seven Years' War and, 136–141
New Frontier, 915
New Granada (Colombia). *See also* Colombia
New Harmony, Indiana, 421
New Jersey
  colonial, 56, 98
  voting rights of women in, 209
New Jersey Plan, 233
New Left, 956
  formation of, 938–939
  Vietnam War protest, 939–940
New Mexico, 23, 441
  Hispanic Americans in, 447–448, 466–467
  independence from Mexico, 445, 447–448
  slavery issue and, 474, 475
New Nationalism, 720
*New Negro, The* (Locke), 770
New Netherland colony, 50, 52, 55–56, 81–82. *See also* New York colony
New Orleans, Louisiana
  in the Civil War, 510
  Spanish seizure of, 223, 306
  War of 1812 in, 323, 324
*New Orleans* (steamboat), 280
New Right, 992, 997
New South, 547–550, 578–586. *See also* Southern states
  blacks in, 582–586
  industrialization of, 579–581
  need for change and, 578–579
New Spain, 22–23
Newspapers, 669–670
  colonial, 100, 127
  Federalist influence on, 251
  nineteenth-century growth of, 278–279
  postrevolutionary growth of, 205
Newton, Huey, 929
Newton, Isaac, 115
New World, 4, 5, 9
  Catholicism in, 3, 17, 23
New York, 416–417, 420, 423
  agriculture in nineteenth-century, 264–265, 266

Articles of Confederation and, 165–166
colonial. *See* New York colony
Erie Canal, 337, 353, 417
Niagara movement in, 715
ratification of Constitution by, 238
Seneca Nation in, 930, 988
settlement of western, 275–276
tenant rent war, 158, 225
New York, New York
British occupation of, 168, 178–179, 180
as colonial trade center, 109
as first United States capital, 240–241, 244
Harlem Renaissance, 770–771
New York colony, 50, 52. *See also* New Netherland colony
agriculture in, 98
Glorious Revolution of 1688 in, 81–82
Leisler's Rebellion in, 81–82
prerevolutionary fervor in, 157–158
slaves in, 71, 72
Stamp Act riots in, 144
Niagara movement, 715
Nicaragua, 480, 663, 664, 680, 681, 732, 779, 822
Nicholson, Francis, 81
Nicolet, Jean, 15
*Nineteen Eighty-four* (Orwell), 858
Nineteenth Amendment, 433, 749
Nixon, E. D., 907
Nixon, Richard, 543, 803, 855, 877, 966
election of 1960, 914–915
election of 1968, 946–948
Hiss case and, 876
presidency of, 948, 949–952, 954, 956–960, 968
as vice-president, 871
Watergate incident, 960–962
Nixon Doctrine, 949
Noble Order of the Knights of Labor, 556, 584, 617–618
Nomadic tribes, 4–6
Non-Importation Act of 1806, 319
Non-Intercourse Act of 1809, 321
Noriega, José, 908
Norris, Frank, 693
Norris, George, 736, 799–800
Norsemen, 14

North Atlantic Treaty Organization (NATO), 862
North Carolina
antebellum agriculture in, 378, 379
colonial. *See* Carolina colonies; North Carolina colony
Reconstruction era, 554–555, 556
North Carolina colony, 52–54
Bacon's Rebellion aftermath in, 78
prerevolutionary fervor in, 157
Northern Securities Company, 711
Northern states. *See also* Civil War
cultural differences with antebellum southern states, 484–488
Kansas Territory and, 486–487
nineteenth-century agriculture in, 264–267, 277
preindustrial manufacturing in, 269–273
proposed secession of (1814), 323
Reconstruction era in, 534, 555–557
regional characteristics of, 277
secession plan under Jefferson, 307–308
Northrop, Solomon, 395
Northwestern Confederacy, 309
Northwest Ordinance of 1787, 221, 277, 329, 473
Norton, Elijah, 270
Nova Scotia, 24, 88, 99, 132
Noyes, John Humphrey, 419–420
Nuclear power, 969, 990–991, 994
Nuclear weapons
development of, 825–826, 849, 859, 873–874
Japan and, 849–850
proliferation of, 872–874, 995–996
under Reagan, 995–996
Nullification, 410
Nye, Gerald P., 824

Oberlin College, 427
Occupational mobility
education and, 622–623, 644–645
nineteenth-century, 610–611, 622–623
Occupational safety and health, 610–611
O'Connor, Sandra Day, 984
*Octopus, The* (Norris), 693
O'Donnell, Thomas, 595

Office of Price Administration (OPA), 829, 885–886
Office of War Information, 831, 839
Oglethorpe, James, 135
Oil embargo, 953–954
Oil industry, 600, 823
Ohio
black laws of, 361–362
settlement of, 276, 277–278, 308
Shawnee armed resistance in, 315
Ohio Valley
Seven Years' War and, 136–138, 140
western expansion and, 277, 278, 280
Oklahoma, 575, 585
Older persons, 982–983
Old Northwest
industrialization in, 350–352
Native Americans in, 315–316
settlement of, 364–366
transportation systems and, 337, 339
Olds, Ransom E., 762
Old World, 4
Oligopoly, 891
Olive Branch Petition, 151
Oliver, Andrew, 131, 144
Olney, Richard, 620, 665, 668
Olson, Floyd, 801
*One Flew Over the Cuckoo's Nest* (Kesey), 941
Oneida, New York, 420
*On the Beach* (Shute), 873
*On the Road* (Kerouac), 898
Op art, 941
OPEC (Organization of Petroleum Exporting Countries), 953–954
Opechancanough, 3–4, 28, 37
Open Door policy, 683
Operation Overlord, 845–846
Operation Wetback, 908
Operation Vittles, 862
*O Pioneers!* (Cather), 570–571
Oppenheimer, J. Robert, 849
Ordinance of Nullification, 410
Oregon, 440
joint United States–British claims on, 438, 441, 448–449
land policy of, 453
O'Reilly, Leonora, 702
O'Reilly, Rose, 702
*Origin of Species* (Darwin), 646

Ortiz, Rudy, 988
Orwell, George, 858
Osborn, Danvers, 126
Ostend Manifesto, 481
O'Sullivan, John L., 441
Oswald, Lee Harvey, 922
Oswald, Richard, 172
Oswego Council, 189–190
*Other America, The* (Harrington), 903
Otis, Harrison Gray, 254
Ottawa tribe, 222
*Our Country* (Strong), 669
*Out of Work* (Kellor), 691
Outworkers, 351
Overseers, 394
Ovington, Mary White, 714
Owen, Robert, 420–421

Pacific Northwest. *See also* Oregon
    exploration of, 308
Pacific Ocean, 15
Pacific Railroad Act of 1862, 527
Pacifism
    Quaker, 55, 56–57, 156
    World War I, 727–728, 736, 739, 751
    World War II, 824
Packard, Vance, 893
Paine, Thomas, 151, 152, 154, 156, 187, 201–202, 207, 214, 252
Painting, 898, 941
Paleo-Indian phase, 5
Palestine, 870
Pallares, Jesus, 808
Palmer, A. Mitchell, 758
*Palmer* v. *Mulligan*, 340
Panama, 514, 663–664, 732, 936
    independence of, 682
    taking of canal in, 679, 681–682
Panama Canal, 679, 681–682, 993
Pan-American Conference, 664
Panic of 1819, 274–275, 286, 304, 309
Panic of 1837, 412–413
Panic of 1893, 636
Paris, Treaty of (1763), 139, 153, 222
Paris Peace Conference of 1918, 750–751
Parker, John and Lizzie, 755
Parker, Theodore, 476
Parks, Rosa, 906–907
Parochial schools, 634, 651

Parris, Betty, 84
Parris, Samuel, 84
Parrish, Isaac, 354
Party system. *See also* specific parties
    compromises over slavery and, 472–474
    factions in, 216
    nineteenth-century
        breakdown of, 477–483
        growth of, 405–406, 413–415
        political participation and, 632–634
Pastor, Rose, 756–757
Paterson, William, 233
*Pathfinder, The* (Cooper), 345
Patriotism
    international expansionism and, 667–668
    in World War I, 736–738
    in World War II, 831–832
Patriots, 176, 178
    postrevolutionary treatment of Loyalists, 196, 216–217
Patriots of '76, 201
Patronage
    in appointment of colonial governors, 125–126
    in the Gilded Age, 629, 631, 632, 650–652
    Lincoln and, 524
Patton, George, 855
Paul, Alice, 749, 774
Payne, Daniel, 585
Payne-Aldrich Tariff, 715
Peace Corps, 933
Peace of Paris (1763), 131
Peace of Utrecht, 88, 95, 97, 132
Peale, Charles Wilson, 289, 327
Pearl Harbor, 664, 827–828, 832–833
Peckham, George, 28
Peckham, Miriam, 569–570
Pena, Federico, 988
Pendleton Act of 1883, 632
Penn, William, 55–59
Pennington, J. W. C., 394
Pennsylvania. *See also* Philadelphia, Pennsylvania
    abolitionism in, 194
    agriculture in nineteenth-century, 264–265, 266, 267
    colonial. *See* Pennsylvania colony

state constitution of, 214
    Whiskey Rebellion in, 246–247
Pennsylvania colony, 176
    agriculture in, 98
    German immigrants to, 95
    population growth of, 95–96
    Quaker settlement of, 56–59
Pensions
    for Civil War veterans, 634, 635
    social security, 803, 924, 982
    Townsend Plan, 801, 803
Pentagon Papers, 950
People's Republic of China, 865, 866
    Carter administration and, 993
    Nixon administration and, 951–952
Pepper, Claude, 982
Pequot tribe, 31–32, 46
Perkins, Frances, 704, 793, 795, 803, 805, 809
Perkins, George, 598–599
Perry, Oliver Hazard, 323
Pershing, John J., 733, 742–743
Peru, 18, 20, 22
Peters, Thomas, 191–192
Philadelphia, Pennsylvania
    artisans in, 111–112
    British occupation of, 169–170, 178, 179
    colonial growth of, 58
    as colonial trade center, 109
    Constitutional Convention of 1787, 232–235, 243
    Continental Congresses in, 150–153, 220–228, 240
    prerevolutionary fervor in, 155–156
    riot of 1834 in, 359–360
    slaves in, 71
    as United States capital, 244–245
    urbanization process and, 353–355
    yellow fever epidemic in, 284, 285
*Philadelphia Negro, The* (Du Bois), 714
Philip II (king of Spain), 3, 24–25
Philippines
    Filipino-American War, 659–660, 674–676
    independence from Spain, 659, 674, 677
    naval fortification of, 671–672, 674
    in World War II, 845, 847

Phillips, David Graham, 693, 705
Phillips, Wendell, 429
Phips, William, 84, 89
Pickering, John, 302
Pickering, Timothy, 320–321
Pickett's Charge, 518
Pierce, Franklin, 478, 480, 485, 505
Pike, Zebulon, 308
Pike's Peak, 308
Pilgrims, 31, 41–42
Pinchot, Gifford, 713, 715
Pinckney, C. C., 321
Pinckney, Charles, 233, 253
Pinckney, Eliza Lucas, 106
Pingree, Hazen, 652, 706
Pioneers, The (Cooper), 345
Pitt, William, 138
Pizarro, Francisco, 18, 23
Platt, Orville, 666
Platt Amendment, 680, 823
Plessy v. Ferguson, 583, 905
Plunkitt, George Washington, 633
Plymouth, Massachusetts, 31
  King Philip's War and, 75–76
  Pilgrims in, 41–42
Pocahontas, 37
Poland, 825–826, 848, 858–859
Pole, Cleveland, 621
Police. See Law enforcement
Political participation
  election of 1896, 654, 655
  nineteenth-century growth of, 632–634, 650–652
Politics
  Hispanic Americans in, 988
  women in, 984, 997
Polk, James K., 445–450, 465
  presidency of, 465
Polk, Leonidas, 589, 590
Pollock, Jackson, 898
Pollution Act of 1924, 778
Poll tax, 219
Polygamy, 461–462
Ponce de León, Juan, 23
Pontiac, (Ottawa chief), 140
Pooling arrangements, 599
Poor Richard's Almanack (Franklin), 100, 343
Pop art, 941
Popé, 23
Popular sovereignty, 473–474
  Kansas-Nebraska Act and, 479

Population
  birthrate of the 1970s and 1980s, 981–982
  black slave, 67, 69, 70, 71, 94, 97–98, 103, 159
  characteristics of 1980, 979
  colonial explosion of, 94–98
  immigrant. See Immigrants
  industrialization and growth of, 601–604
  life expectancy, 767, 888
  nineteenth-century growth of, 280–281, 336–337
  post–World War II, 888–891
Populist party, 590–592
  dissolution of, 652–653, 655
  election of 1892, 590–592
  election of 1896, 652–653
  formation of, 590
  growth of, 591–592
  Omaha platform of 1892, 590–591
Pork, 379, 566
Porter, Peter, 321
Portugal
  Catholicism of, 17
  emergence of nation-state, 12
  era of conquest of New World, 18, 20
  expansionist impulse of, 13–14, 15
  slave trade of, 65
Post, Louis, 758
Postal system, 278–279
Potsdam Conference, 858
Potts, Jonathan, 177
Poverty
  in colonial cities, 112–114
  Great Society program, 923, 924–927, 954–955, 981
  nineteenth-century efforts to relieve, 288–289
  post–World War II, 903
  in preindustrial society, 285–286
  among present-day blacks, 986–987
  among present-day Hispanic Americans, 987
  settlement houses and. See Settlement houses
  social Darwinism and, 647
  in the Southern backcountry, 107
Poverty (Hunter), 693
Powderly, Terence V., 617–618
Powell, Adam Clayton, 904

Powell, Lewis F., Jr., 957
Power
  balancing liberty with, 203–204
  Federalist view of, 236
  postrevolutionary redistribution of, 213–216
Power, Mary, 454
Power Shift: The Rise of the Southern Rim and Its Challenge to the Eastern Establishment (Sale), 978
Powhatan Confederacy, 3, 34–37, 63, 77, 78
Pownall, Thomas, 141
Pragmatism, 647–648
Prairie, The (Cooper), 345
Pratt, Brenda, 462
Preindustrial period
  economic developments, 262–276
  social characteristics, 277–286
Prendergast, William, 158
Presbyterianism, 119
Presley, Elvis, 898
Price, J. C., 585
Price, Sterling, 509–510
Price controls
  Revolutionary War and, 219–220
Pringle, Virgil, 450–451
Printing press
  in Protestant Reformation, 16
  Puritan use of, 43
Prisons, 426
Privateers, 140, 182
Proclamation of 1763, 140, 190
Productivity
  methods of increasing, 341
Professions
  education and rise of, 644–645
  women in, 642, 774, 984
Profiles in Courage (Kennedy), 915
Progress and Poverty (George), 647, 692, 707
Progressive era
  municipal reform in, 695–696, 705–708
  post–World War I, 780–782
  racial issues in, 714–715
  social reform in. See Social justice movement
  state government reform in, 708–709
  trade unions in, 701–705, 720
  working conditions, 699–701

Progressive party, 734
    second, 777–778, 900
    under Theodore Roosevelt, 716–
        718
Prohibition
    nineteenth-century, 633–634
    post–World War I, 781–782
    progressivism and, 697–698, 781–
        782
    repeal of, 796
Promise of American Life, The
    (Croly), 717
Property rights
    preindustrial period, 285
    of Reconstruction era blacks, 537,
        538, 543–544, 546–549, 551
    of women, 102, 432, 433
Prosser, Gabriel, 291–292, 396
Prostitution, 652
    California gold rush, 458
    industrialization process and, 613
    progressivism and, 699
    urbanization process and, 602
    World War I and, 748
Protectionism. See Tariffs
Protestantism, 16–17
    England's westward expansion
        and, 24–25, 31, 40–50
    Great Awakening and. See Great
        Awakening
    of the Moral Majority, 992
    nineteenth-century immigrants
        and, 481–483
    urban revival movements, 649–
        650
Providence, Rhode Island, 44
Public schools
    establishment of first, 342
    urbanization process and, 358
Public Utility Holding Company Act
    of 1935, 804
Public Works Administration
    (PWA), 797
Publishing industry
    industrialization process in, 343,
        344–345
    newspapers in. See Newspapers
    paperback revolution in, 898
    printing press in, 16, 43
    socializing role of, 358
Pueblo tribe, 6, 23
Puerto Rico, 18, 673, 677
Pujo, Arsène, 719
Pulitzer, Joseph, 669

Pullman, George, 620
Pullman Palace Car Company, 619–
    620, 638
Pullman strike, 620, 638
Pure Food and Drug Act of 1906,
    713
Puritans, 31–32, 40–41, 55, 116
    arrival in the New World, 42
    changing values among, 99–100
    desire for land, 45, 46, 47–48,
        50
    family life of, 46–50, 102–103
    ideological difficulties of, 43–45
    Native Americans and, 43, 45–46,
        75–76
    New England predecessors, 41–
        42
    political structure of colonies, 50
    social rank among, 83
    utopian views of, 42–43
Putnam, Thomas, Jr., 85
Puzo, Mario, 839
Pyle, Ernest, 838

Quadrant, 13
Quakers, 54–59, 116
    abolitionist sentiments of, 97–98,
        158, 194
    colony formed by, 55–59
    family life of, 58, 102–103
    formation of, 54
    ideological bases for, 54–55, 56–
        57
    ideological problems of, 58–59
    Native Americans and, 56–57
    pacifism of, 55, 56–57, 156
Quartering Act of 1765, 145
Quay, Matt, 635
Queen Anne's War, 88, 89, 90, 115,
    132
Quincy, Josiah, Jr., 147

Radio, 764–765, 766
    in the 1930s, 816–817
    World War II and, 838
Railroads, 353
    Civil War and, 525, 527
    construction of eastern, 337–340
    farmer protests against, 587–588,
        591
    government regulation of, 587–
        588, 709, 711–712, 715
    industrialization process and, 597,
        598–599

land of, 573
    in modernization of agriculture,
        564, 566, 567, 573–574
    of the New South, 573, 579
    transcontinental, 556, 557
        growth of, 597
        Native Americans and, 576, 577
        worker strikes and, 615–616,
            617, 619–620
    during World War I, 745–746
Rain-in-the-Face, 576
Raleigh, Walter, 26, 32, 51
Ramirez, Francisco, 468
Randolph, A. Philip, 834
Randolph, Edmund, 151, 233
Randolph, John, 328, 408
Rankin, Jeannette, 751, 828
Rauschenbusch, Walter, 650
Reagan, Ronald, 839, 973, 984, 992
    election of 1980, 995
    presidency of, 995–998
Reaganomics, 996
Reconstruction Acts of 1867, 542,
    552
Reconstruction era, 531–560
    end of, 557–558
    formal plans in, 539–545
        congressional, 540–545
        Freedmen's Bureau, 541, 545–546
        presidential, 539–540
    in the North, 534, 555–557
    property rights of blacks during,
        537, 538, 543–544, 546–549,
        551
    Republican rule in the South,
        534–535, 552–555
    status of United States at begin-
        ning of, 532–535
    white Southerners in, 537–539
Reconstruction Finance Corpora-
    tion, 791, 795, 812
Recreation, 815–816
    drugs in, 898, 941, 955, 992
    nineteenth-century forms of,
        640
    sports, 765, 904, 913, 992
    television as. See Television
    World War II and, 838–839
Reddy, Helen, 963
Red Eagle, 317
Red Scare
    Chicanos and, 908
    early twentieth-century, 756–757
    McCarthy and, 853, 876–878

of the 1940s and 1950s, 853, 876–878

worker protests in, 757–758

Reed, Charles, 573

Reed, John, 757

Reed, Esther DeBerdt, 210

Reese, Don, 992

Reformation, 16–17

Reformers

nineteenth-century

Millerites, 421–422

Mormons, 422, 459–462

utopian, 419–421

problems of, 418

social. *See* Social reform

Refrigerators, 814

Regulators, 157

Rehnquist, William, 957

Religion. *See also* specific religions

African, 11

as basis of revolutionary spirit, 154–155

of blacks, 73, 293–294, 390–392, 399, 550, 606–607

conformity in, 895

evolution and, 767–768

of the Moral Majority, 992

mystical movements, 970, 983

Native American, 6, 7–9

postrevolutionary politics and, 205–206

revival movements

Great Awakening. *See* Great Awakening

urban, 649–650

separation of church and state, 217–218

on the Western frontier, 455

Republicanism, 200–205

Anti-Federalist, 237, 240

balancing liberty and power in, 203–204

creation of new identity in, 200–202

political equality in, 204–205, 287–288

rejection of monarchy and, 202

separation of church and state in, 217–218

social aspects, 286–295

education, 289

equality, 287–288

individualism, 288

race and slavery, 291–294

reform efforts, 288–294

role of women, 289–291

youthful focus, 286–287

Republican party

under Andrew Johnson, 534, 539–540

under Coolidge, 775, 777–780

under Eisenhower, 885–856, 864, 901–903

election of 1896, 653–655

formation of, 482–483

under Franklin Roosevelt, 822–849

in the Gilded Age, 629–636

under Grant, 555–558

under Harding, 776–777

under Hayes, 558

under Hoover, 776, 780, 783

under Lincoln, 493–496, 524, 526, 534

under Nixon, 946–948

under Reagan, 995–998

Reconstruction era, 534–535, 552–554

under Taft, 715–717, 718

under Theodore Roosevelt, 709–715

Republicans. *See* Jeffersonian Republicans; National Republicans

Republic Steel, 806

Resettlement Administration (RA), 803–804

Revenue Act of 1942, 830

Revenue (Sugar) Act of 1764, 142

Revolutionary War, 151–153, 163–197

American casualties in, 177–178

British surrender in, 164, 172

civilian involvement in, 178–180

Declaration of Independence, 152–153, 168, 200–201

demobilization of army after, 220–221

economic impact of, 181–188, 218–220, 224–227

agricultural disruption, 183–185

financial chaos, 186–188, 224–227

inflation, 186–188, 219

interruption of trade, 182–183, 224

stimulation of manufacturing, 185–186

war debt, 186–187, 224–225, 243–244

France and, 172–173, 174, 225, 243

French Revolution compared with, 248–249

Loyalists and, 167, 168, 170, 173, 174, 178, 179, 194–196

Native Americans and, 180, 188–191

Netherlands and, 225, 243

northern operations of, 167–170, 174

peace negotiations after, 172–173

political system after, 205–211

preliminary skirmishes, 150–153, 167

reasons for American victory in, 173–175

recruitment of army for, 175–177, 192

slaves in, 170, 191–194

southern operations of, 170–172

Reynolds, George, 545

Reynolds, Malvina, 890–891

Rhode Island colony, 43

attack of British warship by, 148

Massachusetts Bay dissidents in, 44, 45

slave trade of, 68

Stamp Act riots in, 144

Ribicoff, Abraham, 947

Rice

Carolina colony cultivation of, 53–54, 106–107

postrevolutionary export of, 184

slaves in production of, 380–382, 385–386

Rice, Sally, 346

Richardson, Francis, 111

Richmond, Virginia

in the Civil War, 507–508, 517, 522

Riis, Jacob, 695, 708, 710

Ripley, George, 421

*Rise of Silas Lapham, The* (Howells), 640

Road system, 280, 304, 887

Roanoke Island colony, 26, 32–33

Robbins, Harriet, 348

Robeson, Paul, 878

Robins, Margaret, Dreier, 749

Robinson, Chris, 272
Robinson, Emily and Marius, 403, 427, 428
Robinson, Jackie, 904
Robinson, William, 119
Rochester, New York
    Second Great Awakening in, 416–417
    temperance movement in, 423
Rock and roll music, 898
Rockefeller, John D., 521, 600
Rockefeller, John D., Jr., 647, 704
Rock music, 955–956
Rockwell, Norman, 841
Rodriguez, Richard, 987
*Roe* v. *Wade*, 957, 985
Rolfe, John, 37
Rolling Stones, 941, 955–956
Rolvaag, O. E., 570
Roman Empire, 11, 12
Rommel, Erwin, 842
Roosevelt, Eleanor, 795, 797, 801, 807, 808, 809
Roosevelt, Franklin D., 704, 719, 777
    death of, 849
    election of 1932, 793
    as governor of New York, 791, 793–794
    inaugurations of, 794, 810
    presidency of, 793–809
        election of 1936, 810
        election of 1940, 826
        election of 1944, 847–848
    first New Deal, 793, 795–801, 810
    foreign policy in the 1930s, 822–827
    second New Deal, 801–814
    World War II in. *See* World War II
    Yalta Conference in, 848–849
Roosevelt, Theodore, 577, 642, 654, 668. *See also* Progressive era
    as Assistant Secretary of State, 671–672
    election of 1912 and, 716–718
    election of 1916 and, 734
    Filipino-American War and, 671–672, 674–676
    as governor of New York, 677–678
    presidency of, 678–687, 709–715
    in the Spanish-American War, 672–674
    World War I and, 728, 738

Root, Elihu, 677, 678, 684
Root-Takahira Agreement of 1908, 684
Roper, Elmo, 915
Rosenberg, Julius and Ethel, 877
Ross, John, 314
Rowson, Susanna Haswell, 290, 327
Royall, Anne, 283
Roybal, Edward, 909
Rubin, Jerry, 946
Ruggles, David, 430
Rum, 68, 283
Runaway and Homeless Youth Act of 1974, 982
Runaway children, 982
Rural Electrification Administration (REA), 804
Rush, Benjamin, 156, 232, 239, 288, 290
Rusk, Dean, 916
Russell, Edward, 756
Russell, William, 506
Russia. *See also* Soviet Union
    Bolshevik Revolution, 735, 741, 751, 756–757
    invasion of Manchuria, 683
    purchase of Alaska from, 663
    in the Russo-Japanese War, 678, 683–684
    in World War I, 726, 729, 735, 741, 744, 750
Russo-Japanese War, 678, 683–684
Rutledge, John, 233

Sacajawea, 308
Sacco, Nicola, 760
Sacco-Vanzetti case, 760
Sadat, Anwar el, 993
St. Augustine, Florida, 23
St. Christopher, 26
St. Clair, Arthur, 315
St. Lawrence River, 139
Sale, Kirkpatrick, 978
Salem, Massachusetts, 83–85
Salinger, J. D., 898
Saloons, 697–698
Salt Lake City, Utah
    Mormons in, 460–462
Samoan Islands, 665
Sánchez, David, 967
Sand Creek massacre, 575
San Francisco, California
    gold rush and, 458, 459
San Jacinto, Texas, 443–444

San Salvador (Holy Savior), 14, 15, 27
Santa Anna, Antonio López de, 443–444
Santa Fe, New Mexico, 23
Santa Fe Railroad, 573
Santa Fe Trail, 441
Santanta, 575
Santo Domingo (Hispaniola), 663
Sassamon, John, 76
Satellites, 873
Savannah, Georgia
    British occupation of, 170–171, 178
Savio, Mario, 939
*Scarlet Letter* (Hawthorne), 345, 421
Schine, G. David, 877–878
Schlafly, Phyllis, 966, 986
Schmidt, Peter, 571
Schneiderman, Rose, 702
Schools. *See also* Education
    bilingual education in, 968, 987
    busing and, 958–960, 997
    Great Society aid to, 924–927
    impact of World War I on, 736–737
    integration of, 905–906, 958–960
    nineteenth-century reforms, 426
    parochial, 634, 651
    public, 342, 358, 918
Schramm, Jacob, 365
Schurz, Carl, 493
Schwenkenfelders, 17
Schwerner, Michael, 923
Scientific management, 701–702, 763
Scopes, John, 767–768
Scott, Dred, 488–490
Scott, Emmett J., 741
Scott, Long Bill, 286
Scott, William, 163
Scott, Winfield, 478, 506, 507
Scudder, Vida, 648–649
Seabury, Samuel, 195
Sears, Isaac, 145
Sectionalism, 329–330
Sedition Act of 1798, 254–255, 303
Seeger, Alan, 728
Segregation. *See also* Civil rights movement; Discrimination
    legalization of, 583–584
Selective Service Act of 1917, 738–739, 740

Selective Service Act of 1940, 826
Seminole tribe, 188, 192, 438–440,
    930
Senate, 234
Seneca Falls, New York
    women's rights conference, 433,
        643
Seneca tribe, 138, 297, 309, 930, 988
Separatists, 42
Settlement houses, 648–649
    Henry Street, 697, 708
    Hull House, 641, 643, 649, 691,
        697, 698, 708, 714
    racial issues and, 714–715
Sevareid, Eric, 838, 920
Seven Cities of Cíbola, 23
Seventeenth Amendment, 234
Seventh Day Adventists, 422
Seven Years' War (French and In-
    dian War), 131, 132, 133,
    136–141, 224
    consequences of, 139–141
    outbreak of hostilities in, 136–
        139
    taxes after, 142–147
Sewall, Arthur, 653
Sewall, Samuel, 99
Seward, William, 476, 478, 483,
    484, 486, 487, 490, 492, 495,
    505, 511, 514, 663–664
Sewing machine, 351
Sex roles. See also Women's rights
    movement
    in antebellum South, 381–382
    among black slaves, 74
    in colonial society, 101–103
    feminism of the 1970s and,
        966
    industrialization and, 346–349,
        351
    middle class, 640–642, 644–645
    Native American, 6, 8–9
    post–World War II, 895–898
    Puritan, 49–50
    Quaker, 55
    in the Southern colonies, 108
    urbanization process and, 356–
        358
    westward movement and, 453,
        454
Sexual Behavior in the Human Fe-
    male (Kinsey), 897
Sexual Behavior in the Human Male
    (Kinsey), 897

Sexuality. See also Prostitution
    changes of the 1960s, 940–941
    female autonomy and, 432
    homosexual, 989
    Mormon polygamy, 461–462
    nineteenth-century reform move-
        ment, 424–425
    of the 1920s, 772
    post–World War II, 897–898
    utopian community, 420, 421,
        422
Shakers, 420
Shakespeare, William, 25, 40
Shame of the Cities, The (Steffens),
    692
Shannon, William, 894
Sharecropping, 547–550
Shawnee tribe, 166, 188
    nineteenth-century armed resis-
        tance of, 315–316
Shays, Daniel, 227
Shays's Rebellion, 226–227, 228
Sheldon, Charles, 650
Shepherd, Randall, 293
Sheppard, Morris, 781
Sheppard-Towner Maternity Act of
    1921, 781
Sheridan, Philip, 576
Sherman, Phyllis, 261, 263
Sherman, William Tecumseh, 519,
    575–576, 577
Sherman Anti-Trust Act of 1890,
    634–635, 711, 720
Sherman Silver Purchase Act, 635,
    636, 638, 652
Shipbuilding, 224, 264
    ironclad ships, 510
    Revolutionary War impact on, 185
    World War I, 745
Shippen, William, 284
Shoe industry, 269, 272
Shopping, 640, 815, 893
Shopping centers, 891
Shoup, David, 934
Shultz, George, 995
Shute, Nevil, 873
Siberia, 4
Sierra Club, 714
Silent Spring (Carson), 969
Sill, Joseph, 355, 446
Silver
    as basis for currency
        Gilded Age, 632, 635, 636, 638,
            652–654

coinage of, 591
New World discovery of, 21
Simmons, William J., 759
Simonton, S. R., 582
Simpson, Ben, 385
Simpson, "Sockless" Jerry, 636
Sims, Thomas, 477
Sinatra, Frank, 875
Sinclair, Upton, 693, 712–713, 801
Singleton, Benjamin "Pap," 551, 585
Sioux tribe, 465, 576
    Wounded Knee massacre, 578
Sirica, John, 961
Sister Carrie (Dreiser), 602
Sit-ins, 430
    of the 1960s, 918
Sitting Bull, 576
Sixteenth Amendment, 715, 719
Skinner, Catherine, 365, 366
Skipwith, George, 385
Skyscrapers, 764
Slater, Samuel, 273
Slave drivers, 394–395
Slaves, 53–54, 63–74, 369–401. See
    also Abolitionism
    in African culture, 11
    bondage system of, 68–69
    California and, 474, 475
    in the Carolina colonies, 52–53,
        57, 67, 70, 106
    Cherokee tribe use of, 315
    Chesapeake Bay colony, 67, 68,
        69–70, 103
    Christianity of, 390–392, 399
    Civil War impact on, 522–523
    as Civil War soldiers, 519, 526
    in the colonial South, 108
    concerns of owners of, 380–385
    Constitution and, 234
    in cotton production process, 193,
        268–269, 277, 371–376
    culture of. See Afro-American cul-
        ture
    daily routines and, 380, 385–386,
        390
    Democratic party and, 472–474
    emancipation of, 293–294, 514–
        515, 524
    family life of, 69–70, 72–74, 388–
        390, 393–394
    free blacks versus, 293–294, 397–
        399
    fugitive, 234, 474, 475–477
    growth of use of, 69–71, 103

Slaves (*Continued*)
　health of, 386–388
　importation from Africa, 64–66,
　　97–98
　indentured servants versus, 35–
　　36, 67
　in industry, 376
　justification for holding, 382–385
　Kansas and, 484–488
　in Latin America, 291, 306–307,
　　396
　legal status of, 388–389
　manumissions, 292–293, 397, 398
　Mexican War and, 472–473
　music of, 390, 392–393, 394
　Native American, 20–21, 23, 53,
　　76, 77
　New Mexico, 474, 475
　in northern colonies, 67–68, 70–
　　71, 72
　Northwest Ordinance and, 221,
　　277, 329, 473
　population size and growth, 67,
　　69, 70, 71, 94, 97–98, 103,
　　159
　precolonial period, 3, 65
　republican ideals versus, 291–294
　resistance by, 72, 291–292, 394–
　　397
　in the Revolutionary War, 170,
　　191–194
　in rice production, 380–382, 385–
　　386
　silver mining by, 21
　in southern colonies, 67, 69–70
　southern social structure and,
　　377–378, 384–385
　in sugar production, 22, 65, 67,
　　385
　in Texas, 443, 444, 474, 475
　trade in, 65–67, 97–98, 192–193,
　　374, 474, 475
　westward movement and, 472–
　　492
Slidell, John L., 445
Slums
　housing issues in, 695–696
　New Deal program, 812
　nineteenth-century, 606
　settlement house movement in,
　　648–649
Smallpox, 20, 46, 284
Smedes, Susan Dabney, 382
Smith, Adam, 275

Smith, Alfred E., 782–783, 800, 914
Smith, Elijah and Albert, 423
Smith, Hoke, 708
Smith, John, 3, 33, 34, 37, 41, 42,
　83
Smith, Joseph, 422, 460, 461
Smith, Walter Bedell, 846
Smith, William French, 981
Smith Act of 1940, 875
Social Darwinism, 646–647
　in foreign policy, 678–679
Social Gospel movement, 650
Socialist party, 853
　election of 1912 and, 718
　post–World War I Communist
　　scare in, 756–757
Social justice movement, 692–699.
　　*See also* Social reform
　child labor in, 693–694, 704, 781
　education in, 696–697
　housing in, 695–696
　movie theatres and, 698–699
　muckrakers in, 692–693, 712–713
　Progressive party and, 716–717
　prohibition in, 697–698, 781–782
　protection for working women in,
　　694–695, 702–703
　World War I and, 727–728, 747–
　　748
Social reform, 640–641, 648–652.
　　*See also* Social justice move-
　　ment
　abolitionism. *See* Abolitionism
　civil rights movement. *See* Civil
　　rights movement
　consumer movement in, 969,
　　989–991
　environmental movement in,
　　968–969, 990–991
　gay rights, 989
　health issues, 424
　institutional, 425–427
　Moral Majority, 992
　New Deal program for, 801–809,
　　812–814
　pragmatism in, 647–648
　progressive era, 705–709
　　municipal-level, 705–708
　　state-level, 708–709
　settlement house movement in.
　　*See* Settlement houses
　sexuality and, 424–425
　student movement in, 955–956
　temperance. *See* Temperance

　trade unions in. *See* Trade unions
　women's rights. *See* Women's
　　rights movement
Social Security Act of 1935, 803, 924
Social security system, 982
Social status
　antebellum, 377–380, 384–385
　colonial, 83, 103–107, 112–114,
　　155–156
　of eighteenth-century immigrants,
　　96–97
　gospel of wealth and, 645–647
　industrialization process and,
　　351–352, 376–377, 605–607,
　　608, 611–612, 622–623
　in the 1920s, 775–776
　occupational mobility and, 645
　in preindustrial society, 285–286
　Puritan, 83
　Reconstruction era, 535–545,
　　546–551
　social equality versus, 287–288
　urbanization process and, 354–
　　358, 377, 607
Society for Propagating the Gospel
　　Among Indians, 313
Society of Friends. *See* Quakers
Sociology, 649
Sons of Liberty, 144, 191, 249
Soulé, Pierre, 481
South Africa, 679
South America, 4, 18
South Carolina
　attack on Fort Sumter, 495–496,
　　500
　colonial. *See* South Carolina col-
　　ony
　cotton production in, 193, 268–
　　269
　postrevolutionary agrarian pro-
　　tests in, 227
　postrevolutionary exports of, 184
　postrevolutionary slavery in, 193
　Reconstruction era, 555–556
　in the Revolutionary War, 170,
　　171, 178
　secession of, 493
　Tariff of Abominations in, 409–
　　410
South Carolina colony, 52–54, 57
　agriculture in, 53–54, 106–107
　British occupation of, 170, 171,
　　178
　slaves in, 70, 72

South Dakota, 575, 577
Southern Farmers' Alliance, 588–
    590
  blacks in, 589
  Ocala Platform of, 589–590
  Populist party and, 590–592
Southern Pacific Railroad, 573
Southern states. *See also* Civil War;
    Confederate States of Amer-
    ica; New South; specific
    states
  cultural differences with antebel-
    lum northern states, 484–488
  Kansas Territory and, 487–488
  Ku Klux Klan in, 550, 554, 759–
    760
  nineteenth-century agriculture in,
    267–269, 277, 578–579, 581–
    582, 588–592
  regional characteristics of, 277
  school desegregation and, 905–
    906
  secession of, 493–495
Soviet Union, 853. *See also* Russia
  Carter administration and, 993–
    994
  China and, 865
  Cold War and. *See* Cold War
  containment policy toward. *See*
    Containment
  Cuba and, 933–935
  détente with, 951–952, 993–994
  fear of Germany, 858
  Iran and, 869–870
  Korea and, 866
  in the Middle East, 869–871
  nuclear weapons and, 862, 871–
    874
  Reagan administration and, 995–
    996
  recognition of government of, 822
  in World War II, 825–826, 827,
    841, 842, 843, 847, 849–850
  in the Yalta conference of 1945,
    848
Space exploration, 873, 933
Spain, 112
  Catholicism of, 17, 18, 23
  cession of Florida to the United
    States, 308
  cession of Louisiana to France, 306
  civil war in, 824–825
  closing the Mississippi River out-
    let by, 223, 306

Cuba and, 14, 18, 480–481, 669–
    670, 672
emergence of nation-state, 12, 14
English challenge to, 24–25, 88,
    132, 133, 135
era of conquest of New World, 18–
    23
expansionist impulse of, 14–15
ouster of Moors from Africa by,
    15
Philippines and, 659, 674, 677
postrevolutionary trade with, 183
in the Revolutionary War, 172,
    174
Seven Years' War and, 139
sixteenth-century explorers, 3
Spanish-American War, 672–674
trans-Mississippi territory of, 438,
    442, 480–481
in World War II, 843
Spanish-American War, 672–674
Specie Circular, 412
Specie Resumption Act of 1875,
    632
*Spelling Book* (Webster), 327
Spencer, Herbert, 646, 648
Spice Islands, 15
Spinning jennies, 273
Spock, Benjamin, 897
Sports, 765, 815, 913, 914, 992
*Sputnik* (satellite), 873
Squatter, 453
Stalin, Joseph, 842, 845–846, 847,
    848, 857–859
Stamp Act of 1765, 131, 142–145
Standard Oil of New Jersey, 600
Stanton, Edwin, 542–543
Stanton, Elizabeth Cady, 433, 515,
    544, 545, 643, 644, 749
State government
  child labor laws of, 694, 704
  economics of Revolutionary War
    and, 181–188, 218–220
  Eisenhower administration and,
    902–903
  Federal Constitution versus, 234–
    235
  labor laws for women, 695, 704
  postrevolutionary, 212–216
    constitutions of, 212, 214–216,
      218
    Loyalism and, 216–217
    political mobilization and, 207–
      208

redistribution of power in, 213–
    216
separation of church and state,
    217–218
varying approaches to, 213–216
Progressive era reforms, 708–709
Reagan administration and, 996–
    997
Reconstruction era, 539–540,
    552–553
Revolutionary era, 211–212
Revolutionary War debts, 225–
    227, 243–244
segregation laws of, 583–584
universal white suffrage and, 330–
    331
voting restrictions, 907
State militia
  in the Civil War, 501, 505
  in the Revolutionary War, 175–
    176, 180, 199
States' rights, 409–410
States' Rights party, 900
Stay laws, 226
Stead, W. T., 638
Steamboats, 280
Steam power, 353, 597
Steel industry, 597, 711, 806, 917
Steffens, Lincoln, 692, 709, 757
Steinbeck, John, 812, 816
Steinem, Gloria, 964–965, 966, 985
Stennis, John C., 905, 959
Stephens, Alexander, 513
Stettinius, Edward, 859
Stevens, Thaddeus, 540, 543
Stevenson, Adlai, 897, 901, 922
Stewart, John, 313
Still, William, 430
Stimson, Henry L., 829, 834, 872
Stocks, 598
  Crash of 1929, 783, 788, 790
Stoddard, Solomon, 117
Stokes, J. G. Phelps, 756–757
Story, Joseph, 408
Stowe, Harriet Beecher, 477
Straight, Willard, 684
Strategic Arms Limitation Talks
    (SALT), 952
  SALT II, 994, 996
Strauss, Lewis, 873
Strong, Josiah, 649, 669
Strunsky, Anna, 714
Stuart, Archibald, 206
Stuart, Gilbert, 327

Student Nonviolent Coordinating Committee (SNCC), 918, 919, 923, 927, 928, 929
Students
conformity of 1950s, 894–895
New Left and, 938–940, 956
of the 1970s and 1980s, 983
Nixon administration and, 956–957
Vietnam War protests, 950
Students for a Democratic Society (SDS), 938–940, 956
Stump, Margaret, 983
*Sturges* v. *Crowninshield*, 341
Submarine warfare, 730–731, 827
Submerged Lands Act of 1953, 902
*Substitutes for the Saloon* (Caulkins), 698
Suburbs
automobile and growth of, 763
nineteenth-century, 607
post–World War II population shifts, 888–891
Suez Canal, 870–871
Suffrage
black, 208–209, 495, 542, 543, 582, 583, 635, 907, 924, 958
colonial period, 123–124
Native American, 208
postrevolutionary rights, 208–211
property requirement, 214, 215, 330–331
universal white, 330–331
woman, 209–211, 433, 544–545, 642–644, 774, 777
election of 1912 and, 716–717
Nineteenth Amendment, 748–749
progressivism and, 695, 716–717
Sugar
Cuba and, 671
European production of, 65
Hawaiian Islands and, 664–665
New World production of, 21, 22
slaves in production of, 22, 65, 67, 385
Sugar Act of 1764, 142
Sullivan, "Big Tim," 633
Sullivan, John, 190
Sullivan, Louis, 597
Sullivan, Max, 991
Sully, Thomas, 327

Sumner, Charles, 483, 485–486, 540–541, 557–558
Sumner, William Graham, 647
*Sun Also Rises, The* (Hemingway), 771
Sun Belt states, 978–979
Sunday, Billy, 758
Sung, Kim Il, 866
Supreme Court
bus segregation and, 907
contract law and, 341
Franklin Roosevelt and, 811
Great Society programs and, 925
nineteenth-century impeachment trial, 302
in the Nixon administration, 957, 959
school integration and, 905–906, 959
Susquehannock tribe, 57, 77
Sutton, Marjorie, 896
Switzerland
Calvinism in, 17–18
colonial emigrants from, 94
Syria, 953–954

Taft, Robert A., 826, 877, 899–900
Taft, William Howard, 684, 715
election of 1912 and, 716–718
Taft-Hartley Act of 1947, 900, 976
Taiwan (Formosa), 865
Talleyrand, 253, 255, 306
Taney, Roger B., 412, 489, 503
Tanks, 741, 846
Tanner, Henry Ossawa, 607
Tappan, Arthur and Lewis, 427, 429
Tarbell, Ida, 692–693
Tariffs
first protective, 328
Gilded Age, 631, 635–636, 653
Jackson administration and, 408, 409–410
post–World War I, 780
Tariff of Abominations, 408–410
Trade Agreements Act of 1934, 823
Underwood Tariff bill of 1913, 719
Taxes
in Articles of Confederation, 165
for Civil War, 511, 519
for education, 342
of England on colonies, 142–147, 148–149

excess profits, 778
income. *See* Income taxes
on national banks, 302–303
postrevolutionary, 226–227
religious, 218
Revolutionary War, 219
after the Seven Years' War, 142–147
to support education, 289
Whiskey Tax of 1791, 245, 246–247
Taylor, Frederick, 701, 763
Taylor, Zachary, 445, 474–475, 718
Tea Act of 1773, 148–149, 157
Teapot Dome scandal, 777
Tecumseh, 316, 317, 321
Telephone, 764, 765
Television
advertisements on, 893
conformity and, 894–895
in the political process, 914–915, 997
Teller, Edward, 873
Teller Amendment, 680
Temperance
nineteenth-century, 423–424, 632, 633–634, 697
post–World War I, 781–782
progressivism and, 697–698
Temple, Shirley, 816
Tenant farming, 547–550, 581–582
Tenant rent war (New York), 158, 225
*Ten Days That Shook the World* (Reed), 757
Tennent, Gilbert, 117, 119, 122
Tennessee, 541
as border state in the Civil War, 502–503
Cherokee tribe revitalization in, 314–315
Civil War battles and, 508–509
Creek armed resistance in, 317
settlement of, 278
Tennessee Valley Authority (TVA), 799–800, 902–903
Tenochtitlan, 18
Tenure of Office Act, 542
Texas, 441
annexation of, 442–445
cattle ranching in, 571–572
Hispanic Americans in, 467, 968
independence from Mexico, 442–444

riots of black soldiers in, 714, 740–741

secession of, 493

slavery issue and, 443, 444, 474, 475

Textile industry

British, 156–157

child workers in, 273, 335, 346, 349–350

cotton production and, 268

industrialization and, 343–344, 346–350

in the New South, 579–581

nineteenth-century growth of, 272–273, 343–344

Thayer, Eli, 484

Thieu, Nguyen Van, 937

Third World countries, 933

Thirteenth Amendment, 539, 540, 544

*This Side of Paradise* (Fitzgerald), 772

Thomas, Norman, 739, 810

Thompson, Ben, 261, 291, 293

Thompson, J. Walter, 893

Thoreau, Henry David, 419, 491

Three Mile Island incident, 990–991

Thurber, James, 816–817

Thurmond, J. Strom, 900

Tilden, Samuel J., 558

Tillman, Ben, 676

Tilton, James, 177

Time

industrialization and, 345–346

preindustrial attitudes toward, 282

Times Beach, Missouri, 990

Tinney, James, 989

Tobacco, 26, 184

Chesapeake Bay colony, 32–39, 104–106

colonial export restrictions on, 79

decline of production of, 267–268, 374

postrevolutionary export of, 184

Tocqueville, Alexis de, 416

Toledo, Ohio

social reform in, 651–652

Toombs, Robert, 473, 492

Toomer, Jean, 771

*Tootsie*, 985

Tordesillas, Treaty of, 18

Tories, 176, 217

*Tortilla Flat* (Steinbeck), 816

*Total Woman, The* (Morgan), 966

Tourgée, Albion, 555

Tourist industry, 814

Towner, Horace, 781

Town meetings, 48, 126–127, 206

Townsend, Francis E., 801

Townsend Old Age Revolving Pension Plan, 801, 803

Townshend Acts, 145–147

Trade Agreements Act of 1934, 823

Trade unions

Amalgamated Association of Iron, Steel, and Tin Workers, 619

American Federation of Labor, 618, 746, 775–776, 805–807

American Railway Union, 619–620

antebellum formation of, 349, 351, 352

Brotherhood of Railway and Steamship Clerks, 805

decline of, 976

depression of 1837 and, 413

development and growth of, 701–703

Industrial Workers of the World, 704–706, 746

International Ladies' Garment Workers' Union, 618, 703

National Labor Union, 556

New Deal and, 804–807

in the 1920s, 775–776

nineteenth-century formation of, 426–427, 616–622

Noble Order of the Knights of Labor, 556, 584, 617–618

post–World War I benefits, 767

post–World War II strikes, 885–886, 900

problems of forming, 620–621

in the Progressive era, 701–705, 720

Sherman Anti-Trust Act and, 720

United Farmworkers, 930, 931, 968

United Mine Workers, 712, 776, 886

Western Federation of Miners, 618–619

women in, 618, 702–704, 805

during World War I, 746–747

during World War II, 830

Transcendentalists, 418–419

Transcontinental Treaty, 442

Transportation

agriculture and, 337–340, 362–363, 365

in antebellum economic growth, 337–340

automobiles. *See* Automobiles

canal systems, 337, 340, 353, 417

in the Civil War South, 525

federal system for, 328–329

in the modernization of agriculture, 564, 566, 567, 573–574, 587–588

railroads. *See* Railroads

road and highway systems, 280, 304, 887

urbanization process and, 352–353, 605

Transylvania University, 278, 505

Travis, Joseph, 396

*Treason of the Senate, The* (Phillips), 693

Treaty of Brest-Litovsk of 1918, 756

Treaty of Ghent (1814), 323–324

Treaty of Guadalupe Hidalgo, 448, 461

Treaty of Hopewell (1785), 189

Treaty of Paris (1763), 139, 153, 222

Treaty of Paris (1899), 659, 674

Treaty of Portsmouth, 684

Tredegar Iron Works, 520

Trenchard, John, 127

Triangle Shirtwaist Company, 703–704

Trist, Nicholas, 447, 448

*Triumphant Democracy* (Carnegie), 646

Truck farming, 581

Truman, Harry

presidency of, 849–850

atomic bomb in, 825–826, 859, 871–874

domestic policy, 899–901, 904–905

election of 1948, 900–901

foreign policy in, 854–856, 858–863, 866–874

loyalty programs in, 874–876

post–World War II adjustments, 885–886

Red Scare in, 876–879

as vice-president, 847–848

Truman Doctrine, 860–861

Trumbull, Jonathan, 320, 327

Truth, Sojourner, 477

Tryon, William, 157
Tuberculosis, 284
Tubman, Harriet, 395–396
Tugwell, Rexford, 795
Turkey, 860–861, 934
Turner, Frederick Jackson, 665
Turner, Henry McNeal, 399, 551, 585
Turner, Nat, 374, 388, 396
Turnpike system, 280
Tuskegee Institute, 585
Twain, Mark, 629
Tweed Ring, 556
Twentieth Amendment, 794
Twenty-first Amendment, 796
Tydings, Millard, 877
Tyler, John, 415, 444, 445
Tyler, Robert, 74

Uncle Tom's Cabin (Stowe), 477
Underground railroad, 395–396
Underwood Tariff bill, 719
UN Educational, Scientific, and Cultural Organization (UNESCO), 849
Unemployment, 873
  black, 986
  in the depression of 1893, 636, 638
  government responsibility for, 778
  in the Great Depression, 788, 790–791, 792
  industrialization process and, 600–601, 611
  New Deal programs, 796–797, 799, 802–803, 811
  in the 1970s, 975–976
  in the recession of 1983–1985, 977–979
Union of Soviet Socialist Republics (USSR). See Soviet Union
Unions. See Trade unions
United Farmworkers, 930–931, 968
United Mine Workers, 712, 776, 886
United Nations
  Atomic Energy Commission, 872–873, 903
  formation of, 848–849
  Korean War and, 867
  Security Council, 849
  Soviet threat to Iran, 870
United Negro Improvement Association, 769–770
United Railway Administration, 746

U. S. Steel, 711, 806
United States v. E. C. Knight, 635
Unsafe at Any Speed: The Designed-in Dangers of the American Automobile (Nader), 969
Urbanization, 352–362, 601–607, 611. See also Cities; Social justice movement
  corrupt politicians in, 632–633, 650–652
  housing and, 355–356
  industrialization process and, 604–605
  process of, 352–353
  Progressive era reforms and, 695–696, 705–708
  racial tensions in, 359–362
  rural-urban move in, 601–603
  social reform and, 648–652
  social status and, 354–358, 377, 607
  in Southern states, 377
  suburbs in, 607, 763, 888–891
  working-class neighborhoods in, 605–607
Urey, Harold C., 873
U. S. A. (Dos Passos), 816
Utah, 5
  Mormons in, 459–462
Utilitarianism, 100
Utopianism
  nineteenth-century, 419–421
  Puritan, 42–43

Vagrancy laws, 538
Valley Forge, Pennsylvania, 176
Van Buren, Martin, 331, 407, 408, 413, 474
  election of 1840 and, 415
  presidency of, 412–415
Vandenberg, Arthur, 860
Van Devanter, Willis, 811
Vann, Joseph, 315
Vanzetti, Bartolomeo, 760
Vasquez, Tiberio, 468
Veiller, Lawrence, 695
Venezuela, 665, 680, 685
Vergennes, 172, 173
Verrazano, Giovanni da, 24, 27
Versialles Treaty of 1919, 823, 824
Vertical integration, 599–600
Vesey, Denmark, 396
Vespucci, Amerigo, 27

Viet Cong, 936–937
Vietnam War, 868–869, 935, 936–937
  amnesty program for draft dodgers, 963
  election of 1968 and, 946–948
  New Left protests against, 939–940
  during the Nixon administration, 949–951
  protests of, 949–950, 956, 968
  refugees from, 981
  veterans of, 913, 991–992
Villard, Oswald Garrison, 714
Virginia, 26, 28, 255, 491–492, 507–508, 517, 522
  Articles of Confederation and, 165–166
  as border state in the Civil War, 502–503
  colonial. See Virginia colony
  postrevolutionary exports of, 184
  postrevolutionary slavery in, 193
  ratification of Constitution by, 238
  Reconstruction era, 553–554
  religious freedom in, 218
  resolution on Federal assumption of state debts, 244
  in the Revolutionary War, 164, 171–172, 179
  slave rebellion of 1800 in, 291–292
Virginia colony, 3–4, 26, 28, 33–37, 43
  Bacon's Rebellion in, 76–78, 83
  Glorious Revolution of 1688 and, 82
  Great Awakening revivalism in, 119–120
  Native Americans in, 3–4
  population growth of, 96
  slaves in, 69, 103
  social rank in, 83
  Stamp Act riots in, 143–144
Virginia Company, 33–37, 79
Virginia Plan, 233
Virginia Resolutions, 255
Virginia (ship), 510
Vision of Columbus, The (Barlow), 327
Volstead Act of 1919, 782
Voltaire, 57
Von Newmann, John, 893

Vorhees, Daniel, 631
Voting. *See also* Suffrage
  election of 1896, 654, 655
  nineteenth-century turnout, 632
Voting Rights Act of 1965, 924, 925, 958, 997

Wagner, Robert, 805
Wagner Act of 1935, 805, 900
Wagner-Steagall Housing Act of 1937, 812
Wainwright, Jonathan, 842
Wald, Lillian, 649, 708, 727, 790
*Walden* (Thoreau), 419
Walker, David, 429
Walker, Francis Amasa, 576, 706
Walker, William, 480
Wallace, George C., 947–948, 959
Wallace, Henry A., 795, 847, 861, 900
Walling, William English, 702, 714, 718, 756
Wampanoag tribe, 75–76
War bonds, 744–745, 831–832
Ward, May, 501
War Department
  Native American relations and, 309–310, 316
Warham, John, 31
War Hawks, 321
War Industries Board, 745
Warner, Charles Dudley, 629
War of 1812, 308, 315, 318, 406
  economic development programs after, 328
  foreign trade decline during, 271–272, 321–325
  preliminary skirmishes, 319–321
War Production Board (WPB), 829
Warren, Earl, 925, 957
War Revenue Act of 1917, 745
Washing machine, 614
Washington, Booker T., 585–586, 714, 715, 719–720, 769
Washington, D. C.
  as capital, 330–332
  slave trade in, 474, 475
  Vietnam Memorial in, 991–992
Washington, George, 151, 208, 223
  Constitution and, 233, 240
  death of, 280
  Federalists and, 227, 228, 232
  presidency of, 240–252, 315

in the Revolutionary War, 167, 168–172, 174, 176, 177, 180, 185
in the Seven Years' War, 137, 138, 141
Washington Temperance Society, 424
Water, 573, 930, 988
Waterworks, 353–354
Watergate incident, 960–962
Watson, Tom, 590, 592, 653, 677
Wayne, Anthony, 315
*Way to Wealth, The* (Franklin), 100
*Wealth of Nations* (Smith), 275
*Weary Blues* (Hughes), 770–771
Weathermen, 956
Weaver, James B. 590, 591
Webster, Daniel, 408, 410, 411, 413, 476, 480
Webster, Noah, 289, 327
Welch, Joseph, 878
Weld, Theodore Dwight, 403, 423, 427, 429, 430, 431
Welles, Orson, 817
Wells, Ida B., 584
Wells, Rachel, 157
Wesley, John, 117
Western Federation of Miners, 618–619
Western Union, 597
West Indies, 26, 27, 35, 67, 68, 69, 72, 98
  English control of shipping to, 251–252
  as market for American products, 182, 183–184, 318–319, 320
Westinghouse, George, 761
West Jersey, 56
Westward movement, 275–276, 286, 437–469
  annexation of Texas in, 442–445
  California and. *See* California
  emigrants in, 450–468
  by England, 25–27
  foreign claims and possessions in, 438
  Hispanic Americans and, 466–468
  Manifest Destiny, 441–442
  Native Americans and, 438–440, 463–466
  New Mexico and. *See* New Mexico

Oregon and, 438, 440, 441, 448–449, 453
post–World War II, 888–889
slavery and, 472–492
traders and trappers in, 440–441
Treaty of Guadalupe Hidalgo in, 448, 461
war with Mexico and, 445–447, 460, 472–473
Weyler, "Butcher," 670, 671
Wheat, 184, 365, 566
Wheeler, Burton K., 796, 827
Wheeless, Zenobia, 589
Whetten, Harriet, 524
Whig ideology, 127, 153–155
Whig party
  characteristics of early, 413–414
  disintegration of, 478–479, 481–482
  formation of, 411
  under Harrison, 415
  slavery and, 472, 474
  under Taylor, 474–475
  under Tyler, 444, 445
Whiskey, 283
Whiskey Rebellion, 246–247
Whiskey Ring affair, 557
Whiskey Tax of 1791, 245, 246–247
White, William Allen, 718, 826
Whyte, William H., 892
Whitefield, George, 93, 117–120
Whitman, Walt, 485
Whitney, Eli, 268, 372
Wicker, Tom, 994–995
Wilhelm II, 686
Wilk, Michael, 979
Wilkerson, Eliza, 210
Willard, Samuel, 81
William of Orange (king of England), 80, 88, 90
Williams, Abigail, 84
Williams, George Washington, 607
Williams, Jesse, 337
Williams, John Skelton, 580
Williams, Peter, 390
Williams, Roger, 43–45, 50, 120
Willkie, Wendell, 826
Wilmot, David, 472–474
Wilmot Proviso, 472–474
Wilson, Charles E., 902
Wilson, Woodrow, 629, 687, 709.
  *See also* Progressivism; World War I

Wilson, Woodrow (*Continued*)
  election of 1912, 716–718
  personal characteristics of, 716
  presidency of, 718–720
    election of 1916, 734
    Latin American foreign policy,
      731–733
    Paris Peace Conference of 1918,
      750–752
    woman suffrage and, 748–749
Wilson, James, 152, 233
Wilson, Luzena, 458
*Winesburg, Ohio* (Anderson), 772
Winthrop, John, 26, 42–44, 45–46,
  50, 101, 661
Winthrop, John II, 115
Wirt, William, 412
Wisconsin, 709
Witchcraft, 83–85
Witherspoon, John, 187
Wolfe, James, 139
Wolfe, Thomas, 816
Wolfe, Tom, 969–970
*Woman's Bible* (Stanton), 644
Woman's Peace party, 727
Women
  alcohol consumption of, 283
  in antebellum South, 381–382
  in the armed forces
    World War I, 739
    World War II, 840–841
  in the Chesapeake Bay colonies,
    38–39, 105
  childbirth process, 284
  Civil War impact on, 522–524
  contraceptive methods of, 358–
    359, 772, 841, 940–941, 957,
    965, 985–986
  discrimination against, 931–933,
    963–965, 985
  divorce and, 289–291
  domesticity and, 357–360, 772–
    773
  education of, 290–291, 641–642,
    896, 945
  employment of, 641–642
    industrialization process, 612–
      614
    limits on working hours, 612–
      614
    in the 1930s, 805, 815
    in the 1970s and 1980s, 979,
      982, 984
    as outworkers, 613, 614

  post–World War II, 896–897
  textile industry, 272–273, 335,
    346–347, 348–350, 580
  World War I, 746–747
  exclusion from postrevolutionary
    politics, 209–211
  free black, 398
  in the Great Depression, 791
  as heads of household, 979, 987
  as indentured servants, 36
  matrilineality, 8, 11
  New Deal and, 802, 809
  of New England colonies, 101–
    103
  in the 1920s, 772–774
  in nineteenth-century cities, 602
  as outworkers, 351
  pacifism of, 727, 751
  in politics, 984, 997
  in prerevolutionary colonies, 156–
    157
  in professions, 642, 774, 984
  property rights of, 102, 432, 433
  prostitution and. *See* Prostitution
  Puritan, 44–45, 49, 55
  Quaker, 55
  Red Scare and, 759
  republicanism and, 289–291
  in the Revolutionary War, 179,
    180
  role in education, 641–642
  sex roles of. *See* Sex roles
  Sheppard-Towner Maternity Act
    of 1921 and, 781
  shopping as responsibility of, 640,
    815
  slave, 73–74, 382, 386, 387, 388–
    390
  social reform and. *See* Social re-
    form
  in the Southern colonies, 108
  in temperance movements, 633–
    634
  in the textile industry, 272–273,
    335, 346–347, 348–350
  in trade unions, 618, 702–704,
    805
  urbanization process impact on,
    356–358
  voting by. *See* Suffrage, woman
  westward movement and, 453,
    454, 458
  World War II impact on, 836–838,
    840–841, 895–898

*Women and Economics* (Gilman),
  696
Women's Christian Temperance
  Union, 640, 697
Women's rights movement
  abolitionism and, 357, 427, 431–
    433, 477
  civil rights movement as basis of,
    931–932
  Equal Rights Amendment and,
    774, 965, 966, 984, 986
  lesbian, 989
  National Organization for Women
    (NOW), 932–933, 965
  of the 1920s, 774
  in the 1970s and 1980s, 963–966,
    983–986
  suffrage and. *See* Suffrage, woman
Women's Trade Union League, 702,
  703
Wood, Leonard, 680, 728–729
Wood, Robert, 826
Woodbury, Levi, 331
Woodmanson, Charles, 107
Woodstock rock festival, 955
Woodward, Robert, 961
Woolman, John, 98
Woolsey, Jane, 500
*Worcester* v. *Georgia*, 440
Work, Robert, 607
Workmen's Compensation Bill,
  734
Works Progress Administration
  (WPA), 797, 802–803
World Health Organization, 849
World War I, 725–753
  aftermath of, 749–752, 755–776
    economic growth in. *See* Eco-
      nomic growth, post–World
      War I
    Ku Klux Klan, 759–760
    Red Scare in, 756–757
    Sacco-Vanzetti case, 760
    working class protest in, 757–
      759, 775–776
  early years, 726–733
  United States involvement in,
    734–749
    domestic impact, 744–749
    election of 1916 and, 734
    patriotic crusade for, 736–738
    raising army for, 738–739
    soldiers' experiences, 739–744
    Wilson's decision for, 735–736

World War II, 821–851
early years, 825–826
economic growth after, 885–894, 903
United States involvement in, 828–848
aims of, 841–842
armed forces and, 839–841, 842–847
battles of 1942 and 1943, 842–845
domestic social impact, 832–841
final battles, 847–848
invasion of Europe, 845–847
mobilization for, 829–831
patriotic fervor and, 831–832
Pearl Harbor attack and, 827–828, 832–833, 841
Yalta agreement, 848–849
Wounded Knee massacre, 578
Wovoka, 578
Wright, Richard, 769
Wyandotte tribe, 188, 222

XYZ affair, 253

Yale College, 120
Yalta conference of 1945, 848–849
Yates, Robert, 233

Yellow fever, 284, 285
Yeoman farmers, 379–380, 520, 549
Yippie organization, 946
York, Alvin, 743–744
Yorktown, Virginia, 164, 172
Young, Brigham, 422, 460–461, 462
Young, Thomas, 156, 214
Young America, 480
Youthfulness of America, 286–287

Zenger, John Peter, 127
Zoot suits, 835
Zou Enlai, 952
Zuni tribe, 6
Zuse, Konrad, 892

## CULTURAL and TECHNOLOGICAL

1866  Atlantic Cable laid
1867  First elevated railway in New York City
1869  First transcontinental railroad link
1870s  Expansion of public schools and higher education begins
1874  First electric streetcar runs in New York City
1876  Centennial Exposition in Philadelphia
1879  Alexander Graham Bell invents telephone
       Henry George, *Progress and Poverty*
       Light bulb perfected
1880s  Social Darwinism and Social Gospel
1881  Tuskegee Institute founded
1883  Brooklyn Bridge
1889  Andrew Carnegie, "The Gospel of Wealth"
1890s  Electric trolleys
1890  Alfred Thayer Mahan, *Influence of Sea Power upon History*
1891  Hamlin Garland, *Main-Travelled Roads*
1893  World's Exposition in Chicago
1895  Elizabeth Cady Stanton, *Woman's Bible*
1898  Charlotte Perkin Gilman, *Women and Economics*
1899  John Dewey, *School and Society*

1901  Frank Norris, *The Octopus*
1903  Wright brothers make first heavier-than-air flight
1906  Upton Sinclair, *The Jungle*
1909  First Model T Ford produced
1911  Frederick Winslow Taylor, *The Principles of Scientific Management*
1913  First assembly line at Ford Motor Company
       Armory Show, New York
1914  Panama Canal completed
1916  Margaret Sanger organizes New York Birth Control League
1920  First commercial radio broadcast
1927  Charles Lindbergh flies alone to Paris
       Sacco and Vanzetti executed
       *The Jazz Singer*, first feature-length talking movie
1934–1938  Radar developed
1935  Walt Disney releases *Flowers and Trees*, first movie in color
1938  Nylon and fiberglass developed
1939  New York World's Fair
       First scheduled television broadcast
1941  Penicillin developed
1942  Jet plane first tested in United States
1944  First electronic calculator developed
       Serviceman's Readjustment Act ("GI Bill")

## SOCIAL and ECONOMIC

1866  National Labor Union founded
1867  National Grange founded
1869  Knights of Labor formed
1870  Wyoming Territory grants female suffrage
1873–1879  Depression
1874  Women's Christian Temperance Union founded
1875–1876  Indian Wars in Black Hills
1877  Nez Percé Indian uprisings
       Black exodusters to Kansas
       Railroad strikes
1880s  "New South"
1883–1885  Depression
1884  Southern Farmers' Alliance founded
1885  "New Immigration"
1886  AFL founded
1887  College Settlement House Association founded
1889  Hull House founded
1890  Battle of Wounded Knee
       National American Women Suffrage Association formed
1892  Homestead strike
1893–1897  Depression
1895  Atlanta Compromise speech

1901  United States Steel Corporation organized
1903–1910  Muckrakers attack social evils and corruption
1905  Industrial Workers of the World (IWW) organized
1907  Panic caused by business failures
1909  NAACP organized
1911  Triangle fire in New York kills 146 textile workers
1913  Federal Reserve System organized
       Department of Labor organized
1914  Clayton Act strengthens antitrust legislation
1917–1918  Espionage Act and Sedition Act
1918–1919  Influenza epidemic kills 500,000 people in United States
1919  United States becomes creditor nation
1921  Immigration restrictions
1925  A & W Root Beer becomes first fast-food franchise
1929  Stock market crash
1934  Indian Reorganization Act
1935  Committee for Industrial Organization (CIO) formed
1942  Congress of Racial Equality (CORE) founded
1944  Bretton Woods Conference sets up World Bank and International Monetary Fund

## POLITICAL

1867  Alaska purchased
1868–1874  "Granger" Laws
1871  Indian Appropriation Act
1875  Specie Resumption Act
       United States–Hawaii commercial treaty
1877  *Munn v. Illinois*
1878  Bland-Allison Act
1880s  Bossism and urban reform
1882  Chinese Exclusion Act
1883  Pendleton Civil Service Act
1887  Dawes Act
       Interstate Commerce Act
1890  Sherman Anti-Trust Act
1890s  Jim Crow laws and disfranchisement attempts in the South
1892  Populist Party formed
1893  Hawaiian coup by American sugar growers
1895  Cuban Revolution
1898  Spanish-American War
       Annexation of Hawaii and the Philippines
1899–1900  Open Door notes
1899–1902  Philippine-American War

1901  Socialist Party of America formed
1906  Hepburn Act
       Pure Food and Drug Act
       Meat Inspection Act
1913  Sixteenth Amendment provides for an income tax
       Seventeenth Amendment provides for direct election of senators
1914  World War I begins in Europe
1917  United States enters World War I
1918  War ends in Europe
1919  Senate defeats League of Nations treaty
       Eighteenth Amendment establishes prohibition
1920  Nineteenth Amendment provides for woman suffrage
1933  TVA, CCC, NIRA, AAA, and other New Deal acts passed
1935  Social Security, WPA, and other New Deal legislation passed
1939  World War II begins in Europe
1941  Japanese attack Pearl Harbor
1944  Invasion of Normandy